CONSTITUTIONAL LAW FOR A CHANGING AMERICA

A SHORT COURSE

CONSTITUTIONAL LAW FOR A CHANGING AMERICA

A SHORT COURSE

LEE EPSTEIN
Washington University

THOMAS G. WALKER
Emory University

A DIVISION OF
CONGRESSIONAL QUARTERLY INC.
WASHINGTON, D.C.

Book design by Kachergis Book Design, Pittsboro, North Carolina.

Library of Congress Cataloging-in-Publication Data
Epstein, Lee, 1958–
    Constitutional law for a changing America :
a short course / Lee Epstein, Thomas G. Walker.
        p.   cm.
    Includes bibliographical references and index.
    ISBN 1-56802-151-8 (alk. paper)
    1. United States—Constitutional law.   2. Civil rights—United States.
3. Judicial process—United States.   I. Walker, Thomas G.   II. Title.
KF4749.E668   1996
342.73—dc20
[347.302]   96-1028
                                                      CIP

To my nephews and niece
    Evin Epstein, Mark and Stephen Kottler,
    and Zach Walsh —L. E.

To Vicki —T. G. W.

CONTENTS

Preface   xv

I   THE U.S. CONSTITUTION

AN INTRODUCTION TO THE U.S. CONSTITUTION   3
The Road to the U. S. Constitution   3
The Underlying Principles of the Constitution   8

1. THE LIVING CONSTITUTION   13
The Amendment Process   17
The Supreme Court and the Living
   Constitution   19
READINGS   23

2. APPROACHES TO SUPREME COURT DECISION MAKING   24
Legal Approaches   24
Extralegal Approaches   35
READINGS   51

II   INSTITUTIONAL AUTHORITY

THE SEPARATION OF POWERS   55
The Origins of the Separation of Powers
   Doctrine   55
Separation of Powers and the Constitution   57

Contemporary Thinking on the Constitutional
   Scheme   58

3. THE JUDICIARY   61
The Establishment of the Federal Judiciary   62
Judicial Review   66
   Marbury v. Madison (1803)   66
Constraints on Judicial Power   79
   Ex parte McCardle (1869)   80
READINGS   94

4. THE LEGISLATURE   96
Article I: Historical Overview   97
Congressional Authority over Internal Affairs   101
   U. S. Term Limits v. Thornton (1995)   105
The Sources and Scope of Legislative Powers   116
   McCulloch v. Maryland (1819)   118
   United States v. Curtiss-Wright Export Corp.
      (1936)   132
The Role of Congress in National Government   136
   Immigration and Naturalization Service v. Chadha
      (1983)   142
READINGS   147

5. THE EXECUTIVE   149
Selection and Formal Powers   150
The Faithful Execution of the Laws   154

Executive Immunity and Privilege   156
  United States v. Nixon (1974)   158
The Power of Appointment and Removal   163
The President and Foreign Policy   168
  United States v. Curtiss-Wright Export Corp.
    (1936)   169
Presidential Power During War and National
  Emergencies   171
  Youngstown Sheet & Tube Company v. Sawyer
    (1952)   177
READINGS   182

III   NATION-STATE RELATIONS

AN INTRODUCTION TO NATION-
STATE RELATIONS   185
The Framers and Federalism   186
Amending the Constitution: The Tenth
  Amendment   187

6.   FEDERALISM   191
The Marshall Court and the Rise of National
  Supremacy   192
  McCulloch v. Maryland (1819)   193
The Taney Court and the (Re)Emergence of States'
  Rights   196
Dual Federalism and Laissez-Faire Economics   201
  Hammer v. Dagenhart (1918)   201
The (Re)Emergence of National Supremacy:
  Cooperative Federalism   206
  United States v. Darby Lumber (1941)   206
  *Garcia v. San Antonio Metropolitan Transit
    Authority* (1985)   210
READINGS   216

7.   THE COMMERCE POWER   218
Constitutional Foundations of the Commerce
  Power   218
  Gibbons v. Ogden (1824)   220
Defining Interstate Commerce   225
The Supreme Court and the New Deal   229

  Schechter Poultry Corp. v. United States
    (1935)   233
  *National Labor Relations Board v. Jones &
    Laughlin Steel Corporation* (1937)   240
Regulating Commerce as a Federal Police
  Power   249
  Heart of Atlanta Motel v. United States
    (1964)   250
The Commerce Power of the States   252
  Cooley v. Board of Wardens (1852)   253
READINGS   258

8.   THE POWER TO TAX AND SPEND   259
The Constitutional Power to Tax and Spend   259
Direct Taxes and the Power to Tax Income   261
  Pollock v. Farmers' Loan and Trust Co.
    (1895)   264
Intergovernmental Tax Immunity   270
Taxation as a Regulatory Power   272
Taxing and Spending for the General Welfare   275
  South Dakota v. Dole (1987)   277
Restrictions on the Revenue Powers of the
  States   280
READINGS   284

IV   ECONOMIC LIBERTIES

ECONOMIC LIBERTIES AND
INDIVIDUAL RIGHTS   287

9.   THE CONTRACT CLAUSE   291
The Framers and the Contract Clause   291
John Marshall and the Contract Clause   293
The Decline of the Contract Clause   296
  Charles River Bridge v. Warren Bridge
    (1837)   297
  Home Building and Loan Association v. Blaisdell
    (1934)   303
The Revitalization of the Contract Clause   307
READINGS   310

10. ECONOMIC SUBSTANTIVE DUE
PROCESS   311

The Development of Substantive Due Process   314
The Roller Coaster Ride of Substantive Due Process:
1898–1923   320
Lochner v. New York (1905)   322
The Heyday of Substantive Due Process:
1923–1936   330
The Depression, the New Deal, and the Decline
of Substantive Due Process   332
West Coast Hotel v. Parrish (1937)   333
READINGS   338

11. THE TAKINGS CLAUSE   339
Protecting Private Property from Government
Seizure   339
What Constitutes a Taking?   341
*Penn Central Transportation Company v. City of
New York* (1978)   342
The Public Use Requirement   347
Hawaii Housing Authority v. Midkiff (1984)   347
Resurrecting the Takings Clause   350
Lucas v. South Carolina Coastal Council
(1992)   352
READINGS   355

V   CIVIL LIBERTIES

APPROACHING CIVIL LIBERTIES   359

12. RELIGION: EXERCISE AND
ESTABLISHMENT   363
Free Exercise of Religion   364
*Employment Division, Department of Human
Resources of Oregon v. Smith* (1990)   378
Religious Establishment   388
Lemon v. Kurtzman, Earley v. DiCenso (1971)   397
Edwards v. Aguillard (1987)   408
Lee v. Weisman (1992)   424
READINGS   433

13. FREEDOM OF SPEECH, ASSEMBLY,
AND ASSOCIATION   434
The Development of Legal Standards:
The Emergence of Law in Times of Crisis   435
Schenck v. United States (1919)   437
Dennis v. United States (1951)   449
Regulating Expression: Content and
Contexts   457
Texas v. Johnson (1989)   463
Chaplinsky v. New Hampshire (1942)   469
R.A.V. v. City of St. Paul, Minnesota (1992)   477
West Virginia Board of Education v. Barnette
(1943)   483
READINGS   488

14. FREEDOM OF THE PRESS   489
Prior Restraint   490
Near v. Minnesota (1931)   490
The Media and Special Rights   497
Branzburg v. Hayes (1972)   498
The Boundaries of Free Press:
Obscenity and Libel   504
Miller v. California (1973)   508
New York Times v. Sullivan (1964)   514
READINGS   524

15. THE RIGHT TO PRIVACY   525
The Right to Privacy: Foundations   526
Griswold v. Connecticut (1965)   529
Private Activities and the Application of
Griswold   535
Bowers v. Hardwick (1986)   536
Cruzan v. Director, Missouri Department of Health
(1990)   542
Reproductive Freedom and the Right to Privacy:
Abortion   547
Roe v. Wade (1973)   549
READINGS   570

VI THE CRIMINAL JUSTICE SYSTEM AND CONSTITUTIONAL RIGHTS

THE RIGHTS OF THE CRIMINALLY ACCUSED 573
Overview of the Criminal Justice System 574
Trends in Court Decision Making 576

16. INVESTIGATIONS AND EVIDENCE 579
Searches and Seizures 579
   Mapp v. Ohio (1961) 586
The Fifth Amendment and Self-Incrimination 594
   Miranda v. Arizona (1966) 596
READINGS 609

17. ATTORNEYS, TRIALS, AND PUNISHMENTS 610
The Right to Counsel 610
   Gideon v. Wainwright (1963) 613
Fair Trials 617
Sentencing and the Eighth Amendment 622
   Gregg v. Georgia (1976) 625
Post-Trial Stages 636
READINGS 639

VII CIVIL RIGHTS

Civil Rights and the Constitution 643
The Constitution and the Concept of Equality 643
The Supreme Court and Equal Protection of the Laws 645
Congressional Enforcement of Civil Rights 649

18. DISCRIMINATION 653
Racial Discrimination 653
   Plessy v. Ferguson (1896) 654
   Brown v. Board of Education of Topeka (1954) 661
Sex Discrimination 666
   Reed v. Reed (1971) 669
   Craig v. Boren (1976) 671

Economic Discrimination 675
   San Antonio Independent School District v. Rodriguez (1973) 676
Remedies for Discrimination 681
   Swann v. Charlotte-Mecklenburg County Board of Education (1971) 683
   Regents of the University of California v. Bakke (1978) 691
   Adarand Constructors, Inc. v. Pena (1995) 700
READINGS 706

19. VOTING AND REPRESENTATION 707
Voting Rights 707
   Louisiana v. United States (1965) 710
   South Carolina v. Katzenbach (1966) 713
Political Representation 718
   Reynolds v. Sims (1964) 721
   Miller v. Johnson (1995) 728
READINGS 734

REFERENCE MATERIAL

Constitution of the United States 737
Federalist, No. 78 747
U.S. Presidents 751
Thumbnail Sketch of the Supreme Court's History 753
The Justices 755
Natural Courts 761
The American Legal System 767
The Processing of Cases 768
Supreme Court Calendar 769
Briefing Supreme Court Cases 770
Glossary 772

Subject Index 777
Case Index 795
Illustration Credits 800

TABLES, FIGURES, AND BOXES

TABLES

I-1   The Virginia Plan, the New Jersey Plan, and the Constitution   7

1-1   The Ratification of the Constitution   14

1-2   The Ratification of the Bill of Rights   16

1-3   Methods of Amending the Constitution   18

1-4   Cases Incorporating Provisions of the Bill of Rights into the Due Process Clause of the Fourteenth Amendment   22

2-1   Precedents Overruled, 1953–1993 Terms   33

2-2   Liberal Voting of the Chief Justices   37

2-3   Votes in Support of and Opposition to Decisions Declaring Legislation Unconstitutional, 1953–1991 Terms   40

2-4   Success Rate of the Solicitor General as an Amicus Curiae, by President, 1952–1990 Terms   47

2-5   Selected Amici Curiae *in Lucas v. South Carolina Coastal Council*   50

2-6   Justices' Citations to Amicus Curiae Briefs, 1953–1991 Terms   51

3-1   A Sample of Congressional Proposals Aimed at Eliminating the U.S. Supreme Court's Appellate Jurisdiction   82

4-1   U. S. Supreme Court Justices with Federal or State Legislative Experience   100

4-2   Duly Elected Members of Congress Excluded   102

4-3   Speech or Debate Clause Cases After *Gravel v. United States*   115

4-4   The Sources of Congressional Power   117

4-5   "Delegated" Powers Held by Major Federal Regulatory Commissions   141

III-1   The Constitutional Allocation of Government Power   188

6-1   A Comparison of Dual and Cooperative Federalism   192

6-2   Doctrinal Cycles of Nation-State Relations   192

6-3   Selected Events Leading to the Civil War   197

6-4   From the Marshall Court to the Taney Court   199

6-5   Supreme Court Federalism Cases Between *National League of Cities* and *Garcia*   211

6-6   Changes in Court Personnel and Nation-State Relations   216

8-1   Federal Tax Revenues: The Impact of the Sixteenth Amendment   269

IV-1   Percentage of Agenda Space Allocated to Economic Cases   289

10-1   The Legal Tools of the Laissez-Faire Courts, 1890s to 1930s: Some Examples   313

10-2   The U.S. Supreme Court: From *Slaughterhouse* to *Mugler*   319

10-3   From *Bunting* to *Adkins*   331

12-1   Major Religious Establishment Cases from *Everson* Through the Warren Court   394

12-2   Religious Establishment Standards Advocated by Members of the Supreme Court, 1971–1993   402

12-3   Aid to Religious Schools: Major Supreme Court Cases, 1947–1994   404

12-4   Variations in Incidence of Bible Reading in Public School by Region, 1960 and 1966   419

13-1   Personnel Changes: *Dennis* to *Yates*   455

13-2   Summary of Legal Standards Governing Free Speech   457

13-3   Public Forum Cases Decided by the Rehnquist Court   475

14-1   *Roth* and *Miller,* Compared   512

15-1   The *Griswold* Splits   535

15-2   The *Roe v. Wade* Trimester Scheme   557

15-3   Cases Involving Consent to Abortions, 1976–1993   560

15-4   Cases Involving Restrictions on Abortions   561

15-5   Diminishing Support for *Roe v. Wade:* The Supreme Court at the Time of *Webster v. Reproductive Health Services*   566

15-6   Approaches to Abortion: The 1994–1995 Supreme Court   569

VI-1   The American Criminal Justice System   574

VII-1   Equal Protection Tests   648

18-1   Admissions Data for the Entering Class of the Medical School of the University of California at Davis, 1973 and 1974   693

19-1   Percentage of Eligible Blacks Registered to Vote, 1940–1984   716

FIGURES

I-1   The Structure and Powers of Government Under the Articles of Confederation   5

I-2   The Separation of Powers/Checks and Balances   9

2-1   Left-Right Continuum of Justices Serving Between 1939 and 1941   36

2-2   Court Decisions on Economics and Civil Liberties Cases, 1953 and 1991 Terms   38

2-3   Provisions of Federal, State, and Local Laws and Ordinances Held Unconstitutional by the Supreme Court, 1789–1992   41

2-4   The Supreme Court and Public Opinion   44

2-5   The Percentage of the Supreme Court's Full Opinion Cases Containing at Least One Amicus Curiae Brief, 1953–1990 Terms   48

II-1   Sequence of Decision Making in Court/ Congress/President Game   59

3-1   The Federal Court System Under the Judiciary Act of 1789   65

3-2   Map of Districts in Tennessee, 1901 and 1950   87

4-1   The History of the First and Second Banks of the United States   121

6-1   Government Spending as a Percentage of GNP, 1929–1991   208

7-1   Public Support for Roosevelt's 1937 Court-Packing Plan   239

IV-1   Percentage of Agenda Space Allocated to Economic Cases   289

V-1   The Supreme Court's Support for First Amendment Claims, 1953–1991 Terms   360

V-2   Percentage of Agenda Space Allocated to Substantive Rights Cases, 1933–1992 Terms   361

12-1   Free Exercise Approaches Advocated by the Justices in *Smith, Lukumi Babalu,* and Beyond   388

12-2   Approval of Supreme Court Decision Preventing Organized Prayer in School   421

15-1   Percentage of Respondents Supporting an Individual's Right to Die   541

15-2   Legislative Action on Abortion Through the Early 1970s   548

15-3   Percentage of Respondents Supporting *Roe v. Wade,* 1974–1991   558

VI-1   Percentage of Supreme Court Criminal Rights Cases Decided in Favor of the Accused, 1953–1991   576

17-1   Support for Capital Punishment, 1971–1991   634

BOXES

1-1 Amendments Proposed by Congress but Rejected by the States 18

1-2 Four Amendments that Overturned Supreme Court Decisions 20

2-1 Hugo Lafayette Black 28

2-2 Amicus Curiae Participation 49

3-1 Jurisdiction of the Federal Courts as Defined in Article III 63

3-2 John Marshall 72

3-3 The Supreme Court and the Political Questions Doctrine: Some Examples 89

3-4 Standing to Sue in the Aftermath of *Flast* 92

3-5 Justice Brandeis, Concurring in *Ashwander v. Tennessee Valley Authority* 94

4-1 Term Limits 104

4-2 Jefferson and Hamilton on the Bank of the United States 119

4-3 Investigations of "Un-Americanism" 129

4-4 Comparison of *Watkins v. United States* and *Barenblatt v. United States* 130

4-5 Court's Decisions in *Panama* and *Schechter Poultry* 139

4-6 Examples of Laws Containing Legislative Vetoes 142

4-7 Recent Separation of Powers Cases 146

5-1 Line of Succession 153

6-1 Roger Brooke Taney 198

6-2 Doubtful Victory 203

6-3 History of the Wage Regulation Leading to *National League of Cities v. Usery* 209

7-1 New Deal Legislation 229

7-2 The Four Horsemen 231

7-3 The Supreme Court and the New Deal 232

7-4 Supreme Court Expansion of the Commerce Powers 247

7-5 The Evolution of Interstate Commerce Doctrine 248

7-6 Supreme Court Decisions Striking Down State Restrictions on Interstate Commerce 257

8-1 Direct and Indirect Taxes: Apportionment Versus Geographical Uniformity 262

9-1 Daniel Webster 298

10-1 Procedural and Substantive Due Process 312

10-2 Louis Dembitz Brandeis 328

12-1 What Did Madison, Jefferson, and the Other Founders Want? 390

12-2 The Roots of the *Lemon* Test 401

12-3 The Scopes Monkey Trial 407

13-1 Oliver Wendell Holmes, Jr. 441

13-2 The American Civil Liberties Union 444

13-3 Hate Speech and the Civil Liberties Community 478

14-1 William Joseph Brennan, Jr. 505

14-2 *Roth, Jacobellis,* and *Memoirs,* Compared 508

15-1 Living Wills 546

15-2 Harry Andrew Blackmun 556

15-3 Proposed Approaches to Restrictive Abortion Laws 564

15-4 Court's Action in *Planned Parenthood of Southeastern Pennsylvania v. Casey* 568

VI-1 Warren Earl Burger 577

17-1 Justices Blackmun and Scalia on the Death Penalty 637

VII-1 The Civil War Amendments 645

VII-2 Major Civil Rights Acts 651

18-1 Thurgood Marshall 660

18-2 Earl Warren 662

18-3 One Child's Simple Justice 663

18-4 Ruth Bader Ginsburg 668

18-5 Affirmative Action/Minority Set-Aside Principles 705

PREFACE

Over the past decade or so, constitutional law texts for political science courses have experienced a radical change. At one time, relatively short volumes, containing either excerpts of landmark cases or narratives of them, dominated the market. Now, large, almost mammoth, books abound—some in a one-volume form, others in two volumes but all designed for a two-semester sequence.

This trend, while fitting compatibly with the needs of many instructors, has bypassed others, including those who teach institutional powers, civil liberties, rights, and justice in a single course and those who prefer a shorter core text. *Constitutional Law for a Changing America: A Short Course* provides an alternative for these instructors.

To accomplish this, *A Short Course* seeks to combine the best features of the traditional, concise volumes: it interweaves excerpts of the Court's most important decisions and narratives of major developments in the law. For example, our discussion of the right to counsel contains the landmark decision, *Gideon v. Wainwright* (1963), along with an account of the critical cases preceding *Gideon*, such as *Powell v. Alabama* (1932), and antedating it, such as *Scott v. Illinois* (1979).

At the same time, we thought it important to move beyond the traditional texts, and write a book that reflected the exciting nature of constitutional law. In so doing, we were not without guidance. Over the past four years, we have been producing *Constitutional Law for a Changing America*, a two-volume book,

which we think provides an accessible yet sophisticated and contemporary take on the subject.

A Short Course, then, while presenting cases and other materials in ways quite distinct from our two-volume book, maintains some of its most desirable features. First, we approach constitutional law, as we do in *Constitutional Law for a Changing America*, from a political science perspective, demonstrating how political and social forces—not just legal factors—influence the development of the law. This approach follows from the fact the justices carry out their duties in the context of the political and social environment that surrounds them. Accordingly, throughout *A Short Course*, we highlight how relevant political events, personnel changes on the Court, interest groups, and even public opinion may have affected the judicial decision-making process.

Second, just as our two-volume set seeks to animate the subject, so too does *A Short Course*. To us and, we suspect, most instructors constitutional law is an exciting subject, but we realize that some students may not (at least initially) share our enthusiasm. So, to whet their appetites, we develop the human side of landmark litigation. Where possible we include photographs of parties to disputes or pictures of places that figured prominently in cases. For each excerpted case, we provide detailed descriptions, in accessible prose, of the disputes that gave rise to the suit. Students are spared the task of digging out facts from Court opinions and can plunge ahead to the ruling with the contours of the dispute firmly in mind. We also present information about the political environment surrounding various cases in tables, figures, and boxes that supplement the narrative and case excerpts.

Third, because many adopters of *Constitutional Law for a Changing America* have commented favorably on the supporting material we provide in those volumes, we maintain that feature in *A Short Course.* Along these lines, Chapter 2, "Approaches to Supreme Court Decision Making," reviews the various legal and extralegal approaches scholars have invoked to understand and explain why the Court reaches the decisions that it does. And the appendices contain a wealth of reference material, including texts of the U.S. Constitution and *Federalist*, No. 78, descriptions of the Court's history and the justices who have served on it, explanations of the Court's procedures and calendar, and even an example of how to brief a case.

Finally, we plan to keep this "short course" up-to-date, just as the volumes of *Constitutional Law for a Changing America* remain wholly contemporary. Our plans now call for maintaining a link, on CQ's Web Site for *A Short Course*, which will take adopters to excerpts of important Court rulings handed down each term. By accessing the site (URL:http://voter96. cqalert.com/cq_mall/books.html), instructors will be able to add newly decided cases to their course syllabi without waiting for us to produce the next edition; and students can download or print out the excerpts for use in their studies. For more information about the Web Site, contact Julianne Rovesti at: (202) 887-6363.

ACKNOWLEDGMENTS

Although *A Short Course* is just now making its appearance, its roots go back to our two-volume book. As a consequence, those who influenced the development of the original version of *Constitutional Law for a Changing America* influenced this project as well. We are particularly grateful to Joanne Daniels and Brenda Carter. Joanne, a former editor at CQ Press, conceived of a constitutional law book that would be accessible, sophisticated, and contemporary. She brought the concept to our attention and helped us develop it. Brenda, our current editor, worked us through the completion of two editions of the two-

volume version of *Constitutional Law for a Changing America* and urged us to go forward with *A Short Course.* Her support for our projects has been constant and strong, and her advice always wise.

Other members of the CQ team also deserve our thanks and praise. Carolyn Goldinger copy edited both editions of the two-volume work and, along the way contributed many ideas for presentation and content that were far superior to our own. By the same token, Nola Healy Lynch, who edited this text, brought new precision and life to our prose. The effectiveness of our work is largely dependent upon the contributions of these two outstanding editors. Finally, David Tarr, Jeanne Ferris, and Megan Campion— all at CQ— brought ideas, enthusiasm, and efficiency to the project.

Over the years, we have also benefited from the suggestions of numerous scholars who read our manuscripts, offered suggestions, and discussed our ideas. We are especially grateful to Judith A. Baer, Ralph Baker, Lawrence Baum, John Brigham, Gregory A. Caldeira, Bradley C. Canon, Robert A. Carp, Phillip J. Cooper, Sue Davis, John Fliter, John B. Gates, James Gibson, Edward Heck, Jack Knight, Joseph A. Kobylka, John A. Maltese, Kevin McGuire, Wayne McIntosh, Susan Mezey, Richard L. Pacelle, Jr., C. K. Rowland, Jeffrey A. Segal, Donald Songer, Harold Spaeth, and Harry P. Stumpf. We are also grateful to those instructors and students who have used *Constitutional Law for a Changing America* and have sent us comments and suggestions.

Finally, we acknowledge the support of our friends and families. We are forever grateful to our former professors for instilling in us their genuine interest in and curiosity about things judicial and legal, and to our parents for their unequivocal support. Walker expresses his special thanks to Vicki, Aimee, Emily and Nicole; and Epstein to her husband Jay for enduring all that he does not have to (but does, anyway), without complaining (much).

Any errors of omission or comission remain our sole responsibility. We encourage students and instructors alike to comment on the book and to inform us of any errors. Contact us at: epstein@wuecon. wustl.edu (Epstein), or postlw@unix.cc.emory.edu (Walker).

PART I
THE U.S. CONSTITUTION

AN INTRODUCTION TO THE U.S. CONSTITUTION

1. THE LIVING CONSTITUTION

2. APPROACHES TO SUPREME COURT DECISION MAKING

AN INTRODUCTION TO THE U.S. CONSTITUTION

ACCORDING TO President Franklin D. Roosevelt, "Like the Bible, it ought to be read again and again."[1] Henry Clay said it was "made not merely for the generation that then existed, but for posterity—unlimited, undefined, endless, perpetual posterity."[2] And William Gladstone once wrote, "I have always regarded [it] as the most remarkable work . . . to have been produced by the human intellect, at a single stroke . . . , in its application to political affairs."[3] Justice Hugo Black carried one with him virtually all the time. The object of all this admiration? The United States Constitution. To be sure, the Constitution has its flaws and its share of detractors, but most Americans take great pride in their charter. And why not? It is, after all, the world's oldest written constitution.

In what follows, we provide a brief introduction to the document—in particular, the circumstances under which it was written, the basic principles underlying it, and some controversies surrounding it. This material may not be new to you, but, as the balance of this book is devoted to the Supreme Court's interpretation of the Constitution and its amendments, we think it is worth reviewing.

THE ROAD TO THE U.S. CONSTITUTION

While the fledgling United States was fighting for its independence from England, it was being run (and the war conducted) by the Continental Congress. Although this body had no formal authority, it met in session from 1774 through the end of the war in 1781, establishing itself as what C. Herman Pritchett called a "de facto" government.[4] But it may have been something more than that. About a year into the Revolutionary War, Congress took steps toward nationhood. On July 2, 1776, it passed a resolution declaring the "United Colonies free and independent states." Two days later, on July 4, it formalized this proclamation in the Declaration of Independence, in which the nation's Founders used the term *United States of America* for the first time.[5] But even before the adoption of the Declaration of Independence, the Continental Congress had "designated a group of delegates to make

---

1. Quoted in Michael Kammen, ed., *The Origins of the American Constitution* (New York: Penguin Books, 1986), vii.

2. Speech to the Senate, January 29, 1850.

3. Letter to the Committee for the Centennial Celebration of the American Constitution, July 20, 1887.

4. *Constitutional Law of the Federal System* (Englewood Cliffs, N.J.: Prentice Hall, 1984), 4.

5. See J. W. Peltason, *Corwin & Peltason's Understanding the Constitution*, 11th ed. (New York: Holt, Rinehart and Winston, 1988), 1.

recommendations for the formation of a national government after independence was achieved."[6] Composed of representatives of each of the thirteen colonies, this committee labored for several months to produce a proposal for a national charter, the Articles of Confederation. Congress passed the proposal and submitted it to the states for ratification in November 1777. Ratification was achieved in March 1781, when Maryland—a two-year holdout—gave its approval.

The Articles of Confederation represented the nation's first written charter, but the document changed the way the government operated very little; it merely "codified the structure and procedures that had emerged in practice in the years since 1774."[7] For example, rather than provide for a compact between the people and the government, the 1781 charter institutionalized "a league of friendship" among the states, one that rested "expressly on state sovereignty."[8] This is not to suggest that the Articles failed to provide for a central government. As we can see in Figure 1-1, which depicts the structure and powers of government, the Articles created a national governing apparatus, however simple and weak. There was a one-house legislature, but no formal federal executive or judiciary. And while the legislature had some power, most notably in the area of foreign affairs, it derived its authority from the states that had created it, not from the people.

Analysts have pointed out the weaknesses of the Articles of Confederation, including the following:

Because it allowed Congress only to "requisition" funds and not to tax, the federal government was virtually broke. Between 1781 and 1783 the national legislature requested $10 million from the states and received only $1.5 million.[9] Given the foreign debts the United States had accumulated during the war, this problem was particularly troublesome.

Because Congress lacked a concrete way to regulate foreign commerce, "treaties between foreign countries and the Confederation were of little value." Some European nations (for example, England and Spain) took advantage by imposing "trade restrictions that narrowed the markets for American exports."[10]

Because the government lacked coercive power over the states, mutual cooperation among them quickly dissipated. They engaged in trading practices that hurt one another economically. In short, the states acted more like thirteen separate countries than a union or even a confederation.

Because the exercise of most national authority required the approval of nine states and the passage of amendments required unanimity, the Articles stymied Congress. One scholar has noted, "Given the divisions among the states at the time, the approval of nine states for any action of substance was rare, and the required unanimity for amendment was never obtained."[11]

Clearly, the United States had problems under the Articles. But scholar Lance Banning points out that "historians have long since given up the old idea that the Confederation years were a period of governmental folly and unmixed disaster."[12] Indeed, under the Articles, the government accomplished many notable objectives: it brought the Revolutionary War to a successful end and paved the way for the 1783 Treaty of Paris, "which gave the United States de jure the status of a nation."[13] Moreover, the charter served an important purpose. It "preserved the idea of a federal na-

6. Thomas G. Walker, *American Politics and the Constitution* (North Scituate, Mass.: Duxbury Press, 1978), 10.

7. Lance Banning, "From Confederation to Constitution: The Revolutionary Context of the Great Convention," in *This Constitution: Our Enduring Legacy* (Washington, D.C.: Congressional Quarterly, 1986), 30.

8. Peltason, *Understanding the Constitution*, 9.

9. Pritchett, *Constitutional Law of the Federal System*, 6.

10. Daniel A. Farber and Suzanna Sherry, *A History of the American Constitution* (St. Paul, Minn.: West, 1990), 24–25.

11. Walker, *American Politics*, 11.

12. "From Confederation to Constitution," 30.

13. Peltason, *Understanding the Constitution*, 10.

FIGURE I-1   The Structure and Powers of Government Under the Articles of Confederation

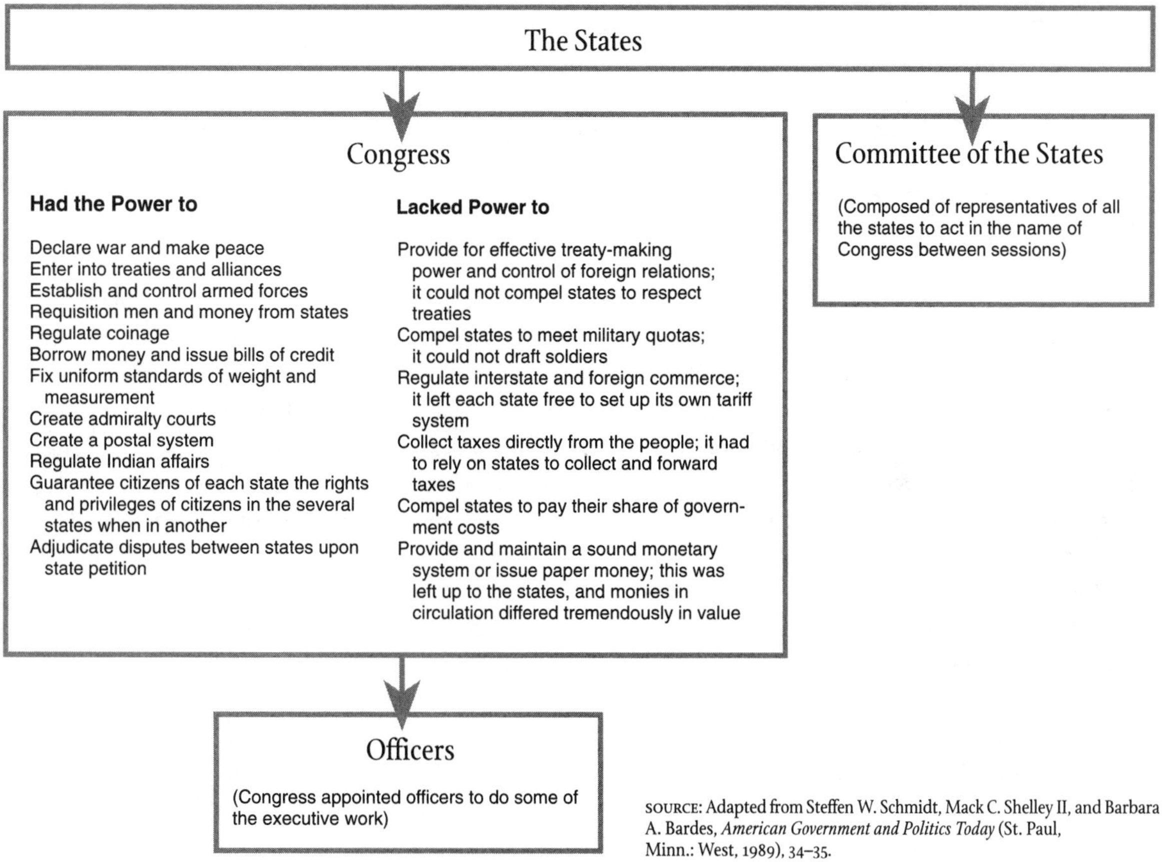

The States

Congress

Had the Power to

Declare war and make peace
Enter into treaties and alliances
Establish and control armed forces
Requisition men and money from states
Regulate coinage
Borrow money and issue bills of credit
Fix uniform standards of weight and
    measurement
Create admiralty courts
Create a postal system
Regulate Indian affairs
Guarantee citizens of each state the rights
    and privileges of citizens in the several
    states when in another
Adjudicate disputes between states upon
    state petition

Lacked Power to

Provide for effective treaty-making
    power and control of foreign relations;
    it could not compel states to respect
    treaties
Compel states to meet military quotas;
    it could not draft soldiers
Regulate interstate and foreign commerce;
    it left each state free to set up its own tariff
    system
Collect taxes directly from the people; it had
    to rely on states to collect and forward
    taxes
Compel states to pay their share of govern-
    ment costs
Provide and maintain a sound monetary
    system or issue paper money; this was
    left up to the states, and monies in
    circulation differed tremendously in value

Committee of the States

(Composed of representatives of all
the states to act in the name of
Congress between sessions)

Officers

(Congress appointed officers to do some of
the executive work)

SOURCE: Adapted from Steffen W. Schmidt, Mack C. Shelley II, and Barbara A. Bardes, *American Government and Politics Today* (St. Paul, Minn.: West, 1989), 34–35.

tional union until national wisdom could adopt a more efficient system."[14]

Nevertheless, the shortcomings of the Articles were becoming more and more apparent to some citizens. By the mid-1780s, in fact, several dissidents, including James Madison of Virginia and Alexander Hamilton of New York, had held a series of meetings to arouse interest in revising the system of government. At one such meeting in Annapolis in September 1786, they urged the states to send delegations to another meet-

ing scheduled for the following May in Philadelphia. Their plea could not have come at a more opportune time. Just the month before, in August 1786, a former Revolutionary War captain, Daniel Shays, had led disgruntled and armed farmers to rebellion in Massachusetts. They were protesting the poor state of the economy, which was taking its toll on farmers, who were jailed for not paying their debts.

Shays's Rebellion was suppressed by state forces, but it was seen as yet another sign that the Articles needed amending. Congress formalized the Annapolis call in February 1787 when it "passed a resolution calling for a convention to reevaluate the state of the

14. J. T. Keenan, *The Constitution of the United States* (Chicago: Dorsey Press, 1988), 11.

national government." [15] It was clear, however, that Congress did not want a whole new charter; in fact, the resolution stated that the delegates were to meet "for the sole and express purpose of revising the Articles of Confederation."

Despite these words, the fifty-five delegates who gathered in Philadelphia quickly realized that they would be doing more than "revising" the Articles: they would be framing a new charter. After examining the records of the convention, scholars Daniel Farber and Suzanna Sherry concluded, "That many delegates were contemplating more than merely revising or amending the Articles is clear throughout the Convention." [16]

We can attribute this change in purpose, at least in part, to the Virginia delegation. When it arrived in Philadelphia on May 14, 1787, the day the convention was supposed to start, only the Pennsylvania delegation was already there. Although lacking a quorum, the Virginia contingent used the eleven-day delay to its advantage, crafting a series of proposals. And, as illustrated in Table 1-1, its "hopes" for the meeting represented far more than just a revision in the existing structure. The Virginians called for a wholly new one, composed of a strong three-branch national government empowered to lead the nation.

Called the Virginia Plan, these proposals were formally introduced to the delegates May 29, just four days after the convention began. And, although it was the target of a counterproposal submitted by the New Jersey delegation, the Virginia Plan set the tone for the convention. It served as the basis for many of the ensuing debates and, as we shall see, for the Constitution itself.

The delegates had much to accomplish during the four-month convention period. Arguments between large states and small states over the structure of the new government and its relationship to the states threatened to deadlock the meeting. In fact, it is al-most a miracle that the delegates were able to frame a new constitution and do so in just a few months. One can speculate that the Founders succeeded in part because they were able to close their meetings to the public, a feat almost inconceivable today. A contemporary convention of the states would be a media circus. Moreover, it is hard to imagine that delegates from fifty states could agree even to frame a new charter, much less do it in four months.

The difficulties facing such an enterprise bring up an important issue. A modern constitutional convention would be hard pressed to reach consensus because the delegates would bring with them diverse interests and aims. What about back in 1787? Who were the Framers and what were their motives? If, as had been recorded, they were such a fractious bunch, how could they have reached accord so rapidly?

These questions have been the subject of lively debates among scholars. Many agree with historian Melvin I. Urofsky, who wrote of the Constitutional Convention, "Few gatherings in the history of this or any other country could boast such a concentration of talent." And, "despite [the Framers'] average age of forty-two [they] had extensive experience in government and were fully conversant with political theories of the Enlightenment." [17] The Framers were an impressive group. Among them were many future leaders: two U.S. presidents, sixteen governors, and two Supreme Court chief justices. Thirty-three had served in the Revolutionary War, forty-two had attended the Continental Congress, and two had signed the Declaration of Independence. [18]

Others would take issue with Urofsky's statement. Because the Framers were a relatively homogeneous lot—all white men, many of whom had been educated at the country's best schools—some suggest that the document they produced was biased in various ways. For example, in 1987 Justice Thurgood Marshall

---

15. Walker, *American Politics*, 13.

16. *A History of the American Constitution*, 37.

17. *A March of Liberty* (New York: Knopf, 1988), 89.

18. Paul E. Johnson et al., *American Government* (Boston: Houghton Mifflin, 1990), 43.

TABLE I-1 The Virginia Plan, the New Jersey Plan, and the Constitution

Item	Virginia Plan	New Jersey Plan	Constitution
Legislature	Two houses	One house	Two houses
Legislative representation	Both houses based on population	Equal for each state	One house based on population; one house with two votes from each state
Legislative power	Veto authority over state legislation	Authority to levy taxes and regulate commerce	Authority to levy tariffs and regulate commerce; authority to compel state compliance with national policies
Executive	Single; elected by legislature for a single term	Plural; removable by majority of state legislatures	Single; chosen by electoral college; removal by national legislature
Courts	National judiciary elected by legislature	No provision	Supreme Court appointed by executive, confirmed by Senate

SOURCE: Paul Johnson et al., *American Government* (Boston: Houghton Mifflin, 1990), 47.

said that the Constitution was "defective from the start," that its first words—"We the People"—excluded "the majority of American citizens," because it left out blacks and women. He further alleged that the Framers "could not have imagined, nor would they have accepted, that the document they were drafting would one day be construed by a Supreme Court to which had been appointed a woman and the descendent of an African slave."[19] Another point of view is expressed by historian Charles Beard in his controversial work, *An Economic Interpretation of the Constitution of the United States,* which depicts the Framers as self-serving. Beard says the Constitution was an "economic document" devised to protect the "property interests" of those who wrote it.

Various scholars have refuted these allegations; Beard's work, in particular, has been largely negated by other studies.[20] Still, by today's standards it is im-

possible to deny that the original Constitution was a racist and sexist document or that the Framers wrote it in a way that benefited them.

Given these charges, how has the Constitution survived for so long, particularly as the U.S. population has become increasingly heterogeneous? The answer lies in part with the Supreme Court, which generally has analyzed the document in light of its contemporary context. That is, some justices have viewed the Constitution as a living document and have sought to adapt it to the times. In addition, the Founders provided for an amending process to keep the document alive. That the Constitution can be altered to fit changing needs and expectations is obviously important. For example, the original document held a slave to be three-fifths of a person for the purposes of representation; as a citizen, a slave had no rights at all. In the aftermath of the Civil War, the country recognized the outrageousness of such a provision and added three amendments to alter the status of blacks and provide full equality under law.

This is not to suggest that controversies surrounding the Constitution no longer exist. To the contrary,

19. Quoted in the *Washington Post*, May 7, 1987.
20. See, for example, Robert E. Brown's *Charles Beard and the Constitution* (Princeton, N.J.: Princeton University Press, 1956). Brown concludes that "we would be doing a grave injustice to the political sagacity of the Founding Fathers if we assumed that property or personal gain was their only motive" (p. 198).

charges abound that the document has retained an elitist or otherwise biased flavor. Some argue that the amending process is too cumbersome, that it is too slanted toward majority will. Others point to the Supreme Court as the culprit, asserting that its interpretation of the document—particularly at certain points in history—has reinforced the biases of the Framers.

Throughout this book, you will have many opportunities to evaluate this controversy. It will be especially evident in cases involving economic and civil liberties—those that ask the Court, in some sense, to adjudicate claims between the privileged and the underdogs in society. For now, let us consider some of the basic features of that controversial document, the U.S. Constitution.

THE UNDERLYING PRINCIPLES OF THE CONSTITUTION

Table 1-1 sets forth the basic proposals considered at the convention and how they got translated into the Constitution. What the table does not show are the fundamental principles underlying, though not necessarily explicit in, the Constitution. Three are particularly important: the separation of powers/checks and balances doctrine, federalism, and individual rights and liberties.

Separation of Powers/Checks and Balances

One of the fundamental weaknesses of the Articles of Confederation was its failure to establish a strong and authoritative federal government. It created a Congress, but that body had few powers, and those it did have were kept in check by the states. The new Constitution overcame this deficiency by creating a national government with three branches—the legislature, the executive, and the judiciary—and by providing each with significant power and authority over its sphere. Moreover, the three newly devised institutions were constitutionally and politically independ-

dent from one another.[21] Urofsky wrote, "Perhaps the most striking feature of the Constitution was how extensively it implemented the prevailing notions of separation of powers. Unlike the Articles and most state constitutions, clear lines divided the executive, legislative, and judicial functions."[22]

The specific powers that each branch was given are spelled out in Articles I, II, and III of the Constitution. Section 8 of Article I is especially explicit, empowering Congress to lay and collect taxes, to regulate commerce, and so forth. Nonetheless, many questions have arisen over the scope of these powers as they are wielded by all three institutions. Consider a few examples:

Article I provides Congress with various authority over the U.S. military, for example, to provide and maintain a navy, to raise and support armies. But it does not specifically empower Congress to initiate and operate a draft. Does that omission mean that Congress may not do so?

Article II provides the president with the power to "nominate, and by and with the Advice and Consent of the Senate, [to] appoint . . . Officers of the United States," but it does not specifically empower the president to fire such officers. May the president independently dismiss appointees or is the "advice and consent" of the Senate also necessary?

Article III provides the federal courts with the authority to hear cases involving federal laws. But it does not specifically empower these courts to strike down such laws if they are incompatible with the Constitution. Does that mean federal courts lack the power of judicial review?

These examples illustrate just a handful of the questions involving institutional powers the U.S. Supreme Court has addressed.

But institutional powers are only one side of the coin. The other side—constraints on those powers—

---

21. Peltason, *Understanding the Constitution*, 21.
22. *A March of Liberty*, 94.

FIGURE I-2 The Separation of Powers/Checks and Balances

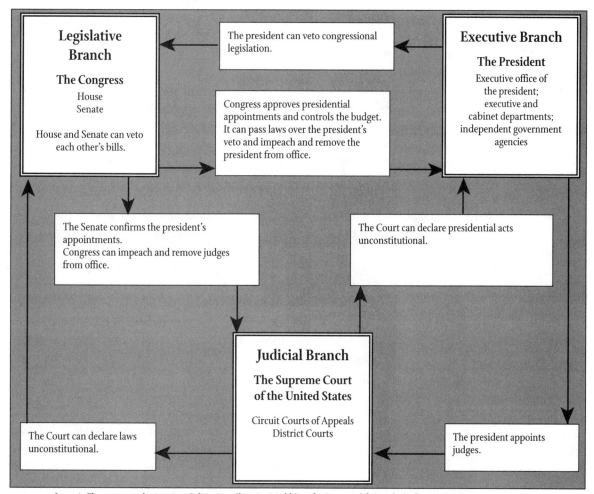

SOURCE: Janet A. Flammang et al., *American Politics in a Changing World* (Pacific Grove, Calif.: Brooks/Cole, 1990), 41.

is also worthy of consideration. The Framers not only gave each branch distinct authority, as depicted in Figure I-2, but also they worked out an intricate system of checks and balances. Because they "feared concentration of powers in a single branch," they provided each branch with mechanisms to rein in the others' authority.[23] They also made the institutions responsible to different sets of constituencies.

23. Peltason, *Understanding the Constitution*, 21.

Although this system has worked, at the same time it has produced numerous constitutional questions. Many of those questions come to the fore when the United States has a politically divided government—for example, a Republican president and a Democratic Congress—and one branch or the other is seeking to assert its authority. What is truly interesting about such cases is that they continue to appear at the Court's doorstep; despite the passage of more than 200 years, the justices have yet to resolve all the "big" constitutional questions. During the past few decades the Court addressed many, including these:

May Congress call for the creation of a commission (whose members, including judges, would be appointed by the president) that would create mandatory sentencing guidelines for federal judges and that would be located within the judicial branch?

May Congress write into laws legislative veto provisions by which to nullify actions of the executive branch?

May Congress pass legislation requiring the attorney general to appoint a special prosecutor to investigate allegations of wrongdoing within the executive branch?

In the cases and narrative that follow, you will see how the Court has addressed these questions.

Federalism

Another weakness of the Articles of Confederation was the way it envisioned the relationship between the federal government and the states. As already noted, the national legislature was not only weak, it was more or less an apparatus controlled by the states. The states had set up the Articles of Confederation and, therefore, they empowered Congress.

The U.S. Constitution overcame this liability in two ways. First, it created three branches of government, all with significant authority. Second, it set out a plan of operation for the exercise of state and federal power. Called federalism, it works today under the following constitutional guidelines:

The Constitution grants certain legislative, executive, and judicial powers to the national government. Those not granted to the national government are reserved to the states.

The Constitution makes the national government supreme. The Constitution, all laws passed in pur-

suance thereof, and treaties are the supreme law of the land. American citizens, most of whom are also state citizens, owe their primary allegiance to the national government; officers of the state governments owe the same allegiance.

The Constitution denies some powers to both national and state governments, some only to the national government, and still others only to the state governments.[24]

By making the national government supreme in its spheres of authority, the Constitution corrected a flaw of the Articles of Confederation. Nevertheless, and in spite of the best efforts of the Framers to spell out the nature of federal–state relations, the Constitution left open many questions. For example, the Constitution authorizes Congress to lay and collect taxes but does not specify whether the states may themselves exercise powers that are reserved to the federal government. States are not expressly prohibited from collecting taxes. Therefore, may Congress and the states both operate taxing systems?

As you know, the answer to this question is yes. However, why that is the case is not explicitly answered by the Constitution. As a result, it has been left largely to elected government bodies through legislation and to the courts through interpretation to define the specifics of state–federal relations. The Supreme Court, in particular, by defining the boundaries of federal and state power, has helped shape the contours of American federalism.

Individual Rights and Liberties

For many of the Framers, the most important purpose of the new Constitution was to safeguard individual rights and liberties. That is why they created a limited government that would wield only those powers delegated to it and would be checked by its own

---

24. Adapted from ibid., 16–17.

component parts—the states and the people. The majority of the Founders felt it unnecessary to load the Constitution with specific individual rights, such as those later spelled out in the Bill of Rights. As Alexander Hamilton put it, "The Constitution is itself . . . a Bill of Rights." Under the Constitution the government could exercise only those functions specifically bestowed upon it; all other rights remained with the people. Hamilton and others felt that adding a list of rights might even be dangerous because it inevitably would leave some out.

For this reason and possibly others—for example, some argue that the Framers were too exhausted to continue—the Constitution was sent to the states without a bill of rights. That omission became the source of major controversy and served as the vehicle by which states exacted a compromise over the Constitution's ratification.

In the next chapter we describe that compromise, which took the form of the first ten amendments to the Constitution—the Bill of Rights. It is enough to note for now that the eventual ratification of the Bill of Rights, on December 15, 1791, quieted those who had voiced objections. But the guarantees it contains continue to serve as fodder for debate and, most relevant here, for Supreme Court litigation. Many of these debates involve the construct of specific guarantees, such as free speech and free exercise of religion, under which individuals seek relief when governments allegedly infringe upon their rights. They also involve clashes between the authority of the government to protect the safety, health, morals, and general welfare of citizens and the right of individuals not to be deprived of their liberty without due process of law. For example, may government force employers to pay their employees a certain wage or does that requirement infringe on the employer's liberty? The answer to this question and others like it reveal the contours of government power in relation to individual rights.

CHAPTER 1

THE LIVING CONSTITUTION

IN MAY OF 1787 the Founders of the United States met in Philadelphia "for the sole and express purpose of revising the Articles of Confederation," but within a month they had dramatically altered their mission. Viewing the articles as unworkable, they decided to start afresh. What emerged just four months later, on September 17, was an entirely new government scheme embodied in the U.S. Constitution.

The Framers were quite pleased with their handiwork; when they had finished, they "adjourned to City Tavern, dined together and took cordial leave of each other."[1] After the long, hot summer in Philadelphia, most of the delegates left for home, confident that the new document would receive speedy passage by the states. At first, it appeared as if their optimism was justified. As Table 1-1 depicts, before the year was out four states had ratified the Constitution—three by unanimous votes. But after January 1788, "the pace . . . slowed considerably."[2] By this time, a movement opposed to ratification was growing and marshaling arguments to deter state convention delegates. Most of all, these opponents, the so-called Anti-Federalists, feared the Constitution's new balance of power. They believed that strong state governments provided the only "sure defense of their liberties against a potentially tyrannical central authority," and that the Constitution tipped the scales in favor of federal power.[3] These fears were countered by the Federalists, who favored passage of the Constitution. Although their arguments and writings took many forms, among the most important was a series of eighty-five articles published in New York newspapers under the pen name Publius. Written by John Jay, James Madison, and Alexander Hamilton, *The Federalist Papers* continue to provide insight into the objectives and intent of the Founders.[4]

Debates between the Federalists and their opponents often were highly philosophical in tone, with emphasis on the appropriate roles and powers of national institutions. In the states, however, ratification drives were full of the stuff of ordinary politics. Massachusetts provides a case in point. According to one account, the following events transpired there:

Of the 355 delegates, 60 percent or more probably came to Boston on January 9 opposed. If the Federalists were to have any chance at all, they would need the hearty support of Samuel Adams, their already legendary Revolutionary

---

1. *1787*, compiled by historians of the Independence National Historical Park (New York: Exeter Books, 1987), 191.

2. Daniel A. Farber and Suzanna Sherry, *A History of the American Constitution* (St. Paul, Minn.: West, 1990), 177.

3. Melvin I. Urofsky, *A March of Liberty* (New York: Knopf, 1988), 96–98.

4. Clinton Rossiter, ed. (New York: New American Library, 1961).

TABLE 1-1 The Ratification of the Constitution

State	Date of Action	Decision	Margin
Delaware	December 7, 1787	ratified	30:0
Pennsylvania	December 12, 1787	ratified	46:23
New Jersey	December 18, 1787	ratified	38:0
Georgia	December 31, 1787	ratified	26:0
Connecticut	January 8, 1788	ratified	128:40
Massachusetts	February 6, 1788	ratified with amendments	187:168
Maryland	April 26, 1788	ratified	63:11
South Carolina	May 23, 1788	ratified with amendments	149:73
New Hampshire	June 21, 1788	ratified with amendments	57:47
Virginia	June 25, 1788	ratified with amendments	89:79
New York	July 26, 1788	ratified with amendments	30:27
North Carolina	August 2, 1788	rejected	184:84
	November 21, 1789	ratified with amendments	194:77
Rhode Island	May 29, 1790	ratified with amendments	34:32

SOURCE: Daniel A. Farber and Suzanna Sherry, *A History of the American Constitution* (St. Paul, Minn.: West, 1990), 216.

hero, and of governor John Hancock, of Declaration immortality. Adams was tepid; Hancock, aloof and cool, preferring to wait and see which way the political tides might flow.

After three weeks of heated debate a delegation headed by Adams climbed Beacon Hill to knock on the door of the wealthy and gouty Hancock. They proposed that the governor declare for ratification on condition that a series of amendments be tacked on for the consideration of the Congress.

The price for Hancock's support? The presidency, if Virginia failed to ratify or if Washington declined to serve. Otherwise, the vice presidency or, some say, the promise of Bowdoin's support in the next governor's race.

Hancock agreed to the bribe and, his feet swathed in bandages, was carried theatrically to the rostrum to make his "Conciliatory Proposition" as though it were his own brainchild. Adams, still the darling of both sides, seconded the resolution to consider the amendments, and a few days later added several of his own.

The Constitution carried on February 6, 187 to 168, making Massachusetts the sixth state to ratify.[5]

This compromise, the call for a bill of rights, caught on. As one scholar noted, "It worked so well that Madison now advocated its use wherever the vote promised to be close."[6] As it turned out, he and other Federalists needed to do so quite often: as Table 1-1 indicates, of the nine states ratifying after January 1788, seven recommended that the new Congress consider amendments. Indeed, New York and Virginia probably would not have agreed to the Constitution without such an addition; Virginia actually called for a second constitutional convention for that purpose. Other states began devising their own wish lists—enumerations of specific rights they wanted put into the document.

Why were states so reluctant to ratify the Constitution without a bill of rights? Some viewed the new government scheme with downright suspicion, bemoaning "the great and extensive powers granted to the new government over the lives, liberties, and property of every citizen."[7] But more tended to agree with Thomas Jefferson's sentiment, expressed in a letter to Madison:

5. J. T. Keenan, *The Constitution of the United States: An Unfolding Story*, 2d ed. (Chicago: Dorsey Press, 1988), 32–33.

6. Alpheus T. Mason, *The States Rights Debate*, 2d ed. (New York: Oxford University Press, 1972), 92–93.

7. Address of the Albany Antifederal Committee, April 26, 1788, quoted in Farber and Sherry, *A History of the American Constitution*, 180.

I like the organization of the government into legislative, Judiciary, and Executive. . . . I will now add what I do not like . . . the omission of a bill of rights providing clearly and without the aid of sophisms for freedom of religion, freedom of press, protection against standing armies. . . . [8]

What Jefferson's remark suggests is that many thought well of the new system of government, but were troubled by the lack of a declaration of rights. Remember that at the time, Americans clearly understood concepts of *fundamental* and *inalienable* rights, those that inherently belonged to them and that no government could deny. Even England, the country with which they had fought a war for their freedom, had such guarantees. The Magna Carta of 1215 and the Bill of Rights of 1689 gave Britons the right to a jury trial, to protection against cruel and unusual punishment, and so forth. Moreover, after the Revolution, virtually every state constitution included a philosophical statement about the relationship between citizens and their government and/or a listing of fifteen to twenty inalienable rights such as religious freedom and electoral independence. Small wonder that the call for such a statement or enumeration of rights became a battle cry for those opposed to ratification. It was so widespread, we might ask why the Framers failed to include it in the original document. Did they not anticipate the reaction?

Records of the 1787 constitutional debates indicate that, in fact, the delegates considered specific individual guarantees on at least four separate occasions.[9] On August 20 Charles Pinckney submitted a proposal that included several guarantees, such as freedom of the press and the eradication of religious tests, but the various committees never considered his plan. On three separate occasions toward the closing days of the convention, September 12, 14, and 16, some tried, again without success, to convince the delegates to enumerate specific guarantees. At one point, George Mason averred that a bill of rights "would give great quiet to the people; and with the aid of the state delegations, a bill might be prepared in a few hours." This motion was unanimously defeated by those remaining in attendance. On the convention's last day, Edmund Randolph made a desperate plea that the delegates allow the states to submit amendments and then convene a second convention. To this, Pinckney responded, "Conventions are serious things, and ought not to be repeated."

Why these suggestions were received unenthusiastically by the majority of delegates is a matter of scholarly debate. Some suggest that the pleas came too late, that the Framers wanted to complete their mission by September 15 and "were not physically or psychologically prepared to stay on in Philadelphia even an extra day."[10] Others disagree, arguing that the Framers were more concerned with the structure of government than with individual rights,[11] and that the plan they devised—one based on enumerated, not unlimited, powers—would foreclose the need for a bill of rights. Hamilton wrote, "The Constitution is itself . . . a Bill of Rights." Under it the government could exercise only those functions specifically bestowed upon it; all remaining rights lay with the people. He also asserted that "independent of those which relate to the structure of government," the Constitution did, in fact, contain some of the more necessary specific guarantees. For example, Article I, Section 9, prohibits bills of attainder, ex post facto laws, and the suspension of writs of habeas corpus. Hamilton and others further argued that the specification of rights was not only unnecessary, but also could "even be dangerous" because no such listing could be inclusive.[12] As James Wilson asserted before the Pennsylvania ratifying convention:

8. Quoted in Alpheus T. Mason and D. Grier Stephenson, Jr., *American Constitutional Law,* 10th ed. (Englewood Cliffs, N.J.: Prentice Hall, 1993), 349.

9. The following discussion relies on Farber and Sherry, *A History of the American Constitution,* 221–222. This book reprints verbatim debates over the Constitution and the Bill of Rights.

10. *1787,* 183.

11. Gerald Gunther, *Individual Rights in Constitutional Law,* 4th ed. (Mineola, N.Y.: Foundation Press, 1986), 72.

12. *The Federalist Papers,* No. 84, Isaac Kramnick, ed. (New York: Penguin Books, 1987), 477, 473, 476.

A Bill of Rights annexed to a constitution is an *enumeration of the powers* reserved. If we attempt an enumeration, everything that is not enumerated is presumed to be given. The consequence is, that an imperfect enumeration would throw all implied power into the scale of government, and the rights of the people would be rendered incomplete.[13]

Despite these misgivings, the reality of the political environment caused many Federalists to change their views on the inclusion of a bill of rights. They realized that if they did not accede to state demands, either the Constitution would not be ratified or a new convention would be necessary. Since neither alternative was particularly attractive, they agreed to amend the Constitution as soon as the new government came into power.

One month after the start of the First Congress, in May 1789, Madison announced to the House of Representatives that he would draft a bill of rights and submit it within the coming month. As it turned out, the task proved a bit more onerous than Madison thought; the states had submitted nearly 200 amendments for Congress's consideration, and some of them would have decreased significantly the power of the national government.[14] After sifting through these lists, Madison at first thought it might be best to incorporate the amendments into the Constitution's text, but he soon changed his mind.[15] Instead, he presented the House with the following statement, echoing the views expressed in the Declaration of Independence: "That there be prefixed to the Constitution a declaration, that all power is originally vested in, and consequently derived from, the people."[16]

The legislators rejected this proposal, preferring a listing of rights to a philosophical statement. Madison returned to his task, eventually fashioning a list of seventeen amendments. When he took it back to the

TABLE 1-2 The Ratification of the Bill of Rights

State	Date of Action	Ratified	Rejected
New Jersey	November 20, 1789	I, III–XII	II
Maryland	December 19, 1789	I–XII	
North Carolina	December 22, 1789	I–XII	
South Carolina	January 19, 1790	I–XII	
New Hampshire	January 25, 1790	I, III–XII	II
Delaware	January 28, 1790	II–XII	I
New York	February 24, 1790	I, III–XII	II
Pennsylvania	March 10, 1790	III–XII	I, II
Rhode Island	June 7, 1790	I, III–XII	II
Vermont	November 3, 1791	I–XII	
Virginia	November 3, 1791	I	
	December 15, 1791	II–XII	
Massachusetts	March 2, 1939	III–XII	I, II
Georgia	March 18, 1939	III–XII	I, II
Connecticut	April 19, 1939	III–XII	I, II

SOURCE: Daniel A. Farber and Suzanna Sherry, *A History of the American Constitution* (St. Paul, Minn.: West , 1990), 244.

NOTE: Roman numerals in the "Ratified" and "Rejected" columns refer to the original articles, not those within the eventual Bill of Rights.

House, however, the list was greeted with suspicion and opposition. Some members of Congress, even those who had argued for a bill of rights, now did not want to be bothered with the proposals, insisting that they had more important business to settle. One suggested that other nations would not see the United States "as a serious trading partner as it was still tinkering with its constitution instead of organizing its government."[17]

Finally, in July 1789, after Madison had prodded and even begged, the House considered his proposals. A special committee scrutinized them and reported a few days later, and the House adopted, with some modification, Madison's seventeen amendments. The Senate, however, considered some and rejected others; by the time President George Washington sub-

13. Quoted in Farber and Sherry, *A History of the American Constitution*, 224.
14. Urofsky, *March of Liberty*, 108.
15. C. Herman Pritchett, *The American Constitution* (New York: McGraw-Hill, 1959), 368.
16. Quoted in Urofsky, *March of Liberty*, 108.

17. Quoted in Farber and Sherry, *A History of the American Constitution*, 231.

mitted the Bill of Rights to the states on October 2, 1789, only twelve remained.[18]

As shown in Table 1-2, the states ratified ten of those twelve. The amendments that did not receive approval were the first two on the list (the original Articles I and II). Article I concerned the number of representatives:

After the first enumeration required by the first article of the Constitution, there shall be one Representative for every thirty thousand, until the number shall amount to one hundred, after which the proportion shall be so regulated by Congress, that there shall be not less than one hundred Representatives, nor less than one Representative for every forty thousand persons, until the number of Representatives shall amount to two hundred; after which the proportion shall be so regulated by Congress, that there shall not be less than two hundred Representatives, nor more than one Representative for every fifty thousand persons.

Article II contained the following provision:

No law varying the compensation for the services of the Senators and Representatives shall take effect, until an election of Representatives shall have intervened.

This article also failed to garner sufficient support from the states in the 1790s and did not become a part of the Bill of Rights. Unlike the original Article I, however, this provision eventually took its place in the Constitution. In 1992, more than 200 years after the amendment was first proposed, it was ratified by the states, thereby becoming the Twenty-seventh Amendment to the U.S. Constitution.

Why the states originally refused to pass this amendment, along with the original Article I, is something of a mystery, for few records of state ratification proceedings exist. What we do know is that two years later, on December 15, 1791, when Virginia ratified, the Bill of Rights became part of the U.S. Constitution.

THE AMENDMENT PROCESS

That Congress proposed and the states ratified the first ten amendments to the Constitution in three years is truly remarkable: since then only seventeen others have been added! Undoubtedly, this reticence would have pleased the writers of the Constitution. They wanted to create a government that would have some permanence, but they also recognized the need for flexibility. One of the major flaws in the Articles of Confederation, some thought, was the amending process: changing that document required the unanimous approval of the thirteen colonies. The Framers imagined an amending procedure that would be "bendable but not trendable, tough but not insurmountable, responsive to genuine waves of popular desire, yet impervious to self-serving campaigns of factional groups."[19] Hence, in Article V, they specified procedures for altering the Constitution (*see Table 1-3*). The Constitution can be amended in four ways. But, perhaps because the First Congress chose the congressional proposing and state legislative ratification method for the Bill of Rights, that way has been used most often. Indeed, all but the Twenty-first Amendment, which repealed prohibition, followed that approach.

That only twenty-seven amendments have made it through Congress and the states and that twenty-six have done so through one route should not be taken to mean that other amendments or other approaches have not been proposed. In fact, through 1995 Congress had considered more than 10,000 amendments and sent 33 of them to the states (*see Box 1-1*). Attempts at using other proposal methods are not unusual.[20] At present, the states are only two votes short of requesting Congress to create a national convention to consider a balanced budget amendment. And, as of this

18. Among those rejected was the one Madison "prized above all others": that the states would have to abide by many of the enumerated guarantees.

19. Keenan, *The Constitution of the United States*, 41.
20. Perhaps the most widely reported was Sen. Everett Dirksen's effort to get the states to request a national convention with the purpose of overturning *Reynolds v. Sims*, the Supreme Court's 1964 reapportionment decision. He failed, by one state, to do so.

TABLE 1-3 Methods of Amending the Constitution

Proposed by	Ratified by	Used for
Two-thirds vote in both houses of Congress	State legislatures in three-fourths of the states	26 amendments
Two-thirds vote in both houses of Congress	Ratifying conventions in three-fourths of the states	1 amendment (21st)
Constitutional convention (called at the request of two-thirds of the states)	State legislatures in three-fourths of the states	Never used
Constitutional convention (called at the request of two-thirds of the states)	Ratifying conventions in three-fourths of the states	Never used

---

BOX 1-1 AMENDMENTS PROPOSED BY CONGRESS BUT REJECTED BY THE STATES

■ The first would have empowered Congress to regulate the proportion of members of the House of Representatives once the population went beyond 100,000 persons per Representative.

■ This amendment, proposed in the second session of the 11th Congress, reflected a suspicion of all things royal dating back to Plymouth Rock. It would have stripped citizenship from anyone who "shall accept, claim, receive or retain any title of nobility or honour, or shall, without the consent of Congress, accept and retain any present pension, office or emolument of any kind whatever, from emperor, king, prince or foreign power. . . ."

■ On March 2, 1861, two days before Abraham Lincoln's inauguration, proslavery forces gathered the votes to propose an amendment that would have "settled" the issue of slavery. It read: "No Amendment shall be made to the Constitution which will authorize or give to Congress the power to abolish or interfere, within any state, with the domestic institutions thereof, including that of persons held to labor or service by the laws of said State."

Five weeks later, Union forces at Fort Sumter were fired upon, and a Civil War was under way over slavery, a domestic institution concerning persons held to labor or service by the laws of certain states.

■ The Child Labor Amendment was proposed June 2, 1924. It would have given Congress power to "limit, regulate, and prohibit the labor of persons under 18 years of age." Section 2 would have suspended any state laws that might contravene regulations established by Congress.

Subsequent federal controls accepted by the Supreme Court, such as the Fair Labor Standards Act of 1938, have pretty much obviated the need for such an amendment. However, a retired top-ranking labor leader said in 1986 that President Ronald Reagan's proposal to establish a lowered minimum wage to help unskilled teenagers obtain summer employment was "proof that a Child Labor Amendment is still needed."

■ The Equal Rights Amendment (ERA), stating that "equality of rights under the law shall not be denied or abridged by the United States or by any State on account of sex," was proposed in March 1972. A seven-year deadline was given an unprecedented three-year extension. That deadline expired in 1982.

■ An amendment to give the District of Columbia representation in Congress was proposed by Congress in 1978. It read: "For purposes of representation in the Congress, election of the President and Vice President, and Article V of this Constitution, the District [of Columbia] . . . shall be treated as though it were a State."

The amendment also would have obviated the Twenty-third Amendment, which gave D.C. residents the right to vote in presidential elections. The measure expired August 22, 1985.

SOURCE: From *The Constitution of the United States: An Unfolding Story*, 2d ed., by J. T. Keenan, 45–46. Copyright © 1988 by The Dorsey Press. Reprinted by permission of the publisher, Brooks/Cole, Pacific Grove, Calif.

writing, it seems possible that the states may clamor for an amendment to limit the terms of members of representatives and senators, should the U.S. Congress continue to lack the votes to propose one.

THE SUPREME COURT AND THE LIVING CONSTITUTION

So far, our discussion of the amendment process has not mentioned the president or the Supreme Court. The reason is that neither has any formal constitutional role in it. We do not want to suggest, however, that these institutions have nothing to do with the process; both have significant, albeit informal, functions. Presidents often instigate and support proposals for constitutional amendments. Indeed, virtually every chief executive has wanted some alteration to the Constitution. In his first inaugural address, George Washington urged adoption of a bill of rights;[21] 200 years later, George Bush urged quick ratification of an amendment to prohibit flag desecration. The Court also has played at least three important roles in the process: instigator, interpreter, and nationalizer.

The Court as an Instigator of Constitutional Amendments

Of the seventeen additions to the Constitution after the Bill of Rights, Congress proposed four specifically to overturn Supreme Court decisions *(see Box 1-2)*. Many consider one of these—the Fourteenth—the single most important addition since 1791.

Many of the 10,000 or so proposals considered by Congress were aimed at similar objectives, among them the failed Child Labor[22] and Equal Rights

Amendments, both of which emanated, at least in part, from Supreme Court rulings rejecting their premises. These two ultimately were passed by Congress, but not ratified by the states. More recently, Congress has considered the following amendments, all of which were aimed at overturning Court decisions: a human life amendment that would make abortion illegal (in response to *Roe v. Wade,* 1973); a school prayer amendment that would allow public school children to engage in prayer (in response to *Engel v. Vitale,* 1962, and *School District of Abington Township v. Schempp,* 1963); and a flag desecration amendment that would prohibit mutilation of the American flag (in response to *Texas v. Johnson,* 1989).

The Court as an Interpreter of the Amendment Process

The Court has been asked to interpret Article V, which deals with the amendment process, but it has been hesitant to do so. Consider *Coleman v. Miller* (1939), which involved the actions of the Kansas legislature over the Child Labor Amendment. Proposed by Congress in 1924, the amendment stated, "The Congress shall have power to limit, regulate, and prohibit the labor of persons under eighteen years of age." In January 1925 Kansas legislators rejected the Child Labor Amendment. The issue arose again, however, when the state senate reconsidered the amendment in January 1937. At that time, the legislative body split 20–20, with the lieutenant governor casting the decisive vote in favor of the amendment. Members of the Kansas legislature (mostly those who had opposed the proposal) challenged the 1937 vote on two grounds: they questioned the ability of the lieutenant governor to break the tie and, more generally, they opposed the reconsideration of an amendment that previously had been rejected. In particular, the legislators asserted that the amendment had "lost its vitality" because "of that rejection and the failure of ratification within a reasonable time limit." Writing for the Court, Chief Justice Charles Evans Hughes refused to

21. See Pritchett, *The American Constitution,* 368.

22. In 1916 Congress passed a child labor law that prohibited the shipment in interstate commerce of anything made by children under age fourteen. When the Court struck down this act (and another like it) as an unconstitutional use of congressional power (*Hammer v. Dagenhart,* 1918), Congress proposed a Child Labor Amendment. See Clement E. Vose, *Constitutional Change* (Lexington, Mass.: Lexington Books, 1972).

BOX 1–2 FOUR AMENDMENTS THAT OVERTURNED SUPREME COURT DECISIONS

THE ELEVENTH

When Chisholm sued Georgia in 1793 and the Supreme Court dropped a bombshell on states-righters by agreeing to hear the case, Anti-Federalists were outraged. Congress responded swiftly by proposing the Eleventh Amendment, which was ratified by the requisite three-fourths of the states within a year, though not declared ratified until 1798. The amendment protects states against suits by citizens of another state or of another country.

THE FOURTEENTH

Congress and the High Court tangled again after the *Dred Scott v. Sandford* (sometimes spelled Dread Scott by abolitionists) case of 1857. Nine separate decisions were rendered on this case, but Chief Justice Roger B. Taney spoke for the "majority" in declaring that slaves could not be citizens and that Congress had exceeded its purview in prohibiting slavery in the territories. A Civil War and a few years of Reconstruction intervened before the Fourteenth Amendment, which conferred citizenship on all persons born or naturalized in the United States, could correct the Scott ruling.

THE SIXTEENTH

Congress next "got around the Supreme Court" through the passage of the Sixteenth Amendment, which legalized the income tax. In 1895 the Court turned down a federal income tax law on grounds that the Constitution requires taxes to be apportioned among the states proportionately according to population. But, in a spirit of cooperation, the Court invited Congress to overthrow the objection by means of an amendment. Congress proposed the Sixteenth Amendment in 1909, and the states ratified it in 1913.

THE TWENTY-SIXTH

President Richard Nixon, although signing a change in the Voting Rights Act that allowed eighteen-year-olds to vote in federal, state, and local elections, expressed doubt that the law was constitutional. Suit was speedily arranged, and the Court confirmed the president's misgivings in a 5–4 rejection that said, in effect: "The Congress does not have jurisdiction over state and local elections."

At a time when eighteen-year-olds were losing their lives in Vietnam, the Twenty-sixth Amendment had wide popular approval. In record time it was proposed by Congress in March 1971 and ratified in June, giving eighteen-year-olds the right to vote in national, state, and local elections.

SOURCE: From *The Constitution of the United States: An Unfolding Story*, 2d ed., by J. T. Keenan, 42–43. Copyright © 1988 by The Dorsey Press. Reprinted by permission of the publisher, Brooks/Cole, Pacific Grove, Calif.

---

address this point. Rather, he asserted that the suit raised questions, particularly those pertaining to recision, that were political and, thus, nonjusticiable. In his words, "the ultimate authority" over the amendment process was Congress, not the Court.

As one authority noted, "From the opinions filed in . . . *Coleman* . . . it would seem that the Court regards all questions relating to the interpretation of [Article V] as 'political questions,' and hence as addressed exclusively by Congress."[23] That observation was borne out in one of the Court's most recent Article V cases, *NOW v. Idaho* (1982). At issue was a 1978 act of Congress that extended the original deadline for state ratification of the Equal Rights Amendment from 1979 to 1982 and rejected a clause "that would have allowed state legislatures to rescind their prior approval."[24] In the wake of a strong anti-ERA movement, Idaho, which had passed the amendment in the early 1970s, decided to ignore federal law and retract its original vote.[25] The National Organization for Women challenged the state's action, and in 1982 the

23. Harold Chase and Craig Ducat, *Edwin Corwin's* The Constitution (Princeton, N.J.: Princeton University Press, 1978), 268.

24. Nancy McGlen and Karen O'Connor, *Women's Rights* (New York: Praeger, 1983), 379.

25. Three other states, Nebraska, Kentucky, and Tennessee, also rescinded.

Court docketed the case for argument. But, upon the request of the U.S. solicitor general, it dismissed the suit as moot: the congressionally extended time period for ratification had run out, and the controversy was no longer viable.

In the near future, the Court may be confronted with even more difficult questions. If the drives for a balanced budget or a term limits amendment succeed in attaining the support of two-thirds of the states, the Court might be in a position to consider issues relating to the creation of a second constitutional convention. Would the delegates to such a convention deliberate only the amendments under consideration, or would they be able to take up any or all parts of the Constitution? Addressing this question might be one of the most significant tasks the Supreme Court has ever faced. Remember that the 1787 Philadelphia delegates met solely to amend the Articles of Confederation, but ended up reframing the entire system of government. Perhaps that is why those same men were so vehemently opposed to the notion of holding another convention to propose a bill of rights. As Jefferson wrote, a second such convention could "endanger the most valuable parts of the system" and significantly weaken the national government.[26]

In an event, it may be a while before the Court must address this delicate issue. Since 1983 no state has passed the balanced budget amendment, a situation some credit to the formation of an anticonvention movement that strongly opposes any organized tinkering with the original document. And any attempt to etch federal term limits into the Constitution may suffer the same fate. In a way, as one writer notes, the success of such countermovements "is testimony to the success of the first convention."[27] Undoubtedly this assertion is so: as the Bill of Rights enters its third century, we have only to remind ourselves that it is the heart of the world's oldest surviving ruling charter.

The Court as a Nationalizer of the Bill of Rights

In 1789, as we have noted, James Madison submitted to the First Congress a list of seventeen articles (amendments), mostly aimed at safeguarding personal freedoms against tyranny by the federal government. In a speech to the House, he suggested that "in revising the Constitution, we may throw into that section, which interdicts the abuse of certain powers of the State legislatures, some other provisions of equal, if not greater importance than those already made." To that end, Madison's fourteenth amendment said that "no State shall violate the equal right of conscience, freedom of the press, or trial by jury in criminal cases."[28] This article failed to garner congressional approval and was never considered by the states.

Although scholars now agree that Madison viewed his fourteenth amendment as the most significant among the seventeen he proposed, Congress's refusal to adopt it may have meant that the Founders of our nation never intended for the Bill of Rights to be applied to the states or their local governments. The language of the amendments lends some support to this interpretation. Consider the First Amendment to the U.S. Constitution: "Congress shall make no law . . . abridging the freedom of speech." Note that the wording specifically and exclusively limits the powers of Congress, reflecting the fact that the Bill of Rights was added to the Constitution because of fear that the *federal* government might become too powerful and encroach upon individual rights.

Does this language mean that state legislatures *may* enact laws curtailing their citizens' free speech? For more than 100 years it did. The U.S. Supreme Court, following historical interpretations and emphasizing

26. Quoted in *The Origins of the American Constitution,* ed. Michael Kammen (New York: Penguin Books, 1986), 372.

27. Richard Lacayo, "Is It Broke: Should We Fix It?" *Time,* July 6, 1987, 55.

28. James Madison, Speech before the House of Representatives, June 7, 1789.

TABLE 1-4 Cases Incorporating Provisions of the Bill of Rights into the Due Process Clause of the Fourteenth Amendment

Constitutional Provision	Case	Year
First Amendment		
Freedom of speech and press	*Gitlow v. New York*	1925
Freedom of assembly	*DeJonge v. Oregon*	1937
Freedom of petition	*Hague v. CIO*	1939
Free exercise of religion	*Cantwell v. Connecticut*	1940
Establishment of religion	*Everson v. Board of Education*	1947
Fourth Amendment		
Unreasonable search and seizure	*Wolf v. Colorado*	1949
Exclusionary rule	*Mapp v. Ohio*	1961
Fifth Amendment		
Payment of compensation for the taking of private property	*Chicago, Burlington and Quincy R. Co. v. Chicago*	1897
Self-incrimination	*Malloy v. Hogan*	1964
Double jeopardy	*Benton v. Maryland*	1969
When jeopardy attaches	*Crist v. Bretz*	1978
Sixth Amendment		
Public trial	*In re Oliver*	1948
Due notice	*Cole v. Arkansas*	1948
Right to counsel (felonies)	*Gideon v. Wainwright*	1963
Confrontation and cross-examination of adverse witnesses	*Pointer v. Texas*	1965
Speedy trial	*Klopfer v. North Carolina*	1967
Compulsory process to obtain witnesses	*Washington v. Texas*	1967
Jury trial	*Duncan v. Louisiana*	1968
Right to counsel (misdemeanor when jail is possible)	*Argersinger v. Hamlin*	1972
Eighth Amendment		
Cruel and unusual punishment	*Louisiana ex rel. Francis v. Resweber*	1947
Ninth Amendment		
Privacy[a]	*Griswold v. Connecticut*	1965

NOTE: Provisions the Court has not incorporated: Second Amendment right to keep and bear arms; Third Amendment right against quartering soldiers; Fifth Amendment right to a grand jury hearing; Seventh Amendment right to a jury trial in civil cases; and Eighth Amendment right against excessive bail and fines.

a. The word *privacy* does not appear in the Ninth Amendment (nor anywhere in the text of the Constitution). In *Griswold* several members of the Court viewed the Ninth Amendment as guaranteeing (and incorporating) that right.

the intention of the Framers of the Constitution, refused to nationalize the Bill of Rights by making its protections as binding on the state governments as they are on the federal government. Not being restricted by the federal Bill of Rights, the states were free to recognize those freedoms they deemed important and to develop their own guarantees against state violations of those rights.

Through a doctrine called selective incorporation, however, this interpretation is no longer valid. Under this doctrine, the Court uses the Fourteenth Amendment's Due Process Clause ("Nor shall any State deprive any person of life, liberty, or property, without due process of law") to apply certain rights to the states. That is, through incorporation the Supreme Court has informed state governments that they too must abide by most guarantees contained in the first eight amendments of the federal Constitution. But, as Table 1-4 shows, the process by which Americans obtained these rights was long; in fact, early litigants who clamored for incorporation (in the major cases) actually lost many of their disputes.

Of course, that is no longer the case: we can now take for granted that the states in which we live must not infringe on our right to exercise our religion freely, to feel safe in our homes against unwarranted government intrusions, and so forth. Seen in this way, Madison may have lost the battle to see his Fourteenth Article become a part of the Constitution but he won the larger war: for all practical purposes and with only a few exceptions *(see Table 1-4)*, a present reading of the Constitution now ensures that the basic civil liberties of the citizens of the United States are uniformly protected against infringement by any government entity—federal, state, or local.

READINGS

Alderman, Ellen, and Caroline Kennedy. *In Our Defense: The Bill of Rights in Action.* New York: William Morrow, 1991.

Cortner, Richard C. *The Supreme Court and the Second Bill of Rights.* Madison: University of Wisconsin Press, 1981.

Farber, Daniel A., and Suzanna Sherry. *A History of the American Constitution.* St. Paul, Minn.: West, 1990.

Glasser, Ira. *Visions of Liberty.* New York: Arcade, 1991.

Hickok, Eugene W., Jr., ed. *The Bill of Rights: Original Meaning and Current Understanding.* Charlottesville: University Press of Virginia, 1991.

Rutland, Robert A. *The Birth of the Bill of Rights, 1776–1791.* Chapel Hill: University of North Carolina Press, 1955.

Vose, Clement E. *Constitutional Change.* Lexington, Mass: Lexington Books, 1972.

CHAPTER 2
APPROACHES TO SUPREME COURT
DECISION MAKING

T HE BALANCE OF THIS BOOK is devoted to narrative and opinion excerpts that show how the U.S. Supreme Court has interpreted the Constitution and its amendments. As a student approaching constitutional law, perhaps for the first time, you may think it is odd that the subject requires hundreds of pages of text. After all, in length, the Constitution and the amendments could fit easily into many Court decisions. Moreover, the document itself— its language—seems so clear.

First impressions, however, can be deceiving. Even apparently clear constitutional scriptures do not necessarily lend themselves to clear constitutional interpretation. For example, according to Article I, Section 2, the president "shall be Commander in Chief of the Army and Navy of the United States." Sounds simple enough. But could you, based on those words, answer the following questions, all of which have been posed to the Court?

• May the president, during times of war, order a blockade of certain American ports?
• May Congress delegate to the president the power to order an arms embargo against nations at war?
• May the president, during times of war, order that "traitors" be tried by military tribunals, rather than civilian courts?
• May the president, during times of international

crisis, authorize the creation of military camps to intern potential "traitors" to prevent sabotage?

What these and other questions arising from the Constitution and its guarantees illustrate is that a gap sometimes exists between the document's words and reality. Although the language may seem explicit, its meaning can be elusive and difficult to follow. Accordingly, justices have developed various approaches to resolving disputes. In this chapter, we consider those approaches, as well as those that have been suggested by generations of scholars who have sought to unravel the mysteries of judicial decision making and to isolate the factors that determine case outcomes.

As you might imagine, there is no shortage of explanations for how the Court makes decisions. Approaches to decision making can be categorized into two groups: the legal and the extralegal. Here, we review these approaches, strains of which appear in the justices' opinions in the chapters that follow.

LEGAL APPROACHES

Legal approaches to U.S. Supreme Court decision making emanate from notions of how society expects justices to behave, particularly what they should and should not consider as they formulate decisions. Under this school of thought, jurists are supposed to shed all their personal biases, preferences, and partisan attachments when they take their seats on the bench, for those things, it is argued, should have no bearing on Court decisions. Rather, justices ought to reach decisions in accord with factors that have some grounding in the law.

Because the justices themselves consider legally relevant factors appropriate criteria for reaching decisions, they often say they use them to resolve disputes. Whether they actually do is for you to determine as you read the cases to come. That is, you will need to think about this question: Do the justices use legal approaches to reach decisions or do they reach their decisions first and then use legal approaches to justify them? Before you can address this question, however, it is important to have some sense of specific factors that comprise the legally relevant category. In the pages that follow, we discuss six of the most important and describe the judicial philosophies that support their use in decision making.

The Doctrine of Original Intent

In an 1833 Supreme Court case, *Barron v. Baltimore,* Chief Justice John Marshall rejected the view that the Bill of Rights covered state actions. His reasoning: the Framers of the Constitution did not intend for it to do so. About 150 years later, Chief Justice William H. Rehnquist used the same grounds to find that cartoon parodies, however obnoxious, constitute protected expression.

Undoubtedly, between Marshall and Rehnquist, other chief justices and associate justices have looked to the intent of the Framers of the Constitution and its amendments to reach conclusions about extant disputes.[1] But why? What possible relevance could bygone intentions have for today's controversies? Advocates of the original intent approach offer several

answers. First, they assert that the Framers acted in a calculated manner. That is, they knew what they were doing, so why should we disregard their precepts? One adherent said, "Those who framed the Constitution chose their words carefully; they debated at great length the most minute points. The language they chose meant something. It is incumbent upon the Court to determine what that meaning was."[2]

Second, if they scrutinize the intent of the Framers, justices can deduce "constitutional truths," which they can apply to cases. Doing so, as Robert Bork and others argue, would produce neutral principles of law and eliminate value-laden decisions.[3] Consider, for example, speech advocating the violent overthrow of the government. Suppose the government enacted a law prohibiting such expression and arrested members of a radical political party for violating it. Justices could scrutinize such a law in several ways. An ideologue—say, a liberal—might conclude solely because of personal liberal values that the First Amendment prohibits such a ban on expression. Conservative jurists might reach the opposite conclusion, again, because their ideology dictates such an outcome.

Neither conclusion would be proper jurisprudence in Bork's opinion, because both are value laden, and ideological preferences should not creep into the law. Bork favors an examination of the Framers' intent as a way to keep the law value free. In 1971 he wrote:

Speech advocating violent overthrow is . . . not [protected] "political speech" . . . as that term must be defined by a Madisonian system of government. It is not political speech because it violates constitutional truths about processes and because it is not aimed at a new definition of political truth by a legislative majority.[4]

Finally, supporters of this mode of analysis argue that it fosters stability in law. According to some observers, the law today is far too fluid; it changes with

---

1. Given the subject of this volume, we deal here exclusively with the intent of the Framers of the U.S. Constitution. One also could apply this approach to statutory construction by considering the intent of those who drafted the laws in question.

2. Edwin Meese III, Address Before the American Bar Association, July 9, 1983, Washington, D.C.

3. See Robert Bork, "Neutral Principles and Some First Amendment Problems," *Indiana Law Journal* 47 (1971): 1–35.

4. Ibid., 31.

the ideological whims of the justices, creating havoc for those who must interpret and implement Court decisions. Lower court judges, lawyers, and even ordinary citizens do not know if today's rights will be there tomorrow. Following a jurisprudence of original intent would eliminate such confusion because "by seeking to judge policies in light of principles, rather than remodel principles in light of policies, the Court could avoid both the charge of incoherence and the charge of being either too conservative or too liberal."[5]

Although many Supreme Court opinions contemplate the original intent of the Framers, and arguments in favor of such an approach seem to have merit, this view is not without its critics. One reason for the controversy is that the doctrine became quite politicized during the Reagan presidency. Those who advocated it, particularly former attorney general Edwin Meese and defeated Supreme Court nominee Bork, were widely viewed as conservatives who were using the doctrine to attain their own ideological ends. The same has been said about Clarence Thomas, who also seems to favor an originalist approach.

Others, however, have raised several more concrete objections to this jurisprudence. Some argue that if the justices employed only this approach, the Constitution would lose its applicability and be rendered useless. In 1985 Justice William J. Brennan, Jr., asserted:

We current Justices read the Constitution in the only way that we can: as Twentieth Century Americans. We look to the history of the time of the framing and to the intervening history of interpretation. But the ultimate question must be, what do the words of the text mean in our time. For the genius of the Constitution rests not in any static meaning it might have had in a world that is dead and gone, but in the adaptability of its great principles to cope with current problems and current needs. What the constitutional fundamentals meant to the wisdom of other times

cannot be their measure to the vision of our time. Similarly, what those fundamentals mean for us, our descendants will learn, cannot be the measure to the vision of their time.[6]

A second criticism is that the Constitution embodies not one intent, but many. Political scientists Jeffrey A. Segal and Harold J. Spaeth pose some interesting questions:

Who were the Framers? All fifty-five of the delegates who showed up at one time or another in Philadelphia during the summer of 1787? Some came and went. . . . Some probably had not read it. Assuredly, they were not all of a single mind. Apart from the delegates who refused to sign, should not the delegates to the various state conventions that were called to ratify the Constitution also be counted as Framers?[7]

Historian Arthur Schlesinger, Jr., provided a poignant example of this ambiguity when he noted that Meese attacked "the Dred Scott decision [holding that blacks did not enjoy the same constitutional status as whites] as a violation of original intent. Yet Chief Justice Roger B. Taney based his decision squarely on 'original intent.'" Such a discrepancy led Schlesinger to ask: "Whose version of original intent are we to believe: Roger Taney's in 1857 or Edwin Meese's in 1985?"[8]

Finally, from which sources should justices divine the original intentions of the Framers? Obviously, they could look at the records of the constitutional debates and at the Founders' journals and papers, but those documents often fail to provide a single clear message. Justice Robert H. Jackson wrote in *Youngstown Sheet & Tube Co. v. Sawyer* (1952):

Just what our forefathers did envision, or would have envisioned had they foreseen modern conditions, must be divined from materials almost as enigmatic as the dreams Joseph was called upon to interpret for Pharaoh. A century and a half of partisan debate and scholarly specification

5. Meese, Address.

6. Address to the Text and Teaching Symposium, Georgetown University, October 12, 1985, Washington, D.C.
7. *The Supreme Court and the Attitudinal Model* (Cambridge: Cambridge University Press, 1993), 39.
8. "On 'Original Intent,'" *Wall Street Journal,* January 17, 1986.

yields no net result but only supplies more or less apt quotations from respected sources on each side of any question. They largely cancel each other.

Literalism

On the surface, literalism resembles the doctrine of original intent: it puts a premium on the Constitution. But this is where the similarity ends. In an effort to prevent the infusion of new meanings from sources outside the text of the Constitution, original intent adherents seek to deduce constitutional truths by examining the intended meanings behind the words. Literalists consider only the plain meaning of the words in the Constitution (their literal meaning) and apply them to disputes. This distinction can lead to some extraordinary differences in case outcomes. If we use again the example of speech aimed at overthrowing the U.S. government, original intent advocates would hold that the meaning behind the First Amendment prohibits such expression. Literalists, on the other hand, would scrutinize the words of the First Amendment—"Congress shall make no law . . . abridging freedom of speech"—and read them literally: *no law* means *no law*. Hence, any statute infringing on speech, even a law that prohibits expression advocating the overthrow of the government, would violate the First Amendment.

Still, these two views sometimes overlap. When it comes to the right to privacy, particularly its use to create other rights, such as legalized abortion, some original intent adherents and literalists would reach the same conclusion: that it does not exist. The former would argue that it was not the intent of the Framers to confer privacy; the latter, that because the Constitution fails to guarantee explicitly such a right, Americans do not automatically possess it.

Although strains of literalism run through the opinions of many justices, Hugo L. Black is most closely associated with this view *(see Box 2-1)*. During his thirty-four-year tenure on the Court, Black reiter-

ated the literalist philosophy.[9] His own words best describe his position:

My view is, without deviation, without exception, without any ifs, buts, or whereases, that freedom of speech means that government shall not do anything to people . . . either for the views they have or the views they express or the words they speak or write. Some people would have you believe that this is a very radical position, and maybe it is. But all I am doing is following what to me is the clear wording of the First Amendment. . . . As I have said innumerable times before I simply believe that "Congress shall make no law" means Congress shall make no law. . . . Thus we have the absolute command of the First Amendment that no law shall be passed by Congress abridging freedom of speech or the press.[10]

As this statement indicates, Black applied literalism most often to cases involving the First Amendment, but he also invoked it to examine other kinds of constitutional disputes. In *Youngstown Sheet & Tube Co. v. Sawyer* the Court was asked to determine whether President Harry S. Truman could order the secretary of commerce to seize the nation's steel mills, which, because of an impending strike, were under threat of being shut down. Truman argued that with the United States at war in Korea, the action was necessary "to avert a national catastrophe." Even so, Black refused to relent. Indeed, his response for the majority was classic literalism:

It is clear that if the President had the authority to issue the order he did, it must be found in some provision of the Constitution. . . . The order cannot properly be sustained [because] . . . the Constitution limits his functions in the lawmaking process to the recommending of laws he thinks wise and the vetoing of laws he thinks bad.

Why did Black advocate literalism? Like original intent adherents, he viewed his approach as a value-

---

9. For an interesting biography of Justice Black, see Tinsley E. Yarbrough, *Mr. Justice Black and His Critics* (Durham: Duke University Press, 1988).

10. *A Constitutional Faith* (New York: Knopf, 1969), 45–46.

BOX 2-1   HUGO LAFAYETTE BLACK
(1937–1971)

THE EIGHTH child of a Baptist storekeeper and farmer, Hugo Black was born February 27, 1886, in Harlan, Alabama, and spent the first years of his life in the hill country near there. When he was still a youngster, his family moved to Ashland, a larger community where his father's business prospered. Black attended the local schools in Ashland and, after trying one year at Birmingham Medical College, decided to study law. At eighteen he entered the University of Alabama Law School at Tuscaloosa.

Receiving his LL.B. in 1906, Black returned to Ashland and set up his first law practice. The following year a fire destroyed his office and library, and Black decided to move to Birmingham. There he quickly established a relationship with labor by defending the United Mine Workers strikers in 1908. Black also developed an expertise for arguing personal injury cases.

BLACK WAS NAMED a part-time police court judge in Birmingham in 1910 and was elected county solicitor (public prosecutor) for Jefferson County in 1914. As solicitor, he gained a measure of local fame for his investigation of reports of the brutal means police employed while questioning suspects at the notorious Bessemer jail. When he left the solicitor's post in 1917 to join the World War I effort, Black had succeeded in emptying a docket that had once held as many as 3,000 pending cases.

His brief military career kept him within the borders of the United States. He returned to practice law in Birmingham in 1918 and continued to expand his practice, still specializing in labor law and personal injury cases. He married Josephine Foster, February 23, 1921. They had two sons and one daughter. In 1923 Black joined the Ku Klux Klan, but resigned from the organization two years later just before he ran for the Democratic nomination for the Senate seat held by Democrat Oscar Underwood. Cam-

paigning as the poor man's candidate, Black won the party's endorsement and the subsequent election. He entered the Senate in 1927 and immediately began to study history and the classics at the Library of Congress to compensate for his lack of a liberal education.

During his two terms in the Senate Black used committee hearings to investigate several areas, including abuses of marine and airline subsidies and the activities of lobbying groups. In 1933 he introduced a bill to create a thirty-hour work week. This legislation, after several alterations, was finally passed in 1938 as the Fair Labor Standards Act. One of the Senate's strongest supporters of President Franklin Roosevelt, Black spoke out in favor of his 1937 Court-packing scheme and other New Deal programs. Black's support for the administration and his strong liberal instincts led the president to pick him as his choice to fill the Supreme Court seat vacated by the retirement of Willis Van Devanter. Black was confirmed by the Senate, 63–16, on August 17, 1937.

Black's previous affiliation with the Ku Klux Klan was widely reported in the national news media after his confirmation. The furor quickly quieted, however, when the new justice admitted in a dramatic radio broadcast that he had indeed been a member of the Klan but added that he had resigned many years before and would comment no further. During his Court career, Black always carried in his a pocket a copy of the United States Constitution.

Black's first wife died in 1951, and he married Elizabeth Seay DeMeritte, September 11, 1957. He retired from the Court September 17, 1971, after suffering an impairing stroke. He died eight days later in Washington.

SOURCE: Adapted from Elder Witt, *Guide to the U.S. Supreme Court*, 2d ed. (Washington, D.C.: Congressional Quarterly, 1990), 860.

free form of jurisprudence. If justices looked only at the words of the Constitution, their decisions would not reflect ideological or political values, but rather those of the document. Black's opinions provide good illustrations. Although he almost always supported claims of free *speech* against government challenges, he refused to extend constitutional protection to expression that was not precisely speech. That is, he asserted that activities such as flag burning and the wearing of armbands, even if designed to express political views, fell outside of the speech protected by the First Amendment.

Despite the high regard scholars have for Black, many have actively attacked his jurisprudence. One asserts that it led him to "quixotic" views, particularly of the coverage of the First Amendment.[11] For example, most analysts and justices—even those considered liberal—agree that obscene materials fall outside of First Amendment protection and that states can prohibit their dissemination. But, in opinion after opinion, Black clung to the view that no publication could be banned on the grounds that it was obscene. In *Smith v. California* (1959) Black wrote separately to express his displeasure with the use of legal standards that may allow for the suppression of obscene material. He asserted:

Certainly the First Amendment's language leaves no room for interference that abridgments of speech and press can be made just because they are slight. That Amendment provides, in simple words, that "Congress shall make no law . . . abridging the freedom of speech, or of the press." I read "no law . . . abridging" to mean no law abridging. The First Amendment, which is the supreme law of the land, has thus fixed its own value on freedom of speech and press by putting these freedoms wholly "beyond the reach" of federal power to abridge. No other provision of the Constitution purports to dilute the scope of the unequivocal commands of the First Amendment. Consequently, I do not believe that any federal agencies, including Congress and the Court, have power or authority to subordinate speech and

press to what they think are "more important interests." The contrary notion is, in my judgment, court-made not Constitution-made.

Even those who generally agreed with literalism thought such a view went a bit too far.

A second objection raised is that literalism can result in wholly inconsistent outcomes. Is it really sensible for a literalist to hold that obscenity is constitutionally protected while the desecration of the flag is not? Moreover, there were times when even Black could not abide by his own approach. During World War II he allowed President Franklin D. Roosevelt to issue an order "excluding all persons of Japanese descent" from certain designated areas on the West Coast, but recall that later he held that President Truman lacked the authority to seize the nation's steel mills. How did he justify the earlier decision? He said, "Because we are at war with the Japanese Empire . . . and . . . because Congress, reposing its confidence in this time of war in our military leaders—as inevitably it must—determined that they should have the power to do just that."[12] The decision may have been reasonable to many in the context of the times, but certainly it is difficult to justify under a literal reading of the Constitution.

Segal and Spaeth raise yet a third problem with literalism: it supposes a precision in the English language that simply does not exist. Not only may words, including those used by the Framers, have multiple meanings, but also the meanings themselves may be quite contrary. For example, the common legal word *sanction*, as Segal and Spaeth note, means both to punish *and* to reward.[13] How, then, would a literalist construe it?

Meaning of the Words

The "meaning of the words" approach to constitutional interpretation, most associated with W. W.

---

11. See John Hart Ely, *Democracy and Distrust* (Cambridge: Harvard University Press, 1980).

12. *Korematsu v. United States* (1944).
13. *The Supreme Court and the Attitudinal Model*, 34.

Crosskey, has its roots in both literalism and original-ism: it emphasizes the words of the Constitution at the time the Framers wrote them.[14] But there are differences. While literalists stress the words themselves, this mode emphasizes their meaning; and while originalism "places a premium upon reasoning that is historically grounded, the meaning of the words focuses on lexicographic skill." In other words, "the 'meaning' mode attempts to define the words of the Constitution according to what they meant at the time the document or its amendment was written."[15]

The merits of this approach are similar to those of literalism and originalism. By focusing on how the Framers defined their own words and then applying their definitions to disputes over those constitutional provisions containing them, this approach seeks to generate value-free and ideology-free jurisprudence. Of even greater importance, its adherents argue, is that it attempts to "preserve some sense of stability and continuity in the agreements and understandings on which legitimate governmental power is based."[16]

Chief Justice Marshall's opinion in *Gibbons v. Ogden* (1824), which, in part, involved a dispute over the congressional power to regulate interstate commerce, provides a particularly good illustration of the value of this approach. As part of his decision, Marshall felt it necessary to determine the meaning of the word *commerce*. Rather than fashion his own definition, Marshall turned to how the Framers defined it at the time they wrote it:

All America understands, and has uniformly understood, the word "commerce" to comprehend navigation. It was so understood, and must have been so understood, when the constitution was framed. The power over commerce, including navigation, was one of the primary objects for

which the people of America adopted their government, and must have been contemplated in forming it.

Even modern-day justices occasionally invoke this approach. In *Nixon v. United States* (1993), the Rehnquist Court considered a challenge to the procedures the Senate used to impeach a federal judge, Walter L. Nixon, Jr. Rather than having the entire Senate try the case, a special twelve-member committee heard it and reported to the full body. Nixon argued that this procedure violated Article I of the Constitution, which states, "The Senate shall have the sole power to try all Impeachments." But before he addressed Nixon's claim, Chief Justice Rehnquist sought to determine whether courts had any business resolving such disputes. In so doing, he used a meaning of the words approach to consider the word *try* in Article I:

Petitioner argues that the word "try" in the first sentence imposes by implication an additional requirement on the Senate in that the proceedings must be in the nature of a judicial trial . . . . There are several difficulties with this position which lead us ultimately to reject it. The word "try," both in 1787 and later, has considerably broader meanings than those to which petitioner would limit it. Older dictionaries define try as "[t]o examine" or "[t]o examine as a judge." See 2 S. Johnson, A Dictionary of the English Language (1785). In more modern usage the term has various meanings. For example, try can mean "to examine or investigate judicially," "to conduct the trial of," or "to put to the test by experiment, investigation. . . ." Webster's Third New International Dictionary (1971).

Like the other modes we have examined, the meaning of the words approach is not without its critics. One objection is similar to that leveled at originalism: the approach is too static. Political scientist C. Herman Pritchett noted that like originalism, the meaning approach can "make a nation the prisoner of its past, and reject any constitutional development save constitutional amendment."[17] Because seafaring vessels were the primary instruments of commerce in 1787, it was easy for Marshall to conclude that com-

14. See *Politics and the Constitution in the History of the United States* (Chicago: University of Chicago Press, 1953).

15. David W. Rohde and Harold J. Spaeth, *Supreme Court Decision Making* (San Francisco: W. H. Freeman, 1976), 41.

16. C. Herman Pritchett, *Constitutional Law of the Federal System* (Englewood Cliffs, N.J.: Prentice Hall, 1984), 37.

17. Ibid.

merce "comprehend[s]" navigation. Although one could try to make an equally compelling case today for, say, airplanes, it would be a far more difficult task.

Another criticism is that the "original meaning may be as difficult to establish as original intent."[18] In our discussion of originalism, we pointed out that it was often impossible to determine the intent of the Framers. Attempting to understand what they meant by each word can be just as daunting, requiring the development of a specialized dictionary, which could take years of research to compile and still not have any value—determinate or otherwise. Even Chief Justice Marshall seemed to recognize this, when he wrote:

A Constitution . . . [which] would partake of the prolixity of a legal code . . . could scarcely be embraced by the human mind. It would, probably, never be understood by the public. Its nature, therefore, requires that only its great outlines should be marked, its important objects designated, and the minor ingredients which compose those objects be deduced from the nature of the objects themselves.[19]

Logical Reasoning

Unlike originalism or the meaning of the words approach, logical reasoning is not necessarily dependent on historical interpretations of particular constitutional provisions. Rather, the logical reasoning approach suggests that judges do "what all intelligent people do when obliged to interpret a document: analyze its terms, then try to discern the premises of its arguments, and the conclusions to which they lead."[20] Logical analysis often takes the form of a syllogism, consisting of a major premise, which "sets forth a proposition"; a minor premise, which "contains an assertion related to the major premise"; and a conclusion, which "logically follows" from both major and minor premises.[21]

Marshall's opinion in *Marbury v. Madison* (1803) provides an oft-cited example of logical reasoning in action:

MAJOR PREMISE: A law repugnant to the Constitution is void.

MINOR PREMISE: This law is repugnant to the Constitution.

CONCLUSION: Therefore, this law is void.

The beauty of logical analysis, as this example illustrates, is that the resulting decision takes on an objective, perhaps even a scientific, aura. In other words, Marshall's syllogism suggests that anybody with a logical mind would reach the same conclusion. But is this necessarily so? Consider another syllogism:

MAJOR PREMISE: Sweden has many storks.

MINOR PREMISE: Storks deliver babies.

CONCLUSION: Therefore, Sweden has many babies.

We know that storks do not deliver babies, and therein lies the major problem with logical analysis: it "exists independently of factual or empirical analysis." Therefore, "almost any conclusion can be given logical form."[22] To understand why this assertion is correct, compare the two syllogisms. If we assume that the major premises of both are accurate, then the soundness of their conclusions rests with the factual accuracy of their minor premises. Obviously, storks do not deliver babies, but is Marshall's minor premise any more believable or, more to the point, logically driven? Put another way, can logic reveal whether a particular law is repugnant to the Constitution?

To many the answer is no. Political scientists David Rohde and Harold Spaeth suggest that logical reasoning "enables judges to make decisions compatibly with their policy preferences and at the same time causing their opinions and decisions to exhibit a sem-

18. Ibid.

19. *McCulloch v. Maryland* (1819).

20. Walter F. Murphy, James E. Fleming, and William F. Harris, *American Constitutional Interpretation* (Mineola, N.Y.: Foundation Press, 1986), 302–303.

21. Rohde and Spaeth, *Supreme Court Decision Making,* 42.

22. Ibid., 43.

blance of order and a quality of connectedness."[23] Justice Oliver Wendell Holmes, Jr., put it this way:

The life of the law has not been logic: it has been experience. The felt necessities of the time, the prevalent moral and political theories, intuitions of public policy, avowed or unconscious, even the prejudices which judges share with their fellow-men, have had a good deal more to do than the syllogism in determining the rules by which men should be governed.[24]

Stare Decisis

Translated from Latin, *stare decisis* means "to abide by, or adhere to, decided cases." What the term suggests is that, as a general rule, jurists should decide cases on the basis of previously established precedent. In shorthand terms, judicial tribunals should "honor prior rulings."[25] Many assert that Chief Justice Earl Warren did just that in *Watkins v. United States* (1957) to resolve one of Watkins's claims, namely that some questions put to him by a congressional committee violated his First Amendment rights. Warren used an earlier precedent, *United States v. Rumely*, to reach a decision favorable to Watkins:

The Court recognized the restraints of the Bill of Rights upon congressional investigations in *United States v. Rumely. . . .* It was concluded that, when First Amendment rights are threatened, the delegation of power to [a] committee [to conduct investigations] must be clearly revealed in its charter.

The benefits of this approach are fairly evident. Ralph Rossum and G. Alan Tarr wrote, "Reliance on precedent . . . adds stability, continuity, and predictability to the entire legal profession."[26] Chief Justice Harlan F. Stone acknowledged the value of prece-

dent in a somewhat more ironic way: "the rule of *stare decisis* embodies a wise policy because it is often more important that a rule of law be settled than that it be settled right."[27] The message, however, is the same: if the Court adheres to past decisions, it provides some direction to all who labor in the legal enterprise. Lower court judges know how they should and should not decide cases; lawyers can frame their arguments in accord with the lessons of past cases; legislators understand what they can and cannot enact or regulate, and so forth. In addition, as Sheldon Goldman notes, the "rule of precedent symbolizes that we are dealing with a court of law as distinguished from a legislative body."[28] It is one of the features that make the judiciary unique.

Precedent, then, is an important and useful factor in Supreme Court decision making. It is interesting to note that the Court rarely reverses itself (only about 250 times over its entire history).[29] Even modern-day Courts, as Table 2-1 shows, have been loath to overrule precedents. In the forty-one terms covered in Table 2-1, the Court has overturned only 111 precedents, or about 2.7 per term. "By comparison," Segal and Spaeth point out, "it declared more than four times as many laws unconstitutional during this same period."[30] What is more, the justices almost always cite previous rulings in their decisions; indeed, it is the rare Court opinion that does not mention other cases.[31] By the same token, several scholars have verified that precedent helps to explain Court decisions in some areas of the law. In one study, analysts found that the Court reacted quite consistently to legal doctrine presented in more than fifteen years of death penalty litigation. Put differently, using prece-

---

23. Ibid.

24. *The Common Law*, quoted by Max Lerner in *The Mind and Faith of Justice Holmes* (New York: Modern Library, 1943), 51–52.

25. Louis Fisher, *Constitutional Dialogues* (Princeton, N.J.: Princeton University Press, 1988), 80.

26. *American Constitutional Law*, 3d ed. (New York: St. Martin's Press, 1991), 4.

27. *United States v. Underwriters Association* (1944).

28. *Constitutional Law*, 2d ed. (New York: HarperCollins, 1991), 13.

29. Stephen L. Wasby, *The Supreme Court in the Federal Judicial System*, 4th ed. (Chicago: Nelson Hall, 1993), 275.

30. *The Supreme Court and the Attitudinal Model*, 50.

31. Wasby, *The Supreme Court in the Federal Judicial System*, 275. It is also the rare justice who says that he or she does not use precedent as a guide. Most unusual, then, was Justice William O. Douglas, who frequently admitted that he would rather create a precedent than follow one.

TABLE 2-1 Precedents Overruled, 1953–1993 Terms

Chief Justice	Number of Terms Served	Number of Overruled Precedents	Average Number of Overrulings Per Term
Warren	16	42	2.6
Burger	17	44	2.6
Rehnquist	8	25	3.1
Total	41	111	2.7

SOURCE: Jeffrey A. Segal and Harold J. Spaeth, *The Supreme Court and the Attitudinal Model* (Cambridge: Cambridge University Press, 1993), 51. Updated by Jeffrey A. Segal.

dent from past cases, the researchers could correctly categorize the outcomes (for or against the death penalty) in 75 percent of sixty-four cases decided since 1972.[32] Scholarly work considering precedent in search and seizure litigation had similar success.[33]

Despite these data, we should not conclude that the justices necessarily follow this approach. Many allege that judicial appeal to precedent often is mere window dressing, used to hide ideologies and values, rather than a substantive form of analysis. There are several reasons for this allegation.

First, the Supreme Court has generated so much precedent that it is usually possible to find support for any conclusion. By way of proof, turn to any page of any opinion in this book and you probably will find the writers—both for the majority and the dissenters—citing precedent.

Second, it may be difficult to locate the rule of law emerging in a majority opinion. "Technically, a court is bound to follow not everything stated in a relevant precedent, but only the rule of law that was necessary for decision in that case, what is called the holding" or *ratio decidendi*.[34] Other points made in a given opinion—*obiter dicta*—have no legal weight, and judges are not bound by it. It is up to courts to separate the *ratio decidendi* from *dicta*. Doing so can be difficult, but it provides a way for justices to skirt precedent with which they do not agree. All they need to do is declare "portions of the reasoning upon which the previous decision was based to be *dicta*."[35] So too, justices can brush aside even the *ratio decidendi* when it suits their interests. Because the Supreme Court, at least today, is so selective about the cases it chooses to decide, it probably would not hear a case for which clear precedent existed. Even in the past, two cases that were identical probably would not both have been accepted.

What this means is that justices can always deal with "problematic" *ratio decidendi* by distinguishing the case at hand from those that have already been decided. The Court's later interpretation of the *Watkins* decision provides a good example. Just two years after it ruled in favor of John Watkins, the Court heard *Barenblatt v. United States* (1959), in which it looked again at whether a congressional committee could question an individual about his political beliefs and associations. Like Watkins, Barenblatt alleged that he could refuse to answer such questions because they infringed on his First Amendment rights. Nonetheless, the Court "distinguished the *Watkins* precedent by authorizing investigating committees to 'balance' the competing . . . interests."[36]

Third, and most interesting, many justices recognize the limits of *stare decisis* in cases involving constitutional interpretation. As Justice William O. Douglas once wrote, a judge should support the Constitution, "not the gloss which his predecessors may have put on it."[37] But Justice Black may have said it best:

32. Tracey E. George and Lee Epstein, "On the Nature of Supreme Court Decision Making," *American Political Science Review* 86 (1992): 323–337.

33. Jeffrey A. Segal, "Predicting Supreme Court Cases Probabilistically: The Search and Seizure Cases, 1962–1984," *American Political Science Review* (1984): 891–900.

34. Lawrence Baum, *The Supreme Court*, 4th ed. (Washington, D.C.: CQ Press, 1992), 132.

35. Rohde and Spaeth, *Supreme Court Decision Making*, 36.

36. Ibid, 37.

37. "Stare Decisis," *Columbia Law Review* 49 (1949), 736.

Ordinarily it is sound policy to adhere to prior decisions but this practice has quite properly never been a blind, inflexible rule. Courts are not omniscient. Like every other human agency, they too can profit from trial and error, from experience and reflection. As others have demonstrated, the principle commonly referred to as *stare decisis* has never been thought to extend so far as to prevent the courts from correcting their own errors. . . . Indeed, the Court has a special responsibility where questions of constitutional law are involved to review its decisions from time to time and where compelling reasons present themselves to refuse to follow erroneous precedents; otherwise mistakes in interpreting the Constitution are extremely difficult to alleviate and needlessly so.[38]

And, in fact, of the 111 precedents overruled between the 1953 and 1993 terms *(see Table 2-1)*, about 68 percent involved constitutional issues.

Balancing Approaches

So far we have examined five modes of analysis that are not case specific, meaning that conclusions reached by literalists and original intent advocates, for example, on points of law would not waiver with the facts of a given case. Presumably, the original intent advocates would always hold that the First Amendment does not protect speech advocating the violent overthrow of the government, and the literalists would always reach precisely the opposite conclusion, regardless of the specific controversy at hand. Supporters of a balancing approach take a position that is more case specific than philosophical; that is, in each case they balance the interests of the individual against those of the government. Their decisions can vary because at some times an individual's activity outweighs the government's interest in prohibiting it, while at other times the reverse holds true.

The balancing approach, however, is not monolithic. Some justices take a very strict view of balancing, giving the interests of individuals and governments equal weight. They justify doing so on

constitutional and philosophical grounds, saying, for example, that while the First Amendment protects individual speech, the text of the Constitution gives legislatures the power to enact laws, which may sometimes interfere with such speech. The Court, according to this view, should initially give equal weight to both and then balance them to determine which should fall. Justice John Marshall Harlan's opinion in *Barenblatt* demonstrates this theory in practice. Among the issues raised was whether a congressional committee could question an individual about his political beliefs and associations. Barenblatt alleged that he could refuse to answer such questions because they infringed on his First Amendment rights. Harlan wrote: "Where First Amendment rights are asserted to bar governmental interrogation, resolution of the issue always involves a balancing by the courts of the competing private and public interests at stake in the particular circumstances shown." He held that, in this instance, the scale favored the government over Barenblatt.

Balancing also can take at least two other forms. While some opinions, such as Harlan's in *Barenblatt*, weigh equally the claims of governments and individuals, others give preference to one above the other. In accordance with a philosophy of judicial restraint, Justice Felix Frankfurter often balanced government interests versus individual interests but with a finger on the scale: he gave preference to the state over the individual. He did so in the belief that a body made up of unelected judges should not lightly overturn laws passed by legislatures composed of representatives elected by the populace. In his view,

the framers of the Constitution denied. . . legislative powers to the federal judiciary. They chose instead to insulate the judiciary from the legislative function. They did not grant to this Court supervision over legislation. . . . [Thus,] the removal of unwise laws from the statute books . . . lies not to the court but to the ballot and to the processes of democratic government.[39]

---

38. *Green v. United States* (1958).

39. *West Virginia v. Barnette* (1943).

In contrast to Frankfurter's perspective is the preferred freedoms position, which also balances interests, but tips the scale to favor the individual's rights and liberties.[40] According to this view, "freedom of expression is so vital in its relationship to the objectives of the Constitution that inevitably it must stand in a preferred position . . . [and, therefore,] legislation claimed to impinge on rights of free speech and thought should be inspected more critically by the judiciary."[41] In other words, the Court should regard any laws touching upon First Amendment rights with a good deal of suspicion. Why? In *West Virginia v. Barnette* (1943) Justice Jackson provided some justifications:

The very purpose of a Bill of Rights was to withdraw certain subjects from the vicissitudes of political controversy, to place them beyond the reach of majorities and officials and to establish them as legal principles to be applied by the courts. One's right to life, liberty, and property, to free speech, a free press, freedom of worship and assembly, and other fundamental rights may not be submitted to vote: they depend on the outcome of no elections.

Critiques of the various forms of balancing are often less pointed than those we have already examined and more philosophical in orientation. Debates over this mode of analysis generally have centered on views about the role of the Supreme Court in a democratic society. Those opposed to the equal balancing of Harlan and to the judicial restraint of Frankfurter contend that each ignores the Court's role of protecting minority interests. According to this argument, justices, because they are not elected officials, are in the best position to protect groups and individuals who hold unpopular views. As Justice Brennan wrote in *NAACP v. Button* (1963):

Groups which find themselves unable to achieve their objectives through the ballot frequently turn to the courts. . . . *And, under the conditions of modern government, litigation may well be the sole practicable avenue open to a minority to petition for redress of grievances* . . . For such a group, association for litigation may be the most effective form of political association. (Emphasis added.)

Brennan opposed doctrines like absolute balancing because they almost always lead to decisions in favor of the majority. Consider the outcome in *Barenblatt:* Would it have been possible for Justice Harlan to weigh the interests of all against those of one man and reach any other conclusion?

Frankfurter and others chastise adherents of a position giving special treatment to individual rights and liberties. In Frankfurter's view, that posture is "mischievous" because its application gives the Court too much power. When Congress and other legislative bodies enact laws that reflect the will of the people, why should the Court—composed of unelected officials—strike them down? In this light, the Court should be seen as part of the ruling regime, willing to reflect its wishes.

EXTRALEGAL APPROACHES

Thus far in our discussion we have not mentioned the justices' ideologies, their political party affiliations, or their personal views on various public policy issues. The reason is that legal approaches to Supreme Court decision making do not admit that such factors play a role in how the Court arrives at its decisions. Instead, they suggest that justices divorce themselves from their personal and political biases and settle disputes based upon the law.

Extralegal approaches posit a quite different vision of Supreme Court decision making. They argue that the forces that drive the justices are anything but legal in composition. Put in different terms, extralegal approaches suggest that it is unrealistic to expect justices to shed all their preferences and values and to ignore

40. As Pritchett wrote: "Advocates of the preferred position . . . also allowed for balancing, but [put] freedom's thumb on the scale." *Constitutional Civil Liberties* (Englewood Cliffs, N.J.: Prentice Hall, 1984), 30.

41. Robert B. McKay, "The Preference for Freedom," *New York University Law Review* 34 (1959): 1182.

FIGURE 2-1　Left-Right Continuum of Justices Serving Between 1939 and 1941

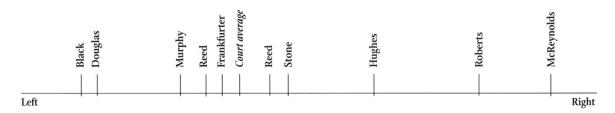

SOURCE: C. Herman Pritchett, "Divisions of Opinion Among Justices of the U.S. Supreme Court, 1939–1941," *American Political Science Review* 35 (1941): 894.

NOTE: Reed appears twice because his dissents were "equally divided" between the liberal and conservative wings of the Court. See Pritchett, "Divisions of Opinion Among Justices," 895.

public opinion when they put on their black robes. Rather, under those black robes remains a person, a person—like all of us—whose biases and partisan attachments are strong and pervasive.

Justices usually do not admit that they are swayed by the public or that they vote the way they do because of their ideologies. Hence, our discussion of extralegal approaches is distinct from the section on legal factors. In it you will find little in the way of supporting statements from the justices, for it is an unusual justice indeed who admits to following anything but legal criteria in deciding cases. Instead, we have included the results of decades of research by scholars who think that extralegal forces shape judicial decisions. We organize these approaches into three categories: policy-based, strategic, and political. Whether you are persuaded by these scholarly accounts is a question to consider not only as you read the discussion that follows but also as you turn to the opinion excerpts in the later chapters.

Policy-Based Approaches

Adherents of policy-based approaches argue that justices hold certain values they would like to see reflected in the outcomes of Court cases. The two most prevalent policy-based approaches stress the importance of judicial *attitudes* and *roles*.

Attitudes. Attitudinal approaches emphasize the importance of the justices' ideologies. Typically, scholars examining the ideologies of the justices discuss the degree to which a justice is conservative or liberal—as in "Justice X has conservative views on issues of criminal law" or "Justice Y has liberal views on free speech." This school of thought holds that when a case comes before the Court each justice evaluates the facts of the dispute and arrives at a decision consistent with his or her personal ideology.

One of the first scholars to study the importance of the personal attitudes of the justices was C. Herman Pritchett.[42] Examining the Court during the New Deal period, Pritchett was not satisfied with traditional legal explanations of judicial decisions. If the law drove Court rulings, why did various justices in interpreting the same legal provisions consistently reach different conclusions on the important legal questions of the day? Pritchett concluded that the law alone was unable to explain why the justices voted the way they did. He found that personal attitudes have a strong influence on judicial decisions. Based on their voting patterns, Pritchett was able to place the justices of that era on a left-right continuum *(see Figure 2-1).*

42. C. Herman Pritchett, *The Roosevelt Court* (New York: Macmillan, 1948); and Pritchett, "Divisions of Opinion Among Justices of the U.S. Supreme Court, 1939–1941," *American Political Science Review* 35 (1941): 890–898.

TABLE 2-2 Liberal Voting of the Chief Justices, 1953–1991

	Issue Areas					
	Civil Liberties		Economics		Federalism	
	Number of cases	Percentage liberal	Number of cases	Percentage liberal	Number of cases	Percentage liberal
Warren	771	78.5	443	81.9	94	69.1
Burger	1,430	29.6	423	42.6	111	63.1
Rehnquist	1,665	20.4	413	42.2	155	38.7

SOURCE: Lee Epstein, Jeffrey A. Segal, Harold J. Spaeth, and Thomas G. Walker, *The Supreme Court Compendium: Data, Decisions, and Developments* (Washington, D.C.: Congressional Quarterly, 1994), Table 6-1. This source can be consulted for voting data over twelve issue areas for all of the justices who sat on the Court from 1953 to 1991.

NOTE: The data in this table are based on decisions reached during the following tenures: Earl Warren, 1953–1968; Warren Burger, 1969–1985; William Rehnquist, justice, 1972–1986; chief justice, 1986– .

Pritchett's findings touched off an explosion of research on the influence of attitudes on Supreme Court decision making.[43] Much of this scholarship describes how liberal or conservative the various justices have been and attempts to predict their voting behavior based on their attitudinal preferences. To understand some of these differences, consider the material in Table 2-2. This table presents the voting records of the present chief justice, William Rehnquist, and his two immediate predecessors, Warren Burger and Earl Warren. The data report the percentage of times each voted in the liberal direction in three different issue areas: civil liberties, economic liberties, and federalism.

The data show dramatic differences among these three important jurists, especially in civil liberties. Cases in this category include disputes over issues such as the First Amendment freedoms of religion, speech, and press; the right to privacy; the rights of the criminally accused; and illegal discrimination. The liberal position in such cases is a vote in favor of the individual who is claiming a denial of these basic

rights. Warren supported the liberal side almost 80 percent of the time, but Burger and Rehnquist did so in less than 30 percent of such cases.

Economics cases involve challenges to the government's authority to regulate the economy. The liberal position supports an active role by the government in controlling business and economic activity. Here again the three justices represent different ideological positions. Warren is the most liberal of the three, ruling in favor of government regulatory activity in better than 80 percent of the cases, while Burger and Rehnquist support such government activity in less than half the cases.

Finally, there are the federalism cases, which deal with disputes between the federal government and the states. Warren and Burger favor the federal government in about two-thirds of such cases, but Rehnquist does so in less than 40 percent. These data are representative of the findings of most such studies. Within given issue areas, individual justices tend to show consistent ideological predispositions.

Moreover, we often hear that a particular Court is ideologically predisposed toward one side or the other. For example, in 1993 the *Wall Street Journal* ran a story entitled "The Right Rules Supreme: America's

43. The classic works in this area are Pritchett, *The Roosevelt Court;* Glendon Schubert, *The Judicial Mind* (Evanston, Ill.: Northwestern University Press, 1965); and Rohde and Spaeth, *Supreme Court Decision Making.* For a lucid, modern-day treatment, see Segal and Spaeth, *The Supreme Court and the Attitudinal Model,* chap. 6.

FIGURE 2-2   Court Decisions on Economics and Civil Liberties Cases, 1953 and 1991 Terms

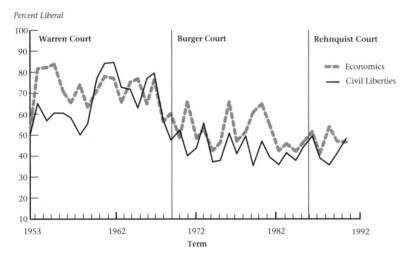

Percent Liberal

SOURCE: Lee Epstein, Jeffrey A. Segal, Harold J. Spaeth, and Thomas G. Walker, *The Supreme Court Compendium: Data, Decisions, and Developments* (Washington, D.C.: Congressional Quarterly, 1994), Table 3-8.

Highest Court Was Dominated by Conservatives in the '92–'93 Term."[44] Sometimes an entire Court era is described in attitudinal terms, such as the "liberal" Warren Court or the "conservative" Rehnquist Court. Figure 2-2 confirms that these labels have some basis in fact. Looking at the two lines from left to right, from the 1950s through the 1990s, you will note the downward trend, indicating the increased conservatism of the Court in economics and civil liberties cases.

How valuable are the ideological terms used to describe particular justices or Courts in helping us understand judicial decision making? On the one hand, knowledge of justices' ideologies can lead to fairly accurate predictions about their voting behavior. Suppose, for example, that the Rehnquist Court hands down a decision dealing with the death penalty and that the vote in the case is 8–1 in favor of the criminal defendant. The most conservative member of the Court (at least on death penalty cases) is Justice An-

tonin Scalia—he almost always votes against the defendant. If we were to predict that Justice Scalia was the dissenter in our hypothetical death penalty case, we would almost certainly be right.[45]

On the other hand, preference-based approaches are not foolproof. First, how do we know if a particular justice is liberal or conservative? The answer is that we know a justice is liberal or conservative because he or she casts liberal or conservative votes. For example, Justice Scalia favors conservative positions on the Court because he is a conservative; we know he is a conservative because he favors conservative positions in the cases he decides. This is circular reasoning indeed.[46] Second, knowing that a justice is liberal or conservative or that the Court decided a case in a lib-

45. We adopt this example from Segal and Spaeth, *The Supreme Court and the Attitudinal Model*, 223.

46. Some scholars have sought to determine justices' ideology from sources independent of their votes. Jeffrey A. Segal and Albert D. Cover, for example, used newspaper editors' assessments of judicial candidates to derive ideological scores for some of the more recent justices. See "Ideological Values and the Votes of U.S. Supreme Court Justices," *American Political Science Review* 83 (1989): 557. This approach works, but because editors paid little attention to judicial nominations prior to the 1930s, it cannot be extended very far back in time.

44. Robert Rice, "The Right Rules Supreme," *Wall Street Journal*, September 14, 1993, 14.

eral or conservative way does not tell us much about the Court's (or the country's) policy positions. To say that *Roe v. Wade* (1973) is a liberal decision is to say little about the policies governing abortion in the United States. If it did, this book would be nothing more than a list of cases labeled liberal or conservative. But such labels would give us no sense of 200 years of constitutional interpretation.

Finally, we must understand that ideological labels are occasionally time dependent, that they are bound to particular historical eras. Consider *Muller v. Oregon* (1908), in which the Supreme Court upheld a state law that set a maximum number on the hours women (but not men) could work. How would you, today's student, view such an opinion? You might classify it as conservative because it seems to patronize and protect women. But in the context of the early 1900s, most considered *Muller* to be a liberal ruling that permitted the government to put an end to the sweatshop conditions women faced in the workplace.

A related problem is that some decisions do not fall neatly on a single conservative-liberal dimension. Think about *Wisconsin v. Mitchell* (1993) in which the Court upheld a state law that increased the sentence for crimes if the defendant "intentionally selects the person against whom the crime is committed" on the basis of race, religion, national origin, sexual orientation, and other similar criteria. Is this ruling liberal or conservative? If you view the law as penalizing racial or ethnic hatred, you would likely see it as a liberal decision. However, if you see the law as treating criminal defendants more harshly and penalizing a person because of what he or she believes or says, the ruling is conservative.

Roles. Another concept within the policy-based category of preferences is the judicial role, which scholars have defined as the "norms of behavior which constrain the activities of the role occupant."[47] In oth-

er words, some students of the Court argue that each jurist has a view of his or her role, a view that is based upon fundamental beliefs of what a good judge should do or what the proper role of the Court should be. The belief is that jurists vote in accordance with these role conceptions.

Analysts typically discuss judicial roles in terms of activism and restraint. An activist justice believes that the proper role of the Court is to assert independent positions in deciding cases, to review the actions of the other branches vigorously, to strike down unconstitutional acts willingly, and to impose far-reaching remedies for legal wrongs whenever necessary. Restraint-oriented justices take the opposite position. Courts should not become involved in the operations of the other branches unless absolutely necessary. The benefit of the doubt should be given to actions taken by elected officials. Courts should impose remedies that are narrowly tailored to correct a specific legal wrong.

Based on these definitions, we might expect to find activist justices more willing than their opposites to strike down legislation. Therefore, a natural question to ask is this: To what extent have specific jurists practiced judicial activism or restraint? The data in Table 2-3 address this question by reporting the votes of justices on the Court between 1953 and 1991 in cases in which the majority declared federal, state, or local legislation unconstitutional. Note the wide variation among the justices, even for those who sat together and therefore heard many of the same cases. For example, compare Justice Powell's rate of nearly 90 percent (meaning that he almost always voted with the majority to strike down laws) with Chief Justice Burger's 68 percent—a difference of more than 20 percentage points, despite the fact that Burger's and Powell's tenures on the Court almost completely overlapped! Perhaps most interesting is the behavior of Justice Frankfurter. In many Supreme Court opinions, Frankfurter declared his adherence to the doctrine of judicial restraint. But the data—although limited to the last nine years of his service on the

47. James L. Gibson, "Judges' Role Orientations, Attitudes, and Decisions," *American Political Science Review* 72 (1978): 917.

TABLE 2-3 Votes in Support of and Opposition to Decisions Declaring Legislation Unconstitutional, 1953–1991 Terms

Justice	Votes on State, Local Laws	Percentage	Votes on Federal Laws	Percentage
Black	128–33	79.5	24–6	80.0
Blackmun	224–69	76.5	22–9	71.0
Brennan	370–12	96.9	51–3	94.4
Burger	154–72	68.1	20–8	71.4
Burton	16–7	69.6	0–3	0.0
Clark	88–23	79.3	6–8	42.9
Douglas	225–10	95.7	30–3	90.9
Fortas	35–3	92.1	11–0	100.0
Frankfurter	32–8	80.0	3–3	50.0
Goldberg	49–3	94.2	6–0	100.0
Harlan	98–56	63.6	16–14	53.3
Jackson	8–0	100.0	0–0	—
Kennedy	35–3	92.1	4–0	100.0
Marshall	271–14	95.1	35–5	87.5
Minton	11–2	84.6	0–0	—
O'Connor	70–33	68.0	15–1	93.8
Powell	171–20	89.5	20–3	87.0
Reed	13–2	86.7	0–0	—
Rehnquist	87–146	37.3	14–14	50.0
Scalia	30–18	62.5	7–0	100.0
Souter	11–1	91.7	2–0	100.0
Stevens	148–22	87.1	14–7	66.7
Stewart	235–45	83.9	29–10	74.4
Thomas	4–4	50.0	1–0	100.0
Warren	129–6	95.6	18–6	75.0
White	297–73	80.3	30–22	57.7
Whittaker	20–3	87.0	2–2	50.0

SOURCE: Lee Epstein, Jeffrey A. Segal, Harold J. Spaeth, and Thomas G. Walker, *The Supreme Court Compendium: Data, Decisions, and Developments* (Washington, D.C.: Congressional Quarterly, 1994), Table 6-7.

NOTE: Includes only those cases in which a majority voted to declare legislation unconstitutional. Figures to the left of the dash indicate the number of votes in favor of striking down legislation; figures to the right indicate the number of votes in favor of upholding the legislation. The other columns give the percentages of cases in which the justice voted with the majority to declare legislation unconstitutional.

bench—reveal a justice who did not hesitate to vote with the majority to overturn legislation.

The Frankfurter example should make clear that what justices say they do and what they actually do may be two different things.[48] But it also illustrates a less obvious point: judicial activism and restraint do not necessarily equal judicial liberalism and conservatism. An activist judge need not be liberal, and a judge who practices restraint need not be conservative. As for Frankfurter, Segal and Spaeth argue that in his voting behavior he was "a staunch economic conservative" who was willing to strike down laws that impinged on his policy preferences.[49] Among the twenty-seven justices who served on the Court between 1953 and 1994, only two—Harlan and Whittaker—supported liberal outcomes in economic cases at a rate lower than Frankfurter's 39 percent. In other words, in some areas of the law, Frankfurter was a conservative activist.

It is also true that so-called liberal Courts are no more likely to strike down legislation than are conservative Courts. Consider Figure 2-3, which shows the number of federal, state, and local laws struck down since 1789. Note the relatively high numbers of statutes declared unconstitutional during the 1920s and by the Burger and Rehnquist Courts. We have already learned that the 1970s and 1980s were periods of relative conservatism on the Court; the 1920s, as we shall see throughout the book, was also a conservative period. Such activism calls into question whether there is a strong relationship between ideology and judicial role.

We have shown that one can use measures, such as the number of laws struck down, to assess the extent to which justices practice judicial activism or restraint. But does such information help us understand Supreme Court decision making? This question is difficult to answer because few scholars have stud-

48. For a more detailed examination of Frankfurter's voting, see Harold J. Spaeth, "The Judicial Restraint of Mr. Justice Frankfurter—Myth or Reality," *American Journal of Political Science* 8 (1964): 22.
49. See *The Supreme Court and the Attitudinal Model*, 236–237.

FIGURE 2-3 Provisions of Federal, State, and Local Laws and Ordinances Held Unconstitutional by the Supreme Court, 1789–1992

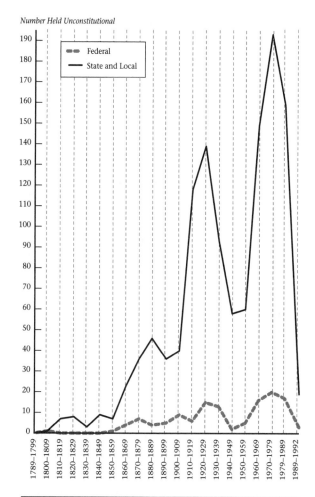

Number Held Unconstitutional

SOURCE: Harold W. Stanley and Richard G. Niemi, *Vital Statistics on American Politics*, 4th ed. (Washington, D.C.: CQ Press, 1994), 308.

NOTE: The last period includes only three years rather than a full decade, which may explain the apparent decline.

ied the relationship between roles and voting in a systematic way.

The paucity of scholarly work on judicial roles leads to one criticism of the approach: it is virtually impossible to separate roles from attitudes. When Justice Frankfurter voted to uphold an economically conservative law, can we necessarily conclude that he was practicing restraint? The answer, quite clearly, is no. It may have been his conservative attitude toward economic cases—not restraint—that led him to uphold the law.

Another criticism of role approaches is similar to that leveled at attitudinal factors—they tell us very little about the resulting policy in a case. Again, to say that *Roe v. Wade* was an activist decision (it did, after all, strike down abortion laws in all fifty states) is to say nothing about the policy content of the opinion.

Strategic Approaches

As a class, strategic approaches argue that justices are rational decision makers who have certain preferences about the outcomes of Court decisions and seek to join opinions that reflect those preferences. While policy-based approaches focus on the individual justice, suggesting that he or she reaches decisions alone, strategic approaches contend that we ought to consider that each justice operates in a setting with eight colleagues. As a consequence, a justice's vote may well depend upon what the other justices do or what they are expected to do.[50]

Such approaches to Supreme Court decision making seem to be sensible: after all, justices can do very little on their own. It takes a majority vote to decide a case and a majority agreeing on a single opinion to set precedent. Under such conditions, human interaction is important and case outcomes—not to mention the rationale of decisions—can be influenced by relations among the members of the group.

Although strategic approaches have not been studied as thoroughly as, say, judicial attitudes, a number of influential works point to their importance. Research conducted by Walter F. Murphy, David J. Danelski, and J. Woodford Howard into the private papers of the former justices consistently has shown

50. Strategic approaches are not limited to what a justice expects his or her colleagues to do. They also take into account expectations concerning other political institutions (for example, the president, Congress). We take these up later in the chapter.

that through intellectual persuasion, effective bargaining over opinion writing, informal lobbying, and so forth, justices have influenced the actions of their colleagues.[51]

How does strategic behavior manifest itself? One way is the frequency of vote changes. During the deliberations that occur shortly after oral argument, the justices discuss the case and vote on it. But these votes do not become final until the opinions are completed and the decision is made public *(see Appendix 8 for information on Court procedures)*. Research has shown that between the initial vote on the merits of cases and the official announcement of the decision at least one vote switch occurs in more than half of all cases.[52] This figure indicates that justices change their minds—a phenomenon that attitudinal-based approaches cannot explain.

Consider an example unearthed from the papers of Justice Thurgood Marshall. During the 1990 term the justices unanimously voted in conference to affirm the lower court judgment in *Owen v. Owen,* a bankruptcy case. Chief Justice Rehnquist assigned the majority opinion to Justice Scalia. Scalia circulated his draft on December 3 with an accompanying memo: "I was as firm as any of you in my opinion that the judgment in this case had to be an affirmance. I found it impossible, however, to write it that way. . . . I hope that you may agree with me, but otherwise the opinion will have to be reassigned." In other words, Scalia was telling his colleagues that he had changed his mind and written to reverse the lower court opinion.

Justice Marshall scribbled NO!!! and WAIT in large letters across the Scalia draft; the chief justice responded with a rather curt note to Scalia, asserting that he should not have written the opinion since he had changed his mind; rather, he should have asked to have it reassigned immediately. Rehnquist decided to have a go at it himself. In the meantime, just four days later Justice O'Connor indicated that she could "join something along [the] lines" Scalia proposed. Suddenly, the nine-person majority to affirm had dwindled to seven.

Another defection from the majority came in February, when Rehnquist sent the following memo to the others:

After Nino [Scalia] circulated his draft opinion coming out to "reverse" rather than to "affirm," I reassigned this case to myself. . . . After having made this effort, I have decided that Nino was correct. . . . Anyone else wishing to do so, of course, is free to try their hand at the same task which I attempted. . . . I therefore assign the case back to Nino and join his revised opinion.

By the end of March, every justice, save John Paul Stevens, had agreed to sign Scalia's opinion. And even Stevens was open to persuasion. During the early days of April he and Scalia exchanged several memos on possible revisions to the opinion. In the end, Scalia could not accommodate Stevens, and Stevens ended up writing a lone dissent that took the position the entire group of nine originally had expressed in conference.

Over a few short months, a 9–0 vote to affirm became an 8–1 decision to reverse. Surely, such a large vote shift is unusual. But our perusal of the Thurgood Marshall papers leads us, like previous scholars, to conclude that it is not unusual for justices to reevaluate their initial positions or to succumb to the persuasion of their colleagues. Nor is it atypical for colleagues to attempt to persuade each other of the merits of their positions.

Vote shifts are just one manifestation of the interdependence of the Court's decision-making process. Another is the revision of opinions that occurs in almost every Court case. As opinion writers seek to ac-

---

51. Walter F. Murphy, *Elements of Judicial Strategy* (Chicago: University of Chicago Press, 1964); David J. Danelski, "The Influence of the Chief Justice in the Decisional Process of the Supreme Court," in *The Federal Judicial System,* ed. Thomas P. Jahnige and Sheldon Goldman (New York: Holt, Rinehart and Winston, 1968); J. Woodford Howard, "On the Fluidity of Judicial Choice," *American Political Science Review* 62 (1968): 43–56.

52. Saul Brenner, "Fluidity on the Supreme Court, 1956–1967," *American Journal of Political Science* 26 (1982): 388; and Brenner, "Fluidity on the United States Supreme Court: A Re-examination," *American Journal of Political Science* 24 (1980): 526. His data are for the Vinson and Warren Courts only.

commodate their colleagues' wishes, their drafts may undergo five, ten, even fifteen revisions. Such bargaining over the content of an opinion is quite important because it can alter significantly the policy ultimately expressed. *Griswold v. Connecticut* (1965), in which the Court considered the constitutionality of a state law that prohibited the dissemination of birth control devices and information, even to married couples, provides a clear example. In his initial draft of the majority opinion, Justice Douglas struck down the law on the grounds that it interfered with the First Amendment's right to association. A memorandum from Justice Brennan, however, convinced Douglas to alter his rationale and to establish the foundation for a right to privacy. "Had the Douglas draft been issued as the *Griswold* opinion of the Court, the case would stand as a precedent on the freedom of association," rather than serve as the landmark ruling it became.[53]

Although strategic approaches have their uses, *Griswold* points to a problem with them: to date, scholarly treatments have been ad hoc or case specific. We do not know the extent to which a case like *Griswold* represents the rule or the anomaly. Until analysts begin to study interdependent decision making more systematically, using manuscript collections such as Marshall's, the general value of this approach will remain unknown.

Political Factors

In the previous section we considered how strategic approaches take into account internal bargaining on the Court. But they also consider political pressures that come from outside the Court. In what follows, we consider three sources of such influence: public opinion, partisan politics, and interest groups.

For these factors, it is important to keep in mind that the justices do not have to face reelection. Indeed, one of the fundamental differences between the Supreme Court and the political branches is that there is

no direct electoral connection between the justices and the public. Once appointed, justices may serve for life. They are not accountable to the public and are not required to undergo any periodic reevaluation of their decisions. Therefore, an ever-present question is why they would let the stuff of ordinary politics, such as public opinion and interest groups, influence their opinions.

Public Opinion. The president and members of Congress are always trying to keep in touch with what the people are thinking. Conducting and analyzing public opinion polls are never-ending tasks. There is good reason for these activities. The political branches are supposed to represent the people, and the incumbents' reelection prospects can be jeopardized by straying too far from what the public wants. But federal judges—including Supreme Court justices—are not dependent upon pleasing the public to stay in office, and they do not serve in the same kind of representative capacity as legislators do.

Does that mean, however, that the justices are not affected by public opinion? Certainly, we can think of times when the Court has handed down rulings that fly in the face of what the public wants. The most obvious example occurred after Franklin Roosevelt's 1932 election to the presidency. By choosing Roosevelt (as well as electing many Democrats to Congress), the people were sending a clear signal that they wanted the government to take vigorous action to end the Great Depression. The president and Congress responded with many laws—the so-called New Deal legislation—but the Court remained unmoved by the public's endorsement of Roosevelt and his legislation. In case after case (at least until 1937), the justices struck down many of the laws and administrative programs designed to get the economy moving again.

In contrast, there have been times when the Court seems to have embraced public opinion, especially under conditions of extreme national stress. One example occurred during World War II. In *Korematsu v. United States* (1944) the justices endorsed the govern-

53. See Bernard Schwartz, *The Unpublished Opinions of the Warren Court* (New York: Oxford University Press, 1985), chap. 7.

FIGURE 2-4 The Supreme Court and Public Opinion

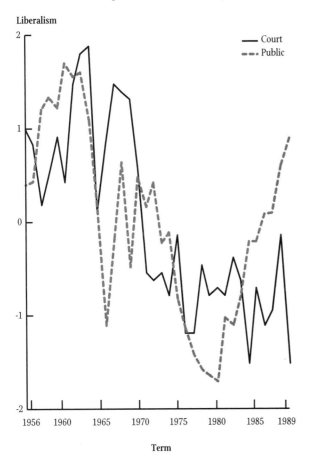

SOURCE: William Mishler and Reginald S. Sheehan, "The Supreme Court as a Counter-Majoritarian Institution? The Impact of Public Opinion on Supreme Court Decisions," *American Political Science Review* 87 (1993): 91.

NOTE: The two series are a public mood score and percentage of Supreme Court decisions decided in the liberal direction. For purposes of presentation, we have standardized the two series.

ment's program to move all Japanese-Americans from the Pacific Coast states to inland relocation centers. The justices clearly were swept away by the same tide of wartime apprehension as the rest of the nation.

In addition to studying specific cases, scholars also conduct more systematic research. Many analysts indicate that particular Court rulings do not deviate significantly from the views of the citizenry. As politi-

cal scientist Thomas Marshall wrote, "Most modern Court decisions reflect public opinion. When a clear-cut poll majority or plurality exists, over three-fifths of the Court's decisions reflect the polls. By all arguable evidence the modern Supreme Court appears to reflect public opinion about as accurately as other policy makers."[54] Moreover, some argue that Court decisions also may reflect more general societal trends. Figure 2-4 plots the ideological mood of the public against the ideological direction of Supreme Court decisions. Two researchers claim a correspondence between decision and mood trends: the justices "are broadly aware of fundamental trends in the ideological tenor of public opinion, and that at least some justices, consciously or not, may adjust their decisions at the margins to accommodate such fundamental trends."[55] However, as you look at the figure, note that the relationship is not exact; in other words, public opinion and Court decisions are not the same at any given time. Rather, the Court seems to lag behind public opinion.

Let us assume that these scholars are correct and that Supreme Court decisions track the public opinion polls. That assumption raises a question: Why do justices consider the views of the public in deciding cases when their jobs do not depend upon winning public approval?[56] Scholars offer a number of reasons. First, because they are political appointees, nominated and approved by popularly elected officials, it is logical that the justices will reflect, however subtly, the views of the majority. It is probably true, for example, that an individual radically out of step with either the president or the Senate would not be nominated, much less confirmed. A second reason relates to the institutional setting of the Court. Put sim-

54. Thomas Marshall, *Public Opinion and the Supreme Court* (New York: Unwin Hyman, 1989), 97.

55. William Mishler and Reginald S. Sheehan, "The Supreme Court as a Counter-Majoritarian Institution? The Impact of Public Opinion on Supreme Court Decisions," *American Political Science Review* 87 (1993): 89.

56. We adopt this discussion from Lee Epstein and Joseph F. Kobylka, *The Supreme Court and Legal Change: Abortion and the Death Penalty* (Chapel Hill: University of North Carolina Press, 1992), 21–22.

ply, the justices lack any real mechanism for enforcing their decisions. Instead, they depend not only on other political officials to support their positions but also on general public compliance, especially when controversial Court opinions will have ramifications well beyond the particular concerns of the parties to the suit. Finally, the Court, at least occasionally, views public opinion as a legitimate guide for decisions. It has even gone so far as to incorporate that dimension into some of its jurisprudential standards. For example, in evaluating whether certain kinds of punishments violate the Eighth Amendment's prohibition against cruel and unusual punishment, the Court proclaimed that it would look toward "evolving standards of decency," as defined by public sentiment.[57]

Some scholars, however, remain unconvinced of the role of public opinion in Court decision making. In part, this disbelief emanates from a concern about the nature of the research that has been conducted. Helmut Norpoth and Jeffrey Segal, for example, criticized the study that produced the data depicted in Figure 2-4.[58] In reexamining that study's methodology, they reasoned as follows: "Does public opinion influence Supreme Court decisions? If the model of influence is of the sort where the justices set aside their own (ideological) preferences and abide by what they divine as the vox populi, our answer is a resounding no." What Norpoth and Segal find, instead, is that Court appointments made by Richard Nixon in the early 1970s caused a "sizable ideological shift" in the direction of Court decisions. Therefore, it was the entry of conservative justices that created the illusion that the Court was echoing public opinion.

Partisan Politics. As Jonathan Casper wrote, we cannot overestimate "the importance of the political context in which the Court does its work." In his view, the statement that the Court follows the election returns "recognizes that the choices the Court makes are related to developments in the broader political system."[59] In other words, the political environment has an effect on Court behavior. In fact, many assert that the Court is responsive to the influence of partisan politics, both internally and externally.

On the inner workings of the Court, social scientists long have argued that political creatures inhabit the Court, that justices are not simply neutral arbiters of the law. Since 1789, the beginning of constitutional government in the United States, those who have ascended to the bench have come from the political institutions of government or, at the very least, have affiliated with a particular political party. Judicial scholars recognize that justices bring with them the philosophies of those partisan attachments. Just as the members of the present Court tend to reflect the views of the Republican or Democratic parties, so too did the justices who came from the ranks of the Federalist and Jeffersonian parties. As one might expect, justices who affiliate with the Democratic party tend to be more liberal in their decision making than those who are Republicans.[60]

The Court also faces political pressure from the outside. Although the justices have no electoral connection or mandate of responsiveness, we recognize that the other institutions of government have some influence on judicial behavior; and, naturally, the direction of that influence will reflect the partisan composition of those branches. For example, the Court has always had a "multifaceted relationship" with the president, a relationship that provides the president with "several sources of potential influence."[61] Some of those sources directly link the president and the Court, including (1) the president's power to nominate justices and, thereby, the ability to shape the Court; (2) the relationships many presidents have en-

---

57. *Trop v. Dulles* (1958).

58. "Popular Influence in Supreme Court Decisions," *American Political Science Review* 88 (September 1994): 711–716.

59. *The Politics of Civil Liberties* (New York: Harper and Row, 1972), 293.

60. See C. Neal Tate, "Personal Attribute Models of Voting Behavior of U.S. Supreme Court Justices: Liberalism in Civil Liberties and Economics Decisions, 1946–1978," *American Journal of Political Science* 75 (1981): 355–367.

61. Baum, *The Supreme Court*, 4th ed., 143.

joyed with sitting justices, including Franklin Roosevelt's with James Byrnes, Lyndon Johnson's with Abe Fortas, and Richard Nixon's with Warren Burger; and (3) the notion that the president, having been elected within the previous four years, may carry a popular mandate, reflecting the preferences of the people, which would affect the environment within which the Court operates.[62]

A less direct source of influence is the executive branch, which operates under the president's command. The bureaucracy can assist the Court in implementing its policies, or it can hinder the Court by refusing to do so, a fact of which the justices are well aware. As a judicial body, the Supreme Court cannot implement or execute its own decisions. The Court often must depend on the executive branch to give its decisions legitimacy through action. The Court, therefore, may act strategically, anticipating the wishes of the executive branch and responding accordingly to avoid a confrontation that could threaten its legitimacy. Along these lines, *Marbury v. Madison* (1803), in which the Court enunciated the doctrine of judicial review, provides a classic example. Some scholars suggest that the justices knew if they ruled in a certain direction, the administration would not carry out their orders. Because the Court felt that such a failure would threaten the legitimacy of judicial institutions, it crafted its opinion in a way that would not force the administration to take any action, but would send a message about its displeasure with the administration's politics.

Another indirect source of presidential influence is the U.S. solicitor general, a presidential appointee whose office presents the position of the federal government in written briefs and oral arguments and represents the interests of the United States in Supreme Court litigation. The solicitor general's office can affect two aspects of Supreme Court decision making. First, the office may express an opinion on whether the Court should grant an appealed case a full hearing. The Court relies on these arguments as a preconference screening device, as a way to filter out insignificant petitions. To the extent that the office helps the Court set its agenda, the solicitor general is able to ensure that the justices consider the administration's political goals and priorities. Second, through written briefs and oral arguments, the justices expect that solicitors general will share their expertise with them, thereby becoming the Court's "tenth justice." This participation occurs both when the federal government is an actual party to an appeal and when the solicitor general acts as an amicus curiae (friend of the Court) expressing views on an appeal in which the government has an interest but is not a formal litigant. In fact, as Table 2-4 indicates, the solicitor general is a most successful amicus in Supreme Court litigation, regardless of the particular administration in office at the time. Data on the government's participation as a party also point to its ability to convince the justices to adopt its preferred positions.[63]

That the president and the executive branch are in a position to affect Supreme Court decision making is undoubtedly true. What also seems to be the case is that the particular party affiliation of the president has a great deal to do with the ideological direction of that influence. Presidents want to see their views, usually reflecting those of their party, translated into law. Such motivation tells us a great deal about the justices they nominate and reflects a partisan pattern of judicial selection politics that began with George Washington's packing the Court with Federalists and carried through Bill Clinton's appointments.

Presidential influence is also demonstrated in the kinds of arguments their solicitors general bring into the Court. That is, solicitors general representing Democratic administrations tend to present more liberal arguments; those from the ranks of the Republi-

---

62. For more on the relationship between the president and the justices, see Henry J. Abraham, *Justices and Presidents*, 3d ed. (New York: Oxford University Press, 1992).

63. See Lee Epstein et al., *The Supreme Court Compendium: Data, Decisions, and Developments* (Washington, D.C.: Congressional Quarterly, 1994), Tables 7-10 and 7-11.

TABLE 2-4 Success Rate of the Solicitor General as an Amicus Curiae, by President, 1952–1990 Terms

President	Total Number of Cases[a]	Percentage Won
Eisenhower	42	83.3
Kennedy	48	87.5
Johnson	41	82.9
Nixon	79	70.9
Ford	38	71.1
Carter	86	65.1
Reagan[b]	123	67.5
Bush[c]	99	75.8

SOURCE: Lee Epstein, Jeffrey A. Segal, Harold J. Spaeth, and Thomas G. Walker, *The Supreme Court Compendium: Data, Decisions, and Developments* (Washington, D.C.: Congressional Quarterly, 1994), Table 7-12.

a. Includes all cases where the solicitor general filed amicus curiae briefs and the Court decided the case with an opinion on the merits.

b. Includes 1980–1982 and 1986–1987 terms.

c. Includes 1988–1990 terms.

can party, more conservative arguments. The transition from the Bush administration to Clinton's provides an interesting illustration. Bush's solicitor general had filed amicus curiae briefs—many of which took a conservative position—in a number of cases heard by the Court during the 1993–1994 term. Drew S. Days III, Clinton's solicitor general, rewrote at least four of those briefs to reflect the new administration's more liberal posture. For example, Days argued that the Civil Rights Act of 1991 should be applied retroactively, whereas the Bush administration suggested that it should not be; in another case, Days claimed that jurors cannot be dismissed on the basis of sex; his predecessor argued that such dismissals were constitutional.[64]

Congress, too—or so some argue—can influence Supreme Court decision making. Like the president, the legislature has many powers over the Court that the justices cannot ignore.[65] Some of these resemble those of the president—the Senate's role in confirmation proceedings, the implementation of judicial decisions—but there are others. Congress can restrict the Court's jurisdiction to hear cases, enact legislation or even propose constitutional amendments to recast Court decisions, and hold judicial salaries constant. In addition, the "goal of deterring or ending a congressional attack on the Court may influence the Court's policy choices."[66] Often cited examples include the Court's willingness to defer to the Radical Republican Congress after the Civil War and to approve New Deal legislation after Roosevelt proposed his Court-packing plan in 1937. (He proposed to appoint one new justice for every sitting justice who had attained the age of seventy, thus adding a number of justices to the Court.) As these—and many other—examples illustrate, relations between the Court and Congress are hardly random. The partisan composition of the legislature vis-à-vis the Court plays a major role in determining whether those relations are antagonistic or amiable.

The effect partisan politics has on the Court has been widely explored. For the most part, analysts agree that politics influences the justices or, at least, the environment in which they work. Still, the criticism leveled against public opinion research may apply here: partisan politics only indirectly affects the Court through presidential appointments and, perhaps, through the office of the solicitor general. What is more, some would argue that the Court has no reason to respond strategically to Congress, in particular, since it is so rare that the legislature threatens, much less takes action, against the judiciary. Only once, for example, has Congress retaliated against the Court by removing its jurisdiction over a class of cases—and that occurred more than 100 years ago.[67] This argument needs to be kept in mind as you read the cases that pit the Court against Congress and the president.

64. William H. Freivogel, "Ginsburg May Alter Balance in Key Civil Rights Cases," *St. Louis Post-Dispatch*, October 3, 1993, 1B.

65. Baum, *The Supreme Court*, 4th ed., 141. See also William N. Eskridge, Jr., "Overriding Supreme Court Statutory Interpretation Decisions," *Yale Law Journal* 101 (1991): 331.

66. Baum, *The Supreme Court*, 4th ed., 142.

67. For a different view, see Eskridge, "Overriding Supreme Court Statutory Interpretation Decisions," and Lee Epstein and Thomas G. Walker, "The Role of the Supreme Court in American Society: Playing the Reconstruction Game," in *Contemplating Courts*, ed. Lee Epstein (Washington, D.C.: CQ Press, 1995).

Interest Groups. In *Federalist*, No. 78, Alexander Hamilton wrote that the U.S. Supreme Court was "to declare the sense of the law" through "inflexible and uniform adherence to the rights of the constitution and individuals." Despite this expectation, Supreme Court litigation has become political over time.[68] We see manifestations of politics in virtually every aspect of the Court's work, from the nomination and confirmation of justices to the factors that influence their decisions. But perhaps the most striking example of this politicization is the incursion of organized interests into the judicial process.

Naturally, interest groups may not attempt to persuade the Supreme Court with the methods lobbyists use to deal with Congress. It would be grossly improper for the representatives of an interest group to approach a Supreme Court justice directly. Instead, interest groups try to influence Court decisions by submitting written legal arguments called amicus curiae briefs *(see Box 2-2)*. This procedure allows interest groups to make their views known to the Court, even when the group is not a direct party to the litigation. As Figure 2-5 shows, interest groups are now a major presence in Supreme Court litigation. The data indicate that the majority of cases contain at least one amicus curiae brief filed by an organized interest. On average, 84.4 percent of all full opinion cases decided between 1986 and 1991 contained at least one amicus curiae brief, and the average amicus case contained 4.4 briefs. During the 1990 term more than 4.5 amici cosigned the typical amicus curiae brief, for a total of about 1,800 organized participants. In addition to participating as amici, groups are sponsoring cases— that is, providing litigants with attorneys and the money necessary to pursue their cases—in record numbers.

The explosion of interest group participation in Supreme Court litigation raises two questions. First,

FIGURE 2-5 The Percentage of the Supreme Court's Full Opinion Cases Containing at Least One Amicus Curiae Brief, 1953–1990 Terms

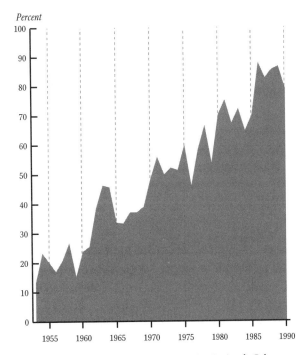

SOURCE: Lee Epstein, "Interest Group Litigation During the Rehnquist Court Era," *The Journal of Law and Politics* 9 (1993): 645.

why do groups, in ever-increasing numbers, go to the Court? One answer is obvious: they want to influence the Court's decisions. But groups also go to the Supreme Court to achieve other, more subtle ends. One of these is the setting of institutional agendas. In other words, by filing amicus curiae briefs at the case-selection stage or by simply bringing cases to the Court's attention, organizations seek to influence the justices' decisions on which disputes they will hear.[69] Group participation also may serve as a counterbalance to other interests that have competing goals. Table 2-5 lists some of the interests participating as amici in *Lucas v. South Carolina Coastal Council* (1992), in which

68. Some of the views expressed in this section come from Lee Epstein, "Interest Group Litigation During the Rehnquist Court Era," *Journal of Law and Politics* 9 (1993): 639–717.

69. See Gregory A. Caldeira and John R. Wright, "Organized Interests and Agenda Setting in the U.S. Supreme Court," *American Political Science Review* 82 (1988): 1109–1127.

BOX 2-2   AMICUS CURIAE PARTICIPATION

No. 91-453

In the Supreme Court of the United States
OCTOBER TERM, 1991

DAVID H. LUCAS,

Petioner,

v.

SOUTH CAROLINA COASTAL COUNCIL,

Respondent,

ON WRIT OF CERTIORARI TO THE
SUPREME COURT OF SOUTH CAROLINA

BRIEF *AMICI CURIAE* OF SIERRA CLUB,
THE HUMANE SOCIETY OF THE UNITED STATES,
AND THE AMERICAN INSTITUTE OF BIOLOGICAL
SCIENCES IN SUPPORT OF RESPONDENT

Of Counsel:

LAURENS H. SILVER
Sierra Club Defense
    Fund
180 Montgomery Street
Suite 140
San Francisco, CA 94104

CHARLES M. CHAMBERS
    Counsel
American Institute of
    Biological Sciences
730 11th Street, N.W.
Washington, D.C. 20001-4521

February 3, 1992

LAWRENCE N. MINCH
Counsel of Record
CAROLE L. MORRELL
LILLICK & CHARLES
Two Embarcadero Center
San Francisco, CA 94111
(415) 984-8200

Attorneys for Amici Curiae

The amicus curiae practice probably originates in Roman law. A judge would often appoint a *consilium* (officer of the court) "to advise him on points on which he [was] in doubt."[1] That may be why the term amicus curiae translates from the Latin as "friend of the court." But today it is the rare amicus who is a friend of the court. Rather, contemporary briefs almost always are a friend of a party, supporting one side over the other.[2] Consider the brief filed in *Lucas v. South Carolina Coastal Council* (1992), the cover of which is reprinted here. In that case attorneys for the Sierra Club and other organizations supported the Coastal Council, which had prohibited Lucas from undertaking any new construction on oceanfront lots he owned. They argued that the council acted properly, for it was seeking to protect shoreline areas against erosion and other environmental dangers. In other words, these groups were anything but neutral participants.

How does an organization become an amicus curiae participant in the Supreme Court of the United States? Under the Court's rules, groups wishing to file an amicus brief must obtain the written consent of the parties to the litigation (the federal and state governments are exempt from this requirement). If the parties refuse to give their consent, the group can file a motion with the Court asking for its permission. The Court today almost always grants these motions.

1. Frank Covey, Jr., "Amicus Curiae: Friend of the Court," *De Paul Law Review* 9 (1959): 33.
2. See Samuel Krislov, "The Amicus Curiae Brief: From Friendship to Advocacy," *Yale Law Journal* 72 (1963): 694–721, for a history of amicus curiae practice in the United States.

---

the Rehnquist Court considered whether David Lucas could build houses on two vacant oceanfront lots—construction the state prohibited to protect the shoreline against erosion and other environmental dangers *(see Box 2-2)*. While the interests listed here represent only a small fraction of the approximately 100 groups and individuals participating in *Lucas,* the goal of balancing is evident: supporters of Lucas and the state matched constituency for constituency, at least in the areas of government, environment/public interest, and land use.

Finally, groups go to the Court to publicize their causes and their organizations. The NAACP Legal Defense Fund's (LDF) legendary litigation campaigns in

TABLE 2-5   Selected Amici Curiae in *Lucas v. South Carolina Coastal Council*

Interest	Supporters of Lucas	Supporters of the State
Governments	United States 4 U.S. Senators	27 States U.S. Conference of Mayors, Council of State Governments, National League of Cities
Environment/ Public Interest	Environmental Conservation Organization Institute for Justice Pacific Legal Foundation Washington Legal Foundation	Sierra Club Environmental Defense Fund National Audubon Society Natural Resources Defense Council
Land Use/ Property	Property Rights Preservation Association National Association of Realtors	National Trust for Historic Preservation Massachusetts Conservation Commission

housing access and school desegregation cases provide excellent examples: not only did they result in favorable policy decisions and moved civil rights issues to the forefront of the policy agenda, they also established the LDF as the foremost organizational litigant of these issues.

A second and more relevant question is this: Can groups influence the outcomes of Supreme Court decisions? This question is difficult to answer. On the one hand, there is evidence that cases sponsored by interest groups have a greater chance of success than those brought by private parties. This seems to be the lesson of the litigation campaigns of the LDF and, more recently, of those conducted by the Women's Rights Project of the American Civil Liberties Union (ACLU), which has had an unusual degree of success in sex discrimination litigation. Some scholars argue that groups help shape the way the Court resolves issues and can set the context in which the justices do their work.[70] Perhaps the justices, like members of Congress, view groups as the sources of important information that otherwise would not have come to their attention. Table 2-6 lists the number of times justices cited amicus curiae briefs in their opinions from 1953 to 1991. It is interesting to note that the propor-

tion of written opinions citing at least one brief has grown appreciably over the past few decades. The average citation rate for the Warren Court justices was .42; that figure rose to .66 for those serving on the Burger Court; and to .68 for Rehnquist Court jurists.[71] Why this increase has occurred is open to speculation; what is clear is that the justices—now more than ever—are at least learning enough from amicus curiae briefs to cite them in their opinions.

On the other hand, there is equally compelling evidence suggesting that groups are no more successful than other interests. One study paired similar cases decided by the same district court judge, the same year, with the only major difference being that one case was sponsored by a group, the other was not. The study found no major differences between the two types.[72] Research by Donald Songer and Reginald Sheehan reached almost the same conclusion about the effectiveness of amicus curiae briefs in Supreme Court litigation. In seeking to assess the impact of amicus curiae briefs on all written Court decisions from 1967 to 1987, Songer and Sheehan devised a statistical model that considered many factors, such as the

70. See Susan E. Lawrence, *The Poor in Court* (Princeton, N.J.: Princeton University Press, 1990).

71. This figure excludes Thomas and Souter, who had not written enough opinions for meaningful analysis.

72. Lee Epstein and C. K. Rowland, "Debunking the Myth of Interest Group Invincibility in the Courts," *American Political Science Review* 85 (1991): 205–217.

TABLE 2-6 Justices' Citations to Amicus Curiae Briefs, 1953–1991 Terms

Justice	Number of Citations to Amicus Curiae Briefs	Number of Citations to Amicus Curiae Briefs Divided by Total Opinions Written
Black	297	.53
Blackmun	531	.69
Brennan	755	.65
Burger	337	.68
Burton	17	.21
Clark	109	.36
Douglas	416	.45
Fortas	43	.44
Frankfurter	74	.29
Goldberg	87	.39
Harlan	252	.37
Jackson	10	.63
Kennedy	82	.65
Marshall	505	.71
Minton	8	.20
O'Connor	292	.77
Powell	458	.77
Reed	20	.33
Rehnquist	453	.53
Scalia	157	.62
Souter	10	.29
Stevens	607	.71
Stewart	363	.51
Thomas	7	.35
Warren	99	.40
White	660	.66
Whittaker	28	.25

SOURCE: Lee Epstein, Jeffrey A. Segal, Harold J. Spaeth, and Thomas G. Walker, *The Supreme Court Compendium: Data, Decisions, and Developments* (Washington, D.C.: Congressional Quarterly, 1994), Table 7-22.

NOTE: Justices' opinions include opinions of the Court, judgments, and dissenting and concurring opinions. Data for the justices cover the terms from 1953 to 1991. Therefore, for those justices joining the Court prior to 1953, data are not completely descriptive of their careers.

Court's ideological makeup, relevant to decision making.[73] Ultimately, they found that the effects of briefs depended on who filed them.

73. "The Impact of Amicus Briefs on Decisions on the Merits" (Paper presented at the annual meeting of the American Political Science Association, San Francisco, August 30, 1990).

Briefs filed by state and local governments appear to have little effect on the outcome of cases heard by the Supreme Court. Briefs filed by other amicus parties have the potential for a moderate impact on the chances for litigant success as long as they are not opposed by the United States as either a direct party or as amicus curiae. In contrast briefs filed for the United States by the solicitor general were shown to have a major impact on Court decisions even after the effects of [other variables] were taken into account.[74]

In short, the debate over the influence of interest groups continues. And it is one that you will be able to enter, for within the case excerpts we often provide information on the arguments of amici and attorneys. Accordingly, you will be able to assess the extent to which they influence the justices.

There is, as you now know, considerable disagreement in the scholarly and legal communities over why justices decide cases the way they do. As you read the narrative and opinion excerpts that follow, try to keep these different approaches in mind. They and variations of them show up in many of the Court's opinions. Ask yourself which of the approaches the justices seem to be adopting. And, when it comes to legal approaches in particular, consider whether the justices use them to reach decisions or whether the justices— as extralegal approaches would suggest—reach conclusions first and then invoke legal factors to justify them.

READINGS

Barnum, David G. *The Supreme Court and American Democracy.* New York: St. Martin's Press, 1993.

Baum, Lawrence. *The Supreme Court,* 5th ed. Washington, D.C.: CQ Press, 1995.

Carter, Lief H. *Contemporary Constitutional Lawmaking.* New York: Pergamon Press, 1985.

Casper, Jonathan D. *The Politics of Civil Liberties.* New York: Harper and Row, 1972.

Crosskey, W. W., and William Jeffrey, Jr. *Politics and the Constitution in the History of the United States.* Chicago: University of Chicago Press, 1980.

74. Ibid., 12.

Emerson, Thomas I. *Toward a General Theory of the First Amendment.* New York: Random House, 1966.

Epstein, Lee, ed. *Contemplating Courts.* Washington, D.C.: CQ Press, 1995.

Epstein, Lee, Jeffrey A. Segal, Harold J. Spaeth, and Thomas G. Walker. *The Supreme Court Compendium: Data, Decisions, and Developments.* Washington, D.C.: Congressional Quarterly, 1994.

Eskridge, William N., Jr., and John Ferejohn. "The Article I, Section 7 Game." *Georgetown Law Journal* 80 (1992): 523–564.

Fisher, Louis. *Constitutional Dialogues.* Princeton, N.J.: Princeton University Press, 1988.

Goldstein, Leslie Friedman. *In Defense of the Text.* Savage, Md.: Rowman and Littlefield, 1991.

Lawrence, Susan E. *The Poor in Court.* Princeton, N.J.: Princeton University Press, 1990.

Marshall, Thomas. *Public Opinion and the Supreme Court.* New York: Unwin Hyman, 1989.

Murphy, Walter J. *Elements of Judicial Strategy.* Chicago: University of Chicago Press, 1964.

Pritchett, C. Herman. *The Roosevelt Court.* New York: Macmillan, 1948.

Segal, Jeffrey A., and Harold J. Spaeth. *The Supreme Court and the Attitudinal Model.* Cambridge: Cambridge University Press, 1993.

Walker, Thomas G., and Lee Epstein. *The Supreme Court of the United States: An Introduction.* New York: St. Martin's Press, 1992.

Wasby, Stephen L. *The Supreme Court in the Federal Judicial System,* 4th ed. Chicago: Nelson Hall, 1993.

PART II
INSTITUTIONAL AUTHORITY

THE SEPARATION OF POWERS

3. THE JUDICIARY

4. THE LEGISLATURE

5. THE EXECUTIVE

THE SEPARATION OF POWERS

ONE OF THE FIRST THINGS anyone learns in an American government course is that the Constitution prescribes a government consisting of three branches: the legislative, the executive, and the judicial. Each plays a distinct role: the legislature makes the laws, the executive implements those laws, and the judiciary interprets them.

This view of the American political system is not wrong, but it is overly simplified. It tells us of the relative powers of the branches of government, but not of their limits. It ignores the fact that policy in the United States emanates not from the separate actions of the branches of government, but from the interaction among them.

To move beyond the basics of the powers and constraints of institutions requires a consideration of two important subjects. First, we must understand the separation of powers doctrine and why the Framers adopted it, a subject we take up in the following pages. Second, because of the unique role played by the judiciary in the American government system, we must grasp the importance of the Supreme Court's decisions relating to the authority of the three branches of government as well as the constitutional constraints placed upon those institutions. We consider these matters in the next three chapters.

THE ORIGINS OF THE SEPARATION OF POWERS DOCTRINE

Even a casual comparison of the Articles of Confederation with the Constitution reveals major differences in the way the two documents structured the national government. Under the Articles, the powers of government were concentrated in the legislature, a unicameral Congress, with the states having equal voting powers. There was no executive or judicial branch separate and independent from the legislature. Issues of separation of powers and checks and balances were not particularly relevant to the Articles, largely because the national government had little power that might be abused. The states were capable of checking anything the central government proposed and provided whatever restraints the newly independent nation needed.

The government under the Articles failed for the most part because it lacked sufficient power and authority to cope with the problems of the day. The requirements for amending the document were so restrictive that fundamental change within the Articles proved impossible. When the Constitutional Convention met in Philadelphia in 1787, the delegates soon concluded that the Articles had to be scrapped and replaced with a charter that would provide more effective power for the national government. The Framers had experienced conditions of economic decline, crippling taxation policies, interstate barriers to commerce, and isolated but alarming insurrections among the lower economic classes. A newly structured national government was seen as the only method of dealing with the problems besetting the nation in the aftermath of the Revolution. But allocating significant power to the national government was not without its risks. Many of the Framers feared the creation of a federal power capable of dominating the states and abusing individual liberties. It was apparent to all that the new government would have to be structured in a way that the potential for abuse and excess would be minimized. The concept of the separation of powers and its twin, the idea of checks and balances, appealed to the Framers as the best way to accomplish these necessary restraints.

The theory of separation of powers was not new to the Framers. They were introduced to it by the political philosophy of the day and by their own political experiences. The theories of James Harrington and Charles de Montesquieu were particularly influential in this respect. Harrington (1611–1677) was an English political philosopher whose emphasis on the importance of property found a sympathetic audience among the former colonists. Harrington's primary work, *Oceana,* published in 1656, was a widely read description of a model government. Incorporated into Harrington's ideal state was the notion that government powers ought to be divided into three parts. A Senate made up of the intellectual elite would propose laws; the people, guided by the Senate's wisdom, would enact the laws; and a magistrate would execute the laws. This system, Harrington argued, would impose an important balance that would maintain a stable government and protect rights to property.

Harrington's concept of a separation of powers was less well developed than that later proposed by Montesquieu (1689–1755), a French political theorist. Many scholars consider his *Spirit of the Laws* (1748),

widely circulated during the last half of the eighteenth century, to be the classic treatise on the separation of powers philosophy. Montesquieu was concerned about government abuse of liberty. In his estimation, liberty could not long prevail if too much power accrued to a single ruler or a single branch of government. He flatly warned, "When the legislative and executive powers are united in the same person, or the same body of magistrates, there can be no liberty. . . . Again, there is no liberty if the judicial power be not separated from the legislative and executive." Although Montesquieu's message was directed at the citizens of his own country, he found a more receptive audience in the United States.

The influence of these political thinkers was reinforced by the political experiences of the Framers. The settlers came to the New World largely to escape the abuses of the European governments. The treatment of the colonies by George III taught them that executives were not to be trusted with too much power. They also feared an independent and powerful judiciary, especially if it were not answerable to the people. While the legislature was undoubtedly the institution in which the Framers had the most confidence, they knew it too had the potential of exceeding proper bounds. The English experience during the reign of Oliver Cromwell was lesson enough that muting the power of the king did not necessarily lead to the elimination of government abuse. What the Framers sought was balance, a system in which each branch of government would be strong enough to stop excessive power flowing into the hands of any other single branch. This necessary balance, as John Adams pointed out in his *Defense of the Constitutions of Government of the United States of America,* would also have the advantage of being able to keep the power-hungry aristocracy in check and prevent the majority from taking the rights away from the minority.

SEPARATION OF POWERS AND THE CONSTITUTION

The debates at the Constitutional Convention and the various plans that were presented for the delegates' consideration all focused on the issue of dividing government power among the three branches as well as between the national government and the states. A general fear of a concentration of power permeated all the discussions. James Madison noted, "The truth is, all men having power ought to be distrusted to a certain degree." The Framers' solution to the exceedingly difficult problem of expanding government power, while at the same time reducing the probability of abuse, was found in their proposed new Constitution of the United States.

Although the term *separation of powers* is nowhere to be found in the document, the Constitution plainly adopts the central tenets of the theory. A reading of the first lines of each of the first three articles makes this point clearly.

All legislative Powers herein granted shall be vested in a Congress of the United States, which shall consist of a Senate and House of Representatives. (Article I)

The executive Power shall be vested in a President of the United States of America. (Article II)

The judicial Power of the United States, shall be vested in one supreme Court, and in such inferior Courts as the Congress may from time to time ordain and establish. (Article III)

In the scheme of government incorporated into the Constitution, the legislative, executive, and judicial powers each resided in a separate branch of government. Unless otherwise specified in the document, each branch was limited to the political function granted to it, and that function could not be exercised by either of the other two branches. In addition to the separation concept, the Framers placed into the Constitution a number of mixed powers. That is, while the document reserves certain functions for specific branches, it also provides explicit checks on the exercise of those powers. As a consequence, each branch of government imposes limits on the primary functions of the others. A few examples illustrate this point.

Congress has the right to pass legislation, but the president may veto those bills.

The president may veto bills passed by Congress, but the legislature may override that veto.

The president may make treaties with foreign powers, but the Senate must ratify those treaties.

The president is commander in chief of the army and navy, but Congress must pass legislation to raise armies, regulate the military, and declare war.

The president may nominate federal judges, but the Senate must confirm them.

The judiciary may interpret the law and even strike down laws as being in violation of the Constitution, but Congress may pass new legislation or propose constitutional amendments.

Congress may pass laws, but the executive must enforce them.

In addition to these offsetting powers, the Framers structured each branch so that the criteria and procedures for selecting the officials of each institution differed, as did their tenures. Consequently, each branch has a slightly different source of political power. In the original scheme these differences were even more pronounced than they are today.

In the original version of the Constitution, for example, the two houses of Congress were politically dependent upon different selection processes. Members of the House were, as they are today, directly elected by the people, and the seats were apportioned among the states on the basis of population. With terms of only two years, the representatives were required to go back to the people for review on a frequent and regular basis. Senators, on the other hand, were, and still are, representatives of whole states, with each state having two members in the upper chamber. But senators originally were selected by the state legislatures, a system that was not changed until the Seventeenth Amendment, which imposed popular election of senators, was ratified in 1913. The six-year, staggered terms of senators were intended to make the upper house less immediately responsive to the volatile nature of public opinion.

The Constitution dictated that the president be selected by an electoral college, a group of political elites selected by the people or their representatives who would exercise judgment in casting their ballots among presidential candidates. Although the electors over time have ceased to perform any truly independent selection function, presidential selection remains a step away from direct popular election. The president's four-year term places the office squarely between the tenures conferred on representatives and senators. The original Constitution placed no limits on the number of terms a president could serve, but a traditional two-term limit was observed until 1940 and was then imposed by constitutional amendment in 1951.

Differing altogether from the other two branches is the judiciary, which was assigned the least democratic selection system. The people have no direct role in the selection or retention of federal judges. Instead, the president nominates individuals for the federal bench, and the Senate confirms them. Once in office, federal judges serve for terms of good behavior, removable against their will only through impeachment. The intent of the Framers was to make the judiciary independent. To do so they created a system in which judges would not depend on the mood of the masses or on a single appointing power. Furthermore, judges would be accountable only to their own philosophies and consciences, with no periodic review or reassessment required.

Through a division of powers, an imposition of checks, and a variation in selection and tenure requirements, the Framers hoped to achieve the balanced government they desired. This structure, they thought, would be the greatest protection against abuses of power and government violations of personal liberties and property rights. Many delegates to the Constitutional Convention considered this system of separation of powers a much more effective method of protecting civil liberties than the formal pronouncements of a bill of rights.

Most political observers would conclude that the Framers' invention has worked remarkably well. As the government has evolved through the years, the relative strengths of the branches have changed back and forth. At certain times, for example, the judiciary was exceptionally weak, such as during the pre-Marshall era and before the Civil War. At other times, however, the judiciary has been criticized as being too powerful, such as when it repeatedly blocked New Deal legislation in the 1930s or expanded civil liberties during the Warren Court era. The executive also has led the other branches in political power. Beginning with the tenure of Franklin Roosevelt, for example, and extending into the 1970s, one often heard references to the "imperial presidency." But when one branch gains too much power and abuses occur, as in the case of Richard Nixon and the Watergate crisis, the system tends to reimpose the balance intended by the Framers.

CONTEMPORARY THINKING ON THE CONSTITUTIONAL SCHEME

As you read the three chapters in this part and consider the original understandings of the separation of powers doctrine, you might also want to take into account contemporary thinking about the relationships among the three branches of government. The past decade or so has witnessed a resurgence of interest in this area of study, with scholars offering novel frameworks to examine federal policy making.

FIGURE II-1 Sequence of Decision Making in Court/Congress/President Game

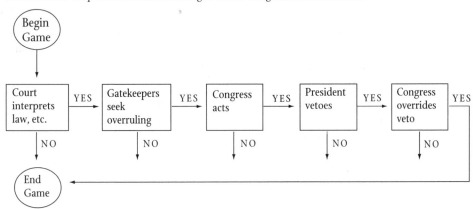

SOURCE: William N. Eskridge, Jr., "Reneging on History: Playing the Court/Congress/President Civil Rights Game," *California Law Review* 79 (1991): 644.

Among the most useful are the "separation of powers games" offered by law professor William Eskridge, among many others.[1] These games typically operate under some simple assumptions about the goals of the various institutions of government and the way the political process works.[2] According to some adherents of this school of thought, the aims of the institutions of government are to see the government's policy—for our purposes, the ultimate state of the law—reflect their positions. Or, to put it in more technical terms, the branches want policy set as close as possible to their ideal or most preferred point. The problem—and here is where assumptions about the nature of the process, including the separation of powers doctrine, come in—is that the political institutions do not make policy in isolation from one another. Rather, policy is set (or the game is played out)

along the lines set out in Figure II-1. In this example, the Supreme Court makes the first "move" when it interprets a congressional statute, a constitutional provision, and so forth. Congressional "gatekeepers" (relevant committees and majority party leaders) then must decide whether they want to introduce legislation or a constitutional amendment to override the Court's decision; if they do, Congress must act by adopting the gatekeepers' recommendation, adopting a different version of it, or rejecting it. If Congress acts, then the president has the option of vetoing the law. The last move rests again with Congress, which must decide whether to override the president's veto.

From these premises about the institutions' goals and about the sequence of play, perhaps you can see why the separation of powers doctrine is so important. Think about it this way. If the Supreme Court were the only American institution, it would merely set policy at its preferred point; it would not need to consider the positions of congressional gatekeepers, Congress as a whole, or the president. We know, however, the Court is but one of several players in the game, and therefore, it may take into account the preferences of others. If it sets the policy too far away from

1. William N. Eskridge, Jr., "Reneging on History: Playing the Court/Congress/President Civil Rights Game," *California Law Review* 79 (1991): 613–684; Eskridge, "Overriding Supreme Court Statutory Interpretation Decisions, *Yale Law Journal* 101 (1991): 331–455. See also William N. Eskridge, Jr., and John A. Ferejohn, "The Article I, Section 7 Game," *Georgetown Law Journal* 80 (1992): 523–563 and Lee Epstein and Thomas G. Walker, "The Role of the Supreme Court in American Society: Playing the Reconstruction Game," in *Contemplating Courts*, ed. Lee Epstein (Washington, D.C.: CQ Press, 1995).

2. We adopt this discussion from Eskridge, "Reneging on History."

the position of, say, Congress, it could face an override.

In the next three chapters, as we explore the constitutional separation of powers and review the basic grants of authority extended to each branch of the government and the limitations placed on those powers, keep in mind these contemporary studies of the system of separation of powers. To what extent do the justices' perceptions of Congress influence their decisions? You will have ample opportunity to think about this question, for in the coming pages we also examine the significant political and legal clashes among the executive, legislative, and judicial branches, focusing on how the justices of the Supreme Court have interpreted and applied the Constitution to settle these disputes. Throughout these constitutional controversies, fundamental issues of institutional powers and the constraints placed on those powers have taken center stage.

CHAPTER 3
THE JUDICIARY

B ETWEEN 1932 and 1983 Congress attached legislative veto provisions to more than 200 laws. Although these provisions took different forms, among the more common were those that authorized one house of Congress to invalidate a decision of the executive branch. For example, under the Immigration and Nationality Act, Congress gave the U.S. attorney general power to suspend the deportation of aliens. However, it reserved the authority to veto, by a majority vote in either house, any such suspension.

In *Immigration and Naturalization Service v. Chadha* (1983) the Court held that this device violated specific clauses as well as general principles contained in the U.S. Constitution. In doing so, as Justice Byron R. White wrote in his dissent, the Court sounded the "death knell" for the legislative veto.[1]

In many ways, the Court's action was less than startling. For nearly two centuries federal courts have exerted the power of judicial review, the power to review acts of government to determine their compatibility with the U.S. Constitution. And, despite the fact that the Constitution does not explicitly give them such power, the courts' authority to do so has been challenged only occasionally. Today we take for granted the notion that federal courts may review government actions and strike them down if they violate constitutional mandates.

Nevertheless, when courts do exert this power, as the U.S. Supreme Court did in *Chadha*, they provoke controversy. Look at it from this perspective: Congress, composed of *elected* officials, passed these legislative veto provisions, which were then rendered invalid by a Supreme Court of nine *unelected* judges. Such an occurrence strikes some people as quite odd, perhaps even antidemocratic. Why should Americans allow a branch of government over which there is no electoral control to review and nullify the actions of elected government officials?

The alleged antidemocratic nature of judicial review is just one of many controversies surrounding the practice. In this chapter, we review others—both in theory and in practice. First, however, we explore the circumstances leading to the adoption of Article III, which outlines the contours of judicial power. To understand the cases that follow—all of which examine the parameters of the judiciary's authority—it is important to consider the framing of Article III. Next,

---

1. It is worth noting that this is true in theory but not in practice. Since *Chadha*, Congress has passed more than 200 new laws containing legislative vetoes. See Louis Fisher, "The Legislative Veto: Invalidated, It Survives," *Law and Contemporary Problems* 56 (1993): 288.

we turn to the development of judicial review in the United States. Many of the early justifications for the practice are still fueling contemporary debates.

Judicial review is the primary weapon, the check that federal courts have on other branches of government. Because this power can be awesome in scope, many tend to emphasize it to the neglect of factors that constrain its use, as well as other checks on the power of the Court. In the second part of this chapter, we explore the limits on judicial power.

THE ESTABLISHMENT OF THE FEDERAL JUCICIARY

The federal judicial system is built on a foundation created by two major statements of the 1780s: Article III of the U.S. Constitution and the Judiciary Act of 1789. In this section, we consider both, with an emphasis on their content and the debate they provoked. Note, in particular, the degree to which the major controversies reflect more general concerns about federalism. Designing and fine-tuning the U.S. system of government required many compromises over the balance of power between the federal government and the states, and Article III and the Judiciary Act are no exceptions.

Article III

While the Framers of the Constitution spent days upon days debating the contents of Article I (dealing with the legislature) and Article II (centering on the executive), they had comparatively little trouble drafting Article III. Indeed, it caused the least controversy of any major constitutional provision. Why? One reason is that the states and Great Britain had well-entrenched court systems, and the Founders had firsthand knowledge about the workings of courts—knowledge they lacked about the other political institutions they were establishing. Second, thirty-four of the fifty-five delegates to the Constitutional Conven-

tion were lawyers or, at least, had some training in the law. They held a common vision of the general role courts should play in the new polity.[2]

That vision was expressed by Alexander Hamilton in *Federalist,* No. 78. Hamilton specifically referred to the judiciary as the "least dangerous branch" of government; he (and virtually all of the Founders) saw the courts as legal, not political, bodies. He wrote, "If judges should be disposed to exercise *will* instead of *judgment,* the consequences would equally be the substitution of their pleasure to that of the legislative body."[3] To ensure that judges did not become legislators, the Framers agreed on the need for judicial independence—a goal they sought to accomplish by giving jurists life tenure rather than subjecting them to periodic public checks through the electoral process.

That the Framers shared a fundamental view of the role of the federal judiciary does not mean that they agreed on all the specifics. They had many debates over the structure of the American legal system. They agreed that there would be at least one federal court, the Supreme Court of the United States, but disagreed over the establishment of federal tribunals inferior to the Supreme Court. The Virginia Plan, which served as the basis for many of the proposals debated at the Convention, suggested that Congress should establish lower federal courts. Delegates who favored a strong national government agreed with this plan, and some of them wanted to use Article III to create such courts.[4]

But delegates who favored states' rights over those of the national government vehemently objected to the creation of any federal tribunals, other than the U.S. Supreme Court. As one put it, "The people will not hear of such an innovation. The states will revolt

2. See Daniel A. Farber and Suzanna Sherry, *A History of the American Constitution* (St. Paul, Minn.: West, 1990), 51.

3. For more on this point, see Kermit L. Hall, *The Magic Mirror* (New York: Oxford University Press, 1989), 72.

4. Ibid.

at such encroachments."[5] Instead of creating new federal courts, they proposed that the existing state courts should hear cases in the first instance, with an allowance for appeals to the U.S. Supreme Court. In the end, as one scholar wrote, "They agreed by not agreeing, leaving the entire matter of the lower federal courts to Congress."[6] In other words, Article III does not create lower federal courts; rather, it gives Congress the option of doing so.

The First Congress (with its Federalist majority) took full advantage of Section 1 by immediately passing the Judiciary Act of 1789, which established lower federal courts. That Congress would take such an action was not a surprise: the majority of the Founders anticipated the law because much of Article III—specifically Section 2, the longest part—defines the jurisdiction of these federal courts that they had not yet created! By spelling out their jurisdiction, the Framers provided the courts with the authority to hear cases involving certain subjects or brought by certain parties. The Framers also defined the jurisdiction of the U.S. Supreme Court, the one judicial body they did create. Its jurisdiction was defined in terms of original and appellate authority *(see Box 3-1)*.

A second area of contention at the 1787 convention was the appointment of federal judges. Again, the Virginia Plan's suggestion—that Congress appoint these judges—served as the focus of debate. Some of the delegates wanted the language of Article III to reflect the Virginia Plan, while others suggested that appointments be left to the Senate. In the end, the delegates decided that the appointment power should be given to the president, with the "advice and consent" of the Senate. Accordingly, the power to appoint federal judges is located in Article II rather than Article III.

Another source of debate was the proposal by James Madison for the creation of a Council of Revi-

5. Quoted in Farber and Sherry, *A History of the American Constitution.*

6. Hall, *The Magic Mirror,* 7. Quoted in Farber and Sherry, *A History of the American Constitution,* 55.

BOX 3-1   JURISDICTION OF THE FEDERAL COURTS AS DEFINED IN ARTICLE III

Jurisdiction of the Lower Federal Courts

Subjects Falling Under Their Authority

- Cases involving the U.S. Constitution, federal laws, and treaties
- Cases affecting ambassadors, public ministers, and consuls
- Cases of admiralty and maritime jurisdiction

Parties Falling Under Their Authority

- United States
- Controversies between two or more states
- Controversies between a state and citizens of another state[a]
- Controversies between citizens of different states
- Controversies between citizens of the same state claiming lands under grants of different states
- Controversies between a state, or the citizens thereof, and foreign states, citizens, or subjects

Jurisdiction of the Supreme Court

Original Jurisdiction

- Cases affecting ambassadors, public ministers, and consuls
- Cases to which a state is a party

Appellate Jurisdiction

- Cases falling under the jurisdiction of the lower federal courts, "with such Exceptions, and under such Regulations as the Congress shall make."

a. In 1795, this was modified by the Eleventh Amendment, which removed from federal jurisdiction those cases in which a state is sued by the citizens of another state.

sion, which would be composed of Supreme Court justices and the president of the United States and have the power to veto legislative acts. But, as Farber and Sherry write, "Madison or one of his fellow nationalists proposed this Council of Revision four separate times, and each time it was soundly defeated."[7] In *Marbury v. Madison* (1803), the first case in this chapter, Chief Justice Marshall in essence articulated such veto power for the Court. Those who take a dim view of Marshall's decision occasionally point to the delegates' rejection of the Council of Revision as proof that Marshall skirted the Founders' intent.

At the end of the section on *Marbury v. Madison,* we consider debates over Marshall's holding. Here, we underscore that Article III—for the reasons just stated—did not establish any federal courts other than the U.S. Supreme Court. It was left up to Congress to create (or not) more federal courts. Dominated by Federalists, the First Congress created new courts, to give some flesh to the skeleton that was Article III.[8]

The Judiciary Act of 1789

The Judiciary Act of 1789 is a long and relatively complex law that, at its core, had two purposes. First, it sought to establish a federal court structure, which it accomplished by providing for a Supreme Court, circuit courts, and district courts. Under the law, the Supreme Court was to have one chief justice and five associate justices. That the Court initially had only six members illustrates an important point: Congress, not the U.S. Constitution, determines the number of justices on the Supreme Court. That number has been fixed at nine since 1869.

As Figure 3-1 shows, the act also created thirteen district courts. Each of the eleven states that had ratified the Constitution received a court, with separate tribunals created for Maine and Kentucky, which were

then parts of Massachusetts and Virginia, respectively. District courts, then as now, were presided over by one judge. But the three newly established circuit courts were quite extraordinary in composition. Congress grouped the district courts—except Kentucky and Maine—geographically into the eastern, middle, or southern circuits and put one district court judge and two Supreme Court justices in charge of each. In other words, three judges would hear cases in the circuits. Today, courts of appeals continue to hear cases in panels of three, but district or Supreme Court judges do not sit on these panels. Instead, the president now appoints judges specifically to the courts of appeals.

A second goal of the Judiciary Act was to specify the jurisdiction of the federal courts. Section 2 of Article III speaks broadly about the authority of federal courts, giving them jurisdiction over cases involving particular parties or subjects or, in the case of the Supreme Court, original and appellate jurisdiction *(see Box 3-1).* The Judiciary Act provided more specific information, defining the parameters of authority for each of the newly established courts and for the U.S. Supreme Court. The district courts were to serve as trial courts, hearing cases involving admiralty issues, forfeitures and penalties, petty federal crimes, and minor U.S. civil cases. Congress recognized that some of these courts would be busier than others and fixed judicial salaries accordingly. For example, Delaware judges received only $800 for their services, while their counterparts in South Carolina, a coastal state that would generate many admiralty disputes, earned $1,800.[9]

Unlike today's courts, the original circuit courts were trial courts with jurisdiction over cases involving citizens from different states and over major federal criminal and civil cases. Congress also gave these courts limited appellate authority to hear major civil and admiralty disputes coming out of the district courts.

---

7. *A History of the American Constitution,* 66.

8. Russell R. Wheeler and Cynthia Harrison, *Creating the Federal Judicial System* (Washington, D.C.: Federal Judicial Center, 1989), 2.

9. Ibid., 6.

FIGURE 3-1 The Federal Court System Under the Judiciary Act of 1789

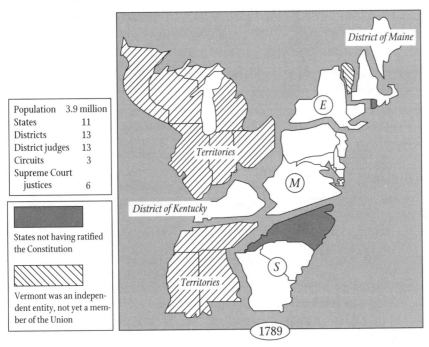

Population	3.9 million
States	11
Districts	13
District judges	13
Circuits	3
Supreme Court justices	6

States not having ratified the Constitution

Vermont was an independent entity, not yet a member of the Union

The first Judiciary Act created thirteen districts and placed eleven of them in three circuits: the eastern, middle, and southern. Each district had a district court, a trial court with a single district judge and primarily admiralty jurisdiction. Each circuit had a circuit court, which met in each district of the circuit and was composed of the district judge and two Supreme Court justices. The circuit courts exercised primarily diversity and criminal jurisdiction and heard appeals from the district courts in some cases. The districts of Maine and Kentucky (parts of the states of Massachusetts and Virginia, respectively) were part of no circuit; their district courts exercised both district and circuit court jurisdiction.

SOURCE: Russell R. Wheeler and Cynthia Harrison, *Creating the Federal Judicial System* (Washington, D.C.: Federal Judicial Center, 1989), 5.

Finally, the 1789 act contained several important provisions concerning the jurisdiction of the U.S. Supreme Court. Section 13 reiterated the Court's authority over suits in the first instance (its original jurisdiction) and gave the justices appellate jurisdiction over major civil disputes, those involving more than $2,000—a good deal of money back then. Section 13 also spoke about the Court's authority to issue writs of *mandamus*, which command a public official to carry out a particular act or duty:

The Supreme Court . . . shall have the power to issue . . . writs of *mandamus*, in cases warranted by the principles and usages of law, to any courts appointed, or persons holding office, under the authority of the United States.

This may seem a trivial matter but, as we shall see, the Court's interpretation of this particular provision formed the centerpiece of *Marbury v. Madison.*

Another part of the act, Section 25, expanded the Court's appellate authority under Article III, enabling it to review certain kinds of cases coming out of the states. Specifically, the Supreme Court could now hear appeals from the highest state courts if those tribunals upheld a state law against claims that the law violated the Constitution or denied some claim based on the U.S. Constitution, federal laws, or treaties.

At first glance, the components of the 1789 act—its establishment of a federal court system and of rules governing that system—appear to favor the Federalists' position. Recall that Anti-Federalist delegates at the Constitutional Convention did not want the document to even mention lower federal tribunals, much less to give Congress the authority to establish them. The 1789 act does that and more: it goes so far as to give the Supreme Court the power to review state supreme court cases—surely an Anti-Federalist's worst nightmare! But it would be a mistake to believe that the act did not take into account the position taken by states' rights advocates. For example, the 1789 act used state lines as the boundaries for the district and circuit courts. It has been noted that using state lines was "not the only way that federal court boundaries could be defined. The creators of the federal judiciary might have established separate judicial administrative divisions that would ensure roughly equal allocation of workload and would be subject to realignment to maintain the allocation."[10] Congress tied the boundaries to the states, which some scholars argue was a concession to the Anti-Federalists who wanted the judges of the federal courts to have bonds "to the states in which they [sat]," to feel a part of the state's legal and political culture.[11]

Whichever side won or lost, it is true that passage of the 1789 Judiciary Act was a defining moment in American legal history. It established the first federal court system, one that is strikingly similar to that in effect today. And, as the following pages reveal, it paved the way for landmark constitutional cases, including *Marbury v. Madison*, which centered on judicial review—the major power of the federal judiciary.

JUDICIAL REVIEW

Even though judicial review is the most powerful tool of federal courts and there is evidence that the Framers intended for courts to have it *(see pages 62–64)*, it is not mentioned in the Constitution. Early in U.S. history, federal courts claimed it for themselves. In *Hylton v. United States* (1796), Daniel Hylton challenged the constitutionality of a 1793 federal tax on carriages. According to Hylton, the act violated the constitutional mandate that direct taxes must be apportioned on the basis of population. With only three

10. Ibid., 9.
11. Ibid.

justices participating, the Court upheld the act. But even by considering the matter, the Court in effect used its authority to review acts of Congress.

Not until 1803, however, did the Court invoke judicial review to strike down legislation deemed incompatible with the U.S. Constitution. That decision came in the landmark case *Marbury v. Madison*. How does Chief Justice Marshall justify the Court's power to strike down legislation in light of the failure of the newly framed Constitution to confer on it judicial review?

Marbury v. Madison

1 Cr. 137 (1803)

Vote: 4 (Chase, Marshall, Paterson, Washington)

0

Opinion of the Court: Marshall
Not participating: Cushing, Moore

When voting in the presidential election of 1800 was over, it was apparent that Federalist president John Adams had lost after a long and bitter campaign, but it was not known who had won. The voting resulted in a tie between Republican candidate Thomas Jefferson and his running mate, Aaron Burr, and the election had to be settled in the House of Representatives. In February 1801 the House elected Jefferson. Because the Federalists had lost both the presidential election and their majority in Congress, they took steps to maintain control of the third branch of government, the judiciary. The lame-duck Congress enacted the Circuit Court Act of 1801, which created six new circuit courts and several district courts to accommodate the new states of Kentucky, Tennessee, and Vermont. These new courts required judges and support staff such as attorneys, marshals, and clerks. As a result, during the last six months of his term in office, Adams made more than 200 nominations,

President John Adams signing judicial commissions, the so-called "midnight appointments," on his last night in office. Several appointees, including William Marbury, did not receive their commissions. The Jefferson administration's refusal to deliver them led to the famous case of *Marbury v. Madison* (1803) in which the Supreme Court clearly asserted its power of judicial review.

with sixteen judgeships (the "midnight appointments") approved by the Senate during his last two weeks in office.

An even more important opportunity arose in December 1800, when the third chief justice of the United States, Federalist Oliver Ellsworth, resigned so that Adams—not Jefferson—could name his replacement. Adams first offered the post to John Jay, who had served as the first chief justice before leaving to take the more prestigious office of governor of New York. When Jay refused, Adams turned to his secretary of state, John Marshall, an ardent Federalist. Marshall was confirmed by the Senate in January 1801, while he continued as secretary of state.

In addition, the Federalist Congress passed the Organic Act, which authorized Adams to appoint forty-two justices of the peace for the District of Columbia. It was this seemingly innocuous law that set the stage for the dramatic case of *Marbury v. Madison*. In the confusion of the Adams administration's last days in office, Marshall, the outgoing secretary of state, failed

to deliver some of these commissions. When the new administration came into office, James Madison, the new secretary of state, acting under orders from Jefferson, refused to deliver at least five commissions.[12] Indeed, some years later, Jefferson explained the situation in this way:

I found the commissions on the table of the Department of State, on my entrance into office, and I forbade their delivery. Whatever is in the Executive offices is certainly deemed to be in the hands of the President, and in this case, was actually in my hands, because when I countermanded them, there was as yet no Secretary of State.[13]

As a result, in 1801 William Marbury and three others who were denied their commissions went directly to the Supreme Court and asked it to issue a writ of mandamus, ordering Madison to deliver the

12. Historical accounts differ, but it seems that Jefferson decreased the number of Adams's appointments to justice of the peace positions to thirty from forty-two. Twenty-five of the thirty appointees received their commissions, but five—including William Marbury—did not. See Francis N. Stites, *John Marshall* (Boston: Little, Brown, 1981), 84.

13. Quoted in Charles Warren, *The Supreme Court in United States History*, vol. 1 (Boston: Little, Brown, 1922), 244.

William Marbury, whose suit against James Madison led to a landmark decision in 1803. John Marshall's opinion in *Marbury v. Madison* established the Court's authority to review the constitutionality of acts of Congress.

commissions. Marbury thought he could take his case directly to the Court because Section 13 of the 1789 Judiciary Act gives the Court the power to issue writs of mandamus to anyone holding federal office.

In this volatile political climate, Marshall, now serving as chief justice, was perhaps in the most tenuous position of all. On the one hand, he had been a supporter of the Federalist party, which now looked to him to "scold" the Jefferson administration. On the other, Marshall wanted to avoid a confrontation between the Jefferson administration and the Supreme Court, which not only seemed imminent, but also would end in disaster for the struggling nation. Note the year in which *Marbury* was handed down by the Court the case was not decided until two years after Marbury filed suit because Congress and the Jefferson administration had abolished the 1802 term of the Court.

The following of the Court was delivered by the *Chief Justice.*

Opinion of the Court.

The peculiar delicacy of this case, the novelty of some of its circumstances, and the real difficulty attending the points which occur in it, require a complete exposition of the principles, on which the opinion to be given by the court, is founded . . .

In the order in which the court has viewed this subject, the following questions have been considered and decided.

1st. Has the applicant a right to the commission he demands?

2dly. If he has a right, and that right has been violated, do the laws of his country afford him a remedy?

3dly. If they do afford him a remedy, is it a *mandamus* issuing from this court?

The first object of enquiry is,

1st. Has the applicant a right to the commission he demands . . .

In order to determine whether he is entitled to this commission, it becomes necessary to enquire whether he has been appointed to the office. For if he has been appointed, the law continues him in office for five years, and he is entitled to the possession of those evidences of office, which, being completed, became his property. . . .

It is . . . decidedly the opinion of the court, that when a commission has been signed by the President, the appointment is made; and that the commission is complete, when the seal of the United States has been affixed to it by the secretary of state. . . .

Mr. Marbury, then, since his commission was signed by the President, and sealed by the secretary of state, was appointed; and as the law creating the office, gave the officer a right to hold for five years, independent of the executive, the appointment was not revocable; but vested in the officer legal rights, which are protected by the laws of his country.

To withhold his commission, therefore, is an act deemed by the court not warranted by law, but violative of a vested legal right.

This brings us to the second enquiry; which is,

2dly. If he has a right, and that right has been violated, do the laws of his country afford him a remedy?

The very essence of civil liberty certainly consists in the right of every individual to claim the protection of the laws, whenever he receives an injury. One of the first duties of government is to afford that protection. . . .

The government of the United States has been emphatically termed a government of laws, and not of men. It will certainly cease to deserve this high appellation, if the laws furnish no remedy for the violation of a vested legal right . . . .

It is then the opinion of the court,

1st. That by signing the commission of Mr. Marbury, the president of the United States appointed him a justice of peace, for the county of Washington in the district of Columbia; and that the seal of the United States, affixed thereto by the secretary of state, is conclusive testimony of the verity of the signature, and of the completion of the appointment; and that the appointment conferred on him a legal right to the office for the space of five years.

2dly. That, having this legal title to the office, he has a consequent right to the commission; a refusal to deliver which, is a plain violation of that right, for which the laws of his country afford him a remedy.

It remains to be enquired whether,

3dly. He is entitled to the remedy for which he applies. . . .

The act to establish the judicial courts of the United States authorizes the supreme court "to issue writs of mandamus, in cases warranted by the principles and usages of law, to any courts appointed, or persons holding office, under the authority of the United States."

The secretary of state, being a person holding an office under the authority of the United States, is precisely within the letter of the description; and if this court is not authorized to issue a writ of mandamus to such an officer, it must be because the law is unconstitutional, and therefore absolutely incapable of conferring the authority, and assigning the duties which its words purport to confer and assign.

The constitution vests the whole judicial power of the United States in one supreme court, and such inferior courts as congress shall, from time to time, ordain and establish. This power is expressly extended to all cases arising under the laws of the United States; and consequently, in some form, may be exercised over the present case; because the right claimed is given by a law of the United States.

In the distribution of this power it is declared that "the supreme court shall have original jurisdiction in all cases affecting ambassadors, other public ministers and consuls, and those in which a state shall be a party. In all other cases, the supreme court shall have appellate jurisdiction."

It has been insisted, at the bar, that as the original grant of jurisdiction, to the supreme and inferior courts, is general, and the clause, assigning original jurisdiction to the supreme court, contains no negative or restrictive words; the power remains to the legislature, to assign original jurisdiction to that court in other cases than those specified in the article which has been recited; provided those cases belong to the judicial power of the United States.

If it had been intended to leave it in the discretion of the legislature to apportion the judicial power between the supreme and inferior courts according to the will of that body, it would certainly have been useless to have proceeded further than to have defined the judicial power, and the tribunals in which it should be vested. The subsequent part of the section is mere surplussage, is entirely without meaning, if such is to be the construction. If congress remains at liberty to give this court appellate jurisdiction, where the constitution has declared their jurisdiction shall be original; and original jurisdiction where the constitution has declared it shall be appellate; the distribution of jurisdiction, made in the constitution, is form without substance.

Affirmative words are often, in their operation, negative of other objects than those affirmed; and in this case, a negative or exclusive sense must be given to them or they have no operation at all.

It cannot be presumed that any clause in the constitution is intended to be without effect; and therefore such a construction is inadmissible, unless the words require it.

If the solicitude of the convention, respecting our peace with foreign powers, induced a provision that the supreme court should take original jurisdiction in cases which might be supposed to affect them; yet the clause would have proceeded no further than to provide for such cases, if no further restriction on the powers of congress had been intended. That they should have appellate jurisdiction in all other cases, with such exceptions as congress might make, is no restriction; unless the words be deemed exclusive of original jurisdiction.

When an instrument organizing fundamentally a judicial system, divides it into one supreme, and so many inferior courts as the legislature may ordain and establish; then enumerates its powers, and proceeds so far to distribute them, as to define the jurisdiction of the supreme court by declaring the cases in which it shall take original jurisdiction, and that in others it shall take appellate jurisdiction; the plain import of the words seems to be, that in one class of cases its jurisdiction is original, and not appellate; in the other it is appellate, and not original. If any other construction would render the clause inoperative, that is an additional reason for rejecting such other construction, and for adhering to their obvious meaning.

To enable this court then to issue a mandamus, it must be shewn to be an exercise of appellate jurisdiction, or to be necessary to enable them to exercise appellate jurisdiction.

It has been stated at the bar that the appellate jurisdiction may be exercised in a variety of forms, and that if it be the will of the legislature that a mandamus should be used for that purpose, that will must be obeyed. This is true, yet the jurisdiction must be appellate, not original.

It is the essential criterion of appellate jurisdiction, that it revises and corrects the proceedings in a cause already instituted, and does not create that cause. Although, therefore, a mandamus may be directed to courts, yet to issue such a writ to an officer for the delivery of a paper, is in effect the same as to sustain an original action for that paper, and therefore seems not to belong to appellate, but to original jurisdiction. Neither is it necessary in such a case as this, to enable the court to exercise its appellate jurisdiction.

The authority, therefore, given to the supreme court, by the act establishing the judicial courts of the United States, to issue writs of mandamus to public officers, appears not to be warranted by the constitution; and it becomes necessary to enquire whether a jurisdiction, so conferred, can be exercised.

The question, whether an act, repugnant to the constitution, can become the law of the land, is a question deeply interesting to the United States; but, happily, not of an intricacy proportioned to its interest. It seems only necessary to recognise certain principles, supposed to have been long and well established, to decide it.

That the people have an original right to establish, for their future government, such principles as, in their opinion, shall most conduce to their own happiness, is the basis, on which the whole American fabric has been erected. The exercise of this original right is a very great exertion; nor can it, nor ought it to be frequently repeated. The principles, therefore, so established, are deemed fundamental. And as the authority, from which they proceed, is supreme, and can seldom act, they are designed to be permanent.

This original and supreme will organizes the government, and assigns, to different departments, their respective powers. It may either stop here; or establish certain limits not to be transcended by those departments.

The government of the United States is of the latter description. The powers of the legislature are defined, and limited; and that those limits may not be mistaken, or forgotten, the constitution is written. To what purpose are powers limited, and to what purpose is that limitation committed to writing, if these limits may, at any time, be passed by those intended to be restrained? The distinction, between a government with limited and unlimited powers, is abolished, if those limits do not confine the persons on whom they are imposed, and if acts prohibited and acts allowed, are of equal obligation. It is a proposition too plain to be contested, that the constitution controls any legislative act repugnant to it; or, that the legislature may alter the constitution by an ordinary act.

Between these alternatives there is no middle ground. The constitution is either a superior, paramount law, unchangeable by ordinary means, or it is on a level with ordinary legislative acts, and like other acts, is alterable when the legislature shall please to alter it.

If the former part of the alternative be true, then a legislative act contrary to the constitution is not law: if the latter part be true, then written constitutions are absurd attempts, on the part of the people, to limit a power, in its own nature illimitable.

Certainly all those who have framed written constitutions contemplate them as forming the fundamental and paramount law of the nation, and consequently the theory of every such government must be, that an act of the legislature, repugnant to the constitution, is void.

This theory is essentially attached to a written constitution, and is consequently to be considered, by this court, as one of the fundamental principles of our society. It is not therefore to be lost sight of in the further consideration of this subject.

If an act of the legislature, repugnant to the constitution, is void, does it, notwithstanding its invalidity, bind the courts, and oblige them to give it effect? Or, in other words, though it be not law, does it constitute a rule as operative as if it was a law? This would be to overthrow in fact what was established in theory; and would seem, at first view, an absurdity too gross to be insisted on. It shall, however, receive a more attentive consideration.

It is emphatically the province and duty of the judicial department to say what the law is. Those who apply the rule to particular cases, must of necessity expound and interpret that rule. If two laws conflict with each other, the courts must decide on the operation of each.

So if a law be in opposition to the constitution; if both the law and the constitution apply to a particular case, so that the court must either decide that case conformably to the law, disregarding the constitution; or conformably to the constitution, disregarding the law; the court must determine which of these conflicting rules governs the case. This is of the very essence of judicial duty.

If then the courts are to regard the constitution; and the constitution is superior to any ordinary act of the legislature; the constitution, and not such ordinary act, must govern the case to which they both apply.

Those then who controvert the principle that the constitution is to be considered, in court, as a paramount law, are reduced to the necessity of maintaining that courts must close their eyes on the constitution, and see only the law.

This doctrine would subvert the very foundation of all written constitutions. It would declare that an act, which, according to the principles and theory of our government, is entirely void; is yet, in practice, completely obligatory. It would declare, that if the legislature shall do what is expressly forbidden, such act, notwithstanding the express prohibition, is in reality effectual. It would be giving to the legislature a practical and real omnipotence, with the same breath which professes to restrict their powers within narrow limits. It is prescribing limits, and declaring that those limits may be passed at pleasure.

That it thus reduces to nothing what we have deemed the greatest improvement on political institutions—a written constitution—would of itself be sufficient, in America,

where written constitutions have been viewed with so much reverence, for rejecting the construction. But the peculiar expressions of the constitution of the United States furnish additional arguments in favour of its rejection.

The judicial power of the United States is extended to all cases arising under the constitution.

Could it be the intention of those who gave this power, to say that, in using it, the constitution should not be looked into? That a case arising under the constitution should be decided without examining the instrument under which it arises?

This is too extravagant to be maintained.

In some cases then, the constitution must be looked into by the judges. And if they can open it at all, what part of it are they forbidden to read, or to obey?

There are many other parts of the constitution which serve to illustrate this subject.

It is declared that "no tax or duty shall be laid on articles exported from any state." Suppose a duty on the export of cotton, of tobacco, or of flour; and a suit instituted to recover it. Ought judgment to be rendered in such a case? ought the judges to close their eyes on the constitution, and only see the law?

The constitution declares that "no bill of attainder or *ex post facto* law shall be passed."

If, however, such a bill should be passed and a person should be prosecuted under it; must the court condemn to death those victims whom the constitution endeavours to preserve?

"No person," says the constitution, "shall be convicted of treason unless on the testimony of two witnesses to the same overt act, or on confession in open court."

Here the language of the constitution is addressed especially to the courts. It prescribes, directly for them, a rule of evidence not to be departed from. If the legislature should change that rule, and declare *one* witness, or a confession *out* of court, sufficient for conviction, must the constitutional principle yield to the legislative act?

From these, and many other selections which might be made, it is apparent, that the Framers of the constitution contemplated that instrument, as a rule for the government of *courts,* as well as of the legislature.

Why otherwise does it direct the judges to take an oath to support it? This oath certainly applies, in an especial

BOX 3-2 JOHN MARSHALL
(1801–1835)

THE ELDEST of fifteen children, John Marshall was born September 24, 1755, in a log cabin on the Virginia frontier near Germantown. His father, descended from Welsh immigrants, was an assistant surveyor to George Washington and member of the Virginia House of Burgesses. His mother was the daughter of an educated Scottish clergyman.

As a youth, Marshall was tutored by two clergymen, but his primary teacher was his father, who introduced him to the study of English literature and Blackstone's *Commentaries on the Laws of England.*

During the Revolutionary War, young Marshall participated in the siege of Norfolk as a member of the Culpeper Minute Men and was present at Brandywine, Monmouth, Stony Point, and Valley Forge as a member of the third Virginia Regiment. In 1779 he returned home to await another assignment but was never recalled. He left the Continental Army with the rank of captain in 1781.

Marshall was self-taught in the law; his only formal instruction came in 1780 when he attended George Wythe's course of law lectures at the College of William and Mary. He was admitted to the bar that same year and gradually developed a lucrative practice, specializing in defending Virginians against their pre–Revolutionary War British creditors.

On January 3, 1783, Marshall married Mary Willis Ambler, daughter of the Virginia state treasurer, and established a home in Richmond. The couple had ten children, only six of whom survived to maturity. Marshall spent many years attending to the needs of his wife, who suffered from a chronic illness. She died December 25, 1831.

From 1796 until about 1806, Marshall's life was dominated by the pressures of meeting debts incurred by a land investment he had made in the northern neck of Virginia. It has been speculated that his need for money motivated him to write *The Life of George Washington*, which appeared

in five volumes from 1804 to 1807. He later condensed the work into a schoolbook, but it proved not to be the answer to his financial difficulties.

Marshall was elected to the Virginia House of Delegates from Fauquier County in 1782 and 1784. He reentered the House in 1787 and was instrumental in Virginia's ratification of the new U.S. Constitution. At the state ratifying convention his primary attention was directed to the need for judicial review. By 1789 Marshall was considered to be a leading Federalist in the state.

Marshall refused many appointments in the Federalist administrations of George Washington and John Adams, including U.S. attorney general in 1795, associate justice of the Supreme Court in 1798, and secretary of war in 1800. In 1796 he refused an appointment by President Adams as minister to France, but the following year agreed to serve as one of three special envoys sent to smooth relations with that country. This mission, known as the "XYZ Affair," failed when French diplomats demanded a bribe as a condition for negotiation. Congress, however, was greatly impressed by the stubborn resistance of the American emissaries, and Marshall received a generous grant as a reward for his participation.

In 1799 Washington persuaded Marshall to run for the U.S. House of Representatives as a Federalist from Richmond. His career in the House was brief, however, for in 1800 he became secretary of state under Adams. When Adams retired to his home in Massachusetts for a few months that year, Marshall served as the effective head of government.

Chief Justice Oliver Ellsworth resigned in 1800, and Adams offered the position to John Jay, who had been the Court's first chief justice. Jay declined, and the Federalists urged Adams to elevate Associate Justice William Paterson. But on January 20, 1801, Adams nominated Marshall instead. The Senate confirmed Marshall January 27 by a voice vote.

As the primary founder of the American system of constitutional law, including the doctrine of judicial review, Marshall participated in more than 1,000 Supreme Court decisions, writing more than 500 of them himself. In 1807 he presided over the treason trial of Aaron Burr in the Richmond circuit court, locking horns with Thomas Jefferson, who sought an absolute conviction. Burr was acquitted.

In 1831, at age seventy-six, Marshall underwent successful surgery in Philadelphia for the removal of kidney stones. Three years later, he developed an enlarged liver, and his health declined rapidly. When Marshall died in Philadelphia on July 6, 1835, three months short of his eightieth birthday, the Liberty Bell cracked as it tolled in mourning.

SOURCE: Adapted from Elder Witt, *Guide to the U.S. Supreme Court*, 2d ed. (Washington, D.C.: Congressional Quarterly, 1990), 810–811.

---

manner, to their conduct in their official character. How immoral to impose it on them, if they were to be used as the instruments, and the knowing instruments, for violating what they swear to support!

The oath of office, too, imposed by the legislature, is completely demonstrative of the legislative opinion on this subject. It is in these words, "I do solemnly swear that I will administer justice without respect to persons, and do equal right to the poor and to the rich; and that I will faithfully and impartially discharge all the duties incumbent on me as according to the best of my abilities and understanding, agreeably to *the constitution*, and laws of the United States."

Why does a judge swear to discharge his duties agreeably to the constitution of the United States, if that constitution forms no rule for his government? if it is closed upon him, and cannot be inspected by him?

If such be the real state of things, this is worse than solemn mockery. To prescribe, or to take this oath, becomes equally a crime.

It is also not entirely worthy of observation, that in declaring what shall be the *supreme law* of the land, the *consti-*

tution itself is first mentioned; and not the laws of the United States generally, but those only which shall be made in *pursuance* of the constitution, have that rank.

Thus, the particular phraseology of the constitution of the United States confirms and strengthens the principle, supposed to be essential to all written constitutions, that a law repugnant to the constitution is void; and that *courts*, as well as other departments, are bound by that instrument.

The rule must be discharged.

Many scholars consider Marshall's opinion in *Marbury* stunning, even brilliant. Think about the way the chief justice dealt with a most delicate political situation. By ruling against Marbury, he avoided a potentially devastating clash with the new president; but, by exerting the power of judicial review, he sent a clear signal to Jefferson that the Court had a major role to play in the American government.

The decision helped to establish John Marshall's reputation as perhaps the greatest justice in Supreme Court history *(see Box 3-2)*. As will be shown throughout this book, *Marbury* was just the first in what would be a long line of seminal Marshall decisions. But most important here, *Marbury* fully established the Court's authority to review and strike down government actions that were incompatible with the Constitution. In Marshall's view, such authority, while not explicit in the Constitution, was clearly intended by the Framers of that document. Was he correct? His opinion makes a plausible argument, but some judges and scholars have suggested otherwise. We review their assertions later in this chapter *(see pages 74–78)*.

For now, note that in *Marbury*, the Court addressed only the power to review acts of the federal government. Could the Court exert judicial review over the states? According to Section 25 of the 1789 Judiciary Act, indeed, it could. Recall from our discussion of the act that Congress expanded the Supreme Court's appellate jurisdiction to encompass appeals from the highest state courts, if those tribunals upheld a state law against challenges of unconstitutionality or denied some claim based on the U.S. Constitution, federal laws, or treaties. But the mere existence of this statute did not necessarily mean that either state courts or the Supreme Court would follow it. Because Section 25 expanded the Supreme Court's jurisdiction, it was always possible that the justices might question Congress's authority to do so, even though the section involved appellate, not original, jurisdiction.

More important was the potentially hostile reaction from the states, which in the 1780s and 1790s zealously guarded their power from federal encroachment. Even if the Court were to take advantage of its ability to review state court decisions, it was more than likely that state courts would disregard its rulings. Still, threats from the states did not deter the Court: In two cases coming out of Virginia, *Martin v. Hunter's Lessee* (1816) and *Cohens v. Virginia* (1821), the justices asserted their power to review state court decisions by upholding Section 25 of the Judiciary Act. In so doing, they took the opportunity to refute claims that allowing the Court to review state courts decisions would destroy the independence of state court judges. As Justice Story wrote in *Martin*:

[S]uch a right [cannot be] deemed to impair the independence of state judges. It is assuming the very ground in controversy to assert that they possess an absolute independence of the United States. In respect to the powers granted to the United States, they are not independent; they are expressly bound to obedience by the letter of the constitution; and if they should unintentionally transcend their authority, or misconstrue the constitution, there is no more reason for giving their judgments an absolute and irresistible force, than for giving it to the acts of the other coordinate departments of state sovereignty. . . .

Story also offered a "motive of another kind" for the Court's ruling—a motive he called "perfectly compatible with the most sincere respect for state tribunals":

That motive is the importance, and even necessity of *uniformity* of decisions throughout the whole United States, upon all subjects within the purview of the constitution.

Judges of equal learning and integrity, in different states, might differently interpret a statute, or a treaty of the United States, or even the constitution itself: If there were no revising authority to control these jarring and discordant judgments, and harmonize them into uniformity, the laws, the treaties, and the constitution of the United States would be different in different states, and might, perhaps, never have precisely the same construction, obligation, or efficacy, in any two states. The public mischiefs that would attend such a state of things would be truly deplorable; and it cannot be believed that they could have escaped the enlightened convention which formed the constitution. What, indeed, might then have been only prophecy, has now become fact; and the appellate jurisdiction must continue to be the only adequate remedy for such evils. . . .

Judicial Review: Some Controversies

Marbury, *Martin*, and *Cohens* firmly established the power of federal courts to exert judicial review over national and state actions. What they did not do, and perhaps could not do, was put an end to the controversies surrounding judicial review.

Some of the complaints with the Court's decisions emerged while Marshall was still on the bench. Jefferson, for one, griped about *Marbury* until his last days. In an 1823 letter, he wrote:

This practice of Judge Marshall, of travelling out of his case to prescribe what the law would be in a moot case not before the court, is very irregular and very censurable. . . . [In *Marbury v. Madison*] the Court determined at once, that being an original process, they had no cognizance of it; and therefore the question before them was ended. But the Chief Justice went on to lay down what the law would be, had they jurisdiction of the case, to wit: that they should command the delivery. The object was clearly to instruct any other court having the jurisdiction, what they should do if *Marbury* should apply to them. Besides the impropriety of this gratuitous interference, could anything exceed the perversion of law? . . . *Yet this case of* Marbury and Madison *is continually cited by bench and bar, as if it were settled law, without any animadversion on its being merely an obiter dissertation of the Chief Justice.* (Emphasis added.)[14]

---

14. Quoted in Andrew A. Lipscomb, *The Writings of Thomas Jefferson*, vol. 15 (Washington, D.C.: Thomas Jefferson Memorial Association, 1905), 447–448.

Strong words from one of our nation's most revered presidents!

But Jefferson was not the last to complain about Marshall's opinion. Some critics pick apart specific aspects of the ruling. Jefferson's comment also falls into this category. He argued that once Marshall ruled that the Court did not have jurisdiction to hear the case, he should have dismissed it. Another criticism of Marshall's opinion is that Section 13 of the 1789 Judiciary Act— which *Marbury* held unconstitutional—did not "even remotely suggest an expansion of the Supreme Court's original jurisdiction." If this is so, then Marshall "had nothing to declare unconstitutional"![15]

Other debates center on the Court's holding. In fact, while most Americans now accept the fact that courts have the power of judicial review, many legal analysts still argue over whether they should. Let's consider some of the theoretical debates surrounding judicial review, debates that political scientist David Adamany puts into five categories: Framers' intent, judicial restraint, democratic checks on the Court, public opinion, and protection of minority rights.[16]

Framers' Intent. Perhaps the oldest debate concerns whether the Framers intended the federal courts to exercise judicial review. Chief Justice Marshall's affirmative view was a major justification in *Marbury* and *Cohens,* and there is some historical evidence to support it. Most important is that the Framers had knowledge of judicial review. Although Marshall often is credited with its first full enunciation, there is evidence that the concept originated in England in *Dr. Bonham's Case* (1610). At issue here was an act of Parliament that enabled physicians of the London College to authorize medical licenses and to punish those practicing without one. Convicted of violating the act, Dr. Bonham appealed his case to England's high court, the King's Bench. Writing for the court, Lord Chief Justice Sir Edward Coke struck down the act, noting in *dictum,* "It appears in our books, that in many cases, the common law will control acts of Parliament, and sometimes adjudge them to be utterly void." Coke's resounding declaration of the authority of the court to void parliamentary acts came at a critical point in British history. At a time when King James I was claiming tremendous authority, the court, in an otherwise trivial case, took the opportunity to assert its power.

By the early 1700s the concept of judicial review had fallen out of favor in England. Coke's writings, however, had a profound impact on the development of the American legal system, as best illustrated by the *Writs of Assistance Case* (1761), involving the legality of sweeping search warrants issued by the British Parliament in the name of the king. In arguing against such writs, James Otis, a Boston lawyer, relied on Coke's opinion in *Bonham.* as precedent for his request. Otis lost the case, but his argument was not forgotten. Between 1776 and 1787, eight of the thirteen colonies incorporated judicial review into their constitutions, and by 1789 various state courts had struck down as unconstitutional eight acts passed by their legislatures.

This background makes the question of why the Framers left judicial review out of the Constitution even more perplexing. Some historians argue that the Framers omitted it because they did not want to heighten controversy over Article III by inserting judicial review, not because they opposed the practice. To the contrary, they may have implicitly accepted it. First, historians have established that more than half of the delegates to the Constitutional Convention approved of judicial review, including those generally considered to be the most influential. Second, in *The Federalist Papers,* Hamilton adamantly defended the concept, arguing that one branch of government must

15. Jeffrey A. Segal and Harold J. Spaeth, *The Supreme Court and the Attitudinal Model* (Cambridge: Cambridge University Press, 1993), 16. A counter to this argument is that people of the day must have considered Section 13 as expanding the Court's original jurisdiction, or else why did Marbury bring his suit directly to the Supreme Court?

16. David Adamany, "The Supreme Court," in *The American Courts: A Critical Assessment,* ed. John B. Gates and Charles A. Johnson (Washington, D.C.: CQ Press, 1991).

safeguard the Constitution and that the courts would be in the best position to undertake that important responsibility.

Even with all this evidence, many still argue that the Framers did not intend for courts to review acts of the other branches. As Adamany summarizes, "The Constitutional Convention rejected a proposed Council of Revision, including judges, to reject or revise laws that did not conform to the Constitution." Furthermore, even though some states adopted judicial review, their courts rarely exercised the power. And "the outrage that followed some of those [state] decisions showed that judicial review was not widely accepted."[17] What, then, can we conclude about the intent of the Framers? Perhaps legal scholar Edward S. Corwin said it best: "The people who say the framers intended it are talking nonsense, and the people who say they did not intend it are talking nonsense."[18]

Judicial Restraint. Another controversy surrounding judicial review involves the notion of judicial restraint. Many legal analysts and justices have asserted that courts generally should defer to the elected institutions of government and "avoid conflicts" with those branches. An early statement of this position came in *Eakin v. Raub* (1825) in which Justice John Gibson, a Pennsylvania Supreme Court justice, took issue with the *Marbury* decision: He wrote:

The constitution and the *right* of the legislature to pass [an] act may be in collision; but is that a legitimate subject for judicial determination? If it be, the judiciary must be a peculiar organ, to revise the proceedings of the legislature and to correct its mistakes. . . . [I]t is by no means clear, that to declare a law void which has been enacted according to the forms prescribed in the constitution, is not a usurpation of legislative power. It is an act of sovereignty; and sovereignty and legislative power are . . . to be controvertible terms. It is the business of the judiciary to interpret the laws, not scan the authority of the law giver; and without the latter, it cannot take cognizance of a collision between a law and the Constitution. So that to affirm that the judiciary has a right

to judge the existence of such collision, is to take for granted the very thing to be proved.

It is worth noting that twenty years after *Raub*, Gibson had something of a change of heart. In an 1845 opinion he suggested that *state courts* should exercise judicial review over the acts of political institutions located within their jurisdictions.[19] But if we take *Raub* on its face, the use of judicial review belies this notion of judicial restraint for which Gibson clamors. Recall, for example, the legislative veto case described in the introduction to this chapter. By even considering the issue, the Court placed itself squarely in the middle of an executive-legislative dispute; when it nullified the veto, it showed no deference to the wishes of the legislature. To this argument, supporters of judicial review point to Marshall's decision in *Marbury*, Hamilton's assertion in *The Federalist Papers,* and so forth. They suggest that the government needs an umpire who will act neutrally and fairly in interpreting the constitutional strictures.

Again, the question of which posture is correct has no absolute answer, only opinion. But what we do know is that U.S. Supreme Court justices—with a few exceptions, such as Felix Frankfurter—have not taken seriously the dictate of judicial restraint or, at the very least, have not let it interfere in their voting.[20] Even those who profess a basic commitment to judicial deference have tended to allow their attitudes and values to dictate their decisions. Still, there is a tendency even today to equate judicial restraint with conservatism and judicial activism with liberalism. Former president Ronald Reagan often asserted the need for judicial restraint, saying that, if he could, he would appoint a Court of Felix Frankfurters. But many note that what Reagan really wanted was a Court that

17. Ibid., 13.
18. Quoted in ibid.

19. Melvin I. Urofsky, ed., *Documents of American Constitutional History,* vol. 1 (New York: Knopf, 1989), 183.
20. But see Segal and Spaeth, who argue that Frankfurter was "nothing more than a stalwart economic conservative who, along with his other economically oriented colleagues, used judicial restraint and judicial activism with equal facility to achieve his substantial policy objectives" (*Supreme Court and the Attitudinal Model,* 318).

would defer to legislatures if the laws in question reflected conservative values and would overturn them otherwise.

Democratic Checks. A third controversy involves what Adamany calls "democratic checks on the Court." According to one side of this debate, judicial review is defensible on the grounds that the Supreme Court—while lacking an explicit electoral connection—is "subject to potential checks by the elected branches." That is, if the Court exercises judicial review in a way repugnant to the best interests of the people, Congress, the president, and even the states have a number of recourses. Acting in different combinations they can, for example, ratify a constitutional amendment to overturn a decision, change the size of the Court, or remove the Court's appellate jurisdiction. The problem with these checks, in the eyes of some analysts, is that they are very rarely invoked: only four amendments have explicitly overturned Court decisions; the Court's size has not been changed since 1869; and only once has Congress removed the Court's appellate jurisdiction.

We do not mean to imply that Congress, in particular, has no control over the federal courts and their decisions. Although Congress does not often take direct action against the Court, the mere fact that the legislature has weapons to use against the judiciary may influence the justices.[21] In other words, if the justices care about the ultimate state of the law, they might seek to accommodate the wishes of Congress rather than face the wrath of the legislators, which could lead to the reversal of a ruling. It is the existence of congressional threat—not its actual invocation—that may affect how the Court rules in a given case.

Some scholars suggest that this dynamic explains why the justices rarely strike down congressional acts. Specific Court decisions may illustrate the extent to which Congress influences the Court. In *Mistretta v.*

United States (1989) the Supreme Court scrutinized a congressional act that sought to minimize judicial discretion in sentencing. The law created a sentencing commission charged with promulgating guidelines for federal judges to follow in handing down criminal sentences. Although some lower court judges refused to adopt the guidelines, arguing that they undermined judicial independence, the Supreme Court upheld the law. It is possible that the justices upheld the law because they agreed with it ideologically, because precedent led them to that conclusion, and so forth. But it also may be true that the justices feared a congressional backlash—a fear that was sufficiently real for them to act in accord with legislative wishes.

Public Opinion. A fourth debate surrounding judicial review concerns public opinion and the Court. Those who support judicial review argue that Court decisions are usually in harmony with public opinion; that is, even though the Court faces no real pressure to do so, it generally "follows the elections." Therefore, Americans need not fear that the Court will usurp their power. Empirical evidence, however, is mixed. After conducting an extensive investigation of the relationship of public opinion and the Court, Thomas Marshall concluded that "the evidence suggests that the modern Court has been an essentially majoritarian institution. Where clear poll margins exist, three-fifths to two-thirds of Court rulings reflect the polls."[22] Yet, as he and others concede, the Court at times has handed down decisions well out of line with public preferences, such as its prohibition of prayer in school and its short-lived ban on the death penalty.[23]

The other side of this controversy involves the "legitimacy-conferring" power of the Court. According to this view, when the Court reviews and upholds legislation, it plays the role of republican schoolmaster, educating the public and conferring some mea-

---

21. See, generally, William N. Eskridge, Jr., "Overriding Supreme Court Statutory Interpretation Decisions," *Yale Law Journal* 101 (1991): 331–455.

22. *Public Opinion and the Supreme Court* (Boston: Unwin Hyman, 1989), 192.

23. For an excellent review of this literature, see Gregory A. Caldeira, "Courts and Public Opinion," in *The American Courts.*

sure of acceptance for government policies. Again, evidence suggests that the Court does not and cannot serve this function, that too few people actually know about any given Court decision and, even if they do know, they do not necessarily shift their ideas to conform to the Court's opinions.

Research by Charles H. Franklin and Liane Kosaki provides an interesting example of the last point.[24] They examined whether the Court's decision in *Roe v. Wade* (1973) changed citizens' opinions on abortion, reasoning that if the Court acted as a republican schoolmaster then the public would adopt more liberal attitudes. Their data indicate, however, that no such change occurred. Instead, those who supported abortion rights before *Roe* became more liberal, while those opposed became more firmly anti-abortion. In other words, the Court's decision served to solidify existing views and not to change attitudes.

Role of the Court. A final controversy—perhaps the most hotly debated—concerns what role the Supreme Court should play in the U.S. system of government. Those who support judicial review assert that the Court must have this power if it is to fulfill its most important constitutional assignment: protection of minority rights. By their very nature—the fact that they are elected—legislatures and executives reflect the interests of the majority. Those interests may take action that is blatantly unconstitutional. So that the majority cannot tyrannize a minority, it is necessary for the one branch of government that lacks any electoral connection to have the power of judicial review. This is a powerful argument, the truth of which has been demonstrated many times throughout American history. For example, when the legislatures of southern states continued to enact segregation laws, it was the U.S. Supreme Court that struck them down as violative of the Constitution.

This position also has its share of problems. One is

that it conflicts with the notion of the Court as a body that defers to the elected branches. Another is that empirical evidence suggests that some Supreme Courts have not used judicial review in this manner. According to Robert Dahl, many of the acts struck down by the Supreme Court before the 1960s were those that harmed a "privileged class," not disadvantaged minorities.[25] We have seen similar decisions by the Rehnquist Court as well. For example, in *City of Richmond v. J. A. Croson Co.* (1989) and *Adarand Constructors v. Pena* (1995), the justices struck down affirmative action programs designed to help minority interests.

Judicial Review in Action

These controversies are important to the extent that they place the subject of judicial review into a theoretical context for debate. But they present debates that probably never will be resolved: as one side finds support for its position, the other always seems to follow suit.

Let us consider instead several issues arising from the way the Court actually has exercised the power of judicial review: the number of times it has invoked the power to strike laws, and the significance of those decisions. As Lawrence Baum suggests, investigation of these issues can help us achieve a better understanding of judicial review and place it in a realistic context.[26] First, how often has the Court overturned a federal, state, or local law or ordinance? Figure 2-3 *(page 40)* depicts those numbers over time. The data seem to indicate that the Court has made frequent use of the power, striking down close to 1,500 government acts since 1790. However, as Baum notes, those acts are but a "minute fraction" of the laws enacted at various levels of government. Between the 1790s and 1990s, for example, Congress passed more than

24. "The Republican Schoolmaster: The U.S. Supreme Court, Public Opinion, and Abortion," *American Political Science Review* 83 (1989): 751–771.

25. "Decision-Making in a Democracy: The Supreme Court as a National Policy-Maker," *Journal of Public Law* 6 (1957): 279–295
26. *The Supreme Court*, 4th ed. (Washington, D.C.: CQ Press, 1992), 185–192.

60,000 laws, with the Court striking far less than 1 percent of them.

The more important question, then, may be that of significance: Does the Court tend to strike down important laws or relatively minor laws? Using the case of *Scott v. Sandford* (1857) as an illustration, some argue that the Court, in fact, often strikes significant legislation. Undoubtedly, that opinion had major consequences. By ruling that Congress could not prohibit slavery in the territories and by striking down a law, the Missouri Compromise, that had already been repealed, the Court fed the growing divisions between the North and South, providing a major impetus for the Civil War. The decision also tarnished the prestige of the Court and the reputation of Chief Justice Taney.

But how representative is *Scott*? Some other Court opinions striking down government acts have been almost as important; those nullifying state abortion and segregation laws, the federal child labor acts, and many pieces of New Deal legislation come to mind. Yet, as Baum astutely notes, "A good many of the Court's decisions declaring [state and federal] measures unconstitutional, perhaps a majority . . . were minor."[27] Consider *Monongahela Navigation Co. v. United States* (1893). Here the Court struck down, on Fifth Amendment grounds, a law concerning the amount of money to be paid to the United States by companies for the "purchase or condemnation of a certain lock and dam in the Monongahela River."

Despite the rather ambiguous record, we can reach two conclusions about the Court's use of judicial review. First, "while judicial review has helped the Court to play a major role in policy making, it certainly has not made the Court the dominant national policy maker."[28] Second, it is not necessarily the Court's use of judicial review that is significant. Rather, as is true with the presidential veto, the threat to invoke review may be its power. In either case, judicial review has provided federal courts with their most significant political weapon.

CONSTRAINTS ON JUDICIAL POWER

Given all the attention paid to judicial review, it is easy to forget that the power of courts to exercise it and their judicial authority, more generally, have substantial limits. Article III—or the Court's interpretation of it—places three major constraints on the ability of federal tribunals to hear and decide cases: the court must have authority to hear a case (jurisdiction); the case must be appropriate for judicial resolution (justiciability); and the appropriate party must be bringing the case (standing).[29] In what follows, we review doctrine surrounding these constraints. As you read this discussion, consider not only the Court's interpretation of its own limits but also the justifications it offers. Note, in particular, how fluid these can be: some Courts tend to construe the rules loosely, while others are anxious to enforce them. What factors might explain these different tendencies? Or, to put it another way, to what extent do these constraints limit the Court's authority?

Jurisdiction

According to Chief Justice Salmon P. Chase, "Without jurisdiction the court cannot proceed at all in any cause. Jurisdiction is power to declare the law, and when it ceases to exist, the only function remaining to the court is that of announcing the fact and dismissing the cause."[30] In other words, a court cannot hear a case unless it has the authority—the jurisdiction—to do so.

Article III, Section 2, defines the jurisdiction of U.S. federal courts. Lower courts have the authority to hear disputes involving particular parties and subject matter. The U.S. Supreme Court's jurisdiction is divided into original and appellate: the former are classes of cases that originate in the Court; the latter are those it hears after a lower court.

---

27. Ibid., 176.   28. Ibid., 191.

29. See Stephen L. Wasby, *The Supreme Court in the Federal Judicial System*, 4th ed. (Chicago: Nelson Hall, 1993), 166.

30. *Ex parte McCardle* (1869).

To what extent does jurisdiction actually constrain the federal courts? *Marbury v. Madison* provides some answers, although contradictory, to this question. Chief Justice Marshall informed Congress that it could not alter the original jurisdiction of the Court. Having reached this conclusion, perhaps Marshall should have merely dismissed the case on the grounds that the Court lacked authority to hear it, but that is not what he did.

Marbury remains an authoritative ruling on original jurisdiction. The issue of appellate jurisdiction is a bit more complex. Article III explicitly states that for those cases over which the Court does not have original jurisdiction, it "shall have appellate Jurisdiction . . . with such Exceptions, and under such Regulations as the Congress shall make." In other words, the Exceptions Clause seems to give Congress authority to alter the Court's appellate jurisdiction.

Has the Supreme Court allowed Congress to do so? We know from *Martin v. Hunter's Lessee* that the Supreme Court has allowed Congress to expand its appellate jurisdiction; in those cases, the Court upheld the additions made to its appellate jurisdiction under Section 25 of the Judiciary Act. The question the Court addresses in *Ex parte McCardle* is a bit different. Here the justices must determine if Congress can use its power under the Exceptions Clause to remove the Court's appellate jurisdiction over a particular category of cases.

Ex parte McCardle

7 WALL. 506 (1869)

Vote: 8   (Chase, Clifford, Davis, Field, Grier, Miller, Nelson, Swayne)

0

Opinion of the Court: Chase

After the Civil War the radical Republican Congress imposed a series of restrictions on the South.[31] Known

as the Reconstruction laws, they in effect placed the region under military rule. Journalist William McCardle opposed these measures and wrote editorials urging resistance to them. As a result, he was arrested for publishing allegedly "incendiary and libelous articles" and held for a trial before a military tribunal, established under Reconstruction.

Because he was a civilian, not a member of any militia, McCardle alleged that he was being illegally held. He petitioned for a writ of habeas corpus—an order issued to determine if a person held in custody is being unlawfully detained or imprisoned—under an 1867 act, which "gave federal judges power to grant habeas corpus to any person restrained in violation" of the U.S. Constitution.[32] When this effort failed, McCardle appealed to the U.S. Supreme Court.

In early March 1868 *McCardle* "was very thoroughly and ably [presented] upon the merits" to the U.S. Supreme Court. It was clear to most observers that "no Justice was still making up his mind": the Court's sympathies, as was widely known, lay with McCardle.[33] But before the justices issued their decision, Congress, on March 27, 1868, enacted a law repealing the 1867 Habeas Corpus Act and removing the Supreme Court's authority to hear appeals emanating from it. This move was meant to punish the Court or, at the very least, to send it a strong message. Two years before *McCardle*, in 1866, the Court had invalidated Lincoln's use of military tribunals in certain areas, and Congress did not want to see the Court take similar action in this dispute.[34] The legislature felt so strongly on this issue that after President Andrew Johnson vetoed the 1868 repealer act, Congress overrode the veto.

The Court responded by redocketing the case for oral arguments in March 1869. During the arguments

the Reconstruction Game," in *Contemplating Courts,* ed. Lee Epstein (Washington, D.C.: CQ Press, 1995), 315–346.

32. C. Herman Pritchett, *The American Constitution* (New York: McGraw-Hill, 1959), 109.

33. Charles Fairman, *History of the Supreme Court of the United States,* vol. 7: *Reconstruction and Reunion* (New York: Macmillan, 1971), 456.

34. That action came in *Ex parte Milligan* (1866), discussed in Chapter 5.

31. For more information on *McCardle,* see Lee Epstein and Thomas G. Walker, "The Role of the Supreme Court in American Society: Playing

and in its briefs, the government made its position clear: "When the jurisdiction of a court to determine a case or a class of cases depends upon a statute and that statute is repealed, the jurisdiction ceases absolutely." In short, the government contended that the Court no longer had authority to hear the case and should dismiss it.

THE CHIEF JUSTICE delivered the opinion of the Court.

It is unnecessary to consider whether, if Congress had made no exceptions and no regulations, this court might not have exercised general appellate jurisdiction under rules prescribed by itself. From among the earliest Acts of the first Congress, at its first session, was the Act of September 24th, 1789, to establish the judicial courts of the United States. That Act provided for the organization of this court, and prescribed regulations for the exercise of its jurisdiction. . . .

The exception to appellate jurisdiction in the case before us . . . is not an inference from the affirmation of other appellate jurisdiction. It is made in terms. The provision of the Act of 1867, affirming the appellate jurisdiction of this court in cases of habeas corpus, is expressly repealed. It is hardly possible to imagine a plainer instance of positive exception.

We are not at liberty to inquire into the motives of the Legislature. We can only examine into its power under the Constitution; and the power to make exceptions to the appellate jurisdiction of this court is given by express words.

What, then, is the effect of the repealing Act upon the case before us? We cannot doubt as to this. Without jurisdiction the court cannot proceed at all in any cause. Jurisdiction is power to declare the law, and when it ceases to exist, the only function remaining to the court is that of announcing the fact and dismissing the cause. And this is not less clear upon authority than upon principle. . . .

It is quite clear, therefore, that this . . . court cannot proceed to pronounce judgment in this case, for it has no longer jurisdiction of the appeal; and judicial duty is not less fitly performed by declining ungranted jurisdiction than in exercising firmly that which the Constitution and the laws confer. . . .

The appeal of the petitioner in this case must be dismissed for want of jurisdiction.

As we can see, the Court acceded and declined to hear the case. *McCardle* suggests that Congress has the authority to remove the Court's appellate jurisdiction as it deems necessary. Since *McCardle*, however, Congress has only considered, but not enacted, legislation—at least legislation aimed directly at the Court—to limit the Court's appellate jurisdiction. Table 3-1 lists some of the proposals members of Congress have offered. As noted, many involve controversial issue areas—abortion, prayer in school, busing—leading to the conclusion that modern Congresses are no different from the one that passed the 1868 repealer act: they would like to use the Exceptions Clause as a political tool, as a way to restrain the Court, but they have yet to do so successfully.

In spite of *McCardle*, there are several reasons to believe that the Court might not uphold the sorts of proposals depicted in Table 3-1. One is that *McCardle* was something of an odd case. According to many scholars, the Court had no choice but to acquiesce to Congress if it wanted to retain its legitimacy in post–Civil War America. The pressures of the day, rather than the Constitution or the beliefs of the justices, may have led to the decision.

Another reason is that a case subsequent to *McCardle* cast some doubt on the precedent it seemed to set. In *United States v. Klein* (1872) the Court considered an 1870 law in which Congress sought to impinge on the president's authority to issue executive amnesties. In particular, it required those who wished to recover property taken by the government during the Civil War to prove their loyalty, even if they had received a presidential pardon. Moreover, the law withdrew the U.S. Supreme Court's (and a lower appellate court's) jurisdiction to hear such cases. Although the justices acknowledged that the Exceptions Clause gave Congress the right to remove their appellate jurisdiction

TABLE 3-1 A Sample of Congressional Proposals Aimed at Eliminating the U.S. Supreme Court's Appellate Jurisdiction

Issue	Supreme Court Decision Provoking Proposal	Proposal
Communist infiltration/ Security programs	*Schware v. Board of Bar Examiners* (1957) in which the Supreme Court refused to allow states to use "inferences regarding moral character" (i.e., past association with a subversive cause) to exclude applicants for admission to the bar.	1958 proposal that would have eliminated the Court's appellate jurisdiction over any "regulation pertaining to the admission of persons to the practice of law."
Criminal confessions	*Miranda v. Arizona* (1966) in which the Court required police to read those under arrest a series of rights.	1968 proposal that removed the Court's jurisdiction to hear state cases involving the admissibility of confessions.
School busing	*Swann v. Charlotte-Mecklenburg County* (1971) in which the Court permitted district courts to fashion their own school desegregation plans, which may include the busing of students to other schools.	During the 1970s and 1980s many proposals were offered to curb the Court's authority to hear busing cases and to limit the authority of courts to order busing.
School prayer	*Engel v. Vitale* (1962) and *Abington School District v. Schempp* (1963), which eliminated voluntary and mandatory prayer in school.	Several proposals, with a major effort coming in 1979, that would have eliminated the Supreme Court's as well as all other federal courts' ability to hear any cases involving voluntary school prayer.
Abortion	*Roe v. Wade* (1973) in which the Supreme Court struck down state laws criminalizing abortion. Roe legalized abortion during the first two trimesters of pregnancy.	During the 1970s and 1980s several proposals to remove the Court's authority to hear abortion cases.

SOURCE: Adopted from Gerald Gunther, *Constitutional Law* (Mineola, N.Y.: Foundation Press, 1985), 48–49.

"in a particular class of cases," it could not do so only as "a means to an end." That is, in previous cases, the Court had stated that the president had the power to grant pardons. Therefore, Congress was using the Exceptions Clause to skirt those decisions. If the Court allowed this, it would then permit Congress to "prescribe rules of decision to the Judicial Department . . . in cases pending before it," in violation of constitutional mandates requiring the separation of powers.[35]

Still, *Klein* did not settle the issue. Compare, for example, the views of two twentieth-century justices. In 1948 Justice Frankfurter wrote, "Congress need not give this Court any appellate power; it may withdraw appellate jurisdiction once conferred and it may do so even while a case is *sub judice*" [before a judge].[36] Thirteen years later, Justice Douglas remarked, "There is a serious question whether the *McCardle* case could command a majority view today."[37]

Whether the Court would allow Congress to use the Exceptions Clause remains an open question until such litigation occurs. Until then, Chief Justice Chase perhaps summed up the situation best when he noted, after *McCardle* had been decided, that use of the Exceptions Clause was "unusual and hardly to be justified except upon some imperious public exigency."[38]

35. See, generally, Gerald Gunther, *Constitutional Law,* 11th ed. (Mineola, N.Y.: Foundation Press, 1985), 43.

36. *National Mutual Insurance Co. v. Tidewater Transfer Co.* (1949).
37. *Glidden Co. v. Zdanok* (1962).
38. *Ex parte Yerger* (1869).

Justiciability

According to Article III, judicial power of the federal courts is restricted to "cases" and "controversies." Taken together, these words mean that a litigation must be justiciable—appropriate or suitable for a federal tribunal to hear or to solve. As Chief Justice Warren asserted, cases and controversies are two complementary but somewhat different limitations. In part those words limit the business of federal courts to questions presented in an adversary context and in a form historically viewed as capable of resolution through the judicial process. And in part those words define the role assigned to the judiciary in a tripartite allocation of power to assure that the federal courts will not intrude into areas committed to the other branches of government. Justiciability is the term of art employed to give expression to this dual limitation placed upon federal courts by the case-and-controversy doctrine.[39]

Although Warren also suggested that "justiciability is itself a concept of uncertain meaning and scope," he elucidated several characteristics of litigation that would render it nonjusticiable. In this section, we treat five: advisory opinions, collusion, mootness, ripeness, and political questions. In the following section we deal with another concept related to justiciability—standing to sue.

Advisory Opinions. Put simply, federal courts will not issue advisory opinions. They will not render advice in hypothetical suits because if litigation is abstract, it possesses no real controversy. The language of the Constitution does not prohibit advisory opinions as opinions, but it is worth noting that the Framers rejected a proposal that would have permitted the other branches of government to request judicial rulings "upon important questions of law, and upon solemn occasions." Madison was critical of this proposal on the grounds that the judiciary should

have jurisdiction only over "cases of a Judiciary Nature."[40]

The Supreme Court agreed with Madison; quite early on it understood the case-or-controversy restriction to prohibit it from rendering advisory opinions. In July 1793 Secretary of State Thomas Jefferson asked the justices if they would be willing to address questions concerning the appropriate role America should play in the ongoing British-French war. Jefferson wrote that President Washington "would be much relieved if he found himself free to refer questions [involving the war] to the opinions of the judges of the [Court], whose knowledge . . . would secure us against errors dangerous to the peace of the United States."[41] Less than a month later the justices denied Jefferson's request:

[The] three departments of government [being] in certain respects checks upon each other, and our being judges of a court in the last resort, are considerations which afford strong arguments against the propriety of our extra judicially deciding the questions alluded to, especially as the power given by the Constitution to the President, of calling on the heads of departments for opinions, seems to have been *purposely* as well as expressly united to the *executive* departments.[42]

With these words, the justices sounded the death knell for advisory opinions: they would violate the separation of powers principle embedded in the Constitution. The subject has resurfaced only a few times in U.S. history; in the 1930s, for example, President Roosevelt considered a proposal that would require the Court to issue advisory opinions on the constitutionality of federal laws. According to Gerald Gunther, "That plan was soon abandoned, partly because of its obvious unconstitutionality."[43]

Nevertheless, scholars still debate the Court's 1793 letter to Washington. Some agree with the justices'

---

39. *Flast v. Cohen* (1968).

40. Quoted by Farber and Sherry in *A History of the American Constitution,* 65.

41. Quoted in Gunther, *Constitutional Law,* 1535.

42. Quoted in ibid.

43. Ibid., 1536.

logic. Others assert that more institutional concerns were at work; perhaps the Court sought to avoid being "thrust" into disputes "too early and too often." [44] Whatever the reason, all subsequent Courts have followed that 1793 precedent: requests for advisory opinions to the U.S. Supreme Court present nonjusticiable disputes. [45]

Collusive Suits. A second corollary of justiciability is collusion. The Court will not decide cases in which the litigants (1) want the same outcome, (2) evince no real adversity between them, or (3) are merely testing the law. Why the Court deems collusive suits nonjusticiable is well illustrated in *Muskrat v. United States* (1911). At issue here were several federal laws involving land distribution and appropriations to Native Americans. To determine whether these laws were constitutional, Congress enacted a statute authorizing David Muskrat and other Native Americans to challenge the land distribution law in court. This legislation also ordered the courts to give priority to Muskrat's suit and allowed the attorney general to defend his claim. Furthermore, Congress agreed to pay Muskrat's legal fees if his suit was successful. When the dispute reached the U.S. Supreme Court, the panel dismissed it. Justice William Day wrote:

[T]here is neither more nor less in this [litigation] than an attempt to provide for a judicial determination, final in this court, of the constitutional validity of an act of Congress. Is such a determination within the judicial power conferred by the Constitution, as the same has been interpreted and defined in the authoritative decisions to which we have referred? We think it is not. That judicial power, as we have seen, is the right to determine actual controversies arising between adverse litigants, duly instituted in courts of proper jurisdiction. The right to declare a law unconstitutional arises because an act of Congress relied upon by one or the other of such parties in determining their rights is in conflict with the fundamental law. The exercise of this, the most important and delicate duty of this court, is not given

to it as a body with revisory power over the action of Congress, but because the rights of the litigants in justiciable controversies require the court to choose between the fundamental law and a law purporting to be enacted within constitutional authority, but in fact beyond the power delegated to the legislative branch of the Government. This attempt to obtain a judicial declaration of the validity of the act of Congress is not presented in a "case" or "controversy," to which, under the Constitution of the United States, the judicial power alone extends. It is true the United States is made a defendant to this action, but it has no interest adverse to the claimants. The object is not to assert a property right as against the Government, or to demand compensation for alleged wrongs because of action upon its part. The whole purpose of the law is to determine the constitutional validity of this class of legislation, in a suit not arising between parties concerning a property right necessarily involved in the decision in question, but in a proceeding against the Government in its sovereign capacity, and concerning which the only judgment required is to settle the doubtful character of the legislation in question.

However, the Court has not always followed the *Muskrat* precedent. To the contrary, as C. Herman Pritchett noted, "several significant pieces of constitutional litigation" were the result of collusive suits. [46] Two examples include:

Pollock v. Farmers' Loan and Trust Co. (1895), in which the Court struck down as unconstitutional a federal income tax. The litigants in this dispute, a bank and a stockholder in the bank, both wanted the same outcome—the demise of the tax.

Carter v. Carter Coal Co. (1936), in which the Court struck down as unconstitutional a major piece of New Deal legislation. The litigants in this dispute, a company president and the company, which included the president's father, both wanted the same outcome—the eradication of the New Deal legislation.

Why did the Court resolve these disputes evincing collusion but dismiss *Muskrat*? Elder Witt provides a reasonable explanation: "The Court's decision to hear or dismiss such a test case usually turns on whether it

---

44. For a discussion of this debate, see ibid., 1536–1538.

45. We emphasize the Supreme Court because some state courts do, in fact, issue advisory opinions.

46. Pritchett, *The American Constitution*, 144.

presents an actual conflict of legal rights."[47] In other words, the Court might overlook some element of collusion if the suit itself presents a real controversy or the potential for one.

Mootness. In general, the Court will not decide cases in which the controversy is no longer live by the time the case reaches its doorstep. *DeFunis v. Odegaard* (1974) provides one example. Rejected for admission to the University of Washington Law School, Marco DeFunis, Jr., brought suit against the school, alleging that it had engaged in reverse discrimination, that it had denied him a place while accepting statistically less qualified minority students. In 1971 a trial court found merit in his claim and ordered that the university admit him. While DeFunis was in his second year of law school, the state's high court reversed the trial judge's ruling. DeFunis then appealed to the U.S. Supreme Court. By that time, DeFunis had registered for his final quarter in school. In a per curiam opinion, the Court refused to rule on the merits of DeFunis's claim, asserting that it was moot:

Because [DeFunis] will complete his law school studies at the end of the term for which he has now registered regardless of any decision this Court might reach on the merits of this litigation, we conclude that the Court cannot, consistently with the limitations of Art. III of the Constitution, consider the substantive constitutional issues tendered by the parties.

Still, the rules governing mootness are a bit fuzzier than the *DeFunis* opinion characterized them. A well-known case is *Roe v. Wade* (1973), in which the Court legalized abortions performed during the first two trimesters of pregnancy. Norma McCorvey, also known as Roe, was pregnant when she filed suit in 1970. When the Court handed down the decision in 1973, she had long since given birth and put her baby up for adoption. But the justices did not declare this case moot.

Why not? What made *Roe* different from *DeFunis?* The justices provided two legal justifications. First, DeFunis brought the litigation in his own behalf; *Roe* was a class action—a lawsuit brought by one or more persons who represent themselves and all others similarly situated. Second, DeFunis had been admitted to law school, and he would "never again be required to run the gauntlet." Roe could become pregnant again; that is, pregnancy is a situation capable of repetition or recurrence. Are these reasonable points? Or is it possible, as some suspect, that the Court developed them to avoid particular legal issues? In either case, it is clear that mootness may be a rather slippery concept, open to interpretation by different justices and Courts.

Ripeness. Related to the concepts of advisory opinions and mootness is that of ripeness. Under existing Court interpretation a case is nonjusticiable if the controversy is premature—has insufficiently gelled—for review. *International Longshoreman's Union v. Boyd* (1954) provides an illustration. In 1952 Congress passed a law mandating that all aliens seeking admission into the United States from Alaska be "examined" as if they were entering from a foreign country. Believing that the law might affect seasonal American laborers working in Alaska temporarily, a union challenged the law. Writing for the Court, Justice Frankfurter dismissed the suit. In his view,

Appellants in effect asked [the Court] to rule that a statute the sanctions of which had not been set in motion against individuals on whose behalf relief was sought, because an occasion for doing so had not arisen, would not be applied to them if in the future such a contingency should arise. That is not a lawsuit to enforce a right; it is an endeavor to obtain a court's assurance that a statute does not govern hypothetical situations that may or may not make the challenged statute applicable. Determination of the . . . constitutionality of the legislation in advance of its immediate adverse effect in the context of a concrete case involves too remote and abstract an inquiry for the proper exercise of the judicial function.

47. *Guide to the U.S. Supreme Court*, 2d ed. (Washington, D.C.: Congressional Quarterly, 1990), 288.

Political Questions. Another type of nonjusticiable suit involves a political question. Chief Justice Marshall stated in *Marbury v. Madison:*

The province of the court is, solely, to decide on the rights of individuals, not to inquire how the executive, or executive officers, perform duties in which they have a discretion. Questions in their nature political, or which are, by the constitution and laws, submitted to the executive, can never be made in this court.

In other words, there is a class of questions that may be constitutional in nature but that the Court will not address because they are better solved by other branches of government.

But what exactly constitutes a political question? In the 1849 case of *Luther v. Borden* the Court provided a partial answer. *Luther* involved a dispute between the existing government of Rhode Island and a group—the "Dorrites"—that was trying to institute a new constitution (at the time Rhode Island had no constitution but continued under a royal charter) and a new government. Believing that the Dorrites' activities amounted to insurrection, the government sought to suppress the rebels through arrests made, in some instances, by police who entered homes without search warrants. Martin Luther, one of the Dorrites who had been arrested, sued state officials for trespass. He argued that the royal charter denied citizens a republican form of government, as mandated by the Guarantee Clause of Article IV: "The United States shall guarantee to every State in this Union a Republican From of Government, and shall protect each of them against Invasion; and on Application of the Legislature, or the Executive (when the Legislature cannot be convened) against domestic Violence."

But the Supreme Court refused to go along with Luther. Writing for the majority, Chief Justice Taney held that the Court should avoid deciding any question arising out of the Guarantee Clause because such questions are inherently "political." He based the opinion largely on the words of Article IV, which he believed governed relations between the states and the federal government, not governments and courts. In other words, since the clause omits mention of the Court, it is enforceable only by the president or Congress.

During the next 100 years or so, the Court adopted Taney's position: any case involving the Guarantee Clause constituted a nonjusticiable dispute. In the 1940s an issue came before the Court that presented an opportunity to rethink *Luther.* The issue was reapportionment, the manner in which states draw legislative districts. Under the U.S. Constitution, each state is allotted a certain number of seats in the House of Representatives based on the population of the state. Once that figure has been established, it is up to the state to determine specific congressional districts. Article I specifies:

Representatives ... shall be apportioned among the several States which may be included within this Union, according to their respective Numbers.... The actual Enumeration shall be made within three Years after the first Meeting of the Congress of the United States, and within every subsequent Term of ten Years, in such Manner as they shall by Law direct. The Number of Representatives shall not exceed one for every thirty Thousand, but each State shall have at Least one Representative.

In other words, Article I makes clear that a ten-year census determines the number of representatives each state receives. But no guidelines exist as to how those representatives are to be allocated or apportioned within a given state.

As population shifts occurred within states in the mid-1900s, some redrew their congressional district lines. For most, the new maps meant creating greater parity for urban centers as citizens moved out of rural areas. Others, however, ignored these shifts and refused to reapportion seats. Over time, the results of their failure to do so became readily apparent. It was possible for two districts within the same state, with large differences in populations, each to elect one member to the House.

Because malapportionment generally had the greatest effect on urban voters, grossly undervaluing their voting power, reform groups representing their interests began to bring litigation to force legislatures to reapportion. In one of the most important of these efforts, *Colegrove v. Green* (1946), they did so under Article IV. They argued that the failure to reapportion legislative districts deprived some voters of their right to a republican form of government. By way of proof, plaintiffs indicated that a large statistical discrepancy existed between the voting power of urban and rural dwellers because the Illinois legislature had not reapportioned since 1901.

Writing for the Court, Justice Frankfurter dismissed *Colegrove.* He invoked the logic of *Luther v. Borden* to hold that the question of legislative reapportionment within states was left open by the Constitution. If the Court intervened in this matter, it would be acting in a way "hostile to a democratic system." Put in different terms, reapportionment constituted a "political thicket" into which "courts ought not enter."

As a result of the Court's decision in *Colegrove,* disparities between the voting power of urban and rural citizens continued to grow. Consider, for example, Figure 3-2, which shows that a rural vote for the Tennessee legislature counted nearly four times as much as an urban vote. Naturally, many citizens and organizations wanted to force legislatures to reapportion, but under *Colegrove* they could not do so using the Guarantee Clause. They looked, therefore, to another section of the Constitution, the Fourteenth Amendment's Equal Protection Clause, which says, no state shall "deny to any person within its jurisdiction the equal protection of the laws." From this clause, they made the argument, in *Baker v. Carr* (1962), that the failure to reapportion led to unequal treatment of voters.

Although this strategy represented a clever legal attempt to reframe the issue of reapportionment, when

FIGURE 3-2   Map of Districts in Tennessee, 1901 and 1950

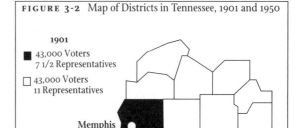

1901
■ 43,000 Voters
   7 1/2 Representatives
□ 43,000 Voters
   11 Representatives

Battle of the ballot: In 1901 Memphis, Tennessee, had as many people as eight nearby counties together and elected nearly the same number of representatives.

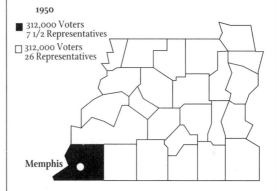

1950
■ 312,000 Voters
   7 1/2 Representatives
□ 312,000 Voters
   26 Representatives

By 1950 Memphis's population equaled that of twenty-four counties. Under the state constitution the city should have gained more representatives, but did not; so the rural vote counted almost four times as much as the urban. Reviewing city voters' complaint that this situation denied them equal protection of the laws, the Court in 1962 held that judges should hear and decide such claims under the Fourteenth Amendment (***Baker v. Carr***). Chief Justice Earl Warren looked back upon this decision as the most important and influential in his sixteen years on the Court. It opened the way to enunciation (in ***Reynolds v. Sims***) of the "one person, one vote" principle and its enforcement by court order in many related cases across the nation.

SOURCE: *Equal Justice Under Law* (Washington, D.C.: Foundation of the Federal Bar Association, 1965), 108.

attorneys sought to apply it to the Tennessee situation, a lower federal district court dismissed their suit.[48] Relying on *Colegrove* and other cases, that court held reapportionment to constitute a political question on which it could not rule.

The Supreme Court, however, disagreed. In a landmark opinion for the majority in *Baker*, Justice Brennan first set out a definition of a political question:

Prominent on the surface of any case held to involve a political question is found a textually demonstrable constitutional commitment of the issue to a coordinate political department; or a lack of judicially discoverable and manageable standards for resolving it; or the impossibility of deciding without an initial policy determination of a kind clearly for nonjudicial discretion; or the impossibility of a court's undertaking independent resolution without expressing lack of the respect due coordinate branches of government; or an unusual need for unquestioning adherence to a political decision already made; or the potentiality of embarrassment from multifarious pronouncements by various departments on one question.

Based on this definition, he offered illustrations of the kinds of questions that would and would not meet the criteria. Cases grounded in the Guarantee Clause, like *Luther*, for example, met the criteria of a political question:

Clearly, several factors were thought by the Court in Luther [v. Borden] to make the question there "political": the commitment to the other branches of the decision as to which is the lawful state government; the unambiguous action by the President, in recognizing the charter government as the lawful authority; the need for finality in the executive's decision; and the lack of criteria by which a court could determine which form of government was republican.

But *Baker* did not. For, in Brennan's opinion, the case did not implicate the Guarantee Clause; it rested on Fourteenth Amendment claim. And that claim was justiciable because it failed to meet the definition of a political question. As Brennan wrote:

48. For more on this, see Richard C. Cortner, "Strategies and Tactics of Litigants in Constitutional Cases," *Journal of Public Law* 17 (1968): 287–307; and Cortner, *The Apportionment Cases* (Knoxville: University of Tennessee Press, 1970).

We come, finally, to the ultimate inquiry whether our precedents as to what constitutes a nonjusticiable "political question" bring the case before us under the umbrella of that doctrine. A natural beginning is to note whether any of the common characteristics which we have been able to identify and label descriptively are present. We find none: The question here is the consistency of state action with the Federal Constitution. We have no question decided, or to be decided, by a political branch of government coequal with this Court. Nor do we risk embarrassment of our government abroad, or grave disturbance at home if we take issue with Tennessee as to the constitutionality of her action here challenged. Nor need the appellants, in order to succeed in this action, ask the Court to enter upon policy determinations for which judicially manageable standards are lacking. Judicial standards under the Equal Protection Clause are well developed and familiar, and it has been open to courts since the enactment of the Fourteenth Amendment to determine, if on the particular facts they must, that a discrimination reflects no policy, but simply arbitrary and capricious action.

To put it another way, had the case been brought under the Guarantee Clause, "it could not have succeeded." But, as Brennan argued, "the nonjusticiability of claims resting on the Guaranty Clause which arises from their embodiment of questions that were thought 'political,' can have no bearing upon the justiciability of the equal protection claim presented in this case."

The author of *Colegrove*, Justice Frankfurter, took great issue with Brennan's opinion. He began his dissent with these words:

The present case involves all of the elements that have made the Guarantee Clause cases non-justiciable. It is, in effect, a Guarantee Clause claim masquerading under a different label. But it cannot make the case more fit for judicial action that appellants invoke the Fourteenth Amendment rather than [the Guarantee Clause], where, in fact, the gist of their complaint is the same. . .

Whether or not you agree with Frankfurter, it is important to recognize that *Baker* is a significant decision for a number of reasons. One is that it opened the window for judicial resolution of reapportionment

Examples of Its Use

1. *Gilligan v. Morgan* (1973). In the aftermath of the shootings at Kent State, students asked the Court to hold that there was "a pattern of training, weaponry, and orders" in the National Guard that made the events of Kent State inevitable. They asked the Court to restrain the governor from "prematurely ordering Guard troops in civil disorders."

The Court found that no justiciable controversy existed. Control of military forces is something the Constitution leaves explicitly to the control of legislatures and executives. In the words of the Court, "It would be difficult to think of a clearer example of the type of governmental action that was intended by the Constitution to be left to the political branches directly responsible . . . to the electoral process."

2. In *Goldwater v. Carter* (1979), which presented a challenge to President Carter's unilateral termination of a U.S. treaty with Taiwan, Justice Rehnquist held the case presented a political question. In his view, it involved a foreign policy matter on which the Constitution provided no definitive answer. As such, it "should be left for resolution by the Executive and Legislative branches."

3. In *Nixon v. United States* (1993), a federal district court judge asked the Court to review procedure used by the Senate to impeach him. The Court ruled that the procedure used by Congress to handle impeachments is not subject to judicial review. The Constitution grants the Senate the sole power to try all impeachments, and how the Senate organizes itself to discharge that duty constitutes a political question.

Examples of Its Rejection

1. In *Powell v. McCormack* (1969) the Court examined the issue of whether the House of Representatives could vote to exclude a member—Rep. Adam Clayton Powell—on the grounds that he allegedly engaged in unethical activities. Respondents asked the Court to dismiss the suit because it asked a political question, meeting several of the criteria set out in *Baker v. Carr.*

The Court refused to do so. In particular, it rejected the contention that the dispute was one in which a "textually demonstrable constitutional commitment" to the House existed, enabling it to determine its own membership. Rather, the Constitution permits the House only to judge the "qualifications expressly set forth in the Constitution," which Powell met. It also rejected *Baker*'s potentially embarrassing criteria, noting that: "Our system of government requires that the federal courts on occasion interpret the Constitution in a manner at variance with a construction given the document by another branch."

2. In *Goldwater v. Carter*, Justice Powell argued that the dispute did not present a political question under *Baker*. In his view, the case only "touched" foreign affairs, with the major issue being "constitutional division of power between Congress and the President." He wrote, "Interpretation of the Constitution does not imply lack of respect for a coordinate branch. If the President and the Congress had reached irreconcilable positions, final disposition of the question presented by this case would eliminate, rather than create, multiple constitutional interpretations."

3. In *Davis v. Bandemer* (1986) the Court held that political gerrymandering constituted a justiciable issue. Though they had been urged to find that it inherently asked the Court to address a political question, the justices found "none of the identifying characteristics of a nonjusticiable political question" dispute to exist.

cases. Another, and more relevant here, is that it established a clear doctrinal base for determining political questions. We demonstrate the vitality of *Baker* in Box 3-3, which depicts how the Court has used that framework. Note that Brennan's opinion did not lead to the demise of the political questions doctrine. Over the years, the Court has used it to dismiss a range of substantive disputes. Indeed, as recently as 1993, in the case of *Nixon v. United States* the Court relied heavily on *Baker v. Carr* to rule that the procedures used by Congress to handle impeachments are not subject to judicial review.

Standing to Sue

Another constraint on federal judicial power is standing: if the party bringing the litigation is not the appropriate party, the courts will not resolve the dispute. Put in somewhat different terms, "not every person with the money to bring a lawsuit is entitled to litigate the legality or constitutionality of government action in the federal courts."[49] Rather, as Justice Brennan noted in *Baker,* Article III requires that litigants demonstrate "such a personal stake in the outcome of the controversy as to assure that concrete adverseness which sharpens the presentation of issues upon which the Court so largely depends for illumination of difficult constitutional questions."

In most private disputes, the litigants have no difficulty demonstrating a personal stake or injury. The more interesting constitutional questions have arisen in suits that involve parties who wish to challenge some government action on the grounds that they are taxpayers. Such claims raise an important question: Does the mere fact that one pays taxes provide a sufficiently personal stake in litigation to meet the requirement for standing?

The Court first addressed this question in *Frothingham v. Mellon* (1923). At issue was the Sheppard-Towner Maternity Act, in which Congress provided federal maternity aid to the states to fund programs designed to reduce infant mortality rates. Although many progressive groups had lobbied for the law, other organizations viewed it as an unconstitutional intrusion into the family and into the rights of states.[50] They decided to challenge it and enlisted one among their ranks, Harriet Frothingham, to serve as a plaintiff. She was not receiving Sheppard-Towner Maternity Act aid; she was a taxpayer who did not want to see her tax dollars spent on the program. Her attorneys argued that she had sufficient grounds to bring suit.

It has been held with practical uniformity by the Courts of the various states that a taxpayer has a sufficient interest to entitle him to maintain a suit against a public officer for the purpose of enjoining an unauthorized payment of public funds.... The appellant maintains ... [that if] these payments are made [she] will suffer a direct injury in that she will be subjected to taxation to pay her proportionate part of such unauthorized payments. She, therefore, has an interest sufficient ... to maintain a proceeding to enjoin the making of these payments. Her relation to these funds is exactly that of a *cestui que trust* [trust beneficiary] to funds held by his trustee. Her injury would be irreparable because it cannot be calculated. She can resort only to equity to maintain her right.

The Court refused to adopt this position. Rather, it held that Frothingham lacked standing to bring the litigation. Justice George Sutherland wrote for the majority:

If one taxpayer may champion and litigate such a cause, then every other taxpayer may do the same, not only in respect of the statute here under review but also in respect of every other appropriation act and statute whose administration requires the outlay of public money, and whose validity may be questioned. The bare suggestion of such a result, with its attendant inconveniences, goes far to sustain the conclusion which we have reached, that a suit of this character cannot be maintained.

---

49. Pritchett, *The American Constitution*, 145.

50. We adopt this discussion from Lee Epstein, *Conservatives in Court* (Knoxville: University of Tennessee Press, 1985), 31–36.

He also outlined an approach to standing:

The party . . . must be able to show not only that the statute is invalid but that he has sustained or is immediately in danger of sustaining some direct injury as the result of its enforcement, and not merely that he suffers in some indefinite way in common with people generally.

For the next forty years, *Frothingham* served as a major bar to taxpayer suits. Unless litigants could demonstrate that a government program injured them or threatened to do so— beyond the mere expenditure of tax dollars—they could not bring suit. In *Flast v. Cohen*, however, the Court substantially relaxed that rule. *Flast* involved seven taxpayers who sought to challenge federal expenditures made under the Elementary and Secondary Education Act of 1965. Under this law, states could apply to the federal government for grants to assist in the education of children from low-income families. They could, for example, obtain funds for the acquisition of textbooks, school library materials, and so forth. The taxpayers alleged that some of the funds disbursed under this Act were used to finance "instruction in reading, arithmetic, and other subjects and for guidance in religious and sectarian schools." Such expenditures, they argued, violated the First Amendment's prohibition on religious establishment ("Congress shall make no law respecting an establishment of religion").

A three-judge district court dismissed their complaint. It reasoned that because the plaintiffs had suffered no real injury and because their only claim of standard rested "solely on their status as federal taxpayers," they failed to meet the criteria established in *Frothingham.*

Writing for the Court, Chief Justice Warren disagreed. And, in so doing, he completely revamped the *Frothingham* standard. To determine whether or not a taxpayer has the requisite "personal stake" to bring suit, Warren wrote:

[I]t is both appropriate and necessary to look to the substantive issues for another purpose, namely, to determine whether there is a logical nexus between the status asserted and the claim sought to be adjudicated. . . . The nexus demanded of federal taxpayers has two aspects to it. First, the taxpayer must establish a logical link between that status and the type of legislative enactment attacked. Thus, a taxpayer will be a proper party to allege the unconstitutionality only of exercises of congressional power under the taxing and spending clause of Art. I, § 8, of the Constitution. It will not be sufficient to allege an incidental expenditure of tax funds in the administration of an essentially regulatory statute . . . Secondly, the taxpayer must establish a nexus between that status and the precise nature of the constitutional infringement alleged. Under this requirement, the taxpayer must show that the challenged enactment exceeds specific constitutional limitations imposed upon the exercise of the congressional taxing and spending power and not simply that the enactment is generally beyond the powers delegated to Congress by Art. I, § 8. When both nexuses are established, the litigant will have shown a taxpayer's stake in the outcome of the controversy and will be a proper and appropriate party to invoke a federal court's jurisdiction.

Applying this standard to the dispute at hand, Warren found that the Flast taxpayers had standing.

Their constitutional challenge is made to an exercise by Congress of its power under Art. I, § 8, to spend for the general welfare, and the challenged program involves a substantial expenditure of federal tax funds. In addition, appellants have alleged that the challenged expenditures violate the Establishment and Free Exercise Clauses of the First Amendment.

Would Harriet Frothingham have met this new, more relaxed standard? To this question, Warren answered no:

The allegations of the taxpayer in Frothingham v. Mellon were quite different from those made in this case, and the result in *Frothingham* is consistent with the test of taxpayer standing announced today. The taxpayer in *Frothingham* attacked a federal spending program and she, therefore, established the first nexus required. However, she lacked standing because her constitutional attack was not based on an allegation that Congress, in enacting the Maternity Act of 1921, had breached a specific limitation upon its taxing and spending power. . . . In essence, Mrs. Frothingham

BOX 3-4 STANDING TO SUE IN THE AFTERMATH OF *FLAST*

Examples of Cases Limiting Standing Concepts

United States v. Richardson (1974)

Question: Does a taxpayer have standing to challenge a congressional law allowing the CIA to avoid a public "accounting of agency expenditures" as a violation of Article I, Section 9?

The Court: Richardson fails to meet the criteria established in *Flast* and "neatly . . . falls within the *Frothingham* holding." In short, because the law was not enacted under Article I, Section 8, the taxpayer cannot demonstrate a "logical nexus" between his status and the law.

Schlesinger v. Reservists Committee to Stop the War (1974)

Question: Do members of an organization (and taxpayers) have standing to launch an attack on the Vietnam War? In particular, can they challenge the fact that members of Congress have commissions in the military reserves, as a violation of Article I, Section 6?

The Court: No. They have suffered an insufficiently concrete injury. Further, the suit does not meet *Flast*'s nexus test because they did not challenge an Article I, Section 8, power.

Warth v. Seldin (1975)

Question: Do individuals and organizations have sufficient standing to sue a town zoning board on the grounds that its regulations discriminate against low and moderate income persons in violation of several constitutional guarantees?

The Court: No. They failed to demonstrate that they each had suffered some personal, actual, or concrete injury.

Valley Forge Christian College v. Americans United for Separation of Church and State (1982)

Question: Can an organization challenge, on First Amendment grounds, a decision by the Department of Health, Education and Welfare—made under a congressional law—to transfer surplus government property to a religious college?

The Court: No. The organization failed to demonstrate some personal injury. And, the "property transfer . . . was not an exercise of authority conferred by the taxing and spending clause of Article I, Section 8." The organization fails the *Flast* nexus test.

Allen v. Wright (1984)

Question: Do parents of black children have standing to challenge the IRS's alleged failure to deny tax-exempt status to schools that engage in racial discrimination on the grounds that such inaction diminished the quality of education their children were receiving and thus constituted a violation of the Equal Protection Clause?

The Court: No. Although an injury existed, the injury was not "fairly traceable" to IRS conduct. Further, it was unclear whether the injury would, in fact, be removed if the policy changed. The majority opinion also expressed concern that the principle of separation of powers might be violated if the Court granted standing in this suit. In its view, federal courts are "not the proper forum for general complaints about how government does its business."

Karcher v. May (1987)

Question: Do public officials (here, former presiding officers of the New Jersey state legislature) "who have participated in a lawsuit solely in their official capacities" have standing to appeal a judgment after they have left office?

The Court: No. Because they no longer hold office, they "lack the authority to pursue [the] appeal on behalf of the legislature."

Lujan v. Defenders of Wildlife (1992)

Question: Do members of an environmental organizatio have standing to challenge the Interior Department's reinterpretation of the Endangered Species Act of 1973, which said that the law would no longer be applied to federally financed projects overseas?

The Court: No. The environmentalists have failed to show how Interior's policy would produce "imminent" injury to them.

Examples of Cases Expanding Standing Concepts

Sierra Club v. Morton (1972)

Question: Does an interest group have standing to bring a suit seeking to restrain the federal government from approving the development of a ski resort in a valley of a national park?

The Court: No. The group lacks standing because it failed to demonstrate sufficient injury to it or its members. However, the Court expanded the concept of injury to include harm to "aesthetic and environmental well-being."

United States v. SCRAP (1973)

Question: Does an interest group have standing to challenge an order of the Interstate Commerce Commission on the grounds that the order adversely affected the environment and the economic interests and recreational pursuits of the organization and its members?

The Court: Yes. The allegations made by SCRAP, though unproven, were sufficient to indicate that perceptible harm might occur. Moreover, SCRAP demonstrated a more "attenuated line of causation to the eventual injury" than did the Sierra Club in *Morton*.

Arlington Heights v. Metropolitan Housing Corporation (1977)

Question: Does a developer have standing to challenge a town's refusal to rezone an area (from a single-family to multifamily category) as racially discriminatory, despite the fact that zoning was not the only obstacle to its housing project? Does an individual black plaintiff have standing to challenge the town's decision on the grounds that he would want to live in the proposed housing project.

The Court: Yes to both questions. Both had specific, not "generalized," complaints. And, both had indicated a "fairly traceable" causal link between the injury and the town's denial sufficient to demonstrate an "actionable causal relationship."

---

was attempting to assert the States' interest in their legislative prerogatives and not a federal taxpayer's interest in being free of taxing and spending in contravention of specific constitutional limitations imposed upon Congress' taxing and spending power.

In the end, thus, *Flast* did not overrule *Frothingham;* in fact, as the above quote indicates, the Court was careful to indicate that had the 1968 ruling been applied to *Frothingham*, the plaintiff still would have been unable to attain standing. But Flast substantially revised the 1923 precedent. If taxpayers could indicate a logical link between their status and the legislation, and one between their status and a specific constitutional infringement, then they might have standing.

In theory, this standard appears to be relatively straightforward; in practice, however, it is open to a significant amount of interpretation. Box 3-4 compares Warren Court and early Burger Court rulings on standing with some later rulings. As we can see,

the earlier Court read *Flast* to relax significantly standing barriers. That reading has changed yet again; some suggest that doctrine governing standing now resembles *Frothingham* more than *Flast*.

Those who hold that view may be overstating the case, but it is true that standing, like the other "constraints" on judicial power—jurisdiction and justiciability—is open to interpretation. Article III may place certain limits on the power of the federal judiciary. However, its language is vague enough to allow for a good deal of judicial latitude.

In the final analysis, then, we are left with many questions centering on judicial power and constraints on its exercise. We shall ask just one. Box 3-5 is an excerpt from Justice Louis D. Brandeis's concurring opinion in *Ashwander v. Tennessee Valley Authority* (1936), in which he outlined the constraints on judicial decision making we reviewed in this chapter. Given the cases and material you have just read, to what

---

BOX 3-5   JUSTICE BRANDEIS, CONCURRING IN *ASHWANDER V. TENNESSEE VALLEY AUTHORITY*

In 1936 Justice Louis D. Brandeis delineated, in a concurring opinion in *Ashwander v. Tennessee Valley Authority*, a set of Court-formulated rules useful in avoiding constitutional decisions. A portion of his opinion setting forth those rules, minus case cites and footnotes, follows:

The Court developed, for its own governance in the cases confessedly within its jurisdiction, a series of rules under which it has avoided passing upon a large part of all the constitutional questions pressed upon it for decision. They are:

1. The Court will not pass upon the constitutionality of legislation in a friendly, non-adversary, proceeding, declining because to decide such questions "is legitimate only in the last resort, and as a necessity in the determination of real, earnest and vital controversy between individuals. It never was the thought that, by means of a friendly suit, a party beaten in the legislature could transfer to the courts an inquiry as to the constitutionality of the legislative act."

2. The Court will not "anticipate a question of constitutional law in advance of the necessity of deciding it." "It is not the habit of the Court to decide questions of a constitutional nature unless absolutely necessary to a decision of the case."

3. The Court will not "formulate a rule of constitutional law broader than is required by the precise facts to which it is to be applied."

4. The Court will not pass upon a constitutional question although properly presented by the record, if there is also present some other ground upon which the case may be disposed of. This rule has found most varied application. Thus, if a case can be decided on either of two grounds, one involving a constitutional question, the other a question of statutory construction or general law, the Court will decide only the latter. Appeals from the highest court of a state challenging its decision of a question under the Federal Constitution are frequently dismissed because the judgment can be sustained on an independent state ground.

5. The Court will not pass upon the validity of a statute upon complaint of one who fails to show that he is injured by its operation. Among the many applications of this rule, none is more striking than the denial of the right of challenge to one who lacks a personal or property right. Thus, the challenge by a public official interested only in the performance of his official duty will not be entertained. . . .

6. (Omitted)

7. "When the validity of an act of the Congress is drawn in question, and even if a serious doubt of constitutionality is raised, it is a cardinal principle that this Court will first ascertain whether a construction of the statute is fairly possible by which the question may be avoided."

---

extent are those limitations real or open to interpretation?

READINGS

Adamany, David. "Legitimacy, Realigning Elections, and the Supreme Court." *Wisconsin Law Review* (1973): 790–846.

Bickel, Alexander M. *The Least Dangerous Branch.* New York: Bobbs-Merrill, 1962.

Caldeira, Gregory A. "Courts and Public Opinion," in *The American Courts: A Critical Assessment.* John B. Gates and Charles A. Johnson, eds. Washington, D.C.: CQ Press, 1991.

Casper, Jonathan D. "The Supreme Court and National Policy Making." *American Political Science Review* 70 (1976): 50–63.

Choper, Jesse H. *Judicial Review and the National Political Process.* Chicago: University of Chicago Press, 1980.

Clinton, Robert Lowry. *Marbury v. Madison and Judicial Review.* Lawrence: University of Kansas Press, 1989.

Dahl, Robert. "Decision Making in a Democracy: The

Supreme Court as a National Policy-Maker." *Journal of Public Law* 6 (1957): 279–295.

Ely, John Hart. *Democracy and Distrust.* Cambridge, Mass.: Harvard University Press, 1980.

Fisher, Louis. *Constitutional Dialogues.* Princeton, N.J.: Princeton University Press, 1988.

Funston, Richard. *A Vital National Seminar.* Palo Alto, Calif.: Mayfield, 1978.

Lasser, William. *The Limits of Judicial Power.* Chapel Hill: University of North Carolina Press, 1988.

Orren, Karen. "Standing to Sue: Interest Group Conflict in the Federal Courts." *American Political Science Review* 70 (1976): 723–741.

Radcliffe, James E. *The Case-or-Controversy Provision.* University Park: Pennsylvania State University Press, 1978.

Strum, Philippa. *The Supreme Court and Political Questions.* Tuscaloosa: University of Alabama Press, 1974.

Wolfe, Christopher. *The Rise of Modern Judicial Review.* New York: Basic Books, 1986.

———. *Judicial Activism.* Pacific Grove, Calif.: Brooks/Cole, 1991.

CHAPTER 4

THE LEGISLATURE

ARTICLE I of the U.S. Constitution is its longest and most explicit. The Founders established Congress's authority to make laws and spelled out in great detail the powers Congress did and did not have over its own operations. Reading through Article I, we might assume that this part of the Constitution would not have been the source of much litigation. After all, given its specificity, how much room for interpretation could there be?

For cases involving Congress's authority over its internal affairs, this assumption would be accurate. The Supreme Court has heard relatively few cases touching upon the first seven sections of Article I, which deal with the various qualifications for membership in Congress, the ability of the chambers to punish members, and certain privileges enjoyed by the members. When the Court has ruled, it generally, though not always, has given the legislature great latitude over its own business.

That assumption, however, is incorrect when we consider cases that deal directly with Congress's most basic power, the enactment of laws, and with its role in American government. Article I, Section 8, enumerates specifically the substantive areas in which Congress may legislate. But is it too specific, failing to foresee how congressional powers might need to be exercised in areas it does not cover? For example, Section 8 provides Congress with the power to borrow and coin money, but not with the "authority to make paper money legal tender for the payment of debts."[1] Since 1792 congressional committees have held investigations and hearings, but no clause in Section 8 authorizes them to do so. In general, the Supreme Court has had to determine whether legislative action that is not explicitly covered in Article I falls within Congress's authority, and that is why the Court so often has examined statutes passed by Congress.

There is another reason. As we saw earlier, and as we shall see throughout this book, basic (and purposeful) tensions were built into the design of the government. Sometimes disputes occur between the branches of the federal government; in other instances, between the federal government and the states; and often, between government and individuals. Emanating from the basic principles underlying the structure of government—federalism, the separation of powers, and checks and balances—these conflicts have provided the stuff of myriad legal disputes, and the Court has been right in the middle of many of them.

1. J. W. Peltason, *Understanding the Constitution*, 11th ed. (New York: Holt, Rinehart and Winston, 1988), 17.

This chapter examines how the justices have interpreted Article I of the Constitution.[2] It is divided into four sections: the first provides a historical overview of Article I; the second explores cases involving Congress's authority over its own structure and operations; the third looks at the sources and scope of its lawmaking power; and the fourth examines its role within the larger American government system.

ARTICLE I: HISTORICAL OVERVIEW

Many factors led the colonists in America to rebel against England. An important one, sometimes neglected in treatments of the American Revolution, was the different ways the British and the colonists thought about legislative bodies such as Parliament. The British viewed legislatures as "deliberative bodies whose allegiance was to the nation rather than specific constituencies."[3] Underlying this view is the notion of "virtual" representation: "since the interests of all British citizens were represented in Parliament, the citizens themselves did not need to be." Therefore, the British reasoned, the colonists did not have to vote for members of Parliament because they were "virtually represented" within it. The Americans took a quite different stance. To them, legislators "were nothing more and nothing less than agents of their constituents." As John Adams wrote in 1776, the ideal legislature "should be in miniature an exact portrait of the people at large. It should think, feel, reason and act like them."

During the founding period, the American states created legislatures that reflected some of Adams's views of representation. Most states provided for very short terms of office, with elections typically occurring every other year. They also mandated that leg-islatures have open sessions and publish their proceedings. Finally, many states actually gave their inhabitants the right to "instruct" their representatives on how to vote on certain issues. These and other measures were designed to keep legislators responsive to their constituents.

Concerns about representation at the federal level also were present, as were suspicions about a powerful national government like England's. The unicameral Congress that had been created under the Articles of Confederation had few important powers; and many of those it had, it could not exercise without state compliance, which was often lacking.

The problems Congress and the nation faced under the Articles of Confederation made it clear to the delegates attending the Constitutional Convention of 1787 that a very different kind of legislature was necessary if the United States was to endure. But what form would that legislature take? And what powers would it have? These questions produced a great deal of discussion during the convention; indeed, debates over the structure and powers of Congress occupied more than half of the Framers' time.[4]

The Structure and Composition of Congress

The Virginia Plan set the tone for the Constitutional Convention and became the backbone for Article I. Essentially, the plan called for a bicameral legislature, with the number of representatives in each house apportioned on the basis of state population. Under this scheme, the lower house (now the House of Representatives) would be elected by the people; the upper house (the Senate) would be chosen by the lower based on recommendations from state legislatures.

The Framers dealt with two aspects of the Virginia Plan with relative ease. Almost all agreed on the need

2. This chapter focuses generally on the scope of Article I and related issues. Chapters 7 and 8 consider specific congressional powers such as the ability to regulate interstate commerce.

3. The discussion in this paragraph has been adopted from Daniel A. Farber and Suzanna Sherry, *A History of the American Constitution* (St. Paul, Minn.: West, 1990), 110–111.

4. Michael Malbin, "Framing a Congress to Channel Ambition," in *This Constitution: Our Enduring Legacy,* ed. American Political Science Association and American Historical Association (Washington, D.C.: Congressional Quarterly, 1986), 55.

for a bicameral legislature. Accord on this point was not surprising; by 1787 only four states had a one-house legislature. The plan for selecting the upper house provoked more discussion. Some thought that having the lower house elect the upper would make the Senate subservient to the House and upset the delicate checks and balances system. Instead, the delegates agreed that the Senate should be selected by state legislatures. (The Seventeenth Amendment to the Constitution, ratified in 1913, changed this method of selection. Senators, like representatives, are now elected by the people.)

The third aspect of the Virginia Plan—the composition of the houses of Congress—generated some of the most acrimonious debates of the convention. As historians Alfred Kelly, Winfred Harbison, and Herman Belz put it: "Would the constituent units be the states, represented equally by delegates chosen by state legislatures, as the small-state group desired? Or would the constituent element be the people of the United States . . . with representation in both chambers apportioned according to population, as the large-state group wished?"[5] On one level, the answer to this question involved the straightforward motivation of self-interest. Naturally, the large states wanted both chambers to be based on population; they would send more representatives to the new Congress. The smaller states thought all states should have equal representation in the houses; they regarded their plan as the only way to avoid tyranny by a majority. On another level, the issue of composition went to the core of the Philadelphia enterprise. The approach advocated by the small states would "imply state sovereignty," while that put forth in the Virginia Plan "would signify that the central government rested directly upon individuals rather than states and was truly sovereign in character."[6]

It is no wonder, then, that the delegates had so

much trouble resolving this issue: it defined the basic character of the new government. In the end they took the course of action that characterized many of their decisions—they agreed to disagree. Specifically, the delegates reached a compromise under which the House of Representatives would be constituted on the basis of population, and the Senate would have two delegates from each state.

Reaching this compromise was crucial to the success of the convention. Without it, the delegates might have left without framing a constitution. But because the Founders split the difference between the demands of the small and large states, they never fully dealt with the critical underlying issue: Do the people or do the states empower the federal government? The impact of this lingering question on the development of the country is addressed in Chapter 6. Here, we note that not only has this question been at the center of many disputes brought to the Supreme Court, but it also was a leading cause of the Civil War.

Powers of Congress

With the important exception of term limits for members of Congress, Americans today rarely debate issues concerning the structure and composition of Congress: most simply accept the arrangements outlined in the Constitution. Instead, we tend to concern ourselves with what Congress does or does not do, with its ability to change our lives—sometimes dramatically—through the exercise of its lawmaking powers. Should Congress increase taxes? Pass health care reform? Provide aid for the homeless? Such questions—not structural points—generate heated debate among Americans.

In 1787 the situation was reversed. While the Framers fiercely debated issues involving the makeup of the legislature, they generally agreed about what particular powers it would have. This consensus probably reflected their experience under the Articles of Confederation: severe economic problems due in no

---

5. *The American Constitution: Its Origins and Development,* 7th ed. (New York: W. W. Norton, 1991), 90.
6. Ibid.

small part, as the Framers knew, to "congressional impotence."[7]

To correct these problems, Article I, Section 8, which lists seventeen specific powers given to Congress by the delegates, contains many provisions relating to the economy. Consider, for example, the problem of raising money. Under the Articles of Confederation the legislature could not collect taxes from the people; instead it had to rely on the less than dependable states to collect and forward taxes (between 1781 and 1783, the legislature requested $10 million from the states but received only $1.5 million).[8] In response, the first power given to Congress in the newly minted Constitution was to "lay and collect taxes." More generally, six of the seventeen specific congressional powers enumerated in Section 8 deal with economic issues. The rest center on foreign relations, the military, and internal matters, such as the creation of courts, post offices, and so forth.

Although the Framers agreed on these powers, two others provoked heated discussions. The first concerned a proposal in the Virginia Plan to give Congress veto authority over state legislation. This idea had the strong support of James Madison, who argued that "the propensity of the States to pursue their particular interests in opposition to the general interest . . . will continue to disturb the system, unless effectually controuled."[9] Madison and others who supported the veto proposal were once again reacting to the problems produced by the Articles of Confederation. Because the federal government lacked any coercive power over the states, mutual cooperation among them was virtually nonexistent. They engaged in practices that hurt one another economically and, in general, acted more like thirteen separate countries than a union or even a confederation. But the majority of delegates thought that a congressional veto would "disgust all the States." Accordingly, they compromised with Article VI, the Supremacy Clause, which made the Constitution, U.S. laws, and treaties "the supreme law of the land," binding all judges in all the states to follow them.

The second source of controversy was this question: Would Congress be able to exercise powers that were not listed in Article I, Section 8, or was Congress limited to those explicitly named? Some analysts would argue that the last clause of Article I, Section 8, the Necessary and Proper Clause, addressed this question by granting Congress the power "To make all Laws which shall be necessary and proper for carrying into Execution the foregoing Powers." But is that interpretation correct? Even after they agreed on the wording of that clause (with little discussion), the delegates continued to raise the issue in various debates. Delegate James McHenry wrote about a conversation that occurred on September 6: "Spoke to Gov. Morris Fitzsimmons . . . to insert a power . . . enabling the legislature to erect piers for protection of shipping in winter. . . . Mr. Gov.: thinks it may be done under the words of the 1 clause 1 sect 7 art. amended—'and provide for the common defense and general welfare.'"[10] In other words, Fitzsimmons was arguing that one of Congress's enumerated powers (to provide for the common defense and general welfare) implied the power to erect piers. Under this argument, then, Congress could assert powers beyond those that were enumerated.

A majority of the Founders may have agreed with Fitzsimmons. Because the question of congressional power is central to understanding the role Congress plays in American society, we shall consider it. At this point, however, we turn to the Court's interpretation of the first parts of Article I, which lay out the structure of Congress and its authority over its internal affairs.

7. Farber and Sherry, *A History of the American Constitution,* 134.

8. C. Herman Pritchett, *Constitutional Law of the Federal System* (Englewood Cliffs, N.J.: Prentice Hall, 1984), 6.

9. Ibid., 15.

10. Farber and Sherry, *A History of the American Constitution,* 141.

TABLE 4-1 U.S. Supreme Court Justices with Federal or State Legislative Experience

| | Legislative Service | | | |
| | Federal | | | |
Justice	House	Senate	State	Court Service
John Rutledge			S.C. (1776–78; 98–99)	1789–91
John Blair, Jr.			Va. (1766–70)	1789–96
William Paterson		1789–90	N.J. (1775–76)	1793–1806
Samuel Chase			Md. (1776–84)	1796–1811
Oliver Ellsworth		1789–96	Conn. (1773–76)	1796–1800
Bushrod Washington			Va. (1787)	1798–1829
Alfred Moore			N.C. (1782, 1792)	1799–1804
John Marshall	1799–1800		Va. (1782–85; 87–90; 95–96)	1801–35
William Johnson			S.C. (1794–98)	1804–34
Henry B. Livingston			N.Y. (3 sessions)	1806–23
Joseph Story	1808–09		Mass. (1805–08)	1811–45
Gabriel Duvall	1794–96		Md. (1787–94)	1811–35
Smith Thompson			N.Y. (1800)	1823–43
Robert Trimble			Ky. (1802)	1826–28
John McLean	1813–16			1829–61
Henry Baldwin	1817–22			1830–44
James M. Wayne	1829–35		Ga. (1815–16)	1835–67
Roger B. Taney			Md. (1799–1800; 16–21)	1836–64
Phillip P. Barbour	1814–25		Va. (1812–14)	1836–41
John McKinley	1837	1826–31; 1837	Ala. (1820, 1831, 1836)	1837–52
Peter Daniel			Va. (1809–12)	1841–60
Levi Woodbury		1825–31; 41–45	N.H. (1825)	1846–51
Benjamin R. Curtis			Mass. (1849–51)	1851–57
John A. Campbell			Ala. (1837, 1843)	1853–61
Nathan Clifford	1839–43		Maine (1830–34)	1858–81
Noah H. Swayne			Ohio (1830, 1836)	1862–81
David Davis		1877–85	Ill. (1845–47)	1862–77
Stephen J. Field			Calif. (1850–51)	1863–97
Salmon P. Chase		1849–55		1864–73
William Strong	1847–51			1870–80
Ward Hunt			N.Y. (1839)	1873–82
Morrison R. Waite			Ohio (1850–52)	1874–88
William B. Woods			Ohio (1858–62)	1880–87
Stanley Matthews		1877–79	Ohio (1855–58)	1881–89
Lucius Q. C. Lamar	1857–60; 73–77	1877–85	Ga. (1853)	1888–93
Melville W. Fuller			Ill. (1863–64)	1888–1910
Howell E. Jackson		1881–86	Tenn. (1880)	1893–95
Edward D. White		1891–94	La. (1874)	1894–1921
Joseph McKenna	1885–92		Calif. (1875–76)	1898–1925
William Moody	1895–1902			1906–10
Willis Van Devanter			Wyo. (1888)	1910–37
Joseph R. Lamar			Ga. (1886–89)	1910–16
Mahlon Pitney	1895–99		N.J. (1899–1901)	1912–22
George Sutherland	1901–03	1905–17	Utah (1896–1900)	1922–38
Hugo L. Black		1927–37		1937–71
James F. Byrnes	1911–25	1931–41		1941–42
Harold H. Burton		1941–45	Ohio (1929)	1945–58
Fred M. Vinson	1924–29			1946–53
Sherman Minton		1935–41		1949–56
Sandra Day O'Conner			Ariz. (1969–75)	1981–

SOURCE: Adapted from Elder Witt, *Guide to the U.S. Supreme Court*, 2d ed. (Washington, D.C.: Congressional Quarterly, 1990), 171.

CONGRESSIONAL AUTHORITY OVER INTERNAL AFFAIRS

While the Framers were debating Congress's structure and composition, they were also thinking about ways to safeguard the independence and integrity of the institution. Included in Article I are provisions dealing with the ability of the chambers to control who joins them and to punish those who do not behave in accord with their norms. Another section, the Speech or Debate Clause, protects members from "harassment" by other institutions.

Before we discuss how the Court has interpreted these sections, look at the data in Table 4-1. We often think about the Court and Congress as wholly separate entities, but they are connected in an interesting way. Table 4-1 lists the justices who served in Congress or a state legislature prior to their appointment to the bench. Almost half of all those who have sat on the Supreme Court have had legislative experience. Some might conclude that those justices would empathize with the claims of Congress regarding the need for authority over its own affairs, and, indeed, the Court generally has acceded to legislative wishes—but not always. As you read what follows, think about the reasons the Court offers for its decisions. Further, take note of the various coalitions emerging on different Courts. Do the justices with legislative experience exhibit a greater willingness to defer to Congress than those who never were legislators?

Membership in Congress: Seating and Discipline

In addition to specifying the structure and composition of Congress, Article I contains the requirements that must be met by all prospective members of the institution:

• A senator must be at least thirty years old and have been a citizen of the United States not less than nine years (Section 3, Clause 3).
• A representative must be at least twenty-five years old and have been a citizen not less than seven years (Section 2, Clause 2).
• Every member of Congress must be, when elected, an inhabitant of the state that he or she is to represent (Section 2, Clause 2, and Section 3, Clause 3).
• No one may be a member of Congress who holds any other "Office under the United States" (Section 6, Clause 2).

Finally, Section 3 of the Fourteenth Amendment states that no person may be a senator or a representative who, having previously taken an oath as a member of Congress to support the Constitution, has engaged in rebellion against the United States or given aid or comfort to its enemies, unless Congress has removed such disability by a two-thirds vote of both houses.

With only a few exceptions, these standards in themselves have not caused much controversy or litigation. Some legal questions, however, have arisen with respect to their relationship to Article I, Section 5, which reads: "Each House shall be the Judge of the Elections, Returns and Qualifications of its own Members." Several interpretations are possible. One is that this clause ought to be read in conjunction with the Article I requirements for members. That is, Congress cannot deny a duly elected person a seat in the institution unless that person fails to meet the specified criteria. Another interpretation is that Congress is free to develop additional qualifications, independent of those specified elsewhere.

For the better part of the nation's history, the Court stayed away from such disputes, even though Congress occasionally acted "as if it were entitled to add qualifications as well as wink at failure to meet them."[11] For example, during the Civil War, Congress enacted the Test Oath Law (1862), which required incoming members to "swear . . . that they had never voluntarily borne arms against the United States."

11. *Guide to Congress*, 4th ed. (Washington, D.C.: Congressional Quarterly, 1991), 762.

TABLE 4-2   Duly Elected Members of Congress Excluded

Chamber (Year)	Member-Elect (Party-State)	Grounds for Exclusion
Senate (1793)	Albert Gallatin (D-Pa.)	Citizenship
House (1823)	John Bailey (Ind.-Mass.)	Residence
House (1867)	John Y. Brown (D-Ky.)	Loyalty
House (1867)	John D. Young (D-Ky.)	Loyalty
House (1867)	John A. Wimpy (Ind.-Ga.)	Loyalty
House (1867)	W. D. Simpson (Ind.-S.C.)	Loyalty
Senate (1867)	Phillip F. Thomas (D-Md.)	Loyalty
House (1870)	Benjamin F. Whittemore (R-S.C.)	Malfeasance
House (1900)	Brigham H. Roberts (D-Utah)	Polygamy
House (1919)	Victor L. Berger (Socialist-Wis.)	Sedition
House (1920)	Victor L. Berger (Socialist-Wis.)	Sedition
House (1967)	Adam C. Powell, Jr. (D-N.Y.)	Misconduct

SOURCE: *Guide to Congress*, 3d ed. (Washington, D.C.: Congressional Quarterly, 1982), 823, 825.

Moreover, as shown in Table 4-2, both the House and the Senate have refused to seat properly elected individuals, sometimes on extraconstitutional grounds. The Senate excluded Phillip Thomas on loyalty grounds when it was discovered that he had "given $100 to his son when the son entered Confederate military service."[12] The House refused to seat Brigham H. Roberts because he had been convicted of violating an antipolygamy law.

Investigating the Roberts case, a congressional committee concluded that the Framers "had not foreclosed the right of Congress to establish qualifications for membership other than those mentioned in the Constitution."[13] As Table 4-2 shows, both houses subscribed to this theory. The question of whether the Supreme Court would follow suit remained largely unaddressed until 1969. In that year, the Court decided *Powell v. McCormack*, in which it squarely responded to Congress's traditional approach to seating qualifications.

Rep. Adam Clayton Powell, Jr., was "one of the most interesting and controversial figures ever to serve in the United States Congress."[14] As pastor of the Abyssinian Baptist Church in Harlem, one of the nation's largest congregations, Powell had been a force within that New York City community since the 1930s. This influence only increased when he was elected to the House in 1944 (he received nominations from both the Democratic and Republican parties) and continued to be reelected by wide margins for the next twenty-five years.

Powell never had problems with his constituents; but his relations with his colleagues were another matter. By the early 1960s he had acquired enough seniority to assume the chairmanship of the House Committee on Education and Labor, but he had become unpopular. Other House members disliked his opulent, unconventional lifestyle, his unpredictable leadership, and his use of the media to suit his political ends. Moreover, by that time, Powell had become entangled in various legal controversies; for example, he refused to pay damages assessed against him in a defamation of character suit and actively sought to avert efforts to compel him to pay.

12. Ibid., 763.
13. Ibid., 764.

14. Thomas G. Walker, *American Politics and the Constitution* (North Scituate, Mass.: Duxbury Press, 1978), 132. We derive our account largely from this source.

It came has no great surprise, then, when Congress launched several inquiries into Powell's activities. The first yielded two major violations of House rules: Powell had used federal monies to fly a woman staff member with him on trips to his vacation home in the Bahamas and to pay his former wife a salary of $20,000, even though she did not work in his district or Washington office, in accordance with law. With these violations in hand, the House refused to seat Powell pending further investigation and despite the fact that he had been reelected in November 1966.

The new investigation reached two conclusions: (1) from a constitutional standpoint, Powell met the requirements for office: he was older than twenty-five, had been a citizen of the United States for seven years, and he lived in New York; and (2) Powell had sought to evade the fine associated with the defamation of character offense, had misused public funds, and filed false expenditure reports. The committee recommended "that Powell be sworn and seated as a member of . . . Congress but that he be censured by the House, fined $40,000 and be deprived of his seniority." The House, however, rejected that recommendation and instead adopted by a vote of 307–116 a resolution that excluded Powell from the House and directed House Speaker John McCormack to "notify the Governor of New York that the seat was vacant."

Powell, not one to accept this decision lying down, responded. He and thirteen constituents filed a lawsuit against McCormack and other members of Congress, claiming that Congress's refusal to seat him violated the letter of the Constitution. In other words, because he met the requirements for office, the House had no choice but to seat him. In his view, Article I, Section 5—"Each House shall be the judge of the Elections, Returns and Qualifications of its own Members"—was not implicated: it gave Congress no authority to exclude members who met the constitutional standards for office. McCormack's attorneys thought otherwise. In their opinion and in accord with institutional tradition, the Court should read separately the Qualifications Clause and Section 5. They argued that the House has the authority to exclude members, even if they meet constitutional standards.

The justices, however, held for Powell. In his opinion for the majority, Chief Justice Warren relied heavily on the records of the constitutional debates—"viewed in the context of the bitter struggle for the right to freely choose representatives which had recently concluded in England"—to conclude that the framers intended to "deny either branch of Congress the authority to add or to otherwise vary the membership qualifications expressly set forth in the Constitution." Warren also asserted that even if the intent of the framers had been less clear, the Court would "nevertheless have been compelled to resolve any ambiguity in favor of a narrow construction of the scope of Congress' power to exclude members-elect." Why? Warren put it this way:

A fundamental principle of our representative democracy is, in Hamilton's words, "that the people should choose whom they please to govern them." As Madison pointed out at the Convention, this principle is undermined as much by limiting whom the people can select as by limiting the franchise itself. In apparent agreement with this basic philosophy, the Convention adopted his suggestion limiting the power to expel. To allow essentially that same power to be exercised under the guise of judging qualifications, would be to ignore Madison's warning, against "vesting an improper & dangerous power in the Legislature.". . . Unquestionably, Congress has an interest in preserving its institutional integrity, but in most cases that interest can be sufficiently safeguarded by the exercise of its power to punish its members for disorderly behavior and, in extreme cases, to expel a member with the concurrence of two-thirds. In short, both the intention of the Framers, to the extent it can be determined, and an examination of the basic principles of our democratic system persuade us that the Constitution does not vest in the Congress a discretionary power to deny membership by a majority vote.

BOX 4-1 TERM LIMITS

Before the Supreme Court decided *U.S. Term Limits v. Thornton* (1995), a national debate took place over term limits. In what follows we detail the arguments for and against them.

Arguments in Support of Term Limits

Supporters of term limits marshal a number of arguments. First, they assert that incumbents are not responsive to their constituents. With reelection rates hovering in the 90 percent vicinity for the past four decades, members of Congress—or so the argument goes—have no fear of electoral reprisal if they ignore constituents' interests. And, in fact, they are better off acceding to the demands of special interests, for it is they and not constituents who fund congressional campaigns. Capping terms, under this school of thought, would have the dual effect of ending almost automatic reelection and forcing greater representation of the public's interest.

Second, term-limit supporters claim that members of Congress spend too much time worrying about being reelected and not enough on conducting legislative business. Term limits would generate a shift in members' priorities, as they would no longer need to concern themselves with reelection after a specified period of time.

Third, term-limit advocates suggest that more electoral races among nonincumbents will increase the opportunities for those not in power. Groups underrepresented in Congress, including blacks and women, will have a greater chance of obtaining seats.

Finally, supporters point to the current lack of public confidence in Congress. When asked, just before the 1994 election, if they approved of the way Congress was handling its job, only 23 percent of Americans responded positively. Such a lack of support, according to some term-limit proponents, explains why—in nonpresidential election years—voter turnout typically has been low (in 1994, for example, only about 40 percent of the voting-age population went to the polls). Term limits would stimulate interest in and increase attention paid to Congress.

Arguments Against Term Limits

Opponents of term limits advance four major claims. The first is obvious: frequent periodic elections give citizens the ability to limit terms. They can simply vote incumbents out of office.

The second suggests that the wish to limit terms focuses on the wrong problem. Supporters argue that the limits will make Congress more responsive to the American public. Research by political scientists, however, shows that members are actually "hyperresponsive" to constituent desires, which is why senators and representatives—no matter how remote their chances of defeat—continue to concern themselves with reelection and, as a by-product, listen closely to their constituents. It also explains why 52 percent of Americans approve of the job their representative is doing (compared with 23 percent support for Congress as a whole) and why most incumbents are reelected: they represent well—perhaps too well—their constituents' interests. Greater accountability is just not needed.

Third, opponents assert that term limits will have only a minimal effect. For example, today the typical member of Congress serves no longer than twelve years, the maximum specified by some term limit initiatives. Therefore, they would have no more than a symbolic impact, mandating limits that already exist in practice.

Finally, and most relevant for our purposes, opponents claim that term limits violate the U.S. Constitution. They point to the Arkansas Supreme Court's decision striking down the state's initiative on the grounds that it violated the Constitution's Qualifications Clauses found in Article I. According to the court: "The qualifications clauses fix the sole requirements for congressional service. This is not a power left to the states." In support of its ruling, the Arkansas court cited *Powell v. McCormack,* in which the justices ruled that Congress could not add or change the qualifications for office listed in the U.S. Constitution.

What's Next?

Supporters of term limits counter the *Powell* argument by pointing to Section 4 of Article I, which says: "The Times, Places and Manner of holding Elections for Senators and Representatives, shall be prescribed in each State by the Legislature thereof." In their view, this section—and not the Qualifications Clauses—is applicable because term limits seek to regulate access to the ballot, not qualifications for office. And, in any event, incumbents could still seek reelection as write-in candidates. They also point out that *Powell* spoke only about the ability of the House, not the states, to set qualifications.

As *Thornton* indicates, the Court rejected this claim and held that term limits violate the Qualifications Clauses. Still, the issue is unlikely to vanish; the public strongly supports twelve-year term limits for all members of Congress. Supporters will no doubt turn their sights to a constitutional amendment to accomplish the same end.

SOURCES: Janet Hook, "Arkansas Case a Crucible in Term Limit Debate," *Congressional Quarterly Weekly Report*, June 25, 1994, 1679; Marjorie Randon Hershey, "The Congressional Elections," in *The Election of 1992*, ed. Gerald Pomper (Chatham, N.J.: Chatham House, 1993), 157–189; Bill Frenzel and Thomas E. Mann, "Term Limits for Congress: Arguments Pro and Con," in *Readings for American Government*, ed. Theodore J. Lowi, Benjamin Ginsberg, and Alice Hearst (New York: W. W. Norton, 1994), 88–99; Terry Eastand, "The Limits of Term Limits," in *Annual Editions: American Government 94/95*, ed. Bruce Stinebrickner (Guilford, Conn.: Dushkin, 1994), 109–111; Linda Greenhouse, "In Debate on Term Limits, Justices Take Up a 'Very Hard' Arkansas Case," *New York Times*, November 30, 1994, 13.

Chief Justice Warren's holding in *Powell* is indisputable: because Powell was duly elected and because he met the constitutional standards for membership, the House could not refuse to seat him. Or, as Warren emphatically noted, "Congress is limited to the standing qualifications prescribed in the Constitution."

An important question to ask yourself about *Powell* concerns its relevance to one of the more interesting contemporary debates about Article I: Does the U.S. Constitution give states the power to enact term limits for members of the U.S. Congress? In *U.S. Term Limits v. Thornton*, excerpted here, the Court addressed this question. But before considering the Court's response, you may want to consult Box 4-1, which provides details about the term limits movement and how *Powell* was implicated in the debate when the Supreme Court joined the fray in 1995.

Then, as you read the majority opinion, compare it to Chief Justice Warren's in *Powell v. McCormack:* Does the rationale used by the majority in *Thornton* square with the reasoning in *Powell?* Also pay close attention to the way that both the majority and dissenting opinions deal with the intent of the Framers. Is *Thornton* yet another example of the difficulty of applying this mode of analysis to actual cases? Finally, consider this question: Do you think that the Court would have arrived at a different answer had Congress mustered the votes to propose a term limits amendment?

U.S. Term Limits v. Thornton

___ U.S. ___ (1995)
Vote: 5 *(Breyer, Ginsburg, Kennedy, Souter, Stevens)*
    4 *(O'Connor, Rehnquist, Scalia, Thomas)*
Opinion of the Court: Stevens
Concurring opinion: Kennedy
Dissenting opinion: Thomas

Since 1990, when Colorado became the first state to limit terms for federal officeholders, twenty-three states have passed term limit initiatives. *Thornton* involved one of those initiatives—Amendment 73 to the Arkansas state constitution, which prohibited from the ballot anyone seeking reelection who previously had served two terms in the U.S. Senate or three terms in the U.S. House of Representatives. It permitted anyone to be elected as a write-in candidate, presumably as a way of allowing for the reelection of a popular incumbent.

Arkansas voters approved the amendment in 1992, and it was to apply to all persons seeking reelection after January 1, 1993. But about two months before that date, various citizens of Arkansas, including U.S. Representative Ray Thornton, and the League of Women Voters filed suit asking a state court to declare the amendment unconstitutional. Among the arguments they made in this court and, later, in the Arkansas Supreme Court was that Amendment 73 violated Article I of the U.S. Constitution. In particular, based on *Powell v. McCormack* (1969), they claimed that the federal Constitution establishes the sole qualifications for federal office, and the states may not alter them. In response, the state and U.S. Term Limits (an organization supporting the amendment) made a number of arguments. First, they pointed to Section 4 of Article I, which says: "The Times, Places and Manner of holding Elections for Senators and Representatives, shall be prescribed in each State by the Legislature thereof." In their view, this section—and not the Qualifications Clauses—is applicable because term limits seek to regulate access to the ballot, not qualifications for office. Second, they suggested that *Powell* spoke only about the ability of the U.S. House of Representatives, not of the states, to set qualifications. Finally, and relatedly, since the Constitution does not explicitly prohibit the states from setting qualifications for office, it is a power reserved to them under the Tenth Amendment.

The Arkansas courts disagreed. The lower court struck down the amendment as a violation of Article I of the U.S. Constitution and, in 1994, the Arkansas Supreme Court affirmed. According to the justices, "The qualifications clauses fix the sole requirement for congressional service. This is not a power left to the states." With this defeat in hand, amendment proponents appealed to the U.S. Supreme Court, which agreed to hear the case.

In the meantime, the topic of term limits was getting even more national attention. In the Contract with America, a majority of Republicans seeking election in 1994 promised that they would guarantee a vote on a term limits initiative if their party gained control of the House. Of course, this pledge made a good deal of political sense: about 80 percent of Americans favored placing limits on congressional tenures.

After they gained control of Congress, the Republi-

can leadership tried to make good on the promise. In March of 1995, before the Supreme Court issued its opinion in *Thornton*, the House considered four constitutional amendment proposals. Although they differed in their specific provisions, each would have limited the number of terms that senators and representatives could serve. Because these proposals were framed as constitutional amendments, a two-thirds vote was required for any one to gain approval. After several days of debate, the House voted. None of the proposals obtained sufficient support to pass. Clearly, and perhaps not so surprisingly, the members of the House were unwilling to pass self-imposed limits on the number of terms they could serve.

With these losses, the Republican leaders still held out hope that the Supreme Court would uphold state term limit initiatives; after all, the justices had yet to issue their opinion in *Thornton*. That Republicans pinned their hopes on the Court was somewhat ironic since they had deliberately chosen the constitutional amendment route (as opposed to a term limits law) to supersede an anti–term limits Supreme Court ruling. But, when the Supreme Court issued its opinion on May 22, 1995, it was clear that the Republican leadership had suffered another setback: in a 5–4 decision, the justices struck down the Arkansas amendment.

JUSTICE STEVENS delivered the opinion of the Court.

Today's cases present a challenge to an amendment to the Arkansas State Constitution that prohibits the name of an otherwise-eligible candidate for Congress from appearing on the general election ballot if that candidate has already served three terms in the House of Representatives or two terms in the Senate. The Arkansas Supreme Court held that the amendment violates the Federal Constitution. We agree with that holding. Such a state-imposed restriction is contrary to the "fundamental principle of our representative democracy," embodied in the Constitution, that "the people should choose whom they please to govern them." *Powell v. McCormack* (1969). Allowing individual States to adopt their own qualifications for congressional service would be inconsistent with the Framers' vision of a uniform National Legislature representing the people of the United States. If the qualifications set forth in the text of the Constitution are to be changed, that text must be amended.

As the opinions of the Arkansas Supreme Court suggest, the constitutionality of Amendment 73 depends critically on the resolution of two distinct issues. The first is whether the Constitution forbids States from adding to or altering the qualifications specifically enumerated in the Constitution. The second is, if the Constitution does so forbid, whether the fact that Amendment 73 is formulated as a ballot access restriction rather than as an outright disqualification is of constitutional significance. Our resolution of these issues draws upon our prior resolution of a related but distinct issue: whether Congress has the power to add to or alter the qualifications of its Members.

Twenty-six years ago, in *Powell v. McCormack,* we reviewed the history and text of the Qualifications Clauses in a case involving an attempted exclusion of a duly elected Member of Congress. The principal issue was whether the power granted to each House in Art. I, § 5, to judge the "Qualifications of its own Members" includes the power to impose qualifications other than those set forth in the text of the Constitution. In an opinion by Chief Justice Warren for eight Members of the Court, we held that it does not. Because of the obvious importance of the issue, the Court's review of the history and meaning of the relevant constitutional text was especially thorough. We therefore begin our analysis today with a . . . statement of what we decided in that case. . . . *Powell* . . . establishes two important propositions: first, that the "relevant historical materials" compel the conclusion that, at least with respect to qualifications imposed by Congress, the Framers intended the qualifications listed in the Constitution to be exclusive; and second, that that conclusion is equally compelled by an understanding of the "fundamental principle of our representative democracy . . . 'that the people should choose whom they please to govern them.'" Petitioners argue somewhat halfheartedly that the narrow holding in *Powell,* which involved the power of the House to exclude a member pursuant to Art. I, § 5, does not control the more general question whether Congress has the power to add qualifications. *Powell,* however, is not susceptible to such a narrow reading. Our conclusion that Congress may not alter or add to the qualifications in the Constitution was integral to our analysis and outcome. Only two Terms ago we confirmed this understanding of *Powell* in *Nixon v. United States* (1993). After noting that the three qualifications for membership specified in Art. I, § 2, are of "a precise, limited nature" and "unalterable by the legislature," we explained:

"Our conclusion in Powell was based on the fixed meaning of 'qualifications' set forth in Art I, § 2. The claim by the House that its power to 'be the Judge of the Elections, Returns and Qualifications of its own Members' was a textual commitment of unreviewable authority was defeated by the existence of this separate provision specifying the only qualifications which might be imposed for House membership."

Unsurprisingly, the state courts and lower federal courts have similarly concluded that *Powell* conclusively resolved the issue whether Congress has the power to impose additional qualifications. In sum, after examining *Powell's* historical analysis and its articulation of the "basic principles of our democratic system," we reaffirm that the qualifications for service in Congress set forth in the text of the Constitution are "fixed," at least in the sense that they may not be supplemented by Congress.

Our reaffirmation of *Powell,* does not necessarily resolve the specific questions presented in these cases. For petitioners argue that whatever the constitutionality of additional qualifications for membership imposed by Congress, the historical and textual materials discussed in *Powell* do not support the conclusion that the Constitution prohibits additional qualifications imposed by States. In the absence of such a constitutional prohibition, petitioners argue, the Tenth Amendment and the principle of reserved powers require that States be allowed to add such qualifications.

Before addressing these arguments, we find it appropriate to take note of the striking unanimity among the courts that have considered the issue. None of the overwhelming array of briefs submitted by the parties and amici has called to our attention even a single case in which a state court or federal court has approved of a State's addition of qualifications for a member of Congress. To the contrary, an impressive number of courts have determined that States lack the authority to add qualifications. . . . This impressive and uniform body of judicial decisions . . . indicates that the obstacles confronting petitioners are formidable indeed. Petitioners argue that the Constitution contains no express prohibition against state-added qualifications, and that Amendment 73 is therefore an appropriate exercise of a State's reserved power to place additional restrictions on the choices that its own voters may make. We disagree for two independent reasons. First, we conclude that the power to add qualifications is not within the "original powers" of the States, and thus is not reserved to the States by the Tenth Amendment. Second, even if States possessed some original power in this area, we conclude that the Framers intended the Constitution to be the exclusive source of qualifications for members of Congress, and that the Framers thereby "divested" States of any power to add qualifications. . . .

Contrary to petitioners' assertions, the power to add qualifications is not part of the original powers of sovereignty that the Tenth Amendment reserved to the States. Petitioners' Tenth Amendment argument misconceives the nature of the right at issue because that Amendment could only "reserve" that which existed before. As Justice Story recognized, "the states can exercise no powers whatsoever, which exclusively spring out of the existence of the national government, which the constitution does not delegate to them. . . . No state can say, that it has reserved, what it never possessed.". . .

With respect to setting qualifications for service in Congress, no such right existed before the Constitution was ratified. The contrary argument overlooks the revolutionary character of the government that the Framers conceived. Prior to the adoption of the Constitution, the States joined together under the Articles of Confederation. In that system, "the States retained most of their sovereignty, like independent nations bound together only by treaties." After the Constitutional Convention convened, the Framers were presented with, and eventually adopted a variation of, "a plan not merely to amend the Articles of Confederation but to create an entirely new government with a National Executive, National Judiciary, and a National Legislature." In adopting that plan, the Framers envisioned a uniform national system, rejecting the notion that the Nation was a collection of States, and instead creating a direct link between the National Government and the people of the United States. In that National Government, representatives owe primary allegiance not to the people of a State but to the people of a Nation. . . .

In short, as the Framers recognized, electing representatives to the National Legislature was a new right, arising from the Constitution itself. The Tenth Amendment thus provides no basis for concluding that the States possess reserved power to add qualifications to those that are fixed in the Constitution. Instead, any state power to set the qualifications for membership in Congress must derive not from the reserved powers of state sovereignty, but rather from the delegated powers of national sovereignty. In the absence of any constitutional delegation to the States of power to add qualifications to those enumerated in the Constitution, such a power does not exist.

Even if we believed that States possessed as part of their original powers some control over congressional qualifications, the text and structure of the Constitution, the relevant historical materials, and, most importantly, the "basic principles of our democratic system" all demonstrate that the Qualifications Clauses were intended to preclude the States from exercising any such power and to fix as exclusive the qualifications in the Constitution.

Much of the historical analysis was undertaken by the Court in *Powell*. There is, however, additional historical evidence that pertains directly to the power of States. That evidence, though perhaps not as extensive as that reviewed in *Powell*, leads unavoidably to the conclusion that the States lack the power to add qualifications.

The available affirmative evidence indicates the Framers' intent that States have no role in the setting of qualifications. In Federalist Paper No. 52, dealing with the House of Representatives, Madison addressed the "qualifications of the electors and the elected." Madison first noted the difficulty in achieving uniformity in the qualifications for electors, which resulted in the Framers' decision to require only that the qualifications for federal electors be the same as those for state electors. Madison argued that such a decision "must be satisfactory to every State, because it is comfortable to the standard already established, or which may be established, by the State itself." Madison then explicitly contrasted the state control over the qualifications of electors with the lack of state control over the qualifications of the elected:

"The qualifications of the elected, being less carefully and properly defined by the State constitutions, and being at the same time more susceptible of uniformity, have been very properly considered and regulated by the convention. A representative of the United States must be of the age of twenty-five years; must have been seven years a citizen of the United States; must, at the time of his election be an inhabitant of the State he is to represent; and, during the time of his service must be in no office under the United States. Under these reasonable limitations, the door of this part of the federal government is open to merit of every description, whether native or adoptive, whether young or old, and without regard to poverty or wealth, or to any particular profession of religious faith.". . .

We also find compelling the complete absence in the ratification debates of any assertion that States had the power to add qualifications. In those debates, the question whether to require term limits, or "rotation," was a major source of controversy. The draft of the Constitution that was submitted for ratification contained no provision for rotation. In arguments that echo in the preamble to Arkansas' Amendment 73, opponents of ratification condemned the absence of a rotation requirement, noting that "there is no doubt that senators will hold their office perpetually; and in this situation, they must of necessity lose their dependence, and their attachments to the people." Even proponents of ratification expressed concern about the "abandonment in every instance of the necessity of rotation in office." At several ratification conventions, participants proposed amendments that would have required rotation.

The Federalists' responses to those criticisms and proposals addressed the merits of the issue, arguing that rotation was incompatible with the people's right to choose. . . . Hamilton argued that the representatives' need for reelection rather than mandatory rotation was the more effective way to keep representatives responsive to the people, because "when a man knows he must quit his station, let his merit be what it may, he will turn his attention chiefly to his own emolument." Regardless of which side has the better of the debate over rotation, it is most striking that nowhere in the extensive ratification debates have we found any statement by either a proponent or an opponent of rotation that the draft constitution would permit States to require rotation for the representatives of their own citizens. If the participants in the debate had be-

lieved that the States retained the authority to impose term limits, it is inconceivable that the Federalists would not have made this obvious response to the arguments of the pro-rotation forces. The absence in an otherwise freewheeling debate of any suggestion that States had the power to impose additional qualifications unquestionably reflects the Framers' common understanding that States lacked that power.

In short, if it had been assumed that States could add additional qualifications, that assumption would have provided the basis for a powerful rebuttal to the arguments being advanced. The failure of intelligent and experienced advocates to utilize this argument must reflect a general agreement that its premise was unsound, and that the power to add qualifications was one that the Constitution denied the States. . . .

Our conclusion that States lack the power to impose qualifications vindicates the same "fundamental principle of our representative democracy" that we recognized in *Powell*, namely that "the people should choose whom they please to govern them."

. . . .[T]he *Powell* Court recognized that an egalitarian ideal—that election to the National Legislature should be open to all people of merit—provided a critical foundation for the Constitutional structure. This egalitarian theme echoes throughout the constitutional debates. In The Federalist No. 57, for example, Madison wrote:

"Who are to be the objects of popular choice? Every citizen whose merit may recommend him to the esteem and confidence of his country. No qualification of wealth, of birth, of religious faith, or of civil profession is permitted to fetter the judgment or disappoint the inclination of the people.". . .

Similarly, we believe that state-imposed qualifications, as much as congressionally imposed qualifications, would undermine the second critical idea recognized in *Powell*: that an aspect of sovereignty is the right of the people to vote for whom they wish. Again, the source of the qualification is of little moment in assessing the qualification's restrictive impact.

Finally, state-imposed restrictions, unlike the congressionally imposed restrictions at issue in *Powell*, violate a third idea central to this basic principle: that the right to choose representatives belongs not to the States, but to the people. From the start, the Framers recognized that the "great and radical vice" of the Articles of Confederation was "the principle of LEGISLATION for STATES or GOVERN-MENTS, in their CORPORATE or COLLECTIVE CAPACI-TIES, and as contradistinguished from the INDIVIDUALS of whom they consist." The Federalist No. 15 (Hamilton). Thus the Framers, in perhaps their most important contribution, conceived of a Federal Government directly responsible to the people, possessed of direct power over the people, and chosen directly, not by States, but by the people. The Framers implemented this ideal most clearly in the provision, extant from the beginning of the Republic, that calls for the Members of the House of Representatives to be "chosen every second Year by the People of the several States." Art. I, § 2, cl. 1. Following the adoption of the 17th Amendment in 1913, this ideal was extended to elections for the Senate. The Congress of the United States, therefore, is not a confederation of nations in which separate sovereigns are represented by appointed delegates, but is instead a body composed of representatives of the people. As Chief Justice John Marshall observed: "The government of the union, then, . . . is, emphatically, and truly, a government of the people. In form and in substance it emanates from them. Its powers are granted by them, and are to be exercised directly on them, and for their benefit." *McCulloch v. Maryland.* Ours is a "government of the people, by the people, for the people." A. Lincoln, Gettysburg Address (1863). The Framers deemed this principle critical when they discussed qualifications. For example, during the debates on residency requirements, Morris noted that in the House, "the people at large, not the States, are represented." Similarly, George Read noted that the Framers "were forming a National Government and such a regulation would correspond little with the idea that we were one people." James Wilson "enforced the same consideration.". . .

Petitioners attempt to overcome this formidable array of evidence against the States' power to impose qualifications by arguing that the practice of the States immediately after the adoption of the Constitution demonstrates their understanding that they possessed such power. One may properly question the extent to which the States' own practice is a reliable indicator of the contours of restrictions that the Constitution imposed on States, especially when no

court has ever upheld a state-imposed qualification of any sort. . . . But petitioners' argument is unpersuasive even on its own terms. At the time of the Convention, "almost all the State Constitutions required members of their Legislatures to possess considerable property." Despite this near uniformity, only one State, Virginia, placed similar restrictions on members of Congress, requiring that a representative be, inter alia, a "freeholder." Just 15 years after imposing a property qualification, Virginia replaced that requirement with a provision requiring that representatives be only "qualified according to the constitution of the United States.". . .

In sum, the available historical and textual evidence, read in light of the basic principles of democracy underlying the Constitution and recognized by this Court in *Powell*, reveal the Framers' intent that neither Congress nor the States should possess the power to supplement the exclusive qualifications set forth in the text of the Constitution.

Petitioners argue that, even if States may not add qualifications, Amendment 73 is constitutional because it is not such a qualification, and because Amendment 73 is a permissible exercise of state power to regulate the "Times, Places and Manner of Holding Elections." We reject these contentions.

Unlike §§ 1 and 2 of Amendment 73, which create absolute bars to service for long-term incumbents running for state office, § 3 merely provides that certain Senators and Representatives shall not be certified as candidates and shall not have their names appear on the ballot. They may run as write-in candidates and, if elected, they may serve. Petitioners contend that only a legal bar to service creates an impermissible qualification, and that Amendment 73 is therefore consistent with the Constitution. . . .

We need not decide whether petitioners' narrow understanding of qualifications is correct because, even if it is, Amendment 73 may not stand. As we have often noted, "'constitutional rights would be of little value if they could be . . . indirectly denied.'" The Constitution "nullifies sophisticated as well as simple-minded modes" of infringing on Constitutional protections.

In our view, Amendment 73 is an indirect attempt to accomplish what the Constitution prohibits Arkansas from accomplishing directly. As the plurality opinion of the

Arkansas Supreme Court recognized, Amendment 73 is an "effort to dress eligibility to stand for Congress in ballot access clothing," because the "intent and the effect of Amendment 73 are to disqualify congressional incumbents from further service." We must, of course, accept the State Court's view of the purpose of its own law: we are thus authoritatively informed that the sole purpose of § 3 of Amendment 73 was to attempt to achieve a result that is forbidden by the Federal Constitution. Indeed, it cannot be seriously contended that the intent behind Amendment 73 is other than to prevent the election of incumbents. The preamble of Amendment 73 states explicitly: "The people of Arkansas . . . herein limit the terms of elected officials." Sections 1 and 2 create absolute limits on the number of terms that may be served. There is no hint that § 3 was intended to have any other purpose. Petitioners do, however, contest the Arkansas Supreme Court's conclusion that the Amendment has the same practical effect as an absolute bar. They argue that the possibility of a write-in campaign creates a real possibility for victory, especially for an entrenched incumbent. One may reasonably question the merits of that contention. Indeed, we are advised by the state court that there is nothing more than a faint glimmer of possibility that the excluded candidate will win. Our prior cases, too, have suggested that write-in candidates have only a slight chance of victory. But even if petitioners are correct that incumbents may occasionally win reelection as write-in candidates, there is no denying that the ballot restrictions will make it significantly more difficult for the barred candidate to win the election. In our view, an amendment with the avowed purpose and obvious effect of evading the requirements of the Qualifications Clauses by handicapping a class of candidates cannot stand. . . .

Petitioners make the related argument that Amendment 73 merely regulates the "Manner" of elections, and that the Amendment is therefore a permissible exercise of state power under Article I, § 4, cl. 1 (the Elections Clause) to regulate the "Times, Places and Manner" of elections. We cannot agree. A necessary consequence of petitioners' argument is that Congress itself would have the power to "make or alter" a measure such as Amendment 73. That the Framers would have approved of such a result is unfathomable. As our decision in *Powell* and our discussion above make clear, the Framers were particularly concerned that a

grant to Congress of the authority to set its own qualifications would lead inevitably to congressional self-aggrandizement and the upsetting of the delicate constitutional balance. Petitioners would have us believe, however, that even as the Framers carefully circumscribed congressional power to set qualifications, they intended to allow Congress to achieve the same result by simply formulating the regulation as a ballot access restriction under the Elections Clause. We refuse to adopt an interpretation of the Elections Clause that would so cavalierly disregard what the Framers intended to be a fundamental constitutional safeguard. . . .

The merits of term limits, or "rotation," have been the subject of debate since the formation of our Constitution, when the Framers unanimously rejected a proposal to add such limits to the Constitution. The cogent arguments on both sides of the question that were articulated during the process of ratification largely retain their force today. Over half the States have adopted measures that impose such limits on some offices either directly or indirectly, and the Nation as a whole, notably by constitutional amendment, has imposed a limit on the number of terms that the President may serve. Term limits, like any other qualification for office, unquestionably restrict the ability of voters to vote for whom they wish. On the other hand, such limits may provide for the infusion of fresh ideas and new perspectives, and may decrease the likelihood that representatives will lose touch with their constituents. It is not our province to resolve this longstanding debate.

We are, however, firmly convinced that allowing the several States to adopt term limits for congressional service would effect a fundamental change in the constitutional framework. Any such change must come not by legislation adopted either by Congress or by an individual State, but rather—as have other important changes in the electoral process—through the Amendment procedures set forth in Article V. The Framers decided that the qualifications for service in the Congress of the United States be fixed in the Constitution and be uniform throughout the Nation. That decision reflects the Framers' understanding that Members of Congress are chosen by separate constituencies, but that they become, when elected, servants of the people of the United States. They are not merely delegates appointed by separate, sovereign States; they occupy offices that are integral and essential components of a single National Government. In the absence of a properly passed constitutional amendment, allowing individual States to craft their own qualifications for Congress would thus erode the structure envisioned by the Framers, a structure that was designed, in the words of the Preamble to our Constitution, to form a "more perfect Union."

The judgment is affirmed.

It is so ordered.

JUSTICE THOMAS, with whom THE CHIEF JUSTICE, JUSTICE O'CONNOR, and JUSTICE SCALIA join, dissenting.

It is ironic that the Court bases today's decision on the right of the people to "choose whom they please to govern them." Under our Constitution, there is only one State whose people have the right to "choose whom they please" to represent Arkansas in Congress. The Court holds, however, that neither the elected legislature of that State nor the people themselves (acting by ballot initiative) may prescribe any qualifications for those representatives. The majority therefore defends the right of the people of Arkansas to "choose whom they please to govern them" by invalidating a provision that won nearly 60% of the votes cast in a direct election and that carried every congressional district in the State.

I dissent. Nothing in the Constitution deprives the people of each State of the power to prescribe eligibility requirements for the candidates who seek to represent them in Congress. The Constitution is simply silent on this question. And where the Constitution is silent, it raises no bar to action by the States or the people.

Because the majority fundamentally misunderstands the notion of "reserved" powers, I start with some first principles. Contrary to the majority's suggestion, the people of the States need not point to any affirmative grant of power in the Constitution in order to prescribe qualifications for their representatives in Congress, or to authorize their elected state legislators to do so.

Our system of government rests on one overriding principle: all power stems from the consent of the people. To phrase the principle in this way, however, is to be imprecise about something important to the notion of "reserved" powers. The ultimate source of the Constitution's authority is the consent of the people of each individual State, not the consent of the undifferentiated people of the Nation as a whole. . . . When they adopted the Federal Constitution, of course, the people of each State surrendered some of their authority to the United States (and hence to entities accountable to the people of other States as well as to themselves). They affirmatively deprived their States of certain powers and they affirmatively conferred certain powers upon the Federal Government. Because the people of the several States are the only true source of power, however, the Federal Government enjoys no authority beyond what the Constitution confers: the Federal Government's powers are limited and enumerated. In the words of Justice Black, "the United States is entirely a creature of the Constitution. Its power and authority have no other source."

In each State, the remainder of the people's powers—"the powers not delegated to the United States by the Constitution, nor prohibited by it to the States,"—are either delegated to the state government or retained by the people. The Federal Constitution does not specify which of these two possibilities obtains; it is up to the various state constitutions to declare which powers the people of each State have delegated to their state government. As far as the Federal Constitution is concerned, then, the States can exercise all powers that the Constitution does not withhold from them. The Federal Government and the States thus face different default rules: where the Constitution is silent about the exercise of a particular power—that is, where the Constitution does not speak either expressly or by necessary implication—the Federal Government lacks that power and the States enjoy it.

These basic principles are enshrined in the Tenth Amendment, which declares that all powers neither delegated to the Federal Government nor prohibited to the States "are reserved to the States respectively, or to the people." With this careful last phrase, the Amendment avoids taking any position on the division of power between the state governments and the people of the States: it is up to the people of each State to determine which "reserved" powers their state government may exercise. . . .

The majority begins by announcing an enormous and untenable limitation on the principle expressed by the Tenth Amendment. According to the majority, the States possess only those powers that the Constitution affirmatively grants to them or that they enjoyed before the Constitution was adopted; the Tenth Amendment "could only 'reserve' that which existed before." From the fact that the States had not previously enjoyed any powers over the particular institutions of the Federal Government established by the Constitution, the majority derives a rule precisely opposite to the one that the Amendment actually prescribes: "'The states can exercise no powers whatsoever, which exclusively spring out of the existence of the national government, which the constitution does not delegate to them.'". . . Given the fundamental principle that all governmental powers stem from the people of the States, it would simply be incoherent to assert that the people of the States could not reserve any powers that they had not previously controlled.

The Tenth Amendment's use of the word "reserved" does not help the majority's position. If someone says that the power to use a particular facility is reserved to some group, he is not saying anything about whether that group has previously used the facility. He is merely saying that the people who control the facility have designated that group as the entity with authority to use it. The Tenth Amendment is similar: the people of the States, from whom all governmental powers stem, have specified that all powers not prohibited to the States by the Federal Constitution are reserved "to the States respectively, or to the people."

The majority is therefore quite wrong to conclude that the people of the States cannot authorize their state governments to exercise any powers that were unknown to the States when the Federal Constitution was drafted. Indeed, the majority's position frustrates the apparent purpose of the Amendment's final phrase. The Amendment does not pre-empt any limitations on state power found in the state constitutions, as it might have done if it simply had said that the powers not delegated to the Federal Government are reserved to the States. But the Amendment also does not prevent the people of the States from amending their state constitutions to remove limitations that were in effect when the Federal Constitution and the Bill of Rights were ratified. . . .

I take it to be established, then, that the people of Arkansas do enjoy "reserved" powers over the selection of their representatives in Congress. . . . Whatever one might think of the wisdom of this arrangement, we may not override the decision of the people of Arkansas unless something in the Federal Constitution deprives them of the power to enact such measures.

The majority settles on "the Qualifications Clauses" as the constitutional provisions that Amendment 73 violates. . . . [T]he Qualifications Clauses are merely straightforward recitations of the minimum eligibility requirements that the Framers thought it essential for every Member of Congress to meet. They restrict state power only in that they prevent the States from abolishing all eligibility requirements for membership in Congress. . . .

To the extent that they bear on this case, the records of the Philadelphia Convention affirmatively support my unwillingness to find hidden meaning in the Qualifications Clauses, while the surviving records from the ratification debates help neither side. As for the postratification period, five States supplemented the constitutional disqualifications in their very first election laws. The historical evidence thus refutes any notion that the Qualifications Clauses were generally understood to be exclusive. Yet the majority must establish just such an understanding in order to justify its position that the Clauses impose unstated prohibitions on the States and the people. In my view, the historical evidence is simply inadequate to warrant the majority's conclusion that the Qualifications Clauses mean anything more than what they say.

The decision in *U.S. Term Limits v. Thornton*, coupled with the *Powell* ruling, authoritatively settles the issue of qualifications for congressional office. The Constitution's age, residency, and citizenship requirements are a complete statement of congressional eligibility standards. Neither Congress nor the states may add to or delete from those requirements. The topic of term limits, however, remains hot. The public continues to support them and the Republican leadership in Congress remains committed to keeping the issue on its political agenda. Given the Court's ruling, however, term limits could be imposed only by constitutional amendment.

The Speech or Debate Clause

The Constitution provides mechanisms for Congress to discipline its members, but it also contains a safeguard against harassment or intimidation. Article I, Section 6, specifies:

The Senators and Representatives . . . shall in all Cases, except Treason, Felony, and Breach of the Peace, be privileged from Arrest during their Attendance at the Session of their respective Houses, and in going to and returning from the same; and for any Speech or Debate in either House, they shall not be questioned in any other Place.

Called the Speech or Debate Clause, this privilege of membership emanates from British practice. C. Herman Pritchett noted, "Immunity from arrest during sessions of the legislature was one of the protections asserted by the English Parliament in its struggle with the Crown, and embodied in the English Bill of Rights."[15] The importance of the Speech or Debate Clause's protection is undeniable: without it, a president could order the arrest of, or otherwise intimidate, members of Congress who disagreed with the administration. The Framers thought the protection was necessary "to protect the integrity of the legislative process by insuring the independence of individual legislators."[16]

The language of Section 6 has generated two kinds of constitutional questions: What is protected and who is protected? The reach of the clause was first addressed by the Court in *Kilbourn v. Thompson* (1881). In *Kilbourn* the Court dealt primarily with the scope of congressional investigations, but it also noted that the clause extends to

written reports presented . . . by its committees, to resolutions offered, which, though in writing, must be reproduced in speech, and to the act of voting, whether it is done vocally or by passing between the tellers. In short, to things generally done in a session [of Congress] by one of its members in relation to the business before it.

With only some minor modifications, *Kilbourn* remained the Court's most significant statement on the Speech or Debate Clause until 1972, when *Gravel v. United States* was decided. This case had important implications for both dimensions of Section 6: Who and what are protected?

Gravel began on June 29, 1971, when Sen. Mike Gravel, D-Alaska, held a public meeting of the Subcommittee on Buildings and Grounds, of which he was the chair. Before the hearing began, Gravel made a statement about the Vietnam War, noting that it was "relevant to his subcommittee . . . because of its effects upon the domestic economy and . . . the lack of federal funds to provide for adequate public facilities." He then read portions of a classified government document, now known as the Pentagon Papers, which provided details of U.S. involvement in the war. After he finished, Gravel introduced the forty-seven-volume document into the committee's record and "arranged, without any personal profit to himself, for its verbatim publication by Beacon Press," a publishing division of the Unitarian Universalist Association.

The Justice Department began an investigation to determine how the Pentagon Papers were released. It requested a district court judge to convene a grand jury, which in turn subpoenaed Dr. Leonard Rodberg, an aide to Gravel; Howard Webber, director of MIT Press; and, later, the publisher of Beacon Press. Rodberg and Gravel asked the court to quash the subpoena. In their view, U.S. attorneys "intended to interrogate Dr. Rodberg" about "the actions of Senator Gravel and his aides in making available" the Pentagon Papers. Such interrogation, they argued, would violate the Speech or Debate Clause because its scope extended to aides. As Gravel's attorney noted, "Given the realities of the modern-day legislative process, congressmen must seek the advice and assistance of persons outside the immediate staff." Forcing Rod-

---

15. *Constitutional Law of the Federal System*, 177.

16. *United States v. Brewster* (1972). See Louis Fisher, *American Constitutional Law* (New York: McGraw-Hill, 1990), 235.

TABLE 4-3 Speech or Debate Clause Cases After *Gravel v. United States*

Case	Legal Question	Court's Response
United States v. Brewster (1972)	Does the Speech or Debate Clause protect members from prosecution for alleged bribery to perform a legislative act?	The Speech or Debate Clause protects members from inquiry into legislative acts; it does not protect all conduct relating to the legislative process.
Doe v. McMillan (1973)	Does the Speech or Debate Clause protect members of Congress (and their staff) and other persons who were involved in the investigating, disseminating, and distributing of a report of the D.C. school system, which identified, by name, specific children and did so in a negative way?	The Speech or Debate Clause offers absolute immunity to members of Congress and staff, but not to individuals who, acting under congressional authority, distributed the materials.
Eastland v. U.S. Servicemen's Fund (1975)	Does the Speech or Debate Clause protect members of Congress against a suit brought by an organization to stop the implementation of a subpoena ordering a bank to produce certain records?	The Speech or Debate Clause offers absolute protection because the activities fall within the "legitimate legislative" sphere.
Davis v. Passman (1979)	Does the Speech or Debate Clause protect a member of Congress against charges of sex discrimination?	The Supreme Court decided the case on Fifth Amendment grounds and reached no result on the member of Congress's claim that he was protected by the Speech or Debate Clause.
United States v. Helstoski (1979)	Does the Speech or Debate Clause protect a member of Congress against prosecution (for accepting bribes), when evidence introduced in that action hinges on past legislative acts?	The Speech or Debate Clause does not permit the introduction of evidence involving past legislative acts.
Hutchinson v. Proxmire (1979)	Does the Speech or Debate Clause protect a member of Congress from a civil suit in response to negative statements made to the press and in newsletters about a government grant awardee's research?	The Speech or Debate Clause does not protect a member of Congress from a libel judgment when information is disseminated to the press and the public through newsletters.

berg to testify would be tantamount to having Gravel do so: they were both protected. He made a similar claim when prosecutors sought to force Webber and the publisher of Beacon Press to testify. He asserted that his arrangements for private publication of the documents also came under the protection of the Speech or Debate Clause, since those documents had been introduced in Congress.

At first, the government rejected all those claims; it even argued that Gravel's actions remained outside of constitutional protections. By the time the case reached the Supreme Court, however, the government had limited its arguments to Gravel's aide and the publisher. It asserted that the language of the Speech or Debate Clause, past precedents, and the intent of the Framers all pointed to the same conclusion: its reach covered neither congressional aides nor arrangements with private publishers, even for material introduced into a subcommittee record. *Gravel* presented the Court with the two classic questions: Who and what are covered under the Speech or Debate Clause?

As for who was protected, Justice White—the author of the majority opinion—held that Clause gave similar protection to both the senator and his aide. For

it is literally impossible, in view of the complexities of the modern legislative process, . . . for Members of Congress to perform their legislative tasks without the help of aides and assistants; the day-to-day work of such aides is so critical to the Members' performance that they must be treated as the latter's alter egos; and that if they are not so recognized, the central role of the Speech or Debate Clause—to prevent intimidation of legislators by the Executive and accountability before a possibly hostile judiciary—will inevitably be diminished and frustrated. . . .

At the same time, though, White asserted that Speech or Debate Clause protection was not absolute. Both the senator and the aide could be questioned for activities that had no direct connection to or "impinged upon" the legislative process. Thus, because "private publication by Senator Gravel through the cooperation of Beacon Press was in no way essential to the deliberations of the Senate," the Speech or Debate Clause did not provide immunity to Rodberg from testifying before the grand jury about the publishing arrangement between Senator Gravel and Beacon Press "or about his own participation, if any, in the alleged transaction, so long as legislative acts of the Senator are not impugned."

Despite the specificity of the Court's ruling in *Gravel*, it did not put an end to controversies under the Speech or Debate Clause. Indeed, as illustrated in Table 4-3, in the 1970s the Court decided several important issues that were left open by *Gravel*. In *United States v. Helstoski* (1979) the justices refused to allow prosecutors to introduce evidence into a court proceeding against a former member of Congress involving legislative activities. *Hutchinson v. Proxmire* (1979),

however, was a defeat for congressional authority. Here the Court examined a dispute arising when Sen. William Proxmire, D-Wis., on the floor of the Senate and later in a newsletter and on television, labeled Ronald R. Hutchinson's federally funded research virtually worthless and a waste of taxpayers' money. Hutchinson brought a libel suit against Proxmire. When the case reached the Court, the justices addressed the issue of whether the Speech or Debate Clause immunized the senator from a libel proceeding on the grounds that he had first made the remarks on the chamber's floor. The Court held that it did not:

A speech by Proxmire in the Senate would be wholly immune and would be available to other Members of Congress and the public in the Congressional Record. But neither the newsletters nor the press release was "essential to the deliberations of the Senate," and neither was part of the deliberative process.

THE SOURCES AND SCOPE OF LEGISLATIVE POWERS

As noted earlier, Article I, Section 8, contains a virtual laundry list of Congress's powers. These enumerated powers, covered in seventeen clauses, establish congressional authority to regulate commerce, to lay and collect taxes, to establish post offices, and so forth. The enumerated powers pose few constitutional problems: those that the Constitution names, Congress clearly has.

But questions have arisen over other aspects of congressional power. First, does the legislative branch have powers beyond those specified by the Constitution? Despite the fact that the Framers left this question unaddressed, as noted in Table 4-4, the Court has not hesitated to answer it affirmatively, suggesting that Congress has implied and inherent powers in addition to those listed in Article I. In this section, we examine the cases in which the Court located those sources.

We also focus on a second, more complex, ques-

TABLE 4-4 The Sources of Congressional Power

Power[a]	Defined	Example
Enumerated powers	Those that the Constitution expressly grants	See Article I, Section 8. Includes the power to borrow money, raise armies, regulate commerce.
Implied powers	Those that may be inferred from power expressly granted	Read Article I, Section 8, Clauses 2–17, in conjunction with Clause 18, the Necessary and Proper Clause. For example, the enumerated power of raising and supporting armies leads to the implied power of operating a draft.
Inherent powers	Those that do not depend on constitutional grants but grow out of the very existence of the national government	Encompasses field of foreign affairs. That is, foreign affairs powers are those that the national government would have even if the Constitution was silent, because they are powers that all nations have under international law. For example, the federal government can issue orders prohibiting U.S. businesses from selling arms to particular nations.

SOURCE: Adopted from J. W. Peltason, *Understanding the Constitution*, 11th ed. (New York: Holt, Rinehart and Winston, 1988), 19.
   a. Some analysts suggest that Congress also possesses resulting powers (those that result when several enumerated powers are added together) and inherited powers (those that Congress inherited from the British Parliament).

tion: What constraints are there on Congress's ability to exercise these powers? For example, the Court has permitted Congress to conduct hearings and investigations, but it also has asserted that the power is not unlimited, that certain restrictions apply.

As you read the next cases, keep in mind not only the sources of legislative power but also the scope of that power. How has the Court sought to constrain Congress and, more important, why? What pressures have been brought to bear on the justices in making their decisions?

Enumerated and Implied Powers

The Constitution's specific list of congressional powers leaves no doubt that Congress has these powers. In *Gibbons v. Ogden* (1824), when the Court was asked to interpret one of them, the power to regulate interstate commerce, Chief Justice John Marshall said:

The words [of the Constitution] are, "Congress shall have power to regulate commerce with foreign nations, and among the several States. . . ." The subject to be regulated is commerce, and our constitution being . . . *one of enumeration, and not of definition,* to ascertain the extent of the pow-

er, it becomes necessary to settle the meaning of the word. (Emphasis added.)

In these two sentences, Marshall asserted that Congress indeed has the enumerated power to regulate commerce, but that the Court needed to define what that power entails. This point is important because, as we shall see later, the fact that a power is written into the Constitution does not necessarily make the Court's task easier: often it must define how Congress can and cannot make appropriate use of that power. For now, we can conclude that virtually no debate ever occurs over whether, in fact, Congress has the powers contained in Article I, Section 8.

Where debate has occurred is over the question of whether Congress has more powers, or was intended to have more powers, than those specifically granted. And if so, how broad should they be? Those who look to the plain language of the Constitution or to the intent of the Framers would find few concrete answers, although both camps would point to the same clause. Article I, Section 8, Clause 18, provides that Congress shall have the power to make all Laws which shall be necessary and proper for carrying into Execution the foregoing Powers, and all other Powers vested by this Constitution in the Government of the United States, or in any Department or Officer thereof.

Called by various names—the Necessary and Proper Clause, the Elastic Clause, or the Sweeping Clause—this provision was the subject of heated debate early in the nation's history. Many affiliated with the Federalist party, which favored a strong national government, argued for a loose construction of the clause. In their view, the Framers inserted it into the Constitution to provide Congress with some "flexibility"; in other words, Congress could exercise powers beyond those listed in the Constitution, those that were "necessary and proper" for implementing legislative activity. In contrast, the Jeffersonians asserted the need for a strict interpretation of the clause; in their view, it constricted congressional powers, rather than expanded them. In other words, congressional exercise of power under the Necessary and Proper Clause could be only that power necessary to carry out its enumerated functions.

Which view would the Supreme Court adopt? Would it interpret the Necessary and Proper Clause strictly or loosely? This was one of two major questions at the core of *McCulloch v. Maryland* (1819), which many consider the Court's most important explication of congressional powers.[17] Indeed, some suggest that this opinion was Chief Justice Marshall's finest. As you read this case, consider not only the Court's holding, but also the language and logic of *McCulloch*. Why is it such an extraordinary statement?

McCulloch v. Maryland

4 Wheat. 316 (1819)

Vote: 6   (Duvall, Johnson, Livingston, Marshall, Story, Washington)

0

Opinion of the Court: Marshall
Not participating: Todd

Although we now take for granted the ability of the federal government to operate a banking system—today called the Federal Reserve System—in the 1700s and into the 1800s this topic was a political battleground. The first sign of controversy came as early as 1790, when George Washington's secretary of the Treasury, Alexander Hamilton, asked Congress to adopt a series of proposals amounting to a "comprehensive financial and economic" plan.[18] Among the proposals was the creation of a Bank of the United States, which would receive deposits, disburse funds, and make loans; and Congress enacted a bill authorizing the founding of the first federal bank.

When the bill arrived at President Washington's desk, however, he did not sign it immediately. He wanted to ascertain whether in fact Congress could create a bank since it lacked explicit constitutional authority to do so. To this end he asked Hamilton, Secretary of State Thomas Jefferson, and Attorney General Edmund Randolph for their opinions on the bank's constitutionality.

Box 4-2 provides excerpts of Hamilton's and Jefferson's responses. We offer them not only because they reached different conclusions—Hamilton argued that it was constitutional, Jefferson that it was not—but also because they represent the "classical expositions of divergent theories" of congressional power.[19] Moreover, they illustrate the limits of the Framers' in-

---

17. The other question involved federalism. See Chapter 6.

18. Jethro Lieberman, *Milestones!* (St. Paul, Minn.: West, 1976), 117–118.
19. Pritchett, *Constitutional Law of the Federal System.*

BOX 4-2 JEFFERSON AND HAMILTON ON THE
BANK OF THE UNITED STATES

OPINION ON THE CONSTITUTIONALITY OF A NATIONAL BANK (1791)

Thomas Jefferson

To take a single step beyond the boundaries . . . specially drawn around the powers of Congress, is to take possession of a boundless field of power, no longer susceptible of any definition.

The incorporation of a bank, and other powers assumed by this bill have not, in my opinion, been delegated to the U.S. by the Constitution.

I. They are not among the powers specially enumerated, for these are

1. A power to *lay taxes* for the purpose of paying the debts of the U.S. But no debt is paid by this bill, nor any tax laid. . . .

2. "to borrow money." But this bill neither borrows money, nor ensures the borrowing of it. . . .

3. "to regulate commerce with foreign nations, and among the states, and with the Indian tribes." To erect a bank, and to regulate commerce, are very different acts. . . .

II. Nor are they within either of the general phrases, which are the two following.

1. "To lay taxes to provide for the general welfare of the U.S." that is to say "to lay taxes *for the purpose* of providing for the general welfare." For the laying of taxes is the *power* and the general welfare the *purpose* for which the power is to be exercised. They are not to lay taxes ad libitum *for any purpose they please;* but only to *pay the debts or provide for the welfare of the Union.* In like manner they are not *to do anything they please* to provide for the general welfare, but only *to lay taxes* for that purpose. To consider the latter phrase, not as describing the purpose of the first, but as giving a distinct and independent power to do any act they please, which might be for the good of the Union, would render all the preceding and subsequent enumerations of power completely useless. It would reduce the whole instrument to a single phrase, that of instituting a Congress with power to do whatever would be for the good

of the U.S. and as they would be the sole judges of the good or evil, it would be also a power to do whatever evil they pleased. . . . Certainly no such universal power was meant to be given them. It was intended to lace them up straitly within the enumerated powers, and those without which, as means, these powers could not be carried into effect. It is known that the very power now proposed *as a means,* was rejected *as an end,* by the Convention which formed the constitution. . . .

2. The second general phrase is "to make all laws *necessary* and proper or carrying into execution the enumerated powers." But they can all be carried into execution without a bank. A bank therefore is not *necessary,* and consequently not authorised by this phrase.

It has been much urged that a bank will give great facility, or convenience in the collection of taxes. Suppose this were true: yet the constitution allows only the means which are "necessary" not those which are merely "convenient" for effecting the enumerated powers. If such a latitude of construction be allowed to this phrase as to give any non-enumerated power, it will go to every one, for there is no one which ingenuity may not torture into a *convenience, in some way or other,* to *some one* of so long a list of enumerated powers. It would swallow up all the delegated powers, and reduce the whole to one phrase as before observed. Therefore it was that the constitution restrained them to the *necessary* means, that is to say, to those means without which the grant of the power would be nugatory.

OPINION AS TO THE CONSTITUTIONALITY OF THE BANK OF THE UNITED STATES (1791)

Alexander Hamilton

Now it appears to the Secretary of the Treasury that this *general principle* is *inherent* in the very *definition* of government, and *essential* to every step of the progress to be made by that of the United States, namely: That every power vested in a government is in its nature *sovereign,* and includes, by *force* of the *term*, a right to employ all the *means* requisite and fairly applicable to the attainment of the *ends* of such power, and which are not precluded by restrictions and exceptions specified in the Constitution, or not immoral, or not contrary to the *essential ends* of political society.

This principle, in its application to government in general, would be admitted as an axiom; and it will be incumbent upon those who may incline to deny it, to prove a distinction, and to show that a rule which, in the general system of things, is essential to the preservation of the social order, is inapplicable to the United States. . . .

This general and indisputable principle puts at once an end to the *abstract* question, whether the United States have power to erect a corporation; that is to say, to give a *legal* or *artificial capacity* to one or more persons, distinct from the *natural*. For it is unquestionably incident to *sovereign power* to erect corporations, and consequently to *that* of the United States, in *relation* to the *objects* intrusted to the management of the government. . . .

Another argument made use of by the Secretary of State is, the rejection of a proposition by the Convention to empower Congress to make corporations, either generally, or for some special purpose.

What was the precise nature or extent of this proposition, or what the reasons for refusing it, is not ascertained by any authentic document, or even by accurate recollection. . . .

But whatever may have been the nature of the proposition, or the reasons for rejecting it, it includes nothing in

respect to the real merits of the question. The Secretary of State will not deny that, whatever may have been the inten-

tion of the framers of a constitution or of a law, that intention is to be sought for in the instrument itself, according to the usual and established rules of construction. Nothing is more common than for laws to *express* and *effect* more or less than was intended. If, then, a power to erect a corporation in any case be deducible, by fair inference, from the whole or any part of the numerous provisions of the Constitution of the United States, arguments drawn from extrinsic circumstances, regarding the intention of the Convention, must be rejected. . . .

To establish such a right, it remains to show the relation of such an institution to one or more of the specified powers of the government. Accordingly it is affirmed that it has a relation, more or less direct, to the power of collecting taxes, to that of borrowing money, to that of regulating trade between the States, and to those of raising and maintaining fleets and armies. To the two former the relation may be said to be immediate; and in the last place it will be argued, that it is clearly within the provision which authorizes the making of all *needful rules and regulations* concerning the *property* of the United States, as the same has been practised upon the government.

A bank relates to the collection of taxes in two ways— *indirectly*, by increasing the quantity of circulating medium and quickening circulation, which facilitates the means of paying directly, by creating a *convenient species* of medium in which they are to be paid. . . .

SOURCE: Melvin I. Urofsky, ed., *Documents of American Constitutional and Legal History*, vol. I (New York: Knopf, 1989), 132–139.

tent mode of constitutional interpretation. Does it seem odd that just four years after the founding of the country, two of its foremost leaders could have such different views? In his argument, Hamilton, in fact, noted that there was a "conflicting recollection" of a convention debate highly relevant to the bank issue.[20]

20. One scholar notes that the Framers rejected a proposal that would have allowed Congress to establish corporations; in fact, they did so in part because of the possibility that Congress would create banks.

In the end, the president was persuaded by Hamilton and signed the bill. Congress then created the First Bank of the United States in 1791, chartering it for a twenty-year period.

Nevertheless, the bank controversy did not disappear. As we illustrate in Figure 4-1, which superimposes the bank's history (and that of its successor) against

See Lieberman, *Milestones!* 118. Still Hamilton argued that debate was unclear.

FIGURE 4-1 The History of the First and Second Banks of the United States

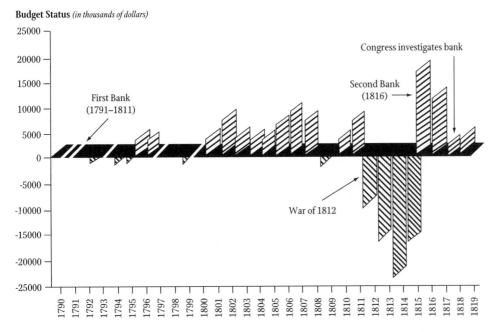

Budget Status *(in thousands of dollars)*

DATA SOURCE: U.S. Department of Commerce, *Historical Statistics of the United States* (Washington D.C.: U.S. Bureau of the Census, 1975), 1104.

political and economic events, it is clear why the bank remained in the spotlight. Most important was that it became a symbol of the nationally oriented Federalist party, which had lost considerable power from its heyday in the 1790s. Indeed, by the turn of the century, "strict construction of congressional authority became a central plank in the opposition platform of the Jeffersonian Republicans."[21] To no one's surprise, and despite the fact the bank "had performed its functions in an orderly [and honest] manner"—the Republican Congress refused to renew its charter in 1811.[22]

After the War of 1812, it became apparent even to the Republicans that Congress should recharter the bank. During the war "the administration had been embarrassed by the lack of a national bank, both as a source for borrowing and as a means of transferring funds from one part of the country to another."[23] Moreover, with the absence of a federal bank, state-chartered institutions flooded the market with worthless notes, contributing to economic problems throughout the country. Amid renewed controversy and cries for strict constructionism, Congress in 1816 created the second Bank of the United States, granting it a twenty-year charter and $35 million in capital.

According to historian Melvin I. Urofsky, "No one doubted that a court challenge to the new Bank would eventually arise . . . [for] the Supreme Court had never passed on the legitimacy of the first Bank."[24] It is possible, however, that litigation would not have materialized had the second bank performed its function as well as its predecessor did, but it did not. It flourished during the postwar economic boom, mainly because

21. Gerald Gunther, *Constitutional Law* (Mineola, N.Y.: Foundation Press, 1985), 86.
22. Lieberman, *Milestones!* 120.

23. Melvin I. Urofsky, *A March of Liberty* (New York: Knopf, 1988), 211.
24. Ibid.

it was fiscally aggressive and encouraged speculative investing.[25] These practices caught up to bank officials when, in 1818, in anticipation of a recession, they began calling in the bank's outstanding loans. As a result, they brought down banks throughout the South and West, which had overextended themselves.[26] To make matters worse, accusations of fraud and embezzlement were rampant within several of the bank's eighteen branches, particularly those in Maryland, Pennsylvania, and Virginia. Among those most seriously implicated was James McCulloch, the cashier of the Baltimore branch bank and its main lobbyist in Washington.[27] According to some accounts, his illegal financial schemes had cost the branch more than $1 million.

As a result of these allegations, Congress began to hold hearings on the bank. In addition, some states reacted by attempting to regulate branches located within their borders. For example, Maryland mandated that branches of the bank in the state pay either a 2 percent tax on all bank notes or a fee of $15,000. When a state official came to collect from the Baltimore branch, McCulloch refused to pay and, by refusing, set the stage for a monumental confrontation between the United States and Maryland on not one, but two, major issues. The first involved the bank itself: Did Congress, in the absence of an explicit constitutional authorization, have the power to charter the bank? Second, did the state exceed its powers by seeking to tax a federal entity?

By the time the case reached the Supreme Court, it was clear that something significant was going to happen. The Court reporter noted that *McCulloch* involved "a constitutional question of great importance." The justices waived their rule that permitted only two attorneys per side "and allowed three each."[28] Oral arguments took nine days.

Both sides were ably represented. Some commentators praise Daniel Webster's oratory for the federal government's side as extraordinary, but it was former attorney general and Maryland senator William Pinkney with whom the Court was most taken. Justice Joseph Story said later, "I never, in my whole life, heard a greater speech."[29] The gist of his arguments (and those of his colleagues) was familiar stuff; Pinkney largely reiterated Hamilton's original defense of the bank, particularly his interpretation of the Necessary and Proper Clause.

Maryland's legal representation may have appeared less astute. According to one account, "it has been rumored" that one of the state's lawyers, Attorney General Luther Martin, "was drunk when he made his two-day-long argument. If he was, it apparently did not affect his acuity." For his side, he reiterated parts of Jefferson's argument against the bank, added some on the subject of state's rights, and "closed his argument by reading from John Marshall's own speeches in the Virginia convention."[30]

CHIEF JUSTICE MARSHALL delivered the opinion of the Court.

The constitution of our country, in its most interesting and vital parts, is to be considered; the conflicting powers of the government of the Union and of its members, as marked in that constitution, are to be discussed; and an opinion given, which may essentially influence the great operations of the government. No tribunal can approach such a question without a deep sense of its importance, and of the awful responsibility involved in its decision. But it must be decided peacefully, or remain a source of hostile legislation, perhaps of hostility of a still more serious nature; and if it is to be so decided, by this tribunal alone can the decision be made. On the Supreme Court of the United States has the constitution of our country devolved this important duty.

25. Gunther, *Constitutional Law,* 89.
26. Urofsky, *A March of Liberty,* 211.
27. Gunther, *Constitutional Law,* 89.
28. Fred W. Friendly and Martha J. H. Elliot, *The Constitution—That Delicate Balance* (New York: Random House, 1984), 256.
29. Quoted in Lieberman, *Milestones!* 122.
30. Farber and Sherry, *A History of the American Constitution,* 251.

The first question . . . is, has Congress power to incorporate a bank? . . .

This government is acknowledged by all to be one of enumerated powers. The principle, that it can exercise only the powers granted to it, would seem too apparent to have required to be enforced by all those arguments which its enlightened friends, while it was depending before the people, found it necessary to urge. That principle is now universally admitted. But the question respecting the extent of the powers actually granted, is perpetually arising, and will probably continue to arise, as long as our system shall exist. . . .

Among the enumerated powers, we do not find that of establishing a bank or creating a corporation. But there is no phrase in the instrument which, like the articles of confederation, excludes incidental or implied powers; and which requires that everything granted shall be expressly and minutely described. Even the 10th amendment, which was framed for the purpose of quieting the excessive jealousies which had been excited, omits the word "expressly," and declares only that the powers "not delegated to the United States, nor prohibited to the states, are reserved to the states or to the people;" thus leaving the question, whether the particular power which may become the subject of contest has been delegated to the one government, or prohibited to the other, to depend on a fair construction of the whole instrument. . . . A constitution, to contain an accurate detail of all the subdivisions of which its great powers will admit, and of all the means by which they may be carried into execution, would partake of a prolixity of a legal code, and could scarcely be embraced by the human mind. It would probably never be understood by the public. Its nature, therefore, requires, that only its great outlines should be marked, its important objects designated, and the minor ingredients which compose those objects be deduced from the nature of the objects themselves. That this idea was entertained by the framers of the American constitution, is not only to be inferred from the nature of the instrument, but from the language. Why else were some of the limitations, found in the ninth section of the 1st article, introduced? It is also, in some degree, warranted by their having omitted to use any restrictive term which might prevent its receiving a fair and just interpretation. In considering this question, then, we must never forget that it is a constitution we are expounding.

Although, among the enumerated powers of government, we do not find the word "bank" or "incorporation," we find the great powers to lay and collect taxes; to borrow money; to regulate commerce; to declare and conduct a war; and to raise and support armies and navies. The sword and the purse, all the external relations, and no inconsiderable portion of the industry of the nation, are entrusted to its government. It can never be pretended that these vast powers draw after them others of inferior importance, merely because they are inferior. Such an idea can never be advanced. But it may with great reason be contended, that a government, entrusted with such ample powers, on the due execution of which the happiness and prosperity of the nation so vitally depends, must also be entrusted with ample means for their execution. The power being given, it is the interest of the nation to facilitate its execution. It can never be their interest, and cannot be presumed to have been their intention, to clog and embarrass its execution by withholding the most appropriate means. . . .

The government which has a right to do an act, and has imposed on it the duty of performing that act, must, according to the dictates of reason, be allowed to select the means; and those who contend that it may not select any appropriate means, that one particular mode of effecting the object is excepted, take upon themselves the burden of establishing that exception. . . .

But the constitution of the United States has not left the right of Congress to employ the necessary means for the execution of the powers conferred on the government to general reasoning. To its enumeration of powers is added that of making "all laws which shall be necessary and proper, for carrying into execution the foregoing powers, and all other powers vested by this constitution, in the government of the United States, or in any department thereof."

The counsel for the State of Maryland have urged various arguments, to prove that this clause, though in terms a grant of power, is not so in effect; but is really restrictive of the general right, which might otherwise be implied, of selecting means for executing the enumerated powers. . . .

The word "necessary" is considered as controlling the whole sentence, and as limiting the right to pass laws for the execution of the granted powers, to such as are indispensable, and without which the power would be nugatory. That it excludes the choice of means, and leaves to Congress, in each case, that only which is most direct and simple.

Is it true that this is the sense in which the word "necessary" is always used? Does it always import an absolute physical necessity, so strong that one thing, to which another may be termed necessary, cannot exist without that other? We think it does not. If reference be had to its use, in the common affairs of the world, or in approved authors, we find that it frequently imports no more than that one thing is convenient, or useful, or essential to another. To employ the means necessary to an end, is generally understood as employing any means calculated to produce the end, and not as being confined to those single means, without which the end would be entirely unattainable. . . . This word, . . . like others, is used in various senses; and, in its construction, the subject, the context, the intention of the person using them, are all to be taken into view.

Let this be done in the case under consideration. The subject is the execution of those great powers on which the welfare of a nation essentially depends. It must have been the intention of those who gave these powers, to insure, as far as human prudence could insure, their beneficial execution. This could not be done by confiding the choice of means to such narrow limits as not to leave it in the power of Congress to adopt any which might be appropriate, and which were conducive to the end. This provision is made in a constitution intended to endure for ages to come, and, consequently, to be adapted to the various crises of human affairs. To have prescribed the means by which government should, in all future time, execute its powers, would have been to change, entirely, the character of the instrument, and give it the properties of a legal code. It would have been an unwise attempt to provide, by immutable rules, for exigencies which, if foreseen at all, must have been seen dimly, and which can be best provided for as they occur. To have declared that the best means shall not be used, but those alone without which the power given would be nugatory, would have been to deprive the legislature of the capacity to avail itself of experience, to exercise its reason, and to accommodate its legislation to circumstances. . . .

The baneful influence of this narrow construction on all the operations of the government, and the absolute impracticability of maintaining it without rendering the government incompetent to its great objects, might be illustrated by numerous examples drawn from the constitution, and from our laws. . . .

In ascertaining the sense in which the word "necessary" is used in this clause of the constitution, we may derive some aid from that with which it is associated. Congress shall have power "to make all laws which shall be necessary and proper to carry into execution" the powers of the government. If the word "necessary" was used in that strict and rigorous sense for which the counsel for the state of Maryland contend, it would be an extraordinary departure from the usual course of the human mind, as exhibited in composition, to add a word, the only possible effect of which is to qualify that strict and rigorous meaning; to present to the mind the idea of some choice of means of legislation not straightened and compressed within the narrow limits for which gentlemen contend.

But the argument which most conclusively demonstrates the error of the construction contended for by the counsel for the state of Maryland, is founded on the intention of the convention, as manifested in the whole clause. To waste time and argument in proving that without it Congress might carry its powers into execution, would be not much less idle than to hold a lighted taper to the sun. As little can it be required to prove, that in the absence of this clause, Congress would have some choice of means. That it might employ those which, in its judgment, would most advantageously effect the object to be accomplished. That any means adapted to the end, any means which tended directly to the execution of the constitutional powers of the government, were in themselves constitutional. This clause, as construed by the state of Maryland, would abridge, and almost annihilate this useful and necessary right of the legislature to select its means. That this could not be intended, is, we should think, had it not been already controverted, too apparent for controversy. We think so for the following reasons:

1st. The clause is placed among the powers of Congress, not among the limitations on those powers.

2d. Its terms purport to enlarge, not to diminish the powers vested in the government. . . .

We admit, as all must admit, that the powers of the government are limited, and that its limits are not to be transcended. But we think the sound construction of the constitution must allow to the national legislature that discretion, with respect to the means by which the powers it confers are to be carried into execution, which will enable that body to perform the high duties assigned to it, in the manner most beneficial to the people. Let the end be legitimate, let it be within the scope of the constitution, and all means which are appropriate, which are plainly adapted to that end, which are not prohibited, but consist with the letter and spirit of the constitution, are constitutional.

That a corporation must be considered as a means not less usual, not of higher dignity, not more requiring a particular specification than other means, has been sufficiently proved. If we look to the origin of corporations, to the manner in which they have been framed in that government from which we have derived most of our legal principles and ideas, or to the uses to which they have been applied, we find no reason to suppose that a constitution, omitting, and wisely omitting, to enumerate all the means for carrying into execution the great powers vested in government, ought to have specified this. Had it been intended to grant this power as one which should be distinct and independent, to be exercised in any case whatever, it would have found a place among the enumerated powers of the government. But being considered merely as a means, to be employed only for the purpose of carrying into execution the given powers, there could be no motive for particularly mentioning it. . . .

If a corporation may be employed indiscriminately with other means to carry into execution the powers of the government, no particular reason can be assigned for excluding the use of a bank, if required for its fiscal operations. To use one, must be within the discretion of Congress, if it be an appropriate mode of executing the powers of government. That it is a convenient, a useful, and essential instrument in the prosecution of its fiscal operations, is not now a subject of controversy. All those who have been concerned in the administration of our finances, have concurred in representing the importance and necessity; and so strongly have they been felt, that statesmen of the first class, whose previous opinions against it had been confirmed by every circumstance which can fix the human judgment, have yielded those opinions to the exigencies of the nation. Under the confederation, Congress, justifying the measure by its necessity, transcended perhaps its powers to obtain the advantage of a bank; and our own legislation attests the universal conviction of the utility of this measure. The time has passed away when it can be necessary to enter into any discussion in order to prove the importance of this instrument, as a means to effect the legitimate objects of the government.

But, were its necessity less apparent, none can deny its being an appropriate measure; and if it is, the degree of its necessity, as has been very justly observed, is to be discussed in another place. Should Congress, in the execution of its powers, adopt measures which are prohibited by the constitution; or should Congress, under the pretext of executing its powers, pass laws for the accomplishment of objects not entrusted to the government, it would become the painful duty of this tribunal, should a case requiring such a decision come before it, to say that such an act was not the law of the land. But where the law is not prohibited, and is really calculated to effect any of the objects entrusted to the government, to undertake here to inquire into the degree of its necessity, would be to pass the line which circumscribes the judicial department, and to tread on legislative ground. This court disclaims all pretensions to such a power. . . .

After the most deliberate consideration, it is the unanimous and decided opinion of this court that the act to incorporate the bank of the United States is a law made in pursuance of the constitution, and is a part of the supreme law of the land.

As we can see, Marshall fully adopted Hamilton's reasoning and the government's claims. Some even felt his opinion "sounded almost like recitations" of the oral arguments presented by the federal attorneys.[31] Given that Marshall issued *McCulloch* just three days after the case had been presented, it is more likely, as others suspect, that he had written the opinion the previous summer.

Either way, *McCulloch* stands as a landmark decision. By holding that Congress has powers beyond those enumerated, that it has implied powers, Marshall set into law a largely Hamiltonian version of congressional authority:

31. Friendly and Elliot, *The Constitution*, 259.

Let the end be legitimate, let it be within the scope of the constitution, and all means which are appropriate, which are plainly adapted to that end, which are not prohibited, but consist with the letter and spirit of the constitution, are constitutional.

And in so doing, he might very well have accomplished his stated objective: to allow the Constitution "to endure for ages to come."

The immediate reaction to Marshall's opinion was interesting in that it focused less on the portion we have dealt with here—congressional powers—and more on the federalism dimension, which we take up in Chapter 6. Nonetheless, the long-term effect of his interpretation of the Necessary and Proper Clause has been significant: Congress now exercises many powers not named in the Constitution but implied from it.

Congressional Investigations

Of all the implied powers now asserted by Congress, the power to investigate merits close examination. Many think it is one of the most important congressional powers. As Woodrow Wilson noted: "The informing function of Congress should be preferred even to its legislative function." Another president, Harry Truman, concurred: "The power of investigation is one of the most important powers of Congress. The manner in which that power is exercised will largely determine the position and prestige of the Congress in the future."[32] In addition, the scope of congressional authority in this area has been the subject of some rather interesting, perhaps conflicting, and most definitely controversial, Supreme Court opinions.

What has never been controversial, however, is Congress's ability to conduct investigations. After all, to legislate effectively requires the gathering of information to determine if new laws are necessary and, if so, how the new statutes can best be written. Al-

though this power is not an enumerated power, there is little question that legislatures can hold inquiries. Some analysts refer to it as an incidental power that legislatures have by virtue of being legislatures.[33] Others call it an inherited power that the British Parliament willed to Congress or, alternatively, an implied power.[34] In any event, Congress took advantage of this privilege virtually from the beginning, holding its first investigation in 1792. Since then "no period of American history has been without" investigations.[35]

If the power of Congress to investigate is so well entrenched, what is controversial about the practice? For one thing, questions arise over the scope of the power—into what subjects may Congress inquire? For another, may Congress summon witnesses and punish, by holding in contempt, those who do not cooperate with the investigating body? And, if so, what sorts of rights, if any, do witnesses have? Some argue that the power to call and punish witnesses may be implied from the inherent nature of legislative authority. Congress is, by definition, *the* lawmaking institution, and an inherent quality of such an institution is the power to investigate. To function, therefore, it is necessary for Congress to have the authority to summon witnesses and punish those who do not comply, and both chambers have always availed themselves of this authority. As early as 1795 Congress jailed for contempt a man who had tried to bribe a member of Congress. The Supreme Court theoretically approved of the contempt practice as early as 1821.[36] But it was not until *Kilbourn v. Thompson* (1881) that the justices attempted to provide firm answers to the questions of Congress's power to summon and punish witnesses and on the scope of congressional investigations.

Kilbourn involved a House investigation into a pri-

---

32. Quoted in *Guide to Congress*, 3d ed. (Washington, D.C.: Congressional Quarterly, 1982), 161.

33. Peter Woll, *Constitutional Law* (Englewood Cliffs, N.J.: Prentice Hall, 1981), 193.
34. Pritchett, *Constitutional Law of the Federal System*, 191.
35. *Guide to Congress*, 4th ed., 221.
36. *Anderson v. Dunn* (1821).

vate banking firm. An important witness, Hallett Kilbourn, refused to produce documents demanded by the inquiring committee. By a House order, Kilbourn was held in contempt and jailed. When he was released, he sued various officials and representatives for false arrest. In his view, the investigation was not legitimate because it concerned private, not public, matters and, as such, he would resist "the naked, arbitrary power of the House to investigate private businesses in which nobody but me and my customers have concern."[37]

The Supreme Court agreed. In what some have called a rather narrow ruling on legislative powers, the justices said that Congress could punish witnesses only if the inquiry itself was within the "legitimate cognizance" of the institution. With this ruling, the Court seemed to establish several limits on the scope of investigations. Inquiries (1) must not "invade areas constitutionally reserved to the courts or the executive"; (2) must deal "with subjects on which Congress could validly legislate"; and (3) must suggest, in the resolutions authorizing the investigation, a "congressional interest in legislating on that subject."[38] In general, then, *Kilbourn* said that Congress could hold inquiries only into subjects that are specifically grounded within its constitutional purview and, in particular, that the "private affairs of individuals," where the inquiry could result in "no valid legislation," did not fall into that category.

Four decades later, in *McGrain v. Daugherty* (1927), the Court was once again called on to examine the scope of congressional investigative authority. In 1922 Congress began an investigation of the so-called Teapot Dome Scandal, which involved the alleged bribery of public officials by private companies to obtain leasing rights to government-held oil reserves, including the Teapot Dome reserves in Wyoming. Although initial inquiries centered on employees of the

Department of the Interior, Congress soon turned its attention to the Justice Department. It was thought that Attorney General Harry M. Daugherty was involved in fraudulent activities because he failed to prosecute wrongdoers. As part of that inquiry, a Senate committee ordered the attorney general's brother, Mally S. Daugherty, to appear before it and to produce documents. Mally Daugherty was a bank president, and the committee suspected that he was involved in the scandal.

This suspicion grew stronger with the resignation of the attorney general and the subsequent refusal of his brother to appear before the committee. The Senate had Mally arrested. He, in turn, challenged the committee's authority to compel him—through arrest—to testify against his brother. Picking up on one of the limits of investigation emanating from *Kilbourn,* Mally's lawyer argued that "the arrest of Mr. Daugherty is the result of an attempt of the Senate to vest its committee with judicial power." The U.S. government's brief also used *Kilbourn* to frame its arguments: "The investigation ordered by the Senate, in the course of which the testimony of the Appellee [Daughertry] and the production of books and records of the bank of which he is President were required, was legislative in its character."

The Court agreed with the government. Writing for the majority, Justice Van Devanter held that "the power of inquiry—with process to enforce it—is an essential and appropriate auxiliary to the legislative function. . . ." In other words, he firmly established Congress's power to inquire and to enforce that power with the ability to punish as an implied power. This was an important affirmation of a longstanding practice. Since 1795, congressional committees had often invoked their power to punish, issuing more than 380 contempt citations over the years. When a committee does so, and, if the parent chamber approves by a simple majority, the case is forwarded to a U.S. attorney for possible prosecution. Still, in *McGrain,* the justices were unwilling to allow a virtually limitless use of that

37. Quoted in *Guide to Congress,* 4th ed., 224.
38. Pritchett, *Constitutional Law of the Federal System,* 191.

The House Un-American Activities Committee holds a press conference December 3, 1948, after a closed session. Standing are two committee investigators. Seated are several reporters and, left to right, Richard Nixon, R-Calif., John Rankin, D-Miss., and John Mc-Dowell, R-Pa.

power. Although they ruled for the government and backed away from the rigid stance of *Kilbourn,* they continued to assert that Congress could not inquire, generally speaking, into private affairs. It was just that, in this case, "the object of the investigation and of the effort to secure the witness's testimony was to obtain information for legislative purposes."

In addition to shedding light on Congress's ability to "inquire," *McGrain* provides some insight into a controversial area of congressional inquiries: the rights of witnesses. While the Court ruled against Daugherty, it held that witnesses may refuse to answer "where the bounds of the power are exceeded or the questions are not pertinent to the matter under inquiry."

McGrain's window of opportunity for witnesses to refuse to testify became quite important during World War II and in the postwar period when, out of fear of an influx of foreign ideologies into the United

States, Congress embarked on a new type of investigation: the "inquisitorial panel." In short, the "overriding purpose of the anti-subversive hearings was exposure," not necessarily "information."[39]

As discussed in Box 4-3, this kind of "investigation" is similar to those held by the House Special Committee to Investigate Un-American Activities in the 1930s. However, the investigations carried on in the Senate by Joseph McCarthy and by the House Committee on Un-American Activities (HUAC) in the 1940s and 1950s produced the most controversy and criticism. At that time, the fear of communism was so pervasive that even being called to testify before McCarthy or HUAC created such suspicion that individuals lost their jobs, were placed on blacklists, and so forth. Moreover, many witnesses were sufficiently scared of being branded a communist sympathizer or support-

39. *Guide to Congress,* 3d ed., 148, 151.

BOX 4-3 INVESTIGATIONS OF "UN-AMERICANISM"

ONE OF THE MOST significant expansions of congressional investigative powers beyond direct legislative matters was the study of subversive movements after World War II. Instead of pursuing traditional lines of congressional inquiry—government operations and national social and economic problems—committees probed into the thoughts, actions, and associations of individuals and institutions.

The House Committee on Un-American Activities was the premier example of these investigative panels. The committee was abolished in January 1975, ending thirty years of controversy over its zealous pursuit of subversives. Its long survival surprised many observers. From the outset the panel, renamed the Internal Security Committee in 1969, was attacked by liberals and civil libertarians. Throughout the 1960s it withstood court suits challenging the constitutionality of its mandate and attempts in the House to end its funding. The death blow finally came when the House Democratic Caucus, by voice vote in January 1975, transferred its functions to the House Judiciary Committee.

EARLY HISTORY

The first congressional investigation of un-American activities was authorized September 19, 1918, toward the close of World War I. That original mandate was to investigate the activities of German brewing interests. The investigation, conducted by the Senate Judiciary Committee, was expanded in 1919 to cover "any efforts . . . to propagate in this country the principles of any party exercising . . . authority in Russia . . . and . . . to incite the overthrow" of the U.S. government.

The House on May 12, 1930, set up a Special Committee to Investigate Communist Activities in the United States—the Fish Committee, so called after its chairman, Rep. Hamilton Fish, Jr., R-N.Y. On March 20, 1934, the House created a Special Committee on Un-American Activities, under Chairman John W. McCormack, D-Mass. On May 26, 1938, three years after McCormack's committee submitted its report, which covered Nazi as well as communist activities in the United States, the House set up another Special Committee on Un-American Activities, under Chairman Martin Dies, Jr., D-Texas. The committee, whose chairman was avowedly anticommunist and anti-New Deal, was given a broad mandate to investigate subversion.

Dies focused his early investigations on organized labor groups, especially the Congress of Industrial Organizations, and set a tactical pattern that would guide the permanent Un-American Activities Committee, which was created in 1945.

Friendly witnesses, who often met in secret with Dies as a one-man subcommittee, accused hundreds of people of supporting communist activities, but few of the accused were permitted to testify in rebuttal. The press treated Dies's charges sensationally, a practice that was to continue after World War II.

The Dies Committee was reconstituted in succeeding Congresses until 1945. That January, at the beginning of the Seventy-ninth Congress, it was renamed the House Committee on Un-American Activities and made a standing committee.

The next five years marked the peak of the committee's influence. In 1947 it investigated communism in the motion picture industry, with repercussions that lasted almost a decade. Its hearings resulted in the Hollywood blacklist that kept many writers and actors suspected of communist leanings out of work.

The committee's investigation in 1948 of State Department official Alger Hiss, and Hiss's subsequent conviction for perjury, established communism as a leading political issue and the committee as an important political force. The case against Hiss was vigorously developed by a young member of the committee, Richard Nixon.

The committee's tactics during this period included extensive use of contempt citations against unfriendly witnesses, some of whom pleaded their Fifth Amendment right against self-incrimination. In 1950, for example, the House voted fifty-nine contempt citations, of which fifty-six had been recommended by the committee.

SENATE INVESTIGATIONS

In the early 1950s the Un-American Activities Committee was overshadowed by Senate investigations conducted by Joseph R. McCarthy, R-Wis., chairman (1953–1954) of the Senate Government Operations Committee's Permanent Investigations Subcommittee. McCarthy's investigation into alleged subversion in the U.S. army—televised nationwide in 1954—intensified concern over the use by Congress of its investigating powers and led to his censure by the Senate in 1954.

During the same period, the Senate Judiciary Committee's Internal Security Subcommittee, established in 1951, also investigated subversive influences in various fields, including government, education, labor unions, the United Nations, and the press.

SOURCE: *Guide to Congress*, 4th ed., ed. Mary Cohn (Washington, D.C.: Congressional Quarterly, 1991), 240.

BACKGROUND

When the House Un-American Activities Committee was made a standing committee in 1945, Congress defined its authority in Rule XI as follows:

The Committee on Un-American Activities, as a whole or by subcommittee, is authorized to make from time to time investigations of (1) the extent, character, and objects of un-American propaganda activities in the United States, (2) the diffusion within the United States of subversive and un-American propaganda that is instigated from foreign countries or of a domestic origin and attacks the principle of the form of government as guaranteed by our Constitution, and (3) all other questions in relation thereto that would aid Congress in any necessary remedial legislation.

FACTS

Watkins. *Watkins v. United States* crystallized when the committee invoked one of its favored modus operandi: asking a witness before it to "name names," to implicate others as Communist party members. Two witnesses told the committee that John T. Watkins, who had been involved in various labor organizations, including the United Electrical, Radio and Machine Workers and the United Auto Workers, was not only a Communist party member but also a recruiter for the party.

When the committee subpoenaed Watkins in April 1954, he answered questions pertaining to his own activities "freely and without reservation." But when he refused to answer questions about the activities of others because he thought they were not pertinent to HUAC's work, the chair of the committee reported the matter to the full House, which held Watkins in contempt and presented the case to a U.S. attorney for criminal prosecution. Watkins was found guilty of "contempt of Congress," fined $100, and given a one-year suspended prison sentence.

In his brief to the Supreme Court, Watkins's lawyer made two interrelated arguments centering on the committee's authority. First, he complained that "the very idea of congressional committee exposure for the sake of exposure unrelated to a legislative purpose is incompatible with our constitutional system." Second, he suggested that the ques-

tions his client refused to answer fell beyond "the language of the Committee's authorization" in part because that "authorization is so vague and indefinitive of purpose" as to deprive Watkins of his rights.

Barenblatt. On February 25, 1953, a subcommittee of HUAC, operating under the same authority it had before the Watkins case (Rule XI), initiated a series of hearings called "Communist Methods of Infiltration (Education)." Before the hearings got under way, HUAC's chair stated that their purpose would be to "ascertain the character, extent and objects of Communist Party activities . . . carried on by [teachers] who are subject to the directives and discipline of the Communist Party." More generally, he observed that:

It has been fully established in testimony before congressional committees and before the courts of our land that the Communist Party of the United States is part of an international conspiracy which is being used as a tool or weapon by a foreign power to promote its own foreign policy and which has for its object the overthrow of the governments of all non-Communist countries, resorting to the use of force and violence, if necessary.

Based on information the subcommittee had obtained from another witness, in June 1954 it subpoenaed Lloyd Barenblatt to testify before it. Barenblatt answered a few preliminary questions but then refused to tell the Committee whether he was then or ever had been a member of the Communist Party. Accordingly, the House held him in contempt for unlawfully refusing to answer these questions, and a U.S. attorney sought and obtained a conviction against him.

On appeal to the Supreme Court, Barenblatt's American Civil Liberties Union lawyers raised three claims. First, "on the basis of . . . *Watkins,* it is clear that the language of the legislation purportedly granting investigative authority to the House Committee was not sufficiently definite and specific to constitute a delegation of power, and thus there is a complete lack of authority in the Committee to investigate by compulsory process." In other words, they reiterated Warren's reasoning in *Watkins* that, first, the authority of the committee rested on a rule (Rule XI) that was too vague; second, the questions lacked pertinency; and, third, the questions infringed on Barenblatt's First Amendment right to expression and association.

MAJORITY OPINION

Watkins. The Court held for Watkins. In his opinion, Chief Justice Warren asserted that committees cannot force witnesses to "make disclosures" on matters outside of their jurisdictions. The problem here is that HUAC's authority, as defined by Rule XI, is so "excessively broad" that the Committee could ask almost anything and claim statutory pertinency. This is unfair to witnesses, like Watkins, for they are "entitled to have knowledge of the subject to which the interrogation is deemed pertinent."

Barenblatt. The Court held for the United States. The majority opinion, written by Justice Harlan, differentiated *Barenblatt* from *Watkins* along the following lines. First, even though the same Rule was still operative (Rule XI), it now comes to the Court with the "persuasive gloss of legislative history." In other words, at the time the Court decided *Watkins* it was unclear whether the Committee would limit its investigations to Communist activities in the United States; by 1959, it seemed that this was the sole interest of HUAC. And, if there was any doubt about the subcommittee's investigation in *Barenblatt,* HUAC's chair clarified it with his statement prior to the onset of the hearings. Second, unlike Watkins—who was willing to testify about his own activities—Barenblatt refused to answer questions about his own Communist Party activities, "whose pertinency of course was beyond doubt."

DISSENTING OPINIONS

Watkins. Justice Clark dissented on the grounds that the Committee was "acting entirely within its scope and that the purpose of the inquiry was set out with 'indisputable clarity.'"

Barenblatt. Justices Black, Brennan, Douglas, and Warren dissented. In his dissenting opinion, Black reiterated the majority's conclusion in *Watkins:* "Rule XI is too broad to be meaningful and cannot support [Barenblatt's] conviction."

er that they refused to testify or asserted a constitutional protection against so doing, which resulted in an unusually high number of contempt citations. Between 1792 and 1942 Congress issued 108 citations; from 1945 to 1957, fourteen committees presented 226 contempt citations to their respective chambers.[40] HUAC alone held 144 "uncooperative" witnesses in contempt.[41]

In the late 1950s the Supreme Court decided two major cases involving the rights of witnesses to refuse to answer questions, *Watkins v. United States* (1957) and *Barenblatt v. United States* (1959). Despite the fact that these cases were quite similar, as Box 4-4 shows, the Court reached very different conclusions: In *Watkins,* the Court ruled for the witness; in *Barenblatt,* against him. This has led scholars to ask whether the Court treated the claims of Barenblatt and Watkins consistently. The majority in *Barenblatt* went to great lengths to indicate that it did—indeed, that *Barenblatt* amounted to nothing more or less than a "clarification" of *Watkins.* But many legal analysts, along with Justice Black, who wrote a dissenting opinion in *Barenblatt,* suggest that at minimum the justices backed away from *Watkins,* and others say that *Barenblatt* signaled a reversal of sorts of the earlier ruling.

If *Barenblatt* was a reversal, how can we explain the shift, which occurred within a two-year period? There are two possibilities. The first is that *Barenblatt* constituted "a strategic withdrawal" because at the time the Court was under "pressure of Congress and some sectors of public opinion."[42] In particular, *Watkins* and other "liberal" decisions on subversive activity and on discrimination such as *Brown v. Board of Education* (1954) made the Court the target of numerous congressional proposals. A few even sought to remove the Court's jurisdiction to hear cases involving

40. Ibid., 163.
41. Ralph A. Rossum and G. Alan Tarr, *American Constitutional Law,* 3d ed. (New York: St. Martin's Press, 1991), 94.
42. C. Herman Pritchett, *Congress Versus the Supreme Court* (Minneapolis: University of Minnesota Press, 1961), 12.

subversive activities. According to some observers, the justices felt the heat and acceded to congressional pressure.

Another explanation is that personnel changes produced a more conservative Court, that *Barenblatt* represented a move "back toward a more conservative position" ushered in by President Dwight Eisenhower's appointments of Charles Whittaker and Potter Stewart.[43] By way of support, scholars point to the voting alignments in the two cases and to the general trend in the disposition of civil liberties cases. As Walter F. Murphy noted, during the 1956 term, which included *Watkins,* the Court ruled in favor of the civil liberties claim in 74 percent of the cases; that figure fell to 59 percent and 51 percent in the 1957 and 1958 terms, respectively.[44]

Either way, the explanations indicate the susceptibility of the Court to political influences outside and inside its chambers. As the dangers associated with the cold war began to ebb, the justices again had a change of heart on the rights of witnesses. In case after case in the 1960s, they reversed the convictions of many whom Congress had cited for contempt. In so doing, the Court has sought to strike a balance between the rights of individuals and those of legislatures, no easy task because of the substantive nature of the power to investigate. Certainly, as HUAC's activities illustrate, there are ample opportunities for abuse. But, "responsibly used, the power to investigate is a vital safeguard against both governmental and private wrongdoing."[45] We have only to consider congressional hearings into the Watergate scandal, which we shall examine in Chapter 5, to see the truth in this.

Inherent Powers

As we have seen, Congress has enumerated powers as well as powers that can be implied or inferred from,

or are incidental to, its role as the lawmaking institution. In addition, many analysts argue that Congress has certain inherent powers that are neither explicit nor even implied by the Constitution, but which somehow attach themselves to sovereign states *(see Table 4-4, page 117).*

As Justice Story defined them, inherent powers are those that result "from the whole mass of the powers of the National Government, and from the nature of political society, [not as] a consequence or incident of the powers specifically enumerated."[46] For example, as noted earlier, some analysts suggest that the congressional power to investigate is an inherent, rather than implied, power. The argument suggests that Congress is the lawmaking body, and an inherent quality of such an institution is the power to investigate.

Although theorists had long espoused this concept, it found its way into constitutional law in *United States v. Curtiss-Wright Export Corp.* (1936). As you read this case, pay particular attention to Justice Sutherland's explication of inherent powers. How does he define them? More important, how does he square the existence of inherent powers with the idea of a government based on enumeration?

United States v. Curtiss-Wright Export Corp.

299 U.S. 304 (1936)

Vote: 7   (*Brandeis, Butler, Cardozo, Hughes, Roberts, Sutherland, Van Devanter*)

1   (*McReynolds*)

Opinion of the Court: Sutherland
Not participating: Stone

After Charles Lindbergh's 1927 transatlantic flight, the aviation industry began to boom. Americans were convinced that "flying . . . would take its place as the

---

43. Ibid.

44. *Congress and the Supreme Court* (Chicago: University of Chicago Press, 1962), 246.

45. Pritchett, *Constitutional Law of the Federal System,* 195.

46. *Commentaries on the Constitution,* vol. 3 (New York: Da Capo Press reprint of 1833 edition, 1970), 124.

new mode of transportation."[47] As a result, many new companies formed to build aircraft. Among them was Curtiss-Wright.

Although it started off on a strong footing, Curtiss-Wright soon fell prey to the Great Depression: between 1930 and 1931, it lost $13 million. To avoid going bankrupt, it looked beyond the United States into the foreign market, where money still could be made. However, Curtiss-Wright was selling its wares not to other private companies but to foreign governments involved in military conflicts and in need of war planes.

The company found a ready buyer in Bolivia, which since 1932 had been at war with Paraguay over the Chaco, a region east of Bolivia. Landlocked Bolivia was determined to take control of the Chaco to gain access to the Atlantic Ocean. Bolivia became an excellent customer of Curtiss-Wright's, buying thirty-four planes in the early 1930s. The Chaco war, in turn, enabled the company to survive the depression.

Things began to turn sour in 1934. Books and articles appeared attacking companies like Curtiss-Wright as "merchants of death." More important, the League of Nations wanted to put an end to the Chaco war and asked the United States to help. In response, President Roosevelt asked Congress to enact a resolution enabling him to prohibit the sale of arms to the warring countries. It did so on May 28, 1934.

[I]f the President finds that the prohibition of the sale of arms and munitions of war in the United States to those countries now engaged in armed conflict in the Chaco may contribute to the reestablishment of peace between those countries, and if after consultation with the governments of other American Republics and with their cooperation, as well as that of such other governments as he may deem necessary, he makes proclamation to that effect, it shall be unlawful to sell, except under such limitations and exceptions as the President prescribes, any arms or munitions of war in any place in the United States to the countries now engaged in that armed conflict, or to any person, company, or association acting in the interest of either country, until otherwise ordered by the President or by Congress.

Whoever sells any arms or munitions of war . . . shall . . . be punished by a fine not exceeding $10,000 or by imprisonment not exceeding two years, or both.

Shortly after the resolution was enacted, Roosevelt issued an order embargoing weapon sales to Bolivia and Paraguay. Curtiss-Wright refused to comply with the order and tried to get around it by disguising bombers as passenger planes. Eventually, the company got caught and was charged with violating the order.

The company challenged the government's action. Among its arguments when the case reached the Court, the most pertinent was the contention that the 1934 resolution was invalid because it gave "uncontrolled" lawmaking "discretion" to the president. On this score, the company's reasoning appeared strong: in *Panama Refining Company v. Ryan* (1935) the Court had struck down a congressional act on the grounds that the legislature had delegated lawmaking authority to the president without sufficient guidelines *(see Box 4-5, page 139)*. In the company's view, the 1934 resolution was no different from the law struck down in *Panama Refining*.

The U.S. government tried to distinguish the facts in this case from those in the 1935 decision. In its view, the congressional delegation of power in *Panama Refining*, as we shall see, involved domestic, not international, affairs. This distinction was important, in the government's opinion, because "from the beginning of the government, in the conduct of foreign affairs, Congress has followed the practice of conferring upon the President power similar to that conferred by the present resolution." By way of example, U.S. attorneys indicated that as early as 1794, Congress had given the president the "duty of determining" when embargoes should be laid "upon vessels in ports of the United States bound for foreign ports."

---

47. We adopt this and what follows from Robert A. Divine, "The Case of the Smuggled Bombers," in *Quarrels That Have Shaped the Constitution*, by John A. Garraty (New York: Harper and Row, 1987).

MR. JUSTICE SUTHERLAND delivered the
opinion of the Court.

It is contended that by the Joint Resolution, the going
into effect and continued operation of the resolution was
conditioned (a) upon the President's judgment as to its
beneficial effect upon the reestablishment of peace between the countries engaged in armed conflict in the Chaco; (b) upon the making of a proclamation, which was left
to his unfettered discretion, thus constituting an attempted
substitution of the President's will for that of Congress; (c)
upon the making of a proclamation putting an end to the
operation of the resolution, which again was left to the
President's unfettered discretion; and (d) further, that the
extent of its operation in particular cases was subject to
limitation and exception by the President, controlled by no
standard. In each of these particulars, appellees urge that
Congress abdicated its essential functions and delegated
them to the Executive.

Whether, if the Joint Resolution had related solely to internal affairs it would be open to the challenge that it constituted an unlawful delegation of legislative power to the
Executive, we find it unnecessary to determine. The whole
aim of the resolution is to affect a situation entirely external
to the United States, and falling within the category of foreign affairs. The determination which we are called to
make, therefore, is whether the Joint Resolution, as applied
to that situation, is vulnerable to attack under the rule that
forbids a delegation of the law-making power. In other
words, assuming (but not deciding) that the challenged
delegation, if it were confined to internal affairs, would be
invalid, may it nevertheless be sustained on the ground
that its exclusive aim is to afford a remedy for a hurtful condition within foreign territory?

It will contribute to the elucidation of the question if we
first consider the differences between the powers of the
Federal government in respect of foreign or external affairs
and those in respect of domestic or internal affairs. That
there are differences between them, and that these differences are fundamental, may not be doubted.

The two classes of powers are different, both in respect
of their origin and their nature. The broad statement that
the Federal government can exercise no powers except
those specifically enumerated in the Constitution, and such

implied powers as are necessary and proper to carry into effect the enumerated powers, is categorically true only in respect of our internal affairs. In that field, the primary purpose of the Constitution was to carve from the general mass
of legislative powers *then possessed by the states* such portions as it was thought desirable to vest in the Federal government, leaving those not included in the enumeration
still in the states. That this doctrine applies only to powers
which the states had, is self-evident. And since the states
severally never possessed international powers, such powers could not have been carved from the mass of state powers but obviously were transmitted to the United States
from some other source. During the colonial period, those
powers were possessed exclusively by and were entirely under the control of the Crown. By the Declaration of Independence, "the Representatives of the United States of
America" declared the United [not the several] Colonies to
be free and independent states, and as such to have "full
Power to levy War, conclude Peace, contract Alliances, establish Commerce and to do all other Acts and Things
which Independent States may of right do."

As a result of the separation from Great Britain by the
colonies, acting as a unit, the powers of external sovereignty passed from the Crown not to the colonies severally, but
to the colonies in their collective and corporate capacity as
the United States of America. Even before the Declaration,
the colonies were a unit in foreign affairs, acting through a
common agency—namely the Continental Congress, composed of delegates from the thirteen colonies. That agency
exercised the powers of war and peace, raised an army, created a navy, and finally adopted the Declaration of Independence. Rulers come and go; governments end and
forms of government change; but sovereignty survives. A
political society cannot endure without a supreme will
somewhere. Sovereignty is never held in suspense. When,
therefore, the external sovereignty of Great Britain in respect of the colonies ceased, it immediately passed to the
Union. . . .

The Union existed before the Constitution, which was
ordained and established among other things to form "a
more perfect Union." Prior to that event, it is clear that the
Union, declared by the Articles of Confederation to be "perpetual," was the sole possessor of external sovereignty, and
in the Union it remained without change save in so far as

the Constitution in express terms qualified its exercise. The Framers' Convention was called and exerted its powers upon the irrefutable postulate that though the states were several their people in respect of foreign affairs were one. . . .

It results that the investment of the Federal government with the powers of external sovereignty did not depend upon the affirmative grants of the Constitution. The powers to declare and wage war, to conclude peace, to make treaties, to maintain diplomatic relations with other sovereignties, if they had never been mentioned in the Constitution, would have vested in the Federal government as necessary concomitants of nationality. Neither the Constitution nor the laws passed in pursuance of it have any force in foreign territory unless in respect of our own citizens . . . and operations of the nation in such territory must be governed by treaties, international understandings and compacts, and the principles of international law. As a member of the family of nations, the right and power of the United States in that field are equal to the right and power of the other members of the international family. Otherwise, the United States is not completely sovereign. . . .

Practically every volume of the United States Statutes contains one or more acts or joint resolutions of Congress authorizing action by the President in respect of subjects affecting foreign relations, which either leave the exercise of the power to his unrestricted judgment, or provide a standard far more general than that which has always been considered requisite with regard to domestic affairs. . . .

The result of holding that the joint resolution here under attack is void and unenforceable as constituting an unlawful delegation of legislative power would be to stamp this multitude of comparable acts and resolutions as likewise invalid. And while this court may not, and should not, hesitate to declare acts of Congress, however many times repeated, to be unconstitutional if beyond all rational doubt it finds them to be so, an impressive array of legislation such as we have just set forth, enacted by nearly every Congress from the beginning of our national existence to the present day, must be given unusual weight in the process of reaching a correct determination of the problem. A legislative practice such as we have here, evidenced not by only occasional instances, but marked by the movement of a steady stream for a century and a half of time, goes a long way in the direction of proving the presence of unassailable ground for the constitutionality of the practice, to be found in the origin and history of the power involved, or in its nature, or in both combined. . . .

The uniform, long-continued and undisputed legislative practice just disclosed rests upon an admissible view of the Constitution which, even if the practice found far less support in principle than we think it does, we should not feel at liberty at this late day to disturb.

We deem it unnecessary to consider, seriatim, the several clauses which are said to evidence the unconstitutionality of the Joint Resolution as involving an unlawful delegation of legislative power. It is enough to summarize by saying that, both upon principle and in accordance with precedent, we conclude there is sufficient warrant for the broad discretion vested in the President to determine whether the enforcement of the statute will have a beneficial effect upon the reestablishment of peace in the affected countries; whether he shall make proclamation to bring the resolution into operation; whether and when the resolution shall cease to operate and to make proclamation accordingly; and to prescribe limitations and exceptions to which the enforcement of the resolution shall be subject.

Curtiss-Wright was a landmark ruling. As we shall see later in this chapter, the decision ran directly counter to what the Court was doing in other areas of the law. While it was striking down many segments of Roosevelt's New Deal, in part on the ground that the laws were unconstitutional delegations of power, here the Court upheld congressional authority to delegate power. Why it did so brings us to another important, and for present purposes more relevant, aspect of the decision: the distinction between foreign and domestic affairs. Sutherland justified the delegation of power here on the grounds that it involved external affairs, whereas the Court's rulings on the New Deal programs involved domestic programs.

In this dichotomy the majority found the concept of inherent powers. In its view, the U.S. Constitution transferred some domestic powers from the states to the federal government, leaving some with the states or the people. That is why Congress cannot exercise authority over internal affairs beyond that which is explicitly enumerated or can be implied from that document. In contrast, no such transfer occurred or could have occurred for authority over foreign affairs. Because the states never had such power to begin with, they could not have bestowed it on the federal government. Rather, "authority over foreign affairs is an inherent power, which attaches automatically to the federal government as a sovereign entity, and derives from the Constitution only as the Constitution is the creator of that sovereign entity."[48] It is not Congress specifically but the federal government that enjoys complete authority over foreign relations, which is an inherent power of sovereign nations, one that is derived not from their charters but from their status. Louis Henkin summarized: "Foreign affairs are national affairs. The United States is a single nation-state, and it is the United States (not the States of the Union, singly or together) that has relations with other nations, and the United States Government that conducts these relations and makes foreign policy."[49]

What are we to make of the majority opinion? Some support certainly exists for its distinction between domestic and foreign affairs. We will explore this subject in greater detail in Chapter 5, but here we can say that some of the Framers would have approved of *Curtiss-Wright*. As Hamilton wrote in *Federalist*, No. 23, "The circumstances that endanger the safety of nations are infinite, and for this reason no constitutional shackles can wisely be imposed on the power to which the care of it is committed." In short, the idea was not novel, and Sutherland had espoused it during his Senate career.

But *Curtiss-Wright* also has been the subject of some criticism. Historians and legal scholars assert that Sutherland's historical analysis was inaccurate: "There is evidence that, after independence, at least

some of the erstwhile colonies . . . considered themselves sovereign, independent states."[50] More relevant here, however, is the argument that the entire notion of "inherent powers" cannot possibly conform with theories underlying the Constitution. The Tenth Amendment states: "The powers not delegated to the United States by the Constitution, nor prohibited by it to the States, are reserved to the States respectively, or to the people." Can it be that this language applies only to domestic powers and not foreign affairs? *Curtiss-Wright* seems to teach this lesson, and it makes some analysts squirm.

Even so, Sutherland's opinion remains authoritative doctrine. Its conceptualization of the federal government's inherent power over foreign affairs provides that entity with considerable leeway. And it is a doctrine to which the Court continues, generally speaking, to subscribe.

THE ROLE OF CONGRESS IN NATIONAL GOVERNMENT

In our discussion so far, you may have noted a pattern in the Court's decisions dealing with the sources and scope of congressional power. On the whole, with a few scattered exceptions, the Court has allowed Congress a good deal of leeway in exercising enumerated and extraconstitutional power, especially in disputes involving that body's power to regulate its own affairs and to enact legislation, even if a law intrudes on state operations. Where the Court has wavered and, at times, has reined Congress in is over its authority vis-à-vis the other national institutions, particularly the executive. In other words, during certain periods of the nation's history, the Court has taken a hard line on the separation of powers doctrine, limiting both friendly and unfriendly relations between Congress and the president.

In this section, we explore Court rulings in both ar-

---

48. Pritchett, *Constitutional Law of the Federal System*, 305.

49. *Foreign Affairs and the Constitution* (New York: W. W. Norton, 1975), 15.

50. Ibid., 23.

eas, beginning with a discussion of Congress's authority to interact with the president in a cooperative sense. Many times throughout the nation's history, Congress has sought to delegate some of its authority to a president who wants such power or has requested it. In the section on delegation of powers, we shall see whether the Court has agreed to such cooperation. Next, we look at congressional authority to oversee executive power, to act as an unwanted check on the president.

Although these sections deal with different substantive material, you may note some commonalties in Court rulings. Pay careful attention to how the Court delineates constitutional interactions from the unconstitutional. Has it acted in a consistent manner? Have the justices grounded their opinions in constitutional language or philosophy, or have other factors had a greater impact?

The Delegation of Powers

Almost all discussions of the ability of Congress to delegate its lawmaking power begin with the old Latin maxim: *delegata potestas non potest delegari,* which means "a power once delegated cannot be redelegated." We could apply this statement to Congress in the following way: because the Constitution delegates to that institution all legislative powers—lawmaking authority—it cannot give such power to another body or person.

Why not? To answer that question, suppose that after you take the final examination in this course, your instructor delegates the responsibility of grading the test papers to a teaching assistant. Being busy with other work, the TA then delegates that task to a roommate who has never taken a constitutional law course. Who would be responsible—the professor, the TA, or the roommate—when your final grade did not fairly reflect your work?[51] The same argument could be applied to delegations of lawmaking power to a president in charge of executing laws who in turn hands authority over to a bureaucrat.

However, no political institution has accepted fully the principle expressed in the Latin maxim. From the First Congress on, the legislature has delegated its power to other branches or even to nongovernmental entities. But why would Congress want to give away some of its power? One reason is that, like the professor in the example, Congress is often busy with other matters and must delegate some authority if it is to fulfill all of its responsibilities. Another is that Congress might "succeed well enough in the task of formulating general policies, but [might] lack the time and expert information needed to prescribe specific methods for carrying out those policies."[52] As the job of governance grows increasingly technical and complex, this reason becomes even more valid. *Curtiss-Wright* provides yet another reason: the need for flexibility. In *Curtiss-Wright* Congress had given the president authority to issue an arms embargo if such an action would help to bring peace to warring South American nations. Congress recognized that once it enacts legislation it may have difficulty amending it, "whereas the problems with which legislation aims to deal," such as in the *Curtiss-Wright* example, "may be constantly changing."[53] Finally, there are political reasons why Congress might want to delegate. Sotirios Barber noted, "A Congress of buck passers is one of the results of the electorate's tendency to reward politicians who are responsive to its [the public's] immediate wants, not its [Congress's] considered constitutional duties."[54] In other words, to avoid dealing with certain "hot potato" issues, Congress might hand them off to others. The delegation of powers issue is tricky: it is accepted, theoretically, that Congress should not dole out its lawmaking authority, but it is a matter of practical and reasonable politics that it does so.

51. Craig R. Ducat and Harold W. Chase, *Constitutional Interpretation,* 4th ed. (St. Paul, Minn.: West, 1988), use a similar example, centering on a school principal delegating authority to a teacher, who delegates it to a groundskeeper, who in turn passes it off to a student.
52. Pritchett, *Constitutional Law of the Federal System,* 184.
53. Ibid.
54. *On What the Constitution Means* (Baltimore: Johns Hopkins University Press, 1984), 177.

Not surprisingly, the Supreme Court has found itself enmeshed in this debate. As we saw in *Curtiss-Wright*, the Court has been asked to determine whether a particular delegation of power is appropriate, constitutionally speaking. As in *Curtiss-Wright*, the Court generally has upheld such delegations, even if they involve domestic issues. *Wayman v. Southard* (1825) was the Court's first major ruling on the delegation of domestic powers. This dispute, unlike most in this area, involved a congressional grant of lawmaking authority to the courts, not to the executive. The case asked the justices to determine whether a section of the 1789 Judiciary Act, which gave the courts power to "make and establish all necessary laws" for the conduct of judicial business, constituted a violation of the separation of powers doctrine and, as such, an unconstitutional delegation of power.

Writing for the Court in *Wayman*, Chief Justice Marshall responded pragmatically. He sought to balance the letter of the Constitution with the practical concerns facing Congress when he formulated the following standard: the legislature must itself "entirely" regulate "important subjects"; but for "those of less interest," it can enact a general provision and authorize "those who are to act under such general provisions to fill up the details." Put simply, Marshall established a different set of rules for the delegation of power, varying by the importance of the subject under regulation.[55] Applying this standard to the delegation of power contained in the 1789 Judiciary Act, he found that Congress could grant courts authority to promulgate their own rules.

Wayman—in theory—created an important precedent for subsequent Courts to follow. We say "in theory" because, although for the next century or so the Supreme Court never struck down a congressional delegation of power, it did not quite follow Marshall's standard. Rather, it took an even broader approach to this kind of case. For example, in *Hampton*

& *Co. v. United States* (1928) it let stand a grant of authority to the president that some suggest failed Marshall's standard. The Court examined the Fordney-McComber Act, in which Congress established a tariff commission within the executive branch and permitted the president to increase or decrease tariffs on imported goods by as much as 50 percent. Because Congress gave the president (and the commission) virtually unlimited discretion to adjust rates, an import company challenged the act as a violation of the separation of powers doctrine. The company argued that Congress had provided the president with what was essentially lawmaking power. Writing for a unanimous Court, Chief Justice William Howard Taft—a former president of the United States—disagreed: "In determining what [Congress] may do in seeking assistance from another branch, the extent and character of that assistance must be fixed according to common sense and the inherent necessities of the governmental coordination." So long as Congress "shall lay down by legislative act an intelligible principle to which the person or body authorized to [exercise the delegated authority] is directed to conform," according to Taft, "such legislative action is not a forbidden delegation of legislative power."

For nearly a decade, the Court seemed quite willing to accept the so-called "intelligible principle" approach to congressional delegations. But in 1935 the Court dealt Congress and the president major blows when it struck down provisions of the National Industrial Recovery Act (NIRA) as excessive delegations of power. In Box 4-5 we describe the circumstances surrounding these cases—*Panama Refining Company v. Ryan* and *Schechter Poultry v. United States*—and the Court's rulings in them. *(For full details, see Chapter 7.)* The NIRA was a major piece of New Deal legislation designed to pull the nation out of the economic depression. In *Panama Refining*, Congress had allowed the president to prohibit the shipment in interstate commerce of oil produced in excess of state quotas; in *Schechter*, Congress had authorized the president to

55. Pritchett, *The American Constitution*, 175.

BOX 4-5   COURT'S DECISIONS IN *PANAMA* AND *SCHECHTER POULTRY*

	PANAMA REFINING CO. V. RYAN (January 7, 1935)	*SCHECHTER POULTRY V. UNITED STATES* (May 27, 1935)
Problem	The oil industry, as a result of overproduction to meet the demand for oil in the 1920s, began to ship "hot oil" (that which had been produced in excess of state quotas) across state lines as a way of dealing with falling prices.	The depression indicated the need for greater regulation of various industries, particularly prohibitions on certain kinds of "unfair" competition.
Congressional solution	A provision of the National Industrial Recovery Act (NIRA), which permitted the president to prohibit the shipment of hot oil in interstate commerce.	The NIRA, which allowed the president, at the request of industrial trade associations, to approve codes for the entire industry.
FDR's action	Issued an order prohibiting the shipment of oil produced in excess of state established quotas.	Approved industry codes.
The specific dispute	Small oil companies challenged the quota system, alleging that it hurt independent, small producers.	The Schechter brothers challenged the Live Poultry Code, which established industry standards and set work hours.
Delegation of powers question	Did challenged sections of the NIRA constitute overly broad (and thus unconstitutional) congressional delegations of power to the president?	
Majority opinion	Struck down challenged section of the NIRA: "in every case in which the question has been raised, the Court has recognized that there are limits of delegation which there is no constitutional authority to transcend. We think [the challenged section of the NIRA] goes beyond those limits. As to the transportation of oil production in excess of state permission the Congress has declared no policy, has established no standard, has laid down no rule."	Struck down parts of the NIRA: "In view of the scope of [the] broad declaration and of the nature of the restrictions that are imposed, the discretion of the President in approving or prescribing codes, and thus enacting laws for the government of trade and industry throughout the country, is virtually unfettered. We think that the code-making authority . . . is an unconstitutional delegation of legislative power."
Cardozo's opinion	In dissent: "My point of difference with the majority is narrow. I concede that to uphold the delegation there is a need to discover in the terms of the act a standard reasonably clear whereby discretion must be governed. I deny that such a standard is lacking in respect of the prohibitions permitted by this section when the act is considered as a whole."	Concurring: This is "delegation running riot."

approve fair competition codes and standards if representatives of a particular industry recommended he do so. In both instances, the Court struck down the delegations of power as unconstitutional.

Why did the Court decide *Panama Refining* and *Schechter* that way? Because Congress passed the NIRA under its power to regulate interstate commerce, we take up this question from a somewhat different angle in Chapter 7. For now, let us first consider it from a doctrinal perspective: Did earlier precedent, particularly *Wayman* and *Hampton*, necessarily lead to these outcomes? The Court undoubtedly thought so: it justified its opinions in *Panama Refining* and *Schechter* as being firmly grounded in past decisions and it did so by wide margins. Eight of the nine justices agreed with the majority opinion in *Panama Refining*, and the one dissenting justice, Benjamin Cardozo, joined the others in *Schechter*, noting that this law constituted "delegation running riot."

Was the Court on firm legal ground? One way to think about this question is to compare the Court's rulings here with those in *Wayman* and *Hampton*. Were the NIRA delegations of power more onerous than that in *Hampton*? Or did they not meet Marshall's standard in *Wayman*? Another is to consider the briefs and arguments in the 1935 cases. Before the Supreme Court decided *Panama Refining*, a federal court of appeals had upheld the law as a constitutional use of congressional commerce powers and, in so doing, gave "very casual treatment to the delegation issue," noting simply that it met previously set standards. When the oil company appealed the decision, U.S. attorneys responded with a 195-page brief filed with the Supreme Court. Apparently, "lulled . . . into a false sense of security" by the lower court ruling and believing that "precedent [was] uniformly on their side," the United States devoted only 3 of those 195 pages to the delegation of powers issue. Indeed, the issue probably would not have been seriously raised had it not been for oral arguments. There, the lawyers for the oil company hammered away at both issues,

the delegation of powers and the Commerce Clause, arguing that Congress had "laid down no rule or criterion to guide or limit the President in the orders that he may promulgate."[56]

Based on this sort of analysis, many scholars suggest that the justices were merely using the delegation of powers as an excuse to strike down New Deal legislation that they fundamentally and ideologically opposed. Whether this is true we leave for you to decide. More important for now is that the rulings in *Panama Refining* and *Schechter* represent anomalies. For reasons we offer later, by 1937 the Court had begun to uphold New Deal legislation, and by the end of the decade it was allowing for all sorts of congressional delegations of powers to a diverse range of executive agencies, some of which are listed in Table 4-5.

What can we conclude about congressional delegations of power? Some analysts suggest that the Court's rulings in 1935 had an effect on Congress, forcing it to be more specific in the guidelines it sets out. Is that accurate? As noted in Table 4-5, some executive agencies wield power just as enormous as that which the Court struck in the mid-1930s, but since 1936 the Supreme Court has not overturned a law on such grounds (although a few of the most suspect never have reached the Court). Many have concluded that "Congress now as a matter of fact can delegate as it pleases."[57]

Unfriendly Relations: The Legislative Veto

The cases we discussed in the last section share a common thread: they involved cooperative relations between Congress and another branch of government, usually the executive. Congress was delegating some of its lawmaking authority—in these cases, the establishment of tariff rates or the prohibition of the shipment of "hot" oil—to an executive who wanted, perhaps even requested, such authority. But Congress

56. Peter H. Irons, *The New Deal Lawyers* (Princeton, N.J.: Princeton University Press, 1982), 69, 70, 71, 93.

57. Ducat and Chase, *Constitutional Interpretation*, 140.

TABLE 4-5 "Delegated" Powers Held by Major Federal Regulatory Commissions

Commission	Examples of the Scope of Power
Interstate Commerce Commission	Fixes rates for railroads and related carriers Sets standards for reasonable service Controls consolidations and mergers of carriers Regulates safety devices and services
Federal Trade Commission	Prevents practices leading to monopoly and restraint of trade such as unfair methods of competition and price discrimination Investigates and issues cease-and-desist orders
Federal Communications Commission	Regulates telegraph carriers Allocates radio frequencies Licenses radio and television stations Monitors broadcasts
National Labor Relations Board	Adjudicates charges of unfair labor practices on the part of employers or unions Enforces collective bargaining agreements

SOURCE: *Guide to Congress*, 3d ed. (Washington, D.C.: Congressional Quarterly, 1982), 198.

is not always so eager to give away its powers; indeed, on many occasions and through different devices, it has sought to exercise authority over the executive branch. One of those devices is the so-called legislative veto.

This kind of veto is a constitutional oddity because it flips the mandated lawmaking process. Rather than follow Article I procedures—both houses of Congress pass bills and the president signs or vetoes them—under this practice, the executive branch makes policies that Congress can veto by a vote of both houses, one house, or even a committee. It should come as no surprise that the legislative veto has been the source of contention between presidents and Congresses, with the former suggesting that they violate constitutional principles and the latter arguing that they represent a way to check the lawmaking power Congress has delegated to the executive branch.

When it was first developed, the legislative veto was not all that contentious; to the contrary, it was part of a quid pro quo between Congress and President Herbert Hoover, who wanted "authority to reor-

ganize the executive branch without having to submit a bill to Congress." The legislature agreed to go along "only on the condition that either House could reject a reorganization plan by passing a resolution of disapproval."[58] When Congress passed the 1933 legislative appropriations bill with that condition attached to it, the legislative veto was born.

Although Hoover had agreed to it, he was less than pleased when Congress used it the following year to veto part of the reorganization plan. In fact, his attorney general, William D. Mitchell, decried the device as a violation of the separation of powers doctrine. That sort of sparring over the legislative veto continued through the early 1980s, but the patterns of debate were somewhat contradictory and confusing. On the one hand, until 1972 Congress had used the device rather sparingly, attaching it to only fifty-one laws (*see Box 4-6 for some examples*).[59] Moreover, the legislative veto did not seem to be taken very seriously by either

58. Fisher, *American Constitutional Law*, 230.
59. Urofsky, *A March of Liberty*, 945.

BOX 4-6   EXAMPLES OF
LAWS CONTAINING
LEGISLATIVE VETOES

International Development and Food Assistance Act of 1975. Foreign assistance to countries not meeting human rights standards may be terminated by concurrent resolution.

Nuclear Non-Proliferation Act of 1978. Cooperative agreements concerning storage and disposition of spent nuclear fuel, proposed export of nuclear facilities, materials, or technology, and proposed agreements for international cooperation in nuclear reactor development may be disapproved by concurrent resolution.

Civil Rights of Institutionalized Persons. Attorney General's proposed standards for resolution of grievances of adults confined in correctional facilities may be disapproved by resolution of either House.

Full Employment and Balanced Growth Act of 1978. Presidential timetable for reducing unemployment may be superseded by concurrent resolution.

War Powers Resolution. Absent declaration of war, president may be directed by concurrent resolution to remove United States armed forces engaged in foreign hostilities.

the president or Congress. Research by political scientist Dennis Simon indicates that presidents have rejected only a handful of laws solely because they contained legislative vetoes and that in those few instances Congress almost always repassed the bill without the veto provision.[60]

On the other hand, presidents have complained about the practice. Dwight D. Eisenhower loathed the legislative veto, claiming that it violated "fundamental constitutional principles." Complaints grew louder after the Nixon presidency, when Congress sought

to reassert itself over the executive, enacting sixty-two statutes with legislative vetoes between 1972 and 1979. In fact, in 1976 the House of Representatives "came within two votes of approving a proposal to make every rule and regulation of every executive agency subject to legislative review."[61]

This issue came to a head during the Carter administration. Jimmy Carter, like Eisenhower, despised legislative vetoes. Suggesting that he did not consider them binding, he had the Justice Department join *Immigration and Naturalization Service v. Chadha*, to test it. The result was the first U.S. Supreme Court ruling centering specifically on the constitutionality of the legislative veto. On what grounds did the Court strike down the practice? There were two strenuous dissents. Why did Justice White, in particular, believe that the Court had committed a grave error?

Immigration and Naturalization Service v. Chadha

462 U.S. 919 (1983)
Vote: 7   *(Blackmun, Brennan, Burger, Marshall, O'Connor, Powell, Stevens)*
        2   *(Rehnquist, White)*
Opinion of the Court: Burger
Concurring opinion: Powell
Dissenting opinions: Rehnquist, White

Jagdish Rai Chadha, an East Indian born in Kenya and holder of a British passport, was admitted into the United States in 1966 on a six-year student visa. More than a year after his visa expired, in October 1973, the Immigration and Naturalization Service ordered Chadha to attend a deportation hearing and show cause why he should not be deported. After two hearings, an immigration judge in June 1974 ordered a suspension of Chadha's deportation, which meant

---

60. "Presidential Vetoes," research in progress.

61. Urofsky, *A March of Liberty*, 946.

that Chadha could stay in the United States, because he was of "good moral character" and would "suffer extreme hardship" if deported.

Acting under a provision of the Immigration and Nationality Act, the U.S. attorney general recommended to Congress that Chadha be allowed to remain in the United States in accordance with the judge's opinion. The act states:

Upon application by any alien who is found by the Attorney General to meet the requirements of . . . this section the Attorney General may in his discretion suspend deportation of such alien. If the deportation of any alien is suspended . . . a complete and detailed statement of the facts and pertinent provisions of the law in the case shall be reported to the Congress with the reasons for such suspension. Such reports shall be submitted on the first day of each calendar month in which Congress is in session.

Congress, in turn, had the authority to veto—by a resolution passed in either house—the attorney general's decision. The act specifies:

[I]f during the session of the Congress at which a case is reported, or prior to the close of the session of the Congress next following the session at which a case is reported, either the Senate or the House of Representatives passes a resolution stating in substance that it does not favor the suspension of such deportation, the Attorney General shall thereupon deport such alien or authorize the alien's voluntary departure at his own expense under the order of deportation in the manner provided by law. If, within the time above specified, neither the Senate nor the House of Representatives shall pass such a resolution, the Attorney General shall cancel deportation proceedings.

For a while it appeared as if Chadha's suspension of deportation was secure, but at the last moment Congress asserted its veto power. Congress had until December 19, 1975, to take action, and on December 12 the chairman of a House committee introduced a resolution opposing the "granting of permanent residence in the United States to [six] aliens," including Chadha. Four days later the House of Representatives passed the motion. No debate or recorded vote occurred; indeed, it was never really clear why the chamber took the action.

That vote set the stage for a major showdown between Congress and the executive branch. Chadha filed a suit, first with the Immigration Court and then with a federal court of appeals, asking that they declare the legislative veto unconstitutional. The Carter administration joined him to argue likewise. The president agreed with Chadha's basic position, and administration attorneys thought his suit provided a great test case because it "pointed up the worst features of the legislative veto—no debate, no recorded vote, no approval by the other chamber, and no chance for presidential review."[62] Given the importance of the dispute, the court of appeals asked both the House and the Senate to file amicus curiae briefs supporting the veto practice, but in 1980 it ruled against their position, finding that the device violated separation of powers principles.

By the time the case was first argued before the Supreme Court in February 1982, the Carter administration was out and the Reagan administration was in. During his 1980 campaign, Reagan claimed to support the legislative veto, but, once in office, he instructed the attorney general to go forward with the *Chadha* case. The Justice Department presented the Court with several reasons why the legislative veto violated the Constitution:

The Constitution explicitly requires that all congressional actions constituting the exercise of legislative power receive the concurrence of both Houses and be presented to the President for his approval or disapproval.

[The veto] violated the constitutional principle of separation of powers because it authorizes one House of Congress to participate in the execution of a previously enacted law.

The House and Senate, which had become parties to the suit, responded this way:

The Constitution provides separately for each of the three Branches, and describes each Branch as vested with the respective functions of legislating, executing, and judging. But the Constitution does not say that the three great func-

62. Ibid., 947.

tions shall at all times be kept separate and independent of each other, or that the three functions can never be blended or mixed or delegated as among the three Branches. The notion of total separation of the powers "central or essential" to the operation of the three great departments is an illogical and impractical formulation of the separation doctrine, not a constitutional command.

They also noted that the legislative veto was a "pragmatic" and necessary device reflecting the realities of modern government.

The Court apparently had some difficulty ferreting through these claims. After the first round of oral arguments, on the last day of the term, it ordered new arguments, which were held on the first day of the following term. But it took the Court until June 23—virtually the end of the term—to issue its decision.

CHIEF JUSTICE BURGER delivered the opinion of the Court.

We granted certiorari [to consider] the constitutionality of the provision in § 244(c)(2) of the Immigration and Nationality Act, authorizing one House of Congress, by resolution, to invalidate the decision of the Executive Branch, pursuant to authority delegated by Congress to the Attorney General of the United States, to allow a particular deportable alien to remain in the United States. . . .

. . . We begin, of course, with the presumption that the challenged statute is valid. Its wisdom is not the concern of the courts; if a challenged action does not violate the Constitution, it must be sustained. . . .

By the same token, the fact that a given law or procedure is efficient, convenient, and useful in facilitating functions of government, standing alone, will not save it if it is contrary to the Constitution. Convenience and efficiency are not the primary objectives—the hallmarks—of democratic government and our inquiry is sharpened rather than blunted by the fact that congressional veto provisions are appearing with increasing frequency in statutes which delegate authority to executive and independent agencies. . . .

Justice White undertakes to make a case for the proposition that the one-House veto is a useful "political invention," and we need not challenge that assertion. . . . But

policy arguments supporting even useful "political inventions" are subject to the demands of the Constitution which defines powers and . . . sets out just how those powers are to be exercised.

Explicit and unambiguous provisions of the Constitution prescribe and define the respective functions of the Congress and of the Executive in the legislative process. . . .

Just as we relied on the textual provision of Art II, § 2, cl 2, to vindicate the principle of separation of powers in Buckley [v. Valeo, 1976], we see that the purposes underlying the Presentment Clauses, Art I, § 7, cls 2, 3, and the bicameral requirement of Art I, § 1, and § 7, cl 2, guide our resolution of the important question present in these cases. . . .

The records of the Constitutional Convention reveal that the requirement that all legislation be presented to the President before becoming law was uniformly accepted by the Framers. Presentment to the President and the Presidential veto were considered so imperative that the draftsmen took special pains to assure that these requirements could not be circumvented. . . .

The decision to provide the President with a limited and qualified power to nullify proposed legislation by veto was based on the profound conviction of the Framers that the powers conferred on Congress were the powers to be most carefully circumscribed. It is beyond doubt that lawmaking was a power to be shared by both Houses and the President. . . .

The bicameral requirement of Art I, §§ 1, 7, was of scarcely less concern to the Framers than was the Presidential veto and indeed the two concepts are interdependent. By providing that no law could take effect without the concurrence of the prescribed majority of the Members of both Houses, the Framers reemphasized their belief . . . that legislation should not be enacted unless it has been carefully and fully considered by the Nation's elected officials. . . .

We see therefore that the Framers were acutely conscious that the bicameral requirement and the Presentment Clauses would serve essential constitutional functions. The President's participation in the legislative process was to protect the Executive Branch from Congress and to protect the whole people from improvident laws. The division of the Congress into two distinctive bodies assures that the legislative power would be exercised only after opportunity for full study and debate in separate settings. The President's unilateral veto power, in turn, was limited by the power of two-thirds of both Houses of Congress to overrule a veto thereby precluding final arbitrary action of one person. It emerges clearly that the prescription for legislative action in Art I, §§ 1, 7, represents the Framers' decision that the legislative power of the Federal Government be exercised in accord with a single, finely wrought and exhaustively considered, procedure. . . .

Examination of the action taken here by one House pursuant to § 244(c)(2) reveals that it was essentially legislative in purpose and effect. In purporting to exercise power defined in Art I, § 8, cl 4, to "establish an uniform Rule of Naturalization," the House took action that had the purpose and effect of altering the legal rights, duties, and relations of persons, including the Attorney General, Executive Branch officials and Chadha, all outside the Legislative Branch. . . .

The legislative character of the one-House veto in these cases is confirmed by the character of the congressional action it supplants. Neither the House of Representatives nor the Senate contends that, absent the veto provision in § 244(c)(2), either one of them, or both of them acting together, could effectively require the Attorney General to deport an alien once the Attorney General, in the exercise of legislatively delegated authority, had determined the alien should remain in the United States. Without the challenged provision in § 244(c)(2), this could have been achieved, if at all, only by legislation requiring deportation. Similarly, a veto by one House of Congress . . . cannot be justified as an attempt at amending the standards set out in § 244(c)(2), or as a repeal of § 244 as applied to Chadha. Amendment and repeal of statutes, no less than enactment, must conform with Art I.

The nature of the decision implemented by the one-House veto in these cases further manifests its legislative character. . . . Congress made a deliberate choice to delegate to the Executive Branch . . . the authority to allow deportable aliens to remain in this country in certain specified circumstances. Congress must abide by its delegation of authority until that delegation is legislatively altered or revoked. . . .

Since it is clear that the action by the House . . . was an exercise of legislative power, that action was subject to the standards prescribed in Art I. . . . To accomplish what has been attempted by one House of Congress in this case requires action in conformity with the express procedures of the Constitution's prescription for legislative action: passage by a majority of both Houses and presentment to the President.

The veto authorized by § 244(c)(2) doubtless has been in many respects a convenient shortcut; the "sharing" with the Executive by Congress of its authority over aliens in this manner is, on its face, an appealing compromise. In purely practical terms, it is obviously easier for action to be taken by one House without submission to the President; but it is crystal clear from the records of the Convention, contemporaneous writings and debates, that the Framers ranked other values higher than efficiency. . . .

The choices we discern as having been made in the Constitutional Convention impose burdens on governmental processes that often seem clumsy, inefficient, even unworkable, but those hard choices were consciously made by men who had lived under a form of government that permitted arbitrary governmental acts to go unchecked. There is no support in the Constitution or decisions of this Court for the proposition that the cumbersomeness and delays often encountered in complying with explicit constitutional standards may be avoided, either by the Congress or by the President. With all the obvious flaws of delay, untidiness, and potential for abuse, we have not yet found a better way to preserve freedom than by making the exercise of power subject to the carefully crafted restraints spelled out in the Constitution.

We hold that the congressional veto provision . . . is severable from the Act and that it is unconstitutional.

JUSTICE WHITE, dissenting.

Today the Court not only invalidates § 244(c)(2) of the Immigration and Nationality Act, but also sounds the death knell for nearly 200 other statutory provisions in which Congress has reserved a "legislative veto." For this reason, the Court's decision is of surpassing importance. And it is for this reason that the Court would have been well advised to decide the cases, if possible, on the narrower grounds of separation of powers, leaving for full consideration the constitutionality of other congressional review statutes operating on such varied matters as war powers

BOX 4-7   RECENT SEPARATION OF POWERS CASES

During the 1970s and 1980s the Supreme Court found itself unusually busy reviewing acts of Congress that were challenged as infringing on the separation of powers implicit in the Constitution. More often than not, the Court agreed with the challenge and struck down the law as infringing too far on the sphere of the executive or the courts.

The Court's decision in these cases included:

—*Buckley v. Valeo* (424 U.S. 1, 1976). The 1974 Federal Election Campaign Act Amendments infringed executive power by giving Congress the power to appoint four of the five members of the Federal Election Commission, which would enforce the law.

—*Nixon v. General Services Administration* (433 U.S. 425, 1977). The Presidential Recordings and Materials Preservation Act of 1974, placing the papers and tapes of the Nixon administration in federal custody, did not violate the separation of powers.

—*Bowsher v. Synar, United States Senate v. Synar, O'Neill v. Synar* (478 U.S. 714, 1986). Congress infringed too far on the prerogatives of the president when it included in the 1985 Balanced Budget and Emergency Deficit Control Act a provision giving the comptroller general, an officer removable from office only at the initiative of Congress, the power to tell the president where to cut federal spending.

—*Morrison v. Olson* (487 U.S. 654, 1988). The 1978 Ethics in Government Act did not usurp executive power when it authorized a panel of judges to appoint independent prosecutors to investigate charges of misconduct by high government officials.

One explanation for the increase in this kind of litigation during the 1970s and 1980s centers on the fact that this was largely a period of divided government, meaning that the president and Congress were of different political parties. Still, even when President Clinton and Congress were both Democratic they had their share of squabbles. Some of these had been leftovers from previous administrations but had implications for the Clinton presidency. For example, in *Dalton v. Specter* (1994), the Court considered a challenge, launched by Sen. Arlen Specter, R-Pa., to a 1991 decision, reached by an independent commission and finalized by the Bush administration, to close a Philadelphia naval base. By the time the case reached the Supreme Court, the battle pitted Specter against the Clinton administration, which supported the base-closing law under issue in *Dalton*. In fact, when the Court agreed with the administration's argument (that congressional law had not contemplated judicial review of base-closing decisions), the press reported that President Clinton had won a major victory.

Dalton will not be the only legislative-executive battle of the 1990s. The Court has already agreed to decide another one, this time involving the composition of the Federal Elections Commission. In *FEC v. National Rifle Association Political Victory Fund*, the justices will determine if the separation of powers doctrine is violated when an executive agency (the FEC) includes two employees of Congress (the secretary of the Senate and the clerk of the House) as nonvoting members.

SOURCE: Excerpted from Elder Witt, *Guide to the U.S. Supreme Court*, 2d ed. (Washington, D.C.: Congressional Quarterly, 1990), 65; and Holly Idelson and Pat Towell, "House and Supreme Court Take Hands-Off Stance," *Congressional Quarterly Weekly Report*, May 28,

and agency rulemaking, some of which concern the independent regulatory agencies.

The prominence of the legislative veto mechanism in our contemporary political system and its importance to Congress can hardly be overstated. It has become a central means by which Congress secures the accountability of executive and independent agencies. Without the legislative

veto, Congress is faced with a Hobson's choice: either to refrain from delegating the necessary authority, leaving itself with a hopeless task of writing laws with the requisite specificity to cover endless special circumstances across the entire policy landscape, or in the alternative, to abdicate its lawmaking function to the Executive Branch and independent agencies. To choose the former leaves major national problems unresolved; to opt for the latter risks unaccountable policymaking by those not elected to fill that role. Accordingly, over the past five decades, the legislative veto has been placed in nearly 200 statutes. The device is known in every field of governmental concern: reorganization, budgets, foreign affairs, war powers, and regulation of trade, safety, energy, the environment, and the economy. . . .

I do not suggest that all legislative vetoes are necessarily consistent with separation-of-powers principles. A legislative check on an inherently executive function . . . poses an entirely different question. But the legislative veto device here—and in many other settings—is far from an instance of legislative tyranny over the Executive. It is a necessary check on the unavoidably expanding power of the agencies, both Executive and independent, as they engage in exercising authority delegated by Congress.

I regret that I am in disagreement with my colleagues on the fundamental questions that these cases present. But even more I regret the destructive scope of the Court's holding. It reflects a profoundly different conception of the Constitution than that held by the courts which sanctioned the modern administrative state. Today's decision strikes down in one fell swoop provisions in more laws enacted by Congress than the Court has cumulatively invalidated in its history. I fear it will now be more difficult to "insur[e] that the fundamental policy decisions in our society will be made not by an appointed official but by the body immediately responsible to the people," Arizona v. California (1963) (Harlan, J., dissenting in part). I must dissent.

In theory, the Court banished legislative vetoes from the government system because they undermined the spirit and letter of the Constitution. In practice, however, the Court's decision had a negligible effect on congressional-executive relations. Since Chadha, Congress has passed more than 200 new laws containing legislative vetoes. But even more important is that the practice continues even in the absence of specific legislation—agencies and departments still pay heed to congressional rejections of policy.[63]

Why has the Court's opinion resulted in such blatant noncompliance? More to the point, why do executive agencies and departments continue to respect the wishes of Congress, even though they need not? One reason is purely pragmatic: because departments and agencies depend on Congress for fiscal support, they relent out of "fear of budgetary retaliation."[64] Another reason was implied by Justice White in his dissenting opinion: Chadha "did not, and could not, eliminate the conditions that gave rise to the legislative veto: the desire of executive officials for broad delegations of power, and the insistence of Congress that it control those delegations without having to pass another public law."[65]

In this particular instance, then, the president may have won the battle, but surely lost the war, as the legislative veto continues to operate. Perhaps the U.S. Supreme Court was the biggest loser: its decision offered a "solution" that was obviously "unacceptable to the political branches" and, as result, will continue to "be eroded by open defiance and subtle evasion."[66] But, as we shall see in the next chapter and as touched on in Box 4-7, in many other separation of powers cases in which the president has sought to assert his power over Congress, the Court has ruled for one side over the other, and has done so authoritatively. As you read the cases in Chapter 5, think about the difference between them and Chadha. Why is it that in some instances Congress and the president accept the authority of the Court, but in others—like Chadha—they pay no heed?

READINGS

Barber, Sotirios A. *The Constitution and the Delegation of Congressional Power*. Chicago: University of Chicago Press, 1975.

Craig, Barbara H. Chadha: *The Story of an Epic Constitutional Struggle*. New York: Oxford University Press, 1988.

---

63. Louis Fisher, "The Legislative Veto: Invalidated, It Survives," *Law and Contemporary Problems* 56 (1993): 288.

64. Urofsky, *A March of Liberty*, 948.

65. Fisher, *American Constitutional Law*, 231. For another perspective on this case, see William N. Eskridge, Jr., and John Ferejohn, "The Article I, Section 7 Game," *Georgetown Law Journal* 80 (1992): 523–563.

66. Ibid., 281.

Elliott, Ward E. Y. *The Rise of Guardian Democracy: The Supreme Court's Role in Voting Rights Disputes, 1845–1969.* Cambridge, Mass.: Harvard University Press, 1974.

Eskridge, William N., Jr., and John Ferejohn. "The Article I, Section 7 Game." *Georgetown Law Journal* 80 (1992): 523–563.

Goodman, Walter. *The Committee: The Extraordinary Career of the House Committee on Un-American Activities.* New York: Farrar, Straus and Giroux, 1968.

Henkin, Louis. *Foreign Affairs and the Constitution.* New York: W. W. Norton, 1975.

Ignagni, Joseph, and James Meernik. "Explaining Congressional Attempts to Reverse Supreme Court Decisions." *Political Research Quarterly* 47 (1994): 353–371.

Irons, Peter H. *The New Deal Lawyers.* Princeton, N.J.: Princeton University Press, 1982.

Katzmann, Robert A., ed. *Judges and Legislators: Toward Institutional Comity.* Washington, D.C.: Brookings Institution, 1988.

Murphy, Walter F. *Congress and the Court.* Chicago: University of Chicago Press, 1962.

Pritchett, C. Herman. *Congress Versus the Supreme Court, 1957–1960.* Minneapolis: University of Minnesota Press, 1961.

Schmidhauser, John R., and Larry L. Berg. *The Supreme Court and Congress.* New York: Free Press, 1972.

CHAPTER 5
THE EXECUTIVE

T HE FRAMERS would have great trouble recognizing today's presidency. The sentiment of the Philadelphia Convention was that the Articles of Confederation were flawed because they did not provide for an executive, but few delegates would have approved of the extent of the powers wielded by our modern presidents. After suffering under the British monarch, many delegates had serious reservations about awarding too much authority to the executive branch. Those who supported the New Jersey Plan even envisioned a plural executive arrangement under which two individuals would share the chief executive position so that excessive power would not accrue to a single person. The Framers would be astonished at the vast military resources over which the president serves as commander in chief, to say nothing of the hundreds of departments, agencies, and bureaus that constitute the executive branch.

The rather loose wording of Article II has permitted this amazing growth in the presidency. The article has neither the detail nor the precision of the Framers' Article I description of the legislature; instead, it is dominated by issues of selection and removal, and less attention is devoted to powers and limitations. The wording is quite broad. For example, presidents are given the undefined "executive power" of the United States and are admonished to take care that the laws are "faithfully executed." Other grants of authority, such as the president's role as "Commander in Chief of the Army and Navy" and the preferential position given the chief executive in matters of foreign policy, allow for significant expansion.

The presidency also has grown in response to the world's changing conditions. Over the years American society has increased in complexity, and the number of matters that require government action has mushroomed. Because Congress has been overwhelmed by the nation's demands, the legislature has delegated to the executive branch authority that was not anticipated by the Framers. In addition, the expanding importance of defense and foreign policy has demanded a more powerful presidency.

As these changes took place, the Supreme Court frequently was called upon to referee disputes over the constitutional limits of executive authority. The Court's decisions have contributed significantly to the way the presidency has evolved, allowing considerable growth in authority and yet imposing necessary restraints.

SELECTION AND FORMAL POWERS

In Article II the Framers developed a novel way to select the chief executive. Until then the executives of most nations were chosen by bloodline, military power, or legislative selection. No other country had experimented with a system like the electoral college apparatus created at the Philadelphia Convention. Perhaps because it had never been tried, the system was plagued with defects that required correction over time.

Presidential Selection and Constitutional Change

The Framers designed the electoral college system to allow the general electorate to have some influence on the selection of the chief executive without resorting to direct popular election. The original blueprint called for each state to select presidential electors equal in number to the state's delegates to the Senate and House of Representatives. The Constitution empowered the state legislatures to decide the method of choosing the electors. Popular election was always the most common method, but in the past some state legislatures voted for the electors. Article II disqualifies those who hold federal office, but otherwise there are no specified qualifications for being an elector. The electoral college system was based on the theory that the states would select their most qualified citizens, who would exercise their best judgment in the selection of the president.

The Constitution mentions only three qualifications for presidential eligibility—citizenship, age, and residency. First, Article II requires that only individuals who are natural-born citizens may become president.[1] Naturalized citizens—those who attain citizenship after birth—may not hold the nation's highest office. Second, to be president a person must have reached the age of thirty-five. Third, the president must have been a resident of the United

States for fourteen years. Although the original version of the Constitution made no mention of qualifications for vice president, this oversight was corrected with the 1804 ratification of the Twelfth Amendment, which said that no person could serve as vice president who was not eligible to be president.

Under the original procedures set forth in Article II, the electors were to assemble in their respective state capitals on election day and cast votes for their presidential preferences. Each elector had two votes, no more than one of which could be cast for a candidate from the elector's home state. The states' votes were sent to the federal capital, where the president of the Senate opened them. The candidate who received the most votes would be declared president, provided that the number of votes received was a majority of the number of electors. Article II anticipated two possible problems with this procedure. First, because the electors each cast two votes, it was possible for the balloting to result in a tie between two candidates. In this event, the Constitution stipulated that the House of Representatives should select one of the two. Second, if multiple candidates sought the presidency, it would be possible for no candidate to receive the required majority. In this case the House was to decide among the top five finishers in the electoral college voting. In settling such disputed elections, each state delegation was to cast a single vote, rather than allowing the individual members to vote independently.

In the original scheme the vice president was selected right after the president. The formula for choosing the vice president was simple—the vice president was the presidential candidate who received the second highest number of electoral votes. If two or more candidates tied for second in the electoral college voting, the Senate would select the vice president from among them.

The first two elections took place with no difficulty. In 1789 George Washington received one ballot from each of the 69 electors who participated and was elected president. John Adams became vice president be-

---

1. The Constitution also allowed individuals who were citizens at the time the Constitution was adopted to be eligible to hold the presidency.

cause he got the next highest number of electoral votes (34). History repeated itself in the election of 1792, with Washington receiving one vote from each of the 132 electors. Adams again gathered the next highest number of votes (77) and returned to the vice presidency.

The first defects in the electoral system became apparent with the election of 1796. By this time political parties had begun to develop, and this election was a contest between the incumbent Federalists and the Democratic-Republicans. With Washington declining to run for a third term, John Adams became the candidate of the Federalists, and Thomas Jefferson was the choice of those who wanted political change. When the ballots were counted, Adams had won the presidency with seventy-one electoral votes; Jefferson, with sixty-eight, became vice president. For the first time, the nation had a divided executive branch, with the president and vice president of different political parties.

Matters got even worse with the 1800 election. The Democratic-Republicans were now the more popular of the two major parties, and they backed Jefferson for president and Aaron Burr for vice president. The electors committed to the Democratic-Republican party candidates each cast one ballot for Jefferson and one for Burr. Although it was clear which man was running for which office, the method of selection did not allow for such distinctions. The result was that Jefferson and Burr each received seventy-three votes, and the election moved to the House of Representatives for settlement. Each of the sixteen states had a single vote, and a majority was required for election. On February 11, 1801, the first vote in the House was taken. Jefferson received eight votes, Burr six. Two states, Maryland and Vermont, were unable to register a preference because their state delegations were evenly divided. Votes continued to be taken over the next several days, until finally, on February 17, after thirty-six ballots, Jefferson received the support of ten

state delegations and was named president, with Burr becoming vice president.

It was clear that the Constitution had to be changed to avoid such situations. Congress proposed the Twelfth Amendment in 1803, and the states ratified it the next year. The amendment altered the selection system by separating the offices of president and vice president. Rather than casting two votes for president, electors would vote for a presidential candidate and then vote separately for a vice presidential candidate. The House and Senate continued to settle presidential and vice presidential elections in which no candidate received a majority, although the procedures for such elections also were modified by the amendment.

Presidential and vice presidential elections are still governed by the Twelfth Amendment. However, the evolution of political parties and the reduction in the degree of independence exercised by presidential electors have resulted in huge changes in the way the system operates. The electoral college persists, although there has always been considerable support for replacing it with direct popular election. Proponents of this reform have never achieved enough strength to prompt Congress or the state legislatures to propose the necessary constitutional amendment. Historically, opposition to popular election has come from the smaller states, which enjoy more influence within the electoral college system than they would under popular election reforms.

Tenure and Succession

The Constitution sets the presidential term at four years. Originally, there was no restriction on the number of terms a president could serve; George Washington began the tradition of a two-term limit when he announced at the end of his second administration that he would not run again. This tradition was honored by every president until Franklin Roosevelt sought election to a third term in 1940 and further vi-

President Lyndon B. Johnson, surrounded by congressional leaders, signing the Twenty-fifth Amendment on February 23, 1967. The Amendment authorized the president to nominate a new vice president when a vacancy in that office occurred and also provided for an orderly transition of authority should the president become disabled. At the time, the vice presidency was vacant. If Johnson had died or become disabled, seventy-four-year-old Speaker John McCormack (far right) would have assumed the presidency. Next in line of succession was president pro tempore of the Senate, eighty-eight-year-old Carl Hayden (third from left, standing).

olated the custom by running for a fourth term in 1944. In reaction, Congress proposed the Twenty-second Amendment, which held that no person could run for president after having served more than six years in that office. The states ratified the amendment in 1951.

If an incumbent president or vice president abuses the office, the Constitution provides for impeachment as the method of removal. Impeachment is a two-stage process. First, the House of Representatives investigates the charges against the incumbent. The Constitution stipulates that impeachment can occur only upon charges of "Treason, Bribery, or other High Crimes and Misdemeanors." Once convinced that there is sufficient evidence of such misconduct, the House passes articles of impeachment specifying the crimes charged and authorizing a trial. The second stage, the trial, takes place in the Senate, but the chief justice of the United States presides. Conviction requires the agreement of two-thirds of the voting sena-

tors. Congress can impose no penalties on a convicted official other than removal from office. However, the officeholder may still be subject to a separate criminal prosecution in the courts. No president has been removed from office by Congress, although two barely escaped such a fate. Andrew Johnson was impeached by the House in 1868, but he survived his trial in the Senate by one vote; and Richard Nixon was well on his way to being impeached in 1974 when he resigned from office.

Eight other sitting presidents failed to complete their terms. Four (William Henry Harrison, Zachary Taylor, Warren G. Harding, and Franklin Roosevelt) died of natural causes, and four (Abraham Lincoln, James A. Garfield, William McKinley, and John F. Kennedy) were assassinated. The Framers provided in Article II that in the event of the president's death or disability, the vice president assumes the powers and responsibilities of the office. In section 1 of Article II, the Constitution authorizes Congress to determine

BOX 5-1   LINE OF SUCCESSION

O N MARCH 30, 1981, President Ronald Reagan was shot by would-be assassin John Hinckley outside a Washington hotel and rushed to an area hospital for surgery. Vice President George Bush was on a plane returning to Washington from Texas. Presidential aides and cabinet members gathered at the White House, where questions arose among them and the press corps about who was "in charge."[1] Secretary of State Alexander M. Haig, Jr., rushed to the press briefing room and, before an audience of reporters and live television cameras, said, "As of now, I am in control here in the White House, pending the return of the vice president. . . . Constitutionally, gentlemen, you have the president, the vice president, and the secretary of state."

Haig was, as many gleeful critics subsequently pointed out, wrong. The Constitution says nothing about who follows the vice president in the line of succession. The Succession Act of 1947 (later modified to reflect the creation of new departments) establishes congressional leaders and the heads of the departments, in the order the departments were created, as filling the line of succession that follows the vice president.

The line of succession is:

vice president
Speaker of the House of Representatives
president pro tempore of the Senate
secretary of state
secretary of the Treasury
secretary of defense
attorney general
secretary of the interior
secretary of agriculture

secretary of commerce
secretary of labor
secretary of health and human services
secretary of housing and urban development
secretary of transportation
secretary of energy
secretary of education
secretary of veterans affairs

A different "line"—not of succession to the presidency, but of National Command Authority in situations of wartime emergency—was created according to the National Security Act of 1947. The command rules are detailed in secret presidential orders that each new president signs at the outset of the term. Among other things, the orders authorize the secretary of defense to act as commander in chief in certain specific, limited situations in which neither the president nor the vice president is available. Presumably, such situations would follow a nuclear attack on Washington.

1. "Confusion over Who Was in Charge Arose Following Reagan Shooting," *Wall Street Journal*, April 1, 1981.

SOURCE: *Guide to the Presidency*, ed. Michael Nelson (Washington, D.C.: Congressional Quarterly, 1989), 339.

presidential succession if there is no sitting vice president when a vacancy occurs.

In 1965 Congress recommended some additional changes in the Constitution to govern presidential succession. The need became apparent after Lyndon Johnson assumed the presidency following Kennedy's assassination in 1963. Johnson's ascension left the vice presidency vacant. If anything had happened to Johnson, the federal succession law dictated that next in

line was the Speaker of the House, followed by the president pro tempore of the Senate *(see Box 5-1)*. In 1965 the Speaker was John McCormack, D-Mass., who was seventy-four years old, and the president of the Senate was Carl Hayden, D-Ariz., who was eighty-eight. Neither was capable of handling the demands of the presidency. Congress proposed that the Constitution be amended to provide that when a vacancy occurs in the office of vice president, the president nominates a new vice president who takes office upon confirmation by majority vote in both houses of Congress. The proposal also clarified procedures governing those times when a president is temporarily unable to carry out the duties of the office. The change was ratified by the states as the Twenty-fifth Amendment in 1967.

It was not long before the country needed the procedures outlined in the Twenty-fifth Amendment. In 1973 Vice President Spiro Agnew resigned when he was charged with income tax evasion stemming from alleged corruption during his years as governor of Maryland. Nixon nominated, and Congress confirmed, Rep. Gerald R. Ford of Michigan to become vice president. Just one year later, Nixon resigned the presidency, and Ford became the nation's first unelected chief executive. Ford selected Nelson Rockefeller, former governor of New York, to fill the new vacancy in the vice presidency.

Constitutional Powers

Despite the constitutional changes dealing with presidential selection and succession, the president's formal powers are the same today as when they were drafted by the Philadelphia Convention. Those formal grants of authority fall into four categories.

General Executive Powers
  To execute and enforce the laws
  To appoint and remove executive branch officials
Military and Foreign Policy Powers
  To be commander in chief of the armed forces
  To appoint ambassadors
  To receive foreign ambassadors
  To make treaties
Powers Related to the Legislative Branch
  To veto bills passed by Congress
  To convene special sessions of Congress
  To advise Congress on the state of the nation

Powers Related to the Judicial Branch
  To appoint federal judges
  To grant pardons to those convicted of federal crimes

These formal grants of authority form the constitutional basis of presidential power, but many of the specific provisions conferring executive power are vaguely worded and open to interpretation. In the course of American history, the struggle for political power among the three branches of government has led to many legal disputes over the nature and extent of presidential authority, and it has fallen to the Supreme Court to determine the contours of presidential power. This chapter examines the constitutional disputes that have shaped the presidency.

THE FAITHFUL EXECUTION OF THE LAWS

At the heart of executive power is the enforcement of the law; Article II, Section 3, states that the president shall be given the responsibility to "take Care that the Laws be faithfully executed." Undoubtedly, the Take Care Clause means that the provisions of the Constitution and the laws enacted by Congress are entrusted to the president for administration and enforcement. Presidents may use the substantial powers of the executive branch to see that the law is followed.

The Constitution obliges the president to enforce all the laws, not just those the administration supports. While a number of presidents have been criticized for failing to carry out certain laws enthusiastically, it would be difficult to prove that the chief executive had not satisfied the constitutional mandate of faithful execution. On rare occasions, however, a president has openly refused to execute a law validly passed by Congress. In such cases court challenges are to be expected.

What happened when Congress passed the Federal

Water Pollution Control Act Amendments of 1972 over President Nixon's veto is a good illustration. The act made federal money available to local governments for sewers and clean water projects. After losing the legislative battle, the president instructed the appropriate officials of his administration not to allot to local governments the full funds authorized by Congress.

New York City, which expected to be a recipient of these funds, filed suit against Russell Train, head of the Environmental Protection Agency, to force the administration to release the impounded money. In interpreting the legislation, the Supreme Court in *Train v. City of New York* (1975) found no congressional grant of discretion to the executive that would allow the president to decide how much of the appropriated money to allocate. In the absence of such a grant, the president's obligation was to carry out the terms of the statute. The Court held that the funds must be distributed according to the intent of Congress. Faithful execution of the laws requires the executive branch to enforce and administer the policies enacted by the legislature even if the president opposes them.

The Constitution unambiguously gives the president the responsibility and authority to enforce the laws. But is this power given exclusively to the president, or may the other branches also exercise enforcement? This question has been at the root of several important battles between Congress and the president.

One of the more important and controversial of these disputes evolved into the case of *Bowsher v. Synar* (1986). The suit involved a challenge to the constitutionality of certain provisions of the Balanced Budget and Emergency Deficit Control Act of 1985, better known as the Gramm-Rudman-Hollings Act, which President Reagan signed into law December 12, 1985. The legislation attempted to control the federal budget deficit by imposing automatic budget cuts when members of Congress were unable or unwilling to ex-

ercise sufficient fiscal restraint. The law established maximum budget deficit levels for each year beginning in 1986. The size of the deficit was to decrease each year until fiscal 1991 when no deficit would be allowed. If the federal budget deficit in any year exceeded the maximum allowed, across-the-board budget cuts would automatically be imposed.

Triggering the cuts involved steps to be taken by several government officials. First, the director of the Office of Management and Budget (OMB) and the director of the Congressional Budget Office (CBO) would independently estimate the projected deficit, with program-by-program calculations. Second, these estimates would be jointly reported to the comptroller general of the United States. Third, the comptroller general would review the reports submitted by OMB and CBO and issue a final report with recommendations. Fourth, the comptroller general would send the report to the president, who would issue an order mandating the automatic budget cuts recommended by the comptroller.

The statute's reliance on the comptroller general for the execution of this law presented a potential constitutional problem. The comptroller general heads the General Accounting Office (GAO), an agency created by Congress in 1921 to provide independent audits of the financial activities of executive agencies. The GAO, however, is located within the legislative branch, and the comptroller general, although appointed by the president, is an employee of Congress, not the White House. Under traditional views of the separation of powers, no legislative officer may exercise executive authority.

Just hours after the bill was signed, Rep. Mike Synar, D-Okla., who had voted against it, filed suit against Comptroller General Charles A. Bowsher to have the law declared unconstitutional. A three-judge district court struck down the statutory provisions that permitted an enforcement role for the comptroller general.

The Supreme Court agreed that the statute was defective. Important to the justices' decision was the fact that the comptroller general is a legislative officer. The organization of the national government clearly places the office under the authority of Congress. The legislative branch makes laws but does not enforce them. That function is the duty of the executive branch.

Once Congress makes its choice in enacting laws, its participation ends. Thereafter, Congress can only control the execution of the law indirectly—by passing new legislation. As a member of the legislative branch, the comptroller general is restricted by these limitations. To the extent that the Balanced Budget and Emergency Deficit Control Act gave enforcement powers to the comptroller general, it is unconstitutional. The execution and enforcement of the law must be left to the executive branch.

The *Bowsher* decision supplied an authoritative declaration of the boundaries between legislative and executive authority and, as such, provided guidelines for the future. The decision, however, had little impact on the legislation. Congress, anticipating the constitutional challenge, had written into the law certain "fallback" mechanisms to enforce the budget restrictions if any part of the original plan failed a constitutional challenge. This secondary plan removed the comptroller general from any enforcement activity, and the Supreme Court allowed this procedure to become operative.

EXECUTIVE IMMUNITY AND PRIVILEGE

At the center of the checks and balances philosophy is the debate over how far the other branches of government can intrude into executive affairs. The problems flowing from this issue divide into two related categories: immunity and privilege.

Protecting the President from Lawsuit

Immunity deals with the extent to which the president is protected from lawsuits while in office, and the subject raises many interesting questions. May a president be ordered by a court to carry out certain executive actions, which are discretionary, or ministerial actions, which are performed as a matter of legal duty? Or, conversely, may a president be restrained by a court from taking such actions? May a private party sue the president for damages that might have been suffered because of the president's actions or omissions? If so, may a court order the president to pay damages or provide some other restitution? These questions place us in quandary. To grant the president immunity from such legal actions may remove needed accountability. But to allow the chief executive to be subject to suit could make the execution of presidential duties impossible.

The Supreme Court's first significant venture into the area of executive immunity came in the aftermath of the Civil War in *Mississippi v. Johnson* (1867). Following the Civil War, Congress passed a number of laws "for the more efficient government of the rebel states." More commonly known as the Reconstruction Acts, they imposed military rule over the southern states until such time as loyal republican governments could be established. Andrew Johnson, a southerner from Tennessee, who had assumed the presidency after Lincoln's assassination, vetoed the legislation, but the Radical Republicans in Congress had sufficient votes to override him. Once the acts were part of federal law, the president had little choice but to enforce them, despite his belief that they were unconstitutional.

The state of Mississippi joined the fray. Applying directly to the Supreme Court, Mississippi sued Johnson, asking the justices to issue an order prohibiting him from enforcing the laws, which the state argued were unconstitutional.

The Supreme Court rejected Mississippi's petition.

The Court drew the distinction between ministerial and executive actions. A ministerial act is one over which there is no discretion. It occurs when a statute clearly directs the performance of a specific act. An executive act, on the other hand, is one that allows discretion. The enforcement of a statute, such as the Reconstruction Act, is undoubtedly an executive action. A president enforces a law using judgment and discretion. It is not a simple ministerial act, but one that involves a number of political and administrative decisions. The judiciary is without power to enjoin the president in carrying out his executive authority. This stems not only from the separation of power principle, but also as a practical matter. If the courts enjoined the president and he refused to comply, how would the judiciary enforce its order? The Court concluded, as Chief Justice Chase wrote, ". . . this court has no jurisdiction of a bill to enjoin the President in the performance of his official duties."

While the decision in *Johnson* settles the issue of whether the president may be personally sued with respect to executive functions, it does not answer the question of civil suits brought by private individuals who have been harmed by a president's actions. If an incumbent president engages in unlawful activities that harm private individuals, can the president be held accountable in a court of law? Or is the president immune from such suits?

These questions were answered by the Court in *Nixon v. Fitzgerald* (1982). This legal action was initiated by A. Ernest Fitzgerald, who had been employed as a civilian management analyst for the U.S. Air Force. Fitzgerald blew the whistle in congressional testimony on some $2 billion in cost overruns for the development of the C-5A transport plane. His testimony was not well received by the Defense Department or military contractors. Thirteen months later Fitzgerald lost his job in what Defense officials claimed was a necessary departmental reorganization. Fitzgerald, however, believed the elimination of his job was an illegal re-

taliation for his congressional testimony. He was able to gather some evidence to support his claim, including Richard Nixon's admission that the president was aware of the firing and approved it. Fitzgerald sued a number of executive branch officials, including the president (who resigned during the early stages of the lower court proceedings). The former president's lawyers asserted that he should be removed from the suit on the grounds of absolute executive immunity from legal actions based on his official conduct as president. The lower courts rejected the absolute immunity claim, and Nixon appealed.

By a 5–4 vote, the justices supported the president, and extended immunity from lawsuit to cases such as this. Justice Powell explained:

Because of the singular importance of the President's duties, diversion of his energies by concern with private lawsuits would raise unique risks to the effective functioning of government. . . . In view of the special nature of the President's constitutional office and functions, we think it appropriate to recognize absolute Presidential immunity from damages liability for acts within the "outer perimeter" of his official responsibility.

In spite of the decisions in *Mississippi v. Johnson* and *Nixon v. Fitzgerald*, presidential immunity issues continue to appear. In 1994, for example, Paula Jones, a former Arkansas state employee, filed suit against President Bill Clinton claiming that, while he was governor, he had made improper and illegal sexual advances toward her. In this case, the chief executive was charged in a civil suit with wrongdoing that allegedly occurred before he became president. Should the doctrine of immunity extend only to actions taken by presidents while in office? Clinton's attorneys argued that allowing such a suit to go forward would set a dangerous precedent. It would encourage individuals to file civil suits, regardless of merit, against a sitting president. The time and effort necessary to mount a defense could cripple the president's ability to carry out the duties of the office. At a minimum, Clinton argued, such suits should not be heard until after the president leaves office. Would the nation be better served if the president were spared the obligation of responding? Or does it violate principles of justice to bar individuals with legitimate legal claims from using the courts to seek legal redress? The trial court judge refused to dismiss the suit on executive immunity grounds, but did hold that the nature of the Presidency required the delay of the trial until after Clinton left office.

Protecting Presidential Confidentiality

Executive privilege is a variation on the notion that the president should be immune from liability for official acts. The privilege argument asserts that there are certain conversations, documents, and records that are so closely tied to the sensitive duties of the president that they should remain confidential. Neither the legislature nor the judiciary should be allowed access to these materials without presidential consent; nor should the other branches be empowered to compel the president to hand over such items. Matters concerning national security or foreign policy especially fall under this protection. Executive privilege, it is argued, is inherent to the office of the president.

Although infrequently invoked, the privilege doctrine has been part of American history since the beginning of the nation. In some early disputes between the president and Congress, chief executives refused to provide certain information to the legislature. George Washington balked at giving the House of Representatives certain documents pertaining to negotiations over the Jay Treaty. During the investigation and trial of Aaron Burr, Thomas Jefferson cooperated with congressional information requests, but only up to a point. He refused to produce some items and later declined to testify at the trial even though he was subpoenaed. Presidents through the years have refused to comply with congressional requests for testimony. It is generally accepted that Congress does not have the power to compel the president to come

before it to answer questions. Other executive department officials generally are not covered by claims of privilege.

In most instances, disputes over executive privilege are handled through negotiation between the executive branch and the institution requesting information. Only rarely have such disputes led to major court cases. When pushed to the limit, executive privilege claims rarely prevail, but when sensitive military or diplomatic matters requiring secrecy are involved, a president can expect to be on relatively safe ground in asserting executive privilege.

No case involving executive privilege has been more important than *United States v. Nixon* (1974). It occurred at a time of great constitutional stress, when all three branches were locked in a fight about fundamental separation of powers issues. The conflict ultimately was resolved when Nixon resigned. Much of the impetus for breaking the constitutional deadlock came from the unanimous decision of the justices in the *Nixon* case. Chief Justice Burger's opinion for the Court reviewed the issues surrounding the executive privilege controversy and then rejected Nixon's invocation of the doctrine.

===

United States v. Nixon

418 U.S. 683 (1974)
Vote: 8 *(Blackmun, Brennan, Burger, Douglas, Marshall, Powell, Stewart, White)*

0

Opinion of the Court: Burger
Not participating: Rehnquist

This case was one of many court actions spawned by the Watergate scandal. The controversy began on June 17, 1972, when seven men broke into the Democratic National Committee headquarters located in the Watergate complex in Washington, D.C. The seven were apprehended and charged with criminal offenses. All had ties either to the White House or to the

This subpoena *duces tecum* was issued July 23, 1973. It ordered President Nixon or his representatives to appear before the federal grand jury on July 26 and to bring taped conversations relevant to the investigation of the Watergate affair.

Committee to Re-elect the President. Five of the seven pleaded guilty, and two were convicted. At the end of the trial, one of the defendants, James McCord, Jr., claimed that he had been pressured to plead guilty and that there were others involved in the break-in who had not been prosecuted. It was clear to many that the break-in was only the tip of a very large iceberg of shady dealings and cover-ups engaged in by influential persons closely tied to the Nixon administration.

In response to these events, the Senate began an investigation of the Watergate incident and the activities related to it. The star witness was John Dean III, special counsel to the president, who testified under a grant of immunity. Dean implicated high officials in the president's office, and he claimed that Nixon had known about the events and the subsequent cover-ups. As surprising as this testimony was, the most shocking revelation was made by presidential aide Alexander Butterfield, who testified that the president

had installed a secret taping system that automatically recorded all conversations in the Oval Office. Obviously, the tape recordings held information that would settle the dispute between the witnesses claiming White House involvement in the Watergate affair and the denial issued by administration officials.

In addition to the Senate investigation, a special prosecutor was appointed to look into the Watergate affair. The first person to hold this position, Archibald Cox, asked Nixon to turn over the tapes. When Nixon declined, Cox went to court to get an order compelling him to deliver the materials. The district and appeals courts ruled in favor of the prosecutor. Nixon then offered to release summaries of the recordings, but that did not satisfy Cox, who continued to pursue the tapes. In response, Nixon ordered that Cox be fired. When the two highest officials in the Justice Department resigned rather than comply with the order, Solicitor General Robert Bork became the acting attorney general and dismissed Cox. The firing of the prosecutor, popularly known as the "Saturday Night Massacre," enraged the American people, and many began calling for the president's impeachment.

A new special prosecutor, Leon Jaworski, was appointed. The Houston attorney pursued the tapes with the same zeal as had Cox. Finally, Nixon relented and agreed to produce some of the materials. But when he did so, the prosecutor found that the tapes had been heavily edited. One contained eighteen and one-half minutes of mysterious buzzing at a crucial point, indicating that conversation had been erased.

Jaworski obtained criminal indictments against several Nixon aides. Although no criminal charges were brought against the president, he was named in the indictment as a co-conspirator. At about the same time, the House Judiciary Committee began an investigation into whether the president should be impeached.

Both the Judiciary Committee and Jaworski sought more of the tapes to review. Nixon steadfastly refused to comply, claiming that it was his right under executive privilege to decide what would be released and what would remain secret. The district court issued a final subpoena *duces tecum* (a judicial command to bring forth physical evidence); thus the president was ordered to produce the tapes and other documents. Both the United States and Nixon requested that the Supreme Court review the case, and the justices accepted the case on an expedited basis, bypassing the court of appeals.

MR. CHIEF JUSTICE BURGER delivered the opinion of the Court.

[W]e turn to the claim that the subpoena should be quashed because it demands "confidential conversations between a President and his close advisors that it would be inconsistent with the public interest to produce." The first contention is a broad claim that the separation of powers doctrine precludes judicial review of a President's claim of privilege. The second contention is that if he does not prevail on the claim of absolute privilege, the court should hold

as a matter of constitutional law that the privilege prevails over the subpoena *duces tecum*.

In the performance of assigned constitutional duties each branch of the Government must initially interpret the Constitution, and the interpretation of its powers by any branch is due great respect from the others. The President's counsel, as we have noted, reads the Constitution as providing an absolute privilege of confidentiality for all Presidential communications. Many decisions of this Court, however, have unequivocally reaffirmed the holding of *Marbury v. Madison* (1803) that "[i]t is emphatically the province and duty of the judicial department to say what the law is."

No holding of the Court has defined the scope of judicial power specifically relating to the enforcement of a subpoena for confidential Presidential communications for use in a criminal prosecution, but other exercises of power by the Executive Branch and the Legislative Branch have been found invalid as in conflict with the Constitution. *Powell v. McCormack* (1969); *Youngstown Sheet & Tube Co. v. Sawyer* (1952). . . . .

Notwithstanding the deference each branch must accord the others, the "judicial Power of the United States" vested in the federal courts by Art. III, § 1, of the Constitution can no more be shared with the Executive Branch than the Chief Executive, for example, can share with the Judiciary the veto power, or the Congress share with the Judiciary the power to override a Presidential veto. Any other conclusion would be contrary to the basic concept of separation of powers and the checks and balances that flow from the scheme of a tripartite government. We therefore reaffirm that it is the province and duty of this Court "to say what the law is" with respect to the claim of privilege presented in this case.

In support of his claim of absolute privilege, the President's counsel urges two grounds, one of which is common to all governments and one of which is peculiar to our system of separation of powers. The first ground is the valid need for protection of communications between high Government officials and those who advise and assist them in the performance of their manifold duties; the importance of this confidentiality is too plain to require further discussion. Human experience teaches that those who expect public dissemination of their remarks may well temper candor with a concern for appearances and for their own interests

This drawing illustrates Richard Nixon's attorney, James St. Clair, arguing the president's case before the Supreme Court in *United States v. Nixon* (1974). The four justices are (left to right): Chief Justice Warren Burger, William J. Brennan, Jr., Byron R. White, and Harry A. Blackmun.

to the detriment of the decisionmaking process. Whatever the nature of the privilege of confidentiality of Presidential communications in the exercise of Art. II powers, the privilege can be said to derive from the supremacy of each branch within its own assigned area of constitutional duties. Certain powers and privileges flow from the nature of enumerated powers; the protection of the confidentiality of Presidential communications has similar constitutional underpinnings.

The second ground asserted by the President's counsel in support of the claim of absolute privilege rests on the doctrine of separation of powers. Here it is argued that the independence of the Executive Branch within its own sphere insulates a President from a judicial subpoena in an ongoing criminal prosecution, and thereby protects confidential Presidential communications.

However, neither the doctrine of separation of powers, nor the need for confidentiality of high-level communications, without more, can sustain an absolute, unqualified Presidential privilege of immunity from judicial process under all circumstances. The President's need for complete candor and objectivity from advisers calls for great deference from the courts. However, when the privilege depends solely on the broad, undifferentiated claim of public interest in the confidentiality of such conversations, a confrontation with other values arises. Absent a claim of need to protect military, diplomatic, or sensitive national security secrets, we find it difficult to accept the argument that even the very important interest in confidentiality of Presidential communications is significantly diminished by production of such material for *in camera* inspection with all the protection that a district court will be obliged to provide.

The impediment that an absolute, unqualified privilege would place in the way of the primary constitutional duty of the Judicial Branch to do justice in criminal prosecutions would plainly conflict with the function of the courts under Art. III. In designing the structure of our Government and dividing and allocating the sovereign power among three co-equal branches, the Framers of the Constitution sought to provide a comprehensive system, but the separate powers were not intended to operate with absolute independence. . . . To read the Art. II powers of the President as providing an absolute privilege as against a subpoena essential to enforcement of criminal statutes on no more than a generalized claim of the public interest in confidentiality of nonmilitary and nondiplomatic discussions would upset the constitutional balance of "a workable government" and gravely impair the role of the courts under Art. III.

Since we conclude that the legitimate needs of the judicial process may outweigh Presidential privilege, it is necessary to resolve those competing interests in a manner that preserves the essential functions of each branch. The right and indeed the duty to resolve that question does not free the Judiciary from according high respect to the representations made on behalf of the President.

The expectation of a President to the confidentiality of his conversations and correspondence, like the claim of confidentiality of judicial deliberations, for example, has all the values to which we accord deference for the privacy of all citizens and, added to those values, is the necessity for protection of the public interest in candid, objective, and even blunt or harsh opinions in Presidential decisionmaking. A President and those who assist him must be free to explore alternatives in the process of shaping policies and making decisions and to do so in a way many would be unwilling to express except privately. These are the considerations justifying a presumptive privilege for Presidential communications. The privilege is fundamental to the operation of Government and inextricably rooted in the separation of powers under the Constitution. . . .

But this presumptive privilege must be considered in light of our historic commitment to the rule of law. This is nowhere more profoundly manifest than in our view that "the twofold aim [of criminal justice] is that guilt shall not escape or innocence suffer." We have elected to employ an adversary system of criminal justice in which the parties contest all issues before a court of law. The need to develop all relevant facts in the adversary system is both fundamental and comprehensive. The ends of criminal justice would be defeated if judgments were to be founded on a partial or speculative presentation of the facts. The very integrity of the judicial system and public confidence in the system depend on full disclosure of all the facts, within the framework of the rules of evidence. To ensure that justice is done,

it is imperative to the function of courts that compulsory process be available for the production of evidence needed either by the prosecution or by the defense. . . .

In this case the President challenges a subpoena served on him as a third party requiring the production of materials for use in a criminal prosecution; he does so on the claim that he has a privilege against disclosure of confidential communications. He does not place his claim of privilege on the ground they are military or diplomatic secrets. As to these areas of Art. II duties the courts have traditionally shown the utmost deference to Presidential responsibilities. . . . No case of the Court, however, has extended this high degree of deference to a President's generalized interest in confidentiality. Nowhere in the Constitution, as we have noted earlier, is there any explicit reference to a privilege of confidentiality, yet to the extent this interest relates to the effective discharge of a President's powers, it is constitutionally based.

The right to the production of all evidence at a criminal trial similarly has constitutional dimensions. The Sixth Amendment explicitly confers upon every defendant in a criminal trial the right "to be confronted with the witnesses against him" and "to have compulsory process for obtaining witnesses in his favor." Moreover, the Fifth Amendment also guarantees that no person shall be deprived of liberty without due process of law. It is the manifest duty of the courts to vindicate those guarantees, and to accomplish that it is essential that all relevant and admissible evidence be produced.

In this case we must weigh the importance of the general privilege of confidentiality of Presidential communications in performance of the President's responsibilities against the inroads of such a privilege on the fair administration of criminal justice. The interest in preserving confidentiality is weighty indeed and entitled to great respect. However, we cannot conclude that advisers will be moved to temper the candor of their remarks by the infrequent occasions of disclosure because of the possibility that such conversations will be called for in the context of a criminal prosecution.

On the other hand, the allowance of the privilege to withhold evidence that is demonstrably relevant in a criminal trial would cut deeply into the guarantee of due process of law and gravely impair the basic function of the courts. A

President's acknowledged need for confidentiality in the communications of his office is general in nature, whereas the constitutional need for production of relevant evidence in a criminal proceeding is specific and central to the fair adjudication of a particular criminal case in the administration of justice. Without access to specific facts a criminal prosecution may be totally frustrated. The President's broad interest in confidentiality of communications will not be vitiated by disclosure of a limited number of conversations preliminarily shown to have some bearing on the pending criminal cases.

We conclude that when the ground for asserting privilege as to subpoenaed materials sought for use in a criminal trial is based only on the generalized interest in confidentiality, it cannot prevail over the fundamental demands of due process of law in the fair administration of criminal justice. The generalized assertion of privilege must yield to the demonstrated, specific need for evidence in a pending criminal trial.

The Court's ruling was clear. The people's interest in the fair administration of criminal justice outweighed the president's interest in confidentiality. Executive privilege was rejected as a justification for refusing to make the tapes available to the prosecutor.

Nixon complied with the Court's ruling, knowing full well that it meant the end of his presidency. In obeying the Court order, he avoided provoking what many feared would be the most serious of all constitutional confrontations. What if Nixon had refused to comply? What if he had destroyed the tapes rather than turn them over? Who could have enforced sanctions on the president for doing so? Remember that in *Mississippi v. Johnson* the Court cited these possible noncompliance and enforcement questions as reasons for not permitting the president personally to be sued for official conduct. Impeachment and conviction of the president probably would have been the only way to handle such a crisis. Whatever Nixon's culpability in Watergate and related matters, he spared the nation an unprecedented crisis by bowing

```
                              AUGUST 9, 1974

        Office of the White House Press Secretary
    - - - - - - - - - - - - - - - - - - - - - - - - - - - - - - - - - -

                        THE WHITE HOUSE

    The following letter was delivered by General Alexander M. Haig Jr.
    to the Secretary of State in his White House office at 11:35 a.m. today:


                          The White House
                            Washington

                          August 9, 1974


        Dear Mr. Secretary:

        I hereby resign the Office of President of the
        United States.

                              Sincerely,

                          /s/   Richard Nixon


        The Honorable Henry A. Kissinger
        The Secretary of State
        Washington, D.C. 20520
```

With this one-sentence letter Richard Nixon became the first American president to resign from office.

to the Supreme Court's interpretation of the Constitution.

The Nixon tapes revealed substantial wrongdoing. It was obvious to all that if Nixon had not voluntarily relinquished his position, the House of Representatives would have presented articles of impeachment, and a Senate trial would have taken place, resulting in his removal from office. Rather than put himself and the nation through such an ordeal, Nixon resigned.

THE POWER OF APPOINTMENT AND REMOVAL

For presidents to carry out the executive duties of the government effectively, they must be able to staff the various departments and offices with administrators who share their views and in whom they have confidence. This duty implies the power to appoint and the power to remove. The Constitution is relatively clear on the president's appointment power but is silent on the right to remove.

Appointing Executive Officials

Article II, Section 2, contains what is known as the Appointments Clause. It details the president's authority to appoint major administrative and judicial officials, but also allows Congress to allocate that authority to other bodies for minor administrative positions:

[The President] shall nominate, and by and with the Advice and Consent of the Senate, shall appoint Ambassadors, other public Ministers and Consuls, Judges of the supreme Court, and all other Officers of the United States, whose Appointments are not herein otherwise provided for, and which shall be established by Law: but the Congress may by Law vest the Appointment of such inferior Officers, as they think proper, in the President alone, in the Courts of Law, or in the Heads of Departments.

From time to time Congress has established government positions that, for various reasons, were to be filled by an appointing authority other than the president. When the executive has objected, legal disputes have arisen. In many cases the issue is whether the official holds a major position as an officer of the United States or is an inferior official. The former, according to the Appointments Clause, must be filled by presidential nomination and Senate confirmation, but the latter may be chosen by some other means as determined by Congress.

Buckley v. Valeo (1976) illustrates this point. The justices heard a challenge to the constitutionality of the 1974 amendments to the Federal Election Campaign Act. The appeal involved a complex set of issues regarding the regulation of federal election campaigns, including the question of who should enforce the law. The statute created the Federal Election Commission (FEC) to police the new regulations. In light of the just-

concluded Watergate controversy, Congress did not want the eight members of the commission to be appointed exclusively by the president, so it devised a plan for choosing them. The secretary of the Senate and the clerk of the House were ex officio members without the right to vote. The president pro tempore of the Senate, the Speaker of the House, and the president each appointed two members, one Democrat and one Republican. The six voting members had to be confirmed by both houses of Congress.

This arrangement was challenged as a violation of the Appointments Clause. The argument was that the commissioners were officers of the United States who should be appointed by the president only and confirmed by the Senate, with no House involvement. Furthermore, the commission's appointment procedures were attacked because as the body given responsibility to enforce the campaign laws (an executive function) the members should not be appointed by the legislature. To construct the commission this way was to violate the principle of separation of powers.

The Supreme Court, unanimously on this point, found the FEC to be unconstitutionally structured. The commissioners were not inferior officers; they were officers entrusted with major enforcement and administrative duties. As such, they belonged to the executive branch and should not be appointed by the legislature.

The Court reached a different conclusion in *Morrison v. Olson* (1988). Because of the problems encountered in prosecuting the Watergate case, Congress included a provision in the Ethics in Government Act of 1978 dealing with the position of special prosecutor. The law provided for an independent counsel to investigate and, when necessary, to prosecute high-ranking officials of the government for violations of federal criminal laws. The special prosecutor was to be chosen by a group of three federal judges, appointed by the chief justice for two years and known as the special division. The selection of special prosecutors and the description of the prosecutor's jurisdiction were the special division's only functions. It carried out these responsibilities only after a preliminary investigation by the attorney general indicated that a special prosecutor would be needed.

Once appointed, the special prosecutor could exercise all of the powers of the Justice Department. A prosecutor appointed under the act could be removed by the attorney general, but only for cause or disabilities that substantially impaired the counsel from completing the required duties. Such dismissals could be reviewed by the federal district court. The special prosecutor's tenure otherwise ended when he or she declared the work to be completed, or the special division concluded that the independent counsel's assigned tasks had been accomplished.

In 1985, a special prosecutor was appointed to investigate Theodore B. Olson, an assistant attorney general, and two other Justice Department officials on the grounds that they may have presented false information to Congress and otherwise obstructed congressional investigations. Olson and the others refused to cooperate with orders to produce evidence on the grounds that the special prosecutor provision of the Ethics in Government Act violated the Constitution's Appointments Clause. They claimed that the special prosecutor was not an "inferior officer" and therefore had to be appointed by the president, not by a group of three judges. The federal district court upheld the validity of the act, but the court of appeals reversed.

The Supreme Court upheld the law with only one justice dissenting. Although acknowledging that the line between inferior and principal officers is blurred one, the majority found that the special prosecutor clearly fell into the inferior officer category. Chief Justice Rehnquist's opinion cites four reasons for this. First, the special prosecutor can be removed by the attorney general. Second, the special prosecutor is authorized to perform only certain, limited duties. Third, the jurisdiction of the special prosecutor is limited to the investigation of specified federal officials.

And finally, the special prosecutor's tenure is temporary; once the investigation is completed the special prosecutor leaves office. In addition, the Court could find no substantial reason to believe that the special prosecutor in any way infringed on the rights and powers of the president; nor was the law an attempt by Congress to increase its power at the expense of the president.

The independent counsel statute, upheld in *Morrison v. Olson*, expired at the end of 1992. It was not reenacted because of partisan differences over an investigation into the Iran-Contra affair, a controversy involving members of the Reagan administration who allegedly offered to trade arms in return for Americans held hostage in Iran. The special prosecutor, Lawrence E. Walsh, aggressively pursued the case, but was viewed by Republicans as excessively partisan. In addition, investigations such as that headed by Walsh had no effective spending limitations and had become unreasonably expensive. President George Bush, a Republican, threatened to veto reauthorization legislation.

In June 1994, however, a new independent counsel statute became law. The act received bipartisan support in Congress and was endorsed by President Clinton, the first chief executive to back independent counsel legislation. The new law imposed procedures modeled after the earlier statute: following a preliminary investigation by the Justice Department into alleged wrongdoing by top administration officials, the attorney general petitions a special three-judge federal court to appoint an independent counsel to pursue the matter. The new law incorporated certain reform provisions, including effective spending guidelines.

Dismissing Executive Officials

The president's need to have executive branch officials who support the administration's policy goals is only partially satisfied by the power to appoint. What is also required is the corollary—the discretionary right to remove administrative officials from office. This need may arise when a president's appointees do not carry out their duties the way the president wishes. It also applies when an official appointed by a previous administration will not voluntarily step aside to make way for a nominee of the new president's choosing.

Although an established removal procedure is obviously necessary, the Framers neglected to mention it in the Constitution. In the absence of constitutional guidelines, a lingering controversy has centered on whether administrative officials can be removed at the discretion of the president alone or whether Congress may play a role.

The argument supporting presidential discretion holds that the chief executive must be free to remove subordinates who fail to meet the president's expectations or who are not loyal to the administration's policy objectives. It would be unreasonable to require the approval of Congress before such officials could be dismissed. Such a requirement might well paralyze the executive branch, particularly when the legislature and the presidency are under the control of different political parties.

The argument for legislative participation in the process holds that the Constitution anticipates Senate action. If the president can appoint major executive department officials only with senatorial approval, it is reasonable to infer that the chief executive can remove administrators only by going through the same process and obtaining the advice and consent of the Senate. This view was supported by Alexander Hamilton in *The Federalist Papers'* only reference to the removal powers. Hamilton flatly stated, "The consent of that body [the Senate] would be necessary to displace as well as to appoint."[2] Hamilton argued that if the president and the Senate agreed that an official should be removed, the decision would be much better accepted than if the president acted alone. Furthermore,

Hamilton asserted that a new president should be restrained from removing an experienced official who had conducted his duties satisfactorily just because the president preferred to have a different person in the position.

Historical practice generally has rejected Hamilton's position. From the very beginning, Congress allowed the chief executive to remove administrative officials without Senate consent. In the First Congress James Madison proposed that three executive departments be created: Foreign Affairs, Treasury, and War. The creation of the Foreign Affairs (later State) Department received the most legislative attention. According to Madison's recommendation, the department was to have a secretary to be appointed by the president with the approval of the Senate who could be removed by the president alone. The House and the Senate held long comprehensive debates on the removal power at that time and passed legislation allowing the secretary of state to be removed at the president's discretion without Senate approval.

At times, however, the legislature has asserted a right to participate in the process. The most notable example occurred with the passage of the Tenure of Office Act in 1867. This statute was enacted to restrict the powers of President Johnson, who took office after Lincoln's assassination in 1865. Following the Civil War, the Radical Republicans dominated Congress and had little use for Johnson, a Democrat from Tennessee. Congress did not want Johnson to be able to remove Lincoln's appointees. The Tenure of Office Act stipulated that the president could not remove high-ranking executive department heads without first obtaining the approval of the Senate. Johnson blatantly defied the statute by dismissing Secretary of War Edwin M. Stanton in August 1867 and appointing Ulysses S. Grant as interim secretary. The Senate reacted by ordering Stanton reinstated. Grant left office and Stanton returned in January 1868. The next month Johnson fired Stanton again. The president's failure to comply with the Tenure of Office Act consti-

2. "Federalist No. 77" in *The Federalist Papers*, by Alexander Hamilton, James Madison, and John Jay, ed. Clinton L. Rossiter (New York: New American Library, 1961), 459.

tuted one of the grounds upon which the House impeached him.

The Tenure of Office Act never had a judicial test. Once Johnson's term expired, the statute was weakened by amendment and then repealed in 1887. Consequently, as the nation entered the twentieth century there had yet to be an authoritative declaration of the constitutional parameters of the removal power, although some statutes remained on the books asserting a role for the Senate in the dismissal of administrative officials.

The Supreme Court finally faced this issue in *Myers v. United States* (1926). The case began when President Wilson fired Frank Myers, a Portland, Oregon, postmaster, who had refused the president's requests to step down. Federal law stipulated that postmasters could "be removed by the President by and with the advice and consent of the Senate." Since the Senate had not approved the dismissal, Myers claimed the firing was illegal and sued the government for lost compensation.

The Court's opinion was written by Chief Justice Taft, who had one of the nation's most spectacular résumés. Among the positions he had held were solicitor general, governor of the Philippines, secretary of war, president of the United States, and, finally, chief justice of the United States. Given Taft's rich experience in the executive branch and the fact that he had not served in the legislature, we would expect, correctly, that he would support a broad interpretation of the president's removal powers and reject the notion that the Senate had the right to limit that discretion.

Taft's opinion stressed the fact that the power to remove is an incident of the power to appoint. It is an executive power that resides with the president. That the Constitution limits the appointment power by Senatorial consent does not necessarily mean that the removal power is also to be limited by Senate participation. The president is entrusted with taking care that the laws are faithfully executed. To accomplish this goal, the president must have an administration in which he has confidence. To allow the Senate to participate in the removal of administrative officials would severely limit the chief executive's ability to carry out the constitutional obligations of the office. As a result of this reasoning, the Court declared unconstitutional the Tenure of Office Act of 1876 and any subsequent legislation having the same purpose.

In later years the Court partially backed away from the strong support of presidential power expressed in *Myers. Humphrey's Executor v. United States* (1935), decided just nine years after *Myers,* focused on President Franklin Roosevelt's dismissal of Commissioner William E. Humphrey of the Federal Trade Commission (FTC). Humphrey had been appointed to that post by President Hoover and certainly did not have policy preferences consistent with Roosevelt's New Deal. After Humphrey repeatedly ignored Roosevelt's demands that he resign, the president ordered him removed from office. This action ran directly counter to legislation creating the FTC, which allowed for the removal of a commissioner only for reasons of inefficiency, neglect of duty, or malfeasance in office. Humphrey sued.

The Supreme Court rejected Roosevelt's actions. In doing so it drew a sharp distinction between officials who exercise purely executive powers and those who carry out quasi-legislative or quasi-judicial functions. The former serve at the pleasure of the president and may be removed at his discretion. The latter may be removed only with procedures consistent with statutory conditions enacted by Congress. Wilson's removal of the postmaster in *Myers* was an example of the firing of an executive official. The members of the Federal Trade Commission were of an entirely different nature. The commission was established by Congress as a nonpartisan agency independent of the president. The commission had no enforcement or executive powers, but was charged with developing and adjudicating administrative regulations. Consequently, the commissioners were not administrative officials whom the president had the sole constitutional authority to remove.

This classification scheme was reaffirmed in *Wiener v. United States* (1958). The case involved a member of the War Claims Commission, a body established by Congress in 1948 to receive and adjudicate claims for compensating certain parties who suffered damages at the hands of the enemy in World War II. When President Eisenhower dismissed Myron Wiener, a Truman appointee, from the commission, Wiener sued.

Justice Frankfurter, writing for a unanimous bench, rebuked the president. The justices concluded that Wiener had been fired illegally. The war claims commissioners exercised quasi-judicial functions, and therefore the position was governed by the decision in *Humphrey's Executor* rather than *Myers.* Because Wiener did not exercise purely executive powers, Eisenhower had no power under the Constitution or the statute creating the commission to remove him. The *Wiener* decision is important because, by reaffirming *Humphrey's Executor,* it brought an authoritative end to questions regarding the extent of the president's power to remove officeholders at his discretion alone.

THE PRESIDENT AND
FOREIGN POLICY

There can be no doubt that the Constitution confers on the president special authority over matters of foreign policy. A review of the powers granted to the chief executive by the Constitution demonstrates why this is the case.

First, Article II, Section 2, assigns to the president the role of commander in chief of the army and navy. The military capability of a nation clearly is tied to its foreign policy. Military power not only enables a nation to deter hostile actions from other countries, but it also can be used as a credible threat to persuade oth-

er nations to follow certain preferred courses of action. Armed interventions and full-scale wars can be major elements in executing a nation's foreign policy. Modern military actions, both small and large, taken by the United States in Grenada, Panama, and the Persian Gulf, demonstrate the use of this power.

Second, Article II gives the president the sole authority to make treaties on behalf of the United States. These international agreements may cover almost any area of interaction among nations, including defense pacts, economic understandings, and human rights accords.

Third, the president selects the individuals to represent the United States in contacts with other nations. The power to appoint ambassadors and ministers influences U.S. relations with the leaders of other states.

Fourth, Article II, Section 3, provides that the president is the appropriate official to receive ambassadors and ministers from foreign nations. When the president accepts the credentials of foreign emissaries, the act confers U.S. recognition on the governments they represent. This provision also means that when foreign diplomats communicate with the United States they must do so through the president.

The Supreme Court has endorsed the notion that by the sum of these powers the Constitution has entrusted the president with the primary responsibility for creating and implementing foreign policy. For the most comprehensive statement of this position we need to refer once again to the Court's decision in *United States v. Curtiss-Wright Export Corp.* As you recall, we discussed this case in Chapter 4 for what it demonstrated about the constitutional limits on the delegation of legislative power to the executive branch. But Justice Sutherland's opinion for the Court also develops nicely the president's constitutional position in matters of foreign policy. A brief review of the essential facts appears below to remind you of the issues involved in this dispute.

United States v. Curtiss-Wright Export Corp.

299 U.S. 304 (1936)

Vote: 7 (Brandeis, Butler, Cardozo, Hughes, Roberts,
Sutherland, Van Devanter)
1 (McReynolds)
Opinion of the Court: Sutherland
Not participating: Stone

On May 28, 1934, Congress passed a joint resolution aimed at quelling the war between Bolivia and Paraguay over the Chaco region. The resolution gave the president the power to prohibit arms sales to the warring parties if that would help to reestablish peace. Once the president issued a proclamation to that effect, the sale of any arms and ammunition to the hostile nations would constitute a crime punishable by a fine and/or imprisonment. The day after passage of the joint resolution, President Roosevelt announced the arms sale prohibition and the criminal sanctions immediately went into effect. On November 14, 1935, Roosevelt issued a second proclamation revoking the first.

On January 27, 1936, a grand jury returned an indictment against Curtiss-Wright Export Corporation, charging that the company conspired to sell military equipment to Bolivia during the period covered by the first proclamation. Curtiss-Wright moved to quash the indictment and received a favorable ruling from the federal district court on one of the three points it asserted. The United States appealed. After explaining that Congress had not engaged in an unconstitutional delegation of powers to the executive branch, Justice Sutherland described the role the Constitution prescribes for the president in the area of foreign policy.

MR. JUSTICE SUTHERLAND delivered the opinion of the Court.

Not only, as we have shown, is the federal power over external affairs in origin and essential character different from that over internal affairs, but participation in the exercise of the power is significantly limited. In this vast external realm, with its important, complicated, delicate and manifold problems, the President alone has the power to speak or listen as a representative of the nation. He *makes* treaties with the advice and consent of the Senate; but he alone negotiates. Into the field of negotiation the Senate cannot intrude; and Congress itself is powerless to invade it. As Marshall said in his great argument of March 7, 1800, in the House of Representatives, "The President is the sole organ of the nation in its external relations, and its sole representative with foreign nations." The Senate Committee on Foreign Relations at a very early day in our history (February 15, 1816), reported to the Senate, among other things, as follows:

"The President is the constitutional representative of the United States with regard to foreign nations. He manages our concerns with foreign nations and must necessarily be most competent to determine when, how, and upon what subjects negotiation may be urged with the greatest prospect of success. For his conduct he is responsible to the Constitution. The committee consider this responsibility the surest pledge for the faithful discharge of his duty. They think the interference of the Senate in the direction of foreign negotiations calculated to diminish that responsibility and thereby to impair the best security for the national safety. The nature of transactions with foreign nations, moreover, requires caution and unity of design, and their success frequently depends on secrecy and dispatch."

It is important to bear in mind that we are here dealing not alone with an authority vested in the President by an exertion of legislative power, but with such an authority plus the very delicate, plenary and exclusive power of the President as the sole organ of the federal government in the field of international relations—a power which does not require as a basis for its exercise an act of Congress, but which, of course, like every other governmental power, must be exercised in subordination to the applicable provisions of the Constitution. It is quite apparent that if, in the maintenance of our international relations, embarrassment—perhaps serious embarrassment—is to be avoided and success for our aims achieved, congressional legislation which is to be made effective through negotiation and inquiry within the international field must often accord to the President a degree of discretion and freedom from statutory restriction which would not be admissible were domestic affairs alone involved. Moreover, he, not Congress, has the better opportunity of knowing the conditions which prevail in foreign countries, and especially is this true in time of war. He has his confidential sources of information. He has his agents in the form of diplomatic, consular and other officials. Secrecy in respect of information gathered by them may be highly necessary, and the premature disclosure of it productive of harmful results. Indeed, so clearly is this true that the first President refused to accede to a request to lay before the House of Representatives the instructions, correspondence and documents relating to the negotiation of the Jay Treaty—a refusal the wisdom of which was recognized by the House itself and has never since been doubted. In his reply to the request, President Washington said:

"The nature of foreign negotiations requires caution, and their success must often depend on secrecy; and even when brought to a conclusion a full disclosure of all the measures, demands, or eventual concessions which may have been proposed or contemplated would be extremely impolitic: for this might have a pernicious influence on future negotiations, or produce immediate inconveniences, perhaps danger and mischief, in relation to other powers. The necessity of such caution and secrecy was one cogent reason for vesting the power of making treaties in the President, with the advice and consent of the Senate, the principle on which that body was formed confining it to a small number of members. To admit, then, a right in the House of Representatives to demand and to have as a matter of course all the papers respecting a negotiation with a foreign power would be to establish a dangerous precedent."

The marked difference between foreign affairs and domestic affairs in this respect is recognized by both houses of Congress in the very form of their requisitions for information from the executive departments. In the case of every department except the Department of State, the resolution *directs* the official to furnish the information. In the case of the State Department, dealing with foreign affairs, the President is *requested* to furnish the information "if not incompatible with the public interest." A statement that to furnish the information is not compatible with the public interest rarely, if ever, is questioned.

When the President is to be authorized by legislation to act in respect of a matter intended to affect a situation in foreign territory, the legislator properly bears in mind the important consideration that the form of the President's action—or, indeed, whether he shall act at all—may well depend, among other things, upon the nature of the confidential information which he has or may thereafter receive, or upon the effect which his action may have upon our foreign relations. This consideration, in connection with what we have already said on the subject, discloses the unwisdom of requiring Congress in this field of governmental power to lay down narrowly definite standards by which the President is to be governed. As this court said in *Mackenzie v. Hare* [1915], "As a government, the United States is invested with all the attributes of sovereignty. As it has the character of nationality it has the powers of nationality, especially those which concern its relations and intercourse with other countries. *We should hesitate long before limiting or embarrassing such powers."* (Italics supplied.)

In the light of the foregoing observations, it is evident that this court should not be in haste to apply a general rule which will have the effect of condemning legislation like that under review as constituting an unlawful delegation of legislative power. The principles which justify such legislation find overwhelming support in the unbroken legislative practice which has prevailed almost from the inception of the national government to the present day.

The Constitution does not leave the president completely unfettered in the pursuit of the nation's foreign policy. In fact, the Framers were sufficiently concerned about the distribution of these foreign policy prerogatives that they gave the legislative branch certain powers to counterbalance those of the executive.

Although the president is commander in chief of the military, Congress has the power to raise and support the army and the navy, to make rules for the military, and to call up the militia. According to Article I, only Congress may declare war. The president has the constitutional authority to make treaties, but a treaty cannot take effect unless the Senate ratifies it by a two-thirds vote. The president's appointments of ambassadors and other foreign policy ministers must be confirmed by the Senate.

PRESIDENTIAL POWER DURING WAR AND NATIONAL EMERGENCIES

Questions concerning the constitutional authority to make and wage war have plagued the nation from the very beginning. Even today many questions remain unresolved. Because war and conditions of national emergency customarily demand quick action, there is rarely sufficient time for the dispassionate consideration of legal questions. When national survival is at risk, the country is usually in an emotionally heightened state and may be willing to ignore the limitations on government power that would be insisted upon in peacetime.[3] Once the crisis has passed, the country turns to other matters and questions of war do not again capture the nation's attention until the next threat occurs.

The Constitutional War Powers

The constitutional authority to send troops into combat has always sparked controversy. The root of the problem is that both the legislative and the executive branches have powers that can be interpreted as controlling the commitment of military forces to combat.[4] The case for presidential control is based on the following passage from Article II, Section 2: "The President shall be Commander in Chief of the Army and Navy of the United States, and of the Militia of the several States, when called into actual Service of the Unit-

ed States." Proponents of congressional dominance over the making of war rest their case on these words from Article I, Section 8:

The Congress shall have Power . . . to declare War, grant Letters of Marque and Reprisal, and make Rules concerning Captures on Land and Water; To raise and support Armies, but no Appropriation of Money to that Use shall be for a longer Term than two Years; To provide and maintain a Navy; To make Rules for the Government and Regulation of the land and naval Forces; To provide for calling forth the Militia to execute the Laws of the Union, suppress Insurrections, and repel Invasions.

The distribution of war-making powers as determined by the Framers envisioned a situation in which Congress would raise and support military forces when necessary and provide the general rules governing them. By granting Congress the power to declare war, the Constitution anticipates that the legislature should determine when military force is to be used. Once the military is raised and war is declared, executive power will be dominant, consistent with the philosophy that to wage war successfully requires that a single official be in charge.

This allocation of powers was more realistic at the end of the eighteenth century than it is today. At the time the Framers considered these issues, the United States was a remote nation far removed from the frequent wars in Europe. It took weeks for vessels to cross the Atlantic, allowing plenty of time for Congress to debate the question of initiating hostilities. Most delegates at the Constitutional Convention did not even anticipate the establishment of a standing military.

Today, with the rapid deployment of troops, air power, and intercontinental missiles, hostile conditions demand quick and decisive actions. The nation expects the president to act immediately to repel a hostile attack and to worry about congressional approval later.

Hundreds of military actions have been initiated by the United States without a declaration of war. The

<hr>

3. Clinton L. Rossiter, *Constitutional Dictatorship: Crisis Government in the Modern Democracies* (Princeton, N.J.: Princeton University Press, 1948).

4. See Joan Biskupic, "Constitution's Conflicting Clauses Underscored by Iraq Crisis," *Congressional Quarterly Weekly Report*, January 5, 1991, 33–36.

first such action was taken by President John Adams when he authorized military strikes against French privateers.[5] Most such undeclared actions have been quick rather than prolonged conflicts. However, both the Korean War and the Vietnam War were major long-term military efforts that were conducted without the benefit of Congress's having declared war. In fact, Congress has taken the positive action of declaring a state of war only five times in the nation's history.[6]

1. The War of 1812 against Great Britain
2. The Mexican War in 1846
3. The Spanish-American War in 1898
4. World War I in 1917
5. World War II in 1941

Occasionally, military force is begun and ended so quickly that the president's actions permit no opportunity for congressional approval, such as President Reagan's overnight air strike against Libya. When military actions extend over greater periods of time, Congress often has given approval through means other than a formal declaration of war. This approval may come in the form of a resolution authorizing the president to conduct some form of military action, such as the 1964 Tonkin Gulf Resolution, which granted President Johnson authority to use force to repel attacks on U.S. forces and to prevent future aggression. Similarly, on January 12, 1991, Congress passed a joint resolution authorizing President Bush to use force against Iraq; Congress gave its approval to the Persian Gulf conflict in words just short of a formal declaration of war. Indirect approval also may take the form of continuing congressional appropriations to support the military action.

But Congress has not abdicated its constitutional authority to approve war; in fact, the legislature has been adamant that the president consult it on all military actions. In 1973 Congress passed the War Powers Act over Nixon's veto. This legislation acknowledges the right of the president to undertake limited military action without first obtaining formal approval from Congress. However, the statute requires the president to file a formal report with Congress within forty-eight hours of initiating hostilities. Military action under this act is limited to sixty days with a possible thirty-day extension. If the president wishes to pursue military activity beyond these limits, prior congressional consent is required. While the legislature intended to impose restrictions on the president with the passage of the War Powers Act, most experts believe the law actually expands the chief executive's right to employ military force.

Because the courts must wait for an appropriate case to be filed before acting, and because its procedures are slow and deliberative, the judicial branch is least capable of taking a role in matters of war and national emergency. Furthermore, the Constitution gives the courts no specified authority in these areas. However, the judiciary is sometimes called upon to decide when government power is used legitimately and when constitutional limits have been exceeded. In times of war and national emergency the executive branch may find it necessary to take actions that would be unlawful at other times. The limits of the Constitution may be stretched to respond to the crisis. When legal disputes arise from such situations, the courts become active participants in determining the government's legitimate authority.

Civil War Disputes

It is a generally recognized constitutional doctrine that government may exercise more power during times of war and national emergency than during times of peace and security. What is not evident is when the extraordinary powers of the government are

---

5. For a good review of the history of undeclared military engagements, see Ronald D. Elving, "America's Most Frequent Fight Has Been the Undeclared War," *Congressional Quarterly Weekly Report*, January 5, 1991, 37–40.

6. Congress also declared a state of war during the Civil War, but this conflict is technically classified as an internal rebellion rather than a true war between independent nations.

to be activated. This question came to the Supreme Court in the *Prize Cases* in 1863, the first of several major constitutional rulings related to questionable actions taken by President Lincoln. The disputes giving rise to these cases present the most fundamental questions of the constitutional allocation of the war powers. When does war begin? Who has the power to initiate war? What war powers may the president pursue without a formal declaration from Congress?

Abraham Lincoln was elected president in November 1860. Before his inauguration on March 4, 1861, seven southern states seceded from the Union, and Lincoln knew that he had to act quickly and decisively to restore the nation. Beginning in mid-April, shortly after the first shots were fired at Fort Sumter, Lincoln imposed a naval blockade of southern ports. He took this action unilaterally without seeking the prior approval of Congress, which did not enact a formal declaration of hostilities until July 13. Before Congress could act, Union war vessels seized a number of ships that were trading with the Confederate states. The owners of the captured ships brought suit to recover their property, claiming that Lincoln had no authority to institute a blockade in the absence of a congressional declaration of war and that the seizures were illegal. Among other matters, the justices confronted this important constitutional issue: Did the president have the right to institute a blockade of ports under the control of persons in armed rebellion against the government?

The Court upheld the president's actions. It ruled that the chief executive is bound to resist force or invasion from any hostile party without waiting to receive special authorization from the legislature. Regardless of whether the military action is initiated by a foreign nation or a rebelling state, a condition of war exists when hostilities are initiated. The lack of a formal declaration does not mean that a war has not begun. In fulfilling his duties, the president is bound to suppress insurrections. The commander in chief is the appropriate person to determine when a military response is necessary.

Lincoln's actions were supported by the barest of majorities. Three of the justices who voted to endorse the validity of the blockade were his own appointees, Samuel Miller, Noah Swayne, and David Davis. They were joined by two Democrats, Robert Grier of Pennsylvania and James Wayne, a Georgian who remained loyal to the Union. The decision is significant for expanding the right of the president to take military action without waiting for congressional approval. It further established that a state of war comes into existence when certain conditions are present, not when the legislature declares that it exists. The decision, however, did not fully settle the issue. The arguments raised in the majority and dissenting opinions in this case seem to reappear whenever a controversy over the power to conduct war arises.

The blockade was only the first of Lincoln's acts that were of questionable constitutionality. More severely criticized were his actions suppressing civil liberties. The Civil War was unlike other wars Americans had faced: the enemies were fellow Americans, not foreigners. The conflict touched every part of the nation, and Lincoln particularly worried about the presence of Confederate supporters in the northern and border states. These individuals were capable of aiding the southern forces without joining the Confederate Army. Of special concern were the large numbers of southern sympathizers, known as Copperheads, active especially in Indiana, Illinois, Ohio, and Missouri. Combating these civilian enemies posed a difficult problem for the president. He decided that the Union was more important than the procedural rights of individuals. Consequently, Lincoln gave his military commanders broad powers to arrest civilians suspected of engaging in traitorous activities. These suspects were to be tried in military courts.

In those areas of the country where hostilities were not occurring, however, the army had no legal authority to arrest and try civilians. State and federal courts were in full operation and were capable of trying civilians charged with treason or any other crime. To allow arrests and military trials for civilians a state of martial law had to be declared, and to do that, the right of habeas corpus had to be suspended. Habeas corpus is a legal procedure with roots extending far back into English legal history; it permits an arrested person to have a judge determine whether the detention is legal. If the court determines that there are no legal grounds for the arrest, it may order the release of the detained individual. Habeas corpus is essential to the doctrine of checks and balances because it gives the judiciary the right to intervene if the executive branch abuses the law enforcement power.

Article I, Section 9, of the Constitution provides for the suspension of habeas corpus in the following words: "The Privilege of the Writ of Habeas Corpus shall not be suspended, unless when in Cases of Rebellion or Invasion the public Safety may require it." This provision posed two problems for Lincoln. First, the suspension provision is found in Article I, which outlines legislative, not executive, powers. And second, if the civilian courts are in full operation and no armed hostilities are taking place in the area, the public safety probably does not demand a suspension of habeas corpus procedures.

These obstacles did not stop the president. Several times during the war he issued orders expanding military control over civilian areas, permitting military arrests and trials of civilians, and suspending habeas corpus. Congress later endorsed some of these actions. Arrests of suspected traitors and conspirators were common and often based on little evidence. Were such actions constitutional under the war powers doctrine? The Court addressed this question in *Ex parte Milligan* (1866), a decision of great importance in defining the wartime powers of the chief executive.[7]

Lambdin Milligan was an attorney who lived in southern Indiana. He had strong states' rights beliefs, and his sympathies lay with the Confederate cause during the war. He openly organized groups and gave speeches in support of the South. He also was involved in efforts to persuade men not to join the Union army. At one point Milligan and his fellow Copperheads were suspected of hatching a plan to raid prisoner of war camps in Illinois, Indiana, and Ohio and release the imprisoned Confederate soldiers, who would then take control of the three states. Federal military investigators followed Milligan closely and kept records of his activities and contacts.

On October 5, 1864, under orders from Gen. Alvin Hovey, commander of the Union armies in Indiana, federal agents arrested Milligan at his home. They also arrested four of Milligan's fellow Confederate sympathizers. Sixteen days later Hovey placed Milligan on trial before a military tribunal in Indianapolis. He was found guilty and sentenced to be hanged on May 19, 1865. On May 2, less than a month after the war ended with General Lee's surrender at Appomattox, President Johnson sustained the order that Milligan be executed. In response, Milligan's attorneys filed for a writ of habeas corpus in federal circuit court. Uncertain of how to apply the law, the circuit judges requested that the Supreme Court resolve certain questions regarding the legal authority of a military commission to try and sentence Milligan.

Nine months later, in March 1866, the Court heard the *Milligan* case. Oral arguments took place at a time of heightened political tension. Relations were strained between Johnson, who supported a moderate position toward the reintroduction of the southern states into the Union, and the Radical Republicans in Congress, who demanded a more severe Reconstruction policy. A majority of the justices opposed the military trials at issue in *Milligan*, but there

---

7. For a description of the events leading up to the Court's decision, see Allan Nevins, "The Case of the Copperhead Conspirator," in *Quarrels That Have Shaped the Constitution*, ed. John A. Garraty (New York: Harper Colophon Books, 1964). See also Lee Epstein and Thomas G. Walker, "The

Role of the Supreme Court in American Society: Playing the Reconstruction Game," in *Contemplating Courts*, ed. Lee Epstein (Washington: CQ Press, 1995).

was concern about possible congressional retaliation if the justices struck a blow against military authority. The Court at this point was quite vulnerable, having suffered a decline in prestige following the infamous *Scott* case. But the justices had a potential ally in Johnson. The president opposed the use of military tribunals, and the Radicals had not yet gained sufficient strength to override a veto of a congressional act. On April 3, 1866, the Court announced its decision in *Milligan,* but formal opinions were not issued until eight months later.

The Court condemned Lincoln's actions. It held that the military was without authority to try Milligan on the charges against him. The federal courts were in full operation in Indiana and open to adjudicate charges of criminal misconduct. Indiana was not in the theater of war and Milligan was not a member of the military. Consequently, with the civilian courts in full operation and Milligan undeniably having civilian status, jurisdiction over his alleged misdeeds rested with the normal federal courts, not with a military tribunal. Milligan's constitutional rights had been violated.

Although the Court's decision was unanimous as to Milligan's claim of illegal imprisonment, the justices split on the power of the government to suspend habeas corpus under conditions presented in the case. A majority of five (Clifford, Davis, Field, Grier, and Nelson) held that neither the president nor Congress, acting separately or in agreement, could suspend the writ of habeas corpus as long as the civilian courts were in full operation and the area was not a combat zone. In a concurring opinion joined by Miller, Swayne, and Wayne, Chief Justice Chase argued that, although the president did not have the power to establish these military tribunals, Congress did.

Before the Court handed down its ruling in this case, President Johnson commuted Milligan's sentence to life in prison, a sentence he was serving under

General Hovey in an Ohio prison when the case was decided. Milligan was released from custody in April 1866.

World War II and the Korean Conflict

The restriction of civil liberties during time of war is not uncommon. Nations pressed for their very survival may feel compelled to deny basic liberties to insure against the efforts of traitors and saboteurs. The most infamous of such actions in the United States was the World War II internment of Japanese-Americans.

The Japanese bombing of Pearl Harbor on December 7, 1941, touched off a wave of anti-Japanese hysteria. In the early weeks of the Pacific war the Japanese fleet showed remarkable strength and power, and the United States feared that Japanese forces were planning an invasion of the West Coast. There was also a great deal of concern about the large numbers of people of Japanese ancestry who lived on the coast. Many thought that among the Japanese-American population were significant numbers of people sympathetic to the Japanese war effort, people who might aid the enemy in an invasion of the United States.

To prevent such an occurrence President Roosevelt on February 19, 1942, issued the first of several orders affecting all people of Japanese background residing on the West Coast. His initial command placed all Japanese-Americans under a tight curfew that required them to stay in their homes between 8:00 P.M. and 6:00 A.M. and to register for future relocation. This act was followed by the much harsher orders to evacuate Japanese-Americans from the Pacific Coast area and move them to inland detention centers. Congress later enacted these orders into law. The program made no attempt to distinguish the loyal from the disloyal or the citizen from the noncitizen. The orders affected all persons of Japanese ancestry. The government interned an estimated 110,000 Japanese-American citizens and resident aliens, some

Japanese-Americans at the federal detention center in Owens Valley, California. In 1990, more than four decades after the war, Congress appropriated $20,000 in compensation for each of the 75,000 relocation camp survivors.

for as long as four years.[8] These programs spawned a number of important lawsuits.

In 1943 the Supreme Court heard a challenge to the curfew regulations that was brought by Gordon Hirabayashi, an American citizen of Japanese descent. He was a native of Washington State and a pacifist of the Quaker faith. At the time he challenged the government actions, he was a senior at the University of Washington. In *Hirabayashi v. United States* (1943) the Supreme Court unanimously upheld the constitutionality of the curfew program. For the Court, Chief Justice Stone explained that the war powers doctrine gave the government ample authority to impose the restrictions. The grave and threatening conditions of war made the racially based program constitutionally acceptable.

The following year the Court heard *Korematsu v. United States* (1944), an appeal attacking the most serious denial of the civil liberties of Japanese-Americans—the orders removing them to detention camps. Fred Korematsu was arrested May 30, 1942, by San Le-

andro, California, police for being on the public streets in violation of the government's evacuation orders. Korematsu had been born in the United States of Japanese-American parents. He grew up in the San Francisco area. He had been rejected for military service for health reasons, but had obtained employment in the defense industry as a welder. When arrested, he tried to convince police that he was of Spanish-Hawaiian origin. He had undergone plastic surgery to make his racial characteristics less pronounced in an effort to avoid the anti-Japanese discrimination he feared because of his engagement to an Italian-American woman.[9]

By a 6–3 vote the Supreme Court upheld the government's authority to remove Japanese-Americans on the West Coast to inland detention centers. Justice Black's opinion for the Court acknowledges that any legal restriction on a single racial group is immediately suspect. However, not all such government actions are unconstitutional. Sometimes public necessity is sufficiently strong to justify such restrictions. Here the

8. See Peter H. Irons, *Justice at War: The Story of the Japanese-American Internment Cases* (New York: Oxford University Press, 1983).

9. Ibid., 93–99.

exclusion of those of Japanese origin was deemed necessary because of the presence of an unascertained number of disloyal members of the racial group. Since it was not possible to bring about an immediate segregation of the loyal from the disloyal, the order's application to all Japanese-Americans was required. The real military danger present at such times triggers the use of war powers which would not be tolerable in times of peace.

The decision to sustain the government's evaluation of Japanese-Americans to relocation centers received sharp criticism from Justices Jackson, Murphy, and Roberts. In Justice Murphy's words, the decision "falls into the ugly abyss of racism." Later, after the war had ended, even members of the majority generally acknowledged that the decision was a misguided one, emanating from the passions of a war-torn nation.

The *Korematsu* decision was softened, but only slightly, by *Ex parte Endo* (1944), a ruling handed down the same day. In this case Mitsuye Endo had been caught escaping from a detention center. However, she had gone through the appropriate government procedures and had been classified as loyal to the United States. The justices ruled in her favor, holding that the government does not have the authority to detain persons whose loyalty has been established.

During the Korean conflict the justices were called upon to decide the constitutional validity of another executive action taken in the name of the war powers doctrine. This case involved property rights rather than civil liberties. As you read Justice Black's opinion for the Court in *Youngstown Sheet & Tube Company v. Sawyer* (1952), compare it with *Korematsu*. Both involved actions taken by the president to strengthen war efforts. Does it make sense to you that the Court approved the detention of more than 110,000 individuals on the basis of national origin but ruled that the government could not take nominal possession of the steel mills? Note the analysis provided in Justice Jackson's concurring opinion, in which he lays out a formula for deciding questions of presidential power in relation to congressional action. Consider, too, the dissenting opinion of Chief Justice Vinson, who concludes that the national emergency justified the president's actions.

Youngstown Sheet & Tube Company v. Sawyer

343 U.S. 579 (1952)
Vote: 6 (Black, Burton, Clark, Douglas, Frankfurter,
        Jackson)
     3 (Minton, Reed, Vinson)
Opinion of the Court: Black
Concurring opinions: Burton, Clark, Douglas, Frankfurter,
Jackson Dissenting opinion: Vinson

In 1951 a labor dispute began in the steel industry. In December the United Steelworkers Union announced that it would call a strike at the end of that month, when its contract with the steel companies expired. For the next several months the Federal Mediation and Conciliation Service and the Federal Wage Stabilization Board tried to work out a settlement, but the efforts were unsuccessful. On April 4, 1952, the union said that its strike would begin on April 9.

President Truman was not about to let a strike hit the steel industry. The nation was engaged in a war in Korea, and steel production was necessary to produce the arms and other military equipment. Only hours before the strike was to begin, Truman issued an executive order commanding Secretary of Commerce Charles Sawyer to seize the nation's steel mills and keep them in operation. Sawyer in turn ordered the mill owners to continue to run their facilities as operators for the United States.

Truman's seizure order cited no statutory authority for his action because there was none. There were federal statutes permitting the seizure of industrial plants for certain specified reasons, but the settlement of a labor dispute was not one of them. In fact, the

The attorney representing the steel industry, John W. Davis, Jr., (left) arriving at the Supreme Court May 13, 1952, with acting attorney general Philip B. Perlman. Davis was the Democratic nominee for the presidency in 1924, capturing 29 percent of the popular vote in a loss to Calvin Coolidge. He later represented the school board defendants in the 1954 school desegregation cases.

Taft-Hartley Act of 1946 rejected the idea that labor disputes could be resolved by such means. Instead, the act authorized the president to impose an eighty-day cooling-off period as a way to postpone any strike that seriously threatened the public interest. Truman, however, had little regard for the Taft-Hartley Act, which Congress had passed over his veto. The president ignored the cooling-off period alternative and took the direct action of seizing the mills. The inherent powers of the chief executive, he maintained, were enough to authorize the action.

Congress might have improved the president's le-

gal ground by immediately passing legislation authorizing such seizures retroactively, but it did not. The mill owners complied with the seizure orders under protest and filed suit in federal court to have Truman's action declared unconstitutional. The district court ruled in favor of the steel industry, enjoining the secretary from seizing the plants, but the same day the court of appeals stayed the injunction.

MR. JUSTICE BLACK delivered the opinion of the Court.

We are asked to decide whether the President was acting within his constitutional power when he issued an order directing the Secretary of Commerce to take possession of and operate most of the Nation's steel mills. The mill owners argue that the President's order amounts to lawmaking, a legislative function which the Constitution has expressly confided to the Congress and not to the President. The Government's position is that the order was made on findings of the President that his action was necessary to avert a national catastrophe which would inevitably result from a stoppage of steel production, and that in meeting this grave emergency the President was acting within the aggregate of his constitutional powers as the Nation's Chief Executive and the Commander in Chief of the Armed Forces of the United States. . . .

The President's power, if any, to issue the order must stem either from an act of Congress or from the Constitution itself. There is no statute that expressly authorizes the President to take possession of property as he did here. Nor is there any act of Congress to which our attention has been directed from which such a power can fairly be implied. Indeed, we do not understand the Government to rely on statutory authorization for this seizure. . . .

It is clear that if the President had authority to issue the order he did, it must be found in some provision of the Constitution. And it is not claimed that express constitutional language grants this power to the President. The contention is that presidential power should be implied from the aggregate of his powers under the Constitution. Particular reliance is placed on provisions in Article II which say that "The executive Power shall be vested in a President. . ."; that "he shall take Care that the Laws be faithfully executed"; and that he "shall be Commander in Chief of the Army and Navy of the United States."

The order cannot properly be sustained as an exercise of the President's military power as Commander in Chief of the Armed Forces. The Government attempts to do so by citing a number of cases upholding broad powers in military commanders engaged in day-to-day fighting in a theater of war. Such cases need not concern us here. Even though "theater of war" be an expanding concept, we cannot with faithfulness to our constitutional system hold that the Commander in Chief of the Armed Forces has the ultimate power as such to take possession of private property in order to keep labor disputes from stopping production. This is a job for the Nation's lawmakers, not for its military authorities.

Nor can the seizure order be sustained because of the several constitutional provisions that grant executive power to the President. In the framework of our Constitution, the President's power to see that the laws are faithfully executed refutes the idea that he is to be a lawmaker. The Constitution limits his functions in the lawmaking process to the recommending of laws he thinks wise and the vetoing of laws he thinks bad. And the Constitution is neither silent nor equivocal about who shall make laws which the President is to execute. The first section of the first article says that "All legislative Powers herein granted shall be vested in a Congress of the United States. . . ." After granting many powers to the Congress, Article I goes on to provide that Congress may "make all Laws which shall be necessary and proper for carrying into Execution the foregoing Powers, and all other Powers vested by this Constitution in the Government of the United States, or in any Department or Officer thereof."

The President's order does not direct that a congressional policy be executed in a manner prescribed by Congress— it directs that a presidential policy be executed in a manner prescribed by the President. The preamble of the order itself, like that of many statutes, sets out reasons why the President believes certain policies should be adopted, proclaims these policies as rules of conduct to be followed, and again, like a statute, authorizes a government official to promulgate additional rules and regulations consistent with the policy proclaimed and needed to carry that policy into execution. The power of Congress to adopt such public policies as those proclaimed by the order is beyond question. It can authorize the taking of private property for public use. It can make laws regulating the relationships between employers and employees, prescribing rules designed to settle labor disputes, and fixing wages and working conditions in certain fields of our economy. The Constitution does not subject this lawmaking power of Congress to presidential or military supervision or control.

It is said that other Presidents without congressional authority have taken possession of private business enterprises in order to settle labor disputes. But even if this be true, Congress has not thereby lost its exclusive constitutional authority to make laws necessary and proper to carry out the powers vested by the Constitution "in the Government of the United States, or any Department or Officer thereof."

The Founders of this Nation entrusted the lawmaking power to the Congress alone in both good and bad times. It would do no good to recall the historical events, the fears of power and the hopes for freedom that lay behind their choice. Such a review would but confirm our holding that this seizure order cannot stand.

The judgment of the District Court is

Affirmed.

MR. JUSTICE JACKSON, concurring in the judgment and opinion of the Court.

A judge, like an executive adviser, may be surprised at the poverty of really useful and unambiguous authority applicable to concrete problems of executive power as they actually present themselves. Just what our forefathers did envision, or would have envisioned had they foreseen modern conditions, must be divined from materials almost as enigmatic as the dreams Joseph was called upon to interpret for Pharaoh. A century and a half of partisan debate and scholarly speculation yields no net result but only supplies more or less apt quotations from respected sources on each side of any question. They largely cancel each other. And court decisions are indecisive because of the judicial practice of dealing with the largest questions in the most narrow way.

. . . We may well begin by a somewhat over-simplified grouping of practical situations in which a President may doubt, or others may challenge, his powers, and by distinguishing roughly the legal consequences of this factor of relativity.

1. When the President acts pursuant to an express or implied authorization of Congress, his authority is at its maximum, for it includes all that he possesses in his own right plus all that Congress can delegate. . . .

2. When the President acts in absence of either a congressional grant or denial of authority, he can only rely upon his own independent powers, but there is a zone of twilight in which he and Congress may have concurrent authority, or in which its distribution is uncertain. Therefore, congressional inertia, indifference or quiescence may sometimes, at least as a practical matter, enable, if not invite, measures on independent presidential responsibility. In this area, any actual test of power is likely to depend on the imperatives of events and contemporary imponderables rather than on abstract theories of law.

3. When the President takes measures incompatible with the expressed or implied will of Congress, his power is at its lowest ebb, for then he can rely only upon his own constitutional powers minus any constitutional powers of Congress over the matter. . . .

Into which of these classifications does this executive seizure of the steel industry fit? It is eliminated from the first by admission, for it is conceded that no congressional authorization exists for this seizure. That takes away also the support of the many precedents and declarations which were made in relation, and must be confined, to this category.

Can it then be defended under flexible tests available to the second category? It seems clearly eliminated from that class because Congress has not left seizure of private property an open field but has covered it by three statutory policies inconsistent with this seizure. . . .

This leaves the current seizure to be justified only by the severe tests under the third grouping, where it can be supported only by any remainder of executive power after subtraction of such powers as Congress may have over the subject. In short, we can sustain the President only by holding that seizure of such strike-bound industries is within his domain and beyond control by Congress. Thus, this Court's first review of such seizures occurs under circumstances which leave presidential power most vulnerable to attack and in the least favorable of possible constitutional postures. . . .

The Solicitor General, acknowledging that Congress has never authorized the seizure here, says practice of prior Presidents has authorized it. He seeks color of legality from claimed executive precedents, chief of which is President Roosevelt's seizure on June 9, 1941, of the California plant of the North American Aviation Company. Its superficial similarities with the present case, upon analysis, yield to distinctions so decisive that it cannot be regarded as even a precedent, much less an authority for the present seizure.

The appeal, however, that we declare the existence of inherent powers *ex necessitate* to meet an emergency asks us to do what many think would be wise, although it is something the forefathers omitted. They knew what emergencies were, knew the pressures they engender for authoritative action, knew, too, how they afford a ready pretext for usurpation. We may also suspect that they suspected that emergency powers would tend to kindle emergencies. Aside from suspension of the privilege of the writ of habeas corpus in time of rebellion or invasion, when the public safety may require it, they made no express provision for exercise of extraordinary authority because of a crisis. I do not think we rightfully may so amend their work, and, if we could, I am not convinced it would be wise to do so, although many modern nations have forthrightly recognized that war and economic crises may upset the normal balance between liberty and authority. . . .

The essence of our free Government is "leave to live by no man's leave, underneath the law"—to be governed by those impersonal forces which we call law. Our Government is fashioned to fulfill this concept so far as humanly possible. The Executive, except for recommendation and veto, has no legislative power. The executive action we have here originates in the individual will of the President and represents an exercise of authority without law. No one, perhaps not even the President, knows the limits of the power he may seek to exert in this instance and the parties affected cannot learn the limit of their rights. We do not know today what powers over labor or property would be claimed to flow from Government possession if we should legalize it, what rights to compensation would be claimed or recognized, or on what contingency it would end. With all its defects, delays and inconveniences, men have discovered no technique for long preserving free government except that the Executive be under the law, and that the law be made by parliamentary deliberations.

Such institutions may be destined to pass away. But it is the duty of the Court to be last, not first, to give them up.

MR. CHIEF JUSTICE VINSON, with whom MR. JUSTICE REED and MR. JUSTICE MINTON join, dissenting.

The President of the United States directed the Secretary of Commerce to take temporary possession of the Nation's steel mills during the existing emergency because "a work stoppage would immediately jeopardize and imperil our national defense and the defense of those joined with us in resisting aggression, and would add to the continuing danger of our soldiers, sailors, and airmen engaged in combat in the field.". . .

In passing upon the question of Presidential powers in this case, we must first consider the context in which those powers were exercised.

Those who suggest that this is a case involving extraordinary powers should be mindful that these are extraordinary times. A world not yet recovered from the devastation of World War II has been forced to face the threat of another and more terrifying global conflict.

Accepting in full measure its responsibility in the world community, the United States was instrumental in securing adoption of the United Nations Charter, approved by the Senate by a vote of 89 to 2. The first purpose of the United Nations is to "maintain international peace and security, and to that end: to take effective collective measures for the prevention and removal of threats to the peace, and for the suppression of acts of aggression or other breaches of the peace. . . ." In 1950, when the United Nations called upon member nations "to render every assistance" to repel aggression in Korea, the United States furnished its vigorous support. For almost two full years, our armed forces have been fighting in Korea, suffering casualties of over 108,000 men. Hostilities have not abated. The "determination of the United Nations to continue its action in Korea to meet the aggression" has been reaffirmed. Congressional support of the action in Korea has been manifested by provisions for increased military manpower and equipment and for economic stabilization. . . .

Congress recognized the impact of these defense programs upon the economy. Following the attack in Korea, the President asked for authority to requisition property and to allocate and fix priorities for scarce goods. In the Defense Production Act of 1950, Congress granted the powers requested and, *in addition*, granted power to stabilize prices and wages and to provide for settlement of labor disputes arising in the defense program. The Defense Production Act was extended in 1951, a Senate Committee noting that in the dislocation caused by the programs for purchase of military equipment "lies the seed of an economic disaster that might well destroy the military might we are straining to build." Significantly, the Committee examined the problem "in terms of just one commodity, steel," and found "a graphic picture of the over-all inflationary danger growing out of reduced civilian supplies and rising incomes." Even before Korea, steel production at levels above theoretical 100% capacity was not capable of supplying civilian needs alone. Since Korea, the tremendous military demand for steel has far exceeded the increases in productive capacity. This Committee emphasized that the shortage of steel, even with the mills operating at full capacity, coupled with increased civilian purchasing power, presented grave danger of disastrous inflation. . . .

A review of executive action demonstrates that our Presidents have on many occasions exhibited the leadership contemplated by the Framers when they made the President Commander in Chief, and imposed upon him the trust to "take Care that the Laws be faithfully executed." With or without explicit statutory authorization, Presidents have at such times dealt with national emergencies by acting promptly and resolutely to enforce legislative programs, at least to save those programs until Congress could act. Congress and the courts have responded to such executive initiative with consistent approval. . . .

The broad executive power granted by Article II to an officer on duty 365 days a year cannot, it is said, be invoked to avert disaster. Instead, the President must confine himself to sending a message to Congress recommending action. Under this messenger-boy concept of the Office, the President cannot even act to preserve legislative programs from destruction so that Congress will have something left to act upon. There is no judicial finding that the executive action was unwarranted because there was in fact no basis for the President's finding of the existence of an emergency for, under this view, the gravity of the emergency and the immediacy of the threatened disaster are considered irrelevant as a matter of law.

Seizure of plaintiffs' property is not a pleasant undertaking. Similarly unpleasant to a free country are the draft which disrupts the home and military procurement which causes economic dislocation and compels adoption of price controls, wage stabilization and allocation of materials. The President informed Congress that even a temporary Government operation of plaintiffs' properties was "thoroughly distasteful" to him, but was necessary to prevent immediate paralysis of the mobilization program. Presidents have been in the past, and any man worthy of the Office should be in the future, free to take at least interim action necessary to execute legislative programs essential to survival of the Nation. A sturdy judiciary should not be swayed by the unpleasantness or unpopularity of necessary executive action, but must independently determine for itself whether the President was acting, as required by the Constitution, to "take Care that the Laws be faithfully executed."

Times of national crisis test the nation's commitment to constitutional rights. When the nation's security is in jeopardy and passions are running high, it is not uncommon for the chief executive to place the highest priority on the country's survival. The Supreme Court has responded to such situations by acknowledging the existence of certain war powers that enhance governmental authority in crisis situations. Nevertheless, the justices have held that there are limitations to these expanded powers as well as specified conditions under which they may be exercised. *Youngstown Sheet & Tube* provides useful guidelines concerning the application of the war powers. In spite of the Court's war powers jurisprudence, however, the limits of executive authority will be always be tested when the nation's survival is at stake.

READINGS

Berger, Raoul. *Executive Privilege: A Constitutional Myth.* Cambridge, Mass.: Harvard University Press, 1974.

Bessette, Joseph, and Jeffrey Tulis. *The Presidency in the Constitutional Order.* Baton Rouge: Louisiana State University Press, 1981.

Corwin, Edward S. *The President: Office and Powers.* 5th rev. ed. New York: New York University Press, 1984.

Crovitz, L. Gordon, and Jeremy A. Rabkin, eds. *The Fettered Presidency: Legal Constraints on the Executive Branch.* Washington, D.C.: American Enterprise Institute, 1989.

Harriger, Katy J. *Independent Justice: The Federal Special Prosecutor in American Politics.* Lawrence: University Press of Kansas, 1992.

Henkin, Louis. *Foreign Affairs and the Constitution.* Mineola, N.Y.: Foundation Press, 1972.

Irons, Peter. *Justice at War: The Story of the Japanese-American Internment Cases.* New York: Oxford University Press, 1983.

Koenig, Louis. *The Chief Executive.* 3d ed. New York: Harcourt Brace Jovanovich, 1975.

Marcus, Maeva. *Truman and the Steel Seizure Case: The Limits of Presidential Power.* New York: Columbia University Press, 1987.

May, Christopher. *In the Name of War: Judicial Review and the War Powers Since 1918.* Cambridge, Mass.: Harvard University Press, 1989.

McKenzie, G. Calvin. *The Politics of Presidential Appointments.* New York: Free Press, 1981.

Randall, James. *Constitutional Problems Under Lincoln.* Urbana: University of Illinois Press, 1964.

Reveley, W. Taylor III. *War Powers of the President and Congress.* Charlottesville: University Press of Virginia, 1981.

Rossiter, Clinton L. *Constitutional Dictatorship: Crisis Government in the Modern Democracies.* Princeton, N.J.: Princeton University Press, 1948.

Westin, Alan F. *Anatomy of a Constitutional Law Case.* New York: Macmillan, 1958.

PART III
NATION–STATE RELATIONS

AN INTRODUCTION TO NATION-STATE
RELATIONS

6. FEDERALISM

7. THE COMMERCE POWER

8. THE POWER TO TAX AND SPEND

AN INTRODUCTION TO NATION-STATE RELATIONS

I F WE CATALOGED the types of governments existing in the world today, we would have a fairly diverse list. Some are unitary systems in which power is located in a central authority that may or may not mete out some power to its subdivisions. Others are virtually the opposite: authority rests largely with local governments with only certain powers reserved to national authority. When the Framers drafted the Constitution, they had to make some basic decisions about the balance between the states and the national government they were creating. Their choice, generally speaking, was federalism: a system in which "a constitution divides governmental power between a central government and one or more subdivisional governments, giving each substantial functions."[1]

That decision turned out to be a good one, and we reap the advantages of it today. For example, because the government is multitiered and layered, Americans have many points of access to the system. Moreover, the system provides for numerous checks on the exercise of government power because federal, state, and even local systems are all involved in policy making.

Finally, federalism encourages experimentation and provides for flexibility. Justice Brandeis once wrote, "It is one of the happy incidents of the federal system that a single courageous State may, if its citizens choose, serve as a laboratory; and try novel social and economic experiments without risk to the rest of the country."[2] While "experimenting with policy on the national level poses great risks," states are uniquely poised to fashion solutions for their own localized problems, some of which may be applicable to the nation.[3] The states were first to implement tougher drinking-and-driving laws, policies protecting workers' rights, and so forth.

But federalism is not perfect. For one thing, it can be costly. In some countries citizens pay a single (and often very large) tax; Americans may pay local property taxes, state sales and income taxes, and federal assessments. For another, the system lacks efficiency. The implementation of certain kinds of policies might require the coordination of the national government, fifty states, and numerous subdivisions, which inevitably slows down the process.

1. J. W. Peltason, *Understanding the Constitution*, 11th ed. (New York: Holt, Rinehart and Winston, 1988), 16.

2. Dissent in *New State Ice Co. v. Liebmann* (1932).
3. Paul Johnson et al., *American Government* (Boston: Houghton Mifflin, 1990), 77.

For our purposes, the most relevant concern about federalism is its complexity. The system "makes it difficult for citizens to keep informed about their government."[4] People may not understand which level of government makes specific policies, and some citizens may have so little interest that they do not know the names of their state representatives. At the other end of the spectrum, governments sometimes do not well understand the boundaries of their own power. Often throughout American history states have charged that the federal government went too far in regulating "their" business; indeed, this was one issue over which the Civil War, the most extreme disagreement, was fought.

Since the nation's founding, the U.S. Supreme Court has played the major role in delineating and defining the contours of American federalism. Why and how it has done so are the subjects of the chapters that follow. Chapter 6 focuses on the various and general theories of federal–state relations with which the Court has dealt. Chapters 7 and 8 consider the exercise of government power over the most contentious of issues: commerce and taxing and spending.

But first, let us explore several issues emanating from our discussion so far: the kind of system the Framers adopted, the amending of that system, and its complexity. The resulting conflicts often require the involvement of "neutral" arbiters—judges and Supreme Court justices.

THE FRAMERS AND FEDERALISM

We have already mentioned that the Framers selected federalism from among several alternative forms of government, although the word *federalism* does not appear in the Constitution. The Founders had some general vision of the sort of government they wanted—or, more aptly, of what sorts they did not want. They rejected a unitary system as wholly in-

compatible with basic values and traditions already existing within the states. They also rejected a confederation in which power would reside with the states; after all, that is what they had under the Articles of Confederation, the charter they came to Philadelphia to revise.

How to divide power, then, became the delegates' central concern. In the end, they wrote into the document a rather elaborate "pattern of allocation." Nevertheless, ambiguity resulted.[5] A most important source of this confusion was the question of constitutional relationships; that is, in the parlance of the eighteenth century, the Framers looked at the Constitution as a contract, but a contract between whom? Some commentators argue that it specifies the relationship between the people and the national government and that the former empower the latter. Justice Story wrote:

The constitution of the United States was ordained and established, not by the states in their sovereign capacities, but emphatically, as the preamble of the constitution declares, by "the people of the United States.". . . The constitution was not, therefore, necessarily carved out of existing state sovereignties, nor a surrender of powers already existing in state institutions.[6]

Others suggest that the contract is between the states and the nation. In a 1798 resolution of the Virginia Assembly, James Madison wrote:

That this Assembly doth explicitly and peremptorily declare that it views the powers of the Federal Government as resulting from the compact, to which the States are parties, as limited by the plain sense and intention of the instrument constituting that compact; as no further valid than they are authorized by the grants enumerated in that compact; and that in case of deliberate, palpable, and dangerous exercise of other powers not granted by the said compact, the States, who are the parties thereto, have the right, and are in duty bound, to interpose for arresting the progress of the evil, and for maintaining within their re-

---

4. Ibid., 75.

5. C. Herman Pritchett, *Constitutional Law of the Federal System* (Englewood Cliffs, N.J.: Prentice Hall, 1984), 58.
6. *Martin v. Hunter's Lessee*, (1816).

spective limits, the authorities, rights, and liberties appertaining to them.[7]

This is not merely an abstract debate, but one with real consequences. In its most violent incarnation, the Civil War, southern leaders took Madison's logic to its limit. They argued that because the Constitution represented a contract between the states and the federal government, with the states creating the national government, when the latter—the North—abrogated its end of the contract, the contract was no longer valid. The Civil War ended that particular dispute, but the principle continued to flare up in less extreme, but no less important, forms. The refusal of some southern states to abide by federal civil rights laws is one example.

This problem continues to manifest itself largely because the Constitution supports both sides and therefore neither. Those who favor the argument that the national government is beholden to the people point to the document's preamble: *We the people* of the United States . . . do ordain and establish this Constitution." To support the argument that the states create the national government, proponents turn to Article VII's language, that the ratification of nine states "shall be sufficient for the Establishment of this Constitution *between the States* so ratifying." When the issue of the contractual nature of the Constitution arises, therefore, many look to the Supreme Court to resolve it. As we shall see in Chapter 6, different Courts have approached this debate in varying ways, adopting one view over the other at distinct points in American history.

AMENDING THE CONSTITUTION: THE TENTH AMENDMENT

Arguments over which entities are the parties to the contract, the U.S. Constitution, may never be fully

resolved, but another point of ambiguity was thought so onerous that it could not be left up to mere interpretation. That area is the balance of power between the states and the federal government. The original charter, in the view of many, placed too much authority with the federal government. In particular, states' rights advocates pointed to two sections of the Constitution as working against their interests.

The first section is the Necessary and Proper Clause: Congress has the power "To make all Laws which shall be necessary and proper for carrying into Execution [its] Powers, and all other Powers vested by this Constitution in the Government of the United States, or in any Department or Officer there of."

The other section is the Supremacy Clause: "This Constitution, and the Laws of the United States which shall be made in Pursuance thereof; and all Treaties made, or which shall be made, under the Authority of the United States, shall be the supreme Law of the Land; and the Judges in every state shall be bound thereby, any Thing in the Constitution or Laws of any State to the Contrary notwithstanding." These clauses seem to allocate a great deal of power to the national government.

Yet, as Madison wrote in *Federalist,* No. 45:

The powers delegated by the proposed Constitution to the Federal Government, are few and defined. Those which are to remain in the State Governments are numerous and indefinite. The former will be exercised principally on external objects, as war, peace, negotiation, and foreign commerce; with which last the power of taxation will for the most part be connected. The powers reserved to the several States will extend to all the objects, which, in the ordinary course of affairs, concern the lives, liberties and properties of the people; and the internal order, improvement, and prosperity of the State.

Nevertheless, states remained concerned that the national government would attempt to cut into their power and sovereignty, and the language of the Constitution did little to allay their fears. At worst, it suggested that the federal institutions always would be

7. Reprinted in *Documents of American Constitutional and Legal History,* vol. 1, ed. Melvin I. Urofsky (New York: Knopf, 1989), 159.

TABLE III-1   The Constitutional Allocation of Government Power

Powers Specified Within the Constitution or by Court Interpretation		
Powers exclusive to the national government	*Powers exclusive to state governments*	*Concurrent powers to both federal and state governments*
Coin money	Run elections	Tax
Regulate interstate and foreign commerce	Regulate intrastate commerce	Borrow money
Tax imports and exports	Establish republican forms of state local governments	Establish courts
Make treaties	Protect public health, safety, and morals	Charter banks and corporations
Make all laws "necessary and proper"	All powers not delegated to the national government or denied to the states by the Constitution	Make and enforce laws
Make war		Take property (power of eminent domain)
Regulate postal system		

Powers Denied by the Constitution or by Court Interpretation		
Expressly prohibited to the national government	*Expressly prohibited to state government*	*Expressly prohibited to both*
Tax state exports	Tax imports and exports	Pass bills of attainder
Change state boundaries	Coin money	Pass ex post facto laws
	Enter into treaties	Grant titles of nobility
	Impair obligation of contracts	Impose religious tests
		Pass laws in conflict with the Bill of Rights and subsequent amendments

SOURCE: Adapted from Paul E. Johnson et al., *American Government* (Boston: Houghton Mifflin, 1990), 84; J. W. Peltason, *Corwin & Peltason's Understanding the Constitution* (New York: Holt, Rinehart and Winston, 1988), 19; and C. Herman Pritchett, *Constitutional Law of the Federal System* (Englewood Cliffs, N.J.: Prentice-Hall, 1984), 58.

supreme; at best, it was highly ambiguous. Even Madison recognized the document's lack of clarity when he wrote in *Federalist*, No. 39:

The proposed Constitution therefore . . . is in strictness neither a national nor a federal Constitution; but a composition of both. In its foundation it is federal, not national; in the sources from which the ordinary powers of the Government are drawn, it is partly federal, and partly national: in the operation of these powers, it is national, not federal. In the extent of them, again, it is federal; not national: And finally in the authoritative mode of introducing amendments, it is neither wholly federal, nor wholly national.

Madison clearly thought this ambiguity an asset of the new system of government, an advantage that made it fit compatibly into the overall philosophies of separation of powers and checks and balances. But his argument proved inadequate; when the perceived unfair balance of power proved to be an obstacle to the ratification of the Constitution, those favoring its adoption promised to remedy the inequality.

This remedy took the form of the Tenth Amendment, which—in terms of the rest of the Bill of Rights—is a constitutional oddity. While the first nine amendments deal mainly with the rights of the people vis-á-vis the federal government (for example, the First Amendment: "Congress shall make no law respecting an establishment of religion," and so forth), the Tenth Amendment states: "The powers not delegated to the United States by the Constitution, nor prohibited by it to the States, are reserved to the States respectively, or to the people." With these words in place, states' rights advocates were mollified, at least temporarily, and the American system of government—that unique brand of federalism—was established.

In the final analysis, what does the system look like? In other words, who gets what? Table III-1 depicts the allocation of powers emanating from the Constitution. As we can see, the different levels of government have some exclusive and some concurrent powers, but they are also prohibited from operating in certain spheres.

The elaborate system of American federalism depicted in Table III-1 seems to belie what we noted at the beginning of this essay. At this point, you may be wondering how such a well-articulated division of power could be the center of so much controversy. In part, the answer takes us back to the contractual nature of the Constitution. As we shall see in Chapter 6, in which we explore general theoretical approaches to federalism, the Court has had some difficulty determining who are the parties to the contract, and its confusion encouraged litigation. In more concrete terms, no matter how elaborate the design, the Constitution does not (and perhaps cannot) address the range of real disputes that arise between nation and state.

Indeed, the irony here is that the complexity of the system coupled with the language of the Constitution is what fosters the need for interpretation. Note the last column in Table III-1, which illustrates concurrent powers. Where do state powers begin and federal powers end and vice versa? For example, states have the authority to regulate intrastate commerce, and the federal government regulates interstate commerce, but is it so easy to delineate those boundaries? Which entity controls the making and selling of goods manufactured in one state and shipped to another? And, more to the point, what happens when the national government and the states have different notions of how to regulate the manufacturing?

If that problem is not enough, compare the constitutional language of the Tenth Amendment with that of the Necessary and Proper and Supremacy Clauses. The last prohibits states from passing laws that directly conflict with the Constitution, federal laws, and so forth. But so often the issues are not clear. For example, is the federal authority supreme only in its sphere of operations (those activities where it has clear constitutional mandates), as some argue the Tenth Amendment states? Or is it the case that every time the federal government enters into a particular realm, it automatically preempts states from acting? Or does the answer depend on the intent of Congress—that is, whether the legislature intended to preempt state action?

It should be clear that American federalism is something of a double-edged sword. On the one side, the balance of power it created not only pacified those who were opposed to ratifying the Constitution but also continues to define the contours of the U.S. system of government. On the other, the complexity of the system has given rise to tensions between the levels of government, in the form of disputes that settlement by the courts. It may be that the system has been so resilient because of the interpretation the Constitution constantly requires. But we will leave that up to you to decide as we now turn to the way the Supreme Court has formulated theories and specific rulings in response to two distinct but interrelated issues: the general contours of state–federal relations and the important powers of commerce and taxing and spending.

CHAPTER 6
FEDERALISM

URING THE 1960s Congress amended a labor standards act and required state governments to pay virtually all their employees a specified minimum wage and to compensate them for overtime work. Were these amendments constitutional or did they interfere with state authority and autonomy? The answer depends on how we view the letter and spirit of the Constitution; we would reach very different conclusions depending on whether we subscribed to the dual approach or the cooperative approach to nation–state relations (see Table 6-1).

Proponents of dual federalism would want the Court to strike down the law. As advocates of states' rights, they would argue that the Constitution represents an agreement between the states and the federal government in which the states empower the central government; states, therefore, are not subservient to the federal government. In other words, because each is supreme within its own sphere, the federal government could no more impose minimum wage requirements on states than the states could on the federal government. To back their theory, dual federalists invoke the Tenth Amendment, arguing that Congress cannot "invade" power reserved to the states and that courts should invalidate any congressional legislation touching traditional state functions.

Cooperative federalism proponents take precisely the opposite view. They argue that the people, not the states, created and animated the federal government. Moreover, they hold that the Supremacy Clause and the Necessary and Proper Clause would settle arguments, not the Tenth Amendment. That amendment, under cooperative federalism, grants no express power to the states. As a result, the law regulating wages would pass constitutional muster.

At present, the Supreme Court seems to subscribe to cooperative federalism, but that has not always been the case. The amendments to the labor standards act, in fact, were struck down by the Court in 1976 in *National League of Cities v. Usery*, only to be upheld in 1985 in *Garcia v. San Antonio Metropolitan Transit Authority*, which effectively overruled the 1976 decision.

The Court's about-face from *National League* to *Garcia* is not an anomaly in this area of the law; rather, it is a symptom of the general confusion that has surrounded American federalism since the eighteenth century. As depicted in Table 6-2, throughout U.S. history different Courts have subscribed to dual federalism, cooperative federalism, or one of their variants. Even more intriguing is that a sort of doctrinal cycle has developed, as the justices have moved between

TABLE 6-1   A Comparison of Dual and Cooperative Federalism

	Dual Federalism	Cooperative Federalism
General view	Operates under the assumption that the two levels of government are co-equal sovereigns, each supreme within its own sphere.	Operates under the assumption that the national government is supreme even if its actions touch state functions. States and the federal government are "partners," but the latter largely sets policy for the nation.
View of the Constitution	It is a compact among the states and a contract between the states and the federal government.	Rejects view of it as a compact; the people, not the states, empower the national government.
Constitutional support	Tenth Amendment reserves certain powers to the states and thus limits the national government to those powers specifically delegated to it.	Tenth Amendment does not provide additional powers to the states.
	Necessary and Proper Clause is to be read literally and narrowly.	Necessary and Proper Clause is to be read expansively and loosely.
		Supremacy Clause means that the national government is supreme within its own sphere, even if its actions touch on state functions.

TABLE 6-2   Doctrinal Cycles of Nation–State Relations

Court Era	General Approach Adopted
Marshall Court (1801–1835)	Cooperative federalism (National supremacy)
Taney Court (1835–1864)	Dual federalism
Civil War/Reconstruction Courts (1865–1895)	Cooperative federalism (National supremacy)
Laissez-faire Courts (1896–1936)	Dual federalism (grounded in laissez-faire philosophy)
Post-New Deal Courts (1937–1975)	Cooperative federalism
Burger Court: *National League of Cities v. Usery* (1976)	Dual federalism (Traditional state functions)
Burger Court: *Garcia v. SAMTA* (1985)	Cooperative federalism
Rehnquist Court	?

states' rights and national supremacy positions over time. This chapter examines the components of that cycle. As you read the cases, consider not only which doctrine governed each decision but also why the philosophies have grown stronger or weaker. What forces—legal, political, and historical—have led the justices to choose one approach over the other? This issue is always important because, as we shall discuss at the end of the chapter, it is possible for future Courts to return to a dualist approach to nation–state questions.

THE MARSHALL COURT AND THE RISE OF NATIONAL SUPREMACY

An ardent Federalist, Chief Justice John Marshall was true to his party's tenets over the course of his long career on the Court. In case after case, he was more than willing to elevate the powers of the federal government above those of the states. Perhaps his most significant statement on national supremacy came in *McCulloch v. Maryland* (1819). In Chapter 4 we saw how he used this case to assert firmly that Congress has implied powers. Here, we shall see that *McCulloch* also served as his vehicle to expound the notion of national supremacy. A brief review of the essential facts is offered to remind you of the issues in this case.

McCulloch v. Maryland

4 WHEAT. 316 (1819)

Vote: 6 (Duvall, Johnson, Livingston, Marshall, Story, Washington)

0

Opinion of the Court: Marshall
Not participating: Todd

Congress established the second Bank of the United States in 1816. Because of inefficiency and corruption, the bank was very unpopular, and many went so far as to blame it for the nation's economic problems. To show its displeasure, the Maryland legislature passed a law saying that banks operating in the state that were not chartered by the state—in other words, the national bank—could issue bank notes only on special paper, which the state taxed.

When James McCulloch, the cashier of the Baltimore branch of the Bank of the United States, refused to pay the tax, Maryland took legal action to enforce its law. The United States challenged the constitutionality of the Maryland tax, and in return Maryland disputed the constitutionality of the bank.[1]

---

1. The first part of the excerpted opinion deals with the question of whether Congress had the power to create the bank. *(See the excerpt in Chapter 3.)* The second part deals with the constitutionality of the Maryland tax. Marshall clearly delineates this division in his opinion.

MR. CHIEF JUSTICE MARSHALL delivered the opinion of the court.

The constitution of our country, in its most interesting and vital parts, is to be considered; the conflicting powers of the government of the Union and of its members, as marked in that constitution, are to be discussed; and an opinion given, which may essentially influence the great operations of the government. . . .

In discussing this . . . the counsel for the state of Maryland have deemed it of some importance, in the construction of the constitution, to consider that instrument not as emanating from the people, but as the act of sovereign and independent states. The powers of the general government, it has been said, are delegated by the states, who alone are truly sovereign; and must be exercised in subordination to the states, who alone possess supreme dominion.

It would be difficult to sustain this proposition. The convention which framed the constitution was indeed elected by the state legislatures. But the instrument, when it came from their hands, was a mere proposal, without obligation, or pretensions to it. It was reported to the then existing Congress of the United States, with a request that it might "be submitted to a convention of delegates, chosen in each state by the people thereof, under the recommendation of its legislature, for their assent and ratification." This mode of proceeding was adopted; and by the convention, by Congress, and by the state legislatures, the instrument was submitted to the people. They acted upon it in the only manner in which they can act safely, effectively, and wisely, on such a subject, by assembling in convention. It is true, they assembled in their several states—and where else should they have assembled? No political dreamer was ever wild enough to think of breaking down the lines which separate the states, and of compounding the American people into one common mass. Of consequence, when they act, they act in their states. But the measures they adopt do not, on that account, cease to be the measures of the people themselves, or become the measures of the state governments. . . .

The government of the Union, then . . . is, emphatically, and truly, a government of the people. . . .

It is the government of all; its powers are delegated by all; it represents all, and acts for all. Though any one state may be willing to control its operations, no state is willing to allow others to control them. The nation, on those subjects on which it can act, must necessarily bind its component parts. But this question is not left to mere reason; the people have, in express terms, decided it by saying, "this constitution, and the laws of the United States, which shall be made in pursuance thereof," "shall be the supreme law of the land," and by requiring that the members of the state legislatures, and the officers of the executive and judicial departments of the states shall take the oath of fidelity to it. The government of the United States, then, though limited in its powers, is supreme; and its laws, when made in pursuance of the constitution, form the supreme law of the land, "anything in the constitution or laws of any State to the contrary notwithstanding."

Among the enumerated powers, we do not find that of establishing a bank or creating a corporation. But there is no phrase in the instrument which, like the articles of confederation, excludes incidental or implied powers; and which requires that everything granted shall be expressly and minutely described. Even the 10th amendment, which was framed for the purpose of quieting the excessive jealousies which had been excited, omits the word "expressly," and declares only that the powers "not delegated to the United States, nor prohibited to the states, are reserved to the states or to the people;" thus leaving the question, whether the particular power which may become the subject of contest has been delegated to the one government, or prohibited to the other, to depend on a fair construction of the whole instrument. The men who drew and adopted this amendment had experienced the embarrassments resulting from the insertion of this word in the articles of confederation, and probably omitted it to avoid those embarrassments. A constitution, to contain an accurate detail of all the subdivisions of which its great powers will admit, and of all the means by which they may be carried into execution, would partake of a prolixity of a legal code, and could scarcely be embraced by the human mind. It would probably never be understood by the public. Its nature, therefore, requires, that only its great outlines should be marked, its important objects designated, and the minor ingredients which compose those objects be deduced from the nature of the objects themselves. That this idea was entertained by the framers of the American constitution, is not only to be

inferred from the nature of the instrument, but from the language. . . .

After this declaration, it can scarcely be necessary to say that the existence of state banks can have no possible influence on the question. No trace is to be found in the constitution of an intention to create a dependence of the government of the Union on those of the states, for the execution of the great powers assigned to it. Its means are adequate to its ends; and on those means alone was it expected to rely for the accomplishment of its ends. To impose on it the necessity of resorting to means which it cannot control, which another government may furnish or withhold, would render its course precarious; the result of its measures uncertain, and create a dependence on other governments, which might disappoint its most important designs and is incompatible with the language of the constitution. But were it otherwise, the choice of means implies a right to choose a national bank in preference to state banks, and Congress alone can make the election.

After the most deliberate consideration, it is the unanimous and decided opinion of this court that the act to incorporate the bank of the United States is a law made in pursuance of the constitution, and is part of the supreme law of the land. . . .

It being the opinion of the court, that the act incorporating the bank is constitutional; and that the power of establishing a branch in the State of Maryland might be properly exercised by the bank itself, we proceed to inquire . . . whether the State of Maryland may, without violating the constitution, tax that branch? . . .

The argument on the part of the State of Maryland, is, not that the States may directly resist a law of Congress, but that they may exercise their acknowledged powers upon it, and that the constitution leaves them this right in the confidence that they will not abuse it.

That the power to tax involves the power to destroy; that the power to destroy may defeat and render useless the power to create; that there is a plain repugnance, in conferring on one government a power to control the constitutional measures of another, which other, with respect to those very measures, is declared to be supreme over that which exerts the control, are propositions not to be denied. But all inconsistencies are to be reconciled by the magic of the word CONFIDENCE. Taxation, it is said, does not necessarily and unavoidably destroy. To carry it to the excess of destruction would be an abuse, to presume which, would banish that confidence which is essential to all government.

But is this a case of confidence? Would the people of any one State trust those of another with a power to control the most insignificant operations of their State government? We know they would not. Why, then, should we suppose that the people of any one State should be willing to trust those of another with a power to control the operations of a government to which they have confided their most important and most valuable interests? In the legislature of the Union alone, are all represented. The legislature of the Union alone, therefore, can be trusted by the people with the power of controlling measures which concern all, in the confidence that it will not be abused. This, then, is not a case of confidence, and we must consider it as it really is.

If we apply the principle for which the State of Maryland contends, to the constitution generally, we shall find it capable of changing totally the character of that instrument. We shall find it capable of arresting all the measures of the government, and of prostrating it at the foot of the States. The American people have declared their constitution, and the laws made in pursuance thereof, to be supreme; but this principle would transfer the supremacy, in fact, to the States.

If the States may tax one instrument, employed by the government in the execution of its powers, they may tax any and every other instrument. They may tax the mail; they may tax the mint; they may tax patent rights; they may tax the papers of the custom-house; they may tax judicial process; they may tax all the means employed by the government, to an excess which would defeat all the ends of government. This was not intended by the American people. They did not design to make their government dependent on the States. . . .

It has also been insisted, that, as the power of taxation in the general and State governments is acknowledged to be concurrent, every argument which would sustain the right of the general government to tax banks chartered by the States, will equally sustain the right of the States to tax banks chartered by the general government.

But the two cases are not on the same reason. The people of all the States have created the general government, and have conferred upon it the general power of taxation. The people of all the States, and the States themselves, are represented in Congress, and, by their representatives, exercise this power. When they tax the chartered institutions of the States, they tax their constituents; and these taxes must be uniform. But, when a State taxes the operations of the government of the United States, it acts upon institutions created, not by their own constituents, but by people over whom they claim no control. It acts upon the measures of a government created by others as well as themselves, for the benefit of others in common with themselves. The difference is that which always exists, and always must exist, between the action of the whole on a part, and the action of a part on the whole—between the laws of a government declared to be supreme, and those of a government which, when in opposition to those laws, is not supreme.

But if the full application of this argument could be admitted, it might bring into question the right of Congress to tax the State banks, and could not prove the right of the States to tax the Bank of the United States.

The court has bestowed on this subject its most deliberate consideration. The result is a conviction that the states have no power, by taxation or otherwise, to retard, impede, burden, or in any manner control the operations of the constitutional laws enacted by Congress to carry into execution the powers vested in the general government. This is, we think, the unavoidable consequence of that supremacy which the constitution has declared.

We are unanimously of opinion that the law passed by the legislature of Maryland, imposing a tax on the Bank of the United States, is unconstitutional and void.

Constitutional scholars regard *McCulloch* as an unequivocal statement of national power over the states. Its strength lies in Marshall's treatment of the three relevant constitutional provisions: the Necessary and Proper Clause, the Tenth Amendment, and the Supremacy Clause.

First, according to *McCulloch*, the Necessary and Proper Clause permits Congress to pass legislation implied by its enumerated functions, bounded only in this way:

Let the end be legitimate, let it be within the scope of the constitution, and all means which are appropriate, which are plainly adapted to that end, which are not prohibited, but consist with the letter and spirit of the constitution, are constitutional.

Second, because the Tenth Amendment reserves to the states or to the people only power that has not been delegated to Congress (and not *expressly* delegated), it stands as no significant bar to Congress's exercise of its powers, including those that are implied. Given Marshall's treatment of the Necessary and Proper Clause, implied powers are quite broad. Third, the Supremacy Clause places the national government at the top within its sphere of operation, a sphere that again, according to Marshall's interpretation of the Necessary and Proper Clause, is expansive. If the Supremacy Clause means anything, it means that no state may "retard, impede, burden, or in any manner control, the operations of the constitutional laws enacted by Congress." Note, too, Marshall's view of the constitutional arrangement; as one would expect, he fully endorsed the position that the charter represents a contract between the people—not the states—and the federal government.

McCulloch's holdings—supporting congressional creation of the bank and negating state taxation of it—were not particularly surprising. Most observers thought the Marshall Court would rule the way it did. It was the chief justice's language and the constitutional theories he offered that sparked a "fierce ideological" debate in a states' rights newspaper, the *Richmond Enquirer.*[2] It began just weeks after *McCulloch* was decided, when a barrage of state rights' advocates wrote in to condemn the ruling. Apparently concerned that if their views took hold "the constitution would be converted into the old confederation," Marshall took an unusual step for a Supreme Court justice: he re-

sponded to his critics. Initially, he wrote two articles, carried by a Philadelphia newspaper, defending *McCulloch.* But when an old enemy, Spence Roane, a Virginia Supreme Court judge, launched an unbridled attack, Marshall responded with nine "elaborate essays," published under the pseudonym "A Friend of the Constitution."

THE TANEY COURT AND THE (RE)EMERGENCE OF STATES' RIGHTS

While Marshall was chief justice of the United States, his view of nation–state relations, not Roane's, prevailed. But their argument foreshadowed a series of events that took place between the 1830s and 1860s, events that would change the country forever *(see Table 6-3).* The first occurred in November 1832. After Congress passed a tariff act that the South thought unfairly burdensome, South Carolina adopted an ordinance that nullified the federal law. Several days later, the state said it was prepared to enforce its nullification by military force and, if necessary, secession from the Union. It is not surprising that South Carolina took the lead in the battle for state sovereignty. The state was the home of John C. Calhoun, a former vice president of the United States and a most outspoken proponent of slavery and states' rights. Indeed, Calhoun is best remembered as an advocate of the doctrine of concurrent majorities, a view that would provide states with a veto over federal policies. This doctrine was the underpinning for South Carolina's ordinance of nullification.

The president, Andrew Jackson, was no great nationalist; rather, he believed that states' rights were not incompatible with those of the federal government. But even he took issue with South Carolina's ordinance. Just a month after the state acted, as Table 6-3 illustrates, Jackson issued a proclamation, warning the state that it could not secede from the Union. The president's action infuriated South Carolina, but it

---

2. This discussion is based on Gerald Gunther, *Constitutional Law,* 12th ed. (Mineola, N.Y.: Foundation Press, 1991), 84. For records of Marshall's essays, see Gerald Gunther, ed., *John Marshall's Defense of* McCulloch v. Maryland (Stanford, Calif.: Stanford University Press, 1969).

TABLE 6-3   Selected Events Leading to the Civil War

Year	Event	Significance
November 1832	South Carolina ordinance of nullification.	Suggests that states can nullify acts of the federal government and, if necessary, secede from the Union.
December 1832	Jackson issues proclamation warning South Carolina against secession.	Temporarily halts secession crisis, as no state follows South Carolina's lead.
December 1835	Jackson nominates Taney to be chief justice of U.S. Supreme Court.	Senate delays confirming Taney, a former slaveholder, until 1836.
May 1854	Congress repeals the Missouri Compromise.	Allows territories to enter the Union with or without slavery.
March 1857	*Scott v. Sandford.*	Increases tension between the North and South, as the former loudly denounces the decision.
November 1860	Lincoln is elected president.	South proclaims that secession is inevitable.
December 1860	South Carolina ordinance of secession.	South Carolina votes to secede from the Union. Within a few weeks, six other states follow suit.

temporarily averted a major crisis, as no other state attempted to act on the nullification doctrine.

Another event that would have major implications was Chief Justice Marshall's death in 1835 and Roger Taney's ascension to the chief justiceship *(see Box 6-1)*. In some ways, Marshall and Taney were alike. Both had begun their political careers in their respective states—Virginia and Maryland—and then held major positions within the executive branch of the national government. Both were committed partisan activists. The difference was that they were committed to completely opposite conceptions of government structure, particularly with regard to nation–state relations. In contrast to Marshall, the Federalist, Taney was a Jacksonian Democrat, a full believer in those ideas espoused by President Jackson, under whom he had served as attorney general, secretary of war, and secretary of the Treasury, and who had appointed him chief justice. The two chief justices' views on the Bank of the United States provide a clear example of their

political ideas in action. In *McCulloch* Marshall lent his full support to the bank; in 1832 Taney helped write President Jackson's veto message in which he "condemned the Second Bank of the United States" and refused to recharter it.[3]

Had Taney been Jackson's only appointment to the Court, he might not have been able to change the course of federalism. But that was not the case. Table 6-4 shows that by 1841 Joseph Story was the only justice remaining from the Marshall Court that decided *McCulloch*. The others, like Taney, were schooled in Jacksonian democracy. It was, R. Kent Newmyer noted, no longer "the Marshall Court. But, then again it was not the age of Marshall."[4] This observation holds on two levels: doctrinally and politically. The Taney Court ushered in substantial legal changes, especially in federal–state relations. Although there is no true

3. R. Kent Newmyer, *The Supreme Court Under Marshall and Taney* (New York: Crowell, 1968), 93.
4. Ibid., 94.

BOX 6-1 ROGER BROOKE TANEY (1836-1864)

ROGER TANEY WAS descended on both sides from prominent Maryland families. His mother's family, named Brooke, first arrived in the state in 1650, complete with fox hounds and other trappings of aristocracy. The first Taney arrived about 1660 as an indentured servant but was able to acquire a large amount of property and became a member of the landed Maryland tidewater gentry.

Taney was born March 17, 1777, on his father's tobacco plantation in Calvert County. He was educated in local rural schools and privately tutored by a Princeton student. In 1795, at the age of eighteen, he graduated first in his class from Dickinson College in Pennsylvania.

As his father's second son, Taney was not in line to inherit the family property and so decided on a career in law and politics. For three years, he was an apprentice lawyer in the office of Judge Jeremiah Chase of the Maryland General Court in Annapolis. He was admitted to the bar in 1799.

Taney married Anne Key, daughter of a prominent farmer and the sister of Francis Scott Key, on January 7, 1806. Since Taney was a devout Roman Catholic and his wife an Episcopalian, they agreed to raise their sons as Catholics and their daughters as Episcopalians. The couple had six daughters and a son who died in infancy. In 1855, the year *Scott v. Sandford* came before the Supreme Court, Taney's wife and youngest daughter died of yellow fever.

TANEY BEGAN his political career as a member of the Federalist party, serving one term in the Maryland legislature from 1799 to 1800. After being defeated for reelection, he moved from Calvert County to Frederick, where he began to develop a profitable law practice. In 1803 Taney was beaten again in an attempt to return to the House of Delegates. Despite this setback, he began to achieve prominence in the Frederick community as a lawyer and politician. He lived there for twenty years.

In supporting the War of 1812, Taney split with the ma-

jority of Maryland Federalists. But in 1816, as a result of shifting political loyalties, he was elected to the state senate and became a dominant figure in party politics. Taney's term expired in 1821. In 1823 he settled in Baltimore, where he continued his successful law practice and political activities. By this time, the Federalist party had virtually disintegrated, and Taney threw his support to Andrew Jackson's Democrats. He led Jackson's 1828 presidential campaign in Maryland and served as the state's attorney general from 1827 until 1831. At that time, he was named U.S. attorney general for the Jackson administration and left Baltimore for Washington.

It was at this stage in his career that Taney played a leading role in the controversy over the second Bank of the United States, helping to write President Jackson's message in 1832 vetoing the bank's recharter. The next year, when Treasury secretary William Duane refused to withdraw federal deposits from the national bank, Duane was dismissed and replaced by Taney, who promptly carried out the action.

Taney held the Treasury job for nine months, presiding over a new system of state bank depositories called "pet banks." Jackson, who had delayed as long as he could, was eventually forced to submit Taney's nomination as Treasury secretary to the Senate, which rejected it. Taney was forced to resign.

In 1835 Jackson named Taney to replace aging Supreme Court justice Gabriel Duvall, but the nomination was indefinitely postponed by a close Senate vote. Ten months later, on December 28, Jackson proposed Taney's name again, this time to fill the seat left vacant by the death of Chief Justice John Marshall. To the horror of the Whigs, who considered him much too radical, Taney was confirmed as chief justice on March 15, 1836. He served until his death in Washington, October 12, 1864.

SOURCE: Elder Witt, *Guide to the U.S. Supreme Court*, 2d ed. (Washington, D.C.: Congressional Quarterly, 1990), 819–820.

Taney corollary to Marshall's opinion in *McCulloch*, examples of his views abound: in many opinions he explicated the doctrine of dual federalism, that national and state government are equivalent sovereigns within their own spheres of operation. Unlike Marshall, he read the Tenth Amendment in a broad sense: that it did, in fact, reserve to the states certain powers and limit the power of the federal government over them. In the *License Cases* (1847), Taney wrote: "Every power delegated to the federal government must be in coincidence with a perfect right in the states to all that they have not been delegated; in coincidence, too, with the possessing of every power and right necessary for their existence and preservation."

Early Taney Court decisions, such as the *License Cases*, were not controversial. They may have represented a break from previous doctrine, but they matched the tenor of the times. Although Jackson had his feuds with the states (as his battle with South Carolina illustrated), his general philosophical approach to federalism and to governance were those popularly held. The issue of slavery was another matter. It had been the cause of acrimony at the Philadelphia convention in 1787, and animosity between the North and the South had continued. Only through compromises, such as the "three-fifths" plan in the U.S. Constitution (in which people who were not free were counted as three-fifths of a person for purposes of determining state populations) and the Missouri Compromise of 1820, which provided a plan for where slavery would be allowed in newly admitted states and the territories, did the country remain united. But by the 1850s old battles began heating up; for example, after California was admitted as a free state, South Carolina once again issued a secession call.

Slavery, therefore, represented the most immediate concern of the day, splitting the nation into two ideological camps. On a different level, however, it was a symptom of a larger problem: the growing resistance of southern states to federal supremacy. As the North grew increasingly critical of slavery, calls for se-

TABLE 6-4 From the Marshall Court to the Taney Court

Marshall Court (1819)	Taney Court (1841)
Marshall	Taney
Livingston	Thompson
Story	Story
Washington	Baldwin
Duval	Daniel
Johnson	Wayne
Todd	McLean
	Catron
	McKinley

cession—or, at the very least, for adoption of Calhoun's "concurrent majority" doctrine—became more widespread in the South.

It was at this critical moment that the Taney-led Supreme Court interceded in both issues—slavery and federal supremacy. When, in the infamous case of *Scott v. Sandford* (1857), the Court planted its feet firmly in the states' rights camp, it may have contributed to the collapse of the Union.

Dred Scott, a slave bought in Missouri, was the property of Dr. John Emerson, an army surgeon. In 1834 Emerson took Scott to the free state of Illinois and in 1836, to the Upper Louisiana territory, which was to remain free of slavery under the Missouri Compromise of 1820. Eventually, Scott and Emerson returned to Missouri, but the doctor died shortly thereafter, leaving title to Scott to his brother-in-law, John Sanford, a citizen of New York.[5] Believing that he no longer had slave status because he had lived on free soil, Scott sued for his freedom in a Missouri state court in 1846. He received a favorable decision at the trial court level but lost in the Missouri Supreme Court. Several years later, Scott and his lawyer decided to try again. This time, however, they brought the case to a federal district court, contending that they had a diversity suit—Scott was a citizen of Missouri

5. The party's name, Sanford, was misspelled Sandford in the official records.

and Sanford of New York. Sanford argued that the suit should be dismissed because blacks could not be citizens. The federal courts seemed perplexed by the issue. In the end, they ruled in favor of Sanford but suggested that for legal purposes Scott may be a citizen.

By the time the case arrived at the U.S. Supreme Court for final judgment in 1856, the facts and the political situation had grown increasingly complex. In 1854, under mounting pressure, Congress had repealed the Missouri Compromise, replacing it with legislation declaring congressional neutrality on the issue of slavery. Given this new law and the growing tensions between the North and the South and the free and slave states, some observers speculated that the Court would decline to decide the case: it had become highly controversial and overtly political.

For at least a year, the Court chose that route. In fact, historians have suggested that after hearing the case the justices wanted simply to affirm the state court's decision, thereby evading the issue of slavery and citizenship for blacks. But when Justice Wayne insisted that the Court deal with these concerns, the majority of the others—including Chief Justice Taney, a former slaveholder—went along.[6] Waiting until after the presidential election, a very divided Court (nine separate opinions were written) announced its decision.

At the end of the day, a majority of the Court held that Scott was still a slave. In his majority opinion, Chief Justice Taney offered several reasons for this holding.[7] First, although Scott could become a citizen of a state, he could not be considered, in a legal sense, to be a citizen of the United States; the nation's history and the words of the Constitution and other documents foreclosed that possibility. As a result, Scott could not sue in federal courts. As Taney put it:

The question before us is, whether the class of persons described in the plea in abatement compose a portion of this people, and are constituent members of this sovereignty. We think they are not, and that they are not included, and were not intended to be included, under the word "citizens" in the Constitution, and can, therefore, claim none of the rights and privileges which that instrument provides for and secures to citizens of the United States. On the contrary, they were at that time considered as a subordinate and inferior class of beings, who had been subjugated by the dominant race, and whether emancipated or not, yet remained subject to their authority, and had no rights or privileges but such as those who held the power and the government might choose to grant them.

Second, Congress had no constitutional power to regulate slavery in the territories (in reaching this result, the Court struck down the Missouri Compromise, which already had been repealed by Congress), and the Constitution protects the right to property, a category into which slaves, according to Taney, fell. Third, the status of slaves depended on the law of the state to which they voluntarily returned, regardless of where they had been. Because the Missouri Supreme Court ruled that Scott was a slave, the U.S. Supreme Court would follow suit.

Scott could not have come at a worse time for nationalists or a better one for states' rights advocates. The nation was on the verge of collapse (see Table 6-3). Taney's holding, coupled with his vision of the nature of the federal–state relationship, rather than calming matters, probably added fuel to the fire. From the perspective of northerners and abolitionists, the opinion was among the most evil and heinous ever issued by the Court. Opponents of slavery used the ruling to rally support for their position; they took aim at Taney and the Court, claiming that the institution was so pro-South that it could not be taken seriously. Northern newspapers aroused anti-Court sentiment around the country, with stories about the decision. As one wrote, "The whole slavery agitation was reopened by the proceedings in the Supreme Court today, and that tribunal voluntarily introduced itself into the political

---

6. Melvin I. Urofsky, *A March of Liberty* (New York: Knopf, 1988), 387.

7. We adopt this discussion from ibid., 384–391, and Walter Ehrlich, "Scott v. Sandford," *The Oxford Companion to the Supreme Court*, ed. Kermit L. Hall (New York: Oxford University Press, 1992), 760–761.

arena. . . . Much feeling is excited by this decree, and the opinion is freely expressed that a new element of sectional strife has been wantonly imposed upon the country."[8] Members of Congress lambasted the Court for the raw and unnecessary display of judicial power it had exercised in striking down the Missouri Compromise. In short, historians of the day asserted that "never has the Supreme Court been treated with such ineffable contempt, and never has that tribunal so often cringed before the clamor of the mob."[9] As for the chief justice, his reputation was forever tarnished. Even after his death, Congress resisted commissioning a bust of him to sit beside those of other chief justices in the Capitol's Supreme Court room. At the time, Sen. Charles Sumner said: "I object that an emancipated country should make a bust to the author of the Dred Scott decision," because "the name of Taney is to be hooted down the page of history."[10]

To southerners, *Scott* was a cause for celebration. Indeed, Taney's notions of slavery and dual federalism appeared in a more energized form just a few years later when South Carolina issued its Declaration of the Causes of Secession. President Abraham Lincoln presented precisely the opposite view—the Marshall approach—in his 1861 inaugural address, but his words were not enough to stop the outbreak of war.

Thus, at its core the Civil War was about not only slavery but also the supremacy of the national government over the states. It was the culmination of the debates between the Federalists and Anti-Federalists, between Marshall and Roane, and so forth. When the Union won the war, it seemed to have also won the debate over the nature of federal–state relations. In the immediate aftermath of the battle, the Court acceded,

although not willingly, to congressional power over the defeated region.

DUAL FEDERALISM AND LAISSEZ-FAIRE ECONOMICS

Did the end of the war and the rise of national supremacy mean that Taney's dual federalism had seen its last days? Indeed, the doctrine remained under wraps for several decades but then resurfaced in a somewhat different form in the courts from the 1890s to the 1930s. The most vivid example of its revival came in *Hammer v. Dagenhart* (1918). Some analysts think that this Court's version of dual federalism differed from Taney's in *Dred Scott*. Do you see the distinction? Or do Day's words echo the sentiment Taney expressed?

═══════════════════════════

Hammer v. Dagenhart

247 U.S. 251 (1918)

Vote: 5 (Day, McReynolds, Pitney, Van Devanter, White)
*   4 (Brandeis, Clarke, Holmes, McKenna)*
Opinion of the Court: Day
Dissenting opinion: Holmes

In the 1880s America entered the industrial age, which was characterized by the unfettered growth of the private-sector economy. The industrial revolution changed the United States for the better in countless ways, but it also had a down side. Lacking any significant government controls, many businesses treated their workers less than benevolently. Some forced employees to work more than fourteen hours a day at absurdly low wages and under awful conditions. They also had no qualms about employing children under the age of sixteen.

Americans were divided over these practices. On one side were the entrepreneurs, stockholders, and others who gained from worker exploitation. By em-

8. Quoted in Charles Warren, *The Supreme Court in United States History*, vol. 2 (Boston: Little, Brown, 1926), 304.

9. Quoted in Bernard Schwartz, *A History of the Supreme Court* (New York: Oxford University Press, 1993), 154.

10. It was not until 1874 that busts of Chase and Taney were approved and approved "without debate." See Warren, *The Supreme Court in United States History*, 393–394.

Young girls working in a clothing factory. Congressional attempts to curb child labor by taxing the items produced were repeatedly rebuffed by the Supreme Court.

ploying children, paying low wages, and providing no benefits, business owners were able to minimize expenses and maximize profits. On the other side were the Progressives, reformist groups, and individuals who sought to convince the states and the federal government to enact laws to protect workers. These two camps repeatedly clashed in their struggle to attain diametrically opposed policy ends.[11]

One of the first battles came in 1915 when Congress was considering the Federal Child Labor Act. The bill prohibited shipment in interstate commerce of factory products made by children under the age of fourteen or by children aged fourteen to sixteen who worked more than eight hours a day. Supported by numerous progressive groups, the legislation faced substantial opposition from employer associations,

including the Executive Committee of Southern Cotton Manufacturers. The committee was made up of militant mill owners who organized in 1915 solely to defeat federal child labor legislation. But its first attempt failed, and in 1916 Congress passed the child labor law. The committee's leader, David Clark, vowed that his group would challenge the constitutionality of the act in court. He retained the services of a corporate law firm that held a laissez-faire philosophy and had successfully placed this argument before the Supreme Court. He then sought the right test case to challenge the law. Eventually, he decided on a suit against the Fidelity Manufacturing Company.

The case he brought was perfect for the committee's needs. Roland Dagenhart and his two minor sons were employed by Fidelity, a cotton mill in North Carolina. Under state law, both of Dagenhart's sons were permitted to work up to eleven hours a day *(see Box 6-2)*. Under the new federal act, however, the older boy could work only eight hours, and the younger one

---

11. We derive what follows from Lee Epstein, *Conservatives in Court* (Knoxville: University of Tennessee Press, 1985); and Stephen B. Wood, *Constitutional Politics in the Progressive Era* (Chicago: University of Chicago Press, 1968).

could not work at all. Not only were the facts relating to the Dagenharts advantageous, but also Clark secured the cooperation of the company, which had equal disdain for the law, in planning the litigation. One month before the effective date of the law, the company posted the new federal regulations on its door, and "explained" to affected employees that they would be unable to continue to work. A week later, having already secured the consent of the Dagenharts and of the factory, the committee's attorneys filed an injunction against the company and William C. Hammer, a U.S. attorney, to prevent enforcement of the law.

Within a month, the district court heard arguments and ruled the act unconstitutional. The judge did not write an opinion, but when he handed down his decision, he fully agreed with the committee's arguments, suggesting that the federal government had usurped state power.

Once the district court stayed enforcement of the act, both the committee and the U.S. Justice Department began to plan the strategies they would use before the U.S. Supreme Court. The committee argued that Congress had no authority to impose its policies on the states. The government's defense was led by Solicitor General John W. Davis. One of the great attorneys of the day, he made a strong case for the law, although he probably opposed it. Not only did he argue that the regulation of child labor fell squarely within Congress's purview, but he also supplied the Court with data indicating that the states themselves had sought to eliminate such practices. His brief pointed out that only three states placed no age limit on factory employees, and only ten allowed those between the ages of fourteen and sixteen to work.

MR. JUSTICE DAY delivered the opinion of the court.

It is . . . contended that the authority of Congress may be exerted to control interstate commerce in the shipment of child-made goods because of the effect of the circulation

---

BOX 6-2   DOUBTFUL VICTORY

Five years after the Supreme Court's decision in *Hammer v. Dagenhart* striking down the child labor law, a journalist interviewed Reuben Dagenhart, whose father had sued to prevent Congress from interfering with his sons' jobs in a North Carolina cotton mill. Reuben was twenty when he was interviewed. Excerpts follow:

"What benefit . . . did you get out of the suit which you won in the United States Supreme Court?"

"I don't see that I got any benefit. I guess I'd be a lot better off if they hadn't won it.

"Look at me! A hundred and five pounds, a grown man, and no education. I may be mistaken, but I think the years I've put in the cotton mills have stunted my growth. They kept me from getting any schooling. I had to stop school after the third grade and now I need the education I didn't get."

"Just what did you and John get out of that suit then?" he was asked.

"Why, we got some automobile rides when them big lawyers from the North was down here. Oh yes, and they bought both of us a Coca-Cola! That's all we got out of it."

"What did you tell the judge when you were in court?"

"Oh, John and me was never in court. Just Paw was there. John and me was just little kids in short pants. I guess we wouldn't have looked like much in court. . . . We were working in the mill while the case was going on."

Reuben hasn't been to school in years, but his mind has not been idle.

"It would have been a good thing for all the kids in this state if that law they passed had been kept. Of course, they do better now than they used to. You don't see so many babies working in the factories, but you see a lot of them that ought to be going to school."

SOURCE: *Labor*, November 17, 1923, 3, quoted in Leonard F. James, *The Supreme Court in American Life*, 2d ed. (Glenview, Ill.: Scott, Foresman, 1971), 74.

of such goods in other states where the evil of this class of labor has been recognized by local legislation, and the right to thus employ child labor has been more rigorously restrained than in the state of production. In other words, that the unfair competition thus engendered may be controlled by closing the channels of interstate commerce to manufacturers in those states where the local laws do not meet what Congress deems to be the more just standard of other states.

There is no power vested in Congress to require the states to exercise their police power so as to prevent possible unfair competition. Many causes may co-operate to give one state, by reason of local laws or conditions, an economic advantage over others. The commerce clause was not intended to give to Congress a general authority to equalize such conditions. In some of the states laws have been passed fixing minimum wages for women; in others the local law regulates the hours of labor of women in various employments. Business done in such states may be at an economic disadvantage when compared with states which have no such regulations; surely, this fact does not give Congress the power to deny transportation in interstate commerce to those who carry on business where the hours of labor and the rate of compensation for women have not been fixed by a standard in the use in other states and approved by Congress.

The grant of power to Congress over the subject of interstate commerce was to enable it to regulate such commerce, and not to give it authority to control the states in their exercise of the police power over local trade and manufacture.

The grant of authority over a purely Federal matter was not intended to destroy the local power always existing and carefully reserved to the states in the 10th Amendment to the Constitution. . . .

That there should be limitations upon the right to employ children in mines and factories in the interest of their own and the public welfare, all will admit. That such employment is generally deemed to require regulation is shown by the fact that the brief of counsel states that every state in the Union has a law upon the subject, limiting the right to thus employ children. In North Carolina, the state wherein is located the factory in which the employment was had in the present case, no child under twelve years of age is permitted to work.

. . . The maintenance of the authority of the states over matters purely local is as essential to the preservation of our institutions as is the conservation of the supremacy of the Federal power in all matters intrusted to the nation by the Federal Constitution.

In interpreting the Constitution it must never be forgotten that the nation is made up of states, to which are intrusted the powers of local government. And to them and to the people the powers not expressly delegated to the national government are reserved. The power of the states to regulate their purely internal affairs by such laws as seem wise to the local authority is inherent, and has never been surrendered to the general government. To sustain this statute would not be, in our judgment, a recognition of the lawful exertion of congressional authority over interstate commerce, but would sanction an invasion by the Federal power of the control of a matter purely local in its character, and over which no authority has been delegated to Congress in conferring the power to regulate commerce among the states.

We have neither authority nor disposition to question the motives of Congress in enacting this legislation. The purposes intended must be attained consistently with constitutional limitations, and not by an invasion of the powers of the states. This court has no more important function than that which devolves upon it the obligation to preserve inviolate the constitutional limitations upon the exercise of authority, Federal and state, to the end that each may continue to discharge, harmoniously with the other, the duties intrusted to it by the Constitution.

In our view the necessary effect of this act is, by means of a prohibition against the movement in interstate commerce of ordinary commercial commodities, to regulate the hours of labor of children in factories and mines within the states,—a purely state authority. Thus the act in a twofold sense is repugnant to the Constitution. It not only transcends the authority delegated to Congress over commerce, but also exerts a power as to a purely local matter to which the Federal authority does not extend. The far-reaching result of upholding the act cannot be more plainly indicated than by pointing out that if Congress can thus regulate matters intrusted to local authority by prohibition of the movement of commodities in interstate commerce, all freedom of commerce will be at an end, and the power of the states over local matters may be eliminated, and thus our system of government be practically destroyed.

For these reasons we hold that this law exceeds the constitutional authority of Congress. It follows that the decree of the District Court must be affirmed.

MR. JUSTICE HOLMES, dissenting.

The act does not meddle with anything belonging to the states. They may regulate their internal affairs and their domestic commerce as they like. But when they seek to send their products across the state line they are no longer within their rights. If there were no Constitution and no Congress their power to cross the line would depend upon their neighbors. Under the Constitution such commerce belongs not to the states, but to Congress to regulate. It may carry out its views of public policy whatever indirect effect they may have upon the activities of the states. Instead of being encountered by a prohibitive tariff at her boundaries, the state encounters the public policy of the United States which it is for Congress to express. The public policy of the United States is shaped with a view to the benefit of the nation as a whole. . . . The national welfare as understood by Congress may require a different attitude within its sphere from that of some self-seeking state. It seems to me entirely constitutional for Congress to enforce its understanding by all the means at its command.

Day's decision was a total victory for the Executive Committee; in fact, C. Herman Pritchett has called *Hammer* the Court's "clearest statement" of dual federalism. But the opinion rested on tenuous grounds. Pritchett points out that Justice Day misquoted the Tenth Amendment: it does not contain the word *expressly*.[12] In so doing, Day ignored Marshall's reasoning in *McCulloch*. It was critical to Marshall's interpretation of congressional powers that the word *expressly* did not appear. When Congress considered the Tenth Amendment, one representative proposed to "add the word 'expressly' so as to read 'the powers not expressly delegated by this Constitution.'" James Madison

and others objected and the motion was defeated.[13] So Day assumed "a position that was historically inaccurate."[14]

Although this error seemed to undermine Day's logic, a more important question may be this: Was Day's explication of dual federalism the same as Taney's? Many scholars think not; in fact, they argue that *Hammer*—taken in conjunction with other opinions of that Court era—diverges from Taney's philosophy. While Taney viewed dual federalism as a way to equalize state and federal power, it may be that the Supreme Court between 1890 and 1930 was not concerned with the rights of states as states. Rather, the justices were bent on prohibiting any state *or* federal interference with the growth of the nation's booming private-sector economy. They used dual federalism as a vehicle to strike down federal regulation of the sort at issue in *Hammer*. At the same time, the Court limited the ability of states to pass similar legislation under the guise that it would restrict individual liberties. *(See Chapter 10 for a discussion of limits on state regulatory efforts during this time.)* The Court's approach was quite distinct from Taney's. For the Courts from the 1890s through the 1930s, dual federalism and the Tenth Amendment were masks to hide their laissez-faire philosophy.

The justices' frame of reference, their wholehearted support of business, was as well suited to their day as Taney's was to his, or so some have argued. At the very least, the Court's willingness to embrace a free enterprise philosophy reflected the general mood of Americans, some of whom were benefiting financially from the growth of the economy. When the economic boom of the 1920s turned into the Great Depression of the 1930s, however, citizens and their newly elected leaders clamored for the sort of regulation struck down in *Hammer.* Yet, as we saw in the delegation of powers section of Chapter 4, the Court was still set in a

---

12. *Constitutional Law of the Federal System* (Englewood Cliffs, N.J.: Prentice Hall, 1984), 60.

13. Daniel A. Farber and Suzanna Sherry, *A History of the American Constitution* (St. Paul, Minn.: West, 1990), 239.

14. Pritchett, *Constitutional Law of the Federal System*, 60–61.

1920s mold. It struck down one New Deal program after another on various grounds that included the unconstitutional delegation of power and the impermissible congressional use of its authority to regulate commerce *(see Chapter 7)*. It also invoked the Tenth Amendment. In *Schechter Poultry Corporation v. United States* (1935), involving the constitutionality of the National Industrial Recovery Act—a major piece of New Deal legislation—the Court noted:

Extraordinary conditions do not create or enlarge constitutional power. The Constitution established a national government with powers deemed to be adequate, as they have proved to be both in war and peace, but these powers of the national government are limited by the constitutional grants. Those who act under these grants are not at liberty to transcend the imposed limits because they believe that more or different power is necessary. *Such assertions of extra-constitutional authority were anticipated and precluded by the explicit terms of the Tenth Amendment.* (Emphasis added.)

THE (RE)EMERGENCE OF NATIONAL SUPREMACY: COOPERATIVE FEDERALISM

Despite the Court's language, the days of dual federalism were numbered. Amid increasing pressure for change, including President Roosevelt's Court-packing scheme, came the famous "switch in time that saved nine" and with it the demise of broad interpretations of the Tenth Amendment *(see Chapter 7)*. Although this process began in 1937, the death knell rang most loudly with the decision in *United States v. Darby Lumber* (1941).[15] As you read Chief Justice Stone's opinion, think about Marshall's in *McCulloch*. Are they making similar claims, or can you detect distinctions?

15. See Joseph F. Kobylka, "The Court, Justice Blackmun, and Federalism," *Creighton Law Review* 19 (1985–1986): 21.

United States v. Darby Lumber

312 U.S. 100 (1941)

Vote: 8   (Black, Douglas, Frankfurter, Hughes, Murphy, Reed, Roberts, Stone)

   0

Opinion of the Court: Stone

In 1938 Congress, under its power to regulate interstate commerce, enacted an important piece of New Deal legislation, the Fair Labor Standards Act (FLSA). It provided that all employers "engaged in interstate commerce, or in the production of goods for that commerce" must pay all their employees a minimum wage of twenty-five cents per hour and not permit employees to work longer than forty-four hours per week without paying them one and one-half times their regular pay. In November 1939 the federal government sought and obtained an indictment against Fred W. Darby for violating the FLSA. The indictment alleged that Darby, the owner of a lumber company, was engaged in the production and manufacturing of goods shipped out of state, but that he had not abided by either of FLSA's major pay requirements.

Darby did not dispute the charges. Rather, invoking the logic of Hammer, his brief argued: "The Fair Labor Standards Act ... is an unconstitutional attempt to regulate conditions in production of goods and commodities and it can not be sustained as a regulation of interstate commerce within the delegated power of Congress under the commerce clause. It violated the Tenth Amendment."

The government responded more pragmatically than legally, stating:

State legislators, Congressional committees, federal commissions, and businessmen over a period of time have realized that no state, acting alone, could require labor standards substantially higher than those obtained in other states whose producers and manufacturers competed in the interstate market.

The reiterated conclusion that the individual states were helpless gained added force during the prolonged economic depression of the 1930's. The . . . National Industrial Recovery Act . . . and the Fair Labor Standards Act itself each reflect a great volume of testimony adduced at congressional hearings and elsewhere to the effect that employers with lower labor standards possess an unfair advantage in interstate competition, and that only the national government could deal with the problem.

The lumber industry, the government asserted, well illustrated "the inability of the particular states to ensure adequate labor standards; over 57 percent of the lumber produced enters into interstate or foreign commerce from 45 of the states."

MR. JUSTICE STONE delivered the opinion of the Court.

The motive and purpose of the present regulation are plainly to make effective the Congressional conception of public policy that interstate commerce should not be made the instrument of competition in the distribution of goods produced under substandard labor conditions, which competition is injurious to the commerce and to the states from and to which the commerce flows. The motive and purpose of a regulation of interstate commerce are matters for the legislative judgment upon the exercise of which the Constitution places no restriction and over which the courts are given no control. . . . Whatever their motive and purpose, regulations of commerce which do not infringe some constitutional prohibition are within the plenary power conferred on Congress by the Commerce Clause. Subject only to that limitation, presently to be considered, we conclude that the prohibition of the shipment interstate of goods produced under the forbidden substandard labor conditions is within the constitutional authority of Congress. . . .

Our conclusion is unaffected by the Tenth Amendment which provides: "The powers not delegated to the United States by the Constitution nor prohibited by it to the states are reserved to the states respectively or to the people." The amendment states but a truism that all is retained which has not been surrendered. There is nothing in the history of its adoption to suggest that it was more than declaratory of the relationship between the national and state governments as it had been established by the Constitution before

the amendment or that its purpose was other than to allay fears that the new national government might seek to exercise powers not granted, and that the states might not be able to exercise fully their reserved powers.

From the beginning and for many years the amendment has been construed as not depriving the national government of authority to resort to all means for the exercise of a granted power which are appropriate and plainly adapted to the permitted end. . . .

Reversed.

Justice Stone's opinion in *Darby Lumber* brought the Court full circle, from Marshall's nationalism to Taney's dual federalism and back. Not only did *Darby Lumber* explicitly overrule *Hammer* and uphold the FLSA, it also gutted the Tenth Amendment: it denied that the amendment constituted an "affirmative base of power from which states may challenge the wide-ranging effects of national legislation."[16]

For the next thirty-five years dual federalism was out and Stone's cooperative federalism was in. Under this doctrine, at least theoretically, the various levels of government shared policy-making responsibilities. In practice, it meant, as Stone's opinion implies, that the national government took the lead in formulating policy goals, which it expected state and local officials to implement. Tremendous changes in government followed, not the least of which was that, as depicted in Figure 6-1, a huge shift occurred in the balance between national and state spending. As the federal government took advantage of its new constitutional freedom—creating more and more programs and projects covering all aspects of American life—it began to account for greater and greater percentages of government spending. By the 1960s the federal government reigned supreme.

Although federal supremacy was a fact of American life, it was not universally applauded or even accepted. Some opposition came from familiar sources:

16. Craig R. Ducat and Harold W. Chase, *Constitutional Interpretation,* 4th ed. (St. Paul, Minn.: West, 1988), 360.

FIGURE 6-1 Government Spending as a Percentage of GNP, 1929–1991

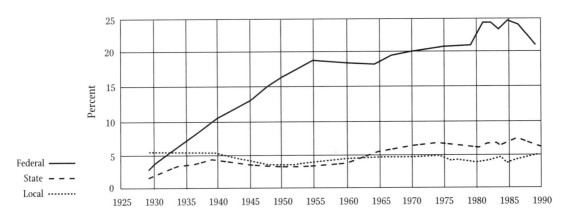

SOURCE: Harold W. Stanley and Richard G. Niemi, *Vital Statistics on American Politics*, 4th ed. (Washington, D.C.: CQ Press, 1994), 334.
NOTE: State and local figures unavailable after 1988. Shown is "own source" spending, i.e., before intergovernmental transfers.

politicians in southern states, who vehemently opposed congressional (and Court) efforts to force integration of schools and other public facilities. Governors, like Alabama's George Wallace, simply refused to relent, making arguments similar to those their counterparts had made in the 1860s. He and others even formed their own political party to advocate states' rights.

Other opposition was more national in scope. President Nixon lamented the tremendous growth of the federal government and the concomitant demise of states' authority over their own affairs. To restore some balance he proposed a "new federalism" plan. Under the plan, states and localities would have increased authority to determine how they spent their money because they would participate in a revenue-sharing arrangement with the federal government, which would allocate money to the states to spend as they saw fit. New federalism, however, was not dual federalism. Nixon may have wanted to give the states and localities greater authority in certain policy arenas, but he was not one to argue that the federal government, particularly the executive branch, and the states were "co-equal sovereigns." Moreover, issues of

federalism were never the most important items on the president's agenda, particularly when it came to nominations to the Supreme Court. Nixon looked for jurists who would be inclined toward judicial restraint generally and to a law and order posture, in particular.

When "Nixon's" Supreme Court handed down its decision in *National League of Cities v. Usery* (1976), therefore, it took many legal scholars by surprise. A greater concern with states' rights was certainly within the realm of the politics of the day, but the Court took that concern to a rather extreme level.

To understand why the *National League* ruling was so surprising and controversial, let us first consider the facts of the case. At issue was the Federal Labor Standards Act, which the Court had upheld in *United States v. Darby Lumber*. Since the decision in 1941, Congress had amended the act to cover public employees, and those amendments, along with other attempts to regulate state employment, were themselves the subject of several major Supreme Court rulings. As noted in Box 6-3, the Court had upheld those regulations.

This case crystallized when Congress in 1974 once again expanded the scope of the FLSA, this time bringing virtually all state public employees, who were ex-

BOX 6-3   HISTORY OF THE WAGE REGULATION
LEADING TO *NATIONAL LEAGUE OF CITIES V. USERY*

CONGRESSIONAL ACTION	COURT RESPONSE
Federal Labor Standards Act of 1938 (FLSA): requires employers to pay employees a minimum wage and one and one-half times their regular pay for overtime work. States and localities are excluded from the act.	Upheld in *United States v. Darby Lumber* (1941).
1966 Extension of the FLSA: extended the law to workers in publicly operated schools, hospitals, and institutions. The extension covered employees of transit companies insofar as their public employers had to pay them minimum wage. But the 1966 extension did not provide overtime pay protection.	Upheld in *Maryland v. Wirtz* (1968). Congress can prescribe wage regulations for employees, even if their employer is a state.
Economic Stabilization Act of 1970: limited wage increases for state employees.	Upheld in *Fry v. United States* (1975). This decision falls under Congress's commerce power. However, Congress cannot use its "power in a fashion that impairs the States' integrity or their ability to function effectively in a federal system."

SOURCE: Adapted from Joseph F. Kobylka, "The Court, Justice Blackmun, and Federalism," *Creighton Law Review* 19 (1985–1986): 22–23.

cluded in the original legislation, under its reach. As a result, various cities and states and two organizations representing their collective interests, the National League of Cities and the National Governors' Conference, challenged the constitutionality of the new amendments. In particular, they argued that the amendments represented a "collision" between federal expansion and states' rights in violation of the Tenth Amendment. As one litigant claimed, the Tenth Amendment should protect the powers states already possessed, including authority over public workers. It is interesting to note that in representing the federal government Solicitor General Robert Bork did not take issue with this analysis. Rather, he argued that the Tenth Amendment was inapplicable because Congress had passed the 1974 amendments under its power to regulate commerce.

In his opinion for the majority (the Nixon appointees, plus Justice Stewart), Justice Rehnquist invoked the underlying "dual federalism" logic of cases like *Hammer* and *Scott* to hold for the National League of Cities and to overrule *Wirtz (see Box 6-3).* For he suggested that the Court had "repeatedly recognized that there are attributes of sovereignty attaching to every state government which may not be impaired by Congress, not because Congress may lack an affirmative grant of legislative authority to reach the matter, but because the Constitution prohibits is from exercising the authority in that manner."

Yet Rehnquist's opinion did not and could not stop there because he needed to address this critical question: Where is the line separating constitutional from unconstitutional federal intrusions into state business? He provided one answer when he wrote: "Congress may not exercise that power so as to force directly upon the States its choices as to how essential decisions regarding the conduct of integral governmental functions are to be made."

To be sure, a majority of the justices believed that "[o]ne undoubted attribute of state sovereignty is the States' power to determine the wages which shall be paid to those whom they employ in order to carry out their governmental functions." That's why they held for the National League of Cities and overturned *Wirtz*. But were there other functions so "essential to [the] separate and independent existence of the states" that Congress could not "abrogate the States' otherwise plenary authority to make them"? While the Court did not clearly delineate these functions, it did provide some examples of activities outside congressional authority and within the area of "traditional operations of state and local governments, including firefighting, police protection, sanitation, public health, and parks and recreation."[17]

In his concurrence, Justice Blackmun argued that the Court was adopting a moderate "balancing approach" to federal–state relations. But others saw it quite differently. *National League*, in fact, provoked numerous scholarly articles, many of which agreed with points raised by Justice Brennan in his dissenting opinion. Like the dissenters, some scholars criticized the Court for elevating the Tenth Amendment and for reasserting the "discredited" doctrine of dual federalism. Others focused on the "uncertainties raised by the ruling." In particular, what would the justices define as "essential to the separate and independent existence of the states," beyond firefighting, police protection, sanitation, and so forth?[18] *(See Table 6-5.)* This was not a question of mere academic interest: between 1976 and 1978 litigants filed some forty-five cases asking the Court to address it.

As noted in the table, the Court issued several decisions designed to clarify its 1976 ruling. But almost from the start the justices began to chip away at its core. In *Hodel v. Virginia Surface Mining & Reclamation Assn.* (1981) and *United Transportation Union v. Long Island Rail Road* (1982) a unanimous Court rejected invitations to apply and thus expand the 1976 ruling. Major breaks with the decision, however, came in 1982 and 1983, when sharply divided Courts so whittled down *National League* as to make it almost invisible.

In theory, *National League* remained on the books as good law, at least until 1985. In *Garcia v. San Antonio Metropolitan Transit Authority*, the justices officially overruled *National League*.

Garcia v. San Antonio Metropolitan Transit Authority

469 U.S. 528 (1985)
Vote: 5 (Blackmun, Brennan, Marshall, Stevens, White)
       4 (Burger, O'Connor, Powell, Rehnquist)
Opinion of the Court: Blackmun
Dissenting opinions: Powell, O'Connor, Rehnquist

Garcia was virtually a carbon copy of *National League*. Once again litigation centered on amendments to the FLSA that required states to pay public employees minimum wages and overtime. The facts, however, were a bit more complicated.

In 1959 San Antonio created a mass transit system called SATS (San Antonio Transit System). For almost a decade SATS was a money-making venture, but by 1969 it was operating at a loss and turned to the federal government for assistance. The federal Urban Mass Transit Administration (UMTA) provided a $4 million grant. When the city replaced SATS with SAMTA (San Antonio Metropolitan Transit Authority) in 1978, federal grants continued to subsidize transit operations. Between 1970 and 1980, the transit system received

17. Kobylka, "The Court, Justice Blackmun, and Federalism," 24–25.
18. Pritchett, *Constitutional Law of the Federal System*, 235.

TABLE 6-5   Supreme Court Federalism Cases Between *National League of Cities* and *Garcia*

Case	Question	Holding (Vote)
Hodel v. Virginia Surface Mining & Reclamation Assn. (1981)	Is the Surface Mining and Reclamation Act of 1977, which sets minimum federal standards with which states had to comply and imposed federal standards on those that did not, an impermissible regulation of interstate commerce under *National League of Cities*?	No (9–0). Marshall, for the majority, read *National League* to provide a three-prong test (now the *Hodel* test): "First, there must be a showing that the challenged statute regulates the 'States as States.' . . . Second, the federal regulation must address matters that are indisputably 'attribute[s] of state sovereignty.' . . . And third, it must be apparent that the States' compliance with the federal law would directly impair their ability 'to structure integral operations in areas of traditional governmental functions.'" Since this act fails to meet the first prong, it is a permissible regulation.
United Transportation Union v. Long Island Rail Road (1982)	Does the Federal Railway Act, as applied to employees of a state-operated railroad, transgress the limitations of national power?	No (9–0). The Court held that the act did not "directly impair [the state's] ability 'to structure integral operations in areas of traditional governmental functions'" and therefore was within the bounds of national power.
Federal Energy Regulatory Commission v. Mississippi (1982)	Is the Public Utility Regulatory Policies Act, which provided for the guidance and regulation of state utility regulatory commissions by FERC and the states, beyond the limits of federal power enunciated in *National League*?	No (5–4). Since *National League* did not hold that "all aspects of a State's sovereign authority are immune from federal control," the nature of the federal interest can overcome state sovereignty, and the interest here does not act to "impair the ability of the States."
Equal Employment Opportunity Commission v. Wyoming (1983)	Is the Age Discrimination Act, which sets the mandatory retirement age of state game wardens at 55, unconstitutional under *National League*?	No. (5–4) Although the act did regulate the "States as States," it did not "'directly impair' the State's ability to 'structure integral operations in areas of traditional governmental functions.'"

SOURCE: Adapted from Joseph F. Kobylka, "The Court, Justice Blackmun, and Federalism," *Creighton Law Review* 19 (1985–1986); 26–31.

more than $51 million, or 40 percent of its costs, from the federal government. The case started in 1979 when, "in response to a specific inquiry about the applicability of the FLSA to employees of SAMTA," the Department of Labor issued an opinion holding that SAMTA must abide by the act's wage provisions. SAMTA filed a challenge to the department's holding, and Joe G. Garcia and other SAMTA employees, in turn, initiated a suit against their employer for overtime pay.

When the case reached the U.S. Supreme Court, SAMTA relied heavily on *National League*. SAMTA argued, for example, that "transit is a traditional [city] function" and that, as the operator of that function, it was not covered by FLSA amendments. The U.S. government and Garcia countered by arguing that National League was not necessarily applicable. In their view, application of the FLSA to public transit did not violate the Tenth Amendment because (1) operation of a transit system is not a traditional government function, and (2) operation of a transit system is not a core government function that must be exempted from federal commerce power legislation to preserve the states' independence. To demonstrate these points, attorneys emphasized the fact that SAMTA received significant funding from the federal government. This, in their view, indicated that "the growth of public transit service reflects cooperative federalism, not independent state initiatives."

JUSTICE BLACKMUN delivered the opinion of the Court.

We revisit in these cases an issue raised in National League of Cities v. Usery (1976). In that litigation, this Court, by a sharply divided vote, ruled that the Commerce Clause does not empower Congress to enforce the minimum-wage and overtime provisions of the Fair Labor Standards Act (FLSA) against the States "in areas of traditional government functions." Although National League of Cities supplied some examples of "traditional governmental functions," it did not offer a general explanation of how a "traditional" function is to be distinguished from a "nontraditional" one. Since then, federal and state courts have struggled with the task, thus imposed, of identifying a traditional function for purposes of state immunity under the Commerce Clause.

In the present cases, a Federal District Court concluded that municipal ownership and operation of a mass-transit system is a traditional governmental function and thus, under National League of Cities, is exempt from the obligations imposed by the FLSA. Faced with the identical question, three Federal Courts of Appeals and one state appellate court have reached the opposite conclusion.

Our examination of this "function" standard applied in these and other cases over the last eight years now persuades us that the attempt to draw the boundaries of state regulatory immunity in terms of "traditional governmental function" is not only unworkable but is also inconsistent with established principles of federalism and, indeed, with those very federalism principles on which National League of Cities purported to rest. That case, accordingly, is overruled. . . .

The central theme of National League of Cities was that the States occupy a special position in our constitutional system and that the scope of Congress' authority under the Commerce Clause must reflect that position. Of course, the Commerce Clause by its specific language does not provide any special limitation on Congress' actions with respect to the States. It is equally true, however, that the text of the Constitution provides the beginning rather than the final answer to every inquiry into questions of federalism, for "[b]ehind the words of the constitutional provisions are postulates which limit and control." National League of Cities reflected the general conviction that the Constitution precludes "the National Government [from] devour[ing] the essentials of state sovereignty." In order to be faithful to the underlying federal premises of the Constitution, courts must look for the "postulates which limit and control."

What has proved problematic is not the perception that the Constitution's federal structure imposes limitations on the Commerce Clause, but rather the nature and content of those limitations. One approach to defining the limits on Congress' authority to regulate the States under the Commerce Clause is to identify certain underlying elements of political sovereignty that are deemed essential to the States' "separate and independent existence." This approach obviously underlay the Court's use of the "traditional governmental function" concept in National League of Cities. It also has led to the separate requirement that the challenged federal statute "address matters that are indisputably 'attribute[s]' of state sovereignty.'" In National League of Cities itself, for example, the Court concluded that decisions by a State concerning the wages and hours of its employees are an "undoubted attribute of state sovereignty." The opinion did not explain what aspects of such decisions made them such an "undoubted attribute," and the Court since then has remarked on the uncertain scope of the concept. The point of the inquiry, however, has remained to single out particular features of a State's internal governance that are deemed to be intrinsic parts of state sovereignty.

We doubt that courts ultimately can identify principled constitutional limitations on the scope of Congress' Commerce Clause powers over the States merely by relying on a priori definitions of state sovereignty. In part, this is because of the elusiveness of objective criteria for "fundamental" elements of state sovereignty, a problem we have witnessed in the search for "traditional governmental functions." There is, however, a more fundamental reason:

the sovereignty of the States is limited by the Constitution itself. A variety of sovereign powers, for example, are withdrawn from the States by Article I, § 10. Section 8 of the same Article works an equally sharp contraction of state sovereignty by authorizing Congress to exercise a wide range of legislative powers and (in conjunction with the Supremacy Clause of Article VI) to displace contrary state legislation. . . .

The States unquestionably do "retai[n] a significant measure of sovereign authority." They do so, however, only to the extent that the Constitution has not divested them of their original powers and transferred those powers to the Federal Government. In the words of James Madison to the Members of the First Congress: "Interference with the power of the States was no constitutional criterion of the power of Congress. If the power was not given, Congress could not exercise it; if given, they might exercise it, although it should interfere with the laws, or even the Constitution of the states." . . .

As a result, to say that the Constitution assumes the continued role of the States is to say little about the nature of that role. Only recently, this Court recognized that the purpose of the constitutional immunity recognized in National League of Cities is not to preserve "a sacred province of state autonomy." With rare exceptions, like the guarantee, in Article IV, § 3, of state territorial integrity, the Constitution does not carve out express elements of state sovereignty that Congress may not employ its delegated powers to displace. . . . The power of the Federal Government is a "power to be respected" as well, and the fact that the States remain sovereign as to all powers not vested in Congress or denied them by the Constitution offers no guidance about where the frontier between state and federal power lies. In short, we have no license to employ freestanding conceptions of state sovereignty when measuring congressional authority under the Commerce Clause. . . .

Insofar as the present cases are concerned, then, we need go no further than to state that we perceive nothing in the overtime and minimum-wage requirements of the FLSA, as applied to SAMTA, that is destructive of state sovereignty or violative of any constitutional provision. SAMTA faces nothing more than the same minimum-wage and overtime obligations that hundreds of thousands of other employers, public as well as private, have to meet.

In these cases, the status of public mass transit simply underscores the extent to which the structural protections of the Constitution insulate the States from federally imposed burdens. When Congress first subjected state mass-transit systems to FLSA obligations in 1966, and when it expanded those obligations in 1974, it simultaneously provided extensive funding for state and local mass transit through UMTA. In the two decades since its enactment, UMTA has provided over $22 billion in mass-transit aid to States and localities. In 1983 alone, UMTA funding amounted to $3.7 billion. . . . In short, Congress has not simply placed a financial burden on the shoulders of States and localities that operate mass-transit systems, but has provided substantial countervailing financial assistance as well, assistance that may leave individual mass-transit systems better off than they would have been had Congress never intervened at all in the area. Congress' treatment of public mass transit reinforces our conviction that the national political process systematically protects States from the risk of having their functions in that area handicapped by Commerce Clause regulation.

This analysis makes clear that Congress' action in affording SAMTA employees the protections of the wage and hour provisions of the FLSA contravened no affirmative limit on Congress' power under the Commerce Clause. The judgment of the District Court therefore must be reversed.

Of course, we continue to recognize that the States occupy a special and specific position in our constitutional system and that the scope of Congress' authority under the Commerce Clause must reflect that position. But the principal and basic limit on the federal commerce power is that inherent in all congressional action—the built-in restraints that our system provides through state participation in federal governmental action. The political process ensures that laws that unduly burden the States will not be promulgated. In the factual setting of these cases the internal safeguards of the political process have performed as intended.

These cases do not require us to identify or define what affirmative limits the constitutional structure might impose on federal action affecting the States under the Commerce Clause. . . .

Though the separate concurrence providing the fifth vote in National League of Cities was "not untroubled by certain possible implications" of the decision, the Court in that case attempted to articulate affirmative limits on the Commerce Clause power in terms of core governmental functions and fundamental attributes of state sovereignty. But the model of democratic decisionmaking the Court there identified underestimated, in our view, the solicitude of the national political process for the continued vitality of the States. Attempts by other courts since then to draw guidance from this model have proved it both impracticable and doctrinally barren. In sum, in National League of Cities the Court tried to repair what did not need repair.

We do not lightly overrule recent precedent. We have not hesitated, however, when it has become apparent that a prior decision has departed from a proper understanding of congressional power under the Commerce Clause. Due respect for the reach of congressional power within the federal system mandates that we do so now.

National League of Cities v. Usery (1976) is overruled. The judgment of the District Court is reversed, and these cases are remanded to that court for further proceedings consistent with this opinion.

It is so ordered.

JUSTICE O'CONNOR, with whom JUSTICE POWELL and JUSTICE REHNQUIST join, dissenting.

The Court today surveys the battle scene of federalism and sounds a retreat. . . . I would prefer to hold the field and, at the very least, render a little aid to the wounded. . . . I . . . write separately to note my fundamental disagreement with the majority's views of federalism and the duty of this Court.

The Court overrules National League of Cities v. Usery (1976) on the grounds that it is not "faithful to the role of federalism in a democratic society." National League of Cities is held to be inconsistent with this narrow view of federalism because it attempts to protect only those fundamental aspects of state sovereignty that are essential to the States' separate and independent existence, rather than protecting all state activities "equally."

In my view, federalism cannot be reduced to the weak "essence" distilled by the majority today. There is more to federalism than the nature of the constraints that can be imposed on the States in "the realm of authority left open to them by the Constitution." The central issue of federalism,

of course, is whether any realm is left open to the States by the Constitution—whether any area remains in which a State may act free of federal interference. "The issue . . . is whether the federal system has any *legal* substance, any core of constitutional right that courts will enforce." The true "essence" of federalism is that the States as States have legitimate interests which the National Government is bound to respect even though its laws are supreme. If federalism so conceived and so carefully cultivated by the Framers of our Constitution is to remain meaningful, this Court cannot abdicate its constitutional responsibility to oversee the Federal Government's compliance with its duty to respect the legitimate interests of the States.

Due to the emergence of an integrated and industrialized national economy, this Court has been required to examine and review a breathtaking expansion of the powers of Congress. In doing so the Court correctly perceived that the Framers of our Constitution intended Congress to have sufficient power to address national problems. . . .

It would be erroneous, however, to conclude that the Supreme Court was blind to the threat to federalism when it expanded the commerce power. The Court based the expansion on the authority of Congress, through the Necessary and Proper Clause, "to resort to all means for the exercise of a granted power which are appropriate and plainly adapted to the permitted end." It is through this reasoning that an interstate activity "affecting" interstate commerce can be reached through the commerce power. . . .

It is worth recalling the cited passage in McCulloch v. Maryland (1819) that lies at the source of the recent expansion of the commerce power. "Let the end be legitimate, let it be within the scope of the constitution," Chief Justice Marshall said, "and all means which are appropriate, which are plainly adapted to that end, which are not prohibited, but consist with the letter *and spirit* of the constitution, are constitutional" (emphasis added). The *spirit* of the Tenth Amendment, of course, is that the States will retain their integrity in a system in which the laws of the United States are nevertheless supreme.

It is not enough that the "end be legitimate"; the means to that end chosen by Congress must not contravene the spirit of the Constitution. Thus many of this Court's decisions acknowledge that the means by which national power is exercised must take into account concerns for state autonomy. . . . The operative language of these cases varies, but the underlying principle is consistent: state autonomy is a relevant factor in assessing the means by which Congress exercises its powers.

This principle requires the Court to enforce affirmative limits on federal regulation of the States to complement the judicially crafted expansion of the interstate commerce power. National League of Cities v. Usery represented an attempt to define such limits. The Court today rejects National League of Cities and washes its hands of all efforts to protect the States. In the process, the Court opines that unwarranted federal encroachments on state authority are and will remain "'horrible possibilities that never happen in the real world.'" There is ample reason to believe to the contrary.

The last two decades have seen an unprecedented growth of federal regulatory activity, as the majority itself acknowledges. . . . Today, as federal legislation and coercive grant programs have expanded to embrace innumerable activities that were once viewed as local, the burden of persuasion has surely shifted, and the extraordinary has become ordinary. For example, recently the Federal Government has, with this Court's blessing, undertaken to tell the States the age at which they can retire their law enforcement officers, and the regulatory standards, procedures, and even the agenda which their utilities commissions must consider and follow. See EEOC v. Wyoming. The political process has not protected against these encroachments on state activities, even though they directly impinge on a State's ability to make and enforce its laws. With the abandonment of National League of Cities, all that stands between the remaining essentials of state sovereignty and Congress is the latter's underdeveloped capacity for self-restraint.

The problems of federalism in an integrated national economy are capable of more responsible resolution than holding that the States as States retain no status apart from that which Congress chooses to let them retain. The proper resolution, I suggest, lies in weighing state autonomy as a factor in the balance when interpreting the means by which Congress can exercise its authority on the States as States. It is insufficient, in assessing the validity of congressional regulation of a State pursuant to the commerce power, to ask only whether the same regulation would be valid if enforced against a private party. That reasoning, embodied in the

majority opinion, is inconsistent with the spirit of our Constitution. It remains relevant that a State is being regulated, as National League of Cities and every recent case have recognized. . . .

It has been difficult for this Court to craft bright lines defining the scope of the state autonomy protected by National League of Cities. Such difficulty is to be expected whenever constitutional concerns as important as federalism and the effectiveness of the commerce power come into conflict. Regardless of the difficulty, it is and will remain the duty of this Court to reconcile these concerns in the final instance. That the Court shuns the task today by appealing to the "essence of federalism" can provide scant comfort to those who believe our federal system requires something more than a unitary, centralized government. I would not shirk the duty acknowledged by National League of Cities and its progeny, and I share Justice Rehnquist's belief that this Court will in time again assume its constitutional responsibility.

I respectfully dissent.

With his opinion in *Garcia*, Justice Blackmun once again buried dual federalism and returned the Court to its posture in *Darby Lumber*. The timing of the decision also was interesting. Stephen L. Wasby wrote:

If *National League of Cities* came at the end of eight years of a Republican administration that made some efforts to return matters to the states, *Garcia* came during a subsequent Republican administration far more committed not merely to limiting, but to reducing the national government's power. By sustaining national authority, Blackmun helped lead the Court's majority on a path counter to the thrust of contemporary political developments.[19]

President Reagan was, in fact, far more determined to return power to the states than any of his immediate predecessors; *Garcia* put a damper on his plans.[20]

19. "Justice Harry A. Blackmun in the Burger Court," *Hamline Law Review* 11 (1988): 214.

20. Congress softened its impact by enacting legislation in 1985 that allowed states to provide employees with compensation time instead of pay.

TABLE 6-6 Changes in Court Personnel and Nation–State Relations

Justice	Vote in National League	Vote in Garcia	Current View
Blackmun	Majority	Majority	——
Brennan	Minority	Majority	——
Breyer	——	——	Cooperative federalism*
Burger	Majority	Minority	——
Ginsburg	——	——	Cooperative federalism*
Kennedy	——	——	Unclear
Marshall	Minority	Majority	——
O'Connor	——	Minority	Dual federalism
Powell	Majority	Minority	——
Rehnquist	Majority	Minority	Dual federalism
Scalia	——	——	Dual federalism*
Souter	——	——	Cooperative federalism*
Stevens	Minority	Majority	Cooperative federalism
Stewart	Majority	——	——
Thomas	——	——	Dual federalism*
White	Minority	Majority	——

* Based on votes in *United States v. Lopez* (see chapter 7).

J. W. Peltason noted, "It is accurate, even if technically incorrect, to make the generalization that Congress has the power to do whatever it believes necessary and proper to promote the general welfare," and that the most significant constraints on the exercise of national power today are not those "designed to preserve the powers of the individual state governments," but those that emanate from specific liberties and rights guaranteed to the people, such as the freedoms of speech and press.[21] As for the Tenth Amendment, Justice Rehnquist said: "It is illuminating for purposes of reflection, if not for argument, to note that one of the greatest 'fictions' of our federal system is that the Congress exercises only those powers delegated to it, while the remainder are reserved to the States or to the people."[22]

An even more important question emanating from *Garcia*, however, may be how long it survives. As we show in Table 6-6, the ground it rests on may be tenuous. Justice Blackmun's defection from the *National League* majority made *Garcia* possible, but with his departure from the Court, along with those of Brennan, Marshall, and White, *Garcia* may be short-lived, given the postures adopted by some of the more recent appointees (particularly Scalia and Thomas). As such, many argue that it is only a matter of time before the Court restarts the cycle of nation–state relations and adopts the logic of Justice O'Connor's dissent. Given the fluctuations of doctrine in this area, would that surprise you?

READINGS

Corwin, Edward S. "The Passing of Dual Federalism." *Virginia Law Review* 36 (1950): 1–24.

Gunther, Gerald, ed. *John Marshall's Defense of* McCulloch v. Maryland. Stanford, Calif.: Stanford University Press, 1969.

21. *Understanding the Constitution,* 11th ed. (New York: Holt, Rinehart and Winston, 1989), 21.

22. *Hodel v. Virginia Surface Mining* (1981).

Howard, A. E. Dick. "The States and the Supreme Court." *Catholic University Law Review* 31 (1982): 375–438.

Kobylka, Joseph F. "The Court, Justice Blackmun, and Federalism." *Creighton Law Review* 19 (1985–1986): 9–49.

Mason, Alpheus. *The States' Rights Debate: Anti-Federalism and the Constitution.* New York: Oxford University Press, 1972.

Newmyer, R. Kent. *The Supreme Court Under Marshall and Taney.* New York: Crowell, 1968.

Schecter, Stephen. "The State of American Federalism." *Publius* 10 (1980): 3–11. Schmidhauser, John. *The Supreme Court as a Final Arbitrator of Federal-State Relations.* Chapel Hill: University of North Carolina Press, 1958.

Semonche, John E. *Charting the Future: The Supreme Court Responds to a Changing Society, 1890–1920.* Westport, Conn.: Greenwood Press, 1978.

Tarr, G. Alan, and Mary C. Porter. *State Supreme Courts in State and Nation.* New Haven, Conn.: Yale University Press, 1988.

Wasby, Stephen L. "Justice Harry Blackmun in the Burger Court." *Hamline Law Review* 11 (1988): 183–245.

Wood, Stephen B. *Constitutional Politics in the Progressive Era: Child Labor and the Law.* Chicago: University of Chicago Press, 1968.

CHAPTER 7
THE COMMERCE POWER

O F A L L T H E P O W E R S granted to government, perhaps none has caused more controversies and resulted in more litigation than the power to regulate commerce. Concern over the exercise of this power was present at the Constitution's birth and continues today. At each stage of the nation's development from a former colony isolated from the world's commercial centers to a country of vast economic power, legal disputes of great significance tested the powers of government to regulate the economy.

During certain periods, such as John Marshall's chief justiceship, the decisions of the Supreme Court enhanced the role of the federal government in promoting economic development. At other times, however, such as the period immediately following the Great Depression, the Court's interpretations thwarted the government's attempts to overcome economic collapse. From the earliest days of the nation, battles over the commerce power have raised basic questions. What is commerce? What is interstate commerce? What powers of commercial regulation did the Constitution grant to the federal government, and what role remains to be played by the states?

CONSTITUTIONAL FOUNDATIONS OF THE COMMERCE POWER

A primary reason for calling the Constitutional Convention was the inability of the government under the Articles of Confederation to control the country's commercial activity effectively. Economic conditions following the Revolutionary War were dismal. The national and state governments were deeply in debt. The tax base of the newly independent nation was minimal, and commerce was undeveloped, leaving property taxes and customs duties as the primary sources of government funds.

The states were almost exclusively in charge of economic regulation. To raise enough revenue to pay their debts, the states imposed substantial taxes on land, placing farmers in an economically precarious situation. The states also erected trade barriers and imposed duties on the importation of foreign goods. Although such policies were enacted in part to promote the states' domestic businesses, the result was a general strangulation of commercial activity. Several states printed their own money and passed statutes canceling debts. With each of the states working independently, the national economy continued to slide into stagnation; for all practical purposes, the central government was powerless to respond effectively.

When agrarian interests reached their economic breaking point—dramatized in the march on the Massachusetts state capitol in 1787 by a makeshift army of farmers led by Daniel Shays—it was clear that something had to be done. Congress called for a convention to reconsider the status of the Articles, a convention that ultimately resulted in the drafting of the U.S. Constitution.

Commerce and the Constitutional Convention

The delegates to the Constitutional Convention realized the necessity of giving the power to regulate the economy to the central government. The condition of the nation could no longer allow the individual states to pursue independent policies, each having a different impact on the country's economic health. To that end Article I of the Constitution removed certain powers from the states and gave the federal government powers it did not have under the Articles. States were stripped of the ability to print money, to impair the obligation of contracts, or to levy import duties. The federal government obtained the authority necessary to impose uniform regulations for the national economy. Among the powers granted to the central government were the authority to tax and impose customs duties, to spend and borrow, to develop and protect a single monetary system, and to regulate bankruptcies. Most important was the authority to regulate interstate and foreign commerce. Article I, Section 8, states: "The Congress shall have the power . . . to regulate Commerce with foreign Nations, and among the several States, and with the Indian Tribes."

The need for Congress to speak for the nation with a single voice on these matters was clear to the Framers. Even Alexander Hamilton and James Madison, who disagreed on many questions of federalism, were in accord on the need for the central government to control interstate and foreign commerce. Hamilton wrote in *Federalist*, No. 22:

In addition to the defects already enumerated in the existing federal system, there are others of not less importance which concur in rendering it altogether unfit for the administration of the affairs of the Union. The want of a power to regulate commerce is by all parties allowed to be of the number.

Madison took a similar position in *Federalist*, No. 42, arguing that the experience under the Articles, as well as that of the European nations, demonstrated that a central government without broad powers over the nation's commerce was destined to fail.

Congress quickly seized upon the authority to regulate commerce with other nations. Almost immediately, it imposed import duties as a means of raising revenue. The constitutional grant in this area was clear: the power to regulate foreign commerce, as well as other matters of foreign policy, was given unambiguously to the national government, and the role of the states was eliminated. Since ratification, the states have challenged congressional supremacy over foreign commerce only on rare occasions.

The power to regulate interstate commerce, however, was a different story. Congress was slow in responding to this grant of authority, despite its constitutional power to regulate commerce among the states. For the first several decades, federal officials continued to view business as an activity occurring within the borders of the individual states. In fact, Congress did not pass comprehensive legislation governing commerce among the states until the Interstate Commerce Act of 1887.

Marshall Defines Commerce

The history of the Commerce Clause is replete with disputes over definitions. For example, how do we distinguish between commercial activities and noncommercial activities? More important, what is the difference between *inter*state commerce, authority over which the Constitution gave to the federal government, and *intra*state commerce, over which the states retain regulatory power? Problems associated with

Aaron Ogden

Court, Chief Justice Marshall responded to the fundamental problems of defining commerce and allocating the power to control it. His answers to the questions presented in this case are still very much a part of the American constitutional fabric.

Gibbons v. Ogden

9 WHEAT. 1 (1824)
Vote: 6 (Duvall, Johnson, Marshall, Story, Todd,
Washington)
0

Opinion of the Court: Marshall
Concurring opinion: Johnson
Not participating: Thompson

This complicated litigation can be traced back to 1798, when the New York legislature granted the wealthy and prominent Robert R. Livingston a monopoly to operate steamboats on all waters within the state, including the two most important commercial waterways, New York Harbor and the Hudson River. New York officials did not see the monopoly grant as particularly important because no one had yet developed a steamship that could operate reliably and profitably. Livingston, however, joined forces with Robert Fulton, and together they produced a commercially viable steamship. This mode of transportation became extremely popular and very profitable for the partners. When they obtained a similar monopoly over the port of New Orleans in 1811, they had significant control over the nation's two most important harbors.

The rapid westward expansion taking place at that time fueled the need for modern transportation systems. The Livingston-Fulton monopoly, however, put a damper on the use of steam in the evolution of such a system. The New York monopoly was so strong and so vigorously enforced that retaliatory laws were enacted by other states, which refused to let steam-pow-

such distinctions were difficult enough in the early years, but they became even more complex as the economy grew and the country changed from agrarian to industrialized. As many constitutional law cases illustrate, disputes over commercial regulatory authority often involve power struggles between the national government and the states.

Disputes over the meaning of the Commerce Clause came before the Supreme Court even during the early years of nationhood. The justices probed the constitutional definition of commerce and the proper division of federal and state power to regulate it. Of the commerce cases decided by the Supreme Court in those early decades, none was more important than *Gibbons v. Ogden* (1824). This dispute involved some of the nation's most prominent and powerful businessmen and attorneys. A great deal was at stake both economically and politically. In his opinion for the

ered vessels from New York use their waters. Especially hostile relations developed between New York and New Jersey, and violence between the crews of rival companies became common. Livingston died in 1813, followed two years later by Fulton, but their monopoly lived on.

In 1817, Aaron Ogden, a former governor of New Jersey, and Thomas Gibbons, a successful Georgia lawyer, entered into a partnership to carry passengers between New York City and Elizabethtown, New Jersey. Ogden had purchased the right to operate in New York waters from the Livingston-Fulton monopoly, and Gibbons had a federal permit issued under the 1793 Coastal Licensing Act to operate steamships along the coast. With these grants of authority the two partners could carry passengers between New York and New Jersey. The New York monopoly, however, pressured Ogden to terminate his relationship with Gibbons. As a result the partnership dissolved.

Gibbons then joined forces with Cornelius Vanderbilt, and they became fierce competitors with Ogden and the New York monopoly interests. Gibbons and Vanderbilt entered New York waters in violation of the monopoly whenever they could, picking up as much New York business as possible. In response, Ogden successfully convinced the New York courts to enjoin Gibbons from entering New York waters. Gibbons appealed this ruling to the U.S. Supreme Court.

To press their case, Gibbons and Vanderbilt acquired the services of two of the best lawyers of the day, Daniel Webster and William Wirt, who later served as attorney general of the United States. Wirt argued that the federal permit issued to Gibbons took precedence over any state-issued monopoly and therefore Gibbons had the right to enter New York waters. Webster took a more radical position, explicitly stating that the Commerce Clause of the Constitution gave Congress exclusive power over commerce and that the state-granted monopoly was a violation of that clause. Ogden's lawyer responded that navigation was not commerce under the meaning of the

Thomas Gibbons

Constitution, but instead was an intrastate enterprise left to the states to regulate. The arguments in the case lasted four and a half days, an unusually long time.

MR. CHIEF JUSTICE MARSHALL delivered the opinion of the Court.

The appellant contends that this decree is erroneous, because the laws which purport to give the exclusive privilege it sustains, are repugnant to the constitution and laws of the United States.

They are said to be repugnant—

To that clause in the constitution which authorizes Congress to regulate commerce. . . .

The words are, "Congress shall have power to regulate commerce with foreign nations, and among the several States, and with the Indian tribes."

The subject to be regulated is commerce; and our con-

Daniel Webster's 1821 handwritten note to Cornelius Vanderbilt acknowledging receipt of a $500 retainer to represent Thomas Gibbons in the case of *Gibbons v. Ogden*.

stitution being . . . one of enumeration, and not of definition, to ascertain the extent of the power, it becomes necessary to settle the meaning of the word. The counsel for the appellee would limit it to traffic, to buying and selling, or the interchange of commodities, and do not admit that it comprehends navigation. This would restrict a general term, applicable to many objects, to one of its significations. Commerce, undoubtedly, is traffic, but it is something more: it is intercourse. It describes the commercial intercourse between nations, and parts of nations, in all its branches, and is regulated by prescribing rules for carrying on that intercourse. The mind can scarcely conceive a system for regulating commerce between nations, which shall exclude all laws concerning navigation, which shall be silent on the admission of the vessels of the one nation into the ports of the other, and be confined to prescribing rules for the conduct of individuals, in the actual employment of buying and selling, or of barter.

If commerce does not include navigation, the government of the Union has no direct power over that subject, and can make no law prescribing what shall constitute American vessels, or requiring that they shall be navigated by American seamen. Yet this power has been exercised from the commencement of the government, has been exercised with the consent of all, and has been understood by all to be a commercial regulation. All America understands, and has uniformly understood, the word "commerce," to comprehend navigation. It was so understood, and must have been so understood, when the constitution was framed. The power over commerce, including naviga-

tion, was one of the primary objects for which the people of America adopted their government, and must have been contemplated in forming it. The convention must have used the word in that sense, because all have understood it in that sense; and the attempt to restrict it comes too late. . . .

The word used in the constitution, then, comprehends, and has been always understood to comprehend, navigation within its meaning; and a power to regulate navigation, is as expressly granted, as if that term had been added to the word "commerce."

To what commerce does this power extend? The constitution informs us, to commerce "with foreign nations, and among the several States, and with the Indian tribes."

It has, we believe, been universally admitted, that these words comprehend every species of commercial intercourse between the United States and foreign nations. No sort of trade can be carried on between this country and any other, to which this power does not extend. It has been truly said, that commerce, as the word is used in the constitution, is a unit, every part of which is indicated by the term.

If this be the admitted meaning of the word, in its application to foreign nations, it must carry the same meaning throughout the sentence, and remain a unit, unless there be some plain intelligible cause which alters it.

The subject to which the power is next applied, is to commerce "among the several States." The word "among" means intermingled with. A thing which is among others, is intermingled with them. Commerce among the States, cannot stop at the external boundary line of each State, but may be introduced into the interior.

It is not intended to say that these words comprehend that commerce, which is completely internal, which is carried on between man and man in a State, or between different parts of the same State, and which does not extend to or affect other States. Such a power would be inconvenient, and is certainly unnecessary.

Comprehensive as the word "among" is, it may very properly be restricted to that commerce which concerns more States than one. The phrase is not one which would probably have been selected to indicate the completely interior traffic of a State, because it is not an apt phrase for that purpose; and the enumeration of the particular classes of commerce, to which the power was to be extended, would not have been made, had the intention been to extend the power to every description. The enumeration presupposes something not enumerated; and that something, if we regard the language or the subject of the sentence, must be the exclusively internal commerce of a State. The genius and character of the whole government seem to be, that its action is to be applied to all the external concerns of the nation, and to those internal concerns which affect the States generally; but not to those which are completely within a particular State, which do not affect other States, and with which it is not necessary to interfere, for the purpose of executing some of the general powers of the government. The completely internal commerce of a State, then, may be considered as reserved for the State itself.

But, in regulating commerce with foreign nations, the power of Congress does not stop at the jurisdictional lines of the several States. It would be a very useless power, if it could not pass those lines. The commerce of the United States with foreign nations, is that of the whole United States. Every district has a right to participate in it. The deep streams which penetrate our country in every direction, pass through the interior of almost every State in the Union, and furnish the means of exercising this right. If Congress has the power to regulate it, that power must be exercised whenever the subject exists. If it exists within the States, if a foreign voyage may commence or terminate at a port within a State, then the power of Congress may be exercised within a State.

This principle is, if possible, still more clear, when ap-

plied to commerce "among the several States." They either join each other, in which case they are separated by a mathematical line, or they are remote from each other, in which case other States lie between them. What is commerce "among" them; and how is it to be conducted? Can a trading expedition between two adjoining States, commence and terminate outside of each? And if the trading intercourse be between two States remote from each other, must it not commence in one, terminate in the other, and probably pass through a third? Commerce among the States must, of necessity, be commerce with the States. . . .

We are now arrived at the inquiry—What is this power?

It is the power to regulate; that is, to prescribe the rule by which commerce is to be governed. This power, like all others vested in Congress, is complete in itself, may be exercised to its utmost extent, and acknowledges no limitations, other than are prescribed in the constitution. . . . If, as has always been understood, the sovereignty of Congress, though limited to specified objects, is plenary as to those objects, the power over commerce with foreign nations, and among the several States, is vested in Congress as absolutely as it would be in a single government, having in its constitution the same restrictions on the exercise of the power as are found in the constitution of the United States. The wisdom and the discretion of Congress, their identity with the people, and the influence which their constituents possess at elections, are, in this, as in many other instances, as that, for example, of declaring war, the sole restraints on which they have relied, to secure them from its abuse. They are the restraints on which the people must often rely solely, in all representative governments.

The power of Congress, then, comprehends navigation, within the limits of every State in the Union; so far as that navigation may be, in any manner, connected with "commerce with foreign nations, or among the several States, or with the Indian tribes." It may, of consequence, pass the jurisdictional line of New-York, and act upon the very waters to which the prohibition now under consideration applies.

But it has been urged with great earnestness, that, although the power of Congress to regulate commerce with foreign nations, and among the several States, be co-extensive with the subject itself, and have no other limits than are prescribed in the constitution, yet the States may severally exercise the same power, within their respective jurisdictions. In support of this argument, it is said, that they possessed it as an inseparable attribute of sovereignty, before the formation of the constitution, and still retain it, except so far as they have surrendered it by that instrument; that this principle results from the nature of the government, and is secured by the tenth amendment; that an affirmative grant of power is not exclusive, unless in its own nature it be such that the continued exercise of it by the former possessor is inconsistent with the grant, and that this is not of that description.

The appellant, conceding these postulates, except the last, contends, that full power to regulate a particular subject, implies the whole power, and leaves no residuum; that a grant of the whole is incompatible with the existence of a right in another to any part of it. . . .

In discussing the question, whether this power is still in the States, in the case under consideration, we may dismiss from it the inquiry, whether it is surrendered by the mere grant to Congress, or is retained until Congress shall exercise the power. We may dismiss that inquiry, because it has been exercised, and the regulations which Congress deemed it proper to make, are now in full operation. The sole question is, can a State regulate commerce with foreign nations and among the States, while Congress is regulating it?

The counsel for the respondent answer this question in the affirmative, and rely very much on the restrictions in the 10th section, as supporting their opinion. . . .

It has been contended by the general counsel for the appellant, that, as the word "to regulate" implies in its nature, full power over the thing to be regulated, it excludes, necessarily, the action of all others that would perform the same operation on the same thing. That regulation is designed for the entire result, applying to those parts which remain as they were, as well as to those which are altered. It produces a uniform whole, which is as much disturbed and deranged by changing what the regulating power designs to leave untouched, as that on which it has operated.

There is great force in this argument, and the Court is not satisfied that it has been refuted.

Since, however, in exercising the power of regulating their own purely internal affairs, whether of trading or police, the States may sometimes enact laws, the validity of which depends on their interfering with, and being con-

trary to, an act of Congress passed in pursuance of the constitution, the Court will enter upon the inquiry, whether the laws of New-York, as expounded by the highest tribunal of that State, have, in their application to this case, come into collision with an act of Congress, and deprived a citizen of a right to which that act entitles him. Should this collision exist, it will be immaterial whether those laws were passed in virtue of a concurrent power "to regulate commerce with foreign nations and among the several States," or, in virtue of a power to regulate their domestic trade and police. In one case and the other, the acts of New-York must yield to the law of Congress; and the decision sustaining the privilege they confer, against a right given by a law of the Union, must be erroneous. . . .

But the framers of our constitution foresaw this state of things, and provided for it, by declaring the supremacy not only of itself, but of the laws made in pursuance of it. The nullity of any act, inconsistent with the constitution, is produced by the declaration, that the constitution is the supreme law. The appropriate application of that part of the clause which confers the same supremacy on laws and treaties, is to such acts of the State Legislatures as do not transcend their powers, but, though enacted in the execution of acknowledged State powers, interfere with, or are contrary to the laws of Congress, made in pursuance of the constitution, or some treaty made under the authority of the United States. In every such case, the act of Congress, or the treaty, is supreme; and the law of the State, though enacted in the exercise of powers not controverted, must yield to it. . . .

But all inquiry into this subject seems to the Court to be put completely at rest, by the act already mentioned, entitled, "An act for the enrolling and licensing of steam boats."

This act authorizes a steam boat employed, or intended to be employed, only in a river or bay of the United States, owned wholly or in part by an alien, resident within the United States, to be enrolled and licensed as if the same belonged to a citizen of the United States.

This act demonstrates the opinion of Congress, that steam boats may be enrolled and licensed, in common with vessels using sails. They are, of course, entitled to the same privileges, and can no more be restrained from navigating waters, and entering ports which are free to such vessels, than if they were wafted on their voyage by the winds, instead of being propelled by the agency of fire. The one element may be as legitimately used as the other, for every commercial purpose authorized by the laws of the Union; and the act of a State inhibiting the use of either to any vessel having a license under the act of Congress, comes, we think, in direct collision with that act.

Like his opinions in *Marbury* and *McCulloch*, Marshall's opinion in *Gibbons* laid a constitutional foundation that remains in place today. The decision made several important points. First, commerce involves more than buying and selling. It includes the commercial intercourse between nations and states, and therefore transportation and navigation clearly fall within the definition of commerce. Second, the power to regulate commerce that occurs completely within the boundaries of a single state is reserved for the states. Third, commerce among the states begins in one state and ends in another. It does not stop when the act of crossing a state border is completed. Consequently, commerce that occurs within a state may be part of a larger interstate process. Fourth, once an act is considered part of interstate commerce, Congress is empowered by the Constitution to regulate it. The power to regulate interstate commerce is complete and has no limitation other than what may be found in other constitutional provisions.

Gibbons v. Ogden was a substantial victory for national power. It broadly construed the definitions of both commerce and interstate commerce. But Marshall did not go as far as Daniel Webster had urged. The opinion asserts only that Congress has complete power to regulate interstate commerce and that federal regulations are superior to any state laws. The decision does not answer the question of the legitimacy of states regulating interstate commerce in the absence of federal action. That controversy was left for future justices to decide.

DEFINING INTERSTATE COMMERCE

The regulation of commerce by the federal government did not become a major item on the Supreme Court's agenda until the latter half of the nineteenth century. By this time, small intrastate businesses were giving way to large interstate corporations. Industrialization was expanding, and the interstate railroad and pipeline systems were well under way. The infamous captains of industry were creating large monopolistic trusts that dominated huge segments of the national economy, squeezing out small businesses and discouraging new entrepreneurs. The industrial combines that controlled the railroads also, in effect, ruled agriculture and other interests that relied on the rails to transport goods to market. This commercial growth brought great prosperity to some, but also caused horrendous social problems. Unsafe working conditions, sweat shops, child labor, and low wages plagued employees, who eventually formed labor unions.

The Shreveport Doctrine

In light of these developments, it was increasingly necessary for Congress to control interstate commerce. As the nineteenth century drew to a close, Congress passed two major laws based on the commerce power. The first was the Interstate Commerce Act of 1887, which established a mechanism for regulating the nation's interstate railroads. The second was the Sherman Anti-Trust Act of 1890, which was designed to break up monopolies that restrained trade. Critics immediately attacked Congress for exceeding its constitutional authority. While the Commerce Clause and Marshall's interpretation of it clearly established congressional power, discriminating between inter- and intrastate commerce was not easy. The Supreme Court faced a significant number of appeals that asked the justices to clarify whether the national legislature had overstepped its bounds and regulated commerce that was purely intrastate. To say that the Court had difficulty developing a coherent doctrine is an understatement.

The regulation of the railroads provides a case in point. The first railroads were small local operations regulated by the states. But as the interstate systems developed, the justices held that their regulation was rightfully a federal responsibility.[1] Congress responded with the Interstate Commerce Act, which established the Interstate Commerce Commission (ICC) to regulate the railroads and set rates. The Supreme Court approved the constitutionality of the commission, but later stripped it of its rate-setting powers.[2] In 1906 Congress revised the authority and procedures of the commission and reestablished its power to set rates. The Court generally supported this amended version of the regulatory plan.[3]

The Court's decision in *Houston, E. & W. Texas Railway Co. v. United States* (1914), better known as the *Shreveport Rate Case,* firmly established congressional power over the nation's rails. This dispute arose from competition among three railroad companies to serve various cities in Texas. Two were based in Texas, one in Houston and the other in Dallas, and the third competitor operated out of Shreveport, Louisiana. The Texas Railroad Commission regulated the Texas companies because their operations were exclusively intrastate, but the Shreveport company came under the jurisdiction of the ICC. Difficulties arose when the Texas regulators set rates substantially lower than did the ICC. The motive behind these lower rates was clear: the Texas commission wanted to encourage intrastate trade and to discourage companies from taking their business to Shreveport. The rates placed the

Shreveport railroad at a distinct disadvantage in competing for the Texas market. In response, the ICC ordered the intrastate Texas rates to be raised to the interstate levels. When the commission's authority to set intrastate rail rates was challenged, the Supreme Court ruled in favor of the ICC, articulating what became known as the Shreveport Doctrine. The Court held that the federal government had the power to regulate intrastate commerce when a failure to regulate would cripple, retard, or destroy interstate commerce. According to Justice Charles Evans Hughes's opinion for the Court, whenever interstate and intrastate commercial activities are entwined so that the regulation of one controls the other, "it is Congress, and not the State, that is entitled to prescribe the final and dominant rule."

Manufacturing and Direct Effects on Interstate Commerce

The Court's endorsement of the federal power to regulate interstate transportation and distribution did not extend initially to the attempts by Congress to impose effective antitrust legislation. The target of the antitrust statutes were the monopolies that controlled basic industries and choked out all competition. During the late 1800s these trusts grew to capture and exercise dominance over many industries, including oil, meat packing, sugar, and steel. The Sherman Act was Congress's first attempt to break up these anticompetitive combines. It outlawed all contracts and combinations of companies that had the effect of restraining trade and commerce or eliminating competition.

For the antitrust law to be fully effective, however, its provisions had to cover the manufacturing and processing stages of commercial activity, which raised a serious constitutional problem. In earlier cases the Court had ruled that manufacturing was essentially a local activity and not part of interstate commerce. For example, in *Veazie v. Moor* (1853) the Court had la-

---

1. *Wabash, St. Louis & Pacific Railway Co. v. Illinois* (1886).
2. *Interstate Commerce Commission v. Brimson* (1894); *Interstate Commerce Commission v. Cincinnati, New Orleans & Texas Pacific Railway Co.* (1897); *Interstate Commerce Commission v. Alabama-Midland Railway Co.* (1897).
3. See *Illinois Central Railroad Co. v. Interstate Commerce Commission* (1907).

beled it a far-reaching "pretension" to suggest that the federal power over interstate commerce extended to manufacturing. Later, in *Kidd v. Pearson* (1888), the Court took an even stronger stand. Here it held that the production of alcoholic beverages was an intrastate activity even if the resulting products were to be sold in interstate commerce.

Could the new antitrust law be applied to manufacturing? Or had Congress exceeded its constitutional authority in regulating production? These questions were answered in *United States v. E. C. Knight Co.* (1895), a battle over the federal government's attempts to break up the sugar trust. At the end of the nineteenth century six companies dominated the American sugar refining industry. The American Sugar Refining Company was the largest, with control of about 65 percent of the nation's refining capacity. Four Pennsylvania refiners shared 33 percent of the market, and a Boston company had a scant 2 percent. In March 1892 American Sugar entered into agreements that allowed it to acquire the four Pennsylvania refineries, including the E. C. Knight Company, giving American Sugar absolute control over 98 percent of the sugar refining business in the United States.

The federal government sued to have the acquisition agreements canceled. According to Justice Department attorneys, the sugar trust operated as a monopoly in restraint of trade in violation of the Sherman Anti-Trust Law. Attorneys for American Sugar and the acquired companies held that the law did not apply to sugar refining because that activity is manufacturing subject to state, not federal, control.

With only John Marshall Harlan in dissent, the justices rejected the federal government's position and ruled that the antitrust law could not be imposed on the sugar refining industry. Refining was manufacturing. It was production that occurred within the boundaries of a single state. It made no difference that the sugar trust controlled 98 percent of the nation's sugar supply, nor that the processed sugar was destined to be sold in interstate commerce. Manufactur-

ing was not interstate commerce. In Chief Justice Fuller's words on behalf of the Court, "Commerce succeeds to manufacture, and is not a part of it."

In *E. C. Knight* the Court first expressed concern about the effects of various economic activities on interstate commerce. Proponents of federal regulation often argued that if an intrastate economic activity had an effect—any effect—on interstate commerce it could be regulated by Congress. The Supreme Court rejected this position in *E. C. Knight,* holding that federal authority is not activated unless the intrastate activity has a direct effect on interstate commerce. In the sugar trust case, Fuller concluded that the challenged monopoly had only an indirect effect on interstate commerce and therefore was not subject to federal regulation. The distinction between direct and indirect effects is not very clear and can be interpreted various ways. In the hands of the Court's conservative majority, the direct effects test would later be used to strike down other federal regulatory attempts.

Although the decision in *E. C. Knight* removed manufacturing from the authority of the Sherman Act, it did not doom federal antitrust efforts. In fact, when the monopolistic activity was not manufacturing, the Court was quite willing to apply the law. For example, the Court held that companies engaged in production and interstate sale of pipe came under the sections of the Sherman Act.[4] In 1904 the Court went even further, ruling in *Northern Securities Company v. United States* that stock transactions creating a holding company (the result of an effective merger between the Northern Pacific and the Great Northern Railroad companies) were subject to Sherman Act scrutiny. In spite of these applications of the antitrust law, *E. C. Knight* set an important precedent, declaring manufacturing to be outside the definition of interstate commerce. This ruling later would be extended, with serious repercussions, to bar many of the New Deal programs passed to combat the Great Depression.

---

4. *Addystone Pipe and Steel Co. v. United States* (1899).

Only when the economy collapsed did the wisdom expressed in Justice Harlan's *E. C. Knight* dissent became apparent: the federal government must be empowered to regulate economic evils that are injurious to the nation's commerce and that a single state is incapable of eradicating.

The Stream of Commerce Doctrine

Government efforts to break up the meat packing trust presented a different constitutional challenge. The corporations that dominated the meat industry, such as Armour, Cudahy, and Swift, ruled the nation's stockyards, which stood at the throat of the meat distribution process. Western ranchers sent their livestock to the stockyards to be sold, butchered, and packed for shipment to consumers in the East. Livestock brokers, known as commission men, received the animals at the stockyards and sold them to the meat packing companies for the ranchers. Consequently, when the meat packing trust acquired control of the stockyards and the commission men who worked there, it was in a position to direct where the ranchers sent their stock, fix meat prices, demand unreasonably low rates from those who transported stock, and decide when to withhold meat from the market. The government believed these actions constituted a restraint of trade in violation of the Sherman Act. The meat packers argued that their control over the stockyards was an intrastate matter to be regulated by the states.

The Court settled the dispute in *Swift & Company v. United States* (1905) in which Justice Holmes, speaking for a unanimous Court, held that the Sherman Act applied to the stockyards. The commercial sale of beef, Holmes reasoned, began when the cattle left the range and did not terminate until final sale. The fact that the cattle stopped at the stockyards, midpoint in this commercial enterprise, did not mean that they were removed from interstate commerce. Holmes's opinion develops what has become known as the

stream of commerce doctrine, which allows federal regulation of interstate commerce from the point of its origin to the point of its termination. Interruptions in the course of that interstate commerce do not suspend the right of Congress to regulate. Seventeen years later, in *Stafford v. Wallace* (1922), the Court reaffirmed the stream of commerce doctrine, when it upheld the constitutionality of the 1921 Packers and Stockyard Act, a comprehensive regulation of the stockyard industry.

The stream of commerce precedents set in the *Swift* and *Stafford* stockyards cases later were applied to other regulatory schemes. Most notable was *Chicago Board of Trade v. Olsen* (1923), which brought the grain exchanges under the rubric of interstate commerce. Such decisions broadened the power of the federal government to control the economy. But the Court still found that certain commercial activities exerted too little direct impact on interstate commerce to justify congressional control. The most prominent among these were manufacturing and processing. The 1895 sugar trust case of *E. C. Knight* established this principle, and it was reinforced in 1918 by *Hammer v. Dagenhart*, the child labor case discussed in Chapter 6.

As the nation enjoyed the prosperity of the 1920s, the federal government had more power to regulate the economy than it had ever had, but not enough to cope effectively with a full-scale economic collapse. When the stock market crashed, the central government did not have the constitutional authority to impose adequate corrective measures, and the justices of the Supreme Court, at least initially, were unwilling to provide the political branches with that authority. This situation touched off history's most dramatic confrontation between the Court and the president, an episode that permanently altered the distribution of government powers.

THE SUPREME COURT AND
THE NEW DEAL

The New York Stock Exchange crash on October 29, 1929, set in motion a series of events that shook the American economy and drove the nation into a deep depression. For the next two years, the stock market continued to tumble, with the Standard and Poor's Industrial Averages falling 75 percent. The gross national product declined 27 percent over three years, and the unemployment rate rose from a healthy 3.2 percent in 1929 to a catastrophic 24.9 percent in 1933.

The Republican party, which had been victorious in the November 1928 elections, controlled the White House and both houses of Congress. The party attempted to cope with the depression by following philosophies of government that had been successful during the previous years of prosperity, with dismal results. The economic forces against which the Republicans fought were enormous. A different political approach was necessary to battle the collapse, and the American people were demanding such a change.

The Depression and Political Change

In the 1932 presidential election, Democratic candidate Franklin D. Roosevelt was swept into office by a huge margin as the voters rejected incumbent, Herbert Hoover. With new Democratic majorities in the House and Senate, the president began combating the depression with his New Deal policies. The overwhelming Democratic margins in Congress gave Roosevelt all the political clout he needed to gain approval of his radical new approach to boosting the economy. His programs were so popular with the American people that in 1936 they reelected Roosevelt by an even greater margin and provided him with even larger Democratic majorities in Congress, reducing the Republicans almost to minor party status.

The U.S. Supreme Court, however, did not change. In 1929, just before the stock market crashed, the

---

BOX 7-1   NEW DEAL
LEGISLATION

The Roosevelt Democrats moved on the nation's economic problems with great speed. Roosevelt took the oath of office on March 4, 1933. Listed below are the major economic actions passed during his first term. Note how many were enacted within the first 100 days of the new administration.

March 9, 1933	Emergency Banking Act
March 31, 1933	Civilian Conservation Corps created
May 12, 1933	Agricultural Adjustment Act
May 12, 1933	Federal Emergency Relief Act
May 18, 1933	Tennessee Valley Authority created
June 5, 1933	Nation taken off gold standard
June 13, 1933	Home Owners Loan Corporation created
June 16, 1933	Federal Deposit Insurance Corporation created
June 16, 1933	Farm Credit Administration created
June 16, 1933	National Industrial Recovery Act
January 30, 1934	Dollar devalued
June 6, 1934	Securities and Exchange Commission authorized
June 12, 1934	Reciprocal Tariff Act
June 19, 1934	Federal Communications Commission created
June 27, 1934	Railroad Retirement Act
June 28, 1934	Federal Housing Administration authorized
April 8, 1935	Works Progress Administration created
July 5, 1935	National Labor Relations Act
August 14, 1935	Social Security Act
August 26, 1935	Federal Power Commission created
August 30, 1935	National Bituminous Coal Conservation Act
February 19, 1936	Soil Conservation and Domestic Allotment Act

Court had six Republicans and three Democrats. The economic conservatives (Taft, Van Devanter, McReynolds, Butler, Sutherland, and Sanford) held control and clearly outnumbered the justices more sympathetic to political and economic change (Holmes, Brandeis, and Stone). By 1932 the Court had three new justices. Hughes succeeded Taft as chief justice, Benjamin Cardozo took Holmes's seat, and Owen Roberts replaced Edward Sanford. Although these changes reduced the Republican majority to five, there was no appreciable change in the ideological balance of the Court. Hoover had filled all three of these vacancies, which occurred before Roosevelt took office. Inaugurated in March 1933, Roosevelt had no opportunity to name a Supreme Court justice until Willis Van Devanter retired in June 1937. Roosevelt's first appointment, Hugo Black, assumed his seat in August of that year. Not until 1940 did the Court have a majority appointed from the period after Roosevelt's first election.

In the executive branch, Roosevelt assembled a cadre of young, creative people to devise novel ways of approaching the ailing economy, and these New Deal Democrats quickly set out to develop, enact, and implement their programs. Congress passed the first legislation, the Emergency Banking Act of 1933, just five days after Roosevelt's inauguration, and a string of statutes designed to control all major sectors of the nation's economy followed (*see Box 7-1*). In adopting these programs, Congress relied on a number of constitutional powers, including the powers to tax, spend, and regulate interstate and foreign commerce.

The new political majority that dominated the legislative and executive branches espoused philosophies that called for the government to take a significantly more active role in economic regulation. The Supreme Court remained firmly in the control of representatives of the old order, whose views on the relationship of government and the economy were at odds with those of the political branches. A clash between the president and the Court was inevitable.

The Court Attacks the New Deal

As soon as the New Deal programs came into being, conservative business interests began to challenge their constitutional validity. In just two years the appeals started to reach the Court's doorstep. Beginning in 1935 and lasting for two long, tense years, the Court and the New Deal Democrats fought over the constitutionality of an expanded federal role in managing the economy.

During this period, the justices struck down a number of important New Deal statutes. Of ten major programs, the Supreme Court approved only two—the Tennessee Valley Authority and the emergency monetary laws. Four hard-line conservative justices, Willis Van Devanter, James Clark McReynolds, George Sutherland, and Pierce Butler, formed the heart of the Court's opposition. Many thought their obstruction of New Deal initiatives would bring about the nation's ruin. As a consequence, they became known as the Four Horsemen of the Apocalypse, a reference to the end of the world as depicted in the Bible book of Revelations. Two of the four, McReynolds and Butler, were Democrats (*see Box 7-2*).

Naturally, these four justices by themselves could not declare void any act of Congress. They needed the vote of at least one other justice. As Box 7-3 indicates, they had little trouble attracting others to their cause. Of the eight major 1935–1936 decisions in which they were able to strike down congressional policies, three were by 5–4 votes in which the four were able to attract Justice Roberts to their fold. In one additional case, both Roberts and Chief Justice Hughes voted with the conservatives. But in three of these significant decisions, the Court was unanimous, with even the more liberal Brandeis, Cardozo, and Stone voting to strike down the challenged legislation.

The first salvo in the war between the two branches occurred on January 7, 1935, when the Supreme Court by an 8–1 vote in *Panama Refining Company v. Ryan* struck down a section of the National Industrial Recovery Act (NIRA) as an improper delegation of congressional power to the executive branch. The section in question was a major New Deal weapon in regulating the oil industry. It gave the president the power to prohibit interstate shipment of oil and petroleum products that were produced or stored in a manner illegal under state law. The justices found fault with the act because it did not provide sufficiently clear standards to guide the executive branch; rather, it gave the president almost unlimited discretion in applying the prohibitions. *Panama Refining* was the first case in which the Court struck down legislation because it was an improper delegation of power.

Although the decision in *Panama Refining* was restricted to the delegation question and did not focus on Congress's interstate commerce authority, it promised bad days ahead for the administration. Not only was the decision a disappointment for the president, but the vote was lopsided. Only Justice Cardozo voted to approve the law.

The Supreme Court dropped its biggest bomb on the New Deal four months later, in May 1935. The justices voted 5–4 on May 6 to declare the Railroad Retirement Act an unconstitutional violation of the Commerce Clause and the Due Process Clause of the Fifth Amendment.[5] Then on May 27, a date that became known as Black Monday, the justices announced three significant blows to the administration's efforts to fight the depression—all by unanimous votes. First, in *Humphrey's Executor v. United States,* the Court declared that the president did not have the power to remove a member of the Federal Trade Commission. Second, the justices invalidated the Frazier-Lemke Act, which provided mortgage relief, especially to farmers.[6] Finally, in *Schechter Poultry Corp. v. United States* the Court handed the president his most stinging defeat when it declared major portions of the NIRA unconstitutional as an improper delegation of legislative power and a violation of the Commerce Clause.

5. *Railroad Retirement Board v. Alton Railroad Co.* (1935).
6. *Louisville Bank v. Radford* (1935).

BOX 7-3 THE SUPREME COURT AND THE NEW DEAL

Listed below are eight major decisions handed down by the Supreme Court in 1935 and 1936 declaring parts of the New Deal legislative program unconstitutional.

Case/Decision Date	Acts Ruled Unconstitutional/Grounds	Majority	Dissent
Panama Refining Co. v. Ryan (January 7, 1935)	Portions of the National Industrial Recovery Act (improper delegation of congressional powers)	Brandeis, Butler, Hughes, McReynolds, Roberts, Stone, Sutherland, Van Devanter	Cardozo
Railroad Retirement Board v. Alton Railroad Co. (May 6, 1935)	Railroad Retirement Act of 1934 (exceeded Commerce Clause powers; Fifth Amendment due process violations)	Butler, McReynolds, Roberts, Sutherland, Van Devanter	Brandeis, Cardozo, Hughes, Stone
Schechter Poultry Corp. v. United States (May 27, 1935)	Portions of the National Industrial Recovery Act (a regulation of intrastate commerce and improper delegation of congressional power)	Brandeis, Butler, Cardozo, Hughes, McReynolds, Roberts, Stone, Sutherland, Van Devanter	
Louisville Bank v. Radford (May 27, 1935)	Frazier-Lemke Act of 1934 extending bankruptcy relief (Fifth Amendment property rights)	Brandeis, Butler, Cardozo, Hughes, McReynolds, Roberts, Stone, Sutherland, Van Devanter	
Hopkins Savings Association v. Cleary (December 12, 1935)	Home Owners Loan Act of 1933 (Tenth Amendment)	Brandeis, Butler, Cardozo, Hughes, McReynolds, Roberts, Stone, Sutherland, Van Devanter	
United States v. Butler (January 6, 1936)	Agricultural Adjustment Act (taxing and spending power violations)	Butler, Hughes, McReynolds, Roberts, Sutherland, Van Devanter	Brandeis, Cardozo, Stone
Carter v. Carter Coal Co. (May 18, 1936)	Bituminous Coal Conservation Act (a regulation of intrastate commerce; improper delegation of congressional power)	Butler, McReynolds, Roberts, Sutherland, Van Devanter	Brandeis, Cardozo, Hughes, Stone
Ashton v. Cameron County District Court (May 25, 1936)	Municipal Bankruptcy Act (Tenth Amendment; Fifth Amendment property rights)	Butler, McReynolds, Roberts, Sutherland, Van Devanter	Brandeis, Cardozo, Hughes, Stone

Schechter Poultry Corp. v. United States

295 U.S. 495 (1935)

*Vote: 9   (Brandeis, Butler, Cardozo, Hughes, McReynolds,
          Roberts, Stone, Sutherland, Van Devanter)*

    0

Opinion of the Court: Hughes
Concurring opinion: Cardozo

Congress passed the NIRA, the most far-reaching and comprehensive of all the New Deal legislation, June 16, 1933. Applying to every sector of American industry, the NIRA called for the creation of codes of fair competition for business. The codes would regulate trade practices, wages, hours, and other business activities within various industries. Trade associations and other industry groups had the responsibility for drafting the codes, which were submitted to the president for approval. In the absence of the private sector's recommendations, the president was authorized to draft codes himself. Once approved by the president, the codes had the force of law, and violators faced fines and even jail.

The NIRA was vulnerable to constitutional challenge on two grounds. First, it set virtually no standards for the president in approving or drafting the codes. Congress had handed Roosevelt a blank check to bring all of American industry into line with his views of what was best for the recovery of the economy. Second, the law regulated what at that time was considered intrastate commerce.

The *Schechter* case involved a challenge to the NIRA poultry codes, focusing on the industry in New York, the nation's largest chicken market.[7] This market clearly was operating in interstate commerce; 96 percent of the poultry sold in New York came from out-of-state suppliers. The industry was riddled with graft

A. L. A. Schechter (center) of Schechter Poultry Corporation with his attorneys Joseph Heller (left) and Frederick Wood, May 2, 1935.

and plagued by deplorable health and sanitary conditions. The Live Poultry Code approved by President Roosevelt set a maximum work week of forty hours and a minimum hourly wage of fifty cents. In addition, the code established a health inspection system, regulations to govern slaughtering procedures, and compulsory record keeping.

The A. L. A. Schechter Poultry Corporation, owned by Joseph, Martin, Aaron, and Alex Schechter, was a poultry slaughtering business in Brooklyn. Slaughterhouse operators, such as the Schechters, purchased large numbers of live chickens from local poultry dealers who imported the fowl from out of state to be killed and dressed for sale.

Government officials found the Schechters in violation of the Poultry Code on numerous counts. They ignored the code's wage and hour provisions, failed to comply with government record-keeping requirements, and did not conform to the slaughter regulations. Their worst offense, however, was selling unsanitary poultry that the government found unfit for human consumption. For this reason, *Schechter Poultry* was known as the Sick Chicken Case.

The government obtained indictments against the Schechter Poultry Corporation and the four brothers on sixty counts of violating the code, and the jury

7. For an interesting discussion of the *Schechter* case, see Chapter 5 in *The New Deal Lawyers,* by Peter H. Irons (Princeton, N.J.: Princeton University Press, 1982).

found them guilty of nineteen. Each of the brothers was sentenced to a short jail term. They appealed unsuccessfully to the court of appeals and then pressed their case to the U.S. Supreme Court, asserting that the NIRA was unconstitutional because it called for improper delegation of powers and violated the Commerce Clause.

MR. CHIEF JUSTICE HUGHES delivered the opinion of the Court.

The question of the delegation of legislative power. We recently had occasion to review the pertinent decisions and the general principles which govern the determination of this question. The Constitution provides that "All legislative powers herein granted shall be vested in a Congress of the United States, which shall consist of a Senate and House of Representatives." Art I, § 1. And the Congress is authorized "To make all laws which shall be necessary and proper for carrying into execution" its general powers. Art. I, § 8, par. 18. The Congress is not permitted to abdicate or to transfer to others the essential legislative functions with which it is thus vested. . . .

Section 3 of the Recovery Act is without precedent. It supplies no standards for any trade, industry or activity. It does not undertake to prescribe rules of conduct to be applied to particular states of fact determined by appropriate administrative procedure. Instead of prescribing rules of conduct, it authorizes the making of codes to prescribe them. For that legislative undertaking, § 3 sets up no standards, aside from the statement of the general aims of rehabilitation, correction and expansion described in section one. In view of the scope of that broad declaration, and of the nature of the few restrictions that are imposed, the discretion of the President in approving or prescribing codes, and thus enacting laws for the government of trade and industry throughout the country, is virtually unfettered. We think that the code-making authority thus conferred is an unconstitutional delegation of legislative power.

. . . *The question of the application of the provisions of the Live Poultry Code to intrastate transactions.* . . . This aspect of the case presents the question whether the particular provisions of the Live Poultry Code, which the defendants were

convicted for violating and for having conspired to violate, were within the regulating power of Congress.

These provisions relate to the hours and wages of those employed by defendants in their slaughterhouses in Brooklyn and to the sales there made to retail dealers and butchers.

(1) Were these transactions *"in"* interstate commerce? Much is made of the fact that almost all the poultry coming to New York is sent there from other States. But the code provisions, as here applied, do not concern the transportation of the poultry from other States to New York, or the transactions of the commission men or others to whom it is consigned, or the sales made by such consignees to defendants. When defendants had made their purchases, whether at the West Washington Market in New York City or at the railroad terminals serving the City, or elsewhere, the poultry was trucked to their slaughterhouses in Brooklyn for local disposition. The interstate transactions in relation to that poultry then ended. Defendants held the poultry at their slaughterhouse markets for slaughter and local sale to retail dealers and butchers who in turn sold directly to consumers. Neither the slaughtering nor the sales by defendants were transactions in interstate commerce.

The undisputed facts thus afford no warrant for the argument that the poultry handled by defendants at their slaughterhouse markets was in a *"current"* or *"flow"* of interstate commerce and was thus subject to congressional regulation. The mere fact that there may be a constant flow of commodities into a State does not mean that the flow continues after the property has arrived and has become commingled with the mass of property within the State and is there held solely for local disposition and use. So far as the poultry here in question is concerned; the flow in interstate commerce had ceased. The poultry had come to a permanent rest within the State. It was not held, used, or sold by defendants in relation to any further transactions in interstate commerce and was not destined for transportation to other States. Hence, decisions which deal with a stream of interstate commerce—where goods come to rest within a State temporarily and are later to go forward in interstate commerce—and with the regulations of transactions involved in that practical continuity of movement, are not applicable here.

(2) Did the defendants' transactions directly *"affect"* in-

terstate commerce so as to be subject to federal regulation? The power of Congress extends not only to the regulation of transactions which are part of interstate commerce, but to the protection of that commerce from injury. It matters not that the injury may be due to the conduct of those engaged in intrastate operations. Thus, Congress may protect the safety of those employed in interstate transportation "no matter what may be the source of the dangers which threaten it." We said in *Second Employers' Liability Cases,* that it is the "effect upon interstate commerce," not "the source of the injury," which is "the criterion of congressional power." We have held that, in dealing with common carriers engaged in both interstate and intrastate commerce, the dominant authority of Congress necessarily embraces the right to control their intrastate operations in all matters having such a close and substantial relation to interstate traffic that the control is essential or appropriate to secure the freedom of that traffic from interference or unjust discrimination and to promote the efficiency of the interstate service. And combinations and conspiracies to restrain interstate commerce, or to monopolize any part of it, are none the less within the reach of the Anti-Trust Act because the conspirators seek to attain their end by means of intrastate activities. . . .

In determining how far the federal government may go in controlling intrastate transactions upon the ground that they "affect" interstate commerce, there is a necessary and well-established distinction between direct and indirect effects. The precise line can be drawn only as individual cases arise, but the distinction is clear in principle. Direct effects are illustrated by the railroad cases we have cited, as *e.g.,* the effect of failure to use prescribed safety appliances on railroads which are the highways of both interstate and intrastate commerce, injury to an employee engaged in interstate transportation by the negligence of an employee engaged in an intrastate movement, the fixing of rates for intrastate transportation which unjustly discriminate against interstate commerce. But where the effect of intrastate transactions upon interstate commerce is merely indirect, such transactions remain within the domain of state power. If the commerce clause were construed to reach all enterprises and transactions which could be said to have an indirect effect upon interstate commerce, the federal authority would embrace practically all the activi-

ties of the people and the authority of the State over its domestic concerns would exist only by sufferance of the federal government. Indeed, on such a theory, even the development of the State's commercial facilities would be subject to federal control. As we said in the *Minnesota Rate Cases:* "In the intimacy of commercial relations, much that is done in the superintendence of local matters may have an indirect bearing upon interstate commerce. The development of local resources and the extension of local facilities may have a very important effect upon communities less favored and to an appreciable degree alter the course of trade. The freedom of local trade may stimulate interstate commerce, while restrictive measures within the police power of the State enacted exclusively with respect to internal business, as distinguished from interstate traffic, may in their reflex or indirect influence diminish the latter and reduce the volume of articles transported into or out of the State."

The distinction between direct and indirect effects has been clearly recognized in the application of the Anti-Trust Act. Where a combination or conspiracy is formed, with the intent to restrain interstate commerce or to monopolize any part of it, the violation of the statute is clear. But where that intent is absent, and the objectives are limited to intrastate activities, the fact that there may be an indirect effect upon interstate commerce does not subject the parties to the federal statute, notwithstanding its broad provisions. . . .

[T]he distinction between direct and indirect effects of intrastate transactions upon interstate commerce must be recognized as a fundamental one, essential to the maintenance of our constitutional system. Otherwise, as we have said, there would be virtually no limit to the federal power and for all practical purposes we should have a completely centralized government. We must consider the provisions here in question in the light of this distinction.

The question of chief importance relates to the provisions of the Code as to the hours and wages of those employed in defendants' slaughterhouse markets. It is plain that these requirements are imposed in order to govern the details of defendants' management of their local business. The persons employed in slaughtering and selling in local trade are not employed in interstate commerce. Their hours and wages have no direct relation to interstate commerce. The question of how many hours these employees should work and what they should be paid differs in no essential respect from similar questions in other local businesses which handle commodities brought into a State and there dealt in as a part of its internal commerce. This appears from an examination of the considerations urged by the Government with respect to conditions in the poultry trade. Thus, the Government argues that hours and wages affect prices; that slaughterhouse men sell at a small margin above operating costs; that a slaughterhouse operator paying lower wages or reducing his cost by exacting long hours of work, translates his saving into lower prices; that this results in demands for a cheaper grade of goods; and that the cutting of prices brings about a demoralization of the price structure. Similar conditions may be adduced in relation to other businesses. The argument of the Government proves too much. If the federal government may determine the wages and hours of employees in the internal commerce of a State, because of their relation to cost and prices and their indirect effect upon interstate commerce, it would seem that a similar control might be exerted over other elements of cost, also affecting prices, such as the number of employees, rents, advertising, methods of doing business, etc. All the processes of production and distribution that enter into cost could likewise be controlled. If the cost of doing an intrastate business is in itself the permitted object of federal control, the extent of the regulation of cost would be a question of discretion and not of power.

The Government also makes the point that efforts to enact state legislation establishing high labor standards have been impeded by the belief that unless similar action is taken generally, commerce will be diverted from the States adopting such standards, and that this fear of diversion has led to demands for federal legislation on the subject of wages and hours. The apparent implication is that the federal authority under the commerce clause should be deemed to extend to the establishment of rules to govern wages and hours in intrastate trade and industry generally throughout the country, thus overriding the authority of the States to deal with domestic problems arising from labor conditions in their internal commerce.

It is not the province of the Court to consider the economic advantages or disadvantages of such a centralized system. It is sufficient to say that the Federal Constitution does not provide for it. Our growth and development have called for wide use of the commerce power of the federal government in its control over the expanded activities of interstate commerce, and in protecting that commerce from burdens, interferences, and conspiracies to restrain and monopolize it. But the authority of the federal government may not be pushed to such an extreme as to destroy the distinction, which the commerce clause itself establishes, between commerce "among the several States" and the internal concerns of a State. The same answer must be made to the contention that is based upon the serious economic situation which led to the passage of the Recovery Act,—the fall in prices, the decline in wages and employment, and the curtailment of the market for commodities. Stress is laid upon the great importance of maintaining wage distributions which would provide the necessary stimulus in starting "the cumulative forces making for expanding commercial activity." Without in any way disparaging this motive, it is enough to say that the recuperative efforts of the federal government must be made in a manner consistent with the authority granted by the Constitution.

We are of the opinion that the attempt through the provisions of the Code to fix the hours and wages of employees of defendants in their intrastate business was not a valid exercise of federal power.

The other violations for which defendants were convicted related to the making of local sales. Ten counts, for violation of the provision as to "straight killing," were for permitting customers to make "selections of individual chickens taken from particular coops and half coops." Whether or not this practice is good or bad for the local trade, its effect, if any, upon interstate commerce was only indirect. The same may be said of violations of the Code by intrastate transactions consisting of the sale "of an unfit chicken" and of sales which were not in accord with the ordinances of the City of New York. The requirement of reports as to prices and volumes of defendants' sales was incident to the effort to control their intrastate business. . . .

On both the grounds we have discussed, the attempted delegation of legislative power, and the attempted regulation of intrastate transactions which affect interstate commerce only indirectly, we hold the code provisions here in question to be invalid and that the judgment of conviction must be reversed.

The decision in *Schechter* closely paralleled the *E. C. Knight* ruling and rejected the application of the stream of commerce doctrine. In *E. C. Knight* the Court held that sugar refining was a manufacturing stage, not part of interstate commerce, and, therefore, the federal government could not regulate it. Similarly, in *Schechter* the Court classified the slaughtering and local sale of chickens as intrastate commerce. The stream of commerce evident in the stockyards decisions did not apply. In *Schechter* the interstate movement of the poultry had ceased. Once the distributor had sold to local processors like the Schechter company, the chickens had reached their state of final destination and became a part of intrastate commerce. Also consistent with *E. C. Knight,* the justices concluded that the poultry slaughter business had only an indirect effect on interstate commerce.

Through the remaining months of 1935 and into 1936, the Court continued to strike down federal legislation designed to cope with the depression. In some cases the Court found the statutes defective for violating the federal taxing and spending power or for depriving individuals of their right to property without due process of law, topics covered in later chapters. But throughout this period, the Court was concerned with congressional actions that went beyond constitutional authority to regulate interstate commerce. Congress could not constitutionally legislate local business activity, such as manufacturing, processing, or refining, unless it had a direct effect on interstate commerce. The Court supported congressional regulation when the commerce was in movement from one state to another, but, as demonstrated in *Schechter,* the justices were unwilling to allow Congress to act on commerce after it had completed its interstate journey. *Schechter* examined when interstate commerce ends; in May 1936, with its decision in *Carter v. Carter Coal Company,* the Court taught the administration a lesson in when interstate commerce begins.

Congress passed the Bituminous Coal Conservation Act in August 1935, following the *Schechter* decision. This law replaced the NIRA coal codes, which had been reasonably effective in bringing some stability to the depressed coal industry. The new act called for the establishment of a commission empowered to develop regulations regarding fair competition, production, wages, hours, and labor relations. The commission included representatives from the coal producers, coal miners, and the public. To fund the program, Congress imposed a tax at the mines of 15 percent of the value of the coal produced. As was not the case with the NIRA codes, compliance with the new code regulations was voluntary. There was, however, an incentive for joining the program. Companies who participated were given a rebate of 90 percent of the taxes levied by the act.

James W. Carter and other shareholders urged their company not to participate in the program. The board of directors did not want to join, but it believed that the company could not afford to pay the 15 percent tax and forgo the participation rebate. The stockholders sued to prevent the company from joining the program on the grounds that the Coal Act was unconstitutional. Of Carter's several attacks on the law, the most deadly was the charge that coal mining was not in interstate commerce.

By a 5–4 vote the justices struck down the law. The majority held that coal mining was not interstate commerce because the activity occurred within a single state. The stream of commerce doctrine was inapplicable because the movement of the coal to other states had not yet begun. Furthermore, the justices concluded that the production of coal did not have a direct effect on interstate commerce. For these reasons, the Court invalidated federal regulation of coal mining. But *Carter v. Carter Coal* was Roosevelt's last major defeat at the hands of the Four Horsemen and their allies.

The Court-Packing Plan

The Court entered its summer recess in 1936 having completed a year and a half of dealing with Roo-

Editorial cartoon on President Roosevelt's Court-packing plan, *Washington Post*, February 6, 1937.

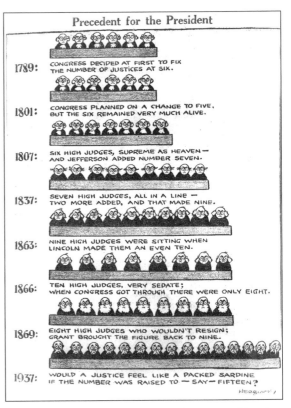

A *Washington Post* Herblock cartoon on the Court-packing plan, February 22, 1937.

sevelt's legislative program and striking down several of the New Deal's most significant programs. The Four Horsemen constituted a solid block, and in important cases they could count on the support of at least one of the other members—usually Owen Roberts. Roosevelt was understandably frustrated with what he viewed as the Court's obstructionism; he was also impatient that no vacancies had occurred that he might fill with appointees sympathetic to the New Deal.

The national elections took center stage during the fall of 1936. There was little doubt that Roosevelt would be reelected and that the Democrats would continue to control Congress. The only question was how big the margin was going to be. Roosevelt won by a landslide, capturing 98 percent of the electoral votes. His Republican opponent, Alf Landon of Kansas, carried only Maine and Vermont. The congressional elections were another triumph for the Democrats. When the legislature reconvened in early 1937, they controlled approximately 80 percent of the seats in both houses. With such an impressive mandate from the people and such strong party support in Congress, Roosevelt was willing to proceed with his planned attack on the Court. If no vacancies on the Supreme Court occurred naturally, Roosevelt would try to create some.

On February 5, 1937, the president announced his plan to reorganize the federal court system. Among other proposals, the president asked Congress to authorize the creation of one new seat on the Supreme Court for every justice who had attained the age of

FIGURE 7-1 Public Support for Roosevelt's 1937 Court-Packing Plan

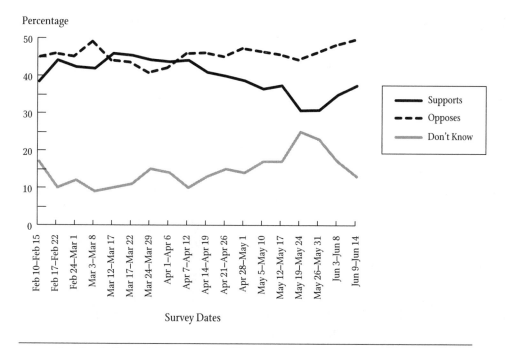

SOURCE: Data from Lee Epstein, Jeffrey A. Segal, Harold Spaeth, and Thomas G. Walker, *The Supreme Court Compendium: Data, Decisions, and Developments* (Washington, D.C.: Congressional Quarterly, 1994), Table 8-26.

seventy but remained in active service. These expanded positions would have an upper limit of six, bringing the potential size of the Court to a maximum of fifteen. At the time of his proposal, six sitting justices were older than seventy. If Roosevelt could appoint six New Deal advocates to the Court, they probably could attract the votes of at least two others and form a majority that would give constitutional approval to the president's programs. Although Roosevelt attempted to justify his Supreme Court proposal on the grounds that the advanced age of several sitting justices called for the addition of younger, more vigorous colleagues, everyone saw the plan for what it was—an attempt to pack the Court.

Reaction was not favorable.[8] Public opinion polls

taken during the course of the debate over the plan revealed that at no time did a majority of Americans support Roosevelt's proposal *(see Figure 7-1)*. Members of the organized bar were overwhelmingly opposed. Even with large Democratic majorities in both houses of Congress, Roosevelt had difficulty selling his proposal to the legislature. Chief Justice Hughes wrote a public letter criticizing the proposal to Sen. Burton Wheeler of Montana, a leader of Democrats opposing the president.[9] The press expressed sharp disapproval. In spite of the general support the people gave Roosevelt and the New Deal, they did not appreciate his tampering with the structure of government to get his way.

8. See Gregory A. Caldeira, "Public Opinion and the U.S. Supreme Court: FDR's Court-Packing Plan," *American Political Science Review* 81 (December 1987): 1139–1153.

9. The letter, dated March 21, 1937, is reprinted in *Guide to the U.S. Supreme Court*, 2d ed., ed. Elder Witt (Washington, D.C.: Congressional Quarterly, 1990), 963–965.

The Switch in Time That Saved Nine

The battle in Congress over the president's plan was closely fought.[10] A continuation of the confrontation, however, was averted in large measure by the actions of the Supreme Court itself. On March 29, the Court signaled that changes were in the making. The first indication was the 5–4 decision in *West Coast Hotel v. Parrish* (1937), which upheld the validity of a Washington State law regulating wages and working conditions for women and children. Although this case involved a state law rather than a federal statute and concerned issues of substantive due process rather than the Commerce Clause, it had great significance. (The doctrinal importance of the case will be discussed in Chapter 10.) The voting coalitions on the Court had changed. Justice Roberts, so long an ally of the Four Horsemen, deserted the conservatives and voted with the liberal bloc to approve the legislation. Just months earlier Roberts had voted with the conservatives in a 5–4 decision striking down a New York law that was nearly a carbon copy of the one he now approved.[11]

Two weeks later Roberts proved that his *West Coast Hotel* vote was not an aberration. On April 12 the Court issued its ruling in *National Labor Relations Board v. Jones & Laughlin Steel Corporation.* Once again Roberts joined Hughes, Brandeis, Cardozo, and Stone to form a majority, this time upholding a major piece of New Deal legislation. The decision may be the most significant economic ruling handed down during the twentieth century. In it the Court announced a break from the past and ushered in a new era in the constitutional relationship between the government and the economy.

10. See William E. Leuchtenburg, "The Origins of Franklin D. Roosevelt's 'Court-Packing' Plan," *Supreme Court Review* 1966 (Chicago: University of Chicago Press, 1966), 347–400; Leuchtenburg, *Franklin D. Roosevelt and the New Deal, 1932–1940* (New York: Harper & Row, 1963).

11. *Morehead v. New York ex rel. Tipaldo* (1936).

National Labor Relations Board v. Jones & Laughlin Steel Corporation

301 U.S. 1 (1937)
Vote: 5 (Brandeis, Cardozo, Hughes, Roberts, Stone)
    4 (Butler, McReynolds, Sutherland, Van Devanter)
Opinion for the Court: Hughes
Dissenting opinion: McReynolds

In 1935 Congress passed the National Labor Relations Act, more commonly known as the Wagner Act. The purpose of the legislation was to help workers achieve gains in wages and working conditions through the collective bargaining process. The act's primary aim was to protect the rights of employees to organize and join labor unions and to provide a means for the enforcement of those rights. The law authorized the creation of the National Labor Relations Board (NLRB), which was empowered to hear complaints of unfair labor practices and impose certain corrective measures. The act was based on the power of Congress to regulate interstate commerce and upon the assertion that labor unrest and strikes caused an interruption in such commerce that Congress had the right to prevent.

Jones & Laughlin was one of the nation's largest steel producers. Its operations were fully integrated, extending into many states and involving every aspect of steel production from mining through production and distribution. Complaints were filed against the company for engaging in unfair labor practices at its plant in Aliquippa, Pennsylvania. The charges included discriminating against workers who wanted to join a labor union. The NLRB ruled against the company and ordered it to reinstate ten workers who had been dismissed because of their union activities. The company refused, claiming that the National Labor Relations Act was unconstitutional. Steel production facilities, according to the company, were engaged in a manufacturing activity that had been declared by the Supreme Court to be intrastate commerce outside the regulatory authority of Congress. The lower courts, applying existing Supreme Court precedent, ruled in favor of the company, and the NLRB appealed.

MR. CHIEF JUSTICE HUGHES delivered the opinion of the Court.

First. The scope of the Act.—The Act is challenged in its entirety as an attempt to regulate all industry, thus invading the reserved powers of the States over their local concerns. It is asserted that the references in the Act to interstate and foreign commerce are colorable at best; that the Act is not a true regulation of such commerce or of matters which directly affect it but on the contrary has the fundamental object of placing under the compulsory supervision of the federal government all industrial labor relations within the nation. . . .

If this conception of terms, intent and consequent inseparability were sound, the Act would necessarily fall by reason of the limitation upon the federal power which inheres in the constitutional grant, as well as because of the explicit reservation of the Tenth Amendment. The authority of the federal government may not be pushed to such an extreme as to destroy the distinction, which the commerce clause itself establishes, between commerce "among the several States" and the internal concerns of a State. That distinction between what is national and what is local in the activities of commerce is vital to the maintenance of our federal system. . . .

We think it clear that the National Labor Relations Act may be construed so as to operate within the sphere of constitutional authority. The jurisdiction conferred upon the Board, and invoked in this instance, is found in § 10 (a), which provides:

"Sec. 10 (a). The Board is empowered, as hereinafter provided, to prevent any person from engaging in any unfair labor practice (listed in section 8) affecting commerce."

The critical words of this provision, prescribing the limits of the Board's authority in dealing with the labor practices, are "affecting commerce." The Act specifically defines the "commerce" to which it refers (§ 2 (6)):

"The term 'commerce' means trade, traffic, commerce, transportation, or communication among the several States, or between the District of Columbia or any Territory of the United States and any State or other Territory, or between any foreign country and any State, Territory, or the District of Columbia, or within the District of Columbia or any Territory, or between points in the same State but through any other State or any Territory or the District of Columbia or any foreign country."

There can be no question that the commerce thus contemplated by the Act (aside from that within a Territory or the District of Columbia) is interstate and foreign commerce in the constitutional sense. The Act also defines the term "affecting commerce" (§ 2 (7)):

"The term 'affecting commerce' means in commerce, or burdening or obstructing commerce or the free flow of commerce or having led or tending to lead to a labor dispute burdening or obstructing commerce or the free flow of commerce."

This definition is one of exclusion as well as inclusion. The grant of authority to the Board does not purport to extend to the relationship between all industrial employees and employers. Its terms do not impose collective bargaining upon all industry regardless of effects upon interstate and foreign commerce. It purports to reach only what may be deemed to burden or obstruct that commerce and, thus qualified, it must be construed as contemplating the exercise of control within constitutional bounds. It is a familiar principle that acts which directly burden or obstruct interstate or foreign commerce, or its free flow, are within the reach of the congressional power. Acts having that effect are not rendered immune because they grow out of labor disputes. It is the effect upon commerce, not the source of the injury, which is the criterion. Whether or not particular action does affect commerce in such a close and intimate fashion as to be subject to federal control, and hence to lie within the authority conferred upon the Board, is left by the statute to be determined as individual cases arise. We are thus to inquire whether in the instant case the constitutional boundary has been passed.

Second. The unfair labor practices in question.—. . .

[T]he statute goes no further than to safeguard the right of employees to self-organization and to select representatives of their own choosing for collective bargaining or other mutual protection without restraint or coercion by their employer.

That is a fundamental right. Employees have as clear a right to organize and select their representatives for lawful purposes as the respondent has to organize its business and select its own officers and agents. Discrimination and coercion to prevent the free exercise of the right of employees to self-organization and representation is a proper subject for condemnation by competent legislative authority. Long ago we stated the reason for labor organizations. We said that they were organized out of the necessities of the situation; that a single employee was helpless in dealing with an employer; that he was dependent ordinarily on his daily wage for the maintenance of himself and family; that if the employer refused to pay him the wages that he thought fair, he was nevertheless unable to leave the employ and resist arbitrary and unfair treatment; that union was essential to give laborers opportunity to deal on an equality with their employer. We reiterated these views when we had under consideration the Railway Labor Act of 1926. Fully recognizing the legality of collective action on the part of employees in order to safeguard their proper interests, we said that Congress was not required to ignore this right but could safeguard it. Congress could seek to make appropriate collective action of employees an instrument of peace rather than of strife. We said that such collective action would be a mockery if representation were made futile by interference with freedom of choice. Hence the prohibition by Congress of interference with the selection of representatives for the purpose of negotiation and conference between employers and employees, "instead of being an invasion of the constitutional right of either, was based on the recognition of the rights of both." We have reasserted the same principle in sustaining the application of the Railway Labor Act as amended in 1934.

Third. The application of the Act to employees engaged in production.—The principle involved.—Respondent says that whatever may be said of employees engaged in interstate commerce, the industrial relations and activities in the manufacturing department of respondent's enterprise are not subject to federal regulation. The argument rests upon the proposition that manufacturing in itself is not commerce.

The Government distinguishes these cases. The various parts of respondent's enterprise are described as interdependent and as thus involving "a great movement of iron ore, coal and limestone along well-defined paths to the steel mills, thence through them, and thence in the form of steel products into the consuming centers of the country—a definite and well-understood course of business." It is urged that these activities constitute a "stream" or "flow" of commerce, of which the Aliquippa manufacturing plant is the focal point, and that industrial strife at that point would cripple the entire government. Reference is made to our decision sustaining the Packers and Stockyards Act. . . .

We do not find it necessary to determine whether these features of defendant's business dispose of the asserted analogy to the "stream of commerce" cases. The instances in which that metaphor has been used are but particular, and not exclusive, illustrations of the protective power which the Government invokes in support of the present Act. The congressional authority to protect interstate commerce from burdens and obstructions is not limited to transactions which can be deemed to be an essential part of a "flow" of interstate or foreign commerce. Burdens and obstructions may be due to injurious action springing from other sources. The fundamental principle is that the power to regulate commerce is the power to enact "all appropriate legislation" for "its protection and advancement"; to adopt measures "to promote its growth and insure its safety"; "to foster, protect, control and restrain." That power is plenary and may be exerted to protect interstate commerce "no matter what the source of the dangers which threaten it." Although activities may be intrastate in character when separately considered, if they have such a close and substantial relation to interstate commerce that their control is essential or appropriate to protect that commerce from burdens and obstructions, Congress cannot be denied the power to exercise that control. . . .

It is thus apparent that the fact that the employees here concerned were engaged in production is not determinative. The question remains as to the effect upon interstate commerce of the labor practice involved. . . .

Fourth. Effects of the unfair labor practice in respondent's enterprise.—Giving full weight to respondent's contention with respect to a break in the complete continuity of the "stream of commerce" by reason of respondent's manufacturing operations, the fact remains that the stoppage of those operations by industrial strife would have a most serious effect upon interstate commerce. In view of respondent's far-flung activities, it is idle to say that the effect would be indirect or remote. It is obvious that it would be immediate and might be catastrophic. We are asked to shut our eyes to the plainest facts of our national life and to deal with the question of direct and indirect effects in an intellectual vacuum. Because there may be but indirect and remote effects upon interstate commerce in connection with a host of local enterprises throughout the country, it does not follow that other industrial activities do not have such a close and intimate relation to interstate commerce as to make the presence of industrial strife a matter of the most urgent national concern. When industries organize themselves on a national scale, making their relation to interstate commerce the dominant factor in their activities, how can it be maintained that their industrial labor relations constitute a forbidden field into which Congress may not enter when it is necessary to protect interstate commerce from the paralyzing consequences of industrial war? We have often said that interstate commerce itself is a practical conception. It is equally true that interferences with that commerce must be appraised by a judgment that does not ignore actual experience.

Experience has abundantly demonstrated that the recognition of the right of employees to self-organization and to have representatives of their own choosing for the purpose of collective bargaining is often an essential condition of industrial peace. Refusal to confer and negotiate has been one of the most prolific causes of strife. This is such an outstanding fact in the history of labor disturbances that it is a proper subject of judicial notice and requires no citation of instances. . . .

These questions have frequently engaged the attention of Congress and have been the subject of many inquiries. The steel industry is one of the great basic industries of the United States, with ramifying activities affecting interstate commerce at every point. The Government aptly refers to the steel strike of 1919–1920 with its far-reaching consequences. The fact that there appears to have been no major disturbance in that industry in the more recent period did not dispose of the possibilities of future and like dangers to interstate commerce which Congress was entitled to foresee and to exercise its protective power to forestall. It is not necessary again to detail the facts as to respondent's enterprise.

Instead of being beyond the pale, we think that it presents in a most striking way the close and intimate relation which a manufacturing industry may have to interstate commerce and we have no doubt that Congress had constitutional authority to safeguard the right of respondent's employees to self-organization and freedom in the choice of representatives for collective bargaining. . . .

Reversed.

MR. JUSTICE MCREYNOLDS delivered the following dissenting opinion in the cases preceding:

MR. JUSTICE VAN DEVANTER, MR. JUSTICE SUTHERLAND, MR. JUSTICE BUTLER and I are unable to agree with the decisions just announced. . . .

Considering the far-reaching import of these decisions, the departure from what we understand has been consistently ruled here, and the extraordinary power confirmed to a Board of three [the NLRB], the obligation to present our views becomes plain. . . .

The precise question for us to determine is whether in the circumstances disclosed Congress has power to authorize what the Labor Board commanded the respondents to do. Stated otherwise, in the circumstances here existing could Congress by statute direct what the Board has ordered? . . .

The argument in support of the Board affirms: "Thus the validity of any specific application of the preventive measures of this Act depends upon whether industrial strife resulting from the practices in the particular enterprise under consideration would be of the character which Federal power could control if it occurred. If strife in that enterprise could be controlled, certainly it could be prevented."

Manifestly that view of Congressional power would extend it into almost every field of human industry. With striking lucidity, fifty years ago, *Kidd v. Pearson* declared: "If it be held that the term [commerce with foreign nations and among the several states] includes the regulation of all such manufactures as are intended to be the subject of commercial transactions in the future, it is impossible to deny that it would also include all productive industries that contemplate the same thing. The result would be that Congress would be invested, to the exclusion of the States, with the power to regulate, not only manufactures, but also agriculture, horticulture, stock raising, domestic fisheries, mining—in short, every branch of human activity." This doctrine found full approval in *United States v. E. C. Knight Co., Schechter Poultry Corp. v. United States,* and *Carter v. Carter Coal Co.,* where the authorities are collected and principles applicable here are discussed. . . .

The Constitution still recognizes the existence of states with indestructible powers; the Tenth Amendment was supposed to put them beyond controversy.

We are told that Congress may protect the "stream of commerce" and that one who buys raw material without the state, manufactures it therein, and ships the output to another state is in that stream. Therefore it is said he may be prevented from doing anything which may interfere with its flow.

This, too, goes beyond the constitutional limitations heretofore enforced. If a man raises cattle and regularly delivers them to a carrier for interstate shipment, may Congress prescribe the conditions under which he may employ or discharge helpers on the ranch? The products of a mine pass daily into interstate commerce; many things are brought to it from other states. Are the owners and miners within the power of Congress in respect of the miners' tenure and discharge? May a mill owner be prohibited from closing his factory or discontinuing his business because so to do would stop the flow of products to and from his plant in interstate commerce? May employees in a factory be restrained from quitting work in a body because this will close the factory and thereby stop the flow of commerce? May arson of a factory be made a Federal offense whenever this would interfere with such flow? If the business cannot continue with the existing wage scale, may Congress command a reduction? If the ruling of the Court just announced is adhered to these questions suggest some of the problems certain to arise. . . .

There is no ground on which reasonably to hold that refusal by a manufacturer, whose raw materials come from states other than that of his factory and whose products are regularly carried to other states, to bargain collectively with employees in his manufacturing plant, directly affects interstate commerce. In such business, there is not one but two distinct movements or streams in interstate transportation. The first brings in raw material and there ends. Then follows manufacture, a separate and local activity.

Upon completion of this, and not before, the second distinct movement or stream in interstate commerce begins and the products go to other states. Such is the common course for small as well as large industries. It is unreasonable and unprecedented to say the commerce clause confers upon Congress power to govern the relations between employers and employees in these local activities. In *Schechter*'s case we condemned as unauthorized by the commerce clause assertion of federal power in respect of commodities which had come to rest after interstate transportation. And, in *Carter*'s case, we held Congress lacked the power to regulate labor relations in respect of commodities before interstate commerce has begun.

It is gravely stated that experience teaches that if an employer discourages membership in "any organization of any kind" "in which employees participate, and which exists for the purpose in whole or in part of dealing with employers concerning grievances, labor disputes, wages, rates of pay, hours of employment or conditions of work," discontent may follow and this in turn may lead to a strike, and as the outcome of the strike there may be a block in the stream of interstate commerce. Therefore Congress may inhibit the discharge! Whatever effect any cause of discontent may ultimately have upon commerce is far too indirect to justify Congressional regulation. Almost anything—marriage, birth, death—may in some fashion affect commerce.

That Congress has power by appropriate means, not prohibited by the Constitution, to prevent direct and material interference with the conduct of interstate commerce is settled doctrine. But the interference struck at must be direct and material, not some mere possibility contingent on wholly uncertain events; and there must be no impairment of rights guaranteed. . . .

The things inhibited by the Labor Act relate to the management of a manufacturing plant—something distinct from commerce and subject to the authority of the state. And this may not be abridged because of some vague possibility of distant interference with commerce. . . .

The right to contract is fundamental and includes the privilege of selecting those with whom one is willing to assume contractual relations. This right is unduly abridged by the Act now upheld. A private owner is deprived of power to manage his own property by freely selecting those to whom his manufacturing operations are to be entrusted.

We think this cannot lawfully be done in circumstances like those here disclosed.

It seems clear to us that Congress has transcended the powers granted.

The decisions in *West Coast Hotel v. Parrish* and *NLRB v. Jones & Laughlin Steel* took the energy out of Roosevelt's drive to pack the Court. It no longer appeared necessary since the Court now had begun to look with greater approval at state and federal legislation to correct the failing economy. In addition, on May 18 Justice Van Devanter, a consistent foe of Roosevelt's New Deal programs, announced that he would retire from the Court at the end of the term. At long last the president would have an opportunity to put a justice of his own choosing on the Court.

Much has been said and written about Justice Roberts's change in position. At the time, it was described as "the switch in time that saved nine," because his move from the conservative to the liberal wing of the Court was largely responsible for killing the Court-packing plan and preserving the Court as a nine-justice institution. Such a characterization is not flattering for a judge, who is not supposed to make decisions on the basis of external political pressures. Nevertheless, it would certainly be understandable for a justice to rethink his views if the future of the Court as an institution were at stake.

More contemporary analyses of Roberts's switch point out that the notion that he caved in to the pressures of the president's plan is simplistic. Although the decision in *West Coast Hotel* was announced after Roosevelt sent his proposal to Congress, it was argued and initially voted upon weeks before the president made his plans public. Roosevelt had kept the Court-packing proposal carefully under wraps before he announced it, and there is little likelihood that the justices had advance knowledge of it. Furthermore, Owen Roberts was not a doctrinaire conservative. Although he joined the Court's right wing in several important decisions, he did not have the laissez-faire zeal

Justice Owen Roberts who cast critical votes in 1937 Supreme Court cases that expanded the authority of the federal government to regulate the economy.

of the Four Horsemen. In fact, Roberts had voted on a number of occasions in support of state efforts to combat economic problems.[12] Some observers now conclude that Roberts's change of position was primarily a matter of his growing disenchantment with the hard-line conservative view and that he followed "his sound judicial intuition to a well-reasoned position in keeping with the public interest."[13] As for Roberts's own explanation, he maintained traditional judicial silence. When asked in a 1946 interview why he had altered his position, he deflected the question by responding, "Who knows what causes a judge to

12. See, for example, his opinion for the Court in *Nebbia v. New York* (1934).

13. Merlo J. Pusey, "Justice Roberts' 1937 Turnaround," *Yearbook of the Supreme Court Historical Society* (Washington, D.C.: Supreme Court Historical Society, 1983), 107.

decide as he does? Maybe the breakfast he had has something to do with it."[14] Whatever the reasons for his switch, it broke the conservatives' domination of the Court.

Consolidating the New Interpretation of the Commerce Power

Van Devanter's retirement was followed over the next four years by the retirements of Justices Sutherland and Brandeis and the deaths of Justices Cardozo and Butler. By 1940 Franklin Roosevelt had appointed a majority of the sitting justices. And in 1941 Justice McReynolds, the last of the Four Horsemen, retired.

With *NLRB v. Jones & Laughlin Steel* showing the way, the increasingly liberal Court upheld a number of New Deal programs. It also continued to expand the concept of interstate commerce. Gone were the old notions that production, manufacturing, mining, and processing were exclusively intrastate affairs with insufficient direct effects on interstate commerce to activate federal commerce powers. Precedents such as *E. C. Knight, Darby Lumber, Panama Refining, Schechter Poultry,* and *Carter Coal* were substantially overruled, discredited, or severely limited *(see Box 7-4)*.

Perhaps *Wickard v. Filburn* (1942) illustrates best how far the Court had moved from its pre-1937 idea of interstate commerce. The 1938 Agricultural Adjustment Act, as amended, allowed the secretary of agriculture to establish production limits for various grains. Under these limits, acreage allotments were assigned to the individual farmer. The purpose of the law was to stop the wild swings in grain prices by eliminating both surpluses and shortfalls.

Roscoe Filburn owned a small farm in Montgomery County, Ohio. For many years he raised dairy cattle and chickens, selling the milk, poultry, and eggs the farm produced. He also raised winter wheat on a small portion of his farm. He sold some of the wheat and used the rest to feed his cattle and chickens, make

flour for home consumption, and produce seeds for the next planting.

In July 1940 Secretary of Agriculture Claude R. Wickard set the wheat production limits for the 1941 crop. Filburn was allotted 11.1 acres to be planted in wheat with a yield of 20.1 bushels per acre. He planted not only his allotted acres but also some other land to produce the wheat for home consumption. In total Filburn planted 23 acres in wheat from which he harvested 239 bushels more than the government allowed him. For this excess planting Filburn was fined $117.11. He refused to pay the fine, claiming that Congress had exceeded its powers under the Commerce Clause by regulating an individual's planting wheat on his own property for on-farm consumption. The lower court ruled in Filburn's favor, and Secretary Wickard appealed.

The Supreme Court unanimously reversed and held that the act applied to Filburn's wheat production. The justices reasoned that wheat grown for on-farm consumption competes with wheat sold in commerce. Filburn's wheat combined with grain grown on other farms for home consumption may have a considerable impact on interstate commerce. Therefore, Congress has the authority to regulate such production—even small amounts produced by individuals. How far the Court had come! Prior to 1937 the justices had held that the 98 percent of the nation's sugar supply and the country's coal production had only an indirect effect on interstate commerce.

With decisions such as *NLRB v. Jones & Laughlin Steel* and *Wickard v. Filburn*, the Court had entered a new era of Commerce Clause interpretation. No longer would the justices grapple with issues such as direct versus indirect effects or stream of commerce concerns *(see Box 7-5)*. Under the modern interpretations very little commercial activity could be defined as purely intrastate. Since 1937, this approach has been considered firmly established in Commerce Clause jurisprudence.

In 1995, however, the Supreme Court seemed to

14. Quoted in ibid., 106.

BOX 7-4   SUPREME COURT EXPANSION OF THE
COMMERCE POWERS, 1937–1941

DECISION	RULING
NLRB v. Friedman-Harry Marks Clothing Company (1937)	The National Labor Relations Act applies to a company engaged in the manufacturing of clothing.
NLRB v. Fruehauf Trailer Company (1937)	The National Labor Relations Act applies to a company engaged in the manufacturing of trailers.
Steward Machine v. Davis (1937)	Unemployment provisions of the Social Security Act are constitutional.
Helvering v. Davis (1937)	Old-age benefits provisions of the Social Security Act are constitutional.
Santa Cruz Fruit Packing v. NLRB (1938)	The National Labor Relations Act applies to a fruit packing company although only 37 percent of its product is sold in interstate commerce.
Consolidated Edison Company v. NLRB (1938)	The National Labor Relations Act applies to a power company although all of its power is sold in state.
NLRB v. Fainblatt (1939)	The National Labor Relations Act applies to a small garment manufacturer even though all of its goods are sold in state.
United States v. Rock Royal Cooperative (1939)	Legislation allowing the secretary of agriculture to set milk prices paid to farmers is constitutional.
Mulford v. Smith (1939)	Tobacco production quotas set by secretary of agriculture under Agricultural Adjustment Act of 1938 are constitutional.
United States v. Darby Lumber Company (1941)	Congressional action prohibiting shipment in interstate commerce of goods in violation of federal wage and hour laws is constitutional.

pull back from the assumption that Congress could regulate almost anything on Commerce Clause grounds. At issue in the case of *United States v. Lopez* (1995) was the constitutionality of the federal Gun-Free School Zones Act. The law made it a crime for any individual knowingly to possess a firearm on school grounds. Alfonzo Lopez, Jr., a twelfth-grade student in San Antonio, was arrested for bringing a concealed .38 caliber revolver to Edison High School. He challenged his conviction on the grounds that education and crime are subjects rightfully left to the states, and not the federal government, to regulate. Although Congress had not specifically stated the constitutional authority upon which the law was passed,

government lawyers defended the statute by claiming that the national legislature had ample power under the Commerce Clause to prohibit the use of guns on school grounds. The connection between education and the economy is a substantial one, they argued, and a social problem, such as violence in the schools, that adversely affects education also has an adverse impact on interstate commerce.

A five-justice majority rejected the government's reasoning. Speaking for the Court, Chief Justice Rehnquist held that carrying a gun on school grounds is not commercial or economic in nature. Congress has no power to regulate such activity unless it "substantially affects" interstate commerce. The majority held

BOX 7-5 THE EVOLUTION OF INTERSTATE COMMERCE DOCTRINE

MARSHALL INTERPRETATION

Gibbons v. Ogden (1824)
Marshall opinion for 6–0 Court

Commerce begins in one state and ends in another. It does not stop when the act of crossing a state border is completed. Commerce occurring within a state may be part of a larger interstate process.

SHREVEPORT DOCTRINE

Shreveport Rate Case (1914)
Hughes opinion for a 7–2 Court

Congress may regulate intrastate commerce when it is intertwined with interstate commerce and a failure to regulate intrastate commerce would injure interstate commerce.

STREAM OF COMMERCE DOCTRINE

Swift and Company v. United States (1905)
Holmes opinion for 9–0 Court

Stafford v. Wallace (1922)
Taft opinion for a 7–1 Court

An article in interstate commerce does not lose its status until it reaches its final destination. The fact that the article may stop along the way to its terminal sale does not remove it from the stream of interstate commerce.

MANUFACTURING EXCLUDED FROM INTERSTATE COMMERCE

United States v. E. C. Knight Co. (1895)
Fuller opinion for an 8–1 Court

Schechter Poultry v. United States (1935)
Hughes opinion for a 9–0 Court

Carter v. Carter Coal Co. (1936)
Sutherland opinion for a 5–4 Court

Manufacturing, processing, and mining activities are local by nature and not a part of interstate commerce. Their effect on interstate commerce is indirect. That an article is intended for interstate commerce does not make the manufacture of that article part of interstate commerce. Commerce succeeds to manufacture, and is not a part of it.

MODERN INTERPRETATION OF INTERSTATE COMMERCE

NLRB v. Jones & Laughlin Steel Corp. (1937)
Hughes opinion for a 5–4 Court

Congress may enact all appropriate legislation to protect, advance, promote, and insure interstate commerce. Although activities may be intrastate in character when separately considered, if they have such a close and substantial relation to interstate commerce that their control is essential or appropriate to protect that commerce from burdens and obstructions, Congress cannot be denied the power to exercise that control.

that this requirement had not been met, and, therefore, in passing the Gun-Free School Zones Act Congress had exceeded its constitutional power.

Just how significant is *United States v. Lopez?* Some have interpreted the decision quite narrowly, as a simple warning to Congress that it must justify legislation by showing the relationship between the activities regulated and interstate commerce. Others view the decision as much more important, as a signal that the Court will no longer allow Congress to regulate whatever it wishes on the ground that all activities somehow affect interstate commerce. At a minimum the *Lopez* decision has introduced an element of instability in an area of the law previous considered settled. Commerce Clause cases clearly merit close watching in the future.

REGULATING COMMERCE AS A FEDERAL POLICE POWER

During the battle over the meaning of interstate commerce, the stakes were almost exclusively economic. The regulation of commerce, however, also can be used as a way to regulate health, safety, and moral matters. If Congress may use the interstate commerce power to regulate essentially noneconomic activities, then the long line of decisions, beginning with the *Jones & Laughlin Steel* case, expands federal power far beyond that envisioned by the Framers. May Congress legitimately use the Commerce Clause as means of exercising an authority at the national level similar to the states' police powers?

The answer to this question is yes. If an activity falls under the definition of commerce among the states, then Congress has the right to regulate it. The Commerce Clause itself imposes no limitations on the motivations for such legislation. As Chief Justice Marshall explained in *Gibbons v. Ogden,* "This power, like all others vested in Congress, is complete in itself, may be exercised to its utmost extent, and acknowledges

no limitations, other than are prescribed in the Constitution." The Commerce Clause, therefore, gives Congress power to regulate some activities that would otherwise be outside the federal purview. An excellent example is Congress's ability to legislate in the field of civil rights.

The constitutional protections against discrimination are found primarily in the Equal Protection Clause of the Fourteenth Amendment and the Due Process Clause of the Fifth, which have erected powerful barriers against invidious discrimination. But their exclusive target is discrimination perpetuated by the government. The words of the Fourteenth Amendment are clear: "Nor shall any state . . . deny to any person within its jurisdiction the equal protection of the laws." Nothing in the Fifth or Fourteenth Amendments prohibits discrimination by private parties. They were not intended to prohibit a private citizen from being discriminatory, but only to bar discriminatory government action. Although the Fourteenth Amendment includes a clause giving Congress the authority to enforce the provision with appropriate legislation, the Supreme Court has ruled that such enforcement legislation may not extend beyond the scope of the amendment itself. Consequently, the amendment does not empower Congress to regulate private discriminatory behavior.

When the civil rights movement of the 1950s and 1960s campaigned for the elimination of discriminatory conditions, high on the list was the eradication of discrimination by private parties who operated public accommodations. The movement targeted the owners of hotels, restaurants, movies, theaters, recreation areas, and transportation systems. In the aftermath of *Brown v. Board of Education* (1954), governments could not maintain laws mandating the segregation of such facilities, but private operators could still impose discrimination on their own. In the South, where segregation was the way of life, no one expected the states to pass civil rights statutes prohibiting private parties from discriminating. Therefore, civil rights advocates pressured Congress to do something about the situation.

Congress responded with passage of the Civil Rights Act of 1964, the most comprehensive legislation of its type ever passed. The act, as amended, is still the nation's most significant statute aimed at eliminating discrimination. However, the primary authority for passing this ground-breaking legislation was not a clause in the Bill of Rights or one of the Civil War amendments, but the Commerce Clause. Because the Court had treated Commerce Clause legislation favorably since 1937, members of Congress had confidence that the Civil Rights Act would withstand a legal challenge. Opponents of the legislation, however, argued that Congress had misused its power to regulate commerce by invoking it as justifying a civil rights law. Obviously, they said, the Framers, many of whom owned slaves, did not intend the power to regulate commerce among the states to be used to enact civil rights legislation.

Was Congress on solid grounds in doing so? The primary test of the law's constitutionality was *Heart of Atlanta Motel v. United States* (1964). As you read this case, note Justice Tom C. Clark's description of how racial discrimination has a negative impact on interstate commerce. Also note the Court's expansive view of interstate commerce and its conclusion that the Commerce Clause can be used to combat moral wrongs.

═══════════════════════════

Heart of Atlanta Motel v. United States

379 U.S. 241 (1964)

Vote: 9 *(Black, Brennan, Clark, Douglas, Goldberg, Harlan, Stewart, Warren, White)*

0

Opinion of the Court: Clark
Concurring opinions: Black, Douglas, Goldberg

Title II of the 1964 Civil Rights Act in its original form prohibited discrimination on the basis of race, color, religion, or national origin by certain public accommodations that operated in or affected interstate commerce. The accommodations specifically included were:

1. Inns, hotels, motels, or other lodging facilities of five rooms or more. Because they served the traveling public, these facilities were considered part of interstate commerce by definition.

2. Restaurants and cafeterias, if they served interstate travelers or if a substantial portion of their food or other products had moved in interstate commerce.

3. Motion picture houses, if they presented films that had moved in interstate commerce.

4. Any facility physically located within any of the other covered accommodations, which included operations such as hotel shops and theater snack bars.

The Heart of Atlanta Motel was a 216-room facility in Atlanta, Georgia. Located near the commercial center of the city, it had easy access to two interstate highways and two major state roads. The motel advertised for business in national publications and maintained more than fifty billboards and highway signs around the state. Both the government and the motel agreed that the facility met the act's definition of a public accommodation in interstate commerce.

The motel admitted that prior to the enactment of the civil rights law it practiced a policy of racial discrimination. Furthermore, it acknowledged that it intended to continue its policy of not serving blacks. To secure its right to do so, the motel filed suit to have the 1964 Civil Rights Act declared unconstitutional.

───────────────────────────

MR. JUSTICE CLARK delivered the opinion of the Court.

The Basis of Congressional Action.

While the Act as adopted carried no congressional findings the record of its passage through each house is replete with evidence of the burdens that discrimination by race or color places upon interstate commerce. This testimony included the fact that our people have become increasingly mobile with millions of people of all races traveling from State to State; that Negroes in particular have been the subject of discrimination in transient accommodations, having to travel great distances to secure the same; that often they have been unable to obtain accommodations and have had to call upon friends to put them up overnight; and that these conditions had become so acute as to require the listing of available lodging for Negroes in a special guidebook which was itself "dramatic testimony to the difficulties" Negroes encounter in travel. These exclusionary practices were found to be nationwide, the Under Secretary of Commerce testifying that there is "no question that this discrimination in the North still exists to a large degree" and in the West and Midwest as well. This testimony indicated a qualitative as well as a quantitative effect on interstate travel by Negroes. The former was the obvious impairment of the Negro traveler's pleasure and convenience that resulted when he continually was uncertain of finding lodging. As for the latter, there was evidence that this uncertainty stemming from racial discrimination had the effect of discouraging travel on the part of a substantial portion of the Negro community. This was the conclusion not only of the Under Secretary of Commerce but also of the Administrator of the Federal Aviation Agency who wrote the Chairman of the Senate Commerce Committee that it was his "belief that air commerce is adversely affected by the denial to a substantial segment of the traveling public of adequate and desegregated public accommodations." We shall not burden this opinion with further details since the voluminous testimony presents overwhelming evidence that discrimination by hotel and motels impedes interstate travel.

The Power of Congress Over Interstate Travel.

The power of Congress to deal with these obstructions depends on the meaning of the Commerce Clause. Its meaning was first enunciated 140 years ago by the great Chief Justice John Marshall in *Gibbons v. Ogden* (1824), in these words:

"The subject to be regulated is commerce; and . . . to ascertain the extent of the power, it becomes necessary to set-

tle the meaning of the word. The counsel for the appellee would limit it to traffic, to buying and selling, or the interchange of commodities . . . but it is something more: it is intercourse . . . between nations, and parts of nations, in all its branches, and is regulated by prescribing rules for carrying on that intercourse.

"To what commerce does this power extend? The constitution informs us, to commerce 'with foreign nations and among the several States, and with the Indian tribes.'

"It has, we believe, been universally admitted, that these words comprehend every species of commercial intercourse. . . . No sort of trade can be carried on . . . to which this power does not extend.

"The subject to which the power is next applied, is to commerce 'among the several States.' The word 'among' means intermingled.". . .

In short, the determinative test of the exercise of power by the Congress under the Commerce Clause is simply whether the activity sought to be regulated is "commerce which concerns more States than one" and has a real and substantial relation to the national interest. Let us now turn to this facet of the problem.

That the "intercourse" of which the Chief Justice spoke included the movement of persons through more States than one was settled as early as 1849, in the *Passenger Cases*, where Mr. Justice McLean stated: "That the transportation of passengers is a part of commerce is not now an open question." Again in 1913 Mr. Justice McKenna, speaking for the Court, said: "Commerce among the States, we have said, consists of intercourse and traffic between their citizens, and includes the transportation of persons and property. . . . Nor does it make any difference whether the transportation is commercial in character.". . .

The same interest in protecting interstate commerce which led Congress to deal with segregation in interstate carriers and the white-slave traffic has prompted it to extend the exercise of its power to gambling; to criminal enterprises; to deceptive practices in the sale of products; to fraudulent security transactions; to misbranding of drugs; to wages and hours; to members of labor unions; to crop control; to discrimination against shippers; to the protection of small business from injurious price cutting; to resale price maintenance; to professional football; and to racial discrimination by owners and managers of terminal restaurants.

That Congress was legislating against moral wrongs in many of these areas rendered its enactments no less valid. In framing Title II of this Act Congress was also dealing with what it considered a moral problem. But that fact does not detract from the overwhelming evidence of the disruptive effect that racial discrimination has had on commercial intercourse. It was this burden which empowered Congress to enact appropriate legislation, and, given this basis for the exercise of its power, Congress was not restricted by the fact that the particular obstruction to interstate commerce with which it was dealing was also deemed a moral and social wrong.

It is said that the operation of the motel here is of a purely local character. But . . . the power of Congress to promote interstate commerce also includes the power to regulate the local incidents thereof, including local activities in both the States of origin and destination, which might have a substantial and harmful effect upon that commerce. One need only examine the evidence which we have discussed above to see that Congress may—as it has—prohibit racial discrimination by motels serving travelers, however "local" their operations may appear. . . .

We, therefore, conclude that the action of the Congress in the adoption of the Act as applied here to a motel which concededly serves interstate travelers is within the power granted it by the Commerce Clause of the Constitution, as interpreted by this Court for 140 years. It may be argued that Congress could have pursued other methods to eliminate the obstructions it found in interstate commerce caused by racial discrimination. But this is a matter of policy that rests entirely with the Congress not with the courts. How obstructions in commerce may be removed—what means are to be employed—is within the sound and exclusive discretion of the Congress. It is subject only to one caveat—that the means chosen by it must be reasonably adapted to the end permitted by the Constitution. We cannot say that its choice here was not so adapted. The Constitution requires no more.

Affirmed.

Employing the same sweeping language as the Court used in *Wickard v. Filburn* to declare wheat grown for home consumption to be in interstate commerce, Justice Clark's opinion gives Congress broad powers to use the Commerce Clause as authority to regulate moral wrongs that occur in interstate commerce. In this way, the Commerce Clause became one of the most powerful weapons in the federal government's arsenal not only to regulate the economy but also to use as a police power.

THE COMMERCE POWER OF THE STATES

Resolving the question of federal power over interstate and foreign commerce leaves unsettled the question of state commercial regulation. Marshall wrote in *Gibbons* that the "completely internal commerce" of a state was reserved for state regulation. This grant of power was substantial prior to the Civil War when most commercial activity was distinctly local and subject to state regulation. But with the industrial revolution and improved transportation systems, business became increasingly interstate in nature. Finally, the Supreme Court's 1937 redefinition of interstate commerce left little that met Marshall's notion of commerce that is "completely internal."

If the regulation of any business activity that affects interstate commerce were the exclusive preserve of the federal government, the role of the states would be minimal indeed. But this is not the case. The decisions of the Supreme Court have left a substantial sphere of authority for the states to regulate commerce. The dividing line between federal and state power, however, has varied over time as the Supreme Court has struggled in building an appropriate doctrine to govern this difficult area of federal-state relations.

Perhaps the Court's most influential ruling on state commerce powers occurred in the case of *Cooley v. Board of Wardens* (1852). Here the justices attempted to balance congressional supremacy over interstate and foreign commerce with the need for the states to regulate the local aspects of such activity. Benjamin Curtis's opinion for the Court establishes a doctrine for handling federal-state commercial conflicts that is still used today.

Cooley v. Board of Wardens

12 How. 299 (1852)
Vote: 7   (Catron, Curtis, Daniel, Grier, McKinley, Nelson, Taney)
　 2   (McLean, Wayne)
Opinion of the Court: Curtis
Concurring opinion: Daniel
Dissenting opinion: McLean

Based on its power over interstate and foreign commerce, Congress passed a statute in 1789 pertaining to the regulation of ports. The legislation said that until Congress acted otherwise, state and local authorities would continue to control the nation's ports and harbors. In 1803 Pennsylvania passed a port regulation law requiring that all vessels hire a local pilot to guide ships in and out of the Port of Philadelphia. Ship owners who did not comply were fined. The money from these fines was placed in a "charitable fund for the distressed or decayed pilots, their widows and children." Aaron Cooley owned a vessel that sailed into Philadelphia without hiring a local pilot. The port's Board of Wardens took legal action against him, and Cooley was fined. He responded by claiming that the Pennsylvania law was unconstitutional; only Congress, he asserted, could regulate the port because the harbor was an integral part of interstate and foreign commerce, and the states had no constitutional authority to set regulations for such commerce. By implication, Cooley also was challenging the 1789 act of Congress that

had delegated such powers to the states. The Pennsylvania Supreme Court upheld the law and the fine, and Cooley pressed his case to the U.S. Supreme Court.

MR. JUSTICE CURTIS delivered the opinion of the Court.

That the power to regulate commerce includes the regulation of navigation, we consider settled. And when we look to the nature of the service performed by pilots, to the relations which that service and its compensations bear to navigation between the several States, and between the ports of the United States and foreign countries, we are brought to the conclusion, that the regulation of the qualifications of pilots, of the modes and times of offering and rendering their services, of the responsibilities which shall rest upon them, of the powers they shall possess, of the compensation they may demand, and of the penalties by which their rights and duties may be enforced, do constitute regulations of navigation, and consequently of commerce, within the just meaning of this clause of the Constitution. . . .

Nor should it be lost sight of, that this subject of the regulation of pilots and pilotage has an intimate connection with, and an important relation to the general subject of commerce with foreign nations and among the several States, over which it was one main object of the Constitution to create a national control. Conflicts between the laws of neighboring States, and discriminations favorable or adverse to commerce with particular foreign nations, might be created by State laws regulating pilotage, deeply affecting that equality of commercial rights, and that freedom from State interference, which those who formed the Constitution were so anxious to secure, and which the experience of more than half a century has taught us to value so highly. . . .

It becomes necessary, therefore, to consider whether this law of Pennsylvania, being a regulation of commerce, is valid.

The act of Congress of the 7th of August, 1789, sect. 4, is as follows:

"That all pilots in the bays, inlets, rivers, harbors, and ports of the United States shall continue to be regulated in conformity with the existing laws of the States, respectively, wherein such pilots may be, or with such laws as the States may respectively hereafter enact for the purpose, until further legislative provision shall be made by Congress."

If the law of Pennsylvania, now in question, had been in existence at the date of this act of Congress, we might hold it to have been adopted by Congress, and thus made a law of the United States, and so valid. Because this act does, in effect, give the force of an act of Congress, to the then existing State laws on this subject, so long as they should continue unrepealed by the State which enacted them.

But the law on which these actions are founded was not enacted till 1803. What effect then can be attributed to so much of the act of 1789, as declares, that pilots shall continue to be regulated in conformity, "with such laws as the States may respectively hereafter enact for the purpose, until further legislative provision shall be made by Congress"?

If the States were divested of the power to legislate on this subject by the grant of the commercial power to Congress, it is plain this act could not confer upon them power thus to legislate. If the Constitution excluded the States from making any law regulating commerce, certainly Congress cannot regrant, or in any manner reconvey to the States that power. And yet this act of 1789 gives its sanction only to laws enacted by the States. This necessarily implies a constitutional power to legislate; for only a rule created by the sovereign power of a State acting in its legislative capacity, can be deemed a law, enacted by a State; and if the State has so limited its sovereign power that it no longer extends to a particular subject, manifestly it cannot, in any proper sense, be said to enact laws thereon. Entertaining these views we are brought directly and unavoidably to the consideration of the question, whether the grant of the commercial power to Congress, did *per se* deprive the States of all power to regulate pilots. This question has never been decided by this court, nor, in our judgment, has any case depending upon all the considerations which must govern this one, come before this court. The grant of commercial power to Congress does not contain any terms which expressly exclude the States from exercising an authority over its subject-matter. If they are excluded it must be because of the nature of the power, thus granted to Congress, requires that a similar authority should not exist in the States. If it were conceded on the one side, that the nature of this power, like that to legislate for the District of Columbia, is ab-

solutely and totally repugnant to the existence of similar power in the States, probably no one would deny that the grant of the power to Congress, as effectually and perfectly excludes the States from all future legislation on the subject, as if express words had been used to exclude them. And on the other hand, if it were admitted that the existence of this power in Congress, lie the power of taxation, is compatible with the existence of a similar power in the States, then it would be in conformity with the contemporary exposition of the Constitution, (Federalist, No. 32,) and with the judicial construction, given from time to time by this court, after the most deliberate consideration, to hold that the mere grant of such a power to Congress, did not imply a prohibition on the States to exercise the same power; that it is not the mere existence of such a power, but its exercise by Congress, which may be incompatible with the exercise of the same power by the States, and that the States may legislate in the absence of congressional regulations.

The diversities of opinion, therefore, which have existed on this subject, have arisen from the different views taken of the nature of this power. But when the nature of a power like this is spoken of, when it is said that the nature of the power requires that it should be exercised exclusively by Congress, it must be intended to refer to the subjects of that power, and to say they are of such a nature as to require exclusive legislation by Congress. Now the power to regulate commerce, embraces a vast field, containing not only many, but exceedingly various subjects, quite unlike in their nature; some imperatively demanding a single uniform rule, operating equally on the commerce of the United States in every port; and some, like the subject now in question, as imperatively demanding that diversity, which alone can meet the local necessities of navigation.

Either absolutely to affirm, or deny that the nature of this power requires exclusive legislation by Congress, is to lose sight of the nature of the subjects of this power, and to assert concerning all of them, what is really applicable but to a part. Whatever subjects of this power are in their nature national, or admit only of one uniform system, or plan of regulation, may justly be said to be of such a nature as to require exclusive legislation by Congress. That this cannot be affirmed of laws for the regulation of pilots and pilotage is plain. The act of 1789 contains a clear and authoritative declaration by the first Congress, that the nature of this subject is such, that until Congress should find it necessary to exert its power, it should be left to the legislation of the States; that it is local and not national; that it is likely to be the best provided for, not by one system, or plan of regulations, but by as many as the legislative discretion of the several States should deem applicable to the local peculiarities of the ports within their limits.

Viewed in this light, so much of this act of 1789 as declares that pilots shall continue to be regulated "by such laws as the States may respectively hereafter enact for that purpose," instead of being held to be inoperative, as an attempt to confer on the States a power to legislate, of which the Constitution had deprived them, is allowed an appropriate and important signification. It manifests the understanding of Congress, at the outset of the government, that the nature of this subject is not such as to require its exclusive legislation. The practice of the States, and of the national government, has been in conformity with this declaration, from the origin of the national government to this time; and the nature of the subject when examined, is such as to leave no doubt of the superior fitness and propriety, not to say the absolute necessity, of different systems of regulation, drawn from local knowledge and experience, and conformed to local wants. How then can we say, that by the mere grant of power to regulate commerce, the States are deprived of all the power to legislate on this subject, because from the nature of the power the legislation of Congress must be exclusive. . . .

It is the opinion of a majority of the court that the mere grant to Congress of the power to regulate commerce, did not deprive the States of power to regulate pilots, and that although Congress has legislated on this subject, its legislation manifests an intention, with a single exception, not to regulate this subject, but to leave its regulation to the several States. To these precise questions, which are all we are called on to decide, this opinion must be understood to be confined. It does not extend to the question what other subjects, under the commercial power, are within the exclusive control of Congress, or may be regulated by the States in the absence of all congressional legislation; nor to the general question how far any regulation of a subject by Congress, may be deemed to operate as an exclusion of all legislation by the States upon the same subject. We decide the precise questions before us, upon what we deem sound principles, applicable to this particular subject in the state in which the legislation of Congress has left it. We go no further. . . .

We are of opinion that this State law was enacted by virtue of a power, residing in the State to legislate; that it is not in conflict with any law of Congress; that it does not interfere with any system which Congress has established by making regulations, or by intentionally leaving individuals to their own unrestricted action; that this law is therefore valid, and the judgment of the Supreme Court of Pennsylvania in each case must be affirmed.

Justice Curtis's opinion in *Cooley* nicely outlines the basic constitutional principles governing the state's power to regulate commerce. From this decision we can begin to build some understanding of how far the states may go in regulating commercial enterprise:

1. The states retain the power to regulate purely intrastate commerce.

2. Congress has the power to regulate interstate and foreign commerce. When it exercises this power any contrary state laws are preempted.

3. The power of Congress to regulate interstate and foreign commerce is exclusive over those elements of commercial activity that are national in scope or require uniform regulation.

4. Those elements of interstate and foreign commerce that are not national in scope or do not require uniformity, and which have not been regulated by Congress, may be subject to state authority including the state's police powers.

This division of authority is known as the doctrine of selected exclusiveness. It designates certain aspects of interstate and foreign commerce over which the powers of Congress are exclusive, allowing no state action. This exclusiveness, however, is not complete; in the absence of federal legislation, states may regulate some business activity affecting interstate commerce. The regulation of the Philadelphia port is an obvious part of interstate and foreign commerce where local harbor conditions require state supervision.

While the states are free to regulate within the general boundaries set in *Cooley,* twentieth-century justices have emphasized two important principles in their state commerce decisions. Both were developed to help achieve the goal of the free movement of commerce and to prohibit the states from erecting barriers to that flow. *(Examples of Supreme Court decisions enforcing these principles may be found in Box 7-6.)*

The first principle is that the state regulations may not place an undue burden on interstate commerce. A good example is provided by the Court's decision in *Southern Pacific Company v. Arizona* (1945). This case involved the validity of a state law making it unlawful to operate in Arizona a railroad train of more than fourteen passenger cars or seventy freight cars. The Southern Pacific Company openly violated the law. When the state took action against the company, Southern Pacific charged that the law was an unconstitutional burden on interstate commerce. Arizona defended its regulation on safety grounds, arguing that trains operating in excess of the state limits threatened the health, safety, and general well-being of the citizens of Arizona. The state's police powers, Arizona claimed, were sufficient to impose such limitations. The company countered by arguing that Arizona's limits were far more restrictive than those of other states. The company encountered considerable expense whenever one of its larger trains crossed into Arizona and the company was forced to reconfigure the cars in order to comply with state law.

The Court ruled in favor of Southern Pacific, holding that the state had placed a serious burden on interstate commerce. The law materially impeded the movement of trains through Arizona and obstructed the flow of interstate commerce. The interest of the nation in establishing an efficient rail system outweighed what marginal improvements in safety might be accomplished by the law. Even in the absence of a federal law imposing uniform train limits,

the state could not impose a policy that obstructed commercial movement.

The second principle is that state policies may not discriminate against interstate commerce. This standard imposes a restraint on states that might wish to protect in-state industries from interstate competition. For example, in *Hunt v. Washington State Apple Advertising Commission* (1977) the Court struck down a North Carolina regulation that required all apples shipped into the state to carry the U.S. Department of Agriculture grade or nothing at all. North Carolina argued that the regulation was meant to ensure that all apples coming into the state used the same grading system. No other state had such a regulation. Washington State apple growers challenged the regulation. Washington's apple industry is the largest in the nation and accounts for about 30 percent of all apples shipped interstate. To enhance its competitive position the Washington growers developed a grading system that was much higher and stricter than the USDA system. The Washington grading system had widespread acceptance in the apple trade. Disallowing the Washington grade to be printed on containers of apples coming into North Carolina was nothing more than a ploy to protect the North Carolina growers from competition from out-of-state producers, Washington argued. The Supreme Court agreed, holding that the North Carolina rules violated the Commerce Clause by discriminating against interstate commerce.

The rules of law developed by the Supreme Court generally have been faithful to the purposes of the Commerce Clause. After the period under the Articles of Confederation in which the national economy suffered because the individual states imposed trade and protective measures, the Framers wanted a system that guaranteed a free flow of business and commerce among the states. State regulations that place undue burdens on interstate commerce or favor in-state enterprises over interstate competition are contrary to the intent of the Commerce Clause.

BOX 7-6 SUPREME COURT DECISIONS STRIKING DOWN STATE RESTRICTIONS ON INTERSTATE COMMERCE

CASE	STATE LAW DECLARED UNCONSTITUTIONAL
Edwards v. California (1941)	California law making it a crime knowingly to bring an indigent into the state.
Dean Milk Company v. Madison (1951)	City ordinance discriminating against milk produced out of state.
Bibb v. Navajo Freight Lines (1959)	Illinois statute requiring a particular mudflap on all trucks and outlawing a conventional mudflap legal in forty-five other states.
Pike v. Bruce Church (1970)	Arizona law commanding that all Arizona-grown cantaloupes be packaged inside the state.
Great Atlantic and Pacific Tea Company v. Cottrell (1976)	Mississippi law banning milk produced in Louisiana in response to Louisiana's refusal to sign a reciprocity agreement.
Raymond Motor Transit v. Rice (1978)	Wisconsin regulation prohibiting from the state's highways double trucks exceeding sixty-five feet in length.
Philadelphia v. New Jersey (1978)	New Jersey ban on the importation and dumping of out-of-state garbage.
Hughes v. Oklahoma (1979)	Law outlawing the transportation of Oklahoma-grown minnows for out-of-state sale.
Kassell v. Consolidated Freightways (1981)	Iowa law banning sixty-five-foot double trucks.
New England Power Company v. New Hampshire (1982)	New Hampshire prohibition against selling domestically produced power to out-of-state interests.
Healy v. Beer Institute (1989)	Connecticut law requiring out-of-state beer distributors to show that the prices charged inside Connecticut are not higher than prices charged in bordering states.
State of Wyoming v. State of Oklahoma (1992)	Oklahoma law mandating that electrical utility companies purchase at least 10 percent of their coal from Oklahoma mining operations.
C & A Carbone, Inc. v. Town of Clarkstown, New York (1994)	City ordinance requiring that all nonhazardous solid waste within the town be sent to a local transfer station, forbidding such waste to be shipped to out-of-state facilities.

READINGS

Baker, Leonard. *Back to Back: The Duel Between FDR and the Supreme Court.* New York: Macmillan, 1967.

Benson, Paul R., Jr. *The Supreme Court and the Commerce Clause, 1937–1970.* New York: Dunellen, 1970.

Cortner, Richard. *The Wagner Act Cases.* Knoxville: University of Tennessee Press, 1964.

Corwin, Edward S. *The Commerce Power versus States' Rights.* Princeton, N.J.: Princeton University Press, 1936.

Dawson, Nelson. *Louis D. Brandeis, Felix Frankfurter, and the New Deal.* Hamden, Conn.: Archon Books, 1980.

Frankfurter, Felix. *The Commerce Clause Under Marshall, Taney and Waite.* Chapel Hill: University of North Carolina Press, 1937.

Himmelberg, Robert. *The Origins of the National Recovery Administration.* New York: Fordham University Press, 1976.

Irons, Peter H. *New Deal Lawyers.* Princeton, N.J.: Princeton University Press, 1982.

McClosky, Robert. *American Conservatism in the Age of Enterprise, 1865–1910.* Cambridge, Mass.: Harvard University Press, 1951.

Pearson, Drew, and Robert S. Allen. *The Nine Old Men.* Garden City, N.Y.: Doubleday, 1936.

Pritchett, C. Herman. *The Roosevelt Court: A Study in Judicial Politics and Values.* New York: Macmillan, 1948.

Wood, Stephen B. *Constitutional Politics in the Progressive Era: Child Labor and the Law.* Chicago: University of Chicago Press, 1968.

CHAPTER 8
THE POWER TO TAX AND SPEND

PERHAPS NO government power affects Americans more directly than the authority to tax and spend. Each year federal, state, and local governments collect billions of dollars in taxes imposed on a wide variety of activities, transactions, and goods. The federal government reminds us of its power to tax when we receive our paychecks, to say nothing of every April 15, the deadline for filing tax returns. Many state governments lay taxes on our incomes as well, and a majority of them also impose a levy each time we make a retail purchase. If we own a house, we must annually pay a tax on its value. We pay state and/or federal excise taxes whenever we make a phone call, put gas in the car, or buy cigarettes or alcoholic beverages. When we buy goods from abroad, the price includes a duty imposed on imports.

Americans have strong opinions about the government's taxing and spending activities. Many people think they pay too much and receive too little from the government in return. The battles over spending priorities are never ending, especially when choices must be made between national defense spending and social programs. In addition, there are constant complaints about the wasting of tax dollars by inefficient and ineffective government agencies. The mere mention of the Internal Revenue Service (IRS) strikes fear in the hearts of many. Minor tax revolts at the state and local level are not unusual. In spite of this general dissatisfaction, however, most Americans pay their taxes honestly and on time and realize that taxation is a fact of modern life.

Today the government's power to tax and spend is firmly established and has reasonably well-defined contours, but this was not always the case. Some of the country's greatest constitutional battles were fought over the fiscal powers. The results of these legal disputes have significantly shaped the powers and constraints of American political institutions. In this chapter, we examine the Supreme Court's interpretations of the twin fiscal powers of taxation and spending.

THE CONSTITUTIONAL POWER TO TAX AND SPEND

The power to tax was a fundamental issue at the Constitutional Convention. The government under the Articles of Confederation was ineffective in part because it had no authority to levy taxes. It could only request funds from the states and had no power to collect payment if the states refused to cooperate. The taxing authority resided solely with the states, which left the national government unable to execute public policies unless the states overwhelmingly supported them, a situation that did not often occur. It was clear that the central government would have to gain some revenue-gathering powers under the new constitution, while the states would retain concurrent authority to impose taxes.

Article I, Section 8, of the Constitution enumerates the powers of the federal government, and the first of those listed is the power to tax and spend:

The Congress shall have the Power to lay and collect Taxes, Duties, Imposts and Excises, to pay the Debts and provide for the common Defence and general Welfare of the United States.

The wording of this grant of authority is quite broad. The revenue function breaks into three categories. The first is the general grant of taxation power. Second is the authority to collect duties and imposts, both of which are taxes levied on imports, the primary source of revenue at that time. The third is the power to impose excises, which are taxes on the manufacture, sale, or use of goods, or on occupational or other activities.

The power to spend is also broadly constructed. The revenues gathered through the various taxing mechanisms may be used to pay government debts, to fund the nation's defense, and to provide for the general welfare. Although James Madison (and others) argued that the Framers intended the spending power to be limited to funding those government activities explicitly authorized in the Constitution, the wording of Article I, Section 8, does not impose any such restriction. The fact that Congress may spend federal funds to provide for the general welfare is indeed a broad grant of authority.

This is not to say that the federal power to tax and spend is without limits. The Framers were sufficiently wary of the dangers of a strong central government that they imposed some restrictions.

First, Article I, Section 8, stipulates that "all Duties, Imposts and Excises shall be uniform throughout the United States." The purpose of this provision was to prevent Congress from imposing different tax rates on various regions or requiring the citizens of one state to pay a tax rate higher than the citizens of other states. Geographical uniformity is the only stated constitutional requirement for excise taxes and taxes on imports. If this standard is met, the tax is likely to be valid.

Second, Article I, Section 9, holds that "No Tax or Duty shall be laid on Articles exported from any State." Consistent with the prevailing philosophy of increased commerce and trade, the Framers wanted to ensure that the products of the states would move freely without the burden of federal taxes being placed on them.

Third, Article I, Section 9, also dictates that "No capitation, or other direct, Tax shall be laid, unless in Proportion to the Census or Enumeration herein before directed to be taken." This same admonition is found in Article I, Section 2, where the Framers wrote, "[D]irect Taxes shall be apportioned among the several States . . . according to their respective Numbers" as determined by the national census. The term *direct tax* is not defined in the Constitution and is a difficult concept to understand. When the Framers referred to direct taxes they most likely meant a head tax—a tax imposed on each person—or a tax on land. As we shall see in the next section of this chapter, the requirement that direct taxes be apportioned on the basis of population has proved troublesome, and Congress has not often resorted to such levies.

The Framers generally allowed the states to retain their taxing authority as it existed prior to the ratification of the Constitution. Consequently, state and local governments today tax a wide array of activities and goods, including individual and corporate incomes, personal property, real estate, retail sales, investment holdings, and inheritances. But the Constitution imposed some new restraints on state taxing authority. These limitations specifically removed from the states any power to place a tax on certain forms of commerce. Article I, Section 10, prohibits them from imposing any duty on imports or exports, as well as any tax on the cargo capacity of vessels using the nation's ports. The Framers were interested in the promotion of commerce, and these provisions meant that states could not retard commerce by using foreign trade as a source of tax revenue.

In addition to these specific restrictions, state and federal taxation must be consistent with the other provisions of the Constitution. It would be a violation of the Constitution, for example, if a state or the federal government taxed the exercise of a constitutional right, such as the freedom of speech or the exercise of religion. By the same token, if the government imposed varying tax rates based on a person's sex or race, such levies would be in violation of the constitutional rights of due process and equal protection of the laws.

DIRECT TAXES AND THE POWER TO TAX INCOME

The Constitution stipulates two standards for assessing federal taxes. The first is geographical uniformity. Duties, imposts, and excise taxes all must be applied according to this standard. If Congress taxes a particular product entering the ports of the United States, the tax rate on the article must be the same regardless of the point of entry. Excise taxes also must be applied uniformly throughout the nation. If an excise is placed on automobiles, for example, the amount assessed must be the same in California as it is in Tennessee.

The second standard for imposing taxes is population distribution. The Constitution says that all direct taxes must be apportioned among the states on the basis of population. The delegates from the sparsely populated states supported this provision because they feared that the larger states, with greater representation in the House of Representatives, would craft tax measures in such a way that the burden would fall disproportionately upon the citizens of the smaller states. Unfortunately, the Framers did not explain what they meant by a direct tax. As Box 8-1 illustrates, whether a tax is levied uniformly or is apportioned on the basis of population greatly affects who pays how much. In *Federalist*, No. 21, Alexander Hamilton claimed that direct taxes were only those imposed on land and buildings, but Hamilton's opinion did not settle the issue. It required a Supreme Court decision to do that.

Defining Direct Taxation

In one of the Court's earliest cases, *Hylton v. United States* (1796), the justices defined the term *direct tax.* The dispute stemmed from a tax on carriages Congress passed June 5, 1794. The statute classified the tax as an excise and, therefore, applied the same rate on carriages nationwide. The Federalist majorities in Congress passed the statute over Anti-Federalist opposition, and the tax was completely partisan. The Federalists generally represented the states in the Northeast with large populations but relatively few carriages; the Anti-Federalist strongholds were the less densely populated and more agricultural states with larger numbers of carriages. Because the carriage tax was deemed an excise, the Anti-Federalist areas would pay a much greater share of it than would the residents of the Northeast. The Anti-Federalists would have preferred to classify the measure as a direct tax and apportion it on the basis of population.

Daniel Hylton, a resident of Virginia, challenged the constitutionality of the assessment, claiming that it was a direct tax, not an excise, and should have been apportioned on the basis of population. The government took the position that, as a tax on an article, the carriage tax was an excise.

By almost every rule of judicial authority developed since that time, the Court should have refused to

---

BOX 8-1   DIRECT AND INDIRECT TAXES:
APPORTIONMENT VERSUS GEOGRAPHICAL UNIFORMITY

This example demonstrates the difference between direct and indirect taxing methods. The facts and figures used are purely hypothetical.

Assume that Congress decides to raise $1 million through a tax on the nation's 100,000 thoroughbred horses. If this tax is considered an excise tax, it must conform to the constitutional requirement of geographical uniformity. Congress would have to require that all thoroughbred horse owners pay a tax of ten dollars per horse. The rate would be the same in Maine as in Oregon. If, however, the tax on thoroughbred horses is classified as a direct tax, a different set of calculations would have to be made to meet the constitutionally required apportionment standard. Three facts would need to be known: first, the amount of money Congress intends to raise; second, the proportion of the national population residing in each state; and, third, the number of thoroughbred horses in each state. Apportionment means that the proportion of the revenue obtained from a state must equal the proportion of the country's population living there.

The impact of apportionment can be seen by the following calculations in applying the $1 million horse tax to three states. State A is a densely populated, urban state with few horses. State B is a moderately populated state with some ranching areas. And State C is a sparsely populated, primarily agricultural state, with a relatively large number of thoroughbreds.

State	Percentage of National Population	Taxes Due from State	Number of Horses in State	Tax Rate per Horse
State A	10	$100,000	100	$1,000
State B	5	$50,000	1,000	$50
State C	1	$10,000	10,000	$1

Obviously, the horse owners in State A would be greatly disadvantaged if the horse tax were classified as a direct tax and apportioned among the states on the basis of population. State C, on the other hand, would be greatly benefited. Because State C has only 1 percent of the nation's population, it would be responsible for raising only 1 percent of the tax revenues. Furthermore, that smaller tax obligation would be distributed over a disproportionately large number of horses.

Horse owners in State A clearly would prefer the tax on thoroughbreds to be defined as an excise tax with its required geographical uniformity. State C's thoroughbred owners obviously would argue for the horse tax to be considered a direct tax and be apportioned among the states on the basis of population.

---

hear the dispute.[1] The evidence showed that the case did not involve adverse parties. In fact, the suit appeared to be little more than a ploy by the government to obtain Court approval of its interpretation of the taxation provisions of the Constitution. Both sides to the dispute agreed that Hylton owned 125 carriages exclusively for his private use. In reality, he owned only 1, but the tax due on a single carriage was insufficient to meet the threshold for federal court jurisdiction. If Hylton owned 125 carriages, the taxes and penalties due would reach $2,000, enough for federal court action. This jurisdictional point was important because Federalist judges dominated the federal courts, and they were likely to give the law a sympathetic hearing. Administration officials also agreed that if the tax were found valid they would demand that Hylton pay only $16. Perhaps an even greater indication of collusion was that the government paid the fees of the attorneys for both sides.

Former secretary of the treasury Alexander Hamilton presented the government's case. Hamilton was one of the most vigorous supporters of a strong na-

1. See Melvin I. Urofsky, *A March of Liberty: A Constitutional History of the United States* (New York: Knopf, 1988), 146–148. See also Robert F. Cushman, *Cases in Constitutional Law,* 7th ed. (Englewood Cliffs, N.J.: Prentice Hall, 1989), 177–178.

tional government and of broad federal taxation powers. He understood the problems associated with apportioning taxes on the basis of population and consequently wanted the Court to set down a very narrow definition of direct taxes.

Hamilton's side was victorious. The three judges who participated in the decision each voted in favor of the statute and in agreement with Congress's determination that the carriage tax was an excise tax.[2] As was the custom in the years before John Marshall became chief justice, each justice wrote a separate opinion explaining his vote.[3] The opinions of James Iredell and Samuel Chase stressed the inappropriateness of attempting to apportion a tax on carriages and the inevitable inequities that would result. William Paterson's opinion emphasized the intention of the Framers. His opinion had particular credibility because Paterson, having been a New Jersey delegate to the Constitutional Convention, was one of the Framers.[4] All three agreed that only two kinds of taxes fell into the direct tax category: capitation (or head) taxes and taxes on land.

Apportioning taxes on the basis of population is very cumbersome and almost inevitably leads to unjust tax burdens. The *Hylton* decision, by limiting the kinds of taxes that fell into the direct taxation category, significantly strengthened federal taxation powers. It freed Congress from having to apply unpopular apportionment standards to most taxes. So difficult is

the apportionment problem that Congress only rarely has attempted to use a direct tax, and such efforts generally have been unsatisfactory.

Hylton was the first case in which the Supreme Court heard a challenge to the constitutionality of a federal statute; the decision predated *Marbury v. Madison* by seven years. It is clear from the arguments before the Court and the justices' opinions that the law was tested for its constitutionality. *Hylton* has not received the notoriety of *Marbury* because the act of Congress was found to be valid.

The Constitutionality of the Income Tax

From *Hylton* to the 1860s federal taxing authority remained generally unchanged. The government financed its activities largely through import duties and excise taxes. The Civil War, however, placed an incredible financial strain on the federal government. Between 1858 and the end of the war, the government ran unusually high budget deficits and needed to find new sources of revenue to fund the war effort. In response, Congress in 1862 and 1864 imposed the first taxes on individual incomes. The 1881 case of *Springer v. United States* involved a challenge to the validity of the income tax. William M. Springer, an attorney, claimed that the income tax was a direct tax and should have been apportioned on the basis of population. The justices unanimously rejected this position, once again holding that only capitation taxes and taxes on land were direct taxes. Although the challenged tax was a levy on the income of individuals, it could not be considered a capitation tax within the normal meaning of that term. *Springer*, then, set precedent that the federal government had the power to tax incomes.

As the government reduced its war debts, Congress in 1872 was able to repeal the income tax law.[5] But the issue of taxing incomes did not go away. The Populist

2. The other three members of the Court were absent for various reasons. Oliver Ellsworth had just been sworn in as chief justice and, because he had missed some of the arguments, did not participate in the decision. Justice James Wilson heard arguments but did not vote in the case because he had participated in the lower court decision upholding the tax. Justice William Cushing was not present for the arguments and therefore did not vote on the merits.

3. Having each justice write a separate opinion explaining his views was a practice borrowed from the British courts. When Marshall became chief justice, he moved away from the use of these seriatim opinions to the current practice of a single opinion explaining the views of the majority. Marshall believed that the presentation of a single opinion increased the Court's status and effectiveness.

4. Justice Wilson was also a delegate at the Constitutional Convention and, therefore, one of the Framers. Although he did not participate at the Supreme Court level, Wilson earlier voted to uphold the tax as an excise in the lower court.

5. For an excellent review of the history of the income tax in the United States, see John F. Witte, *The Politics and Development of the Federal Income Tax* (Madison: University of Wisconsin Press, 1985).

movement favored the use of the income tax as the primary method of raising federal revenues. In addition, labor groups and farm organizations began arguing that new revenue sources should be developed to shift the burden away from reliance on import duties.

Members of the Democratic party criticized the regressive aspects of the tax structure of that time. In response to these demands, Congress enacted an income tax law in 1894. The statute, which was passed as part of the Wilson-Gorman Tariff Act, imposed a 2 percent tax on all corporate profits and on individual incomes.

Income derived from salaries and wages, gifts, inheritances, dividends, rents, and interest, including interest from state and municipal bonds, all were subject to this tax. People with incomes under $4,000 paid no tax. This exemption, set at a figure much higher than what the average worker earned, meant that most of the burden fell upon the wealthy. For this reason, the tax received overwhelming support from rank and file citizens and bitter opposition from businesses and high-income individuals. The wealthy classes, in fact, claimed that the income tax would destroy the very fabric of the nation, replacing the historical principle of respect for private property with communism and socialism.

The income tax law was promptly challenged in Court in an 1895 appeal, *Pollock v. Farmers' Loan & Trust Co.* One of the primary arguments of the law's opponents was that the income tax was a direct tax, and since Congress had not apportioned it, the law was unconstitutional. Given precedents such as *Hylton* and *Springer,* would you anticipate that this position would be successful?

Pollock v. Farmers' Loan & Trust Co.

158 U.S. 601 (1895)

Vote: 5 (Brewer, Field, Fuller, Gray, Shiras)
4 (Brown, Harlan, Jackson, White)

Opinion of the Court: Fuller

Dissenting opinions: Brown, Harlan, Jackson, White

Charles Pollock, a shareholder in the Farmers' Loan & Trust Company of New York, filed suit on behalf of himself and his fellow stockholders to block the company from paying the national income tax on the grounds that the tax was unconstitutional. The lawsuit was obviously collusive: the company no more wanted to pay the tax than did its shareholders. Opponents of the law claimed (1) that taxing income from state and city bonds was an unconstitutional encroachment on the state's power to borrow money; (2) that a tax on income from real property was a direct tax and must be apportioned on the basis of population; and (3) that these taxes were so integral to the entire tax act that the whole law should be declared unconstitutional.

The Court heard arguments on the *Pollock* case twice. In its first decision, the majority declared the tax on state and municipal bonds unconstitutional.[6] It further ruled that a tax on income from land was essentially the same as taxing land itself. Because a tax on land is a direct tax, so too is a tax on the income from land. Therefore, such taxes must be apportioned on the basis of population. But the Court was unable to reach a decision on whether the entire law should be declared unconstitutional. On this question the justices divided 4–4 because Justice Howell Jackson, ill with tuberculosis, was absent.

Pollock filed a petition for a second hearing, and Jackson made it known that he would be present for it. The second decision reviewed much of what the Court concluded in the first, but this time the Court went on

6. *Pollock v. Farmers' Loan & Trust Co.* (1895).

to rule on the question of the general constitutionality of the income tax act.

The *Pollock* decision was one of the most controversial and important of its day. It contained all the elements of high drama. The case pitted the interests of business and wealthy individuals against those supporting social and fiscal reform. Both sides believed that a victory for their opponents would have disastrous consequences for the nation. Newspapers editorialized with enthusiasm. The first decision having ended in a tie, the suspense surrounding the second hearing grew tremendously. The human interest factor was heightened when Justice Jackson was transported to Washington to cast what he thought would be the deciding vote in favor of the tax. (Jackson died three months later.) Oral arguments took place from May 6 to May 8. The justices did not act in a manner consistent with detached objectivity. Loren Beth reports that "Harlan wrote privately that Justice Stephen J. Field acted like a 'madman' throughout the case, but the dissenters' own opinions were similarly emotional."[7] In the end the opponents of the tax were victorious. Although Jackson, as expected, voted to uphold the law, Justice George Shiras, who had supported the tax in the first hearing, changed positions and became the crucial fifth vote to strike it down.

MR. CHIEF JUSTICE FULLER delivered the opinion of the court.

Whenever this court is required to pass upon the validity of an act of Congress as tested by the fundamental law enacted by the people, the duty imposed demands in its discharge the utmost deliberation and care, and invokes the deepest sense of responsibility. And this is especially so when the question involves the exercise of a great governmental power, and brings into consideration, as vitally affected by the decision, that complex system of government,

so sagaciously framed to secure and perpetuate "an indestructible Union, composed of indestructible States."....

As heretofore stated, the Constitution divided Federal taxation into two great classes, the class of direct taxes, and the class of duties, imposts and excises; and prescribed two rules which qualified the grant of power as to each class.

The power to lay direct taxes apportioned among the several States in proportion to their representation in the popular branch of Congress, a representation based on population as ascertained by the census, was plenary and absolute; but to lay direct taxes without apportionment was forbidden. The power to lay duties, imposts, and excises was subject to the qualification that the imposition must be uniform throughout the United States.

Our previous decision was confined to the consideration of the validity of the tax on the income from real estate, and on the income from municipal bonds. The question thus limited was whether such taxation was direct or not, in the meaning of the Constitution; and the court went no farther, as to the tax on the income from real estate, than to hold that it fell within the same class as the source whence the income was derived, that is, that a tax upon the realty and a tax upon the receipts therefrom were alike direct; while as to the income from municipal bonds, that could not be taxed because of want of power to tax the source, and no reference was made to the nature of the tax as being direct or indirect.

We are now permitted to broaden the field of inquiry, and to determine to which of the two great classes a tax upon a person's entire income, whether derived from rents, or products, or otherwise, of real estate, or from bonds, stocks, or other forms of personal property, belongs; and we are unable to conclude that the enforced subtraction from the yield of all the owner's real or personal property, in the manner prescribed, is so different from a tax upon the property itself, that it is not a direct, but an indirect tax, in the meaning of the Constitution. . . .

The reasons for the clauses of the Constitution in respect of direct taxation are not far to seek. The States, respectively, possessed plenary powers of taxation. They could tax the property of their citizens in such manner and to such extent as they saw fit; they had unrestricted powers to impose duties or imposts on imports from abroad, and excises on manufactures, consumable commodities, or oth-

---

7. Loren P. Beth, "*Pollock v. Farmers' Loan & Trust Co.,*" in *The Oxford Companion to the Supreme Court,* ed. Kermit L. Hall (New York: Oxford University Press, 1992), 655.

erwise. They gave up the great sources of revenue derived from commerce; they retained the concurrent power o[f] levying excises, and duties if covering anything other than excises; but in respect of them the range of taxation was narrowed by the power granted over interstate commerce, and by the danger of being put at disadvantage in dealing with excises on manufactures. They retained the power of direct taxation, and to that they looked as their chief resource; but even in respect of that, they granted the concurrent power, and if the tax were placed by both governments on the same subject, the claim of the United States had preference. Therefore, they did not grant the power of direct taxation without regard to their own condition and resources as States; but they granted the power of apportioned direct taxation, a power just as efficacious to serve the needs of the general government, but securing to the States the opportunity to pay the amount apportioned, and to recoup from their own citizens in the most feasible way, and in harmony with their systems of local self-government. If, in the changes of wealth and population in particular States, apportionment produced inequality, it was an inequality stipulated for, just as the equal representation of the States, however small, in the Senate, was stipulated for. The Constitution ordains affirmatively that each State shall have two members of that body, and negatively that no State shall by amendment be deprived of its equal suffrage in the Senate without its consent. The Constitution ordains affirmatively that representatives and direct taxes shall be apportioned among the several States according to numbers, and negatively that no direct tax shall be laid unless in proportion to the enumeration.

The founders anticipated that the expenditures of the States, their counties, cities, and towns, would chiefly be met by direct taxation on accumulated property, while they expected that those of the Federal government would be for the most part met by indirect taxes. And in order that the power of direct taxation by the general government should not be exercised, except on necessity; and, when the necessity arose, should be so exercised as to leave the States at liberty to discharge their respective obligations, and should not be so exercised, unfairly and discriminatingly, as to particular States or otherwise, by a mere majority vote, possibly of those whose constituents were intentionally not sub-

jected to any part of the burden, the qualified grant was made. . . .

It is said that a tax on the whole income of property is not a direct tax in the meaning of the Constitution, but a duty, and, as a duty, leviable without apportionment, whether direct or indirect. We do not think so. Direct taxation was not restricted in one breath, and the restriction blown to the winds in another. . . .

We have unanimously held in this case that, so far as this law operates on the receipts from municipal bonds, it cannot be sustained, because it is a tax on the power of the States, and on their instrumentalities to borrow money, and consequently repugnant to the Constitution. But if, as contended, the interest when received has become merely money in the recipient's pocket, and taxable as such without reference to the source from which it came, the question is immaterial whether it could have been originally taxed at all or not. This was admitted by the Attorney General with characteristic candor; and it follows that, if the revenue derived from municipal bonds cannot be taxed because the source cannot be, the same rule applies to revenue from any other source not subject to the tax; and the lack of power to levy any but an apportioned tax on real and personal property equally exists as to the revenue therefrom.

Admitting that this act taxes the income of property irrespective of its source, still we cannot doubt that such a tax is necessarily a direct tax in the meaning of the Constitution. . . .

We are not here concerned with the question whether an income tax be or be not desirable, nor whether such a tax would enable the government to diminish taxes on consumption and duties on imports, and to enter upon what may be believed to be a reform of its fiscal and commercial system. Questions of that character belong to the controversies of political parties, and cannot be settled by judicial decision. In these cases our province is to determine whether this income tax on the revenue from property does or does not belong to the class of direct taxes. If it does, it is, being unapportioned, in violation of the Constitution, and we must so declare. . . .

We have considered the act only in respect of the tax on income derived from real estate, and from invested personal property, and have not commented on so much of it as bears on gains or profits from business, privileges, or employments, in view of the instances in which taxation on business, privileges, or employments has assumed the guise of an excise tax and been sustained as such.

Being of opinion that so much of the sections of this law as lays a tax on income from real and personal property is invalid, we are brought to the question of the effect of that conclusion upon these sections as a whole.

It is elementary that the same statute may be in part constitutional and in part unconstitutional, and if the parts are wholly independent of each other, that which is constitutional may stand while that which is unconstitutional will be rejected. And in the case before us there is no question as to the validity of this act, except sections twenty-seven to thirty-seven, inclusive, which relate to the subject which has been under discussion; and as to them we think . . . that if the different parts "are so mutually connected with and dependent on each other, as to warrant a belief that the legislature intended them as a whole, and that, if all could not be carried into effect, the legislature would not pass the residue independently, and some parts are unconstitutional, all the provisions which are thus dependent, conditional or connected, must fall with them.". . .

According to the census, the true valuation of real and personal property in the United States in 1890 was $65,037,091,197, of which real estate with improvements thereon made up $39,544,544,333. Of course, from the latter must be deducted, in applying these sections, all unproductive property and all property whose net yield does not exceed four thousand dollars; but, even with such deductions, it is evident that the income from realty formed a vital part of the scheme for taxation embodied therein. If that be stricken out, and also the income from all invested personal property, bonds, stocks, investments of all kinds, it is obvious that by far the largest part of the anticipated revenue would be eliminated, and this would leave the burden of the tax to be borne by professions, trades, employments, or vocations; and in that way what was intended as a tax on capital would remain in substance a tax on occupations and labor. We cannot believe that such was the intention of Congress. We do not mean to say that an act laying by apportionment a direct tax on all real estate and personal property, or the income thereof, might not also lay excise taxes on business, privileges, employments, and vocations. But this is not such an act; and the scheme must be considered as a whole. Being invalid as to the greater part, and falling, as the tax would, if any part were held valid, in a direction which could not have been contemplated except in connection with the taxation considered as an entirety, we are constrained to conclude that sections twenty-seven to thirty-seven, inclusive, of the act, which became a law without the signature of the President on August 28, 1894, are wholly inoperative and void.

Our conclusions may, therefore, be summed up as follows:

First. We adhere to the opinion already announced, that, taxes on real estate being indisputably direct taxes, taxes on the rents or income of real estate are equally direct taxes.

Second. We are of opinion that taxes on personal property, or on the income of personal property, are likewise direct taxes.

Third. The tax imposed by sections twenty-seven to thirty-seven, inclusive, of the act of 1894, so far as it falls on the income of real estate and of personal property, being a direct tax within the meaning of the Constitution, and, therefore, unconstitutional and void because not apportioned according to representation, all those sections, constituting one entire scheme of taxation, are necessarily invalid.

MR. JUSTICE WHITE, with whom concurred MR. JUSTICE HARLAN, dissenting.

My brief judicial experience has convinced me that the custom of filing long dissenting opinions is one "more honored in the breach than in the observance." The only purpose which an elaborate dissent can accomplish, if any, is to weaken the effect of the opinion of the majority, and thus engender want of confidence in the conclusions of courts of last resort. This consideration would impel me to content myself with simply recording my dissent in the present case, were it not for the fact that I consider that the result of the opinion of the court just announced is to overthrow a long and consistent line of decisions, and to deny to the legislative department of government the possession of a power conceded to it by universal consensus for one hundred years, and which has been recognized by repeated adjudications of this court. . . .

... At the very birth of the government a contention arose as to the meaning of the word "direct." The controversy was determined by the legislative and executive departments of the government. Their action came to this court for review, and it was approved. Every judge of this court who expressed an opinion, made use of language which clearly showed that he thought the word "direct" in the Constitution applied only to capitation taxes and taxes directly on land. Thereafter the construction thus given was accepted everywhere as definitive. The matter came again and again to this court, and in every case the original ruling was adhered to. The suggestions made in the *Hylton case* were adopted here, and, in the last case here decided, reviewing all others, this court said that direct taxes within the meaning of the Constitution were only taxes on land and capitation taxes. And now, after a hundred years, after long-continued action by other departments of government, and after repeated adjudications of this court, this interpretation is overthrown, and the Congress is declared not to have a power of taxation which may at some time, as it has in the past, prove necessary to the very existence of the government. . . . In view of all that has taken place and of the many decisions of this court, the matter at issue here ought to be regarded as closed forever. . . .

My inability to agree with the court in the conclusions which it has just expressed causes me much regret. Great as is my respect for any view by it announced, I cannot resist the conviction that its opinion and decree in this case virtually annuls its previous decisions in regard to the powers of Congress on the subject of taxation, and is therefore fraught with danger to the court, to each and every citizen, and to the republic. The conservation and orderly development of our institutions rests on our acceptance of the results of the past, and their use as lights to guide our steps in the future. Teach the lesson that settled principles may be overthrown at any time, and confusion and turmoil must ultimately result. In the discharge of its function of interpreting the Constitution, this court exercises an august power. It sits removed from the contentions of political parties and the animosities of factions. It seems to me that the accomplishment of its lofty mission can only be secured by the stability of its teachings and the sanctity which surrounds them. If the permanency of its conclusions is to depend upon the personal opinions of those who, from time to time, may

WITHOUT A FRIEND.

This 1895 editorial cartoon, published after the Supreme Court's decision in *Pollock v. Farmers' Loan and Trust,* illustrates the defeat of the federal income tax law. In 1913, however, the situation reversed itself when the states ratified the Sixteenth Amendment, which gave the federal government the power to tax incomes regardless of source.

make up its membership, it will inevitably become a theatre of political strife, and its action will be without coherence or consistency. . . . My strong convictions forbid that I take part in a conclusion which seems to me so full of peril to the country. I am unwilling to do so, without reference to the question of what my personal opinion upon the subject might be if the question were a new one, and was thus unaffected by the action of the framers, the history of the government, and the long line of decisions by this court. . . . The fundamental conception of a judicial body is that of one hedged about by precedents which are binding on the

TABLE 8-1 Federal Tax Revenues: The Impact of the Sixteenth Amendment

Source	1800	1850	1900	1950	1993
Customs duties	83.7	91.0	41.1	1.0	1.6
Excises	7.5	—	50.1	18.4	4.2
Gifts and inheritances	—	—	—	1.7	1.1
Individual incomes	—	—	—	38.5	44.2
Corporate incomes	—	—	—	25.5	10.2
Insurance trust (Social Security, etc.)	—	—	—	10.7	37.1
Other income	8.8	9.0	8.8	4.2	1.6

SOURCES: *Historical Statistics of the United States: Colonial Times to 1970* (Washington, D.C.: U.S. Bureau of the Census, 1975); *Statistical Abstract of the United States, 1994* (Washington, D.C.: U.S. Department of Commerce, Bureau of the Census, 1994).

NOTE: The data represent the proportion of total federal revenues for each of seven sources of taxation. The data prior to ratification of the Sixteenth Amendment in 1913 demonstrate the federal government's reliance on customs duties and excise taxes. Data from the period after 1913 illustrate the shift to income taxes as the primary sources for federal tax dollars.

court without regard to the personality of its members. Break down this belief in judicial continuity, and let it be felt that on great constitutional questions this court is to depart from the settled conclusins of its predecessors, and to determine them all according to the mere opinion of those who temporarily fill its bench, and our Constitution will, in my judgment, be bereft of value and become a most dangerous instrument to the rights and liberties of the people.

The Sixteenth Amendment

The decision to invalidate the entire income tax act was quite unpopular. Because that statute had placed a greater obligation on the wealthy, the ruling convinced the middle and working classes that the Supreme Court was little more than the defender of the rich. Various political groups immediately began working to reverse the impact of the Court's decision by means of either a constitutional amendment or revised federal legislation. Labor and farming interests supported a new income tax, as did Progressive Republicans and Democratic populists. Opposition came primarily from conservative Republicans in the Northeast.

Finally, in 1909 Congress began serious work on an income tax measure. There were sufficient votes in the legislature to reform the tax structure, moving the federal government away from excessive reliance on regressive tariffs and excise taxes. The major question was whether to pass another income tax bill or to propose a constitutional amendment. Finding themselves in a minority, conservative Republicans threw their support to an amendment. They hoped the state legislatures would not ratify it; but, even if the states approved, the process would take several years to complete.

Congress proposed a constitutional amendment to authorize a federal income tax in July 1909 by overwhelming votes of 77–0 in the Senate and 318–14 in the House. The amendment received the required number of approvals from the state legislatures in February 1913 and became the Sixteenth Amendment to the United States Constitution:

The Congress shall have power to lay and collect taxes on incomes, from whatever source derived, without apportionment among the several States, and without regard to any census or enumeration.

The amendment, which effectively ended the debate over direct taxation, is one of only four designed to overturn a Supreme Court precedent. It gave Congress sufficient taxing authority to fund the federal government without having to resort to direct taxes. The Constitution now made all sources of income subject to Congress's taxing power and removed any requirement that a tax on income be apportioned on the basis of population.

Congress wasted no time. In 1913 the legislature imposed a 1 percent tax rate on individual incomes in excess of $3,000 and on incomes of married couples over $4,000. Not surprisingly, the statute's constitutionality was challenged in Court, but the justices upheld the law three years later in *Brushaber v. Union Pacific Railroad* (1916) by a 7–2 vote. As shown in Table 8-1, the income tax is now the primary source of federal revenue.

INTERGOVERNMENTAL TAX IMMUNITY

The operation of a federal system carries within it inherent risks of conflict between the national government and the states. When both levels of government are authorized to tax, one government can use the power as a weapon against the other. No specific provision of the Constitution prohibits the federal government from taxing state governments or vice versa, but for the federal system to operate effectively, the entities need to avoid such conflicts.

Establishing the Tax Immunity Doctrine

The issue of intergovernmental tax immunity was first raised in *McCulloch v. Maryland* (1819), which tested the constitutional validity of the national bank. The Supreme Court's decision in *McCulloch* was tremendously important in a number of ways. We have already discussed its significance for the development of congressional power and the concept of federalism, but *McCulloch* also is relevant to the constitutional limitations on the power to tax.

McCulloch involved a challenge to a tax imposed by the state of Maryland on the national bank, a creation of the federal government. Supporters of federal power argued that the union could not be maintained if the states were permitted to place debilitating taxes on the operations of the federal government that they did not approve of. States' rights advocates claimed that the power of the states to tax within their own borders was absolute and there was no constitutional bar to such taxes. The Supreme Court ruled in favor of the federal government, declaring the state tax unconstitutional. Chief Justice Marshall's hard-hitting opinion for a unanimous Court put an immediate stop to a conflict that would have desperately weakened the union if allowed to continue.

In doing so, Marshall created the intergovernmental tax immunity doctrine. He wrote, "[T]he power to tax involves the power to destroy; . . . the power to destroy may defeat and render useless the power to create; . . . there is plain repugnance, in conferring on one government a power to control the constitutional measures of another." The ability of the states to tax the legitimate operations of the federal government is simply incompatible with the Framers' intent of creating viable government units at both the national and state levels.

Marshall's decision in *McCulloch* was consistent with his general philosophy of favoring a strong national government. But was the doctrine of intergovernmental tax immunity a two-way street? Marshall's opinion fell short of proclaiming that the national government was prohibited from taxing the legitimate operations of the states. He was more concerned in this case with reinforcing principles of federal supremacy. Yet a strong case can be made that it would also violate the principles of the Constitution for the federal government to be permitted to destroy the states through its taxing power.

The first case that tested whether the states enjoyed immunity from federal taxation was *Collector v. Day* (1871), which stemmed from an application of the Civil War federal income tax law. Judge J. M. Day of the probate court in Massachusetts objected to paying a federal tax on his income on intergovernmental tax immunity grounds. Three decades earlier the Supreme Court had ruled that the state governments could not tax the income of federal officeholders, and now Day was asking the Court to adopt the converse of that.[8] The Supreme Court, 8–1, held that Day's judicial income was immune from federal taxation. The Court reasoned that the Constitution protects the legitimate functions of the state. The federal government cannot use its taxation powers to curtail or destroy the operations or instruments of the state, and the probate court system is a legitimate and necessary agency of state government. To allow the federal government to tax the income of state judges would be to open the door for Congress to tax all state government functions.

For several decades the justices vigorously maintained the doctrine that the Constitution did not allow one government to tax the essential functions of another. In the *Pollock* income tax decisions, as we have already seen, the Court struck down a federal tax on interest income from state and municipal bonds as an unconstitutional burden on the state's authority to borrow. The Court struck down state taxes on income from federal land leases and federally granted patents and copyrights, and on the sales of petroleum products to the federal government.[9] It also invalidated a federal tax on revenues derived from the sales of goods to state agencies.[10] The only significant standard imposed by the Court in this line of cases was that immunity covered only essential government functions. Consequently, the justices upheld a federal tax on the profits of South Carolina's state-run liquor stores.[11] As a merchant of alcoholic beverages, the state was acting as a private business, not exercising a government function, and therefore was not immune from federal taxation.

The Erosion of the Tax Immunity Doctrine

The Court's general support for the tax immunity doctrine was closely related to its conservatism; it opposed both big government and comprehensive regulation of the economy. When the more activist New Deal justices took control of the Court, however, support for the tax immunity doctrine began to wane. A series of Supreme Court decisions modified or reversed the earlier rulings that had established an almost impenetrable barrier against the taxation by one government of the instruments or operations of another.

For example, in *Helvering v. Gerhardt* (1938) the Court overruled *Dobbins v. Commissioners of Erie County* (1842) and permitted states to tax the income of federal officials. The very next year the justices overruled *Collector v. Day* in *Graves v. New York ex rel. O'Keefe* (1939), holding that there was no constitutional bar to the taxation by the federal government of the income of state employees. "The theory," said the Court, "that a tax on income is legally or economically a tax on its source, is no longer tenable." Also falling were bans on taxing profits from doing business with state or federal government agencies. The Supreme Court went so far as to allow a state to impose taxes on a federal contractor even when those taxes were passed on to the federal government through a cost-plus contract.[12]

Although these rulings seriously weakened the doctrine of intergovernmental tax immunity, the principle still has some vitality. It would be unconstitu-

8. *Dobbins v. Commissioners of Erie County* (1842).
9. *Gillespie v. Oklahoma* (1922) and *Long v. Rockwood* (1928) concerned patents and copyrights; *Panhandle Oil Co. v. Mississippi* (1928) dealt with petroleum sales.
10. *Indian Motorcycle Co. v. United States* (1931).

11. *South Carolina v. United States* (1905).
12. *Alabama v. King and Boozer* (1941).

tional for a state to place a tax on cases filed in the federal courts operating within its boundaries, or for the federal government to impose an excise tax on the tickets issued by a state highway patrol. But aside from these obvious examples, where is the line between permissible and impermissible taxation? The Supreme Court helped answer that question in *South Carolina v. Baker* (1988), which involved a challenge to a federal law taxing the income from long-term state and city bonds.

In 1982 Congress passed a tax act that removed the federal tax exemption for interest earned on publicly offered long-term bonds issued by state and local governments unless the bonds and their owners were registered. The registration requirement was intended to identify owners of such bonds so that capital gains and estate taxes could be better monitored. The taxing of interest from unregistered state and municipal bonds ran directly contrary to the *Pollock* decision. South Carolina objected to the law as a direct violation of the intergovernmental tax immunity doctrine. The federal tax, it argued, placed a direct burden on the ability of state and local governments to raise revenue.

By a 7–1 vote, with only Justice O'Connor in dissent, the Supreme Court upheld the law. For the Court, Justice Brennan explained that precedents since *Pollock* had repudiated the position that a tax on those doing business with the state was the equivalent of a tax on the state. The justices could see no reason for treating persons who receive interest on state bonds any differently than persons receiving income from other kinds of contracts with the state.

South Carolina v. Baker continued a longstanding trend of the Court to erode the doctrine of intergovernmental tax immunity. A statement of the contemporary status of the doctrine, in Justice Brennan's words, is that "the States can never tax the United States directly but can tax any private parties with whom it does business, even though the financial burden falls on the United States, as long as the tax does not discriminate against the United States or those with whom it deals." A similar, although not quite as rigid, prohibition applies to federal taxes on the states.

Even in those cases, like *South Carolina v. Baker*, that have limited intergovernmental tax immunity the Court repeatedly has stressed the principle that taxes must be nondiscriminatory. If a state wishes to tax a company's profits from a business transaction with the federal government, for example, the tax obligation must be the same as that imposed on profits from business with nongovernmental parties. This bar against discriminatory taxation was reinforced in *Davis v. Michigan Department of Treasury* (1989), in which the Court struck down a state law that taxed income residents received from federal retirement plans but exempted income from state retirement programs.

Fourteen other states had similar tax laws. As a result of this decision they were required to revise the laws, choosing between extending the tax exemptions to retired federal employees or eliminating the exemption granted to state and local retirees. The Court's decision in *Davis* reminds us that the tax immunity doctrine remains viable in spite of decisions that have imposed limitations on it.

TAXATION AS A REGULATORY POWER

Normally, we think of taxation as a method of funding the government. Yet Marshall's well-known statement that the "power to tax involves the power to destroy" was an early recognition that taxes can be used for purposes other than raising revenue. Excessive taxation can make the targeted activities so unprofitable that it is no longer feasible to engage in them. The converse also is true. Favorable tax status, including tax exemptions, can encourage a preferred activity. These observations lead us to several important constitutional questions regarding the taxation powers of the federal government. Is it proper for the

United States to impose taxes for reasons other than revenue raising? Is it constitutional for the government to use taxation as a method of regulation? Is it valid for Congress to enact tax laws as means of controlling activities not otherwise within the jurisdiction of the federal government?

From the beginning, Congress has used its authority to tax for purposes other than raising revenue. Before the ratification of the Sixteenth Amendment, the federal government relied heavily on customs duties. In deciding what imported products to tax and at what level, the legislators clearly were guided by their policy preferences. Certain industries received protection from imports and were able to grow with little foreign competition. The practice of combining revenue gathering with other policy objectives continues to this day.

Deciding that Congress may impose import duties with regulatory purposes does not necessarily answer a similar question with respect to excise taxes. Customs, after all, have a limited range. They can be applied only to those goods that are brought into the country from abroad. Excise taxes can be applied to the broad spectrum of domestic goods, services, and activities. The only restriction on such taxes explicitly mentioned in the Constitution is that they be geographically uniform. But is there an implied requirement that excise taxes be generated only by revenue objectives, or can Congress regulate through the use of the excise? If Congress is allowed to regulate domestic activities through the power to tax, does that not give the federal government the equivalent of a police power that the Framers reserved to the states?

Shortly after the Civil War, the Court heard *Veazie Bank v. Fenno* (1869), which presented a challenge to a federal excise tax that was imposed far more to regulate the economy than to raise revenue. In 1866 Congress passed a law placing a 10 percent tax on notes issued by state banks. The law was intended to protect the newly chartered national bank from state competition by making notes far too costly for state banks to issue. Veazie Bank paid the tax under protest, claiming that Congress had no authority to issue such an excise. But in a 5–2 decision, the Court held that the tax was proper given the constitutional power of Congress to regulate the monetary system.

Did the *Veazie Bank* decision mean that Congress may impose excise taxes for any regulatory purpose or only as a means of promoting a power already granted to the federal government? The first major case to confront this question was *McRay v. United States* (1904), which concerned a federal excise tax placed on margarine.

In the latter half of the nineteenth century, food producers developed a commercially marketable oleomargarine. The product was made of oleo oil, lard, milk, cream, and salt. It had a taste and consistency similar to butter but was less expensive. Especially successful was a margarine that was artificially colored to make the naturally white product look like butter. As margarine grew in popularity, the dairy industry became concerned and demanded protection. In response, Congress passed the Oleomargarine Act of 1886 and amended it in 1902. In addition to licensing producers and retailers of margarine, the statute imposed an excise tax of one-quarter cent per pound on uncolored margarine and a tax of ten cents per pound on artificially colored margarine. The manufacturers of the product were responsible for payment of the tax. Although the act raised revenue, its central purpose was to protect the dairy industry by raising the price of margarine and discouraging the sale of the artificially colored product.

McCray, a licensed retail seller of margarine, was assessed a $50 penalty for knowingly purchasing from the Ohio Butterine Company a fifty-pound package of margarine for resale upon which sufficient taxes had not been paid. McCray challenged his fine, claiming that the federal tax was unconstitutional. Its defect, according to McCray, was that the law was a regulation on the intrastate manufacture of margarine, a sphere of authority reserved for the states. The federal government countered with the argument that the margarine tax was an excise tax and as such the Constitution required only that it meet the standard of geographical uniformity. The lower courts upheld the validity of the tax.

The Supreme Court affirmed. The justices refused to examine the motives of the legislators in passing the act. In the words of Justice Edward White, "The decisions of this court from the beginning lend no support whatever to the assumption that the judiciary may restrain the exercise of lawful power on the assumption that a wrongful purpose or motive has caused the power to be exerted." The tax was clearly an excise tax, and as such was subject to only one constitutional limitation—geographical uniformity. That requirement having been met, the federal tax on margarine was constitutional.

With decisions such as *Veazie, McCray,* and others, Congress reasonably concluded that the power to tax could be employed as a regulatory weapon. The Court seemed committed to a policy of approving legislation that took the proper form of an excise tax and met the geographical uniformity requirement, regardless of the congressional motives behind it. If motives were not to be probed by the judiciary, the legislative branch would have a free hand in using taxation to regulate or even destroy certain activities considered by Congress to be detrimental to the nation. As a consequence, Congress became more aggressive in using the taxing power for regulatory purposes.

Among Congress's targets was child labor. As we saw in our earlier discussions, Congress first attempted to regulate child labor in the 1916 Keating-Owen Act, which prohibited articles produced by child labor from being shipped in interstate and foreign commerce. Just two years after that law was enacted, the Supreme Court in *Hammer v. Dagenhart* struck it down on the grounds that Congress, under the guise of interstate commerce regulation, was actually controlling manufacturing and mining, considered at that time to be intrastate activities, the regulation of which was reserved to the states.

After suffering this defeat at the hands of the Supreme Court, Congress drafted a second statute to attack child labor, this time using the power to tax. The Child Labor Tax Act of 1919 imposed an excise tax of 10 percent on the net profits of any company hiring child labor. The Act's constitutionality was challenged in *Bailey v. Drexel Furniture Co.* (1922).

Drexel was a furniture manufacturing company in North Carolina. On September 20, 1921, it received from J. W. Bailey, the IRS collector for the Western District of North Carolina, a notice that it had been assessed $6,312.79 in excise taxes for having employed a boy under the age of fourteen during the 1919 tax year. The company paid the tax under protest and sued for a refund. Drexel argued that the tax was nothing more than an unconstitutional attempt to regulate manufacturing. The United States defended the statute as an excise tax that need meet no standard but geographical uniformity.

The Supreme Court ruled in favor of the company and struck down the act. In doing so the justices took into consideration the motives behind the legislation. They concluded that the legislature was using the power to tax as a means of regulating activities that were outside Congress's proper authority. As Chief Justice Taft explained, "So here the so-called tax is a penalty to coerce the people of a State to act as Congress wishes them to act in respect of a matter completely the business of the state government under the Federal Constitution."

The decision in *Drexel* was a reversal of the position on excise taxes the Court had held since the early 1800s. It generally proved to be out of line with Supreme Court rulings both before and after. The Court repeatedly has faced the question of taxation and regulation and generally has ruled in favor of the federal power to tax and even acknowledged that all taxes to some degree have regulatory effects. For example, in *United States v. Doremus* (1919) and *Nigro v. United States* (1928) the Court upheld federal excise taxes on narcotics, and in *United States v. Sanchez* (1950) it upheld a tax on marijuana. Similarly, an excise tax on objectionable firearms was declared valid in *Sonzinsky v. United States* (1937), even though the Court admitted that the law had an unmistakable "legislative purpose to regulate rather than to tax." The justices found no constitutional defects with an excise levied on professional gamblers in *United States v. Kahriger* (1953). These taxes expand federal regulatory powers. If Congress has the power to impose the tax, then the federal government also has the power to enforce the tax laws, creating, to an extent, "police powers" within the federal government that originally resided with the states.

TAXING AND SPENDING FOR THE GENERAL WELFARE

The Constitution authorizes Congress to tax and spend for the general welfare. Whether the term *general welfare* was intended to expand the powers of Congress beyond those explicitly stated in the Constitution is subject to debate. James Madison, for example, argued that general welfare was only a reference to the other enumerated powers. Because the United States is a government of limited and specified powers, he asserted, the authority to tax and spend must be confined to those spheres of authority the Constitution explicitly granted. Alexander Hamilton took the opposite position. He interpreted the power to tax and spend for the general welfare to be a separate power altogether. For Hamilton taxing and spending authority was given in addition to the other granted powers, not limited by them. The conflict between these two opposing interpretations was the subject of legal disputes throughout much of the nation's history. During the constitutional crisis over legislation passed during the New Deal, however, the final battle between the two was waged.

Many of the programs recommended by Franklin Roosevelt to reestablish the nation's economic strength involved regulatory activity far more extensive than ever before proposed. Several depended on the power of the federal government to tax and spend for the general welfare. Opponents of the New Deal claimed that these programs, while ostensibly based upon the taxing and spending authority, in reality were regulations of matters the Constitution reserved for the states.

During the Great Depression, agriculture was one of the hardest hit sectors of the economy. The nation's farmers were overproducing, which caused prices for farm products to drop. In many cases the cost of production was higher than the income from crop sales, leaving farmers in desperate straits. Most had their farms mortgaged, and all owed taxes on their lands. The more the farmers got behind economically, the more they attempted to produce to improve their situation. This strategy further increased production, making matters even worse. At that time agriculture was responsible for a much larger proportion of the nation's economy than it is today, and conditions in the farming sector had dire effects on the general welfare of the entire country.

In response, Roosevelt proposed and Congress passed the Agricultural Adjustment Act (AAA), a statute that combined the taxing and spending powers to combat the agricultural crisis. The central purpose of the plan was to reduce the amount of acreage being farmed. To accomplish this goal, the federal government would "rent" a percentage of the nation's farmland and leave this acreage unplanted. In effect, the government would pay the farmers not to farm. If the plan succeeded, production would drop, prices would rise, and the farmer would have a sufficient income. Making payments to the nation's farmers was an expensive proposition, and to fund these expenditures the AAA imposed an excise tax on the processing of agricultural products.

The program was a success until William M. Butler

William M. Butler, receiver for Hoosac Mills, objected to paying the federal tax on processing cotton. His lawsuit successfully challenged the constitutionality of the Agricultural Adjustment Act of 1933.

challenged the constitutionality of the law. Butler was the bankruptcy receiver for Hoosac Mills Corporation, a cotton processor. When the government imposed the processing tax on Hoosac, Butler took legal action to avoid payment, claiming that the AAA exceeded the taxing and spending powers granted to the federal government.

The Court concluded that the federal government had broad powers to tax and spend for the general welfare. The justices decided, consistent with the posi-

tion previously articulated by Alexander Hamilton, that Congress's fiscal authority was not limited to those subjects specifically enumerated in Article I. However, this philosophy did not mean that congressional powers had no limits. The majority in *Butler* ruled that the law was unconstitutional because what it imposed was not truly a tax. Instead, the government was taking money from one group (the processors) to give to another (the farmers), and doing this to regulate farm production, a matter of intrastate commerce reserved for state regulation. The decision dealt a severe blow to the New Deal.

The impact of the *Butler* case was short-lived. Following the Court's dramatic change in position after Roosevelt's threat to add new members, the justices ruled that agriculture could be regulated under the commerce power.[13] As for the power to tax and spend for the general welfare, the position taken in *Butler* was reevaluated the very next year in *Steward Machine Co. v. Davis* (1937) and *Helvering v. Davis* (1937), challenges to the constitutionality of the newly formed Social Security system. The Social Security Act shared several characteristics with the Agricultural Adjustment Act the Court had condemned in *Butler*. Both used the taxing and spending powers to combat the effects of the depression; both took money from one group of people to give to another; and both regulated areas previously thought to be reserved to the states. The radical change in position occurred largely because Chief Justice Hughes and Justice Roberts deserted the *Butler* majority and joined with the liberal wing of the Court to forge a new constitutional interpretation.

The Social Security Cases firmly established that the taxing and spending powers are to be broadly construed. If Congress decides that the general welfare of the United States demands a program requiring the use of these fiscal powers, the Supreme Court likely will find it constitutionally valid unless parts of the

13. See *Mulford v. Smith* (1939); and *Wickard v. Filburn* (1942).

law violate specific provisions of the Constitution. In fact, *United States v. Butler* was the last major case in which the Supreme Court ruled that Congress had exceeded its spending powers. Since these 1937 decisions, Congress has used the spending authority to expand greatly the role of the federal government.

Serious challenges to a federal spending program are now unusual. Yet a battle over federal and state authority with respect to spending programs does occasionally flare up. One such case was *South Dakota v. Dole* (1987). This dispute involved a conflict over federal spending power and the state's authority to regulate highway safety and alcoholic beverages. The use of federal funds to coerce the states into taking particular policy positions was attacked in much the same manner as *Steward Machine* attacked the establishment of state unemployment compensation programs. It is interesting to note that Chief Justice Rehnquist, normally considered a strong defender of states' rights, wrote the majority opinion upholding the exercise of federal authority over the states. A dissenting vote was cast by Justice Brennan, another surprise because Brennan usually could be counted on to support federal power. Not surprising was the stinging dissent registered by Justice O'Connor on behalf of state interests.

South Dakota v. Dole

483 U.S. 203 (1987)
Vote: 7 (Blackmun, Marshall, Powell, Rehnquist, Scalia,
    Stevens, White)
    2 (Brennan, O'Connor)
Opinion of the Court: Rehnquist
Dissenting opinions: Brennan, O'Connor

In 1984 Congress passed a statute directing the secretary of transportation to withhold a portion of federal highway funds from any state that did not estab-lish a minimum drinking age of twenty-one years. The purpose of the law was to decrease the number of serious automobile accidents among a group that statistics showed had a high percentage of accidents. The legislators correctly believed that withholding federal dollars would be an effective way of encouraging the states to comply with the federal program.

South Dakota, which allowed the purchase of beer containing 3.2 percent alcohol by persons nineteen years or older, objected to the statute, arguing that Congress was infringing on the rights of the states. The Twenty-first Amendment, which repealed prohibition in 1933, gave full authority to the states to regulate alcoholic beverages; therefore, South Dakota claimed that Congress had no authority to set minimum drinking ages. According to the state, the federal government was using its considerable spending power to coerce the states into enacting laws that were otherwise outside congressional authority.

The state sued Secretary of Transportation Elizabeth Dole, asking the courts to declare the law unconstitutional. Both the district court and the court of appeals ruled against the state and upheld the law.

CHIEF JUSTICE REHNQUIST delivered the opinion of the Court.

The Constitution empowers Congress to "lay and collect Taxes, Duties, Imposts, and Excises, to pay the Debts and provide for the common Defence and general Welfare of the United States." Art. I, § 8, cl. 1. Incident to this power, Congress may attach conditions on the receipt of federal funds, and has repeatedly employed the power "to further broad policy objectives by conditioning receipt of federal moneys upon compliance by the recipient with federal statutory and administrative directives." The breadth of this power was made clear in *United States v. Butler* (1936), where the Court, resolving a longstanding debate over the scope of the Spending Clause, determined that "the power of Congress to authorize expenditure of public moneys for public purposes is not limited by the direct grants of legislative power found in the Constitution." Thus, objectives not thought to be within Article I's "enumerated legislative fields" may nevertheless be attained through the use of the spending power and the conditional grant of federal funds.

The spending power is of course not limited, but is instead subject to several general restrictions articulated in our cases. The first of these limitations is derived from the language of the Constitution itself: the exercise of the spending power must be in pursuit of "the general welfare." In considering whether a particular expenditure is intended to serve general public purposes, courts should defer substantially to the judgment of Congress. Second, we have required that if Congress desires to condition the States' receipt of federal funds, it "must do so unambiguously . . . , enabl[ing] the States to exercise their choice knowingly, cognizant of the consequences of their participation." Third, our cases have suggested (without significant elaboration) that conditions on federal grants might be illegitimate if they are unrelated "to the federal interest in particular national projects or programs." Finally, we have noted that other constitutional provisions may provide an independent bar to the conditional grant of federal funds.

South Dakota does not seriously claim that § 158 is inconsistent with any of the first three restrictions mentioned above. We can readily conclude that the provision is designed to serve the general welfare, especially in light of the fact that "the concept of welfare or the opposite is shaped by Congress. . . ." Congress found that the differing drinking ages in the States created particular incentives for young persons to combine their desire to drink with their ability to drive, and that this interstate problem required a national solution. The means it chose to address this dangerous situation were reasonably calculated to advance the general welfare. The conditions upon which States receive the funds, moreover, could not be more clearly stated by Congress. And the State itself, rather than challenging the germaneness of the condition to federal purposes, admits that it "has never contended that the congressional action was . . . unrelated to a national concern in the absence of the Twenty-first Amendment." Indeed, the condition imposed by Congress is directly related to one of the main purposes for which highway funds are expended—safe interstate travel. This goal of the interstate highway system had been frustrated by varying drinking ages among the States. . . . By enacting § 158, Congress conditioned the receipt of federal funds in a way reasonably calculated to address this particular impediment to a purpose for which the funds are expended.

The remaining question about the validity of § 158— and the basic point of disagreement between the parties— is whether the Twenty-first Amendment constitutes an "independent constitutional bar" to the conditional grant of federal funds. Petitioner, relying on its view that the Twenty-first Amendment prohibits *direct* regulation of drinking ages by Congress, asserts that "Congress may not use the spending power to regulate that which it is prohibited from regulating directly under the Twenty-first Amendment." But our cases show that this "independent constitutional bar" limitation on the spending power is not of the kind petitioner suggests. *United States v. Butler,* for example, established that the constitutional limitations on Congress when exercising its spending power are less exacting than those on its authority to regulate directly. . . .

[T]he "independent constitutional bar" limitation on the spending power is not, as petitioner suggests, a prohibition on the indirect achievement of objectives which Congress is not empowered to achieve directly. Instead, we think that the language in our earlier opinions stands for the unexceptionable proposition that the power may not be used to induce the States to engage in activities that would themselves be unconstitutional. Thus, for example, a grant of federal funds conditioned on invidiously discriminatory state action or the infliction of cruel and unusual punishment would be an illegitimate exercise of the Congress' broad spending power. But no such claim can be or is made here. Were South Dakota to succumb to the blandishments offered by Congress and raise its drinking age to 21, the State's action in so doing would not violate the constitutional rights of anyone.

Our decisions have recognized that in some circumstances the financial inducement offered by Congress might be so coercive as to pass the point at which "pressure turns into compulsion." Here, however, Congress has directed only that a State desiring to establish a minimum drinking age lower than 21 lose a relatively small percentage of certain federal highway funds. Petitioner contends that the coercive nature of this program is evident from the degree of success it has achieved. We cannot conclude, however, that a conditional grant of federal money of this sort is unconstitutional simply by reason of its success in achieving the congressional objective.

When we consider, for a moment, that all South Dakota would lose if she adheres to her chosen course as to a suitable minimum drinking age is 5% of the funds otherwise obtainable under specified highway grant programs, the argument as to coercion is shown to be more rhetoric than fact. . . .

Here Congress has offered relatively mild encouragement to the States to enact higher minimum drinking ages than they would otherwise choose. But the enactment of such laws remains the prerogative of the States not merely in theory but in fact. Even if Congress might lack the power to impose a national minimum drinking age directly, we conclude that encouragement to state action found in § 158 is a valid use of the spending power. Accordingly, the judgment of the Court of Appeals is

Affirmed.

JUSTICE O'CONNOR, dissenting.

The Court today upholds the National Minimum Drinking Age Amendment, 23 U.S.C. § 158, as a valid exercise of the spending power conferred by Article I, § 8. But § 158 is not a condition on spending reasonably related to the expenditure of federal funds and cannot be justified on that ground. Rather, it is an attempt to regulate the sale of liquor, an attempt that lies outside Congress' power to regulate commerce because it falls within the ambit of § 2 of the Twenty-first Amendment. . . .

When Congress appropriates money to build a highway, it is entitled to insist that the highway be a safe one. But it is not entitled to insist as a condition of the use of highway funds that the State impose or change regulations in other areas of the State's social and economic life because of an attenuated or tangential relationship to highway use or safety. Indeed, if the rule were otherwise, the Congress could effectively regulate almost any area of a State's social, political, or economic life on the theory that use of the interstate transportation system is somehow enhanced. If, for example, the United States were to condition highway moneys upon moving the state capital, I suppose it might argue that interstate transportation is facilitated by locating local governments in places easily accessible to interstate high-

ways—or, conversely, that highways might become overburdened if they had to carry traffic to and from the state capital. In my mind, such a relationship is hardly more attenuated than the one which the Court finds supports § 158.

There is a clear place at which the Court can draw the line between permissible and impermissible conditions on federal grants. It is the line identified in the Brief for the National Conference of State Legislatures et al. as *Amici Curiae:*

"Congress has the power to spend for the general welfare, it has the power to legislate only for the delegated purposes.". . .

This approach harks back to *United States v. Butler* (1936), the last case in which this Court struck down an Act of Congress as beyond the authority granted by the Spending Clause. . . .

While *Butler's* authority is questionable insofar as it assumes that Congress has no regulatory power over farm production, its discussion of the spending power and its description of both the power's breadth and its limitations remain sound. The Court's decision in *Butler* also properly recognizes the gravity of the task of appropriately limiting the spending power. If the spending power is to be limited only by Congress' notion of the general welfare, the reality, given the vast financial resources of the Federal Government, is that the Spending Clause gives "power to the Congress to tear down the barriers, to invade the states' jurisdiction, and to become a parliament of the whole people, subject to no restrictions save such as are self-imposed." This, of course, as *Butler* held, was not the Framers' plan and it is not the meaning of the Spending Clause. . . .

The immense size and power of the Government of the United States ought not obscure its fundamental character. It remains a Government of enumerated powers. Because 23 U.S.C. § 158 cannot be justified as an exercise of any power delegated to the Congress, it is not authorized by the Constitution. The Court errs in holding it to be the law of the land, and I respectfully dissent.

Rehnquist's opinion gave strong support to the federal spending power. The majority held that there are only four basic requirements that must be met for a federal spending statute to be valid: (1) the expenditure must be for the general welfare; (2) any conditions imposed on the expenditure must be unambiguous; (3) the conditions must be reasonably related to the purpose of the expenditure; and (4) the legislation must not violate any independent constitutional provision. These are minimal requirements indeed, especially since the Court acknowledged a policy of deferring to the legislature's determinations of what promotes the general welfare. O'Connor's dissent, which praised much of what the Court concluded in *Butler,* is not likely to find a great deal of support today; rather, since 1937 the Court repeatedly has given approval to an expansive interpretation of the powers of the federal government to tax and spend for the general welfare.

Decisions such as *South Dakota v. Dole* give wide latitude to Congress in using the taxing and spending power to "encourage" states to comply with federal policy preferences. If Congress uses this power effectively, it can extend its policy influence well beyond the customary limits. Congress simply enlists the states to regulate areas where the federal government may not constitutionally act on its own. States may resent what they consider to be "coercive" federal action, and, as exemplified by South Dakota's opposition to the federal government's intrusion into alcohol regulation, it is not uncommon for states to challenge these federal incentive programs.

RESTRICTIONS ON THE REVENUE POWERS OF THE STATES

Taxation is a concurrent power, one that can be exercised by both the federal government and the states. The states exercised the power to tax prior to the ratification of the Constitution and retain that authority today. The powers of the states to tax are very broad, limited primarily by provisions in their own constitutions and laws. Taxes on property, income, and sales provide the bulk of funds for state government activities.

The federal Constitution, however, removed certain sources of revenue from the states. Article I, Section 10, explicitly prohibits the states from taxing imports. In addition, the Commerce Clause blocks the states from imposing taxes that place an unreasonable burden on interstate or foreign commerce. Aside from these limitations, the states remain free to develop their own tax structures and sources of revenue.

State Taxes on Foreign Commerce

In *Brown v. Maryland* (1827) the Supreme Court first faced a question of the validity of state taxes on imports. The dispute centered on a Maryland law that required importers of foreign goods to pay a license fee. The Supreme Court struck down the statute as a tax on imports and as infringing on the authority of the federal government to regulate foreign commerce. An important part of the Court's opinion, however, dealt with the following question: When does an imported article cease to be an import and become part of the taxable goods within a state? The Court's answer to this question was the "original package" doctrine. For the majority, John Marshall wrote, "While [the imported article remains] the property of the importer, in his warehouse, in the original form or package in which it was imported, a tax upon it is too plainly a duty on imports to escape the prohibition in the constitution."

The original package doctrine meant that goods flowing into the United States remained within the federal government's taxing and regulating power until they were sold, processed, or broken out of their original packaging. Once any of those events took place, the articles became normal property within the state and subject to state taxation. The impact of this interpretation was that large warehouses filled with imported goods ready for shipment to other parts of the United States were free from state taxation as long as no sale took place and the materials remained in their original packages. The states balked at this rule, arguing that they should be able to levy property taxes on such goods as long as the tax was nondiscriminatory—that is, if imported articles stored in warehouses were taxed on exactly the same basis as other property within the state.

Although attacked by legal scholars and those promoting the interests of the states, the original package doctrine survived until 1976, when the justices accepted an appeal from a decision by the Georgia Supreme Court that approved certain nondiscriminatory taxes on warehoused imports. The case, *Michelin Tire Corp. v. Georgia* (1976), prompted the Court to alter a rule of law that had been in effect for more than a century.

The Michelin Tire Corporation operated a warehouse in Gwinnett County, Georgia, just outside of Atlanta. The company imported tires and tire products into the United States from France and Nova Scotia and stored them in the Georgia warehouse for later distribution to retail outlets. When the county tax assessors levied a nondiscriminatory ad valorem property tax on the inventory, the company sued W. L. Wages, the county tax commissioner, for relief, claiming that, except for some tire tubes that had been removed from their original containers, the warehouse contents were constitutionally free from state taxation.

The local court granted the relief requested, and the Georgia Supreme Court heard the county's appeal. The state high court ruled that the tires were subject to tax because after being imported in bulk they had been sorted and arranged for sale. Michelin sought a reversal by the U.S. Supreme Court, which ignored subtle questions regarding the application of the original package doctrine and instead focused on the fundamental issue of whether any warehoused imports are subject to state taxation.

The justices unanimously decided in favor of the state. After conducting its own independent study, the Court concluded the Framers did not intend the ban on state imposts and duties to apply to nondiscriminatory warehouse taxes. An impost or a duty is a tax on the act of bringing articles into the country. Warehouse taxes do not fit this definition. Rather, the act of importing has stopped and the goods in the warehouse have become goods inside the state. Although such articles may be intended for interstate shipment, they are subject to property taxation by the state as long as those taxes are nondiscriminatory. The warehouse in question operated in the same fashion as a warehouse storing domestic goods and could be taxed in the same manner.

State Taxes on Interstate Commerce

State taxes on interstate commerce have provided another source of constitutional disputes. A state has the right to tax commerce that occurs within its borders, but it cannot impose taxes that discriminate against or place an undue burden on interstate commerce. In the nation's formative years this rule of constitutional interpretation was relatively easy to apply. But, given the changes in economic realities and the significant alterations in the definition of interstate commerce, the situation is now much more complex.

Relatively little commercial activity today is purely intrastate. Consequently, whenever a state imposes a tax on business activity, it can be charged that the state is placing a burden on interstate commerce. The Supreme Court has attempted to fashion a rule that copes with modern economic conditions and yet is mindful of three important considerations. First, if the states are to remain viable entities, they must retain the ability to tax commercial activities. Second, true burdens on interstate commerce, as well as taxes that discriminate against it, must be avoided. Third, simply engaging in an interstate commercial activity should not suffice to exempt a company from paying its fair share of in-state taxes. Naturally, these principles are far easier to state than to apply to real situations.

In *Complete Auto Transit v. Brady* (1977) the justices

concluded that their previous decisions were inconsistent with contemporary conditions and that a new statement on the authority of states to tax activities affecting interstate commerce was required. Complete Auto Transit was a Michigan corporation doing business in Mississippi. Under its contract with General Motors, Complete trucked new vehicles manufactured out of state and brought into Mississippi by rail. The automobiles were loaded onto Complete's trucks in the Jackson, Mississippi, rail yards and delivered to GM dealerships around the state. There is no doubt that Complete's business was interstate commerce. The company provided the last segment in the transportation of goods manufactured out of state to their retail destinations within the state.

Mississippi imposed a tax on transportation companies for the privilege of doing business in the state at a rate of 5 percent of gross income from state business. The state applied the tax to businesses operating in intra- and interstate commerce. In 1971 the Mississippi Tax Commission informed Complete that it owed $122,160.59 in taxes for a three-year period beginning in 1968. In 1972 Complete received a second bill for $42,990.89 for taxes due over the previous year. Complete paid the taxes under protest and sued for a refund. The Mississippi Supreme Court upheld the tax, holding that Complete enjoyed the various services of the state and should be obliged to pay its fair share of state taxes. Because the tax did not discriminate against interstate commerce and was based exclusively on income derived from Mississippi sources, it was not constitutionally defective.

The Supreme Court agreed, but in doing so was forced to reject earlier precedents and replace them with a new set of criteria for state taxation systems. That the Court was unanimous in its decision indicates a strong feeling among the justices that the law was in need of improvement.

The *Complete Auto Transit* decision established four criteria that must be met for a state tax on interstate commerce to be valid: (1) the targeted activity must be sufficiently connected to the state to justify a tax; (2) the tax must be fairly apportioned so that the levy is based on intrastate activity or income not subject to taxation by other states; (3) the tax must not discriminate against interstate commerce; and (4) the tax must be fairly related to the services provided by the state. These criteria assume that Congress has not preempted the state tax by imposing conflicting regulations on the interstate commerce activities involved.

The four-pronged test established in *Complete Auto Transit* constitutes the Court's current policy on state taxation of interstate activities. It has been consistently applied in subsequent cases in which parties have challenged state taxes as being unconstitutional. The test appears to provide a workable compromise between the needs of the states to secure revenue and the Constitution's mandate that interstate commerce not be unreasonably burdened.

Taxing and Spending for the Protection of Intrastate Interests

In decisions such as *Complete Auto Transit* states attempted to tax interstate commerce activities that occurred within their boundaries. The goal was simply to gather revenue. Given today's economic conditions, states are continually searching for new revenue sources. Imposing taxes on out-of-state corporations is a politically appealing strategy because revenue can be raised without directly affecting the state's residents (or upsetting its voters).

Sometimes the goal of a state taxation policy is not just to raise revenue. States can create tax policies to protect intrastate businesses or to promote intrastate development. When such policies place a burden on interstate commerce and give an advantage to intrastate enterprises, constitutional challenges are common. Tax policies that discriminate against interstate commerce often meet the same fate as we saw discriminatory commerce regulation suffer in Chapter 7. The Court takes a dim view of state laws that place a financial obligation on interstate commerce that is not equally placed on intrastate business—no matter if those obligations take the form of taxes, fees, tariffs, duties, or similar assessments.

Today the states share a zeal to raise their revenues, improve their economic climates, increase employment for their citizens, and protect their resources from encroachment by other states. In attempting to achieve these goals, legislatures on occasion use their taxing powers in a way that invites legal challenge. One recent example is *Oregon Waste Systems v. Department of Environmental Quality of the State of Oregon* (1994).

The state of Oregon has a comprehensive policy for the management, reduction, and recycling of solid waste. Its landfill operations received and processed waste from both Oregon and out-of-state sources. In 1989 the state legislature decided to revise its fee structure for the handling of solid waste. The result was to assess a fee of $2.25 per ton on waste brought into Oregon from other states and to charge $.85 per ton for waste generated in Oregon. Oregon Waste Systems was in the business of transporting solid waste from Washington State by barge to landfills in Oregon. The company filed suit over the surcharge, claiming that the assessment discriminated against interstate commerce in violation of the Commerce Clause. State courts upheld the Oregon law, concluding that the surcharge was not a discriminatory tax but a compensatory fee that was reasonably related to the cost of the services rendered.

The Supreme Court saw the case differently. As Justice Clarence Thomas said for the Court, ". . . the fact remains that the differential charge favors shippers of Oregon waste over their counterparts handling waste generated in other States. In making that geographical distinction, the surcharge patently discriminates against interstate commerce." Although states may charge out-of-state businesses higher rates to compen-

sate for additional costs incurred in providing services, there was no proof in this case that the state of Oregon had incurred special costs that would justify charging fees for non-Oregon firms that were three times higher than the assessment on solid waste generated in Oregon.

Despite the Court's position that discriminatory taxation is unconstitutional, states continue to search for systems that might survive legal challenge. In *West Lynn Creamery v. Healy* (1994), for example, the Court reviewed a Massachusetts law that used the state's taxing and spending powers to promote local producers. The problem began in the 1980s when milk producers in Massachusetts lost market share to lower-cost producers in neighboring states. Prices paid to Massachusetts producers decreased while the cost of production increased. Between 1980 and 1991 approximately one-half of the dairy farms in the state went out of business. As a result, Massachusetts farmers produced only about one-third of the milk sold in the state. The Massachusetts commissioner of food and agriculture declared that emergency conditions existed in the state's milk industry and issued a special pricing order to combat the problem. That order required all dealers of milk products to make a monthly "premium payment" to the "Massachusetts Dairy Equalization Fund." The premiums were based on all milk sold in Massachusetts regardless of the state in which the raw milk was produced. The state then distributed those moneys exclusively to Massachusetts dairy farmers. The goal was to subsidize their operations and to keep Massachusetts dairy farmers in business.

West Lynn Creamery was a milk dealer licensed to do business in Massachusetts. It purchased raw milk from producers and then processed, packaged, and sold milk products to dealers in the state. About 97 percent of the milk it handled was produced out of state. At first West Lynn complied with the law and paid the required premiums. Beginning in July of 1992, however, it stopped making the payments and filed suit against state commissioner Jonathan Healy, claiming that the state was using its taxing and spending powers to discriminate against interstate commerce. The state courts upheld the pricing and premium payment policy, saying that it did not discriminate against out-of-state producers and placed only an incidental burden on interstate commerce.

The Supreme Court found the state law unconstitutional as discriminating against interstate commerce for the purposes of protecting Massachusetts producers. It is not necessarily unconstitutional for a state to place a tax on the sale of such commodities as milk; nor is instituting policies to promote local interests necessarily invalid. However, in this case the state places a tax, the majority of which comes from interstate sales, and uses the proceeds to subsidize intrastate producers. The net result is a state policy that benefits in-state economic interests by burdening out-of-state competitors. This, according to the Court's majority, is a violation of a "cardinal principle" of constitutional law.

Although the Court has developed relatively clear guidelines on federal and state taxing and spending powers, each term brings new disputes for resolution. It is not likely that this tendency will change in the near future. Policies that impose taxes and distribute funds are among the most politically and emotionally charged of all government programs. They not only give rise to questions of constitutional philosophy, but they also affect people's pocketbooks. It is not surprising, therefore, that when government uses its powers to tax and spend, legal challenges are common.

READINGS

Carson, Gerald. "The Income Tax and How It Grew." *American Heritage,* December 1973, 4–7, 79–88.

Corwin, Edward S. "The Spending Power of Congress—Apropos the Maternity Act." *Harvard Law Review* 36 (1923): 548–582.

Dakin, Melvin G. "The Protective Cloak of the Export-Import Clause: Immunity for the Goods or Immunity for the Process?" *Louisiana Law Review* 19 (1959): 747–776.

Dunne, Gerald T. *Monetary Decisions of the Supreme Court.* New Brunswick, N.J.: Rutgers University Press, 1960.

Early, Alexander R., and Robert G. Weitzman. "A Century of Dissent: The Immunity of Goods Imported for Resale from Nondiscriminatory State Personal Property Taxes." *Southwestern University Law Review* 7 (1975): 247–272.

Hurst, James Willard. *A Legal History of Money in the United States, 1774–1970.* Lincoln: University of Nebraska Press, 1973.

Lund, Nelson. "Congressional Power over Taxation and Commerce: The Supreme Court's Lost Chance to Devise a Consistent Doctrine." *Texas Tech Law Review* 18 (1987): 729–760.

McCoy, Thomas R., and Barry Friedman. "Conditional Spending: Federalism's Trojan Horse." *Supreme Court Review* (1988): 85–127.

Powell, Thomas Reed. "State Taxation of Imports: When Does an Import Cease to Be an Import?" *Harvard Law Review* 58 (1945): 858–876.

Witte, John F. *The Politics and Development of the Federal Income Tax.* Madison: University of Wisconsin Press, 1985.

PART IV
ECONOMIC LIBERTIES

**ECONOMIC LIBERTIES AND
INDIVIDUAL RIGHTS**

9. THE CONTRACT CLAUSE

**10. ECONOMIC SUBSTANTIVE DUE
PROCESS**

11. THE TAKINGS CLAUSE

ECONOMIC LIBERTIES AND INDIVIDUAL RIGHTS

I F AMERICANS WERE ASKED what they admire about the United States, many would answer: the freedoms of speech, press, and religion. But when asked to make political decisions—to choose elected officials, for example—Americans may put other considerations ahead of the cherished freedoms. As the old adage goes, people tend to vote their pocketbooks. Americans might not admit that the state of the economy drives their behavior, but it is perhaps the single most important determinant in their voting decisions.

That Americans hold economic well-being as a priority is not surprising. In Part III we saw that economic issues—commerce, taxing, and spending—were major sources of friction between the federal government and the states virtually from the beginning of U.S. history.

Economic questions, however, are not the exclusive domain of the Supreme Court's federalism cases. Quite the contrary. The Supreme Court often has heard constitutional challenges in which individuals claim that their personal economic liberties have been violated by government actions. In such cases the justices must determine how much power federal and state governments have to seize private property, to alter freely made contracts, and to restrict private employment agreements about wages and hours. Seen in

this way, there is a strong relationship between civil liberties, such as the freedom of speech, and economic liberties, such as the right to own private property. Indeed, both provoke the same fundamental question: To what extent can government enact legislation that infringes on personal rights? Both also involve the same perennial conflict between the interests of the individual and the common good.

Even so, most people, including elected officials and even Supreme Court justices, tend to separate economic liberties from other civil liberties. We consider the right to express our views as significantly different from the right to conduct business. The Framers, however, viewed both as vested rights, "those so fundamental to an individual that they must remain beyond governmental control," and they were very much on the minds of the men who gathered to write the Constitution in 1787.[1] According to James Madison, one of the most important objectives of the Framers was to provide "more effectively for the security of private rights and the steady dispensation of justice within the states. Interference with these were the evils which had, more perhaps than anything else, produced this convention."[2]

1. Ralph A. Rossum and G. Alan Tarr, *American Constitutional Law,* 3d ed. (New York: St. Martin's Press, 1991), 285.
2. Quoted in ibid.

But, as Madison's comment implies, the Framers' conception of liberties and what interfered with their exercise was somewhat different from ours. They equated liberty with the protection of private property, and in their view the states, not the new government, posed the greater threat. Given the economic chaos under the Articles of Confederation, we can easily understand the Founders' concerns. They believed the states had "crippled" both the government and the economy, and they wanted to create a national government strong enough to protect economic liberty from aggressive state governments. We must also keep in mind that many who attended the convention were wealthy men who, "having accumulated property . . . wanted to keep it." In short, the Framers were concerned that the unpropertied masses might succeed in taking control of state legislatures and using "their numerical strength" to advance their interests, "to abrogate debts, tax industry," and so forth.[3] Indeed, in an important (albeit controversial) work, *An Economic Interpretation of the Constitution*, historian Charles A. Beard depicted the Founders as self-serving, even greedy, men, who viewed the Constitution as a vehicle for the protection of their property interests.

Other analysts have taken issue with Beard's interpretation. Some contend that we cannot necessarily equate modern definitions of property with those used by the Framers; that is, the property interests they sought to protect were probably more encompassing than those we envision today. Although we may consider property as something tangible, or of clear monetary value, the Framers—at least some of them—thought of property as "shorthand for an expanse of personal freedoms that need only be tangentially related, if at all, to economic activity."[4]

To protect these paramount property rights, however conceptualized, the Framers inserted several provisions into the Constitution. An important provision, which we examine in Chapter 9, is the Contract Clause. Under Article I, Section 10, "No State shall . . . pass any . . . Law impairing the Obligation of Contracts." To understand the meaning of the clause, we must consider its language within the context of the day. As one source suggests:

> For the generation of 1787, property was a natural right. And if men were to be able to use their property, they had to have an equal right to make pledges about their property—to contract. Thus the right to contract was of the same sacredness as the right to property itself, and the obligation to keep one's contracts was a duty required by the natural right to property.[5]

If the Contract Clause was one of the ways the Framers sought to protect property interests against the "evils" of government interference, it was effective, at least initially. For the Marshall Court the Contract Clause, in particular, "served as one of the most effective instruments for establishing federal control over state actions."[6] That Court read Article I, Section 10, to prohibit state action that infringed on property rights, which in turn impeded economic development.

But this interpretation was short-lived. With the end of the Marshall Court and the ascendancy of the Taney Court in the mid-1830s, use of the Contract Clause as a vehicle to protect property interests waned. Why that occurred is considered fully in Chapter 9; for now, it is important to note that the "death" of the Contract Clause did not mean that courts were no longer interested in protecting economic liberties. They simply turned to another section of the Constitution to do so. The Fourteenth Amendment's Due Process Clause says no state shall "deprive any person of life, liberty, or property, without due process of law." Under a doctrine called sub-

3. Malcolm M. Feeley and Samuel Krislov, *Constitutional Law* (Glenview, Ill.: Scott, Foresman, 1990), 328.

4. Walter F. Murphy, James E. Fleming, and William F. Harris II, *American Constitutional Interpretation* (Mineola, N.Y.: Foundation Press, 1986), 939.

5. Ibid., 940.

6. Elder Witt, *Guide to the U.S. Supreme Court*, 2d ed. (Washington, D.C.: Congressional Quarterly, 1990), 305.

FIGURE IV-1 Percentage of Agenda Space Allocated to Economic Cases

Percentage of Agenda Space

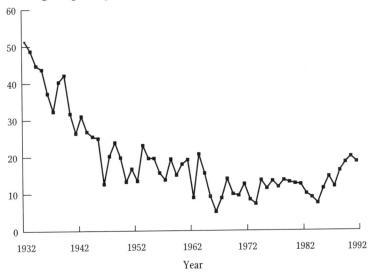

Year

SOURCE: Richard L. Pacelle, Jr., "The Dynamics and Determinants of Agenda Change in the Rehnquist Court," in *Contemplating Courts*, ed. Lee Epstein (Washington, D.C.: CQ Press, 1995).

stantive due process, which is reviewed in Chapter 10, between the 1890s and the 1930s the Supreme Court used the Fourteenth Amendment to prohibit states' interference with "liberty" interests. For example, it struck down legislation mandating maximum work hours on the ground that such legislation interfered with the rights of employers to enter into contracts with their employees. Like the Court's interpretation of the Contract Clause, this treatment of the Fourteenth Amendment eventually fell into disrepute, as we explain in Chapter 10.

More recently, the Court has taken a serious look at yet another provision of the Constitution designed to protect property interests—the Takings Clause of the Fifth Amendment. While in the Contract Clause the Framers sought to prevent governments from infringing on contractual agreements, in the Takings Clause they tried to protect private property from government seizure: "nor shall private property be taken for public use without just compensation." The Found-

ers recognized that the government could confiscate property, for example, to construct roads or erect government buildings, and that property owners should have some form of protection from abusive government practices.

As described in Chapter 11, the Court's interpretation of the Takings Clause has repeatedly twisted and turned. By contrast, its reading of the Contract Clause and its application of the Due Process Clause to economic issues seem almost straightforward. Although the heyday of the Contract Clause and economic substantive due process has long since passed, the Takings Clause is enjoying a renaissance. Some members of the Rehnquist Court, particularly Antonin Scalia, have sought to revitalize the Takings Clause as a significant vehicle for protecting property rights.

Whether the Rehnquist Court will continue to move in the direction advocated by Scalia and others and increase protection for private property interests is one of many questions we consider in Chapter 11. It is enough to note for now that the current Court seems to be taking a greater interest in all kinds of economic issues than did its immediate predecessors. As Figure IV-1 shows, during the past few terms, the Court has allocated nearly 20 percent of its agenda space to cases involving economic issues. This figure pales in comparison with that of the 1930s, a period during which the majority of the cases the Court accepted for review had an economic dimension, or even the 1800s, when fully one-third of the business of the Court involved economic issues.[7] But it represents an increase from the number of economic cases accepted for review during the Warren and Burger Court years, which averaged 13 percent.

Does the increase in agenda space allocated to economic cases represent a real trend or a minor historical blip? This question is worthy of scholarly consideration because the kinds of cases the Court accepts speak to the role it plays in American society.[8] When the justices were deciding mostly economic cases, as they did for the first 150 years of the Court's history, it is not surprising that they exerted great influence in that arena, and not in civil liberties, civil rights, or criminal justice.[9] Moreover, if the Court is seeking to play a greater role in the economic realm, it will be forced to confront the fundamental issue that bedeviled its predecessors: the complex relationship between "vested rights" and "community interests." While, as we suggested, many of the Founders were concerned about individual liberty (such as the protection of private property), we now know that in a mature democratic society the pursuit of such individual interests impinges on the collective good. For example, if a state enacts a law setting a minimum wage, that statute affects the individual liberty of employers: it would be in their best interest, economically speaking, to pay their employees as little as possible. As a result, they may argue that minimum wage laws violate their constitutional guarantees. But is there another interest at stake? What are the results of paying workers a substandard wage? Does the state have a responsibility to enact legislation for the "health, safety, and welfare" of all its citizens?

The clash between the two interests—individual liberty (vested rights) and the state (community interests)—has been a primary reason for the Court's involvement in this area. As the Rehnquist Court reenters the economic liberties realm, the major questions center less on which interests are to be balanced than on the approaches different Courts have taken to balance them. As we shall see, some Courts exalted liberty interests above those of the community; others took precisely the opposite approach.

And, as we noted earlier, some analysts suggest that the Rehnquist Court may be heading in yet another doctrinal direction. They argue that the Court will use the Takings Clause as a mechanism for protecting property rights. Think about what political, legal, and historical factors contributed to these varying approaches to economic liberties as you read the chapters that follow.

---

7. See Sheldon Goldman, *Constitutional Law* (New York: Harper and Row, 1987), 167.

8. For interesting responses, see Richard L. Pacelle Jr., *The Transformation of the Supreme Court's Agenda* (Boulder, Colo.: Westview Press, 1991); and Pacelle, "The Dynamics and Determinants of Agenda Change in the Rehnquist Court," in *Contemplating Courts,* ed. Lee Epstein (Washington, D.C.: CQ Press, 1995).

9. Witt, *Guide to the U.S. Supreme Court,* 305.

CHAPTER 9
THE CONTRACT CLAUSE

SUPPOSE A FRIEND of yours had accepted a position some years ago with a large corporation. One of the reasons she took this particular job was that the company offered an attractive savings plan as a fringe benefit. Under the terms of the savings plan contract, your friend regularly placed a portion of her income into the fund, and the company matched her contributions. Money deposited in the fund belonged to the individual savers, and the company had no authority to use the funds for any corporate purpose. Over the years her savings account grew steadily. Then, in a national recession, the company's fortunes reversed and it, along with many others, faced bankruptcy. The state rushed to the relief of the troubled businesses by passing a law that allowed them unilaterally to use the assets in employee savings plans to finance operations until the economy regained its strength. The company took advantage of this statute, but, after spending all of the savings plan funds, the company still went under.

This story raises some basic questions. How can the state pass a law that releases a company from its contractual obligations? The company's employees were cheated out of their money, and the state was involved. How can one participate in any investment or commercial activity without some protection against a state's granting similar special considerations to corporations or other parties?

If you were outraged by your friend's fate, your reaction would be understandable. One of the hallmarks of a society that values commercial activity is the right to enter into legally binding contracts. It would be hard to imagine a market-based economy that did not recognize and protect such agreements. In most instances, we would expect the government to enforce contracts and not encourage parties who wished to break them.

The individuals who drafted the Constitution felt much the same way. Disturbed by the actions of state governments in the economic upheaval that followed the Revolution, the delegates to the Constitutional Convention moved to block state interference with contractual obligations. They did this by drafting the Contract Clause, one of the most important provisions of the Constitution during the nation's formative years.

THE FRAMERS AND THE CONTRACT CLAUSE

In fact, it might be difficult to find a group of people more supportive of the right to enter into binding agreements than the delegates to the convention. For the most part, these individuals represented the propertied classes, and they assembled in Philadelphia at a time of economic turmoil. Many of them feared that as the nation coped with its economic problems it might suspend the obligation to honor contracts.

Following the Revolutionary War the economy was very unstable, and the government under the Articles of Confederation was powerless to correct the situation. Hardest hit were small farmers, many of whom had taken out large loans they could not repay. When creditors started foreclosing on real estate and debtors were jailed for failing to pay, farmers and others faced with unmanageable obligations began to agitate for relief. Several states responded by passing laws to help them. Among these acts were bankruptcy laws that erased certain debt obligations or extended the time to pay, legal obstacles that blocked creditors from asserting their contractual rights against their debtors. Also, state currencies of dubious value were declared legal tender to satisfy debt obligations.

These policies hurt the creditors, many of whom were wealthy landowners. They called for a strengthening of the national government to deal with economic problems and a ban on the state governments' practice of nullifying contractual obligations. In response, Congress authorized a convention to propose changes in the Articles of Confederation. Once assembled, the delegates went much further than originally authorized and created the Constitution of the United States. The document drafted in Philadelphia clearly reflected the economic interests of the delegates. Among the provisions they wrote was a protection of contracts against state government infringement. Article I, Section 10, declares: "No State shall . . . pass any . . . Law impairing the obligation of contracts."

The eighteenth century's understanding of the term *contract* was the same as today's. A contract is an agreement voluntarily entered into by two or more parties in which a promise is made and something of value is given or pledged. Contractual agreements are made in almost every commercial transaction, such as a mining company's promise to deliver a quantity of iron ore to a steel mill in return for a particular fee, or a lawyer's promise to represent a client at a specified rate of compensation.

For the Framers, the right to enter into contracts was an important freedom closely tied to the right of private property. The ownership of private property implies the right to buy, sell, divide, occupy, lease, and use it; but one cannot effectively exercise these various property rights without the ability to enter into legally binding arrangements with others. In commercial transactions the parties rely on each other to carry out the contractual provisions. During the nation's formative years, those who failed to live up to contractual promises were dealt with harshly. In the minds of the propertied classes of the eighteenth century, this is how it should be, and the government should not be allowed to intervene in such private arrangements.

Evidence from the convention indicates that the Framers adopted the Contract Clause as a means of protecting agreements between private parties from state interference. However, at that time contracts also were a means of carrying out public policy. Because governments then were much more limited than they are today, the states regularly entered into contracts with individuals or corporations to carry out government policy or to distribute government benefits. These state actions included land grants, commercial monopolies, and licenses to construct roads and bridges. Individuals who entered into a contractual agreement with the state expected it to live up to its obligations and not abrogate the arrangement or unilaterally change the terms. In spite of what the Framers might have intended, the Contract Clause is worded generally and therefore offers protection both to contracts among private parties and to agreements made between private parties and the government.

The debates over ratification of the Constitution made little reference to the Contract Clause. In *The Federalist Papers*, Alexander Hamilton justified the prohibition against state impairment of contract obligations by claiming, "Laws in violation of private contracts . . . may be considered as another probable source of hostility."[1] James Madison declared in *Federalist*, No. 44: "[L]aws impairing the obligation of contracts are contrary to the first principles of the social compact and to every principle of sound legislation."

The Contract Clause became an important legal force in the early years of the nation's development. As political majorities changed from election to election, it was not unusual for state legislatures to enter into contracts with private parties only to break or change those agreements in subsequent legislative sessions. In addition, state governments often would adopt policies that ran contrary to contracts among private individuals. When such actions occurred, injured parties would challenge the state in court. As a result, the Contract Clause was one of the most litigated constitutional provisions in the first decades of U.S. history. One study concluded that roughly 40 percent of all Supreme Court cases prior to 1889 that attacked the validity of state legislation did so on the basis of Contract Clause arguments.[2]

JOHN MARSHALL AND THE CONTRACT CLAUSE

The significance of the Contract Clause increased dramatically through the Marshall Court's interpretations of its meaning. Chief Justice Marshall had strong views on private property, economic development, and the role of the federal government. He consistently supported aggressive policies that would result in vigorous economic expansion. Underlying this position was a philosophy that elevated private property to the level of a natural right that government had little authority to limit. Furthermore, Marshall firmly believed that the nation's interests could be served best if the federal government rather than the states became the primary agent for economic policy making. As we have seen in the areas of federalism and commerce, Marshall could be counted on to uphold actions taken by the federal government and to favor it over competing state interests. Marshall's ideology predisposed him to champion the Contract Clause, which he viewed as essential to the right to private property. Moreover, the clause's restriction of state regulatory powers appealed to his views on federalism. Given Marshall's domination of the Court for more than three decades, it is not surprising that the Contract Clause achieved an elevated status during those years.

Establishing the Importance of the Contract Clause

The first Supreme Court decision to consider the Contract Clause was *Fletcher v. Peck* (1810), which concerned whether a state could nullify a public contract. The suit flowed from one of the most notorious incidents of corruption and bribery in the nation's early history—the Yazoo River land fraud. In this litigation the beneficiaries of the scheme sought to use the Contract Clause to protect their gains.

This dispute had its roots in the 1795 session of the Georgia legislature. Clearly motivated by wholesale bribery, the legislators sold about 35 million acres of public lands to several land companies. The territory in question encompassed most of what is now Mississippi and Alabama. Some of the nation's most prominent public figures, including a number of members of Congress, supported this transaction or invested in it. The citizens of Georgia were outraged by the sale and turned out most of the legislators in the next elec-

---

1. Alexander Hamilton, "Federalist No. 7," in *The Federalist Papers*, ed. Clinton Rossiter (New York: New American Library, 1961).

2. Benjamin F. Wright, *The Contract Clause of the Constitution* (Cambridge, Mass.: Harvard University Press, 1938).

tion. In 1796 the newly elected legislature promptly rescinded the sales contract and moved to repossess the land. Unfortunately, by this time the land companies had sold numerous parcels to third-party investors and settlers. A massive and complicated set of legal actions ensued to determine ownership of the disputed lands. Attempts to negotiate a settlement proved unsuccessful. Even the president, Thomas Jefferson, was drawn into the controversy as he tried to work out a compromise settlement that would satisfy the state of Georgia as well as the investors.

Fletcher v. Peck was a lawsuit filed to obtain a judicial determination of the ownership question. John Peck acquired a parcel of the land in question from James Gunn, one of the original buyers in the Georgia land sales. Peck in turn sold the land to Robert Fletcher. When the state repealed the sale and resumed control of the land, Fletcher sued Peck for return of the purchase price. The real issue, however, rested squarely on the meaning of the Contract Clause: May a state that has entered into a valid contract later rescind that contract?

Joseph Story, who was to become the youngest man appointed to the Supreme Court, represented those who had purchased the land and wanted clear title to it. He argued that the Contract Clause barred the state from rescinding the original sales agreements. Attorneys supporting Georgia's repudiation of the land sale held that the state was empowered to declare it void because the original transaction was based on fraud. Furthermore, they contended that the Contract Clause was intended to protect against the abrogation of private contracts, not those made by the states.

Chief Justice Marshall was caught in a bind. To give force to the Contract Clause would be to rule in favor of those who profited from state government corruption. To rule against the unpopular fraudulent transactions would be to hand down a precedent significantly curtailing the meaning of the provision.

Marshall's choice, supported by each of the other four justices participating in the decision, was to uphold the land sales. The Court did not question the general ability of a legislature to repeal what a previous legislature had done. However, when the law is in the form of "a contract, when absolute rights have vested under that contract, a repeal of the law cannot devest those rights." To do so would be to impair the obligation of contracts in violation of Article I, Section 10.

Marshall's opinion gave considerable force to the Contract Clause. Although he acknowledged that the original transactions were based on bribery and corruption, Marshall concluded that such matters are beyond the power of the courts to control. He concentrated instead on the validity of a state's rescinding a previously passed, binding agreement. According to the Court's holding in this case, the Constitution prohibits the states from impairing the obligation of any contract, even those contracts contrary to the public good. In striking down the 1796 Georgia statute, the Supreme Court for the first time nullified a state law on constitutional grounds. *Fletcher v. Peck* established the Contract Clause as an important provision of the new Constitution and encouraged its use in challenging the states' economic regulations.

In 1819 the Marshall Court heard *Sturges v. Crowninshield,* an appeal that presented issues hitting squarely on the concerns expressed by the delegates at the Constitutional Convention. Richard Crowninshield, whose business enterprises had suffered hard times, received two loans from Josiah Sturges totaling approximately $1,500. The loans were secured by promissory notes. When Crowninshield became insolvent, he sought relief from his debts by invoking New York's recently passed bankruptcy law. Sturges objected, claiming that the New York law was a state impairment of the obligation of contracts in violation of the Constitution. The New York bankruptcy law was an example of just what the Framers had intended to prohibit—states interfering with debtor-creditor agreements.

The case presented two issues to the Supreme Court. The first was whether a state may enact a bankruptcy law at all. Article I, Section 8, Clause 4, of the Constitution expressly gave the federal government power to enact such legislation. Did this power preclude the states' acting? A unanimous Court, again through an opinion written by Chief Justice Marshall, held that in the absence of any federal action the states were free to enact bankruptcy laws. The second issue was whether the New York law was invalid as an impairment of contracts. Here the Court found the law defective. The New York law discharged Crowninshield's contractual indebtedness entered into prior to the passage of the statute, which, according to the Court, was beyond the power of the State.[3]

Corporate Charters as Contracts

The same year the Court decided *Sturges,* the justices announced their decision in *Trustees of Dartmouth College v. Woodward* (1819), perhaps the most famous of the Marshall-era Contract Clause cases. The Dartmouth College case presented a question of particular significance to the business community: Is a corporation charter a contract protected against state impairment? The case had added intrigue because it involved a bitter partisan battle between the Republicans and the Federalists.

In 1769 King George III issued a corporate charter establishing Dartmouth College in New Hampshire. The charter designated a board of trustees as the ultimate governing body, and the board's authority extended to the college president. The board was self-perpetuating with the power to fill its own vacancies. The founder and first president of Dartmouth was Eleazar Wheelock, who also had authority to designate his own successor. He chose his son, John Wheelock, who assumed the presidency upon Eleazar's death. John Wheelock was ill-suited for the position,

and for years friction existed between him and the board.

To shore up his position, Wheelock made political alliances with the Jeffersonian Republicans who had gained control of the state legislature in 1816. The Republicans gladly took his side in the dispute with the Federalist-dominated board of trustees and passed a law radically changing the governing structure of the college. The law called for an expansion of the board from twelve to twenty-one members to be appointed by the governor, and it created a supervisory panel with veto power over the actions of the trustees. The new officials removed the old trustees from office. In effect, the legislature had converted Dartmouth College, renamed Dartmouth University under the new law, from a private to a public institution. The result was chaos. The students and faculty for the most part remained loyal to the old trustees, but the state essentially took over the buildings and records of the college. As might be expected, the college soon found itself on the edge of fiscal collapse.

To resolve the situation, the old trustees hired Daniel Webster to represent them. Webster, an 1801 Dartmouth graduate, agreed to take the case for a fee of $1,000, a considerable sum of money in those days. The trustees sued William Woodward, the secretary of the college, who had in his possession the college charter, records, and seal. Webster and the old trustees lost in the state courts and then appealed to the U.S. Supreme Court. When the case was argued in March 1818, Webster engaged in four hours of brilliant oratory before the justices. At times his argument was quite emotional, and he is said to have brought tears to the eyes of those present when he spoke his often quoted line, "It is, sir, as I have said, a small college, and yet there are those that love it." The justices, however, did not act in the heat of emotion. Instead, almost a full year went by before the Court announced its decision. By the time the opinion was released, both John Wheelock and William Woodward had died.

3. Eight years later, however, the Court held in *Ogden v. Saunders* (1827) that state bankruptcy laws did not violate the Contract Clause if the contract was entered into after the enactment of the bankruptcy statute.

With only one justice dissenting, the Court supported Webster's position. The grant by the English Crown setting up the college was a contract, Marshall declared, and the governing structure of the college was part of that contract. When the state of New Hampshire restructured the college with the 1816 legislation, it impaired the original contract. The statute was repugnant to the Contract Clause and therefore void.

As a result of this decision the old trustees regained control of the college, and Webster's reputation as one of the nation's leading legal advocates was firmly established. The decision was also a victory for business interests. By holding that corporate charters were contracts under the meaning of Article I, Section 10, the Court gave businesses considerable protection against state regulation. The decision, however, was not totally one-sided. Marshall acknowledged the power of the state to include within its contracts and charters provisions reserving the right to make future changes.

The importance of the Contract Clause reached its zenith under the Marshall Court. These early decisions protecting contractual agreements helped spur economic development and expansion. But an inevitable battle was on the horizon, a battle between the constitutional sanctity of contracts and a state's authority to regulate for the public good.

THE DECLINE OF THE CONTRACT CLAUSE

The Marshall years ended when the chief justice died July 6, 1835, at the age of seventy-nine. Marshall had been appointed in 1801 in one of the last acts of the once-dominant Federalist party, and he had imposed his political philosophy on the Court's constitutional interpretations for more than three decades. His decisions in Contract Clause disputes, as well as in other areas of federalism and economic regulation, encouraged economic development and fostered entrepreneurial activity.

Elevating the Public Good

The days of the Federalist philosophy sympathetic to the interests of business and the economic elite had passed. Andrew Jackson now occupied the White House. Jackson came from the American frontier and was committed to policies beneficial to ordinary citizens; he had little sympathy for the moneyed classes of the Northeast. Within a short period, Jackson had the opportunity to change the course of the Supreme Court. He filled not only the center chair left vacant by Marshall's death, but also those of five associate justices during his presidency.[4] The new appointees all held ideologies consistent with principles of Jacksonian democracy, especially the new chief justice, Roger Brooke Taney, a Maryland Democrat who had served in a number of posts in the Jackson administration. Changes in constitutional interpretation were inevitable, although in the final analysis the Taney Court did not veer as far from Marshall precedents as many had predicted.

Given the differences between Federalist and Jacksonian values, however, the Court was likely to reevaluate the Contract Clause. The Taney Court's first opportunity to do so came in *Charles River Bridge v. Warren Bridge* (1837). As you read the Court's opinion, compare it to the positions taken by the Court during the Marshall era. While Taney certainly did not repudiate Marshall's rulings, his opinion in *Charles River Bridge* struck a new balance between the inviolability of contracts and the power of the state to legislate for the public good. The Court also held that contracts should be strictly construed, a position at odds with Marshall's rather expansive interpretations of contractual obligations. Justice Story, who had appeared as an attorney in *Fletcher* and had supported Marshall's views of the Contract Clause since he joined the Court in 1811, dissented from this change in doctrine.

---

4. This number includes Associate Justice John Catron, who was nominated on Jackson's last day in office and whose appointment is often credited to Jackson's successor, Martin Van Buren.

The Charles River Bridge ran from Prince Street in Boston to Charlestown. The bridge, considered a very advanced design at the time of its construction, was built on seventy-five oak piers and was more than 1,500 feet long.

Charles River Bridge v. Warren Bridge

11 PET. 420 (1837)

Vote: 5 (Baldwin, Barbour, McLean, Taney, Wayne)
2 (Story, Thompson)
Opinion of the Court: Taney
Concurring opinion: McLean
Dissenting opinions: Story, Thompson

In 1785 the Massachusetts legislature created by charter the Charles River Bridge Company. The charter gave the company the right to construct a bridge between Boston and Charlestown and to collect tolls for its use. This agreement replaced a ferry franchise between the two cities that the colonial legislature had granted to Harvard College in 1650. In 1792 the legislature extended the charter. Because of the population growth in the Boston area, the bridge received heavy use, and its investors prospered. In 1828, when traffic congestion on the bridge became a significant prob-

lem, the legislature decided that a second bridge was needed. Consequently, the state incorporated the Warren Bridge Company and authorized it to construct a bridge to be located about a hundred yards from the first. The Warren Bridge investors had authority to collect tolls to pay for the expense of construction plus an agreed-upon profit. However, in no more than six years the state was to assume ownership of the Warren Bridge and then operate it on a toll-free basis.

The Charles River Bridge Company opposed the construction of a second bridge. It claimed that its charter conferred the exclusive right to build and operate a bridge between Boston and Charlestown. A second bridge, eventually to be operated without tolls, would deprive the company of the profits from its investment. The second charter, the company claimed, was a violation of the Contract Clause. To represent it, the Charles River Bridge Company hired Daniel Webster, who had won the Dartmouth College

BOX 9-1   DANIEL WEBSTER
(1782-1852)

Daniel webster played an influential role in the development of American law and politics during a public career that spanned almost fifty years. He was born in Salisbury, New Hampshire, January 18, 1782, and educated at Phillips Exeter Academy and Dartmouth College. He was admitted to the bar in 1805 and immediately began the practice of law in his home state.

In 1813 Webster was first elected to Congress as a Federalist representative from New Hampshire. This office was only the beginning of an illustrious series of important positions:

United States representative, New Hampshire,
   1813–1817

Monroe delegate to Electoral College, 1820

United States representative, Massachusetts,
   1823–1827

United States senator, Massachusetts, 1827–1841

Presidential candidate, 1836

Secretary of state (Harrison-Tyler administrations),
   1841–1843

United States senator, Massachusetts, 1845–1850

Secretary of state (Fillmore administration), 1850–1852

Webster was perhaps best known for his role as an advocate before the Supreme Court and the brilliant oratorical skills he displayed in both Congress and the courts. Webster appeared before the Supreme Court in 168 cases, winning about half of them. In twenty-four of his appearances he was an advocate in a major constitutional dispute. Among his most celebrated cases were:

McCulloch v. Maryland (1819)
Dartmouth College v. Woodward (1819)
Cohens v. Virginia (1821)
Gibbons v. Ogden (1824)
Osborn v. Bank of the United States (1824)
Ogden v. Saunders (1827)
Wheaton v. Peters (1834)
Charles River Bridge v. Warren Bridge (1837)
Swift v. Tyson (1842)
West River Bridge v. Dix (1848)
Luther v. Borden (1849)

NOTE: For a review of Webster's legal career, see Maurice G. Baxter, *Daniel Webster and the Supreme Court* (Amherst: University of Massachusetts Press, 1966).

---

case two decades earlier *(see Box 9-1)*. When the Massachusetts courts failed to grant relief, Charles River Bridge took its case to the U.S. Supreme Court.

The case was first argued in March 1831. John Marshall still led the Court at that time, and Webster understandably felt confident of victory. However, the justices could not agree on a decision, and the case was scheduled for reargument in 1833. Once again, no decision was reached. Before a third hearing could be

scheduled, deaths and resignations had changed the ideological complexion of the Court. When Jackson announced Taney as his choice for chief justice, Webster is said to have proclaimed, "The Constitution is gone." From Webster's perspective perhaps that was true. The Taney justices scheduled arguments on the bridge case in 1837, and Webster no longer had a sympathetic audience for his strong Contract Clause position.

MR. CHIEF JUSTICE TANEY delivered the
opinion of the Court.

The plaintiffs in error insist . . . [t]hat . . . the acts of the
legislature of Massachusetts . . . by their true construction,
necessarily implied that the legislature would not authorize
another bridge, and especially a free one, by the side of this,
and placed in the same line of travel, whereby the franchise
granted to the "proprietors of the Charles River Bridge"
should be rendered of no value; and the plaintiffs in error
contend, that the grant of the ferry to the college, and of the
charter to the proprietors of the bridge, are both contracts
on the part of the state; and that the law authorizing the
erection of the Warren Bridge in 1828, impairs the obligation of one or both of these contracts. . . .

[W]e are not now left to determine, for the first time, the
rules by which public grants are to be construed in this
country. The subject has already been considered in this
Court . . . and the principle recognized, that in grants by
the public, nothing passes by implication. . . .

[T]he object and end of all government is to promote the
happiness and prosperity of the community by which it is
established; and it can never be assumed, that the government intended to diminish its power of accomplishing the
end for which it was created. And in a country like ours,
free, active, and enterprising, continually advancing in
numbers and wealth; new channels of communication are
daily found necessary, both for travel and trade; and are essential to the comfort, convenience, and prosperity of the
people. A state ought never to be presumed to surrender
this power, because, like the taxing power, the whole community have an interest in preserving it undiminished. And
when a corporation alleges, that a state has surrendered for
seventy years, its power of improvement, and public accommodation, in a great and important line of travel, along
which a vast number of its citizens must daily pass; the
community have a right to insist, in the language of this
Court above quoted, "that its abandonment ought not to be
presumed, in a case, in which the deliberate purpose of the
state to abandon it does not appear." The continued existence of a government would be of no great value, if by implications and presumptions, it was disarmed of the powers
necessary to accomplish the ends of its creation; and the
functions it was designed to perform, transferred to the

hands of privileged corporations. The rule of construction
announced by the Court, was not confined to the taxing
power; nor is it so limited in the opinion delivered. On the
contrary, it was distinctly placed on the ground that the interests of the community were concerned in preserving,
undiminished, the power then in question; and whenever
any power of the state is said to be surrendered or diminished, whether it be the taxing power or any other affecting
the public interest, the same principle applies, and the rule
of construction must be the same. No one will question that
the interests of the great body of the people of the state,
would, in this intance, be affected by the surrender of this
great line of travel to a single corporation, with the right to
exact toll, and exclude competition for seventy years. While
the rights of private property are sacredly guarded, we must
not forget that the community also have rights, and that the
happiness and well being of every citizen depends on their
faithful preservation.

Adopting the rule of construction above stated as the
settled one, we proceed to apply it to the charter of 1785, to
the proprietors of the Charles River Bridge. This act of incorporation is in the usual form, and the privileges such as
are commonly given to corporations of that kind. It confers
on them the ordinary faculties of a corporation, for the purpose of building the bridge; and establishes certain rates of
toll, which the company are authorized to take. This is the
whole grant. There is no exclusive privilege given to them
over the waters of Charles river, above or below their
bridge. No right to erect another bridge themselves, nor to
prevent other persons from erecting one. No engagement
from the state, that another shall not be erected; and no undertaking not to sanction competition, nor to make improvements that may diminish the amount of its income.
Upon all these subjects the charter is silent; and nothing is
said in it about a line of travel, so much insisted on in the argument, in which they are to have exclusive privileges. No
words are used, from which an intention to grant any of
these rights can be inferred. If the plaintiff is entitled to
them, it must be implied, simply, from the nature of the
grant; and cannot be inferred from the words by which the
grant is made.

The relative position of the Warren Bridge has already
been described. It does not interrupt the passage over the
Charles River Bridge, nor make the way to it or from it less

convenient. None of the faculties or franchises granted to that corporation, have been revoked by the legislature; and its right to take the tolls granted by the charter remains unaltered. In short, all the franchises and rights of property enumerated in the charter, and there mentioned to have been granted to it, remain unimpaired. But its income is destroyed by the Warren Bridge; which, being free, draws off the passengers and property which would have gone over it, and renders their franchise of no value. This is the gist of the complaint. For it is not pretended, that the erection of the Warren Bridge would have done them any injury, or in any degree affected their right of property; if it had not diminished the amount of their tolls. In order then to entitle themselves to relief, it is necessary to show, that the legislature contracted not to do the act of which they complain; and that they impaired, or in other words, violated that contract by the erection of the Warren Bridge.

The inquiry then is, does the charter contain such a contract on the part of the state? Is there any such stipulation to be found in that instrument? It must be admitted on all hands, that there is none—no words that even relate to another bridge or to the diminution of their tolls, or to the line of travel. If a contract on that subject can be gathered from the charter, it must be by implication; and cannot be found in the words used. Can such an agreement be implied? The rule of construction before stated is an answer to the question. In charters of this description, no rights are taken from the public, or given to the corporation, beyond those which the words of the charter, by their natural and proper construction, purport to convey. There are no words which import such a contract as the plaintiffs in error contend for, and none can be implied. . . .

Indeed, the practice and usage of almost every state in the Union, old enough to have commenced the work of internal improvement, is opposed to the doctrine contended for on the part of the plaintiffs in error. Turnpike roads have been made in succession, on the same line of travel; the later ones interfering materially with the profits of the first. These corporations have, in some instances, been utterly ruined by the introduction of newer and better modes of transportation, and travelling. In some cases, rail roads have rendered the turnpike roads on the same line of travel so entirely useless, that the franchise of the turnpike corporation is not worth preserving. Yet in none of these cases have the corporations supposed that their privileges were invaded, or any contract violated on the part of the state. Amid the multitude of cases which have occurred, and have been daily occurring for the last forty or fifty years, this is the first instance in which such an implied contract has been contended for, and this Court called upon to infer it from an ordinary act of incorporation, containing nothing more than the usual stipulations and provisions to be found in every such law. The absence of any such controversy, when there must have been so many occasions to give rise to it, proves that neither states, nor individuals, nor corporations, ever imagined that such a contract could be implied from such charters. It shows that the men who voted for these laws, never imagined that they were forming such a contract; and if we maintain that they have made it, we must create it by a legal fiction, in opposition to the truth of the fact, and the obvious intention of the party. We cannot deal thus with the rights reserved to the states; and by legal intendments and mere technical reasoning, take away from them any portion of that power over their own internal police and improvement, which is so necessary to their well being and prosperity. . . .

The judgment of the supreme judicial court of the commonwealth of Massachusetts, dismissing the plaintiff's bill, must, therefore, be affirmed, with costs.

MR. JUSTICE STORY, dissenting.

I maintain, that, upon the principles of common reason and legal interpretation, the present grant carries with it a necessary implication that the legislature shall do no act to destroy or essentially to impair the franchise; that, (as one of the learned judges of the state court expressed it,) there is an implied agreement that the state will not grant another bridge between Boston and Charlestown, so near as to draw away the custom from the old one; and, (as another learned judge expressed it,) that there is an implied agreement of the state to grant the undisturbed use of the bridge and its tolls so far as respects any acts of its own, or of any persons acting under its authority. In other words, the state, impliedly, contracts not to resume its grant, or to do any act to the prejudice or destruction of its grant. I maintain, that there is no authority or principle established in relation to the construction of crown grants, or legislative grants; which does not concede and justify this doctrine. Where the thing is given, the incidents, without which it cannot be enjoyed, are also given. . . . I maintain that a different doctrine is utterly repugnant to all the principles of the common law, applicable to all franchises of a like nature; and that we must overturn some of the best securities of the rights of property, before it can be established. I maintain, that the common law is the birthright of every citizen of Massachusetts, and that he holds the title deeds of his property, corporeal, and incorporeal, under it. I maintain, that under the principles of the common law, there exists no more right in the legislature of Massachusetts, to erect the Warren Bridge, to the ruin of the franchise of the Charles River Bridge than exists to transfer the latter to the former, or to authorize the former to demolish the latter. If the legislature does not mean in its grant to give any exclusive rights, let it say so, expressly; directly; and in terms admitting of no misconstruction. The grantees will then take at their peril, and must abide the results of their overweening confidence, indiscretion, and zeal.

My judgment is formed upon the terms of the grant, its nature and objects, its design and duties; and, in its interpretation, I seek for no new principles, but I apply such as are as old as the very rudiments of the common law.

In spite of Justice Story's protest that the majority had rendered the Contract Clause meaningless, the Taney Court continued to allow the states more leeway in regulating for the public good. As Taney noted in *Charles River Bridge*, "While the rights of private property are sacredly guarded, we must not forget that the community also have rights, and that the happiness and well being of every citizen depends on their faithful preservation."

The Taney justices, however, did not totally abandon the Marshall Court's posture favoring business, nor did they repeal the Contract Clause by judicial fiat; the Court instead took a more balanced position. In a number of cases, especially when the contractual provisions were clear, the Taney Court struck down state regulations on Contract Clause grounds. For example, in *Bronson v. Kinzie* (1843) the Court invalidated Illinois laws that expanded the rights of debtors.

The challenged statutes placed certain limits on mortgage debt, including protecting the rights of owners to repurchase properties lost to foreclosure. To the extent that these laws were applied to contracts in existence before their passage, the laws were unconstitutional. In *Piqua Branch of the State Bank of Ohio v. Knoop* (1854) the justices declared void the assessment of state taxes on a bank because, in calculating the taxes, Ohio had used a basis different from that specified under the state charter establishing the bank.

Decline in the Post–Civil War Period

After the Taney years, the Court continued to move away from strong enforcement of the Contract Clause and to accord the states increased freedom to exercise their police powers. *Fertilizing Company v. Hyde Park* (1878) provides a good illustration. The Illinois state legislature passed a statute March 8, 1867, creating the Northwest Fertilizing Company. The charter authorized the company within a designated territory to operate a facility that converted dead animals to fertilizer and other products. The charter also gave the company the right to transport dead animals and animal parts (offal) through the territory. Based on this authority, the company operated its plant in a sparsely populated, swampy area.

However, the facility was located within the boundaries of the village of Hyde Park, which was beginning to experience considerable population growth. In 1869 the legislature upgraded the village charter, giving it full powers of local government including the authority to "define or abate nuisances which are, or may be, injurious to the public health." Recognizing its charter with Northwest, the legislature stipulated that no village regulations could be applied to the company for at least two years. At the end of the two years, the village passed an ordinance that said, "No person shall transfer, carry, haul, or convey any offal, dead animals, or other offensive or unwholesome matter or material, into or through the village of Hyde Park." Parties in violation of the law were subject to fines. In 1873, following the arrest and conviction of railroad workers hauling dead animals to its plant, Northwest filed suit claiming that their original charter was a contract that could not be abrogated by the state or its local governments. The company was unsuccessful in the state courts and appealed to the U.S. Supreme Court.

Justice Swayne's opinion made clear at the outset that the company faced a difficult task in its attempt to convince the justices:

The rule of construction in this class of cases is that it shall be most strongly against the corporation. Every reasonable doubt is to be resolved adversely. Nothing is to be taken as conceded but what is given in unmistakable terms, or by an implication equally clear. The affirmative must be shown. Silence is negation, and doubt is fatal to the claim. This doctrine is vital to the public welfare.

The Court then went on to rule against the Contract Clause arguments of the company. The justices had no doubt that the transportation of offal was a public nuisance. Nor was there any doubt that the state had ample police power to combat such an offensive practice. According to Swayne, "That power belonged to the States when the Federal Constitution was adopted. They did not surrender it, and they all have it now. . . . It rests upon the fundamental principle that every one shall so use his own as not to wrong and injure another. To regulate and abate nuisances is one of its ordinary functions." The states, the Court was implying, could not contract away their inherent powers to regulate for their citizens' health, safety, and welfare.

Two years following the *Northwest Fertilizing Company* case, the justices addressed a similar appeal, this time dealing with questions of public morality. *Stone v. Mississippi* (1880) focused on the use of the state's police power to combat lotteries, a form of gambling that much of the population considered evil at that time.

In 1867 the post–Civil War provisional state legislature chartered the Mississippi Agricultural, Educational, and Manufacturing Aid Society. In spite of its name, the society's only purpose was to operate a lottery. The charter gave the society authority to run a lottery in Mississippi for twenty-five years, and, in return, the society paid an initial sum of cash to the state, an additional annual payment for each year of operation, plus a percentage of the lottery receipts. In 1868, however, a state convention drafted a new constitution, which the people ratified the next year. This constitution contained provisions explicitly outlawing lotteries. On July 16, 1870, the legislature passed a statute providing for enforcement of the antilottery provisions, and four years later, on March 17, 1874, the state attorney general filed charges against John B. Stone and others associated with the Mississippi Agricultural, Educational, and Manufacturing Aid Society for being in violation of state law. The state admitted that the company was operating within the provisions of its 1867 charter, but contended that the new constitution and subsequent enforcement legislation effectively repealed that grant. Stone countered that the federal Contract Clause explicitly prohibits the state from negating the provisions of the charter.

A unanimous Supreme Court ruled in favor of the state. The states possess police powers that allow them to regulate for the health, safety, morals, and general welfare of their citizens. The legislature, by means of a contract, cannot bargain away the state's police powers. Lotteries are proper subjects for police power regulation. Anyone contracting with the state to conduct a lottery does so with the implied understanding that the people, through their properly constituted state agencies, may later exercise the power to regulate or even prohibit such gambling.

Following *Stone v. Mississippi* it was clear that the Court would no longer be sympathetic to Contract Clause attacks on state regulatory statutes. With Contract Clause avenues closing, opponents of the state regulation of business and commercial activities turned to another provision of the Constitution, the Due Process Clause of the Fourteenth Amendment.

From the late 1880s to the 1930s—a period of Court history discussed in Chapter 10—the Court heard and often responded favorably to these substantive due process arguments.

The Depression and the Abrogation of Contracts

The Contract Clause reached its lowest status during the Great Depression of the 1930s. With the stock market crash of 1929, the nation entered its worst economic crisis; most Americans were placed in serious financial jeopardy. The 1932 election of Franklin Roosevelt ushered in the New Deal, and the federal government began innovative economic programs to combat the depression. At the same time, various states were developing their own programs to protect their citizens against the economic ravages the country was experiencing.

What people feared most during the depression was losing the family home. Homeowners did what they could to meet their mortgage obligations, but, because so many were out of work, they were unable to make their payments. Financial institutions had little choice but to foreclose on these properties as stipulated in the mortgage contracts. To provide relief, several states passed statutes to increase homeowners' chances of saving their houses. Banks and other creditors opposed these assistance measures. For them, intervention by the state was a direct violation of the constitutional ban against impairment of contracts.

The showdown between the Contract Clause and the government's authority to cope with economic crisis occurred in *Home Building and Loan Association v. Blaisdell* (1934). As you read Chief Justice Hughes's opinion for the Court, think about the Constitutional Convention and the concerns that led the Framers to adopt the Contract Clause. Would they agree with the Court that the Constitution should bend in the face of national crises; or would they side with Justice Sutherland's dissent that the provisions of the Constitution should be interpreted the same way regardless of the conditions of the times?

Home Building and Loan Association v. Blaisdell

290 U.S. 398 (1934)
Vote: 5 (Brandeis, Cardozo, Hughes, Roberts, Stone)
        4 (Butler, McReynolds, Sutherland, Van Devanter)
Opinion of the Court: Hughes
Dissenting opinion: Sutherland

During the Great Depression, people faced high unemployment, low prices for agricultural and manufactured products, a stagnation of business, and a scarcity of credit. In response to these conditions, the Minnesota legislature declared that a state of economic emergency existed that demanded the use of extraordinary police powers for the protection of the people. One of the legislature's actions was passage of the Minnesota Mortgage Moratorium Act, which was designed to protect homeowners when they could not make their mortgage payments. The act allowed homeowners who were behind in their payments to petition a state court for an extension of time to meet their mortgage obligations. During the period of the extension, the homeowners would not make normal mortgage payments but instead would pay a reasonable rental amount to the mortgage holder. The maximum extension was two years. The act was to be in effect only as long as the economic emergency continued. Its provisions applied to all mortgages, including those signed prior to the passage of the statute.

John and Rosella Blaisdell owned a house in Minneapolis that was mortgaged to the Home Building and Loan Association. They lived in one part of the house and rented out the other part. When the Blaisdells were unable to keep their payments current or to obtain additional credit, they requested an extension in accordance with the moratorium law. After initially denying the request and then being reversed by the state supreme court, the trial court granted the Blaisdells a two-year moratorium on mortgage payments. During this period the Blaisdells were ordered to pay

$40.00 per month, which would be applied to taxes, insurance, interest, and mortgage principal. The Home Building and Loan Association opposed the extension and appealed to the Minnesota Supreme Court on the grounds that the law was an impairment of contracts in violation of the Contract Clause of the federal Constitution. The Minnesota court conceded that the law impaired the obligation of contracts, but concluded that the statute was within the police powers of the state because of the severe economic emergency. Home Building and Loan appealed to the U.S. Supreme Court.

MR. CHIEF JUSTICE HUGHES delivered the opinion of the Court.

In determining whether the provision for this temporary and conditional relief exceeds the power of the State by reason of the clause in the Federal Constitution prohibiting impairment of the obligations of contracts, we must consider the relation of emergency to constitutional power, the historical setting of the contract clause, the development of the jurisprudence of this Court in the construction of that clause, and the principles of construction which we may consider to be established.

Emergency does not create power. Emergency does not increase granted power or remove or diminish the restrictions imposed upon power granted or reserved. The Constitution was adopted in a period of grave emergency. Its grants of power to the Federal Government and its limitations of the power of the States were determined in the light of emergency and they are not altered by emergency. What power was thus granted and what limitations were thus imposed are questions which have always been, and always will be, the subject of close examination under our constitutional system.

While emergency does not create power, emergency may furnish the occasion for the exercise of power. "Although an emergency may not call into life a power which has never lived, nevertheless emergency may afford a reason for the exertion of a living power already enjoyed." The constitutional question presented in the light of an emergency is whether the power possessed embraces the particular exercise of it in response to particular conditions. Thus, the war power of the Federal Government is not created by the emergency of war, but it is a power given to meet that emergency. It is a power to wage war successfully, and thus it permits the harnessing of the entire energies of the people in a supreme coöperative effort to preserve the nation. But even the war power does not remove constitutional limitations safeguarding essential liberties. When the provisions of the Constitution, in grant or restriction, are specific, so particularized as not to admit of construction, no question is presented. Thus, emergency would not permit a State to have more than two Senators in the Congress, or permit the election of President by a general popular vote without regard to the number of electors to which the States are respectively entitled, or permit the States to "coin money" or to "make anything but gold and silver coin a tender in payment of debts." But where constitutional grants and limitations of power are set forth in general clauses, which afford a broad outline, the process of construction is essential to fill in the details. That is true of the contract clause. The necessity of construction is not obviated by the fact that the contract clause is associated in the same section with other and more specific prohibitions. Even the grouping of subjects in the same clause may not require the same application to each of the subjects, regardless of differences in their nature.

In the construction of the contract clause, the debates in the Constitutional Convention are of little aid. But the reasons which led to the adoption of that clause, and of the other prohibitions of Section 10 of Article I, are not left in doubt and have frequently been described with eloquent emphasis. The widespread distress following the revolutionary period, and the plight of debtors, had called forth in the States an ignoble array of legislative schemes for the defeat of creditors and the invasion of contractual obligations. Legislative interferences had been so numerous and extreme that the confidence essential to prosperous trade had been undermined and the utter destruction of credit was threatened. "The sober people of America" were convinced that some "thorough reform" was needed which would "inspire a general prudence and industry, and give a regular course to the business of society." *The Federalist,*

No. 44. It was necessary to impose the restraining power of a central authority in order to secure the foundations even of "private faith.". . .

But full recognition of the occasion and general purpose of the clause does not suffice to fix its precise scope. Nor does an examination of the details of prior legislation in the States yield criteria which can be considered controlling. To ascertain the scope of the constitutional prohibition we examine the course of judicial decisions in its application. These put it beyond question that the prohibition is not an absolute one and is not to be read with literal exactness like a mathematical formula. . . .

The legislature cannot "bargain away the public health or the public morals." Thus, the constitutional provision against the impairment of contracts was held not to be violated by an amendment of the state constitution which put an end to a lottery theretofore authorized by the legislature. The lottery was a valid enterprise when established under express state authority, but the legislature in the public interest could put a stop to it. A similar rule has been applied to the control by the State of the sale of intoxicating liquors. The States retain adequate power to protect the public health against the maintenance of nuisances despite insistence upon existing contracts. Legislation to protect the public safety comes within the same category of reserved power. This principle has had recent and noteworthy application to the regulation of the use of public highways by common carriers and "contract carriers," where the assertion of interference with existing contract rights has been without avail. . . .

It is manifest from this review of our decisions that there has been a growing appreciation of public needs and of the necessity of finding ground for a rational compromise between individual rights and public welfare. The settlement and consequent contraction of the public domain, the pressure· of a constantly increasing density of population, the interrelation of the activities of our people and the complexity of our economic interests, have inevitably led to an increased use of the organization of society in order to protect the very bases of individual opportunity. Where, in earlier days, it was thought that only the concerns of individuals or of classes were involved, and that those of the State itself were touched only remotely, it has later been found

that the fundamental interests of the State are directly affected; and that the question is no longer merely that of one party to a contract as against another, but of the use of reasonable means to safeguard the economic structure upon which the good of all depends.

It is no answer to say that this public need was not apprehended a century ago, or to insist that what the provision of the Constitution meant to the vision of that day it must mean to the vision of our time. If by the statement that what the Constitution meant at the time of its adoption it means to-day, it is intended to say that the great clauses of the Constitution must be confined to the interpretation which the framers, with the conditions and outlook of their time, would have placed upon them, the statement carries its own refutation. It was to guard against such a narrow conception that Chief Justice Marshall uttered the memorable warning—"We must never forget that it is *a constitution* we are expounding": *(McCulloch v. Maryland)*—"a constitution intended to endure for ages to come, and consequently, to be adapted to the various *crises* of human affairs." When we are dealing with the words of the Constitution, said this Court in *Missouri v. Holland,* "we must realize that they have called into life a being the development of which could not have been foreseen completely by the most gifted of its begetters. . . . The case before us must be considered in the light of our whole experience and not merely in that of what was said a hundred years ago."

Nor is it helpful to attempt to draw a fine distinction between the intended meaning of the words of the Constitution and their intended application. When we consider the contract clause and the decisions which have expounded it in harmony with the essential reserved power of the States to protect the security of their peoples, we find no warrant for the conclusion that the clause has been warped by these decisions from its proper significance or that the founders of our Government would have interpreted the clause differently had they had occasion to assume that responsibility in the conditions of the later day. The vast body of law which has been developed was unknown to the fathers, but it is believed to have preserved the essential content and the spirit of the Constitution. With a growing recognition of public needs and the relation of individual right to public security, the court has sought to prevent the perversion of the clause through its use as an instrument to throttle the capacity of the States to protect their fundamental interests. This development is a growth from the seeds which the fathers planted. . . . The principle of this development is . . . that the reservation of the reasonable exercise of the protective power of the State is read into all contracts and there is no greater reason for refusing to apply this principle to Minnesota mortgages than to New York leases.

Applying the criteria established by our decisions we conclude:

1. An emergency existed in Minnesota which furnished a proper occasion for the exercise of the reserved power of the State to protect the vital interests of the community. . . .

2. The legislation was addressed to a legitimate end, that is, the legislation was not for the mere advantage of particular individuals but for the protection of a basic interest of society.

3. In view of the nature of the contracts in question—mortgages of unquestionable validity—the relief afforded and justified by the emergency, in order not to contravene the constitutional provision, could only be of a character appropriate to that emergency and could be granted only upon reasonable conditions.

4. The conditions upon which the period of redemption is extended do not appear to be unreasonable. . . .

5. The legislation is temporary in operation. It is limited to the exigency which called it forth. . . .

We are of the opinion that the Minnesota statute as here applied does not violate the contract clause of the Federal Constitution. Whether the legislation is wise or unwise as a matter of policy is a question with which we are not concerned. . . .

The judgment of the Supreme Court of Minnesota is affirmed.

MR. JUSTICE SUTHERLAND, dissenting.

Few questions of greater moment than that just decided have been submitted for judicial inquiry during this generation. He simply closes his eyes to the necessary implications of the decision who fails to see in it the potentiality of future gradual but ever-advancing encroachments upon the sanctity of private and public contracts. The effect of the Minnesota legislation, though serious enough in itself, is of trivial significance compared with the far more serious and dangerous inroads upon the limitations of the Constitution which are almost certain to ensue as a consequence naturally following any step beyond the boundaries fixed by that instrument. And those of us who are thus apprehensive of the effect of this decision would, in a matter so important, be neglectful of our duty should we fail to spread upon the permanent records of the court the reasons which move us to the opposite view.

A provision of the Constitution, it is hardly necessary to say, does not admit of two distinctly opposite interpretations. It does not mean one thing at one time and an entirely different thing at another time. If the contract impairment clause, when framed and adopted, meant that the terms of a contract for the payment of money could not be altered . . . by a state statute enacted for the relief of hardly pressed debtors to the end and with the effect of postponing payment or enforcement during and because of an economic or financial emergency, it is but to state the obvious to say that it means the same now. This view, at once so rational in its application to the written word, and so necessary to the stability of constitutional principles, though from time to time challenged, has never, unless recently, been put within the realm of doubt by the decisions of this court. . . .

The provisions of the Federal Constitution, undoubtedly, are pliable in the sense that in appropriate cases they have the capacity of bringing within their grasp every new condition which falls within their meaning. But, their *meaning* is changeless; it is only their *application* which is extensible. . . .

A statute which materially delays enforcement of the mortgagee's contractual right of ownership and possession does not modify the remedy merely; it destroys, for the period of delay, *all* remedy so far as the enforcement of that right is concerned. The phrase, "obligation of a contract," in the constitutional sense imports a legal duty to perform the specified obligation of *that* contract, not to substitute and perform, against the will of one of the parties, a different, albeit equally valuable, obligation. And a state, under the contract impairment clause, has no more power to accomplish such a substitution than has one of the parties to the contract against the will of the other. It cannot do so either by acting directly upon the contract, or by bringing about the result under the guise of a statute in form acting only upon the remedy. If it could, the efficacy of the constitutional restriction would, in large measure, be made to disappear. . . .

I quite agree with the opinion of the court that whether the legislation under review is wise or unwise is a matter with which we have nothing to do. Whether it is likely to work well or work ill presents a question entirely irrelevant to the issue. The only legitimate inquiry we can make is whether it is constitutional. If it is not, its virtues, if it have any, cannot save it; if it is, its faults cannot be invoked to accomplish its destruction. If the provisions of the Constitution be not upheld when they pinch as well as when they comfort, they may as well be abandoned. Being unable to reach any other conclusion than that the Minnesota statute infringes the constitutional restriction under review, I have no choice but to say so.

The Court upheld the Minnesota statute because the majority concluded that the economic emergency justified the state's use of extensive police powers. Does the Contract Clause retain any vitality under such an interpretation? Or did the *Home Building and Loan Association* decision render it virtually meaningless? After all, there would be little reason to pass such a statute in good economic times.

THE REVITALIZATION OF THE CONTRACT CLAUSE

For four decades following the Minnesota Mortgage Moratorium Act decision, parties challenging state laws rarely rested their arguments on the Contract Clause. It made little practical sense to do so when the justices were reluctant to use the provision to strike down state legislation designed to promote the economic welfare of the citizens. Litigants who attempted to invoke the clause usually were unsuccessful.

To conclude, however, that the Contract Clause had been erased from the Constitution effectively and forever would be incorrect. In the decades following

the New Deal, the Court was dominated by justices who took generally liberal positions on economic matters. They were philosophically opposed to allowing business interests to use the clause as a weapon to strike down legislation benefiting the people at large. But the Court's liberal majority began to unravel following the retirement of Chief Justice Warren and President Nixon's appointment of Warren Burger to replace him in 1969. As succeeding appointments brought more conservative and business-oriented justices to the Court, the prospects for a revitalized Contract Clause grew. This fact was not lost on enterprising lawyers, who began to consider raising Contract Clause issues once again.

Finally, in 1977 and 1978 the Court handed down two Contract Clause decisions: *United States Trust Co. v. New Jersey* and *Allied Structural Steel Co. v. Spannaus.* In both cases the justices struck down state legislation intended to promote the general welfare because the statutes were found to impair the obligation of contracts. Each time the Court's liberal justices voiced strong objections.

In *United States Trust v. New Jersey* (1977) the justices confronted a dispute stemming from an agreement for the financing of transportation systems. In 1921 the states of New York and New Jersey entered into a compact to establish the Port Authority of New York, a body responsible for developing and coordinating transportation and commerce. The Port Authority was financially independent, with funds primarily derived from private investors. It had the power to mortgage its facilities and to pledge its revenues as payment for bonds issued to its investors. In 1962, in response to increased interest in mass transit, the Port Authority took control of the financially ailing Hudson & Manhattan Railroad. As part of the acquisition, the states agreed that none of the authority's revenues pledged as security for existing bonds would be used for any additional railroad expenditures.

Between 1972 and 1974, with the nation in the midst of an energy crisis and under intense pressure to develop mass transit, New York and New Jersey moved to expand their system. Because money was difficult to raise, the states decided that they would use revenues previously pledged as security for existing bonds. To free such funds both state legislatures passed statutes in 1974 repealing retroactively their pledge not to use these moneys for increased mass transit expenditures. United States Trust Company, a holder of the affected bonds, sued to invalidate the repeal as an unconstitutional impairment of the obligation of contracts. The New Jersey courts ruled against the company on the grounds that the repeal was a proper exercise of state police powers.

The Supreme Court reversed by a 4–3 vote. The state had clearly abrogated a contractual obligation by repealing its pledge to the bondholders. In spite of decisions such as *Home Building and Loan Association,* it would be a mistake, the majority explained, to conclude that the Contract Clause was without meaning in modern constitutional jurisprudence. The Minnesota mortgage moratorium legislation had been a response to an unanticipated and extreme emergency which furnished the opportunity to exercise emergency powers. Although transportation and energy are significant national problems, they do not pose an immediate enough emergency to justify the total repeal of contractual obligations. Less extreme alternatives for financing mass transit could have been used. The retroactive repeal of the 1962 covenant violated the Contract Clause.

The legislation challenged in *United States Trust* was passed for the general welfare of the people of New York and New Jersey and in large measure was a response to a national energy crisis. These factors seemed similar to the conditions that had prompted the Court to approve the Minnesota Mortgage Moratorium Act. Therefore, many observers were surprised by the Court's resurrection of the Contract Clause, and there was considerable interest in what the case meant for the future. Although the decision used the Contract Clause to invalidate state laws, the opinion was a moderate one without the absolutist tones of the Marshall era. Did the Court's decision signal a change in policy or was it an aberration? How solid was this newly expressed support for the Contract Clause? After all, only seven justices participated in the decision, and the majority consisted of just four. Would the outcome have been different had the full Court voted? The justices provided some answers to these questions the very next year in *Allied Structural Steel Co. v. Spannaus* (1978).

The *Allied Steel* case involved complicated pension legislation. Although its principal place of business was Illinois, Allied Structural Steel Company maintained an office with thirty employees in Minnesota. In 1963 the company adopted a general pension plan, in which employees became vested after working the required number of years and reaching the specified age. Employees who quit or were terminated before meeting these requirements did not acquire pension rights. The company, which made annual payments to a pension trust fund, was the sole contributor to the plan. The company retained a virtually unrestricted right to modify the plan or to terminate it at any time.

On April 9, 1974, Minnesota enacted the Private Pension Benefits Protection Act. Under the provisions of that law, a company that terminated a pension plan or closed down its Minnesota operations would be subject to a charge to the extent that its retirement funds did not assure full pensions to all workers employed by the company for ten or more years. During the summer of 1974, Allied began closing its Minnesota office and discharged a number of its employees. Nine of the terminated workers had been with the company longer than ten years, but they did not qualify for a pension under Allied's plan. The state invoked the Private Pension Benefits Protection Act and assessed Allied $185,000 for the employees' pensions. Claiming that the Minnesota law impaired the obligation of its pension contract with its employees, Allied filed suit in federal district court against Warren

Spannaus, the state attorney general. The court ruled in favor of the state.

On appeal, the Supreme Court reversed. A six-justice majority held that the state had impaired the contractual obligations Allied had agreed to with its employees. Minnesota had not imposed modest changes on those obligations, but had severely changed the contractual arrangement in retroactive fashion. Furthermore, the state's action was not in response to an emergency remotely approaching the desperate economic conditions of the 1930s that justified the Minnesota mortgage legislation. The state had imposed a sudden, totally unanticipated financial liability on Allied Steel while entering an area in which it had not previously regulated. According to Justice Stewart's opinion for the Court, "If the Contract Clause means anything at all, it means that Minnesota could not constitutionally do what it tried to do to the company in this case."

Justice Stewart's opinion provides insight into the meaning of the Contract Clause in the contemporary era. First, although the Court invalidated the charges assessed against Allied Steel, the Court did not restore the Contract Clause to the prominence it had during the Marshall era. Second, the Contract Clause places some limits on the exercise of the state's police powers, but it does not obliterate those powers. Third, the Contract Clause applies to laws that either increase or decrease the duties of a party to a contract. Fourth, the clause is not limited to creditor-debtor contracts. Fifth, in applying the Contract Clause, the Court will first examine the extent of the impairment of contractual obligations, and "the severity of the impairment measures the height of the hurdle the state legislation must clear." If there has been substantial impairment of a contractual relationship, the Court will consider with care the nature and purpose of the legislation. In short, the majority assumed a position that balanced the importance of contractual relationships against the need of the state to exercise its police powers for the public welfare. Such a position neither returns the Contract Clause to the preferred position it enjoyed during the Marshall era nor substantially strips it of its meaning as occurred in later years.

In the years following *Allied Structural Steel* the Court has continued to take a moderate approach. In Stewart's terms, it has interpreted the Contract Clause not as a "dead letter," but also not applying it in an absolute "Draconian" fashion. The justices have generally expressed a sensitivity to the need of the states to use their police powers to combat social problems. For example, in *Energy Reserves Group, Inc. v. Kansas Power and Light Company* (1983) the justices unanimously upheld a Kansas act that dictated an energy pricing system in conflict with existing contracts. The Court held that the Contract Clause prohibits only state actions that "substantially impair the contractual arrangement." And even such substantial impairments can be justified if there is a significant and legitimate public purpose behind the regulation, such as remedying a broad and general social or economic problem.[5] In 1987 the justices upheld a Pennsylvania law that required coal mine operators to leave 50 percent of the coal in the ground beneath certain structures to provide surface support.[6] This provision was at odds with contracts between the mining companies and the landowners that allowed the companies to extract a much higher proportion of coal in the ground. The justices, however, upheld the right of the state, pursuant to its police powers, to impose such a regulation, explaining that the Contract Clause "is not to be read literally."

Decisions such as these have signaled potential litigants that successfully challenging state laws on Contract Clause grounds—although success is more likely today than it was in the years immediately following the New Deal—remains a difficult task. As a consequence, parties wishing to defend private property

5. See also *Exxon Corporation v. Eagerton* (1983).
6. *Keystone Bituminous Coal Association v. DeBenedictis* (1987).

rights against state regulation have begun to turn to other constitutional provisions. Most often, the Fifth Amendment Takings Clause has served as a vehicle for such challenges. This subject is addressed in Chapter 11.

READINGS

Ackerman, Bruce. *Private Property and the Constitution.* New Haven, Conn.: Yale University Press, 1977.

Dowd, Morgan D. "Justice Story, the Supreme Court, and the Obligation of Contract." *Case Western Reserve Law Review* 19 (1968): 493–527.

Hagin, Horace H. "Fletcher vs. Peck." *Georgetown Law Journal* 16 (November 1927): 1–40.

Horowitz, Morton J. *The Transformation of American Law, 1780–1860.* Cambridge, Mass.: Harvard University Press, 1977.

Hunting, Warren B. *The Obligation of Contracts Clause of the United States Constitution.* Baltimore: Johns Hopkins University Press, 1919.

Isaacs, Nathan. "John Marshall on Contracts: A Study in Early American Juristic Theory." *Virginia Law Review* 7 (March 1921): 413–428.

Magrath, C. Peter. *Yazoo: Law and Politics in the New Republic.* Providence, R.I.: Brown University Press, 1966.

Schwartz, Bernard. "Old Wine in New Bottles? The Renaissance of the Contract Clause." *Supreme Court Review* 1979 (1980): 95–121.

Stites, Francis N. *Private Interest and Public Gain: The Dartmouth College Case.* Amherst: University of Massachusetts Press, 1972.

Trimble, Bruce. "Chief Justice Waite and the Limitations on the Dartmouth College Decision." *University of Cincinnati Law Review* 9 (January 1935): 41–66.

Wright, Benjamin F. *The Contract Clause of the Constitution.* Cambridge, Mass.: Harvard University Press, 1938.

CHAPTER 10
ECONOMIC SUBSTANTIVE DUE PROCESS

SUPPOSE THAT FEDERAL and state agents receive a tip that the owners of a factory are violating the federal law that prohibits the employment of children younger than fourteen. Without stopping to obtain a warrant, the agents enter the factory and observe that underage employees are indeed working there. The agents arrest the owners, and a court convicts them. But the factory owners challenge their conviction on two similarly named but distinct grounds—procedural due process and substantive due process.

Citing the first ground, the factory owners allege that the procedure the agents used—entering the factory without a warrant—violated guarantees in the Constitution, including sections of the Fifth and Fourteenth Amendments that prohibit government from depriving persons of life, liberty, and property without due process of law. For many, the term *due process* is synonymous with fairness. The American system of justice is based on the idea that even people guilty of violating the law deserve fair treatment. What fair treatment means is often in dispute, but what is not in dispute is this particular characterization of due process. Known as *procedural due process*, it is the most traditional and widely accepted use of the term. Procedural due process suggests that governments must proceed in fair ways, but it does not bar their action

completely. If the government had proceeded fairly against the factory owners, their conviction was justified.

What is the second ground on which the factory owners base their appeal? None other than due process. Under this approach to the Due Process Clause, the owners argue that the law prohibiting the employment of minors violates due process guarantees because, in an unreasonable way, it takes away their "liberty," their right to do business. In their appeal, the owners say that due process implies something more than procedural fairness; they seek to inject into it some substantive meaning. In other words, in their view, the term not only covers the way government operates, but it also provides a concrete right that government cannot violate. Under this interpretation, often called *substantive due process*, the guarantee places a limit on government activity: it suggests, using the factory example, that the federal law cannot stand because it "is inherently unfair and unjust and therefore can never meet the requirement of due process of law. The substance of the law must be just and must not unfairly deny persons their life, liberty, or property."[1] *(See Box 10-1.)*

1. Sheldon Goldman, *Constitutional Law*, 2d ed. (New York: Harper-Collins, 1991), 378.

BOX 10-1 PROCEDURAL AND SUBSTANTIVE DUE PROCESS

THE U.S. CONSTITUTION contains two clauses—in the Fifth and Fourteenth Amendments—prohibiting the federal government and the states from depriving any person of life, liberty, or property without due process of law. When James Madison included the clause in the Fifth Amendment—part of the Bill of Rights—the meaning of the words "due process" was considered in its literal sense as guaranteeing only that government would follow fair and proper procedure in its dealings with private individuals. This became known in law as procedural due process—essentially a requirement that

Justice Stephen J. Field

those who were adversely affected by particular government action had to be given fair notice, as well as proper opportunity to be heard, before the government could take action against them. Observance of procedural due process, or fair procedure, was actually as old as Magna Carta, if not older. As an English judge noted in 1723: "Even God himself did not pass sentence upon Adam, before he [Adam] was called upon to make his defence. Adam [says God] where art thou? Has thou not eaten of the tree, whereof I commanded thee that thou shouldst not eat?"

In the years prior to the Civil War, state courts also began to interpret due process as a protection against arbitrary or unjust laws. In other words, even where the fairest procedure was followed, legislation could deprive a person of life, liberty, or property unless he were protected by limitations imposed by due process on the substance of that legislation. As Supreme Court Justice John Marshall Harlan defined this aspect of due process at a later time, substantive due process "includes a freedom from all substantial arbitrary impositions."

Since arbitrary action is synonymous with unreasonable action, due process requires a determination of reasonableness. Substantive due process thus allowed courts to decide on the reasonableness of challenged government action in relation to the ends which may be legitimately

furthered by government, a procedure that permitted judges to substitute their own opinions for those of legislatures on the question of what constituted reasonable government acts. This, in fact, is what occurred toward the close of the nineteenth century when the Supreme Court, at the urging of Justices Stephen J. Field and Joseph P. Bradley, adopted the substantive due process approach in its decisions. Particularly after the turn of the century, in cases following that of *Lochner v. New York* in 1905, the Court relied on its independent judgment to determine the reasonableness of challenged statutes. In those cases, the Court came close to exercising the functions of what dissenting Justice Louis D. Brandeis called a "superlegislature," setting itself up as virtual supreme censor of the wisdom of legislation.

Under the *Lochner* approach, substantive due process became the great instrument of judicially imposed laissez faire and was employed to invalidate a host of laws, particularly those seeking to regulate economic abuses. As the twentieth century went on, the justices themselves came to see that *Lochner* went too far and that due process was not intended to make them judges of the wisdom or desirability of government measures. Eventually, they adopted a view urged by Justice Oliver Wendell Holmes on the proper judicial role in due process cases. The Holmes test was whether a reasonable legislator—the legislative version of the "reasonable man"—could have adopted the law at issue. The legislative judgment might well be debatable. But that was the whole point about the Holmes approach. Under it, the courts left debatable issues, as respects business, economic, and social affairs, to legislative decision.

SOURCE: Bernard Schwartz, *The Law in America* (New York: McGraw-Hill, 1974), 137.

TABLE 10-1 The Legal Tools of the Laissez-Faire Courts, 1890s to 1930s: Some Examples

	1890–1899	1900–1909	1910–1919	1920–1929	1930–1939
Used to Strike State Laws					
Substantive Due Process	*Allgeyer v. Louisiana* (1897)	*Lochner v. New York* (1905)			*Morehead v. Tipaldo* (1936)
Used to Strike Federal Laws					
Delegation of Powers					*Panama Refining Co. v. Ryan* (1935)
					Schechter Poultry v. United States (1935)
Commerce Clause			*Hammer v. Dagenhart* (1918)		*Panama Refining Co. v. Ryan* (1935)
					Schechter Poultry v. United States (1935)
					Carter v. Carter Coal (1936)
Taxing and Spending				*Bailey v. Drexel Furniture* (1922)	*United States v. Butler* (1936)
Tenth Amendment			*Hammer v. Dagenhart* (1918)		

This chapter examines whether the substantive due process argument is a reasonable reading of the Due Process Clauses. We shall see that modern Supreme Courts, for the most part, have rejected substantive due process as it applies to laws governing economic relationships. However, for approximately forty years between the 1890s and the 1930s, the Court read due process in substantive terms and used the principle to strike down many laws that allegedly infringed on economic rights. In our hypothetical example, even if the agents had obtained a search warrant, these earlier Courts might have ruled in favor of the factory owners.

If economic substantive due process is now a discredited doctrine, why should we devote an entire chapter to it? There are several reasons. First, its rise in and fall from the Court's grace are an intriguing part of legal history. The adoption of substantive due

process came about gradually and resulted from the push and pull of the legal and political environment of the day. Second, looking at economic substantive due process provides us with an opportunity to revisit the concept of judicial activism. Today activism is most often associated with liberalism, with Courts that overturned restrictive government laws and practices, such as those requiring the segregation of public facilities or prohibiting seditious speech. But, as we pointed out in Chapter 1, activism does not always mean liberalism. Indeed, the Courts of the 1890s to 1930s were activist in overturning many laws, but that activism was conservative, not liberal.

Third, substantive due process is a way to reexamine the cycles of history we have already discussed. As depicted in Table 10-1, substantive due process was another weapon in the Court's laissez-faire arsenal. While it was using delegation of power doctrines

(Chapter 4), the Tenth Amendment (Chapter 6), the Commerce Clause (Chapter 7), and taxing and spending provisions (Chapter 8) to strike down federal regulations of business, the Court also invoked substantive due process to hold against similar legislation passed by the states. This use was particularly ironic because, at the time, the Court was espousing notions of dual federalism and invoking the Tenth Amendment. In other words, the Court found ways to strike down all sorts of economic regulation, even though, in so doing, it often took contradictory stances. Therefore, substantive due process provides a way to tie together much of what has been covered in this book.

Finally, the doctrine of substantive due process has relevance today, even if it no longer governs economic relationships. The Court continues to apply due process guarantees to noneconomic relations, legislation that allegedly infringes on privacy rights. Moreover, it always is possible that the Court will return to endorsing a laissez-faire philosophy. Should the justices be so inclined, they may find economic substantive due process or other constitutional provisions equally useful. We shall consider these issues at the end of the chapter, but first let us review substantive due process chronologically—how it developed, why the Court embraced it, and what led to its demise.

THE DEVELOPMENT OF SUBSTANTIVE DUE PROCESS

In general terms, prior to the adoption of the Fourteenth Amendment, judges interpreted due process guarantees contained in the Fifth Amendment and in state constitutions as procedural in intent and nature. Historian Kermit L. Hall wrote, "Before the Civil War [due process] had essentially one meaning," that people were "entitled" to fair and orderly proceedings, particularly criminal proceedings.[2]

There were some exceptions. Writing in *Scott v. Sandford*, (1857), Chief Justice Taney invoked the specter of due process to strike government interference in "property rights": "An act of Congress which deprives a citizen of the United States of his liberty or property [a slave], merely because he came himself or brought his property into a particular Territory . . . could hardly be dignified with the name of due process of law."

Around the same time, a New York court in *Wynehamer v. People* (1856) invoked a substantive interpretation of the state's due process requirement in striking down an alcohol prohibition law. It asserted that due process guarantees "prohibit, regardless of the matter of procedure, a certain kind or degree of exertion of legislative power altogether" and that the "substantive content of legislation" is covered, not simply the "mode of procedure."[3]

But decisions like *Wynehamer* represented the exception, not the rule. Neither state court judges interpreting their states' due process clauses nor their federal court counterparts treating the Fifth Amendment read the clauses to possess a substantive right and, therefore, to be a bar on interventionist government legislation. Rather, they viewed them through a procedural lens because it was not clear that due process clauses were meant to have substance. More to the point, some argue that the country needed the kinds of regulations that would be unlikely to survive substantive due process. As the United States changed from an agrarian to an industrial society, economic abuses called for limits. In Chapter 9 we saw that this perceived need provided one reason why the Contract Clause—as a mechanism for protecting economic interests—vanished from the legal scene.

---

2. Kermit L. Hall, *The Magic Mirror* (New York: Oxford University Press, 1989), 232.

3. See Gerald Gunther, *Constitutional Law* (Mineola, N.Y.: Foundation Press, 1991), 436.

Initial Interpretation of the Fourteenth Amendment's Due Process Clause

The federal and state governments' recognition of the need for limits on individual liberties, especially economic liberties, caused at least one sector of American life, business, intense displeasure. As the Court weakened its major source of protection—the Contract Clause—business was subjected to increasing regulation by the states, and these regulations decreased profits. Not surprisingly, business interests looked to other parts of the Constitution for protection.

As *The Slaughterhouse Cases* (1873) reveal, business thought it had found an answer in the newly ratified Fourteenth Amendment. The context for this litigation was the industrial revolution, an economic diversification that touched the entire country in the aftermath of the Civil War. While industrialization had many benefits, it also had some unpleasant side effects. For example, the Louisiana state legislature claimed that the Mississippi River had become polluted because New Orleans butchers dumped garbage into it. To remedy this problem (or, as some have suggested, to use it as an excuse to create a monopolistic enterprise), the legislature created a company—the Crescent City Live Stock Landing & Slaughter House Company—to receive and slaughter all city livestock for twenty-five years.

Because the butchers were forced to use the company facilities and to pay top dollar for the privilege, they formed their own organization, the Butchers' Benevolent Association, and hired an attorney, former U.S. Supreme Court justice John A. Campbell, to sue the corporation. In his arguments, Campbell sought to apply the Fourteenth Amendment to the butchers' cause. In general terms, he asserted that the amendment, although passed in the wake of the Civil War, was not meant solely to protect blacks. Rather, its language was broad enough to encompass all citizens. He used that point as a base from which to launch his more specific argument, that Louisiana's law deprived his clients of their right to pursue their business, a basic guarantee granted by the Fourteenth Amendment's Privileges and Immunities Clause:

No State shall make or enforce any law which shall abridge the privileges or immunities of citizens of the United States.

For good measure, he noted that the Louisiana law also violated the amendment's two other central guarantees, due process and equal protection:

[N]or shall any State deprive any person of life, liberty, or property, without *due process of law;* nor deny to any person within its jurisdiction the *equal protection* of the laws. (Emphasis added.)

Writing for the Court's majority, though, Justice Miller rejected all of these claims. He relied on history to confirm the true purpose of the Fourteenth Amendment—to protect blacks—and to refute Campbell's basic position. Miller focused his opinion on showing why the primary claim of privileges and immunities (truly weakening the clause) was inapplicable to the current dispute, but he also rejected the substantive Due Process Clause claim. As he asserted:

[I]t is sufficient to say that under no construction of that provision that we have ever seen, or any that we deem admissible, can the restraint imposed by the state of Louisiana upon the exercise of their trade by the butchers of New Orleans be held to be a deprivation of property within the meaning of that provision.

Why did he take such a hard-line position? In large measure, he did not want to see the Court become a "super legislature," a censor imposing its judgment on what state legislatures—composed of elected officials—could and could not do.

In dissenting opinions, Justices Bradley, Field, and Swayne took great issue with Miller's claims. Bradley, in particular, refuted the majority's position that the Due Process Clause was inapplicable to the extant dispute:

In my view, a law which prohibits a large class of citizens

from adopting a lawful employment, or from following a lawful employment previously adopted, does deprive them of liberty as well as property, without due process of law. Their right of choice is a portion of their liberty; their occupation is their property.

The Beginning of Substantive Due Process: The Court Opens a Window

Miller's opinion in *Slaughterhouse*, taken in conjunction with Bradley's (and Field's) dissent, are clear statements of the Court's initial rejection and acceptance of substantive due process. Indeed, the Miller and Bradley-Field opinions are considered to represent the distillation of opposing views on the subject *(see Box 10-1).*

It was Miller's view, however, that for the moment carried the day—there was no substance in due process. Given the definitive nature of his opinion, we might suspect that it closed the book on the subject forever. But that was not the case. Miller observed just five years later:

It is not a little remarkable, that while [due process] has been in the Constitution . . . as a restraint upon the authority of the Federal government, for nearly a century . . . its powers ha[ve] rarely been invoked in the judicial forum or the more enlarged theatre of public discussion. But while it has been a part of the Constitution, as a restraint upon the power of the States, only a very few years, the docket of this court is crowded with cases in which we are asked to hold that State courts and State legislatures have deprived their own citizens of life, liberty, or property without due process of law. There is here abundant evidence that there exists some strange misconception of the scope of this provision as found in the fourteenth amendment.[4]

Why was it necessary for Miller to write this? Had not *Slaughterhouse* eradicated the notion of the Fourteenth Amendment's Due Process Clause as a prohibition of state economic regulation?

It had, but that did not prevent attorneys, representing increasingly desperate business interests, from continuing to make substantive due process ar-

guments. From their perspective, the current environment held promise for the eventual adoption of such arguments. Within legal circles, for example, there was much discussion of several theories that lent themselves to Bradley's dissenting position in *Slaughterhouse.* One was expressed in Thomas M. Cooley's influential *Constitutional Limitations,* which singled out the word *liberty* within the Due Process Clause as an important constitutional right. The protection of this right, in Cooley's eyes, required a substantive reading of the Fourteenth Amendment, which, in turn, would serve as a mechanism for protecting property rights and for restricting government regulation. While Cooley's theory was specific, Herbert Spencer offered a more general view. Called social Darwinism, it treated social evolution in the same terms as Darwin wrote about biological evolution: "If left to themselves, the best of mankind, 'the fittest' would survive and prosper."[5] This proposition had a natural compatibility with laissez-faire economic theories: if government leaves business alone, the best will prosper. Applying substantive due process would persuade government to leave business alone.

But perhaps the most important factor contributing to the vitality of substantive due process was the Court. Social Darwinism may have influenced some scholars, the social elite, and business, but most Americans did not buy its tenets.[6] If they had, states would not have kept on trying to regulate businesses; the public would have demanded policies of noninterference. But they did continue. To a large extent, the crowded docket to which Miller referred was the Court's own doing.

An important, and certainly vivid, example of how the Court encouraged substantive due process arguments came in *Munn v. Illinois.* In this case, the Court considered an 1871 Illinois law that sought to regulate

---

4. *Davidson v. New Orleans* (1878).

5. Walter F. Murphy, James E. Fleming, and William F. Harris II, *American Constitutional Interpretation* (Mineola, N.Y.: Foundation Press, 1986), 942.
6. Ibid.

the grain storage industry, which had grown increasingly corrupt. The state justified the law as compatible with its constitution, which specified that public warehouses were subject to regulation. But companies forced to comply with the law disliked it and one challenged it as a violation of the Fourteenth Amendment's Due Process Clause.

In his opinion for the Court, Chief Justice Waite upheld the law and, in so doing, seemed to reject substantive due process completely, asserting that most regulatory legislation should be presumed valid. The decision, in fact, elicited an acrimonious dissent from Justice Field, which largely reflected Bradley's in *Slaughterhouse:* the law was "nothing less than a bold assertion of absolute power by the state to control at its discretion the property and business of the citizen." So it is not surprising that Waite's majority opinion "has generally been regarded as a great victory for liberalism and a judicial refusal to recognize due process as a limit on the substance of legislative regulatory power."[7]

But that description is not exactly accurate. Although Waite could have taken the same approach as Miller in *Slaughterhouse*—the complete rejection of the due process claim—he did not. Instead, Waite qualified his opinion, asserting first that state regulations of private property were "not supposed" to deprive owners of their right to due process, but that "under some circumstances they may." What differentiated "some circumstances" from others? In Waite's opinion, the answer lay in the nature of the subject of the regulation: "We find that when private property is 'affected with a public interest it ceases to be [of private right] only.'" Waite used this doctrine, often called the business-affected-with-a-public-interest doctrine (BAPI), to find against Munn's claim.

But isn't the doctrine also the source of a problem? Couldn't it be used to support the claim as well? Justice Field thought so, for in his dissent he found:

"There is hardly an enterprise or business engaging the attention and labor of any considerable portion of the community, in which the public has not an interest in the sense in which that term is used by the court." Waite's opinion (with Field's dissent) thus unwittingly provided the loophole that lawyers representing business clients who were unhappy with state regulation attempted to open even further. By avoiding a hard-line stance of the sort taken by Miller in *Slaughterhouse,* Waite's "maybe yes, maybe no" approach in the end provided some elbow room for the concept of substantive due process.[8]

In two cases, coming a decade or so after *Munn,* the Court moved closer to the concession only implied by Waite. In the first, *Mugler v. Kansas* (1887), the Court considered a state law that prohibited the manufacture and sale of liquor. Although the majority upheld the regulation against a substantive due process challenge, the Court's opinion represented something of a break from *Munn.* First, it articulated the view that not "every statute enacted ostensibly for the promotion of [the public interest] is to be accepted as a legitimate exertion of police powers of the state." This opinion was far more explicit than Waite's: there were clear limits of state regulatory power. Second, and more important, it took precisely the opposite position from the majority in *Slaughterhouse.* Recall that Justice Miller wanted to avoid having the Court be placed in the position of a "super legislature," scrutinizing and perhaps censoring state action. But in *Mugler,* that is precisely what the Court said it would do:

There are . . . limits beyond which legislation cannot rightfully go. . . . If, therefore, a statute purporting to have been enacted to protect the public health, the public morals, or the public safety, has no real or substantial relation to those objects, or is a palpable invasion of rights secured by the fundamental law, *it is the duty of the courts to so adjudge,* and thereby give effect to the Constitution. (Emphasis added.)

In *Mugler* the Court did not fully adopt the doctrine

7. C. Herman Pritchett, *The American Constitution* (New York: McGraw-Hill, 1959), 557.

8. See Goldman, *Constitutional Law,* 385.

of substantive due process; it even upheld the state regulation on liquor. Yet the Court established its intent to review legislation to determine whether a law was a "reasonable" exercise of state power. In essence, the Court would balance the interests of the state against those of individual due process guarantees—a course of action *Slaughterhouse* rejected.

The legislation tested in *Mugler* was deemed reasonable, but in *Chicago, Milwaukee & St. Paul Railway v. Minnesota* (1890), decided three years after *Mugler*, the Court went the other way: the justices struck down a state regulation on the grounds that it interfered with due process guarantees. At first glance, *Chicago, Milwaukee & St. Paul Railway* bears a distinct resemblance to *Munn v. Illinois*. Strong lobbying efforts by farm groups led Minnesota in 1887 to establish a commission to set "equal and reasonable" rates for railroad transportation of goods and for warehouse storage. The commission received a complaint that the Chicago, Milwaukee, and St. Paul Railway Company was charging dairy farmers unreasonable rates to ship their milk. It held hearings to investigate the claim and ruled against the railroad. When the company refused to abide by the ruling and reduce its rates, the commission went to the state supreme court. In the opinion of that tribunal, the commission's enabling legislation intended that the rates it "recommended and published" were to be "not simply advisory . . . but final and conclusive as to what are equal and reasonable charges." The railroad took its case to the U.S. Supreme Court, where it argued that the commission had interfered with "its property" without providing it with due process of law.

Writing for the majority, Justice Samuel Blatchford held for the railroad on two grounds, both centering on the Fourteenth Amendment's Due Process Clause. Procedurally, he found the law—at least as construed by the state supreme court—defective. Because courts could not review the rates the commission set, the law deprived the railroad of a certain degree of fairness. On this point, the Court took a "traditional"

approach to due process, asserting that "procedural safeguards" must be "attached to public expropriations of private property."[9] But Blatchford did not stop there; rather, he examined the law in terms of the reasonableness standard promulgated in *Mugler:*

The question of the reasonableness of a rate of charge for transportation by a railroad company . . . is eminently a question for judicial investigation, requiring due process of law for its determination.

Blatchford found the law deprived the company of its property in an unfair way:

If the company is deprived of the power of charging reasonable rates . . . and such deprivation takes place in the absence of an investigation by judicial machinery, it is deprived of the lawful use of its property, and thus, in substance and effect, of the property itself, without due process of law.

The *Chicago, Milwaukee & St. Paul Railway* case was not extraordinary: it merely applied the standard articulated in *Mugler*, a standard that obviously cut both ways. Sometimes the Court, in its attempt to inquire (balance interests), would find a law a "reasonable" use of state power (*Mugler*), and sometimes it would find that it violated substantive due process guarantees, as it did here. But this case and, to a lesser extent, *Mugler*, were remarkable if we consider how different they were from *Slaughterhouse*. Over a seventeen-year period, the Court had moved from a refusal to inject substance into due process to a near affirmation of the doctrine of substantive due process; it had moved from the assertion that it would not become a censor to one arguing that judicial inquiry was necessary, if not mandated, by the Constitution. And although, as we shall see, the Court did not fully endorse Thomas Cooley's position defining due process "liberty" in economic terms until seven years later, Blatchford's ruling laid the groundwork for exactly that.

This change in position prompts us to ask why the

9. Hall, *The Magic Mirror*, 236.

Court did such a turnabout over two decades. The most obvious answer is personnel changes. As Table 10-2 shows, by the time the Court decided *Mugler*, only one member of the *Slaughterhouse* majority, Miller, remained. By 1890 Miller also was gone, as was Chief Justice Waite, who, despite the loophole in the *Munn* opinion, generally favored state regulatory power. Their replacements were quite different. Some had been corporate attorneys schooled in the philosophies of Cooley and Spencer and quite willing to borrow from the briefs of their former colleagues who argued against state regulation. Justice David J. Brewer, who replaced Stanley Matthews (a moderate-conservative states' rights advocate), had refused to follow *Munn* as a court of appeals judge. It is not surprising that many eagerly awaited the *Chicago, Milwaukee & St. Paul Railway* decision as to see how membership changes might affect the direction of this area of the law.[10] Given the backgrounds of the new appointees, it also is not surprising to find that the views of the *Slaughterhouse* dissenters—especially field and Bradley—went on to rule the day.

But there may have been more to it. By asserting the standard they did, the Court was engaging in extreme judicial activism. Peter Woll wrote:

By substituting its judgment for that of state legislators in determining the fairness of regulations of property and liberty under the due process clause of the Fourteenth Amendment, the Court was acting contrary to the public opinion that spurred state regulation. Political pressures upon state legislatures throughout the country had resulted in laws regulating business which courts were unwilling to sustain.[11]

It seems fair to say that the justices did not see it this way. Rather, they viewed these "political pressures" as particularized, radical "socialistic" elements that did not reflect majority interests. If this was their

TABLE 10-2 The U.S. Supreme Court: From *Slaughterhouse* to *Mugler*

The *Slaughterhouse* Court (1873)	The Mugler *Court* (1887)
Chase[a]	Waite
Hunt	Blatchford
Clifford	Gray
Strong	Woods
Miller	Miller
Bradley[a]	Bradley
Swayne[a]	Matthews
Davis	Harlan
Field[a]	Field

a. In minority in *Slaughterhouse*.

perception, it had a solid foundation. Some legislation had resulted from the lobbying efforts of farm and labor movements and later, as we shall see, of the Progressives and New Dealers. In the minds of many conservatives of the day, including some of the justices, such pressures were illegitimate because they sought to subvert the free enterprise system. In short, while the Populists, Progressives, and New Dealers, in the opinion of conservatives, tried to put the brakes on businesses and inculcate the government with socialistic legislation, the conservatives strongly believed that the best interests of the country lay with "an utterly free market, unfettered by governmental regulation." This, not the plans of radicals, was "more just and socially useful" because in the end all would benefit financially.[12]

A fundamental change was in the wind, and many point to the Court's decision in *Allgeyer v. Louisiana* (1897) as the turning point. This case involved a Louisiana law that barred its citizens and corporations from doing business with out-of-state insurance companies, unless the companies complied with a specified set of requirements. State attorneys alleged

10. See Arnold M. Paul, *Conservative Crisis and the Rule of Law* (Ithaca, N.Y.: Cornell University Press, 1960), 42.

11. Peter Woll, *Constitutional Law* (Englewood Cliffs, N.J.: Prentice Hall, 1981), 486.

12. Craig R. Ducat and Harold W. Chase, *Constitutional Interpretation* (St. Paul, Minn.: West, 1988), 559.

that the Allgeyer Company had violated the law by maintaining an insurance policy with a New York mail order agency.

The state argued that the purpose of the law was to prevent fraud. But Allgeyer did not see it that way; it challenged the constitutionality of the law on Fourteenth Amendment due process grounds. In its view, the term *liberty* included the right to use and enjoy all "endowments" without constraint and that the term *property* included the right to acquire it and engage in business. Here, Allgeyer's attorney alleged, the law acts as a significant and unconstitutional curtailment of the business activity of the company.

In some ways, the opinion Justice Peckham wrote for the Court was not so different from the majority's opinion in *Chicago, Milwaukee & St. Paul Railway*. He struck down the state law in part on the grounds that it was not reasonable. But he went much further: He merged substantive due process with freedom of contract, by reading the term *liberty* to mean economic liberty, encompassing the right to "enter into all contracts." As he wrote:

Has not a citizen of a state, under the [Due Process Clause of the Fourteenth Amendment], a right to contract outside of the state for insurance on his property—a right of which state legislation cannot deprive him? We are not alluding to acts done within the state by an insurance company or its agents doing business therein, which are in violation of the state statutes . . . and would be controlled by it. When we speak of the liberty to contract for insurance or to do an act to effectuate such a contract already existing, we refer to and have in mind the facts of this case, where the contract was made outside the state, and as such was a valid and proper contract. The act done within the limits of the state under the circumstances of this case and for the purpose therein mentioned, we hold a proper act, one which the defendants were at liberty to perform and which the state legislature had no right to prevent, at least with reference to the Federal Constitution. To deprive the citizen of such a right as herein described without due process of law is illegal. Such a statute as this in question is not due process of law, because it prohibits an act which under the Federal Constitution the defendants had a right to perform. This

does not interfere in any way with the acknowledged right of the state to enact such legislation in the legitimate exercise of its police or other powers as to it may seem proper. In the exercise of such right, however, care must be taken not to infringe upon those other rights of the citizen which are protected by the Federal Constitution.

In other words, he adopted the position that businesses had been pressing since the demise of the Contract Clause as a source of protection. Now their right to do business, to set their own rates and enter into contracts with other businesses and perhaps even with employees, had the highest level of legal protection. In just under twenty-five years, business interests had pushed the Court from *Slaughterhouse*, in which it refused to review state legislation for its compatibility with due process guarantees, to *Munn*, in which legislation was presumed valid generally, but was open to judicial inquiry into its "reasonableness." The Court then moved from a balancing of state versus individual interests (*Chicago, Milwaukee & St. Paul Railway*) to placing state regulations in a less exalted position than the fundamental liberty of contract (*Allgeyer*).

THE ROLLER COASTER RIDE OF SUBSTANTIVE DUE PROCESS: 1898–1923

However explicit *Allgeyer* was, the true test of its importance would come in its application. Some read the decision to mean that the Court would not uphold legislation that infringed on economic "liberty," but *Holden v. Hardy*, decided the very next year, dispelled this notion. In this case, the Court examined a Utah law prohibiting companies engaged in the excavation of mines from working their employees more than eight hours a day, except in emergency situations. Attorneys challenging the law claimed that

[i]t is . . . not within the power of the legislature to prevent persons who are . . . perfectly competent to contract, from

After Joseph Lochner, the owner of a bakery located in Utica, New York, was convicted of violating a state maximum hour work law, he asked the U.S. Supreme Court to strike it down as violative of his constitutional rights. In *Lochner v. New York* (1905), the justices agreed. The majority found that the law impermissibly interfered with the right of employers to enter into contracts with their employees.

entering into employment and voluntarily making contracts in relation thereto merely because the employment . . . may be considered by the legislature to be dangerous or injurious to the health of the employee; and if such right to contract cannot be prevented, it certainly cannot be restricted by the legislature to suit its own ideas of the ability of the employee to stand the physical and mental strain incident to the work.

The state asserted that the challenged statute was a "health regulation" and within the state's power because it was aimed at "preserving to a citizen his ability to work and support himself."

In *Holden* the Court reiterated its *Mugler* position: "The question in each case is whether the legislature has adopted the statute in exercise of a reasonable discretion or whether its actions be a mere excuse for an unjust discrimination." The Supreme Court, now acting as the nation's "super legislature," deemed the legislation "reasonable"; that is, it did not impinge on the liberty of contract because the state had well justified

its interest protecting the unique health problems caused by working in mines.

Holden was a victory for emerging labor groups and the still-forming Progressive movement, which were vigorously lobbying state legislatures to pass laws protecting workers. As the industrial revolution wore on, they argued, such laws were becoming increasingly important because corporations were even more profit-oriented and, as a result, more likely to exploit employees. While they succeeded in convincing many state legislatures to enact laws like Utah's, the possibility that courts would strike them down remained a threat. *Holden* had proven otherwise.

That ruling, however, took on a different gloss once the Court decided *Lochner v. New York* (1905). Although the law at issue varied only slightly from Utah's, the justices reached a wholly different conclusion. Why? Does the case fit compatibly with the logic of *Holden*, as Justice Peckham implies, or does it reveal the true reach of his ruling in *Allgeyer?*

Lochner v. New York

198 U.S. 45 (1905)

Vote: 5 *(Brewer, Brown, Fuller, McKenna, Peckham)*
    4 *(Day, Harlan, Holmes, White)*

Opinion of the Court: Peckham

Dissenting opinions: Harlan, Holmes

In 1897 New York enacted a law that limited employees of bakeries to no more than ten hours per day and sixty hours per week of work. The state justified the law on the following grounds:

1. Police power is necessarily invoked to control work conditions in a "great commercial and manufacturing State" like New York. The police power here reflects community standards and is properly exercised by an elected body that is aware of unique local conditions.

2. New York, through its use of the police power, protects both consumers and workers from bad health and sickness; therefore, this law is a health measure.

After he was convicted of violating the law, Joseph Lochner, the owner of a New York bakery, challenged it on Fourteenth Amendment due process grounds. In part, he alleged that

1. Employees and employer have the right to agree upon hours and wages, and the use of the police power by New York to interfere with such agreements is so "paternal" as to violate the Fourteenth Amendment.

2. Regardless of the state's asserted interests, the "most cherished rights of American citizenship"— freedom of contract and property rights—"should be most closely and jealously scrutinized by this court." Since the interests here are not sufficiently "clear and apparent," the Court should strike the law.

MR. JUSTICE PECKHAM . . . delivered the opinion of the court.

The mandate of the statute, that "no employee shall be required or permitted to work," is the substantial equivalent of an enactment that "no employee shall contract or agree to work," more than ten hours per day; and, as there is no provision for special emergencies, the statute is mandatory in all cases. It is not an act merely fixing the number of hours which shall constitute a legal day's work, but an absolute prohibition upon the employer permitting, under any circumstances, more than ten hours' work to be done in his establishment. The employee may desire to earn the extra money which would arise from his working more than the prescribed time, but this statute forbids the employer from permitting the employee to earn it.

The statute necessarily interferes with the right of contract between the employer and employees, concerning the number of hours in which the latter may labor in the bakery of the employer. The general right to make a contract in relation to his business is part of the liberty of the individual protected by the 14th Amendment of the Federal Constitution. *Allgeyer v. Louisiana.* Under that provision no state can deprive any person of life, liberty, or property without due process of law. The right to purchase or to sell labor is part of the liberty protected by this amendment, unless there are circumstances which exclude the right. There are, however, certain powers, existing in the sovereignty of each state in the Union, somewhat vaguely termed police powers, the exact description and limitation of which have not been attempted by the courts. Those powers, broadly stated, and without, at present, any attempt at a more specific limitation, relate to the safety, health, morals, and general welfare of the public. Both property and liberty are held on such reasonable conditions as may be imposed by the governing power of the state in the exercise of those powers, and with such conditions the 14th Amendment was not designed to interfere.

The state, therefore, has power to prevent the individual from making certain kinds of contracts, and in regard to them the Federal Constitution offers no protection. If the contract be one which the state, in the legitimate exercise of its police power, has the right to prohibit, it is not prevented from prohibiting it by the 14th Amendment. Contracts in violation of a statute, either of the Federal or state government, or a contract to let one's property for immoral purposes, or to do any other unlawful act, could obtain no protection from the Federal Constitution, as coming under the liberty of person or of free contract. Therefore, when the state, by its legislature, in the assumed exercise of its police powers, has passed an act which seriously limits the right to labor or the right of contract in regard to their means of livelihood between persons who are *sui juris* (both employer and employee), it becomes of great importance to determine which shall prevail,—the right of the individual to labor for such time as he may choose, or the right of the state to prevent the individual from laboring, or from entering into any contract to labor, beyond a certain time prescribed by the state.

This court has recognized the existence and upheld the exercise of the police powers of the states in many cases which might fairly be considered as border ones, and it has, in the course of its determination of questions regarding the asserted invalidity of such statutes, on the ground of their violation of the rights secured by the Federal Constitution, been guided by rules of a very liberal nature, the application of which has resulted, in numerous instances, in upholding the validity of state statutes thus assailed. Among the later cases where the state law has been upheld by this court is that of *Holden v. Hardy*. A provision in the act of the legislature of Utah was there under consideration, the act limiting the employment of workmen in all underground mines or workings, to eight hours per day, "except in cases of emergency, where life or property is in imminent danger." It also limited the hours of labor in smelting and other institutions for the reduction or refining of ores or metals to eight hours per day, except in like cases of emergency. The act was held to be a valid exercise of the police powers of the state . . . [because the] law applies only to the classes subjected by their employment to the peculiar conditions and effects attending underground mining and work in smelters, and other works for the reduction and refining of ores. Therefore it is not necessary to discuss or decide whether the legislature can fix the hours of labor in other employments. . . .

It must, of course, be conceded that there is a limit to the valid exercise of the police power by the state. There is no dispute concerning this general proposition. Otherwise the 14th Amendment would have no efficacy and the legislatures of the states would have unbounded power, and it would be enough to say that any piece of legislation was enacted to conserve the morals, the health, or the safety of the people; such legislation would be valid, no matter how absolutely without foundation the claim might be. The claim of the police power would be a mere pretext,—become another and delusive name for the supreme sovereignty of the state to be exercised free from constitutional restraint. This is not contended for. In every case that comes before this court, therefore, where legislation of this character is concerned, and where the protection of the Federal Constitution is sought, the question necessarily arises: Is this a fair, reasonable, and appropriate exercise of the police power of the state, or is it an unreasonable, unnecessary, and arbitrary interference with the right of the individual to his personal liberty, or to enter into those contracts in relation to labor which may seem to him appropriate or necessary for the support of himself and his family? Of course the liberty of contract relating to labor includes both parties to it. The one has as much right to purchase as the other to sell labor.

This is not a question of substituting the judgment of the court for that of the legislature. If the act be within the power of the state it is valid, although the judgment of the court might be totally opposed to the enactment of such a law. But the question would still remain: Is it within the police power of the state? and that question must be answered by the court.

The question whether this act is valid as a labor law, pure and simple, may be dismissed in a few words. There is no reasonable ground for interfering with the liberty of person or the right of free contract, by determining the hours of labor, in the occupation of a baker. There is no contention that bakers as a class are not equal in intelligence and capacity to men in other trades or manual occupations, or that they are not able to assert their rights and care for themselves without the protecting arm of the state, interfering with their independence of judgment and of action. They are in no sense wards of the state. Viewed in the light of a purely labor law, with no reference whatever to the question of health, we think that a law like the one before us involves neither the safety, the morals, nor the welfare, of the public, and that the interest of the public is not in the slightest degree affected by such an act. The law must be upheld, if at all, as a law pertaining to the health of the individual engaged in the occupation of a baker. It does not affect any other portion of the public than those who are engaged in that occupation. Clean and wholesome bread does not depend upon whether the baker works but ten hours per day or only sixty hours a week. The limitation of the hours of labor does not come within the police power on that ground.

It is a question of which of two powers or rights shall prevail,—the power of the state to legislate or the right of the individual to liberty of person and freedom of contract. The mere assertion that the subject relates, though but in a remote degree, to the public health, does not necessarily render the enactment valid. The act must have a more direct relation, as a means to an end, and the end itself must be appropriate and legitimate, before an act can be held to be valid which interferes with the general right of an individual to be free in his person and in his power to contract in relation to his own labor. . . .

We think the limit of the police power has been reached and passed in this case. There is, in our judgment, no reasonable foundation for holding this to be necessary or appropriate as a health law to safeguard the public health, or the health of the individuals who are following the trade of a baker. If this statute be valid, and if, therefore, a proper case is made out in which to deny the right of an individual, *sui juris,* as employer or employee, to make contracts for the labor of the latter under the protection of the provisions of the Federal Constitution, there would seem to be no length to which legislation of this nature might not go. The case differs widely, as we have already stated, from the expressions of this court in regard to laws of this nature, as stated in *Holden v. Hardy.* . . .

We think that there can be no fair doubt that the trade of a baker, in and of itself, is not an unhealthy one to that degree which would authorize the legislature to interfere with the right to labor, and with the right of free contract on the part of the individual, either as employer or employee. In looking through statistics regarding all trades and occupations, it may be true that the trade of a baker does not appear to be as healthy as some other trades, and is also vastly more healthy than still others. To the common understanding the trade of a baker has never been regarded as an unhealthy one. Very likely physicians would not recommend the exercise of that or of any other trade as a remedy for ill health. Some occupations are more healthy than others, but we think there are none which might not come under the power of the legislature to supervise and control the hours of working therein, if the mere fact that the occupation is not absolutely and perfectly healthy is to confer that right upon the legislative department of the government. It might be safely affirmed that almost all occupations more or less affect the health. There must be more than the mere fact of the possible existence of some small amount of unhealthiness to warrant legislative interference with liberty. It is unfortunately true that labor, even in any department, may possibly carry with it the seeds of unhealthiness. But are we all, on that account, at the mercy of legislative majorities? A printer, a tinsmith, a locksmith, a carpenter, a cabinetmaker, a dry goods clerk, a bank's, a lawyer's, or a physician's clerk, or a clerk in almost any kind of business, would all come under the power of the legislature, on this assumption. No trade, no occupation, no mode of earning one's living, could escape this all-pervading power, and the acts of the legislature in limiting the hours of labor in all employments would be valid, although such limitation might seriously cripple the ability of the laborer to support himself and his family. In our large cities there are many buildings into which the sun penetrates for but a short time in each day, and these buildings are occupied by people carrying on the business of bankers, brokers, lawyers, real estate, and many other kinds of business, aided by many clerks, messengers, and other employees. Upon the assumption of the validity of this act under review, it is not possible to say that an act, prohibiting lawyers' or bank clerks, or others, from contracting to labor for their employers more than eight hours a day would be invalid. It might be said that it is unhealthy to work more than that number of hours in an apartment lighted by artificial light during the working hours of the day; that the occupation of the bank clerk, the lawyer's clerk, the real-estate clerk, or the broker's clerk, in such offices is therefore unhealthy, and the legislature, in its paternal wisdom, must, therefore, have the right to legislate on the subject of, and to limit, the hours for such labor; and, if it exercises that power, and its validity be questioned, it is sufficient to say, it has reference to the public health; it has reference to the health of the employees condemned to labor day after day in buildings where the sun never shines; it is a health law, and therefore it is valid, and cannot be questioned by the courts.

It is also urged, pursuing the same line of argument, that it is to the interest of the state that its population should be strong and robust, and therefore any legislation which may be said to tend to make people healthy must be valid as health laws, enacted under the police power. If this be a valid argument and a justification for this kind of legislation, it follows that the protection of the Federal Constitution from undue interference with liberty of person and freedom of contract is visionary, wherever the law is sought to be justified as a valid exercise of the police power. Scarcely any law but might find shelter under such assumptions, and conduct, properly so called, as well as contract, would come under the restrictive sway of the legislature. Not only the hours of employees, but the hours of employers, could be regulated, and doctors, lawyers, scientists, all professional men, as well as athletes and artisans, could be forbidden to fatigue their brains and bodies by prolonged hours of exercise, lest the fighting strength of the state be impaired. We mention these extreme cases because the contention is extreme. We do not believe in the soundness of the views which uphold this law. On the contrary, we think that such a law as this, although passed in the assumed exercise of the police power, and as relating to the public health, or the health of the employees named, is not within that power, and is invalid. The act is not, within any fair meaning of the term, a health law, but is an illegal interference with the rights of individuals, both employers and employees, to make contracts regarding labor upon such terms as they may think best, or which they may agree upon with the other parties to such contracts. Statutes of the nature of that under review, limiting the hours in which grown and intelligent men may labor to earn their living, are mere meddlesome interferences with the rights of the individual and they are not saved from condemnation by the claim that they are passed in the exercise of the police power and upon the subject of the health of the individual whose rights are interfered with, unless there be some fair ground, reasonable in and of itself, to say that there is material danger to the public health, or to the health of the employees, if the hours of labor are not curtailed. If this be not clearly the case, the individuals whose rights are thus made

the subject of legislative interference are under the protection of the Federal Constitution regarding their liberty of contract as well as of person; and the legislature of the state has no power to limit their right as proposed in this statute. All that it could properly do has been done by it with regard to the conduct of bakeries, as provided for in the other sections of the act, above set forth. These several sections provide for the inspection of the premises where the bakery is carried on, with regard to furnishing proper wash rooms and watercloset, apart from the bake room, also with regard to providing proper drainage, plumbing, and painting; the sections, in addition, provide for the height of the ceiling, the cementing or tiling of floors, where necessary in the opinion of the factory inspector, and for other things of that nature; alterations are also provided for and are to be made where necessary in the opinion of the inspector, in order to comply with the provisions of the statute. These various sections may be wise and valid regulations, and they certainly go to the full extent of providing for the cleanliness and the healthiness, so far as possible, of the quarters in which bakeries are to be conducted. Adding to all these requirements a prohibition to enter into any contract of labor in a bakery for more than a certain number of hours a week is, in our judgment, so wholly beside the matter of a proper, reasonable, and fair provision as to run counter to that liberty of person and of free contract provided for in the Federal Constitution.

It was further urged on the argument that restricting the hours of labor in the case of bakers was valid because it tended to cleanliness on the part of the workers, as a man was more apt to be cleanly when not overworked, and if cleanly then his "output" was also more likely to be so. What has already been said applies with equal force to this contention. We do not admit the reasoning to be sufficient to justify the claimed right of such interference. The state in that case would assume the position of a supervisor, or pater familias, over every act of the individual, and its right of governmental interference with his hours of labor, his hours of exercise, the character thereof, and the extent to which it shall be carried would be recognized and upheld. In our judgment it is not possible in fact to discover the connection between the number of hours a baker may work in the bakery and the healthful quality of the bread made by the workman. The connection, if any exist, is too shadowy and thin to build any argument for the interference of the legislature. If the man works ten hours a day it is all right, but if ten and a half or eleven his health is in danger and his bread may be unhealthy, and, therefore, he shall not be permitted to do it. This, we think, is unreasonable and entirely arbitrary. When assertions such as we have adverted to become necessary in order to give, if possible, a plausible foundation for the contention that the law is a "health law," it gives rise to at least a suspicion that there was some other motive dominating the legislature than the purpose to subserve the public health or welfare.

This interference on the part of the legislatures of the several states with the ordinary trades and occupations of the people seems to be on the increase. . . .

It is impossible for us to shut our eyes to the fact that many of the laws of this character, while passed under what is claimed to be the police power for the purpose of protecting the public health or welfare, are, in reality, passed from other motives. We are justified in saying so when, from the character of the law and the subject upon which it legislates, it is apparent that the public health or welfare bears but the most remote relation to the law. The purpose of a statute must be determined from the natural and legal effect of the language employed; and whether it is or is not repugnant to the Constitution of the United States must be determined from the natural effect of such statutes when put into operation, and not from their proclaimed purpose.

It is manifest to us that the limitation of the hours of labor provided for in this section of the statute under which the indictment was found, and the plaintiff in error convicted, has no such direct relation to, and no such substantial effect upon, the health of the employee, as to justify us in regarding the section as really a health law. It seems to us that the real object and purpose were simply to regulate the hours of labor between the master and his employees (all being men, sui juris), in a private business, not dangerous in any degree to morals, or in any real and substantial degree to the health of the employees. Under such circumstances the freedom of master and employee to contract with each other in relation to their employment, and in defining the same, cannot be prohibited or interfered with, without violating the Federal Constitution.

The judgment of the Court of Appeals of New York, as well as that of the Supreme Court and the County Court of Oneida County, must be reversed and the case remanded to the County Court for further proceedings not inconsistent with this opinion.

Reversed.

MR. JUSTICE HOLMES dissenting.

This case is decided upon an economic theory which a large part of the country does not entertain. If it were a question whether I agreed with that theory I should desire to study it further and long before making up my mind. But I do not conceive that to be my duty, because I strongly believe that my agreement or disagreement has nothing to do with the right of a majority to embody their opinions in law. It is settled by various decisions of this court that state constitutions and state laws may regulate life in many ways which we as legislators might think as injudicious or if you like as tyrannical as this, and which equally with this interfere with the liberty to contract. Sunday laws and usury laws are ancient examples. A more modern one is the prohibition of lotteries. The liberty of the citizen to do as he likes so long as he does not interfere with the liberty of others to do the same, which has been a shibboleth for some well-known writers, is interfered with by school laws, by the Post Office, by every state or municipal institution which takes his money for purposes thought desirable, whether he likes it or not. The Fourteenth Amendment does not enact Mr. Herbert Spencer's Social Statics. . . . United States and state statutes and decisions cutting down the liberty to contract by way of combination are familiar to this court. Two years ago we upheld the prohibition of sales of stock on margins or for future delivery in the constitution of California. *Otis v. Parker.* The decision sustaining an eight hour law for miners is still recent. *Holden v. Hardy.* Some of these laws embody convictions or prejudices which judges are likely to share. Some may not. But a constitution is not intended to embody a particular economic theory, whether of paternalism and the organic relation of the citizen to the State or of *laissez faire.* It is made for people of fundamentally differing views, and the accident of our finding certain opinions natural and familiar or novel and even shocking ought not to conclude our judgment upon the question whether statutes embodying them conflict with the Constitution of the United States.

General propositions do not decide concrete cases. The

decision will depend on a judgment or intuition more subtle than any articulate major premise. But I think that the proposition just stated, if it is accepted, will carry us far toward the end. Every opinion tends to become a law. I think that the word liberty in the Fourteenth Amendment is perverted when it is held to prevent the natural outcome of a dominant opinion, unless it can be said that a rational and fair man necessarily would admit that the statute proposed would infringe fundamental principles as they have been understood by the traditions of our people and our law. It does not need research to show that no such sweeping condemnation can be passed upon the statute before us. A reasonable man might think it a proper measure on the score of health. Men whom I certainly could not pronounce unreasonable would uphold it as a first instalment of a general regulation of the hours of work. Whether in the latter aspect it would be open to the charge of inequality I think it unnecessary to discuss.

Many scholars have called *Lochner* the Court's strongest expression of economic substantive due process. Although the Court said the question to be asked in this case is the same one it had been addressing since *Mugler*—Is the law a fair, reasonable, and appropriate exercise of police power?—its answer is quite different. By distinguishing *Holden* to the point of nonexistence and by narrowing the scope of reasonable state regulations, the Court moved away from a strict "reasonableness" approach to one that reflected *Allgeyer*: an employer's right "to make a contract" with employees is virtually sacrosanct.

That the Court, although divided 5–4, accomplished this feat not by changing the legal question but by changing the answer creates something of a puzzle, particularly with regard to the immediate subject of the dispute—maximum work hours. Think about it this way: the Court upheld the Utah law at issue in *Holden* on the grounds that the "kind of employment . . . and the character of the employees . . . were such as to make [the state law] reasonable and proper"; it struck the *Lochner* law because bakers can

"care for themselves" (despite evidence to the contrary) and that the production of "clean and wholesome bread" is not affected. Was this distinction significant? Or was it merely a way to mask what the Court wanted to do: narrow the grounds on which states could reasonably regulate and, thereby, strike protective legislation as a violation of the right to contract? Justice Holmes's dissent certainly implies the latter. He goes so far as to accuse the Court of using the Fourteenth Amendment to "enact Mr. Herbert Spencer's Social Statics." While many scholars agree with Holmes's assessment and argue that the justices in the *Lochner* majority were "motivated by their own policy preferences favoring laissez-faire economics and Social Darwinism,"[13] other analysts present a somewhat different picture.[14] They suggest that the Court was seeking to remain faithful to "a long-standing constitutional ideology that distinguished between valid economic regulation and invalid 'class,' or factional legislation."[15] In other words, *Lochner* represented a "principled effort" on the part of the justices to keep this area of the law consistent and coherent, and not merely a statement of their ideological predilections.

Regardless of who is right, these issues moved to the fore in *Muller v. Oregon* (1908). This case began when the state of Oregon brought charges against Curt Muller for working his female laundry workers longer than the state maximum of ten hours per day. Once convicted, Muller decided to challenge the law. In the view of his attorneys, Oregon's regulation, which prohibited the employment of women, but not men, in laundries for more than ten hours a day, violated his right to enter into a contract with his employees.

Recognizing that, in light of *Lochner*, Muller's argu-

13. C. Ian Anderson, "Courts and the Constitution," *Michigan Law Review* 92 (1994): 1438.

14. See, especially, Howard Gillman, *The Constitution Besieged: The Rise and Demise of Lochner Era Police Powers Jurisprudence* (Durham, N.C.: Duke University Press, 1993).

15. Anderson, "Courts and the Constitution," 1439.

BOX 10-2   LOUIS DEMBITZ BRANDEIS (1916–1939)

LOUIS DEMBITZ BRANDEIS, born November 13, 1856, in Louisville, Kentucky, was the son of Adolph and Fredericka Dembitz Brandeis, Jews who had emigrated from Bohemia after the unsuccessful democratic revolts of 1848. His father was a prosperous grain merchant who provided his family with comfort, education, and culture. Having completed two years of preparatory studies at the Annen-Realschule in Dresden, but without a college degree, Brandeis enrolled at Harvard Law School when he was eighteen years of age. He graduated in 1877 with the highest average in the law school's history. After eight months practicing law in St. Louis, Brandeis returned to Cambridge—for him "the world's center"—and with Bostonian Samuel D. Warren, Jr., second in their law school class, opened a one-room office downtown.

Warren and Brandeis and the successor firm Brandeis, Dunbar, and Nutter handled a variety of cases and were highly successful. By the time he was thirty-five, Brandeis was earning more than $50,000 a year. He married Alice Goldmark of New York, March 23, 1891, and the couple had two daughters. Despite his earnings, the family preferred to live simply, setting a ceiling on their personal expenditures of $10,000 a year. As a young lawyer Brandeis devoted many hours to his alma mater. He helped raise funds for a teaching post for Oliver Wendell Holmes, Jr., and was one of the founders of the *Harvard Law Review.*

The turn of the century marked the rapid growth in America of corporate monopolies—the "curse of bigness," as Brandeis described it. He chose to protect the rights not of special interest groups but of the general public, and usually without a fee for his services. Brandeis initiated sliding scale gas rates in Boston that lowered consumer costs while raising corporate dividends, and he instituted savings bank insurance policies, another reform later implemented in the rest of the country. He defended municipal control of Boston's subway system and opposed the monopolistic practices of the New Haven Railroad. He arbitrated labor disputes in New York's garment industry, serving as chairman of an arbitration board from 1910 to 1916, and established the constitutionality of state maximum hour and minimum wage statutes. For thirty-seven years Brandeis devoted his time, energy, and talents to a host of public causes. He called himself an "attorney for the situation," but the press adopted the popular title "people's attorney."

President Wilson respected Brandeis and often sought his opinion. He nominated him associate justice of the Supreme Court January 28, 1916, to fill the vacancy left by Justice Joseph R. Lamar's death. Vicious opposition to his appointment ensued. One particularly vituperative critic described Brandeis as a "business-baiter, stirrer up of strife, litigious lover of hate and unrest, destroyer of confidence, killer of values, commercial coyote, spoiler of pay envelopes."

Factory owners paying higher wages, New Haven Railroad stockholders, moguls in the Boston transit system, insurance and gas industries—in short, all the losers in court—united to voice their objections to the appointment. Among those seeking satisfaction for past injuries was William Howard Taft. His administration had been embarrassed by an investigation led in part by Brandeis of the conservation practices of Secretary of the Interior Richard A. Ballinger.

The former president, ambitious for a justiceship himself, described the nomination as "one of the deepest wounds that I have had as an American and a lover of the Constitution" and spoke of the "indelible stain" on the Wilson administration that confirmation would bring.

Another critic, Clarence W. Barron, editor and publisher of the *Wall Street Journal*, also felt the choice was unwise: "There is only one redeeming feature in the nomination and that is that it will assist to bury Mr. Wilson in the next Presidential election." The president viewed the political climate differently. He believed Brandeis was a smart choice who would attract the needed Progressive vote. Wilson could not count on a divided Republican party to ensure his re-election.

During four months of acrimonious debate over his appointment, Brandeis quietly pursued his legal practice. He went to the office every day and did not resort to personal attacks against his opponents. "Your attitude while the wolves yelp is sublime," his young nephew wrote.

The hearings in the Senate Judiciary Committee turned up no valid grounds for rejection. According to Senator Thomas J. Walsh, Brandeis's only "real crime" was that "he had not stood in awe of the majesty of wealth." One of his supporters from the Harvard Law School, Arthur Hill, attributed the opposition to the fact that "Mr. Brandeis is an outsider, successful and a Jew."

Brandeis was confirmed by the Senate on June 1, 1916, by a vote of 47–22, becoming the first Jewish justice.

On February 13, 1939, Brandeis, aged eighty-two, resigned from the Court but not from public service. After twenty-two years on the bench, he devoted the last years of his life to the Zionist movement and a boycott of German products. As the *New York Times* noted upon his retirement in 1939, "the storm against him . . . seems almost incredible now." He died October 5, 1941, in Washington, D.C.

SOURCE: Elder Witt, *Guide to the U.S. Supreme Court*, 2d ed. (Washington, D.C.: Congressional Quarterly, 1990), 852–853.

ment rested on strong legal grounds, the National Consumers' League (NCL)—a group that had pressed states to pass maximum hour legislation—grew concerned. The organization was reluctant to see its hard work to attain passage of the Oregon law nullified by the Supreme Court. To defend the law, the NCL contacted Louis Brandeis, a well-known attorney of the day and a future U.S. Supreme Court justice *(see Box 10-2)*.

Because of the decision in *Lochner* and the stability of the Court's membership, Brandeis decided that bold action was necessary. Instead of filling his brief with legal arguments, he would provide the Court with "*facts,* published by anyone with expert knowledge of industry in its relation to women's hours of labor," which indicated the evils of Muller's actions. In particular, the brief pointed out that forcing women to work long hours affected their health and their reproductive systems.[16] In the end, with the help of the NCL, Brandeis produced an incredible document. Known in legal history as the Brandeis Brief, it contained 113 pages of sociological data and only 2 pages of legal argument.

To the surprise of some, the justices ruled in the NCL's favor. Why, given *Lochner,* did the Court affirm the Oregon law? One answer is that, in its opinion, the Court did not depart from *Lochner:* it merely found that Oregon's regulations, unlike New York's, were a reasonable use of the state's power. But the Court applied the reasonableness approach in both *Lochner* and *Holden* and came to completely different conclusions. So, despite the Court's attempt to distinguish *Lochner,* how much can the application of that standard possibly explain about *Muller's* outcome? Another possibility is that Brandeis forced the Court to see the reasonableness of the Oregon regulation. By presenting such a mass of statistical data, he kept the justices riveted on the law and diverted their attention from a substantive due process approach. The strate-

16. Clement E. Vose, *Constitutional Change* (Lexington, Mass.: Lexington Books, 1972), 172.

gy worked: the justices even commended the Brandeis Brief. Finally, *Muller* was different from *Lochner* in at least one important way: the law applied solely to women. This was a point stressed by Brandeis and by the Court. As the majority opinion put it:

That woman's physical structure and the performance of maternal functions place her at a disadvantage in the struggle for subsistence is obvious. This is especially true when the burdens of motherhood are upon her. Even when they are not, by abundant testimony of the medical fraternity continuance for a long time on her feet at work, repeating this from day to day, tends to injurious effects upon the body, and, as healthy mothers are essential to vigorous offspring, the physical well-being of woman becomes an object of public interest and care in order to preserve the strength and vigor of the race.

Winning *Muller* gave a big boost to organizations like the NCL. Those who favored maximum-hour work laws worried, however, that the decision depended on the fact that the law covered only women and that, when the Court had an opportunity to review a law covering all workers, it would apply *Lochner*. This fear increased when the Court agreed to review *Bunting v. Oregon* (1917), which involved another Oregon law providing that "no person shall be employed in any mill, factory, or manufacturing establishment in this state more than ten hours in any one day." Compounding the NCL's concern was that Brandeis now sat on the Supreme Court and, since he had participated in oral argument, would almost certainly disqualify himself from the case.

In 1917, however, the Supreme Court dispelled their concerns. In a 5–3 decision, with Brandeis not participating, the majority upheld the Oregon law. Writing for the Court, Justice Joseph McKenna explained that, although Bunting contended that "the law . . . is not either necessary or useful 'for the preservation of the health of employees,'" no evidence was provided to support that contention. Moreover, the judgment of the Oregon legislature and supreme court was that "'it cannot be held, as a matter of law,

that the legislative requirement is unreasonable or arbitrary.'" McKenna concluded, therefore, that no further discussion was "necessary" and upheld the law.

Once again the Court failed even to mention *Lochner*. But, given its holding, many predicted the death of that decision; after all, it was wholly incompatible with *Bunting*. Perhaps the demise of substantive due process would follow. Indeed, throughout the period between *Mugler* (1890) and up to about *Bunting*, it appeared that *Lochner* was more the exception than the rule. Between 1887 and 1910, the Court decided 558 cases involving due process claims challenging state regulations and upheld 83 percent of the laws. It seemed that *Lochner*, not *Muller*, was the unusual case.[17]

THE HEYDAY OF SUBSTANTIVE DUE PROCESS: 1923–1936

The *Bunting* funeral for *Lochner* proved to be premature. Within six years, not only did the Court virtually overrule *Bunting*, but also it seemed to be more committed to the *Lochner* version of due process than ever before. *Adkins v. Children's Hospital* (1923) provides an excellent illustration of the magnitude of this resurgence. At issue here was a 1918 federal law that fixed minimum wages for women and children in the District of Columbia.[18] Children's Hospital of the District of Columbia, which employed many women, refused to comply. In its opinion, the law violated the Due Process Clause of the Fifth Amendment encompassing the liberty to enter into salary contracts with employees.[19] Once again, the NCL defended the law by offering the Court "impressive documentation on the cost of living and the desirability of good wages."

17. Alfred H. Kelly, Winfred A. Harbison, and Herman Belz, *The American Constitution*, 7th ed. (New York: W. W. Norton, 1991), 405.
18. We adopt this account from Vose, *Constitutional Change*, 190–196.
19. Because the District of Columbia is not a state, the Due Process Clause of the Fourteenth Amendment did not apply.

TABLE 10-3   From *Bunting* to *Adkins*

Justice	Bunting *Vote* (1917)	Justice	Adkins *Vote* (1923)
McKenna	Uphold Law	McKenna	Strike Law
Holmes	Uphold Law	Holmes	Uphold Law
Day	Uphold Law	Butler[a]	Strike Law
Pitney	Uphold Law	Sanford[a]	Uphold Law
Clarke	Uphold Law	Sutherland[a]	Strike Law
White	Strike Law	Taft[a]	Uphold Law
Van Devanter	Strike Law	Van Devanter	Strike Law
McReynolds	Strike Law	McReynolds	Strike Law
Brandeis	No participation	Brandeis	No participation

a. Harding appointments (1921–1922)

But, in *Adkins*—unlike *Muller*—the Court was not persuaded by the NCL's evidence. In his opinion for the majority, Justice Sutherland wrote:

> The statute now under consideration is attacked upon the ground that it authorizes an unconstitutional interference with the freedom of contract included within the guaranties of the due process clause of the 5th Amendment. That the right to contract about one's affairs is a part of the liberty of the individual protected by this clause is settled by the decisions of this court, and is no longer open to question. . . .
>
> There is, of course, no such thing as absolute freedom of contract. It is subject to a great variety of restraints. But freedom of contract is, nevertheless, the general rule and restraint the exception; and the exercise of legislative authority to abridge it can be justified only by the existence of exceptional circumstances. . . .
>
> [The statute under consideration] is simply and exclusively a price-fixing law, confined to adult women . . . who are legally as capable of contracting for themselves as men. It forbids two parties having lawful capacity—under penalties as to the employer—to freely contract with one another in respect of the price for which one shall render service to the other in a purely private employment. . . .

Adkins, thus, represented the return of substantive due process; indeed, it made clear that *Muller* and *Bunting* were not major breaks from that doctrine. If anything, as Justice Holmes wrote in his *Adkins* dissent, it had come back stronger than ever with the term "due process of law" evolving into the "dogma, Liberty of Contract."

Why the change? In large measure, it can be traced back to the political climate of the day. Following World War I, the U.S. economy boomed, and voters elected one president after another who were committed to a free market economy. These presidents, in turn, appointed justices, at least some of whom shared their economic point of view. As Table 10-3 indicates, one president, Warren Harding, made the first four of these new Supreme Court appointments. Clement E. Vose notes that "the most important single fact about the Harding appointments was that he named two ardent conservatives of the old school—Sutherland and Butler—to serve along with two justices similarly committed who were already sitting—Van Devanter and McReynolds."[20] By 1922 the Four Horsemen were all in place.

The entrenchment of substantive due process, as we mentioned at the beginning of this chapter, was but one manifestation of the impact of Republican appointments to the Court. With their stronger commit-

20. *Constitutional Change,* 194.

ment to an "utterly free market," these conservative justices also invoked creative theories of the limits of national power, especially dual federalism, to strike down federal regulatory efforts. "Taken together" the doctrines of dual federalism and substantive due process constituted "a lethal sequence of knock-out punches which killed all [regulatory] legislation."[21]

THE DEPRESSION, THE NEW DEAL, AND THE DECLINE OF SUBSTANTIVE DUE PROCESS

The laissez-faire approach of the Court through the 1920s was in keeping with the times. The nation continued to boom and to elect politicians—President Herbert Hoover, for example—who were committed to a private sector–based economy that they were convinced would remain successful if left free from regulation. The Great Depression, triggered by the stock market crash of 1929, and the subsequent election of Franklin Roosevelt demonstrate just how quickly that perception changed. The depression "shattered the dream of a self-correcting free economy."[22] Roosevelt's election indicated the desire of the citizenry for greater regulation to get the nation back on its feet.

At first, it appeared as if the Court, although dominated by Republican-appointed justices, might go along with the depression-fighting regulatory efforts of the new administration and of the states, which in part would require a repudiation of substantive due process. How could states exercise any control on employers if the Court continued to strike down the legislatures' efforts on "liberty of contracts" grounds?

In the 1934 case of *Nebbia v. New York*, the Court seemed willing to relent. At issue here was the authority of the New York Milk Control Board to fix milk prices. The owner of a grocery store, Leo Nebbia, sold

milk at a rate higher than allowed and was convicted of violating the Board's order. In arguing against the law, Nebbia invoked the Fourteenth Amendment's Due Process Clause: the establishment of maximum prices interfered with his ability to conduct business.

In a 5–4 decision, the Court rejected this claim. Writing for the majority, Justice Owen Roberts seemed to return in earnest to Waite's business-affected-with-a-public-interest doctrine:

> The phrase "affected with a public interest" can, in the nature of things, mean no more than that an industry, for adequate reason, is subject to control for the public good. [There] can be no doubt that upon proper occasion and by appropriate measures the state may regulate a business in any of its aspects, including prices to be charged for the products or commodities it sells.

Although *Nebbia*, in retrospect, was a sign that the heyday of substantive due process was drawing to a close, that was hardly the case in the context of the day. As you will recall from the chapters on the Commerce Clause (7) and federalism (6), for the next two years the Court generally continued along its laissez-faire path of the 1920s—seemingly in ignorance of the political, economic, and social events transpiring around it. In particular, the Court refused to let go of the doctrine of substantive due process.

Just two years after *Nebbia*, it decided another New York case, but in quite a different way. At issue in *Morehead v. New York ex rel. Tipaldo* (1936) was a 1933 minimum wage law that "declared it to be against public policy for any employer to employ any woman at an oppressive and unreasonable wage." It defined as unreasonable a wage that was "both less than the fair and reasonable value of the services rendered and less than sufficient to meet the minimum cost of living necessary for health."[23] If a woman thought that her employer was paying her inadequate wages, she could file a complaint with a state board. Women employees of a laundry invoked this procedure against

---

21. Ducat and Chase, *Constitutional Interpretation*, 554.

22. Louis Fisher, *American Constitutional Law* (New York, McGraw-Hill, 1990), 476.

23. See Vose, *Constitutional Change*, 204.

Joseph Tipaldo, the manager of the operation. In 1934 Tipaldo was found guilty: he paid his employees only $7.00 to $10.00 per week, when the board had set $12.40 as a minimum wage.

When the case reached the Supreme Court, Tipaldo received some support from an unexpected source: the feminist National Woman's Party (NWP). Although it did not agree with his substantive due process claim, the NWP argued that the New York law violated the Constitution on the grounds that it treated the sexes differently and fostered inequality. As NWP leaders explained:

The Woman's Party stands for equality between men and women in all laws. This includes laws affecting the position of women in industry as well as all other laws. The Woman's Party does not take any position with regard to the merits of minimum wage legislation, but it does demand that such legislation, if passed, shall be for both sexes. It is opposed to all legislation having a sex basis and applying to one sex alone.[24]

Attorneys defending the state's action, including National Consumers' League representatives, therefore, faced a difficult challenge. The constituency benefiting from the law—women—was divided over the issue, but more important, the attorneys had to deal with the *Adkins* precedent. In part, they did so by trying to distinguish this law from the one at issue in *Adkins;* they also tried to demonstrate that economic conditions had changed considerably since 1923 and required this kind of regulation. Moreover, they had the *Nebbia* ruling in hand. It was just possible that the Court might go along with the state. But it was not to be. In keeping with their rulings on federal New Deal legislation and as a result of Justice Roberts's defection from the *Nebbia* majority, the Court struck the New York law. Writing for a majority of five, Justice Butler was just as emphatic on the subject of substantive due process as the *Adkins* Court had been: "Freedom of contract is the general rule and restraint the exception."

24. Quoted in ibid., 212.

West Coast Hotel v. Parrish:
The End of Substantive Due Process

The Court's refusal to uphold federal New Deal legislation, as you recall from Chapter 7, angered President Roosevelt. Its ruling in *Morehead* cut even deeper. Peter Irons wrote, "More than any other decision by the Court during the New Deal period, *Morehead* unleashed a barrage of criticism from conservatives as well as from liberals" who sympathized with the plight of women and children workers.[25] Even the Republican party's 1936 platform included a plank supporting adoption of minimum wage and maximum hour laws of the sort struck in *Morehead.*

Amid all this pressure, including Roosevelt's Court-packing scheme, the Court did a major about-face on the constitutionality of New Deal programs. As part of that change came what would be the demise of the doctrine of substantive due process in *West Coast Hotel v. Parrish.*

===

West Coast Hotel v. Parrish

300 U.S. 379 (1937)
Vote: 5 (Brandeis, Cardozo, Hughes, Roberts, Stone)
    4 (Butler, McReynolds, Sutherland, Van Devanter)
Opinion of the Court: Hughes
Dissenting opinion: Sutherland

Elsie Parrish had worked as a chambermaid in a hotel in Washington State for a wage of 22 cents to 25 cents per hour.[26] When she was discharged in 1935, she asked the management for back pay of $216.19, "the difference between what she had received and what she would have gotten" if the hotel had abided by the Washington wage board's minimum wage rate of $14.30 per week.

25. *The New Deal Lawyers* (Princeton, N.J.: Princeton University Press, 1982), 278.
26. We derive this account from William E. Leuchtenburg, "The Case of the Wenatchee Chambermaid," in *Quarrels That Have Shaped the Constitution,* John A. Garraty, ed. (New York: Harper & Row, 1987).

The hotel offered her $17.00, but Parrish refused to settle and brought suit against it. She found an attorney willing to represent her, but the attorney could not generate much interest in her case among outside organizations. Even the National Consumers' League declined to participate, viewing the effort as a waste of time in light of *Morehead*.

MR. CHIEF JUSTICE HUGHES delivered the opinion of the Court.

This case presents the question of the constitutional validity of the minimum wage law of the State of Washington. . . .

The appellant relies upon the decision of this Court in Adkins v. Children's Hospital, which held invalid the District of Columbia Minimum Wage Act which was attacked under the due process clause of the Fifth Amendment. On the argument at bar, counsel for the appellees attempted to distinguish the Adkins Case upon the ground that the appellee was employed in a hotel and that the business of an innkeeper was affected with a public interest. That effort at distinction is obviously futile, as it appears that in one of the cases ruled by the Adkins opinion the employee was a woman employed as an elevator operator in a hotel.

The recent case of Morehead v. New York came here on certiorari to the New York court which had held the New York minimum wage act for women to be invalid. A minority of this Court thought that the New York statute was distinguishable in a material feature from that involved in the Adkins Case and that for that and other reasons the New York statute should be sustained. But the Court of Appeals of New York had said that it found no material difference between the two statutes and this Court held that the "meaning of the statute" as fixed by the decisions of the state court "must be accepted here as if the meaning had been specifically expressed in the enactment." That view led to the affirmance by this Court of the judgment in the Morehead Case, as the Court considered that the only question before it was whether the Adkins Case was distinguishable and that reconsideration of that decision had not been sought. Upon that point the Court said: "The petition for the writ sought review upon the ground that this case [Morehead] is distinguishable from that one [Adkins]. No application has been made for reconsideration of the constitutional question there decided. The validity of the principles upon which that decision rests is not challenged. This court confines itself to the ground upon which the writ was asked or granted. . . . Here the review granted was no broader than that sought by the petitioner. . . . He is not entitled and does not ask to be heard upon the question whether the Adkins Case should be overruled. He maintains that it may be distinguished on the ground that the statutes are vitally dissimilar."

We think that the question which was not deemed to be open in the Morehead Case is open and is necessarily presented here. The Supreme Court of Washington has upheld the minimum wage statute of that State. It has decided that the statute is a reasonable exercise of the police power of the State. In reaching that conclusion the state court has invoked principles long established by this Court in the application of the Fourteenth Amendment. The state court has refused to regard the decision in the Adkins Case as determinative and has pointed to our decisions both before and since that case as justifying its position. We are of the opinion that this ruling of the state court demands on our part a reexamination of the Adkins Case. The importance of the question, in which many States having similar laws are concerned, the close division by which the decision in the Adkins Case was reached, and the economic conditions which have supervened, and in the light of which the reasonableness of the exercise of the protective power of the State must be considered, make it not only appropriate, but we think imperative, that in deciding the present case the subject should receive fresh consideration. . . .

The principle which must control our decision is not in doubt. The constitutional provision invoked is the due process clause of the Fourteenth Amendment governing the States, as the due process clause invoked in the Adkins Case governed Congress. In each case the violation alleged by those attacking minimum wage regulation for women is deprivation of freedom of contract. What is this freedom? The Constitution does not speak of freedom of contract. It speaks of liberty and prohibits the deprivation of liberty without due process of law. In prohibiting that deprivation the Constitution does not recognize an absolute and uncontrollable liberty. Liberty in each of its phases has its history and connotation. But the liberty safeguarded is liberty in a social organization which requires the protection of law against the evils which menace the health, safety, morals and welfare of the people. Liberty under the Constitution is thus necessarily subject to the restraints of due process, and regulation which is reasonable in relation to its subject and is adopted in the interests of the community is due process.

This essential limitation of liberty in general governs freedom of contract in particular. More than twenty-five years ago we set forth the applicable principle in these words after referring to the cases where the liberty guaranteed by the Fourteenth Amendment had been broadly described:

"But it was recognized in the cases cited, as in many others, that freedom of contract is a qualified and not an absolute right. There is no absolute freedom to do as one wills or to contract as one chooses. The guaranty of liberty does not withdraw from legislative supervision that wide department of activity which consists of the making of contracts, or deny to government the power to provide restrictive safeguards. Liberty implies the absence of arbitrary restraint, not immunity from reasonable regulations and prohibitions imposed in the interests of the community."

This power under the Constitution to restrict freedom of contract has had many illustrations. That it may be exercised in the public interest with respect to contracts between employer and employee is undeniable. . . . In dealing with the relation of employer and employed, the legislature has necessarily a wide field of discretion in order that there may be suitable protection of health and safety, and that peace and good order may be promoted through regulations designed to insure wholesome conditions of work and freedom from oppression.

The point that has been strongly stressed that adult employees should be deemed competent to make their own contracts was decisively met nearly forty years ago in Holden v. Hardy, where we pointed out the inequality in the footing of the parties. . . .

It is manifest that this established principle is peculiarly applicable in relation to the employment of women in whose protection the State has a special interest. That phase of the subject received elaborate consideration in Muller v. Oregon (1908). . . . In later rulings this Court sustained the regulation of hours of work of women employees.

This array of precedents and the principles they applied were thought by the dissenting Justices in the Adkins Case to demand that the minimum wage statute be sustained. The validity of the distinction made by the Court between a minimum wage and a maximum of hours in limiting liberty of contract was especially challenged. That challenge persists and is without any satisfactory answer. . . .

One of the points which was pressed by the Court in supporting its ruling in the Adkins Case was that the standard set up by the District of Columbia Act did not take appropriate account of the value of the services rendered. In the Morehead Case, the minority thought that the New York statute had met that point in its definition of a "fair wage" and that it accordingly presented a distinguishable feature which the Court could recognize within the limits which the Morehead petition for certiorari was deemed to present. The Court, however, did not take that view and the New York Act was held to be essentially the same as that for the District of Columbia. The statute now before us is like the latter, but we are unable to conclude that in its minimum wage requirement the State has passed beyond the boundary of its broad protective power.

The minimum wage to be paid under the Washington statute is fixed after full consideration by representatives of employers, employees and the public. It may be assumed that the minimum wage is fixed in consideration of the services that are performed in the particular occupations under normal conditions. Provision is made for special licenses at less wages in the case of women who are incapable of full service. The statement of Mr. Justice Holmes in the Adkins Case is pertinent: "This statute does not compel anybody to pay anything. It simply forbids employment at rates below those fixed as the minimum requirement of health and right living. It is safe to assume that women will not be employed at even the lowest wages allowed unless they earn them, or unless the employer's business can sustain the burden. In short the law in its character and operation is like hundreds of so-called police laws that have been upheld.". . .

We think that the views thus expressed are sound and that the decision in the Adkins Case was a departure from the true application of the principles governing the regulation by the State of the relation of employer and employed. Those principles have been reenforced by our subsequent decisions. . . .

With full recognition of the earnestness and vigor which characterize the prevailing opinion in the Adkins Case, we find it impossible to reconcile that ruling with these well-considered declarations. What can be closer to the public interest than the health of women and their protection from unscrupulous and overreaching employers? And if the protection of women is a legitimate end of the exercise of state power, how can it be said that the requirement of the payment of a minimum wage fairly fixed in order to meet the very necessities of existence is not an admissible means to that end? The legislature of the State was clearly entitled to consider the situation of women in employment, the fact that they are in the class receiving the least pay, that their bargaining power is relatively weak, and that they are the ready victims of those who would take advantage of their necessitous circumstances. The legislature was entitled to adopt measures to reduce the evils of the "sweating system," the exploiting of workers at wages so low as to be insufficient to meet the bare cost of living, thus making their very helplessness the occasion of a most injurious competition. The legislature had the right to consider that its minimum wage requirements would be an important aid in carrying out its policy of protection. The adoption of similar requirements by many States evidences a deep-seated conviction both as to the presence of the evil and as to the means adapted to check it. Legislative response to the conviction cannot be regarded as arbitrary or capricious and that is all we have to decide. Even if the wisdom of the policy be regarded as debatable and its effects uncertain, still the legislature is entitled to its judgment.

There is an additional and compelling consideration which recent economic experience has brought into a strong light. The exploitation of a class of workers who are in an unequal position with respect to bargaining power and are thus relatively defenceless against the denial of a living wage is not only detrimental to their health and well-being but casts a direct burden for their support upon the community. What these workers lose in wages the taxpayers are called upon to pay. The bare cost of living must be met. We may take judicial notice of the unparalleled demands for relief which arose during the recent period of depression and still continue to an alarming extent despite the degree of economic recovery which has been achieved. It is unnecessary to cite official statistics to establish what is of common knowledge through the length and breadth of the land. While in the instant case no factual brief has been presented, there is no reason to doubt that the State of Washington has encountered the same social problem that is present elsewhere. The community is not bound to provide what is in effect a subsidy for unconscionable employers. The community may direct its law-making power to correct the abuse which springs from their selfish disregard of the public interest. The argument that the legislation in question constitutes an arbitrary discrimination, because it does not extend to men, is unavailing. This Court has frequently held that the legislative authority, acting within its proper field, is not bound to extend its regulation to all cases which it might possibly reach. The legislature "is free to recognize degrees of harm and it may confine its restrictions to those classes of cases where the need is deemed to be clearest.". . .

Our conclusion is that the case of Adkins v. Children's Hospital should be, and it is, overruled. The judgment of the Supreme Court of the State of Washington is affirmed.

The Aftermath of West Coast Hotel

West Coast Hotel was an explicit repudiation of economic substantive due process. In one fell swoop, the justices overruled *Adkins* and changed the way the Court would view state regulatory efforts. But the period stretching from 1890 through 1936 continues to have an impact on Supreme Court rulings. Although the Court has not revitalized economic due process, neither has it returned to the hard-line position of Justice Miller in *Slaughterhouse*. How, then, does it examine state regulatory efforts? In some ways, its approach is not all that different, at least in theory, from Waite's in *Munn*. Recall that he promulgated a standard by which the Court should presume state legislation valid. Today's Court has adopted a rational basis test that also "starts with the assumption that legislation bears some rational relation to a state's legitimate powers and places the burden on opponents to prove there is no conceivable rational relationship between the statute or regulation and a legitimate function of government."[27] The difference between Waite's standard and that of today's Court lies generally in application. The Waite Court and its successors allowed incursions into their standard, and we should remember that the standard was amenable to exceptions; modern Courts have not done so. Indeed, since 1937, the Court has rejected virtually all challenges to state economic regulatory efforts. One reason for these decisions is the nature of the current legal test: it is extremely difficult for attorneys to demonstrate "no conceivable rational relationship." Another reason is the Court's reluctance to apply even that standard to state regulation. Unlike the Waite Court, for example, it simply refuses to determine what is and is not in the public interest or what is and is not rational.[28]

Williamson v. Lee Optical Company (1955) provides a good example of how the Court now treats Fourteenth Amendment economic claims. Here the Court upheld a 1953 Oklahoma law that made it "unlawful for any person . . . to fit, adjust, adapt, or to apply . . . lenses, frames . . . or any other optical appliances to the face," unless that person was a licensed ophthalmologist, "a physician who specializes in the care of eyes," or an optometrist, "one who examines eyes for refractory error . . . and fills prescriptions." It did so even though the justices thought that the "law may exact a needless, wasteful requirement in many cases." But, as Justice Douglas noted in his majority opinion, "it is for the legislature, not the courts, to balance the advantages and disadvantages of the new requirement." That is because, "[t]he day is gone when this Court uses the Due Process Clause of the Fourteenth

Amendment to strike down state laws, regulatory of business and industrial conditions, because they may be unwise, improvident, or out of harmony with a particular school of thought. . . ." The Court even quoted from Waite's opinion in *Munn:* "For protection against abuses by legislatures the people must resort to the polls, not to the courts."

Although *Williamson* was decided in 1955, it continues to characterize the Court's thinking on substantive due process. In *Pennell v. City of San Jose* (1988), the Court rejected the claims of a landlord who sought to invalidate a city rent control scheme on substantive due process grounds. In applying a rational basis standard, Chief Justice Rehnquist concluded, "We have long recognized that a legitimate and rational goal of price or rate regulation is the protection of consumer welfare."

For the moment, therefore, individual economic claims against state regulation lack the protection they once had under the Contract Clause and later under the Fourteenth Amendment. We say "for the moment" because some observers suggest that the justices of the Rehnquist Court have uncovered a new source for the elevation of such "rights": the Takings Clause. For now, we can safely assume that the days of *Lochner* have come to a close, at least as they bear on economic rights.

But the demise of the doctrine of substantive due process may have another effect. The doctrine may no longer apply to individual economic–state relations, but it currently remains alive as a mode of governance of individual privacy–state relations. Indeed, at least some of the justices in the majority of *Griswold v. Connecticut* (1965), in which the Court struck a Connecticut law prohibiting the disbursement of birth control and established a right to privacy, did so on substantive due process grounds. Justice Harlan wrote in a concurring opinion:

In my view, the proper constitutional inquiry in this case is whether this Connecticut statute infringes the Due Process

27. Malcolm M. Feeley and Samuel Krislov, *Constitutional Law,* 2d ed. (Glenview, Ill.: Scott, Foresman, 1990), 336.

28. Ralph A. Rossum and G. Alan Tarr, *American Constitutional Law* (New York: St. Martin's Press, 1991), 315.

Clause of the Fourteenth Amendment because the enactment violates basic values "implicit in the concept of ordered liberty.". . . The Due Process Clause of the Fourteenth Amendment stands, in my opinion, on its own bottom.

Furthermore, Justice Blackmun's 1973 opinion in *Roe v. Wade* legalizing abortion during the first two trimesters of pregnancy also invoked the Due Process Clause:

[The] right of privacy, whether it be founded in the Fourteenth Amendment's concept of personal liberty and restrictions upon state action, as we feel it is, or [another clause] . . . is broad enough to encompass a woman's decision whether or not to terminate her pregnancy.

That the *Roe* right rests, in part, on the Due Process Clause has been a source of contention among legal scholars. There are those, like John Hart Ely, who accuse Blackmun of "*Lochner*-ing," of returning to a discredited theory of individual rights as the peg on which to hang abortion rights. Others point out the difference between *Lochner* and *Roe* in the nature of the rights at issue.

Either way, it is true that the doctrine—so exalted at the turn of the century and so despised by its middle—has had a significant effect on the course of the law. What could have simply faded out of existence with Miller's *Slaughterhouse* opinion became the source of one of the most interesting episodes in constitutional law.

READINGS

Berger, Raoul. *Government by Judiciary.* Cambridge, Mass.: Harvard University Press, 1977.

Beth, Loren P. *The Development of the American Constitution.* New York: Harper and Row, 1971.

Gillman, Howard. *The Constitution Besieged: The Rise and Demise of* Lochner *Era Police Powers Jurisprudence.* Durham, N.C.: Duke University Press, 1993.

Jacobs, Clyde E. *Law Writers and the Courts.* Berkeley: University of California Press, 1954.

Keller, Morton. *Affairs of State.* Cambridge, Mass.: Harvard University Press, 1977.

Paul, Arnold M. *Conservative Crisis and the Rule of Law.* Ithaca, N.Y.: Cornell University Press, 1960.

Swindler, William F. *Court and Constitution in the Twentieth Century.* 3 vols. Indianapolis: Bobbs-Merrill, 1970.

Twiss, Benjamin R. *Lawyers and the Constitution.* Princeton, N.J.: Princeton University Press, 1942.

Vose, Clement E. *Constitutional Change.* Lexington, Mass.: Lexington Books, 1972.

Wolfe, Christopher. *The Rise of Modern Judicial Review.* New York: Basic Books, 1986.

CHAPTER 11

THE TAKINGS CLAUSE

O NE DAY a certified letter arrives at your house informing you that the government has decided to construct a new highway and your property lies directly in its path. The letter further states that in return for your property the government will pay you $100,000, an amount it considers "fair market value" for your home. Finally, the letter instructs you to vacate the house within six months.

Does the government have the right to seize your property in this fashion? What if this house has been in your family for five generations and you do not want to sell? What if this is your dream house, just completed after years of saving and sacrificing? If you believe the government has offered much less than the property is worth, can you challenge the amount offered? What about your rights to private property? Don't they mean anything?

The general answer to these questions is that the government indeed has the right to seize private property for a public purpose, such as a new roadway. This authority is referred to as the power of eminent domain. When federal, state, or local governments embark on new construction projects for roads, schools, military bases, or government offices, private proper-

ty usually must be acquired. Sometimes only a single parcel or two needs to be obtained, but at other times the massive condemnation of property is necessary. Although the property owner may feel mistreated when the government seizes the land, such government power is generally regarded as justified. Moreover, property owners have an important protection. The Constitution contains a provision, known as the Takings Clause, that checks the authority of the government against the individual's right to property.

PROTECTING PRIVATE PROPERTY FROM GOVERNMENT SEIZURE

When the Bill of Rights is mentioned, we almost automatically think of liberties such as freedom of speech, press, and religion, or the protections against unfair criminal procedures. But when the members of the First Congress proposed a listing of those rights considered important enough to merit constitutional protection, they included in the Fifth Amendment a significant private property guarantee—the Takings Clause—which states: "nor shall private property be taken for public use, without just compensation."

That the Framers would have protected private

property in this way is not surprising. The men who fashioned the U.S. Constitution were firm believers in private property rights, but they also supported a national government that would be stronger than it had been under the Articles of Confederation. The Takings Clause acknowledges that government projects sometimes require the seizure of private property. Without the power of eminent domain, individuals could block government programs, such as the interstate highway system, by refusing to sell property to the government or demanding unreasonable compensation, holding the government project for ransom. But James Madison, the primary author of the Bill of Rights, rejected the notion that government should have the absolute power to confiscate private property.[1] The Takings Clause was intended to moderate that authority by ensuring that property owners will not be unduly disadvantaged when the government seizes their land. It guarantees that the owner will be fairly compensated for the loss. As Justice Black explained, the Takings Clause "was designed to bar Government from forcing some people to bear public burdens which, in all fairness and justice, should be borne by the public as a whole." [2]

Because many states already protected private property against state government seizures, the Takings Clause was intended to apply only to federal government confiscations. This interpretation was endorsed by the Supreme Court in the case of *Barron v. Baltimore* in 1833. The dispute arose when the city of Baltimore initiated a series of street improvements, which also necessitated the alteration of several small streams. As a result, large amounts of sand and dirt were swept downstream into Baltimore Harbor, causing serious problems for the owners of wharves operating in the harbor. John Barron and John Craig were particularly damaged. Their wharf had been very profitable because it was located in deep water and

was capable of servicing large ships. The accumulation of silt and waste near their wharf was so great that the water became too shallow for large vessels, and Barron and Craig lost considerable business. They demanded compensation from the city for their loss. When the city refused, they sued, asking for $20,000 in damages. The local court awarded them $4,500, but a state appellate court reversed, and Barron and Craig appealed to the U.S. Supreme Court.

They claimed that the city's construction caused their loss of profitability. That constituted a "taking" under the meaning of the Fifth Amendment, and they deserved "just compensation." The justices, however, were not concerned with questions of whether a taking had occurred or what constituted just compensation. Instead, the Court focused on a more fundamental issue: Did the Fifth Amendment apply to state actions at all? The Court concluded that it did not. In the words of Chief Justice Marshall:

> We are of opinion that the provision in the fifth amendment to the constitution, declaring that private property shall not be taken for public use without just compensation, is intended solely as a limitation on the exercise of power by the government of the United States, and is not applicable to the legislation of the states.[3]

For the next half century this interpretation remained the law of the land. The Takings Clause applied only to the federal government. If states did not impose similar restraints on themselves, they were free to exercise the power of eminent domain without providing adequate compensation to landowners whose property had been seized.

In the late 1800s, prompted by the ratification of the Fourteenth Amendment, the Court began to re-

---

1. James W. Ely, Jr., *The Guardian of Every Other Right: A Constitutional History of Property Rights* (New York: Oxford University Press, 1992), 55.

2. *Armstrong v. United States* (1960).

3. The implications of this decision went far beyond the Takings Clause issue. In ruling as it did, the Supreme Court held that the states did not have to abide by any of the provisions of the Bill of Rights: those sections of the Constitution limited federal government actions only. The states were governed only by their own bills of rights. Over time the Court incrementally changed its position, but it took more than 130 years for it to conclude that the states were bound by almost all the provisions of the Bill of Rights.

consider this position. The Due Process Clause of the Fourteenth Amendment, you will recall, states: "nor shall any state deprive any person of life, liberty, or property, without due process of law." Lawyers began arguing that when states confiscated private property without giving the owners adequate compensation they were depriving the owners of property without due process of law, a violation of the Fourteenth Amendment.

The Supreme Court adopted this position in *Chicago, Burlington, and Quincy Railroad Company v. Chicago* (1897). The justices held that the Takings Clause of the U.S. Constitution was binding not only upon the federal government but also upon state and local governments. It affirmed the government's power of eminent domain, but required the payment of adequate compensation whenever that power was exercised.[4] With this ruling, the Takings Clause became the first provision of the Bill of Rights to be made binding on the states.

The authority of government to take private property in order to carry out legitimate projects is now well established. The most common issue that flows from government takings cases is the question of what constitutes "just compensation." In the normal course of events, the government attempts to buy the necessary land from the owners. If negotiations fail, the government may declare the power of eminent domain and take the property, giving the owners what it thinks is a fair price. Usually fair market value is the appropriate standard. It is not uncommon, however, for the owners to argue that the government's offer is inadequate. In such situations the owners may go to court to challenge the amount. Questions of just compensation normally are settled through negotiation or trial court action and rarely involve issues of significance beyond the specific land under dispute.[5] While

legal battles may be fought over whether the offered compensation is just, there is no doubt about the power of the government to seize the property.

Of greater importance are two questions of more general significance in understanding the meaning of the Fifth Amendment Takings Clause: What is a taking and what constitutes a public use? Both questions have required authoritative answers by the Supreme Court.

WHAT CONSTITUTES A TAKING?

In most cases it is relatively easy to determine that a taking has occurred. If the federal government decides to build a new post office and must acquire a piece of privately owned property upon which to build, a taking is necessary if a voluntary sale is not negotiated. Similarly, a taking occurs when, to complete a water control project, the government will need to dam certain streams and cause privately owned land to become permanently flooded. In these situations private land is totally taken by the government and is used for a public purpose. There is no question that the individual has been deprived of ownership rights over the property.

But a taking may also occur if the government engages in some activity that destroys the use of private property without physically seizing it. *United States v. Causby* (1946) provides an appropriate example. In this case the federal government built a military airfield within 2,300 feet of a North Carolina couple's chicken farm. The planes flew just 67 feet above the farmhouse. The constant noise and commotion as the planes took off and landed caused considerable disruption on the farm. The chickens became much less

---

4. See David A. Schultz, *Property, Power and American Democracy* (New Brunswick, N.J.: Transaction Books, 1992).

5. Although disputes over compensations levels normally are settled at the trial court level, occasionally such controversies involve significant issues and large amounts of money. For example, in *United States v. Sioux*

Nation of Indians (1980), the Supreme Court settled a longstanding dispute over the abrogation of the Fort Laramie Treaty of 1868. The treaty had established the right of the Sioux nation to the Black Hills, but an 1877 act of Congress essentially took back those lands. The Supreme Court ruled that the treaty abrogation was governed by the Takings Clause and that the Sioux were entitled to the value of the land in 1877 plus 5 percent annual interest since that year, amounting to a total claim of some $100 million.

productive, and many died when they flew into the walls of their coops out of fear and panic. The property was no longer suitable for raising chickens.

The Supreme Court held that government had "taken" this property. The path of the airplanes was so low and so close to the farm and residence as to deprive the owners of the use and enjoyment of their land. There was a diminution of the property's value that was directly and immediately attributable to the government's actions. Under such circumstances a taking has occurred and the land owners deserve compensation.

How far can the definition of a taking be legitimately extended? After all, every time the government passes a law regulating the use of property, the rights of owners are diminished. Does regulation constitute a taking? Justice Holmes addressed this question in *Pennsylvania Coal Co. v. Mahon* (1922). For Holmes, the answer depended upon the extent of the regulation: "The general rule at least is, that while property may be regulated to a certain extent, if regulation goes too far it will be recognized as a taking." Holmes feared that given too much discretion the government might regulate "until the last private property disappears."[6]

Generally, government regulation that only incidentally infringes on the owner's use of property is not considered a taking; nor is regulation that outlaws the noxious or dangerous use of property. Obvious examples are zoning laws or other regulatory ordinances that make certain uses unlawful.[7] Owners may be distressed that they can no longer use their property in particular ways, but the Supreme Court has held that such statutes do not constitute a Fifth Amendment taking that deserves compensation. For example, the justices ruled that takings did not occur when a state ordered property owners to cut down standing cedar trees because a disease they carried threatened nearby apple orchards, when a local government passed an ordinance removing an individual's right to use his land as a brickyard—a use seen as inconsistent with the surrounding neighborhood, and when for safety reasons a city prohibited a person from mining sand and gravel on his land.[8] In these and numerous similar cases the government's action significantly reduced the way the land could be used and decreased its commercial value; yet the Court held that a taking had not occurred. Instead, these government policies were instituted in response to social, economic, or environmental problems that could be addressed through the use of the government's police powers.

The questions of how far such regulation may go and for what reasons were addressed in *Penn Central Transportation Company v. City of New York* in 1978. The issue is important. If the government imposes regulations that seriously curtail the economic use of the property, has a taking occurred? Although Justice Brennan's opinion acknowledges that this area of the law has proved to be one of "considerable difficulty," it presents a good review of the principles the Court has developed to determine when a taking has occurred.

Penn Central Transportation Company v. City of New York

438 U.S. 104 (1978)

Vote: 6 *(Blackmun, Brennan, Marshall, Powell, Stewart, White)*

3 *(Burger, Rehnquist, Stevens)*

Opinion of the Court: Brennan

Dissenting opinion: Rehnquist

New York City passed the Landmarks Preservation Law in 1965 as part of an effort to protect historic buildings and districts. Each of the fifty states and

---

6. See Ely, *The Guardian of Every Other Right*, chap. 6.
7. See *Agins v. City of Tiburon* (1980).

8. *Miller v. Schoene* (1928); *Hadacheck v. Los Angeles* (1915); *Goldblatt v. Hempstead* (1962), respectively.

more than 500 cities had similar statutes. The law was administered by the Landmarks Preservation Commission. The task of the commission was to identify buildings and areas that held special historic or aesthetic value. The buildings were then discussed in hearings to determine whether landmark status should be conferred. If a building or area was designated historic, the owner's ability to change the property was restricted. For example, owners of landmark buildings were required to keep the exterior in good repair and not alter the building without securing approval from the commission. Owners of such buildings received no direct compensation, but they were accorded enhanced development rights for other properties.

This case involved the application of the preservation law to the Grand Central Terminal, owned by the Penn Central Transportation Company. The station opened in 1913 and is widely regarded as an example of ingenious engineering in response to problems presented by modern urban rail stations. It is also cited as a magnificent example of French beaux arts style. The terminal was designated a historic landmark in 1967, although Penn Central initially opposed the action.

In 1968, to increase revenue, Penn Central entered into an agreement with UGP Properties to build a multistory office building above the terminal. UGP and Penn Central presented two separate plans to the commission for its approval. One of the plans proposed a change in the facade of the building and the construction of a fifty-three-story office tower above it. The other envisioned a fifty-five-story office building cantilevered above the existing facade and resting on the roof of the terminal. The commission rejected both proposals.

In response, Penn Central and UGP filed suit claiming that the application of the Landmark Preservation Law to the terminal constituted a taking of their property without just compensation. The New York courts denied their claims, with the state's high-

Artist's conception of a fifty-five story office building to be floated over the waiting room of New York's Grand Central Terminal, which had been designated a historic landmark. Plans for this building, and several others, were rejected by the Landmarks Preservation Commission, and the Supreme Court ruled that such a rejection did not constitute a taking.

est court rejecting the notion that the property had been "taken" under the meaning of the Fifth Amendment.

MR. JUSTICE BRENNAN delivered the opinion of the Court.

Before considering appellants' specific contentions, it will be useful to review the factors that have shaped the jurisprudence of the Fifth Amendment injunction "nor shall private property be taken for public use, without just compensation." The question of what constitutes a "taking" for purposes of the Fifth Amendment has proved to be a problem of considerable difficulty. . . . [T]his Court, quite simply, has been unable to develop any "set formula" for determining when "justice and fairness" require that economic injuries caused by public action be compensated by the government, rather than remain disproportionately concentrated on a few persons. Indeed, we have frequently observed that whether a particular restriction will be rendered invalid by the government's failure to pay for any losses proximately caused by it depends largely "upon the particular circumstances [in that] case."

In engaging in these essentially ad hoc, factual inquiries, the Court's decisions have identified several factors that have particular significance. The economic impact of the regulation on the claimant and, particularly, the extent to which the regulation has interfered with distinct investment-backed expectations are, of course, relevant considerations. So, too, is the character of the government action. A "taking" may more readily be found when the interference with property can be characterized as a physical invasion by the government than when interference arises from some public program adjusting the benefits and burdens of economic life to promote the common good.

"Government hardly could go on if to some extent values incident to property could not be diminished without paying for every such change in the general law," *Pennsylvania Coal Co. v. Mahon* (1922), and this Court has accordingly recognized, in a wide variety of contexts, that government may execute laws or programs that adversely affect recognized economic values. Exercises of the taxing power are one obvious example. A second are the decisions in which this Court has dismissed "taking" challenges on the ground that, while the challenged government action caused economic harm, it did not interfere with interests that were sufficiently bound up with the reasonable expectations of the claimant to constitute "property" for Fifth Amendment purposes.

More importantly for the present case, in instances in which a state tribunal reasonably concluded that "the health, safety, morals, or general welfare" would be promoted by prohibiting particular contemplated uses of land, this Court has upheld land-use regulations that destroyed or adversely affected recognized real property interests. Zoning laws are, of course, the classic example. . . .

Zoning laws generally do not affect existing uses of real property, but "taking" challenges have also been held to be without merit in a wide variety of situations when the challenged governmental actions prohibited a beneficial use to which individual parcels had previously been devoted and thus caused substantial individualized harm. . . .

Pennsylvania Coal Co. v. Mahon (1922) is the leading case for the proposition that a state statute that substantially furthers important public policies may so frustrate distinct investment-backed expectations as to amount to a "taking." There the claimant had sold the surface rights to particular parcels of property, but expressly reserved the right to remove the coal thereunder. A Pennsylvania statute, enacted after the transactions, forbade any mining of coal that caused the subsidence of any house, unless the house was the property of the owner of the underlying coal and was more than 150 feet from the improved property of another. Because the statute made it commercially impracticable to mine the coal, and thus had nearly the same effect as the complete destruction of rights claimant had reserved from the owners of the surface land, the Court held that the statute was invalid as effecting a "taking" without just compensation. . . .

In contending that the New York City law has "taken" their property in violation of the Fifth and Fourteenth Amendments, appellants make a series of arguments, which, while tailored to the facts of this case, essentially urge that any substantial restriction imposed pursuant to a landmark law must be accompanied by just compensation if it is to be constitutional. Before considering these, we emphasize what is not in dispute. Because this Court has recognized in a number of settings, that States and cities may enact land-use restrictions or controls to enhance the quality of life by preserving the character and desirable aesthetic features of a city, appellants do not contest that New York City's objective of preserving structures and areas with special historic, architectural, or cultural significance is an entirely permissible governmental goal. They also do not dispute that the restrictions imposed on its parcel are appropriate means of securing the purposes of the New York City law. Finally, appellants do not challenge any of the specific factual premises of the decision below. They accept for present purposes both that the parcel of land occupied by Grand Central Terminal must, in its present state, be regarded as capable of earning a reasonable return, and that the transferable development rights afforded the appellants by virtue of the Terminal's designation as a landmark are valuable, even if not as valuable as the rights to construct above the Terminal. In appellants' view none of these factors derogate from their claim that New York City's law has effected a "taking."

They first observe that the airspace above the Terminal is a valuable property interest, citing *United States v. Causby.* They urge that the Landmarks Law has deprived them of any gainful use of their "air rights" above the Terminal and that, irrespective of the value of the remainder of their parcel, the city has "taken" their right to this superadjacent airspace, thus entitling them to "just compensation" measured by the fair market value of these air rights.

Apart from our own disagreement with appellants' characterization of the effect of the New York City law, the submission that appellants may establish a "taking" simply by showing that they have been denied the ability to exploit a property interest that they heretofore had believed was available for development is quite simply untenable. . . . "Taking" jurisprudence does not divide a single parcel into discrete segments and attempt to determine whether rights in a particular segment have been entirely abrogated. In deciding whether a particular governmental action has effected a taking, this Court focuses rather both on the character of the action and on the nature and extent of the interference with rights in the parcel as a whole—here, the city tax block designated as the "landmark site."

Secondly, appellants, focusing on the character and impact of the New York City law, argue that it effects a "taking" because its operation has significantly diminished the value of the Terminal site. Appellants concede that the decisions sustaining other land-use regulations, which, like the New York City law, are reasonably related to the promotion of the general welfare, uniformly reject the proposition that diminution in property value, standing alone, can establish a "taking.". . . [B]ut appellants argue that New York City's regulation of individual landmarks is fundamentally different from zoning or from historic-district legislation because the controls imposed by New York City's law apply only to individuals who own selected properties.

Stated baldly, appellants' position appears to be that the only means of ensuring that selected owners are not singled out to endure financial hardship for no reason is to hold that any restriction imposed on individual landmarks pursuant to the New York City scheme is a "taking" requiring the payment of "just compensation." Agreement with this argument would, of course, invalidate not just New York City's law, but all comparable landmark legislation in the Nation. We find no merit in it. . . .

Equally without merit is the related argument that the decision to designate a structure as a landmark "is inevitably arbitrary or at least subjective, because it is basically a matter of taste," thus unavoidably singling out individual landowners for disparate and unfair treatment. The argument has a particularly hollow ring in this case. . . . [A] landmark owner has a right to judicial review of any Commission decision, and, quite simply, there is no basis whatsoever for a conclusion that courts will have any greater difficulty identifying arbitrary or discriminatory action in the context of landmark regulation than in the context of classic zoning or indeed in any other context. . . .

In any event, appellants' repeated suggestions that they are solely burdened and unbenefited is factually inaccurate. This contention overlooks the fact that the New York City law applies to vast numbers of structures in the city in addition to the Terminal—all the structures contained in the 31 historic districts and over 400 individual landmarks, many of which are close to the Terminal. Unless we are to reject the judgment of the New York City Council that the preservation of landmarks benefits all New York citizens and all structures, both economically and by improving the quality of life in the city as a whole—which we are unwilling to do—we cannot conclude that the owners of the Terminal have in no sense been benefited by the Landmarks Law. . . .

. . . [T]he New York City law does not interfere in any way with the present uses of the Terminal. Its designation as a landmark not only permits but contemplates that appellants may continue to use the property precisely as it has been used for the past 65 years: as a railroad terminal containing office space and concessions. So the law does not interfere with what must be regarded as Penn Central's primary expectation concerning the use of the parcel. More importantly, on this record, we must regard the New York City law as permitting Penn Central not only to profit from the Terminal but also to obtain a "reasonable" return on its investment. . . .

On this record, we conclude that the application of New York City's Landmarks Law has not effected a "taking" of appellants' property. The restrictions imposed are substantially related to the promotion of the general welfare and not only permit reasonable beneficial use of the landmark site but also afford appellants opportunities further to enhance not only the Terminal site proper but also other properties.

Affirmed.

MR. JUSTICE REHNQUIST, with whom the CHIEF JUSTICE, and MR. JUSTICE STEVENS join, dissenting.

Of the over one million buildings and structures in the city of New York, appellees have singled out 400 for designation as official landmarks. The owner of a building might initially be pleased that his property has been chosen by a distinguished committee of architects, historians, and city planners for such a singular distinction. But he may well discover, as appellant Penn Central Transportation Co. did here, that the landmark designation imposes upon him a substantial cost, with little or no offsetting benefit except for the honor of the designation. The question in this case is whether the cost associated with the city of New York's desire to preserve a limited number of "landmarks" within its borders must be borne by all of its taxpayers or whether it can instead be imposed entirely on the owners of the individual properties. . . .

The Fifth Amendment provides in part: "nor shall private property be taken for public use, without just compen-

sation." In a very literal sense, the actions of appellees violated this constitutional prohibition. Before the city of New York declared Grand Central Terminal to be a landmark, Penn Central could have used its "air rights" over the Terminal to build a multistory office building, at an apparent value of several million dollars per year. Today, the Terminal cannot be modified in any form, including the erection of additional stories, without the permission of the Landmark Preservation Commission, a permission which appellants, despite good-faith attempts, have so far been unable to obtain. . . .

As Mr. Justice Holmes pointed out in *Pennsylvania Coal Co. v. Mahon,* "the question at bottom" in an eminent domain case "is upon whom the loss of the changes desired should fall." The benefits that appellees believe will flow from preservation of the Grand Central Terminal will accrue to all the citizens of New York City. There is no reason to believe that appellants will enjoy a substantially greater share of these benefits. If the cost of preserving Grand Central Terminal were spread evenly across the entire population of the city of New York, the burden per person would be in cents per year—a minor cost appellees would surely concede for the benefit accrued. Instead, however, appellees would impose the entire cost of several million dollars per year on Penn Central. But it is precisely this sort of discrimination that the Fifth Amendment prohibits. . . .

Over 50 years ago, Mr. Justice Holmes, speaking for the Court, warned that the courts were "in danger of forgetting that a strong public desire to improve the public condition is not enough to warrant achieving the desire by a shorter cut than the constitutional way of paying for the change." The Court's opinion in this case demonstrates that the danger thus foreseen has not abated. The city of New York is in a precarious financial state, and some may believe that the costs of landmark preservation will be more easily borne by corporations such as Penn Central than the overburdened individual taxpayers of New York. But these concerns do not allow us to ignore past precedents construing the Eminent Domain Clause to the end that the desire to improve the public condition is, indeed, achieved by a shorter cut than the constitutional way of paying for the change.

THE PUBLIC USE REQUIREMENT

Although the Fifth Amendment recognizes the government's power to take private property, it does not allow all such seizures. Quite explicitly, the Takings Clause stipulates that the government may take private property only for a "public use." Even if the government provides adequate compensation, it may not take property against the owner's will for the sole benefit of a private individual or organization. When the government plans to build a new courthouse, road, or park, the public use is clear; but it would be of doubtful constitutionality, for example, if a state seized a piece of private property under the power of eminent domain and gave it to a fraternal organization to construct a new lodge.

Throughout most of the nation's history, the justices were relatively insistent about the public use requirement.[9] Beginning in the New Deal period, however, the Court initiated a policy of deferring to Congress's authority to determine what constitutes a public purpose. For example, in 1954, the Court upheld a federal urban renewal project in Washington, D.C., in which private property was seized, improved, and then transferred to another private party.[10] In spite of the fact that private property was taken and then given to another private party, the Court accepted the conclusion of Congress that the program had a public purpose.

The Court's deference to the legislature on questions of what constitutes a public purpose was extended to the state level in *Hawaii Housing Authority v. Midkiff*. Attacked here was Hawaii's plan to redistribute land, using the power of eminent domain to force large landowners to sell their properties to the people who leased them. The transfer of land was clearly from one private owner to another. Was this program a benefit to the public generally, or did it serve only the private interests of those who now were able to become landowners?

9. See Schultz, *Property, Power and American Democracy.*
10. *Berman v. Parker* (1954).

Hawaii Housing Authority v. Midkiff

467 U.S. 229 (1984)
Vote: 8 *(Blackmun, Brennan, Burger, O'Connor, Powell, Rehnquist, Stevens, White)*

0

Opinion of the Court: O'Connor
Not participating: Marshall

The Hawaiian Islands were settled by Polynesians who developed an economic system based upon principles of feudalism. Ownership and control of the land rested with the islands' high chief, who distributed parcels to various lower-ranking chiefs. At the end of the chain, tenant farmers and their families lived on the land and worked it. Private ownership of real property was not permitted. Ultimate ownership of all lands rested with the royal family.

The monarchy was overthrown in 1893, and, after a brief period as a republic, the islands were annexed by the United States in 1898. When Hawaii became the fiftieth state in 1959, the land still remained in the hands of a few. In the mid-1960s the federal government owned 49 percent of the land in the Hawaiian Islands, and just seventy-two private landowners held another 47 percent. On Oahu, the most commercially developed island, twenty-two landowners controlled more than 72 percent of the private real estate. The Hawaiian legislature determined that this concentration of land ownership was detrimental to the state's economy and general welfare.

The legislature first decided to compel landowners to sell a large portion of their holdings to those individuals who leased the land from them. The landowners opposed this plan because it would result in exceedingly high capital gains that would be subject to significant federal taxation. The legislature then revised its plans and enacted the Land Reform Act of 1967. This legislation allowed the state to condemn tracts of residential real estate. The Hawaii Housing Authority (HHA) would then seize the condemned property, compensate the landowners for their loss, and resell the parcels to the private individuals who had been leasing the land. Compensation for land seized by the government enjoyed a more favorable tax status than did profits from outright sales, making the legislation more acceptable to the landowners.

Frank Midkiff and others owned a large tract of land that was condemned under the land reform program, but Midkiff and the HHA could not agree on a fair price. He and his co-owners filed suit in federal district court to have the Land Reform Act declared unconstitutional as a violation of Takings Clause. Among the arguments presented was the claim that redistributing land ownership was not an appropriate "public use" under the meaning of the Fifth Amendment. The district court rejected this argument, but the Court of Appeals for the Ninth Circuit reversed. The housing authority appealed to the Supreme Court.

JUSTICE O'CONNOR delivered the
opinion of the Court.

The Fifth Amendment of the United States Constitution provides, in pertinent part, that "private property [shall not] be taken for public use, without just compensation." These cases present the question whether the Public Use Clause of that Amendment, made applicable to the States through the Fourteenth Amendment, prohibits the State of Hawaii from taking, with just compensation, title in real property from lessors and transferring it to lessees in order to reduce the concentration of ownership of fees simple in the State. We conclude that it does not. . . .

The majority of the Court of Appeals . . . determined that the Act violates the "public use" requirement of the Fifth and Fourteenth Amendments. On this argument, however, we find ourselves in agreement with the dissenting judge in the Court of Appeals.

The starting point for our analysis of the Act's constitutionality is the Court's decision in *Berman v. Parker* (1954). In *Berman*, the Court held constitutional the District of Columbia Redevelopment Act of 1945. That Act provided both for the comprehensive use of the eminent domain power to redevelop slum areas and for the possible sale or lease of the condemned lands to private interests. In discussing whether the takings authorized by that Act were for a "public use," the Court stated:

"We deal . . . with what traditionally has been known as the police power. An attempt to define its reach or trace its outer limits is fruitless, for each case must turn on its own facts. The definition is essentially the product of legislative determinations addressed to the purposes of government, purposes neither abstractly nor historically capable of complete definition. Subject to specific constitutional limitations, when the legislature has spoken, the public interest has been declared in terms well-nigh conclusive. In such cases the legislature, not the judiciary, is the main guardian of the public needs to be served by social legislation, whether it be Congress legislating concerning the District of Columbia . . . or the States legislating concerning local affairs. . . . This principle admits of no exception merely because the power of eminent domain is involved. . . ."

The Court explicitly recognized the breadth of the principle it was announcing, noting:

"Once the object is within the authority of Congress, the right to realize it through the exercise of eminent domain is clear. For the power of eminent domain is merely the means to the end. . . . Once the object is within the authority of Congress, the means by which it will be attained is also for Congress to determine. Here one of the means chosen is the use of private enterprise for redevelopment of the area. Appellants argue that this makes the project a taking from one businessman for the benefit of another businessman. But the means of executing the project are for Congress and Congress alone to determine, once the public purpose has been established."

The "public use" requirement is thus coterminous with the scope of a sovereign's police powers.

There is, of course, a role for courts to play in reviewing a legislature's judgment of what constitutes a public use, even when the eminent domain power is equated with the police power. But the Court in *Berman* made clear that it is "an extremely narrow" one. The Court in *Berman* cited with approval the Court's decision in *Old Dominion Co. v. United*

States (1925), which held that deference to the legislature's "public use" determination is required "until it is shown to involve an impossibility." The *Berman* Court also cited to *United States ex rel. TVA v. Welch* (1946), which emphasized that "[a]ny departure from this judicial restraint would result in courts deciding on what is and is not a governmental function and in their invalidating legislation on the basis of their view on that question at the moment of decision, a practice which has proved impracticable in other fields." In short, the Court has made clear that it will not substitute its judgment for a legislature's judgment as to what constitutes a public use "unless the use be palpably without reasonable foundation."

To be sure, the Court's cases have repeatedly stated that "one person's property may not be taken for the benefit of another private person without a justifying public purpose, even though compensation be paid." Thus, in *Missouri Pacific R. Co. v. Nebraska* (1896), where the "order in question was not, *and was not claimed to be*, . . . a taking of private property for a public use under the right of eminent domain," the Court invalidated a compensated taking of property for lack of a justifying public purpose. But where the exercise of the eminent domain power is rationally related to a conceivable public purpose, the Court has never held a compensated taking to be proscribed by the Public Use Clause.

On this basis, we have no trouble concluding that the Hawaii Act is constitutional. The people of Hawaii have attempted, much as the settlers of the original 13 Colonies did, to reduce the perceived social and economic evils of a land oligopoly traceable to their monarchs. The land oligopoly has, according to the Hawaii Legislature, created artificial deterrents to the normal functioning of the State's residential land market and forced thousands of individual homeowners to lease, rather than buy, the land underneath their homes. Regulating oligopoly and the evils associated with it is a classic exercise of a State's police powers. We cannot disapprove of Hawaii's exercise of this power.

Nor can we condemn as irrational the Act's approach to correcting the land oligopoly problem. The Act presumes that when a sufficiently large number of persons declare that they are willing but unable to buy lots at fair prices the land market is malfunctioning. When such a malfunction is signalled, the Act authorizes HHA to condemn lots in the relevant tract. The Act limits the number of lots any one tenant can purchase and authorizes HHA to use public funds to ensure that the market dilution goals will be achieved. This is a comprehensive and rational approach to identifying and correcting market failure.

Of course, this Act, like any other, may not be successful in achieving its intended goals. But "whether *in fact* the provision will accomplish its objectives is not the question: the [constitutional requirement] is satisfied if . . . the . . . [state] Legislature *rationally could have believed* that the [Act] would promote its objective." When the legislature's purpose is legitimate and its means are not irrational, our cases make clear that empirical debates over the wisdom of takings—no less than debates over the wisdom of other kinds of socioeconomic legislation—are not to be carried out in the federal courts. Redistribution of fees simple to correct deficiencies in the market determined by the state legislature to be attributable to land oligopoly is a rational exercise of the eminent domain power. Therefore, the Hawaii statute must pass the scrutiny of the Public Use Clause. . . .

The mere fact that property taken outright by eminent domain is transferred in the first instance to private beneficiaries does not condemn that taking as having only a private purpose. The Court long ago rejected any literal requirement that condemned property be put into use for the general public. "It is not essential that the entire community, nor even any considerable portion, . . . directly enjoy or participate in any improvement in order [for it] to constitute a public use." As the unique way titles were held in Hawaii skewed the land market, exercise of the power of eminent domain was justified. The Act advances its purposes without the State's taking actual possession of the land. In such cases, government does not itself have to use property to legitimate the taking; it is only the taking's purpose, and not its mechanics, that must pass scrutiny under the Public Use Clause. . . .

The State of Hawaii has never denied that the Constitution forbids even a compensated taking of property when executed for no reason other than to confer a private benefit on a particular private party. A purely private taking could not withstand the scrutiny of the public use requirement; it would serve no legitimate purpose of government and would thus be void. But no purely private taking is involved in these cases. The Hawaii Legislature enacted its

Land Reform Act not to benefit a particular class of identifiable individuals but to attack certain perceived evils of concentrated property ownership in Hawaii—a legitimate public purpose. Use of the condemnation power to achieve this purpose is not irrational. Since we assume for purposes of these appeals that the weighty demand of just compensation has been met, the requirements of the fifth and Fourteenth Amendments have been satisfied. Accordingly, we reverse the judgment of the Court of Appeals, and remand these cases for further proceedings in conformity with this opinion.

It is so ordered.

Decisions such as *Midkiff* made significant changes in the way the Court deals with Takings Clause appeals. No longer do the justices examine the nature of the public purpose of the taking. Instead, the Court gives wide latitude to legislatures to determine what constitutes public use. To this extent private property rights have become political as well as legal questions, increasing the power of the legislature at the expense of traditional property considerations. These decisions also reduce the extent to which "public use" objections can be employed to thwart the legislative redistribution of wealth and property for the public good.[11]

RESURRECTING THE TAKINGS CLAUSE

The Court's Takings Clause jurisprudence began to change in 1986 when William Rehnquist was elevated to the chief justiceship and Antonin Scalia joined the Court. Both were strong advocates of private property rights. Rehnquist previously had been on the losing side of important Takings Clause cases. His dissenting opinion in the *Penn Central Trans-*

11. Schultz, *Property, Power and American Democracy,* 73–74.

portation case clearly indicated that he had views at odds with the way the majority was handling Takings Clause appeals. It was also an area of the law in which he had a special interest.

The first signs of change appeared in 1987, when the Court handed down three Takings Clause decisions. The first, decided in March, was *Keystone Bituminous Coal Association v. DeBenedictis.* The majority upheld a state regulation of coal mining operations against Takings Clause and Contract Clause attacks, but a dissenting opinion by the new chief justice attracted the support of three other justices, indicating that the more conservative members of the Court were poised to make a major assault on existing Takings Clause interpretations.

The second 1987 decision, *First English Evangelical Lutheran Church of Glendale v. County of Los Angeles,* was decided in June. Although this case involved a relatively minor point regarding the recovery of damages in Takings Clause cases, the Court voted 6–3 to support the property owners who claimed compensation. Chief Justice Rehnquist wrote the majority opinion in support of the property rights position. This decision was a clear signal that the Rehnquist Court was open to new Takings Clause appeals. This fact was acknowledged in Justice Stevens's dissenting opinion, in which he said: "One thing is certain. The Court's decision today will generate a great deal of litigation."

The final 1987 decision, *Nollan v. California Coastal Commission,* decided in late June, was the most important indication that the Rehnquist Court was about to resurrect property rights under the Takings Clause. James and Marilyn Nollan owned a beachfront lot in Ventura County, California. The property was located between two public beaches. The Nollans had a small bungalow on the property that they rented to summer vacationers. When the bungalow fell into serious disrepair and could no longer be rented, the Nollans decided to replace it with a new structure. To do so,

David Lucas purchased two oceanfront lots on the Isle of Palms with the intention of building homes on them. Shortly after the sale was completed, the South Carolina Coastal Council determined that future home-building would be detrimental to the environment and issued an order prohibiting future development. In 1992, the Supreme Court agreed with Lucas that the state's action was a violation of the Takings Clause.

they needed a building permit from the California Coastal Commission.

The commission granted the Nollans permission to build their new house, but with one significant condition: a strip of their property was to be set aside for public use as a passage between the two public beaches. The Nollans protested, but the Commission remained firm. The Nollans then filed suit claiming that the public access condition constituted a taking under the Fifth Amendment. The Supreme Court, in an opinion written by Justice Scalia for a five justice majority, ruled that the condition attached to the building permit was in fact a taking for which the Nollans must be compensated. In dissent, Brennan condemned the decision as being out of step with the complex reality of natural resource protection in the twentieth century.

Brennan's hope that *Nollan* would be an aberra-

tion did not come to pass. In the years following *Nollan* the personnel on the Court continued to change. Justices Brennan and Marshall retired. Both had been firm supporters of public interests over private property rights. Joining the Court were two supporters of private property, Justices Anthony Kennedy and Clarence Thomas. These changes gave increased strength to Chief Justice Rehnquist's efforts to breathe new life into the Constitution's private property protections.

The importance of these personnel changes can be seen in *Lucas v. South Carolina Coastal Council* (1992), a case that pitted private property rights against a state's attempts to protect its coastal environment. As might be predicted, the Court's conservative majority sided with the landowner, holding that the state may not deprive the owner of the value of his property without proper compensation. In dissent, Justice Blackmun decried the Court's changing policies.

Lucas v. South Carolina Coastal Council

505 U.S. 1003 (1992)

Vote: 6 (Kennedy, O'Connor, Rehnquist, Scalia, Thomas,
    White)
    3 (Blackmun, Souter, Stevens)

Opinion of the Court: Scalia

Opinion concurring in the judgment: Kennedy

Dissenting opinions: Blackmun, Stevens

Separate statement: Souter

In 1986 David Lucas paid $975,000 for two vacant oceanfront lots on the Isle of Palms, a barrier island near Charleston, South Carolina. He acquired the property with the intention of building single-family homes similar to those already built on adjacent lots. When Lucas bought the land there were no regulations prohibiting such use. Shortly thereafter, however, the state passed the Beachfront Management Act, an environmental law that gave the state coastal council increased authority to protect certain shoreline areas against erosion and other dangers. The council decided that the Lucas lots were in a "critical area" and prohibited any new construction.

There is no doubt that under its police powers the state has the right to pass such legislation, but Lucas claimed that the new regulations amounted to a taking of his property for a public purpose. The Fifth Amendment, he argued, required the state to pay him for the loss of his property. A state trial judge agreed that the regulations had made the Lucas property essentially worthless and ordered the state to pay him $1.23 million as just compensation for the loss. On appeal the South Carolina Supreme Court reversed, holding that the environmental legislation was not a taking under the meaning of the Constitution. Lucas appealed to the U.S. Supreme Court.

JUSTICE SCALIA delivered the opinion
of the Court.

Prior to Justice Holmes' exposition in *Pennsylvania Coal Co. v. Mahon* (1922), it was generally thought that the Takings Clause reached only a "direct appropriation" of property or the functional equivalent of a "practical ouster of [the owner's] possession." Justice Holmes recognized in *Mahon,* however, that if the protection against physical appropriations of private property was to be meaningfully enforced, the government's power to redefine the range of interests included in the ownership of property was necessarily constrained by constitutional limits. If, instead, the uses of private property were subject to unbridled, uncompensated qualification under the police power, "the natural tendency of human nature [would be] to extend the qualification more and more until at last private property disappear[ed]." These considerations gave birth in that case to the oft-cited maxim that, "while property may be regulated to a certain extent, if regulation goes too far it will be recognized as a taking."

Nevertheless, our decision in *Mahon* offered little insight into when, and under what circumstances, a given regulation would be seen as going "too far" for purposes of the Fifth Amendment. . . . We have, however, described at least two discrete categories of regulatory action as compensable without case-specific inquiry into the public interest advanced in support of the restraint. The first encompasses regulations that compel the property owner to suffer a physical "invasion" of his property. In general (at least with regard to permanent invasions), no matter how minute the intrusion, and no matter how weighty the public purpose behind it, we have required compensation. . . .

The second situation in which we have found categorical treatment appropriate is where regulation denies all economically beneficial or productive use of land. As we have said on numerous occasions, the Fifth Amendment is violated when land-use regulation "does not substantially advance legitimate state interests or *denies an owner economically viable use of his land.*". . .

We think . . . that there are good reasons for our frequently expressed belief that when the owner of real property has been called upon to sacrifice *all* economically beneficial uses in the name of the common good, that is, to leave his property economically idle, he has suffered a taking.

The trial court found Lucas's two beachfront lots to have been rendered valueless by respondent's enforcement of the coastal-zone construction ban. Under Lucas's theory of the case, which rested upon our "no economically viable use" statements, that finding entitled him to compensation. . . . The South Carolina Supreme Court, however, thought otherwise. In its view, the Beachfront Management Act was no ordinary enactment, but involved an exercise of South Carolina's "police powers" to mitigate the harm to the public interest that petitioner's use of his land might occasion. . . .

It is correct that many of our prior opinions have suggested that "harmful or noxious uses" of property may be proscribed by government regulation without the requirement of compensation. For a number of reasons, however, we think the South Carolina Supreme Court was too quick to conclude that that principle decides the present case. The "harmful or noxious uses" principle was the Court's early attempt to describe in theoretical terms why government may, consistent with the Takings Clause, affect property values by regulation without incurring an obligation to compensate—a reality we nowadays acknowledge explicitly with respect to the full scope of the State's police power. . . . "Harmful or noxious use" analysis was, in other words, simply the progenitor of our more contemporary statements that "land-use regulation does not effect a taking if it 'substantially advance[s] legitimate state interests'. . . ."

The transition from our early focus on control of "noxious" uses to our contemporary understanding of the broad realm within which government may regulate without compensation was an easy one, since the distinction between "harm-preventing" and "benefit-conferring" regulation is often in the eye of the beholder. It is quite possible, for example, to describe in *either* fashion the ecological, economic, and aesthetic concerns that inspired the South Carolina legislature in the present case. One could say that imposing a servitude on Lucas's land is necessary in order to prevent his use of it from "harming" South Carolina's ecological resources; or, instead, in order to achieve the "benefits" of an ecological preserve. . . . Whether Lucas's construction of single-family residences on his parcels should be described

as bringing "harm" to South Carolina's adjacent ecological resources thus depends principally upon whether the describer believes that the State's use interest in nurturing those resources is so important that any competing adjacent use must yield.

When it is understood that "prevention of harmful use" was merely our early formulation of the police power justification necessary to sustain (without compensation) *any* regulatory diminution in value; and that the distinction between regulation that "prevents harmful use" and that which "confers benefits" is difficult, if not impossible, to discern on an objective, value-free basis; it becomes self-evident that noxious-use logic cannot serve as a touchstone to distinguish regulatory "takings"—which require compensation—from regulatory deprivations that do not require compensation. A fortiori the legislature's recitation of a noxious-use justification cannot be the basis for departing from our categorical rule that total regulatory takings must be compensated. If it were, departure would virtually always be allowed. . . .

Where the State seeks to sustain regulation that deprives land of all economically beneficial use, we think it may resist compensation only if the logically antecedent inquiry into the nature of the owner's estate shows that the proscribed use interests were not part of his title to begin with. This accords, we think, with our "takings" jurisprudence, which has traditionally been guided by the understandings of our citizens regarding the content of, and the State's power over, the "bundle of rights" that they acquire when they obtain title to property. It seems to us that the property owner necessarily expects the uses of his property to be restricted, from time to time, by various measures newly enacted by the State in legitimate exercise of its police powers; "[a]s long recognized, some values are enjoyed under an implied limitation and must yield to the police power." And in the case of personal property, by reason of the State's traditionally high degree of control over commercial dealings, he ought to be aware of the possibility that new regulation might even render his property economically worthless (at least if the property's only economically productive use is sale or manufacture for sale). In the case of land, however, we think the notion pressed by the Council that title is somehow held subject to the "implied limitation" that the State may subsequently eliminate all economically valuable use is inconsistent with the historical compact recorded in the Takings Clause that has become part of our constitutional culture.

Where "permanent physical occupation" of land is concerned, we have refused to allow the government to decree it anew (without compensation), no matter how weighty the asserted "public interests" involved. . . . We believe similar treatment must be accorded confiscatory regulations, *i.e.*, regulations that prohibit all economically beneficial use of land: Any limitation so severe cannot be newly legislated or decreed (without compensation), but must inhere in the title itself, in the restrictions that background principles of the State's law of property and nuisance already place upon land ownership. A law or decree with such an effect must, in other words, do no more than duplicate the result that could have been achieved in the courts—by adjacent landowners (or other uniquely affected persons) under the State's law of private nuisance, or by the State under its complementary power to abate nuisances that affect the public generally, or otherwise.

On this analysis, the owner of a lake bed, for example, would not be entitled to compensation when he is denied the requisite permit to engage in a landfilling operation that would have the effect of flooding others' land. Nor the corporate owner of a nuclear generating plant, when it is directed to remove all improvements from its land upon discovery that the plant sits astride an earthquake fault. Such regulatory action may well have the effect of eliminating the land's only economically productive use, but it does not proscribe a productive use that was previously permissible under relevant property and nuisance principles. The use of these properties for what are now expressly prohibited purposes was always unlawful, and (subject to other constitutional limitations) it was open to the State at any point to make the implication of those background principles of nuisance and property law explicit. . . . When, however, a regulation that declares "off-limits" all economically productive or beneficial uses of land goes beyond what the relevant background principles would dictate, compensation must be paid to sustain it.

The "total taking" inquiry we require today will ordinarily entail (as the application of state nuisance law ordinarily entails) analysis of, among other things, the degree of harm to public lands and resources, or adjacent private property, posed by the claimant's proposed activities, the social value of the claimant's activities and their suitability to the locality in question, and the relative ease with which the alleged harm can be avoided through measures taken by the claimant and the government (or adjacent private landowners) alike. The fact that a particular use has long been engaged in by similarly situated owners ordinarily imports a lack of any common-law prohibition (though changed circumstances or new knowledge may make what was previously permissible no longer so). So also does the fact that other landowners, similarly situated, are permitted to continue the use denied to the claimant.

It seems unlikely that common-law principles would have prevented the erection of any habitable or productive improvements on petitioner's land; they rarely support prohibition of the "essential use" of land. The question, however, is one of state law to be dealt with on remand. We emphasize that to win its case South Carolina must do more than proffer the legislature's declaration that the uses Lucas desires are inconsistent with the public interest, or the conclusory assertion that they violate a common-law maxim. . . . As we have said, a "State, by *ipse dixit*, may not transform private property into public property without compensation. . . ." Instead, as it would be required to do if it sought to restrain Lucas in a common-law action for public nuisance, South Carolina must identify background principles of nuisance and property law that prohibit the uses he now intends in the circumstances in which the property is presently found. Only on this showing can the State fairly claim that, in proscribing all such beneficial uses, the Beachfront Management Act is taking nothing.

The judgment is reversed and the cause remanded for proceedings not inconsistent with this opinion.

So ordered.

JUSTICE BLACKMUN, dissenting.

Today the Court launches a missile to kill a mouse.

The state of South Carolina prohibited petitioner Lucas from building a permanent structure on his property from 1988 to 1990. Relying on an unreviewed (and implausible) state trial court finding that this restriction left Lucas' property valueless, this Court granted review to determine whether compensation must be paid in cases where the State prohibits all economic use of real estate. According to the Court, such an occasion never has arisen in any of our prior cases, and the Court imagines that it will arise "relatively rarely" or only in "extraordinary circumstances." Almost certainly it did not happen in this case.

Nonetheless, the Court presses on to decide the issue, and as it does, it ignores its jurisdictional limits, remakes its traditional rules of review, and creates simultaneously a new categorical rule and an exception (neither of which is rooted in our prior case law, common law, or common sense). I protest not only the Court's decision, but each step taken to reach it. More fundamentally, I question the Court's wisdom in issuing sweeping new rules to decide such a narrow case. Surely, . . . the Court could have reached the result it wanted without inflicting this damage upon our Takings Clause jurisprudence. . . .

The Court makes sweeping and, in my view, misguided and unsupported changes in our takings doctrine. While it limits these changes to the most narrow subset of government regulation—those that eliminate all economic value from land—these changes go far beyond what is necessary to secure petitioner Lucas' private benefit. One hopes they do not go beyond the narrow confines the Court assigns them to today. I dissent.

Justice Blackmun's hope that the Court's decision in *Lucas* would not be extended beyond the narrow confines of that particular case was quickly dashed. In *Dolan v. City of Tigard* (1994) the Court again upheld the rights of a property owner over the regulatory authority of the state. At issue in *Dolan* was a petition by Florence Dolan to expand her plumbing and electrical supply store and pave its parking lot. The local government in Tigard, Oregon, approved the application, but only on the condition that Dolan convert part of her land for public green space and set aside a fifteen-foot strip across her property for the city's pedestrian/bicycle pathway. Dolan objected to these conditions. The Supreme Court upheld Dolan's position. A state may impose conditions on a building permit that are reasonably related to proposed construction, but in this case a five-justice majority, in an opinion by Chief Justice Rehnquist, held that there was not a rea-

sonable relationship between the alterations Dolan proposed and the conditions attached to its approval by the city. Therefore, the conditions constituted a taking.

The *Dolan* decision was cheered by advocates of private property rights and criticized by supporters of government policies to regulate land for the public good. It once again demonstrated Chief Justice Rehnquist's intention to put more life into the Takings Clause. As successful as Rehnquist's attempts have been, note that this case was decided by the narrowest of margins. The Court's Takings Clause jurisprudence is clearly subject to modification. Given the ideologically driven voting that has occurred in these disputes, a single change in justices could easily tip the balance. The Takings Clause remains an unstable area of the law that merits close watching in the future.

READINGS

Ackerman, Alan T. *Current Condemnation Law: Takings, Compensation, and Benefits.* Chicago: American Bar Association, 1994.

Ackerman, Bruce. *Economic Foundations of Property Law.* Boston: Little, Brown, 1975.

———. *Private Property and the Constitution.* New Haven: Yale University Press, 1977.

Ely, James W., Jr. *The Guardian of Every Other Right: A Constitutional History of Property Rights.* New York: Oxford University Press, 1992.

Epstein, Richard A. *Takings: Private Property and the Power of Eminent Domain.* Cambridge, Mass.: Harvard University Press, 1985.

Mercuro, Nicholas. *Taking Property and Just Compensation.* Boston: Kluwer, 1992.

Paul, Ellen Frankel. *Liberty, Property, and the Foundations of the American Constitution.* Albany: State University of New York Press, 1988.

———. *Property Rights and Eminent Domain.* New Brunswick, N.J.: Transaction Publishers, 1987.

Schultz, David A. *Property, Power and American Democracy.* New Brunswick, N.J.: Transaction, 1992.

Stoebuck, William B. *Nontrespassory Takings in Eminent Domain.* Charlottesville, Va.: Michie, 1977.

PART V
CIVIL LIBERTIES

APPROACHING CIVIL LIBERTIES

12. RELIGION: EXERCISE AND ESTABLISHMENT

13. FREEDOM OF SPEECH, ASSEMBLY, AND ASSOCIATION

14. FREEDOM OF THE PRESS

15. THE RIGHT TO PRIVACY

APPROACHING CIVIL LIBERTIES

T HE NEXT FOUR CHAPTERS explore Supreme Court interpretation of guarantees contained in the First Amendment and those that have been seen as relating to the right of privacy. As a student approaching civil liberties, perhaps for the first time, you might be wondering why we devote so much space in Chapter 12 (Religion) and Chapters 13 and 14 (Expression) to the following few phrases:

Congress shall make no law respecting an establishment of religion, or prohibiting the free exercise thereof; or abridging the freedom of speech, or of the press; or the right of the people peaceably to assemble, and to petition the Government for a redress of grievances.

After all, the guarantees contained in the First Amendment seem specific enough—or do they? Suppose we read about a religion that required its members to ingest LSD before religious services, or about students who were so fed up with university policies they burned down the administration building, or about a radio station that regularly allowed its announcers to use profanity. Taking the words of the First Amendment, "Congress shall make *no* law," to heart, we might conclude that its language—the guarantees of freedom of religion, speech, and press—protects these activities. Is that conclusion correct? Is society obliged to condone forms of expression such as those in our examples? What these and the subse-

quent case examples illustrate is that a gap sometimes exists between the words of the First Amendment and reality. Although the language of the amendment may seem straightforward, its meaning can be elusive and therefore difficult to apply to actual circumstances.

The Supreme Court's formulation and interpretation of a right to privacy, as we shall see in Chapter 15, present even more difficulties, primarily because the Constitution contains no explicit mention of such a guarantee. Even though most justices agree that a right to privacy exists, they have disagreed over various questions, including from what provision of the Constitution the right arises and how far it extends.

It is the gap between what the Constitution says (or does not say) and the kinds of questions litigants ask the Court to address that explains why we devote so much space to civil liberties. Because the meaning of those rights is less than crystal clear, the institution charged with interpreting and applying them—the Supreme Court of the United States—has approached its task in a somewhat erratic way. Throughout the Court's history, different justices have brought different modes of interpretation to the guarantees of freedom of religion, expression, and the press, and to the right to privacy, which in turn have significantly affected the way citizens enjoy those rights.

Figure v-1 provides one way of looking at how dif-

FIGURE V-1 The Supreme Court's Support for First Amendment Claims, 1953–1991 Terms

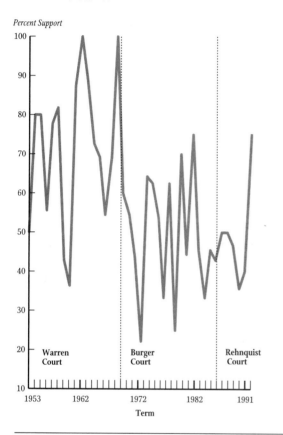

Percent Support

Warren Court

Burger Court

Rehnquist Court

Term

SOURCE: Lee Epstein, Jeffrey A. Segal, Harold J. Spaeth, and Thomas G. Walker, *The Supreme Court Compendium: Data, Decisions, and Developments* (Washington, D.C.: Congressional Quarterly, 1994), Table 3-8.

NOTE: First Amendment cases include all disputes involving free expression and religious liberty.

ferently the Court has treated First Amendment claims over a period of forty years. The Court led by Earl Warren was generally supportive of such claims; in more than two-thirds of such cases, his Court ruled in favor of persons who alleged that their rights had been abridged in some way. The Court under Chief Justice Warren Burger moved in the opposite direction, supporting the individual rights position far less often. It may be too soon to reach any conclusions about the Rehnquist Court, but, based on the data displayed in Figure v-1, it seems that the present jus-

tices may be about as supportive of First Amendment rights as those who sat on the Burger Court.

Figure v-1 helps to reinforce the point that the First Amendment is open to interpretation, that the words of the Constitution alone do not necessarily provide a solid guidepost for the justices as they go about resolving cases. Even so, the data raise many questions. Why are the Burger Court's—and perhaps the Rehnquist Court's—patterns of decision making distinctly different from those of the Warren Court? Have recent Courts simply had more conservative members? Or have the cases and the precedent governing their resolution changed? Perhaps the more recent justices have invoked different modes of analysis to resolve such disputes. Might it also be that the Court has responded to the public or to the other institutions of government? Another possibility is that the Warren Court was far more supportive of First Amendment claims than its predecessors, so that the Burger and Rehnquist Courts have rebalanced the scales. Finding the answers to these questions will require careful study of the cases to come.

This task is important because since 1942 more of the Court's docket has been taken up by civil liberties disputes. Figure v-2 details this growth, showing the percentage of the agenda the Court has allocated to cases involving First Amendment and privacy claims. In the 1930s these disputes took up a paltry 2 to 3 percent of the Court's time; today that figure is around 15 percent, but it reached as high as 25 percent in the early 1970s.

What accounts for this emphasis on civil liberties? Scholars have offered many different answers: they have pointed to the changes in legal standards governing this area; the growing presence of interest groups; the fact that states, under the selective incorporation of the Bill of Rights *(see Chapter 1)*, must now guarantee all First Amendment rights to their citizens, and so forth.

Another answer is that the legal standards in this area have changed. Changes occur when scholars and

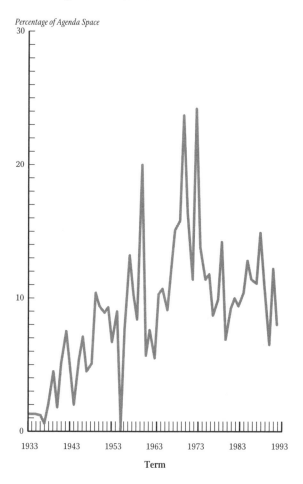

FIGURE V-2 Percentage of Agenda Space Allocated to Substantive Rights Cases, 1933–1992 Terms

Percentage of Agenda Space

Term

SOURCES: 1933–1987: Richard L. Pacelle, Jr., *The Transformation of the Supreme Court's Agenda* (Boulder, Colo.: Westview Press, 1991), Figure 6-3. 1988–1992: Provided to the authors by Richard L. Pacelle, Jr.

NOTE: Substantive rights cases center on First Amendment and privacy (including abortion) issues.

attorneys develop new ways of framing old problems; occasionally, governments codify these new approaches and/or lawyers present them to the Court for its consideration. The so-called hate speech laws provide an example. In the belief that certain kinds of expression pose a threat to compelling societal inter-

ests, some state and local governments have passed laws forbidding racist and sexist language, the placement of symbols (such as a swastika or burning cross) that might arouse anger, and so forth. However well intended such laws might be, they pose complex problems for the Supreme Court because they can run counter to the First Amendment's guarantee of freedom of speech.

Another illustration comes from the writings of one of the Court's most recent additions, Ruth Bader Ginsburg. Eight years before she took her seat on the Supreme Court, Ginsburg advocated a distinct approach to abortion jurisprudence. Rather than locating the right to obtain an abortion in privacy or due process guarantees (the course, as you shall see, that the Court had taken), she argued that the right could be based in notions of equality. This approach may be reasonable, but to adopt it the justices would have to rethink at least twenty years of constitutional litigation.

In the coming pages, we examine hate speech laws, Ginsburg's arguments, and several other newer approaches to older problems. For now, we remind you that the recent spate of frameworks within which to (re)consider issues of civil liberties provides another explanation for the length of this section of the book. Every now and then, new approaches have provided the fodder for litigation, causing the Court to rethink previously well-entrenched principles of law. And while the justices do not always adopt these approaches, it is important for us to think about them. Not only does the rejection (or acceptance) of new approaches have bearing on the ultimate state of the law in a given area, but also they provide a unique window from which to view some of the most interesting legal, societal, and political controversies of our day.

CHAPTER 12
RELIGION: EXERCISE AND ESTABLISHMENT

O N MY ARRIVAL in the United States," wrote Alexis de Tocqueville in the 1830s,

the religious aspect of the country was the first thing that struck my attention; and the longer I stayed there, the more I perceived the great political consequences resulting from this new state of things. In France I had almost always seen the spirit of religion and the spirit of freedom marching in opposite directions. But in America I found they were intimately united and that they reigned in common over the same country.[1]

Writing in the 1990s, political commentator Garry Wills asserted:

We may not realize that we live in the most religious nation in the developed world. But nine out of ten Americans say that they have never doubted the existence of God, and internationally, Americans rank second (behind only Malta) when rating the importance of God in their lives. So why is it surprising when the decisions we make in the voting booth reflect our basic religious values?[2]

Two of the most astute observers of American politics, writing 155 years apart, reached similar conclusions: religion plays an important role in the lives of most Americans. In a nation where 60 percent to 75

percent of the population belong to one of the more than 340,000 churches, temples, and synagogues, it is not surprising, therefore, to find chaplains reading invocations before legislative sessions, states erecting Christmas displays, or members of the Supreme Court singing carols.[3]

Indeed, as Tocqueville observed, Americans have always been a religious people. Americans learn in elementary school that the first settlers came to the New World to escape religious persecution in Europe and to practice their religion freely in a new land. What Americans often forget, however, is that as the colonies developed during the seventeenth century, they too became intolerant toward "minority" religions: many passed anti-Catholic laws or imposed ecclesiastical views on their citizens. Prior to the adoption of the Constitution, only two states (Maryland and Rhode Island, later joined by Virginia) provided full religious freedoms—the remaining eleven had some restrictive laws, and six of those had established state religions. Puritanism was the official faith of the Massachusetts Bay Colony, for instance, while Virginia established itself under the Church of England.

1. Alexis de Tocqueville, *Democracy in America*, vol. 1 (New York: Vintage Books, 1954), 319.
2. *Under God* (New York: Simon and Schuster, 1990), book jacket.

3. For excellent reviews of the role religion plays in American political culture, see Kenneth D. Wald, *Religion and Politics in the United States*, 2d ed. (Washington, D.C.: CQ Press, 1992); and Wills, *Under God*.

More tolerant attitudes toward religious liberty developed with time. After independence was declared, some states adopted constitutions that contained guarantees of religious freedom. For example, North Carolina's 1776 constitution proclaimed that "All men have a natural and unalienable right to worship Almighty God according to the dictates of their own consciences." But other constitutions continued to favor some religions over others. While Delaware provided that "[t]here shall be no establishment of any religious sect in this State in preference to another," it forced all state officers to "profess faith in God the Father, and in Jesus Christ His Only Son."

It would be fair to say that when the Framers gathered in Philadelphia, they—like modern-day Americans—held divergent views about the relationship between religion and the state. Even so, the subject of religion arose only occasionally during the course of the debates. After one particularly difficult session, Benjamin Franklin moved that the delegates pray "for the assistance of Heaven, and its blessings on our deliberations." With virtual unanimity, the delegates attacked Franklin, arguing that a prayer session might offend some members and that it would require them to pay a minister "to officiate in [the] service."[4] In the end, the Founders mentioned religion only once in the Constitution. Article VI provides that all government officials must take an oath to "support this Constitution; but no religious Test shall ever be required as a Qualification to any Office or public Trust under the United States."

Opponents of the new Constitution objected to its lack of any guarantees of religious liberty. New York Anti-Federalists, for example, condemned the document for "not securing the rights of conscience in matters of religion, of granting the liberty of worshipping God agreeable to the mode thereby dictated."[5]

Many states proposed amendments to the Constitution that centered on religious liberty. When James Madison drew up what would become the Bill of Rights, he included a section on religion: "The Civil Rights of none shall be abridged on account of religious belief or worship, nor shall any national religion be established, nor shall the full and equal rights of conscience be in any manner, or on any pretext, infringed." After several rounds of changes, the following phrases became the first two guarantees contained in the First Amendment of the Constitution:

Congress shall make no law respecting an establishment of religion, or prohibiting the free exercise thereof. . . .

About 150 years after the Bill of Rights was ratified, a Supreme Court justice wrote: "No provision of the Constitution is more closely tied to or given content by its generating history than the religious clause of the First Amendment. It is at once the refined product and the terse summation of that history."[6] Surely, this assessment accurately describes attitudes toward religion yesterday and today: religion motivated many to come to America, and it continues to play a major role in our political culture.

But how has the Court interpreted the Religious Establishment and Free Exercise Clauses? Are their meanings the same today as when the Framers wrote them? In this chapter, we examine these and other questions associated with the First Amendment's Religion Clauses.

FREE EXERCISE OF RELIGION

Imagine a religious sect that forced its members to handle poisonous snakes in the belief that such activity served two purposes: to test the sincerity of members and to help recruit new members. Should a court of law prohibit such activity because it is dangerous? Or should the court rule that snake handling falls un-

---

4. Quoted in *A History of the American Constitution* by Daniel A. Farber and Suzanna Sherry (St. Paul, Minn.: West, 1990), 122–123.

5. Address of the Albany Antifederal Committee, April 26, 1788, excerpted in Farber and Sherry, *A History of the American Constitution*, 181.

6. Dissenting opinion of Justice Wiley B. Rutledge in *Everson v. Board of Education* (1947).

der the umbrella of the free exercise of religion and thus constitutes legitimate behavior?[7] A literal approach to the Free Exercise Clause would suggest the latter; that is, religious denominations can pursue any exercise of their religion they desire. It seems clear that the majority of Americans did not think the free exercise of religion meant any such thing at the time the clause was framed. While we do not know specifically what the Framers intended by the words "free exercise" (congressional debates over religious guarantees tended to focus on the Establishment, rather than the Free Exercise Clause), writings and documents of the day point to a universally accepted limit.[8] As Thomas Jefferson set it out in an 1802 letter to the Danbury Baptist Association: "[I believe] that religion is a matter which lies solely between man and his God; that he owes account to none other for his faith or his worship; that the legislative powers of the Government reach actions only, and not opinion."[9] In other words, the free exercise of religion is not limitless, as a literal reading of the amendment would suggest. Rather, at least under Jefferson's interpretation, governments can regulate "actions."

Like Jefferson, the Court has never taken a literal approach to the Free Exercise Clause. Rather, in its first major decision in this area, it seized on his words to proclaim that some religious activities lie beyond First Amendment protection.[10] That case was *Reynolds*

v. United States, (1879), which involved the Mormon practice of polygamy. Mormons believed that men "had the duty . . . to practice polygamy" and that failure to do so would result in "damnation in the life to come." Word of this practice found its way to the U.S. Congress, which was charged with governing the Utah territory, where many Mormons lived. In 1874 Congress outlawed polygamy. After he took his second wife, Mormon follower George Reynolds was charged with violating the law. In his defense, Reynolds argued that he was following the dictates of his faith, a right reserved to him under the Free Exercise Clause.

The U.S. Supreme Court disagreed. In a unanimous opinion, the justices rejected an absolutist interpretation of the clause and instead sought to draw a distinction between behavior it did and did not protect. Chief Justice Waite's opinion for the Court asserted: "Congress was deprived of all legislative power over mere opinion, but was left free to reach actions which were in violation of social duties or subversive of the good order." This distinction between opinions (or beliefs) and actions (or practices) became, as we shall see, the centerpiece for several future religion cases. Some suggest that the Court used it here as a means to strike down the unpopular practice of polygamy. Constitutional law scholar John Brigham notes, "More significant than the distinction between belief and action . . . seems to be the fact that the Mormon practice was not viewed with equanimity by the rest of the population including the Supreme Court."[11]

Because it involved a practice considerably less problematic than polygamy, and an older, more established religion than the Mormon church, *Pierce v. Society of Sisters* (1925) illustrates the validity of Brigham's observation. In 1922 Oregon passed a compulsory public school education act, requiring children between the ages of eight and sixteen to attend public school. A diverse body of interests supported this measure for equally varying reasons: Progressives

---

7. In *Harden v. Tennessee* (1949), the Tennessee Supreme Court decided to outlaw such activity on the grounds that it was "dangerous to the life and health of people." We draw this example from M. Glenn Abernathy, *Civil Liberties Under the Constitution*, 3d ed. (New York: Harper and Row, 1977).

8. For an interesting view, see Michael W. McConnell, "Free Exercise as the Framers Understood It," in *The Bill of Rights* by Eugene W. Hickok, Jr. (Charlottesville: University of Virginia Press, 1991).

9. Letter to the Danbury Baptist Association, 1802, quoted in *Reynolds v. United States* (1879).

10. As we shall soon see, in its religious establishment cases the Court also seized upon another phrase used in Jefferson's Danbury Baptist Association letter—a "wall of separation." The Court's reliance on Jefferson's thinking has been questioned by some analysts because he was in France at the time the First Amendment was drafted. See John S. Baker, Jr., "The Establishment Clause as Intended" in Hickok, *The Bill of Rights.* On the other hand, Jefferson and Madison, the author of the Bill of Rights, corresponded frequently during this period. See Leonard W. Levy, *Constitutional Opinions* (New York: Oxford University Press, 1986).

11. *Civil Liberties and American Democracy* (Washington, D.C.: CQ Press, 1984), 77.

hailed it as a necessary step for the assimilation of immigrants, while the Ku Klux Klan backed it because it was viewed as anti-Catholic. Indeed, the ultimate effect of the Oregon law was to force closure of the state's privately run schools, several of which were Roman Catholic. The Society of Sisters, organized in 1880 to provide secular and religious instruction to children, faced dissolution because it derived more than $30,000 a year from its school. Rather than shut its doors, the society chose to sue the state, arguing that the law impinged on its free exercise rights. The sisters received support from organizations representing the spectrum of religions in the United States. Jews, Lutherans, Episcopalians, and Seventh-Day Adventists also had a vested interest in the case's outcome—most ran private schools. In addition, they wanted to show their unified distaste for the Klan-backed law, believing it repressed "pluralism in education."[12]

In a unanimous opinion, the Court held for the Society of Sisters. But the Court virtually ignored the *Reynolds* belief–action distinction; instead, it rested its ruling on the view that the society (as opposed to the Mormons) engaged in a "useful and meritorious" undertaking. In the eyes of the justices,

The inevitable practical result of enforcing the act . . . would be the destruction of appellees' primary schools. . . . Appellees are engaged in a kind of undertaking not inherently harmful but long regarded as useful and meritorious. Certainly, there is nothing in the present record to indicate that they have failed to discharge their obligations to patrons, students, or the state.

It was not until 1940, in *Cantwell v. Connecticut*, that the Court returned to and embellished upon the belief–action dichotomy. Here, the Court considered a Connecticut law that required those who wanted to solicit money to obtain a "certificate of approval" from the state's secretary of the Public Welfare Council. The state charged this official with determining whether "the cause is a religious one" or one of a "*bona fide* object of charity."[13] If the official found neither, he was authorized to withhold the necessary certificate.

Although this law was neutral—that is, it applied to all those engaging in solicitation—the Jehovah's Witnesses challenged it as a restriction on their free exercise rights. This denomination considers itself "ministers of the gospel to the 'gentiles,'" and, as such, distributes pamphlets and solicits money, activities regulated by the Connecticut law. Accordingly the Witnesses argued that the state regulation deprived them of "their right of freedom to worship Almighty God."

In a unanimous decision, the Court held for the Witnesses. Yet Justice Roberts's majority opinion was something less than a complete victory for them. Not only did Roberts return to the belief–action dichotomy—he claimed that the Free Exercise Clause covered belief and action, although "The first is absolute but, in the nature of things, the second cannot be"—but he went further, explaining how the Court distinguishes protected action from illegal action. He said that Court will look at the particular legislation or policy adopted by the government.[14] If the policy serves a legitimate nonreligious governmental goal, not directed at any particular religion, the Court will uphold it, even if the legislation has the effect of conflicting with religious practices. Applying this principle, which some analysts refer to as the "valid secular policy" test, to *Cantwell*, Roberts asserted that the state could regulate the collection of funds, even if those funds were for a religious purpose, because it has a valid interest in protecting its citizens from fraudulent solicitation. The major defect in the law? It empowered a government official to determine whether a cause was religious or not. Had the law not

12. For more details on this case, see Clement E. Vose, *Constitutional Change* (Lexington, Mass.: Lexington Books, 1972).

13. For more details, see Henry J. Abraham, *Freedom and the Court*, 5th ed. (New York: Oxford University Press, 1988), 298, and Richard E. Morgan, *The Law and Politics of Civil Rights and Liberties* (New York: Knopf, 1985), 185.

14. See Richard C. Cortner, *The Supreme Court and Civil Liberties Policy* (Palo Alto, Calif.: Mayfield, 1975), 145–147.

contained such a provision, the Court probably would have upheld it as a legitimate secular policy.

If the Court had upheld the law, the Jehovah's Witnesses would have found it more difficult to carry out the dictates of their religion. By the same token, all other would-be solicitors—charitable organizations and the like—would have been similarly affected. In other words, the religious and the nonreligious would have been subject to the regulations. Looking at *Cantwell* this way reveals an important underpinning of the logic of the valid secular policy test: neutrality. If the government has a valid secular reason for its policy, then in the eyes of the justices, religions should not be exempt from its coverage simply because they are religions. Exempting them would be to give religion an elevated position in society. One could argue that there is a difference between making it more difficult for a religion to carry out its mandate and for a charity to collect funds. But by adopting the valid secular policy test, the Court suggested that the effect on the Jehovah's Witnesses would amount to only an incidental intrusion on religion that would come about as the government pursued a legitimate interest.

Application of the Valid Secular Policy Test

How has this test worked? In particular, what constitutes a valid secular policy, a legitimate state interest? In *Cantwell,* Justice Roberts provided some clues about what these concepts might encompass: the prevention of fraud, the regulation of the time and manner of solicitation, and actions involving the interest of "public safety, peace, comfort or convenience." Shortly after *Cantwell,* the Court added to Roberts's list when it reviewed cases involving mandatory flag salutes and child labor laws.

At issue in the first flag salute case, *Minersville School District v. Gobitis* (1940), were the recitation of the Pledge of Allegiance and the hand gesture or salute that accompanied it. For most individuals, particularly school children, the pledge and salute are noncontroversial routines that illustrate their loyalty to the basic tenets of American society. Such is not the case for the Jehovah's Witnesses, who exalt religious laws over all others. They claim that the salute and the pledge violate a teaching from Exodus:

Thou shalt not make unto thee any graven image, or any likeness of anything that is in heaven above, or that is in earth beneath, or that is in the water under the earth; thou shalt not bow down thyself to them, nor serve them.

Accordingly, Jehovah's Witnesses do not want their children to recite the pledge and salute the flag. The problem, at the time of this case, was that schools made the pledge and salute to the flag mandatory for all public school children. Flag salute laws became particularly pervasive after World War I as a show of patriotism. Before the war only five states required flag salutes; by 1935 that figure had risen to eighteen, with many local school boards compelling the salute in the absence of state legislation.[15]

Beginning in the mid-1930s, the Witnesses actively campaigned to do away with the salutes. The campaign began in Nazi Germany, where Jehovah's Witnesses refused to salute Hitler with raised palms and were punished by imprisonment in concentration camps. Joseph Rutherford, who was the Witnesses' leader in the United States, spoke out against the American flag salute, which, at the time, was regularly done with a straight, extended arm, resembling the Nazi-Fascist salute. He asserted that Witnesses "do not 'Heil Hitler' nor any other creature."

After Rutherford's speech, some members of the Jehovah's Witnesses asked their children not to salute the flag. Among these was Walter Gobitas,[16] whose two children—twelve-year-old Lillian and her younger brother William—attended a Pennsylvania public school with a mandatory flag salute policy. When they refused to salute the flag, they were expelled. Represented by attorneys from the Witnesses, Gobitas brought suit against the school board, arguing that

15. We derive this account from Peter Irons, *The Courage of Their Convictions* (New York: Free Press, 1988), 16–24.

16. The family name, Gobitas, was misspelled in the records.

the expulsion violated his children's free speech and free exercise of religion rights. In Chapter 13, we explore the free speech component of Gobitas's claim. For now, it is important to note that the Supreme Court rejected these arguments. Writing for the Court, Justice Frankfurter asserted that:

[T]he ultimate foundation of a free society is the binding tie of cohesive sentiment. . . . The flag is the symbol of our national unity, transcending all internal differences. . . . To stigmatize legislative judgment in providing for this universal gesture of respect for the symbol of our national life . . . would amount to no less than the pronouncement of pedagogical and psychological dogma in a field where courts possess . . . no controlling competence.

To put it in terms of the valid secular policy test, Frankfurter was claiming that the state had a legitimate secular reason for requiring flag salutes: to foster patriotism. That the law affected the religious practice of the Jehovah's Witnesses did not, in Frankfurter's view, detract from its constitutionality. Besides, Frankfurter believed that the Court should not interfere with local policies because that "would in effect make [the Court] the school board for the country."

Some of these same arguments—particularly those centered on national unity—were raised in the 1980s by attorneys seeking to convince the Court to uphold state regulations prohibiting the desecration of the American flag. (We shall consider these cases in the next chapter.) Here, it is worth noting that there were extraordinary repercussions from the Court's decision in *Gobitis*. Not surprisingly, after the ruling many states either retained or passed laws requiring flag salutes and pledges for all public school children and threatening to expel anyone who did not comply. What was startling was the violence against Jehovah's Witnesses. "Within two weeks of the Court's decision," two federal officials later wrote, "hundreds of attacks upon the Witnesses were reported to the Department of Justice."[17] Viewing their refusal to salute the flag as unpatriotic—especially as the country fought in World War II—mobs throughout the United States stoned, kidnapped, beat, and even castrated Jehovah's Witnesses.

These episodes of violence prompted many newspapers and major organizations, such as the American Bar Association, to condemn the Court's ruling. They also propelled the Witnesses to look for yet another suit by which to mount a constitutional challenge to the mandatory flag salutes. They located the Barnette family—Jehovah's Witnesses who had been harassed by the West Virginia school system for failure to participate in the flag salute ritual. One of the Barnette children had been expelled.[18]

Despite the Supreme Court's decision in *Gobitis*, which said the flag salute laws were constitutional, a three-judge district court, in *West Virginia Board of Education v. Barnette*, (1943) sympathized with the Barnette family's plight. According to John J. Parker, the well-respected circuit court judge:

The salute to the United States' flag is an expression of the homage of the soul. To force it upon one who has conscientious scruples against giving it is petty tyranny unworthy of the spirit of the Republic, and forbidden, we think, by the United States Constitution.[19]

The Supreme Court agreed. In a 6–3 decision, handed down on Flag Day in 1943, the Court overturned *Gobitis*. The Court centered its decision squarely in free expression, rather than free exercise, guarantees. Justice Jackson wrote for the majority:

[The issue does not] turn on one's possession of particular religious views or the sincerity with which they are held.

---

17. Irons, *The Courage of Their Convictions*, 22–23.

18. For more details on this case, see David Manwaring, *Render Unto Caesar: The Flag Salute Controversy* (Chicago: University of Chicago Press, 1962).

19. Chief Judge John Parker of the Fourth Circuit, as Henry J. Abraham notes, was a "prominent and distinguished Republican leader in North Carolina for many years and an outstanding jurist." Parker was nominated to the Supreme Court, but a coalition of organized interests (most notably the AFL-CIO and NAACP) and anti-Hoover Progressive senators blocked his appointment by a two-vote margin. See Abraham, *Justices and Presidents*, 3d ed. (New York: Oxford University Press, 1992), 42–43.

While religion supplies appellees' motive for enduring the discomforts of making the issue in this case, many citizens who do not share these religious views hold such a compulsory rite to infringe constitutional liberty of the individual. It is not necessary to inquire whether non-conformist beliefs will exempt from the duty to salute unless we first find power to make the salute a legal duty.

Because the Court found that the state did not have the power to impose a flag salute on public school children, it did not need to make such an inquiry.

We revisit *Barnette* in the next chapter because it is important to an understanding of the development of free expression guarantees. Two questions, however, should be addressed here. The first is obvious: Why did the Court undergo a major change of heart, overruling *Gobitis* just three years after it had been announced? Some scholars suggest that extrajudicial factors were at work. For example, the legal community widely criticized the *Gobitis* opinion: of the twenty-two articles published about the case in law reviews and similar journals between 1940 and 1941, only two agreed with the justices. In addition, state courts generally did not follow the precepts of *Gobitis;* none that heard related cases affirmed the expulsion of children against challenges on religious grounds. Some rejected the Court's logic outright.[20] Moreover, the Court may have been reacting to the atrocities of Nazi Germany, where patriotism was taken to obscene ends. Justice Frankfurter, in *Gobitis,* viewed patriotism as a legitimate government end. But in *Barnette,* Jackson had a different point of view. Note, in particular, his implicit reference to Nazism and fascism:

National unity as an end which officials may foster by persuasion and example is not in question. The problem is whether under our Constitution compulsion as here employed is a permissible means for its achievement. Struggles to coerce uniformity of sentiment in support of some end thought essential to their time and country have been waged by many good as well as by evil men. . . . Those who begin coercive elimination of dissent soon find themselves exterminating dissenters. Compulsory unification of opinion achieves only the unanimity of the graveyard. It seems trite but necessary to say that the First Amendment . . . was designed to avoid these ends by avoiding these beginnings.

Finally, the Court experienced some turnover in membership between *Gobitis* and *Barnette.* Two members of the *Gobitis* majority were replaced by Jackson and Wiley Rutledge. Also, Hugo Black, William Douglas, and Frank Murphy—all of whom had joined *Gobitis*—indicated in 1942 that they had changed their thinking on the issue.[21]

A second question concerns the valid secular policy test. The Court used it to uphold mandatory flag salutes in *Gobitis,* so did the justices banish it in *Barnette* by striking down the same laws? The answer is no, as you may be able to see from the excerpt of Jackson's opinion. In fact, the very next year in *Prince v. Massachusetts* (1944), the Court invoked the valid secular policy test to rule against the Witnesses.

Prince involved a Massachusetts law that said minors (girls under eighteen and boys under twelve) could not sell "upon the streets or in other public places, any newspaper, magazines, periodicals, or other articles of merchandise." It further specified that any parent or guardian who allowed a minor to perform such activity would be engaging in criminal behavior. Sarah Prince, a Jehovah's Witness, allowed her nine-year-old niece, Betty Simmons, for whom Prince was the legal guardian, to help her distribute religious pamphlets. Prince knew she was violating the law— she had been warned by school authorities—but she continued and was arrested.

At the trial court level, there was some doubt about whether the child actually had sold materials, but the Supreme Court dealt exclusively with this question:

---

20. See the amicus curiae brief filed by the Bill of Rights Committee of the American Bar Association in *Barnette.* Also, in note 15 of his opinion, Jackson cites some of the writings critical of *Gobitis.*

21. As Henry J. Abraham notes, the trio filed a memorandum (in another Jehovah's Witness case, *Jones v. Opelika,* 1942) stating that "since we joined in the opinion in the *Gobitis* case, we think this is an appropriate occasion to state that we now believe that it was also wrongly decided." See *Freedom and the Court,* 303.

Did the state law violate First Amendment principles? A divided Court held that it did not. Writing for a five-person majority, Justice Rutledge asserted:

The State's authority over children's activities is broader than over like actions of adults. This is peculiarly true of public activities and in matters of employment. A democratic society rests ... upon the healthy, well-rounded growth of young people into full maturity as citizens. . . . It may secure this against impeding restraints and dangers, within a broad range of selection. Among evils most appropriate for such action are the crippling effects of child employment . . . and the possible harms arising from other activities subject to all the diverse influences of the street. It is too late now to doubt that legislation appropriately designed to reach such evils is within the state's police power, whether against the parent's claim to control of the child or one that religious scruples dictate contrary action.

Clearly, legislatures can regulate religious practices of potential harm to children as well as those of questionable morality and safety. Such laws, in the eyes of the justices, present a reasonable use of state police power, which is the ability of states to regulate in the best interests of their citizens. In other words, child labor laws represent a valid secular policy and, when in opposition to a free exercise claim, the free exercise claim falls.

The Demise of the Valid Secular Policy Test

Most of the cases we have examined have several traits in common: they were brought by Jehovah's Witnesses, a minority religion; they were decided during the 1940s, a period when the Court was neither particularly conservative nor liberal in ideological outlook; and they involved arguments that combined free expression and free exercise claims. By the same token, the Court's approaches to the cases were relatively consistent. The Court remained true to the belief–action dichotomy set out in *Reynolds* and, when a religion's actions were at stake, it invoked the valid secular policy test to resolve the disputes. These approaches occasionally led the justices to strike down

state policies *(Cantwell)*, as well as to uphold them *(Gobitis, Prince)*.

In the 1960s, however, major changes began to occur in the direction of precedent governing free exercise claims and in the kinds of cases the Court decided. The first signs came in *Braunfeld v. Brown,* which was one of several cases the Court heard in 1961 involving "blue" or Sunday closing laws. At issue in *Braunfeld* was Pennsylvania's blue law, which allowed only certain kinds of stores to remain open on Sunday. Abraham Braunfeld, an Orthodox Jew, owned a retail clothing and home furnishing store in Philadelphia. Because such stores were not among those permitted to remain open on Sunday, Braunfeld wanted the Court to issue a permanent injunction against the law. His religious principles dictated that he could not work on Saturday, the Jewish Sabbath, but he needed to be open six days a week for economic reasons. He challenged the law as a violation of, among other things, his right to exercise his religion.

In a judgment, Chief Justice Earl Warren upheld the constitutionality of blue laws and restated the belief-action dichotomy:

Certain aspects of religious exercise cannot, in any way, be restricted or burdened by either federal or state legislation. Compulsion by law of the acceptance of any creed or the practice of any form of worship is strictly forbidden. The freedom to hold religious beliefs and opinions is absolute. . . .
However, the freedom to act, even where the action is in accord with one's religious convictions, is not totally free from legislative restrictions. . . . [L]egislative power over mere opinion is forbidden but it may reach people's action when they are found to be in violation of important social duties or subversive of good order, even when the actions are demanded by one's religion.

But, according to many observers, Warren's opinion veered significantly from established precedent. Consider the following passage:

Of course, to hold unassailable all legislation regulating conduct which imposes solely an indirect burden on the observance of religion would be a gross oversimplification. If the purpose or effect of a law is to impede the observance of one or all religions or is to discriminate invidiously between religions, that law is constitutionally invalid even though the burden may be characterized as being only indirect. But if the State regulates conduct by enacting a general law within its power, the purpose and effect of which is to advance the State's secular goals, the statute is valid despite its indirect burden on religious observance *unless the State may accomplish its purpose by means which do not impose such a burden.* (Emphasis added.)

In some ways, this statement merely restates the logic of *Cantwell* and the valid secular policy test. But note the italicized phrase: this statement represents an important addition to the test because it suggests that the state must show that its legislation achieves an important secular end *and* that it could not have achieved those ends with less restrictive legislation, that is, legislation that would place less of a burden on religious freedom.

Sunday closing laws, Warren reasoned, met both these standards. According to the chief justice, in passing blue laws, the state intended to set up a day of "rest, repose, recreation and tranquillity—a day which all members of the family and community have the opportunity to spend and enjoy together." In other words, the Sunday closing laws reflect a valid secular purpose. They also are the least restrictive way of accomplishing that purpose. Even though the laws indirectly burden members of some religions (for example, Orthodox Jews), Warren reasoned that the states had adopted a relatively unburdensome way of accomplishing their goal of creating a uniform "weekly respite from all labor."

Other members of the Court took issue with Warren's analysis; as a judgment, after all, his opinion represented the views of only a plurality of the justices. Especially memorable were dissents by William Brennan and Potter Stewart. Brennan thought the Court had taken a misguided approach to the issue: "I would approach this case differently, from the point of view of the individuals whose liberty is—concededly—

curtailed by these enactments. For the values of the First Amendment . . . look primarily towards the preservation of personal liberty, rather than towards the fulfillment of collective goals."

In a one-paragraph dissent, Stewart put the issue even more starkly:

Pennsylvania has passed a law which compels an Orthodox Jew to choose between his religious faith and his economic survival. That is a cruel choice. It is a choice which I think no State can constitutionally demand. For me this is not something that can be swept under the rug and forgotten in the interest of enforced Sunday togetherness. I think the impact of this law upon the appellants grossly violates their constitutional right to free exercise of their religion.

The divided opinion over *Braunfeld* created something of a quandary for legal scholars: Was the Court—through its adoption of a least restrictive means approach—signaling a change in the way it would resolve free exercise disputes? Or was *Braunfeld* an aberration? In *Sherbert v. Verner* (1963), the Court provided some answers.

Adell Sherbert was spool tender in a Spartanburg, South Carolina, textile mill, a job she had held for thirty-five years. Sherbert worked Monday though Friday from 7 A.M. to 3 P.M. She had the option of working Saturdays, but chose not to. Sherbert was a member of the Seventh-Day Adventist church, which held that no work be performed between sundown on Friday and sundown on Saturday. In other words, Saturday was her church's Sabbath.

On June 5, 1959, Sherbert's employer informed her that, beginning June 6, work on Saturdays would no longer be voluntary: to retain her job she would need to report to the mill every Saturday. Sherbert continued to work Monday through Friday but, in accord with her religious beliefs, failed to show up on six successive Saturdays. Her employer fired her July 27.

Between June 5 and July 27, Sherbert had tried to find a job at three other textile mills, but they too operated on Saturdays. Sherbert filed for state unemployment benefits. Under South Carolina law, a claimant who is eligible for benefits must be "able to work . . . and available for work"; a claimant is ineligible for benefits if he or she has "failed, without good cause . . . to accept available suitable work when offered him by the employment office or the employer." The benefits examiner in charge of Sherbert's claim turned her down on the grounds that she failed, without good cause, to accept "suitable work when offered" by her employer. In other words, her religious preference was an insufficient justification for her refusal of a job.

Sherbert and her lawyers filed suit in a state court, which ruled in favor of the employment office, as did the state supreme court. When Sherbert's attorneys asked the U.S. Supreme Court to review the case, they raised several claims emanating from the Court's previous rulings on the free exercise of religion. First, after reviewing the belief–action distinction of *Reynolds* and *Cantwell,* they tried to show that the state's denial actually impinged on the forbidden territory of beliefs. They illustrated the fine line that separates beliefs from actions: the South Carolina law

conditions [Sherbert's] eligibility for benefits . . . upon being willing to accept work on Saturday and disqualified her for her refusal to accept a job involving work on Saturday. In effect this requires her to repudiate her religious belief by professing a willingness to do something in conflict with the tenets of her church. This is not mere regulation of conduct. It invades the sphere of belief and intellect.

In essence, the attorneys were adopting a page out of Stewart's dissent in *Braunfeld:* the state was using economic coercion to force Sherbert to give up a religious belief.

Second, Sherbert's attorneys tried to use *Braunfeld,* a precedent seemingly adverse to their client's interests, by flipping *Braunfeld* so that it worked for her.

The right to observe the Sabbath by abstaining from labor is of the essence. Take away that right or stifle it, and there is no freedom of religion so far as a Saturday Sabbatarian is concerned. Most Sunday-observing Christians probably feel as strongly with respect to their right similarly to refrain from labor in observance of Sunday as the Lord's Day.

The state had an easier task, or so it seemed. It could rely on *Braunfeld* to show that South Carolina, just like Pennsylvania, had not criminalized religious beliefs. Moreover, it offered—as did Pennsylvania in *Braunfeld*—a secular and, in its view, "legitimate governmental purposes for the law." According to the state, it sought to encourage "stable employment" and to discourage fraudulent behavior in those seeking unemployment benefits. Finally, while the state admitted that its denial of benefits financially burdened Sherbert, it argued that the burden was no more direct or greater than the economic hardship Braunfeld had alleged.

So the question for the Court to settle was the following: May a state deny unemployment benefits to persons whose religious beliefs preclude working on Saturdays? And, to it, the Court said no. In writing for the majority, Justice Brennan set out the problem in this way:

The door of the Free Exercise Clause stands tightly closed against any governmental regulation of religious beliefs as such, *Cantwell v. Connecticut.* . . . On the other hand, the Court has rejected challenges under the Free Exercise Clause to governmental regulation of certain overt acts prompted by religious beliefs or principles, for "even when the action is in accord with one's religious convictions, [it] is not totally free from legislative restrictions." *Braunfeld v. Brown.* The conduct or actions so regulated have invariably posed some substantial threat to public safety, peace or order. See, *e.g., Reynolds v. United States; Prince v. Massachusetts.* . . .

Plainly enough, appellant's conscientious objection to Saturday work constitutes no conduct prompted by religious principles of a kind within the reach of state legislation. If, therefore, the decision of the South Carolina Supreme Court is to withstand appellant's constitutional challenge, it must be either because her disqualification as a beneficiary represents no infringement by the State of her constitutional rights of free exercise, or because any incidental burden on the free exercise of appellant's religion may be justified by a "compelling state interest in the regulation of a subject within the State's constitutional power to regulate.". . .

The answers to both these questions, in Brennan's eyes, favored Sherbert. The disqualification from benefits clearly imposed a burden on the free exercise of her religion. And that state had failed to provide a compelling interest for the "substantial infringement her First Amendment right."

The question remains: Does Brennan's majority opinion represent a significant break from past free exercise claims? Some analysts suggest that it does. Although—as the above quotation reveals—Brennan affirmed the belief–action dichotomy, he agreed with Sherbert's attorney that the lines were blurred. Accordingly, he made it far more difficult for states to regulate "action." No longer would a secular legislative purpose suffice; rather, under *Sherbert*, when the government enacts a law that burdens the free exercise of religion, it must show that it was protecting an important, compelling government interest and in the least restrictive manner possible. *Sherbert* also represented a step away from previous free exercise cases in which the Court insisted on neutrality, for here the Court was striking down a law that was neutral in application on the grounds that it burdened the free exercise of religion with a less than compelling interest. Other analysts argue that *Sherbert* represented a logical step from *Braunfeld*. It was in *Braunfeld* that Warren first articulated the least restrictive manner standard on which Brennan relied to strike the South Carolina law.

Either way, *Sherbert* perhaps raises even more questions than it answers. First, if *Braunfeld* and *Sherbert*, taken together, indicated a turning point in the standards governing free exercise cases, why did the Court decide the cases so differently? In *Braunfeld*, the Court found against the religious claimant to uphold Sunday closing laws, but in *Sherbert* it struck down the state's unemployment benefits policy. How can we explain the inconsistency? Some of the justices (for example, Harlan in dissent and Stewart in concurrence) argued that because this discrepancy could not be resolved, *Sherbert* effectively overruled *Braunfeld*. But the majority claimed that the difference between the two was obvious: Pennsylvania had achieved its goal of creating a uniform day of rest in the least intrusive way possible, while South Carolina could have protected its interest in preventing fraud in other, less restrictive ways.

Second, how would the Court use the new standard? In theory, the Court would now balance the interests of the state against those of the free exercise claimant. In practice, according to some analysts, such balancing—given the compelling interest–least restrictive means approach—would almost always result in a victory for the free exercise claimant. After all, governments would have to demonstrate that policies burdening religion are of "sufficient magnitude to override the interest claiming protection"[22] and cast in the least restrictive possible manner, a difficult task, as indicated by *Sherbert*. The next section examines whether this prediction—that governments would be unable to prevail in these cases—accurately describes the Court's resolution of the post-*Sherbert* cases.

Free Exercise Claims During the Burger Court, 1969–1986

The Warren Court ushered in the change in free exercise standards in *Braunfeld* and *Sherbert*, but that Court heard very few free exercise cases after *Sherbert*. It was up to the justices of the Court led by Chief Justice Warren Burger to apply those standards.

The opportunity for the Burger Court to put its stamp on this area of the law arose early in the new chief's tenure. In 1972, with two of the four Nixon appointees (Burger and Harry A. Blackmun) participating, the Court decided *Wisconsin v. Yoder*. At issue here

22. *Wisconsin v. Yoder* (1972).

was a Wisconsin law mandating that children attend public or private schools until the age of sixteen. This kind of compulsory education law violated the norms of the Amish, who had been among the first religious groups to arrive in the United States. As a simple people, who eschew technology, including automobiles and electricity, they do not permit their children to attend school after the eighth grade, believing that they will be adversely exposed "to worldly influences in terms of attitudes, goals, and values contrary to their beliefs."

In challenging the Wisconsin law, attorneys representing the parents of Amish children raised two fundamental claims. First, they asserted that the Amish did not want their children to be uneducated or ignorant. In fact, the teenagers pursued rigorous home study after their public school education. Second, because education was continuing at home, the state could demonstrate no compelling reason to require the children to attend public school. In contrast, the attorney general of Wisconsin compared this case to *Prince v. Massachusetts (see pages 369–370)*, in which the Court upheld child labor regulations. He claimed that the two laws were similar because both were enacted out of a legitimate "concern for the welfare of" children.

Chief Justice Burger's opinion for the Court held for the Amish. In so doing, he cited *Sherbert* with approval:

The essence of all that has been said and written on the subject is that only those interests of the highest order and those not otherwise served can overbalance legitimate claims of free exercise of religion. We can accept it as settled, therefore, that, however strong the State's interest in universal compulsory education, it is by no means absolute to the exclusion or subordination of all other interests. *E.g., Sherbert v. Verner* (1963). . . .

Burger invoked *Sherbert*'s approach to find that the state's interest was not sufficiently compelling to outweigh the free exercise claim.

That Burger found for the religious claimants

lends support to those analysts who argue that the *Sherbert* standard would almost always lead to such a conclusion. But some scholars allege that Burger grounded his opinion on respect for the history and the practices of the Amish rather than on the logic of *Sherbert*. Consider this passage from his opinion:

Giving no weight to . . . secular considerations . . . we see that the record in this case abundantly supports the claim that the traditional way of life of the Amish is not merely a matter of personal preference, but one of deep religious conviction, shared by an organized group, and intimately related to daily living. . . .

. . . The conclusion is inescapable that secondary schooling, by exposing Amish children to worldly influences in terms of attitudes, goals, and values contrary to beliefs, and by substantially interfering with the religious development of the Amish child and his integration into the way of life of the Amish faith community at the crucial adolescent stage of development, contravenes the basic religious tenets and practice of the Amish faith, both as to the parent and the child. . . .

If Burger did follow such a course, he would not be the first—and probably not the last—to do so. Remember Chief Justice Waite's opinion in *Reynolds*? Did it not rest as much on his Court's perception of the Mormons as a strange and bizarre sect as on legal factors?

Whatever Burger's motivation, it seemed as if the Court would continue to apply the compelling interest standard to free exercise claims. Less than a decade after *Yoder*, the justices decided *Thomas v. Review Board of Indiana Employment Security Division* (1981), the facts of which a bore a marked resemblance to *Sherbert*. Thomas was a Jehovah's Witness who worked in a steel mill. When the owners closed the mill down, they transferred Thomas to another plant. Because his new job required him to make tanks for use by the military, Thomas quit on religious grounds and filed for unemployment benefits, which the state denied. Writing for the Court, Chief Justice Burger acknowledged the parallels between *Sherbert* and this dispute: "Here, as in *Sherbert*, the employee was put to a choice between fidelity to his religious beliefs or cessation of work; the coercive impact on Thomas is indistinguishable from *Sherbert*. . . ." Accordingly, he said, "Unless we are prepared to overrule *Sherbert*, Thomas can not be denied the benefits due him."

The Demise of Sherbert *and the Compelling Interest Standard?*

Despite the Burger Court's apparent adoption of the compelling interest standard, there were signs in the early to mid-1980s that some of the justices wanted to rethink that standard or, at the very least, make it easier for the state to respond to free exercise challenges. *United States v. Lee*, decided in 1982, was the first of these signs.

Lee, a member of the Amish faith, owned a farm and a carpentry shop. In violation of federal law, he refused to withhold Social Security taxes or pay the employer's share of those taxes, arguing that the payment of taxes and the receipt of Social Security benefits violated his religious tenets. To support his argument, Lee's attorneys pointed out that Congress had provided a Social Security tax exemption to self-employed Amish. Although Lee did not fall under that specific exemption—he employed others—the very existence of the exemption demonstrated Congress's sensitivity toward the Amish.

In a short opinion for the Court, Chief Justice Burger disagreed. To be sure, Burger conceded, "compulsory participation" in the Social Security system interferes with the free exercise rights of the Amish. But the government was able to justify that burden on religion by showing that compulsory participation is "essential to accomplish an overriding governmental interest" in the maintenance of the Social Security system in the United States. As Burger put it: "To maintain an organized society that guarantees religious freedom to a great variety of faiths requires that some religious practices yield to the common good."

Why do some scholars cite *Lee* as a first cut into the compelling interest standard of *Sherbert?* After all,

Burger did adopt the standard to resolve the dispute. What they see is a discrepancy between *Lee* and *Yoder*. Why was Burger willing to exempt the Amish from mandatory education laws but unwilling to exempt them from compulsory participation in the Social Security system? In *Lee*, Burger tried to address this question when he wrote: "It would be difficult to accommodate the comprehensive Social Security system with myriad exceptions flowing from a wide variety of religious beliefs." But this point led observers to suggest that the Burger Court was willing to override an important governmental interest if only a few groups would be affected or if the impact of the religious exemption would be fairly negligible, as was the case in *Yoder*.

Goldman v. Weinberger (1986), one of the last major free exercise cases of the Burger Court era, did little to quell these and other suspicions about the direction of Court doctrine. S. Simcha Goldman was an Orthodox Jew, an ordained rabbi, and a captain in the Air Force. He was stationed at March Air Force Base in Riverside, California, as a clinical psychologist in the base hospital. From the time Goldman began his service at the base, he wore a yarmulke (skull cap) while in and out of uniform. Goldman did so because his religion requires its adherents to keep their heads covered at all times.

After a superior told him that the yarmulke violated Air Force Dress Code Regulation (AFR) 35-10, a 190-page regulation "that describes in minute detail all of the various items of apparel that constitute the Air Force Uniform," Goldman brought suit against the secretary of defense, arguing that the Air Force regulation violated his First Amendment free exercise rights. A U.S. district court agreed, but a panel of judges on the Court of Appeals for the District of Columbia reversed. When Goldman asked for an en banc hearing,[23] the appellate court denied the request

---

23. U.S. Courts of Appeals typically hear cases in panels of three judges. An *en banc* hearing is one in which all the judges of the court participate.

above the dissents of only three judges.[24] But what an interesting trio they made! Judge Kenneth Starr, who would later serve as solicitor general, said, "The treatment of Dr. Goldman seems to me patently unconscionable." Two future Supreme Court justices, Ruth Bader Ginsburg and Antonin Scalia, wrote in dissent:

S. Simcha Goldman . . . has long served his country as an Air Force officer with honor and devotion. A military commander has now declared intolerable the yarmulke Dr. Goldman has worn without incident throughout his several years of military service. At the least, the declaration suggests "callous indifference" to Dr. Goldman's faith, and it runs counter to "the best of our traditions" to "accommodate the public service to the spiritual needs [of our people]." . . . *cf.* Braunfeld v. Brown [(Stewart, J., dissenting) (commenting on state law exposing Orthodox Jew to "cruel choice" between "his religious faith and his economic survival"). . . . I believe that the court en banc should measure the command suddenly and lately championed by the military against the restraint imposed even on an armed forces commander by the Free Exercise Clause of the First Amendment.]

With the court of appeals' rejection, Goldman brought the case to the Supreme Court. There, his attorneys argued that Goldman's conduct was of a nonintrusive nature that "interferes with no one else, does not harm the public health, and imposes no burden on accommodation." They were attempting to show that Goldman's behavior was markedly different from activities the Court had struck down in *Reynolds* (polygamy) and *Prince* (solicitation by children in violation of child labor laws). They also maintained that the Air Force lacked any overriding governmental interest that would justify such a major intrusion into Goldman's religious practice.

The government's response was that "[t]here can be no serious doubt that uniform dress and appearance standards serve the military interest in maintaining discipline, moral, and esprit de corps" and that enforcement of the dress code "is a necessary

means to the undeniably critical ends of molding soldiers into an effective fighting force." The government also urged the justices to consider what might happen if they allowed Goldman to wear his yarmulke: adherents of other religions could request exemptions to wear turbans, dreadlocks, kum kums (red dots on foreheads), and so forth.

Writing for the majority, Justice Rehnquist agreed with the government and ruled against Goldman. As he said:

Petitioner argues that AFR 35-10, as applied to him, prohibits religiously motivated conduct and should therefore be analyzed under the standard enunciated in *Sherbert v. Verner* (1963). . . . But we have repeatedly held that "the military is, by necessity, a specialized society separate from civilian society." . . . "[T]he military must insist upon a respect for duty and a discipline without counterpart in civilian life" . . . in order to prepare for and perform its vital role. . . .

Our review of military regulations challenged on First Amendment grounds is far more deferential than constitutional review of similar laws or regulations designed for civilian society. The military need not encourage debate or tolerate protest to the extent that such tolerance is required of the civilian state by the First Amendment; to accomplish its mission the military must foster instinctive obedience, unity, commitment, and esprit de corps. . . . The essence of military service "is the subordination of the desires and interests of the individual to the needs of the service." . . .

These aspects of military life do not, of course, render entirely nugatory in the military context the guarantees of the First Amendment. . . . But "within the military community there is simply not the same [individual] autonomy as there is in the larger civilian community." . . . In the context of the present case, when evaluating whether military needs justify a particular restriction on religiously motivated conduct, courts must give great deference to the professional judgment of military authorities concerning the relative importance of a particular military interest. . . . Not only are courts "'ill-equipped to determine the impact upon discipline that any particular intrusion upon military authority might have,'". . . but the military authorities have been charged by the Executive and Legislative Branches with carrying out our Nation's military policy. "[J]udicial deference . . . is at its apogee when legislative action under

24. *Goldman v. Secretary of Defense*, 739 F. 2d 657 (1984).

the congressional authority to raise and support armies and make rules and regulations for their governance is challenged.". . .

The Court's decision in *Goldman* fueled debate in political and academic circles. Taking up an invitation issued by Justice Brennan in a dissenting opinion ("The Court and the military have refused these servicemen their constitutional rights; we must hope that Congress will correct this wrong"), members of Congress introduced legislation to overturn the ruling. The bill allowed members of the armed forces "to wear an item of religious apparel while in uniform" so long the item is "neat and conservative" and does not "interfere with the performance" of military duties. In the debate over the bill supporters made poignant arguments about religious freedom. As Rep. Benjamin Gilman, R-N.Y., put it, "To deny religious individuals the opportunity to serve because of the necessity of wearing an unobtrusive part of their apparel would be a disservice to so many loyal, patriotic Americans." Opponents were equally adamant. Sen. John Glenn, D-Ohio, put into the record letters from the secretary of defense and the joint chiefs of staff expressing serious reservations about the legislation. They feared that officers would have difficulty determining whether attire was "neat and conservative."[25] But Congress, unlike the Supreme Court, resisted military claims and passed the law in September 1987. *Goldman* was effectively overturned.

Debate in academic and legal circles centered less on the Court's holding in *Goldman* than on the rationale the Court invoked to resolve the dispute. Was *Goldman* a substantial break from the *Sherbert* standard? Clearly, the four dissenters (Blackmun, Brennan, Marshall, and O'Connor) saw it that way. O'Connor's opinion is particularly interesting. After noting that Court cases in this area adopted slightly different versions of a similar standard, she set out the "two

consistent themes" running through Court precedent from *Sherbert* to *Lee*. First, the government "must show that an unusually important interest is at stake, whether that interest is denominated 'compelling.'" Second, "the government must show that granting the requested exemption will do substantial harm to that interest, whether by showing that the means adopted is the 'least restrictive' or 'essential.'" O'Connor saw no reason to jettison this two-pronged standard—as she thought the majority had done—simply because the military was involved. In contrast, some scholars (along with a few members of the Court) did not think *Goldman* represented a significant shift in Court opinion. They argued that *Goldman* was an exceptional case: it involved the interests of the armed forces, interests to which the justices traditionally defer. Accordingly, they asserted that the Court would return to the compelling interest–least restrictive means standard, mentioned in the dissents, in future cases.

Free Exercise Claims During the Rehnquist Court, 1986–

In the first year or so of the Rehnquist Court, it appeared that those scholars who argued that *Goldman* was an anomalous ruling were correct. In *Hobbie v. Unemployment Appeals Commission of Florida* (1987) the Court returned to the compelling interest standard. The facts of *Hobbie* were similar to those of *Sherbert* and *Thomas*: a Seventh-Day Adventist was fired from her job for refusing to work certain hours, and the state denied her claim for unemployment benefits. The state claimed Hobbie had failed to meet the standard that she became "unemployed through no fault of her own." The only significant difference between *Hobbie* and *Sherbert/Thomas* was that Hobbie had converted to the Seventh-Day Adventist church after working at the company for two and a half years.

This distinction, however, was trivial to the majority, which wrote:

25. See Louis Fisher, *American Constitutional Law* (New York: McGraw-Hill, 1990), 740–746.

We see no meaningful distinction among the situations of Sherbert, Thomas, and Hobbie. We again affirm, as we stated in Thomas: "Where the state conditions receipt of an important benefit upon the conduct proscribed by a religious faith, or where it denies such a benefit because of conduct mandated by a religious belief, thereby putting substantial pressure on an adherent to modify his behavior and to violate his beliefs, a burden upon religion exists."

In writing for a majority of eight, Justice Brennan also used the logic of Sherbert and similar cases to find for Hobbie: "Both Sherbert and Thomas held that such infringements [on the free exercise of religion] must be subjected to strict scrutiny and could be justified only by proof by the State of a compelling interest."

Hobbie seemed to indicate the willingness of most of the justices to return to the Sherbert standard. Whether they feared congressional retaliation (the justices knew that Congress was considering legislation to overturn Goldman) or because they never had really abandoned Sherbert is open to speculation. What is clear, however, is that one member of the Rehnquist Court—the chief justice himself—was unhappy with the Sherbert standard. He had written the Court's opinion in Goldman, in which he abstained from applying that standard, and he dissented in Thomas. Indeed, in that case, Rehnquist specifically stated his agreement with Justice Harlan's dissent in Sherbert. As Rehnquist put it:

Where . . . the State has enacted a general statute, the purpose and effect of which is to advance the State's secular goals, the Free Exercise Clause does not in my view require the State to conform that statute to the dictates of religious conscience of any group. As Justice Harlan recognized in his dissent in Sherbert: "Those situations in which the Constitution may require special treatment on account of religion are . . . few and far between."

Applying this logic to Hobbie, Rehnquist voted in favor of Florida: the state had not discriminated against Hobbie because she was a Seventh-Day Adventist.

The chief justice may not have prevailed in Hobbie. But in a subsequent case, it appeared as if he won the larger war to dismantle, if not completely eradicate, the Sherbert standard. That case was Employment Division, Department of Human Resources of Oregon v. Smith (1990). In Smith the Court seemed to turn its back on nearly three decades of free exercise cases—those from Braunfeld and Sherbert through Hobbie. How did the majority justify its position? Do you find its logic compelling? Keep these questions in mind as you read the facts and excerpts in this highly controversial case.

=====

Employment Division, Department of Human Resources of Oregon v. Smith

494 U.S. 872 (1990)

Vote: 6 (Kennedy, O'Connor, Rehnquist, Scalia, Stevens, White)
        3 (Blackmun, Brennan, Marshall)

Opinion of the Court: Scalia
Concurring opinion: O'Connor
Dissenting opinion: Blackmun

This case centers on the use of peyote, which is a controlled substance under Oregon law. In other words, it is illegal to possess the drug unless it is prescribed by a doctor. Peyote is a hallucinogen produced by certain cactus plants found in the southwestern United States and northern Mexico. Unlike other hallucinogenic drugs (such as LSD), peyote has never been widely used or problematic. One reason is that peyote is taken by eating the buds of certain cactus plants, which are "tough, bitter, and frequently cause nausea and vomiting."[26]

There is, however, one group of citizens who regularly ingest peyote—members of a bona fide religion, the Native American Church. To them "peyote is a sacramental substance, an object of worship, and a source of divine protection." They use the substance during religious rituals.

26. The discussion of peyote is drawn from Douglas Laycock, "The Remnants of Free Exercise," The Supreme Court Review (1990): 7–8.

The spiritual nature of the church's use of peyote has been acknowledged by various governments. Although they have laws (like the one in Oregon) criminalizing the general use of peyote, twenty-three states (those with large Native American populations) and the federal government exempt the religious use of peyote from such laws. The federal government even provides licenses to grow peyote for sacramental purposes.

The dispute at issue in *Smith* arose when two members of the Native American Church, Alfred Smith and Galen Black, were fired from their jobs as counselors at a private drug and alcohol abuse clinic for ingesting peyote at a religious ceremony. Smith and Black applied for unemployment benefits but were turned down by the state. Oregon found them ineligible because they had been fired for "misconduct"; under state law, workers discharged for that reason cannot obtain benefits.

Smith and Black brought suit in state court, arguing that under the U.S. Supreme Court's precedents of *Sherbert* and *Thomas* (they later added *Hobbie*, which had yet to be handed down by the Court), the state could not deny them benefits. The issue for them was not that the state had criminalized peyote: they had not been charged with committing a criminal offense. Rather, they pointed to the Supreme Court's previous rulings, which indicated that states may not deny unemployment benefits because of an individual's unwillingness to forgo activity mandated by religion. The state argued that it could deny the benefits—regardless of Smith and Black's free exercise claim—because the use of peyote was prohibited by a general criminal statute, which was not aimed at inhibiting religion. Oregon also noted that it—like all other government entities—has a compelling interest in regulating drug use and that the state's law represented the least intrusive means of achieving that interest.

The Oregon Supreme Court thought otherwise, however, and relied on *Sherbert* and *Thomas* to find in favor of Smith and Black. The state appealed to the U.S. Supreme Court, which heard arguments in the case in 1987. But because the Oregon Supreme Court had not determined whether peyote use at religious ceremonies violated the state's criminal laws, the justices remanded the case back to Oregon for a decision.

That court ruled that the state law's prohibition against the use of peyote did not exempt the sacramental use of peyote, but it also said that the prohibition violated the Free Exercise Clause. The state brought its case back to the Supreme Court, where both sides assumed that the Court would use the *Sherbert* standard to resolve the dispute.

JUSTICE SCALIA delivered the opinion of the Court.

The free exercise of religion means, first and foremost, the right to believe and profess whatever religious doctrine one desires. Thus, the First Amendment obviously excludes all "governmental regulation of religious *beliefs* as such.". . .

But the "exercise of religion" often involves not only belief and profession but the performance of (or abstention from) physical acts: assembling with others for a worship service, participating in sacramental use of bread and wine, proselytizing, abstaining from certain foods or certain modes of transportation. It would be true, we think (though no case of ours has involved the point), that a state would be "prohibiting the free exercise [of religion]" if it sought to ban such acts or abstentions only when they are engaged in for religious reasons, or only because of the religious belief that they display. It would doubtless be unconstitutional, for example, to ban the casting of "statues that are to be used for worship purposes," or to prohibit bowing down before a golden calf.

Respondents in the present case, however, seek to carry the meaning of "prohibiting the free exercise [of religion]" one large step further. They contend that their religious motivation for using peyote places them beyond the reach of a criminal law that is not specifically directed at their religious practice, and that is concededly constitutional as applied to those who use the drug for other reasons. . . .

. . . We have never held that an individual's religious beliefs excuse him from compliance with an otherwise valid law prohibiting conduct that the State is free to regulate.

On the contrary, the record of more than a century of our free exercise jurisprudence contradicts that proposition. . . . We first had occasion to assert that principle in *Reynolds v. United States* (1879), where we rejected the claim that criminal laws against polygamy could not be constitutionally applied to those whose religion commanded the practice. . . .

Subsequent decisions have consistently held that the right of free exercise does not relieve an individual of the obligation to comply with a "valid and neutral law of general applicability on the ground that the law proscribes (or prescribes) conduct that his religion prescribes (or proscribes)." *United States v. Lee* (1982). . . . In *Prince v. Massachusetts* (1944) we held that a mother could be prosecuted under the child labor laws for using her children to dispense literature in the streets, her religious motivation notwithstanding. We found no constitutional infirmity in "excluding [these children] from doing there what no other children may do." In *Braunfeld v. Brown* (1961) (plurality opinion) we upheld Sunday-closing laws against the claim that they burdened the religious practices of persons whose religions compelled them to refrain from work on other days. . . .

The only decisions in which we have held that the First Amendment bars application of a neutral, generally applicable law to religiously motivated action have involved not the Free Exercise Clause alone, but the Free Exercise Clause in conjunction with other constitutional protections, such as freedom of speech and of the press, see *Cantwell v. Connecticut.* . . .

The present case does not present such a hybrid situation, but a free exercise claim unconnected with any communicative activity or parental right. Respondents urge us to hold, quite simply, that when otherwise prohibitable conduct is accompanied by religious convictions, not only the convictions but the conduct itself must be free from governmental regulation. We have never held that, and decline to do so now. There being no contention that Oregon's drug law represents an attempt to regulate religious beliefs, the communication of religious beliefs, or the raising of one's children in those beliefs, the rule to which we have adhered ever since *Reynolds* plainly controls. "Our cases do not at their farthest reach support the proposition that a stance of conscientious opposition relieves an objec-tor from any colliding duty fixed by a democratic government.". . .

Respondents argue that even though exemption from generally applicable criminal laws need not automatically be extended to religiously motivated actors, at least the claim for a religious exemption must be evaluated under the balancing test set forth in *Sherbert v. Verner* (1963). Under the *Sherbert* test, governmental actions that substantially burden a religious practice must be justified by a compelling governmental interest. . . . Applying that test we have, on three occasions, invalidated state unemployment compensation rules that conditioned the availability of benefits upon an applicant's willingness to work under conditions forbidden by his religion. See *Sherbert v. Verner*; *Thomas v. Review Bd. of Indiana Employment Security Div.* (1981); *Hobbie v. Unemployment Appeals Comm'n of Florida* (1987). We have never invalidated any governmental action on the basis of the *Sherbert* test except the denial of unemployment compensation. Although we have sometimes purported to apply the *Sherbert* test in contexts other than that, we have always found the test satisfied. . . . In recent years we have abstained from applying the *Sherbert* test (outside the unemployment compensation field) at all. . . . In *Goldman v. Weinberger* (1986) we rejected application of the *Sherbert* test to military dress regulations that forbade the wearing of yarmulkes. . . .

Even if we were inclined to breathe into *Sherbert* some life beyond the unemployment compensation field, we would not apply it to require exemptions from a generally applicable criminal law. The *Sherbert* test, it must be recalled, was developed in a context that lent itself to individualized governmental assessment of the reasons for the relevant conduct. . . .

Whether or not the decisions are that limited, they at least have nothing to do with an across-the-board criminal prohibition on a particular form of conduct. Although, as noted earlier, we have sometimes used the *Sherbert* test to analyze free exercise challenges to such laws . . . we have never applied the test to invalidate one. We conclude today that the sounder approach, and the approach in accord with the vast majority of our precedents, is to hold the test inapplicable to such challenges. The government's ability to enforce generally applicable prohibitions of socially harmful conduct, like its ability to carry out other aspects of public policy, "cannot depend on measuring the effects of a governmental action on a religious objector's spiritual development.". . . To make an individual's obligation to obey such a law contingent upon the law's coincidence with his religious beliefs, except where the State's interest is "compelling"—permitting him, by virtue of his beliefs, "to become a law unto himself," *Reynolds v. United States*— contradicts both constitutional tradition and common sense.

The "compelling government interest" requirement seems benign, because it is familiar from other fields. But using it as the standard that must be met before the government may accord different treatment on the basis of race . . . or before the government may regulate the content of speech . . . is not remotely comparable to using it for the purpose asserted here. What it produces in those other fields—equality of treatment and an unrestricted flow of contending speech—are constitutional norms; what it would produce here—a private right to ignore generally applicable laws—is a constitutional anomaly.

Nor is it possible to limit the impact of respondents' proposal by requiring a "compelling state interest" only when the conduct prohibited is "central" to the individual's religion. . . . It is no more appropriate for judges to determine the "centrality" of religious beliefs before applying a "compelling interest" test in the free exercise field, than it would be for them to determine the "importance" of ideas before applying the "compelling interest" test in the free speech field. What principle of law or logic can be brought to bear to contradict a believer's assertion that a particular act is "central" to his personal faith? Judging the centrality of different religious practices is akin to the unacceptable "business of evaluating the relative merits of differing religious claims.". . . Repeatedly and in many different contexts, we have warned that courts must not presume to determine the place of a particular belief in a religion or the plausibility of a religious claim. . . .

If the "compelling interest" test is to be applied at all, then, it must be applied across the board, to all actions thought to be religiously commanded. Moreover, if "compelling interest" really means what it says (and watering it down here would subvert its rigor in the other fields where it is applied), many laws will not meet the test. Any society adopting such a system would be courting anarchy, but

that danger increases in direct proportion to the society's diversity of religious beliefs, and its determination to coerce or suppress none of them. Precisely because "we are a cosmopolitan nation made up of people of almost every conceivable religious preference," *Braunfeld v. Brown,* and precisely because we value and protect that religious divergence, we cannot afford the luxury of deeming *presumptively invalid,* as applied to the religious objector, every regulation of conduct that does not protect an interest of the highest order. The rule respondents favor would open the prospect of constitutionally required religious exemptions from civic obligations of almost every conceivable kind— ranging from compulsory military service . . . to the payment of taxes . . . to health and safety regulation such as manslaughter and child neglect laws . . . compulsory vaccination laws . . . drug laws . . . and traffic laws . . . to social welfare legislation such as minimum wage laws . . . child labor laws . . . animal cruelty laws, see, *e.g., Church of the Lukumi Babalu Aye Inc. v. City of Hialeah,* 723 F.Supp. 1467 (SD Fla. 1989) . . . environmental protection laws . . . and laws providing for equality of opportunity for the races. . . . The First Amendment's protection of religious liberty does not require this.

Values that are protected against government interference through enshrinement in the Bill of Rights are not thereby banished from the political process. Just as a society that believes in the negative protection accorded to the press by the First Amendment is likely to enact laws that affirmatively foster the dissemination of the printed word, so also a society that believes in the negative protection accorded to religious belief can be expected to be solicitous of that value in its legislation as well. It is therefore not surprising that a number of States have made an exception to their drug laws for sacramental peyote use. . . . But to say that a nondiscriminatory religious-practice exemption is permitted, or even that it is desirable, is not to say that it is constitutionally required, and that the appropriate occasions for its creation can be discerned by the courts. It may fairly be said that leaving accommodation to the political process will place at a relative disadvantage those religious practices that are not widely engaged in; but that unavoidable consequence of democratic government must be preferred to a system in which each conscience is a law unto itself or in which judges weigh the social importance of all laws against the centrality of all religious beliefs.

Because respondents' ingestion of peyote was prohibited under Oregon law, and because that prohibition is constitutional, Oregon may, consistent with the Free Exercise Clause, deny respondents unemployment compensation when their dismissal results from use of the drug. The decision of the Oregon Supreme Court is accordingly reversed.

It is so ordered.

JUSTICE O'CONNOR, with whom JUSTICE BRENNAN, JUSTICE MARSHALL, and JUSTICE BLACKMUN join as to Parts I and II, concurring in the judgment.*

Although I agree with the result the Court reaches in this case, I cannot join its opinion. In my view, today's holding dramatically departs from well-settled First Amendment jurisprudence, appears unnecessary to resolve the question presented, and is incompatible with our Nation's fundamental commitment to individual religious liberty.

[Part I omitted]
II
The Court today extracts from our long history of free exercise precedents the single categorical rule that "if prohibiting the exercise of religion . . . is . . . merely the incidental effect of a generally applicable and otherwise valid provision, the First Amendment has not been offended." Indeed, the Court holds that where the law is a generally applicable criminal prohibition, our usual free exercise jurisprudence does not even apply. To reach this sweeping result, however, the Court must not only give a strained reading of the First Amendment but must also disregard our consistent application of free exercise doctrine to cases involving generally applicable regulations that burden religious conduct.

The Free Exercise Clause of the First Amendment commands that "Congress shall make no law . . . prohibiting the free exercise [of religion]." In *Cantwell v. Connecticut* (1940) we held that this prohibition applies to the States by incorporation into the Fourteenth Amendment and that it categorically forbids government regulation of religious beliefs. As the Court recognizes, however, the "free *exercise*" of religion often, if not invariably, requires the performance of (or abstention from) certain acts. . . . Because the First Amendment does not distinguish between religious belief and religious conduct, conduct motivated by sincere religious belief, like the belief itself, must be at least presumptively protected by the Free Exercise Clause.

The Court today, however, interprets the Clause to permit the government to prohibit, without justification, conduct mandated by an individual's religious beliefs, so long as that prohibition is generally applicable. But a law that prohibits certain conduct—conduct that happens to be an act of worship for someone—manifestly does prohibit that person's free exercise of his religion. A person who is barred from engaging in religiously motivated conduct is barred from freely exercising his religion. Moreover, that person is barred from freely exercising his religion regardless of whether the law prohibits the conduct only when engaged in for religious reasons, only by members of that religion, or by all persons. It is difficult to deny that a law that prohibits religiously motivated conduct, even if the law is generally applicable, does not at least implicate First Amendment concerns.

The Court responds that generally applicable laws are "one large step" removed from laws aimed at specific religious practices. The First Amendment, however, does not distinguish between laws that are generally applicable and laws that target particular religious practices. Indeed, few States would be so naive as to enact a law directly prohibiting or burdening a religious practice as such. Our free exercise cases have all concerned generally applicable laws that had the effect of significantly burdening a religious practice. If the First Amendment is to have any vitality, it ought not be construed to cover only the extreme and hypothetical situation in which a State directly targets a religious practice. . . .

To say that a person's right to free exercise has been burdened, of course, does not mean that he has an absolute right to engage in the conduct. Under our established First Amendment jurisprudence, we have recognized that the freedom to act, unlike the freedom to believe, cannot be absolute. See, *e.g., Cantwell; Reynolds v. United States* (1879). Instead, we have respected both the First Amendment's ex-

*Although JUSTICE BRENNAN, JUSTICE MARSHALL, and JUSTICE BLACKMUN join Parts I and II of this opinion, they do not concur in the judgment.

press textual mandate and the governmental interest in regulation of conduct by requiring the government to justify any substantial burden on religiously motivated conduct by a compelling state interest and by means narrowly tailored to achieve that interest. . . .

The Court attempts to support its narrow reading of the Clause by claiming that "[w]e have never held that an individual's religious beliefs excuse him from compliance with an otherwise valid law prohibiting conduct that the State is free to regulate." But as the Court later notes, as it must, in cases such as *Cantwell* and *Yoder* we have in fact interpreted the Free Exercise Clause to forbid application of a generally applicable prohibition to religiously motivated conduct. . . . Indeed, in *Yoder* we expressly rejected the interpretation the Court now adopts. . . .

The Court endeavors to escape from our decisions in *Cantwell* and *Yoder* by labeling them "hybrid" decisions, but there is no denying that both cases expressly relied on the Free Exercise Clause . . . and that we have consistently regarded those cases as part of the mainstream of our free exercise jurisprudence. Moreover, in each of the other cases cited by the Court to support its categorical rule, we rejected the particular constitutional claims before us only after carefully weighing the competing interests. See *Prince v. Massachusetts* . . . *Braunfeld v. Brown.* . . . That we rejected the free exercise claims in those cases hardly calls into question the applicability of First Amendment doctrine in the first place. Indeed, it is surely unusual to judge the vitality of a constitutional doctrine by looking to the win-loss record of the plaintiffs who happen to come before us.

Respondents, of course, do not contend that their conduct is automatically immune from all governmental regulation simply because it is motivated by their sincere religious beliefs. The Court's rejection of that argument might therefore be regarded as merely harmless dictum. Rather, respondents invoke our traditional compelling interest test to argue that the Free Exercise Clause requires the State to grant them a limited exemption from its general criminal prohibition against the possession of peyote. The Court today, however, denies them even the opportunity to make that argument, concluding that "the sounder approach, and the approach in accord with the vast majority of our precedents, is to hold the [compelling interest] test inapplicable to" challenges to general criminal prohibitions.

In my view, however, the essence of a free exercise claim is relief from a burden imposed by government on religious practices or beliefs, whether the burden is imposed directly through laws that prohibit or compel specific religious practices, or indirectly through laws that, in effect, make abandonment of one's own religion or conformity to the religious beliefs of others the price of an equal place in the civil community. . . . A State that makes criminal an individual's religiously motivated conduct burdens that individual's free exercise of religion in the severest manner possible, for it "results in the choice to the individual of either abandoning his religious principle or facing criminal prosecution.". . . I would have thought it beyond argument that such laws implicate free exercise concerns.

Indeed, we have never distinguished between cases in which a State conditions receipt of a benefit on conduct prohibited by religious beliefs and cases in which a State affirmatively prohibits such conduct. The *Sherbert* compelling interest test applies in both kinds of cases. . . . I would reaffirm that principle today: a neutral criminal law prohibiting conduct that a State may legitimately regulate is, if anything, *more* burdensome than a neutral civil statute placing legitimate conditions on the award of a state benefit.

Legislatures, of course, have always been "left free to reach actions which were in violation of social duties or subversive of good order.". . . Yet because of the close relationship between conduct and religious belief, "[i]n every case the power to regulate must be so exercised as not, in attaining a permissible end, unduly to infringe the protected freedom.". . . Once it has been shown that a government regulation or criminal prohibition burdens the free exercise of religion, we have consistently asked the Government to demonstrate that unbending application of its regulation to the religious objector "is essential to accomplish an overriding governmental interest," or represents "the least restrictive means of achieving some compelling state interest.". . . To me, the sounder approach—the approach more consistent with our role as judges to decide each case on its individual merits—is to apply this test in each case to determine whether the burden on the specific plaintiffs before us is constitutionally significant and whether the particular criminal interest asserted by the State before us is compelling. Even if, as an empirical matter, a government's criminal laws might usually serve a compelling interest in health, safety, or public order, the First Amendment at least requires a case-by-case determination of the question, sensitive to the facts of each particular claim. . . . Given the range of conduct that a State might legitimately make criminal, we cannot assume, merely because a law carries criminal sanctions and is generally applicable, that the First Amendment *never* requires the State to grant a limited exemption for religiously motivated conduct. . . .

The Court today gives no convincing reason to depart from settled First Amendment jurisprudence. There is nothing talismanic about neutral laws of general applicability or general criminal prohibitions, for laws neutral toward religion can coerce a person to violate his religious conscience or intrude upon his religious duties just as effectively as laws aimed at religion. Although the Court suggests that the compelling interest test, as applied to generally applicable laws, would result in a "constitutional anomaly," the First Amendment unequivocally makes freedom of religion, like freedom from race discrimination and freedom of speech, a "constitutional nor[m]," not an "anomaly.". . . The Court's parade of horribles not only fails as a reason for discarding the compelling interest test, it instead demonstrates just the opposite: that courts have been quite capable of applying our free exercise jurisprudence to strike sensible balances between religious liberty and competing state interests.

Finally, the Court today suggests that the disfavoring of minority religions is an "unavoidable consequence" under our system of government and that accommodation of such religions must be left to the political process. In my view, however, the First Amendment was enacted precisely to protect the rights of those whose religious practices are not shared by the majority and may be viewed with hostility. The history of our free exercise doctrine amply demonstrates the harsh impact majoritarian rule has had on unpopular or emerging religious groups such as the Jehovah's Witnesses and the Amish. . . .

III

The Court's holding today not only misreads settled First Amendment precedent; it appears to be unnecessary to this case. I would reach the same result applying our established free exercise jurisprudence.

There is no dispute that Oregon's criminal prohibition of peyote places a severe burden on the ability of respondents to freely exercise their religion. Peyote is a sacrament of the Native American Church and is regarded as vital to respondents' ability to practice their religion. . . .

There is also no dispute that Oregon has a significant interest in enforcing laws that control the possession and use of controlled substances by its citizens. . . . As we recently noted, drug abuse is "one of the greatest problems affecting the health and welfare of our population" and thus "one of the most serious problems confronting our society today.". . .

Thus, the critical question in this case is whether exempting respondents from the State's general criminal prohibition "will unduly interfere with fulfillment of the governmental interest.". . . Although the question is close, I would conclude that uniform application of Oregon's criminal prohibition is "essential to accomplish" . . . its overriding interest in preventing the physical harm caused by the use of a . . . controlled substance. Oregon's criminal prohibition represents that State's judgment that the possession and use of controlled substances, even by only one person, is inherently harmful and dangerous. Because the health effects caused by the use of controlled substances exist regardless of the motivation of the user, the use of such substances, even for religious purposes, violates the very purpose of the laws that prohibit them. . . . Moreover, in view of the societal interest in preventing trafficking in controlled substances, uniform application of the criminal prohibition at issue is essential to the effectiveness of Oregon's stated interest in preventing any possession of peyote. . . .

I would therefore adhere to our established free exercise jurisprudence and hold that the State in this case has a compelling interest in regulating peyote use by its citizens and that accommodating respondents' religiously motivated conduct "will unduly interfere with fulfillment of the governmental interest.". . .

Accordingly, I concur in the judgment of the Court.

JUSTICE BLACKMUN, with whom JUSTICE BRENNAN and JUSTICE MARSHALL join, dissenting.

This Court over the years painstakingly has developed a consistent and exacting standard to test the constitutionality of a state statute that burdens the free exercise of religion. Such a statute may stand only if the law in general, and the State's refusal to allow a religious exemption in particular, are justified by a compelling interest that cannot be served by less restrictive means.

Until today, I thought this was a settled and inviolate principle of this Court's First Amendment jurisprudence. The majority, however, perfunctorily dismisses it as a "constitutional anomaly." As carefully detailed in JUSTICE O'-CONNOR's concurring opinion, the majority is able to arrive at this view only by mischaracterizing this Court's precedents. The Court discards leading free exercise cases such as *Cantwell v. Connecticut* (1940) and *Wisconsin v. Yoder* (1972), as "hybrid." The Court views traditional free exercise analysis as somehow inapplicable to criminal prohibitions (as opposed to conditions on the receipt of benefits), and to state laws of general applicability (as opposed, presumably, to laws that expressly single out religious practices). The Court cites cases in which, due to various exceptional circumstances, we found strict scrutiny inapposite, to hint that the Court has repudiated that standard altogether. In short, it effectuates a wholesale overturning of settled law concerning the Religion Clauses of our Constitution. One hopes that the Court is aware of the consequences, and that its result is not a product of overreaction to the serious problems the country's drug crisis has generated.

This distorted view of our precedents leads the majority to conclude that strict scrutiny of a state law burdening the free exercise of religion is a "luxury" that a well-ordered society cannot afford, and that the repression of minority religions is an "unavoidable consequence of democratic government." I do not believe the Founders thought their dearly bought freedom from religious persecution a "luxury," but an essential element of liberty—and they could not have thought religious intolerance "unavoidable," for they drafted the Religion Clauses precisely in order to avoid that intolerance.

For these reasons, I agree with JUSTICE O'CONNOR's analysis of the applicable free exercise doctrine, and I join parts I and II of her opinion. As she points out, "the critical question in this case is whether exempting respondents from the State's general criminal prohibition 'will unduly interfere with fulfillment of the governmental interest.'" I do disagree, however, with her specific answer to that question.

In weighing respondents' clear interest in the free exercise of their religion against Oregon's asserted interest in enforcing its drug laws, it is important to articulate in precise terms the state interest involved. It is not the State's broad interest in fighting the critical "war on drugs" that must be weighed against respondents' claim, but the State's narrow interest in refusing to make an exception for the religious, ceremonial use of peyote. . . .

The State's interest in enforcing its prohibition, in order to be sufficiently compelling to outweigh a free exercise claim, cannot be merely abstract or symbolic. The State cannot plausibly assert that unbending application of a criminal prohibition is essential to fulfill any compelling interest, if it does not, in fact, attempt to enforce that prohibition. In this case, the State actually has not evinced any concrete interest in enforcing its drug laws against religious users of peyote. Oregon has never sought to prosecute respondents, and does not claim that it has made significant enforcement efforts against other religious users of peyote. The State's asserted interest thus amounts only to the symbolic preservation of an unenforced prohibition. But a government interest in "symbolism, even symbolism for so worthy a cause as the abolition of unlawful drugs," cannot suffice to abrogate the constitutional rights of individuals. . . .

Similarly, this Court's prior decisions have not allowed a government to rely on mere speculation about potential harms, but have demanded evidentiary support for a refusal to allow a religious exception. . . . In this case, the State's justification for refusing to recognize an exception to its criminal laws for religious peyote use is entirely speculative.

To some, *Smith* represents a change in the standards governing free exercise disputes. For the first time since it was articulated, the Court explicitly rejected the *Sherbert* test. To be sure, the justices had failed to apply it in cases such as *Goldman,* but here the Court was eradicating the *Sherbert-Yoder* lineage of cases and returning to the kind of analysis it used in *Reynolds v. United States.* As Scalia wrote:

To make an individual's obligation to obey . . . a law contingent upon the law's coincidence with his religious beliefs, except where the State's interest is "compelling"—permitting him, by virtue of his beliefs, "to become a law unto himself," *Reynolds v. United States*—contradicts both constitutional tradition and common sense.

In place of the *Sherbert* test, the Court would now use a standard it hinted at in *United States v. Lee:*

If prohibiting the exercise of religion . . . is . . . merely the incidental effect of a generally applicable and otherwise valid provision, the First Amendment has not been offended. . . . [T]he right of free exercise does not relieve an individual of the obligation to comply with a 'valid and neutral law of general applicability.'[27]

In other words, under the *Smith* rule, the Court will not necessarily apply the compelling interest standard to state laws that are neutral and generally applicable. The articulation of this new standard meant, as one scholar put it, that the Court had "brought free exercise jurisprudence full circle by reaffirming the . . . doctrine of *Reynolds*" and rejecting the compelling interest approach of *Sherbert*.[28]

On what grounds did Scalia justify this alteration in Free Exercise doctrine? One of his justifications is that the precedential cases, such as *Cantwell* and *Barnette*, were "hybrids" involving "the Free Exercise Clause in conjunction with other constitutional protections, such as freedom of speech and of the press, or the right of parents . . . to direct the education of their children." Therefore, it was reasonable for the Court to use a compelling interest approach. *Smith* was—at least in Scalia's view—a pure free exercise case involving a neutral and generally applicable law that the Court did not need to balance against the competing religious interests.

As you might expect, *Smith* was the subject of enormous controversy. O'Connor and Blackmun made

clear their displeasure with the majority's break from precedent, asserting that the Court should stick with the compelling interest–least restrictive means approach. Yet the two justices reached different conclusions about how *Smith* should be resolved: O'Connor would have ruled against Smith and Black, while Blackmun would have found in their favor.

Congress also voiced its disapproval. Soon after the justices handed down *Smith,* interest groups began to lobby Congress to overturn the decision. As Sen. Edward M. Kennedy, D-Mass., put it, these interests feared that, under the new standard "dry communities could ban the use of wine in communion services, Government meat inspectors could require changes in the preparation of kosher food and school boards could force children to attend sex education classes [contrary to their religious beliefs]."[29] With support from politicians as varied in ideological approach as Kennedy and Orrin Hatch, R-Utah, the bill—called the Religious Freedom Restoration Act—was enacted into law in 1993. It says government cannot burden religion unless the government offers a compelling interest and that interest is pursued in the least restrictive manner. In other words, the act codifies the *Sherbert* standard.

While Congress was debating the Religious Freedom Restoration Act, the Supreme Court heard yet another free exercise case. In *Church of the Lukumi Babalu Aye v. City of Hialeah* (1993) the justices considered whether a the Florida city of Hialeah's ordinances prohibiting animal sacrifice for religious purposes violated the Free Exercise Clause. The particular targets of the law were adherents of the Santeria religion. Central to this religion is animal sacrifice. Practitioners sacrifice chickens, pigeons, doves, ducks, guinea pigs, goats, sheep, and turtles at various events, including the initiations of new priests, weddings, births, and deaths, and as cures for the ailing. The an-

27. Ibid., 8–9.

28. Frederick Mark Gedicks, "Religion," in *The Oxford Companion to the Supreme Court,* ed. Kermit L. Hall (New York: Oxford University Press, 1992), 725.

29. Quoted by Adam Clymer in "Congress Moves to Ease Curb on Religious Acts," *New York Times,* May 10, 1993, A9.

Santeria priest Rigoberto Zamora cooks the lamb and goat he sacrificed in a religious ritual the previous day. Zamora and other members of his church celebrated the Supreme Court's decision striking down city attempts to prohibit animal sacrifices in religious worship.

imals, which are killed by cutting the carotid arteries in the neck, are cooked and eaten after some of the rituals. Santerians sacrifice as many as thirty animals during a given ritual.

Members of the Hialeah community—who apparently were less than enthusiastic about the practice of animal sacrifice— enacted six ordinances limiting animal sacrifice, which it defined as "to unnecessarily kill, torment, or mutilate an animal in a public or private ritual or ceremony not for the primary purpose of food consumption."

In his opinion in *Smith*, Scalia listed the Lukumi Babalu dispute in his "parade of horribles," as O'Connor called it, even though the religious sacrifice case had not yet come to the Supreme Court. That is, Scalia used this law as one example of legislation that should be permissible but would not necessarily be so if the Court continued to use the compelling interest standard. However, he and other members of the *Smith* majority voted to strike down such laws. Why?

Several explanations come to mind. The first is that the facts of *Smith* and *Lukumi Babalu* were different in at least one important respect. It is clear that Oregon did not pass its prohibition on peyote use to hinder the religious practice of the Native American church, while it is equally clear that Hialeah aimed its ordinance directly at the Santerians. Accordingly, as Justice Blackmun put it in a concurring opinion, "Because the respondent [Hialeah] here does single out religion in this way, the present case is an easy one to decide." A second reason is that the Court feared yet another rebuke from Congress. By the time the justices handed down *Lukumi Babalu*, Congress had overturned their decision in *Goldman* and was on its way to doing the same with *Smith*. Finally, keep in mind that *Lukumi Babalu* gives only the appearance of unanimity and that underneath the surface (assuming that the justices do not alter their views) lay some very serious disagreements, as Figure 12-1 illustrates.

What does the future hold for Free Exercise cases? With Justice White's departure and Ginsburg's ascension, the *Smith* rule may have lost a vote: as a circuit

FIGURE 12-1 Free Exercise Approaches Advocated by the Justices in *Smith*, *Lukumi Babalu*, and Beyond

Smith	*Lukumi Babalu*	*Post Lukumi, Post-Congressional Act*
Blackmun ⟶ (*Sherbert-Yoder* standard)	Blackmun ⟶ (*Sherbert-Yoder* standard)	Breyer (?)
Brennan ⟶ (*Sherbert-Yoder* standard)	Souter (reconsider *Smith; Smith* fails to consider substantive neutrality)	same
Kennedy ⟶ (*Smith* rule)	Kennedy ⟶ (*Smith* rule)	same
Marshall ⟶ (*Sherbert-Yoder* standard)	Thomas ⟶ (*Smith* rule)	same
O'Connor ⟶ (*Sherbert-Yoder* standard)	O'Connor ⟶ (*Sherbert-Yoder* standard)	same
Rehnquist ⟶ (*Smith* rule)	Rehnquist ⟶ (*Smith* rule, without considering legislators' motives)	same
Scalia ⟶ (*Smith* rule)	Scalia ⟶ (*Smith* rule, without considering legislators' motives)	same
Stevens ⟶ (*Smith* rule)	Stevens ⟶ (*Smith* rule)	same
White ⟶ (*Smith* rule)	White ⟶ (*Smith* rule)	Ginsburg (*Sherbert-Yoder* standard?)

court judge Ginsburg favored Goldman's free exercise claim.[30] This change in membership, especially coupled with passage of the Religious Freedom Restoration Act, may bode poorly for future application of *Smith*. But with what will the justices replace it? That issue remains unsettled, for the Court has not yet agreed to hear another Free Exercise Clause case. What is clear, as our review of the key cases has shown, is that this area of the law is subject to change. Just consider how many decisions the Court later

overturned (such as *Minersville School District*) or the political branches of government sought to negate (such as *Employment Division*).

RELIGIOUS ESTABLISHMENT

In a letter he wrote in 1802 to the Danbury Baptist Association, Thomas Jefferson proclaimed that the First Amendment built "a wall of separation between Church and State." But what sort of wall did Jefferson conceive of? Was it to be flimsy, connoting, as some suggest, that commingling between church and state is constitutional so long as government does not es-

---

30. On the other hand, perhaps we should not make too much of this, for Scalia joined Ginsburg's dissent and he has not proven a great champion of Free Exercise claims.

tablish a national religion? Or was it to be a solid wall that bars all cooperative interactions between church and state? Or something in between?

Underlying the cases involving the Religious Establishment Clause is that question: What is the nature of the wall that separates church from state? To answer it, many Court opinions, as we shall see, look to the intent of the Framers, a highly elusive concept, particularly in this area of the law. As the nation's Founders were of many minds, it is possible to find evidence supporting the following interpretations of the Establishment Clause:

1. The Religious Establishment Clause erects a solid wall of separation between church and state, prohibiting most, if not all, forms of public aid for or support of religion.

2. The Religious Establishment Clause may erect a wall of separation between church and state, but that wall of separation forbids only the favoring by the state of one religion over another—not nondiscriminatory support or aid for all religions.

3. The Religious Establishment Clause simply prohibits the establishment of a national religion.

In a detailed analysis of the intent of the Framers, Michael J. Malbin found that the *majority* of the Founders ascribed to views 2 or 3 (*accommodationist* positions), but not view 1 (a *separationist* position), which erects the highest wall. [31]

Other scholars, however, argue that we must look to the views of Jefferson and Madison to understand the Establishment Clause because they were largely responsible for its inclusion in the Constitution. Such an examination, some analysts argue, leads to a wholly different conclusion: Madison and Jefferson agreed with view 1—government should have little or nothing to do with organized religion. Still others suggest that Madison was far more tolerant of commingling between church and state than is typically assumed

and that he was more likely to have agreed with view 2 than with view 1. Box 12-1 provides some details about how Madison, Jefferson, and other Founders thought about religion.

The information in Box 12-1 will be useful because, as the cases to come indicate, the Court often refers to the views of Jefferson and Madison when it interprets the Establishment Clause. As we shall see, the Supreme Court generally has adhered to the position that Jefferson and Madison advocated view 1. Accordingly, the Court has prohibited many forms of public support of or aid to religion. We say *generally* and *many* for the following reasons. First, while most justices have adopted Jefferson's metaphor of the wall of separation, under some circumstances (those that passed a well-entrenched test) they allow aid to religious institutions. Therefore, the Court has not subscribed to a strict version of view 1, which would eliminate *all* aid to religion. Second, several justices of the Burger and Rehnquist Courts take the position that the Framers of the First Amendment, including Madison, supported view 2, not 1. They have advocated a far different approach to Establishment Clause cases, one that would permit a good deal more public support for religion.

Do these justices now command a majority on the Court? Will they bring about a major change in the way the Court approaches religious establishment cases? What will that new policy be? These questions are on the minds of many lawyers, judges, and legal scholars. You might consider them as you read the narrative and cases that follow.

Religious Establishment Cases: Origins

In 1899, the Supreme Court decided its first major religious establishment case, *Bradfield v. Roberts*, which involved a congressional grant of $30,000 to a hospital run by Catholic nuns. Here, the justices agreed that the Establishment Clause did not negate the law because the hospital was not a religious institution:

---

31. *Religion and Politics: The Intentions of the Authors of the First Amendment* (Washington, D.C.: American Enterprise Institute, 1978).

BOX 12-1 WHAT DID MADISON, JEFFERSON, AND THE OTHER FOUNDERS WANT?

For many years, legal scholars have sought to throw light on Thomas Jefferson's, James Madison's, and the other Founders' views on the relationship between church and state. Why they have devoted so much time to this enterprise is not difficult to explain. From its first major decision on religious liberty, *Reynolds v. United States (see page 385)* through its more recent cases (see, for example, *Wallace v. Jaffree, page 422),* the Supreme Court has used the intent of the Founders—particularly Madison and Jefferson—as a guide to resolving religious establishment disputes. The search for original intent escalated during the Reagan administration, when members of the administration and Chief Justice Rehnquist, among others, argued that the Court's (and scholars') previous interpretations of that intent were historically incorrect. Here we summarize the positions of both sides and the major sources of support they use to justify them.

	Wall of Separation	*Nonpreferential Treatment*
Position	Jefferson and Madison advocated a wall of separation between church and state that prohibited most, if not all, forms of public aid or support of religion.	Jefferson, Madison, and the majority of the Founders merely argued that the state could not establish a national religion or give preference to one religion over another
Notable Adherents	Constitutional law scholar Leonard W. Levy, Justice Hugo Black, political commentator Garry Wills	Constitutional law scholar Walter Berns, Chief Justice William Rehnquist, former attorney general Edwin Meese
Support (Examples)	1. In 1779 the Virginia legislature considered a bill that would have used tax dollars to support churches. At that time, Jefferson introduced a "Bill for Religious Freedom," which said that "no man shall be compelled to frequent or support any religious worship, place, or ministry whatsoever." Neither bill received majority support. Debate resumed in 1784, when Patrick Henry introduced the General Assessment Bill, which would have used tax dollars to support the "Christian religion." Jefferson was in Paris at the time this bill was introduced, but when Madison wrote him of this new attempt to use public monies Jefferson responded: "What we have to do is devoutly to pray for [Henry's] death" (Alley, 10). Madison took less drastic, but not less effective measures. Through clever political maneuvers, Madison rid the Virginia legislature of Henry (he became governor) and got the legislature to postpone the vote on the bill for one year. In the meantime, Madison distributed a pamphlet called "Memorial and Remonstrance Against Religious Assessments." It was a *tour de force* on the need for separation of church and state so that both could remain strong. Madison's arguments were so persuasive that the Assessment Bill died without consideration, while Jefferson's proposal was passed. 2. In 1802 Jefferson wrote a letter to the Danbury Baptist Association asserting that the religious Establishment Clause built a "wall of separation" between church and state. As president, Jefferson refused to proclaim Thanksgiving Day on religious establishment grounds.	1. Madison may have pushed for Virginia's Bill for Religious Freedom, but he did not advocate its incorporation into the U.S. Consitution. Indeed, he thought a Bill of Rights completely unnecessary. But, being an astute politician, Madison realized that the Constitution might not be ratified without a Bill of Rights. So he took on the task of drafting one. Madison's original version of the Establishment Clause said only that Congress shall not establish "any national religion." This, as Rehnquist wrote in *Wallace v. Jaffree,* "obviously does not conform to the 'wall of separation' between church and State idea which latter-day commentators have ascribed to him." Rather, his language and his comments during congressional debate over the amendment in 1789 make it clear that he thought it prohibited Congress from establishing a national religion and from giving preference to particular religions. There is simply no evidence that Madison attempted to get Congress to enact anything resembling Virginia's Bill for Religious Freedom. Whatever he and Jefferson did in Virginia is irrelevant to understanding his intent for the Bill of Rights. 2. Jefferson was in France when Congress passed the Bill of Rights. His letter to the Danbury Baptist Association, as Rehnquist claims, was "a short note of courtesy, written fourteen years after the Amendments were passed by Congress." It is not an "ideal source" for understanding the intent of the Framers.

BOX 12-1 *(continued)*

Wall of Separation	*Nonpreferential Treatment*
	Jefferson's two predecessors, Washington and Adams, issued Thanksgiving Day proclamations.
3. Madison, as Wills presents it, devoted much of his life to campaigning for separation of church and state. A partial list (Wills, 374) includes: 1774: Madison, denouncing the jailing of Baptist preachers in Virginia, concluded that "ecclesiastical establishments tend to great ignorance and corruption." 1776: At Virginia's revolutionary convention, Madison tried to amend George Mason's preamble to the new Virginia constitution, in order to remove all "emoluments or privileges" from religion. He failed at that, but substituted "free exercise of religion" for "fullest toleration in the exercise of religion." His first important legislative act, undertaken when he was only twenty-five, struck a blow for religious freedom. 1785: Madison published his major statement on religious freedom, "Memorial and Remonstrance against Religious Assessments." 1789: Drafting what will become the First Amendment, Madison proposed not only disestablishment at a national level but that "no *state* shall violate the equal rights of conscience." Although disestablishment at the federal level was all he could accomplish in his lifetime, he regularly referred to the First Amendment as opposing "establishments," reflecting his original intent.	3. To understand the intent of the Framers, one also ought to look at the actions of early Congresses: 1789: On the same day Madison introduced his Amendments, the House enacted the Northwest Ordinance, which gave federal land grants to sectarian schools. 1789: The day after the House passed the version of the Religious Establishment Clause that was ratified by the states, it proposed a resolution asking President Washington to issue a Thanksgiving Day proclamation. 1789: Washington issued the proclamation: "I do recommend and assign Thursday ... to be devoted by the people of these States to the service of that great and glorious Being, who is the beneficent author of all the good that was, that is, or that will be; that we may then all unite in rendering unto Him our sincere and humble thanks." 1789–1823: Congress provided public land grants to the Society of the United Brethren for "propagating the Gospel among the Heathen." Early 1800s: Congress approved treaties with Native American tribes requiring financial support of tribes' religious education programs, churches, and clergy.
The Bottom Line	"If Madison is any guide, our churches are not, even now, too separated from political support." "Though he is called the father of the Constitution, [Madison] has an even better claim as the father of disestablishment." (Wills, 373, 380) An establishment of religion in America at the time of the framing of the Bill of Rights meant government aid and sponsorship of religion, principally by impartial tax support of the institutions of religion, the churches. (Levy, 161)	"It is impossible to build sound constitutional doctrine upon a mistaken understanding of constitutional history, but unfortunately the Establishment Clause has been expressly freighted with Jefferson's misleading metaphor for nearly 40 years." (Rehnquist) "Probably at the time of the adoption of the Constitution ... the general if not universal sentiment in America was that Christianity ought to receive encouragement from the State so far as was not incompatible with ... the freedom of religious worship. An attempt to level all religions, and to make it a matter of state policy to hold all in utter indifference, would have created universal disapprobation." (Story, 630–632)

WORKS CITED: Robert S. Alley, *The Supreme Court on Church and State,* (New York: Oxford University Press, 1988); Leonard W. Levy, *Constitutional Opinions* (New York: Oxford University Press, 1986); William H. Rehnquist, dissenting opinion in *Wallace v. Jaffree,* 472 U.S. 38 (1985); Joseph Story, *Commentaries on the Constitution of the United States,* vol. 2, 5th ed., 1891; Garry Wills, *Under God* (New York: Simon and Schuster, 1990).

NOTE: Material in the "Strict Separation" column draws heavily on Levy, *Constitutional Opinions,* and Levy, *The Establishment Clause* (New York: Macmillan, 1986); material in the "Nonpreferential" column comes largely from Rehnquist's dissent in *Wallace v. Jaffree* (1985).

Whether the individuals who compose a corporation . . . happen to be all Roman Catholics, or all Methodists . . . or members of any religious organization or of no organization at all is [of] the slightest consequence. . . . [This does] not in the least change the legal character of the hospital, or make a religious corporation out of a purely secular one.

Bradfield was important because it demonstrated from the start the Court's willingness to allow some aid, but it did not establish any legal standards by which to adjudicate future claims.

Almost fifty years elapsed between *Bradfield* and the next important religious establishment case, *Everson v. Board of Education* (1947). This litigation involved a 1941 New Jersey law authorizing local school boards that provided "any transportation for public school children to and from school" to also supply transportation to school children living in the district who attended nonprofit private schools. Ewing Township decided to use tax dollars to reimburse parents for transportation costs incurred in sending their children to school. Because the township had no public high schools of its own, the reimbursement policy covered transportation expenses to parents sending their children to three neighboring public high schools. It also covered four private schools, all of which were affiliated with the Roman Catholic church and provided "regular religious instruction conforming to the religion's tenets and modes of worship of the Catholic faith." The average payment to parents sending their children to public or Catholic schools was $40 per student. Arch Everson, a taxpayer living in the district, challenged the reimbursements to parents sending their children to private religious schools. He argued that they supported religion in violation of the Establishment Clause of the First Amendment.

In his opinion for a divided Court, Justice Black held for the state. As he wrote:

[W]e cannot say that the First Amendment prohibits New Jersey from spending tax-raised funds to pay the bus fares of parochial school pupils as a part of a general program

under which it pays the fares of pupils attending public and other schools. It is undoubtedly true that children are helped to get to church schools. There is even a possibility that some of the children might not be sent to the church schools if the parents were compelled to pay their children's bus fares out of their own pockets when transportation to a public school would have been paid for by the State. The same possibility exists where the state requires a local transit company to provide reduced fares to school children including those attending parochial schools, or where a municipally owned transportation system undertakes to carry all school children free of charge. Moreover, state-paid policemen, detailed to protect children going to and from church schools from the very real hazards of traffic, would serve much the same purpose and accomplish much the same result as state provisions intended to guarantee free transportation of a kind which the state deems to be best for the school children's welfare. And parents might refuse to risk their children to the serious danger of traffic accidents going to and from parochial schools, the approaches to which were not protected by policemen. Similarly, parents might be reluctant to permit their children to attend schools which the state had cut off from such general government services as ordinary police and fire protection, connections for sewage disposal, public highways and sidewalks. Of course, cutting off church schools from these services, so separate and so indisputably marked off from the religious function, would make it far more difficult for the schools to operate. But such is obviously not the purpose of the First Amendment. That Amendment requires the state to be a neutral in its relations with groups of religious believers and non-believers; it does not require the state to be their adversary. State power is no more to be used so as to handicap religions, than it is to favor them.

Beyond this basic holding, the Court's decision in *Everson* is notable for a number of reasons. First, even though Black ruled for the state, his opinion etches into law that interpretation of Madison's and Jefferson's philosophies that suggests their desire for a strong wall of separation of church and state. As he noted, in an often-cited passage from the opinion:

The "establishment of religion" clause of the First Amendment means at least this: Neither a state nor the Federal Government can set up a church. Neither can pass laws which aid one religion, aid all religions, or prefer one religion over another. Neither can force nor influence a person to go to or to remain away from church against his will or force him to profess a belief or disbelief in any religion. No person can be punished for entertaining or professing religious beliefs or disbeliefs, for church attendance or non-attendance. No tax in any amount, large or small, can be levied to support any religious activities or institutions, whatever they may be called, or whatever form they may adopt to teach or practice religion. Neither a state nor the Federal Government can, openly or secretly, participate in the affairs of any religious organizations or groups and vice versa. In the words of Jefferson, the clause against establishment of religion by law was intended to erect "a wall of separation between Church and State."

Black's quotation of Jefferson's comment "constitutionalized" the phrase.[32]

Second, although Black's opinion does not lay down a concrete legal standard, it stresses several fundamental ideas, most notably that the aid was secular in purpose (it was going to parents, not a religious body, for a nonreligious expense); that the beneficiaries of the aid were children (not churches); and that the state was "neutral in its relations with groups of religious believers and non-believers" (all school children were eligible for aid). As we shall see, these themes recur in later Court opinions and foreshadow aspects of a legal standard the Court eventually formulated.

Finally, and perhaps most important, *Everson* indicates the divisive and complex nature of religious establishment questions. On the one hand, all the justices—the majority and dissenters alike—agreed with Black's portrayal of the intent of the Framers. In other words, the entire Court believed that Jefferson and Madison preferred strict separation of church and state. On the other hand—and this is the crux of the matter—the justices applied that historical framework to reach wholly disparate conclusions about the reimbursement plan. The majority, as Frank Sorauf

put it, "succeeded . . . in combining the strictest separationist rhetoric with an accommodationist outcome."[33] That is, Black's opinion, while adopting Jefferson's metaphor, found in favor of the township. The dissenters also advocated the same general approach, but they thought it led to a disposition against the township. Indeed, they took Black to task for heading in one direction and landing in another. As Justice Jackson wrote in the opening paragraph of his dissent, the disparity between Black's rhetoric and outcome reminded him of Byron's Julia, who "whispering 'I will ne'er consent'—consented."[34]

That the adoption of a similar historical vision of religious establishment could lead to such disparate outcomes is a problem that continued to confound this area of the law at least through the Warren Court (and, as we shall see, crops up today). As Table 12-1 illustrates, between 1947 and 1968 the Court decided seven major cases involving the Establishment Clause. Three led to an accommodationist outcome (upholding a government policy challenged as a violation of the Establishment Clause), and four to a separationist outcome (striking down a government policy as a violation of the Establishment Clause). Many of these cases will be discussed in detail, but here we simply underscore several points.

The first is a reiteration: while the Court continued to adhere to Black's historical account of the separation between church and state, it was willing to uphold some kinds of support for religion, as it had in *Everson*, while ruling others unconstitutional. But, as Table 12-1 shows, a pattern began to emerge from the Court's rulings. The justices seemed more willing to tolerate *some* public support of private education, such as transporting children to school (*Everson*) and loaning textbooks (*Board of Education v. Allen*, 1968) than it was to legitimize the entry of religion into public education, such as prayer in school (*Abington School*

---

32. It is interesting to note that the Court, in *Reynolds v. United States*, also quoted Jefferson on this point. Scholars and other justices, however, point to Black's opinion as etching this into law because the *Reynolds* Court was more interested in applying another part of Jefferson's passage.

33. *The Wall of Separation* (Princeton: Princeton University Press, 1976), 20.

34. Ibid.

TABLE 12-1 Major Religious Establishment Cases from *Everson* Through the Warren Court

Case	Issue	Vote (Outcome)	Rationale
Everson v. Board of Education (1947)	Reimbursement for transportation costs incurred by parents sending their children to private schools	5–4 (accommodationist)	Secular purpose; child benefits; neutral
Illinois ex rel. McCollum v. Board of Education (1948)	Time-release program in which religious instructors come to public school weekly and provide religious training	8–1 (separationist)	State provides "invaluable aid" to religion
Zorach v. Clauson (1952)	Time-release program in which students are released an hour or so early each week to obtain religious instruction off school premises	6–3 (accommodationist)	State and religion need not be "hostile, suspicious, and even unfriendly"
Engel v. Vitale (1962)	Prayer, recited by public school children each morning, written by state's board of regents	8–1 (separationist)	Government cannot be in the prayer-writing business
School District of Abington Township v. Schempp (1963)	Reading of the Lord's Prayer and verses from the Bible in public schools	8–1 (separationist)	Public school prayer does not have (1) a secular legislative purpose or (2) a primary purpose that neither advances nor inhibits religion
Board of Education v. Allen (1968)	Public school loans of secular textbooks to students attending private schools	6–3 (accommodationist)	Primary purpose of the law furthers education, not religion
Epperson v. Arkansas (1968)	Barring the teaching of evolutionary theory in public schools	9–0 (separationist)	Not neutral; nonsecular purpose

District v. Schempp, 1963) and the teaching of creationism (*Epperson v. Arkansas,* 1968). Whether this trend continued during the Burger Court is a subject we consider in the next section.

Another point highlighted in Table 12-1 is this: after *Everson,* the Court began to formulate a test, flowing from Jefferson's metaphor and Black's decision in *Everson,* to determine whether government actions violated the Establishment Clause. During the Warren Court era, that test received its fullest articulation in *Abington Township.* (Near the end of this chapter, we examine in some detail the Court's important decisions involving prayer in school.) Writing for the majority, Justice Tom C. Clark explained that standard:

The test may be stated as follows: What are the purpose and primary effect of the enactment? If either is the advancement or inhibition of religion then the enactment exceeds the scope of legislative power as circumscribed by the Constitution. That is to say that to withstand the strictures of the Establishment Clause there must be a secular legislative purpose and a primary effect that neither advances nor inhibits religion.

With these words, Clark did what Black had failed to do in *Everson*—provide attorneys and lower court judges with a benchmark for future litigation and decisions.

Early on, some analysts argued that this standard would always lead to separationist outcomes. These scholars thought it would be difficult for government attorneys to show that their policies met the two-pronged standard reached in *Abington*: that the policy had a secular legislative purpose and that its primary effect neither advanced nor inhibited religion. But, as Table 12-1 shows, those commentators were wrong. In *Allen*, for example, the Court considered a New York state requirement that public schools lend, upon request, secular books to private school students in the seventh through twelfth grades. Attorneys challenging the state argued that the requirement violated the Establishment Clause, but the Court disagreed. Writing for a six-person majority, Justice Byron R. White asserted:

The express purpose [of the law] was stated by the New York legislature to be furtherance of the educational opportunities available to the young. Appellants have shown us nothing about the necessary effects of the statute that is contrary to this stated purpose. The law merely makes available to all children the benefits of a general program to lend school books free of charge. Perhaps free books make it more likely that some children choose to attend a sectarian school, but that was true of the state-paid bus fare in *Everson* and does not alone demonstrate an unconstitutional degree of support for a religious institution.

In other words, White used the *Abington* "purpose" prong to reach an accommodationist outcome. Three justices, Douglas, Fortas, and Black (the author of *Everson*), dissented. Both Black and Douglas differentiated the kind of aid at issue in *Everson* (reimbursement for transportation costs) from that in *Allen* (book loans). As Douglas put it:

Whatever may be said of *Everson*, there is nothing ideological about a bus. . . . [But] the textbook goes to the very heart of education in a parochial school. It is the chief, although not solitary, instrumentality for propagating a particular religious creed or faith. How can we possibly approve such state aid to a religion?

Apparently there was some truth to this perspective. Several years before the Court handed down *Allen*, Professor George La Noue published a study examining books used in Catholic schools. The following are extracts he took from textbooks used to teach mathematics, presumably a secular course:

- How much money must I have to buy these four books? *Poems About the Christ Child*, $1.85; *Story of Our Lady*, $2.25; *Saint Joseph*, $1.05; *Saint Theresa*, $2.00?
- The children of St. Francis School ransomed 125 pagan babies last year. This year they hope to increase this number by 20%. If they succeed, how many babies will they ransom this year?
- David sells subscriptions to the *Catholic Digest* on a commission basis of 20%. If the subscription is $2.50 a year what is David's commission on each sale?[35]

The third point about the Warren Court's handling of religious establishment cases is that although the justices generally adopted Jefferson's "wall of separation" metaphor and agreed on the test for adjudicating Establishment Clause cases, they continued to split on case outcomes. Note the votes depicted in Table 12-1: with the exception of cases centering on prayer and teaching religious principles in schools, from *Everson* through *Allen*, the justices were divided over the resolution of cases.

The Burger Court's "New" Legal Standard

By the time Warren Burger became chief justice in 1969, observers predicted that the Court would change its approach to adjudicating Establishment Clause cases. Although the justices generally coalesced around the *Everson* historical understanding and the *Abington* standard, they were divided over how to apply those approaches to particular disputes.

---

35. Quoted in *Religion, State, and the Burger Court* by Leo Pfeffer (Buffalo, N.Y.: Prometheus Books, 1984), 35. The article was published in a 1962 edition of the *Harvard Education Review*.

Moreover, some analysts expected that the new chief justice, Warren Burger, would be more inclined than his predecessor, Earl Warren, to rule with the government in many areas of the law. They predicted that Burger would push for wholesale changes in the Court's approaches to cases involving liberties, rights, and justice. Most of this speculation centered on criminal law because one of the primary reasons President Nixon appointed Burger was to turn back the Warren Court's liberal rulings in this area. But, as it turned out, the new chief justice had a strong interest in taking a leadership role in religion cases. In fact, Burger was so determined to exert influence over this area of the law that during his tenure on the Court (1969–1985 terms), he wrote 69 percent (eighteen of twenty-six) of the Court's majority opinions dealing with religion, a much higher percentage than his overall rate of 20 percent in all formally decided cases.[36]

What was Burger's "understanding" of the Establishment Clause? How did he seek to change the law? Was he successful? We can begin to address these questions by considering Burger's first two religious establishment cases, *Walz v. Tax Commission of the City of New York* (1970) and *Lemon v. Kurtzman* (1971).

Walz involved the property tax exemptions enjoyed by religious institutions. Frederick Walz bought a small, useless lot on Staten Island, New York, for the sole purpose of challenging the state's tax laws, which gave religious organizations exemptions from property taxes. Walz contended that the tax exemptions in effect forced property owners to make involuntary contributions to churches in violation of the Establishment Clause. After losing in the lower courts, Walz appealed to the U.S. Supreme Court, arguing that both the majority and dissenting opinions in *Everson* supported his position: "The First Amendment's objective was to create a complete and permanent separation of the sphere of religious activity and

civil authority by comprehensively . . . forbidding any form of . . . support for religion." New York pointed to the fact that all fifty states had property tax exemptions for religious organizations. It also asserted that "Religious property exemptions have played an integral part of public policy in New York. The role of religious organizations as charitable associations, in furthering the state, has become a fundamental concept in our society."[37]

Writing for a seven-person majority (only Justice Douglas dissented), Chief Justice Burger found in favor of the state. The outcome was not so surprising; after all, had the Court ruled the other way, the tax status of every religious institution in the United States would have been dramatically altered. The startling aspect of *Walz* was that Burger, in his first writing on the Establishment Clause, sought to usher in a major change. The opinion started traditionally enough, with an examination of the "purpose" prong of *Abington*:

The legislative purpose of property tax exemptions is neither the advancement nor the inhibition of religion; it is neither sponsorship nor hostility. New York, in common with the other States, has determined that certain entities that exist in a harmonious relationship to the community at large, and that foster its "moral or mental improvement," should not be inhibited in their activities by property taxation or the hazard of loss of those properties for nonpayment of taxes.

But instead of exploring whether the effect of the legislation inhibited or advanced religion, as the *Abington* standard specified, Burger suggested the following:

Determining that the legislative purpose of tax exemption is not aimed at establishing, sponsoring, or supporting religion does not end the inquiry, however. We must also be sure that the end result—the effect—is not *an excessive government entanglement* with religion. (Emphasis added.)

He went on to hold that property tax exemptions did not create an excessive entanglement with reli-

---

36. Joseph F. Kobylka, "Leadership in the Supreme Court: Chief Justice Burger and Establishment Clause Litigation," *Western Political Quarterly* 42 (December 1989): 545.

37. For more on *Walz*, see Sorauf, *The Wall of Separation*.

gion: to the contrary, even though tax exemptions to churches "necessarily operate to afford an indirect economic benefit," involvement with religion would be far greater if the exemptions did not exist. State officials might occasionally want to examine church records, or they might need to speak with clergy about expenditures, and so forth. As Burger concluded, the tax exemption "restricts the fiscal relationship between church and state, and tends to complement and reinforce the desired separation insulating each from the other."

In the end, then, *Walz* probably raised more questions about Burger and the fate of Establishment Clause litigation than it answered. Did Burger seek to redesign the *Abington* standard—through adoption of an "excessive entanglement" criterion—as a way to bring down the wall of separation between church and state? Would excessive entanglement now become a part of the Court's analytic toolbag for examining establishment claims? Or would the majority of the justices favor a return to a strict reading of *Abington?* Consider these questions as you read *Lemon v. Kurtzman* and its companion case, *Earley v. DiCenso.*

===

Lemon v. Kurtzman
Earley v. DiCenso

403 U.S. 602 (1971)
Vote in Lemon: 8 (Black, Blackmun, Brennan, Burger,
                    Douglas, Harlan, Stewart, White)
                 0
Opinion of the Court: Burger
Concurring opinions: Brennan, White
Not participating: Marshall

Vote in DiCenso: 8 (Black, Blackmun, Brennan, Burger,
                      Douglas, Harlan, Marshall, Stewart)
                    1 (White)
Opinion of the Court: Burger
Concurring opinion: Douglas
Dissenting opinion: White

Lemon v. Kurtzman (The Pennsylvania Program). Alton Lemon brought suit against David Kurtzman, state superintendent of schools. Lemon wanted the court to declare unconstitutional a Pennsylvania law that authorized Kurtzman to "purchase" secular educational services from nonpublic schools. Under this law, the superintendent would use state taxes levied on cigarettes to reimburse nonpublic schools for expenses incurred for teachers' salaries, textbooks, and instructional materials. The state authorized such funding with certain restrictions: it would pay for secular expenses only, that is, secular books and teachers' salaries for the same courses taught in public schools. To receive payments, schools had to keep separate records, identifying secular and nonsecular expenses.

The act took effect in July 1968. Up to the time the Court heard the case, Pennsylvania had spent about $5 million annually. It reimbursed expenses at 1,181 nonpublic elementary and secondary schools attended by about a half million students, around 20 percent of the school population. About 96 percent of the nonpublic school students attended religious schools, primarily Roman Catholic.

Earley v. DiCenso (The Rhode Island Program). This case involved a challenge to the Rhode Island Salary Supplement Act. Aimed at improving the quality of private education, this law supplemented the salaries of teachers of secular subjects in private elementary schools by up to 15 percent of their current salaries with the restriction that payments could be made only to those who agreed in writing not to teach religious subjects and salaries could not exceed the maximum salaries paid to public school instructors. Attorneys claimed that this law violated the Establishment Clause, in part because 95 percent of the schools falling under the terms of the act were affiliated with the Roman Catholic church. Moreover, all of the 250 teachers who had applied for salary supplements worked at Roman Catholic schools. And, as evidence submitted at trial indicated, about two-thirds of them "were nuns of various religious orders."[38]

MR. CHIEF JUSTICE BURGER delivered the opinion of the Court.

These two appeals raise questions as to Pennsylvania and Rhode Island statutes providing state aid to church-related elementary and secondary schools. Both statutes are challenged as violative of the Establishment and Free Exercise Clauses of the First Amendment and the Due Process Clause of the Fourteenth Amendment. . . .

In Everson v. Board of Education (1947), this Court upheld a state statute that reimbursed the parents of parochial school children for bus transportation expenses. There MR. JUSTICE BLACK, writing for the majority, suggested that the decision carried to "the verge" of forbidden territory under the Religion Clauses. Candor compels acknowledgment, moreover, that we can only dimly perceive the lines of demarcation in this extraordinarily sensitive area of constitutional law.

The language of the Religion Clauses of the First Amendment is at best opaque, particularly when compared with other portions of the Amendment. Its authors did not simply prohibit the establishment of a state church or a state religion, an area history shows they regarded as very important and fraught with great dangers. Instead they commanded that there should be "no law *respecting* an establishment of religion." A law may be one "respecting" the forbidden objective while falling short of its total realization. A law "respecting" the proscribed result, that is, the establishment of religion, is not always easily identifiable as one violative of the Clause. A given law might not establish a state religion but nevertheless be one "respecting" that end in the sense of being a step that could lead to such establishment and hence offend the First Amendment.

In the absence of precisely stated constitutional prohibitions, we must draw lines with reference to the three main evils against which the Establishment Clause was intended to afford protection: "sponsorship, financial sup-

port, and active involvement of the sovereign in religious activity." Walz v. Tax Commission (1970).

Every analysis in this area must begin with consideration of the cumulative criteria developed by the Court over many years. Three such tests may be gleaned from our cases. First, the statute must have a secular legislative purpose; second, its principal or primary effect must be one that neither advances nor inhibits religion; finally, the statute must not foster "an excessive government entanglement with religion."

Inquiry into the legislative purposes of the Pennsylvania and Rhode Island statutes affords no basis for a conclusion that the legislative intent was to advance religion. On the contrary, the statutes themselves clearly state that they are intended to enhance the quality of the secular education in all schools covered by the compulsory attendance laws. There is no reason to believe the legislatures meant anything else. A State always has a legitimate concern for maintaining minimum standards in all schools it allows to operate. As in *Allen*, we find nothing here that undermines the stated legislative intent; it must therefore be accorded appropriate deference.

In *Allen* the Court acknowledged that secular and religious teachings were not necessarily so intertwined that secular textbooks furnished to students by the State were in fact instrumental in the teaching of religion. The legislatures of Rhode Island and Pennsylvania have concluded that secular and religious education are identifiable and separable. In the abstract we have no quarrel with this conclusion.

The two legislatures, however, have also recognized that church-related elementary and secondary schools have a significant religious mission and that a substantial portion of their activities is religiously oriented. They have therefore sought to create statutory restrictions designed to guarantee the separation between secular and religious educational functions and to ensure that State financial aid supports only the former. All these provisions are precautions taken in candid recognition that these programs approached, even if they did not intrude upon, the forbidden areas under the Religion Clauses. We need not decide whether these legislative precautions restrict the principal or primary effect of the programs to the point where they do not offend the Religion Clauses, for we conclude that the

38. See Pfeffer, *Religion, State, and the Burger Court*, 27.

cumulative impact of the entire relationship arising under the statutes in each State involves excessive entanglement between government and religion.

In Walz v. Tax Commission, the Court upheld state tax exemptions for real property owned by religious organizations and used for religious worship. That holding, however, tended to confine rather than enlarge the area of permissible state involvement with religious institutions by calling for close scrutiny of the degree of entanglement involved in the relationship. The objective is to prevent, as far as possible, the intrusion of either into the precincts of the other. . . .

In order to determine whether the government entanglement with religion is excessive, we must examine the character and purposes of the institutions that are benefited, the nature of the aid that the State provides, and the resulting relationship between the government and the religious authority. . . . Here we find that both statutes foster an impermissible degree of entanglement.

Rhode Island program

The District Court made extensive findings on the grave potential for excessive entanglement that inheres in the religious character and purpose of the Roman Catholic elementary schools of Rhode Island, to date the sole beneficiaries of the Rhode Island Salary Supplement Act.

The church schools involved in the program are located close to parish churches. This understandably permits convenient access for religious exercises since instruction in faith and morals is part of the total educational process. The school buildings contain identifying religious symbols such as crosses on the exterior and crucifixes, and religious paintings and statues either in the classrooms or hallways. Although only approximately 30 minutes a day are devoted to direct religious instruction, there are religiously oriented extracurricular activities. Approximately two-thirds of the teachers in these schools are nuns of various religious orders. Their dedicated efforts provide an atmosphere in which religious instruction and religious vocations are natural and proper parts of life in such schools. Indeed, as the District Court found, the role of teaching nuns in enhancing the religious atmosphere has led the parochial school authorities to attempt to maintain a one-to-one ratio between nuns and lay teachers in all schools rather than to permit some to be staffed almost entirely by lay teachers.

On the basis of these findings the District Court concluded that the parochial schools constituted "an integral part of the religious mission of the Catholic Church." The various characteristics of the schools make them "a powerful vehicle for transmitting the Catholic faith to the next generation." This process of inculcating religious doctrine is, of course, enhanced by the impressionable age of the pupils, in primary schools particularly. In short, parochial schools involve substantial religious activity and purpose. . . .

The dangers and corresponding entanglements are enhanced by the particular form of aid that the Rhode Island Act provides. Our decisions from *Everson* to *Allen* have permitted the States to provide church-related schools with secular, neutral, or nonideological services, facilities, or materials. Bus transportation, school lunches, public health services, and secular textbooks supplied in common to all students were not thought to offend the Establishment Clause. We note that the dissenters in *Allen* seemed chiefly concerned with the pragmatic difficulties involved in ensuring the truly secular content of the textbooks provided at state expense. . . .

In our view the record shows these dangers are present to a substantial degree. The Rhode Island Roman Catholic elementary schools are under the general supervision of the Bishop of Providence and his appointed representative, the Diocesan Superintendent of Schools. In most cases, each individual parish, however, assumes the ultimate financial responsibility for the school, with the parish priest authorizing the allocation of parish funds. With only two exceptions, school principals are nuns appointed either by the Superintendent or the Mother Provincial of the order whose members staff the school. By 1969 lay teachers constituted more than a third of all teachers in the parochial elementary schools, and their number is growing. They are first interviewed by the superintendent's office and then by the school principal. The contracts are signed by the parish priest, and he retains some discretion in negotiating salary levels. Religious authority necessarily pervades the school system.

The schools are governed by the standards set forth in a "Handbook of School Regulations," which has the force of synodal law in the diocese. It emphasizes the role and importance of the teacher in parochial schools: "The prime factor for the success or the failure of the school is the spirit and personality, as well as the professional competency, of the teacher. . . ." The Handbook also states that: "Religious formation is not confined to formal courses; nor is it restricted to a single subject area." Finally, the Handbook advises teachers to stimulate interest in religious vocations and missionary work. Given the mission of the church school, these instructions are consistent and logical.

Several teachers testified, however, that they did not inject religion into their secular classes. And the District Court found that religious values did not necessarily affect the content of the secular instruction. But what has been recounted suggests the potential if not actual hazards of this form of state aid. The teacher is employed by a religious organization, subject to the direction and discipline of religious authorities, and works in a system dedicated to rearing children in a particular faith. These controls are not lessened by the fact that most of the lay teachers are of the Catholic faith. Inevitably some of a teacher's responsibilities hover on the border between secular and religious orientation. . . .

We do not assume, however, that parochial school teachers will be unsuccessful in their attempts to segregate their religious beliefs from their secular educational responsibilities. But the potential for impermissible fostering of religion is present. The Rhode Island Legislature has not, and could not, provide state aid on the basis of a mere assumption that secular teachers under religious discipline can avoid conflicts. The State must be certain, given the Religion Clauses, that subsidized teachers do not inculcate religion—indeed the State here has undertaken to do so. To ensure that no trespass occurs, the State has therefore carefully conditioned its aid with pervasive restrictions. An eligible recipient must teach only those courses that are offered in the public schools and use only those texts and materials that are found in the public schools. In addition the teacher must not engage in teaching any course in religion.

A comprehensive, discriminating, and continuing state surveillance will inevitably be required to ensure that these restrictions are obeyed and the First Amendment otherwise respected. Unlike a book, a teacher cannot be inspected once so as to determine the extent and intent of his or her personal beliefs and subjective acceptance of the limitations imposed by the First Amendment. These prophylactic contacts will involve excessive and enduring entanglement between state and church. . . .

Pennsylvania program

The Pennsylvania statute also provides state aid to church-related schools for teachers' salaries. The complaint describes an educational system that is very similar to the one existing in Rhode Island. According to the allegations, the church-related elementary and secondary schools are controlled by religious organizations, have the purpose of propagating and promoting a particular religious faith, and conduct their operations to fulfill that purpose. . . .

As we noted earlier, the very restrictions and surveillance necessary to ensure that teachers play a strictly nonideological role give rise to entanglements between church and state. The Pennsylvania statute, like that of Rhode Island, fosters this kind of relationship. Reimbursement is not only limited to courses offered in the public schools and materials approved by state officials, but the statute excludes "any subject matter expressing religious teaching, or the morals or forms of worship of any sect." In addition, schools seeking reimbursements must maintain accounting procedures that require the State to establish the cost of the secular as distinguished from the religious instruction.

The Pennsylvania statute, moreover, has the further defect of providing state financial aid directly to the church-related schools. This factor distinguishes both *Everson* and *Allen,* for in both those cases the Court was careful to point out that state aid was provided to the student and his parents—not to the church-related school. . . . The history of government grants of a continuing cash subsidy indicates that such programs have almost always been accompanied by varying measures of control and surveillance. The government cash grants before us now provide no basis for predicting that comprehensive measures of surveillance and controls will not follow. In particular the government's post-audit power to inspect and evaluate a church-related school's financial records and to determine which expenditures are religious and which are secular creates an intimate and continuing relationship between church and state. . . .

The sole question is whether state aid to these schools can be squared with the dictates of the Religion Clauses. Under our system the choice has been made that government is to be entirely excluded from the area of religious instruction and churches excluded from the affairs of government. The Constitution decrees that religion must be a private matter for the individual, the family, and the institutions of private choice, and that while some involvement and entanglements are inevitable, lines must be drawn.

The judgment of the Rhode Island District Court . . . is affirmed. The judgment of the Pennsylvania District Court . . . is reversed, and the case is remanded for further proceedings consistent with this opinion.

What is the significance of *Lemon* and *DiCenso,*? First, the duo cleared up some of the confusion creat-

---

BOX 12-2   THE ROOTS OF THE *LEMON* TEST

Test	Everson (1947)	Abington (1963)	Walz (1970)	Lemon (1971)
Secular Purpose	The state ⟶ has a legitimate, general interest in helping "parents get their children, regardless of their religion, safely and expeditiously to and from accredited schools."	"What [is] ⟶ the purpose . . . of the enactment? If [it] is the advancement or inhibition of religion then the enactment exceeds the scope of legislative power. . . . That is to say that to withstand the strictures of the Establishment Clause there must be secular legislative purpose."	"The ⟶ legislative purpose of a property tax exemption is neither the advancement nor the inhibition of religion."	"The statute must have a secular legislative pupose."
Primary Effect	Governments cannot ⟶ "pass laws which aid one religion, aid all religions, or prefer one religion over another."	"What [is] . . . the primary effect of the enactment? If [it] is the advancement or inhibition of religion then the enactment exceeds the scope of legislative power. . . . That is to say that to withstand the strictures of the Establishment Clause there must be a . . . primary effect that neither advances nor inhibits religion."	⟶	The statute's "principal or primary effect must be one that neither advances nor inhibits religion."
Excessive Entanglement			"We ⟶ must . . . be sure that the end result—the effect—is not an excessive government entanglement with religion."	"The statute must not foster an excessive government entanglement with religion."

TABLE 12-2 Religious Establishment Standards Advocated by Members of the Supreme Court, 1971–1993

Standard	Definition	Chief Supporters	Occasional Adherents
Lemon (1971)	"Every analysis in this area must begin with consideration of the cumulative criteria developed by the Court over many years. Three tests may be gleaned from our cases. First, the statute must have a secular legislative purpose; second, its principal or primary effect must be one that neither advances nor inhibits religion; finally, the statute must not foster an excessive government entanglement with religion." (Burger, majority opinion in Lemon v. Kurtzman)	Powell, Stewart	Burger, *Stevens*, *O'Connor*, Douglas, Marshall, *Blackmun*
Nonpreferentialism (1983)	"[T]he Establishment Clause . . . [forbids] establishment of a national religion, and [forbids] preference among religious sects or denominations." (Rehnquist, dissenting in Wallace v. Jaffree)	*Rehnquist*	*Scalia, Thomas*, White, Burger
Endorsement Approach to Lemon (1984)	"The Establishment Clause prohibits government from making adherence to a religion relevant in any person's standing in the political community. Government can run afoul of that prohibition in two principal ways. One is excessive entanglement with religious institutions. . . . The second and more direct infringement is government endorsment or disaproval of religion. . . . Under this view, Lemon's inquiry as to the purpose and effect of a statute requires courts to consider whether government's purpose is to endorse religion and whether the statute actually conveys a message of endorsement." (O'Connor, concurring in Lynch v. Donnelly and in Wallace v. Jaffree)	*O'Connor*	*Blackmun*, *Stevens, Souter*, White
Coercion	"Our cases disclose two limiting principles: government may not coerce anyone to support or participate in any religion or its exercise; and it may not, in the guise of avoiding hostility or callous indifference, give direct benefits to a religion in such a degree that it in fact 'establishes a religion or religious faith, or tends to do so.'"	*Kennedy*	*Scalia, Thomas, Rehnquist*, White

NOTE: Justices in italic are members of the current Court. Ginsburg and Breyer are not depicted because (at the time of this writing) they had yet to write opinions in a religious establishment case. Also keep in mind that justices adhering to a particular approach do not always agree on its application in a given case. For example, Justices Scalia and Kennedy, who generally agree with the "coercion" standard, have vehemently disagreed over the kinds of coercion (such as psychological as the Founders understood it, and so forth) the Court should consider.

ed by *Walz* over legal standards governing Establishment Clause cases. It now seemed that the justices planned to adhere to a tripartite test, usually called the *Lemon* test: secular legislative purpose, primary effect, and excessive entanglement. None of these prongs is new. As Box 12-3 illustrates, they had their genesis in early Supreme Court cases. Second, because the *Lemon* test finds its roots in earlier Court decisions that were based on the belief that Madison and Jefferson envisioned a strict wall of separation be-

tween church and state, it seemed that the Court was not only following precedent but also reinforcing the historical understanding from which that precedent flowed. Yet, with the adoption of the *Lemon* test, that precedent led it to the separationist outcome it had not reached in *Everson* or *Allen*, the two major cases on aid to public schools.

Still, the enunciation of a legal standard by which to judge religious establishment claims raises questions: Would the justices of the Burger Court and their successors continue to apply the *Lemon* test? Would it stand the test of time? In 1996 *Lemon* was still good law, although many commentators would argue that its days are numbered. The three-pronged standard may continue to dominate Court adjudication of Establishment Clause claims, but this does not mean that the Court always applies *Lemon,* or that all of the justices subscribe to it and its historical underpinnings, or that different approaches have not been offered. Even when it has applied *Lemon,* the Court has not reached particularly consistent decisions.

The problem is that *Lemon* hangs on because a majority of justices have yet to coalesce behind an alternative standard, even though other standards have been proposed *(Table 12-2)*. You will have further opportunities to consider these alternate standards and their proponents. In the pages to come, we explore how the Court has approached four categories of religious establishment cases in the aftermath of *Lemon:* aid to religious schools, religion in public schools, holiday displays, and prayer in school. Because the Court delved into some of these areas prior to *Lemon,* you will discover trends in Court decision making in particular issues, such as prayer, over the past four decades.

Aid to Religious Schools

Questions concerning "parochiaid"—aid to religious schools—are among the most enduring of those raised in religious establishment litigation. Since *Everson,* the Court has struggled to define the region where government and nonpublic education may interact.

Everson, Allen, and *Lemon-DiCenso* provide early indications of the boundaries of that region. But what has the Court done since 1971? At first it seemed that the Court would continue to apply the *Lemon* test, but not without dissent. For example, in *Committee for Public Education and Religious Liberty v. Nyquist* (1973), one of the first post-*Lemon* cases, separationist groups challenged a New York state law providing maintenance and repair funds for private schools on a per

pupil basis and establishing tuition grants and tax credits. Writing for the Court's majority, Justice Lewis F. Powell, Jr., struck down the law on the basis of the effect prong of *Lemon,* saying the law had "the impermissible effect of advancing the sectarian activities of religious schools." But Chief Justice Burger (along with Justices White and Rehnquist) dissented in part. Burger wrote:

While there is no straight line running through our decisions interpreting the Establishment . . . Clause . . . our cases do, it seems . . . lay down one solid, basic principle: that the Establishment Clause does not forbid governments . . . to enact a program of general welfare . . . even though many . . . elect to use those benefits in ways that "aid" religious instruction. . . . This fundamental principle which I see running through our prior decisions . . . is premised more on experience and history than logic.

This dissent illustrates Burger's second thoughts about the three-pronged test he helped to create and so eagerly applied in *Walz* and *Lemon.* What he now realized is that if the Court adhered strictly to it, as it did in *Nyquist,* his accommodationist approach to religion would not prevail. The test was too rigid to allow for many forms of intermingling between church and state, particularly in areas involving the funding of elementary and secondary schools.

That Burger began to have doubts about the *Lemon* test, however, did not deter a majority of the justices from applying it, at least in the parochiaid cases coming after *Nyquist.* As Table 12-3, which lists all the important aid cases, indicates, *Lemon* dominates this category of Establishment Clause litigation. But because of their use of the three-pronged standard, the justices have come in for much criticism from scholars. Some criticize the Court for its inability to achieve consensus over the application of *Lemon.* This area of the law is marked by dissenting and concurring opinions, and judgments of the Court, rather than majority opinions. Others label this area of the law a mess, marred by disagreement and inconsistencies. For example, is it reasonable to allow public schools to loan books to

TABLE 12-3 Aid to Religious Schools: Major Supreme Court Cases, 1947–1994

Case	Outcome (Opinion Type)[a]	Aid Upheld	Aid Struck	Standard Used
Everson v. Board of Education (1947)	accommodation (majority, 5–4)	transportation reimbursements		neutrality, child benefit, secular purpose
Board of Education v. Allen (1968)	accommodation (majority, 6–3)	textbook loans		*Abington*
Lemon v. Kurtzman (1971)	separation (majority, 8–0)		reimbursements for teacher salaries, textbooks, instructional materials	*Lemon*
Earley v. DiCenso (1971)	separation (majority, 8–1)		teacher salary supplements	*Lemon*
Tilton v. Richardson (1971)	accommodation (judgment, 5–4)	funds for secular buildings (colleges and universities)		*Lemon*
Hunt v. McNair (1973)	accommodation (majority, 6–3)	aid for construction, financing academic buildings (colleges and universities) obtained from revenue bonds		*Lemon*
Levitt v. CPEARL (1973)	separation (majority, 8–1)		reimbursements for administering and grading tests and examinations required by state	*Lemon*
CPEARL v. Nyquist (1973)	separation (majority, 6–3)		grants for maintenance and building repair, tax benefits, tuition reimbursements	*Lemon*
Meek v. Pittenger (1975)	mixed (majority/ judgment, 6–3)	textbook loans	"auxiliary services" such as counseling, testing, speech therapy loans of "instructional materials and equipment" such as maps, films, photographs, periodicals	*Lemon*
Roemer v. Maryland Public Works Board (1976)	accommodation (judgment, 5–4)	general-purpose funds to colleges and universities for secular purposes		*Lemon*
Wolman v. Walter (1977)	mixed (majority/ judgment, various votes)	textbook purchases, testing services, speech and hearing diagnostic services, therapeutic, guidance, and remedial services	instructional material purchases and loans, field trip transportation	*Lemon*

Case	Outcome (Opinion Type)[a]	Aid Upheld	Aid Struck	Standard Used
New York v. Cathedral Academy (1977)	separation (majority, 6–3)		direct reimbursement for record keeping and testing	*Lemon*
CPEARL v. Regan (1980)	accommodation (majority, 5–4)	reimbursements for meeting state requirements for regents examinations, "pupil attendance reporting" and so forth		*Lemon*
Mueller v. Allen (1983)	accommodation (majority, 5–4)	tax deductions for tuition, textbooks, transportation		*Lemon*
Grand Rapids School District v. Ball (1985)	separation (majority, 7–2 and 5–4)		Community Education Program offering courses (chess, home economics, languages) at end of school day; employing private school teachers and using public and private school facilities Shared Time Program offering secular classes to private school children in private school facilities (leased by the state) during regular school hours and taught by public school teachers, many of whom had previously taught in private schools	*Lemon*
Aguilar v. Felton (1985)	separation (majority, 5–4)		teacher/counselor salaries and supplies/materials for remedial instruction to private school students in private school facilities	*Lemon*
Witters v. Washington Department for Services for the Blind (1986)	accommodation (majority, 9–0)	Disabled student at Christian college cannot be denied state vocational rehabilitation assistance		*Lemon*
Zobrest v. Catalina Foothills School District (1993)	accommodation (majority, 5–4)	Disabled student at Roman Catholic high school can be furnished with a state-funded sign-language interpreter		neutrality; child benefit
Board of Education of Kiryas Joel Village School Dist. v. Grumet (1994)	separation (majority, 6–3)		school district created to accommodate handicapped children of particular sect	neutrality

a. A judgment represents the views of a plurality, not a majority, of the Court's members. Unlike a majority opinion, a judgment lacks precedential value.

students (for example, *Meek v. Pittenger*) but not instructional materials and equipment to schools (for example, *Wolman v. Walter; see Table 12-3*)? The Court justified making a distinction, in part, on the grounds that the books were going directly to the students while the equipment was going to the schools. But, to many commentators, this distinction is trivial and overly technical; after all, in both instances it is the child who ultimately benefits.

Still, and despite all the alleged inconsistencies and zigzag lines the Court has drawn in this area, we can identify some common themes that continue to be important in the resolution of these disputes. First, in the area of parochiaid, rarely has the Court veered from *Lemon:* in virtually every case listed in Table 12-3, the majority used *Lemon* to reach conclusions about the specific program under challenge. This consistency, as we shall see, is not the case in other areas of establishment law (particularly prayer), where the Court has seemed on the verge of abandoning *Lemon* since the 1980s.

A second common theme concerns the justices' application of *Lemon* and the different results reached. These differences seem to depend on the nature of the institution receiving the support. As Table 12-3 shows, the justices have been more willing to tolerate aid to colleges and universities than to primary and secondary schools. Why? One reason offered by the Court is that "the symbolism of union between church and state is most likely to influence children of tender years, whose experience is limited and whose beliefs consequently are the function of environment as much as of free and voluntary choice."[39] Another is that religious primary and secondary schools tend to be more "pervasively sectarian" than their college counterparts.[40]

Finally, the Court has made distinctions based on the recipient of the aid. Hearkening back to *Everson*,

the justices are more likely to uphold support that goes directly to parents and children than to the private schools, which explains why the Court usually allows public schools to lend secular textbooks: the books go to the students, not the schools.

These are some general rules, but there are exceptions. For example, the Court has not always upheld all forms of aid to colleges and universities. Nor has it always applied *Lemon* to the letter. To put it somewhat differently, despite these common themes there is no denying that parochiaid remains a troubled area of establishment case law. Even casual study of Table 12-3 attests to this.

Religion in the Public Schools: Teaching Ideas Associated with Particular Religions

While parochiaid litigation centers on whether public moneys should in any way support students at religious schools and their parents or the schools themselves, another category of cases asks the Court to assess the extent to which the teaching and practice of religion can be incorporated into public schools. Although the Court has decided many cases involving this central question, we consider two major types: (1) the recitation of prayers and (2) the teaching of ideas associated with particular religions. At the end of this chapter, we discuss the prayer in school cases; for now, we turn to the second type.

At the onset, it is important to keep in mind that nonpublic schools are free to teach secular subjects couched in religious terms. Remember the book titles that were used for a math problem? Public schools use secular books to teach subjects like math, so we would expect to find only nonreligious examples. However, some public schools have sought to disseminate tenets held by particular religions by slanting the curriculum to favor religious views about secular subjects. The best known and most enduring example is the way teachers address the origins of human life. Did humankind evolve, as scientists suggest (evolu-

39. *Grand Rapids School District v. Ball* (1985).
40. See Tribe, *American Constitutional Law*, 1220.

BOX 12-3 THE SCOPES MONKEY TRIAL

"The law is a ass," observed Charles Dickens's character, Mr. Bumble, in *Oliver Twist*. In 1925 many Americans, watching with amazement the circus-like proceedings of the dramatic Scopes trial in Tennessee, found themselves echoing the same sentiments. "Isn't it difficult to realize that a trial of this kind is possible in the twentieth century in the United States of America?" demanded the lawyer for the defense, the famed Clarence Darrow. In truth, the case appeared a vestigial survival from an earlier day when people were prosecuted for witchcraft or for offenses like imagining the king's death. Headlined in the press as the Great Monkey Trial, it pitted the Biblical version of creation against the teachings of Charles Darwin, and did so in a courtroom atmosphere more closely resembling that of a revival meeting than a hall of justice.

The defendant, John T. Scopes, was a twenty-four-year-old high school teacher in Dayton, Tennessee, who was prosecuted for teaching evolution in violation of a state statute that prohibited the teaching in any public school of "any theory that denies the story of the divine creation of man as taught in the Bible, and to teach instead that man has descended from a lower order of animals." Conducted in the heat of July, the trial was a parody of all that a legal proceeding should be. Dayton was ready for what it hoped would be the Waterloo of science. "One was hard put . . . ," an observer wrote, "to know whether Dayton was holding a camp meeting, a Chautauqua, a street fair, a carnival or a belated Fourth of July celebration. Literally, it was drunk on religious excitement."

The courtroom itself was decked with a large banner, exhorting everyone to "Read your Bible daily." Darrow finally got it removed by demanding equal space for a banner urging, "Read your Evolution." The stars of the trial were the lawyers: Clarence Darrow, perhaps the best known criminal lawyer in American history (Lincoln Steffens had called him "the attorney for the damned") representing Scopes and, indirectly, Darwin and evolution and, against him, William Jennings Bryan, the Great Commoner, orator of the famed "Cross of Gold" speech in 1896, three-time candidate for President, and Secretary of State under Woodrow Wilson,

who had volunteered to direct the prosecution. Aging and sanctimonious, Bryan was the leading Fundamentalist of the day. "I am more interested in the Rock of Ages than in the age of rocks," he proclaimed.

At the trial's beginning, Darrow said later, "the judge . . . with great solemnity and all the dignity possible announced that Brother Twitchell would invoke the Divine blessing. This was new to me. I had practiced law for more that forty years, and had never before heard God called in to referee a court trial." Darrow's objection to the blessing was overruled, and each day's session began with a prayer by a different preacher. The high point of the trial saw Darrow put Bryan himself on the stand as an expert on "religion." The *New York Times* described this as the most amazing court scene in history, and out-of-state reporters and observers like the iconoclast H. L. Mencken had a field day conveying the incongruous proceedings to the nation. Bryan stuck doggedly to his insistence on the literal truth of the Bible, refusing, in Darrow's phrase, "to choose between his crude beliefs and the common intelligence of modern times."

In the end, the local population felt it won a righteous victory when the jury found Scopes guilty. But the judge imposed only a $100 fine, and, on appeal, the Tennessee Supreme Court reversed the decision on a technicality: the court, rather than the jury, had set the fine. The case itself was more dramatic than significant—unless it deserved remembrance as an example of the law at its worst. "I think," said Darrow during the trial, "this case will be remembered because it is the first case of this sort since we stopped trying people in America for witchcraft." On another plane, Darrow's withering examination during the trial went far to discredit Fundamentalist dogma. Though anti-evolution laws remained on the books in what Mencken referred to as "the Bible Belt" of the South, they were never again enforced. And in 1968, the U.S. Supreme Court finally struck down an Arkansas anti-evolution law, though admitting that by then "the statute is presently more of a curiosity than a vital fact of life."

SOURCE: Bernard Schwartz, *The Law in America* (New York: McGraw Hill, 1974), 224. Reprinted by permission of the author.

tionary theory), or did it come about as a result of some divine intervention, as various religions argue (creationism)?

This debate received an unusual amount of attention in 1925 when attorney Clarence Darrow led a legal challenge to a Tennessee law that made it a crime to teach evolutionary principles or any theory denigrating the biblical version of the creation. That case, which culminated in the Scopes "monkey trial," never made it to the Supreme Court *(see Box 12-3)*. But two other similar challenges did reach the Court.

The first such case to reach the Court was *Epperson v. Arkansas,* a 1968 case in which the Court considered the constitutionality of a 1928 state "anti-evolution" law that was an "adaptation" of Tennessee's 1925 version. The Arkansas law made it a crime for any state university or public school instructor "to teach the theory or doctrine that mankind ascended or descended from a lower order of animals" or to "adopt or use . . . a textbook that teaches" evolutionary theory. The history of the law's adoption makes it clear that its purpose was to further religious beliefs about the beginning of life. For example, an advertisement placed in an Arkansas newspaper to drum up support for the act said: "The Bible or atheism, which? All atheists favor evolution. . . . Shall conscientious church members be forced to pay taxes to support teachers to teach evolution which will undermine the faith of their children?"

Epperson began in the mid-1960s when the school system in Little Rock, Arkansas, decided to adopt a biology book that contained a chapter on evolutionary theory. Susan Epperson, a biology teacher in a Little Rock high school, wanted to use the new book but was afraid—in light of the 1928 law—that she could face criminal prosecution if she did so. She asked the Arkansas courts to nullify the law, and, when the Arkansas Supreme Court turned down her request, she appealed her case to the U.S. Supreme Court.

Writing for a unanimous Court, Justice Abe Fortas reversed the state supreme court's ruling. Relying heavily on *Everson* (the *Lemon* test had yet to be established), Fortas said, "The First Amendment mandates governmental neutrality between religion and religion, between religion and nonreligion." Under this standard the outcome was clear to the justices:

Arkansas' law cannot be defended as an act of religious neutrality. Arkansas did not seek to excise from the curricula of its schools . . . all discussion of the origin of man. The law's effort was confined to an attempt to blot out a particular theory because of its supposed conflict with the Biblical account, literally read. Plainly, the law is contrary to the mandate of the First . . . Amendment.

Despite the Court's clear statement about the constitutional violation posed by anti-evolutionary laws, some states devised other ways to teach creationism. In *Edwards v. Aguillard* (1987) the Court reviewed one of these attempts. This case was decided after the *Lemon* test had been established and during the chief justiceship of William Rehnquist, who—along with Antonin Scalia—sought greater accommodation between church and state. As you read this case, then, consider the difference between the Court's opinion and the dissent filed by Scalia and joined by Rehnquist.

Edwards v. Aguillard

482 U.S. 578 (1987)
Vote: 7 (Blackmun, Brennan, Marshall, O'Connor, Powell,
   Stevens, White)
   2 (Rehnquist, Scalia)
Opinion of the Court: Brennan
Concurring opinions: Powell, White
Dissenting opinion: Scalia

After *Epperson,* organized interests—particularly religious groups—lobbied state legislatures to pass new laws. Louisiana enacted the Balanced Treatment for Creation-Science and Evolution-Science in Public School Instruction Act in 1981. This law differed from the one struck down in *Epperson* because it did not outlaw the teaching of evolution. Rather, it prohibited schools from teaching evolutionary principles unless theories of creationism also were taught.

The state and various organizations offered two major lines of argument in support of this legislation. One is that evolutionary theory is a religion, the religion of secular humanism. If evolution is taught then so should creationism be, as found in a literal reading of Genesis. In other words, public school teachers must give equal time to the two primary "religious" views of the origin of humankind.[41] The second argument states that creationism is as much a science as evolutionary theory is and, therefore, deserves equal treatment in public school curriculums.

Represented by the American Civil Liberties Union (ACLU)—an organization committed to the separation of church and state—Assistant Principal Don Aguillard, and several teachers, parents, and religious groups thought otherwise and challenged the act as a violation of the Establishment Clause. Attorneys and amici attacked the argument that creationism is a science. As amicus curiae the National Academy of Sciences put it:

The explanatory power of a scientific hypothesis or theory is, in effect, the medium of exchange by which the value of a scientific theory is determined in the market place of ideas that constitutes the scientific community. Creationists do not compete in the marketplace, and creation-science does not offer scientific value.

From this base, attorneys found it easy to reject notions of academic freedom and fairness, at least as it pertained to this debate. All the legislature had done, in the eyes of the ACLU, was to give equal time to a particular religion's view of the origins of humankind, which, the ACLU argued, violated the Establishment Clause

41. For more on this point, see Pfeffer, *Religion, State, and the Burger Court*, 73-75.

Don Aguillard, assistant principal at Acadiana High School in Scott, Louisiana, filed suit against the state's creation science law in 1981. Six years later, in *Edwards v. Aguillard*, the Supreme Court found that law to be in violation of the Establishment Clause.

JUSTICE BRENNAN delivered the opinion of the Court.

The Establishment Clause forbids the enactment of any law "respecting an establishment of religion." The Court has applied a three-pronged test to determine whether legislation comports with the Establishment Clause. First, the legislature must have adopted the law with a secular purpose. Second, the statute's principal or primary effect must be one that neither advances nor inhibits religion. Third, the statute must not result in an excessive entanglement of government with religion. State action violates the Establishment Clause if it fails to satisfy any of these prongs.

In this case, the Court must determine whether the Establishment Clause was violated in the special context of the public elementary and secondary school system. States and local school boards are generally afforded considerable discretion in operating public schools. . . .

The Court has been particularly vigilant in monitoring compliance with the Establishment Clause in elementary and secondary schools. Families entrust public schools with the education of their children, but condition their trust on the understanding that the classroom will not purposely be used to advance religious views that may conflict with the private beliefs of the student and his or her family. Students in such institutions are impressionable and their attendance is involuntary. The State exerts great authority and coercive power through mandatory attendance requirements, and because of the students' emulation of teachers as role models and the children's susceptibility to peer pressure. . . .

Therefore, in employing the three-pronged *Lemon* test, we must do so mindful of the particular concerns that arise in the context of public elementary and secondary schools. We now turn to the evaluation of the Act under the *Lemon* test.

Lemon's first prong focuses on the purpose that animated adoption of the Act. . . . If the law was enacted for the purpose of endorsing religion, "no consideration of the second or third criteria [of *Lemon*] is necessary." In this case, the petitioners have identified no clear secular purpose for the Louisiana Act.

True, the Act's stated purpose is to protect academic freedom. This phrase might, in common parlance, be understood as referring to enhancing the freedom of teachers to teach what they will. The Court of Appeals, however, correctly concluded that the Act was not designed to further that goal. We find no merit in the State's argument that the "legislature may not [have] use[d] the terms 'academic freedom' in the correct legal sense. They might have [had] in mind, instead, a basic concept of fairness; teaching all of the evidence." Even if "academic freedom" is read to mean "teaching all of the evidence" with respect to the origin of human beings, the Act does not further this purpose. The goal of providing a more comprehensive science curriculum is not furthered either by outlawing the teaching of evolution or by requiring the teaching of creation science.

While the Court is normally deferential to a State's articulation of a secular purpose, it is required that the statement of such purpose be sincere and not a sham. . . .

It is clear from the legislative history that the purpose of the legislative sponsor, Senator Bill Keith, was to narrow the science curriculum. During the legislative hearings, Senator Keith stated: "My preference would be that neither [creationism nor evolution] be taught." Such a ban on teaching does not promote—indeed, it undermines—the provision of a comprehensive scientific education.

It is equally clear that requiring schools to teach creation science with evolution does not advance academic freedom. The Act does not grant teachers a flexibility that they did not already possess to supplant the present science curriculum with the presentation of theories, besides evolution, about the origin of life. Indeed, the Court of Appeals found that no law prohibited Louisiana public schoolteachers from teaching any scientific theory. As the president of the Louisiana Science Teachers Association testified, "[a]ny scientific concept that's based on established fact can be included in our curriculum already, and no legislation allowing this is necessary." The Act provides Louisiana schoolteachers with no new authority. Thus the stated purpose is not furthered by it. . . .

Furthermore, the goal of basic "fairness" is hardly furthered by the Act's discriminatory preference for the teaching of creation science and against the teaching of evolution. While requiring that curriculum guides be developed for creation science, the Act says nothing of comparable guides for evolution. Similarly, research services are supplied for creation science but not for evolution. Only "creation scientists" can serve on the panel that supplies the resource services. The Act forbids school boards to discriminate against anyone who "chooses to be a creation-scientist" or to teach "creationism," but fails to protect those who choose to teach evolution or any other non-creation science theory, or who refuse to teach creation science.

If the Louisiana legislature's purpose was solely to maximize the comprehensiveness and effectiveness of science instruction, it would have encouraged the teaching of all scientific theories about the origins of humankind. But under the Act's requirements, teachers who were once free to teach any and all facets of this subject are now unable to do so. Moreover, the Act fails even to ensure that creation science will be taught, but instead requires the teaching of this theory only when the theory of evolution is taught. Thus we agree with the Court of Appeals' conclusion that the Act does not serve to protect academic freedom, but has the distinctly different purpose of discrediting "evolution by counterbalancing its teaching at every turn with the teaching of creation science."....

[W]e need not be blind in this case to the legislature's preeminent religious purpose in enacting this statute. There is a historic and contemporaneous link between the teachings of certain religious denominations and the teaching of evolution. It was this link that concerned the Court in *Epperson v. Arkansas* (1968), which also involved a facial challenge to a statute regulating the teaching of evolution. In that case, the Court reviewed an Arkansas statute that made it unlawful for an instructor to teach evolution or to use a textbook that referred to this scientific theory. Although the Arkansas anti-evolution law did not explicitly state its predominant religious purpose, the Court could not ignore that "[t]he statute was a product of the upsurge of 'fundamentalist' religious fervor" that has long viewed this particular scientific theory as contradicting the literal interpretation of the Bible. After reviewing the history of anti-evolution statutes, the Court determined that "there can be no doubt that the motivation for the [Arkansas] law was the same [as other anti-evolution statutes]: to suppress the teaching of a theory which, it was thought, 'denied' the divine creation of man." The Court found that there can be no legitimate state interest in protecting particular religions from scientific views "distasteful to them" and concluded "that the First Amendment does not permit the State to require that teaching and learning must be tailored to the principles or prohibitions of any religious sect or dogma."

These same historic and contemporaneous antagonisms between the teachings of certain religious denominations and the teaching of evolution are present in this case. The preeminent purpose of the Louisiana legislature was clearly to advance the religious viewpoint that a supernatural being created humankind. The term "creation science" was defined as embracing this particular religious doctrine by those responsible for the passage of the Creationism Act. Senator Keith's leading expert on creation science, Edward Boudreaux, testified at the legislative hearings that the theory of creation science included belief in the existence of a supernatural creator. Senator Keith also cited testimony from other experts to support the creation-science view that "a creator [was] responsible for the universe and everything in it." The legislative history therefore reveals that the term "creation science," as contemplated by the legislature that adopted this Act, embodies the religious belief that a supernatural creator was responsible for the creation of humankind.

Furthermore, it is not happenstance that the legislature required the teaching of a theory that coincided with this religious view. The legislative history documents that the Act's primary purpose was to change the science curriculum of public schools in order to provide persuasive advantage to a particular religious doctrine that rejects the factual basis of evolution in its entirety. The sponsor of the Creationism Act, Senator Keith, explained during the legislative hearings that his disdain for the theory of evolution resulted from the support that evolution supplied to views contrary to his own religious beliefs.... The legislation therefore sought to alter the science curriculum to reflect endorsement of a religious view that is antagonistic to the theory of evolution.

In this case, the purpose of the Creationism Act was to restructure the science curriculum to conform with a particular religious viewpoint. Out of many possible science subjects taught in the public schools, the legislature chose to affect the teaching of the one scientific theory that historically has been opposed by certain religious sects. As in *Epperson*, the legislature passed the Act to give preference to those religious groups which have as one of their tenets the creation of humankind by a divine creator. The "overriding fact" that confronted the Court in *Epperson* was "that Arkansas' law selects from the body of knowledge a particular segment which it proscribes for the sole reason that it is deemed to conflict with . . . a particular interpretation of the Book of Genesis by a particular religious group." Similarly, the Creationism Act is designed *either* to promote the theory of creation science which embodies a particular religious tenet by requiring that creation science is taught whenever evolution is taught *or* to prohibit the teaching of a scientific theory disfavored by certain religious sects by forbidding the teaching of evolution when creation science is not also taught. The Establishment Clause, however, "forbids *alike* the preference of a religious doctrine *or* the prohibition of theory which is deemed antagonistic to a particular dogma." Because the primary purpose of the Creationism Act is to advance a particular religious belief, the Act endorses religion in violation of the First Amendment.

We do not imply that a legislature could never require

that scientific critiques of prevailing scientific theories be taught. . . . But because the primary purpose of the Creationism Act is to endorse a particular religious doctrine, the Act furthers religion in violation of the Establishment Clause. . . .

The Louisiana Creationism Act advances a religious doctrine by requiring either the banishment of the theory of evolution from public school classrooms or the presentation of a religious viewpoint that rejects evolution in its entirety. The Act violates the Establishment Clause of the First Amendment because it seeks to employ the symbolic and financial support of government to achieve a religious purpose. The judgment of the Court of Appeals therefore is

Affirmed.

JUSTICE SCALIA, with whom THE CHIEF JUSTICE joins, dissenting.

Even if I agreed with the questionable premise that legislation can be invalidated under the Establishment Clause on the basis of its motivation alone, without regard to its effects, I would still find no justification for today's decision. The Louisiana legislators who passed the "Balanced Treatment for Creation-Science and Evolution-Science Act" (Balanced Treatment Act), each of whom had sworn to support the Constitution, were well aware of the potential Establishment Clause problems and considered that aspect of the legislation with great care. After seven hearings and several months of study, resulting in substantial revision of the original proposal, they approved the Act overwhelmingly and specifically articulated the secular purpose they meant it to serve. Although the record contains abundant evidence of the sincerity of that purpose (the only issue pertinent to this case), the Court today holds, essentially on the basis of "its visceral knowledge regarding what must have motivated the legislators," that the members of the Louisiana Legislature knowingly violated their oaths and then lied about it. I dissent. Had requirements of the Balanced Treatment Act that are not apparent on its face been clarified by an interpretation of the Louisiana Supreme Court, or by the manner of its implementation, the Act might well be found unconstitutional; but the question of its constitutionality cannot rightly be disposed of on the gallop, by impugning the motives of its supporters. . . .

It is important to stress that the purpose forbidden by *Lemon* is the purpose to "advance religion." . . . Our cases in no way imply that the Establishment Clause forbids legislators merely to act upon their religious convictions. We surely would not strike down a law providing money to feed the hungry or shelter the homeless if it could be demonstrated that, but for the religious beliefs of the legislators, the funds would not have been approved. Notwithstanding the majority's implication to the contrary, we do not presume that the sole purpose of a law is to advance religion merely because it was supported strongly by organized religions or by adherents of particular faiths. . . . To do so would deprive religious men and women of their right to participate in the political process. Today's religious activism may give us the Balanced Treatment Act, but yesterday's resulted in the abolition of slavery, and tomorrow's may bring relief for famine victims. . . .

With the foregoing in mind, I now turn to the purposes underlying adoption of the Balanced Treatment Act.

We have relatively little information upon which to judge the motives of those who supported the Act. About the only direct evidence is the statute itself and transcripts of the seven committee hearings at which it was considered. . . . Nevertheless, there is ample evidence that the majority is wrong in holding that the Balanced Treatment Act is without secular purpose.

At the outset, it is important to note that the Balanced Treatment Act did not fly through the Louisiana Legislature on wings of fundamentalist religious fervor—which would be unlikely, in any event, since only a small minority of the State's citizens belong to fundamentalist religious denominations. The Act had its genesis (so to speak) in legislation introduced by Senator Bill Keith in June 1980. . . .

Most of the testimony in support of Senator Keith's bill came from the Senator himself and from scientists and educators he presented, many of whom enjoyed academic credentials that may have been regarded as quite impressive by members of the Louisiana Legislature. . . .

Senator Keith and his witnesses testified essentially as set forth in the following numbered paragraphs:

(1) There are two and only two scientific explanations for the beginning of life—evolution and creation science. . . .

(2) The body of scientific evidence supporting creation science is as strong as that supporting evolution. . . .

(3) Creation science is educationally valuable. Students exposed to it better understand the current state of scientific evidence about the origin of life. . . .

(4) Although creation science is educationally valuable and strictly scientific, it is now being censored from or misrepresented in the public schools. Evolution, in turn, is misrepresented as an absolute truth. . . .

(5) The censorship of creation science has at least two harmful effects. First, it deprives students of knowledge of one of the two scientific explanations for the origin of life and leads them to believe that evolution is proven fact; thus, their education suffers and they are wrongly taught that science has proved their religious beliefs false. Second, it violates the Establishment Clause. The United States Supreme Court has held that secular humanism is a religion. . . .

We have no way of knowing, of course, how many legislators believed the testimony of Senator Keith and his witnesses. But in the absence of evidence to the contrary, we have to assume that many of them did. Given that assumption, the Court today plainly errs in holding that the Louisiana Legislature passed the Balanced Treatment Act for exclusively religious purposes. . . .

I have to this point assumed the validity of the *Lemon* "purpose" test. In fact, however, I think the pessimistic evaluation that THE CHIEF JUSTICE made of the totality of *Lemon* is particularly applicable to the "purpose" prong: it is "a constitutional theory [that] has no basis in the history of the amendment it seeks to interpret, is difficult to apply and yields unprincipled results. . . ."

Our cases interpreting and applying the purpose test have made such a maze of the Establishment Clause that even the most conscientious governmental officials can only guess what motives will be held unconstitutional. We have said essentially the following: Government may not act with the purpose of advancing religion, except when forced to do so by the Free Exercise Clause (which is now and then); or when eliminating existing governmental hostility to religion (which exists sometimes); or even when merely accommodating governmentally uninhibited religious practices, except that at some point (it is unclear where) intentional accommodation results in the fostering of religion, which is of course unconstitutional.

But the difficulty of knowing what vitiating purpose one is looking for is as nothing compared with the difficulty of knowing how or where to find it. For while it is possible to discern the objective "purpose" of a statute (*i.e.,* the public good at which its provisions appear to be directed), or even the formal motivation for a statute where that is explicitly set forth (as it was, to no avail, here), discerning the subjective motivation of those enacting the statute is, to be honest, almost always an impossible task. The number of possible motivations, to begin with, is not binary, or indeed even finite. In the present case, for example, a particular legislator need not have voted for the Act either because he wanted to foster religion or because he wanted to improve education. He may have thought the bill would provide jobs for his district, or may have wanted to make amends with a faction of his party he had alienated on another vote, or he may have been a close friend of the bill's sponsor, or he may have been repaying a favor he owed the Majority Leader, or he may have hoped the Governor would appreciate his vote and make a fundraising appearance for him, or he may have been pressured to vote for a bill he disliked by a wealthy contributor . . . or, of course, he may have had (and very likely did have) a combination of some of the above and many other motivations. To look for *the sole purpose* of even a single legislator is probably to look for something that does not exist.

Putting that problem aside, however, where ought we to look for the individual legislator's purpose? We cannot of course assume that every member present (if, as is unlikely, we know who or even how many they were) agreed with the motivation expressed in a particular legislator's pre-enactment floor or committee statement. Quite obviously, "[w]hat motivates one legislator to make a speech about a statute is not necessarily what motivates scores of others to enact it.". . . Can we assume, then, that they all agree with the motivation expressed in the staff-prepared committee reports they might have read—even though we are unwilling to assume that they agreed with the motivation expressed in the very statute that they voted for? Should we consider post-enactment floor statements? Or post-enactment testimony from legislators, obtained expressly for the lawsuit? Should we consider media reports on the realities of the legislative bargaining? All of these sources, of course, are eminently manipulable. . . .

Given the many hazards involved in assessing the subjective intent of governmental decisionmakers, the first prong of *Lemon* is defensible, I think, only if the text of the Establishment Clause demands it. That is surely not the case. The Clause states that "Congress shall make no law respecting an establishment of religion." One could argue, I suppose, that any time Congress acts with the *intent* of advancing religion, it has enacted a "law respecting an establishment of religion"; but far from being an unavoidable reading, it is quite an unnatural one. . . . It is, in short, far from an inevitable reading of the Establishment Clause that it forbids all governmental action intended to advance religion; and if not inevitable, any reading with such untoward consequences must be wrong.

In the past we have attempted to justify our embarrassing Establishment Clause jurisprudence on the ground that it "sacrifices clarity and predictability for flexibility.". . . One commentator has aptly characterized this as "a euphemism . . . for . . . the absence of any principled rationale." I think it time that we sacrifice some "flexibility" for "clarity and predictability." Abandoning *Lemon*'s purpose test—a test which exacerbates the tension between the Free Exercise and Establishment Clauses, has no basis in the language or history of the Amendment, and, as today's decision shows, has wonderfully flexible consequences—would be a good place to start.

Writing for the Court, Brennan had little trouble applying *Lemon* to rule against the state. The majority found that the law lacked a secular purpose; rather, its purpose was to "endorse a particular religious view." But Justice Scalia's dissent is a sign of things to come. Not only does Scalia adopt the state's argument that there is "ample uncontradicted testimony" to indicate that "creation science is a body of scientific knowledge rather than a revealed belief," but also he criticizes the purpose prong of *Lemon* as "indefensible" and as a main contributor to the Court's "embarrassing Estab-

lishment Clause jurisprudence." This may have been Scalia's first attack on *Lemon*, but it would not be his last. Since *Edwards v. Aguillard*, Scalia has become more adamant in his view that *Lemon* should be discarded in favor of a standard that would bring more "clarity and predictability" to this area of the law.

Although the Court has yet to take the route advocated by Scalia, in one of its more recent cases addressing religion in public schools, *Rosenberger v. University of Virginia* (1995), it all but ignored the *Lemon* test. In a 5–4 decision, the Court held that the university (a publicly financed institution) was required to subsidize the printing costs of an explicitly Christian magazine, produced by students, in the same way that it would underwrite any other student publication. In writing for the Court, Justice Kennedy relied heavily on the free speech clause of the First Amendment to reach his decision. As he said, "vital First Amendment speech principles are at stake here" because the state was seeking to "silence the expression of selected viewpoints." The dissenters (Breyer, Ginsburg, Souter, and Stevens) did not see it that way. Rather, they thought the decision approved "direct funding of core religious activities by an arm of the state" for the first time in history.

Rosenberger may be an interesting case, but it gives little guidance for those seeking clarification of legal standards in this area. The majority opinion, although it did not overturn *Lemon*, barely mentioned the 1971 test. On the other hand, it may provide some indication of the direction into which the Rehnquist Court seems to be heading in this complex area: toward greater accommodation of church and state.

Government Endorsement of Religion: Holiday Displays

In *Epperson* Justice Fortas wrote, "The First Amendment mandates governmental neutrality between religion and religion, between religion and nonreligion." His statement provides a theoretical way to think about the relationship between church and state, but as citizens we are confronted with daily reminders that the United States does not follow Fortas's words. For example, all U.S. currency carries the words: "In God We Trust." Does that motto represent government endorsement of religion over nonreligion? What about the national Christmas tree? It stands in front of the White House, the home of the head of our secular nation. Yet the tree is a symbol associated with Christianity. Its annual appearance seems to violate Fortas's principle because it represents government endorsement of one religion over another. In fact, the presence (and general acceptance) of religious mottoes and symbols supports Justice Douglas's classic statement: "We are a religious people whose institutions presuppose a Supreme Being."

That Americans "are a religious people," the majority of whom accept "In God We Trust" on currency or even a national Christmas tree, however, should not be taken to mean that all symbolic endorsements of religion are legally acceptable. The problem is separating the permissible from the impermissible. This issue has not been easy for the Court to resolve, as its holiday display cases demonstrate.

When the owners of retail stores place religious symbols in their windows, no constitutional questions arise. But when governments pay for the erection of such symbols or allow their property to be used for the placement of religious displays, questions concerning the separation of church and state abound.

The Court first considered these questions in *Lynch v. Donnelly* (1984), which involved the constitutionality of state-sponsored Christmas nativity scenes (créches). For more than forty years, the city of Pawtucket, Rhode Island, and its Retail Merchants Association erected a Christmas display in a park owned by a nonprofit organization. The display included a Santa Claus house, reindeer, a Christmas tree, a clown, colored lights, a Season's Greetings banner, and a créche

with the infant Jesus, Mary and Joseph, angels, animals, and so forth. In 1973 the city spent $1,365 for a new créche, and it cost $20 to set it up and take it down each year. Believing that these annual expenditures for the créche constituted a violation of the Establishment Clause, the state Civil Liberties Union brought suit against the city. City officials and area business people countered that the Christmas display had a secular purpose: to attract customers to the city's downtown shopping area.

Writing for a five-person majority, Chief Justice Burger found that the display was not an impermissible breach of the Establishment Clause. In one of his more strongly worded accommodationist opinions, he pointed to many examples indicating "an unbroken history of official acknowledgment by all three branches of government of the role of religion in American life": executive orders proclaiming Christmas and Thanksgiving as national holidays, "In God We Trust" on currency, publicly supported art galleries full of religious paintings. This examination led him to conclude that

the créche is identified with one religious faith. . . . [But] to forbid the use of this one passive symbol—the créche—at the very time people are taking note of the season with Christmas hymns and carols in public schools and other public places, and while the Congress and legislatures open session with prayers by paid chaplains, would be a stilted overreaction contrary to our history and to our holdings. If the presence of the créche violates the Establishment Clause, a host of other forms of taking official note of Christmas, and our religious heritage, are equally offensive to the Constitution.

In short, Burger implied that Christmas was so much a part of the American heritage that it came close to representing a national, nonsectarian celebration, rather than a religious holiday.

Burger's opinion is interesting because, although he applied *Lemon* to find that there was a secular purpose for the créche, he also said, "We have repeatedly emphasized our unwillingness to be confined to any single test." This modifying statement did not go unnoticed; it was, after all, the first time a majority opinion hinted at the demise of *Lemon*. In dissent, Brennan (joined by Marshall, Blackmun, and Stevens) wrote, "The Court's less-than-vigorous application of the *Lemon* test suggests that its commitment to those standards may only be superficial." He then went on to assert that applying a more vigorous version of *Lemon* to the case leads to the conclusion that the créche's inclusion in the display "does not reflect a clearly secular purpose."

The dissenters wanted the Court to apply *Lemon* strictly, but O'Connor, in a concurring opinion, suggested a new way to frame the three-pronged standard. She proposed to focus *Lemon*'s purpose prong on "whether the government's actual purpose is to endorse or disapprove religions" and the effect prong on "whether, irrespective of government's actual purpose, the practice under review in fact conveys a message of endorsement or disapproval." Invocation of this endorsement standard led her to conclude that the city did not "intend to convey any message of endorsement of Christianity or disapproval of non-Christian religions." She based this conclusion mainly on the fact that the créche was a small part of a larger holiday display. "Celebration of public holidays," O'Connor reasoned, "which have cultural significance even if they also have religious aspects, is a legitimate secular purpose."

It was this endorsement standard that Justice Blackmun invoked to resolve the next major "display" case, *County of Allegheny v. ACLU* (1989). *County of Allegheny* involved the constitutionality of two holiday displays erected every year in downtown Pittsburgh, Pennsylvania. The first is a créche that belongs to a Roman Catholic group, the Holy Name Society. Beginning with the Christmas season of 1981, the city allowed the society to place the créche on the grand staircase of the county courthouse, which is, by all accounts, the "main," "most beautiful," and "most public" part of the courthouse. The second challenged display was a Hanukkah menorah located outside of the City-County Building, where the mayor and other city officials have their offices. For much of its history, the city erected only a Christmas tree outside this building, but, beginning in the 1980s, it began to include the menorah. By 1986 the entire display included a forty-five-foot Christmas tree complete with lights and ornaments; an eighteen-foot Hanukkah menorah, owned by a Jewish group, but stored and erected by the city; and a sign with a statement proclaiming the city's "Salute to Liberty."

Do these displays violate the Religious Establishment Clause? This question gave the Court a good deal of trouble: a majority of justices simply could not agree on the appropriate standard by which to answer it. So, in the end, the best the Court could muster was a judgment, written by Justice Blackmun.

In that judgment, Blackmun began by outlining the approach he would take to the case:

In the course of adjudicating specific cases, this Court has come to understand the Establishment Clause to mean that government may not promote or affiliate itself with any religious doctrine or organization, may not discriminate among persons on the basis of their religious beliefs and practices, may not delegate a governmental power to a religious institution, and may not involve itself too deeply in such an institution's affairs. Although "the myriad, subtle ways in which Establishment Clause values can be eroded" are not susceptible to a single verbal formulation, this Court has attempted to encapsulate the essential precepts of the Establishment Clause. . . .

In *Lemon v. Kurtzman* (1971) the Court sought to refine these principles by focusing on three "tests" for determining whether a government practice violates the Establishment Clause. . . .

Our subsequent decisions further have refined the definition of governmental action that unconstitutionally advances religion. In recent years, we have paid particularly close attention to whether the challenged governmental practice either has the purpose or effect of "endorsing" religion, a concern that has long had a place in our Establishment Clause jurisprudence.

As part of its holiday decorations, Allegheny County, Pennsylvania, erected on public property a nativity scene and a combined Christmas tree and menorah display. In *County of Allegheny v. ACLU* (1989) the Supreme Court ruled that the crèche violated the separation of church and state principle, but that the combined exhibit did not.

Applying these "general principles" to the case at hand, Blackmun set out the Court's 'task': to determine whether the display of the crèche and the menorah, in their respective "particular physical settings," has the effect of endorsing or disapproving religious beliefs. In the end, he found that "the display of the crèche in the County Courthouse has this unconstitutional effect." This crèche, unlike the one at issue in *Lynch*, did not contain "objects of attention" (such as Santa's house and his reindeer) that were "separate from the crèche, and had their specific visual story to tell." Rather the crèche at issue here "stands alone: it is the single element of the display on the Grand Staircase. . . ." Thus, in Blackmun's mind, "by permitting the 'display of the crèche in this particular physical setting,' the county sends an unmistakable message that it supports and promotes the Christian praise to God. . . ."

The display of the menorah in front of the City-County Building, however, did not—in Blackmun's view—have this unconstitutional effect. Why? Blackmun offered several reasons, with an important one being that the "the menorah here stands next to a Christmas tree and a sign saluting liberty. . . . The necessary result of placing a menorah next to a Christmas tree [which is 'not itself a religious symbol'] is to create an 'overall holiday setting' that represents both Christmas and Chanukah—two holidays, not one." Accordingly, Blackmun found that "it is not 'sufficiently likely' that residents of Pittsburgh will perceive the combined display of the tree, the sign, and the menorah as an 'endorsement' or 'disapproval . . . of their individual religious choices.'"

Throughout this chapter, we have noted that scholars criticize the Court for reaching inconsistent, puzzling, and even amusing decisions. *County of Allegheny* provides ammunition for these critics. Because Blackmun's judgment centers on the kinds of objects, in juxtaposition to one another, that holiday displays may or may not contain, it has been the source of some ridicule. As one federal judge put it, holiday displays have come to "require scrutiny more commonly associated with interior decorators than with the judiciary."[42] Moreover, public school teachers, city officials, firefighters, and the like must now give careful consideration to the kinds of symbols they can erect. And even after careful consideration they may be unable to derive sure answers. As a 1993 newspaper article put it:

Pity the public school principal in December. Between Hanukkah, Christmas and Kwanzaa [a holiday celebrated by African Americans to honor family and community], this long last month lays a minefield of grand proportions for educators trying to acknowledge the holidays without bridging the separation of church and state. Every decoration is fraught with peril. Every lesson and every song must pass the "does not promote religion" test. Red and green cookies? Maybe. "A Christmas Carol?" Maybe. "Silent Night?" Definitely not.[43]

County of Allegheny also sends mixed signals about the appropriate legal standards by which to adjudicate religious establishment claims. Blackmun's judgment adopted O'Connor's endorsement standard from her concurrence in *Lynch*. But this standard does not end reliance on *Lemon;* it merely gives another way to apply parts of it *(see Table 12-2)*. In an opinion concurring in judgment in part and dissenting in part, Kennedy (joined by Rehnquist, White, and Scalia) attacked the endorsement standard as "an unwelcome addition to our tangled Establishment Clause jurisprudence." In its (and *Lemon's*) place, he would adopt a "coercion" standard. Under this approach, the justices would prohibit government activities only if they "coerce anyone to support or participate in any religion" or if they "give direct benefits to religion in such a degree" that it in fact "established a

religion . . . or tends to do so." Applying this standard to holiday displays, Kennedy found the crèche and the menorah permissible under the Establishment Clause because they do not foster even subtle coercion.[44]

Has the Court provided any indication, since *County of Allegheny*, of which of these approaches may move to the fore? The answer is no. In its most recent decision in this area, *Capitol Square Review Board v. Pinette* (1995), the justices held that Ohio violated the free speech rights of the Ku Klux Klan when it denied the KKK the right to erect a cross— during the Christmas season—in a state-owned park in Columbus. Yet the justices could not agree over an appropriate standard of review. O'Connor (joined in this case by Souter and Breyer) continued to press her endorsement standard; Scalia (joined by Rehnquist, Thomas, and Kennedy) rejected O'Connor's approach and seemed to advocate a rule that would hold all religious expression in public places (such as state-owned parks) permissible under the Establishment Clause; and, finally, Stevens and Ginsburg (the only dissenters in the case) took a somewhat different tact to the endorsement standard. They argued that a passerby would not know that the cross was the KKK's private expression and, instead, "identify the state either as the messenger, or, at the very least, as the one who has endorsed the [private religious] message."

Prayer in Public School

Throughout this section we have seen the Court change the standards by which it adjudicates religious establishment claims, reason through cases in seemingly inconsistent ways, divide over the resolution of major issues, and cause public consternation and debate. The subject of prayer magnifies all of these observations. Moreover, prayer is a topic that has steadily occupied part of the Court's agenda since the 1960s. It therefore provides us with an excellent vehicle by which to reexamine and summarize what we have

---

42. Judge Easterbrook dissenting in *American Jewish Congress v. Chicago*, 827 F. 2d 120, at 129; quoted in *Lee v. Weisman* by Justice Scalia.

43. Kimberly J. McLarin, "Holiday Dilemma at Schools: Is That a Legal Decoration?" *New York Times*, Dec. 16, 1993, 1, 15.

44. See Sherry, "Lee v. Weisman: Paradox Redux," 131.

learned about how the Court, under Chief Justices Warren, Burger, and Rehnquist, has approached establishment questions.

Prayer and the Warren Court. Throughout most of the nation's history, almost all public schools engaged in religious practices of some kind: they may have held devotional services, distributed Bibles, or taught about religion. Particularly prevalent was prayer. Even into the 1960s, as Table 12-4 indicates, the Bible was read regularly in most public schools in the South and East; in other schools, students recited state-written prayers. Separationist groups—groups, such as the ACLU, that oppose intermingling between church and state—believed that these practices violated the Establishment Clause and set out to convince the Court to eradicate them. Their initial suit, *Engel v. Vitale* (1962), challenged a New York practice that each morning had public school children reciting a prayer written by the state's board of regents: "Almighty God, we acknowledge our dependence upon Thee, and we beg Thy blessings upon us, our parents, our teachers and our country." New York representatives argued that this prayer was innocuous and purposefully drafted so that it would not favor one religion over another. They also argued that recitation was voluntary: students who did not want to participate could remain silent or leave the room. The New York Civil Liberties Union, representing parents from a Long Island school district, claimed the religious neutrality of the prayer and the voluntary aspect were irrelevant. What mattered was that the state had written it and, therefore, that it violated the Establishment Clause.

Writing for the Court, Justice Black adopted the separationist argument:

We think the constitutional prohibition against laws respecting the establishment of religion must at least mean that in this country it is no part of the business of government to compose official prayers for any group of the American people to recite as a part of a religious program carried out by the government.

TABLE 12-4 Variations in Incidence of Bible Reading in Public School by Region, 1960 and 1966

| | Percentage of Schools Reporting Bible Reading | |
Region	1960	1966
East	67.6	4.3
Midwest	18.3	5.2
South	76.8	49.5
West	11.0	2.3

SOURCE: Frank J. Sorauf, *The Wall of Separation* (Princeton: Princeton University Press, 1976), 297.

Only Justice Stewart dissented from the Court's opinion. After citing many examples of congressional approval of religion, including the legislation placing the words "In God We Trust" on currency, he quoted Justice Douglas's statement, written a decade before in *Illinois ex rel. McCollum v. Board of Education* (1948): "We are a religious people whose institutions presuppose a Supreme Being." What New York "has done has been to recognize and to follow the deeply entrenched and highly cherished spiritual traditions of our Nation," he said.

Despite the majority's strong words, the decision was not a complete victory for separationists. The Court failed to enunciate a strict legal definition of establishment (it announced no standard), and it dealt with only one aspect of prayer in school—state-written prayers—and not the more widespread practice of Bible readings. Moreover, *Engel* generated a tremendous public backlash. Less than 20 percent of the public supported the Court's decision; Congress considered constitutional amendments to overturn it; and church leaders condemned it. Most of the justices described themselves as "surprised and pained" by the negative reaction. Chief Justice Warren later wrote: "I vividly remember one bold newspaper headline, 'Court outlaws God.' Many religious leaders in this same spirit condemned the Court." Justice Clark defended the Court's opinion in a public address:

Here was a state-written prayer circulated by the school district to state-employed teachers with instructions to have their pupils recite it. [The Constitution] provides that both state and Federal governments shall take no part respecting the establishment of religion. . . . "No" means "No." That was all the Court decided.[45]

With all this uproar, it is no wonder that separationist groups were concerned when the Court agreed to hear arguments in a case, *School District of Abington Township v. Schempp* (1963) involving the more prevalent practice of Bible readings in public schools. They questioned whether the justices would cave in to public pressure and reverse their stance in *Engel*. But, as it turned out, their fears were misplaced, for the Court used *Abington* to reinforce its *Engel* decision.

In striking down a Pennsylvania law that mandated "at least ten verses from the Holy Bible shall be read, without comment, at the opening of each public school on each school day," Justice Clark's majority opinion set out a standard of law, a two-pronged test that served as the forerunner of *Lemon*. And, in applying this test to *Abington*, Clark found that the Bible reading

exercises are prescribed as part of the curricular activities of students who are required by law to attend school. They are held in the school buildings under the supervision and with the participation of teachers employed in those schools. . . . The trial court in [*Schempp*] has found that such an opening exercise is a religious ceremony and was intended by the State to be so. We agree with the trial court's finding as to the religious character of the exercises. Given that finding, the exercises and the law requiring them are in violation of the Establishment Clause. . . .

Clearly, then, the Court indicated that it would stand behind its ruling in *Engel*, despite the public backlash. However, if the justices thought that *Abington* would quell the school prayer controversy they had ignited in *Engel*, they could not have been more wrong. Opinion polls taken after *Abington* indicated

that only 24 percent of the public supported the Court's decision. As shown in Figure 12-1, that number has remained relatively stable over the past two decades; at the very least, support has never reached the 50 percent mark. Given public antipathy for *Abington* and *Engel*, it is not surprising to find widespread noncompliance with the Court's decisions. Several years after *Abington* came down, political scientist Robert Birkby asked school officials in Tennessee whether prayer had been eliminated from their schools.[46] One would suspect that Birkby's respondents would "overestimate compliance,"[47] since the practice at issue was unconstitutional. But only 1 of the 121 respondents admitted to having totally eliminated Bible readings and the like. Note the 1966 data in Table 12-4: the schools in the South continued to allow Bible readings, despite the Court's decision in *Abington*.

The lack of public support for the Court's rulings in *Engel* and *Abington* also helps to explain why Congress considered nearly 150 proposals to overturn the decisions through a constitutional amendment. One introduced by Rep. Frank Becker, R-N.Y., was typical:

Nothing in this Constitution shall be deemed to prohibit the offering, reading from, or listening to prayers of Biblical Scriptures, if participation therein is on a voluntary basis, in any governmental or public school, institution or place.

In 1966 and 1971 simple majorities passed versions of a prayer-in-school amendment. But these votes were insufficient to send the amendment to the states (a two-thirds vote is required), and the proposals died in Congress.[48]

Prayer and the Burger Court. With the death of the prayer-in-school constitutional amendment in 1971, the issue moved to the back burner of American politics. But not for long. The election of Ronald Reagan,

---

45. Quotes from the justices come from Bernard Schwartz, *Super Chief* (New York: New York University Press, 1983), 441–442.

46. "The Supreme Court in the Bible Belt: Tennessee Reaction to the *Schempp* Decision," *American Journal of Political Science* (1966) 10: 304.

47. Jeffrey A. Segal and Harold J. Spaeth, *The Supreme Court and the Attitudinal Model* (Cambridge: Cambridge University Press, 1993), 339.

48. See David G. Barnum, *The Supreme Court and American Democracy* (New York: St. Martin's Press, 1993), 145.

FIGURE 12-2 Approval of Supreme Court Decision
Preventing Organized Prayer in School

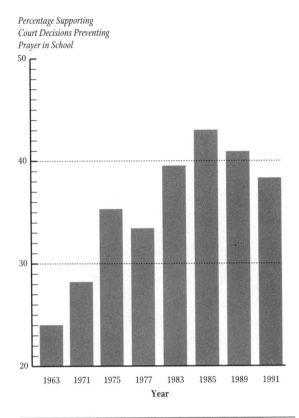

Percentage Supporting
Court Decisions Preventing
Prayer in School

SOURCES: 1971: Harold W. Stanley and Richard G. Niemi, *Vital Statistics on American Politics*, 3d ed. (Washington, D.C.: CQ Press, 1992), 21; all other years: Lee Epstein, Jeffrey A. Segal, Harold J. Spaeth, and Thomas G. Walker, *The Supreme Court Compendium: Data, Decisions, and Developments* (Washington, D.C.: Congressional Quarterly, 1994), Table 8-22.

NOTE: The question was: "The U.S. Supreme Court has ruled that no state or local government may require the reading of the Lord's prayer or Bible verses in public schools. What are your views on this?"

Nothing in this Constitution shall be construed to prohibit individual or group prayer in public schools or other public institutions. No person shall be required by the United States or any state to participate in prayer.

In 1984 the Republican-dominated Senate came close to approving Reagan's proposal, but the vote of 56–44 again fell short of the necessary two-thirds.[49]

Once the proposal was defeated, all eyes turned to the Burger Court, which gave signs of being sympathetic to the use of prayer in public places. Consider its ruling in *Marsh v. Chambers* (1983), issued while the Senate was debating Reagan's prayer-in-school amendment. Chambers, a member of the Nebraska legislature, challenged that body's use of a legislative chaplain to open each session with a prayer, as had been the practice since 1965. For his services, the chaplain, a Presbyterian minister, received $319.75 for each month the legislature was in session. Applying the three-pronged *Lemon* standard, a court of appeals held for Chambers, noting that the use of legislative chaplains violated all three parts. The legislature then appealed to the U.S. Supreme Court.

That the Court would eventually hear such a case was predicted by Justice Douglas in 1963. When Justice Black circulated his majority opinion in *Engel v. Vitale*, the first school prayer case, Douglas wrote the following memo to Black:

As you know I have had troubles with . . . *Engel v. Vitale*. . . . I am inclined to reverse if we are prepared to disallow public property and public funds to be used to finance religious exercise.

If, however, we would strike down a New York requirement that public school teachers open each day with a prayer, I think we could not consistently open each of our sessions with prayer. That's the kernel of my problem.[50]

Black did not adjust his opinion, and Douglas ended up filing a concurring opinion in which he stated

a vocal opponent of the Court's decisions, in 1980 once again brought prayer to the forefront. In one of his State of the Union addresses, Reagan proclaimed that "God should never have been expelled from America's classrooms." He also began a new movement to amend the Constitution with this proposal, introduced into Congress in 1982:

49. See Pfeffer, *Religion, State, and the Burger Court*, 99–103; and Barnum, *The Supreme Court and American Democracy*, 146.

50. Memo of June 11, 1962. In *The Douglas Letters* by Melvin I. Urofsky (Bethesda, Md.: Adler and Adler, 1987), 200.

his opposition to government funding of any religious activity, including the use of legislative chaplains.

But times had changed. Black and Douglas had long since departed the Court. They, and many other members of the Warren Court, had been replaced by jurists, such as Rehnquist and Burger, who, as we know, were far more sympathetic to accommodationist claims. It is not surprising that the Supreme Court reversed the court of appeals and upheld the use of legislative chaplains. What was surprising, however, was that Burger—writing for Justices Blackmun, O'-Connor, Powell, Rehnquist, and White—ignored the *Lemon* test, substituting instead a reliance on history. He justified this substitution on the grounds that the intent of the Framers was all too clear:

[T]he first Congress, as one of its early items of business, adopted the policy of selecting a chaplain to open each session with prayer. . . . Clearly the men who wrote the First Amendment Religion Clauses did not view paid legislative chaplains and opening prayers as a violation of that Amendment, for the practice of opening sessions with prayer has continued without interruption ever since. . . . In light of the unambiguous and unbroken history of more than 200 years, there can be no doubt that the practice of opening legislative sessions with prayer has become part of the fabric of society. To invoke Divine guidance on a public body entrusted with making the laws is not, in these circumstances, an "establishment" of religion or a step toward establishment; it is simply a tolerable acknowledgment of beliefs widely held among the people of this country.

In short, *Marsh* represents the first (though, as we know from *County of Allegheny,* not the last) time the Court failed to use *Lemon* since its articulation in 1971.

The dissenters, Brennan, Marshall, and Stevens, argued that Burger's substitution of the intent of the Framers for the *Lemon* test was disingenuous, for, in their eyes, he did so because the three-pronged standard would have led him to a conclusion he did not want to reach: legislative chaplains violated the First Amendment. One might also argue that the intent of the Framers was less clear than Burger suggested. Recall, for example, how the delegates to the constitu-

tional convention reacted to Benjamin Franklin's proposal to bring in clergy for prayer.

For the Reagan administration, Burger's opinion was cause for optimism. The chief justice had invoked originalism, an approach to adjudication Reagan and his colleagues advocated. In light of the defeat of Reagan's amendment, the decision provided some indication that the Court might be ready to reconsider prayer in school.

Would the Court take this step and overturn *Abington* and *Engel?* Would it continue its reliance on the intent of the Framers, instead of *Lemon,* to adjudicate prayer-in-school cases? These were some of the questions observers asked when the Court agreed to hear *Wallace v. Jaffree* (1985).

Wallace involved a challenge to an Alabama law, authorizing a period of silence in all public schools "for meditation or voluntary prayer." Though a federal district court upheld the law, a U.S. court of appeals overturned the decision on the grounds that the law "advance[s] and encourage[s] religious activity" in ways that were inconsistent with Supreme Court precedent.

When the case got to the Supreme Court, opponents of the law argued that it was unconstitutional because it lacked a secular purpose as required by *Lemon;* its legislative sponsors clearly viewed it as a way to return prayer to school. The state countered that the law does not "in any way offend the constitution" because it "neither proscribes prayer; nor affirms religious belief; nor coerces religious exercise." The Reagan administration supported this position. In an amicus curiae brief, the solicitor general argued that the law was "perfectly neutral with respect to religious practices. It neither favors one religion over another nor conveys endorsement of religion."

Despite public opinion *(see Figure 12-2)* and the clear preferences of the Reagan administration, the Court did not overturn *Engel* or *Abington.* To the contrary, by invoking the *Lemon* test to strike down the Alabama law, it reaffirmed its commitment to those decisions and to the standards of law on which they were based—the forerunners of *Lemon*. As Justice Stevens wrote for the majority:

When the Court has been called upon to construe the breadth of the Establishment Clause, it has examined the criteria developed over a period of many years. Thus, in *Lemon v. Kurtzman*, we wrote:

"Every analysis in this area must begin with consideration of the cumulative criteria developed by the Court over many years. Three such tests may be gleaned from our cases. First, the statute must have a secular legislative purpose; second, its principal or primary effect must be one that neither advances nor inhibits religion . . . ; finally, the statute must not foster 'an excessive government entanglement with religion.'"

It is the first of these three criteria that is most plainly implicated by this case. . . . [N]o consideration of the second or third criteria is necessary if a statute does not have a clearly secular purpose. For even though a statute that is motivated in part by a religious purpose may satisfy the first criterion . . . the First Amendment requires that a statute must be invalidated if it is entirely motivated by a purpose to advance religion.

In applying the purpose test, it is appropriate to ask "whether government's actual purpose is to endorse or disapprove of religion." In this case, the answer to that question is dispositive. For the record not only provides us with an unambiguous affirmative answer, but it also reveals that the enactment of [law] was not motivated by any clearly secular purpose—indeed, the statute had *no* secular purpose.

Still, while the majority opinion invoked *Lemon*, the justices were not unanimous in their support for the three-pronged test. Powell expressed concern over some justices' criticism of the test, and O'Connor continued to press for her endorsement approach to *Lemon*. In dissent, Burger lamented that the majority's "extended treatment" of the *Lemon* test "suggests a naive preoccupation with an easy, bright-line approach for addressing constitutional issues." But it was Rehnquist's dissenting opinion that raised the most eyebrows because it questioned the Court's en-

tire approach to Establishment Clause cases beginning with *Everson*. He said the Court was wrong to "concede" Jefferson's metaphor of a "wall of separation," or to etch into law such a strict separation. In other words, he asserted that for the four decades since *Everson*, the Court had operated under a misguided understanding of what the Framers meant by religious establishment. The truth, according to Rehnquist, was that the Founders, particularly Madison, intended something more in line with view 2 *(see page 389)* or the nonpreferential position that the Establishment Clause simply "forbade the establishment of a national religion and forbade preference among religious sects or denominations. . . . [I]t did not prohibit the federal government from providing nondiscriminatory aid to religion." Justice White, who admitted that he had "been out of step" with the Court's rulings in this area, was happy to "appreciate" Rehnquist's reexamination of history.

Whether Rehnquist was correct or whether he "flunked history," as one scholar put it,[51] is a question that is probably unresolvable. What is true, however, is that *Wallace* was the Burger Court's last major religious establishment case; a year or so after the opinion was handed down, the chief justice retired. As we noted at the beginning of this section, Burger had sought to influence this area of the law, first by establishing the *Lemon* test and, then, after realizing that *Lemon* might lead to a stronger wall of separation than he envisioned, through the adoption of a Framers' intent approach (used in *Marsh*), or of a softened version of *Lemon*. In light of *Wallace*, should we conclude that Burger failed to achieve his goals? Probably not. As political scientist Joseph Kobylka notes, "This area of the law is heavy with his legacy," even in cases Burger lost.[52] At the very least, Burger convinced many of his colleagues that *Lemon* should be applied with a soft hand or, perhaps, abandoned entirely. Note, in

51. Levy, *The Establishment Clause*, xii.
52. "Leadership in the Supreme Court."

particular, his influence on Rehnquist, whose opinion in *Wallace* was largely devoted to an explication of the intent of the Framers, which he used as a launching pad to call for the demise of *Lemon*. This legacy is especially important because Rehnquist, who succeeded Burger, could play some role in determining whether Burger's influence continues to be felt.

Prayer and the Rehnquist Court. It is no secret that Chief Justice Rehnquist wants the Court to move in a more accommodationist direction and to overrule *Lemon*. The problem he faces is that his colleagues do not agree on a standard of law by which to adjudicate these cases. Indeed, as shown in Table 12-2, by 1993 members of the Court had endorsed at least three different standards for Establishment Clause litigation.

When the Rehnquist Court faced its first major school prayer case, *Lee v. Weisman,* a great deal of speculation arose over what the justices would do. Some observers thought the Court would overturn *Lemon,* a position advocated by President Bush's solicitor general. Did the Court take this step? Note, too, how fractured the Court was. How did the dissenters and concurrers' positions differ from that proposed by the majority? Pay special attention to Justice David Souter's concurring opinion, as this was his first independent statement in a religious establishment case.

Lee v. Weisman

505 U.S. 577 (1992)
Vote: 5 (Blackmun, Kennedy, O'Connor, Souter, Stevens)
      4 (Rehnquist, Scalia, Thomas, White)
Opinion of the Court: Kennedy
Concurring opinions: Blackmun, Souter
Dissenting opinion: Scalia

Each June the Nathan Bishop Middle School, a public school in Providence, Rhode Island, holds for-mal graduation exercises on school grounds. Attendance is voluntary. For years, it has been the practice of the school district to allow principals to invite local clergy to give invocations and benedictions at the middle and high school graduation exercises. Typically, what happens is this: school principals contact members of the clergy and ask them to give an invocation/benediction; if the clergy agree, principals give them a copy of a pamphlet entitled "Guidelines for Civic Occasions." Prepared by the National Conference of Christians and Jews, the guidelines stress "inclusiveness and sensitivity" in writing nonsectarian prayers.

For the June 1989 graduation, Principal Robert E. Lee followed this procedure. He contacted Rabbi Leslie Gutterman and, once the rabbi agreed to give the invocation and benediction, Lee gave him a copy of the guidelines. Lee also advised Rabbi Gutterman that any prayers should be nonsectarian.

At the graduation the rabbi gave the following invocation:

God of the Free, Hope of the Brave:
For the legacy of America where diversity is celebrated and the rights of minorities are protected, we thank You. May these young men and women grow up to enrich it.
For the liberty of America, we thank You. May these new graduates grow up to guard it.
For the political process of America in which all its citizens may participate, for its court system where all may seek justice, we thank You. May those we honor this morning always turn to it in trust.
For the destiny of America, we thank You. May the graduates of Nathan Bishop Middle School so live that they might help to share it.
May our aspirations for our country and for these young people, who are our hope for the future, be richly fulfilled.
AMEN

In his benediction, the rabbi said:

O God, we are grateful to You for having endowed us with the capacity for learning which we have celebrated on this joyous commencement.

Happy families give thanks for seeing their children achieve an important milestone. Send Your blessings upon the teachers and administrators who helped prepare them.

The graduates now need strength and guidance for the future. Help them to understand that we are not complete with academic knowledge alone. We must each strive to fulfill what You require from all of us: To do justly, to love mercy, to walk humbly.

We give thanks to You, Lord, for keeping us alive, sustaining us and allowing us to reach this special, happy occasion. AMEN

Daniel Weisman, whose daughter, Deborah, was in the graduating class, challenged as a violation of the First Amendment the school's allowing invocations and benedictions at graduation exercises. He asked a federal trial court to issue an order to Lee and other Providence officials prohibiting them from continuing this practice. The trial court found for Weisman, and a federal appellate court affirmed. As a result, Lee and the school board appealed to the U.S. Supreme Court. Joined by the Bush administration's solicitor general as an amicus curiae, they argued, as one justice later put it, "that these short prayers . . . are of profound meaning to many students and parents throughout this country who consider that due respect and acknowledgment for divine guidance and for the deepest spiritual aspirations of our people ought to be expressed at an event as important in life as a graduation." The school board and the solicitor general also asked the Supreme Court to reconsider the *Lemon* test, which the district court had used to find against Principal Lee.

Daniel Weisman and his daughter, Debbie, challenged the practice of having a member of the clergy deliver invocation and benediction prayers at public junior high school graduation exercises in Providence, Rhode Island. The Supreme Court ruled in their favor in *Lee v. Weisman*.

JUSTICE KENNEDY delivered the opinion of the Court.

These dominant facts mark and control the confines of our decision: State officials direct the performance of a formal religious exercise at promotional and graduation ceremonies for secondary schools. Even for those students who object to the religious exercise, their attendance and participation in the state-sponsored religious activity are in a fair and real sense obligatory, though the school district does not require attendance as a condition for receipt of the diploma.

This case does not require us to revisit the difficult questions dividing us in recent cases, questions of the definition and full scope of the principles governing the extent of permitted accommodation by the State for the religious beliefs and practices of many of its citizens. See *Allegheny County v. Greater Pittsburgh ACLU* (1989); *Wallace v. Jaffree* (1985); *Lynch v. Donnelly* (1984). For without reference to those principles in other contexts, the controlling precedents as they relate to prayer and religious exercise in primary and secondary public schools compel the holding here that the policy of the city of Providence is an unconstitutional one. We can decide the case without reconsidering the general constitutional framework by which public schools' efforts to accommodate religion are measured. Thus we do not accept the invitation of petitioners and *amicus* the United States to reconsider our decision in *Lemon v. Kurtzman.* The government involvement with religious activity in this case is pervasive, to the point of creating a state-sponsored and state-directed religious exercise in a public school. Conducting this formal religious observance conflicts with settled rules pertaining to prayer exercises for students, and that suffices to determine the question before us.

The principle that government may accommodate the free exercise of religion does not supersede the fundamental limitations imposed by the Establishment Clause. It is beyond dispute that, at a minimum, the Constitution guarantees that government may not coerce anyone to support or participate in religion or its exercise, or otherwise act in a way which "establishes a [state] religion or religious faith, or tends to do so.". . . The State's involvement in the school prayers challenged today violates these central principles.

That involvement is as troubling as it is undenied. A school official, the principal, decided that an invocation and a benediction should be given; this is a choice attributable to the State, and from a constitutional perspective it is as if a state statute decreed that the prayers must occur. The principal chose the religious participant, here a rabbi, and that choice is also attributable to the State. The reason for the choice of a rabbi is not disclosed by the record, but the potential for divisiveness over the choice of a particular member of the clergy to conduct the ceremony is apparent.

Divisiveness, of course, can attend any state decision respecting religions, and neither its existence nor its potential necessarily invalidates the State's attempts to accommodate religion in all cases. The potential for divisiveness is of particular relevance here though, because it centers around an overt religious exercise in a secondary school environment where, as we discuss below, subtle coercive pressures exist and where the student had no real alternative which would have allowed her to avoid the fact or appearance of participation.

The State's role did not end with the decision to include a prayer and with the choice of clergyman. Principal Lee provided Rabbi Gutterman with a copy of the "Guidelines for Civic Occasions," and advised him that his prayers should be nonsectarian. Through these means the principal directed and controlled the content of the prayer. Even if the only sanction for ignoring the instructions were that the rabbi would not be invited back, we think no religious representative who valued his or her continued reputation and effectiveness in the community would incur the State's displeasure in this regard. It is a cornerstone principle of

our Establishment Clause jurisprudence that it is "no part of the business of government to compose official prayers for any group of the American people to recite as a part of a religious program carried on by government," *Engel v. Vitale* (1962), and that is what the school officials attempted to do.

Petitioners argue, and we find nothing in the case to refute it, that the directions for the content of the prayers were a good-faith attempt by the school to ensure that the sectarianism which is so often the flashpoint for religious animosity be removed from the graduation ceremony. The concern is understandable, as a prayer which uses ideas or images identified with a particular religion may foster a different sort of sectarian rivalry than an invocation or benediction in terms more neutral. The school's explanation, however, does not resolve the dilemma caused by its participation. The question is not the good faith of the school in attempting to make the prayer acceptable to most persons, but the legitimacy of its undertaking that enterprise at all when the object is to produce a prayer to be used in a formal religious exercise which students, for all practical purposes, are obliged to attend.

We are asked to recognize the existence of a practice of nonsectarian prayer, prayer within the embrace of what is known as the Judeo-Christian tradition, prayer which is more acceptable than one which, for example, makes explicit references to the God of Israel, or to Jesus Christ, or to a patron saint. There may be some support, as an empirical observation, to the statement of the Court of Appeals for the Sixth Circuit, picked up by Judge Campbell's dissent in the Court of Appeals in this case, that there has emerged in this country a civic religion, one which is tolerated when sectarian exercises are not. If common ground can be defined which permits once conflicting faiths to express the shared conviction that there is an ethic and a morality which transcend human invention, the sense of community and purpose sought by all decent societies might be advanced. But though the First Amendment does not allow the government to stifle prayers which aspire to these ends, neither does it permit the government to undertake that task for itself. . . .

These concerns have particular application in the case of school officials, whose effort to monitor prayer will be perceived by the students as inducing a participation they might otherwise reject. Though the efforts of the school officials in this case to find common ground appear to have been a good-faith attempt to recognize the common aspects of religions and not the divisive ones, our precedents do not permit school officials to assist in composing prayers as an incident to a formal exercise for their students. *Engel v. Vitale.* And these same precedents caution us to measure the idea of a civic religion against the central meaning of the Religion Clauses of the First Amendment, which is that all creeds must be tolerated and none favored. The suggestion that government may establish an official or civic religion as a means of avoiding the establishment of a religion with more specific creeds strikes us as a contradiction that cannot be accepted.

The degree of school involvement here made it clear that the graduation prayers bore the imprint of the State and thus put school-age children who objected in an untenable position. We turn our attention now to consider the position of the students, both those who desired the prayer and she who did not. . . .

As we have observed before, there are heightened concerns with protecting freedom of conscience from subtle coercive pressure in the elementary and secondary public schools. . . . Our decisions in *Engel v. Vitale* and *Abington School District,* recognize, among other things, that prayer exercises in public schools carry a particular risk of indirect coercion. The concern may not be limited to the context of schools, but it is most pronounced there. . . . What to most believers may seem nothing more than a reasonable request that the nonbeliever respect their religious practices, in a school context may appear to the nonbeliever or dissenter to be an attempt to employ the machinery of the State to enforce a religious orthodoxy.

We need not look beyond the circumstances of this case to see the phenomenon at work. The undeniable fact is that the school district's supervision and control of a high school graduation ceremony places public pressure, as well as peer pressure, on attending students to stand as a group or, at least, maintain respectful silence during the Invocation and Benediction. This pressure, though subtle and indirect, can be as real as any overt compulsion. Of course, in our culture standing or remaining silent can signify adherence to a view or simple respect for the views of others. And no doubt some persons who have no desire to join a prayer have little objection to standing as a sign of respect for those who do. But for the dissenter of high school age, who has a reasonable perception that she is being forced by the State to pray in a manner her conscience will not allow, the injury is no less real. There can be no doubt that for many, if not most, of the students at the graduation, the act of standing or remaining silent was an expression of participation in the Rabbi's prayer. That was the very point of the religious exercise. It is of little comfort to a dissenter, then, to be told that for her the act of standing or remaining in silence signifies mere respect, rather than participation. What matters is that, given our social conventions, a reasonable dissenter in this milieu could believe that the group exercise signified her own participation or approval of it.

Finding no violation under these circumstances would place objectors in the dilemma of participating, with all that implies, or protesting. We do not address whether that choice is acceptable if the affected citizens are mature adults, but we think the State may not, consistent with the Establishment Clause, place primary and secondary school children in this position. Research in psychology supports the common assumption that adolescents are often susceptible to pressure from their peers towards conformity, and that the influence is strongest in matters of social convention. Brittain, Adolescent Choices and Parent-Peer Cross-Pressures, 28 Am. Sociological Rev. 385 (June 1963); Clasen & Brown, The Multidimensionality of Peer Pressure in Adolescence, 14 J. of Youth and Adolescence 451 (Dec. 1985). . . . To recognize that the choice imposed by the State constitutes an unacceptable constraint only acknowledges that the government may no more use social pressure to enforce orthodoxy than it may use more direct means. . . .

There was a stipulation in the District Court that attendance at graduation and promotional ceremonies is voluntary. Petitioners and the United States, as *amicus,* made this a center point of the case, arguing that the option of not attending the graduation excuses any inducement or coercion in the ceremony itself. The argument lacks all persuasion. Law reaches past formalism. And to say a teenage student has a real choice not to attend her high school graduation is formalistic in the extreme. True, Deborah could elect not to attend commencement without renouncing her diploma; but we shall not allow the case to turn on this point. Everyone knows that in our society and in our culture high school graduation is one of life's most significant occasions. A school rule which excuses attendance is beside the point. Attendance may not be required by official decree, yet it is apparent that a student is not free to absent herself from the graduation exercise in any real sense of the term "voluntary," for absence would require forfeiture of those intangible benefits which have motivated the student through youth and all her high school years. Graduation is a time for family and those closest to the student to celebrate success and express mutual wishes of gratitude and respect, all to the end of impressing upon the young person the role that it is his or her right and duty to assume in the community and all of its diverse parts.

The importance of the event is the point the school district and the United States rely upon to argue that a formal prayer ought to be permitted, but it becomes one of the principal reasons why their argument must fail. Their contention, one of considerable force were it not for the constitutional constraints applied to state action, is that the prayers are an essential part of these ceremonies because for many persons an occasion of this significance lacks meaning if there is no recognition, however brief, that human achievements cannot be understood apart from their spiritual essence. We think the Government's position that this interest suffices to force students to choose between compliance or forfeiture demonstrates fundamental inconsistency in its argumentation. It fails to acknowledge that what for many of Deborah's classmates and their parents was a spiritual imperative was for Daniel and Deborah Weisman religious conformance compelled by the State. While in some societies the wishes of the majority might prevail, the Establishment Clause of the First Amendment is addressed to this contingency and rejects the balance urged upon us. The Constitution forbids the State to exact religious conformity from a student as the price of attending her own high school graduation. This is the calculus the Constitution commands. . . .

We do not hold that every state action implicating religion is invalid if one or a few citizens find it offensive. People may take offense at all manner of religious as well as nonreligious messages, but offense alone does not in every case show a violation. We know too that sometimes to endure social isolation or even anger may be the price of conscience or nonconformity. But, by any reading of our cases,

the conformity required of the student in this case was too high an exaction to withstand the test of the Establishment Clause. The prayer exercises in this case are especially improper because the State has in every practical sense compelled attendance and participation in an explicit religious exercise at an event of singular importance to every student, one the objecting student had no real alternative to avoid. . . .

. . . No holding by this Court suggests that a school can persuade or compel a student to participate in a religious exercise. That is being done here, and it is forbidden by the Establishment Clause of the First Amendment.

For the reasons we have stated, the judgment of the Court of Appeals is

Affirmed.

JUSTICE BLACKMUN, with whom JUSTICE STEVENS and JUSTICE O'CONNOR join, concurring.

In 1971, Chief Justice Burger reviewed the Court's past decisions and found: "Three . . . tests may be gleaned from our cases." *Lemon v. Kurtzman.* . . . After *Lemon*, the Court continued to rely on these basic principles in resolving Establishment Clause disputes.

Application of these principles to the facts of this case is straightforward. There can be "no doubt" that the "invocation of God's blessings" delivered at Nathan Bishop Middle School "is a religious activity." . . . The question then is whether the government has "placed its official stamp of approval" on the prayer. As the Court ably demonstrates, when the government "compose[s] official prayers," selects the member of the clergy to deliver the prayer, has the prayer delivered at a public school event that is planned, supervised and given by school officials, and pressures students to attend and participate in the prayer, there can be no doubt that the government is advancing and promoting religion. As our prior decisions teach us, it is this that the Constitution prohibits.

I join the Court's opinion today because I find nothing in it inconsistent with the essential precepts of the Establishment Clause developed in our precedents. The Court holds that the graduation prayer is unconstitutional because the State "in effect required participation in a religious exercise." Although our precedents make clear that proof of government coercion is not necessary to prove an Establishment Clause violation, it is sufficient. Government pressure to participate in a religious activity is an obvious indication that the government is endorsing or promoting religion.

But it is not enough that the government restrain from compelling religious practices: it must not engage in them either. . . . The Court repeatedly has recognized that a violation of the Establishment Clause is not predicated on coercion. . . . The Establishment Clause proscribes public schools from "conveying or attempting to convey a message that religion or a particular religious belief is favored or preferred," *County of Allegheny v. ACLU* (1989), even if the schools do not actually "impose pressure upon a student to participate in a religious activity.". . .

It is these understandings . . . that underlie our Establishment Clause jurisprudence. We have believed that religious freedom cannot exist in the absence of a free democratic government, and that such a government cannot endure when there is fusion between religion and the political regime. We have believed that religious freedom cannot thrive in the absence of a vibrant religious community and that such a community cannot prosper when it is bound to the secular. And we have believed that these were the animating principles behind the adoption of the Establishment Clause. To that end, our cases have prohibited government endorsement of religion, its sponsorship, and active involvement in religion, whether or not citizens were coerced to conform.

I remain convinced that our jurisprudence is not misguided, and that it requires the decision reached by the Court today. Accordingly, I join the Court in affirming the judgment of the Court of Appeals.

JUSTICE SOUTER, with whom JUSTICE STEVENS and JUSTICE O'CONNOR join, concurring.

I join the whole of the Court's opinion, and fully agree that prayers at public school graduation ceremonies indirectly coerce religious observance. I write separately nonetheless on two issues of Establishment Clause analysis that underlie my independent resolution of this case: whether the Clause applies to governmental practices that do not favor one religion or denomination over others, and whether state coercion of religious conformity, over and above state

endorsement of religious exercise or belief, is a necessary element of an Establishment Clause violation.

Forty-five years ago, this Court announced a basic principle of constitutional law from which it has not strayed: the Establishment Clause forbids not only state practices that "aid one religion . . . or prefer one religion over another," but also those that "aid all religions." *Everson v. Board of Education of Ewing* (1947). Today we reaffirm that principle, holding that the Establishment Clause forbids state-sponsored prayers in public school settings no matter how nondenominational the prayers may be. In barring the State from sponsoring generically Theistic prayers where it could not sponsor sectarian ones, we hold true to a line of precedent from which there is no adequate historical case to depart. . . .

Some have challenged this precedent by reading the Establishment Clause to permit "nonpreferential" state promotion of religion. The challengers argue that, as originally understood by the Framers, "the Establishment Clause did not require government neutrality between religion and irreligion nor did it prohibit the Federal Government from providing nondiscriminatory aid to religion." *Wallace* (REHNQUIST, J., dissenting). While a case has been made for this position, it is not so convincing as to warrant reconsideration of our settled law; indeed, I find in the history of the Clause's textual development a more powerful argument supporting the Court's jurisprudence following *Everson*. . . .

What we . . . know of the Framers' experience underscores the observation of one prominent commentator, that confining the Establishment Clause to a prohibition on preferential aid "requires a premise that the Framers were extraordinarily bad drafters—that they believed one thing but adopted language that said something substantially different, and that they did so after repeatedly attending to the choice of language.". . . We must presume, since there is no conclusive evidence to the contrary, that the Framers embraced the significance of their textual judgment. Thus, on balance, history neither contradicts nor warrants reconsideration of the settled principle that the Establishment Clause forbids support for religion in general no less than support for one religion or some. . . .

Petitioners rest most of their argument on a theory that, whether or not the Establishment Clause permits extensive nonsectarian support for religion, it does not forbid the state to sponsor affirmations of religious belief that coerce neither support for religion nor participation in religious observance. I appreciate the force of some of the arguments supporting a "coercion" analysis of the Clause. See generally *Allegheny County* (opinion of KENNEDY, J.) But we could not adopt that reading without abandoning our settled law, a course that, in my view, the text of the Clause would not readily permit. Nor does the extratextual evidence of original meaning stand so unequivocally at odds with the textual premise inherent in existing precedent that we should fundamentally reconsider our course.

Over the years, this Court has declared the invalidity of many noncoercive state laws and practices conveying a message of religious endorsement. For example, in *Allegheny County* we forbade the prominent display of a nativity scene on public property; without contesting the dissent's observation that the crèche coerced no one into accepting or supporting whatever message it proclaimed, five Members of the Court found its display unconstitutional as a state endorsement of Christianity. Likewise, in *Wallace v. Jaffree* (1985), we struck down a state law requiring a moment of silence in public classrooms not because the statute coerced students to participate in prayer (for it did not), but because the manner of its enactment "conveyed a message of state approval of prayer activities in the public schools.". . .

Our precedents may not always have drawn perfectly straight lines. They simply cannot, however, support the position that a showing of coercion is necessary to a successful Establishment Clause claim. . . .

Petitioners argue from the political setting in which the Establishment Clause was framed, and from the Framers' own political practices following ratification, that government may constitutionally endorse religion so long as it does not coerce religious conformity. The setting and the practices warrant canvassing, but while they yield some evidence for petitioners' argument, they do not reveal the degree of consensus in early constitutional thought that would raise a threat to *stare decisis* by challenging the presumption that the Establishment Clause adds something to the Free Exercise Clause that follows it. . . .

Petitioners contend that because the early Presidents included religious messages in their inaugural and Thanksgiving Day addresses, the Framers could not have meant the Establishment Clause to forbid noncoercive state endorsement of religion. The argument ignores the fact, however, that Americans today find such proclamations less controversial than did the founding generation, whose published thoughts on the matter belie petitioners' claim. President Jefferson, for example, steadfastly refused to issue Thanksgiving proclamations of any kind, in part because he thought they violated the Religion Clauses. . . .

While we may be unable to know for certain what the Framers meant by the Clause, we do know that, around the time of its ratification, a respectable body of opinion supported a considerably broader reading than petitioners urge upon us. This consistency with the textual considerations is enough to preclude fundamentally reexamining our settled law, and I am accordingly left with the task of considering whether the state practice at issue here violates our traditional understanding of the Clause's proscriptions.

While the Establishment Clause's concept of neutrality is not self-revealing, our recent cases have invested it with specific content: the state may not favor or endorse either religion generally over nonreligion or one religion over others. . . . This principle against favoritism and endorsement has become the foundation of Establishment Clause jurisprudence, ensuring that religious belief is irrelevant to every citizen's standing in the political community. . . . Our aspiration to religious liberty, embodied in the First Amendment, permits no other standard. . . .

JUSTICE SCALIA, with whom THE CHIEF JUSTICE, JUSTICE WHITE, and JUSTICE THOMAS join, dissenting.

Three Terms ago, I joined an opinion recognizing that the Establishment Clause must be construed in light of the "[g]overnment policies of accommodation, acknowledgment, and support for religion [that] are an accepted part of our political and cultural heritage." That opinion affirmed that "the meaning of the Clause is to be determined by reference to historical practices and understandings." It said that "[a] test for implementing the protections of the Establishment Clause that, if applied with consistency, would invalidate longstanding traditions cannot be a proper reading of the Clause." *Allegheny County v. Greater Pittsburgh ACLU* (1989) (KENNEDY, J., concurring in judgment in part and dissenting in part).

These views of course prevent me from joining today's opinion, which is conspicuously bereft of any reference to history. In holding that the Establishment Clause prohibits invocations and benedictions at public-school graduation ceremonies, the Court—with nary a mention that it is doing so—lays waste a tradition that is as old as public-school graduation ceremonies themselves, and that is a component of an even more longstanding American tradition of nonsectarian prayer to God at public celebrations generally. As its instrument of destruction, the bulldozer of its social engineering, the Court invents a boundless, and boundlessly manipulable, test of psychological coercion. . . . Today's opinion shows more forcefully than volumes of argumentation why our Nation's protection, that fortress which is our Constitution, cannot possibly rest upon the changeable philosophical predilections of the Justices of this Court, but must have deep foundations in the historic practices of our people. . . .

The history and tradition of our Nation are replete with public ceremonies featuring prayers of thanksgiving and petition. . . . Most recently, President Bush, continuing the tradition established by President Washington, asked those attending his inauguration to bow their heads, and made a prayer his first official act as President. . . .

The Court presumably would separate graduation invocations and benedictions from other instances of public "preservation and transmission of religious beliefs" on the ground that they involve "psychological coercion." I find it a sufficient embarrassment that our Establishment Clause jurisprudence regarding holiday displays . . . has come to "requir[e] scrutiny more commonly associated with interior decorators than with the judiciary.". . . But interior decorating is a rock-hard science compared to psychology practiced by amateurs. A few citations of "[r]esearch in psychology" that have no particular bearing upon the precise issue here cannot disguise the fact that the Court has gone beyond the realm where judges know what they are doing. The Court's argument that state officials have "coerced" students to take part in the invocation and benediction at graduation ceremonies is, not to put too fine a point on it, incoherent. . . .

The deeper flaw in the Court's opinion does not lie in its wrong answer to the question whether there was state-induced "peer-pressure" coercion; it lies, rather, in the Court's making violation of the Establishment Clause hinge on such a precious question. . . .

. . . [W]hile I have no quarrel with the Court's general proposition that the Establishment Clause "guarantees that government may not coerce anyone to support or participate in religion or its exercise," I see no warrant for expanding the concept of coercion beyond acts backed by threat of penalty—a brand of coercion that, happily, is readily discernible to those of us who have made a career of reading the disciples of Blackstone rather than of Freud. The Framers were indeed opposed to coercion of religious worship by the National Government; but, as their own sponsorship of nonsectarian prayer in public events demonstrates, they understood that "speech is not coercive; the listener may do as he likes.". . .

Our religion-clause jurisprudence has become bedeviled (so to speak) by reliance on formulaic abstractions that are not derived from, but positively conflict with, our long-accepted constitutional traditions. Foremost among these has been the so-called *Lemon* test, see *Lemon v. Kurtzman* (1971), which has received well-earned criticism from many members of this Court. . . . The Court today demonstrates the irrelevance of *Lemon* by essentially ignoring it, and the interment of that case may be the one happy byproduct of the Court's otherwise lamentable decision. Unfortunately, however, the Court has replaced *Lemon* with its psycho-coercion test, which suffers the double disability of having no roots whatever in our people's historic practice, and being as infinitely expandable as the reasons for psychotherapy itself.

Another happy aspect of the case is that it is only a jurisprudential disaster and not a practical one. Given the odd basis for the Court's decision, invocations and benedictions will be able to be given at public-school graduations next June, as they have for the past century and a half, so long as school authorities make clear that anyone who abstains from screaming in protest does not necessarily participate in the prayers. All that is seemingly needed is an announcement, or perhaps a written insertion at the beginning of the graduation Program, to the effect that, while all are asked to rise for the invocation and benediction, none is compelled to join in them, nor will be assumed, by rising, to have done so. That obvious fact recited, the graduates and their parents may proceed to thank God, as Americans have always done, for the blessings He has generously bestowed on them and on their country. . . .

For the foregoing reasons, I dissent.

Justice Kennedy may not have applied *Lemon* to resolve *Lee,* but he did not overturn it. To the contrary, he specifically declined to "revisit" *Lemon* on the grounds that the Court's previous cases on prayer in school established clear precedent for this case. Returning to the coercion standard he advocated in *County of Allegheny,* Kennedy noted that *Engel* and *Abington* recognized that "prayer exercises in public schools carry a particular risk of indirect coercion." It was this coercion, however subtle, to which Kennedy took offense. The concurrers, on the other hand, complained that coercion was insufficient: Stevens, Blackmun, and O'Connor continued to advocate an endorsement approach to *Lemon.* Souter, joined by Stevens and O'Connor, explicitly rejected Kennedy's coercion standard and Rehnquist's nonpreferentialism in favor of the endorsement approach. Souter also stressed that the Court should not abandon precedent governing Religious Establishment cases, yet he had very little to say about *Lemon,* in particular.

Most interesting of all may be Scalia's dissent because it indicates that justices can agree over a standard of law but disagree vehemently over its application. Scalia endorsed the coercion standard in *County of Allegheny,* but here he takes issue with the way Kennedy applied it, arguing that the majority opinion is too ahistorical and psychologically grounded. Joined by Rehnquist, Thomas, and White, Scalia lambastes the Court for engaging in amateur psychology and for paying more attention to Freud than to the Framers. About the only thing the dissenters found redeemable in *Lee* was that the majority opinion seemed to "inter" *Lemon.* But they were wrong: as of this writing *Lemon* remains good law.

Scalia and his colleagues also lost on the holding:

the Court once again rejected prayer in school. With White's retirement and Ginsburg's appointment to the Court, prohibitions against prayer in school may be on even firmer ground. Throughout his career, White was one of the more accommodation-oriented justices, and it seems unlikely that Ginsburg would follow suit. But her presence does not ensure the end to litigation on this controversial subject. Indeed, given continued public support for the return of prayer in school, it is virtually assured that the Court will revisit the issue. Just a year after the decision in *Lee,* a Mississippi high school principal, Bishop Knox, became ensnared in controversy for allowing students to read a prayer over the loudspeaker. Knox defended his actions on the ground that the students had voted (490–96) to allow the prayers, but the school's superintendent fired him. That action set off a series of protests and rallies in defense of Knox, some of which were attended by the state's governor. Within three weeks, the school board overturned the superintendent's decision, and Knox was reinstated.[53]

Although the case attracted nationwide attention, the action taken by Knox was not unusual. Various forms of prayer in school may no longer be the norm in the United States, but they are not exceptional. The exceptional part of the Knox case was that an official fired a principal for allowing the prayers. That step is rare, especially in southern states, where noncompliance with Court decisions remains high.

What can we conclude about the Court's handling of prayer-in-school cases and religious liberty litigation in general? At the very least, we can see that this area of the law is unstable: justices call on varying approaches to resolve the cases. As we have observed, each time the Court seems on the verge of eliminating *Lemon,* that test reappears, as Justice Scalia once put it, "like some ghoul in a late-night horror movie. . . ." Whether the Court kills off *Lemon* once and for all

53. See "Principal in a School Prayer Dispute is Reinstated," *New York Times,* Dec. 17, 1993, A14.

seems to hinge on the justices' ability to agree over a replacement and on the application of that replacement, which—as *Lee v. Weisman* illustrates—they have not been able to do.

At its most extreme, religion litigation is an area rife with contradictions and "unprincipled decisions." Lawrence Rosen listed some of those apparent inconsistencies, many of which should be familiar to you by now:

At various times the Court has held that [prayer] in a public school classroom is impermissible but that the erection of a Nativity scene on municipal property is not; that delivery by a clergyman of an opening prayer to the state legislature is allowable but that religious headgear may not be worn if military regulations bar such attire; that the provision from public funds of books to parochial school children or released time for off-campus religious instruction is constitutional but that providing parochial students with remedial aid is not.[54]

Will the Court seek to resolve these and other inconsistencies? What standard or test will it invoke to do so? Having read about many of the significant cases, these are questions on which you might want to speculate, for there are still no easy answers.

READINGS

Alley, Robert S. *The Supreme Court on Church and State.* New York: Oxford University Press, 1988.

Carter, Stephen L. *The Culture of Disbelief.* New York: Basic Books, 1993.

Currey, Thomas J. *The First Amendment Freedoms: Church and State in America to the Passage of the First Amendment.* New York: Oxford University Press, 1986.

Dolbeare, Kenneth M., and Phillip E. Hammond. *The School Prayer Decision.* Chicago: University of Chicago Press, 1971.

Fellman, David. *Religion in American Public Law.* Boston: Boston University Press, 1965.

Howe, Mark Dewolfe. *The Garden and the Wilderness: Religion and Government in American Constitutional History.* Chicago: University of Chicago Press, 1965.

Kurland, Philip B., ed. *Church and State: The Supreme Court and the First Amendment.* Chicago: University of Chicago Press, 1975.

Levy, Leonard W. *The Establishment Clause.* New York: Macmillan, 1986.

Malbin, Michael J. *Religion and Politics.* Washington, D.C.: American Enterprise Institute, 1978.

Manwaring, David B. *Render unto Caesar.* Chicago: University of Chicago Press, 1962.

Morgan, Richard E. *The Politics of Religious Conflict.* New York: Pegasus, 1968.

———. *The Supreme Court and Religion.* New York: Free Press, 1972.

Pfeffer, Leo. *Church, State, and Freedom.* Boston: Beacon Press, 1967.

———. *Religion, State, and the Burger Court.* Buffalo, N.Y.: Prometheus Books, 1985.

Sorauf, Frank J. *The Wall of Separation.* Princeton, N.J.: Princeton University Press, 1976.

Stokes, Anson Phelps, and Leo Pfeffer. *Church and State in America.* New York: Harper and Row, 1964.

Wills, Garry. *Under God.* New York: Simon and Schuster, 1990.

---

54. "Continuing the Conversation: Creationism, the Religious Clauses, and the Politics of Culture," *Supreme Court Review* (1988): 61–62.

CHAPTER 13
FREEDOM OF SPEECH, ASSEMBLY, AND ASSOCIATION

T ONE TIME or another, everyone has criticized someone in government. The president or a state senator has said or done something we thought was wrong. We may have been polite, simply noting our displeasure, or we may have called the official a bum, or worse. Either way, we expressed our views. Speaking our minds is a privilege we enjoy as inhabitants of the United States, but we probably have not thought very seriously about it.

The First Amendment is our most fundamental protection against government encroachment on freedom of expression. We have shown in Chapter 12 how the first Amendment protects religious freedom. In its bold language it accomplishes even more: "Congress shall make no law . . . abridging the freedom of speech, or of the press; or the right of the people peaceably to assemble, and to petition the Government for a redress of grievances." These words seem to provide an absolute shield against government actions that would restrict any of the four components of freedom of expression: speech, press, assembly, and petition. But to what extent *does* the Constitution protect these rights? May mischievous patrons stand

up in a crowded movie theater and shout *fire* when they know there is no fire? May a publisher knowingly print lies about a member of the community in order to destroy that person's reputation? May a radical political party take actions to overthrow the government by force and violence? May a group of protesters storm onto the Senate floor to bring attention to their demands?

Despite the absolute wording of the First Amendment, the answer to each of these questions is no. The Supreme Court never has adhered to a literal interpretation of the expression guarantees; rather, it has ruled that certain expressions—whether communicated verbally, in print, or by actions—may be restricted because of the effect they may have.

This chapter is the first of two dealing with the right of expression. Here we examine the development of constitutional standards for freedom of expression and then the application of those standards to various kinds of expression. In the next we look at issues specific to the freedom of the press and discuss forms of expression that traditionally have been considered outside First Amendment protection.

THE DEVELOPMENT OF LEGAL STANDARDS: THE EMERGENCE OF LAW IN TIMES OF CRISIS

History teaches that governments tend to be more repressive in times of crisis. Such emergencies may be the result of war, economic collapse, natural catastrophes, or internal rebellion. During these times a nation's survival may be at stake, and the government may be unstable. Political dissent and opposition to the government are more likely to occur. The responses of political leaders are predictable: they will put national unity first and take firm action against subversive and opposition groups. Often these reactions take the form of policies that restrict the right of the people to speak, publish, and organize.

The United States is no exception to this rule. In times of peace and general prosperity there is little reason to restrict freedom of expression. The government and the nation are secure, and the people are relatively content. In times of crisis, however, the president and Congress may react harshly, contending that some forms of expression must be curtailed to protect national security. In response, political dissidents may challenge such laws, arguing that repressive government policies are unconstitutional—even in times of war or national emergency.

The justices of the Supreme Court must ultimately decide where constitutional protections end and the government's right to restrict expression begins. These questions have come to the Court during or soon after periods of crisis. At these times the Constitution has been most seriously tested, and the Court has been called upon to develop its most fundamental doctrines regarding freedom of expression.

To demonstrate this point, we have organized this section around times of crisis—the Revolution (1775–1781) and the Civil War (1861–1865), World War I (1917–1918), World War II (1941–1945) and the resultant cold war, and the Vietnam War (1963–1973). As you read the cases associated with each of these times, you will be asked questions about the development of law and legal doctrine. Perhaps the most basic question is this: Had a crisis not existed, would the Court have decided this case the same way? This question should serve as a constant reminder that Supreme Court justices are as vulnerable to public pressures and to waves of patriotism as the average citizen.

The Early Crises: The Revolutionary and Civil Wars

The Founders also were vulnerable to the patriotic atmosphere that seems to permeate society following a major crisis. Not long after the Revolution, Congress passed one of the most restrictive laws in American history, the Sedition Act of 1798:

If any person shall write, print, utter or publish, or shall cause to procure to be written, printed, uttered or published, or shall knowingly and willingly assist or aid in writing, printing, uttering or publishing any false, scandalous and malicious writing or writings against the government of the United States, or either House of the Congress of the United States, or the President of the United States, with intent to defame the said government, or either House of the said Congress, or the said President, or to bring them, or either of them into contempt or disrepute; or to excite against them, or either or any of them, the hatred of the good people of the United States, done in pursuance of any such law, or of the powers in him vested by the Constitution of the United States, or to resist, oppose, or defeat any such law or act, or to aid, encourage or abet any hostile designs of any foreign nation against the United States, their people or government, then such person, being thereof convicted before any court of the United States having jurisdiction thereof, shall be punished by a fine not exceeding $2,000, and by imprisonment not exceeding two years.

The act expired in 1801. But why did our Founding Fathers, who so dearly treasured liberty, ever pass such a repressive law? First, Congress was dominated by the Federalist party, to the extent that some argued that the statute was intended to "suppress political opposition," not plain speech.[1] Indeed, Thomas Jeffer-

1. Peter Woll, *Constitutional Law* (Englewood Cliffs, N.J.: Prentice Hall, 1981), 581.

son, leader of the Anti-Federalist (Democratic-Republican) party, vigorously attacked the law, claiming that it led to witch hunts. Second, it is undoubtedly true that the Framers held a view of free expression different from the present-day view. They had known only the British system, which often imposed laws that severely curtailed free expression.

For the next sixty years, the United States enjoyed relative tranquility; Congress passed no major restrictive legislation, and the Supreme Court decided no major expression cases. In the 1860s, however, peaceful times came to a crashing halt as the nation divided over the issue of slavery. As civil war broke out, President Abraham Lincoln took a number of steps to suppress "treacherous" behavior, believing "that the nation must be able to protect itself in war against utterances which actually cause insubordination."[2] Still, the Supreme Court had no opportunity to rule on the constitutionality of the president's actions, at least on First Amendment grounds.

World War I

The early decades of the twentieth century present a mixed picture of the United States. On the one hand, as a result of efforts by Progressive groups and leaders, Congress and the states enacted legislation aimed at protecting workers and cleaning up American politics. On the other hand, as John Schmidhauser notes, "The thrust of Progressive legislative efforts . . . [was] ultimately overshadowed by the channeling of national efforts into the first World War."[3] That is, as the war in Europe raged and other events ensued, most notably the Russian Revolution in 1917, the country turned its attention toward defending the American system of government and away from domestic reforms.

Today, the emotional and patriotic fervor unleashed by World War I is difficult to imagine. No American was immune, not even Supreme Court justices. Consider Chief Justice Edward D. White's response to an attorney who argued that the military draft, enacted by Congress in 1917, lacked public support: "I don't think your statement has anything to do with legal arguments and should not have been said in this Court. It is a very unpatriotic statement to make."[4] Members of Congress, too, were caught up in the patriotic fervor gripping the nation. They, like the Founders, felt it necessary to enact legislation to ensure that Americans presented a unified front to the world. The Espionage Act of 1917 prohibited any attempt to "interfere with the operation or success of the military or naval forces of the United States . . . to cause insubordination . . . in the military or naval forces . . . or willfully obstruct the recruiting or enlistment service of the United States." One year later, Congress passed the Sedition Act, which prohibited the uttering of, writing, or publishing of anything disloyal to the government, flag, or military forces of the United States.

Although the majority of Americans probably supported these laws, some groups and individuals thought they constituted intolerable infringements on civil liberties guarantees contained in the First Amendment. Dissenters, however, were not of one political voice: some, most notably the American Union Against Militarism (a predecessor of the American Civil Liberties Union), were blatantly pacifist; others, primarily leaders of the Progressive movement, were pure civil libertarians, opposed to any government intrusion into free expressions; and others were radicals, individuals who hoped to see the United States undergo a socialist or communist revolution. Regardless of their motivation, these individuals and groups brought legal challenges to the repres-

2. Zechariah Chafee, Jr., *Free Speech in the United States* (Cambridge: Harvard University Press, 1941), 266.

3. *Constitutional Law in American Politics* (Monterey, Calif.: Brooks/Cole, 1984), 325.

4. Ibid.

Government officers and clerks loading a police ambulance with literature seized at the Communist party headquarters in Cambridge, Massachusetts, in 1919. Such activities against communist organizations were not uncommon during the Red Scare era.

sive laws and pushed the Supreme Court into freedom of expression cases for the first time. The first of the World War I cases, *Schenck v. United States,* was decided by the Court in 1919, followed by three others the same year.

While you read *Schenck,* keep in mind the circumstances surrounding the Court's decision. The United States had just successfully completed a war effort in which more than 4 million Americans were in uniform and more than 1 million troops had been sent to fight in Europe. The number of Americans killed or seriously wounded exceeded 300,000. There had been tremendous national fervor and support for the war effort. In the face of this national unity, a socialist had engaged in active opposition to America's participation in the war. His appeal of an espionage conviction allowed the Supreme Court to make its first major doctrinal statement on freedom of expression. What did the Court decide? What standard did it develop to adjudicate future claims?

Schenck v. United States

249 U.S. 47 (1919)
Vote: 9 (Brandeis, Clarke, Day, Holmes, McKenna, McReynolds, Pitney, Van Devanter, White)
0
Opinion of the Court: Holmes

In 1917 Charles Schenck, the general secretary of the Socialist party of Philadelphia, had 15,000 pamphlets printed, urging resistance to the draft. He sent these leaflets, described by the government's case as "frank, bitter, passionate appeal[s] for resistance to the Selective Service Law," to men listed in a local newspaper as eligible for service. Federal authorities charged him with violating the Espionage Act; specifically, the United States alleged that Schenck had attempted to obstruct recruitment and illegally used the mail to do so.

Henry J. Gibbons, Schenck's attorney, did not dispute the government's charges; rather, he argued that the Espionage Act violated the First Amendment's

Free Speech Clause because it placed a chilling effect on expression. That is, the act prohibited speech or publication before the words are uttered, and not after, as, Gibbons argued, the Constitution mandated.

MR. JUSTICE HOLMES delivered the opinion of the Court.

The document in question upon its first printed side recited the first section of the Thirteenth Amendment, said that the idea embodied in it was violated by the Conscription Act and that a conscript is little better than a convict. In impassioned language it intimated that conscription was despotism in its worst form and a monstrous wrong against humanity in the interest of Wall Street's chosen few. It said "Do not submit to intimidation," but in form at least confined itself to peaceful measures such as a petition for the repeal of the act. The other and later printed side of the sheet was headed "Assert Your Rights." It stated reasons for alleging that any one violated the Constitution when he refused to recognize "your right to assert your opposition to the draft," and went on "If you do not assert and support your rights, you are helping to deny or disparage rights which it is the solemn duty of all citizens and residents of the United States to retain." It described the arguments on the other side as coming from cunning politicians and a mercenary capitalist press, and even silent consent to the conscription law as helping to support an infamous conspiracy. It denied the power to send our citizens away to foreign shores to shoot up the people of other lands, and added that words could not express the condemnation such cold-blooded ruthlessness deserves, &c., &c., winding up "You must do your share to maintain, support and uphold the rights of the people of this country." Of course the document would not have been sent unless it had been intended to have some effect, and we do not see what effect it could be expected to have upon persons subject to the draft except to influence them to obstruct the carrying of it out. The defendants do not deny that the jury might find against them on this point.

But it is said, suppose that that was the tendency of this circular, it is protected by the First Amendment to the Constitution. Two of the strongest expressions are said to be quoted respectively from well-known public men. It may

well be that the prohibition of laws abridging the freedom of speech is not confined to previous constraints, although to prevent them may have been the main purpose. We admit that in many places and in ordinary times the defendants in saying all that was said in the circular would have been within their constitutional rights. But the character of every act depends upon the circumstances in which it is done. The most stringent protection of free speech would not protect a man in falsely shouting fire in a theatre and causing a panic. It does not even protect a man from an injunction against uttering words that may have all the effect of force. The question in every case is whether the words used are used in such circumstances and are of such a nature as to create a clear and present danger that they will bring about the substantive evils that Congress has a right to prevent. It is a question of proximity and degree. When a nation is at war many things that might be said in time of peace are such a hindrance to its effort that their utterance will not be endured so long as men fight and that no Court could regard them as protected by any constitutional right. It seems to be admitted that if an actual obstruction of the recruiting service were proved, liability for words that produced that effect might be enforced. The statute of 1917 in § 4 punishes conspiracies to obstruct as well as actual obstruction. If the act, (speaking, or circulating a paper), its tendency and the intent with which it is done are the same, we perceive no ground for saying that success alone warrants making the act a crime. Indeed that case might be said to dispose of the present contention if the precedent covers all *media concludendi* [the steps of an argument]. But as the right to free speech was not referred to specifically, we have thought fit to add a few words.

It was not argued that a conspiracy to obstruct the draft was not within the words of the Act of 1917. The words are "obstruct the recruiting or enlistment service," and it might be suggested that they refer only to making it hard to get volunteers. Recruiting heretofore usually having been accomplished by getting volunteers the word is apt to call up that method only in our minds. But recruiting is gaining fresh supplies for the forces, as well by draft as otherwise. It is put as an alternative to enlistment or voluntary enrollment in this act. . . .

Judgments affirmed.

Many scholars argue that Holmes's opinion in *Schenck* represents not only his finest work but also a most important and substantial explication of free speech. Why? First, Holmes provided the Court with a mechanism for framing such cases and a standard by which to adjudicate future claims:

The question in every case is whether the words used are used in such circumstances and are of such a nature as to create a clear and present danger that they will bring about the substantive evils that Congress has a right to prevent.

Often called the Clear and Present Danger test, the standard apparently reflected the other justices' views on free speech, as the Court's decision in *Schenck* was unanimous. Second, Holmes's opinion was politically astute. Schmidhauser notes that, given "the political context in which it arose . . . when the emphasis was on 'Americanism,'" the Court could not protect all speech.[5] Yet, in light of the First Amendment, it could not move to the opposite extreme, totally prohibiting controversial language. Seen in this way, Holmes's words created an elegant compromise and avoided a confrontation between the Court and Congress during a crisis period. Finally, that Holmes devised a test by which to adjudicate First Amendment claims provides the earliest example of the justices' willingness to recognize legitimate limits to free speech.

One week after *Schenck,* Holmes applied his Clear and Present Danger standard to two other challenges to the Espionage Act. In *Frohwerk v. United States* a newspaper editor and an editorial writer for the *Missouri Staats Zeitung* urged the Court to overturn their convictions for publishing a series of articles accusing the United States of pursuing an imperialistic policy toward Germany. In *Frohwerk*'s companion case, *Debs v. United States,* Eugene V. Debs, a leader of the Socialist party in the United States, had been convicted for a speech he delivered in Canton, Ohio. Extolling the virtues of socialism and praising the Bolshevik Revolution, Debs said:

5. Ibid., 327.

The Socialist has a great idea. An expanding philosophy. It is spreading over the face of the earth. It is as useless to resist it as it is to resist the rising sunrise. . . . What a privilege it is to serve it. I have regretted a thousand times I can do so little for the movement that has done so much for me. . . . Do not worry over the charge of treason to your masters, but be concerned about the treason that involves yourself. This year we are going to sweep into power . . . and we are going to destroy capitalistic institutions and recreate them.

Federal authorities arrested Debs, charging him with attempting to incite insubordination, a violation of the Espionage Act. They cited as "evidence" not only his words but the timing of his speech, right after Congress passed the Selective Service Act. Writing for the Court in both cases, Justice Holmes relied on the Clear and Present Danger test to uphold the Debs and Frohwerk convictions. In fact, his only new statement of any significance was "that the First Amendment while prohibiting legislation against free speech as such cannot have been, and obviously was not intended to give immunity for every possible use of language."

Such an assertion again underscores the Court's unwillingness to read literally and absolutely First Amendment guarantees. Moreover, because Holmes wrote for the majority in both cases, the future vitality of the Clear and Present Danger test seemed assured; the Court apparently agreed that it provided a reasonable vehicle for judging First Amendment claims. But, just eight months after the *Debs* and *Frohwerk* decisions, the majority of justices banished this test to a legal exile that would last for almost two decades. The first hint of their disaffection came in *Abrams v. United States,* the fourth of the 1919 quartet. Abrams, a twenty-nine-year-old Russian immigrant, also was charged with violating the Espionage Act. The conviction hinged on the publication and distribution of several pamphlets criticizing President Wilson's decision to send U.S. troops into Russia and calling for a general strike to protest that policy.

Writing for the Supreme Court, Justice Clarke upheld Abrams's conviction. In doing so, though, he moved away from the Clear and Present Danger test, and instead asserted:

[T]he plain purpose of their propaganda was to excite, at the supreme crisis of the war, disaffection, sedition, riots, and, as they hoped, revolution, in this country for the purpose of embarrassing and if possible defeating the military plans of the Government in Europe. A technical distinction may perhaps be taken between disloyal and abusive language applied to the *form* of our government or language intended to bring the *form* of our government into contempt and disrepute, and language of like character and intended to produce like results directed against the President and Congress, the agencies through which that form of government must function in time of war. *But it is not necessary to a decision of this case to consider whether such distinction is vital or merely formal, for the language of these circulars was obviously intended to provoke and to encourage resistance to the United States in the war.* . . . (Emphasis added.)

Justice Holmes, joined by Justice Brandeis, wrote a vigorous dissent to counter Clarke's approach:

I never have seen any reason to doubt that the questions of law that alone were before this Court in the cases of *Schenck, Frohwerk* and *Debs* were rightly decided. I do not doubt for a moment that by the same reasoning that would justify punishing persuasion to murder, the United States constitutionally may punish speech that produces or is intended to produce a clear and imminent danger that it will bring about forthwith certain substantive evils that the United States constitutionally may seek to prevent. The power undoubtedly is greater in time of war than in time of peace because war opens dangers that do not exist at other times.

But as against dangers peculiar to war, as against others, the principle of the right to free speech is always the same. It is only the present danger of immediate evil or an intent to bring it about that warrants Congress in setting a limit to the expression of opinion where private rights are not concerned. Congress certainly cannot forbid all effort to change the mind of the country. Now nobody can suppose that the surreptitious publishing of a silly leaflet by an unknown man, without more, would present any immediate danger that its opinions would hinder the success of the government arms or have any appreciable tendency to do so. . . .

Persecution for the expression of opinions seems to me perfectly logical. If you have no doubt of your premises or your power and want a certain result with all your heart you naturally express your wishes in law and sweep away all opposition. To allow opposition by speech seems to indicate that you think the speech impotent, as when a man says that he has squared the circle, or that you do not care whole-heartedly for the result, or that you doubt either your power or your premises. But when men have realized that time has upset many fighting faiths, they may come to believe even more than they believe the very foundations of their own conduct that the ultimate good desired is better reached by free trade in ideas—that the best test of truth is the power of the thought to get itself accepted in the competition of the market, and that truth is the only ground upon which their wishes safely can be carried out. That at any rate is the theory of our Constitution. It is an experiment, as all life is an experiment. Every year if not every day we have to wager our salvation upon some prophecy based upon imperfect knowledge. While that experiment is part of our system I think that we should be eternally vigilant against attempts to check the expression of opinions that we loathe and believe to be fraught with death, unless they so imminently threaten immediate interference with the lawful and pressing purposes of the law that an immediate check is required to save the country. I wholly disagree with the argument of the Government that the First Amendment left the common law as to seditious libel in force. History seems to me against the notion. I had conceived that the United States through many years had shown its repentance for the Sedition Act of 1798, by repaying fines that it imposed. Only the emergency that makes it immediately dangerous to leave the correction of evil counsels to time warrants making any exception to the sweeping command, "Congress shall make no law . . . abridging the freedom of speech." Of course I am speaking only of expressions of opinion and exhortations, which were all that were uttered here, but I regret that I cannot put into more impressive words my belief that in their conviction upon this indictment the defendants were deprived of their rights under the Constitution of the United States.

That the *Abrams* decision marked a turning away from the Clear and Present Danger standard was evident to Holmes. In his dissent he tried to refine the test to show how the *Schenck* rationale could work in a variety of contexts. Many view this dissent as one of Holmes's finest, earning him the sobriquet "the Great Dissenter." *(See Box 13-1.)*

BOX 13-1 OLIVER WENDELL HOLMES, JR. (1902–1932)

OLIVER WENDELL HOLMES, JR., was born March 8, 1841, in Boston. He was named after his father, a professor of anatomy at Harvard Medical School as well as a poet, essayist, and novelist in the New England literary circle that included Longfellow, Emerson, Lowell, and Whittier. Dr. Holmes's wife, Amelia Lee Jackson Holmes, was the third daughter of Justice Charles Jackson of the Supreme Judicial Court of Massachusetts. Young Holmes attended a private Latin school in Cambridge and received his undergraduate education at Harvard, graduating as class poet in 1861 as had his father thirty-two years before him.

Commissioned a second lieutenant in the Massachusetts Twentieth Volunteers, known as the Harvard Regiment, Holmes was wounded three times in battle. Serving three years, he was mustered out a captain in recognition of his bravery and gallant service. After the Civil War, Holmes returned to Harvard to study law despite his father's conviction that "a lawyer can't be a great man."

He was admitted to the Massachusetts bar in 1867 and practiced in Boston for fifteen years, beginning with the firm of Chandler, Shattuck, and Thayer and later forming his own partnership with Shattuck. In 1872 Holmes married Fanny Bowdich Dixwell, the daughter of his former schoolmaster and a friend since childhood. They were married fifty-seven years.

During his legal career Holmes taught constitutional law at his alma mater, edited the *American Law Review,* and lectured on common law at the Lowell Institute. His twelve lectures were compiled in a book called *The Common Law* and published shortly before his fortieth birthday. The London *Spectator* heralded Holmes's treatise as the most original work of legal speculation in decades. *The Common Law* was translated into German, Italian, and French.

IN 1882 THE GOVERNOR of Massachusetts appointed Holmes—then a full professor at the Harvard Law School in a chair established by Boston lawyer Louis D. Brandeis—an associate justice of the Massachusetts Supreme Court. Holmes served on the state court for twenty years, the last three as chief justice, and wrote more than 1,000 opinions, many of them involving labor disputes. Holmes's progressive labor views, criticized by railroad and corporate interests, were considered favorably by President Theodore Roosevelt during his search in 1902 for someone to fill the "Massachusetts seat" on the U.S. Supreme Court, vacated by Bostonian Horace Gray. Convinced of Holmes's compatibility with the administration's national policies, Roosevelt nominated him associate justice December 2 and he was confirmed without objection two days later.

Holmes's twenty-nine years of service on the Supreme Court spanned the tenures of Chief Justices Fuller, White, Taft, and Hughes and the administrations of Presidents Roosevelt, Taft, Wilson, Harding, Coolidge, and Hoover.

For twenty-five years he never missed a session and daily walked the two and a half miles from his home to the Court. Like Justice Brandeis, Holmes voluntarily paid an income tax despite the majority's ruling that exempted federal judges. Unlike the idealistic and often moralistic Brandeis, with whom he is frequently compared, Holmes was pragmatic, approaching each case on its own set of facts without a preconceived notion of the proper result.

Although a lifelong Republican, on the Court Holmes did not fulfill Roosevelt's expectations as a loyal party man. His dissent shortly after his appointment from the Court's decision to break up the railroad trust of the Northern Securities Company surprised the nation and angered the president.

At the suggestion of Chief Justice Hughes and his colleagues on the bench, Holmes retired on January 12, 1932, at the age of ninety. A widower since 1929, he continued to spend his winters in Washington, D.C., and his summers in Beverly Farms, Massachusetts. He died at his Washington home March 6, 1935, two days before his ninety-fourth birthday.

SOURCE: Adapted from Elder Witt, *Guide to the U.S. Supreme Court,* 2d ed. (Washington, D.C.: Congressional Quarterly, 1990), 845–846.

Holmes had failed to convince his colleagues in *Abrams.* Instead, Clarke's majority opinion used a standard known as the Bad Tendency Test, an approach derived from English common law. It asks, "Do the words have a *tendency* to bring about something evil?" rather than, "Do the words bring about an immediate substantive evil?" Why the majority shifted constitutional standards is a mystery. We cannot say that the Clear and Present Danger test produced results markedly different from the Bad Tendency standard. Holmes had not used it in *Schenck, Debs,* or *Frohwerk* to overturn convictions. Some scholars assert that the main drawback of the Holmes standard was its simplicity: it did not solve with certainty the confusing and complicated problems of the day.[6]

Regardless of their motivation, by the early 1920s it was obvious that a majority of justices rejected the Clear and Present Danger standard in favor of more stringent constitutional interpretations, such as the Bad Tendency test. Two cases, *Gitlow v. New York* (1925) and *Whitney v. California* (1927), exemplify this shift but with a slightly different twist. *Gitlow* and *Whitney* involved state prosecutions, not Espionage Act violations. Just as the federal government wanted to foster patriotism during wartime, the states also felt the need to promulgate their own versions of nationalism. The result was the so-called state criminal syndicalism laws, which made it a crime to advocate, teach, aid, or abet in any activity designed to bring about the overthrow of the government by force or violence. The actual effect of such laws was to outlaw any association with views "abhorrent" to the interests of the United States, such as communism and socialism. Would the Court be willing to tolerate such state intrusions into free speech? That was the question with which the justices grappled in *Gitlow* and *Whitney.*

In *Gitlow,* the answer reached by the Court was

somewhat mixed. On the one hand, the Court upheld the conviction of Benjamin Gitlow, a socialist charged with violating New York's criminal anarchy law for his distribution of a pamphlet that called for mass action to overthrow the capitalist system in the United States. The majority held that Gitlow's rights had not been violated, that the state had the authority to punish expression that might lead to the violent overthrow of the government. In dissent, Holmes continued to press his Clear and Present Danger standard, arguing that Gitlow's actions posed no obvious and immediate danger. Whatever danger Gitlow's message might pose, it was too inconsequential and too remote to justify the government's repression of a citizen's right to free expression.

The majority in *Gitlow* made an enduring contribution to constitutional law with its statement that for "present purposes we may and do assume that freedom of speech and of the press—which are protected by the First Amendment from abridgment by Congress—are among the fundamental personal rights and 'liberties' protected by the due process clause of the Fourteenth Amendment from impairment by the States." This sweeping incorporation vastly expanded constitutional guarantees for freedom of expression by ensuring that the states had to abide by guarantees contained in the First Amendment.

The Court's decision in *Whitney v. California* was clearer. This case involved Charlotte Whitney, a well-known California heiress and a niece of former Supreme Court justice Stephen J. Field. She was a member of the Oakland branch of the Socialist party and apparently an active member because she voted for delegates sent by the chapter to a national party meeting held in 1919 in Chicago.[7] At that convention the party ejected its more radical members, including Oakland locals, who in turn formed the Communist party of the United States. Local party chapters from

---

6. Malcolm M. Feeley and Samuel Krislov, *Constitutional Law* (Boston: Little, Brown, 1985), 424.

7. For more on this 1927 case, see Thomas I. Emerson, *The System of Freedom of Expression* (New York: Vintage Books, 1970), 105–107.

California then held a state meeting in Oakland, where they created the Communist Labor party of California.

Although Whitney had opposed the radical platform "urging a revolutionary class struggle" offered at the national convention, she nevertheless served as one of her chapter's delegates to the local meeting and, in fact, became chair of the credentials committee. Based on her association with this group and its predecessor, California authorities charged Whitney with violating the state's syndicalism law. She was found guilty of organizing and associating with a party dedicated to overthrowing the U.S. government.

On appeal to the Supreme Court, her attorneys from the newly formed American Civil Liberties Union *(see Box 13-2)* argued that the California act violated the Free Speech Clause of the First Amendment. But the justices upheld her conviction. They treated her claim just as they had Gitlow's, relying on the Bad Tendency test. The majority asserted in *Whitney:*

> That the freedom of speech which is secured by the Constitution does not confer an absolute right to speak . . . whatever one may choose . . . and that a State in the exercise of its police power may punish those who abuse this freedom by utterances inimical to the public welfare, tending to incite crime, disturb the public peace, or endanger the foundations of organized government and threaten its overthrow by unlawful means, is not open to question.

It has been noted that in *Gitlow* and *Whitney* the justices seem to be operating under "the assumption that the First Amendment . . . was designed to promote the public good," rather than to provide affirmative protection for individual speech.[8]

Brandeis and Holmes filed a concurrence in *Whitney.* Clearly, they favored a return to the Clear and Present Danger standard, but with this modification: that the evil take the form of behavior. Justice Brandeis wrote, "No danger flowing from speech can be deemed clear and present, unless the incidence of evil apprehended is so imminent that it may befall before there is opportunity for full discussions." What is even more curious (and a matter of some scholarly interest) is why the duo concurred rather than dissented. It seems clear that Whitney's behavior did not meet the standard they articulated, making the question all the more intriguing. One reasonable hypothesis is that Brandeis wanted to demonstrate that the Clear and Present Danger test was not necessarily a vehicle created to overturn convictions, but merely a more equitable way to adjudge First Amendment claims.

Regardless of the philosophical debates triggered by the series of cases from *Schenck* to *Whitney,* one fact remains clear: the justices seemed swept away by the wave of nationalism and patriotism in the aftermath of World War I. With but one exception, they acceded to the wishes of Congress and the states, which centered around the complementary goals of promoting nationalism and suppressing radicalism.[9]

The 1930s and 1940s: A Return to Clear and Present Danger?

The United States learned many lessons from World War I; among the most important was to appreciate the resilience of its system of government. As Sheldon Goldman notes, "America became intensely self-conscious of its civil liberties heritage in contrast to its totalitarian enemies."[10] This awareness, plus "distance in time from actual combat brought calmer voices to the debate on seditious speech."[11] In other words, as the war died down, so did the national fervor that had swept the nation over the preceding two decades.

As a microcosm of society, the Supreme Court also

---

8. Ralph A. Rossum and G. Alan Tarr, *American Constitutional Law,* 3d ed. (New York: St. Martin's Press, 1991), 346.

9. The one exception was *Fiske v. Kansas* (1927), decided on the same day as *Whitney.* The Court for the first time overturned a conviction under a state syndicalism law, the justices concluding that there was insufficient evidence to sustain Fiske's conviction.

10. *Constitutional Law and Supreme Court Decision Making* (New York: Harper and Row, 1982), 345.

11. Elder Witt, *The Supreme Court and Individual Rights,* 2d ed. (Washington, D.C.: Congressional Quarterly, 1988), 30.

BOX 13-2 THE AMERICAN CIVIL LIBERTIES UNION

BY ALMOST ALL MEASURES, the American Civil Liberties Union (ACLU) is the largest and most complex organization dedicated to public interest litigation in the United States. Beyond its national organization, the ACLU maintains fifty state and local affiliates and, via its foundation, runs several specialized projects.

Given its current form, the humble origins of the ACLU may come as quite a surprise: the ACLU "was ... very much a phenomenon of the Progressive-Populist era with its concern over government abuse." Indeed, the ACLU's roots lie in a small organization called the Henry Street Group, which was started by several leaders of the Progressive Movement to combat growing militarism. One year later, this group united with another to become the American Union Against Militarism (AUAM).

Between 1915 and 1917 the AUAM tried to lobby against any legislation designed to stimulate the U.S. "war machine." But in 1917, when Germany announced "its intention to resume unrestricted warfare," the AUAM turned its attention to the draft. The organization sought to defend those who had conscientious objections to serving in the military. This goal was handled primarily by an agency within the AUAM, the Bureau of Conscientious Objectors (BCO).

Under the leadership of the young charismatic Roger Baldwin, the BCO eventually dominated the AUAM. Baldwin's BCO doubled the size of AUAM's membership and spent more than 50 percent of its funds. Clearly, Baldwin was an effective leader, but the old-line Progressive leaders of the AUAM disliked Baldwin's strategy of providing direct assistance to conscientious objectors and threatened to resign. To save the AUAM and to show solidarity with its "greater" agenda, Baldwin changed the name of the BCO to the Civil Liberties Bureau (CLB). This last-ditch effort failed, however, and in 1917 the new National CLB split from its parent organization, which expired shortly thereafter.

Between 1917 and 1919, the NCLB continued to defend conscientious objectors. Unfortunately, it could not prevent Baldwin's imprisonment for draft violations in 1918. Ironically, during Baldwin's jail term the seed for what is now known as the American Civil Liberties Union was planted. In prison, Baldwin became acquainted with the activities of a radical labor union, the Industrial Workers of the World, an organization that made no secret of its use of violence and sabotage to achieve its policy needs.

This name alteration and reorganization forever changed the NCLB. After 1920 the newly formed ACLU would never be a single-purpose organization; by 1925 it was involved with labor, pacifists, and the "Red Scare" caused by the Palmer raids.

Defending the right of free speech eventually became the ACLU's major trademark as the organization moved into the 1930s, 1940s, and 1950s. But while cultivating such expertise, ACLU leaders realized they had to "nationalize" the growing group. Such steps included fuller recognition of the growing chain of ACLU affiliates throughout the United States and provision of more information to its membership, which increased by almost 5,000 annually.

Fortunately for the organization, its efforts to build and regroup during the 1950s were quite timely: the 1960s turned out to be critical years for the union. Not only was the decade significant in the development of law governing civil rights and liberties, but the ACLU itself seemed to embody the goals of the nation. The union's stance against the Vietnam War, President Richard Nixon, and racism, and its defense of draft dodgers and student protesters proved to be highly popular. Between 1966 and 1973, the ACLU's membership skyrocketed from 77,200 to 222,000, and its litigation activities exploded.

To deal with its increasing caseload and to focus its energies on specific areas of the law, the ACLU established the ACLU Foundation in 1967. This foundation, in turn, established special national projects, including the National Prison, Women's Rights, and Reproductive Freedom projects. Today, the union has about 250,000 members and affiliates in every state. The organization currently operates on a $12 million budget.

The ACLU has used these financial and personnel resources to build an increasingly vast and active organization. The union and its affiliates employ 225 persons and 5 to 10 student interns per year. Staff attorneys account for 38 of its 125 national employees, and 35 of the 100 affiliated workers. At the state and local levels, ACLU organizations use volunteer attorneys for 65 percent of their legal work.

SOURCE: Adapted from Karen O'Connor and Lee Epstein, *Public Interest Law Groups* (Westport, Conn.: Greenwood Press, 1989).

began to reevaluate its decisions from *Schenck* to *Whitney*. And, beginning in 1931 in *Stromberg v. California*, calmer voices began to prevail. Yetta Stromberg, a nineteen-year-old member of the Young Communist League, served as a counselor at a summer camp for children ages ten to fifteen. Stromberg regularly introduced her campers to various aspects of Marxist theory, including class consciousness and the solidarity of workers. In addition, she would raise a red banner and lead the children in reciting a workers' pledge of allegiance. State authorities prosecuted Stromberg under a California statute making it a felony to raise publicly a red flag or banner as a symbol of opposition to organized government or in support of anarchy. She was convicted over her attorneys' arguments that the California law violated the First Amendment.

Writing for a seven-justice majority, Chief Justice Charles Evans Hughes reversed the conviction. The Court found the California statute to be excessively broad because its wording applied not only to persons advocating the violent overthrow of the government but also to those engaged in orderly and peaceful opposition. Such vagueness and ambiguity do not comport with the demands of the First Amendment.

Stromberg is important because of the Court's ruling, not its reasoning. It sent a message to attorneys that the justices would be willing to listen to First Amendment claims more sympathetically now than they had during the years following World War I. But in *Stromberg* Hughes did not formulate a free speech standard. Such a standard did not appear until nearly six years later in *DeJonge v. Oregon* (1937). As a member of the Communist party in Portland, Oregon, Dirk DeJonge distributed handbills throughout the city, calling for a meeting of all members and other interested parties. The purpose of the gathering was to protest police raids of members' houses. DeJonge held the meeting on July 27, 1934, and between 160 and 200 people attended, only a small percentage of whom belonged to the party. Although the members tried to sell copies of the party's newspaper, the *Daily Worker*, the agenda of the meeting was quite general, with all proceeding in an orderly fashion until the police raided it. They arrested DeJonge for violating Oregon's criminal syndicalism law, which prohibited the organization of the Communist party. Faced with the *Whitney* precedent, DeJonge's ACLU attorney tried to argue that his client neither created a public danger nor advocated any subversive views. State attorneys relied on an earlier Court view: "the right of free speech . . . is not an absolute one."

For a unanimous Court, Hughes wrote:

The right of peaceable assembly is a right cognate to those of free speech and free press and is equally fundamental. . . . [It] follows [that] peaceable assembly for lawful discussion cannot be made a crime. . . . The question . . . is not as to the auspices under which the meeting is held but as to its purpose; not as to the relations of the speakers, but whether their utterances transcend the bounds of the freedom of speech which the Constitution [safeguards]. . . . The state [law] as applied to the particular charge as defined by the state court is repugnant to the [Constitution].

Sound familiar? Hughes's language echoes Holmes's opinion in *Schenck*, for in *DeJonge* the majority tried to revitalize the presumably long-dead doctrine of Clear and Present Danger. Hughes overturned the convictions because the defendant did not engage in "forcible subversion." As he noted, "Legislative intervention can find constitutional justification only by dealing with the abuse."

Surely such reasoning turns the Court's decision in *Whitney* on its head. But even more dramatic was a seemingly insignificant bit of writing—a footnote contained in Justice Harlan F. Stone's opinion in *United States v. Carolene Products* (1938). This case dealt with a federal ban on the shipment of a certain kind of milk—an economic, not a First Amendment, issue. Stone wrote in footnote 4:

There may be narrower scope for operation of the presumption of constitutionality when legislation appears on its face to be within a specific prohibition of the Constitution, such as those of the first ten Amendments, which are deemed equally specific when held to be embraced by the Fourteenth Amendment. . . .

It is unnecessary to consider now whether legislation which restricts those political processes which can ordinarily be expected to bring about repeal of undesirable legislation, is to be subjected to more exacting judicial scrutiny under the general prohibitions of the Fourteenth Amendment than are most other types of legislation. . . .

Nor need we enquire whether similar considerations enter into the review of statutes directed at particular religious, or national, or racial minorities; whether prejudice against discrete and insular minorities may be a special condition, which tends seriously to curtail the operation of those political processes ordinarily to be relied upon to protect minorities, and which may call for a correspondingly more searching judicial inquiry.

What appeared to be an obscure footnote in a relatively insignificant case took on tremendous importance for civil liberties claims, especially those based on First Amendment expression rights. As Alpheus Mason and Grier Stephenson explain, each of the footnote's three paragraphs contained powerful ideas regarding the status of constitutional rights.[12] The first paragraph holds that whenever a government regulation appears on its face to be in conflict with the Bill of Rights the usual presumption that laws are constitutional should be reduced or waived altogether. The second paragraph hints that the judiciary has a special responsibility to defend rights that are essential to the effective functioning of the political process, a class of liberties that clearly includes freedom of expression rights. And finally, the third paragraph suggests a special role for the Court in protecting the rights of minorities and unpopular groups. The standard expressed in footnote 4 has become known as the Preferred Freedoms doctrine. This doctrine has special significance for First Amendment claims, for it means that the judiciary will proceed with a special scrutiny when faced with laws that restrict freedom of

expression, especially as those laws may relate to the articulation of unpopular political views. Put another way, "Laws restricting fundamental rights . . . would be regarded as suspect and potentially dangerous to the functioning of democracy."[13]

The importance of Justice Stone's footnote goes beyond its obvious declaration of a new standard for evaluating First Amendment claims. In *Carolene Products* Stone announces a modification in the fundamental role of the Court. He declares that the Court will assume a special responsibility for protecting civil rights and civil liberties and be particularly vigilant in guarding the rights of minorities and the politically unpopular. Stone's statement marked a major change in course for an institution that had, for its entire history, been tilted toward settling private economic disputes and wrestling with questions of governmental power. From this point forward the civil liberties docket began to grow, and the Court rapidly began to evolve into an institution with a primary focus on civil liberties issues.[14]

But would the majority of the justices adopt Stone's Preferred Freedoms approach to First Amendment claims? Moreover, how would such an approach square with the Clear and Present Danger standard, to which most of the justices seemed to want to return? Attorneys, states, and civil libertarians had to wait only a year until the Court addressed these questions in *Schneider v. Irvington* (1939). This case involved not a radical leader of the Communist party, but a member of the Jehovah's Witnesses. In accordance with her religious tenets, Schneider distributed literature from house to house, leaving residents her card. Town authorities arrested her because she had failed to obtain a solicitation permit, an action Schneider claimed violated her religion, but which the city required in the interest of keeping the streets

12. Alpheus Thomas Mason and Donald Grier Stephenson, Jr., *American Constitutional Law,* 10th ed. (Englewood Cliffs, N.J.: Prentice Hall, 1993), 279.

13. Stanley I. Kutler, ed., *The Supreme Court and the Constitution* (New York: W. W. Norton, 1984), 429.

14. Richard L. Pacelle, *The Transformation of the Supreme Court's Agenda: From the New Deal to the Reagan Administration* (Boulder, Colo.: Westview Press, 1991).

uncluttered. Although this case, and three others decided with it, involved elements of religion, the Court was more interested in Schneider's claim that the permit ordinance violated her free speech guarantees. In an 8–1 decision, it struck down the municipal regulation as an unconstitutional burden on free speech. Justice Roberts stated:

We are of the opinion that the purpose to keep the streets clean [is] insufficient to justify an ordinance which prohibits a person rightfully on a public street from handing literature to one willing to receive it. Any burden imposed upon the city authorities in cleaning . . . the streets . . . results from the constitutional protection of the freedom of speech.

Six years later in *Thomas v. Collins* (1945) the Court moved even closer to embracing the Preferred Freedoms approach. The case arose when R. J. Thomas, president of the United Automobile, Aircraft and Agricultural Workers (UAW) and vice president of the Congress of Industrial Organizations (CIO), arrived in Houston, Texas, to deliver a speech to a group of workers a regional CIO affiliate wanted to organize. Six hours before Thomas was to speak, Texas authorities served him with a restraining order, prohibiting him from making his scheduled address. Believing that the order constituted a violation of his free speech guarantees, Thomas delivered his speech anyway to an audience of 300 people. The meeting was described as "peaceful and orderly," but authorities arrested Thomas. He was sentenced to three days in jail and a $100 fine. On appeal to the U.S. Supreme Court, Thomas's claim of a free speech infringement received reinforcement from several civil liberties organizations including the National Federation for Constitutional Liberties, which argued, "The activities of labor organizations involve the exercise of peaceful assembly, freedom of speech and freedom of the press."

In a 6–3 opinion, the Supreme Court agreed, ruling against the state. Most significant, the Court used a Preferred Freedoms approach to reach that conclu-

sion. Justice Rutledge, writing for the majority, asserted:

[This] case confronts us again with the duty our system places on this Court to say where the individual's freedom ends and the State's power begins. Choice of that border, now as always delicate, is perhaps more so where the usual presumptive supporting legislation is balanced *by the preferred place given in our scheme to the great, the indispensable democratic freedoms secured by the First Amendment.* . . . For [this] reason any attempt to restrict those liberties must be justified by clear public interest, threatened not . . . remotely, but by a *clear and present danger.* (Emphasis added.)

Constitutional experts claim that this decision represented another major breakthrough in the area of freedom of speech, but why? First, it reinforces the majority view in *Schneider* that Preferred Freedoms provides an appropriate solution to First Amendment problems. Second, Rutledge's language—"Any attempt to restrict the liberties of speech and assembly must be justified . . . by a clear and present danger"— indicates that the Court, instead of abandoning Holmes's standard, had combined the Clear and Present Danger standard with the Preferred Freedoms framework. The Preferred Freedoms "concept was never a repudiation of the notion of clear and present danger, but was seen as giving its purposes a firmer base and texture—incorporating it much as Einsteinian physics incorporates Newtonian."[15]

The Aftermath of World War II: Cold War Politics and the Court

As *Thomas* indicates, by the mid-1940s it seemed as if the Court had finally settled on an approach to solve First Amendment problems. Stone's Preferred Freedoms doctrine had gained acceptance among the justices, even though it served as a vehicle by which to overturn many laws restricting speech. Compare it with the Bad Tendency test of the *Gitlow* era, a test under which many restrictions on free speech could pass

15. Feeley and Krislov, *Constitutional Law*, 427.

muster. In short, the Court had altered its position dramatically over three decades.

Like the Bad Tendency test, however, the Preferred Freedoms doctrine was short-lived. By the early 1950s, in fact, the Court had turned to a modified version of the conservative Bad Tendency test—the Clear and Probable Danger standard. Between 1950 and 1956 the application of this stricter standard led the Court to uphold the vast majority of free speech convictions. What caused this sudden change in direction? Three factors may explain it.

First, several changes in Court personnel occurred between 1945 and 1952. Chief Justice Frederick M. Vinson replaced Stone, the author of footnote 4, and two relatively conservative justices, Tom C. Clark and Sherman Minton, took the place of two liberals, Francis W. Murphy and Wiley Rutledge. As we have seen, such changes can have a substantial impact on Court outcomes.

Second, by 1949 it became evident that some of the justices were not satisfied with the Preferred Freedoms framework. Keep in mind that several dissented in *Thomas,* but at the time they offered no alternative standard. This situation changed dramatically in 1949 in the case of *Kovacs v. Cooper,* which involved a challenge to a local ordinance prohibiting the use of sound and amplifying devices on city streets. Writing for the majority, Justice Stanley F. Reed argued that the law withstood the Preferred Freedoms test and was, therefore, constitutional. In a long concurring opinion Justice Frankfurter agreed with the outcome in *Kovacs* but disagreed with Reed's reasoning. Calling Preferred Freedoms a "mischievous phrase," Frankfurter articulated a new standard by which to review First Amendment claims:

So long as a legislature does not prescribe what ideas may be . . . expressed and what may not be, nor discriminate among those who would make inroads upon the public peace, it is not for us to supervise the limits the legislature may impose.

Often called the Ad Hoc Balancing test, it urges the justices to balance, on a case-by-case basis, the individual free speech claim versus the government's reason for regulating the behavior. But, in Frankfurter's judgment, these competing claims were not of equal merit; the latter should be taken more seriously, as legislators had already determined that the law in question met a compelling governmental interest.

A third reason for the Court's dramatic turnaround in the 1950s was the alteration in its external environment. After World War II, the United States entered into a cold war with the Soviet Union. This period was characterized by an intense fear of communism, not unlike the time of the World War I. Some politicians, led by Sen. Joseph McCarthy, R-Wis. (1947–1957), fed the fear by alleging that Communist party sympathizers had infiltrated the upper echelon of government. Others asserted that the Communist party of the United States was growing in strength and numbers and spreading its message through motion pictures and plays. *(For more information on this period, see Chapter 4, pages 128–131).*

The fear of communism manifested itself in a number of ways. Most important was congressional enactment of several pieces of legislation designed to suppress communist and other forms of subversive activity in the United States. For example, a section of the Labor-Management Relations Act of 1947 required union leaders to file affidavits proclaiming nonaffiliation with the Communist party before they could attain the National Labor Relations Board's recognition of their unions. Congress passed this law in recognition of Marxist-Leninist theory, which assumes that it will be the "workers" who lead the "revolution." In *American Communication Association v. Douds* (1950) union leaders mounted a First Amendment challenge to the law. Because this was one of the earliest of the cold war cases, many eagerly awaited the Court's decision: Would the justices, now under the leadership of Chief Justice Vinson, use the Preferred Freedoms approach, or would they adopt Frankfurter's Ad Hoc Balancing test?

Apparently not immune to the pressures of the day, the Court adopted the latter. Writing for the Court, Vinson rejected the heart of the Preferred Freedoms approach, the Clear and Present Danger standard, noting, "It is the considerations that gave birth to the phrase clear and present danger, not the phrase itself, that are vital in our decisions of questions involving . . . the First Amendment." In his view, the Ad Hoc Balancing approach fully encapsulated that genesis: because Congress has determined that communism constitutes harmful conduct carried on by people, then it may regulate subversive activity in the public interest.

Vinson's standard is akin to the Bad Tendency test of the 1920s. Both operate under the assumption that the First Amendment protects the public good, as defined by legislatures, rather than individual expression. In fact, just one year after *Douds*, in *Dennis v. United States*, the Court adopted the Clear and Probable Danger test. At issue in *Dennis* was the Smith Act. Enacted in 1940, this statute prohibited anyone from knowingly or willfully advocating or teaching the overthrow of any government of the United States by force; from organizing any society to teach, advocate, or encourage the overthrow of the United States by force; or from becoming a member of any such society. By covering so many kinds of activities, the law provided authorities with a significant weapon to stop the spread of communism in the United States.

While reading *Dennis*, keep in mind the environment in which the justices operated. Remember that tremendous political pressures influenced the Court just as they did many other sectors of American life. If *Dennis* came before the Court today, would the justices reach the same conclusion?

Dennis v. United States

341 U.S. 494 (1951)
Vote: 6 (Burton, Frankfurter, Jackson, Minton, Reed, Vinson)
　　　2 (Black, Douglas)
Judgment of the Court: Vinson
Concurring opinions: Frankfurter, Jackson
Dissenting opinions: Black, Douglas
Not participating: Clark

On July 20, 1948, twelve leaders of the national board of the Communist party were indicted for conspiring to teach and advocate the overthrow of the government by force and violence, and to organize the Communist party for that purpose.[16] Such actions were in violation of the Smith Act. The trial was a protracted affair, lasting nine months and generating 16,000 pages of evidence. A great deal of the testimony on both sides involved Marxist-Leninist theory and the inner workings of the Communist party. The prosecutor's case read like a spy novel, full of international conspiracies, secret passwords and code books, aliases, and plots to overthrow the U.S. government. The defense was a bit more philosophical as it attempted to demonstrate that the leaders of this particular branch of the party wanted "to work for the improvement of conditions under capitalism and not for chaos and depression."

Not sympathetic to this line of reasoning, the trial court sentenced each defendant to five years in prison and a $10,000 fine. Dennis and the others appealed to the U.S. Supreme Court, requesting it to overturn their convictions and strike down the Smith Act as an unconstitutional infringement on free speech. They said, "The statute and the convictions which are here for review cannot be validated without at the same

---

16. The initial suit involved twelve defendants. The case against William Z. Foster, head of the party, however, was separated from the others when he became ill.

time destroying the constitutional foundations of American democracy."

MR. CHIEF JUSTICE VINSON announced the judgment of the Court.

The obvious purpose of the statute is to protect existing Government, not from change by peaceable, lawful and constitutional means, but from change by violence, revolution and terrorism. That it is within the *power* of the Congress to protect the Government of the United States from armed rebellion is a proposition which requires little discussion. Whatever theoretical merit there may be to the argument that there is a "right" to rebellion against dictatorial governments is without force where the existing structure of the government provides for peaceful and orderly change. We reject any principle of governmental helplessness in the face of preparation for revolution, which principle, carried to its logical conclusion, must lead to anarchy. No one could conceive that it is not within the power of Congress to prohibit acts intended to overthrow the Government by force and violence. The question with which we are concerned here is not whether Congress has such *power,* but whether the *means* which it has employed conflict with the First and Fifth Amendments to the Constitution. . . .

The very language of the Smith Act negates the interpretation which petitioners would have us impose on that Act. It is directed at advocacy, not discussion. Thus, the trial judge properly charged the jury that they could not convict if they found that petitioners did "no more than pursue peaceful studies and discussions or teaching and advocacy in the realm of ideas." He further charged that it was not unlawful "to conduct in an American college and university a course explaining the philosophical theories set forth in the books which have been placed in evidence." Such a charge is in strict accord with the statutory language, and illustrates the meaning to be placed on those words. Congress did not intend to eradicate the free discussion of political theories, to destroy the traditional rights of Americans to discuss and evaluate ideas without fear of governmental sanction. Rather Congress was concerned with the very kind of activity in which the evidence showed these petitioners engaged.

But although the statute is not directed at the hypothetical cases which petitioners have conjured, its application in this case has resulted in convictions for the teaching and advocacy of the overthrow of the Government by force and violence, which, even though coupled with the intent to accomplish that overthrow, contains an element of speech. For this reason, we must pay special heed to the demands of the First Amendment marking out the boundaries of speech.

We pointed out in Douds that the basis of the First Amendment is the hypothesis that speech can rebut speech, propaganda will answer propaganda, free debate of ideas will result in the wisest governmental policies. It is for this reason that this Court has recognized the inherent value of free discourse. An analysis of the leading cases in this Court which have involved direct limitations on speech, however, will demonstrate that both the majority of the Court and the dissenters in particular cases have recognized that this is not an unlimited, unqualified right, but that the societal value of speech must, on occasion, be subordinated to other values and considerations. . . .

Although no case subsequent to . . . Gitlow has expressly overruled the majority . . . there is little doubt that subsequent opinions have inclined toward the Holmes-Brandeis rationale. . . . But . . . neither Justice Holmes nor Justice Brandeis ever envisioned that a shorthand phrase should be crystalized into a rigid rule to be applied inflexibly without regard to the circumstances of each case. Speech is not an absolute, above and beyond control by the legislature when its judgment, subject to review here, is that certain kinds of speech are so undesirable as to warrant criminal sanction. Nothing is more certain in modern society than the principle that there are no absolutes, that a name, a phrase, a standard has meaning only when associated with the considerations which gave birth to the nomenclature. To those who would paralyze our Government in the face of impending threat by encasing it in a semantic straitjacket we must reply that all concepts are relative.

In this case we are squarely presented with the application of the "clear and present danger" test, and must decide what that phrase imports. We first note that many of the cases in which this Court has reversed convictions by use of this or similar tests have been based on the fact that the interest which the State was attempting to protect was itself too insubstantial to warrant restriction of speech. Overthrow of the Government by force and violence is certainly a substantial enough interest for the Government to limit speech. Indeed, this is the ultimate value of any society, for if a society cannot protect its very structure from armed internal attack, it must follow that no subordinate value can be protected. If, then, this interest may be protected, the literal problem which is presented is what has been meant by the use of the phrase "clear and present danger" of the utterances bringing about the evil within the power of Congress to punish.

Obviously, the words cannot mean that before the Government may act, it must wait until the *putsch* is about to be executed, the plans have been laid and the signal is awaited. If Government is aware that a group aiming at its overthrow is attempting to indoctrinate its members and to commit them to a course whereby they will strike when the leaders feel the circumstances permit, action by the Government is required. The argument that there is no need for Government to concern itself, for Government is strong, it possesses ample powers to put down a rebellion, it may defeat the revolution with ease needs no answer. For that is not the question. Certainly an attempt to overthrow the Government by force, even though doomed from the outset because of inadequate numbers or power of the revolutionists, is a sufficient evil for Congress to prevent. The damage which such attempts create both physically and politically to a nation makes it impossible to measure the validity in terms of the probability of success, or the immediacy of a successful attempt. In the instant case the trial judge charged the jury that they could not convict unless they found that petitioners intended to overthrow the Government "as speedily as circumstances would permit." This does not mean, and could not properly mean, that they would not strike until there was certainty of success. What was meant was that the revolutionists would strike when they thought the time was ripe. We must therefore reject the contention that success or probability of success is the criterion.

The situation with which Justices Holmes and Brandeis were concerned in Gitlow was a comparatively isolated event, bearing little relation in their minds to any substantial threat to the safety of the community. They were not confronted with any situation comparable to the instant one—the development of an apparatus designed and dedicated to the overthrow of the Government, in the context of world crisis after crisis.

Chief Judge Learned Hand, writing for the majority below, interpreted the phrase as follows: "In each case [courts] must ask whether the gravity of the 'evil,' discounted by its improbability, justifies such invasion of free speech as is necessary to avoid the danger." We adopt this statement of the rule. As articulated by Chief Judge Hand, it is as succinct and inclusive as any other we might devise at this time. It takes into consideration those factors which we deem relevant, and relates their significances. More we cannot expect from words. . . .

We hold that the Smith Act, do[es] not inherently, or as construed or applied in the instant case, violate the First Amendment and other provisions of the Bill of Rights. . . . Petitioners intended to overthrow the Government of the United States as speedily as the circumstances would permit. Their conspiracy to organize the Communist Party and to teach and advocate the overthrow of the Government of the United States by force and violence created a "clear and present danger" of an attempt to overthrow the Government by force and violence. They were properly and constitutionally convicted for violation of the Smith Act. The judgments of conviction are affirmed.

Affirmed.

MR. JUSTICE BLACK, dissenting.

[M]y basic disagreement with the Court is not as to how we should explain or reconcile what was said in prior decisions but springs from a fundamental difference in constitutional approach. Consequently, it would serve no useful purpose to state my position at length.

At the outset I want to emphasize what the crime involved in this case is, and what it is not. These petitioners were not charged with an attempt to overthrow the Government. They were not charged with overt acts of any kind designed to overthrow the Government. They were not even charged with saying anything or writing anything designed to overthrow the Government. The charge was that they agreed to assemble and to talk and publish certain ideas at a later date: The indictment is that they conspired to organize the Communist Party and to use speech or newspapers and other publications in the future to teach and advocate the forcible overthrow of the Government.

No matter how it is worded, this is a virulent form of prior censorship of speech and press, which I believe the First Amendment forbids. I would hold § 3 of the Smith Act authorizing this prior restraint unconstitutional on its face and as applied.

But let us assume, contrary to all constitutional ideas of fair criminal procedure, that petitioners although not indicted for the crime of actual advocacy, may be punished for it. Even on this radical assumption, the other opinions in this case show that the only way to affirm these convictions is to repudiate directly or indirectly the established "clear and present danger" rule. This the Court does in a way which greatly restricts the protections afforded by the First Amendment. The opinions for affirmance indicate that the chief reason for jettisoning the rule is the expressed fear that advocacy of Communist doctrine endangers the safety of the Republic. Undoubtedly, a governmental policy of unfettered communication of ideas does entail dangers. To the Founders of this Nation, however, the benefits derived from free expression were worth the risk. They embodied this philosophy in the First Amendment's command that "Congress shall make no law . . . abridging the freedom of speech, or of the press. . . ." I have always believed that the First Amendment is the keystone of our Government, that the freedoms it guarantees provide the best insurance against destruction of all freedom. At least as to speech in the realm of public matters, I believe that the "clear and present danger" test does not "mark the furthermost constitutional boundaries of protected expression" but does "no more than recognize a minimum compulsion of the Bill of Rights."

So long as this Court exercises the power of judicial review of legislation, I cannot agree that the First Amendment permits us to sustain laws suppressing freedom of speech and press on the basis of Congress' or our own notions of mere "reasonableness." Such a doctrine waters down the First Amendment so that it amounts to little more than an admonition to Congress. The Amendment as so construed is not likely to protect any but those "safe" or orthodox views which rarely need its protection. . . .

Public opinion being what it now is, few will protest the conviction of these Communist petitioners. There is hope, however, that in calmer times, when present pressures, passions and fears subside, this or some later Court will restore the First Amendment liberties to the high preferred place where they belong in a free society.

MR. JUSTICE DOUGLAS, dissenting.

Free speech has occupied an exalted position because of the high service it has given our society. Its protection is essential to the very existence of a democracy. The airing of ideas releases pressures which otherwise might become destructive. When ideas compete in the market for acceptance, full and free discussion exposes the false and they gain few adherents. Full and free discussion even of ideas we hate encourages the testing of our own prejudices and preconceptions. Full and free discussion keeps a society from becoming stagnant and unprepared for the stresses and strains that work to tear all civilizations apart.

Full and free discussion has indeed been the first article of our faith. We have founded our political system on it. It has been the safeguard of every religious, political, philosophical, economic, and racial group amongst us. We have counted on it to keep us from embracing what is cheap and false; we have trusted the common sense of our people to choose the doctrine true to our genius and to reject the rest. This has been the one single outstanding tenet that has made our institutions the symbol of freedom and equality. We have deemed it more costly to liberty to suppress a despised minority than to let them vent their spleen. We have above all else feared the political censor. We have wanted a land where our people can be exposed to all the diverse creeds and cultures of the world.

There comes a time when even speech loses its constitutional immunity. Speech innocuous one year may at another time fan such destructive flames that it must be halted in the interests of the safety of the Republic. That is the meaning of the clear and present danger test. When conditions are so critical that there will be no time to avoid the evil that the speech threatens, it is time to call a halt. Otherwise, free speech which is the strength of the Nation will be the cause of its destruction.

Yet free speech is the rule, not the exception. The restraint to be constitutional must be based on more than fear, on more than passionate opposition against the speech, on more than a revolted dislike for its contents. There must be some immediate injury to society that is likely if speech is allowed. . . .

Free speech—the glory of our system of government—should not be sacrificed on anything less than plain and objective proof of danger that the evil advocated is imminent. On this record no one can say that petitioners and their converts are in such a strategic position as to have even the slightest chance of achieving their aims.

The First Amendment provides that "Congress shall make no law ... abridging the freedom of speech." The Constitution provides no exception. This does not mean, however, that the Nation need hold its hand until it is in such weakened condition that there is no time to protect itself from incitement to revolution. Seditious conduct can always be punished. But the command of the First Amendment is so clear that we should not allow Congress to call a halt to free speech except in the extreme case of peril from the speech itself. The First Amendment makes confidence in the common sense of our people and in their maturity of judgment the great postulate of our democracy. Its philosophy is that violence is rarely, if ever, stopped by denying civil liberties to those advocating resort to force. The First Amendment reflects the philosophy of Jefferson "that it is time enough for the rightful purposes of civil government, for its officers to interfere when principles break out into overt acts against peace and good order." The political censor has no place in our public debates. Unless and until extreme and necessitous circumstances are shown our aim should be to keep speech unfettered and to allow the processes of law to be invoked only when the provocateurs among us move from speech to action.

Vishinsky wrote in 1938 in The Law of the Soviet State, "In our state, naturally, there is and can be no place for freedom of speech, press, and so on for the foes of socialism."

Our concern should be that we accept no such standard for the United States. Our faith should be that our people will never give support to these advocates of revolution, so long as we remain loyal to the purposes for which our Nation was founded.

Scholars consider Dennis a significant case for several reasons. First, a plurality of the Court accepted Vinson's Clear and Probable Danger test: "In each case courts must ask whether the gravity of the 'evil,' discounted by its improbability, justifies such invasion of free speech as is necessary to avoid the danger."[17] But is this a reasonable interpretation of the test emanating from Schenck; that is, would Holmes have agreed with this language? Or does it more closely resemble the Bad Tendency standard, with which Holmes disagreed? The second reason is what the dissenters, Justices Black and Douglas, had to say. This pair of civil libertarians remained in relative isolation during the early 1950s, but the Warren Court of the late 1950s and 1960s adopted many of their views. Based on their dissents in Dennis, which direction would Black and Douglas like to see the Court take? A third reason Dennis is significant is precedent: between 1951 and 1956 the justices used Vinson's Clear and Probable Danger standard to uphold a number of loyalty programs.[18] Moreover, Dennis served as a benchmark in other areas of the law in which the federal government asked the Court for sweeping powers to investigate the Communist party, other subversive groups, and their alleged adherents.

In sum, once again we see the Supreme Court responding to perceived threats to national security. As was the case during the 1920s, when the justices moved from a Clear and Present Danger test to a Bad Tendency standard, in the 1950s they moved from a Preferred Freedoms approach to a revisionist interpretation of the Holmes standard, Clear and Probable Danger, which itself "marked a return to the 'bad tendency' views of the post–World War I period."[19]

Free Speech During the Warren Court Era

In 1956 and 1957 the Supreme Court heard back-to-back cases involving Communist party prosecutions. In the first, Pennsylvania v. Nelson, the justices considered a state law similar to the Smith Act. As was true

---

17. Vinson adopted this language from Learned Hand's decision from the lower court.

18. See, for example, Adler v. Board of Education (1952) in which the Court upheld a New York law (the so-called Feinberg Act) disqualifying from teaching positions persons affiliated with subversive groups.

19. Kutler, The Supreme Court and the Constitution, 429.

during the World War I years, in the cold war period many states passed or revitalized laws that forbade the organization of subversive groups or parties and the advocacy or teaching of anarchy. Under Pennsylvania's version, the Sedition Act, authorities prosecuted Steve Nelson, a Communist party member, and a trial court sentenced him to twenty years in prison and a $10,000 fine.

On appeal to the U.S. Supreme Court, Nelson argued that the justices should uphold the decision of the Pennsylvania Supreme Court, which ruled that the federal law superseded the state's. Several states, however, filed amicus curiae briefs in support of the Pennsylvania statute. New Hampshire, for example, argued, "Neither expressly nor by implication has federal law attempted to take from the states the power to enact anti-subversive legislation." Massachusetts agreed, noting, "The state is acting to protect itself." Perhaps even more significant was an argument contained in the solicitor general's amicus curiae brief: "The Smith Act does not preclude enforcement of state sedition statutes." Writing for the Court, however, Chief Justice Earl Warren rejected state and federal government arguments. Rather, he asserted that federal legislation, such as the Smith Act, indicated the intent of Congress to retain sole control over subversive activity.

The following year, the Court decided another case, *Yates v. United States,* which closely resembled *Dennis.* In 1951 federal authorities alleged that fourteen second-tier leaders of the Communist party, including Oleta O'Connor Yates, engaged in subversive activities forbidden by the Smith Act. Specifically, they were party members, they organized party units in California, they helped publish the *Daily Worker,* and they conducted courses to recruit and indoctrinate potential members. At their trial, the judge explained the Smith Act to the jurors, but he did not tell them that it prohibited only the advocacy of unlawful activity, not abstract doctrines. Based on this information, the jury found the defendants guilty, and the

court sentenced them to five years in prison and a $10,000 fine. On appeal, Yates's attorneys seized on this discrepancy in the judge's charge. They stated, "Lawful activities and associations not shown to be unlawful cannot by addition or multiplication be cemented into illegality." The government argued that *Dennis* should control the Court's decision.

A majority rejected the government's position. Justice Harlan wrote:

The legislative history of the Smith Act and related bills shows beyond all question that Congress was aware of the distinction between advocacy or teaching of abstract doctrine and the advocacy or teaching of action, and that it did not intend to disregard it. The statute was aimed at the advocacy and teaching of concrete action for the forcible overthrow of the Government, and not of principles divorced from action.

The government's reliance on this Court's decision is misplaced. It is true that at one point in the . . . opinion it is stated that the Smith Act "is directed at advocacy, not discussion," but it is clear that the reference was to *advocacy of action, not ideas.* (Emphasis added.)

With the decision in *Yates,* despite some protestation to the contrary, the Court altered its position: by distinguishing between the advocacy of abstract doctrines (protected) and the advocacy of unlawful action (unprotected), the Court substantially modified the *Dennis* standard. And although *Yates* did not advocate the Preferred Freedoms or absolutist approach favored by Black, it certainly liberalized free speech doctrine, making prosecutions under the Smith Act far more difficult.

Why did the Court alter its view? Some scholars point to changes in Court personnel, as shown in Table 13-1. Dramatic alterations occurred between *Dennis* and *Yates:* the more liberal Earl Warren replaced Fred Vinson as chief justice; John Marshall Harlan, grandson and namesake of another "great dissenter," stepped in for Robert H. Jackson; and President Eisenhower appointed William J. Brennan, Jr., to Sherman Minton's vacant seat.

Perhaps of equal significance was the rapidly declining fear among the American public of communist infiltration. Clearly, the year 1957 was far from the end of the cold war. In fact, certain members of Congress, still under an anticommunist influence, were less than overwhelmed by the Court's rulings and introduced a bill to overturn *Nelson*, which failed to gain approval in the Senate. By the same token, *Yates* was neither the last of the Court's cases on subversive activities nor the end of Court approval of such legislation. Four years later, in *Scales v. United States* (1961), the Court upheld the membership clause of the Smith Act. That same year, it also sustained a clause of the Subversive Activities Control Act of 1950, mandating that all Communist party-affiliated organizations register with the attorney general. Nonetheless, by 1957 the hysteria had substantially subsided. One indication was the rapid decline of Senator McCarthy's influence. As his accusations grew "ever more wild . . . and arrogant," focusing on all sorts of government officials, including senators and President Eisenhower, his "conduct became too destructive for all but his closest associates to tolerate."[20] In 1954 the Senate censured him by a 67–22 vote; the man who symbolized the communist witch hunt had lost his power. He died May 2, 1957, the year the *Yates* decision was handed down.

Once the Red Scare was over, the Supreme Court began taking positions defending freedom of expression and association against the repressive legislation passed during the McCarthy era. It handed down a series of decisions upholding the constitutional rights of communists and other so-called subversives. For example, in *Communist Party v. United States* (1963) and *Albertson v. Subversive Activities Control Board* (1965) the justices repudiated federal laws requiring communist organizations to register with the government. In *Elfbrandt v. Russell* (1966) and *Whitehill v. Elkins* (1967)

20. Arthur M. Schlesinger, Jr., *The Almanac of American History* (New York: Putnam, 1983), 541.

TABLE 13-1 Personnel Changes: *Dennis* to *Yates*

Dennis Court (1951)	Yates Court (1957)
Vinson, chief justice ⟶	Warren, chief justice
Black[a]	Black[b]
Reed ⟶	Whittaker
Frankfurter	Frankfurter
Douglas[a]	Douglas[b]
Jackson ⟶	Harlan
Burton	Burton
Clark	Clark[a]
Minton ⟶	Brennan

a. Dissented from majority opinion.
b. Partial dissent from majority opinion.

loyalty oath requirements directed at subversives were found constitutionally defective. The Court also struck down laws and enforcement actions barring communists from holding office in labor unions (*United States v. Brown*, 1965), prohibiting communists from working in defense plants (*United States v. Robel*, 1967), and stripping passports from Communist party leaders (*Aptheker v. Secretary of State*, 1964). Clearly, these decisions and others handed down during more tranquil years would have been unheard of during the times of anticommunist hysteria.

By the end of the 1960s, then, the Court had turned away from many of its cold war rulings. It struck down as being in violation of the freedom to speak, publish, or associate much of the federal and state anticommunist legislation still on the books. An important representative of this era was *Brandenburg v. Ohio* (1969), one of the Warren Court's last major rulings. Ironically, the *Brandenburg* decision had nothing to do with the Communist party or other groups dedicated to violent overthrow of the U.S. government. Instead, the dispute involved a group with a much different purpose, the racist Ku Klux Klan.

Clarence Brandenburg, the leader of an Ohio affiliate of the KKK, sought to obtain publicity for the group's goals by inviting a Cincinnati reporter and camera crew to attend a rally. Subsequently, local and national television stations aired some of the events that occurred at this gathering; one film "showed 12 hooded figures, some of whom carried firearms. They were gathered around a large wooden cross, which they burned." In another, Brandenburg delivered a speech to the group in which he said, "Personally I believe the nigger should be returned to Africa, the Jew returned to Israel."[21] Based on these films, Ohio authorities arrested Brandenburg for violating the Ohio Criminal Syndicalism law, which was passed in 1919 to prevent the spread of unpatriotic views. Similar to many other state laws of the sort upheld in *Gitlow*, the Ohio act prohibited the advocacy and assembly of individuals to teach criminal syndicalism.

In a per curiam opinion, the Court claimed that "the constitutional guarantees of free speech and free press do not permit a State to forbid or proscribe advocacy of the use of force or of law violation except where such advocacy is directed to inciting or producing imminent lawless action and is likely to incite or produce such action." And that "measured by this test" the Ohio law could not be sustained, for it punishes "mere advocacy."

In so ruling, the justices closed the door on the long series of repressive expression rulings. Indeed, as if to underscore the point, they overruled *Whitney* in *Brandenburg*.

Vietnam, the Civil Rights Movement, and Beyond

As the nation's fear of communist infiltration ebbed, a new international crisis was brewing in Vietnam. Although U.S. involvement in that conflict dated back to the Truman administration, it grew significantly in 1964 when President Johnson announced that the North Vietnamese had attacked American ships in the Gulf of Tonkin. Johnson launched a massive military buildup: by 1968, 541,000 U.S. troops had been sent to Vietnam.[22] Initially, many Americans approved of Johnson's pursuit of the war, but by the late 1960s, approval had turned to criticism. A peace movement, centered on college campuses, arose throughout the country. What is more, another cause was gathering strength. The civil rights movement, which in the 1950s was isolated in the South, by the 1960s had taken hold in all major urban centers. Because of these two social currents, and the resistance to them, the decade was marked by domestic upheaval and turmoil. Although Congress did not respond with any legislation like the Smith Act, these protest movements generated many free expression cases. Some involved the constitutionality of mass demonstrations, "the chief weapon of the civil rights and peace movements."[23] Others involved the issues of political expression associated with that decade—flag desecrations, draft card burnings, and so forth.

The freedom of expression cases flowing from the Vietnam War protests and civil rights movement presented the Court with a host of novel constitutional claims. The character of the Court was also undergoing change. In 1969 Warren Burger, a conservative Nixon appointee, replaced the retiring Earl Warren as chief justice. Burger would soon be followed by three additional Nixon appointees—William H. Rehquist, Harry A. Blackmun, and Lewis F. Powell, Jr. With these appointments the Court began to take on a more conservative posture. This trend continued without interruption for the next twenty-three years as Republican presidents Ford, Reagan, and Bush filled vacancies with an eye to moving the Court to the right.

As the Court confronted new disputes over expression rights, the justices had at their disposal a half century of doctrinal development. The internal security cases beginning with *Schenck* and continuing into

---

21. *Brandenburg v. Ohio (1969).*

22. Schlesinger, *The Almanac of American History*, 508.
23. Kutler, *The Supreme Court and the Constitution*, 455.

TABLE 13-2 Summary of Legal Standards Governing Free Speech

Standard	Major Proponents	Court Usage: Example
Clear and Present Danger test "Whether the words are used in such circumstances and are of such a nature as to create a clear and present danger that they will bring about substantive evils that Congress has a right to prevent."	Holmes, Brandeis	*Schenck v. United States*, 1919
Bad Tendency test Do the words have a tendency to bring about something evil?	Clarke, Sanford	*Abrams v. United States*, 1919
Preferred Freedoms "There may be a narrower scope for operation of the presumption of constitutionality when legislation appears on its face to be within a specific prohibition of the Constitution, such as those of the first ten Amendments."	Douglas, Stone, Rutledge	*United States v. Carolene Products*, 1938; *Thomas v. Collins*, 1945.
Absolutism "The First Amendment, its prohibition in terms absolute, was designed to preclude courts as well as legislatures from weighing values of speech against silence."	Black, Douglas	Never adopted. See Black's dissent in *Dennis v. United States*, 1951; Douglas's dissent in *Roth v. United States*, 1957.
Ad Hoc Balancing "So long as a legislature does not prescribe what ideas may be … expressed and what may not be, nor discriminate among those who would make inroads upon the public peace, it is not for us to supervise the limits the legislature may impose."	Frankfurter	Frankfurter's concurrence in *Kovacs v. Cooper*, 1949
Clear and Probable Danger "Whether the gravity of the 'evil,' discounted by its improbability, justifies such an invasion of free speech as is necessary to avoid danger."	Vinson	*Dennis v. United States*, 1951

the 1960s had given birth to six major tests of how the First Amendment should be interpreted and applied *(see Table 13-2)*. In the years that followed, the justices created no significant additions to this list of competing approaches to First Amendment interpretation, but continued to debate their relative merits as applied to various expressive forms and contexts. Just as the justices before them, modern members of the Court have had to struggle with the perennial conflict between the need for an ordered society and the desire for individual liberty.

REGULATING EXPRESSION: CONTENT AND CONTEXTS

Justice Holmes noted in *Schenck* that the legitimacy of expression often depends upon the nature of the words and the conditions under which they are uttered. The major tests of the First Amendment, developed in the national security cases, provide broad guidelines for determining the boundaries of constitutional protection. Yet even if the justices could agree on a controlling philosophy of what the First Amendment means, they would still have to wrestle with the task of applying that doctrine to specific cases. In the remaining portion of this chapter, we present some of the recurring expression issues that the justices have confronted and the rules of law they developed as a response.

Guiding Principles

Before we turn our attention to specific types of expression, we set forth some of the principles the Court has deemed relevant in deciding freedom of expression issues. Keep in mind that these principles are flexible and may be applied in slightly different ways depending upon the nature of the expression and the forum in which it occurs.

When the Framers drafted the First Amendment they had specific purposes in mind. The goal was to create a society in which expression would thrive and the government could not use its power to repress individuals' expression by speech, publication, or in association with others of similar mind. The Supreme Court has accepted the duty to interpret the First Amendment with these purposes in mind: over the years the justices have referred to the goal of creating a free marketplace of ideas and a society in which a robust exchange of views occurs without government censorship.

While the vibrant exchange of thoughts and opinions might be the goal, the justices have never concluded that the First Amendment absolutely protects all forms of speech. Instead, the Court's decisions have acknowledged that freedom of expression has certain limitations. These limitations are in response to the need for an ordered society that functions well. In general, the Court has recognized that freedom of expression must be balanced against the need to safeguard the rights of others and the right of the government to carry out its legitimate functions in a reasonable fashion.

Although the First Amendment does not make distinctions, the Framers approached freedom of expression with a definite hierarchy in mind. Of primary concern was the need to protect political and social speech. Other forms of expression, such as those primarily for entertainment or commercial gain, ranked lower in the hierarchy. Still others, like libel and obscenity, were viewed as illegitimate and occupied a position outside the scope of First Amendment protections. As we shall see in this section and the next chapter, the Court has often approached freedom of expression disputes with this hierarchy in mind. It is especially vigilant in protecting political and social communication, but allows greater deference to government in regulating other forms.

Under what conditions, then, may the government regulate expression? In general, government may encroach on speech rights if the expression itself or its consequences involve matters of legitimate government concern. Holmes may have defined it best when he referred to "substantive evils that Congress has a right to prevent." The Court has applied this admittedly vague standard by designating certain conditions that justify government's authority to intervene. Although not exhaustive, the following list includes the major categories of conditions that may trigger valid government regulation of expression.

Violence. The government has authority to protect citizens from personal injury. If expression takes a violent form or incites others to violence the government may regulate it.

Property Damage. The government has the right to protect private and public property from being destroyed or damaged. Antiwar protesters, for example, who express themselves by setting fire to a National Guard armory have gone beyond their First Amendment protections and can be arrested for their conduct.

Criminal Speech. Some forms of expression are crimes by their very nature. For example, the Constitution does not protect those who might give military secrets to the enemy or engage in conspiracies to violate valid criminal laws.

Encroaching on the Rights of Others. Freedom of expression does not provide a license to infringe on the rights of others. If animal rights protesters block an entrance to a zoo or prolife groups prevent access to an abortion clinic, the government may intervene. In both cases, the protesters have curtailed the right of the public to move about without interference.

Burdens on Government Functions. Regulation is permissible if expression places a burden on a legitimate government function. If, for example, environmentalists opposed to the construction of a Corps of Engineers dam lie down in front of bulldozers, the government may arrest them.

Trespass. The freedom of expression does not include the right to speak anywhere one wishes. A campaign worker, for example, does not have the right to come into another person's home without permission to promote the candidate's cause. Similarly, some public facilities are not legitimate places for groups of demonstrators to congregate. It would be legitimate, for example, to prohibit antiwar protesters from demonstrating inside a defense facility.

Forms of Expression Considered Outside the Scope of the First Amendment. As indicated above, certain classes of expression from the very beginning have been considered unprotected by the Constitution. Chief among these are obscenity and libel. As we shall see in Chapter 14, if expression meets the Court's rather strict definitions of libel or obscenity, the First Amendment imposes no barrier to government regulation.

These various conditions of legitimate government concern have given rise to the Court's "time, place, and manner" doctrine. By this standard the Court acknowledges that government has the general authority to impose reasonable time, place, and manner restrictions on the freedom of expression. Therefore, the Court would certainly uphold the arrest of demonstrators who gathered in the middle of an expressway or of political zealots who promoted their candidate by driving a sound truck through a residential area at 2:00 A.M.

Although the Court has been sympathetic to the government's need to regulate expression under certain carefully defined conditions, the justices also have been careful to place restraints on the government to insure against abuse. The Court has constructed certain generally accepted criteria to hold the government's power within acceptable bounds. We list here some of the more frequently invoked of those standards.

Legitimate Purpose. Any government restriction on freedom of expression must have a clearly defined, legitimate government purpose. A law that makes inciting to riot a crime, for example, would rest on the legitimate government purpose of curtailing violence. A law prohibiting criticism of the president, motivated by an interest in keeping incumbents in power, would clearly fail this test.

Narrow Construction/Overbreadth. Any regulation of expression must be narrowly tailored to meet the government's objectives. If a legislature, concerned with protests that cause violence, passed a law prohibiting all public demonstrations, the statute would fail the narrow construction requirement. This regulatory scheme would be overbroad, going far beyond what is necessary to deal with the legislature's legitimate concern.

Vagueness. Legislatures must draft laws restricting freedom of expression with sufficient precision to give fair notice of what is being regulated. If normally intelligent people have to guess what a statute means and come to different conclusions about what is prohibited by it, the statute is unconstitutionally vague.

Chilling Effect. A law intended to regulate certain forms of illegitimate expression cannot be written in a way that makes people fearful of engaging in legitimate activity. Often such a "chilling effect" stems from statutes that are vague or overbroad. Assume that a state legislature, concerned about sexual activities that occur in certain nightclubs, passes a statute making it illegal to serve alcoholic beverages in any establishment that also offers nude entertainment. In response to that law, museum officials may be fearful of sponsoring a gathering at which patrons would sip wine while viewing an exhibit of paintings that include some nude figures. Here a statute designed to curb obscenity creates a chilling effect on the exercise of legitimate activities.

Prior Restraint. Government may prosecute individuals who violate legitimate restrictions on expression, but, absent extraordinary circumstances, may not intervene before the fact. For example, the government may not constitutionally require a speaker to submit for review a copy of the speech before its delivery in order to make sure that nothing in it may incite the audience to riot.

Content Discrimination. Laws regulating expression should be content neutral. A local ordinance, for example, enforced in a manner that allowed a Democratic group to conduct a public rally but prohibited a Republican group to engage in the same activity would violate this principle.

As you read the cases and commentary in the remaining portion of this chapter and the next, keep these principles in mind. You will observe many examples of cases in which the justices debated whether the expression in question merited regulation and whether the methods of regulation were proper. You will witness the flexibility of these standards as the Court adjusted them to different contexts. Finally, you will see how individual justices differed in the way they applied these standards based upon their own ideologies and preferences.

Symbolic Speech

The First Amendment specifically protects the freedoms of speech and press, two forms of expression with which the Framers were thoroughly familiar. In the days of the Revolution, political protest customarily took the form of eloquent addresses, sharp-

ly worded editorials, and fiery publications. Verbal expression and published communication were the methods of political debate, and the Framers unambiguously sought to protect them from government encroachment by drafting and ratifying the First Amendment.

But what if someone wishes to communicate a message by means other than word of mouth or printed copy? If a point is made by action rather than by verbal expression, does the First Amendment still grant immunity from government regulation? These questions deal with symbolic speech and whether expressive conduct qualifies as speech under the meaning of the First Amendment.

Most of the symbolic speech cases have occurred in the modern period, but the debate over expressive conduct began much earlier. Recall the discussion of *Stromberg v. California.* In that 1931 case, a camp counselor was convicted not because of anything she said but because of an expressive act that was in conflict with California law. In reversing her conviction on First Amendment grounds, the Supreme Court acknowledged that at least some forms of symbolic speech merit constitutional protection.

In the years that followed, the Court had to decide whether the same principles applied to various forms of picketing in labor disputes. Some states sought to hinder the development and success of labor unions by passing laws prohibiting workers from carrying placards and walking picket lines to protest allegedly unfair labor practices. The most significant case of this era was *Thornhill v. Alabama* (1940), in which Byron Thornhill had been arrested for violating an Alabama law that made picketing a crime. Supporters of the antipicketing statutes argued that picketing was conduct and not speech, but the Supreme Court reversed the conviction on First Amendment grounds. For the Court, Justice Frank Murphy concluded, "In the circumstances of our times the dissemination of information concerning the facts of a labor dispute

On March 31, 1966, David O'Brien and three other anti-war protestors demonstrated their opposition to U.S. military action in Vietnam by burning their draft cards on the steps of the South Boston courthouse. Their convictions for violating the Selective Service Act were affirmed in *United States v. O'Brien*.

must be regarded as within that area of free discussion that is guaranteed by the Constitution."

Decisions such as these established the principle that symbolic actions can qualify as speech and be accorded First Amendment protection. This principle does not mean, however, that the First Amendment shields from government regulation *any* act committed to express an idea or opinion. No one, for example, would seriously claim that assassination is a protected form of expressing political opposition. Perhaps even more than verbal expression, symbolic speech presents especially difficult questions of drawing constitutional boundaries.

The turbulence of the late 1960s brought a number of difficult symbolic expression issues before the Court. The civil rights movement and the Vietnam War protests expanded the ways of communicating political messages. Traditional forms of speech and press gave way to demonstrations, sit-ins, flag desecration, and other varieties of conduct designed to

present the protesters' political messages in a graphic manner. The first of such cases was *United States v. O'Brien* (1968), which crystallized on March 31, 1966, when David O'Brien and three others burned their draft cards on the steps of a South Boston courthouse. A sizable crowd gathered and began attacking O'Brien and his colleagues. FBI agents took the four into the courthouse to protect them and to question them. The agents told O'Brien that he had violated a 1965 amendment to the Selective Service Act, making it illegal to "destroy or mutilate" draft cards. O'Brien replied that he understood, but had burned his card anyway because he was "a pacifist and as such [could not] kill."

After a federal court ruled that O'Brien had acted within the bounds of the Constitution, the United States asked the Supreme Court to hear the case. Solicitor General Thurgood Marshall argued that O'Brien's actions thwarted a valid business of government—to draft men into the armed forces—because his purpose was "to influence others to adopt his anti-war beliefs."[24] The solicitor general also tried to negate the chief argument made by O'Brien's ACLU attorney that his action constituted symbolic speech of the kind upheld by the Court in *Stromberg*. To this, the government argued, "Terming [O'Brien's] conduct 'symbolic speech' does not transform it into activity entitled to the same kind of constitutional protection given to words and other modes of expression."

Writing for the Court, Chief Justice Warren explicitly rejected the notion that conduct used to express an idea automatically merits First Amendment protection. Rather, he wrote that whenever "speech" and "nonspeech" elements are combined, a sufficiently important government interest in regulating the nonspeech element can justify limitations on First Amendment rights. As applied in this case, the Court found that O'Brien's conduct (burning the draft card) placed a burden on a legitimate government activity (the power to raise and support armies). The government had a substantial interest in exercising its military authority, and the draft registration system was a reasonable means of achieving that end. Consequently, the government had the constitutional power to prosecute individuals who violated the Selective Service laws even if the acts in question communicated a message of political protest.

One year later the Court heard another symbolic speech case stemming from protests against the Vietnam War, *Tinker v. Des Moines* (1969). This appeal came out of Des Moines, Iowa, where, in December 1965, a group of adults and secondary school students devised two strategies to demonstrate their opposition to the Vietnam War: they would fast on December 16 and New Year's Day, and they would wear black armbands every day in between. Principals of the students' schools learned of the plan and agreed to suspend any students who wore armbands. Despite the

warning, the parents of five children, among them John and Mary Beth Tinker, allowed them to wear black armbands to school. All five were suspended. Representing the students, ACLU attorneys argued that the armbands constituted legitimate symbolic speech that the principals could not suppress.

Here, the Court ruled in favor of the Tinkers' expression claim, declaring that students and teachers do not "shed their constitutional rights to freedom of speech or expression at the schoolhouse gate." Important to the Court was that the protest was peaceful: there was no violence, no property damage, and no significant disruption of the school day. On this count, *Tinker* differed from *O'Brien*, in which the justices found that the burning of Selective Service documents placed a burden on a legitimate government function. In dissent, Justice Black took issue with the majority, arguing that the freedom of speech does not extend equally to every place and circumstance. School administrators, he said, should be allowed to impose reasonable regulations to ensure conditions conducive to learning.

Although *Tinker* and *O'Brien* are important cases in the development of symbolic expression doctrine, they did not seem to give the Court much trouble. Only one justice dissented in *O'Brien* and two in *Tinker*. This has not been the case for the flag desecration cases; indeed, among all symbolic expression issues none has caused the Court greater difficulty. As a national symbol, the American flag evokes intense emotional feelings, especially among those, like members of the Supreme Court, who have long histories of public service. Even the justices who were most committed to freedom of expression have indicated their discomfort in extending First Amendment protection to those who destroy the flag as a method of political expression.

The Warren Court first grappled with this issue in *Street v. New York* (1969), a case brought to it by the ACLU. In 1966 the appellant heard on his radio that James Meredith, a civil rights activist, had been shot

24. Solicitor General Marshall filed the petition for certiorari. After Marshall's elevation to the Supreme Court, Erwin Griswold took over the litigation, writing the major brief.

in Mississippi. Street took a flag he kept for display on national holidays, went outside, and burned it. He drew attention to his action by yelling, "If they let that happen to Meredith, we don't need an American flag." The police arrested him for violating a New York law that prohibited physical and verbal desecration of the flag. A Supreme Court majority, using a Preferred Freedoms approach, agreed that the verbal part of the New York law violated free speech guarantees, but the justices divided 4–4 on whether states could prohibit the physical desecration of the flag.

It was not until 1974 that the Court, again divided, returned to this issue in *Spence v. Washington.* Harold Spence was a college student living in Washington State. To protest the deaths of antiwar demonstrators at Kent State University and the U.S. invasion of Cambodia, Spence displayed an American flag with a large peace symbol taped to both sides of it. The police informed Spence that his "desecrated" flag violated a state law, forbidding "the exhibition of a U.S. flag to which is attached or superimposed figures, symbols, or other extraneous material." Spence told the officers that he "didn't know there was anything wrong" with the flag; he fully cooperated with them when they seized it from his apartment.

At his trial, Spence explained why he had altered his flag: "I felt there had been so much killing and that this was not what America stood for. I felt that the flag stood for America and I wanted people to know that I thought America stood for peace." Spence's testimony allowed his ACLU attorneys to frame his case differently from *Street.* Because Washington's law did not punish speech per se, the lawyers put the issue of symbolic expression squarely before the justices, arguing, "The First Amendment's protection encompasses visual symbols as well as spoken words."

In a 6–3 per curiam opinion, the justices agreed with the ACLU. In fact, they adopted the same reasoning we have seen time and time again in symbolic speech cases: as long as the action does not "incite violence or even stimulate a public demonstration," it

is protected by the First Amendment. The justices equated Spence's speech with that of the Tinkers— they were both nonviolent forms of expression. The Court also took notice of the tumultuous times during which this case arose. In a footnote, it compared Spence's activity to others occurring during that decade:

Appellant's activity occurred at a time of national turmoil. . . . It is difficult now, more than four years later, to recall vividly the depth of emotion that pervaded most colleges. . . . A spontaneous outpouring of feeling resulted in widespread action. . . . It was against this highly inflamed background that [Spence] chose to express his views in a manner that can fairly be described as gentle.

As the war in Vietnam abated so did the protest cases; in fact, this flag desecration series was among the last decided by the Burger Court. Now that you have read about some of the more important Warren and Burger Court cases associated with that tumultuous era, consider these questions: How do the Court's decisions of the 1960s and 1970s differ from those of the 1920s, 1930s, and 1950s? Does the thesis that the Court is more willing to suppress free speech during times of international crisis hold true for the Vietnam War era? One way of addressing this is to consider Rehnquist Court treatment of the same crisis-related issue, flag burning. Note that *Texas v. Johnson* was decided in 1989, during a period of domestic tranquility. But also keep in mind the conservative leanings of this Court.

***

Texas v. Johnson

491 U.S. 397 (1989)
Vote: 5 (Blackmun, Brennan, Kennedy, Marshall, Scalia)
    4 (O'Connor, Rehnquist, Stevens, White)
Opinion of the Court: Brennan
Concurring opinion: Kennedy
Dissenting opinions: Rehnquist, Stevens

In the summer of 1984 the Republican party held its national convention in Dallas, Texas, and overwhelmingly supported President Ronald Reagan's reelection bid. While the party was meeting, a group of demonstrators marched through the city to protest the Reagan administration's policies. One of the demonstrators gave an American flag to Gregory Lee Johnson, who also was marching. When the march ended, Johnson "unfurled the flag, doused it with kerosene and set it on fire." As it burned, others chanted, "America, the red, white, and blue, we spit on you." Authorities arrested Johnson, charging him with violating the Texas flag desecration law. He was convicted and sentenced to a one-year prison term and a $2,000 fine.

JUSTICE BRENNAN delivered the opinion of the Court.

Johnson was convicted of flag desecration for burning the flag rather than for uttering insulting words. This fact somewhat complicates our consideration of his conviction under the First Amendment. We must first determine whether Johnson's burning of the flag constituted expressive conduct, permitting him to invoke the First Amendment in challenging his conviction. If his conduct was expressive, we next decide whether the State's regulation is related to the suppression of free expression. If the State's regulation is not related to expression, then the less stringent standard we announced in *United States v. O'Brien* for regulations of noncommunicative conduct controls. If it is, then we are outside of *O'Brien*'s test, and we must ask whether this interest justifies Johnson's conviction under a more demanding standard. A third possibility is that the State's asserted interest is simply not implicated on these facts, and in that event the interest drops out of the picture.

The First Amendment literally forbids the abridgement only of "speech," but we have long recognized that its protection does not end at the spoken or written word. While we have rejected "the view that an apparently limitless variety of conduct can be labeled 'speech' whenever the person engaging in the conduct intends thereby to express an idea," we have acknowledged that conduct may be "sufficiently imbued with elements of communication to fall

Gregory Johnson, who has a record of flag burning, holds the American flag while another protestor sets it alight. In 1989 the Supreme Court ruled that the conviction of Johnson for burning a flag during a demonstration in Dallas violated his First Amendment expression rights.

within the scope of the First and Fourteenth Amendments."

In deciding whether particular conduct possesses sufficient communicative elements to bring the First Amendment into play, we have asked whether "[a]n intent to convey a particularized message was present, and [whether] the likelihood was great that the message would be understood by those who viewed it." Hence, we have recognized the expressive nature of students' wearing of black armbands to protest American military involvement in Vietnam. . . .

Especially pertinent to this case are our decisions recognizing the communicative nature of conduct relating to flags. Attaching a peace sign to the flag, saluting the flag, and displaying a red flag, we have held, all may find shelter under the First Amendment. That we have had little difficulty identifying an expressive element in conduct relating to flags should not be surprising. The very purpose of a national flag is to serve as a symbol of our country; it is, one might say, "the one visible manifestation of two hundred years of nationhood.". . .

We have not automatically concluded, however, that any action taken with respect to our flag is expressive. Instead, in characterizing such action for First Amendment purposes, we have considered the context in which it occurred. . . .

Johnson burned an American flag as part—indeed, as the culmination—of a political demonstration that coincided with the convening of the Republican Party and its renomination of Ronald Reagan for President. In these circumstances, Johnson's burning of the flag was conduct "sufficiently imbued with elements of communication" to implicate the First Amendment.

The Government generally has a freer hand in restricting expressive conduct than it has in restricting the written or spoken word. . . . "A law *directed at* the communicative nature of conduct must, like a law directed at speech itself, be justified by the substantial showing of need that the First Amendment requires." It is, in short, not simply the verbal or nonverbal nature of the expression, but the governmental interest at stake, that helps to determine whether a restriction on that expression is valid.

Thus, although we have recognized that where "'speech' and 'nonspeech' elements are combined in the same course of conduct, a sufficiently important governmental interest in regulating the nonspeech element can justify incidental limitations on First Amendment freedoms," we have limited the applicability of *O'Brien*'s relatively lenient standard to those cases in which "the governmental interest is unrelated to the suppression of free expression." In stating, moreover, that *O'Brien*'s test "in the last analysis is little, if any, different from the standard applied to time, place, or manner restrictions," we have highlighted the requirement that the governmental interest in question be unconnected to expression in order to come under *O'Brien*'s less demanding rule.

In order to decide whether *O'Brien*'s test applies here, therefore, we must decide whether Texas has asserted an interest in support of Johnson's conviction that is unrelated to the suppression of expression. If we find that an interest asserted by the State is simply not implicated on the facts before us, we need not ask whether *O'Brien*'s test applies. The State offers two separate interests to justify this conviction: preventing breaches of the peace, and preserving the flag as a symbol of nationhood and national unity. We hold that the first interest is not implicated on this record and that the second is related to the suppression of expression.

Texas claims that its interest in preventing breaches of the peace justifies Johnson's conviction for flag desecration. However, no disturbance of the peace actually occurred or threatened to occur because of Johnson's burning of the flag. . . .

The State's position, therefore, amounts to a claim that an audience that takes serious offense at particular expression is necessarily likely to disturb the peace and that the expression may be prohibited on this basis. Our precedents do not countenance such a presumption. On the contrary, they recognize that a principal "function of free speech under our system of government is to invite dispute. It may indeed best serve its high purpose when it induces a condition of unrest, creates dissatisfaction with conditions as they are, or even stirs people to anger.". . .

Nor does Johnson's expressive conduct fall within that small class of "fighting words" that are "likely to provoke the average person to retaliation, and thereby cause a breach of the peace." No reasonable onlooker would have regarded Johnson's generalized expression of dissatisfaction with the policies of the Federal Government as a direct personal insult or an invitation to exchange fisticuffs.

We thus conclude that the State's interest in maintaining order is not implicated on these facts. The State need not worry that our holding will disable it from preserving the peace. We do not suggest that the First Amendment forbids a State to prevent "imminent lawless action.". . .

The State also asserts an interest in preserving the flag as a symbol of nationhood and national unity. In *Spence [v. Washington,* 1974], we acknowledged that the Government's interest in preserving the flag's special symbolic value "is directly related to expression in the context of activity" such as affixing a peace symbol to a flag. We are equally persuaded that this interest is related to expression in the case of Johnson's burning of the flag. The State, apparently, is concerned that such conduct will lead people to believe either that the flag does not stand for nationhood and national unity, but instead reflects other, less positive concepts, or that the concepts reflected in the flag do not in fact exist, that is, we do not enjoy unity as a Nation. These concerns blossom only when a person's treatment of the flag communicates some message, and thus are related "to the suppression of free expression" within the meaning of *O'Brien*. We are thus outside of *O'Brien*'s test altogether.

It remains to consider whether the State's interest in preserving the flag as a symbol of nationhood and national unity justifies Johnson's conviction. . . .

Johnson's political expression was restricted because of the content of the message he conveyed. We must therefore subject the State's asserted interest in preserving the special symbolic character of the flag to "the most exacting scrutiny."

Texas argues that its interest in preserving the flag as a symbol of nationhood and national unity survives this close analysis. Quoting extensively from the writings of this Court chronicling the flag's historic and symbolic role in our society, the State emphasizes the "'special place'" reserved for the flag in our Nation. The State's argument is not that it has an interest simply in maintaining the flag as a symbol of *something*, no matter what it symbolizes; indeed, if that were the State's position, it would be difficult to see how that interest is endangered by highly symbolic conduct such as Johnson's. Rather, the State's claim is that it has an interest in preserving the flag as a symbol of *nationhood* and *national unity*, a symbol with a determinate range of meanings. According to Texas, if one physically treats the flag in a way that would tend to cast doubt on either the idea that nationhood and national unity are the flag's referents or that national unity actually exists, the message conveyed thereby is a harmful one and therefore may be prohibited.

If there is a bedrock principle underlying the First Amendment, it is that the Government may not prohibit the expression of an idea simply because society finds the idea itself offensive or disagreeable.

We have not recognized an exception to this principle even where our flag has been involved. In *Street v. New York* we held that a State may not criminally punish a person for uttering words critical of the flag. . . .

In short, nothing in our precedents suggests that a State may foster its own view of the flag by prohibiting expressive conduct relating to it. To bring its argument outside our precedents, Texas attempts to convince us that even if its interest in preserving the flag's symbolic role does not allow it to prohibit words or some expressive conduct critical of the flag, it does permit it to forbid the outright destruction of the flag. The State's argument cannot depend here on the distinction between written or spoken words and nonverbal conduct. That distinction, we have shown, is of no moment where the nonverbal conduct is expressive, as it is here, and where the regulation of that conduct is related to expression, as it is here. . . .

Texas' focus on the precise nature of Johnson's expression, moreover, misses the point of our prior decisions: their enduring lesson, that the Government may not prohibit expression simply because it disagrees with its message, is not dependent on the particular mode in which one chooses to express an idea. If we were to hold that a State may forbid flag-burning wherever it is likely to endanger the flag's symbolic role, but allow it wherever burning a flag promotes that role—as where, for example, a person ceremoniously burns a dirty flag—we would be saying that when it comes to impairing the flag's physical integrity, the flag itself may be used as a symbol—as a substitute for the written or spoken word or a "short cut from mind to mind"—only in one direction. We would be permitting a State to "prescribe what shall be orthodox" by saying that one may burn the flag to convey one's attitude toward it and its referents only if one does not endanger the flag's representation of nationhood and national unity. . . .

There is, moreover, no indication—either in the text of the Constitution or in our cases interpreting it—that a separate juridical category exists for the American flag alone. Indeed, we would not be surprised to learn that the persons who framed our Constitution and wrote the Amendment that we now construe were not known for their reverence for the Union Jack. The First Amendment does not guarantee that other concepts virtually sacred to our Nation as a whole—such as the principle that discrimination on the basis of race is odious and destructive—will go unquestioned in the marketplace of ideas. We decline, therefore, to create for the flag an exception to the joust of principles protected by the First Amendment. . . .

We are fortified in today's conclusion by our conviction that forbidding criminal punishment for conduct such as Johnson's will not endanger the special role played by our flag or the feelings it inspires. To paraphrase Justice Holmes, we submit that nobody can suppose that this one gesture of an unknown man will change our Nation's attitude towards its flag. See *Abrams v. United States* (1919) (Holmes, J., dissenting). Indeed, Texas' argument that the burning of an American flag "'is an act having a high likelihood to cause a breach of the peace,'" and its statute's implicit assumption that physical mistreatment of the flag will lead to "serious offense," tend to confirm that the flag's special role is not in danger; if it were, no one would riot or take offense because a flag had been burned.

We are tempted to say, in fact, that the flag's deservedly cherished place in our community will be strengthened, not weakened, by our holding today. Our decision is a reaffirmation of the principles of freedom and inclusiveness that the flag best reflects, and of the conviction that our toleration of criticism such as Johnson's is a sign and source of our strength. Indeed, one of the proudest images of our flag, the one immortalized in our own national anthem, is of the bombardment it survived at Fort McHenry. It is the Nation's resilience, not its rigidity, that Texas sees reflected in the flag—and it is that resilience that we reassert today.

The way to preserve the flag's special role is not to punish those who feel differently about these matters. It is to persuade them that they are wrong. . . . And, precisely because it is our flag that is involved, one's response to the flag-burner may exploit the uniquely persuasive power of the flag itself. We can imagine no more appropriate response to burning a flag than waving one's own, no better way to counter a flag-burner's message than by saluting the flag that burns, no surer means of preserving the dignity even of the flag that burned than by—as one witness here did—according its remains a respectful burial. We do not consecrate the flag by punishing its desecration, for in doing so we dilute the freedom that this cherished emblem represents.

Johnson was convicted for engaging in expressive conduct. The State's interest in preventing breaches of the peace does not support his conviction because Johnson's conduct did not threaten to disturb the peace. Nor does the State's interest in preserving the flag as a symbol of nationhood and national unity justify his criminal conviction for engaging in political expression. The judgment of the Texas Court of Criminal Appeals is therefore

Affirmed.

CHIEF JUSTICE REHNQUIST, with whom JUSTICE WHITE and JUSTICE O'CONNOR join, dissenting.

In holding this Texas statute unconstitutional, the Court ignores Justice Holmes' familiar aphorism that "a page of history is worth a volume of logic." *New York Trust Co. v. Eisner* (1921). For more than 200 years, the American flag has occupied a unique position as the symbol of our Nation, a uniqueness that justifies a governmental prohibition against flag burning in the way respondent Johnson did here. . . .

The American flag . . . has come to be the visible symbol embodying our Nation. It does not represent the views of any particular political party, and it does not represent any particular political philosophy. The flag is not simply another "idea" or "point of view" competing for recognition in the marketplace of ideas. Millions and millions of Americans regard it with an almost mystical reverence regardless of what sort of social, political, or philosophical beliefs they may have. I cannot agree that the First Amendment invalidates the Act of Congress, and the laws of 48 of the 50 States, which make criminal the public burning of the flag. . . .

. . . [T]he public burning of the American flag by Johnson was no essential part of any exposition of ideas, and at the same time it had a tendency to incite a breach of the peace. Johnson was free to make any verbal denunciation of the flag that he wished; indeed, he was free to burn the flag in private. He could publicly burn other symbols of the Government or effigies of political leaders. He did lead a march through the streets of Dallas, and conducted a rally in front of the Dallas City Hall. He engaged in a "die-in" to protest nuclear weapons. He shouted out various slogans during the march, including: "Reagan, Mondale which will it be? Either one means World War III"; "Ronald Reagan, killer of the hour, Perfect example of U.S. power"; and "red, white and blue, we spit on you, you stand for plunder, you will go under." For none of these acts was he arrested or prosecuted; it was only when he proceeded to burn publicly an American flag stolen from its rightful owner that he violated the Texas statute. . . .

. . . The Texas statute deprived Johnson of only one rather inarticulate symbolic form of protest—a form of protest that was profoundly offensive to many—and left him with a full panoply of other symbols and every conceivable form of verbal expression to express his deep disapproval of national policy. Thus, in no way can it be said that Texas is punishing him because his hearers—or any other group of people—were profoundly opposed to the message that he sought to convey. Such opposition is no proper basis for restricting speech or expression under the First Amendment. It was Johnson's use of this particular symbol, and not the idea that he sought to convey by it or by his many other expressions, for which he was punished. . . .

. . . Uncritical extension of constitutional protection to the burning of the flag risks the frustration of the very purpose for which organized governments are instituted. The Court decides that the American flag is just another symbol, about which not only must opinions pro and con be tolerated, but for which the most minimal public respect may not be enjoined. The government may conscript men into the Armed Forces where they must fight and perhaps die for the flag, but the government may not prohibit the public burning of the banner under which they fight. I would uphold the Texas statute as applied in this case.

The Court's decision in *Johnson* is intriguing for a number of reasons. Note, for example, the rather odd alignments: two of the more conservative members of the Rehnquist Court, Antonin Scalia and Anthony M. Kennedy, voted with the majority; John Paul Stevens, usually found with the liberal wing of the Court, dissented.

Perhaps most important was the tremendous—and to some, surprising—uproar created by the Court's ruling. President George Bush immediately condemned it, and public opinion polls indicated that Americans generally favored a constitutional amendment overturning *Johnson*. But, after some politicking by civil liberties groups, senators, and representatives, Congress did not propose an amendment. Instead, it passed the Flag Protection Act of 1989, which penalized by a one-year jail sentence and a $1,000 fine anyone who "knowingly mutilates, defaces, physically defiles, burns, maintains on the floor or ground, or tramples upon any flag of the United States."

Because the federal act differed from the Texas law at issue in *Johnson*—it banned flag desecration regardless of the motivation of the burner, whereas the Texas law did so only if a jury found the activity to be offensive—some thought it would meet approval in the Supreme Court. Others saw this difference as relatively insignificant, and, as it turned out, they were correct. In *United States v. Eichman* (1990) the Court, using the same reasoning expressed in *Johnson* and by the same vote, struck down this law as a violation of the First Amendment.

Public Forums and the Preservation of Order

So far, many of the cases we have examined involve individuals who—either through verbal or symbolic conduct—have tried to relay a "message": Eugene Debs's speech, Yetta Stromberg's red flag, and David O'Brien's draft-card burning were all forms of self-expression. However, "when those seeking to exercise rights of expression choose public forums, their activities move from the realm of 'pure speech' into an arena that creates new questions of restraint."[25] Why? Shouldn't the Court treat speech occurring in a public forum the same way it deals with other forms of expression?

The answer to this question depends on the effect such speech may have rather than with its content. In short, unlike Stromberg's flag raising, an essentially private form of expression, activities conducted in

25. Jerome R. Corsi and Matthew Ross Lippman, *Constitutional Law* (Englewood Cliffs, N.J.: Prentice Hall, 1985), 298.

open forums can threaten the public order, causing others to engage in illegal behavior.

Preserving public order and protecting citizens from injury caused by violence are among the essential duties of government. The Preamble of the Constitution includes insuring "domestic Tranquility" among the six basic purposes for which the new government was formed. Yet in some instances free expression can threaten order. Such a breakdown of order may take the form of bodily injury, property destruction, restricting the free movement of the public, or impeding the government from carrying out its duties. In such cases a conflict arises between the nation's commitment to freedom of expression and the government's duty to maintain order. At what point is government constitutionally justified in repressing expression in order to stop or prevent violence?

To deal with such expression, the justices have promulgated legal criteria distinct from those they use to adjudicate pure speech cases. The Court began to develop these standards in 1942 with *Chaplinsky v. New Hampshire*, but the majority of public order cases did not come to it until the 1960s and 1970s. As you read Justice Murphy's opinion in *Chaplinsky*, try to ascertain the legal standard he articulates and remember it as we look at the later Court decisions in these areas. Did Murphy's approach continue to permeate Court decisions of the civil rights and Vietnam War movements, or did the Court revise it to fit changing times?

Chaplinsky v. New Hampshire

315 U.S. 568 (1942)

Vote: 9 (Black, Byrnes, Douglas, Frankfurter, Jackson,
      Murphy, Reed, Roberts, Stone)
        0
Opinion of the Court: Murphy

On April 6, 1940, Jehovah's Witness member Walter Chaplinsky was selling biblical pamphlets and literature, including *Watchtower* and *Consolation*, on a public street in New Hampshire. While he was announcing the sale of his pamphlets, a crowd began to gather. After one person tried to attack Chaplinsky, the rest joined in. When the police arrived and handcuffed a very agitated Chaplinsky, he demanded to know why they had arrested him and not the mob. An officer replied, "Shut up, you damn bastard," and Chaplinsky in turn called the officer a "damned fascist and a God damned racketeer." For those words, the state charged him with breaking a law prohibiting the use of "any offensive, derisive, or annoying word to any other person who is lawfully in the street."

On appeal to the Supreme Court, Chaplinsky's attorneys asked the Court to overturn the state statute on free speech grounds, arguing that "the fact that speech is likely to cause violence is no grounds for suppressing it." The state countered that the law constituted a valid exercise of its police powers.

MR. JUSTICE MURPHY delivered the opinion of the Court.

Allowing the broadest scope to the language and purpose of the Fourteenth Amendment, it is well understood that the right of free speech is not absolute at all times and under all circumstances. There are certain well-defined and narrowly limited classes of speech, the prevention and punishment of which have never been thought to raise any Constitutional problem. These include the lewd and obscene, the profane, the libelous, and the insulting or "fighting" words—those which by their very utterance inflict injury or tend to incite an immediate breach of the peace. It has been well observed that such utterances are no essential part of any exposition of ideas, and are of such slight social value as a step to truth that any benefit that may be derived from them is clearly outweighed by the social interest in order and morality. . . .

The state statute here challenged comes to us authoritatively construed by the highest court of New Hampshire. It has two provisions—the first relates to words or names addressed to another in a public place; the second refers to noises and exclamations. The court said: "the two provisions are distinct. One may stand separately from the other. Assuming, without holding, that the second were unconstitutional, the first could stand if constitutional." We accept that construction of severability and limit our consideration to the first provision of the statute.

On the authority of its earlier decisions, the state court declared that the state's purpose was to preserve the public peace, no words being "forbidden except such as have a direct tendency to cause acts of violence by the persons to whom, individually, the remark is addressed." It was further said: "The word 'offensive' is not to be defined in terms of what a particular addressee thinks. . . . The test is what men of common intelligence would understand would be words likely to cause an average addressee to fight. . . . The English language has a number of words and expressions which by general consent are 'fighting words' when said without a disarming smile. . . . Such words, as ordinary men know, are likely to cause a fight. So are threatening, profane or obscene revilings. Derisive and annoying words can be taken as coming within the purview of the statute as heretofore interpreted only when they have this characteristic of plainly tending to excite the addressee to a breach of the peace. . . . The statute, as construed, does no more than prohibit the face-to-face words plainly likely to cause a breach of the peace by the addressee, words whose speaking constitutes a breach of the peace by the speaker—including 'classical fighting words,' words in current use less 'classical' but equally likely to cause violence, and other disorderly words, including profanity, obscenity and threats."

We are unable to say that the limited scope of the statute as thus construed contravenes the Constitutional right of free expression. It is a statute narrowly drawn and limited to define and punish specific conduct lying within the domain of state power, the use in a public place of words likely to cause a breach of the peace.

In unanimously affirming Chaplinsky's conviction, the Court agreed with Murphy's enunciation of the so-called Fighting Words doctrine: expressions, "as ordinary men know, which are likely to cause a fight" may be prohibited. But, would its apparent agreement over this doctrine stand the test of time? Or would it unravel, as did the unanimity surrounding

Schenck's Clear and Present Danger standard? Two cases, *Terminiello v. Chicago* (1949) and *Feiner v. New York* (1951), provide us with partial, but perhaps contradictory, answers to those questions. As you read about them, consider not only the Court's rationale and use of the *Chaplinsky* doctrine, but also the differences between the two cases. Why did the justices reach different conclusions in cases presenting similar situations?

Arthur Terminiello, a Catholic priest, was scheduled to give a speech in Chicago. Terminiello was widely regarded as a racist, anti-Semitic, anti–New Deal communist hunter, who would cause turmoil wherever he spoke. At the Chicago auditorium where he was booked, Terminiello found a crowd of more than 1,000 gathered outside to oppose his views; in fact, some of the 800 individuals inside the auditorium felt the same. This hostility did not deter him. True to his reputation, Terminiello played with the angry mob by giving a particularly virulent speech. Among his statements were these:

And nothing I say tonight could begin to express the contempt I have for the slimy scum that got in by mistake. . . . The subject I want to talk to you tonight about is the attempt that is going on outside this hall . . . to destroy America by revolutions. . . .

The tide is changing . . . and if you and I turn and run . . . we will all be drowned in this tidal wave of communism. . . .

We have fifty-seven varieties of pink and reds and pastel shades in this country; and all of it can be traced to the twelve years we spent in the New Deal. . . .

Now this danger that we face—let us call them Zionist Jews. . . . Do you wonder they were persecuted in other countries in the world?. . .

As Terminiello spoke, the people outside grew increasingly hostile. They began to scream, calling him a fascist, and they threw rocks and stones, resulting in seventeen arrests. Eventually, authorities also arrested Terminiello, citing him with a violation of a city ordinance: "All persons who shall make, aid . . . [in] any improper voice, riot or disturbance, breach of peace, or diversion tending to a breach of peace . . . shall be deemed guilty of disorderly conduct." Terminiello appealed his conviction to the Supreme Court, arguing that such breach of peace ordinances violated his First Amendment freedom of speech guarantee. The state countered, noting that the ordinance fell squarely within the bounds of the Fighting Words doctrine.

Writing for the Court in its 5–4 decision, Justice Douglas rejected the state's position, but on a technicality. He noted: "The argument has been focused on the issue of whether the content of [Terminiello's] speech was composed of 'fighting words.'. . . We do not reach that question for there is a preliminary question that is dispositive of the case." That question, in Douglas's view, involved the instructions the court gave to the jury. In his charge, the trial court judge defined "breach of the peace" to include speech that "stirs the public to anger, invites dispute, brings about a condition of unrest, or creates a disturbance." Douglas took issue with the charge:

Speech is often provocative and challenging. It may strike at prejudices and preconceptions and have profound unsettling effects. . . . That is why freedom of speech, though not absolute, is nevertheless protected against censorship . . . unless shown likely to produce a clear and present danger . . . that arises far above public inconvenience, annoyance, or unrest.

Douglas found that the "ordinance as construed by the trial court seriously invaded" free speech guarantees. "It permitted conviction of petitioner if his speech stirred people to anger, invited public dispute, or brought about a condition of unrest. A conviction resting on any of those grounds may not stand."

The second case, *Feiner v. New York,* began in 1949, when the City of Syracuse, New York, issued a permit to the Young Progressives, allowing O. John Rogge, a former assistant attorney general, to speak at a local auditorium. Several days later, the city canceled the permit. Protesting this development, Irving Feiner, a member of the Young Progressives, addressed a crowd of seventy-five blacks and whites outside the auditorium where Rogge was to have spoken. The police were called to investigate complaints about the noise. They found Feiner standing on top of a box and using a microphone to make "derogatory remarks concerning President Truman, the American Legion, and the Mayor of Syracuse." But police made no attempt to arrest Feiner until he began making statements concerning race; according to eye witnesses, he implied that blacks should rise up against whites. Because such comments "stirred up" the racially mixed crowd, and threats of violence were made, police arrested Feiner under a breach of peace ordinance.

Writing for the majority in the 6–3 decision, Chief Justice Vinson upheld the conviction. He noted, "It is one thing to say that police cannot be used as an instrument for the oppression of unpopular views, and another to say that, when as here the speaker passes the bounds of argument or persuasion and undertakes incitement to riot, they are powerless to prevent a breach of the peace."

Feiner and *Terminiello* raised similar issues but evoked wholly different reactions from the Court. In fact, it is somewhat ironic that the justices reversed Terminiello's conviction and upheld Feiner's, given that the former's speech actually created public disorder, while the latter's held only the "imminence of greater disorder."

At this point, the Court seemed to agree that the Fighting Words doctrine provided a reasonable framework by which to decide public order cases. What divided the justices was the appropriate interpretation of that doctrine. During the 1960s the issue took on particular urgency because, as we have seen, the convergence of the civil rights and Vietnam War protest movements produced new expression cases, many of which centered on issues of public order. Would the Court use the *Chaplinsky* doctrine to resolve cases arising out of those movements—for example, convictions resulting from mass demonstrations on college campuses and state capitols and other government buildings, sit-ins on public and private

Mass demonstrations were an important element in the civil rights movement during the 1960s. A huge crowd attended a 1963 demonstration in front of the Lincoln Memorial.

property, and protest rallies? Or, given the novelty of the times, would it seek to handle them in novel ways? These questions dominated many of the Court's expression cases, beginning in 1963 with *Edwards v. South Carolina.*

Edwards has its genesis in March of 1961, when a group of black high school and college students met at a Baptist church in Columbia, South Carolina. At noon they walked toward the state capitol building "to submit a protest to the citizens of South Carolina to show their feelings and dissatisfaction with the present condition of discriminatory actions against Negroes." By marching on the state capitol, these students used a strategy that would become symbolic of the civil rights movement. When they arrived, thirty law enforcement officers were on hand to greet them.

The officers told the protesters they could go onto the capitol grounds as long as they were peaceful. For the next hour, the group walked in an orderly fashion, carrying signs with messages such as "I Am Proud to be a Negro." In time, a peaceful, nonobstructive crowd of 200 to 300 gathered. Although no violence appeared imminent, the officers told the demonstrators to disperse within five minutes or face arrest. "Instead . . . they engaged in what the City Manager described as 'boisterous,' 'loud,' and 'flamboyant' conduct": they held hands and sang, "I shall not be moved." Police eventually arrested 187 of the protesters, and they were convicted under a state breach of peace law.

On appeal to the Supreme Court, attorneys for the protesters stressed the fact that no violence occurred or was ever likely to occur. The state pointed to the *Feiner* precedent. But the justices sided with the protesters and held that the state had infringed on their First Amendment rights. Weighing heavily in the majority's opinion was the fact that the protest was not violent, nor did the protesters threaten to engage in violence. By the same token, the justices took note that the record was "barren of any evidence of 'fighting words.'"

In so ruling, the Court seemed to return to a *Terminiello* approach to public order issues; it overturned the convictions but announced no new doctrine. Justice Stewart's opinion for the Court, in fact, borrowed from Douglas's words in *Terminiello*, which in turn had been influenced by Holmes's opinion in *Schenck.* Only Justice Clark, in a dissenting opinion, seemed to view *Feiner* as controlling precedent, claiming that the possibility of a "public brawl" certainly existed.

Based on the Court's decision in *Edwards,* then, what is required for the lawful suppression of speech in public forums? One criterion clearly is the presence of real violence or a threat of violence. Would this requirement remain viable, or would the growth of the various protest movements force the Court back to its position in *Feiner*? In two 1965 cases emanating from the same event, *Cox v. Louisiana I* and *Cox v. Louisiana II*, a divided Court tried to ferret out further doctrine in this area. As you read about these cases, consider how they square with the original case in this area, *Chaplinsky v. New Hampshire*. Also, remember the social environment: by 1965 the protest movements had gained momentum and strength.

Cox I and *Cox II* began when, as part of a general protest against racial discrimination in the South, the Congress of Racial Equality (CORE) recommended a boycott of stores with segregated lunch counters. On December 14, 1961, authorities in Baton Rouge, Louisiana, arrested twenty-three black students for picketing such stores. That same evening, B. Elton Cox, field secretary of CORE and an ordained minister, spoke at a mass meeting at Southern University, one of the country's historically black colleges. The students agreed to hold a demonstration the next day protesting segregationist policies and the arrest of the picketers.

The next morning 2,000 students, led by Cox, walked from the campus to the old state capitol, two and a half blocks from the courthouse. As they assembled, police asked Cox why they were there, and he replied that they were protesting "the illegal arrest of some of their people who were being held in jail." Cox then led the group to the courthouse where they sang songs but maintained order. The police questioned Cox a second time. Cox said his agenda included a peaceful protest and the singing of certain patriotic songs. An officer told Cox they could proceed as long as they stayed on the sidewalk across the street from the courthouse, approximately 125 feet away from the building. Cox complied, but a crowd of 100 to 300 curious white people, mostly court personnel, gathered to watch the activities, which included singing and the holding of signs, some of which read, "Don't buy discrimination for X-Mas."

At noon Cox obtained a microphone and made the following statement:

All right. It's lunchtime. Let's go eat. There are twelve stores we are protesting. A number of the stores have twenty counters; they accept your money from nineteen. They won't accept it from the twentieth counter. This is an act of racial discrimination. These stores are open to the public. You are members of the public.

Perceiving that Cox's speech would wreak havoc in the city, a sheriff took the microphone and said:

Now you have been allowed to demonstrate. Up until now your demonstration has been more or less peaceful, but what you are doing now is a direct violation of the law . . . and it has to be broken up immediately.

When the demonstrators failed to heed the warning, police exploded tear gas cannisters, which caused the group to disperse. The next day police arrested Cox for violating three state laws: disturbing the peace, obstructing public passage, and interfering with the administration of justice.

In *Cox I* the Court dealt with the validity and applicability of the first two laws; in *Cox II* it scrutinized the last. On the first, the breach of peace violation, Justice Arthur Goldberg, for the majority, compared this case to *Edwards*, saying that "the facts [were] strikingly similar." He used the *Edwards* rationale to find the statute unconstitutional:

[As] in Terminiello and Edwards the conviction under this statute must be reversed as the statute is unconstitutional in that it sweeps within its broad scope activities that are constitutionally protected free speech and assembly. Maintenance of the opportunity for free political discussion is a basic tenet of our constitutional democracy.

Goldberg also reversed Cox's conviction for obstructing public passage, but on somewhat different grounds. Although he agreed with the state that it may regulate the "time, place, duration, or manner of use" of public streets, he took issue with the way the statute was enforced. As he noted, it gave city officials far too much discretion to determine who could conduct parades or hold street meetings.

It is clearly unconstitutional to enable a public official to determine which expressions of view will be permitted and which will not or to engage in invidious discrimination among persons or groups either by use of a statute providing a system of broad discretionary licensing power or . . . the equivalent of such a system by selective enforcement of an extremely broad prohibitory statute.

In *Cox II* Goldberg scrutinized the state's law on impeding the administration of justice. The statute was not constitutionally defective because "there can be no question that a state has a legitimate interest in protecting its judicial system from the pressures which picketing near a courthouse might create." But he found that its application to the circumstances here violated Cox's rights: he was "convicted for demonstrating not 'in,' but 'near' the courthouse."

In *Cox I* the majority reverted to the *Edwards* interpretation of *Chaplinsky:* no violence or threat of violence arose. Nor did Cox utter any fighting words. But Goldberg also asserts in *Cox II* that localities have a "legitimate interest in protecting" their judicial systems. And, even though several factors nullify the application of the law to the Southern University demonstrators, Goldberg is clear in holding that this does not imply that "police cannot call a halt to a meeting which originally peaceful, becomes violent. Nor does it mean that . . . authorities cannot set reasonable time limits for assemblies . . . and then order them dispersed."

This ruling is important because the justices once again reiterate that political expression affecting the public order is not limitless. Indeed, the law emerging in *Edwards* and *Cox* has largely governed the public order cases that were to follow. The justices generally applied the Fighting Words doctrine to adjudicate such claims unless the expressive conduct infringed on a legitimate government activity. In other words, time, place, and manner considerations make a difference.

By the same token, cases such as *Edwards* and *Cox* represent typical public forum disputes. Each involves large numbers of people collectively expressing their political opinions by assembling in a public place. Such gatherings are of concern to local officials who are responsible for maintaining public order and protecting public and private property. When large demonstrations also involve the communication of unpopular political views, the potential for disruption increases.

As we move toward the end of the twentieth century, will new sorts of public forum issues arise? If so, what direction will the Court take? One way to address these questions is to consider several cases decided by the Rehnquist Court that involve speech in public forums. Table 13-3 provides the facts of those disputes, their outcome, and a synopsis of the Court's reasoning. As you can see, the Court continues to face questions of how far the government may go in restricting the manner and place of protests. We also see that civil rights, religion, and foreign policy protests still dominate First Amendment litigation. But the 1990s cases include a new protest issue: abortion. These cases commonly involved a clash between pro-life advocates who protested at abortion clinics and pro-choice groups that wanted the courts to curtail the demonstrations. For the demonstrators the issue was freedom of speech. For their opponents the issue was guaranteeing free access to legal abortion services without undue interference from abortion opponents. Note that in *Madsen v. Women's Health Center, Inc.* (1994) the Court issued a mixed opinion, upholding some regulations but striking others.

Hate Speech

The cases we have discussed so far demonstrate a great diversity in the content and method of communication. Individuals in some of these cases have used conventional forms of protest, such as speeches, parades, and published documents; others have used unconventional methods that are offensive to many, such as Gregory Johnson's desecration of the Ameri-

TABLE 13-3 Public Forum Cases Decided by the Rehnquist Court

Case	Facts	Outcome
Board of Airport Commissioners of the City of Los Angeles v. Jews for Jesus (1987)	Challenge to a resolution of a board of airport commissioners banning all "First Amendment activities" within the terminal.	Regardless of whether an airport is a public or nonpublic forum, the resolution is overly broad and, therefore, violative of the First Amendment.
Boos v. Barry (1988)	Challenge to a District of Columbia ordinance prohibiting the display of any sign within 500 feet of a foreign embassy that brings that foreign government into public disrepute, and prohibiting the congregation of three or more persons within 500 feet of an embassy.	The sign-display provision is an unconstitutional content-based restriction on political expression. The congregation provision is a constitutional manner and place restriction.
Frisby v. Schultz (1988)	Challenge to a city ordinance prohibiting picketing before a particular residence of an individual.	Ordinance serves a legitimate governmental interest. It does not violate the First Amendment.
Ward v. Rock Against Racism (1989)	Challenge to a city regulation requiring bands playing in a city park to use a band shell.	Government may impose reasonable restrictions on speech in public forums. This regulation was reasonable and tailored to meet a significant governmental objective. It does not violate the First Amendment.
United States v. Kokinda (1990)	Challenge to a postal service regulation prohibiting the solicitation of contributions on sidewalks outside of post office.	Sidewalk outside a post office is not a traditional public forum. The regulation does not violate the First Amendment.
International Society for Krishna Consciousness v. Lee (1992)	Challenge to a New York Port Authority regulation forbidding the repetitive solicitation of money or distribution of literature in airport terminals.	An airport terminal is not a public forum. Repetitive, face-to-face solicitation may be disruptive, impede the normal flow of the public, and be fraudulent. The regulation is reasonable. However, the ban on the distribution of literature violates the First Amendment.
Forsyth County, Georgia v. Nationalist Movement (1992)	Challenge to a county ordinance allowing an official to fix the cost of a parade permit based on the estimated cost of providing sufficient security to maintain public order during the gathering.	The ordinance is unconstitutional because it gives excessive discretion to the official and allows the fee to be fixed on the content of the message and the projected public response to it.
Bray v. Alexandria Women's Health Clinic (1993)	An abortion clinic and its supporters sued to enjoin anti-abortion protesters from demonstrating at clinics in the Washington, D.C., area, claiming that such protests are in violation of the Civil Rights Act of 1871 because they reflect an "animus" against women and restrict freedom of interstate travel.	The protests were not directed at women as a class, but were intended to protect victims of abortion, stop its practice, and reverse its legalization. Although many women travel interstate to obtain abortion services, the right to interstate travel was not the focus of the protesters' activity.
National Organization for Women v. Scheidler (1994)	Pro-choice groups sued anti-abortion groups claiming they were in violation of the Racketeer Influenced and Corrupt Organizations Act (RICO) by conspiring to engage in protests designed to shut down abortion clinics and persuade women not to have abortions.	Although the RICO law primarily targets organized crime motivated by hopes of financial gain, the statute is not restricted to crimes having economic motives. RICO laws may be applied to organized criminal activity inspired by noneconomic goals.
Madsen v. Women's Health Center, Inc. (1994)	Anti-abortion groups challenged a state court injunction prohibiting them from protesting within 36 feet of an abortion clinic, restricting noise levels during times abortion surgeries were being conducted, prohibiting protesters from physically approaching clinic clients within 300 feet of the facility, and prohibiting protests within 300 feet of the residences of clinic workers.	The injunction against protests within 36 feet of clinic is generally upheld, as are the noise level restrictions. Banning protest activity within 300 feet of clinic or private residences, however, is unconstitutional.

can flag and O'Brien's burning of his draft card. Their expressions have included a wide array of philosophies and causes—communism, socialism, civil rights, religious beliefs, and opposition to war. In spite of this diversity, however, these cases share some common elements. Each case has involved an individual or group communicating a political or social message, usually expressing dissatisfaction with certain government policies. This speech is the traditional form of political expression that the Framers sought to protect when they approved the First Amendment.

Since the mid-1970s, however, another form of communication, which differs markedly from the traditional, has come before the Court. Expression based on hatred goes well beyond offending our standards of appropriateness or good taste. It arises from hostile, discriminatory, and prejudicial attitudes toward another person's innate characteristics: sex, race, ethnicity, religion, or sexual orientation. When directed at a member of the targeted group, such expression is demeaning and hurtful. Hate speech tends to be devoid of traditional commentary on political issues or on the need for changes in public policy. Instead, its central theme is hostility toward individuals belonging to the target group. May hate speech be banned, or does the First Amendment protect it? If regulation is permissible, under what conditions? And what standard should control?

One of the first modern cases involving these issues was *National Socialist Party v. Skokie* (1977). The National Socialist party was a minor political party with no hope of gaining electoral victories. Minor parties often set their sights a bit lower, viewing activities such as public education and awareness as important tools in achieving their desired policy objectives. *Skokie* concerned the party's desire to exercise its First Amendment right to assemble. More specifically, the party wanted to "educate" the public by marching in Skokie, Illinois, a suburb of Chicago.

Such marches are commonplace in America; almost daily, a political party or other group stages a demonstration or protest somewhere. But this proposed march was anything but commonplace. The National Socialist party is an American version of the Nazi party, which came into power under Adolf Hitler in Germany. A large number of Jews, including survivors of Hitler's concentration camps, live in Skokie. Together the two groups formed a potentially lethal combination. In fact, as soon as the town heard of the Nazis' plan to march in full regalia, it passed a variety of ordinances aimed specifically at stopping it. Believing that these measures abridged their First Amendment rights, party leaders turned to the ACLU for legal assistance. Many of its members objected to representing Nazi interests, but the ACLU agreed to participate because Skokie's prohibitions symbolized just the sorts of laws the organization was founded to fight—abridgements of the First Amendment. Skokie residents saw the matter in a much different light; they felt the presence of Nazi uniforms in their town constituted fighting words.[26] Therefore, Skokie argued that it could legitimately regulate such speech to prevent a riot.

A state circuit court agreed with the town and entered an injunction prohibiting the Nazis from marching in Skokie. The ACLU asked the Illinois Supreme Court for a stay and for an expedited appeal. When both requests were denied, the matter came before the U.S. Supreme Court.

In a short per curiam opinion, five members of the Court reversed the Illinois Supreme Court's denial of the stay. The Court said:

The outstanding injunction will deprive [the Nazis] of rights protected by the First Amendment.... If a State seeks to impose a restraint of this kind, it must provide strict procedural safeguard ... including immediate appellate review.... Absent such review, the State must instead allow a stay. The order of the Illinois Supreme Court constituted a denial of that right.

26. Many ACLU members also agreed with the town: almost half resigned in protest of its decision to defend Nazis. For an interesting account of this episode, see Aryeh Neier's *Defending My Enemy* (New York: Dutton, 1979).

The Court refused to uphold ordinances regulating speech before it occurred, claiming that such laws amounted to censorship. In the Court's eyes, governments can prohibit such expression only after it occurs, an opportunity the Town of Skokie never had, as the party chose instead to march in Chicago.

In the *Skokie* case, and in *Brandenburg* before it, the justices struck down government regulation of racially based hate speech. In both cases, however, the Court's decision rested on defects in the way the government attempted to block the unacceptable expression. In *Brandenburg* the Court found constitutional problems with Ohio's Criminal Syndicalism Act upon which the prosecution of a Ku Klux Klan leader was based. In *Skokie* the Court found that the local government was unconstitutionally attempting to repress speech before it occurred, a form of prior restraint. In neither case did the Court directly confront the question of whether the First Amendment allows government to punish expression based on hatred.

In response to an increase in hate speech incidents, many state and local governments, as well as colleges and universities, passed ordinances in the 1990s making hate speech punishable. Although most Americans consider hate-based expression reprehensible, there is a deep division of opinion over whether it can be constitutionally banned. Individuals concerned with minority rights and elimination of bigotry have argued that laws making hate speech illegal are both necessary and constitutionally permissible.

Free speech advocates, however, contend that such laws run in direct contradiction to the First Amendment. Often this issue has divided groups that have been traditional allies in the attempt to expand personal rights and liberties. *(See Box 13-3.)* The issue first found its way to the Supreme Court in the case of *R. A. V. v. City of St. Paul, Minnesota* (1992).

R. A. V. v. City of St. Paul, Minnesota

505 U.S. 377 (1992)
Vote: 9 (Blackmun, Kennedy, O'Connor, Rehnquist, Scalia, Souter, Stevens, Thomas, White)

    0

Opinion of the Court: Scalia
Concurring opinions: Blackmun, Stevens, White

The City of St. Paul, Minnesota, alleged that between 1:00 A.M. and 3:00 A.M. on June 21, 1990, R. A. V., a seventeen-year-old high school dropout, and several other teenagers "assembled a crudely made cross by taping together broken chair legs" and then burned the cross inside the fenced back yard of a black family across the street from R. A. V.'s house. St. Paul could have prosecuted R. A. V. under several severe criminal laws; for example, it could have charged him with arson, which carries a maximum penalty of five years in prison and a $10,000 fine. Instead, it charged him with violating two laws, including the St. Paul Bias-Motivated Crime Ordinance. This law stated:

Whoever places on public or private property a symbol, object, appellation, characterization or graffiti, including, but not limited to, a burning cross or Nazi swastika, which one knows or has reasonable grounds to know arouses anger, alarm, or resentment in others on the basis of race, color, creed, religion, or gender commits disorderly conduct and shall be guilty of a misdemeanor.

Before R. A. V.'s trial, his attorney asked the judge to dismiss the charge, arguing that the ordinance violated the First Amendment because it was "substantially overbroad and impermissibly content-based." The trial court judge granted the motion, and the city appealed to the Minnesota Supreme Court.

The Minnesota high court reversed the trial court's decision, holding that the ordinance did not violate freedom of expression guarantees contained in the First Amendment. The court found that the ordinance prohibits conduct equivalent to "fighting words," un-

BOX 13-3   HATE SPEECH AND THE CIVIL LIBERTIES COMMUNITY

REGULATING HATE SPEECH is an issue that divides the civil liberties community. Groups that historically have worked together to advance civil liberties and civil rights have found themselves in the uncomfortable position of fighting against each other over the hate speech controversy. Listed below are short excerpts from amicus curiae briefs submitted by traditionally liberal groups in the case of *R.A.V. v. City of St. Paul* (1992). Notice how the briefs emphasize different values. Those in favor of striking down the St. Paul ordinance stress the primacy of the First Amendment. Supporters of the law focus on the significance of equality considerations.

IN SUPPORT OF R.A.V.:

[T]he antibias ordinance cannot be defended on the ground that the State has a compelling interest in banning messages of racial and religious bigotry and intolerance. Although these messages are inconsistent with the Nation's highest aspirations, the Court has repeatedly held that the First Amendment does not permit a State to prohibit the communication of ideas simply because they are offensive or at odds with national policies.

—*Center for Individual Rights*

It is quite clear from the Court's First Amendment jurisprudence that government cannot criminalize such speech simply because it arouses anger, alarm and resentment.

—*Association of American Publishers and the Freedom to Read Foundation*

This society has rested its faith on the proposition that "the remedy [for speech] is more speech, not enforced silence." [Justice Brandeis concurring in *Whitney v. California*] Accordingly, our constitutional tradition demands that even a message of racial supremacy is entitled to be heard so long as it remains in the realm of advocacy. Those who articulated this faith in public debate were not naive about the power of words or symbols. To the contrary, they believed that pernicious ideas were more dangerous when suppressed than when exposed.

—*American Civil Liberties Union, Minnesota Civil Liberties Union, and the American Jewish Congress*

IN SUPPORT OF THE ST. PAUL ORDINANCE:

Crossburnings, of which defendant R.A.V. is accused, should be recognized as a terrorist hate practice of intimidation and harassment, which, contrary to the purposes of the Fourteenth Amendment, works to institutionalize the civil inequality of protected groups.... [T]he statute in question does not violate the First Amendment because social inequality, including through expressive conduct, is a harm for which states are entitled leeway in regulation.

—*National Black Women's Health Project*

When used in a personally threatening or assaultive manner, these symbols [burning cross and NAZI swastika] are part of the marketplace of ideas of which our society is justifiably tolerant; however, when used as a form of a bias-motivated personal attack, they cease to symbolize ideas and become violent tools that inflict injury. This Court has consistently recognized that this type of "expression" should not be afforded First Amendment protection.

—*Anti-Defamation League of B'nai B'rith*

Cross burning is an especially invidious act. A burning cross is an insult and a threat; it carries with it the historical baggage of past terrorism and physical attacks. When a cross burning is targeted against an individual and his family, it is more than just expression; it is a form of violence itself—symbolic violence.

—*Asian American Legal Defense and Education Fund, the Asian Law Caucus, the Asian Pacific American Legal Center, and the National Asian Pacific American Bar Association*

In his brief, [R.A.V.] intones principles of freedom of speech with which, in the abstract, no one will disagree. But the State of Minnesota was not indulging in theory when it charged [him] with a violation of the ordinance in controversy. It was dealing with what can only fairly be described as an act of terrorism. This conduct cannot rationally be viewed as protected by the First Amendment.

—*National Association for the Advancement of Colored People and the Clarendon Foundation*

protected expression under the First Amendment. It also ruled that the ordinance was not impermissibly content-based because it was "a narrowly tailored means toward accomplishing the compelling governmental interest in protecting the community against bias-motivated threats to public safety and order."

JUSTICE SCALIA delivered the opinion of the Court.

In construing the St. Paul ordinance, we are bound by the construction given to it by the Minnesota court. Accordingly, we accept the Minnesota Supreme Court's authoritative statement that the ordinance reaches only those expressions that constitute "fighting words" within the meaning of *Chaplinsky*. Petitioner . . . urge[s] us to modify the scope of the *Chaplinsky* formulation, thereby invalidating the ordinance as "substantially overbroad." We find it unnecessary to consider this issue. Assuming, *arguendo,* that all of the expression reached by the ordinance is proscribable under the "fighting words" doctrine, we nonetheless conclude that the ordinance is facially unconstitutional in that it prohibits otherwise permitted speech solely on the basis of the subjects the speech addresses.

The First Amendment generally prevents government from proscribing speech, *Cantwell v. Connecticut* (1940), or even expressive conduct, see *Texas v. Johnson* (1989), because of disapproval of the ideas expressed. Content-based regulations are presumptively invalid. From 1791 to the present, however, our society, like other free but civilized societies, has permitted restrictions upon the content of speech in a few limited areas, which are "of such slight social value as a step to truth that any benefit that may be derived from them is clearly outweighed by the social interest in order and morality." *Chaplinsky.* We have recognized that "the freedom of speech" referred to by the First Amendment does not include a freedom to disregard these traditional limitations. See, *e.g., Roth v. United States* (1957) (obscenity); *Beauharnais v. Illinois* (1952) (defamation); *Chaplinsky v. New Hampshire* ("fighting words"). Our decisions since the 1960's have narrowed the scope of the traditional categorical exceptions for defamation and for obscenity, but a limited categorical approach has remained an important part of our First Amendment jurisprudence.

We have sometimes said that these categories of expression are "not within the area of constitutionally protected speech" or that the "protection of the First Amendment does not extend" to them. Such statements must be taken in context, however, and are no more literally true than is the occasionally repeated shorthand characterizing obscenity "as not being speech at all." What they mean is that these areas of speech can, consistently with the First Amendment, be regulated *because of their constitutionally proscribable content* (obscenity, defamation, etc.)—not that they are categories of speech entirely invisible to the Constitution, so that they may be made the vehicles for content discrimination unrelated to their distinctively proscribable content. Thus, the government may proscribe libel; but it may not make the further content discrimination of proscribing *only* libel critical of the government. We recently acknowledged this distinction in [*New York v.*] *Ferber* [1982], where, in upholding New York's child pornography law, we expressly recognized that there was no "question here of censoring a particular literary theme. . . ."

Our cases surely do not establish the proposition that the First Amendment imposes no obstacle whatsoever to regulation of particular instances of such proscribable expression, so that the government "may regulate [them] freely." That would mean that a city council could enact an ordinance prohibiting only those legally obscene works that contain criticism of the city government or, indeed, that do not include endorsement of the city government. Such a simplistic, all-or-nothing-at-all approach to First Amendment protection is at odds with common sense and with our jurisprudence as well. It is not true that "fighting words" have at most a *"de minimis"* expressive content, or that their content is *in all respects* "worthless and undeserving of constitutional protection"; sometimes they are quite expressive indeed. We have not said that they constitute *"no* part of the expression of ideas," but only that they constitute "no *essential* part of any exposition of ideas."

The proposition that a particular instance of speech can be proscribable on the basis of one feature (*e.g.,* obscenity) but not on the basis of another (*e.g.,* opposition to the city government) is commonplace, and has found application in many contexts. We have long held, for example, that nonverbal expressive activity can be banned because of the action it entails, but not because of the ideas it expresses— so that burning a flag in violation of an ordinance against outdoor fires could be punishable, whereas burning a flag in violation of an ordinance against dishonoring the flag is not. . . .

In other words, the exclusion of "fighting words" from the scope of the First Amendment simply means that, for purposes of that Amendment, the unprotected features of the words are, despite their verbal character, essentially a "nonspeech" element of communication. Fighting words are thus analogous to a noisy sound truck: Each is, as Justice Frankfurter recognized, a "mode of speech"; both can be used to convey an idea; but neither has, in and of itself, a claim upon the First Amendment. As with the sound truck, however, so also with fighting words: The government may not regulate use based on hostility—or favoritism—towards the underlying message expressed. . . .

Even the prohibition against content discrimination that we assert the First Amendment requires is not absolute. It applies differently in the context of proscribable speech than in the area of fully protected speech. The rationale of the general prohibition, after all, is that content discrimination "rais[es] the specter that the Government may effectively drive certain ideas or viewpoints from the marketplace." *Simon & Schuster.* But content discrimination among various instances of a class of proscribable speech often does not pose this threat.

When the basis for the content discrimination consists entirely of the very reason the entire class of speech at issue is proscribable, no significant danger of idea or viewpoint discrimination exists. Such a reason, having been adjudged neutral enough to support exclusion of the entire class of speech from First Amendment protection, is also neutral enough to form the basis of distinction within the class. To illustrate: A State might choose to prohibit only that obscenity which is the most patently offensive *in its prurience—i.e.,* that which involves the most lascivious displays of sexual activity. But it may not prohibit, for example, only that obscenity which includes offensive *political* messages. . . .

Another valid basis for according differential treatment to even a content-defined subclass of proscribable speech is that the subclass happens to be associated with particular "secondary effects" of the speech, so that the regulation is *"justified* without reference to the content of the . . . speech." A State could, for example, permit all obscene live performances except those involving minors. Moreover,

since words can in some circumstances violate laws directed not against speech but against conduct (a law against treason, for example, is violated by telling the enemy the nation's defense secrets), a particular content-based subcategory of a proscribable class of speech can be swept up incidentally within the reach of a statute directed at conduct rather than speech. Thus, for example, sexually derogatory "fighting words," among other words, may produce a violation of Title VII's general prohibition against sexual discrimination in employment practices. Where the government does not target conduct on the basis of its expressive content, acts are not shielded from regulation merely because they express a discriminatory idea or philosophy. . . .

Applying these principles to the St. Paul ordinance, we conclude that, even as narrowly construed by the Minnesota Supreme Court, the ordinance is facially unconstitutional. Although the phrase in the ordinance, "arouses anger, alarm or resentment in others," has been limited by the Minnesota Supreme Court's construction to reach only those symbols or displays that amount to "fighting words," the remaining, unmodified terms make clear that the ordinance applies only to "fighting words" that insult, or provoke violence, "on the basis of race, color, creed, religion or gender." Displays containing abusive invective, no matter how vicious or severe, are permissible unless they are addressed to one of the specified disfavored topics. Those who wish to use "fighting words" in connection with other ideas—to express hostility, for example, on the basis of political affiliation, union membership, or homosexuality— are not covered. The First Amendment does not permit St. Paul to impose special prohibitions on those speakers who express views on disfavored subjects.

In its practical operation, moreover, the ordinance goes even beyond mere content discrimination, to actual viewpoint discrimination. Displays containing some words— odious racial epithets, for example—would be prohibited to proponents of all views. But "fighting words" that do not themselves invoke race, color, creed, religion, or gender— aspersions upon a person's mother, for example—would seemingly be usable *ad libitum* in the placards of those arguing *in favor* of racial, color, etc. tolerance and equality, but could not be used by that speaker's opponents. One could hold up a sign saying, for example, that all "anti-

Catholic bigots" are misbegotten; but not that all "papists" are, for that would insult and provoke violence "on the basis of religion." St. Paul has no such authority to license one side of a debate to fight freestyle, while requiring the other to follow Marquis of Queensbury Rules.

What we have here, it must be emphasized, is not a prohibition of fighting words that are directed at certain persons or groups (which would be *facially* valid if it met the requirements of the Equal Protection Clause); but rather, a prohibition of fighting words that contain (as the Minnesota Supreme Court repeatedly emphasized) messages of "bias-motivated" hatred and in particular, as applied to this case, messages "based on virulent notions of racial supremacy." One must wholeheartedly agree with the Minnesota Supreme Court that "[i]t is the responsibility, even the obligation, of diverse communities to confront such notions in whatever form they appear," but the manner of that confrontation cannot consist of selective limitations upon speech. St. Paul's brief asserts that a general "fighting words" law would not meet the city's needs because only a content-specific measure can communicate to minority groups that the "group hatred" aspect of such speech "is not condoned by the majority." The point of the First Amendment is that majority preferences must be expressed in some fashion other than silencing speech on the basis of its content. . . .

The content-based discrimination reflected in the St. Paul ordinance comes within neither any of the specific exceptions to the First Amendment prohibition we discussed earlier, nor within a more general exception for content discrimination that does not threaten censorship of ideas. It assuredly does not fall within the exception for content discrimination based on the very reasons why the particular class of speech at issue (here, fighting words) is proscribable. . . . [T]he reason why fighting words are categorically excluded from the protection of the First Amendment is not that their content communicates any particular idea, but that their content embodies a particularly intolerable (and socially unnecessary) *mode* of expressing *whatever* idea the speaker wishes to convey. St. Paul has not singled out an especially offensive mode of expression—it has not, for example, selected for prohibition only those fighting words that communicate ideas in a threatening (as opposed to a merely obnoxious) manner. Rather, it has proscribed fighting words of whatever manner that communicate messages of racial, gender, or religious intolerance. Selectivity of this sort creates the possibility that the city is seeking to handicap the expression of particular ideas. That possibility would alone be enough to render the ordinance presumptively invalid, but St. Paul's comments and concessions in this case elevate the possibility to a certainty. . . .

Finally, St. Paul . . . defend[s] the conclusion of the Minnesota Supreme Court that, even if the ordinance regulates expression based on hostility towards its protected ideological content, this discrimination is nonetheless justified because it is narrowly tailored to serve compelling state interests. Specifically, they assert that the ordinance helps to ensure the basic human rights of members of groups that have historically been subjected to discrimination, including the right of such group members to live in peace where they wish. We do not doubt that these interests are compelling, and that the ordinance can be said to promote them. But the "danger of censorship" presented by a facially content-based statute requires that that weapon be employed only where it is *"necessary* to serve the asserted [compelling] interest.". . . The dispositive question in this case, therefore, is whether content discrimination is reasonably necessary to achieve St. Paul's compelling interests; it plainly is not. An ordinance not limited to the favored topics, for example, would have precisely the same beneficial effect. In fact the only interest distinctively served by the content limitation is that of displaying the city council's special hostility towards the particular biases thus singled out. That is precisely what the First Amendment forbids. The politicians of St. Paul are entitled to express that hostility—but not through the means of imposing unique limitations upon speakers who (however benightedly) disagree.

Let there be no mistake about our belief that burning a cross in someone's front yard is reprehensible. But St. Paul has sufficient means at its disposal to prevent such behavior without adding the First Amendment to the fire.

The judgment of the Minnesota Supreme Court is reversed, and the case is remanded for proceedings not inconsistent with this opinion.

It is so ordered.

The Supreme Court unanimously declared the St. Paul hate speech ordinance to be unconstitutional. The justices found the law defective because it singled out a particular kind of hate speech. The ordinance, therefore, violated the principle that laws regulating expression must not discriminate on the basis of content. The concurring justices also found the law unacceptable, but preferred to strike it down for being unconstitutionally vague.

It would be incorrect, however, to generalize from *R. A. V.* that the Court will strike down any law that imposes a penalty for hateful expression. In the 1993 case of *Wisconsin v. Mitchell*, for example, the justices considered a Wisconsin statute that allowed judges to impose more severe sentences on defendants whose crimes were motivated by prejudicial attitudes based on race, religion, sexual orientation, national origin, and so forth. The Wisconsin penalty "enhancement" law was similar to those enacted by many state and local governments in an attempt to reduce the incidence of hate crimes. Forty-nine states submitted a joint brief urging the Court to uphold Wisconsin's law. The federal government also submitted arguments in support of the constitutionality of the hate crimes provision.

In this instance, the justices ruled in favor of the government. Writing for a unanimous Court, Justice Rehnquist offered several reasons for the decision, with important ones expressed in this passage:

Traditionally, sentencing judges have considered a wide variety of factors in addition to evidence bearing on guilt in determining what sentence to impose on a convicted defendant. The defendant's motive for committing the offense is one important factor. . .

[It is also] permissible for the sentencing court to consider the defendant's racial animus in determining whether he should be sentenced to death, surely the most severe "enhancement" of all. And the fact that the Wisconsin Legislature has decided, as a general matter, that bias-motivated offenses warrant greater maximum penalties across the board does not alter the result here. For the primary responsibility for fixing criminal penalties lies with the legislature. . . .

Rehnquist also sought to distinguish the decision here from the one in *R. A. V.:*

Nothing in our decision last Term in *R. A. V.* compels a different result here. That case involved a First Amendment challenge to a municipal ordinance prohibiting the use of "'fighting words' that insult, or provoke violence, 'on the basis of race, color, creed, religion or gender.'" Because the ordinance only proscribed a class of "fighting words" deemed particularly offensive by the city—i.e., those "that contain . . . messages of 'bias-motivated' hatred," we held that it violated the rule against content-based discrimination. But whereas the ordinance struck down in *R. A. V.* was explicitly directed at expression, *i.e.,* "speech" or "messages," the statute in this case is aimed at conduct unprotected by the First Amendment.

Although the Court took care to distinguish the two cases, it did not settle the hate speech issue, perhaps because the rulings reached somewhat different conclusions: *Mitchell* supported government regulation, while *R. A. V.* did not. Supporters of broad First Amendment protection and those who favor restricting discriminatory expression both can find encouragement in the Court's opinions. As a result, the battle over hateful and harassing expression continues on college campuses, in the workplace, and in legislatures. The Court certainly has not seen its last dispute in this area.

The Right Not to Speak

So far we have discussed the constitutionality of government attempts to restrict or prohibit certain kinds of expression. Although curtailing expression is the most common form of government regulation, there are situations in which the government requires citizens to speak or write. For example, Americans may be ordered to appear as a witness before a court, grand jury, or legislative investigating committee. The government compels people to provide information on income tax returns. It may be necessary to take an oath when we become citizens, provide court testimony, take public office, or apply for a gun permit. Americans generally consider these regulations to be reasonable requirements relevant to legitimate government functions. But what if an individual does not want to comply with a government regulation that requires expression? Other than the Fifth Amendment's protection against the government compelling self-incriminating testimony, is there any restraint on the government's authority to coerce expression? Put another way, does the First Amendment's guarantee of freedom of speech carry with it the freedom not to speak?

To understand this issue we need once again to turn our attention to the famous "flag salute" cases discussed in Chapter 12. As you recall, in 1940 the Court in *Minersville School District v. Gobitis* upheld flag salute regulations against claims that the school system was violating the children's right to free exercise of religion. Three years later, in *West Virginia Board of Education v. Barnette* (1943), the Court again considered the constitutionality of the compulsory flag salute laws, once again in a case brought by Jehovah's Witnesses.

By this time, however, some conditions had changed. First, after American victories on the battlefield, the feverishly patriotic mood so strong at the beginning of World War II had moderated somewhat. Second, the Court had undergone some personnel changes that strengthened its civil libertarian wing. Third, the *Gobitis* decision had been roundly criticized in legal circles. These circumstances encouraged the Witnesses to be more optimistic about their chances of winning in *Barnette*.

But there was one additional factor that distinguished *Gobitis* from *Barnette*. Lawyers supporting the challenge made a significant strategy decision to base the attack not so much on freedom of religion as on the freedom of speech. As you read Justice Jackson's majority opinion in *Barnette*, notice how he weaves religion and expression rights into his explanation for striking down the flag salute laws.

West Virginia Board of Education v. Barnette

319 U.S. 624 (1943)
Vote: 6 *(Black, Douglas, Jackson, Murphy, Rutledge, Stone)*
    3 *(Frankfurter, Reed, Roberts)*
Opinion of the Court: Jackson
Concurring opinions: Black and Douglas (joint), Murphy
Dissenting opinions: Frankfurter, Reed and Roberts (joint)

Following the *Gobitis* decision, the West Virginia legislature amended its laws to require that all public schools teach courses intended to increase students' knowledge of the American system of government and to foster the spirit of Americanism. In support of this policy, the state board of education required that the American flag be saluted and the Pledge of Allegiance be recited each day. Students who refused to participate could be charged with insubordination and expelled. Not attending school because of such an expulsion was grounds for the child's being declared delinquent. Parents of delinquent children were subject to fines and jail penalties of up to thirty days. In some cases officials threatened noncomplying students with reform school.

The Jehovah's Witnesses challenged these regulations in the name of the Barnette family, church members who had been harassed by the school system for failure to participate in the flag salute ritual. One of the Barnette children, in fact, had been expelled.[27]

Despite the Supreme Court's decision in *Gobitis*, a three-judge district court sympathized with the Barnette family's plight. According to the well-respected circuit court judge, John J. Parker: "The salute to the United States' flag is an expression of the homage of the soul. To force it upon one who has conscientious scruples against giving it is petty tyranny unworthy of the spirit of the Republic, and forbidden, we think, by the United States Constitution." After the decision,

27. For more details on this case, see David Manwaring, *Render Unto Caesar: The Flag Salute Controversy* (Chicago: University of Chicago Press, 1962).

the West Virginia School Board appealed to the U.S. Supreme Court.

MR. JUSTICE JACKSON delivered the opinion of the Court.

As the present Chief Justice said in dissent in the Gobitis case, the State may "require teaching by instruction and study of all in our history and in the structure and organization of our government, including the guaranties of civil liberty which tend to inspire patriotism and love of country." Here, however, we are dealing with a compulsion of students to declare a belief. They are not merely made acquainted with the flag salute so that they may be informed as to what it is or even what it means. The issue here is whether this slow and easily neglected route to aroused loyalties constitutionally may be short-cut by substituting a compulsory salute and slogan. . . .

There is no doubt that, in connection with the pledges, the flag salute is a form of utterance. Symbolism is a primitive but effective way of communicating ideas. The use of an emblem or flag to symbolize some system, idea, institution, or personality, is a short cut from mind to mind. Causes and nations, political parties, lodges and ecclesiastical groups seek to knit the loyalty of their following to a flag or banner, a color or design. The State announces rank, function, and authority through crowns and maces, uniforms and black robes; the church speaks through the Cross, the Crucifix, the altar and shrine, and clerical raiment. Symbols of State often convey political ideas just as religious symbols come to convey theological ones. Associated with many of these symbols are appropriate gestures of acceptance or respect: a salute, a bowed or bared head, a bended knee. A person gets from a symbol the meaning he puts into it, and what is one man's comfort and inspiration is another's jest and scorn.

Over a decade ago Chief Justice Hughes led this Court in holding that the display of a red flag as a symbol of opposition by peaceful and legal means to organized government was protected by the free speech guaranties of the Constitution. Stromberg v. California [1931]. Here it is the State that employs a flag as a symbol of adherence to government as presently organized. It requires the individual to communicate by word and sign his acceptance of the political ideas it

thus bespeaks. Objection to this form of communication when coerced is an old one, well known to the framers of the Bill of Rights.

It is also to be noted that the compulsory flag salute and pledge requires affirmation of a belief and an attitude of mind. It is not clear whether the regulation contemplates that pupils forego any contrary convictions of their own and become unwilling converts to the prescribed ceremony or whether it will be acceptable if they simulate assent by words without belief and by a gesture barren of meaning. It is now a commonplace that censorship or suppression of expression of opinion is tolerated by our Constitution only when the expression presents a clear and present danger of action of a kind the State is empowered to prevent and punish. It would seem that involuntary affirmation could be commanded only on even more immediate and urgent grounds than silence. But here the power of compulsion is invoked without any allegation that remaining passive during a flag salute ritual creates a clear and present danger that would justify an effort even to muffle expression. To sustain the compulsory flag salute we are required to say that a Bill of Rights which guards the individual's right to speak his own mind, left it open to public authorities to compel him to utter what is not in his mind.

Whether the First Amendment to the Constitution will permit officials to order observance of ritual of this nature does not depend upon whether as a voluntary exercise we would think it to be good, bad or merely innocuous. Any credo of nationalism is likely to include what some disapprove or to omit what others think essential, and to give off different overtones as it takes on different accents or interpretations. If official power exists to coerce acceptance of any patriotic creed, what it shall contain cannot be decided by courts, but must be largely discretionary with the ordaining authority, whose power to prescribe would no doubt include power to amend. Hence validity of the asserted power to force an American citizen publicly to profess any statement of belief or to engage in any ceremony of assent to one presents questions of power that must be considered independently of any idea we may have as to the utility of the ceremony in question.

Nor does the issue as we see it turn on one's possession of particular religious views or the sincerity with which they are held. While religion supplies appellees' motive for enduring the discomforts of making the issue in this case, many citizens who do not share these religious views hold such a compulsory rite to infringe constitutional liberty of the individual. It is not necessary to inquire whether nonconformist beliefs will exempt from the duty to salute unless we first find power to make the salute a legal duty.

The Gobitis decision, however, *assumed*, as did the argument in that case and in this, that power exists in the State to impose the flag salute discipline upon school children in general. The Court only examined and rejected a claim based on religious beliefs of immunity from an unquestioned general rule. The question which underlies the flag salute controversy is whether such a ceremony so touching matters of opinion and political attitude may be imposed upon the individual by official authority under powers committed to any political organization under our Constitution. We examine rather than assume existence of this power and, against this broader definition of issues in this case, re-examine specific grounds assigned for the Gobitis decision.

1. It was said that the flag-salute controversy confronted the Court with "the problem which Lincoln cast in memorable dilemma: 'Must a government of necessity be too *strong* for the liberties of its people, or too *weak* to maintain its own existence?'" and that the answer must be in favor of strength. Minersville School District v. Gobitis.

We think these issues may be examined free of pressure or restraint growing out of such considerations.

It may be doubted whether Mr. Lincoln would have thought that the strength of government to maintain itself would be impressively vindicated by our confirming power of the state to expel a handful of children from school. Such oversimplification, so handy in political debate, often lacks the precision necessary to postulates of judicial reasoning. If validly applied to this problem, the utterance cited would resolve every issue of power in favor of those in authority and would require us to override every liberty thought to weaken or delay execution of their policies.

Government of limited power need not be anemic government. Assurance that rights are secure tends to diminish fear and jealousy of strong government, and by making us feel safe to live under it makes for its better support. Without promise of a limiting Bill of Rights it is doubtful if

our Constitution could have mustered enough strength to enable its ratification. To enforce those rights today is not to choose weak government over strong government. It is only to adhere as a means of strength to individual freedom of mind in preference to officially disciplined uniformity for which history indicates a disappointing and disastrous end.

The subject now before us exemplifies this principle. Free public education, if faithful to the ideal of secular instruction and political neutrality, will not be partisan or enemy of any class, creed, party, or faction. If it is to impose any ideological discipline, however, each party or denomination must seek to control, or failing that, to weaken the influence of the educational system. Observance of the limitations of the Constitution will not weaken government in the field appropriate for its exercise.

2. It was also considered in the Gobitis case that functions of educational officers in states, counties and school districts were such that to interfere with their authority "would in effect make us the school board for the country."

The Fourteenth Amendment, as now applied to the States, protects the citizen against the State itself and all of its creatures—Boards of Education not excepted. These have, of course, important, delicate, and highly discretionary functions, but none that they may not perform within the limits of the Bill of Rights. That they are educating the young for citizenship is reason for scrupulous protection of Constitutional freedoms of the individual, if we are not to strangle the free mind at its source and teach youth to discount important principles of our government as mere platitudes.

Such Boards are numerous and their territorial jurisdiction often small. But small and local authority may feel less sense of responsibility to the Constitution, and agencies of publicity may be less vigilant in calling it to account. The action of Congress in making flag observance voluntary and respecting the conscience of the objector in a matter so vital as raising the Army contrasts sharply with these local regulations in matters relatively trivial to the welfare of the nation. There are village tyrants as well as village Hampdens, but none who acts under color of law is beyond reach of the Constitution.

3. The Gobitis opinion reasoned that this is a field "where courts possess no marked and certainly no controlling competence," that it is committed to the legislatures as

well as the courts to guard cherished liberties and that it is constitutionally appropriate to "fight out the wise use of legislative authority in the forum of public opinion and before legislative assemblies rather than to transfer such a contest to the judicial arena," since all the "effective means of inducing political changes are left free."

The very purpose of a Bill of Rights was to withdraw certain subjects from the vicissitudes of political controversy, to place them beyond the reach of majorities and officials and to establish them as legal principles to be applied by the courts. One's right to life, liberty, and property, to free speech, a free press, freedom of worship and assembly, and other fundamental rights may not be submitted to vote; they depend on the outcome of no elections.

In weighing arguments of the parties it is important to distinguish between the due process clause of the Fourteenth Amendment as an instrument for transmitting the principles of the First Amendment and those cases in which it is applied for its own sake. The test of legislation which collides with the Fourteenth Amendment, because it also collides with the principles of the First, is much more definite than the test when only the Fourteenth is involved. Much of the vagueness of the due process clause disappears when the specific prohibitions of the First become its standard. The right of a State to regulate, for example, a public utility may well include, so far as the due process test is concerned, power to impose all of the restrictions which a legislature may have a "rational basis" for adopting. But freedoms of speech and of press, of assembly, and of worship may not be infringed on such slender grounds. They are susceptible of restriction only to prevent grave and immediate danger to interests which the state may lawfully protect. It is important to note that while it is the Fourteenth Amendment which bears directly upon the State it is the more specific limiting principles of the First Amendment that finally govern this case. . . .

4. Lastly, and this is the very heart of the Gobitis opinion, it reasons that "National unity is the basis of national security," that the authorities have "the right to select appropriate means for its attainment," and hence reaches the conclusion that such compulsory measures toward "national unity" are constitutional. Upon the verity of this assumption depends our answer in this case.

National unity as an end which officials may foster by persuasion and example is not in question. The problem is whether under our Constitution compulsion as here employed is a permissible means for its achievement.

Struggles to coerce uniformity of sentiment in support of some end thought essential to their time and country have been waged by many good as well as by evil men. Nationalism is a relatively recent phenomenon but at other times and places the ends have been racial or territorial security, support of a dynasty or regime, and particular plans for saving souls. As first and moderate methods to attain unity have failed, those bent on its accomplishment must resort to an ever-increasing severity. . . . Those who begin coercive elimination of dissent soon find themselves exterminating dissenters. Compulsory unification of opinion achieves only the unanimity of the graveyard.

It seems trite but necessary to say that the First Amendment to our Constitution was designed to avoid these ends by avoiding these beginnings. There is no mysticism in the American concept of the State or of the nature or origin of its authority. We set up government by consent of the governed, and the Bill of Rights denies those in power any legal opportunity to coerce that consent. Authority here is to be controlled by public opinion, not public opinion by authority.

The case is made difficult not because the principles of its decision are obscure but because the flag involved is our own. Nevertheless, we apply the limitations of the Constitution with no fear that freedom to be intellectually and spiritually diverse or even contrary will disintegrate the social organization. To believe that patriotism will not flourish if patriotic ceremonies are voluntary and spontaneous instead of a compulsory routine is to make an unflattering estimate of the appeal of our institutions to free minds. We can have intellectual individualism and the rich cultural diversity that we owe to exceptional minds only at the price of occasional eccentricity and abnormal attitudes. When they are so harmless to others or to the State as those we deal with here, the price is not too great. But freedom to differ is not limited to things that do not matter much. That would be a mere shadow of freedom. The test of its substance is the right to differ as to things that touch the heart of the existing order.

If there is any fixed star in our constitutional constellation, it is that no official, high or petty, can prescribe what shall be orthodox in politics, nationalism, religion, or other matters of opinion or force citizens to confess by word or act their faith therein. If there are any circumstances which permit an exception, they do not now occur to us.

We think the action of the local authorities in compelling the flag salute and pledge transcends constitutional limitations on their power and invades the sphere of intellect and spirit which it is the purpose of the First Amendment to our Constitution to reserve from all official control.

The decision of this Court in Minersville School District v. Gobitis and the holdings of those few per curiam decisions which preceded and foreshadowed it are overruled, and the judgment enjoining enforcement of the West Virginia Regulation is affirmed.

Affirmed.

MR. JUSTICE FRANKFURTER, dissenting.

One who belongs to the most vilified and persecuted minority in history is not likely to be insensible to the freedoms guaranteed by our Constitution. Were my purely personal attitude relevant I should wholeheartedly associate myself with the general libertarian views in the Court's opinion, representing as they do the thought and action of a lifetime. But as judges we are neither Jew nor Gentile, neither Catholic nor agnostic. We owe equal attachment to the Constitution and are equally bound by our judicial obligations whether we derive our citizenship from the earliest or latest immigrants to these shores. As a member of this Court I am not justified in writing my private notions of policy into the Constitution, no matter how deeply I may cherish them or how mischievous I may deem their disregard. The duty of a judge who must decide which of two claims before the Court shall prevail, that of a State to enact and enforce laws within its general competence or that of an individual to refuse obedience because of the demands of his conscience, is not that of the ordinary person. It can never be emphasized too much that one's own opinion about the wisdom or evil of a law should be excluded altogether when one is doing one's duty on the bench. . . . [I]t would require more daring than I possess to deny that reasonable legislators could have taken the action which is before us for review. Most unwillingly, therefore, I must differ from my brethren with regard to legislation like this. I cannot bring my mind to believe that the "liberty" secured by the Due Process Clause gives this Court authority to deny to the State of West Virginia the attainment of that which we all recognize as a legitimate legislative end, namely, the promotion of good citizenship, by employment of the means here chosen. . . .

In striking down the West Virginia compulsory flag salute law, the Court ruled that the individual has at least a qualified right to be free of government coercion to express views the individual disavows. This decision does not go so far as to hold that an individual's First Amendment right can be used to avoid obligations such as testifying in a court case or providing information on a tax return, but it precludes certain forms of coerced expression.

For another example of this principle, consider the plight of George and Maxine Maynard of Lebanon, New Hampshire. Like the Gobitas and Barnette families, the Maynards were Jehovah's Witnesses. Their entanglement with the law stemmed from a statute mandating that the state slogan appear on all vehicle license plates. The Maynards considered the slogan, "Live Free or Die," to be repugnant to their moral, religious, and political beliefs. To disassociate himself from the slogan, Maynard cut a portion of the slogan from the plates on his cars and covered the remaining words with tape, but he did not conceal the identifying letters or numbers. In November 1974 local authorities arrested Maynard for obscuring a license plate, a misdemeanor under New Hampshire law. He explained his objections to the slogan, but the court found him guilty. The judge imposed a $25.00 fine, but agreed to suspend it if Maynard would comply with the law. The next month authorities arrested Maynard once again for the same offense. The court found him guilty and sentenced him to six months in jail and a $50.00 fine. The judge again showed leniency by permitting Maynard to avoid jail if he would pay the two fines. Maynard announced that as a matter of conscience, he would pay no fines. The judge ordered him to serve a fifteen-day jail sentence, which he did. The Maynards then sued, challenging the constitutionality of the law. They won and the state appealed.

The case of *Wooley v. Maynard* (1977) presented the justices with a classic conflict between individual and state interests. The Maynards argued that their First Amendment rights protected them from state compulsion. George Maynard filed a statement saying, "I refuse to be coerced by the State into advertising a slogan which I find morally, ethically, religiously, and politically abhorrent." The state responded by contending that its interest in promoting an appreciation of history, individualism, and state pride outweighed the narrow interests of the Maynards.

Speaking for the Court, Chief Justice Burger ruled in favor of the Maynards. He explained:

We begin with the proposition that the right of freedom of thought protected by the First Amendment against state action includes both the right to speak freely and the right to refrain from speaking at all. A system which secures the right to proselytize religious, political, and ideological causes must also guarantee the concomitant right to decline to foster such concepts. The right to speak and the right to refrain from speaking are complementary components of the broader concept of "individual freedom of mind."

The justices concluded that the countervailing interests of the state were insufficiently compelling to outweigh the First Amendment liberties at stake. The state slogan was not ideologically neutral, but proclaimed an official view of such subjects as history, state pride, and individualism. While the state may have an interest in promoting these beliefs, such an interest cannot outweigh an individual's First Amendment right to avoid becoming an unwilling spokesperson for that message.

READINGS

Bollinger, Lee C. *The Tolerant Society.* New York: Oxford University Press, 1986.

Chafee, Zechariah, Jr. *Free Speech in the United States.* Cambridge, Mass.: Harvard University Press, 1941.

Cox, Archibald. *Freedom of Expression.* Cambridge, Mass.: Harvard University Press, 1981.

Emerson, Thomas I. *The System of Freedom of Expression.* New York: Vintage Books, 1970.

Fish, Stanley. *There's No Such Thing as Free Speech, and It's a Good Thing, Too.* New York: Oxford University Press, 1994.

Fortas, Abe. *Concerning Dissent and Civil Disobedience.* New York: New American Library, 1968.

Goldstein, Robert Justin. *Political Repression in Modern America.* Cambridge, Mass.: Schenkman, 1978.

Graber, Mark A. *Transforming Free Speech.* Berkeley: University of California Press, 1991.

Hemmer, Joseph J. *The Supreme Court and the First Amendment.* New York: Praeger, 1986.

Levy, Leonard W. *Legacy of Suppression.* Cambridge, Mass.: Harvard University Press, 1960.

MacKinnon, Catherine A. *Only Words.* Cambridge, Mass.: Harvard University Press, 1993.

Rabban, David M. "The Emergence of Modern First Amendment Doctrine." *University of Chicago Law Review* 50 (Fall 1983): 1205–1355.

Smolla, Rodney A. *Free Speech in an Open Society.* New York: Knopf, 1992.

Sunstein, Cass A. *Democracy and the Problem of Free Speech.* New York: Free Press, 1993.

Telford, Thomas L. *Freedom of Speech in the United States.* New York: Random House, 1985.

Van Alstyne, William W. *Interpretations of the First Amendment.* Durham, N.C.: Duke University Press, 1984.

Washburn, Patrick S. *A Question of Sedition.* New York: Oxford University Press, 1986.

CHAPTER 14
FREEDOM OF THE PRESS

FREEDOM OF THE PRESS is perhaps the most visible manifestation of Americans' expression of their rights. Each day the print and broadcast media bombard the nation with news, editorials, and entertainment from almost every conceivable perspective. Newsstands and bookstores flourish by offering periodicals and books devoted to every imaginable interest. With the emergence of interactive media, such as talk radio, op-ed pages, and letters to the editor, citizens have become participants in the press rather than merely consumers. The result is a robust exchange of information and opinion.

Much of what appears in the press is critical of government and government policies. In contrast to the citizens of some other countries, however, Americans who criticize officials do not face government censorship or possible retaliation. They enjoy protection provided by the First Amendment's stipulation that "Congress shall make no law . . . abridging the freedom . . . of the press."

This constitutional provision reflects the Framers' strong commitment to the rights of the press. They saw the right to publish freely not only as important for its own sake, but also as a significant protection for other political and personal liberties. The press is the watchdog that sounds a warning when other rights

are threatened. The Founders believed, for example, that the rights of speech and religion would be meaningless without a free press. Thomas Jefferson was so certain of this precept that in 1816 he proclaimed, "When the press is free, and every man is able to read, all is safe."

As British colonists, the Framers were well schooled in the values of a free press. But history also taught them that this right could not be taken for granted. They knew that England had controlled the press from the fifteenth through the seventeenth centuries and that repressive measures from that period had become common law. They understood that to remain free, a society must tolerate divergent views and opinions, which can be formed only through the open exchange of ideas. Unless protected from government interference, the press is vulnerable to becoming an extension of the political regime, not an independent observer, a check, or even a source of information.

In the first part of this chapter, we examine the right of the press to be free from government control prior to publication. This is known as the doctrine of prior restraint. Under what conditions, if any, may the government enjoin the press from freely printing and distributing its material? In the second part of this chapter, we explore special privileges claimed by the media. Reporters argue that they should enjoy a unique set of guarantees to perform their jobs. How has the Court reacted to such claims? We conclude the chapter with an analysis of expression that the Supreme Court historically has considered outside the free press protections of the First Amendment: obscenity and libel. To what extent can the government penalize material that contains sexually explicit material or falsehoods?

PRIOR RESTRAINT

No concept is more important to understanding freedom of the press than prior restraint. Prior restraint occurs when the government reviews material to determine whether publication will be allowed. The practice is a form of government censorship and is antithetical to freedom of the press. If the First Amendment means anything, it means that no government has the authority to decide what may and may not be published. The government may punish press activity that violates legitimate criminal laws, but such government sanctions may take place only *after* publication, not before.

The principle that prior restraint runs contrary to the Constitution was established in the formative case of *Near v. Minnesota* (1931). The justices took a strong stance against such censorship. But does their decision imply that the government may never block the publication of material it considers inappropriate or harmful? Are there exceptions to the constitutional prohibition against prior restraint? As you read Chief Justice Charles Evans Hughes's opinion in *Near*, pay close attention to how the justices develop the general principle against prior restraint, and look for any indication that the Court might allow exceptions to it.

Near v. Minnesota

283 U.S. 697 (1931)
Vote: 5 (Brandeis, Holmes, Hughes, Roberts, Stone)
    4 (Butler, McReynolds, Sutherland, Van Devanter)
Opinion of the Court: Hughes
Dissenting opinion: Butler

A 1925 Minnesota law provided for "the abatement, as a public nuisance, of a 'malicious, scandalous, and defamatory newspaper, magazine, or other periodical.'" In the fall of 1927, a county attorney asked a state judge to issue a restraining order banning publication of the *Saturday Press*. In the attorney's view, the newspaper, partly owned by Jay Near, was the epitome of a malicious, scandalous, and defamatory publication.[1] *The Saturday Press* committed itself to exposing corruption, bribery, gambling, and prostitution in Minneapolis. It attacked specific city officials for being in league with gangsters and chided the established press for refusing to uncover the corruption. These attacks were colored by Near's racist, anti-Semitic attitudes. In one issue, Near wrote:

I simply state a fact when I say that ninety per cent of the crimes committed against society in this city are committed by Jew gangsters. . . . It is Jew, Jew, Jew, as long as one cares to comb over the records. I am launching no attack against the Jewish people AS A RACE. I am merely calling attention to a FACT. And if people of that race and faith wish to rid themselves of the odium and stigma THE RODENTS OF THEIR OWN RACE HAVE BROUGHT UPON THEM, they need only to step to the front and help the decent citizens of Minneapolis rid the city of these criminal Jews.[2]

In a piece attacking establishment journalism, Near proclaimed: "Journalism today isn't prostituted so much as it is disgustingly flabby. I'd rather be a louse in the cotton shirt of a nigger than be a journal-

1. For an in-depth account of this case, see Fred W. Friendly, *Minnesota Rag* (New York: Random House, 1981).
    2. Ibid., 47.

istic prostitute."[3] Based on the paper's past record, a judge issued a temporary restraining order prohibiting the sale of printed and future editions of the paper.

Upset by this action, Near contacted the ACLU, which agreed to take his case. But he grew uncomfortable with the organization and instead obtained assistance from the publisher of the *Chicago Tribune.* Together, they challenged the Minnesota law as a violation of the First Amendment freedom of press guarantee, arguing that the law was tantamount to censorship. In their view, states could not issue gag orders to keep newspapers from publishing in the future; newspapers could be punished only after publication through libel or defamation proceedings. The state's attorney thought otherwise, arguing that freedom of the press does not give publishers an unrestricted right to print anything and everything, that they must act responsibly.

The only known photograph of *Saturday Press* editor Jay Near appeared April 19, 1936, in the Minneapolis *Tribune.* Near's successful appeal to the Supreme Court in 1931 marked the first time the Court enforced the First Amendment's guarantee of freedom of the press to strike a state law that imposed a prior restraint on a newspaper.

MR. CHIEF JUSTICE HUGHES delivered the opinion of the Court.

Chapter 285 of the Session Laws of Minnesota for the year 1925 provides for the abatement, as a public nuisance, of a "malicious, scandalous and defamatory newspaper, magazine, or other periodical."...

This statute, for the suppression as a public nuisance of a newspaper or periodical, is unusual, if not unique, and raises questions of grave importance transcending the local interests involved in the particular action. It is no longer open to doubt that the liberty of the press and of speech is within the liberty safeguarded by the due process clause of the Fourteenth Amendment from invasion by state action. It was found impossible to conclude that this essential personal liberty of the citizen was left unprotected by the general guaranty of fundamental rights of person and property. Gitlow v. New York, Whitney v. California, Fiske v. Kansas. In maintaining this guaranty, the authority of the state to enact laws to promote the health, safety, morals, and general welfare of its people is necessarily admitted. The limits of this sovereign power must always be deter-

mined with appropriate regard to the particular subject of its exercise. . . .

It is thus important to note precisely the purpose and effect of the statute as the state court has construed it.

First. The statute is not aimed at the redress of individual or private wrongs. Remedies for libel remain available and unaffected. . . . It is aimed at the distribution of scandalous matter as "detrimental to public morals and to the general welfare," tending "to disturb the peace of the community" and "to provoke assaults and the commission of crime." In order to obtain an injunction to suppress the future publication of the newspaper or periodical, it is not necessary to prove the falsity of the charges that have been made in the publication condemned. In the present action there was no allegation that the matter published was not true. It is alleged, and the statute requires the allegation that the publication was "malicious." But, as in prosecutions for libel, there is no requirement of proof by the state of malice in fact as distinguished from malice inferred from the mere publication of the defamatory matter. The judgment in this case proceeded upon the mere proof of publication. The statute permits the defense, not of the truth alone, but only that the truth was published with good motives and for justifiable ends. It is apparent that under the

3. Ibid., 43.

statute the publication is to be regarded as defamatory if it injures reputation, and that it is scandalous if it circulates charges of reprehensible conduct, whether criminal or otherwise, and the publication is thus deemed to invite public reprobation and to constitute a public scandal. . . .

Second. The statute is directed not simply at the circulation of scandalous and defamatory statements with regard to private citizens, but at the continued publication by newspapers and periodicals of charges against public officers of corruption, malfeasance in office, or serious neglect of duty. Such charges by their very nature create a public scandal. They are scandalous and defamatory within the meaning of the statute, which has its normal operation in relation to publications dealing prominently and chiefly with the alleged derelictions of public officers.

Third. The object of the statute is not punishment, in the ordinary sense, but suppression of the offending newspaper or periodical. The reason for the enactment, as the state court has said, is that prosecutions to enforce penal statutes for libel do not result in "efficient repression or suppression of the evils of scandal." Describing the business of publication as a public nuisance does not obscure the substance of the proceeding which the statute authorizes. It is the continued publication of scandalous and defamatory matter that constitutes the business and the declared nuisance. In the case of public officers, it is the reiteration of charges of official misconduct, and the fact that the newspaper or periodical is principally devoted to that purpose, that exposes it to suppression. . . .

This suppression is accomplished by enjoining publication, and that restraint is the object and effect of the statute.

Fourth. The statute not only operates to suppress the offending newspaper or periodical, but to put the publisher under an effective censorship. When a newspaper or periodical is found to be "malicious, scandalous and defamatory," and is suppressed as such, resumption of publication is punishable as a contempt of court by fine or imprisonment. Thus, where a newspaper or periodical has been suppressed because of the circulation of charges against public officers of official misconduct, it would seem to be clear that the renewal of the publication of such charges would constitute a contempt, and that the judgment would lay a permanent restraint upon the publisher, to escape which

he must satisfy the court as to the character of a new publication. Whether he would be permitted again to publish matter deemed to be derogatory to the same or other public officers would depend upon the court's ruling. . . .

If we cut through mere details of procedure, the operation and effect of the statute in substance is that public authorities may bring the owner or publisher of a newspaper or periodical before a judge upon a charge of conducting a business of publishing scandalous and defamatory matter—in particular that the matter consists of charges against public officers of official dereliction—and, unless the owner or publisher is able and disposed to bring competent evidence to satisfy the judge that the charges are true and are published with good motives and for justifiable ends, his newspaper or periodical is suppressed and further publication is made punishable as a contempt. This is of the essence of censorship.

The question is whether a statute authorizing such proceedings in restraint of publication is consistent with the conception of the liberty of the press as historically conceived and guaranteed. In determining the extent of the constitutional protection, it has been generally, if not universally, considered that it is the chief purpose of the guaranty to prevent previous restraints upon publication. The struggle in England, directed against the legislative power of the licenser, resulted in renunciation of the censorship of the press. The liberty deemed to be established was thus described by Blackstone: "The liberty of the press is indeed essential to the nature of a free state; but this consists in laying no *previous* restraints upon publications, and not in freedom from censure for criminal matter when published. Every freeman has an undoubted right to lay what sentiments he pleases before the public; to forbid this, is to destroy the freedom of the press; but if he publishes what is improper, mischievous or illegal, he must take the consequence of his own temerity." The distinction was early pointed out between the extent of the freedom with respect to censorship under our constitutional system and that enjoyed in England. Here, as Madison said, "the great and essential rights of the people are secured against legislative as well as against executive ambition. They are secured, not by laws paramount to prerogative, but by constitutions paramount to laws. This security of the freedom of the press requires that it should be exempt not only from previous restraint by the Executive, as in Great Britain, but from legislative restraint also.". . .

The criticism upon Blackstone's statement has not been because immunity from previous restraint upon publication has not been regarded as deserving of special emphasis, but chiefly because that immunity cannot be deemed to exhaust the conception of the liberty guaranteed by State and Federal Constitutions. The point of criticism has been "that the mere exemption from previous restraints cannot be all that is secured by the constitutional provisions," and that "the liberty of the press might be rendered a mockery and a delusion, and the phrase itself a by-word, if, while every man was at liberty to publish what he pleased, the public authorities might nevertheless punish him for harmless publications." But it is recognized that punishment for the abuse of the liberty accorded to the press is essential to the protection of the public, and that the common-law rules that subject the libeler to responsibility for the public offense, as well as for the private injury, are not abolished by the protection extended in our Constitutions. The law of criminal libel rests upon that secure foundation. There is also the conceded authority of courts to punish for contempt when publications directly tend to prevent the proper discharge of judicial functions. In the present case, we have no occasion to inquire as to the permissible scope of subsequent punishment. For whatever wrong the appellant has committed or may commit, by his publications, the state appropriately affords both public and private redress by its libel laws. As has been noted, the statute in question does not deal with punishments; it provides for no punishment, except in case of contempt for violation of the court's order, but for suppression and injunction—that is, for restraint upon publication.

The objection has also been made that the principle as to immunity from previous restraint is stated too broadly, if every such restraint is deemed to be prohibited. That is undoubtedly true; the protection even as to previous restraint is not absolutely unlimited. But the limitation has been recognized only in exceptional cases. "When a nation is at war many things that might be said in time of peace are such a hindrance to its effort that their utterance will not be endured so long as men fight and that no Court could regard

them as protected by any constitutional right." No one would question but that a government might prevent actual obstruction to its recruiting service or the publication of the sailing dates of transports or the number and location of troops. On similar grounds, the primary requirements of decency may be enforced against obscene publications. The security of the community life may be protected against incitements to acts of violence and the overthrow by force of orderly government. The constitutional guaranty of free speech does not "protect a man from an injunction against uttering words that may have all the effect of force." These limitations are not applicable here. Nor are we now concerned with questions as to the extent of authority to prevent publications in order to protect private rights according to the principles governing the exercise of the jurisdiction of courts of equity.

The exceptional nature of its limitations places in a strong light the general conception that liberty of the press, historically considered and taken up by the Federal Constitution, has meant, principally although not exclusively, immunity from previous restraints or censorship. The conception of the liberty of the press in this country had broadened with the exigencies of the colonial period and with the efforts to secure freedom from oppressive administration. That liberty was especially cherished for the immunity it afforded from previous restraint of the publication of censure of public officers and charges of official misconduct. . . .

The fact that for approximately one hundred and fifty years there has been almost an entire absence of attempts to impose previous restraints upon publications relating to the malfeasance of public officers is significant of the deepseated conviction that such restraints would violate constitutional right. Public officers, whose character and conduct remains open to debate and free discussion in the press, find their remedies for false accusations in actions under libel laws providing for redress and punishment, and not in proceedings to restrain the publication of newspapers and periodicals. The general principle that the constitutional guaranty of the liberty of the press gives immunity from previous restraints has been approved in many decisions under the provisions of state constitutions.

The importance of this immunity has not lessened.

While reckless assaults upon public men, and efforts to bring obloquy upon those who are endeavoring faithfully to discharge official duties, exert a baleful influence and deserve the severest condemnation in public opinion, it cannot be said that this abuse is greater, and it is believed to be less, than that which characterized the period in which our institutions took shape. Meanwhile, the administration of government has become more complex, the opportunities for malfeasance and corruption have multiplied, crime has grown to most serious proportions, and the danger of its protection by unfaithful officials and of the impairment of the fundamental security of life and property by criminal alliances and official neglect, emphasizes the primary need of a vigilant and courageous press, especially in great cities. The fact that the liberty of the press may be abused by miscreant purveyors of scandal does not make any the less necessary the immunity of the press from previous restraint in dealing with official misconduct. Subsequent punishment for such abuses as may exist is the appropriate remedy, consistent with constitutional privilege.

In attempted justification of the statute, it is said that it deals not with publication per se, but with the "business" of publishing defamation. If, however, the publisher has a constitutional right to publish, without previous restraint, an edition of his newspaper charging official derelictions, it cannot be denied that he may publish subsequent editions for the same purpose. He does not lose his right by exercising it. If his right exists, it may be exercised in publishing nine editions, as in this case, as well as in one edition. If previous restraint is permissible, it may be imposed at once; indeed, the wrong may be as serious in one publication as in several. Characterizing the publication as a business, and the business as a nuisance, does not permit an invasion of the constitutional immunity against restraint. Similarly, it does not matter that the newspaper or periodical is found to be "largely" or "chiefly" devoted to the publication of such derelictions. If the publisher has a right, without previous restraint, to publish them, his right cannot be deemed to be dependent upon his publishing something else, more or less, with the matter to which objection is made.

Nor can it be said that the constitutional freedom from previous restraint is lost because charges are made of derelictions which constitute crimes. With the multiplying pro-visions of penal codes, and of municipal charters and ordinances carrying penal sanctions, the conduct of public officers is very largely within the purview of criminal statutes. The freedom of the press from previous restraint has never been regarded as limited to such animadversions as lay outside the range of penal enactments. Historically, there is no such limitation; it is inconsistent with the reason which underlies the privilege, as the privilege so limited would be of slight value for the purposes for which it came to be established.

The statute in question cannot be justified by reason of the fact that the publisher is permitted to show, before injunction issues, that the matter published is true and is published with good motives and for justifiable ends. If such a statute, authorizing suppression and injunction on such a basis, is constitutionally valid, it would be equally permissible for the Legislature to provide that at any time the publisher of any newspaper could be brought before a court, or even an administrative officer (as the constitutional protection may not be regarded as resting on mere procedural details), and required to produce proof of the truth of his publication, or of what he intended to publish and of his motives, or stand enjoined. If this can be done, the Legislature may provide machinery for determining in the complete exercise of its discretion what are justifiable ends and restrain publication accordingly. And it would be but a step to a complete system of censorship. The recognition of authority to impose previous restraint upon publication in order to protect the community against the circulation of charges of misconduct, and especially of official misconduct, necessarily would carry with it the admission of the authority of the censor against which the constitutional barrier was erected. The preliminary freedom, by virtue of the very reason for its existence, does not depend, as this court has said, on proof of truth.

Equally unavailing is the insistence that the statute is designed to prevent the circulation of scandal which tends to disturb the public peace and to provoke assaults and the commission of crime. Charges of reprehensible conduct, and in particular of official malfeasance, unquestionably create a public scandal, but the theory of the constitutional guaranty is that even a more serious public evil would be caused by authority to prevent publication. . . . There is nothing new in the fact that charges of reprehensible conduct may create resentment and the disposition to resort to violent means of redress, but this well-understood tendency did not alter the determination to protect the press against censorship and restraint upon publication. As was said in New Yorker Staats-Zeitung v. Nolan, "If the township may prevent the circulation of a newspaper for no reason other than that some of its inhabitants may violently disagree with it, and resent its circulation by resorting to physical violence, there is no limit to what may be prohibited." The danger of violent reactions becomes greater with effective organization of defiant groups resenting exposure, and, if this consideration warranted legislative interference with the initial freedom of publication, the constitutional protection would be reduced to a mere form of words.

For these reasons we hold the statute, so far as it authorized the proceedings in this action under clause (b) of section 1, to be an infringement of the liberty of the press guaranteed by the Fourteenth Amendment. We should add that this decision rests upon the operation and effect of the statute, without regard to the question of the truth of the charges contained in the particular periodical. The fact that the public officers named in this case, and those associated with the charges of official dereliction, may be deemed to be impeccable, cannot affect the conclusion that the statute imposes an unconstitutional restraint upon publication.

Judgment reversed.

Chief Justice Hughes's opinion appears definitive. Note his words: "The statute not only seeks to suppress the offending newspaper . . . but to put the publisher under an effective censorship." While Hughes takes a strong position against prior censorship in *Near*, he acknowledges that the protection against "previous restraint is not absolutely unlimited." There may be exceptional circumstances under which government restraint is necessary. Hughes cites three vital interests that may justify the imposition of censorship by the government: protecting national security, regulating obscenity, and prohibiting expression that would incite acts of violence.

In *Near*, Hughes explains that the government may legitimately prohibit the publication of certain material in times of war that it might not constitutionally regulate in times of peace. For example, suppose that during World War II a major newspaper received advanced classified information about the Allied invasion of Normandy, and the editors announced that they would publish that information so the American people would be fully informed about the war effort. Military officials would understandably be concerned because publication would give the enemy advance knowledge of the military operation. Could the government take action to prohibit publication, or would it be confined only to pursuing criminal charges against the paper for illegal dissemination of classified documents after publication? According to *Near*, the courts would likely rule in favor of the government.

Fortunately, the United States has rarely faced a situation in which the press threatened to publish material that would seriously jeopardize vital national security interests. However, the national security issue has come before the justices. The most notable example is the case of *New York Times v. United States* (1971). In this case, the government attempted to stop the *New York Times* and the *Washington Post* from publishing classified documents pertaining to the Vietnam War.

The case began in June 1971, when the *New York Times* and the *Washington Post* began publishing articles based on two government documents: a 1965 Defense Department depiction of the Gulf of Tonkin incident and the 1968 "History of U.S. Decision-Making Process on Viet Nam Policy," a 7,000-page, forty-seven-volume study undertaken by the Pentagon. Known as the Pentagon Papers, the documents constituted a massive history of how the United States went to war in Indochina, a subject of acute interest in the early 1970s.

After the newspapers published several installments, the U.S. government brought action against them, asking a district court judge to restrain them from publishing any more. The government argued that the articles would cause "irreparable injury" to the country's national security. To support this assertion, the government said that the entire 1968 study was top secret, a classification "applied only to that information or material the defense aspect of which is paramount, and the unauthorized disclosure of which could result in *exceptionally grave* damage to the Nation." The newspapers disagreed; they argued that the material was largely of historical, not current, interest, and that nothing in the documents related "to a time period subsequent to early 1968." As such, the government's attempt to enjoin publication amounted to nothing less than prior restraint.

Because the issues in this case were so important and the public controversy so intense, the judicial system responded to the dispute in a very unusual manner. The government first requested that the district court prohibit publication on June 15, 1971. The lower courts handled the case in an expedited fashion, and only nine days later the issue was before the Supreme Court. By then the justices had completed their work for the term and were about to go into their summer recess. To accommodate the case, however, the justices extended their session and heard arguments on June 26. Only four days later, the Court announced its decision. Because of its hurried consideration of the dispute, the Court issued only a short per curiam (unsigned or collectively written) opinion announcing that the majority had voted to reject the government's demands. Then each of the justices submitted an opinion expressing his view. From start to finish, it took the federal judiciary only two weeks to decide this major constitutional dispute.

Six justices supported the claim of the newspapers, but they hardly agreed on the reasons for doing so. Justices Black and Douglas took the most extreme position. Consistent with their views that First Amendment protections are absolute, they argued that the censorship requested by the government was inappropriate. In Justice Black's words:

I believe that every moment's continuance of the injunctions against these newspapers amounts to a flagrant, indefensible, and continuing violation of the First Amendment. . . . Both the history and language of the First Amendment support the view that the press must be left free to publish news, whatever the source, without censorship, injunctions, or prior restraints.

Brennan and Marshall also strongly condemned the injunctions, but without completely foreclosing the possibility that under extreme circumstances such censorship might be allowable. The government simply had failed to show that it was necessary in this case. Brennan wrote: "[T]he First Amendment stands as an absolute bar to the imposition of judicial restraints in circumstances of the kind presented by these cases. . . . Unless and until the Government has clearly made out its case, the First Amendment commands that no injunction may issue."

White and Stewart took the most moderate position of those in the majority. They agreed that the injunctions should not be issued in Pentagon Papers cases, but only because the government had not proven that publication would "result in direct, immediate, and irreparable damage to our Nation or its people." Both expressed concerns about letting the executive branch intervene against the press in this way. They explained that they would have been more open to the action requested by the executive if Congress had passed legislation authorizing prior restraints in circumstances such as those presented by this case.

The three dissenting justices, Blackmun, Burger, and Harlan, stressed two major points. First, they condemned the speed with which the case was decided. The Court, in their view, had been unable to give careful consideration to the difficult issues raised because justices were rushed to arrive at a judgment. Second, they took the position that in matters of foreign policy the Constitution rested primary authority in the executive branch. Therefore, when the executive branch, for foreign policy reasons, claims that it is necessary to impose certain limits on the press, deference should be given to that position. The dissenters preferred to have the case sent back down to the lower courts for more lengthy study and with instructions that the courts should give considerable latitude to the executive branch when it is "operating within the field of its constitutional prerogative."

New York Times has generated a great deal of debate among legal scholars. Some suggest that it was the Court's, or at least individual justices', strongest statement to date on freedom of the press, that the justices virtually eradicated Hughes's national security exception to prior restraint. Others disagree. C. Herman Pritchett noted, "While the result in *New York Times* was clear enough, the Court's opinions do not add up to a sound defense of freedom of the press."[4] At the very least, the justices were divided in their views.

Since *New York Times* the Court has not had another important case dealing with prior restraints and national security concerns. But in 1991, during the war with Iraq, the U.S. government placed many constraints on the media. For example, most reports had to be cleared by a designated representative of the military. Although there were no serious legal challenges to these restrictions, if one had occurred, how do you think the Rehnquist Court would have ruled?

THE MEDIA AND SPECIAL RIGHTS

Challenging restraints on First Amendment rights is not the only battle the media have fought. For many years, the media asked courts for "special rights" not normally accorded average citizens, but which the press considered necessary to provide "full and robust" coverage of local, national, and world events. The most important of these special rights is known as the reporter's privilege, a special protection that prohibits the government from compelling reporters to supply information about their sources. While reading about the controversy surrounding this issue, ask yourself whether, in fact, the media should enjoy a special legal status.

As far back as 1840 reporters asserted the need for unusual legal privileges; that year, the Senate held a secret meeting to debate a proposed treaty to end the Mexican-American War. John Nugent, a reporter for the *New York Herald,* managed to obtain a copy of the proposed draft and mailed it to his editor. The Senate subpoenaed Nugent, and, when he refused to reveal his source of information, it held him in contempt. Nugent was later sent to prison for protecting his source.[5]

Although from time to time others faced the same fate as Nugent, during the 1960s and 1970s a marked increase occurred in the frequency of claims of reporter's privilege. Some credit this increase to the trial of the Chicago Seven, in which the government charged individuals with starting a riot in the streets outside of the Democratic party's 1968 convention. The United States served subpoenas on the major networks, newspapers, and magazines to obtain any information they had on the disturbances. Others suggest that it was the Nixon administration's disdain for the press that led to the increase, and still others argue that the rise in investigative reporting ushered in by Watergate led reporters to assert their right to protect sources absolutely and unconditionally.

Whatever the cause, the debate over reporter's privilege reached its climax in 1972, when the Supreme Court agreed to hear several cases involving such claims. The cases presented somewhat different issues, but the points of view were clear on both sides. The government asserted that reporters were entitled to no special rights or privileges; if ordinary citizens were forced to testify upon subpoena, then so should the media. The media responded that there were, in fact, certain privileged relationships. Doctors, for ex-

---

4. *Constitutional Civil Liberties* (Englewood Cliffs, N.J.: Prentice Hall, 1984), 65.

5. This paragraph and the next draw heavily on Mark Neubauer, "The Newsmen's Privilege after *Branzburg*," *UCLA Law Review* 24 (1976): 160–192.

ample, cannot be forced to reveal information about their patients. Reporters also argued that if they were forced to answer questions about their sources, those sources would dry up, a result that would have a chilling effect on their ability to do their jobs and would violate their free press guarantee.

Branzburg v. Hayes

408 U.S. 665 (1972)
Vote: 5 (Blackmun, Burger, Powell, Rehnquist, White)
    4 (Brennan, Douglas, Marshall, Stewart)
Opinion of the Court: White
Concurring opinion: Powell
Dissenting opinions: Douglas, Stewart

This case involved two articles written by Paul M. Branzburg, a reporter for the *Courier-Journal,* a Louisville, Kentucky, newspaper. In the first, he detailed his observations of two individuals, "synthesizing hashish from Marijuana, an activity which they asserted earned them about $5,000 in three weeks." The article contained this statement:

"I don't know why I am letting you do this story," [one of the individuals] said quietly. "To make the narcs mad, I guess. That's the main reason." However, [the two individuals] *asked for and received a promise that their names would be changed.* (Emphasis added.)

The second piece contained interviews Branzburg conducted with drug users in Frankfort, Kentucky. Branzburg was subpoenaed by a grand jury. He appeared but refused to answer the following questions:

1. Who was the person or persons you observed in possession of Marijuana, about which you wrote an article?
2. Who was the person or persons you observed compounding Marijuana, producing same to a compound known as hashish?

MR. JUSTICE WHITE delivered the opinion of the Court.

The issue in these cases is whether requiring newsmen to appear and testify before state or federal grand juries abridges the freedom of speech and press guaranteed by the First Amendment. We hold that it does not. . . .

Petitioner . . . Branzburg . . . press[es] First Amendment claims that may be simply put: that to gather news it is often necessary to agree either not to identify the source of information published or to publish only part of the facts revealed, or both; that if the reporter is nevertheless forced to reveal these confidences to a grand jury, the source so identified and other confidential sources of other reporters will be measurably deterred from furnishing publishable information, all to the detriment of the free flow of information protected by the First Amendment. Although the newsmen in these cases do not claim an absolute privilege against official interrogation in all circumstances, they assert that the reporter should not be forced either to appear or to testify before a grand jury or at trial until and unless sufficient grounds are shown for believing that the reporter possesses information relevant to a crime the grand jury is investigating, that the information the reporter has is unavailable from other sources, and that the need for the information is sufficiently compelling to override the claimed invasion of First Amendment interests occasioned by the disclosure. Principally relied upon are prior cases emphasizing the importance of the First Amendment guarantees to individual development and to our system of representative government, decisions requiring that official action with adverse impact on First Amendment rights be justified by a public interest that is "compelling" or "paramount," and those precedents establishing the principle that justifiable governmental goals may not be achieved by unduly broad means having an unnecessary impact on protected rights of speech, press, or association. The heart of the claim is that the burden on news gathering resulting from compelling reporters to disclose confidential information outweighs any public interest in obtaining the information.

We do not question the significance of free speech, press, or assembly to the country's welfare. Nor is it suggested that news gathering does not qualify for First

Amendment protection; without some protection for seeking out the news, freedom of the press could be eviscerated. But these cases involve no intrusions upon speech or assembly, no prior restraint or restriction on what the press may publish, and no express or implied command that the press publish what it prefers to withhold. No exaction or tax for the privilege of publishing, and no penalty, civil or criminal, related to the content of published material is at issue here. The use of confidential sources by the press is not forbidden or restricted; reporters remain free to seek news from any source by means within the law. No attempt is made to require the press to publish its sources of information or indiscriminately to disclose them on request.

The sole issue before us is the obligation of reporters to respond to grand jury subpoenas as other citizens do and to answer questions relevant to an investigation into the commission of crime. Citizens generally are not constitutionally immune from grand jury subpoenas; and neither the First Amendment nor any other constitutional provision protects the average citizen from disclosing to a grand jury information that he has received in confidence. The claim is, however, that reporters are exempt from these obligations because if forced to respond to subpoenas and identify their sources or disclose other confidences, their informants will refuse or be reluctant to furnish newsworthy information in the future. This asserted burden on news gathering is said to make compelled testimony from newsmen constitutionally suspect and to require a privileged position for them. . . .

The prevailing constitutional view of the newsman's privilege is very much rooted in the ancient role of the grand jury that has the dual function of determining if there is probable cause to believe that a crime has been committed and of protecting citizens against unfounded criminal prosecutions. Grand jury proceedings are constitutionally mandated for the institution of federal criminal prosecutions for capital or other serious crimes, and "its constitutional prerogatives are rooted in long centuries of Anglo-American history." . . . Although state systems of criminal procedure differ greatly among themselves, the grand jury is similarly guaranteed by many state constitutions and plays an important role in fair and effective law enforcement in the overwhelming majority of the States. Because its task is to inquire into the existence of possible criminal

conduct and to return only well-founded indictments, its investigative powers are necessarily broad. "It is a grand inquest, a body with powers of investigation and inquisition, the scope of whose inquiries is not to be limited narrowly by questions of propriety or forecasts of the probable result of the investigation, or by doubts whether any particular individual will be found properly subject to an accusation of crime." Hence the grand jury's authority to subpoena witnesses is not only historic but essential to its task. Although the powers of the grand jury are not unlimited and are subject to the supervision of a judge, the longstanding principle that "the public . . . has a right to every man's evidence," except for those persons protected by a constitutional, common-law, or statutory privilege, is particularly applicable to grand jury proceedings.

A number of States have provided newsmen a statutory privilege of varying breadth, but the majority have not done so, and none has been provided by federal statute. Until now the only testimonial privilege for unofficial witnesses that is rooted in the Federal Constitution is the Fifth Amendment privilege against compelled self-incrimination. We are asked to create another by interpreting the First Amendment to grant newsmen a testimonial privilege that other citizens do not enjoy. This we decline to do. Fair and effective law enforcement aimed at providing security for the person and property of the individual is a fundamental function of government, and the grand jury plays an important, constitutionally mandated role in this process. On the records now before us, we perceive no basis for holding that the public interest in law enforcement and in ensuring effective grand jury proceedings is insufficient to override the consequential, but uncertain, burden on news gathering that is said to result from insisting that reporters, like other citizens, respond to relevant questions put to them in the course of a valid grand jury investigation or criminal trial.

This conclusion itself involves no restraint on what newspapers may publish or on the type or quality of information reporters may seek to acquire, nor does it threaten the vast bulk of confidential relationships between reporters and their sources. Grand juries address themselves to the issues of whether crimes have been committed and who committed them. Only where news sources themselves are implicated in crime or possess information relevant to the grand jury's task need they or the reporter be concerned about grand jury subpoenas. Nothing before us indicates that a large number or percentage of *all* confidential news sources falls into either category and would in any way be deterred by our holding that the Constitution does not, as it never has, exempt the newsman from performing the citizen's normal duty of appearing and furnishing information relevant to the grand jury's task.

The preference for anonymity of those confidential informants involved in actual criminal conduct is presumably a product of their desire to escape criminal prosecution, and this preference, while understandable, is hardly deserving of constitutional protection. It would be frivolous to assert—and no one does in these cases—that the First Amendment, in the interest of securing news or otherwise, confers a license on either the reporter or his news sources to violate valid criminal laws. Although stealing documents or private wiretapping could provide newsworthy information, neither reporter nor source is immune from conviction for such conduct, whatever the impact on the flow of news. Neither is immune, on First Amendment grounds, from testifying against the other, before the grand jury or at a criminal trial. The Amendment does not reach so far as to override the interest of the public in ensuring that neither reporter nor source is invading the rights of other citizens through reprehensible conduct forbidden to all other persons. . . .

Thus, we cannot seriously entertain the notion that the First Amendment protects a newsman's agreement to conceal the criminal conduct of his source, or evidence thereof, on the theory that it is better to write about crime than to do something about it. Insofar as any reporter in these cases undertook not to reveal or testify about the crime he witnessed, his claim of privilege under the First Amendment presents no substantial question. The crimes of news sources are no less reprehensible and threatening to the public interest when witnessed by a reporter than when they are not. . . .

The argument that the flow of news will be diminished by compelling reporters to aid the grand jury in a criminal investigation is not irrational, nor are the records before us silent on the matter. But we remain unclear how often and to what extent informers are actually deterred from furnishing information when newsmen are forced to testify before a grand jury. The available data indicate that some newsmen rely a great deal on confidential sources and that some informants are particularly sensitive to the threat of exposure and may be silenced if it is held by this Court that, ordinarily, newsmen must testify pursuant to subpoenas, but the evidence fails to demonstrate that there would be a significant constriction of the flow of news to the public if this Court reaffirms the prior common-law and constitutional rule regarding the testimonial obligations of newsmen. Estimates of the inhibiting effect of such subpoenas on the willingness of informants to make disclosures to newsmen are widely divergent and to a great extent speculative. It would be difficult to canvass the views of the informants themselves: surveys of reporters on this topic are chiefly opinions of predicted informant behavior and must be viewed in the light of the professional self-interest of the interviewees. Reliance by the press on confidential informants does not mean that all such sources will in fact dry up because of the later possible appearance of the newsman before a grand jury. The reporter may never be called and if he objects to testifying, the prosecution may not insist. Also, the relationship of many informants to the press is a symbiotic one which is unlikely to be greatly inhibited by the threat of subpoena: quite often, such informants are members of a minority political or cultural group that relies heavily on the media to propagate its views, publicize its aims, and magnify its exposure to the public. Moreover, grand juries characteristically conduct secret proceedings, and law enforcement officers are themselves experienced in dealing with informers, and have their own methods for protecting them without interference with the effective administration of justice. There is little before us indicating that informants whose interest in avoiding exposure is that it may threaten job security, personal safety, or peace of mind, would in fact be in a worse position, or would think they would be, if they risked placing their trust in public officials as well as reporters. We doubt if the informer who prefers anonymity but is sincerely interested in furnishing evidence of crime will always or very often be deterred by the prospect of dealing with those public authorities characteristically charged with the duty to protect the public interest as well as his.

Accepting the fact, however, that an undetermined number of informants not themselves implicated in crime will nevertheless, for whatever reason, refuse to talk to newsmen if they fear identification by a reporter in an official investigation, we cannot accept the argument that the public interest in possible future news about crime from undisclosed, unverified sources must take precedence over the public interest in pursuing and prosecuting those crimes reported to the press by informants and in thus deterring the commission of such crimes in the future.

We note first that the privilege claimed is that of the reporter, not the informant, and that if the authorities independently identify the informant, neither his own reluctance to testify nor the objection of the newsman would shield him from grand jury inquiry, whatever the impact on the flow of news or on his future usefulness as a secret source of information. More important, it is obvious that agreements to conceal information relevant to commission of crime have very little to recommend them from the standpoint of public policy. . . . It is apparent . . . from our history and that of England, that concealment of crime and agreements to do so are not looked upon with favor. Such conduct deserves no encomium, and we decline now to afford it First Amendment protection by denigrating the duty of a citizen, whether reporter or informer, to respond to grand jury subpoena and answer relevant questions put to him.

Of course, the press has the right to abide by its agreement not to publish all the information it has, but the right to withhold news is not equivalent to a First Amendment exemption from the ordinary duty of all other citizens to furnish relevant information to a grand jury performing an important public function. Private restraints on the flow of information are not so favored by the First Amendment that they override all other public interests. . . .

We are admonished that refusal to provide a First Amendment reporter's privilege will undermine the freedom of the press to collect and disseminate news. But this is not the lesson history teaches us. As noted previously, the common law recognized no such privilege, and the constitutional argument was not even asserted until 1958. From the beginning of our country the press has operated without constitutional protection for press informants, and the press has flourished. The existing constitutional rules have not been a serious obstacle to either the development or retention of confidential news sources by the press.

It is said that currently press subpoenas have multiplied, that mutual distrust and tension between press and officialdom have increased, that reporting styles have changed, and that there is now more need for confidential sources, particularly where the press seeks news about minority cultural and political groups or dissident organizations suspicious of the law and public officials. These developments, even if true, are treacherous grounds for a far-reaching interpretation of the First Amendment fastening a nationwide rule on courts, grand juries, and prosecuting officials everywhere. The obligation to testify in response to grand jury subpoenas will not threaten these sources not involved with criminal conduct and without information relevant to grand jury investigations, and we cannot hold that the Constitution places the sources in these two categories either above the law or beyond its reach.

The argument for such a constitutional privilege rests heavily on those cases holding that the infringement of protected First Amendment rights must be no broader than necessary to achieve a permissible governmental purpose. We do not deal, however, with a governmental institution that has abused its proper function, as a legislative committee does when it "expose[s] for the sake of exposure." Nothing in the record indicates that these grand juries were "prob[ing] at will and without relation to existing need." Nor did the grand juries attempt to invade protected First Amendment rights by forcing wholesale disclosure of names and organizational affiliations for a purpose that was not germane to the determination of whether crime has been committed, and the characteristic secrecy of grand jury proceedings is a further protection against the undue invasion of such rights. The investigative power of the grand jury is necessarily broad if its public responsibility is to be adequately discharged. . . .

At the federal level, Congress has freedom to determine whether a statutory newsman's privilege is necessary and desirable and to fashion standards and rules as narrow or broad as deemed necessary to deal with the evil discerned and, equally important, to refashion those rules as experience from time to time may dictate. There is also merit in leaving state legislatures free, within First Amendment limits, to fashion their own standards in light of the conditions and problems with respect to the relations between law enforcement officials and press in their own areas. It goes without saying, of course, that we are powerless to bar state courts from responding in their own way and construing their own constitutions so as to recognize a newsman's privilege, either qualified or absolute.

In addition, there is much force in the pragmatic view that the press has at its disposal powerful mechanisms of communication and is far from helpless to protect itself from harassment or substantial harm. Furthermore, if what the newsman urged in these cases is true—that law enforcement cannot hope to gain and may suffer from subpoenaing newsmen before grand juries—prosecutors will be loath to risk so much for so little. Thus, at the federal level the Attorney General has already fashioned a set of rules for federal officials in connection with subpoenaing members of the press to testify before grand juries or at criminal trials. These rules are a major step in the direction the reporters herein desire to move. They may prove wholly sufficient to resolve the bulk of disagreements and controversies between press and federal officials.

Finally, as we have earlier indicated, news gathering is not without its First Amendment protections, and grand jury investigations if instituted or conducted other than in good faith, would pose wholly different issues for resolution under the First Amendment. Official harassment of the press undertaken not for the purposes of law enforcement but to disrupt a reporter's relationship with his news sources would have no justification. Grand juries are subject to judicial control and subpoenas to motions to quash. We do not expect courts will forget that grand juries must operate within the limits of the First Amendment as well as the Fifth.

The decision . . . in Branzburg v. Hayes . . . must be affirmed. Here, petitioner refused to answer questions that directly related to criminal conduct that he had observed and written about. The Kentucky Court of Appeals noted that marijuana is defined as a narcotic drug by statute and that unlicensed possession or compounding of it is a felony punishable by both fine and imprisonment. It held that petitioner "saw the commission of the statutory felonies of

unlawful possession of marijuana and the unlawful conversion of it into hashish.". . . [I]f what the petitioner wrote was true, he had direct information to provide the grand jury concerning the commission of serious crimes.

Affirmed.

In *Branzburg* the majority emphatically denied the existence of reporter's privilege. The dissenters were distraught; Justice Stewart, who had worked in his youth as a reporter for a Cincinnati newspaper and also edited the *Yale Daily News* while in college, wrote, "The Court's crabbed view of the First Amendment reflects a disturbing insensitivity to the critical role of an independent press in our society." The reaction of the media was even more vehement, with widespread condemnation of *Branzburg* and calls for federal and state statutes that would shield reporters when they felt they could not reveal their sources. As a result of this pressure, some twenty-six states (but not Congress) enacted reporter's privilege laws, which allowed reporters to refuse to divulge information about certain news-gathering activities. Pritchett noted that the laws are "not necessarily effective" because courts have ruled "that the law must yield when it conflicted with fair-trial" rights.[6] Moreover, such laws often limit protections to specific circumstances. Kentucky already had a shield law on the books at the time of Branzburg's grand jury proceedings. Unfortunately for the reporter, it covered only sources of information and not personal observation. Journalists still face the threat of imprisonment if they refuse to answer questions pertaining to their stories.

Immunity from testifying was not the only privilege for which reporters pressed. In *Zurcher v. Stanford Daily* (1978) they also asserted a need for special treatment under the Fourth Amendment. In April 1971 the *Stanford Daily*, a Stanford University student newspaper, published a special edition devoted to an incident

6. Pritchett, *Constitutional Civil Liberties*, 70.

at the university's hospital. A group of demonstrators had seized the hospital's administrative offices and barricaded the doors. When police forced their way in, a riot broke out, which resulted in injuries to the officers. They could not identify their assailants, but one claimed to have seen a photographer in the building. In fact, the *Daily* published several pictures of the incident, none of which fully revealed the identity of the demonstrators. But, because it was reasonable to think that the photographer had more pictures, the day after the special edition, police obtained a warrant to search the *Daily*'s office for the pictures. They found no pictures.

The *Daily* initiated a civil action against all those involved in issuing and executing the warrant. Its lawyers argued that the First Amendment forbade such searches: "Petitioners view this case as if only the Fourth Amendment is implemented. But the search of a newspaper must be judged by the more restrictive standards that apply where First and Fourteenth Amendment interests coalesce." The attorneys suggested that searches of newspapers were not necessarily unconstitutional, but that they should be based on a subpoena rather than a warrant. This distinction, in their view, would eliminate "police scrutiny [of] unrelated material, which may be highly confidential and sensitive, retained in the newspaper's files." The government responded that the warrant had been properly obtained and executed and that newspapers were undeserving of special Fourth Amendment protection.

Writing for a divided Court, Justice White agreed with the government. He relied on the intent of the Framers, noting that they "did not forbid warrants where the press was involved." He also suggested there was no reason to believe that those authorizing search warrants could not "guard against searches of the type, scope, and intrusiveness that would actually interfere with the timely publication of a newspaper." The Court dismissed the *Stanford Daily*'s claim, and

here the alignments were almost identical to those in *Branzburg*. White reiterated the *Branzburg* position that the press is not above the law; and Stewart forcefully reasserted his dissenting view: "It seems to me self-evident that police searches of newspapers burden the freedom of the press."

Several months after *Zurcher* the Court decided *Houchins v. KQED* (1978), which raised another issue involving the press. Of concern in *Houchins* was the right of reporters to have access to inmates in a county jail, which ordinarily would be denied to other individuals. Although this case is different from *Zurcher*, it poses a similar question: Should the justices accord the press rights and privileges beyond those enjoyed by average citizens?

A divided Court ruled that it should not. As Chief Justice Burger explained for the majority:

The media are not a substitute for or an adjunct of the government, and like the courts, are "ill equipped" to deal with the problems of prison administration. We must not confuse the role of the media with that of government; each has special, crucial functions, each complementing—and sometimes conflicting with—the other.

Burger said that the Court would be no more amenable to special access claims than it was to reporter's privilege; indeed, relying on past decisions such as *Branzburg*, Burger called the media's arguments flawed. He held that the First Amendment did not mandate "a right of access to government information or sources of information within the government's control." This was strong language, which could be understood to limit press access to a wide range of state and federal proceedings.

In cases following *Houchins*, however, the Court has not gone so far as Burger's words suggested. In *Richmond Newspapers v. Virginia* (1980), for example, it overruled a trial court judge who had denied the press access to a highly publicized murder trial. Burger wrote, "The right to attend criminal trials is implicit within the guarantees of the First Amendment," and, if such access were denied, "important aspects of freedom of speech and of the press could be eviscerated."

THE BOUNDARIES OF FREE PRESS: OBSCENITY AND LIBEL

The Supreme Court consistently has taught us that the First Amendment is not absolute. This lesson began in *Schenck v. United States,* (1919) where Holmes noted that the First Amendment would not protect a person who falsely yelled "fire" in a crowded theater. Periodically, other justices have reminded us of the limits of First Amendment protection as the Court has developed its freedom of expression doctrines.

First Amendment protection does not mean that people are shielded from government regulation of anything published or expressed verbally. Some varieties of expression are illegitimate and may be punished. Several examples immediately come to mind. One may not communicate military secrets to the enemy or make terrorist threats. One may not provide fraudulent information in commercial transactions or engage in discussions that amount to criminal conspiracies. One may not tell falsehoods under oath, or exchange "insider information" in securities transactions. In each of these cases the expression falls outside the boundaries of First Amendment protection.

In this section we explore the limits of First Amendment protection by examining two varieties of expression, obscenity and libel, that have presented the justices with perplexing freedom of the press questions. There is almost universal agreement that the Framers considered neither to be legitimate expression and did not intend the First Amendment to protect them from government regulation. Accepting this proposition, however, does not settle the matter: other questions remain. How do we define obscenity and libel? What distinguishes obscene and libelous expression from protected speech and press? What standards of evidence should be imposed? How can government regulate obscenity and libel without imposing a "chilling effect" on protected expression?

Obscenity

According to Justice Harlan, "The subject of obscenity has produced a variety of views among the members of the Court unmatched in any other course of constitutional interpretation."[7] Justice Brennan, the member of the Court most associated with the subject, was even more candid *(see Box 14-1)*. Discussing service on the Court, Brennan noted, "It takes a while before you can become even calm about approaching a job like this. Which is not to say you do not make mistakes. In my case, there has been the obscenity area."[8]

What is it about obscenity that has produced such extraordinary statements from these justices? After all, the Court uniformly has held that obscenity is not entitled to First Amendment protection. The problem is determining what makes a work obscene. In other words, how should we define the term? The answer is important because how we differentiate protected from unprotected expression has broad implications for what we see, read, and hear. Consider the movie industry: in the not-so-distant past, strict definitions of obscenity required an actor to keep one foot on the floor when performing a bedroom scene. Imagine the number of contemporary movies the courts would ban under such a standard! Today, the issues are no less important: groups throughout the country try to bar certain books from public schools, to prohibit the sale of particular records to minors, and to stop libraries from subscribing to certain magazines—all on obscenity grounds.

Given the task involved, one might think the Court has set definitive policy in this area, but nothing could be further from reality. For more than four decades the Court has grappled with the issue, particularly

7. *Interstate Circuit v. Dallas* (1968).
8. Nat Hentoff, "Profiles: The Constitutionalists," *New Yorker,* March 12, 1990, 54.

BOX 14-1   WILLIAM JOSEPH BRENNAN, JR. (1956–1990)

William J. Brennan, Jr., was born April 25, 1906, in Newark, New Jersey. He was the second of eight children of Irish parents who immigrated to the United States in 1890. Brennan displayed impressive academic abilities early in life. He was an outstanding student in high school, an honors student at the University of Pennsylvania's Wharton School of Finance, and in the top 10 percent of his Harvard Law School class in 1931.

Brennan married Marjorie Leonard, May 5, 1928, and they had two sons and one daughter. (Marjorie Brennan died in 1982, and Brennan married Mary Fowler, March 9, 1983.) After law school Brennan returned to Newark, where he joined a prominent law firm. Following passage of the Wagner Labor Act in 1935, Brennan began to specialize in labor law.

With the outbreak of World War II, Brennan entered the Army, serving as a manpower trouble-shooter on the staff of the undersecretary of war, Robert B. Patterson. At the conclusion of the war, Brennan returned to his old law firm. But as his practice swelled, Brennan, a dedicated family man, began to resent the demands it placed on his time.

A desire to temper the pace of his work was one of the reasons Brennan accepted an appointment to the newly created New Jersey Superior Court in 1949. Brennan had been a leader in the movement to establish the court as part of a large program of judicial reform. It came as no surprise when Republican governor Alfred E. Driscoll named Brennan, a registered but inactive Democrat, to the court.

During his tenure on the superior court, Brennan's use of pretrial procedures to speed up the disposition of cases brought him to the attention of New Jersey Supreme Court justice Arthur T. Vanderbilt. It was reportedly at Vanderbilt's suggestion that Brennan was moved first in 1950 to the appellate division of the superior court and then in 1952 to the state supreme court.

Late in 1956, when President Eisenhower was looking for a justice to replace Sherman Minton, Vanderbilt and others strongly recommended Brennan for the post, and Eisenhower gave him a recess appointment in October. There was some criticism that Eisenhower was currying favor with voters by nominating a Roman Catholic Democrat to the bench so close to the election, but Brennan's established integrity and nonpolitical background minimized the impact of the charges. He was confirmed by the Senate March 19, 1957. Brennan retired from the Court July 20, 1990.

SOURCE: Adapted from Elder Witt, *Guide to the U.S. Supreme Court,* 2d ed. (Washington, D.C.: Congressional Quarterly, 1990), 871.

---

with fashioning a definition of obscenity. Why has this issue caused such problems? Is there a reasonable solution? Or will the Court continue to flounder among competing schools of thought?

The adjudication of obscenity claims is a modern phenomenon. Before the 1950s the Court generally avoided the issue by adopting the British definition of obscenity. In *Regina v. Hicklin* (1868), which involved a pamphlet questioning the morals of Catholic priests, a British court promulgated the following test: "whether the tendency of the matter charged as obscenity is to deprave and corrupt those whose minds are open to such immoral influences and into whose hands a publication of this sort might fall."

Under this standard, commonly referred to as the *Hicklin* test, the British court found the pamphlet obscene. That it did so is not surprising: three aspects of the *Hicklin* test make it particularly difficult to overcome. First, the test targets "those whose minds are open to such immoral influences and into whose hands a publication of this sort might fall." Although this standard is vague, in practice, prosecutors often asked, "What if this material would fall into the hands of a child?" In other words, the *Hicklin* test used a stringent level of acceptability—whether the material could be seen by a child. Second, the *Hicklin* test did not require that the publication be considered as a whole. Instead, a work could be declared obscene based upon one of its parts. Third, the *Hicklin* test did not direct the courts to consider the social value of the work; rather, it only provided that impact of the offensive sections be examined. As a result, the *Hicklin* standard left a wide range of expression unprotected.

The U.S. Supreme Court not only adopted the standard; it also strengthened it. In *Ex parte Jackson* (1878) the Court upheld the Comstock Act, which made it a crime to send obscene materials, including information on abortion and birth control, through the U.S. mail. The justices applied the *Hicklin* test and extended its coverage to reproduction.

While the Supreme Court clung to *Hicklin,* some lower courts were attempting to liberalize it or even reject it. Among the examples cited most often is *United States v. One Book Called Ulysses* (1933) in which Judge Augustus Hand argued that the proper standard should be whether the author *intended* to produce obscenity. The promulgations of diverse rulings from the lower courts, coupled with the Supreme Court's silence on the issue, started to have an effect. By the 1950s the pornography business was flourishing in this country. "There was a steady increase in the volume and sale of obscene material,"[9] with little restriction on who could buy or view such material. This situation led to a backlash, with irate citizens clamoring for tighter controls. Others, particularly

the ACLU, pressured courts to move in precisely the opposite direction—to rule that the First Amendment covers all materials, including those previously adjudged obscene. By the late 1950s these interests, however diverse, were sending the same signal to the justices: the time had come to deal with the issue.

The Court responded in *Butler v. Michigan* (1957), an appeal challenging a state statute that defined obscenity along *Hicklin* test lines. Specifically, the law made it a crime to distribute material "found to have a potentially deleterious influence on youth." The justices struck down the statute, finding fault with the child standard. It is incompatible with the First Amendment, the justices said, to reduce the reading material available to adults to that which is fit for children. To do so, according to Justice Frankfurter's opinion, is "to burn the house to roast the pig."

The *Butler* decision mortally wounded the *Hicklin* test, but the justices failed to provide an alternative. Later that year, however, the Court took its first stab at creating a contemporary American obscenity standard. The case was *Roth v. United States* (1957). This appeal stemmed from charges that Samuel Roth had sent "obscene, indecent, and filthy matter" through the mail. At Roth's trial the judge instructed the jury with this definition of obscenity: the material

must be calculated to debauch the minds and morals of those into whose hands it may fall and that the test in each case is the effect of the book, picture or publication considered as a whole, not upon any particular class, but upon all those whom it is likely to reach. In other words, you determine its impact upon the average person in the community.

The jury found Roth guilty on four of the counts, and the judge sentenced him to the maximum punishment: five years in prison and a $5,000 fine. Roth challenged his conviction, arguing that the standard imposed was inconsistent with First Amendment freedoms.

Although they were badly divided, a majority of the justices in *Roth* supported a new standard articulated by Justice Brennan in his opinion of the Court.

9. Lucius J. Barker and Twiley W. Barker, Jr., *Freedom, Courts and Politics* (Englewood Cliffs, N.J.: Prentice Hall, 1965), 65.

Now known as the *Roth* test, Brennan's obscenity standard posed the following: "Whether to the average person applying contemporary community standards, the dominant theme of the material, taken as a whole, appeals to prurient interests."

At first glance, Brennan's opinion seems to forge a compromise between competing views. On one hand, he appeased "decency" advocates by rejecting the view that nothing is obscene; on the other, he set a new standard of obscenity that was far less restrictive than *Hicklin*. Yet this new *Roth* test was a significant departure from the *Hicklin* standard. First, *Roth* imposed an "average person" test, replacing *Hicklin*'s child standard with that of an adult. Second, the "contemporary community standards" criterion recognized the evolving nature of society's views of sexual morality. Third, the "dominant theme of the material taken as a whole" approach rejected *Hicklin*'s notion that a work can be declared obscene based on the content of a single part. And finally, the "prurient interests" element ensured that only material with sexual content would potentially fall under the obscenity rubric.

Although a majority of the Court supported Brennan's opinion, the Court remained divided over the proper way to handle the obscenity issue. In the following years, the Court confronted several appeals that provided opportunities for the justices to improve upon *Roth*. Attempts to replace *Roth* were unsuccessful. The justices simply could not agree on an acceptable substitute.

Although *Roth* survived, the justices did amplify and build upon its meaning. Perhaps the most significant of the post-*Roth* decisions were *Jacobellis v. Ohio* (1964) and *Memoirs v. Massachusetts* (1966). In *Jacobellis* the Court considered the appeal of Nico Jacobellis, the manager of a movie theater, who had been charged by Ohio authorities with showing an obscene film. Called *Les Amants* ("The Lovers"), the movie depicts the love affair of an archeologist and a woman who leaves her husband and child. *Les Amants* contains one "explicit love scene."

Brennan's opinion in *Jacobellis* is noteworthy for several reasons. First, Brennan refined his *Roth* test: he stated that contemporary community standards were those of the nation, not of a local community. In doing so, he not only held the film to be protected speech, but also substantially liberalized *Roth*. It is bound to be the case that communities seeking to ban obscenity have stricter standards than those of the country at large. Under Brennan's refinement, Tulsa, Oklahoma, would be bound by the same obscenity standards as New York City. Second, Brennan added a new provision to the *Roth* test. Not only must material meet all of the provisions of the test to be legally obscene, but it also must be found to be "utterly without redeeming social importance."

In *Memoirs v. Massachusetts* (1966) the Court further explained what was required under its new social importance standard. This case reviewed the attempts of Massachusetts to declare obscene John Cleland's *Memoirs of a Woman of Pleasure*. This book, popularly known as *Fanny Hill*, had been written in 1749. A concededly erotic novel, *Memoirs* traces the escapades of a London prostitute. The Massachusetts Supreme Court held that a book need not be "unqualifiedly worthless before it could be deemed obscene"; that is, just because *Memoirs* contained some nonerotic passages did not mean that it had redeeming value. Although divided, the U.S. Supreme Court disagreed. In his judgment for the Court, Brennan expanded the parameters of *Roth*. If a work had a "modicum of social value" it could not be adjudged obscene.

By 1966, then, a divided Court had substantially altered *Roth*, as shown in Box 14-2, which compares the test in 1957 to that articulated in 1966. Would anything be defined as obscene under the *Roth-Jacobellis-Memoirs* test? We might think that hard-core pornography would fall outside of it, but could not a clever movie maker, author, or publisher circumvent it? If a short passage of some merit appears in the middle of an erotic book or pornographic movie, does the product have redeeming value?

BOX 14-2 *ROTH, JACOBELLIS, AND MEMOIRS,* COMPARED

ROTH: "whether to the average person applying contemporary community standards, the dominant theme of the material, taken as a whole, appeals to prurient interests."

ROTH and *JACOBELLIS:* "whether to the average person applying" standards of "the society at large," the material is "utterly without redeeming social importance."

ROTH, JACOBELLIS, and *MEMOIRS:* "whether to the average person applying standards of the society at large, the material is utterly without redeeming social importance," possessing not "a modicum of social value."

The impact of these decisions was predictable. Expanded First Amendment protection prompted an explosion in sexually oriented materials. Adult movies, magazines, and books were more widely distributed than ever before. The reaction to these developments was also predictable. A backlash developed primarily among more conservative citizens who were not pleased with the increasing numbers of adult bookstores, theaters, and nightclubs, and were disturbed that sexually explicit materials had become so widely available.

In the election of 1968 Republican candidate Richard Nixon delivered a campaign message that was quite critical of the Supreme Court. His expressed discontent with the justices covered a wide array of decisions, but the Court's obscenity decisions were primary targets for his campaign rhetoric. He promised the voters that if he became president he would appoint justices to the Court who were more conservative in their orientation. When he took office he kept his promise. He had the opportunity to appoint four new justices to the Court, including a new chief justice,

Warren Burger. Nixon's appointments turned the Court in a more conservative direction, and observers knew that eventually the justices would reconsider the line of liberal obscenity rulings that had begun with *Roth.* The anticipated change became apparent on June 21, 1973, when the justices announced their decision in *Miller v. California.*

Miller v. California

413 U.S. 15 (1973)
Vote: 5 (Blackmun, Burger, Powell, Rehnquist, White)
    4 (Brennan, Douglas, Marshall, Stewart)
Opinion of the Court: Burger
Dissenting opinions: Douglas, Brennan

Marvin Miller, a vendor of so-called adult material, conducted a mass-mail campaign to drum up sales for his books. The pamphlets were fairly explicit: some contained pictures of "men and women in groups of two or more engaging in a variety of sexual activities, with genitals often prominently displayed."[10]

Had Miller sent the brochures to interested individuals only, he might not have been caught. But because he did a mass mailing, some pamphlets ended up in the hands of people who did not want them. Indeed, Miller's arrest came when the manager of a restaurant and his mother opened one of the envelopes and complained to the police.

MR. CHIEF JUSTICE BURGER delivered the opinion of the Court.

This is one of a group of "obscenity-pornography" cases being reviewed by the Court in a re-examination of standards enunciated in earlier cases involving what Mr. Justice Harlan called "the intractable obscenity problem.". . .

10. *Miller v. California* (1973).

This case involves the application of a State's criminal obscenity statute to a situation in which sexually explicit materials have been thrust by aggressive sales action upon unwilling recipients who had in no way indicated any desire to receive such materials. This Court has recognized that the States have a legitimate interest in prohibiting dissemination or exhibition of obscene material when the mode of dissemination carries with it a significant danger of offending the sensibilities of unwilling recipients or of exposure to juveniles. It is in this context that we are called on to define the standards which must be used to identify obscene material that a State may regulate without infringing on the First Amendment as applicable to the States through the Fourteenth Amendment.

The dissent of Mr. Justice BRENNAN reviews the background of the obscenity problem, but since the Court now undertakes to formulate standards more concrete than those in the past, it is useful for us to focus on two of the landmark cases in the somewhat tortured history of the Court's obscenity decisions. In Roth v. United States (1957) the Court sustained a conviction under a federal statute punishing the mailing of "obscene, lewd, lascivious or filthy . . ." materials. The key to that holding was the Court's rejection of the claim that obscene materials were protected by the First Amendment. Five Justices joined in the opinion stating:

"All ideas having even the slightest redeeming social importance—unorthodox ideas, controversial ideas, even ideas hateful to the prevailing climate of opinion—have the full protection of the [First Amendment] guaranties, unless excludable because they encroach upon the limited area of more important interests. But implicit in the history of the First Amendment is the rejection of obscenity as utterly without redeeming social importance. . . .

"'. . . There are certain well-defined and narrowly limited classes of speech, the prevention and punishment of which have never been thought to raise any Constitutional problem. *These include the lewd and obscene.* . . . It has been well observed that such utterances are no essential part of any exposition of ideas, and are of such slight social value as a step to truth that any benefit that may be derived from them is clearly outweighed by the social interest in order and morality. . . .'" [Emphasis by Court in *Roth* opinion.]

Nine years later, in Memoirs v. Massachusetts (1966), the Court veered sharply away from the *Roth* concept and, with only three Justices in the plurality opinion, articulated a new test of obscenity. The plurality held that under the *Roth* definition

"as elaborated in subsequent cases, three elements must coalesce: it must be established that (a) the dominant theme of the material taken as a whole appeals to a prurient interest in sex; (b) the material is patently offensive because it affronts contemporary community standards relating to the description or representation of sexual matters; and (c) the material is utterly without redeeming social value."

The sharpness of the break with *Roth*, represented by the third element of the *Memoirs* test,. . . was further underscored when the *Memoirs* plurality went on to state:

"The Supreme Judicial Court erred in holding that a book need not be 'unqualifiedly worthless before it can be deemed obscene.' A book cannot be proscribed unless it is found to be *utterly* without redeeming social value."

While *Roth* presumed "obscenity" to be "utterly without redeeming social importance," *Memoirs* required that to prove obscenity it must be affirmatively established that the material is "*utterly* without redeeming social value." Thus, even as they repeated the words of *Roth*, the *Memoirs* plurality produced a drastically altered test that called on the prosecution to prove a negative, *i.e.,* that the material was "*utterly* without redeeming social value"—a burden virtually impossible to discharge under our criminal standards of proof. Such considerations caused Mr. Justice Harlan to wonder if the "*utterly* without redeeming social value" test had any meaning at all.

Apart from the initial formulation in the *Roth* case, no majority of the Court has at any given time been able to agree on a standard to determine what constitutes obscene, pornographic material subject to regulation under the States' police power. We have seen "a variety of views among the members of the Court unmatched in any other course of constitutional adjudication." This is not remarkable, for in the area of freedom of speech and press the courts must always remain sensitive to any infringement on genuinely serious literary, artistic, political, or scientific expression. This is an area in which there are few eternal verities.

The case we now review was tried on the theory that the California Penal Code § 311 approximately incorporates the three-stage *Memoirs* test. But now the *Memoirs* test has been abandoned as unworkable by its author, and no Member of the Court today supports the *Memoirs* formulation.

This much has been categorically settled by the Court, that obscene material is unprotected by the First Amendment. We acknowledge, however, the inherent dangers of undertaking to regulate any form of expression. State statutes designed to regulate obscene materials must be carefully limited. As a result, we now confine the permissible scope of such regulation to works which depict or describe sexual conduct. That conduct must be specifically defined by the applicable state law, as written or authoritatively construed. A state offense must also be limited to works which, taken as a whole, appeal to the prurient interest in sex, which portray sexual conduct in a patently offensive way, and which, taken as a whole, do not have serious literary, artistic, political, or scientific value.

The basic guidelines for the trier of fact must be: (a) whether "the average person, applying contemporary community standards" would find that the work, taken as a whole, appeals to the prurient interest; (b) whether the work depicts or describes, in a patently offensive way, sexual conduct specifically defined by the applicable state law; and (c) whether the work, taken as a whole, lacks serious literary, artistic, political, or scientific value. We do not adopt as a constitutional standard the "*utterly* without redeeming social value" test of Memoirs v. Massachusetts; that concept has never commanded the adherence of more than three Justices at one time. If a state law that regulates obscene material is thus limited, as written or construed, the First Amendment values applicable to the States through the Fourteenth Amendment are adequately protected by the ultimate power of appellate courts to conduct an independent review of constitutional claims when necessary.

We emphasize that it is not our function to propose regulatory schemes for the States. That must await their concrete legislative efforts. It is possible, however, to give a few

plain examples of what a state statute could define for regulation under part (b) of the standard announced in this opinion.

(a) Patently offensive representations or descriptions of ultimate sexual acts, normal or perverted, actual or simulated.

(b) Patently offensive representation or descriptions of masturbation, excretory functions, and lewd exhibition of the genitals.

Sex and nudity may not be exploited without limit by films or pictures exhibited or sold in places of public accommodation any more than live sex and nudity can be exhibited or sold without limit in such public places. At a minimum, prurient, patently offensive depiction or description of sexual conduct must have serious literary, artistic, political, or scientific value to merit First Amendment protection. . . .

Under the holdings announced today, no one will be subject to prosecution for the sale or exposure of obscene materials unless these materials depict or describe patently offensive "hard core" sexual conduct specifically defined by the regulating state law, as written or construed. We are satisfied that these specific prerequisites will provide fair notice to a dealer in such materials that his public and commercial activities may bring prosecution. If the inability to define regulated materials with ultimate, god-like precision altogether removes the power of the States or the Congress to regulate, then "hard core" pornography may be exposed without limit to the juvenile, the passerby, and the consenting adult alike. . . .

It is certainly true that the absence, since *Roth,* of a single majority view of this Court as to proper standards for testing obscenity has placed a strain on both state and federal courts. But today, for the first time since *Roth* was decided in 1957, a majority of this Court has agreed on concrete guidelines to isolate "hard core" pornography from expression protected by the First Amendment. Now we . . . attempt to provide positive guidance to federal and state courts alike.

This may not be an easy road, free from difficulty. But no amount of "fatigue" should lead us to adopt a convenient "institutional" rationale—an absolutist, "anything goes" view of the First Amendment—because it will lighten our burdens. "Such an abnegation of judicial supervision in this field would be inconsistent with our duty to uphold the constitutional guarantees." Nor should we remedy "tension between state and federal courts" by arbitrarily depriving the States of a power reserved to them under the Constitution, a power which they have enjoyed and exercised continuously from before the adoption of the First Amendment to this day. "Our duty admits of no 'substitute for facing up to the tough individual problems of constitutional judgment involved in every obscenity case.'"

Under a National Constitution, fundamental First Amendment limitations on the powers of the States do not vary from community to community, but this does not mean that there are, or should or can be, fixed, uniform national standards of precisely what appeals to the "prurient interest" or is "patently offensive." These are essentially questions of fact, and our Nation is simply too big and too diverse for this Court to reasonably expect that such standards could be articulated for all 50 States in a single formulation, even assuming the prerequisite consensus exists. When triers of fact are asked to decide whether "the average person, applying contemporary community standards" would consider certain materials "prurient," it would be unrealistic to require that the answer be based on some abstract formulation. The adversary system, with lay jurors as the usual ultimate fact-finders in criminal prosecutions, has historically permitted triers of fact to draw on the standards of their community, guided always by limiting instructions on the law. To require a State to structure obscenity proceedings around evidence of a *national* "community standard" would be an exercise in futility.

As noted before, this case was tried on the theory that the California obscenity statute sought to incorporate the tripartite test of *Memoirs*. This, a "national" standard of First Amendment protection enumerated by a plurality of this Court, was correctly regarded at the time of trial as limiting state prosecution under the controlling case law. The jury, however, was explicitly instructed that, in determining whether the "dominant theme of the material as a whole . . . appeals to the prurient interest" and in determining whether the material "goes substantially beyond customary limits of candor and affronts contemporary community standards of decency," it was to apply "contemporary community standards of the State of California."

During the trial, both the prosecution and the defense

assumed that the relevant "community standards" in making the factual determination of obscenity were those of the State of California, not some hypothetical standard of the entire United States of America. Defense counsel at trial never objected to the testimony of the State's expert on community standards or to the instructions of the trial judge on "statewide" standards. On appeal to the Appellate Department, Superior Court of California, County of Orange, appellant for the first time contended that application of state, rather than national, standards violated the First and Fourteenth Amendments.

We conclude that neither the State's alleged failure to offer evidence of "national standards," nor the trial court's charge that the jury consider state community standards, were constitutional errors. Nothing in the First Amendment requires that a jury must consider hypothetical and unascertainable "national standards" when attempting to determine whether certain materials are obscene as a matter of fact. . . . It is neither realistic nor constitutionally sound to read the First Amendment as requiring that the people of Maine or Mississippi accept public depiction of conduct found tolerable in Las Vegas, or New York City. People in different States vary in their tastes and attitudes, and this diversity is not to be strangled by the absolutism of imposed uniformity. . . . We hold that the requirement that the jury evaluate the materials with reference to "contemporary standards of the State of California" serves this protective purpose and is constitutionally adequate.

The dissenting Justices sound the alarm of repression. But, in our view, to equate the free and robust exchange of ideas and political debate with commercial exploitation of obscene material demeans the grand conception of the First Amendment and its high purposes in the historic struggle for freedom. It is a "misuse of the great guarantees of free speech and free press. . . ." The First Amendment protects works which, taken as a whole, have serious literary, artistic, political, or scientific value, regardless of whether the government or a majority of the people approve of the ideas these works represent. . . . But the public portrayal of hardcore sexual conduct for its own sake, and for the ensuing commercial gain, is a different matter. . . .

In sum, we (a) reaffirm the *Roth* holding that obscene material is not protected by the First Amendment; (b) hold that such material can be regulated by the States, subject to

TABLE 14-1 *Roth* and *Miller,* Compared

	Warren Court	Burger Court
Relevant audience:	Average person	Average person
Scope of consideration:	Work taken as a whole	Work taken as a whole
Standard:	Sexual material found patently offensive by the national standards of society at large	Sexual conduct found patently offensive by contemporary community standards as specifically defined by applicable state law
Value of the work:	Utterly without redeeming social importance	Lacks serious literary, artistic, political, or scientific value

the specific safeguards enunciated above, without a showing that the material is "*utterly* without redeeming social value"; and (c) hold that obscenity is to be determined by applying "contemporary community standards," not "national standards.". . .

Vacated and remanded.

The same day, the Court also handed down a decision in *Paris Adult Theatre I v. Slaton,* which involved a 1970 complaint filed by Atlanta, Georgia, against the Paris Adult Theatre, asserting that the theater was showing obscene films. The trial court judge viewed two of the offending films, which depicted simulated fellatio, cunnilingus, and group sexual intercourse. The judge ruled in favor of the theater, mainly because the owners did not admit anyone under the age of twenty-one. After the Georgia Supreme Court reversed, the owners appealed to the U.S. Supreme Court. The justices, however, affirmed the ruling, refusing to extend the theater First Amendment protection, even though only consenting adults would be exposed to the films.

Some have suggested that *Miller* (and *Paris Adult Theatre I*) did not substantially alter *Roth,* but we see significant changes. In Table 14-1 we compare the *Roth* test (and its expansions) with the new *Miller* stan-

dard. Although the Court retained three important elements of the *Roth* test (the adult standard, the work taken as a whole, and the restriction of obscenity to sexually oriented materials), two major changes stand out. First, the *Miller* test specifically gives the states the authority to define what is obscene. The Court, therefore, emphasized local values rather than the national standard articulated in *Roth.* Second, the Court did away with the notion that a work merited protection as long as it did not meet the "utterly without redeeming social value" criterion. Instead, the justices held that to receive First Amendment protection, sexually oriented materials had to have serious literary, artistic, political, or scientific value. As a consequence, the new *Miller* test permitted much greater regulation of sexually explicit materials than the *Roth* standard had.

In addition to the significant change in obscenity law ushered in by *Miller* and its companion case, *Paris Adult Theatre I,* liberals from the Warren Court era also expressed a change in approach. Justice Brennan wrote in his dissenting opinion in *Paris Adult Theatre I:*

Our experience since *Roth* requires us not only to abandon the effort to pick out obscene materials on a case-by-case basis, but also to reconsider a fundamental postulate of *Roth:* that there exists a definable class of sexually oriented expression that may be totally suppressed by the Federal and State Governments. Assuming that such a class of expression does in fact exist, I am forced to conclude that the concept of "obscenity" cannot be defined with sufficient specificity and clarity to provide fair notice to persons who create and distribute sexually oriented materials, to prevent substantial erosion of protected speech as a byproduct of the attempt to suppress unprotected speech, and to avoid very costly institutional harms. Given these inevitable side effects of state efforts to suppress what is assumed to be *unprotected* speech, we must scrutinize with care the state interest that is asserted to justify the suppression. For in the absence of some very substantial interest in suppressing such speech, we can hardly condone the ill effects that seem to flow inevitably from the effort. . . .

In short, while I cannot say that the interests of the State—apart from the question of juveniles and unconsenting adults—are trivial or nonexistent, I am compelled to conclude that these interests cannot justify the substantial damage to constitutional rights and to this Nation's judicial machinery that inevitably results from state efforts to bar the distribution even of unprotected material to consenting adults. . . . I would hold, therefore, that at least in the absence of distribution to juveniles or obtrusive exposure to unconsenting adults, the First and Fourteenth Amendments prohibit the State and Federal Governments from attempting wholly to suppress sexually oriented materials on the basis of their allegedly "obscene" contents.

Brennan's opinion, joined by Justices Marshall and Stewart, is remarkable for three reasons. First, after almost two decades of leading the Court in attempts to define obscenity, the author of *Roth* decided finally that it could not be done. Second, the three liberals argued that efforts to regulate "obscene" material inevitably led to unacceptable restrictions on protected expression. Third, Brennan and the others concluded that, except for protecting juveniles and unconsenting adults, state and federal authorities should be banned from regulating sexually oriented expression altogether.

While it would be hard to imagine two more different positions than those taken by the majority and the dissenters in these obscenity cases, they are remarkably alike in one respect: both sides wanted to extricate the Court from the obscenity business. Brennan

and the other dissenters advocated an almost total end to government regulation of obscenity. The *Miller* majority wanted to put an end to federal obscenity cases by shifting authority to the states.

Since 1973, the *Miller* test has remained the authoritative definition of obscenity. The justices generally have refused to accept cases that have asked them to reconsider the definition of obscenity. The *Miller* majority successfully removed the Court from the obscenity area and allowed the state and local governments much more leeway in dealing with the problem.

Libel

On any given day in the United States, we can buy a newspaper or turn on the television and find information on the activities of public officials, well-known figures, and even private citizens who, for various reasons, have made news. Sometimes the reports imply criticism—for instance, a newspaper article about a public official accused of wrongdoing. In other cases, the reports are blatantly false. To see this phenomenon we need go no farther than a supermarket checkout and read the tabloid headlines about the doings of celebrities.

We know from our readings on prior restraint that government generally cannot censor material before it is published. But once a story containing falsehoods is published or broadcast, do the people who have been damaged by it have any recourse? Under U.S. law they do: they can bring a *libel* action against the offender. That is, if individuals believe that falsehoods contained in an article resulted in monetary losses or the defamation of their character, they can attempt to have a court hold the media responsible for their actions.[11] The reason is that, like obscenity, libelous statements remain outside of the reach of the First Amendment.[12]

The lack of First Amendment protection does not

11. Pritchett, *Constitutional Civil Liberties*, 99.
12. See *Chaplinsky v. New Hampshire* (1942).

mean that libel is a simple area of law. The Supreme Court has had a difficult time developing standards for the application of libel. Why? One reason is that before 1964 libel was an undeveloped area of law. Recall that in 1798, the Federalist Congress enacted the Sedition Act, which outlawed seditious libel—criticism of the government and of government officials. Under this act, the government could bring criminal charges against those who made "false, scandalous, and malicious" statements that brought the United States or its representatives into "contempt or disrepute." Because President Thomas Jefferson later pardoned all those who had been convicted under it, the Supreme Court never had an opportunity to rule on the law's constitutionality. For most of our nation's history, therefore, it was unclear whether seditious libel was protected or unprotected speech. Indeed, some scholars argued that the purpose of the First Amendment was to "abolish seditious libel," while others contended the contrary.[13]

What is clear, however, is that until 1964 states were free to determine their own standards for the more typical version of libel: civil actions brought by individuals against other individuals, for example, those running a newspaper. Some variation existed among state laws, but most allowed defamed individuals to seek two kinds of damages: compensatory, which provide money for actual financial loss (an individual loses his or her job because of the story), and punitive, which punish the offender. To collect compensatory damages, all the plaintiff generally had to demonstrate was that the story was false—truth is always a defense against claims of libel—and damaging.

These criteria might sound like simple standards for plaintiffs to meet. In fact, the simplicity further

compounded the Court's problems. Many newspapers, television stations, and other media argued that the traditional standard had a chilling effect on their First Amendment guarantee of a free press. They feared printing anything critical of government or public officials, in particular, because if the story contained even the smallest factual error, they could face a costly lawsuit. Therefore, they felt constrained in their reporting of news.

Until 1964 the Supreme Court ignored this complaint and allowed states to formulate their own libel laws. In the seminal case of *New York Times v. Sullivan*, however, the Court radically departed from this position. What standard did the Court articulate? How did it alter existing libel law?

<hr>

New York Times v. Sullivan

376 U.S. 254 (1964)
Vote: 9 (Black, Brennan, Clark, Douglas, Goldberg, Harlan, Stewart, Warren, White)

0

Opinion of the Court: Brennan
Concurring opinions: Black, Goldberg

The March 29, 1960, edition of the *New York Times* ran an advertisement to publicize the struggle for civil rights and to raise money for the cause. L. B. Sullivan, an elected commissioner of the City of Montgomery, Alabama, took offense at the ad. It did not mention his name, but it gave an account of a racial incident that had occurred in the city. The ad suggested that the police, of whom Sullivan was in charge, participated in some wrongdoing.

Sullivan brought a libel action against the paper, alleging that the ad contained falsehoods—which, in fact, it did. For example, the ad claimed that demonstrating students sang "My Country, 'Tis of Thee," when they actually sang the "Star-Spangled Banner," and so forth. In his charge to the jury, the judge said

13. See Zechariah Chafee, Jr., *Free Speech in the United States* (Cambridge, Mass.: Harvard University Press, 1941); and Leonard W. Levy, *Legacy of Suppression* (Cambridge, Mass.: Harvard University Press, 1960). See also Levy's revised and enlarged edition, *Emergence of a Free Press* (New York: Oxford University Press, 1985). See also Pritchett, *Constitutional Civil Liberties*, for an interesting review of these debates.

" The growing movement of peaceful mass demonstrations by Negroes is something new in the South, something understandable. . . . Let Congress heed their rising voices, for they will be heard."

—New York Times editorial
Saturday, March 19, 1960

Heed Their Rising Voices

As the whole world knows by now, thousands of Southern Negro students are engaged in widespread non-violent demonstrations in positive affirmation of the right to live in human dignity as guaranteed by the U.S. Constitution and the Bill of Rights. In their efforts to uphold these guarantees, they are being met by an unprecedented wave of terror by those who would deny and negate that document which the whole world looks upon as setting the pattern for modern freedom . . .

In Orangeburg, South Carolina, when 400 students peacefully sought to buy doughnuts and coffee at lunch counters in the business district, they were forcibly ejected, tear-gassed, soaked to the skin in freezing weather with fire hoses, arrested en masse and herded into an open barbed-wire stockade to stand for hours in bitter cold.

In Montgomery, Alabama, after students sang "My Country 'Tis of Thee" on the State Capitol steps, their leaders were expelled from school, and truckloads of police armed with shotguns and tear-gas ringed the Alabama State College Campus. When the entire student body protested to state authorities by refusing to re-register, their dining hall was padlocked in an attempt to starve them into submission.

In Tallahassee, Atlanta, Nashville, Savannah, Greensboro, Memphis, Richmond, Charlotte, and a host of other cities in the South, young American teenagers, in face of the entire weight of official state apparatus and police power, have boldly stepped forth as protagonists of democracy. Their courage and amazing restraint have inspired millions and given a new dignity to the cause of freedom.

Small wonder that the Southern violators of the Constitution fear this new, non-violent brand of freedom fighter . . . even as they fear the upswelling right-to-vote movement. Small wonder that they are determined to destroy the one man who, more than any other, symbolizes the new spirit now sweeping the South—the Rev. Dr. Martin Luther King, Jr., world-famous leader of the Montgomery Bus Protest. For it is his doctrine of non-violence which has inspired and guided the students in their widening wave of sit-ins; and it is this same Dr. King who founded and is president of the Southern Christian Leadership Conference—the organization which is spearheading the surging right-to-vote movement. Under Dr. King's direction the Leadership Conference conducts Student Workshops and Seminars in the philosophy and techniques of non-violent resistance.

Again and again the Southern violators have answered Dr. King's peaceful protests with intimidation and violence. They have bombed his home almost killing his wife and child. They have assaulted his person. They have arrested him seven times—for "speeding," "loitering" and similar "offenses." And now they have charged him with "perjury"—a felony under which they could imprison him for ten years. Obviously, their real purpose is to remove him physically as the leader to whom the students and millions of others—look for guidance and support, and thereby to intimidate all leaders who may rise in the South. Their strategy is to behead this affirmative movement, and thus to demoralize Negro Americans and weaken their will to struggle. The defense of Martin Luther King, spiritual leader of the student sit-in movement, clearly, therefore, is an integral part of the total struggle for freedom in the South.

Decent-minded Americans cannot help but applaud the creative daring of the students and the quiet heroism of Dr. King. But this is one of those moments in the stormy history of Freedom when men and women of good will must do more than applaud the rising-to-glory of others. The America whose good name hangs in the balance before a watchful world, the America whose heritage of Liberty these Southern Upholders of the Constitution are defending, is *our* America as well as theirs . . .

We must heed their rising voices—yes—but we must add our own.

We must extend ourselves above and beyond moral support and render the material help so urgently needed by those who are taking the risks, facing jail, and even death in a glorious re-affirmation of our Constitution and its Bill of Rights.

We urge you to join hands with our fellow Americans in the South by supporting, with your dollars, this combined appeal for all three needs—the defense of Martin Luther King—the support of the embattled students—and the struggle for the right-to-vote.

Stella Adler	Dr. Alan Knight Chalmers	Anthony Franciosa	John Killens	L. Joseph Overton	Maureen Stapleton
Raymond Pace Alexander	Richard Coe	Lorraine Hansbury	Eartha Kitt	Clarence Pickett	Frank Silvera
Harry Van Arsdale	Nat King Cole	Rev. Donald Harrington	Rabbi Edward Klein	Shad Polier	Hope Stevens
Harry Belafonte	Cheryl Crawford	Nat Hentoff	Hope Lange	Sidney Poitier	George Tabor
Julie Belafonte	Dorothy Dandridge	James Hicks	John Lewis	A. Philip Randolph	Rev. Gardner C.
Dr. Algernon Black	Ossie Davis	Mary Hinkson	Viveca Lindfors	John Raitt	Taylor
Marc Blitzstein	Sammy Davis, Jr.	Van Heflin	Carl Murphy	Elmer Rice	Norman Thomas
William Branch	Ruby Dee	Langston Hughes	Don Murray	Jackie Robinson	Kenneth Tynan
Marlon Brando	Dr. Philip Elliliott	Morris Iushewitz	John Murray	Mrs. Eleanor Roosevelt	Charles White
Mrs. Ralph Bunche	Dr. Harry Emerson	Mahalia Jackson	A. J. Muste	Bayard Rustin	Shelley Winters
Diahann Carroll	Fosdick	Mordecai Johnson	Frederick O'Neal	Robert Ryan	Max Youngstein

We in the south who are struggling daily for dignity and freedom warmly endorse this appeal

Rev. Ralph D. Abernathy *(Montgomery, Ala.)*	Rev. Matthew D. McCollom *(Orangeburg, S.C.)*	Rev. Walter L. Hamilton *(Norfolk, Va.)*	Rev. A. L. Davis *(New Orleans, La.)*
Rev. Fred L. Shuttlesworth *(Birmingham, Ala.)*	Rev. William Holmes Borders	I. S. Levy *(Columbia, S.C.)*	Mrs. Katie E. Whickham *(New Orleans, La.)*
Rev. Kelly Miller Smith *(Nashville, Tenn.)*	*(Atlanta, Ga.)*	Rev. Martin Luther King, Sr. *(Atlanta, Ga.)*	Rev. W. H. Hall *(Hattiesburg, Miss.)*
Rev. W. A. Dennis *(Chattanooga, Tenn.)*	Rev. Douglas Moore *(Durham, N.C.)*	Rev. Henry C. Bunton *(Memphis, Tenn.)*	Rev. J. E. Lowery *(Mobile, Ala.)*
Rev. C. K. Steele *(Tallahassee, Fla.)*	Rev. Wyatt Tee Walker *(Parkersburg, Va.)*	Rev. S. S. Seay, Sr. *(Montgomery, Ala.)*	Rev. T. J. Jemison *(Baton Rouge, La.)*
		Rev. Samuel W. Williams *(Atlanta, Ga.)*	

COMMITTEE TO DEFEND MARTIN LUTHER KING AND THE STRUGGLE FOR FREEDOM IN THE SOUTH

312 West 125th Street, New York 27, N.Y. UNiversity 6-1700

Chairmen: A. Philip Randolph, Dr. Gardner C. Taylor; *Chairmen of Cultural Division:* Harry Belafonte, Sidney Poitier; *Treasurer:* Nat King Cole; *Executive Director:* Bayard Rustin; *Chairmen of Church Division:* Father George B. Ford, Rev. Harry Emerson Fosdick, Rev. Thomas Kilgore, Jr., Rabbi Edward E. Klein; *Chairman of Labor Division:* Morris Iushewitz

Please mail this coupon TODAY!

Committee To Defend Martin Luther King
and
The Struggle For Freedom in The South
312 West 125th Street, New York 27, N.Y.
UNiversity 6-1700

I am enclosing my contribution of $_____
for the work of the Committee.

Name _____
Address _____
City _____ Zone _____ State ____

☐ I want to help   ☐ Please send further information

Please make checks payable to:
Committee to Defend Martin Luther King

that the ad was "libelous per se," meaning that because it contained lies, it was unprotected speech, and, that if the jury found that the statements were made "of and concerning" Sullivan, it could hold the *Times* liable. Taking these words to heart, the jury awarded Sullivan $500,000 in damages.

The Supreme Court of Alabama affirmed this judgment. In doing so, it specified that words are libelous per se when they "tend to injure a person labeled by them in his reputation, profession, trade or business, or charge him with an indictable offense, or tend to bring the individual into public contempt." This definition was fairly typical. The *New York Times* challenged the decision, arguing that the libel standard "presumes malice and falsity. . . . Such a rule of liability works an abridgment of the free press." The newspaper's attorneys added, "It is implicit in this Court's decisions that speech which is critical of governmental action may not be repressed upon the ground that it diminishes the reputation of those officers whose conduct it deplores."

MR. JUSTICE BRENNAN delivered the opinion of the Court.

We are required in this case to determine for the first time the extent to which the constitutional protections for speech and press limit a State's power to award damages in a libel action brought by a public official against critics of his official conduct. . . .

Because of the importance of the constitutional issues involved, we granted the separate petitions for certiorari of the individual petitioners and of the Times. We reverse the judgment. We hold that the rule of law applied by the Alabama courts is constitutionally deficient for failure to provide the safeguards for freedom of speech and of the press that are required by the First and Fourteenth Amendments in a libel action brought by a public official against critics of his official conduct. We further hold that under the proper safeguards the evidence presented in this case is constitutionally insufficient to support the judgment for respondent.

We may dispose at the outset of [t]he . . . contention . . .

that the constitutional guarantees of freedom of speech and of the press are inapplicable here, at least so far as the Times is concerned, because the allegedly libelous statements were published as part of a paid, "commercial" advertisement. . . .

The publication here was not a "commercial" advertisement in the sense in which the word was used in Chrestensen. It communicated information, expressed opinion, recited grievances, protested claimed abuses, and sought financial support on behalf of a movement whose existence and objectives are matters of the highest public interest and concern. That the Times was paid for publishing the advertisement is as immaterial in this connection as is the fact that newspapers and books are sold. Any other conclusion would discourage newspapers from carrying "editorial advertisements" of this type, and so might shut off an important outlet for the promulgation of information and ideas by persons who do not themselves have access to publishing facilities—who wish to exercise their freedom of speech even though they are not members of the press. The effect would be to shackle the First Amendment in its attempt to secure "the widest possible dissemination of information from diverse and antagonistic sources." To avoid placing such a handicap upon the freedoms of expression, we hold that if the allegedly libelous statements would otherwise be constitutionally protected from the present judgment, they do not forfeit that protection because they were published in the form of a paid advertisement.

Under Alabama law as applied in this case, a publication is "libelous per se" if the words "tend to injure a person . . . in his reputation" or to "bring [him] into public contempt"; the trial court stated that the standard was met if the words are such as to "injure him in his public office, or impute misconduct to him in his office, or want of official integrity, or want of fidelity to a public trust. . . ." The jury must find that the words were published "of and concerning" the plaintiff, but where the plaintiff is a public official his place in the governmental hierarchy is sufficient evidence to support a finding that his reputation has been affected by statements that reflect upon the agency of which he is in charge. Once "libel per se" has been established, the defendant has no defense as to stated facts unless he can persuade the jury that they were true in all their particulars. His privilege of "fair comment" for expressions of opinion depends on the truth of the facts upon which the comment is based. Unless he can discharge the burden of proving truth, general damages are presumed, and may be awarded without proof of pecuniary injury. A showing of actual malice is apparently a prerequisite to recovery of punitive damages, and the defendant may in any event forestall a punitive award by a retraction meeting the statutory requirements. Good motives and belief in truth do not negate an inference of malice, but are relevant only in mitigation of punitive damages if the jury chooses to accord them weight.

The question before us is whether this rule of liability, as applied to an action brought by a public official against critics of his official conduct, abridges the freedom of speech and of the press that is guaranteed by the First and Fourteenth Amendments.

Respondent relies heavily, as did the Alabama courts, on statements of this Court to the effect that the Constitution does not protect libelous publications. Those statements do not foreclose our inquiry here. None of the cases sustained the use of libel laws to impose sanctions upon expression critical of the official conduct of public officials. . . . In deciding the question now, we are compelled by neither precedent nor policy to give any more weight to the epithet "libel" than we have to other "mere labels" of state law. Like insurrection, contempt, advocacy of unlawful acts, breach of the peace, obscenity, solicitation of legal business, and the various other formulae for the repression of expression that have been challenged in this Court, libel can claim no talismanic immunity from constitutional limitations. It must be measured by standards that satisfy the First Amendment.

The general proposition that freedom of expression upon public questions is secured by the First Amendment has long been settled by our decisions. The constitutional safeguard, we have said, "was fashioned to assure unfettered interchange of ideas for the bringing about of political and social changes desired by the people." The First Amendment, said Judge Learned Hand, "presupposes that right conclusions are more likely to be gathered out of a multitude of tongues, than through any kind of authoritative selection. To many this is, and always will be, folly; but we have staked upon it our all." Mr. Justice Brandeis, in his concurring opinion in Whitney v. California, gave the principle its classic formulation:

"Those who won our independence believed . . . that public discussion is a political duty; and that this should be a fundamental principle of the American government. They recognized the risks to which all human institutions are subject. But they knew that order cannot be secured merely through fear of punishment for its infraction; that it is hazardous to discourage thought, hope and imagination; that fear breeds repression; that repression breeds hate; that hate menaces stable government; that the path of safety lies in the opportunity to discuss freely supposed grievances and proposed remedies; and that the fitting remedy for evil counsels is good ones. Believing in the power of reason as applied through public discussion, they eschewed silence coerced by law—the argument of force in its worst form. Recognizing the occasional tyrannies of governing majorities, they amended the Constitution so that free speech and assembly should be guaranteed."

Thus we consider this case against the background of a profound national commitment to the principle that debate on public issues should be uninhibited, robust, and wide-open, and that it may well include vehement, caustic, and sometimes unpleasantly sharp attacks on government and public officials. The present advertisement, as an expression of grievance and protest on one of the major public issues of our time, would seem clearly to qualify for the constitutional protection. The question is whether it forfeits that protection by the falsity of some of its factual statements and by its alleged defamation of respondent.

Authoritative interpretations of the First Amendment guarantees have consistently refused to recognize an exception for any test of truth—whether administered by judges, juries, or administrative officials—and especially one that puts the burden of proving truth on the speaker. The constitutional protection does not turn upon "the truth, popularity, or social utility of the ideas and beliefs which are offered.". . . That erroneous statement is inevitable in free debate, and that it must be protected if the freedoms of expression are to have the "breathing space" that they "need . . . to survive," was . . . recognized by the Court of Appeals for the District of Columbia Circuit in Sweeney v. Patterson. . . .

Injury to official reputation error affords no more warrant for repressing speech that would otherwise be free than does factual error. Where judicial officers are involved, this Court has held that concern for the dignity and reputation of the courts does not justify the punishment as criminal contempt of criticism of the judge or his decision. This is true even though the utterance contains "half-truths" and "misinformation." Such repression can be justified, if at all, only by a clear and present danger of the obstruction of justice. If judges are to be treated as "men of fortitude, able to thrive in a hardy climate," surely the same must be true of other government officials, such as elected city commissioners. Criticism of their official conduct does not lose its constitutional protection merely because it is effective criticism and hence diminishes their official reputations.

If neither factual error nor defamatory content suffices to remove the constitutional shield from criticism of official conduct, the combination of the two elements is no less inadequate. This is the lesson to be drawn from the great controversy over the Sedition Act of 1798, which first crystallized a national awareness of the central meaning of the First Amendment. That statute made it a crime, punishable by a $5,000 fine and five years in prison, "if any person shall write, print, utter or publish . . . any false, scandalous and malicious writing or writings against the government of the United States, or either House of the Congress . . . or the President . . ., with intent to defame . . . or to bring them, or either of them, into contempt or disrepute; or to excite against them, or either or any of them, the hatred of the good people of the United States.". . .

Although the Sedition Act was never tested in this Court, the attack upon its validity has carried the day in the court of history. Fines levied in its prosecution were repaid by Act of Congress on the ground that it was unconstitutional. Calhoun, reporting to the Senate on February 4, 1836, assumed that its invalidity was a matter "which no one now doubts." Jefferson, as President, pardoned those who had been convicted and sentenced under the Act and remitted their fines, stating: "I discharged every person under punishment or prosecution under the sedition law, because I considered, and now consider, that law to be a nulli-

ty, as absolute and as palpable as if Congress had ordered us to fall down and worship a golden image." [This view reflects] a broad consensus that the Act, because of the restraint it imposed upon criticism of government and public officials, was inconsistent with the First Amendment.

There is no force in respondent's argument that the constitutional limitations implicit in the history of the Sedition Act apply only to Congress and not to the States. It is true that the First Amendment was originally addressed only to action by the Federal Government, and that Jefferson, for one, while denying the power of Congress "to controul the freedom of the press," recognized such a power in the States. But this distinction was eliminated with the adoption of the Fourteenth Amendment and the application to the States of the First Amendment's restrictions.

What a State may not constitutionally bring about by means of a criminal statute is likewise beyond the reach of its civil law of libel. The fear of damage awards under a rule such as that invoked by the Alabama courts here may be markedly more inhibiting than the fear of prosecution under a criminal statute. Alabama, for example, has a criminal libel law which subjects to prosecution "any person who speaks, writes, or prints of and concerning another any accusation falsely and maliciously importing the commission by such person of a felony, or any other indictable offense involving moral turpitude," and which allows as punishment upon conviction a fine not exceeding $500 and a prison sentence of six months. Presumably a person charged with violation of this statute enjoys ordinary criminal-law safeguards such as the requirements of an indictment and of proof beyond a reasonable doubt. These safeguards are not available to the defendant in a civil action. The judgment awarded in this case—without the need for any proof of actual pecuniary loss—was one thousand times greater than the maximum fine provided by the Alabama criminal statute, and one hundred times greater than that provided by the Sedition Act. And since there is no double-jeopardy limitation applicable to civil lawsuits, this is not the only judgment that may be awarded against petitioners for the same publication. Whether or not a newspaper can survive a succession of such judgments, the pall of fear and timidity imposed upon those who would give voice to public criticism is an atmosphere in which the First Amendment freedoms cannot survive. Plainly the Alabama law of civil libel is "a form of regulation that creates hazards to protected freedoms markedly greater than those that attend reliance upon the criminal law."

The state rule of law is not saved by its allowance of the defense of truth. A defense for erroneous statements honestly made is no less essential here than was the requirement of proof of guilty knowledge which we held indispensable to a valid conviction of a bookseller for possessing obscene writings for sale. . . . A rule compelling the critic of official conduct to guarantee the truth of all his factual assertions—and to do so on pain of libel judgments virtually unlimited in amount—leads to a comparable "self-censorship." Allowance of the defense of truth, with the burden of proving it on the defendant, does not mean that only false speech will be deterred. Even courts accepting this defense as an adequate safeguard have recognized the difficulties of adducing legal proofs that the alleged libel was true in all its factual particulars. Under such a rule, would-be critics of official conduct may be deterred from voicing their criticism, even though it is believed to be true and even though it is in fact true, because of doubt whether it can be proved in court or fear of the expense of having to do so. They tend to make only statements which "steer far wider of the unlawful zone." The rule thus dampens the vigor and limits the variety of public debate. It is inconsistent with the First and Fourteenth Amendments.

The constitutional guarantees require, we think, a federal rule that prohibits a public official from recovering damages for a defamatory falsehood relating to his official conduct unless he proves that the statement was made with "actual malice"—that is, with knowledge that it was false or with reckless disregard of whether it was false or not. . . .

. . . [A] privilege for criticism of official conduct is appropriately analogous to the protection accorded a public official when *he* is sued for libel by a private citizen. . . . The reason for the official privilege is said to be that the threat of damage suits would otherwise "inhibit the fearless, vigorous, and effective administration of policies of government" and "dampen the ardor of all but the most resolute, or the most irresponsible, in the unflinching discharge of their duties." Analogous considerations support the privilege for the citizen-critic of government. It is as much his duty to criticize as it is the official's duty to administer. As Madison said, "the censorial power is in the people over the Government, and not in the Government over the people." It would give public servants an unjustified preference over the public they serve, if critics of official conduct did not have a fair equivalent of the immunity granted to the officials themselves.

We conclude that such a privilege is required by the First and Fourteenth Amendments.

We hold today that the Constitution delimits a State's power to award damages for libel in actions brought by public officials against critics of their official conduct. Since this is such an action, the rule requiring proof of actual malice is applicable. While Alabama law apparently requires proof of actual malice for an award of punitive damages, where general damages are concerned malice is "presumed." Such a presumption is inconsistent with the federal rule. . . . Since the trial judge did not instruct the jury to differentiate between general and punitive damages, it may be that the verdict was wholly an award of one or the other. But it is impossible to know, in view of the general verdict returned. Because of this uncertainty, the judgment must be reversed and the case remanded.

Since respondent may seek a new trial, we deem that considerations of effective judicial administration require us to review the evidence in the present record to determine whether it could constitutionally support a judgment for respondent. This Court's duty is not limited to the elaboration of constitutional principles; we must also in proper cases review the evidence to make certain that those principles have been constitutionally applied. This is such a case, particularly since the question is one of alleged trespass across "the line between speech unconditionally guaranteed and speech which may legitimately be regulated." In cases where that line must be drawn, the rule is that we "examine for ourselves the statements in issue and the circumstances under which they were made to see . . . whether they are of a character which the principles of the First Amendment, as adopted by the Due Process Clause of the Fourteenth Amendment, protect." We must "make an independent examination of the whole record," so as to assure ourselves that the judgment does not constitute a forbidden intrusion on the field of free expression.

Applying these standards, we consider that the proof presented to show actual malice lacks the convincing clarity which the constitutional standard demands, and hence that it would not constitutionally sustain the judgment for respondent under the proper rule of law. The case of the individual petitioners requires little discussion. Even assuming that they could constitutionally be found to have authorized the use of their names on the advertisement, there was no evidence whatever that they were aware of any erroneous statements or were in any way reckless in that regard. The judgment against them is thus without constitutional support.

As to the Times, we similarly conclude that the facts do not support a finding of actual malice. The statement by the Times' Secretary that . . . he thought the advertisement was "substantially correct," affords no constitutional warrant for the Alabama Supreme Court's conclusion that it was a "cavalier ignoring of the falsity of the advertisement from which, the jury could not have but been impressed with the bad faith of The Times, and its maliciousness inferable therefrom." The statement does not indicate malice at the time of the publication; even if the advertisement was not "substantially correct"—although respondent's own proofs tend to show that it was—that opinion was at least a reasonable one, and there was no evidence to impeach the witness' good faith in holding it. The Times' failure to retract upon respondent's demand, although it later retracted upon the demand of Governor Patterson, is likewise not adequate evidence of malice for constitutional purposes. Whether or not a failure to retract may ever constitute such evidence, there are two reasons why it does not here. *First,* the letter written by the Times reflected a reasonable doubt on its part as to whether the advertisement could reasonably be taken to refer to respondent at all. *Second,* it was not a final refusal, since it asked for an explanation on this point—a request that respondent chose to ignore. Nor does the retraction upon the demand of the Governor supply the necessary proof. It may be doubted that a failure to retract which is not itself evidence of malice can retroactively become such by virtue of a retraction subsequently made to another party. But in any event that did not happen here, since the explanation given by the Times' Secretary for the distinction drawn between respondent and the Governor was a reasonable one, the good faith of which was not impeached.

Finally, there is evidence that the Times published the advertisement without checking its accuracy against the news stories in the Times' own files. The mere presence of the stories in the files does not, of course, establish that the Times "knew" the advertisement was false, since the state of mind required for actual malice would have to be brought home to the persons in the Times' organization having responsibility for the publication of the advertisement. With respect to the failure of those persons to make the check, the record shows that they relied upon their knowledge of the good reputation of many of those whose names were listed as sponsors of the advertisement, and upon the letter from A. Philip Randolph, known to them as a responsible individual, certifying that the use of the names was authorized. There was testimony that the persons handling the advertisement saw nothing in it that would render it unacceptable under the Times' policy of rejecting advertisements containing "attacks of a personal character"; their failure to reject it on this ground was not unreasonable. We think the evidence against the Times supports at most a finding of negligence in failing to discover the misstatements, and is constitutionally insufficient to show the recklessness that is required for a finding of actual malice.

We also think the evidence was constitutionally defective in another respect: it was incapable of supporting the jury's finding that the allegedly libelous statements were made "of and concerning" respondent. Respondent relies on the words of the advertisement and the testimony of six witnesses to establish a connection between it and himself. . . . There was no reference to respondent in the advertisement, either by name or official position. A number of the allegedly libelous statements—the charges that the dining hall was padlocked and that Dr. King's home was bombed, his person assaulted, and a perjury prosecution instituted against him—did not even concern the police; despite the ingenuity of the arguments which would attach this significance to the word "They," it is plain that these statements could not reasonably be read as accusing respondent of personal involvement in the acts in question. The statements upon which respondent principally relies as referring to him are the two allegations that did concern the police or police functions: that "truckloads of police . . . ringed the Alabama State College Campus" after the demonstration on the State Capitol steps, and that Dr. King had been "arrested . . . seven times." These statements were false only in that the police had been "deployed near" the campus but had not actually "ringed" it and had not gone there in connection with the State Capitol demonstration, and in that Dr. King had been arrested only four times. The ruling that these discrepancies between what was true and what was asserted were sufficient to injure respondent's reputation may itself raise constitutional problems, but we need not consider them here. Although the statements may be taken as referring to the police, they did not on their face make even an oblique reference to respondent as an individual. Support for the asserted reference must, therefore, be sought in the testimony of respondent's witnesses. But none of them suggested any basis for the belief that respondent himself was attacked in the advertisement beyond the bare fact that he was in overall charge of the Police Department and thus bore official responsibility for police conduct; to the extent that some of the witnesses thought respondent to have been charged with ordering or approving the conduct or otherwise being personally involved in it, they based this notion not on any statements in the advertisement, and not on any evidence that he had in fact been so involved, but solely on the unsupported assumption that, because of his official position, he must have been. This reliance on the bare fact of respondent's official position was made explicit by the Supreme Court of Alabama. That court, in holding that the trial court "did not err in overruling the demurrer [of the Times] in the aspect that the libelous matter was not of and concerning the [plaintiff,]" based its ruling on the proposition that:

"We think it common knowledge that the average person knows that municipal agents, such as police and firemen, and others, are under the control and direction of the city governing body, and more particularly under the direction and control of a single commissioner. In measuring the performance or deficiencies of such groups, praise or criticism is usually attached to the official in complete control of the body."

This proposition has disquieting implications for criticism of governmental conduct. For good reason, "no court of last resort in this country has ever held, or even suggested, that prosecutions for libel on government have any place in the American system of jurisprudence." The pre-sent proposition would side-step this obstacle by transmuting criticism of government, however impersonal it may seem on its face, into personal criticism, and hence potential libel, of the officials of whom the government is composed. There is no legal alchemy by which a State may thus create the cause of action that would otherwise be denied for a publication which, as respondent himself said of the advertisement, "reflects not only on me but on the other Commissioners and the community." Raising as it does the possibility that a good-faith critic of government will be penalized for his criticism, the proposition relied on by the Alabama courts strikes at the very center of the constitutionally protected area of free expression. We hold that such a proposition may not constitutionally be utilized to establish that an otherwise impersonal attack on governmental operations was a libel of an official responsible for those operations. Since it was relied on exclusively here, and there was no other evidence to connect the statements with respondent, the evidence was constitutionally insufficient to support a finding that the statements referred to respondent.

The judgment of the Supreme Court of Alabama is reversed and the case is remanded to that court for further proceedings not inconsistent with this opinion.

Reversed and remanded.

Many consider Brennan's opinion a tour de force on the subject of libel. By holding the Sedition Act of 1798 unconstitutional, however belatedly, Brennan said that the First Amendment protects seditious libel, that the government cannot criminally punish individuals who speak out, in a true or false manner, against it. But more important was the part of the opinion that dealt with civil actions. The concurrers argued that the press had an absolute and unconditional right to criticize government officials, that states could not permit civil actions in such cases. Brennan and the majority did not go that far, but they radically altered the standards that *public officials* acting in a *public capacity* had to meet before they could prove libel and receive damages. Calling previous

L.B. Sullivan, second from right, poses with his attorneys after winning his libel suit against *The New York Times*. The Supreme Court overturned the decision in 1964. Justice Brennan's opinion stated that public officials are held to a higher standard than private citizens when proving libel.

rules of falsehood and defamation "constitutionally deficient," Brennan asserted that if plaintiffs were public officials, they had to demonstrate that the statement was false, damaging, *and* "made with 'actual malice'—that is, with knowledge that it was false or with reckless disregard of whether it was false or not." In his view, such an exacting standard—now called the *New York Times* test—was necessary because of a "profound national commitment to the principle that debate on public issues should be uninhibited, robust, and wide-open."

Brennan's opinion significantly altered the course of libel law, making it more difficult for public officials to bring actions against the media. But the decision had some gaps. First, who constitutes a public official? In note 23 Brennan wrote, "We have no occasion here to determine how far down into lower ranks of government employees the 'public official' designation would extend." Obviously, such an occasion would present itself shortly, and the Court would have to draw some distinctions. How it did so would

have significant ramifications because, under the *New York Times* test, only public officials had to prove actual malice; other plaintiffs were bound only to the traditional standards that the statements were false and damaging. Second, how could a public official prove actual malice? What did that term encompass?

In 1967 the Supreme Court decided two cases, *Curtis Publishing Company v. Butts* and *Associated Press v. Walker*, in hopes of clarifying its *New York Times* ruling. At issue in Curtis was an article entitled "The Story of a College Football Fix," published by the *Saturday Evening Post*. The author asserted that Wally Butts, the athletic director of the University of Georgia's sports program, had given Paul Bryant, the football coach at the University of Alabama, "the plays, defensive patterns, and all the significant secrets Georgia's football team possessed." He did so, according to the article, to fix a 1962 game between the two schools. The author claimed he had obtained this information from an Atlanta insurance salesman, who accidentally overheard the conversation between

Butts and Bryant. Butts initiated a libel suit against the publishing company, arguing that the article was false and damaging.[14] Further, although the Court had yet to hand down the *New York Times* decision, Butts's suit also alleged that actual malice had occurred because the *Saturday Evening Post* "had departed greatly from the standards of good investigation and reporting." The magazine's attorneys' "were aware of the progress" of the *New York Times* case, but offered only a defense of truth. A jury awarded Butts $3,060,000, which was later reduced by an appeals court. The *Post* asked for a new trial on *New York Times* grounds—that Butts was a public figure and should have to prove malice. The judge refused, asserting that Butts was not a public official and, even if he were, the magazine had demonstrated a "reckless disregard for the truth."

Associated Press v. Walker concerned a 1962 AP story, an eyewitness account of the riots at the University of Mississippi over the government-ordered admission of James Meredith, a black student. According to the story, retired army general Edwin Walker "took command of the violent crowd and . . . led a charge against federal marshals," who were in Mississippi to oversee the desegregation process. It also alleged that Walker gave the segregationists "lessons" on the use of tear gas. Walker sued the Associated Press for $2 million in compensatory and punitive damages, arguing that the article was false and damaging. The jury awarded $500,000 in compensation and $300,000 in punishment, but the judge set aside the latter on the ground that Walker, while not a public official, was a public figure—his views on integration were well known and, as such, he had to prove actual malice under the *New York Times* standard.

Writing for the Court, Justice Harlan ruled in favor of Butts's claim and against Walker's. In reaching

those conclusions, Harlan used the differences between the two cases to clarify *New York Times.* On one hand, he made it somewhat less burdensome for public officials to demonstrate malice: if the media engaged in "highly unreasonable conduct constituting an extreme departure from the standards of investigation and reporting," they could be held liable for their actions. On the other, the Court expanded the coverage of the *New York Times* test to include public figures. That is, even though Walker and Butts were not officials of the government, they would have to meet the *New York Times* test to win their suits because they were individuals in the public eye. Butts met this burden—he demonstrated that the magazine had abandoned professional standards and exhibited a reckless disregard for the truth. Walker failed to prove such press improprieties.

The result of these cases has been special protection given to the press from libel suits filed by public officials or public figures. Before such persons can win a libel case they must show that the press published or broadcast falsehoods and that such publication was done with actual malice. This allows the press greater latitude in covering public persons about whom the people have a legitimate interest.

Private individuals remained covered by traditional libel rules. A person who does not qualify as a public official or figure must only prove that the published statements were false. A showing of malice is not required. Drawing a line between public and private persons is not easy. The Court itself has had a difficult time doing so. In two cases, however, the justices helped draw the line between the two categories. In *Gertz v. Welch* (1974) the justices held that an attorney in private practice was not a public figure even though he represented a plaintiff in a controversial wrongful death suit. And in *Time, Inc. v. Firestone* (1976) the Court ruled that a prominent socialite involved in a scandalous divorce suit retained her status as a private person and had not become a public figure under the *New York Times* test approach to libel.

14. Up to this point, Butts had been a respected figure in coaching ranks and in fact had been negotiating for a coaching position with a professional team. After the *Saturday Evening Post* published the story, he resigned from the University of Georgia for "health" reasons.

In essence, the Court has taken a middle position. It has given the media a significant shield against libel actions when they are carrying out their historic mission of reporting news about public persons. Yet the Court has not imposed any additional burden on private individuals who are damaged by published falsehoods and turn to the judicial system for redress.

READINGS

Adler, Renata. *Reckless Disregard.* New York: Vintage Books, 1986.

Anderson, David A. "The Origins of the Press Clause." *UCLA Law Review* 30 (1983): 456–541.

Berger, Ronald. *Feminism and Pornography.* New York: Praeger, 1991.

Forer, Lois G. *A Chilling Effect.* New York: W. W. Norton, 1987.

Friendly, Fred. *Minnesota Rag.* New York: Random House, 1981.

Gillmor, Donald M. *Power, Publicity, and the Abuse of Libel Law.* New York: Oxford University Press, 1992.

Hopkins, W. Wat. *Actual Malice.* New York: Praeger, 1989.

Kane, Peter E. *Errors, Lies and Libel.* Carbondale: Southern Illinois University Press, 1992.

Kelly, Sean. *Access Denied: The Politics of Press Censorship.* Beverly Hills, Calif.: Sage Publications, 1978.

Kirby, James. *Fumble: Bear Bryant, Wally Butts and the Great College Football Scandal.* San Diego: Harcourt Brace Jovanovich, 1986.

Levy, Leonard W. *Emergence of a Free Press.* New York: Oxford University Press, 1985.

Lewis, Anthony. *Make No Law: The Sullivan Case and the First Amendment.* New York: Random House, 1991.

Neubauer, Mark. "The Newsmen's Privilege after *Branzburg.*" *UCLA Law Review* 24 (1976): 160–192.

Shapiro, Martin. *The Pentagon Papers and the Courts.* San Francisco: Chandler, 1972.

CHAPTER 15
THE RIGHT TO PRIVACY

L ET US SUPPOSE that the semester is drawing to a close, and final examinations are only a week away. Two roommates plan to spend the week studying in their dorm room. Assume that the roommates go to their room, place a Do Not Disturb sign on the door, and close the door. Can't they expect others to leave them alone and respect their privacy?

The answer seems obvious: of course. People have a right to be let alone. To many Americans, privacy is a basic and fundamental part of civil liberties and rights. But the issue is in fact very complicated, primarily because the Constitution makes no explicit mention of this right. The word *privacy* does not appear in the text of the charter or in the Bill of Rights. This omission has led to questions about the existence and nature of this presumed right, questions the Supreme Court has had difficulty answering.

First, do Americans have a constitutional right to privacy? If they do, where does this right originate? Justices of recent Courts have responded affirmatively to the first part of the query, but they have offered different answers to the second. As we shall see, some assert that the right emanates from several specific constitutional guarantees, most notably the following:

1. The First Amendment's right of association

2. The Third Amendment's prohibition against quartering soldiers

3. The Fourth Amendment's Search and Seizure Clause

4. The Fifth Amendment guarantees against self-incrimination

5. The Ninth Amendment

Other justices argue that they need look only at the Ninth Amendment, which says that the "enumeration . . . of certain rights shall not be construed to deny or disparage others retained by the people." Finally, some find that the Fourteenth Amendment's Due Process Clause prohibits government intrusion in ways that infringe upon liberties of citizens.

Second, to what areas does the right extend? Many Americans today equate the right to privacy with reproductive freedom; in fact, the Court has used privacy as a basis for legalizing birth control and abortion. But consider a twist on our opening scenario. Suppose the two roommates, in the privacy of their room, decide to use some cocaine. If possession of this substance is illegal, does someone have the right to use it—engage in criminal activity—in the privacy of his or her home? Or does the government have the right to invade that privacy? In short, where do we draw the line? To what extent should the state limit the right to privacy so that it may act in the best interests of its citizens?

In the end, we are left with many questions concerning the amorphous right to privacy. But, while reading this chapter, also consider these. Have approaches to privacy and those rights encompassed in privacy, such as abortion, changed substantially over the years? If so, why? Do alterations in the membership of the Court generate changes in the reach of the right to privacy? Or has the Court succumbed to pressure from the larger political environment?

THE RIGHT TO PRIVACY: FOUNDATIONS

In today's legal and political context, the right to privacy has become more or less synonymous with reproductive freedom, particularly abortion. The reason may be that the case in which the Court articulated a constitutional right to privacy, *Griswold v. Connecticut* (1965), involved birth control, and a decision that depended on *Griswold, Roe v. Wade* (1973), legalized abortion.

Prior to these decisions, however, members of the Court had contemplated privacy in somewhat different contexts. Following the common law dictates that "a man's home is his castle" and all "have the right to be left alone," future Supreme Court justice Louis Brandeis co-authored an 1890 *Harvard Law Review* article, asserting that privacy rights should be applied to civil law cases of libel.[1] The influence of the article was enormous. As one scholar wrote, "Out of a few fragments of common law, [they] invented a brand new tort, the invasion of privacy...[doing] nothing less than [to] add a chapter to the law."[2]

---

1. Louis Brandeis and Samuel Warren, "The Right of Privacy," *Harvard Law Review* 4 (1890): 193. William L. Prosser notes that they wrote this piece in response to the yellow journalism of the day. See "Privacy," *California Law Review* 48 (1960): 383–423.

2. M. Glenn Abernathy, *Civil Liberties Under the Constitution*, 4th ed. (Columbia: University of South Carolina Press, 1985), 578.

After Brandeis ascended to the bench, he continued his quest to see a right to privacy etched into law. Among his most famous attempts was a dissent in *Olmstead v. United States* (1928), which involved the ability of federal agents to place wiretaps on telephones without warrants. The majority of the justices ruled that neither the Fifth Amendment's protection against self-incrimination nor the Fourth Amendment's search and seizure provision protected individuals against wiretaps. Brandeis, however, thought that the Fourth and Fifth Amendments prohibited such activity. He noted:

The makers of our Constitution undertook to secure conditions favorable to the pursuit of happiness. They recognized the significance of man's spiritual nature, of his feelings and of his intellect. They knew that only a part of the pain, pleasure and satisfactions of life are to be found in material things. They sought to protect Americans in their beliefs, their thoughts, their emotions and their sensations. They conferred, as against the Government, the right to be let alone—the most comprehensive of rights and the right most valued by civilized men. To protect that right, every unjustifiable intrusion by the Government upon the privacy of the individual, whatever the means employed, must be deemed a violation of the Fourth Amendment. And the use, as evidence in a criminal proceeding, of facts ascertained by such intrusion must be deemed a violation of the Fifth.

However persuasive Brandeis's logic might appear, it stood for nearly thirty years as the only serious mention of a right to privacy. Court after Court ignored his dissent in *Olmstead*. However, Courts of earlier eras did pay attention to a concept that would later become associated with privacy—the concept of liberty. The word *liberty* appears in the Due Process Clauses of the Fifth and Fourteenth Amendments. The Fifth Amendment states that Congress shall not deprive any person of "life, liberty, or property, without due process of law," while the Fourteenth Amendment uses the same wording to apply to the states. In the early 1900s, the Supreme Court created a doctrine, called substantive due process, to guide its interpretation of some government policies challenged as violations of the guarantees contained in the Due Process Clauses. *(See Chapter 10 for more details.)*

Under the doctrine of substantive due process, the Court stressed the word *liberty* in the Due Process Clauses to prevent governments from enacting certain kinds of laws, particularly those that regulated business practices. *Lochner v. New York* (1905) illustrates the point. In this case, the Court reviewed an 1897 New York law that prohibited employees of bakeries from working more than ten hours per day and sixty hours per week. Joseph Lochner, the owner of a New York bakery who was convicted of violating the law, challenged it on Fourteenth Amendment due process grounds. He argued that the Due Process Clause gives employers and employees the liberty to enter into contracts specifying the number of hours employees could work. By interfering with that contractual arrangement with no valid reason, the New York law, in his view, violated this guarantee. The justices agreed. They struck down the law on the ground that it was a "meddlesome" and "unreasonable interference with an employer's right of contract protected in the liberty guarantee of the 14th Amendment."[3] *(An excerpt of* Lochner *appears on pages 322–327.)*

The Court also applied the doctrine of substantive due process to regulations outside of business. In *Meyer v. Nebraska* (1923) the justices considered a state law, enacted after World War I, that forbade schools to teach German and other foreign languages to students below the eighth grade. They invoked a substantive due process approach to strike down the law, reasoning that the word *liberty* in the Fourteenth Amendment protects more than the right to enter into contracts. It also covers

the right of the individual . . . to engage in any of the common occupations of life, to acquire useful knowledge, to marry, establish a home and bring up children, to worship God according to the dictates of his own conscience, and generally to enjoy those privileges long recognized at common law as essential to the orderly pursuit of happiness by free men.

According to the Court, government cannot interfere with these liberties, "under the guise of protecting the public interest, by legislative action which is arbitrary or without reasonable relation to some purpose within the competency of the State to that effect." *Meyer* and *Lochner* provide examples of substantive due process in action: under this approach, the Court is free to strike down legislation that interferes with liberty unless governments can demonstrate that they are seeking to achieve an end that is not "arbitrary," "capricious," or "unreasonable." To some analysts, this doctrine was the epitome of judicial activism because it allowed the Court to function "as a self-appointed czar over social and economic legislation."[4]

Through the 1930s the Court used the doctrine of substantive due process to strike down many laws, particularly those—as in *Lochner*—that sought to regulate businesses. The justices subscribed to the principle of laissez faire; they believed that the government should not interfere with the business of business. During the New Deal, however, substantive due process fell into disrepute because the public demanded that the government attempt to straighten out the economy. As a result, the Court changed its approach: states would be "free to adopt whatever economic policy" they wanted so long as it "may reasonably be deemed to promote public welfare."[5] If an economic policy was related to a legitimate government interest, the Court would not strike it down. This reasoning is called the *rational basis* approach to the Fourteenth Amendment. It differs significantly from substantive due process because, under it, courts generally defer to governments and presume the validity of their policies.

---

3. See Louis Fisher and Neal Devins, *Political Dynamics of Constitutional Law* (St. Paul: West, 1992), 199.

4. Ibid.
5. *Nebbia v. New York* (1934).

Application of the rational basis test led the Court to uphold legislation such as maximum hour and minimum wage laws, which it had previously struck down on liberty grounds, even if the laws did not necessarily seem reasonable to the justices. In one case, in fact, the justices characterized a particular state's economic policy as "needless" and "wasteful." They upheld the law anyway, proclaiming that "[t]he day is gone when this Court uses the Due Process Clause of the Fourteenth Amendment to strike down state laws, regulatory of business and industrial conditions, because they may be unwise, improvident, or out of harmony with a particular school of thought."[6] The majority added that if the people did not like the legislation their governments passed they should "resort to the polls, not to the courts." With this declaration, the Court seemed to strike the death knell for substantive due process. It would no longer substitute its "social and economic beliefs for the judgment of legislative bodies, who are elected to pass laws."[7]

What, then, does the discredited doctrine of substantive due process have to do with the right to privacy? It was Justice Harlan who tied these two concepts together. Neither an activist nor a liberal, he took great offense at the Court's handling of a 1961 case, *Poe v. Ullman*. At issue in *Poe* was the constitutionality of an 1879 Connecticut law prohibiting the use of any method of birth control, even by married couples. A physician challenged the act on behalf of two women who wanted to use contraceptives for health reasons.

The majority of the Court voted to dismiss the case on procedural grounds.[8] Several other justices disagreed with the Court, but Harlan's dissent was memorable. He argued that the Fourteenth Amendment's Due Process Clause could be used to strike the law:

I consider that this Connecticut legislation . . . violates the Fourteenth Amendment. . . . [It] involves what, by common understanding throughout the English-speaking world, must be granted to be the fundamental aspect of "liberty," the privacy of the home in its most basic sense, and it is this which requires that the statute be subjected to "strict scrutiny."

In making this claim, Harlan sought to demonstrate that the concepts of liberty and privacy were constitutionally bound together, that the word *liberty*, as used in the Due Process Clauses, "embraced" a right to privacy. And, because that right was fundamental, laws that touched on liberty/privacy interests, such as the one at issue in *Poe*, must be subjected to "strict scrutiny," meaning that the Court should presume that laws infringing on liberty/privacy were unconstitutional unless the state could show that the policies were the least restrictive means to accomplish a *compelling* interest.

Harlan's opinion was extraordinary in two ways.[9] First, some scholars have pointed out that it resurrected the long-dead (and discredited) doctrine of substantive due process, which the Court had buried in the 1930s. Now Harlan wanted to reinject some substance into the word *liberty*, but with a twist. Rather than protecting economic rights, in his view, due process protects fundamental rights, those the Court believes to be important in the concept of ordered liberty.

It is one of these fundamental liberties—privacy—that provides the second novel aspect of Harlan's opinion. As we have indicated, he was not writing on a blank slate; Brandeis had written about a right to privacy in the contexts of libel and search and seizure.

---

6. The case was *Williamson v. Lee Optical Company* (1955). The law at issue prohibited persons other than ophthalmologists and optometrists from fitting, adjusting, adapting, or applying lenses and frames.

7. *Ferguson v. Skrupa* (1963).

8. For an interesting account of this case, see Bernard Schwartz, *Super Chief* (New York: New York University Press, 1983), 378–379.

9. As was Douglas's, which read: "Though I believe that 'due process' as used in the Fourteenth Amendment includes all of the first eight Amendments, I do not think it is restricted . . . to them. The right 'to marry, establish a home and bring up children' was said in *Meyer v. State of Nebraska*, to come within the 'liberty' of the person protected by the Due Process Clause of the Fourteenth Amendment . . . 'liberty' within the purview of the Fifth Amendment includes the right of 'privacy'. . . . This notion of privacy is not drawn from the blue. It emanates from the totality of the constitutional scheme under which we live."

In fact, Harlan cited—with approval—Brandeis's dissent in *Olmstead*. Still, Harlan's application of the doctrine to marital sexual relations was bold. As he (and Justice Douglas) wrote, "it is difficult to imagine what is more private or more intimate than a husband and wife's relations."

Harlan and Douglas's assertion of a constitutional right to privacy proved too much, too soon for the Court; the majority was not yet willing to adopt it. But just four years later in *Griswold v. Connecticut*, a dramatic change took place. Why did the justices suddenly alter their views? More important is what the Court said about the right to privacy: the majority agreed that it existed, but disagreed over where it resided in the Constitution.

Estelle Griswold opened a birth control clinic in New Haven in violation of an 1879 Connecticut law prohibiting the use of contraceptives. She challenged the constitutionality of the statute, and in *Griswold v. Connecticut* (1965) the Supreme Court struck down the law and established a constitutionally protected right to privacy.

Griswold v. Connecticut

381 U.S. 479 (1965)

Vote: 7   (*Brennan, Clark, Douglas, Goldberg, Harlan, Warren, White*)

 2   (*Black, Stewart*)

Opinion of the Court: Douglas
Concurring opinions: Goldberg, Harlan, White
Dissenting opinions: Black, Stewart

Griswold was virtually a carbon copy of *Poe v. Ullman*, with but a few alterations designed to remedy meet some of the shortcomings of the earlier case.[10] Estelle Griswold, the executive director of the Planned Parenthood League of Connecticut, and Dr. C. Lee Buxton (the physician involved in *Poe*) opened a birth control clinic in 1961 with the intent of being arrested for violating the Connecticut law that had been at issue in *Poe*. Three days after the clinic was opening, Griswold was arrested for dispensing contraceptives to a married couple.

In the U.S. Supreme Court, Griswold's attorney, Yale Law School professor Thomas Emerson, challenged the Connecticut law on some of the same grounds as had been set forth in the *Poe* dissent. Emerson took a substantive due process approach to the Fourteenth Amendment, arguing that the law infringed on individual liberty. He strengthened the privacy argument by asserting that it could be found in five amendments: the First, Third, Fourth, Ninth, and Fourteenth.

10. For an interesting account of *Griswold*, see Fred W. Friendly and Martha J. H. Elliot, *The Constitution: That Delicate Balance* (New York: Random House, 1984).

MR. JUSTICE DOUGLAS delivered the opinion of the Court.

[W]e are met with a wide range of questions that implicate the Due Process Clause of the Fourteenth Amendment. . . . We do not sit as a super-legislature to determine the wisdom, need, and propriety of laws that touch economic problems, business affairs, or social conditions. This law, however, operates directly on an intimate relation of husband and wife and their physician's role in one aspect of that relation.

The association of people is not mentioned in the Constitution nor in the Bill of Rights. The right to educate a child in a school of the parents' choice—whether public or private or parochial—is also not mentioned. Nor is the right to study any particular subject or any foreign language. Yet the First Amendment has been construed to include certain of those rights. . . .

Without those peripheral rights the specific rights would be less secure. . . .

. . . [Previous] cases suggest that specific guarantees in the Bill of Rights have penumbras, formed by emanations from those guarantees that help give them life and substance. Various guarantees create zones of privacy. The right of association contained in the penumbra of the First Amendment is one. . . . The Third Amendment in its prohibition against the quartering of soldiers "in any house" in time of peace without the consent of the owner is another facet of that privacy. The Fourth Amendment explicitly affirms the "right of the people to be secure in their persons, houses, papers, and effects, against unreasonable searches and seizures." The Fifth Amendment in its Self-Incrimination Clause enables the citizen to create a zone of privacy which government may not force him to surrender to his detriment. The Ninth Amendment provides: "The enumeration in the Constitution, of certain rights, shall not be construed to deny or disparage others retained by the people."

The Fourth and Fifth Amendments were described in Boyd v. United States as protection against all governmental invasions "of the sanctity of a man's home and the privacies of life." We recently referred to the Fourth Amendment as creating a "right to privacy, no less important than any other right carefully and particularly reserved to the people."

We have had many controversies over these penumbral rights of "privacy and repose." These cases bear witness that the right of privacy which presses for recognition here is a legitimate one.

The present case, then, concerns a relationship lying within the zone of privacy created by several fundamental constitutional guarantees. And it concerns a law which, in forbidding the *use* of contraceptives rather than regulating their manufacture or sale, seeks to achieve its goals by means having a maximum destructive impact upon that relationship. Such a law cannot stand in light of the familiar principle, so often applied by this Court, that a "governmental purpose to control or prevent activities constitutionally subject to state regulation may not be achieved by means which sweep unnecessarily broadly and thereby invade the area of protected freedoms." Would we allow the police to search the sacred precincts of marital bedrooms for telltale signs of the use of contraceptives? The very idea is repulsive to the notions of privacy surrounding the marriage relationship.

We deal with a right of privacy older than the Bill of Rights—older than our political parties, older than our school system. Marriage is a coming together for better or for worse, hopefully enduring, and intimate to the degree of being sacred. It is an association that promotes a way of life, not causes; harmony in living, not political faiths; bilateral loyalty, not commercial or social projects. Yet it is an association for as noble a purpose as any involved in our prior decisions.

Reversed.

MR. JUSTICE GOLDBERG, whom THE CHIEF JUSTICE and MR. JUSTICE BRENNAN join, concurring.

I agree with the Court that Connecticut's birth-control law unconstitutionally intrudes upon the right of marital privacy, and I join in its opinion and judgment. Although I have not accepted the view that "due process" as used in the Fourteenth Amendment includes all of the first eight Amendments, I do agree that the concept of liberty protects those personal rights that are fundamental, and is not confined to the specific terms of the Bill of Rights. My conclusion that the concept of liberty is not so restricted and that it embraces the right of marital privacy though that right is not mentioned explicitly in the Constitution is supported both by numerous decisions of this Court, referred to in the Court's opinion, and by the language and history of the Ninth Amendment. In reaching the conclusion that the right of marital privacy is protected, as being within the protected penumbra of specific guarantees of the Bill of Rights, the Court refers to the Ninth Amendment. . . .

The language and history of the Ninth Amendment reveal that the Framers of the Constitution believed that there are additional fundamental rights, protected from governmental infringement, which exist alongside those fundamental rights specifically mentioned in the first eight constitutional amendments.

The Ninth Amendment reads, "The enumeration in the Constitution, of certain rights, shall not be construed to deny or disparage others retained by the people." The Amendment is almost entirely the work of James Madison. It was introduced in Congress by him and passed the House and Senate with little or no debate and virtually no change in language. It was proffered to quiet expressed fears that a bill of specifically enumerated rights could not be sufficiently broad to cover all essential rights and that the specific mention of certain rights would be interpreted as a denial that others were protected. . . .

While this Court has had little occasion to interpret the Ninth Amendment, "it cannot be presumed that any clause in the constitution is intended to be without effect." The Ninth Amendment to the Constitution may be regarded by some as a recent discovery and may be forgotten by others, but since 1791 it has been a basic part of the Constitution which we are sworn to uphold. To hold that a right so basic and fundamental and so deep-rooted in our society as the right of privacy in marriage may be infringed because that right is not guaranteed in so many words by the first eight amendments to the Constitution is to ignore the Ninth Amendment and to give it no effect whatsoever. Moreover, a judicial construction that this fundamental right is not protected by the Constitution because it is not mentioned in explicit terms by one of the first eight amendments or elsewhere in the Constitution would violate the Ninth Amendment, which specifically states that "the enumera-

tion in the Constitution, of certain rights shall not be *construed* to deny or disparage others retained by the people." (Emphasis added.) . . .

In sum, I believe that the right of privacy in the marital relation is fundamental and basic—a personal right "retained by the people" within the meaning of the Ninth Amendment. Connecticut cannot constitutionally abridge this fundamental right, which is protected by the Fourteenth Amendment from infringement by the States. I agree with the Court that petitioners' convictions must therefore be reversed.

MR. JUSTICE HARLAN, concurring in the judgment.

I fully agree with the judgment of reversal, but find myself unable to join the Court's opinion. . . .

In my view, the proper constitutional inquiry in this case is whether this Connecticut statute infringes the Due Process Clause of the Fourteenth Amendment because the enactment violates basic values "implicit in the concept of ordered liberty." For reasons stated at length in my dissenting opinion in Poe v. Ullman, I believe that it does. While the relevant inquiry may be aided by resort to one or more of the provisions of the Bill of Rights, it is not dependent on them or any of their radiations. The Due Process Clause of the Fourteenth Amendment stands, in my opinion, on its own bottom.

MR. JUSTICE BLACK, with whom MR. JUSTICE STEWART joins, dissenting.

The Court talks about a constitutional "right of privacy" as though there is some constitutional provision or provisions forbidding any law ever to be passed which might abridge the "privacy" of individuals. But there is not. There are, of course, guarantees in certain specific constitutional provisions which are designed in part to protect privacy at certain times and places with respect to certain activities. Such, for example, is the Fourth Amendment's guarantee against "unreasonable searches and seizures." But I think it belittles that Amendment to talk about it as though it protects nothing but "privacy." To treat it that way is to give it a niggardly interpretation, not the kind of liberal reading I think any Bill of Rights provision should be given. The average man would very likely not have his feelings soothed any more by having his property seized openly than by having it seized privately and by stealth. He simply wants his property left alone. And a person can be just as much, if not more, irritated, annoyed and injured by an unceremonious public arrest by a policeman as he is by a seizure in the privacy of his office or home.

One of the most effective ways of diluting or expanding a constitutionally guaranteed right is to substitute for the crucial word or words of a constitutional guarantee another word or words, more or less flexible and more or less restricted in meaning. This fact is well illustrated by the use of the term "right of privacy" as a comprehensive substitute for the Fourth Amendment's guarantee against "unreasonable searches and seizures." "Privacy" is a broad, abstract and ambiguous concept which can easily be shrunken in meaning but which can also, on the other hand, easily be interpreted as a constitutional ban against many things other than searches and seizures. I have expressed the view many times that First Amendment freedoms, for example, have suffered from a failure of the courts to stick to the simple language of the First Amendment in construing it, instead of invoking multitudes of words substituted for those the Framers used. . . . For these reasons I get nowhere in this case by talk about a constitutional "right of privacy" as an emanation from one or more constitutional provisions. I like my privacy as well as the next one, but I am nevertheless compelled to admit that government has a right to invade it unless prohibited by some specific constitutional provision. For these reasons I cannot agree with the Court's judgment and the reasons it gives for holding this Connecticut law unconstitutional.

This brings me to the arguments made by my Brothers HARLAN, WHITE and GOLDBERG for invalidating the Connecticut law. Brothers HARLAN and WHITE would invalidate it by reliance on the Due Process Clause of the Fourteenth Amendment, but Brother GOLDBERG, while agreeing with Brother HARLAN, relies also on the Ninth Amendment. I have no doubt that the Connecticut law could be applied in such a way as to abridge freedom of speech and press and therefore violate the First and Fourteenth Amendments. My disagreement with the Court's opinion holding that there is such a violation here is a narrow one, relating to the application of the First Amendment to the facts and circumstances of this particular case. But my disagreement with Brothers HARLAN, WHITE and

GOLDBERG is more basic. I think that if properly construed neither the Due Process Clause nor the Ninth Amendment, nor both together, could under any circumstances be a proper basis for invalidating the Connecticut law. I discuss the due process and Ninth Amendment arguments together because on analysis they turn out to be the same thing—merely using different words to claim for this Court and the federal judiciary power to invalidate any legislative act which the judges find irrational, unreasonable or offensive.

The due process argument which my Brothers HARLAN and WHITE adopt here is based, as their opinions indicate, on the premise that this Court is vested with power to invalidate all state laws that it considers to be arbitrary, capricious, unreasonable, or oppressive, or on this Court's belief that a particular state law under scrutiny has no "rational or justifying" purpose, or is offensive to a "sense of fairness and justice." If these formulas based on "natural justice," or others which mean the same thing, are to prevail, they require judges to determine what is or is not constitutional on the basis of their own appraisal of what laws are unwise or unnecessary. The power to make such decisions is of course that of a legislative body. Surely it has to be admitted that no provision of the Constitution specifically gives such blanket power to courts to exercise such a supervisory veto over the wisdom and value of legislative policies and to hold unconstitutional those laws which they believe unwise or dangerous. I readily admit that no legislative body, state or national, should pass laws that can justly be given any of the invidious labels invoked as constitutional excuses to strike down state laws. But perhaps it is not too much to say that no legislative body ever does pass laws without believing that they will accomplish a sane, rational, wise and justifiable purpose. While. . . our Court has constitutional power to strike down statutes, state or federal, that violate commands of the Federal Constitution, I do not believe that we are granted power by the Due Process Clause or any other constitutional provision or provisions to measure constitutionality by our belief that legislation is arbitrary, capricious or unreasonable, or accomplishes no justifiable purpose, or is offensive to our own notions of "civilized standards of conduct." Such an appraisal of the wisdom of legislation is an attribute of the power to make laws, not of the power to interpret them. The use by federal courts of such a formula or doctrine or whatnot to veto federal or state laws simply takes away from Congress and States the power to make laws based on their own judgment of fairness and wisdom and transfers that power to this Court for ultimate determination—a power which was specifically denied to federal courts by the convention that framed the Constitution. . . .

My Brother GOLDBERG has adopted the recent discovery that the Ninth Amendment as well as the Due Process Clause can be used by this Court as authority to strike down all state legislation which this Court thinks violates "fundamental principles of liberty and justice," or is contrary to the "traditions and [collective] conscience of our people." He also states, without proof satisfactory to me, that in making decisions on this basis judges will not consider "their personal and private notions." One may ask how they can avoid considering them. Our Court certainly has no machinery with which to take a Gallup Poll. And the scientific miracles of this age have not yet produced a gadget which the Court can use to determine what traditions are rooted in the "[collective] conscience of our people." Moreover, one would certainly have to look far beyond the language of the Ninth Amendment to find that the Framers vested in this Court any such awesome veto powers over lawmaking, either by the States or by the Congress. Nor does anything in the history of the Amendment offer any support for such a shocking doctrine. The whole history of the adoption of the Constitution and Bill of Rights points the other way. . . . That Amendment was passed, not to broaden the powers of this Court or any other department of "the General Government," but, as every student of history knows, to assure the people that the Constitution in all its provisions was intended to limit the Federal Government to the powers granted expressly or by necessary implication. . . . [F]or a period of a century and a half no serious suggestion was ever made that the Ninth Amendment, enacted to protect state powers against federal invasion, could be used as a weapon of federal power to prevent state legislatures from passing laws they consider appropriate to govern local affairs. Use of any such broad, unbounded judicial authority would make of this Court's members a day-to-day constitutional convention. . . .

I realize that many good and able men have eloquently spoken and written, sometimes in rhapsodical strains, about the duty of this Court to keep the Constitution in tune with the times. The idea is that the Constitution must be changed from time to time and that this Court is charged with a duty to make those changes. For myself, I must with all deference reject that philosophy. The Constitution makers knew the need for change and provided for it. Amendments suggested by the people's elected representatives can be submitted to the people or their selected agents for ratification. That method of change was good for our Fathers, and being somewhat old-fashioned I must add it is good enough for me. And so, I cannot rely on the Due Process Clause or the Ninth Amendment or any mysterious and uncertain natural law concept as a reason for striking down this state law. The Due Process Clause with an "arbitrary and capricious". . . formula was liberally used by this Court to strike down economic legislation in the early decades of this century, threatening, many people thought, the tranquility and stability of the Nation. See, e.g., Lochner v. New York. That formula, based on subjective considerations of "natural justice," is no less dangerous when used to enforce this Court's views about personal rights than those about economic rights. I had thought that we had laid that formula, as a means for striking down state legislation, to rest once and for all.

MR. JUSTICE STEWART, whom MR. JUSTICE BLACK joins, dissenting.

Since 1879 Connecticut has had on its books a law which forbids the use of contraceptives by anyone. I think this is an uncommonly silly law. As a practical matter, the law is obviously unenforceable, except in the oblique context of the present case. As a philosophical matter, I believe the use of contraceptives in the relationship of marriage should be left to personal and private choice, based upon each individual's moral, ethical, and religious beliefs. As a matter of social policy, I think professional counsel about methods of birth control should be available to all, so that each individual's choice can be meaningfully made. But we are not asked in this case to say whether we think this law is unwise, or even asinine. We are asked to hold that it violates the United States Constitution. And that I cannot do.

In the course of its opinion the Court refers to no less than six Amendments to the Constitution: the First, the Third, the Fourth, the Fifth, the Ninth, and the Fourteenth.

But the Court does not say which of these Amendments, if any, it thinks is infringed by this Connecticut law.

We *are* told that the Due Process Clause of the Fourteenth Amendment is not, as such, the "guide" in this case. With that much I agree. There is no claim that this law, duly enacted by the Connecticut Legislature, is unconstitutionally vague. There is no claim that the appellants were denied any of the elements of procedural due process at their trial, so as to make their convictions constitutionally invalid. And, as the Court says, the day has long passed since the Due Process Clause was regarded as a proper instrument for determining "the wisdom, need, and propriety" of state laws....

The Court also quotes the Ninth Amendment, and my Brother GOLDBERG's concurring opinion relies heavily upon it. But to say that the Ninth Amendment has anything to do with this case is to turn somersaults with history. The Ninth Amendment, like its companion the Tenth, which this Court held "states but a truism that all is retained which has not been surrendered," was framed by James Madison and adopted by the States simply to make clear that the adoption of the Bill of Rights did not alter the plan that the *Federal* Government was to be a government of express and limited powers, and that all rights and powers not delegated to it were retained by the people and the individual States. Until today no member of this Court has ever suggested that the Ninth Amendment meant anything else, and the idea that a federal court could ever use the Ninth Amendment to annul a law passed by the elected representatives of the people of the State of Connecticut would have caused James Madison no little wonder.

What provision of the Constitution, then, does make this state law invalid? The Court says it is the right of privacy "created by several fundamental constitutional guarantees." With all deference, I can find no such general right of privacy in the Bill of Rights, in any other part of the Constitution, or in any case ever before decided by this Court.

At the oral argument in this case we were told that the Connecticut law does not "conform to current community standards." But it is not the function of this Court to decide cases on the basis of community standards. We are here to decide cases "agreeably to the Constitution and laws of the United States." It is the essence of judicial duty to subordinate our own personal views, our own ideas of what legislation is wise and what is not. If, as I should surely hope, the law before us does not reflect the standards of the people of Connecticut, the people of Connecticut can freely exercise their true Ninth and Tenth Amendment rights to persuade their elected representatives to repeal it. That is the constitutional way to take this law off the books.

Griswold was a landmark decision because it created a constitutional right to privacy and deemed that right fundamental. To put it another way, under *Griswold* governments may place limits on the right to privacy only if those limits survive "strict" constitutional scrutiny, which means that the government must demonstrate that its restrictions are necessary and narrowly tailored to serve a compelling government interest. However, the justices disagreed about where that right existed within the Constitution *(see Table 15-1)*. Douglas's opinion for the Court asserted that specific guarantees in the Bill of Rights have penumbras, formed by emanations from First, Third, Fourth, Fifth, and Ninth Amendment guarantees "that help give them life and substance." In other words, Douglas claimed that even though the Constitution failed to mention privacy, clauses within the document created zones that gave rise to the right. Note that in making this argument, Douglas avoided reliance on the Fourteenth Amendment's Due Process Clause. He apparently believed that grounding privacy in that clause would hark back to the days of *Lochner* and substantive due process, a doctrine he explicitly rejected.[11]

Justice Goldberg, writing for Earl Warren and William Brennan, did not dispute Douglas's penumbra theory, but chose to emphasize the relevance of the Ninth Amendment. In Goldberg's view that amendment, which states, "The enumeration in the Constitution, of certain rights, shall not be construed to deny or disparage others retained by the people,"

11. For an interesting and inside view of the Court's decision-making process in *Griswold*, see Bernard Schwartz, *The Unpublished Opinions of the Warren Court* (New York: Oxford University Press, 1985).

TABLE 15-1 The *Griswold* Splits

Location of the Privacy Right	Justices
First, Third, Fourth, Fifth, and Ninth Amendments	Douglas, Clark
Ninth Amendment	Goldberg, Brennan, Warren
Fourteenth Amendment (Due Process Clause)	Harlan, White
No general right to privacy in the Constitution	Black, Stewart

could be read to contain a right to privacy. His logic was simple: the wording of the amendment, coupled with its history, suggested that it was "proffered to quiet expressed fears that a bill of specifically enumerated rights could not be sufficiently broad to cover all essential rights," including the right to privacy. Harlan took the opportunity to reiterate his stance in *Poe* that the Due Process Clause of the Fourteenth Amendment prohibits such legislation. In holding to his *Poe* opinion, however, Harlan went one step beyond the Goldberg concurrers; he rejected the Douglas penumbra theory, asserting, "While the relevant inquiry may be aided by resort to one or more of the provisions of the Bill of Rights, it is not dependent on them or any of their radiations." Justice White also filed a concurring opinion lending support to Harlan's due process view of privacy.

As important as *Griswold* was and still is, it is clear that the justices did not speak with one voice. Seven agreed, more or less, that a right to privacy existed, but they located that right in three distinct constitutional spheres. The other two—Black and Stewart—argued that the Constitution did not contain a general right to privacy, but they did more than that. They took their colleagues to task for, in their view, reverting back to the days of *Lochner* and substantive due process. From Black and Stewart's vantage point, it

should be the people, not the courts, that pressure legislatures to change "unwise" laws.

Whether a right to privacy existed and where the right was located, however, were not the only questions raised by *Griswold*. Another important issue concerned the areas covered by this newly found right. Clearly, it protected "notions of privacy surrounding the marriage relationship," but beyond that observers could only speculate.

In this chapter we examine the other areas where the Court has applied *Griswold*. We look first at its extensions into private activities and then at its role in the more controversial issue of abortion. Keep the *Griswold* precedent in mind. To which interpretation of the right to privacy has the Court subscribed in the cases that follow? Has the Court's approach changed with its increasing conservatism? Or do the majority of justices continue to adopt its basic tenets?

PRIVATE ACTIVITIES AND THE APPLICATION OF *GRISWOLD*

Many Americans now equate *Griswold*'s right to privacy with reproductive freedom, especially the right to abortion, but one of the first important applications came in a criminal procedure case, *Katz v. United States* (1967). FBI agents suspected Charles Katz of engaging in illegal bookmaking activity; in particular, they thought he was "transmitting wagering information by telephone from Los Angeles to Miami and Boston." To gather evidence, they placed listening and recording devices outside the telephone booth where Katz made his calls and used the transcripts of his conversations to obtain an eight-count indictment.

Katz challenged the use of the transcripts as evidence against him, asserting that his conversations were private and that the government had violated his rights under the Fourth Amendment. The government argued that in previous Fourth Amendment search and seizure cases, the justices had permitted the use of bugs and mikes as long as agents did not "physically penetrate" an individual's space. Here, the FBI had attached listening devices to the *outside* of the booth; it claimed that it had not invaded Katz's space.

The Court disagreed. In his majority opinion, Justice Stewart dealt primarily with existing precedent governing searches and seizures, a topic covered in Chapter 16. But Stewart touched on the privacy issue, asserting that "What a person knowingly exposes to the public, even in his own home or office, is not a subject of Fourth Amendment protection. But what he seeks to preserve as private, even in an area accessible to the public, may be constitutionally protected." Justice Harlan, in a concurring opinion, put it in these terms: if a person has "exhibited an actual (subjective) expectation of privacy," and "the expectation . . . [is] one that society is prepared to recognize as 'reasonable,'" then he or she comes under the protection of the Fourth Amendment. In other words, the justices—even Stewart, who dissented in *Griswold*—were willing to apply the right to privacy to searches and seizures. If citizens expect privacy, as Charles Katz did when he entered the telephone booth, then they are entitled to it. This position was not wholly different from what Justice Brandeis had advocated in *Olmstead v. United States*—about forty years before *Katz!*

Two years later, in *Stanley v. Georgia,* the Court had another occasion to examine the privacy doctrine and its relationship to searches and seizures. While the police were investigating Robert Stanley for illegal bookmaking, they obtained a warrant to search his home. Authorities found little evidence of gambling activity, but they did find three reels of film. They watched the movies and arrested Stanley for possessing obscene material. Stanley's attorney challenged the seizure and arrest on the ground that the law should not "punish mere private possession of obscene material"—that his client had a right of privacy to view whatever he wished in his own home. The state argued that it had the right to seize obscene materials because they are illegal to possess. Indeed, in previous decisions, the Court had said that states could regulate the dissemination of obscene movies, magazines, and so forth.

In a unanimous opinion for the Court, Justice Marshall accepted Stanley's argument. As he put it: "If the First Amendment means anything, it means that a State has no business telling a man, sitting alone in his house, what books he may read or films he may watch." Put somewhat differently, states can regulate obscenity, but cannot prohibit such activity inside someone's house. The First Amendment and privacy rights simply prohibit this kind of intrusion into the home.

This point is important: *Stanley* hinged on an infringement of a fundamental liberty—in this instance, the First Amendment. But would the Court apply *Stanley* to activities forbidden by the state that did not fall under the First Amendment? In *Bowers v. Hardwick* (1986) the Court considered the constitutionality of a man's conviction for engaging in sodomy. As you read *Bowers* think about how the Court applied *Stanley* to the dispute. Some scholars allege that the Court virtually gutted the underpinnings of *Stanley.* Is this assertion accurate? Or did the Court merely seek to limit its application and that of the *Griswold* right to privacy, more generally?

Bowers v. Hardwick

478 U.S. 186 (1986)
Vote: 5 (Burger, O'Connor, Powell, Rehnquist, White)
    4 (Blackmun, Brennan, Marshall, Stevens)
Opinion of the Court: White
Concurring opinions: Burger, Powell
Dissenting opinions: Blackmun, Stevens

In August 1982 a police officer appeared at Michael Hardwick's residence to serve him with an arrest warrant for failure to keep a court date. According to the officer, one of Hardwick's housemates let him in and

Michael Hardwick was arrested for violating the Georgia sodomy statute in 1982. With help from the American Civil Liberties Union, Hardwick sued the state, claiming the law violated his constitutional rights. In *Bowers v. Hardwick* (1986) the Supreme Court rejected Hardwick's privacy argument and upheld the Georgia law.

he then observed Hardwick engaged in sodomy with another man.[12] The officer arrested Hardwick for violating a Georgia law that prohibited the practice of oral or anal sex.[13] The district attorney decided not to pursue the matter, but Hardwick and his ACLU attorneys challenged the law, asserting that it violated the fundamental right to privacy as articulated in *Griswold* and should be subject to strict constitutional scrutiny.

JUSTICE WHITE delivered the opinion of the Court.

The issue presented is whether the Federal Constitution confers a fundamental right upon homosexuals to engage in sodomy and hence invalidates the laws of the many States that still make such conduct illegal and have done so

12. For more on this case, see Peter Irons, *The Courage of Their Convictions* (New York: Free Press, 1988).

13. The majority opinion dealt exclusively with "consensual homosexual sodomy," expressing "no opinion . . . on other acts of sodomy."

for a very long time. The case also calls for some judgment about the limits of the Court's role in carrying out its constitutional mandate.

We first register our disagreement . . . with respondent that the Court's prior cases have construed the Constitution to confer a right of privacy that extends to homosexual sodomy and for all intents and purposes have decided this case. . . .

. . . [N]one of the rights announced in . . . [past] cases bears any resemblance to the claimed constitutional right of homosexuals to engage in acts of sodomy. . . .

Precedent aside, however, respondent would have us announce . . . a fundamental right to engage in homosexual sodomy. This we are quite unwilling to do. It is true that despite the language of the Due Process Clauses of the Fifth and Fourteenth Amendments, which appears to focus only on the processes by which life, liberty, or property is taken, the cases are legion in which those Clauses have been interpreted to have substantive content, subsuming rights that to a great extent are immune from federal or state regulation or proscription. Among such cases are those recognizing rights that have little or no textual support in the constitutional language. . . .

Striving to assure itself and the public that announcing rights not readily identifiable in the Constitution's text involves much more than the imposition of the Justices' own choice of values on the States and the Federal Government, the Court has sought to identify the nature of the rights qualifying for heightened judicial protection. . . . [I]t was said that this category includes those fundamental liberties that are "implicit in the concept of ordered liberty," such that "neither liberty nor justice would exist if [they] were sacrificed.". . . [F]undamental liberties . . . are characterized as those. . . that are "deeply rooted in this Nation's history and tradition."

It is obvious to us that neither of these formulations would extend a fundamental right to homosexuals to engage in acts of consensual sodomy. Proscriptions against that conduct have ancient roots. Sodomy was a criminal offense at common law and was forbidden by the laws of the original thirteen States when they ratified the Bill of Rights. . . . In fact, until 1961, all 50 States outlawed sodomy, and today 24 States and the District of Columbia continue to provide criminal penalties for sodomy performed in private and between consenting adults. Against this background, to claim that a right to engage in such conduct is "deeply rooted in this Nation's history and tradition" or "implicit in the concept of ordered liberty" is, at best, facetious.

Nor are we inclined to take a more expansive view of our authority to discover new fundamental rights imbedded in the Due Process Clause. The Court is most vulnerable and comes nearest to illegitimacy when it deals with judge-made constitutional law having little or no cognizable roots in the language or design of the Constitution. That this is so was painfully demonstrated by the face-off between the Executive and the Court in the 1930's, which resulted in the repudiation of much of the substantive gloss that the Court had placed on the Due Process Clause of the Fifth and Fourteenth Amendments. There should be, therefore, great resistance to expand the substantive reach of those Clauses, particularly if it requires redefining the category of rights deemed to be fundamental. Otherwise, the Judiciary necessarily takes to itself further authority to govern the country without express constitutional authority. The claimed right pressed on us today falls far short of overcoming this resistance.

Respondent, however, asserts that the result should be different where the homosexual conduct occurs in the privacy of the home. He relies on *Stanley v. Georgia* (1969), where the Court held that the First Amendment prevents conviction for possessing and reading obscene material in the privacy of his home. . . .

Stanley did protect conduct that would not have been protected outside the home, and it partially prevented the enforcement of state obscenity laws; but the decision was firmly grounded in the First Amendment. The right pressed upon us here has no similar support in the text of the Constitution, and it does not qualify for recognition under the prevailing principles for construing the Fourteenth Amendment. Its limits are also difficult to discern. Plainly enough, otherwise illegal conduct is not always immunized whenever it occurs in the home. Victimless crimes, such as the possession and use of illegal drugs, do not escape the law where they are committed at home. *Stanley* itself recognized that its holding offered no protection for the possession in the home of drugs, firearms, or stolen goods. And if respondent's submission is limited to the voluntary sexual conduct between consenting adults, it would be difficult, except by

fiat, to limit the claimed right to homosexual conduct while leaving exposed to prosecution adultery, incest, and other sexual crimes even though they are committed in the home. We are unwilling to start down that road. . . .

Accordingly, the judgment of the Court of Appeals is

Reversed.

JUSTICE BLACKMUN, with whom JUSTICE BRENNAN, JUSTICE MARSHALL, and JUSTICE STEVENS join, dissenting.

This case is no more about "a fundamental right to engage in homosexual sodomy," as the Court purports to declare, than *Stanley v. Georgia* (1969), was about a fundamental right to watch obscene movies, or *Katz v. United States* (1967), was about a fundamental right to place interstate bets from a telephone booth. Rather, this case is about "the most comprehensive of rights and the right most valued by civilized men," namely, "the right to be let alone." *Olmstead v. United States* (1928) (Brandeis, J., dissenting). . . .

In its haste to reverse the Court of Appeals and hold that the Constitution does not "confe[r] a fundamental right upon homosexuals to engage in sodomy," the Court relegates the actual statute being challenged to a footnote and ignores the procedural posture of the case before it. A fair reading of the statute and of the complaint clearly reveals that the majority has distorted the question this case presents.

First, the Court's almost obsessive focus on homosexual activity is particularly hard to justify in light of the broad language Georgia has used. Unlike the Court, the Georgia Legislature has not proceeded on the assumption that homosexuals are so different from other citizens that their lives may be controlled in a way that would not be tolerated if it limited the choices of those other citizens. . . . The sex or status of the persons who engage in the act is irrelevant as a matter of state law. . . . Michael Hardwick's standing may rest in significant part on Georgia's apparent willingness to enforce against homosexuals a law it seems not to have any desire to enforce against heterosexuals. But his claim that . . . [the law] involves an unconstitutional intrusion into his privacy and his right of intimate association does not depend in any way on his sexual orientation.

Second, I disagree with the Court's refusal to consider whether: . . . [the law] runs afoul of the . . . Ninth Amendment. . . . Respondent's complaint expressly invoked the Ninth Amendment and he relied heavily before this Court on *Griswold v. Connecticut* (1965), which identifies that Amendment as one of the specific constitutional provisions giving "life and substance" to our understanding of privacy. . . . I believe that Hardwick has stated a cognizable claim that . . . [the law] interferes with constitutionally protected interests in privacy and freedom of intimate association. . . .

The Court concludes today that none of our prior cases dealing with various decisions that individuals are entitled to make free of governmental interference "bears any resemblance to the claimed constitutional right of homosexuals to engage in acts of sodomy that is asserted in this case.". . .

In a variety of circumstances we have recognized that a necessary corollary of giving individuals freedom to choose how to conduct their lives is acceptance of the fact that different individuals will make different choices. For example, in holding that the clearly important state interest in public education should give way to a competing claim by the Amish to the effect that extended formal schooling threatened their way of life, the Court declared:"There can be no assumption that today's majority is 'right' and the Amish and others like them are 'wrong.' A way of life that is odd or even erratic but interferes with no rights or interests of others is not to be condemned because it is different." *Wisconsin v. Yoder* (1972). The Court claims that its decision today merely refuses to recognize a fundamental right to engage in homosexual sodomy; what the Court really has refused to recognize is the fundamental interest all individuals have in controlling the nature of their intimate associations with others.

The behavior for which Hardwick faces prosecution occurred in his own home, a place to which the Fourth Amendment attaches special significance. The Court's treatment of this aspect of the case is symptomatic of its overall refusal to consider the broad principles that have informed our treatment of privacy in specific cases. Just as the right to privacy is more than the mere aggregation of a number of entitlements to engage in specific behavior, so too, protecting the physical integrity of the home is more than merely a means of protecting specific activities that often take place there. . . .

The Court's interpretation of the pivotal case of *Stanley*

v. Georgia (1969) is entirely unconvincing. *Stanley* held that Georgia's undoubted power to punish the public distribution of constitutionally unprotected, obscene material did not permit the State to punish the private possession of such material. According to the majority here, *Stanley* relied entirely on the First Amendment, and thus, it is claimed, sheds no light on cases not involving printed materials. But that is not what *Stanley* said. Rather, the *Stanley* Court anchored its holding in the Fourth Amendment's special protection for the individual in his home. . . .

The central place that *Stanley* gives Justice Brandeis' dissent in *Olmstead*, a case raising no First Amendment claim, shows that *Stanley* rested as much on the Court's understanding of the Fourth Amendment as it did on the First. . . . [T]hus I cannot agree with the Court's statement that "[t]he right pressed upon us here has no . . . support in the text of the Constitution." Indeed, the right of an individual to conduct intimate relationships in the intimacy of his or her own home seems to me to be the heart of the Constitution's protection of privacy.

The Court's failure to comprehend the magnitude of the liberty interests at stake in this case leads it to slight the question whether petitioner, on behalf of the State, has justified Georgia's infringement of these interests. I believe that neither of the two general justifications for . . . [the law] that petitioner has advanced warrants dismissing respondent's challenge for failure to state a claim.

First, petitioner asserts that the acts made criminal by the statute may have serious adverse consequences for "the general public health and welfare," such as spreading communicable diseases or fostering other criminal activity. Inasmuch as this case was dismissed by the District Court on the pleadings, it is not surprising that the record before us is barren of any evidence to support petitioner's claim. . . . Nothing in the record before the Court provides any justification for finding the activity forbidden by . . . [the law] to be physically dangerous, either to the persons engaged in it or to others.

The core of petitioner's defense of . . . [the law], however, is that respondent and others who engage in the conduct prohibited by . . . [it] interfere with Georgia's exercise of the "'right of the Nation and of the States to maintain a decent society.'". . . Essentially, petitioner argues, and the Court agrees, that the fact that the acts described in . . . [the law] "for hundreds of years, if not thousands, have been uniformly condemned as immoral" is a sufficient reason to permit a State to ban them today.

I cannot agree that either the length of time a majority has held its convictions or the passions with which it defends them can withdraw legislation from this Court's scrutiny. . . . As Justice Jackson wrote so eloquently for the Court in *West Virginia Board of Education v. Barnette* (1943), "we apply the limitations of the Constitution with no fear that freedom to be intellectually and spiritually diverse or even contrary will disintegrate the social organization. . . . [F]reedom to differ is not limited to things that do not matter much. That would be a mere shadow of freedom. The test of its substance is the right to differ as to things that touch the heart of the existing order." It is precisely because the issue raised by this case touches the heart of what makes individuals what they are that we should be especially sensitive to the rights of those whose choices upset the majority. . . .

This case involves no real interference with the rights of others, for the mere knowledge that other individuals do not adhere to one's value system cannot be a legally cognizable interest, let alone an interest that can justify invading the houses, hearts, and minds of citizens who choose to live their lives differently.

Both the majority opinions and the dissenting opinions in *Bowers* dealt with privacy concerns. White's opinion found fault with a due process approach to privacy or, at the very least, with using due process to "discover" a new "fundamental right to engage in homosexual sodomy." Nor was he interested in using *Stanley* to find in favor of Hardwick. He read *Stanley* narrowly: the decision protected the exercise of some otherwise illegal activity only if the First Amendment was implicated. Hence, because Hardwick did not raise a First Amendment objection to sodomy laws, *Stanley* was inapplicable. The dissenters (including Marshall, the author of *Stanley*) called this interpretation unconvincing. In their view, *Stanley* took its cues from Brandeis's dissent in *Olmstead* and, accordingly, rested as much on the Fourth Amendment as on the First.

We leave it to you to consider whether the Burger Court, in *Bowers,* began to dismantle the Warren Court's rulings in *Stanley* and *Griswold* or if it merely drew sensible limits around them. Most Americans seem to agree with the latter statement. In surveys conducted during the 1980s and 1990s, about 75 percent of respondents said they believed "sexual relations between two adults of the same sex" are wrong. The justices showed less consensus than the public: the case was decided by a one-vote margin. Moreover, since his retirement, Justice Powell has stated he "probably made a mistake" in voting to uphold the Georgia laws.

Powell's remark provides some indication of the difficulty involved in resolving disputes touching on the amorphous right to privacy. The disputes have become even thornier over time. In *Cruzan v. Director, Missouri Department of Health* (1990), the Court—under the leadership of William Rehnquist—took an initial look at one of the most troublesome of all privacy issues—the right to die.

Right-to-die cases present two levels of questions. The first concerns whether and under what circumstances individuals can make the decision to refuse medical treatment necessary to sustain their lives. Most of the state courts that addressed right-to-die cases in the 1970s—well before the Supreme Court's ruling in *Cruzan*—agreed that the rights of privacy and liberty were broad enough to permit competent individuals to refuse medical treatment. But the issue becomes far more complicated when individuals seek to commit suicide or seek assistance in ending their life ("assisted suicides") when they have terminal illnesses.

A second right-to-die question centers on whether and under what circumstances the family or guardian of an incapacitated individual can make the decision to withdraw treatment. This question has proven the more problematic of the two. In the 1970s and 1980s, most state courts allowed various forms of what are called "substituted judgments," that is, they permitted relatives or guardians to "surmise" what the patient would have wanted or to act in the "best interest" of the patient.[14] A frequently cited example of the use of substituted judgment is the New Jersey Supreme Court's ruling in *In re Quinlan* (1976). As their twenty-two-year-old daughter Karen lay in a coma, the Quinlans sought to have the respirator, which was sustaining her life, removed. When Karen's doctors refused their request, her parents went to court. The state supreme court decided that the right to privacy is broad enough to allow a patient to "decline medical treatment under certain circumstances." And, because Karen could not make that decision for herself, the "only practical way to prevent the destruction of the right [to privacy] is to permit the guardian and family of Karen to render their best judgment as to whether she would exercise it in these circumstances."

Under this decision, the Quinlans could (and did) have Karen's respirator removed without intervention from the state and its courts. Although most state courts endorsed *Quinlan*, the Missouri Supreme Court took a different stance.[15] Viewing the state's interest in preserving life as controlling,[16] it asserted that the family must provide "clear and convincing" evidence that the patient would have wanted medical care terminated. This kind of standard is often difficult for families to meet because they must provide direct evidence about the patient's desires, when the patient can no longer express them.

In any event, rules that permit patients and the families to end treatment have garnered public support. As Figure 15-1 shows, in the 1940s only about 37

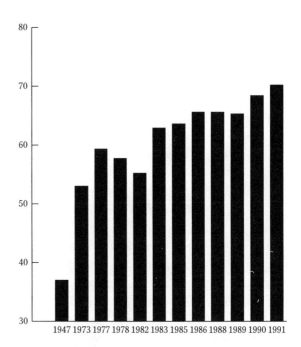

FIGURE 15-1 Percentage of Respondents Supporting an Individual's Right to Die

SOURCE: Lee Epstein, Jeffrey A. Segal, Harold J. Spaeth, and Thomas G. Walker, *The Supreme Court Compendium: Data, Decisions, and Developments* (Washington, D.C.: Congressional Quarterly, 1994), Table 8-23.

NOTE: The question was: Do you believe that doctors should be allowed by law to end an incurable patient's life if the patient and his family request it?

percent of the citizenry agreed that doctors should be allowed to end a terminal patient's life if that patient or the family request it. By 1991 that number had grown to 70.2 percent.

Would the Supreme Court agree with the public? Would it allow even competent patients to end their medical treatment? If so, would it permit families to make these decisions? What kind of proof would it require? These were the questions the Court with which the Court dealt in its first right-to-die case, *Cruzan v. Director, Missouri Health Department.*

14. See Laurence Tribe, *American Constitutional Law* (Mineola, N.Y.: Foundation Press, 1988), 1368.

15. In "Policy Making and State Supreme Courts," *The American Courts: A Critical Assessment,* ed. John B. Gates and Charles A. Johnson (Washington, D.C.: CQ Press, 1990), 108–110, Henry R. Glick provides a list of state right-to-die cases that predate *Cruzan.*

16. Preserving life is only one of several state interests. In *Belchertown v. Saikewicz* (1977), the Massachusetts Supreme Judicial Court offered three others: the maintenance of "ethical integrity of the medical profession," "the prevention of suicide," and the "protection of the interests of innocent third parties." See Tribe, *American Constitutional Law,* 1365.

Cruzan v. Director, Missouri Department of Health

497 U.S. 261 (1990)

Vote: 5   (Kennedy, O'Connor, Rehnquist, Scalia, White)
     4   (Blackmun, Brennan, Marshall, Stevens)

Opinion of the Court: Rehnquist
Concurring opinions: O'Connor, Scalia
Dissenting opinions: Brennan, Stevens

In January 1983 Nancy Beth Cruzan was in a serious car accident. When paramedics found her, she was "lying face down in a ditch without detectable respiratory or cardiac function." Although they were able to restore her breathing and heartbeat, Cruzan remained unconscious and was taken to a hospital. Both short- and long-term medical efforts failed, and, as a result, Cruzan degenerated to a persistent vegetative state, "a condition in which a person exhibits motor reflexes but evinces no indications of significant cognitive function." She required feeding and hydration tubes to stay alive. In short, when her case was before the Court, Nancy Cruzan was not dead, and some experts suggested that she could live another thirty years, but no one predicted any improvement in her condition.

Her parents, Lester and Joyce Cruzan, asked doctors to remove her feeding tubes, a step that would lead to Nancy's death. The hospital staff refused, and the Cruzans sought permission from a state court. They argued that "a person in Nancy's condition had a fundamental right to refuse or direct the withdrawal of 'death prolonging procedures.'" The Cruzans presented as evidence that when Nancy was twenty-five, she had told a friend that "she would not wish to continue her life unless she could live it at least halfway normally."

The trial court ruled in their favor, but the state supreme court reversed. It found no support in common law for a right to die, and it refused to apply privacy doctrines to the Cruzan situation. It also held that because the state had a strong interest in preserving life, the Cruzans would have to provide "clear and convincing evidence" that Nancy would have wanted her feeding tubes withdrawn.

CHIEF JUSTICE REHNQUIST delivered the opinion of the Court.

We granted certiorari to consider the question of whether Cruzan has a right under the United States Constitution which would require the hospital to withdraw life-sustaining treatment from her under these circumstances. . . .

The Fourteenth Amendment provides that no state shall "deprive any person of life, liberty, or property, without due process of law." The principle that a competent person has a constitutionally protected liberty interest in refusing unwanted medical treatment may be inferred from our prior decisions. . . .

But determining that a person has a "liberty interest" under the Due Process Clause does not end the inquiry; "whether respondent's constitutional rights have been violated must be determined by balancing his liberty interests against the relevant state interests."

Petitioners insist that under the general holdings of our cases, the forced administration of life-sustaining medical treatment, and even of artificially-delivered food and water essential to life, would implicate a competent person's liberty interest. Although we think the logic of the cases . . . would embrace such a liberty interest, the dramatic consequences involved in refusal of such treatment would inform the inquiry as to whether the deprivation of that interest is constitutionally permissible. But for purposes of this case, we assume that the United States Constitution would grant a competent person a constitutionally protected right to refuse lifesaving hydration and nutrition.

Petitioners go on to assert that an incompetent person should possess the same right in this respect as is possessed by a competent person. . . .

The difficulty with petitioners' claim is that in a sense it begs the question: an incompetent person is not able to make an informed and voluntary choice to exercise a hypothetical right to refuse treatment or any other right. Such a "right" must be exercised for her, if at all, by some sort of surrogate. Here, Missouri has in effect recognized that under certain circumstances a surrogate may act for the patient in electing to have hydration and nutrition withdrawn in such a way as to cause death, but it has established a procedural safeguard to assure that the action of the surrogate conforms as best it may to the wishes expressed by the patient while competent. Missouri requires that evidence of the incompetent's wishes as to the withdrawal of treatment be proved by clear and convincing evidence. The question, then, is whether the United States Constitution forbids the establishment of this procedural requirement by the State. We hold that it does not.

Whether or not Missouri's clear and convincing evidence requirement comports with the United States Constitution depends in part on what interests the State may properly seek to protect in this situation. Missouri relies on its interest in the protection and preservation of human life, and there can be no gainsaying this interest. As a general matter, the States—indeed, all civilized nations—demonstrate their commitment to life by treating homicide as a serious crime. Moreover, the majority of States in this country have laws imposing criminal penalties on one who assists another to commit suicide. We do not think a State is required to remain neutral in the face of an informed and voluntary decision by a physically-able adult to starve to death.

But in the context presented here, a State has more particular interests at stake. The choice between life and death is a deeply personal decision of obvious and overwhelming finality. We believe Missouri may legitimately seek to safeguard the personal element of this choice through the imposition of heightened evidentiary requirements. It cannot be disputed that the Due Process Clause protects an interest in life as well as an interest in refusing life-sustaining medical treatment. Not all incompetent patients will have loved ones available to serve as surrogate decision-makers. And even where family members are present, "there will, of course, be some unfortunate situations in which family members will not act to protect a patient." A State is entitled to guard against potential abuses in such situations. Similarly, a State is entitled to consider that a judicial proceeding to make a determination regarding an incompetent's wishes may very well not be an adversarial one, with the added guarantee of accurate factfinding that the adversary process brings with it. Finally, we think a State may properly decline to make judgments about the "quality" of life that a particular individual may enjoy, and simply assert an unqualified interest in the preservation of human life to be weighed against the constitutionally protected interests of the individual.

In our view, Missouri has permissibly sought to advance these interests through the adoption of . . . "an intermediate standard of proof—'clear and convincing evidence'—when the individual interests at stake in a state proceeding are both 'particularly important' and 'more substantial than mere loss of money.'"

We think it self-evident that the interests at stake in the instant proceedings are more substantial, both on an individual and societal level, than those involved in a run-of-the-[mill] civil dispute. But not only does the standard of proof reflect the importance of a particular adjudication, it also serves as "a societal judgment about how the risk of error should be distributed between the litigants." The more stringent the burden of proof a party must bear, the more that party bears the risk of an erroneous decision. We believe that Missouri may permissibly place an increased risk of an erroneous decision on those seeking to terminate an incompetent individual's life-sustaining treatment. An erroneous decision not to terminate results in a maintenance of the status quo; the possibility of subsequent developments such as advancements in medical science, the discovery of new evidence regarding the patient's intent, changes in the law, or simply the unexpected death of the patient despite the administration of life-sustaining treatment, at least create the potential that a wrong decision will eventually be corrected or its impact mitigated. An erroneous decision to withdraw life-sustaining treatment, however, is not susceptible of correction. . . .

It is also worth noting that most, if not all, States simply forbid oral testimony entirely in determining the wishes of parties in transactions which, while important, simply do not have the consequences that a decision to terminate a person's life does. At common law and by statute in most States, the parole evidence rule prevents the variations of the terms of a written contract by oral testimony. The statute of frauds makes unenforceable oral contracts to leave property by will, and statutes regulating the making of wills universally require that those instruments be in writing. There is no doubt that statutes requiring wills to be in writing, and statutes of frauds which require that a contract to make a will be in writing, on occasion frustrate the effectuation of the intent of a particular decedent, just as Missouri's requirement of proof in this case may have frustrated the effectuation of the not-fully-expressed desires of Nancy Cruzan. But the Constitution does not require general rules to work faultlessly; no general rule can.

In sum, we conclude that a State may apply a clear and convincing evidence standard in proceedings where a guardian seeks to discontinue nutrition and hydration of a person diagnosed to be in a persistent vegetative state. . . .

The Supreme Court of Missouri held that in this case the testimony adduced at trial did not amount to clear and convincing proof of the patient's desire to have hydration and nutrition withdrawn. In so doing, it reversed a decision of the Missouri trial court which had found that the evidence "suggest[ed]" Nancy Cruzan would not have desired to continue such measures, but which had not adopted the standard of "clear and convincing evidence" enunciated by the Supreme Court. The testimony adduced at trial consisted primarily of Nancy Cruzan's statements made to a housemate about a year before her accident that she would not want to live should she face life as a "vegetable," and other observations to the same effect. The observations did not deal in terms with withdrawal of medical treatment or of hydration and nutrition. We cannot say that the Supreme Court of Missouri committed constitutional error in reaching the conclusion that it did.

Petitioners alternatively contend that Missouri must accept the "substituted judgment" of close family members even in the absence of substantial proof that their views reflect the views of the patient. . . . Here again petitioners would seek to turn a decision which allowed a State to rely on family decisionmaking into a constitutional requirement that the State recognize such decisionmaking. But constitutional law does not work that way.

No doubt is engendered by anything in this record but that Nancy Cruzan's mother and father are loving and caring parents. If the State were required by the United States Constitution to repose a right of "substituted judgment" with anyone, the Cruzans would surely qualify. But we do not think the Due Process Clause requires the State to repose judgment on these matters with anyone but the patient herself. Close family members may have a strong feeling—a feeling not at all ignoble or unworthy, but not entirely disinterested, either—that they do not wish to witness the continuation of the life of a loved one which they regard as hopeless, meaningless, and even degrading. But there is no automatic assurance that the view of close family members will necessarily be the same as the patient's would have been had she been confronted with the prospect of her situation while competent. All of the reasons previously discussed for allowing Missouri to require clear and convincing evidence of the patient's wishes lead us to conclude that the State may choose to defer only to those wishes, rather than confide the decision to close family members.

The judgment of the Supreme Court of Missouri is

Affirmed.

JUSTICE BRENNAN, with whom JUSTICE MARSHALL and JUSTICE BLACKMUN join, dissenting.

"Medical technology has effectively created a twilight zone of suspended animation where death commences while life, in some form, continues. Some patients, however, want no part of a life sustained only by medical technology. Instead, they prefer a plan of medical treatment that allows nature to take its course and permits them to die with dignity."

Nancy Cruzan has dwelt in that twilight zone for six years. She is oblivious to her surroundings and will remain so. . . .

Today the Court, while tentatively accepting that there is some degree of constitutionally protected liberty interest in avoiding unwanted medical treatment, including life-sustaining medical treatment such as artificial nutrition and hydration, affirms the decision of the Missouri Supreme Court. The majority opinion, as I read it, would affirm that decision on the ground that a State may require "clear and convincing" evidence of Nancy Cruzan's prior decision to forgo life-sustaining treatment under circumstances such as hers in order to ensure that her actual wishes are honored. Because I believe that Nancy Cruzan has a fundamental right to be free of unwanted artificial nutrition and hydration, which right is not outweighed by any interests of the State, and because I find that the improperly biased procedural obstacles imposed by the Missouri Supreme Court impermissibly burden that right, I respectfully dissent. Nancy Cruzan is entitled to choose to die with dignity. . . .

The question before this Court is a relatively narrow one: whether the Due Process Clause allows Missouri to require a now-incompetent patient in an irreversible persistent vegetative state to remain on life-support absent rigorously clear and convincing evidence that avoiding the treatment represents the patient's prior, express choice. . . .

Although the right to be free of unwanted medical intervention, like other constitutionally protected interests, may not be absolute, no State interest could outweigh the rights of an individual in Nancy Cruzan's position. Whatever a State's possible interests in mandating life-support treatment under other circumstances, there is no good to be obtained here by Missouri's insistence that Nancy Cruzan remain on life-support systems if it is indeed her wish not to do so. Missouri does not claim, nor could it, that society as a whole will be benefited by Nancy's receiving medical treatment. No third party's situation will be improved and no harm to others will be averted.

The only state interest asserted here is a general interest in the preservation of life. But the State has no legitimate general interest in someone's life, completely abstracted from the interest of the person living that life, that could outweigh the person's choice to avoid medical treatment. . . . Thus, the State's general interest in life must accede to Nancy Cruzan's particularized and intense interest in self-determination in her choice of medical treatment. There is simply nothing legitimately within the State's purview to be gained by superseding her decision. . . .

I do not suggest that States must sit by helplessly if the choices of incompetent patients are in danger of being ignored. Even if the Court had ruled that Missouri's rule of decision is unconstitutional, as I believe it should have, States would nevertheless remain free to fashion procedural protections to safeguard the interests of incompetents under these circumstances. The Constitution provides merely a framework here: protections must be genuinely aimed at ensuring decisions commensurate with the will of the patient, and must be reliable as instruments to that end. Of the many States which have instituted such protec-

tions, Missouri is virtually the only one to have fashioned a rule that lessens the likelihood of accurate determinations. In contrast, nothing in the Constitution prevents States from reviewing the advisability of a family decision, by requiring a court proceeding or by appointing an impartial guardian ad litem.

There are various approaches to determining an incompetent patient's treatment choice in use by the several States today and there may be advantages and disadvantages to each and other approaches not yet envisioned. The choice, in largest part, is and should be left to the States, so long as each State is seeking, in a reliable manner, to discover what the patient would want. But with such momentous interests in the balance, States must avoid procedures that will prejudice the decision. . . .

Finally, I cannot agree with the majority that where it is not possible to determine what choice an incompetent patient would make, a State's role as *parens patriae* permits the State automatically to make that choice itself. Under fair rules of evidence, it is improbable that a court could not determine what the patient's choice would be. Under the rule of decision adopted by Missouri and upheld today by this Court, such occasions might be numerous. But in neither case does it follow that it is constitutionally acceptable for the State invariably to assume the role of deciding for the patient. A State's legitimate interest in safeguarding a patient's choice cannot be furthered by simply appropriating it.

The majority justifies its position by arguing that, while close family members may have a strong feeling about the question, "there is no automatic assurance that the view of close family members will necessarily be the same as the patient's would have been had she been confronted with the prospect of her situation while competent." I cannot quarrel with this observation. But it leads only to another question: Is there any reason to suppose that a State is *more* likely to make the choice that the patient would have made than someone who knew the patient intimately? To ask this is to answer it. . . .

A State's inability to discern an incompetent patient's choice still need not mean that a State is rendered powerless to protect that choice. But I would find that the Due Process Clause prohibits a State from doing more than that. A State may ensure that the person who makes the decision

BOX 15-1   LIVING WILLS

In 1976 California became the first state to adopt living will legislation. Since then almost all the other states have followed suit. Living wills permit individuals various types of control over the use of heroic, life-sustaining medical treatment in the event of a terminal illness. Demand for living will laws is a product of increased social concern with the ability and tendency of modern medicine to keep elderly, terminally ill, and permanently comatose patients alive beyond the natural course of death from age or infirmity. Respirators, cardiac resuscitation, artificial feeding and hydration, drug treatment, and other procedures all have surpassed a natural and easy death, often from pneumonia, known widely in the past as the "old man's friend." Living will laws—and the broader issue of the right to die—affect all age and social groups, although the growing elderly population is disproportionately affected. The issue is similar to abortion because it concerns the preservation of life, but at the opposite end of the life cycle.

NATURAL DEATH ACT DECLARATION
("LIVING WILL")

Virginia's Natural Death Act was enacted in 1983 to permit Virginians to record their wishes regarding extraordinary care in the event of terminal illness. The declaration below is the suggested form developed by the state legislators to implement the Act. Fill out this form and give it to your physician and any relatives and friends you would like to have a copy. You must sign in the presence of two witnesses, and both witnesses must sign in your presence. Blood relatives or spouse may not be witnesses.

DECLARATION

In accordance with the Virginia Natural Death Act, this Declaration was made on _____.
Month/Day/Year

I, _____, willfully and voluntarily make known my desire and do here-
Name of person making declaration
by declare:

You must choose between the following two paragraphs. PARAGRAPH ONE designates a person to make a decision for you. In PARAGRAPH TWO, you make the decision. Cross through the paragraph you do NOT want.

PARAGRAPH ONE:

If at any time I should have a terminal condition and I am comatose, incompetent or otherwise mentally or physically incapable of communication, I designate _____
to make a decision on my behalf as to whether life-prolonging procedures shall be withheld or withdrawn. In the event that my designee decides that such procedures should be withheld or withdrawn, I wish to be permitted to die naturally with only the administration of medication or the performance of any medical procedure deemed necessary to provide me with comfort care or to alleviate pain. (OPTION: I specifically direct that the following procedures or treatments be provided to me:

OR

PARAGRAPH TWO:

If at any time I should have a terminal condition where the application of life-prolonging procedures would serve only to artificially prolong the dying process, I direct that such procedures be withheld or withdrawn, and that I be permitted to die naturally with only the administration of medication or the performance of any medical procedure deemed necessary to provide me with comfort care or to alleviate pain. (OPTION: I specifically direct that the following procedures or treatments be provided to me:

_____

_____

on the patient's behalf is the one whom the patient himself would have selected to make that choice for him. And a State may exclude from consideration anyone having improper motives. But a State generally must either repose the choice with the person whom the patient himself would most likely have chosen as proxy or leave the decision to the patient's family.

I respectfully dissent.

In August 1990, two months after the Court's decision, the Cruzans petitioned a Missouri court for a new hearing. Three of Nancy's former co-workers testified that she had said she would not want to live "like a vegetable." Despite protests from right-to-life groups, a state court judge ruled December 14 that the Cruzans could have Nancy's feeding tube removed. She died December 26.

For the Cruzans the battle was over. But there are approximately 10,000 "Nancy Cruzans" in the United States, a figure that may increase tenfold as medical technology advances. Does the Court's opinion provide guidance for them and their families? Yes and no. On the one hand, the Court clearly ruled that the Fourteenth Amendment's Due Process Clause permits a competent individual to terminate medical treatment. As to incompetent patients, the majority of the justices suggested that states may fashion their own standards, including those that require "clear and convincing evidence" of the patient's interests. Living wills, as Justice O'Connor suggested in a concurring opinion, may be the best form of such evidence *(see Box 15-1)*.

On the other hand, the case did not call for the Court to address squarely another dimension of the right-to-die question, suicides or "assisted suicides" for the terminally ill. May a person take his or her own life or arrange an assisted suicide when suffering from an illness that will surely result in death? In the 1990s this question has taken on unusual importance: the media are full of accounts of people in the advanced stages of AIDS seeking to end their lives and of the as-

sisted suicides conducted by Dr. Jack Kevorkian and others. For the most part, the Court has yet to decide whether the right to privacy or "liberty interest" is broad enough to encompass these practices. While we might speculate on the Court's response, it does seem inevitable that it will have to address this issue within the not too distant future.

REPRODUCTIVE FREEDOM AND THE RIGHT TO PRIVACY: ABORTION

Cruzan's treatment of the right-to-die issue and *Griswold*'s assertion of a right to privacy, more generally, continue to be hotly debated. But those discussions are mild compared with the controversy stirred up by the Court's use of the right-to-privacy doctrine to legalize abortion in *Roe v. Wade* (1973). Since this decision, virtually no other issue has come close to abortion on any political, legal, or emotional scale. Views on abortion have affected the outcome of many political races; occupied preeminent places on legislative, executive, and judicial agendas; and played a role in the nomination proceedings for Supreme Court and lower federal court judges.

What is particularly intriguing about the issue is that the Court generated the furor. Prior to the 1973 decision in *Roe v. Wade,* abortion was not a significant political issue. As Figure 15-2 shows, many states had on their books laws enacted in the late 1800s that permitted abortion only to save the life of the mother. Other states had reformed their legislation in the 1960s to allow for abortion when pregnancy had resulted from incest or when the baby was likely to be severely deformed. The majority of states defined performing or obtaining an abortion, under all other circumstances, as a criminal offense. These conditions do not mean that states were not under pressure to change their laws. During the 1960s a growing pro-choice movement, led by groups such as the ACLU and NARAL, which at that time stood for the National Association for Repeal of Abortion Laws, sought to

FIGURE 15-2 Legislative Action on Abortion Through the Early 1970s

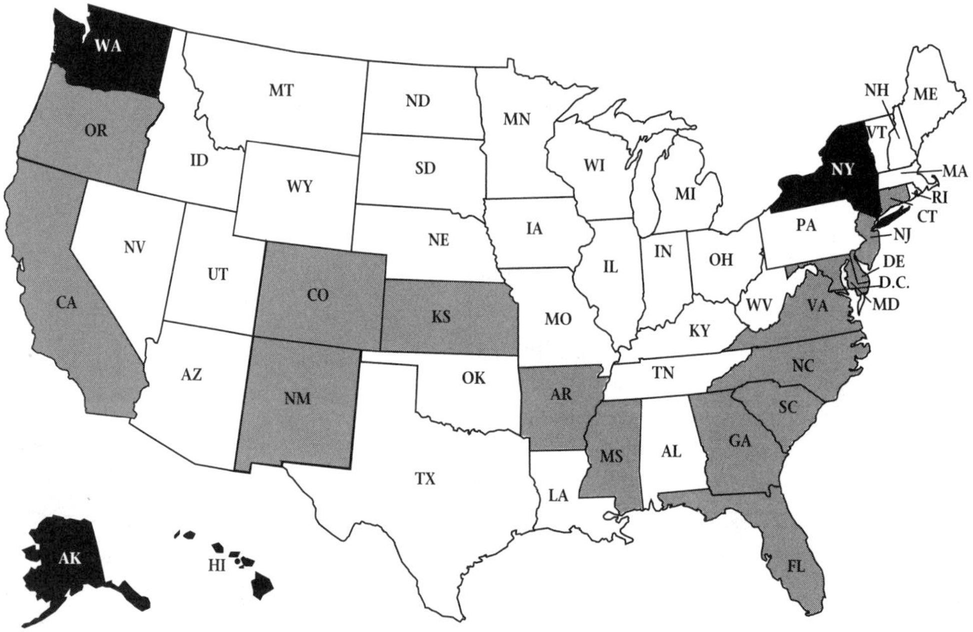

Key:

States in white: retained existing law, which generally permitted abortions to save the life of the mother only.

States in grey: altered existing abortion law, between 1966–1970, to permit abortion under certain circumstances, such as pregnancies resulting from rape or incest.

States in black: repealed existing abortion law in 1970 to allow for some form of "abortion on demand."

convince states to legalize fully the procedure, that is, to allow abortion on demand.

When only a handful of states even considered taking such action, attorneys and leaders of the pro-choice movement supplemented their legislative lobbying with litigation, initiating dozens of suits in federal and state courts. These cases challenged restrictive abortion laws on a number of grounds, including the First Amendment's freedoms of association and speech for doctors (and patients) and the Fourteenth Amendment's Equal Protection Clause (alleging discrimination against women). But the most commonly invoked legal ground was *Griswold*'s right

to privacy. Because it was unclear to attorneys which clause of the Constitution generated the right to privacy *(see Table 15-1)*, in many cases, pro-choice lawyers covered their bases by arguing on all three specific grounds. But their larger point was clear: the right to privacy was broad enough to encompass the right to obtain an abortion. And, because the right to privacy was "fundamental," logic would hold that the right to obtain an abortion was also fundamental, meaning that states could proscribe the procedure only with a compelling interest. Such an interest, pro-choice attorneys asserted, did not exist.

The result of this legal activity was an "avalanche"

of litigation. Pro-choice groups had flooded the U.S. courts with lawsuits—some on behalf of doctors, some for women—challenging both major kinds of abortion laws: those that permitted abortion only to save the life of the mother and those that allowed abortion in cases of rape or incest or to save the life of the mother. They were hoping that the Supreme Court would hear at least one.

Their wish was granted when the Court agreed to hear arguments in December of 1971 in two cases, *Roe v. Wade*, a challenge to a Texas law, representing the most restrictive kinds of abortion laws, and *Doe v. Bolton*, a challenge to a Georgia law, representing the newer, less restrictive laws. As you read *Roe*, pay particular attention to the Court's logic: On what grounds did it strike the Texas law?

Roe v. Wade

410 U.S. 113 (1973)
Vote: 7 (Blackmun, Brennan, Burger, Douglas, Marshall,
        Powell, Stewart)
    2 (Rehnquist, White)
Opinion of the Court: Blackmun
Concurring opinions: Burger, Douglas, Stewart
Dissenting opinions: Rehnquist, White

In August 1969, twenty-one-year-old Norma Mc-Corvey was pregnant; she claimed that the pregnancy was the result of rape.[17] Her doctor refused to perform an abortion, citing an 1857 Texas law, revised in 1879, that made it a crime to "procure an abortion" unless it was necessary to save the life of a mother. He provided her with the name of a lawyer who handled adoptions.

The lawyer, in turn, sent her to two other attorneys, Linda Coffee and Sarah Weddington, whom he knew to be interested in challenging the Texas law.

Coffee and Weddington went after the Texas law with a vengeance, challenging it on all possible grounds: privacy, women's rights, due process, and so forth. Their efforts paid off; a three-judge district court ruled in their favor, mostly on Ninth Amendment privacy grounds. But because the court would not issue an injunction to the state law, McCorvey, using the pseudonym Jane Roe, and her attorneys appealed to the U.S. Supreme Court.

Once the Supreme Court agreed to hear the case, pro-choice and pro-life sides mobilized their forces. On the pro-choice side, the ACLU and other groups helped Weddington and Coffee, who had never appeared before the Court, prepare their briefs and arguments. These groups also lined up numerous amici, ranging from the American College of Obstetricians and Gynecologists to the Planned Parenthood Federation to the American Association of University Women.

In general, the pro-choice side wanted to convince the Court that abortion was a fundamental right under the *Griswold* doctrine. So unless the state could provide a compelling and narrowly drawn interest, the Texas law should fall. It also presented a mass of data indicating that physical and mental health risks are associated with restrictive abortion laws.

The state countered with arguments concerning the rights of fetuses. In its brief, it devoted twenty-four pages, along with nine photographs of fetuses at various stages of development, to depict the "humanness" of the unborn and to support its argument that a state has a compelling interest in protecting human life. The state's position was supported by several pro-life organizations (including the National Right to Life Committee and the League for Infants, Fetuses, and the Elderly) and groups of doctors and nurses.

17. We draw some of this discussion from Marion Faux, *Roe v. Wade* (New York: Macmillan, 1988); and Lee Epstein and Joseph F. Kobylka, *The Supreme Court and Legal Change* (Chapel Hill: University of North Carolina Press, 1992). For other accounts, see Eva Rubin, *Abortion, Politics, and the Courts* (Westport, Conn.: Greenwood Press, 1987); and Richard C. Cortner, *The Supreme Court and Civil Liberties Policy* (Palo Alto, Calif.: Mayfield, 1975).

MR. JUSTICE BLACKMUN delivered the opinion
of the Court.

We forthwith acknowledge our awareness of the sensitive and emotional nature of the abortion controversy, of the vigorous opposing views, even among physicians, and of the deep and seemingly absolute convictions that the subject inspires. One's philosophy, one's experiences, one's exposure to the raw edges of human existence, one's religious training, one's attitudes toward life and family and their values, and the moral standards one establishes and seeks to observe, are all likely to influence and to color one's thinking and conclusions about abortion.

In addition, population growth, pollution, poverty, and racial overtones tend to complicate and not to simplify the problem.

Our task, of course, is to resolve the issue by constitutional measurement, free of emotion and of predilection. We seek earnestly to do this, and, because we do, we have inquired into, and in this opinion place some emphasis upon, medical and medical-legal history and what that history reveals about man's attitudes toward the abortion procedure over the centuries. . . .

The principal thrust of appellant's attack on the Texas statutes is that they improperly invade a right, said to be possessed by the pregnant woman, to choose to terminate her pregnancy. Appellant would discover this right in the concept of personal "liberty" embodied in the Fourteenth Amendment's Due Process Clause in personal, marital, familial, and sexual privacy said to be protected by the Bill of Rights or its penumbras, see Griswold v. Connecticut (1965), or among those rights reserved to the people by the Ninth Amendment, Griswold v. Connecticut. Before addressing this claim, we feel it desirable briefly to survey, in several aspects, the history of abortion, for such insight as that history may afford us, and then to examine the state purposes and interests behind the criminal abortion laws.

It perhaps is not generally appreciated that the restrictive criminal abortion laws in effect in a majority of States today are of relatively recent vintage. Those laws, generally proscribing abortion or its attempt at any time during pregnancy except when necessary to preserve the pregnant woman's life, are not of ancient or even of common-law origin. Instead, they derive from statutory changes effected, for the most part, in the latter half of the 19th century. . . .

Three reasons have been advanced to explain historically the enactment of criminal abortion laws in the 19th century and to justify their continued existence.

It has been argued occasionally that these laws were the product of a Victorian social concern to discourage illicit sexual conduct. Texas, however, does not advance this justification in the present case, and it appears that no court or commentator has taken the argument seriously. . . .

A second reason is concerned with abortion as a medical procedure. When most criminal abortion laws were first enacted, the procedure was a hazardous one for the woman. This was particularly true prior to the development of antisepsis. . . . Thus, it has been argued that a State's real concern in enacting a criminal abortion law was to protect the pregnant woman, that is, to restrain her from submitting to a procedure that placed her life in serious jeopardy.

The modern medical techniques have altered this situation. . . . Consequently, any interest of the State in protecting the woman from an inherently hazardous procedure, except when it would be equally dangerous for her to forgo it, has largely disappeared. Of course, important state interests in the areas of health and medical standards do remain. The State has a legitimate interest in seeing to it that abortion, like any other medical procedure, is performed under circumstances that insure maximum safety for the patient. . . . Moreover, the risk to the woman increases as her pregnancy continues. Thus, the State retains a definite interest in protecting the woman's own health and safety when an abortion is proposed at a late stage of pregnancy.

The third reason is the State's interest—some phrase it in terms of duty—in protecting prenatal life. Some of the argument for this justification rests on the theory that a new human life is present from the moment of conception. The State's interest and general obligation to protect life then extends, it is argued, to prenatal life. Only when the life of the pregnant mother herself is at stake, balanced against the life she carries within her, should the interest of the embryo or fetus not prevail. Logically, of course, a legitimate state interest in this area need not stand or fall on acceptance of the belief that life begins at conception or at some other point prior to live birth. In assessing the State's interest, recognition may be given to the less rigid claim that as long as at least *potential* life is involved, the State may assert interests beyond the protection of the pregnant woman alone. . . .

It is with these interests, and the weight to be attached to them, that this case is concerned.

The Constitution does not explicitly mention any right of privacy. In a line of decisions, however, the Court has recognized that a right of personal privacy, or a guarantee of certain areas or zones of privacy, does exist under the Constitution. In varying contexts, the Court or individual Justices have, indeed, found at least the roots of that right in the First Amendment, in the Fourth and Fifth Amendments, in the penumbras of the Bill of Rights, in the Ninth Amendment, or in the concept of liberty guaranteed by the first section of the Fourteenth Amendment. These decisions make it clear that only personal rights that can be deemed "fundamental" or "implicit in the concept of ordered liberty" are included in this guarantee of personal privacy. They also make it clear that the right has some extension to activities relating to marriage, procreation, family relationships, and child rearing and education.

This right of privacy, whether it be founded in the Fourteenth Amendment's concept of personal liberty and restrictions upon state action, as we feel it is, or, as the District Court determined, in the Ninth Amendment's reservation of rights to the people, is broad enough to encompass a woman's decision whether or not to terminate her pregnancy. The detriment that the State would impose upon the pregnant woman by denying this choice altogether is apparent. Specific and direct harm medically diagnosable even in early pregnancy may be involved. Maternity, or additional offspring, may force upon the woman a distressful life and future. Psychological harm may be imminent. Mental and physical health may be taxed by child care. There is also the distress, for all concerned, associated with the unwanted child, and there is the problem of bringing a child into a family already unable, psychologically and otherwise, to care for it. In other cases, as in this one, the additional difficulties and continuing stigma of unwed motherhood may be involved. All these are factors the woman and her responsible physician necessarily will consider in consultation.

On the basis of elements such as these, appellant and some *amici* argue that the woman's right is absolute and

Norma McCorvey (shown here in 1989) was the real "Jane Roe." She challenged the constitutionality of the Texas anti-abortion statute. The suit was resolved in 1973 when the Supreme Court handed down its decision in *Roe v. Wade*, declaring that the right to privacy protected a woman's freedom to terminate a pregnancy.

that she is entitled to terminate her pregnancy at whatever time, in whatever way, and for whatever reason she alone chooses. With this we do not agree. Appellant's arguments that Texas either has no valid interest at all in regulating the abortion decision, or no interest strong enough to support any limitation upon the woman's sole determination, are unpersuasive. The Court's decisions recognizing a right of privacy also acknowledge that some state regulation in areas protected by that right is appropriate. As noted above, a State may properly assert important interests in safeguarding health, in maintaining medical standards, and in protecting potential life. At some point in pregnancy, these respective interests become sufficiently compelling to sustain regulation of the factors that govern the abortion decision. The privacy right involved, therefore, cannot be said to be absolute. . . .

We, therefore, conclude that the right of personal privacy includes the abortion decision, but that this right is not unqualified and must be considered against important state interests in regulation. . . .

The District Court held that the appellee failed to meet his burden of demonstrating that the Texas statute's infringement upon Roe's rights was necessary to support a compelling state interest, and that, although the appellee presented "several compelling justifications for state presence in the area of abortions," the statutes outstripped these justifications and swept "far beyond any areas of compelling state interest." Appellant and appellee both contest that holding. Appellant, as has been indicated, claims an absolute right that bars any state imposition of criminal penalties in the area. Appellee argues that the State's determination to recognize and protect prenatal life from and after conception constitutes a compelling state interest. As noted above, we do not agree fully with either formulation.

A. The appellee and certain *amici* argue that the fetus is a "person" within the language and meaning of the Fourteenth Amendment. . . .

The Constitution does not define "person" in so many words. Section 1 of the Fourteenth Amendment contains three references to "person." The first, in defining "citizens," speaks of "persons born or naturalized in the United States." The word also appears both in the Due Process Clause and in the Equal Protection Clause. "Person" is used in other places in the Constitution: in the listing of qualifications for Representatives and Senators, Art. I, § 2, cl. 2, and § 3, cl. 3; in the Apportionment Clause, Art. I, § 2, § 3. . . . But in nearly all these instances, the use of the word is such that it has application only postnatally. None indicates, with any assurance, that it has any possible prenatal application.

All this, together with our observation that throughout the major portion of the 19th century prevailing legal abortion practices were far freer than they are today, persuades us that the word "person," as used in the Fourteenth Amendment, does not include the unborn. . . .

This conclusion, however, does not of itself fully answer the contentions raised by Texas, and we pass on to other considerations.

B. The pregnant woman cannot be isolated in her privacy. She carries an embryo and, later, a fetus, if one accepts the medical definitions of the developing young in the human uterus. The situation therefore is inherently different from marital intimacy, or bedroom possession of obscene material, or marriage, or procreation. . . . As we have intimated above, it is reasonable and appropriate for a State to decide that at some point in time another interest, that of health of the mother or that of potential human life, becomes significantly involved. The woman's privacy is no longer sole and any right of privacy she possesses must be measured accordingly.

Texas urges that, apart from the Fourteenth Amendment, life begins at conception and is present throughout pregnancy, and that, therefore, the State has a compelling interest in protecting that life from and after conception. We need not resolve the difficult question of when life begins. When those trained in the respective disciplines of medicine, philosophy, and theology are unable to arrive at any consensus, the judiciary, at this point in the development of man's knowledge, is not in a position to speculate as to the answer. . . .

In view of all this, we do not agree that, by adopting one theory of life, Texas may override the rights of the pregnant woman that are at stake. We repeat, however, that the State does have an important and legitimate interest in preserving and protecting the health of the pregnant woman, whether she be a resident of the State or a non-resident who seeks medical consultation and treatment there, and that it has still another important and legitimate interest in protecting the potentiality of human life. These interests are separate and distinct. Each grows in substantiality as the woman approaches term and, at a point during pregnancy, each becomes "compelling."

With respect to the State's important and legitimate interest in the health of the mother, the "compelling" point, in the light of present medical knowledge, is at approximately the end of the first trimester. This is so because of the now-established medical fact. . . . that until the end of the first trimester mortality in abortion may be less than mortality in normal childbirth. It follows that, from and after this point, a State may regulate the abortion procedure to the extent that the regulation reasonably relates to the preservation and protection of maternal health. Examples of permissible state regulation in this area are requirements as to the qualifications of the person who is to perform the abortion; as to the licensure of that person; as to the facility in which the procedure is to be performed, that is, whether it must be a hospital or may be a clinic or some other place of less-than-hospital status; as to the licensing of the facility; and the like.

This means, on the other hand, that, for the period of pregnancy prior to this "compelling" point, the attending physician, in consultation with his patient, is free to determine, without regulation by the State, that, in his medical judgment, the patient's pregnancy should be terminated. If that decision is reached, the judgment may be effectuated by an abortion free of interference by the State.

With respect to the State's important and legitimate interest in potential life, the "compelling" point is at viability. This is so because the fetus then presumably has the capability of meaningful life outside the mother's womb. State regulation protective of fetal life after viability thus has both logical and biological justifications. If the State is interested in protecting fetal life after viability, it may go so far as to proscribe abortion during that period, except when it is necessary to preserve the life or health of the mother.

Measured against these standards, . . . the Texas [law] . . . , in restricting legal abortions to those "procured or attempted by medical advice for the purpose of saving the life of the mother," sweeps too broadly. The statute makes no distinction between abortions performed early in pregnancy and those performed later, and it limits to a single reason, "saving" the mother's life, the legal justification for the procedure. The statute, therefore, cannot survive the constitutional attack made upon it here. . . .

To summarize and to repeat:

1. A state criminal abortion statute of the current Texas type, that excepts from criminality only a *life-saving* procedure on behalf of the mother, without regard to pregnancy stage and without recognition of the other interests involved, is violative of the Due Process Clause of the Fourteenth Amendment.

(a) For the stage prior to approximately the end of the first trimester, the abortion decision and its effectuation must be left to the medical judgment of the pregnant woman's attending physician.

(b) For the stage subsequent to approximately the end of the first trimester, the State, in promoting its interest in the health of the mother, may, if it chooses, regulate the abortion procedure in ways that are reasonably related to maternal health.

(c) For the stage subsequent to viability, the State in promoting its interest in the potentiality of human life may, if it chooses, regulate, and even proscribe, abortion except where it is necessary, in appropriate medical judgment, for the preservation of the life or health of the mother. . . .

This holding, we feel, is consistent with the relative weights of the respective interests involved, with the lessons and examples of medical and legal history, with the lenity of the common law, and with the demands of the profound problems of the present day. The decision leaves the State free to place increasing restrictions on abortion as the period of pregnancy lengthens, so long as those restrictions are tailored to the recognized state interests. The decision vindicates the right of the physician to administer medical treatment according to his professional judgment up to the points where important state interests provide compelling justifications for intervention. Up to those points, the abortion decision in all its aspects is inherently, and primarily, a medical decision, and basic responsibility for it must rest with the physician. If an individual practitioner abuses the privilege of exercising proper medical judgment, the usual remedies, judicial and intra-professional, are available.[18]

MR. JUSTICE REHNQUIST, dissenting.

The Court's opinion brings to the decision of this troubling question both extensive historical fact and a wealth of legal scholarship. While the opinion thus commands my respect, I find myself nonetheless in fundamental disagreement with those parts of it that invalidate the Texas statute in question, and therefore dissent. . . .

. . . I have difficulty in concluding, as the Court does, that the right of "privacy" is involved in this case. Texas, by the statute here challenged, bars the performance of a medical abortion by a licensed physician on a plaintiff such as

18. In *Doe*, decided the same day as *Roe*, the Court reviewed a challenge to the newer abortion laws, enacted by some states in the 1960s. While Texas permitted abortions only to save a mother's life, Georgia allowed them under the following circumstances: (1) when a "duly licensed Georgia physician" determines in "his best clinical judgment" that carrying the baby to term would injure the mother's life or health; (2) when a high likelihood existed that the fetus would be born with a serious deformity; and (3) when the pregnancy was the result of rape. The law contained other requirements, the most stringent of which was that two other doctors agree with the judgment of the one performing the abortion. Reiterating his opinion in *Roe*, Blackmun struck down the Georgia law as a violation of Fourteenth Amendment guarantees. Once again, six other members of the Court agreed with his conclusion.

Roe. A transaction resulting in an operation such as this is not "private" in the ordinary usage of that word. Nor is the "privacy" that the Court finds here even a distant relative of the freedom from searches and seizures protected by the Fourth Amendment to the Constitution, which the Court has referred to as embodying a right to privacy. Katz v. United States (1967).

If the Court means by the term "privacy" no more than that the claim of a person to be free from unwanted state regulation of consensual transactions may be a form of "liberty" protected by the Fourteenth Amendment, there is no doubt that similar claims have been upheld in our earlier decisions on the basis of that liberty. I agree . . . that the "liberty," against deprivation of which without due process the Fourteenth Amendment protects, embraces more than the rights found in the Bill of Rights. But that liberty is not guaranteed absolutely against deprivation, only against deprivation without due process of law. The test traditionally applied in the area of social and economic legislation is whether or not a law such as that challenged has a rational relation to a valid state objective. . . . The Due Process Clause of the Fourteenth Amendment undoubtedly does place a limit, albeit a broad one, on legislative power to enact laws such as this. If the Texas statute were to prohibit an abortion even where the mother's life is in jeopardy, I have little doubt that such a statute would lack a rational relation to a valid state objective. . . . But the Court's sweeping invalidation of any restrictions on abortion during the first trimester is impossible to justify under that standard, and the conscious weighing of competing factors that the Court's opinion apparently substitutes for the established test is far more appropriate to a legislative judgment than to a judicial one.

The Court eschews the history of the Fourteenth Amendment in its reliance on the "compelling state interest" test. . . . But the Court adds a new wrinkle to this test by transposing it from the legal considerations associated with the Equal Protection Clause of the Fourteenth Amendment to this case arising under the Due Process Clause of the Fourteenth Amendment. Unless I misapprehend the consequences of this transplanting of the "compelling state interest test," the Court's opinion will accomplish the seemingly impossible feat of leaving this area of the law more confused than it found it. . . .

. . . As in *Lochner* and similar cases applying substantive due process standards to economic and social welfare legislation, the adoption of the compelling state interest standard will inevitably require this Court to examine the legislative policies and pass on the wisdom of these policies in the very process of deciding whether a particular state interest put forward may or may not be "compelling." The decision here to break pregnancy into three distinct terms and to outline the permissible restrictions the State may impose in each one, for example, partakes more of judicial legislation than it does of a determination of the intent of the drafters of the Fourteenth Amendment.

The fact that a majority of the States reflecting, after all, the majority sentiment in those States, have had restrictions on abortions for at least a century is a strong indication, it seems to me, that the asserted right to an abortion is not "so rooted in the traditions and conscience of our people as to be ranked as fundamental.". . . Even today, when society's views on abortion are changing, the very existence of the debate is evidence that the "right" to an abortion is not so universally accepted as the appellant would have us believe.

To reach its result, the Court necessarily has had to find within the scope of the Fourteenth Amendment a right that was apparently completely unknown to the drafters of the Amendment. As early as 1821, the first state law dealing directly with abortion was enacted by the Connecticut Legislature. By the time of the adoption of the Fourteenth Amendment in 1868, there were at least 36 laws enacted by state or territorial legislatures limiting abortion. While many States have amended or updated their laws, 21 of the laws on the books in 1868 remain in effect today. Indeed, the Texas statute struck down today was, as the majority notes, first enacted in 1857 and "has remained substantially unchanged to the present time."

There apparently was no question concerning the validity of this provision or of any of the other state statutes when the Fourteenth Amendment was adopted. The only conclusion possible from this history is that the drafters did not intend to have the Fourteenth Amendment withdraw from the States the power to legislate with respect to this matter. . . .

For all of the foregoing reasons, I respectfully dissent.

MR. JUSTICE WHITE, with whom MR. JUSTICE REHNQUIST joins, dissenting.

The Court for the most part sustains this position:During the period prior to the time the fetus becomes viable, the Constitution of the United States values the convenience, whim, or caprice of the putative mother more than the life or potential life of the fetus; the Constitution, therefore, guarantees the right to an abortion as against any state law or policy seeking to protect the fetus from an abortion not prompted by more compelling reasons of the mother.

With all due respect, I dissent. I find nothing in the language or history of the Constitution to support the Court's judgment. The Court simply fashions and announces a new constitutional right for pregnant women and, with scarcely any reason or authority for its action, invests that right with sufficient substance to override most existing state abortion statutes. The upshot is that the people and the legislatures of the 50 States are constitutionally disentitled to weigh the relative importance of the continued existence and development of the fetus, on the one hand, against a spectrum of possible impacts on the mother, on the other hand. As an exercise of raw judicial power, the Court perhaps has authority to do what it does today; but in my view its judgment is an improvident and extravagant exercise of the power of judicial review that the Constitution extends to this Court.

The Court apparently values the convenience of the pregnant mother more than the continued existence and development of the life or potential life that she carries. Whether or not I might agree with that marshaling of values, I can in no event join the Court's judgment because I find no constitutional warrant for imposing such an order of priorities on the people and legislatures of the States. In a sensitive area such as this, involving as it does issues over which reasonable men may easily and heatedly differ, I cannot accept the Court's exercise of its clear power of choice by interposing a constitutional barrier to state efforts to protect human life and by investing mothers and doctors with the constitutionally protected right to exterminate it. This issue, for the most part, should be left with the people and to the political processes the people have devised to govern their affairs.

Justice Blackmun's decisions in *Roe* and *Doe* were a tour de force on the subject of abortion. They provided a comprehensive history of government regulation of abortion and reviewed in some detail arguments for and against the procedure. Most important was his conclusion: the right to privacy "is broad enough to encompass a woman's decision whether or not to terminate a pregnancy." Behind this assertion are several important ideas. First, the Court, while not rejecting a Ninth Amendment theory of privacy, preferred to locate the right in the Fourteenth Amendment's Due Process Clause, an approach suggested by Justices Harlan and White in their concurring opinions in *Griswold (see Table 15-1)*. Second, the Court found the abortion right fundamental and, therefore, would use a compelling state interest test to assess the constitutionality of restrictions on that right—but with something of a twist. For the reasons Blackmun gave in his opinion, the state's interests in protecting the woman's health and in protecting the "potentiality of human life" grow "in substantiality as the woman approaches term and, at a point during pregnancy . . . become compelling." This point led the majority to adopt the trimester scheme *(see Table 15-2)*. Under this scheme, the state's compelling interest arises at the point of viability. It may, however, regulate second trimester abortions in ways that "are reasonably related to the mother's health."

In their dissents, Justices White and Rehnquist lambasted the trimester scheme, as well as almost every other aspect of the opinion. They thought it relied on "raw judicial power" to reach an "extravagant" and "improvident" decision. Rehnquist found that the Court's use of a compelling state interest test to assess statutes under the Fourteenth Amendment's Due Process Clause represented a return to the discredited doctrine of substantive due process as expressed in *Lochner v. New York* (1905), a complaint that echoed Black's dissent in *Griswold*. Rehnquist would have preferred that the Court adopt a "rational basis" ap-

BOX 15-2   HARRY ANDREW BLACKMUN
(1970–1994)

Harry A. Blackmun was born November 12, 1908, in Nashville, Illinois. He spent most of his early life in the Minneapolis- St. Paul area, where his father was an official of the Twin Cities Savings and Loan Company. In grade school Blackmun began a friendship with Warren Burger, with whom he was later to serve on the Supreme Court.

Showing an early aptitude for mathematics, Blackmun attended Harvard University on a scholarship. He majored in mathematics and thought briefly of becoming a physician, but chose the law instead. He graduated Phi Beta Kappa from Harvard in 1929 and entered Harvard Law School, graduating in 1932. During his law school years, Blackmun supported himself with a variety of odd jobs, including tutoring in math and driving the launch for the college crew team.

After law school, Blackmun returned to St. Paul, where he served for a year and a half as a law clerk to Judge John B. Sanborn, whom Blackmun was to succeed on the U.S. Circuit Court twenty-six years later. He left the clerkship in 1933 to enter private practice with a Minneapolis law firm, where he remained for sixteen years. During that time he also taught at the Mitchell College of Law in St. Paul, Chief Justice Burger's alma mater, and at the University of Minnesota Law School.

Blackmun married Dorothy E. Clark, June 21, 1941, and they have three daughters.

In 1950 he accepted a post as "house counsel" for the world-famous Mayo Clinic in Rochester, Minnesota. There, Blackmun quickly developed a reputation among his colleagues as a serious man totally engrossed in his profession.

His reputation followed him to the bench of the Eighth Circuit Court of Appeals, to which Blackmun was appointed by President Dwight D. Eisenhower in 1959. As an appeals court judge, Blackmun became known for his scholarly and thorough opinions.

Blackmun's nomination to the Supreme Court was President Richard Nixon's third try to fill the seat vacated by Justice Abe Fortas's resignation. The Senate had refused to confirm Nixon's first two nominees—Clement F. Haynesworth, Jr., of South Carolina and G. Harrold Carswell of Florida. Nixon remarked that he had concluded from the rejection of his first two nominees that the Senate "as it is presently constituted" would not confirm a southern nominee who was also a judicial conservative.

Nixon then turned to Blackmun, who was confirmed without opposition. During his first years on the Court, Blackmun was frequently linked with Burger as the "Minnesota Twins," who thought and voted alike, but, beginning with his authorship of the Court's 1973 ruling in *Roe v. Wade*, which legalized abortion, Blackmun moved in a steadily more liberal direction, leaving Burger behind in the Court's conservative wing.

Blackmun retired from the Court August 3, 1994.

SOURCE: Adapted from Elder Witt, *Guide to the U.S. Supreme Court,* 2d ed. (Washington, D.C.: Congressional Quarterly, 1990), 876–877.

TABLE 15-2 The *Roe v. Wade* Trimester Scheme

Stage of Pregnancy	Degree of Permissible State Regulation of the Decision to Terminate Pregnancy
Prior to the end of the first trimester (approximately months 1–3)	Almost None: "the abortion and its effectuation must be left to [the woman and] the medical judgment of the pregnant woman's attending physician."
The end of the first trimester through "viability" (approximately months 4–6)	Some: "the state, in promoting its interest in the health of the mother, may, if it chooses, regulate the abortion procedure in ways that are reasonably related to maternal health." But it may not prohibit abortions.
Subsequent to viability (approximately months 7–9)	High: "the state, in promoting its interest in the potentiality of human life, may, if it chooses, regulate, and even proscribe, abortion except where necessary, in appropriate medical judgment, for the preservation of the life or health of the mother."

proach to the abortion right as it had to regulations challenged on due process grounds after the fall of substantive due process. Under this approach, the Court would have to decide only whether the government had acted reasonably to achieve a legitimate government objective. Using a rational basis approach, as you can imagine, the Court generally defers to the government and presumes the validity of the government's action. Had the Court adopted this approach to the abortion right, it would have upheld the Texas and Georgia restrictions. White, joined by Rehnquist, thought the Court had gone well beyond the scope of its powers and of the text and history of the Constitution to generate a policy statement that smacked of judicial activism. To White, it was up to the people and their elected officials to determine the fate of abortion, not the Court.

As Blackmun's opinion was nearly two years in the making, the other justices knew that, if nothing else, it would be a comprehensive statement. Outsiders, however, were shocked; few expected such an opinion from a Nixon appointee and Warren Burger's childhood friend *(see Box 15-2)*. But Blackmun's opinion

was not the only surprise; Burger's decision to go along with the majority startled many observers. Moreover, White and Stewart cast rather puzzling votes in light of their opinions in *Griswold*. Stewart had dissented in *Griswold*, asserting that the Constitution did not guarantee a general right to privacy. If he believed that to be so, then how could he agree to the creation of the right to obtain legal abortions, a right that rested on privacy? White, on the other hand, had been in the majority in *Griswold*. But, for him, apparently, the right to privacy was not broad enough to cover abortion.

The factors that explain the justices' position in *Roe* and *Doe* are matters of speculation, for, as Justice Blackmun once noted, it is always hard to predict how a new justice will come down on the abortion issue. What is not a matter of speculation is that the responses of Americans to *Roe*—both positive and negative—were (and still are) perhaps the strongest in the Court's history.

Reaction came from all quarters of American life. Some legal scholars applauded the *Roe* opinion, asserting that it indicated the Court's sensitivity to

558   CIVIL LIBERTIES

FIGURE 15-3 Percentage of Respondents Supporting *Roe v. Wade*, 1974–1991

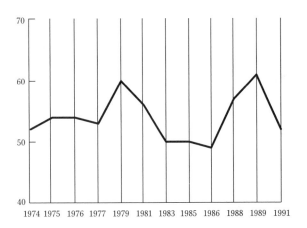

1974 1975 1976 1977 1979 1981 1983 1985 1986 1988 1989 1991

SOURCE: Lee Epstein, Jeffrey A. Segal, Harold J. Spaeth, and Thomas G. Walker, *The Supreme Court Compendium: Data, Decisions, and Developments* (Washington, D.C.: Congressional Quarterly, 1994), Table 8-19.

changing times. Others ripped it to shreds. They called the trimester scheme unworkable and said that, as medical technology advanced, viability would come increasingly earlier in pregnancy. Others attacked the decision's use of the Fourteenth Amendment, agreeing with Justice Rehnquist that the application represented a retreat to pre-New Deal days. Still others claimed that the decision usurped the intention of *Griswold*. John Hart Ely wrote that a right to privacy against "governmental snooping" is legitimate, but a general freedom of "autonomy"—"to live one's life without governmental interference"—goes beyond the scope of *Griswold*.[19]

Roe also divided the political community. Some legislators were pleased that the Court, and not they, had handled a political hot potato. Others were outraged on moral grounds ("abortion is murder") and on constitutional grounds (this is a matter of public policy for legislators, not judges, to determine).

As Figure 15-3 shows, the public was (and remains)

split over its support for the Court's ruling. But divisions over the abortion right did not come about as a result of *Roe*. Since the first public opinion polls taken on abortion in the 1960s, opinion on abortion has been fragmented. For example, in the 1990s nearly 80 percent of survey respondents indicate that a pregnant woman should be able to obtain an abortion if there is a chance of "serious defect" in the baby, while only 41 percent say that a woman should be able to terminate a pregnancy because she "is not married and does not want to marry the man." In the final analysis, all *Roe* did, as political scientists Charles Franklin and Liane Kosaki show, was to intensify basic divisions over abortion: if one was pro-choice before the decision, one became even more so; the converse held true for those favoring the pro-life side.[20]

Although *Roe* may not have changed public opinion on abortion, it had the important effect of mobilizing the right to life movement. Before 1973 groups opposed to legalized abortion had lobbied successfully against efforts to liberalize state laws. When *Roe* nullified these legislative victories, these groups vowed to see the decision overturned. In short, *Roe* and *Doe* fanned the fire, rather than quenched it.

The Aftermath of Roe: *Attempts to Limit the Decision*

Right to life groups are dedicated to the eradication of *Roe v. Wade*, a goal that they can accomplish in one of two ways: they can convince Congress to propose an amendment to the Constitution or convince the Court to overrule its decision. In the immediate aftermath of *Roe*, neither of these options was viable. Despite the public's mixed view of abortion, during the 1970s only about a third of Americans supported a constitutional amendment to proscribe it. The lack of support may explain why Congress, ever cognizant of the polls, did not pass any of the "human life"

19. John Hart Ely, "The Wages of Crying Wolf: A Comment on *Roe v. Wade*," *Yale Law Journal* 82 (1973): 920.

20. "The Republican Schoolmaster: The Supreme Court, Public Opinion, and Abortion," *American Political Science Review* 83 (1989): 751–772.

amendments it considered in the 1970s. And, given the 7-2 vote in *Roe,* wholesale changes in the Court's membership would be required before the Court would reconsider its stance on abortion.

Faced with this situation, pro-life groups determined that their best course of action was to seek limitations on the ways in which women could obtain and pay for abortions. They lobbied legislatures to enact restrictions on *Roe.* Two types of restrictions predominated—those that required the consent of a woman's parents or husband and those that limited government funding for abortion services. These efforts were quite successful. During the 1970s, eighteen states required some form of consent and thirty (along with the federal government) restricted funding. To put it another way, by 1978 only about fifteen states had not enacted laws requiring consent or restricting funding.

Consent. As pro-life forces convinced states to enact these laws, pro-choice forces just as quickly challenged them in court. The first major post-*Roe* battle, *Planned Parenthood v. Danforth* (1976) involved consent, a subject the Court had not considered in *Roe.* The state of Missouri passed legislation that required the written consent of a pregnant woman and her spouse or parents (in the case of an unmarried minor) before an abortion could be performed.

While the Court found no constitutional violation in requiring a woman to give her own consent to the procedure, it struck down parental and spousal consent provisions as violative of the Constitution and inconsistent with *Roe.* However, Justice Blackmun's majority opinion gave pro-life movements a little hope. It struck down Missouri's parental consent requirement, but it also stated: "We emphasize that our holding that parental consent is invalid does not suggest that every minor, regardless of age or maturity, may give effective consent for the termination of her pregnancy." With these words, Blackmun opened the door to the possibility of some form of required parental consent.

As illustrated in Table 15-3, pro-life forces took advantage of Blackmun's statement, convincing states to enact various parental and other consent requirements, many of which were tested by the Court. And, although the Court has continued to strike down laws forcing a woman to obtain the consent of or to notify her spouse prior to obtaining an abortion, as Table 15-3 shows it has been much more willing to permit forms of parental consent or notification.

Funding. Consent laws were not the only way pro-life forces sought to restrict the abortion right in the wake of *Roe.* They also sought to convince states and the federal government to restrict government funding for abortions.[21] To pro-life organizations, this type of restriction was another step toward the eradication of *Roe.* Funding was inextricably bound to implementation: if women could not afford abortions and the government could not pay for them, then either doctors would not perform them or women would be deterred from having them. Pro-choice groups viewed these laws as backdoor attempts to gut *Roe.* From their perspective, *Roe* was a victory not just for doctors or even middle-class women, but for those women who could not afford to travel to other countries or states to obtain abortions. Logically, they assumed, that once the Court established the right to choose, governments had an obligation to protect that right, even if meant funding for the poor through government health insurance programs.

Few governments, however, shared this pro-choice vision, at least in the immediate aftermath of *Roe.* In September 1976, after several years of prodding by pro-life forces, Congress passed the Hyde Amendment (named after its sponsor, Henry Hyde, R-Ill.). In its original form, it stated that no federal funds "shall be used to perform abortions except where the life of the mother would be endangered if the fetus were carried to full term." In 1977 and 1978 Congress altered the language to expand the circumstances under which

---

21. Material in the next two paragraphs draws heavily on Epstein and Kobylka, *The Supreme Court and Legal Change,* 220–221.

TABLE 15-3 Cases Involving Consent to Abortions, 1976–1993

Case	Consent Provision at Issue	Court Holding
Planned Parenthood v. Danforth (1976)	Written consent required of the (1) pregnant woman, (2) her spouse, or (3) her parents.	The Court struck spousal and parental requirements. It upheld the provision requiring the woman's consent.
Bellotti v. Baird II (1979)	Parental consent required prior to abortions performed on unmarried women under eighteen. If one or both parents refuse, the "abortion may be obtained by order of a judge … for good cause shown."	The Court struck the law, but claimed that it was not "persuaded as a general rule" that parental consent "unconstitutionally burdens a minor's right to seek an abortion."
H. L. v. Matheson (1981)	Doctors should "notify, if possible" a minor's parents prior to performing an abortion.	The Court upheld the law on the ground that "the Constitution does not compel a state to fine-tune its statutes as to encourage or facilitate abortions."
Akron v. Akron Center for Reproductive Health (1983)	Parental notification and consent required prior to abortions performed on unmarried minors under fifteen. Doctors must make "certain specified statements" to ensure that consent for all those seeking abortions is "truly informed." Requires a twenty-four-hour waiting period "between the time a woman signs a consent form and the time the abortion is performed."	The Court invalidated all three provisions.
Planned Parenthood v. Ashcroft (1983)	Parental or judicial consent required prior to abortions performed on unmarried minors.	The Court upheld the provision, asserting that judges may give their consent to abortions.
Hodgson v. Minnesota (1990)	Requirement that both parents be notified prior to the performance of an abortion (unless a court orders otherwise). Abortions cannot be performed on minors until forty-eight hours after both parents have been notified.	The Court upheld the two-parent requirement with an exemption option. It upheld the forty-eight hour waiting period.
Ohio v. Akron Center for Reproductive Health (1990)	Requirement that one parent be notified prior to the performance of an abortion on an unmarried, unemancipated minor (unless a court authorizes it).	The Court upheld the law.
Planned Parenthood of Southeastern Pennsylvania v. Casey (1992)	Required three kinds of consent: (1) informed consent of the woman; (2) statement from woman indicating that she has notified her spouse; (3) in the case of minors, informed consent of one parent.	The Court upheld informed consent, struck spousal notifications, and upheld parental consent.

TABLE 15-4 Cases Involving Restrictions on Abortions

Case	Funding Restriction at Issue	Court Holding
Beal v. Doe (1977)	Pennsylvania law limiting Medicaid funding "to those abortions that are certified by physicians as medically necessary."	The Court upheld the restriction against constitutional claims that the law interfered with the fundamental right to obtain an abortion as articulated in *Roe* and that it discriminated on the basis of socioeconomic status and against those choosing abortion over childbirth.
Maher v. Roe (1977)	Connecticut Welfare Department regulation limiting state Medicaid "benefits for first trimester abortions … that are 'medically necessary.'"	The Court upheld the restriction against various constitutional claims (see above).
Poelker v. Doe (1977)	St. Louis policy directive that barred city-owned hospitals from performing abortions.	The Court upheld the restriction against various constitutional claims (see above).
Harris v. McCrae (1980)	Federal government regulation (the Hyde Amendment) limiting Medicaid funding of abortions to those "where the life of the mother would be endangered if the fetus were carried to term."	The Court upheld the restrictions against claims that the law violated due process (impinges on a fundamental right), equal protection (discriminates against women, especially poor women), and First Amendment (burdens religious exercise and constitutes religious establishment) guarantees.

funding could be obtained. Even so, under the Hyde Amendment federal funds paid for only about 10 percent of all abortion services for women.[22] Following the lead of the federal government, more than half the states passed legislation restricting the use of Medicaid funds for abortion procedures. The states were particularly easy targets for pro-life groups: all these organizations needed to do was to point out that funding limits constituted fiscally prudent measures. Before the limitations went into effect, 25 percent of all abortions were funded by state monies.[23]

In response to these pro-life legislative victories, pro-choice groups challenged the funding laws as violations of the fundamental right to obtain an abortion, as articulated in *Roe*. The courts again became battlefields, and the Supreme Court reentered the fray in 1977. As Table 15-4 shows, the Court decided three cases that year, *Maher v. Roe, Beal v. Doe,* and *Poelker v. Doe*—all of which involved state or local restrictions on abortion funding. The Court upheld all of these various restrictions. In the eyes of the justices, the regulations did not infringe significantly on abortion rights and, as Justice Powell wrote in *Maher*, "The State unquestionably has 'a strong and legitimate interest in encouraging normal childbirth.'" In short, the justices found that there is a right to abortion, but states have no obligation to fund it. It is worth emphasizing that these rulings did not *prohibit* the state funding of abortions; rather, they held that, because the Constitution does not mandate such funding, states could enact restrictions.

22. At one point, the Hyde Amendment provided Medicaid funding if two doctors certified that carrying a pregnancy to full term would result in "severe and long lasting physical health damages" or the pregnancy was the result of incest or rape.

23. See Epstein and Kobylka, *The Supreme Court and Legal Change,* 220.

As Table 15-4 indicates, pro-choice groups also failed in their challenge to the Hyde Amendment. Immediately after the amendment was passed, a coalition of pro-choice advocates, including the ACLU, Planned Parenthood, and the Center for Constitutional Rights, challenged its constitutionality. In bringing *Harris v. McCrae* (1980) they marshaled an array of legal arguments and sociological evidence suggesting that poor women might resort to self-abortion or other unsafe procedures if the Hyde Amendment remained law. But, in a 5–4 decision, the Court rejected their arguments, asserting that

regardless of whether the freedom of a woman to choose to terminate her pregnancy for health reasons lies at the core or the periphery of the due process liberty recognized in [*Roe v. Wade*], it simply does not follow that a woman's freedom of choice carries with it a constitutional entitlement to the financial resources to avail herself of the full range of protected choices. . . . [A]lthough government may not place obstacles in the path of a woman's exercise of her freedom of choice, it need not remove those not of its own creation. Indigency falls in the latter category.

Challenges to Roe v. Wade: *The Burger Court in the 1980s*

Harris v. McCrae was a major victory for pro-life forces, which saw it as an indication of the Court's willingness to allow some incursions into the abortion right. Still, this decision only cut into the right to abortion; it did not eradicate it. After *Harris* and the elections of 1980, however, pro-life groups thought that the time might be right to achieve their goal. The elections of 1980 saw both the victory of Ronald Reagan, the first presidential contender ever to support, unequivocally, the goals of the pro-life movement, and the Republican capture of the Senate.

In this environment the pro-life groups thought they could finally eliminate legalized abortion. They continued to lobby states and localities to pass laws that cut into the heart of *Roe*. And when pro-choice groups challenged these laws, the pro-life groups began asking the courts to adopt legal standards that would make it more difficult to obtain abortions. The first of these cases to reach the Supreme Court was *Akron v. Akron Center for Reproductive Health* (1983).

As you read about *Akron Center,* keep in mind that two Court membership changes had occurred since *Roe.* John Paul Stevens had replaced the pro-choice Justice Douglas, and Sandra Day O'Connor had taken the place of another *Roe* majority member, Justice Stewart. Based on his vote in *Planned Parenthood v. Danforth,* (1976) it seemed clear that Stevens was pro-choice. O'Connor's position, however, was far from clear, and *Akron Center* was her first vote in an abortion case. Before her appointment to the Court, some pro-life groups alleged that O'Connor supported the pro-choice side because of votes she had cast in the Arizona state legislature. But during her confirmation proceedings, she refused to answer pointed questions on abortion, saying only that it was "a practice in which [she] would not have engaged," but that she was "over the hill" and "not going to be pregnant any more . . . so perhaps it's easy for me to speak." How would O'Connor come down on the abortion issue? This question was very much on the minds of Court watchers as they waited for the decision in *Akron Center for Reproductive Health.*

The Akron controversy centered on a 1978 ordinance passed by the city council of Akron, Ohio. That ordinance contained the following provisions:

Hospital requirement. All post-first trimester abortions must be performed in a hospital.

Consent for minors. If a minor is under the age of fifteen, she must obtain the informed written consent of a parent or a court before a physician can perform an abortion.

Informed consent. A woman's consent to abortion services must be informed. That is, a physician must tell her (1) the number of weeks she is pregnant; (2) that the "unborn child is a human life form from the moment of conception"; (3) about the "anatomical and physiological characteristics of the particular unborn child" at the gestational point of development at which time the abortion is to be performed; (4) that the "unborn child" may be viable if "more than 22 weeks have elapsed from the time of conception"; and (5) about public and private adoption agencies.

A twenty-four-hour waiting period. A physician cannot perform an abortion until twenty-four hours after the pregnant woman signs a consent form.

Disposal of remains. Doctors who perform abortion "shall insure that the remains of the unborn child are disposed of in a humane and sanitary manner."

A month before the ordinance was to take effect, ACLU attorneys brought suit on behalf of an abortion clinic, the Akron Center for Reproductive Health. When the case reached the Supreme Court, the city of Akron was joined by the Reagan administration's solicitor general, Rex E. Lee. According to one source, some members of the administration "hounded" Lee into asking the justices to use *Akron Center* to overrule *Roe*.[24] Lee did not go quite that far. In his amicus curiae brief, Lee advanced two arguments. First, on abortion, he articulated a constitutional standard that he said derived from previous Court decisions. His reading of *Roe*'s progeny led him to conclude that the justices had never really "applied" *Roe*'s "sweeping" language regarding first-trimester abortions. Instead, he argued that the Court *"has repeatedly adopted an 'unduly burdensome' analysis. . . ."* That is, the Court had permitted state regulations of abortion as long as they did not "unduly burden" that decision. Second, Lee proposed a way to distinguish an *unduly* burdensome regulation from a regulation that was *simply* burdensome. In his view, the justices should generally defer to state legislatures.

But the Supreme Court did not see it Lee's way. Writing for six of the justices (Brennan, Blackmun, Burger, Marshall, and Stevens), Justice Powell firmly stated to the Court's commitment to Roe:

24. Lincoln Caplan, *The Tenth Justice* (New York: Vintage Books, 1987), 107.

[*Akron Center* comes] to us a decade after we held in *Roe v. Wade* (1973) that the right of privacy, grounded in the concept of personal liberty guaranteed by the Constitution, encompasses a woman's right to decide whether to terminate her pregnancy. Legislative responses to the Court's decision have required us on several occasions, and again today, to define the limits of a State's authority to regulate the performance of abortions. And arguments continue to be made, in these cases as well, that we erred in interpreting the Constitution. Nonetheless, the doctrine of *stare decisis*, while perhaps never entirely persuasive on a constitutional question, is a doctrine that demands respect in a society governed by the rule of law. We respect it today, and reaffirm *Roe v. Wade*. . . .

That "respect" for *Roe* led him to strike all of the provisions of the Akron law.

Despite this resounding affirmation of *Roe*, the pro-choice side had apparently lost a vote. In a dissent signed by *Roe*'s two dissenters (Rehnquist and White), O'Connor provided a scathing critique of *Roe*. She cited medical advances—for example, at the time of *Roe*, viability "before 28 weeks was considered unusual," but newer studies indicated viability as early as 25 weeks—to show that (1) because it is "inherently" tied to ever-changing medical technology, "the Roe framework . . . is clearly on a collision course with itself and (2) because lines separating viability from nonviability are fading, "compelling state interests" exist throughout the pregnancy.

This kind of analysis paralleled that which appeared in Solicitor General Lee's amicus brief. So it is hardly surprising that O'Connor agreed to the standard he had proposed: she urged the Court to abandon the trimester framework in favor of one that "protects the woman from unduly burdensome interference with her freedom to decide whether to terminate her pregnancy." O'Connor did, however, part company with Lee on how the Court should determine whether a law "imposes an undue burden." She explicitly rejected Lee's assertion that it simply requires courts to defer to legislatures: "The 'unduly burdensome' standard is appropriate *not* because it incorporates deference to legislative judgment at the

BOX 15-3   PROPOSED APPROACHES TO RESTRICTIVE ABORTION LAWS

APPROACH	EXEMPLARY OPINIONS	DEFINITION
Strict scrutiny	Blackmun in *Roe;* Powell in *Akron*	The right to abortion is fundamental. So laws restricting that right must be the least restrictive means available to achieve a compelling state interest. In the abortion context, a state's interest grows more compelling as the pregnancy passes from the first to second to third trimesters.
Undue burden	O'Connor in *Akron Center*	The right to decide whether to terminate a pregnancy is fundamental. So laws placing an undue burden on the women's decision to terminate her pregnancy may be subject to strict scrutiny; other kinds of laws need only be rationally related to a legitimate state interest (rational basis test).
Rational basis	Rehnquist in *Roe*	The right to abortion is no different from economic rights claimed under the Fourteenth Amendment Due Process Clause. So the law must be a reasonable measure designed to achieve a legitimate state interest.

threshold stage of analysis, but rather because of the limited *nature* of the fundamental right that has been recognized in the abortion cases. . . . [I]t is not appropriate to *weigh* the state interests at the threshold stage."

What, then, would O'Connor count as "unduly burdensome" regulation? The majority claimed that "the dissent would uphold virtually any abortion regulation under a rational-basis test," meaning that it would find constitutional any regulation that was reasonably related to a governmental interest. Such a standard, Powell noted, would gut *Roe.* O'Connor did not go that far. Rather, she suggested that if the law in question "unduly burdened" the fundamental right to seek an abortion, the Court should apply strict scrutiny; if the law does not "unduly burden" the abortion right, then the Court should apply a rational basis test.

Thus, as displayed in Box 15-3, by 1983, the justices

had proposed three different approaches to restrictive abortion laws. While the majority of the justices continued to support *Roe*'s strict scrutiny standard, O'Connor's dissent raised questions. Would she stick with her "undue burden" standard? If so, would she be able to convince other justices to adopt it? And what exactly did she mean by an "undue burden?" These questions were on the minds of observers when the Court agreed to decide *Thornburgh v. American College of Obstetricians and Gynecologists* (1986) because, in this case, the Reagan administration had decided to deemphasize the undue burden approach and to ask the Court to overrule *Roe.*

In many important ways the Pennsylvania law at issue in *Thornburgh* was similar to the law struck in *Akron Center.* It contained various provisions designed to regulate abortion, including a requirement that women give their "voluntary and informed" consent for abortions and that a pregnant woman's physician present her with various kinds of "explicit" information twenty-four hours prior to an abortion, such as the name of the doctor performing the abortion and the "fact" that "there may be" psychological and physical damage, the medical risks associated with abortion.

Not surprisingly, various pro-choice groups joined forces, on behalf of the American College of Obstetricians and Gynecologists, to challenge the act. This challenge was countered by the state of Pennsylvania, various pro-life groups, and the Reagan Justice Department, now under the command of Attorney General Edwin Meese, an avowed opponent of abortion.

Meese instructed Charles Fried, the acting solicitor general, to ask the Court to overrule *Roe*. Fried took this step, but the Court would not. Justice Blackmun's majority opinion blasted legislation designed to undermine *Roe* ("The States are not free, under the guise of protecting maternal health or potential life, to intimidate women into continuing pregnancies"); chastised Pennsylvania for its repeated efforts to circumvent *Roe* (this "was not the Commonwealth's first attempt . . . after . . . *Roe* . . . to impose abortion restraints"); and implicitly refuted the solicitor general's position ("Again today, we reaffirm the general principles laid down in *Roe*. . . . As judges . . . we are sworn to uphold the law even when its content gives rise to bitter dispute").

But the pro-life side had picked up another vote. After thirteen years of generally supporting the abortion right, Chief Justice Burger joined *Roe*'s opponents. In his *Thornburgh* dissent, he wrote:

I based my concurring statements in Roe and Maher on the principle expressed in the Court's opinion in Roe that the right to an abortion "is not unqualified and must be considered against important state interests in regulation." In short, every Member of the Roe Court rejected the idea of abortion on demand. The Court's opinion today, however, plainly undermines that important principle, and I regretfully conclude that some of the concerns of the dissenting Justices in Roe, as well as the concerns I expressed in my separate opinion, have now been realized.

Less surprising were dissents registered by White, O'Connor, and Rehnquist. White, joined by Rehnquist, lambasted the Court's "venture" into abortion as "fundamentally misguided since its conception" and agreed with Fried: *Roe* should go. O'Connor's dissent, also signed by Rehnquist, refrained from arguing that the Court should overrule *Roe*. She continued to press her *Akron Center* position: the justices should move to an "unduly burdensome" standard. And, she remained critical of *Roe*: "This Court's abortion decisions have already worked a major distortion in the Court's constitutional jurisprudence"; the justices were not dealing with abortion "evenhandedly."

The Reversal of Roe v. Wade? *The Rehnquist Court and the Abortion Right*

Although pro-choice advocates won the 1980s cases, they were steadily losing ground. As Table 15-5 shows, the *Roe* majority of seven became six in 1983 and was down to five in 1986. Indeed, diminishing support for *Roe* was widely acknowledged in the popular press and noted by legislative bodies. And it was evident in 1987 when pro-choice forces (among many others) rallied to oppose President Reagan's nomination of Robert Bork, an avowed *Roe* opponent, to replace Justice Powell. Pro-choice advocates, along with the members of the Senate, realized that Bork's appointment to the Court could tip the balance between maintaining *Roe* and overruling it. Undoubtedly Bork's position on abortion, coupled with many of his other controversial stances, contributed to his defeat.[25]

Even with Bork's rejection, pro-choice forces were concerned when the Rehnquist Court agreed to hear *Webster v. Reproductive Health Services*, a case involving a Missouri law, which, like the regulations at issue in *Akron Center* and *Thornburgh*, sought to restrict the

25. There were many reasons for Bork's defeat. Numerous civil rights and civil liberties groups opposed his stances on women's rights and homosexual conduct. Moreover, public opinion was squarely against him. By September 1987, only 29 percent of Americans supported his appointment to the Court.

TABLE 15-5 Diminishing Support for *Roe v. Wade:* The Supreme Court at the Time of *Webster v. Reproductive Health Services*

Roe v. Wade (1973)	*Akron v. Akron Center* (1983)	*Thornburgh v. ACOG* (1986)	*Webster v. Reproductive Health Services* (1989)
Blackmun	**Blackmun**	**Blackmun**	**Blackmun**
Brennan	**Brennan**	**Brennan**	**Brennan**
Burger	**Burger**	*Burger*	*Rehnquist*
Douglas	**Stevens**	**Stevens**	**Stevens**
Marshall	**Marshall**	**Marshall**	**Marshall**
Powell	**Powell**	**Powell**	Kennedy
Rehnquist	*Rehnquist*	*Rehnquist*	Scalia
Stewart	*O'Connor*	*O'Connor*	*O'Connor*
White	*White*	*White*	*White*

Key: justices in boldface support *Roe;* justices in italics oppose *Roe;* justices in regular type had not participated in an abortion case prior to *Webster.*

abortion right. By the time *Webster* got to the Court, the Senate had confirmed Powell's replacement, Anthony Kennedy, whose views on abortion were not known. Moreover, Justice Rehnquist, a persistent critic, had been elevated to chief justice, with Reagan appointee Antonin Scalia taking his place.

These changes led many observers to conclude that *Webster* would be a major ruling on abortion. As Table 15-5 shows, if the two new Reagan appointees, Scalia and Kennedy, opposed *Roe,* the Court would overrule the 1973 decision. Even *Roe*'s author thought it was doomed. In a speech given before the start of the 1988 term, during which the Court would decide *Webster,* Justice Blackmun wondered aloud:"Will *Roe v. Wade* go down the drain? I think there's a very distinct possibility that it will, this term. You can count the votes."[26]

The possibility that *Webster* would reverse *Roe* was not lost on pro-choice and pro-life forces, who filed seventy-eight amicus curiae briefs (the largest number ever submitted to the Court in a single case), representing more than 5,000 individual groups and inter-

ests. The Bush administration's solicitor general not only filed a brief supporting state regulation of abortions but also participated in oral argument, again requesting the Court to overrule *Roe.* Would the newly configured Rehnquist Court accept this invitation? Was the ruling as much of a landmark as many Court watchers expected?

The answer to both these questions is a qualified no. Only one justice, Scalia, explicitly wrote that *Roe* should be overruled. Three others (Rehnquist, White, and Kennedy) came close to agreeing with Scalia when they wrote that *Roe* was a highly problematic decision:

Stare decisis is a cornerstone of our legal system, but it has less power in constitutional cases, where, save for constitutional amendments, this Court is the only body able to make needed changes. We have not refrained from reconsideration of a prior construction of the Constitution that has proved "unsound in principle and unworkable in practice.". . . We think the *Roe* trimester framework falls into that category.

In the first place, the rigid *Roe* framework is hardly consistent with the notion of a Constitution cast in general terms, as ours is, and usually speaking in general principles, as ours does. The key elements of the *Roe* framework—trimesters and viability—are not found in the text of the

26. "Justice Fears for *Roe* Ruling," *New York Times,* September 14, 1988.

Constitution or in any place else one would expect to find a constitutional principle. Since the bounds of the inquiry are essentially indeterminate, the result has been a web of legal rules that have become increasingly intricate, resembling a code of regulations rather than a body of constitutional doctrine . . .

In the second place, we do not see why the State's interest in protecting potential human life should come into existence only at the point of viability, and that there should therefore be a rigid line allowing state regulation after viability but prohibiting it before viability.

Despite these harsh words, the three refused to take the ultimate step and overrule *Roe*. As Rehnquist wrote:

This case therefore affords us no occasion to revisit the holding of *Roe*, which was that the Texas statute unconstitutionally infringed the right to an abortion derived from the Due Process Clause, and we leave it undisturbed. To the extent indicated in our opinion, we would modify and narrow *Roe* and succeeding cases.

With O'Connor continuing to push her "unduly burdensome" approach and the four remaining justices (Blackmun, Brennan, Marshall, and Stevens) clinging to the 1973 precedent, in *Webster* it appeared as if the Court was one short vote of overturning *Roe*. For many commentators thought that Rehnquist, White, and Kennedy would have gone along with Scalia and explicitly overruled *Roe* had they been able to persuade O'Connor to join them. Thus, in the end, it was her advocating the "unduly burdensome" approach that kept *Roe* alive and kept *Webster* from being the landmark decision many had expected. At least this was the argument some analysts made. In any event, it did seem as if *Roe* was operating on borrowed time: President George Bush eventually would have the opportunity to appoint justices who could tip the balance against *Roe*.

It was not long before this view was tested. By the time the Court agreed to hear arguments in *Planned Parenthood of Southeastern Pennsylvania v. Casey*—involving the constitutionality of various restrictions Pennsylvania put on the abortion right, including a twenty-four-hour waiting period and informed con-

sent *(see Box 15-4 on page 568)*—Bush had appointed two justices. David Souter and Clarence Thomas replaced the pro-choice justices Brennan and Marshall, respectively. These membership changes seemed to confirm the greatest hope and fear of the pro-life and pro-choice movements: *Roe* would finally go. Or would it?

Once again, the answer is a qualified no. In a "joint" judgment for the Court, Justices Kennedy, O'-Connor, and Souter were clear that "the essential holding of *Roe v. Wade* should be retained and once again reaffirmed." They went on to say, in contradiction to O'Connor's dissent in *Akron Center*:

The sum of . . . precedential inquiry . . . shows *Roe*'s underpinnings unweakened in any way affecting its central holding. While it has engendered disapproval, it has not been unworkable. An entire generation has come of age free to assume *Roe*'s concept of liberty in defining the capacity of women to act in society, and to make reproductive decisions; no erosion of principle going to liberty or personal autonomy has left *Roe*'s central holding a doctrinal remnant; *Roe* portends no developments at odds with other precedent for the analysis of personal liberty; and no changes of fact have rendered viability more or less appropriate as the point at which the balance of interests tips. Within the bounds of normal *stare decisis* analysis, then, and subject to the considerations on which it customarily turns, the stronger argument is for affirming *Roe*'s central holding, with whatever degree of personal reluctance any of us may have, not for overruling it.

Yet the rest of the joint opinion picked up where O'Connor's *Akron Center* dissent left off: the trio explicitly rejected *Roe*'s trimester framework. As they put it:

A logical reading of the central holding in *Roe* itself, and a necessary reconciliation of the liberty of the woman and the interest of the State in promoting prenatal life, require, in our view, that we abandon the trimester framework as a rigid prohibition on all previability regulation aimed at the protection of fetal life. The trimester framework suffers from these basic flaws: in its formulation it misconceives the nature of the pregnant woman's interest; and in practice it undervalues the State's interest in potential life, as recognized in *Roe*.

In place of the trimester framework, they proposed

BOX 15-4 COURT'S ACTION IN *PLANNED PARENTHOOD OF SOUTHEASTERN PENNSYLVANIA V. CASEY* (1992)

PROVISIONS OF LAW UPHELD ON THE GROUND THAT THEY DO NOT PLACE AN UNDUE BURDEN ON THE ABORTION RIGHT

Informed consent/twenty-four-hour waiting period. At least twenty-four hours before a physician performs an abortion, he or she must inform the woman of "the nature of the procedure, the health risks of the abortion and of childbirth, and the 'probable gestational age of the unborn child.'" The physician also must provide the woman with a list of adoption agencies. Abortions may not be performed unless the woman "certifies in writing" that she has given her informed consent. Twenty-four hours must elapse between the time the woman gives her consent and the abortion procedure is performed.

Parental consent. Unless she exercises a judicial by-pass option, a woman under the age of eighteen must obtain the informed consent of one parent prior to obtaining an abortion.

Reporting and recordkeeping. All facilities performing abortions must file reports containing information about the procedure, including: the physician, the woman's age, the number of prior pregnancies or abortions she has had, "pre-existing medical conditions that would complicate the pregnancy," the weight and age of the aborted fetus, whether or not the woman was married. . . . If the abortion is performed in a facility funded by the state, the information becomes public.

PROVISIONS OF LAW STRUCK DOWN ON THE GROUND THAT THEY PLACE AN UNDUE BURDEN ON THE ABORTION RIGHT

Spousal notice. Before performing an abortion on a married woman, a physician must receive a statement from her stating that she has notified her spouse that she "is about to undergo an abortion." Alternatively, the woman may "provide a statement certifying that her husband is not the man who impregnated her; that her husband could not be located; that the pregnancy is the result of spousal sexual assault which she has reported; or that the women believes that notifying her husband will cause him or someone else to inflict bodily injury upon her."

Reporting and recordkeeping. All facilities performing abortions must file reports containing information about the procedure, including . . . if relevant, the reason(s) the woman has failed to notify her spouse.

---

to use O'Connor's undue burden approach: "Only where state regulation imposes an undue burden on a woman's ability to make this decision does the power of the State reach into the heart of the liberty protected by the Due Process Clause. . . ." And, in applying this standard to the law at hand, they upheld many of the challenged provisions *(see Box 15-4)*, including the kinds of informed consent requirements previously stricken in *Akron Center* and *Thornburgh*. (The trio overruled those parts of *Akron Center* and *Thornburgh* dealing with informed consent.)

It is the enunciation of the undue burden standard, coupled with the Court's application of it, that leads us to suggest a qualified no to the question of whether *Casey* overruled *Roe*. For, on the one hand, the judgment clearly reaffirmed the "central holding" of the

1973 decision that a woman should have "some" freedom to terminate a pregnancy. On the other hand, Kennedy, O'Connor, and Souter gutted the core of *Roe.* The trimester framework was gone. Under *Casey,* states may enact laws—regulating the entire pregnancy—that further their interest in potential life as long as those laws are rationally related to that end and do not put an undue burden on the right to terminate a pregnancy. Laws that do not meet this standard will be subject to strict scrutiny, as was the spousal notification provision at issue in *Casey.*

In general, this undue burden approach, which Justice O'Connor originally proposed in 1983 in her *Akron Center* dissent, *could* lead to very different outcomes in abortion cases. Justice Scalia made this clear in his dissent in *Casey.* He indicated that many of the provisions at issue in *Casey* that the Court had upheld under the undue burden standard—such as a mandatory twenty-four-hour waiting period—would have been struck down under *Roe*'s strict scrutiny approach. Yet, Justice Blackmun's opinion holds out hope that the undue burden standard could be applied, in the future, to strike down restrictive laws. Moreover, as Justice Stevens's writing illustrates, a different treatment of the undue burden would have led the Court to strike down the twenty-four-hour waiting period.

Is *Casey* the Court's final word on abortion? Will undue burden become the standard the justices use to assess regulations on abortion? Perhaps not. As Table 15-6 indicates, in 1993 the justices were truly divided over legal approaches to abortion. Moreover, we cannot forget that a justice can have a change of heart: Burger went from a *Roe* supporter to an opponent; Kennedy signed Rehnquist's opinion in *Webster*, yet provided crucial support for O'Connor's undue burden approach in *Casey*. Justice Ginsburg's ascension to the bench—she replaced White, a *Roe* critic—only complicates the picture. Although Ginsburg supports a woman's right to choose, she has been critical of the *Roe* framework. In a 1985 law review article, she argued that abortion rights should be framed in equal protection terms; that is, the Court should consider whether laws restricting the right discriminate against women. Had the Court adopted this approach, Ginsburg asserted, it would have struck down many state laws, including those that restricted funding for abortions. As she put it, "If the Court had acknowledged a woman's equality aspect [and] not simply a patient-physician autonomy constitutional dimension to the abortion issue, a majority perhaps might have seen the public assistance cases as instances in which . . . the [government] had violated its duty to govern impartially."[27]

TABLE 15-6   Approaches to Abortion: The 1994–1995 Supreme Court

Justice	Favored Approach
Breyer	Unknown
Ginsburg	equal protection analysis[a]
Kennedy	undue burden
O'Connor	undue burden
Rehnquist	rational basis
Scalia	rational basis
Souter	undue burden
Stevens	*Roe*'s strict scrutiny
Thomas	rational basis

[a] In a 1985 law review article, Judge Ginsburg urged courts to acknowledge a "women's equality aspect" to the abortion issue. See Ruth Bader Ginsburg, "Some Thoughts on Autonomy and Equality in Relation to *Roe v. Wade*," *North Carolina Law Review* 63 (1985): 375–386.

Whether Justice Ginsburg will press this position on her colleagues is something on which we can only speculate. What is true is that the political and legal environment surrounding abortion has changed even since *Casey*. During Bill Clinton's presidency, it would be unlikely that a solicitor general would ask the Court to overturn *Roe*. Moreover, pro-choice advocates, discouraged by the Supreme Court, have begun to bring their cases into state courts, asking those judiciaries to protect the abortion right under state constitutional guarantees.

The state-by-state strategy has its advantages. For example, many commentators note that several state courts have held that their constitutions, unlike the federal document, require public funding of abortions. In addition, some state courts have shown a willingness to rule for pro-choice forces. An oft-cited example is *In re T. W.* (1989), a decision of the Florida supreme court striking down a parental consent law.[28] Yet, the use of state courts to secure abortion rights has an obvious drawback: some states will go along with the wishes of pro-choice advocates, while others

27. Ruth Bader Ginsburg, "Some Thoughts on Autonomy and Equality in Relation to *Roe v. Wade*," *University of North Carolina Law Review* 63 (1985): 382.

28. See Fisher and Devins, *Political Dynamics of Constitutional Law*, 238.

will not. Thus, rights will differ on a state-by-state basis, as was the case before *Roe* (with the caveat that under *Casey* states may not proscribe abortion).

In all of these changes, there is one constant, which may be decisive, at least as abortion plays in political branches and in the states: public opinion. In the twenty-year period since *Roe*, the public has remained ambivalent about the scope of the abortion right. Polls taken immediately after *Casey* indicate that the public—like the Court—overwhelmingly (82 percent) favors legalized abortion, but—just as they have since *Roe*—48 percent of Americans support some restrictions on that right.[29] It seems inevitable that Americans (and the Court) will continue to debate the abortion issue, and there will be no easy answers.

READINGS

Craig, Barbara Hinkson, and David M. O'Brien. *Abortion and American Politics.* Chatham, N.J.:Chatham House, 1993.

Ely, John Hart. "The Wages of Crying Wolf: A Comment on Roe v. Wade." *Yale Law Journal* 82 (1973): 920–949.

29. Polls cited in Craig and O'Brien, *Abortion and American Politics,* 327.

Emerson, Thomas I. "Nine Justices in Search of a Doctrine." *Michigan Law Review* 64 (1965): 219–234.

Epstein, Lee, and Joseph F. Kobylka. *The Supreme Court and Legal Change: Abortion and the Death Penalty.* Chapel Hill: University of North Carolina Press, 1992.

Epstein, Richard A. "Substantive Due Process by Any Other Name." *Supreme Court Review* (1973): 159–186.

Faux, Marian. *Roe v. Wade.* New York: Macmillan, 1988.

Glick, Henry R. *The Right to Die: Policy Innovation and Its Consequences.* New York: Columbia University Press, 1992.

Johnson, Charles A., and Bradley C. Canon. *Judicial Policies: Implementation and Impact.* Washington, D.C.: CQ Press, 1984.

Lader, Lawrence. *Abortion.* Indianapolis: Bobbs-Merrill, 1966.

———. *Abortion II.* Boston: Beacon Press, 1973.

Luker, Kristen. *Abortion and the Politics of Motherhood.* Berkeley: University of California Press, 1984.

Mohr, James C. *Abortion in America.* New York: Oxford University Press, 1978.

Rubin, Eva R. *Abortion, Politics, and the Courts.* Westport, Conn.: Greenwood Press, 1987.

Tribe, Laurence H. *Abortion: The Clash of Absolutes.* New York: W. W. Norton, *1990.*

Wardle, Lynn D., and Mary A. Wood. *A Lawyer Looks at Abortion.* Provo, Utah: Brigham Young University Press, 1982.

PART VI
THE CRIMINAL JUSTICE SYSTEM AND CONSTITUTIONAL RIGHTS

THE RIGHTS OF THE CRIMINALLY ACCUSED

16. **INVESTIGATIONS AND EVIDENCE**

17. **ATTORNEYS, TRIALS, AND PUNISHMENTS**

THE RIGHTS OF THE CRIMINALLY ACCUSED

AMERICANS REGARD the Bill of Rights as an enumeration of the nation's most cherished freedoms. The right to speak freely and to practice religion without undue interference from government are the guarantees to which politicians and citizens refer most often when they describe the unique character of the United States. Americans may need to be reminded, therefore, that four of the first eight amendments explicitly guarantee rights for the *criminally accused*. The Framers of the Constitution emphasized criminal rights because they had grown to despise the abusive practices of British criminal procedure. The Founders believed that agents of government should not enter private homes and search personal property without proper justification and that the accused should not be tried without the benefit of public scrutiny.

Consequently, the Fourth Amendment protects Americans from unreasonable searches and prescribes the procedures by which law enforcement officials can obtain warrants. The Fifth Amendment protects individuals from having to testify against themselves and from being tried more than once on the same charges; it provides for grand juries and ensures due process of law. The Sixth Amendment governs criminal proceedings. It calls for speedy and pub-lic jury trials during which defendants can call witnesses and face their accusers. It also provides for the assistance of counsel. The Eighth Amendment prohibits excessive bail and monetary fines as well as "cruel and unusual" punishments. The Framers insisted on constitutional guarantees that would protect the guilty as well as the innocent against the potentially abusive prosecutorial powers of the government.

Just because these rights are not the first that come to mind when we think about the Bill of Rights does not mean that they are any less important or less relevant to society. At least once during your life, you are likely to be a participant in the criminal justice system. You may be the victim of a crime. You may serve as a juror in a criminal trial or become involved as a witness. You may even be accused of a crime. All citizens should understand the rights the Founders established and the procedures that invoke such guarantees.

The two chapters that follow explore the constitutional rights of the criminally accused and the Supreme Court's interpretation of them. To appreciate their importance, however, we first take a brief look at the stages of the criminal justice process. Following that discussion, we describe trends in Supreme Court decision making in this area.

TABLE VI-1 The American Criminal Justice System

Stage	Governing Amendment[a]
Reported or suspected crime ↓	
Investigation by law enforcement officials ↓	Fourth Amendment search and seizure rights Fifth Amendment self-incrimination clause
Arrest ↓	Sixth Amendment right to counsel clause
Booking ↓	
Decision to prosecute ↓	
Pretrial hearings (initial appearance, bail hearing, preliminary hearing, arraignment) ↓	Fifth Amendment grand jury clause Sixth Amendment notification clause Eighth Amendment bail clause
Trial ↓	Fifth Amendment self-incrimination clause Sixth Amendment speedy and public trial, jury, confrontation, and compulsory process clauses
Sentencing ↓	Eighth Amendment cruel and unusual punishment clause
Appeals, postconviction stages	Fifth Amendment double jeopardy clause

[a]The right to due process of law is in effect throughout the process.

OVERVIEW OF THE CRIMINAL JUSTICE SYSTEM

Table VI-1 provides a general overview of the criminal justice system and the constitutional rights effective at each stage. Keep two things in mind. First, because the states are given a degree of latitude in developing their criminal justice systems, these procedures vary from jurisdiction to jurisdiction. Second, fewer than 5 percent of all criminal cases actually proceed through every stage of the system. At some point during the process, most criminal defendants plead guilty, thereby waiving their right to a jury trial, and proceed directly to sentencing. Most of these guilty pleas are the result of plea-bargaining arrangements in which the accused agrees to admit guilt in exchange for reduced charges or a lenient sentence.

This qualification noted, the process normally begins with an alleged or suspected violation of a state or federal criminal law. However, the first step in the criminal justice system is the response of law enforcement officials to the reporting of the offense. Many scholars and lawyers consider this part of the process to be of the utmost importance. The way police conduct their investigation and gather evidence affects all subsequent decisions made by lawyers, judges, and juries. Americans expect police officers to act lawfully, within the confines of the Constitution. No one wants them to break down doors and search houses without proper cause. But society also expects effective law enforcement. The police must make arrests and enforce laws. No one wants to see heinous crimes go unpunished—and criminals out on the streets—because constitutional guarantees have unreasonably tied the hands of police. Law enforcement officers must understand the rules well enough to act without violating them because, when they make mistakes, the consequences can be enormous.

Once police make an arrest and take an individual into custody, the prosecuting attorney joins the process. The prosecutor of state-level crimes, commonly known as the district attorney, is an elected official who has jurisdiction over criminal matters in a particular local jurisdiction, usually a county. The prosecutor of federal offenses is called a United States attorney. U.S. attorneys are appointed by the president and confirmed by the Senate. Their assignments correspond to the geographical jurisdiction of the federal district courts, and they serve at the president's pleasure. State and federal prosecutors decide whether the government will bring charges against the accused. Prosecutors consider, among other factors, whether police acted properly in gathering evidence and making the arrest. If the prosecutor decides not to press charges, the police must release the suspect, and the process ends. If prosecution is indicated, the government brings the individual before a judge, who ensures that the accused has legal representation and understands the charges. The judge also must verify that police were justified in holding the accused in the first place. Further, the judge sets bail, a monetary guarantee that the accused will appear for trial.

The system next provides a step to ensure that the prosecutor is not abusing the power to charge persons with crimes. This check on prosecutorial discretion takes place in one of two ways. Individuals accused of committing federal offenses or of violating the laws of some states will receive grand jury hearings in accordance with the Fifth Amendment. Composed of ordinary citizens, grand juries examine the strength of the prosecutor's case to determine whether the government's evidence can support formal charges. If the grand jury decides that the prosecutor has satisfied the legal requirements, it will issue a formal document, known as an *indictment*, ordering the accused to stand trial on specified charges. If the grand jury concludes that the prosecutor's case is too weak, the defendant will be released.

The right to a grand jury hearing is not one of the provisions of the Bill of Rights that has been incorporated into the Due Process Clause of the Fourteenth Amendment. Accordingly, the states are free to develop other methods of checking the prosecutor. As an alternative to the grand jury, several states use preliminary hearings. Such proceedings more closely resemble trials than does the grand jury process. Both prosecution and defense may present their cases to a judge, who evaluates the adequacy of the government's evidence. If the judge agrees that the prosecutor's case justifies a trial, an *information* is issued. The information is a formal document, roughly the equivalent of an indictment, that orders the accused to stand trial on certain specified violations of the criminal code. If the prosecutor's case is found inadequate to justify a trial, the judge may order the release of the defendant.

After being formally charged, the defendant proceeds to the arraignment stage. At arraignment, a judge reads the indictment or information to ensure that the defendant understands the charges and the applicable constitutional rights. The judge also asks if the defendant is represented by counsel. Because the specific criminal accusations may have changed in seriousness or number of counts since the defendant's initial appearance, the judge reviews and perhaps modifies the bail amount. Finally, the judge accepts the defendant's plea: guilty, *nolo contendere* (no contest), or not guilty. Should the defendant plead either of the first two, a trial is not necessary, and the accused proceeds to sentencing.

A plea of not guilty normally leads to a full trial governed by constitutional provisions found in the Fifth and Sixth Amendments. The accused is entitled to a fair, public, and speedy trial by jury. The judge presides over the trial, and the two opposing lawyers question witnesses and summarize case facts. When both sides have presented their cases, the jury deliberates to reach a verdict. If the individual is found guilty, the judge issues a sentence, which under Eighth Amendment protections cannot be cruel and unusual.

If the defendant is found not guilty, the process ends. The Fifth Amendment prohibition against double jeopardy means that the government cannot try an acquitted defendant a second time for the same offense. The prosecution has no right to appeal an acquittal verdict reached by the trial court. Should the verdict be guilty, however, the defendant has the right to appeal the conviction to a higher court. The appeals court reviews the trial procedures to determine whether any significant errors in law or procedure occurred. If dissatisfied with the findings of the appeals court, either side—the prosecution or the defense—may try for a review by an even higher court. These requests may be denied because the system generally provides for only one appeal as a matter of right. Subsequent appeals are left to the discretion of the appellate courts.

TRENDS IN COURT DECISION MAKING

In what follows, we examine each stage in the criminal justice system vis-á-vis the constitutional rights of the criminally accused. While reading the narrative and cases, keep in mind that the four amendments governing criminal proceedings do not work in isolation. Rather, they fit into a larger scheme that includes law, politics, local custom, and the practical necessities of coping with crime in a contemporary society.

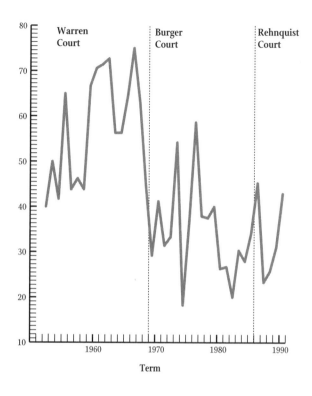

FIGURE VI-1 Percentage of Supreme Court Criminal Rights Cases Decided in Favor of the Accused, 1953–1991

SOURCE: Lee Epstein, Jeffrey A. Segal, Harold J. Spaeth, and Thomas G. Walker, *The Supreme Court Compendium: Data, Decisions, and Developments* (Washington, D.C.: Congressional Quarterly, 1994), Table 3-8.

The rights accorded the criminally accused in the four amendments set limits that, in tandem with the legal system, define the criminal justice process. The system depends heavily upon Supreme Court interpretation of the several clauses contained in those amendments. As we have seen in other legal areas, however, the way the Court interprets constitutional rights is not determined exclusively by traditional legal factors such as precedent, the plain language of the law, or the intent of the Framers. Historical circumstances, ideological stances, and pressure from other institutions and private groups also affect the course of law, which explains why jurisprudence

BOX VI-1 WARRREN EARL BURGER
(1969–1986)

Warren Burger was born September 17, 1907, in St. Paul, Minnesota. He was the fourth of seven children of Swiss and German parents. Financially unable to attend college full time, Burger spent the years following his 1925 graduation from high school attending college and law school evening classes—two at the University of Minnesota and four at St. Paul College of Law. To support himself, Burger sold life insurance.

He graduated magna cum laude from law school in 1931 and joined a respected law firm in Minnesota, where he practiced until 1953. He also taught part time at his alma mater, Mitchell College of Law, from 1931 to 1948.

Burger married Elvera Stromberg, November 8, 1933. They had one son and one daughter.

Burger developed a deep interest in art and was an accomplished sculptor; as chief justice, he served as chairman of the board of the National Gallery of Art. He was also an antiques buff and a connoisseur of fine wines. He also served as chancellor of the Smithsonian Institution.

Soon after beginning his law career in Minnesota, Burger became involved in Republican state politics. In 1938 he helped in Harold E. Stassen's successful campaign for governor of Minnesota.

During Stassen's unsuccessful bid for the Republican presidential nomination ten years later, Burger met a man who was to figure prominently in his future—Herbert Brownell, then campaign manager for GOP presidential nominee Thomas E. Dewey. Brownell, who became attorney general during the Eisenhower administration, brought Burger to Washington in 1953 to serve as assistant attorney general in charge of the Justice Department's Civil Division.

Burger's stint as assistant attorney general from 1953 to 1956 was not without controversy. His decision to defend the government's action in the dismissal of John F. Peters, a part-time federal employee, on grounds of disloyalty—after Solicitor General Simon E. Sobeloff had refused to do so on grounds of conscience—won Burger the enmity of many liberals.

But Burger's overall record as assistant attorney general apparently met with President Dwight D. Eisenhower's approval, and in 1956 Burger was appointed to the U.S. Court of Appeals for the District of Columbia circuit. As an appeals court judge, Burger developed a reputation as a conservative, especially in criminal justice cases.

Off the bench, Burger became increasingly outspoken in his support of major administrative reform of the judicial system—a cause he continued to advocate as chief justice. During Burger's years as chief justice, Congress approved a number of measures to modernize the operations of the federal judiciary.

President Richard Nixon's appointment of Burger as chief justice on May 21, 1969, caught most observers by surprise. Despite Burger's years of service in the Justice Department and the court of appeals, he was little known outside the legal community. But Nixon apparently was impressed by Burger's consistent argument as an appeals judge that the Constitution should be read narrowly—a belief Nixon shared. Burger was confirmed by the Senate, 74–3, June 9, 1969.

Burger served for seventeen years as chief justice, retiring in 1986 to devote full time to the chairmanship of the commission that planned the Constitution's bicentennial celebration celebration in 1987. He died in 1995.

SOURCE: Adapted from Elder Witt, *Guide to the U.S. Supreme Court*, 2d ed. (Washington, D.C.: Congressional Quarterly, 1990), 875–876.

varies from one Court era to the next or even from term to term.

Perhaps no issue illustrates this intersection of law and politics better than criminal rights. In the 1960s the Warren Court revolutionized criminal law by expanding the protections accorded those charged with crimes. The extent to which the Warren Court altered existing law will become clear when you read the cases to come. For now, note the high percentage of decisions favoring the criminally accused during the 1960s, as depicted in Figure VI-1.

This liberal trend did not go unnoticed. President Richard Nixon was among the first to recognize that expanded rights for the criminally accused touched the nerves of a majority of Americans. During his presidential campaign of 1968 (and after his election), Nixon emphasized the law and order theme, proclaiming to the voters that the liberal Warren Court had gone too far.

In a 1968 speech, for example, Nixon said, "And tonight it's time for some honest talk about the problem of order in the United States. Let us always respect, as I do, our courts and those who serve on them, but let us also recognize that some of our courts in their decisions have gone too far in weakening the peace forces as against the criminal forces in this country." All of those who heard these words knew that Nixon was referring only to the Warren Court. Apparently, many voters agreed with the future president. Public opinion polls taken in 1968 show that nearly two-thirds of Americans believed that the courts were not dealing with criminals harshly enough, compared with about 50 percent just three years earlier.[1] In short, Nixon had hit a nerve with U.S. citizens; he placed crime on the public agenda, where it remains.

Nixon also had the opportunity to keep his promise to restore law and order to American communities by changing the composition of the Supreme Court. One year before Nixon took office Earl Warren had resigned to give President Lyndon Johnson the chance to appoint his successor. When Johnson's choice for that position, Associate Justice Abe Fortas, failed to obtain Senate confirmation, the chief justiceship remained vacant for Nixon to fill. His choice was Warren Burger, a court of appeals judge who agreed with Nixon's stance on criminal law (see Box VI-1).

During the 1970s those who sympathized with the liberal decisions of the Warren Court watched in horror as Nixon appointed three more justices to the Court. The American Civil Liberties Union and various legal aid societies predicted that this new Court not only would stop any expansion of criminal rights but also would begin to overturn Warren Court precedents. Figure VI-1 shows there may be some truth to this view. The justices were far less supportive of criminal rights under Burger's leadership than they had been under Warren's.

Chief Justice Burger retired in 1986. Ronald Reagan replaced him by promoting Associate Justice William Rehnquist, a judge whose voting reflected strong law and order attitudes. The Rehnquist Court, with several Burger Court holdovers and Reagan/Bush appointees, continued to interpret the rights of criminal defendants quite narrowly, generally favoring police and prosecutors. However, in 1993 and 1994, President Bill Clinton appointed two new justices to the bench, Ruth Bader Ginsburg and Stephen Breyer. Both were projected to be somewhat more sympathetic to the rights of the criminally accused than the Rehnquist Court majority had been. In fact, based on 1993 and 1994 term data, both Ginsburg and Breyer were moderately more liberal on criminal cases than the Court average.

---

1. Harold W. Stanley and Richard G. Niemi, *Vital Statistics on American Politics*, 5th ed. (Washington, D.C.: CQ Press, 1995), 379.

CHAPTER 16
INVESTIGATIONS AND EVIDENCE

T HE INVESTIGATION is a critical stage in most criminal cases. It is during this early portion of the criminal process that police collect evidence of the crime. How strongly that evidence points to the accused and how lawfully it was obtained largely dictate what will occur at subsequent phases of the criminal process. If the police work is sound and the evidence of guilt is strong, a guilty plea or conviction is likely to result. But if the evidence is weak or gathered illegally, criminal charges may be dropped altogether.

The Framers understood the importance of the investigatory stage. They realized that effective law enforcement required that police be able to collect evidence of criminal behavior, but they also had experienced abusive investigation tactics on the part of law enforcement agents in England and other European countries. As a consequence, the Framers included in the Bill of Rights certain protections for the criminally accused, protections that were meant to safeguard individual liberties without significantly weakening the ability of police to investigate and solve crimes.

Most evidence of criminal behavior is either physical or testimonial. The collection of physical evidence is controlled by the Fourth Amendment, which pro-

hibits unreasonable searches and seizures by the police. The gathering of testimonial evidence is limited by the Fifth Amendment, which protects suspects from having to give testimony against themselves. In this chapter we focus on these two crucial rights and on how the Supreme Court has interpreted and enforced them.

SEARCHES AND SEIZURES

To build a case against a criminal suspect a prosecutor often relies on physical evidence gathered by the police. This evidence may assume many different forms: the money or goods taken during a theft, the weapons or tools used to carry out the crime, the clothing worn during the offense, illegal drugs, hair or blood samples, and so forth. Physical evidence can be a powerful indicator of the guilt or innocence of a suspect. Given contemporary advances in technology (for example, DNA testing) physical evidence today can yield much more information than ever before.

The Founders recognized the importance of physical evidence to the criminal process, but they also understood that people's rights could be abused by overzealous law enforcement efforts to obtain it. As a consequence, the Fourth Amendment, which deals exclusively with searches and seizures, became part of the Bill of Rights.

Like many of the constitutional guarantees accorded the criminally accused, the Fourth Amendment has its genesis in the Framers' resentment of an English institution, the writs of assistance. These writs were general search warrants that did not specify the places or things to be searched. They were authorized by the crown in England beginning in the mid-1600s; by the early 1700s they were used in the colonies primarily to allow customs officials to conduct unrestricted searches. By authorizing these searches, Britain hoped to discourage smuggling by colonial merchants and to enforce existing restrictions on colonial trade.[1]

As general searches became increasingly common, some colonists began to express their distaste for what they felt were major intrusions on their personal privacy and political liberty. James Otis, a Massachusetts lawyer, summed up the situation in a now famous statement. In 1761, when customs officials asked a Massachusetts court for writs of assistance to enforce the "hated Stamp Act," Otis mounted a legal challenge.[2] He argued that the writs went "against the fundamental principles of law," not because the government lacked the power to conduct searches but because it should not be permitted to conduct the open-ended searches—those that did not specify the places and things to be searched—authorized by writs of assistance. In his view, a "man's house is his castle; and whilst he is quiet, he is well guarded as a prince in his castle."

The Massachusetts court ignored Otis's plea and issued the writs. But his concerns were echoed in England by William Pitt. In a speech delivered in the House of Commons, Pitt uttered these equally famous words:

The poorest may, in his cottage, bid defiance to all the forces of the Crown. It may be frail; its roof may shake; the wind may blow through it; the storm may enter; the rain may enter; but the King of England may not enter.

Unlike Otis, Pitt was successful: in 1766 the House of Commons invalidated general warrants.

Still, the damage had been done. Right before the Declaration of Independence was issued, Samuel Adams said that opposition to the general searches was the "Commencement of the Controversy between Great Britain and America."[3] By the time Madison proposed the Bill of Rights to Congress, it was clear that most Americans agreed with the position Otis had advocated: almost all of the newly adopted state constitutions restricted government searches and seizures.

The Fourth Amendment contains two provisions, the first stating the basic right against unreasonable searches and seizures, and the second detailing the requirements for search warrants:

[1] The right of the people to be secure in their persons, houses, papers, and effects, against unreasonable searches and seizures, shall not be violated, and [2] no Warrants shall issue, but upon probable cause, supported by Oath or affirmation, and particularly describing the place to be searched, and the persons or things to be seized.

The amendment clearly balances the government's need to gather evidence with the citizen's right not to suffer unnecessary government intrusions. The amendment does not stop police from searching and seizing, it simply outlaws such activities as are deemed "unreasonable." But what distinguishes reasonable from unreasonable search and seizure? As in so many other areas, the task has fallen on the Supreme Court to apply important principles to concrete cases, that is, to give meaning to the Constitution.

---

1. For more on the origins of the Fourth Amendment see Melvin I. Urofsky, *A March on Liberty* (New York: Knopf, 1988), 36–42.

2. See Marvin Zalman and Larry Siegel, *Criminal Procedure* (St. Paul, Minn.: West, 1991), 99.

3. Ira Glasser, *Visions of Liberty* (New York: Arcade, 1991), 166.

The Supreme Court and the Fourth Amendment

Throughout the twentieth century the justices have struggled to develop rules to govern searches and seizures. To be sure, the Court has wanted to be true to the spirit of the Fourth Amendment, providing protection for all citizens against abusive intrusions by the government, but not restricting police to the extent that effective law enforcement becomes impossible.

In grappling with these often conflicting goals, the Court has been guided by one important principle: the Fourth Amendment requires that searches be *reasonable*. Over the years the justices have designated as reasonable several types of searches and seizures. For each type, the Court has drafted procedures that must be followed for the search and seizure to be valid.

Searches with Warrants. The warrant procedure is the only search authorization method mentioned in the Constitution. Clause 2 of the Fourth Amendment outlines the steps to be followed. A police officer must go before a judge or magistrate and swear under oath that reason exists to believe that a crime has been committed and that evidence of the crime is located in a particular place. This information often is in the form of a sworn written statement called an affidavit. The judge then must determine whether probable cause exists to issue the warrant. If such cause is present, the judge authorizes a search by issuing a warrant that carefully describes the area to be searched and the items that may be seized. Police may then execute the warrant by searching in the area prescribed and seizing the designated evidence, if found.

Warrant-based searches are the preferred method of gathering physical evidence. Because a detached and objective judge issues the warrant, this method ensures the greatest protection of individual rights. However, the warrant procedure is cumbersome. Time constraints or special circumstances may prevent police from going to a judge to apply for a warrant. Immediate action may be necessary. Recognizing this, the Supreme Court has defined certain circumstances under which a search may be deemed reasonable even without a warrant.

Searches Incident to a Valid Arrest. As a general principle of law, police may conduct a search when placing a suspect under a valid arrest. For example, if a law enforcement official checks an apprehended suspect for weapons, the officer is engaging in a search incident to a valid arrest. The Supreme Court has allowed such searches for three reasons: to protect the safety of the police officer in case the suspect is armed, to remove any means of escape, and to prevent the suspect from disposing of evidence.

The Court also has imposed two types of limits—temporal and spatial—on searches incident to a valid arrest. The temporal limit means that police can conduct such a search only at the time of the arrest. If the arresting officers forget to check something or someone, they cannot later return to conduct a search unless they have some other justification. This rule makes sense in light of the original purposes for allowing searches incident to arrest: an individual can place a police officer in jeopardy or attempt escape at the time of an arrest, but no danger exists once police remove the individual from the scene. The spatial limitation means that searches made incident to a valid arrest may include only the arrested suspect and the area under the suspect's immediate control.

Loss of Evidence Searches. The Supreme Court has held that police can conduct warrantless searches and seizures to prevent the loss of evidence. Frequently officers come upon situations in which they must act quickly to preserve evidence that is in danger of being destroyed—as, for example, when a drug dealer is about to flush narcotics down the toilet or an armed robber is intent on throwing the weapon into the river. It would not be reasonable to require an officer faced with such a situation to find a judge to issue a search warrant. By the time the law enforcement official complied with this requirement, the evidence would be gone. Therefore, the Supreme Court has allowed police considerable latitude in acting without a warrant under such circumstances.

Like other searches and seizures, evidence-loss searches are limited; the search and seizure may extend no farther than necessary to preserve the evidence from loss or destruction. Searches justified under evidence-loss conditions, therefore, may not be full evidence-seeking procedures because they must focus exclusively on the evidence at risk.

Consent Searches. As a rule, law enforcement officials can conduct searches upon consent. To be considered valid, consent searches must satisfy two criteria. First, permission must be freely and voluntarily granted. Second, the individual granting consent must have the authority to do so. Once permission is obtained police may legitimately search, but that search may not extend beyond limits imposed by person giving consent.

The required voluntary nature of the consent means that permission cannot be granted as a result of coercion. If police extract consent by actual or threatened physical force or by means of trickery, the permission is invalid and so is the resulting search. For example, *Bumper v. North Carolina* (1968) involved the investigation of a rape in which Bumper was the primary suspect. Police went to his house and told his grandmother, with whom he lived, that they had a search warrant when in fact they did not. Believing the police, Bumper's grandmother granted her permission for the search, which yielded a .22-caliber rifle used in the rape. At the trial the state asserted that the search and seizure were valid because permission was granted. Bumper's attorney argued otherwise, noting that police tricked and, in essence, coerced the grandmother to give consent. The U.S. Supreme Court agreed with Bumper's counsel. The justices found the grant of consent to have been coerced and therefore not voluntary.

The second requirement is that only an authorized person can give permission to search. Normally such permission can be given only by an adult who owns, occupies, or otherwise legally controls the house, automobile, office, or whatever other area the police desire to search.

Questions of rightful authority often have presented themselves to the Court. For example, in *Stoner v. California* (1964), the justices considered a disputed police search of a hotel room. The case involved a grocery store robbery. At the scene of the crime police found a checkbook belonging to Joey Stoner. The checkbook showed payments made to a local hotel. The desk clerk there told police that Stoner was not in his room. Police then asked and received permission from the clerk to search the room, where they found substantial evidence of Stoner's participation in the robbery. According to the Supreme Court, however, this search was invalid because the desk clerk did not have the proper authority to grant police permission to enter the room. In the absence of any waiver of that right, a person who rents or leases property is the only one who may grant permission to enter it.[4] The hotel room was an area in which Stoner had an expectation of privacy, and a warrantless intrusion into that room could not be authorized by anyone but Stoner.

Safety Searches. The decisions of the Supreme Court have recognized that in the conduct of their duties police officers frequently find themselves in dangerous situations. What action may a police officer take upon confronting a person who may pose a danger to the officer or to the public more generally? Suppose the officer fears the person may be armed, but none of the conditions justifying a search and seizure is present (that is, no warrant, insufficient evidence to justify an arrest, no consent, and so on). The response of the Court has been to allow safety searches. The Court first permitted such searches in *Terry v. Ohio*

---

4. Several exceptions to this general rule exist; for example, some tenant–landlord agreements contain clauses that allow superintendents to search residences or give permission to police to do so.

(1968); consequently, safety searches are often referred to as Terry stops.

Under the Court's safety search rulings, a police officer may stop and pat down a suspect believed to be dangerous in order to find and remove any weapons or other threatening objects. Similar to the other justifications we have discussed, safety searches are limited by the reasons the Court has allowed them. For such searches to be valid, two conditions must be met. First, there must be reason to believe that the suspect poses a threat to safety. And second, the search may be only for the purposes of removing the danger. As a consequence, the officer may not probe beyond a place where a hidden weapon is likely to be.

Plain View Doctrine. Our discussion so far has described circumstances under which police may search and the guidelines the Court has established to determine reasonableness. Under each justification for a search there are limitations: searches based on a warrant must be confined to the place specified in the document; consent searches may go no farther than the grant of permission stipulates; and safety searches can extend only far enough to discover or remove the possible danger. But what if, while conducting a valid search, police come upon seizable articles that are outside the scope of the search authorization? For example, suppose law enforcement officials have a valid warrant to search a house for stolen goods and, in the course of their investigation, come across illegal narcotics. What should they do? Must they ignore such items? Or may they seize the drugs? These questions are addressed by the plain view doctrine, a controversial rule that expands the powers of police to gather evidence. This doctrine holds that if police officers are lawfully present and they come upon openly visible items subject to seizure, the officers may take possession of those articles without additional authorization.

Some analysts refer to the plain view doctrine as yet another exception to the Fourth Amendment's warrant requirement. This interpretation is reasonable because the doctrine provides officers with some freedom to seize contraband and other evidence of a crime without necessarily having a warrant. Still, it is important to understand that at the heart of the doctrine is the requirement that police must be acting lawfully when seizable items come into plain view. Accordingly, the plain view doctrine often supplements other searches. Suppose, for example, that two officers come to a student's apartment and the student allows them to enter. Walking into the apartment, police spot marijuana on a table. Under the plain view doctrine, the officers can seize the marijuana because the student has *consented* to the search. Had the student denied the officers permission and they entered anyway, the plain view doctrine would not apply unless the officers had some other legitimate reason for conducting a search or they had a search warrant.

Hot Pursuit. Suppose a police officer witnesses a mugging on a city street and chases the perpetrators.[5] The muggers run into an apartment building and close the door. Must the police officer obtain a warrant to enter the building? As a general rule of law, the answer is no, and the reason is that the Supreme Court has carved out yet another exception to the Fourth Amendment's warrant requirement: hot pursuit. In other words, the Court has said that it would be reasonable for the police officer to enter the apartment without a search warrant, because evidence could be destroyed and lives could be endangered. And, if the officer found evidence of a crime—for example, the wallet of the person the officer saw being mugged—under the hot pursuit exception, the evidence could be used against the defendant.

As with all other exceptions to the warrant requirement, the Court has placed limits on the hot pursuit exception—limits that, as always, reflect the original justifications for permitting the exception. These limits were laid out by the justices in *Warden v. Hayden* (1967), a Warren Court case that provides an impor-

5. We adopt this discussion from Zalman and Siegel, *Criminal Procedure,* 258–259.

tant example of the hot pursuit exception. Hayden robbed a taxi company and fled on foot. Hearing yells of "Holdup!" from company employees, two cab drivers followed Hayden and saw him enter a house. One of the drivers radioed the cab dispatcher with a description of Hayden and where he was hiding. The police arrived immediately, entered the house, and found Hayden in a bedroom pretending to be asleep. In the meantime, another officer found—in an adjoining bathroom—two guns and the clothing that witnesses had said the robber was wearing. These and other items were introduced as evidence against Hayden.

Even though police officers had entered the house without a warrant, the Supreme Court ruled that the search was constitutional on the grounds that they were in hot pursuit of a suspect. It is reasonable to allow warrantless searches in such circumstances, as Justice Brennan put it for the majority, because the

Fourth Amendment does not require police officers to delay in the course of an investigation if to do so would gravely endanger their lives or the lives of others. Speed here was essential, and only a thorough search of the house for persons and weapons could have ensured that Hayden was the only man present and the police had control of all weapons which could be used against them or to effect an escape.

The "exigencies of the situation"—the fact that lives were in danger, that evidence could have been lost, and so forth—made the warrantless entry into Hayden's house "imperative."

Place Searches. So far we have addressed questions of when and under what circumstances police may conduct searches and seizures. The Court has also examined a number of cases that presented different questions: Where can law enforcement officials search and seize without a warrant? Do certain places require special consideration? These questions assume that not all places deserve equal levels of Fourth Amendment protection. The level of protection accorded a particular place depends upon the degree of privacy people expect there. The greater the expectation of privacy, the greater the constitutional protection. The home, for example, merits the highest degree of protection; it is in our residences that we expect to be the most secure against government intrusion.

The Court has specified a number of places, however, that merit low levels of constitutional protection. For example, the justices have ruled that open fields merit almost no constitutional protection. Police may search an open field, even if privately owned, with little justification.[6] The reason for this is that in an open field little privacy is expected. Similarly, minimal protection is given to jails and prisons.[7] If corrections officials believe it necessary to search for weapons, articles that may be used in escape attempts, or illegal substances, they may do so without obtaining authorizaton. Since prisons are places in which those convicted of crimes forfeit their freedoms, it is not surprising that the Court has held that inmates deserve little in the way of Fourth Amendment rights.

Perhaps the most controversial of the Court's decisions in this area deals with the automobile. The justices have ruled that motor vehicles deserve little protection. This has been the case since the Court's ruling in *Carroll v. United States* in 1925 and has generally continued to the present.[8] The Court has given the police broad latitude in searching cars without warrants because (1) cars are mobile and, as such, can quickly leave the jurisdiction of the police; (2) automobile windows allow outsiders to look in, and drivers have a lower expectation of privacy inside a car than they do in their homes; and (3) the government has a pervasive interest in regulating cars.

The Fourth Amendment was intended to be a barrier against unjustified violations of privacy by the police or other government officials. Consequently, the Court's search and seizure doctrine has repeatedly

6. See, for example, *Oliver v. United States* (1984).
7. See, for example, *Hudson v. Palmer* (1984).
8. See *Chambers v. Maroney* (1970); *United States v. Ross* (1982).

emphasized that whenever a person is in circumstances in which privacy is reasonably expected, the Fourth Amendment applies.[9] The higher the degree of expected privacy, the more stringent the Court's requirements for establishing the reasonableness of the search.

Enforcing the Fourth Amendment: The Exclusionary Rule

So far, we have focused on the constitutional rules governing searches and seizures. We showed that the Court has carved out numerous exceptions to the general principle that police should obtain warrants to conduct searches. At the same time, we saw that the Court has placed limits on those exceptions. For example, assume that police arrest a person at his home. If they wish to use the "incident to arrest" exception to conduct the warrantless search of the person and his immediate surroundings, then they must conduct that search *at the time* of the arrest. If police return after the suspect has been removed to the police station and conduct a warrantless search of his house, the Court would not allow them to use the "incident to arrest" exception to justify their search. The search would fail the requirement that such searches be contemporaneous with the arrest. The search would be declared unconstitutional.

But suppose that the police did go back to the house a day later, found evidence, and tried to justify the search under the incident to arrest exception. We know that such a search would be illegal, but what is to prevent the police from doing it anyway? In England, if the police conduct an illegal search and seizure, the evidence they obtain *may* be used in court against the accused, although the person whose privacy rights have been violated can sue the police for damages. This system of police liability enables the British to enforce search and seizure rights.

The United States imposes a different remedy for police infractions. In this country the Fourth Amendment is enforced through the application of the exclusionary rule, a judicially created principle that removes any incentive police might otherwise have for violating search and seizure rights. The exclusionary rule holds that evidence gathered illegally may not be admitted into court. It is excluded from use by prosecutors in attempting to establish the suspect's guilt. The rationale behind the rule is straightforward: if police know that evidence produced by an illegal search will be of no use, they have no motive for violating the Constitution.

At one time, law enforcement officials faced no federal punitive measures for conducting illegal searches and seizures. Unless individual state laws imposed some form of redress, the police were not held liable for their activities, nor was evidence obtained unconstitutionally excluded from trials. In 1914, however, the Supreme Court decided *Weeks v. United States,* a case that arose from a federal investigation into the business practices of Freemont Weeks. Police officers went to Weeks's office, placed him under arrest, and conducted a search. Later, the police and a U.S. marshal went to Weeks's house and, without a warrant, carried off boxes of his papers and documents, a clear violation of search and seizure rules. In addition, the materials seized were not narrowly selected for their relevance but were voluminous business records on which authorities could conduct a fishing expedition in search of possible incriminating evidence.

Should the documents be used as evidence against Weeks, even though police and the marshal had gathered the materials in an illegal manner? Writing for the Court, Justice William R. Day proclaimed:

If letters and private documents can thus be seized and held and used as evidence against a citizen accused of an offense, the protection of the Fourth Amendment declaring his right to be secure against such searches and seizures is of no value, and, so far as those thus placed are concerned, might as well be stricken from the Constitution.

With this conclusion, the Court, through Justice Day, created the exclusionary rule: judges must ex-

9. See *Katz v. United States* (1967).

clude from trial any evidence gathered in violation of the Fourth Amendment. Although *Weeks* constituted a major decision, it was limited in scope, applying only to federal agents and federal judges in federal criminal cases. It was clear, however, that eventually the Court would be asked to apply the exclusionary rule to the states because that is where most criminal prosecutions take place. But it was also the case that many states or their judges resisted adopting an exclusionary rule. *People v. Defore* (1926) provides perhaps the most famous example. In that case, Benjamin Cardozo, then a judge on the New York Court of Appeals, rejected the adoption of *Weeks* to New York. In his opinion he wrote the now famous lines disparaging the exclusionary rule: "The criminal is to go free because the constable has blundered. . . . A room is searched against the law, and the body of a murdered man is found. . . . The privacy of the home has been infringed, and the murderer goes free."

The issue first reached the Supreme Court in 1949 in *Wolf v. Colorado.* This case involved a Colorado physician who was suspected to be performing illegal abortions. Because the police were unable to obtain any solid evidence against him, a deputy sheriff surreptitiously took Dr. Wolf's appointment book and followed up on the names in it. The police gathered enough evidence to convict him. Wolf's attorney argued that because the case against his client rested on illegally obtained evidence, the Court should dismiss it. To implement his arguments, however, the justices would have to apply or incorporate the Fourth Amendment and impose the exclusionary rule on the states.

Writing for the Court, Justice Frankfurter agreed that the states had to obey the Fourth Amendment. The right to be secure from unreasonable searches and seizures was deemed a fundamental right, "basic to a free society," and the provisions of the amendment was applied to the states through the Due Process Clause of the Fourteenth Amendment. However, the Court refused to hold that the exclusionary rule was a necessary part of the Fourth Amendment. The rule was one method of enforcing search and seizure rights, but not the only one. In other words, although state law enforcement officials must abide by the guarantees contained in the Fourth Amendment, judges need not use a particular mechanism, such as the exclusionary rule, to ensure compliance. Frankfurter noted that the law in England, where there was no exclusionary rule, and in the states, the majority of which rejected the rule, proved that justice could be served without this check on police behavior. States were left free to adopt whatever procedures they wished to enforce search and seizure rights. The exclusionary rule was not mandatory.

Growing conflicts between state and federal search and seizure rules, coupled with changes in Court personnel, caused the Court to reconsider the applicability of the exclusionary rule to states in *Mapp v. Ohio* (1961). As you read *Mapp,* can you discern why it is such a significant, yet controversial, opinion? Does Justice Clark's majority opinion leave any room for exceptions?

Mapp v. Ohio

367 U.S. 643 (1961)
Vote: 6 (Black, Brennan, Clark, Douglas, Stewart, Warren)
    3 (Frankfurter, Harlan, Whittaker)
Opinion of the Court: Clark
Concurring opinions: Black, Douglas, Stewart
Dissenting opinion: Harlan

Dollree Mapp, a woman in her early twenties, was involved in myriad illegal activities, ranging from gambling to prostitution, which she carried on in her Cleveland home. For several months the police had attempted to shut down her operations, but apparently Mapp was tipped off because each time police planned a raid, she managed to elude them.

On May 23, 1957, police officers, led by Sgt. Carl

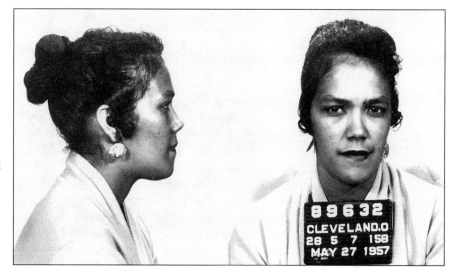

In 1957 Dollree Mapp was arrested for possession of obscene materials. The police seized vital evidence against her during an unconstitutional search. In *Mapp v. Ohio* (1961) the Supreme Court reversed her conviction, holding that evidence obtained through an illegal search could not be admitted in court.

Delau, tried to enter Mapp's house, this time on the grounds that she was harboring a fugitive from justice. (The fugitive was suspected of bombing the house of an alleged Cleveland numbers racketeer, Don King, who was later to become a prominent boxing promoter.)[10] When the police arrived, Mapp refused to let them in because they did not have a search warrant. Delau returned to his car, radioed for a search warrant, and kept the house under surveillance. Three hours later, and with additional police officers, Delau again tried to enter. This time Mapp did not come to the door, so police forced it open.

At this point several events occurred almost simultaneously. Mapp's attorney, whom she had called when police first appeared, arrived and tried to see her. Police would not let him in. Hearing the police break in, Mapp came downstairs and began arguing with them. Delau held up a piece of a paper, which he claimed was a search warrant. Mapp grabbed it and stuffed it down her blouse. A fight broke out, during which police handcuffed Mapp, retrieved the paper, and searched the house. The police seized some allegedly obscene pictures, which were illegal to possess under Ohio law. The existence of a valid search warrant was never established by the state. Mapp was found guilty of possession of obscene materials and sentenced to prison. Her attorney appealed to the U.S. Supreme Court, asking the justices to review Mapp's claim on First Amendment grounds, but the justices were more interested in exploring the search and seizure issue.[11]

MR. JUSTICE CLARK delivered the opinion of the Court.

Seventy-five years ago, in Boyd v. United States . . . [t]he Court noted that

"constitutional provisions for the security of person and property should be liberally construed. . . . It is the duty of courts to be watchful for the constitutional rights of the citizen, and against any stealthy encroachments thereon."

10. See Fred W. Friendly and Martha J. H. Elliott, *The Constitution: That Delicate Balance* (New York: Random House, 1984), 128–133.

11. Indeed, both Mapp's and the state's attorneys argued this case on First Amendment grounds because she was convicted for possessing obscene material. The ACLU, in an amicus curiae brief, raised the Fourth Amendment issue on which the Court ultimately decided. *Mapp*, therefore, presents an excellent illustration of the effect amicus curiae briefs can have on the justices. It also is used as an example of the uneven quality of state attorneys general. During oral argument, a justice asked Ohio's attorney about the applicability of *Wolf* to *Mapp*. The attorney responded that he did not know anything about *Wolf*, even though it was the leading case in the area.

In this jealous regard for maintaining the integrity of individual rights, the Court gave life to Madison's prediction that "independent tribunals of justice . . . will be naturally led to resist every encroachment upon rights expressly stipulated for in the Constitution by the declaration of rights.". . .

Less than 30 years after Boyd, this Court, in Weeks v. United States, 1914, . . . stated that use of the seized evidence involved "a denial of the constitutional rights of the accused." Thus, in the year 1914, in the Weeks case, this Court "for the first time" held that "in a federal prosecution the Fourth Amendment barred the use of evidence secured through an illegal search and seizure." This Court has ever since required of federal law officers a strict adherence to that command which this Court has held to be a clear, specific, and constitutionally required—even if judicially implied—deterrent safeguard without insistence upon which the Fourth Amendment would have been reduced to "a form of words." It meant, quite simply, that "conviction by means of unlawful seizures and enforced confessions . . . should find no sanction in the judgments of the courts . . . ," that such evidence "shall not be used at all."

There are in the cases of this Court some passing references to the Weeks rule as being one of evidence. But the plain and unequivocal language of Weeks—and its later paraphrase in Wolf—to the effect that the Weeks rule is of constitutional origin, remains entirely undisturbed. . . .

In 1949, 35 years after Weeks was announced, this Court, in Wolf v. People of State of Colorado, again for the first time, discussed the effect of the Fourth Amendment upon the states through the operation of the Due Process Clause of the Fourteenth Amendment. It said:

"[W]e have no hesitation in saying that were a State affirmatively to sanction such police incursion into privacy it would run counter to the guaranty of the Fourteenth Amendment."

Nevertheless, after declaring that the "security of one's privacy against arbitrary intrusion by the police" is "implicit in 'the concept of ordered liberty' and as such enforceable against the States through the Due Process Clause," and announcing that it "stoutly adhere[d]" to the Weeks decision, the Court decided that the Weeks exclusionary rule would not then be imposed upon the States as "an essential ingredient of the right." The Court's reasons for not considering essential to the right to privacy, as a curb imposed upon the

States by the Due Process Clause, that which decades before had been posited as part and parcel of the Fourth Amendment's limitation upon federal encroachment of individual privacy, were bottomed on factual considerations.

While they are not basically relevant to a decision that the exclusionary rule is an essential ingredient of the Fourth Amendment as the right it embodies is vouchsafed against the States by the Due Process Clause, we will consider the current validity of the factual grounds upon which Wolf was based.

The Court in Wolf first stated that "[t]he contrariety of views of the States" on the adoption of the exclusionary rule of Weeks was "particularly impressive" and, in this connection that it could not "brush aside the experience of States which deem the incidence of such conduct by the police too slight to call for a deterrent remedy . . . by overriding the [States'] relevant rules of evidence." While in 1949, prior to the Wolf case, almost two-thirds of the States were opposed to the use of the exclusionary rule, now, despite the Wolf case, more than half of those since passing upon it, by their own legislative or judicial decision, have wholly or partly adopted or adhered to the Weeks rule. Significantly, among those now following the rule is California, which, according to its highest court, was "compelled to reach that conclusion because other remedies have completely failed to secure compliance with the constitutional provisions. . . . " In connection with this California case, we note that the second basis elaborated in Wolf in support of its failure to enforce the exclusionary doctrine against the States was that "other means of protection" have been afforded "the right to privacy." The experience of California that such other remedies have been worthless and futile is buttressed by the experience of other States. . . .

Likewise, time has set its face against . . . Wolf. . . . [T]he force of that reasoning has been largely vitiated by later decisions of this Court. These include the recent discarding of the "silver platter" doctrine which allowed federal judicial use of evidence seized in violation of the Constitution by state agents; the relaxation of the formerly strict requirements as to standing to challenge the use of evidence thus seized, so that now the procedure of exclusion, "ultimately referable to constitutional safeguards," is available to anyone even "legitimately on [the] premises" unlawfully searched; and finally, the formulation of a method to prevent state use of evidence unconstitutionally seized by federal agents. Because there can be no fixed formula, we are admittedly met with "recurring questions of the [r]easonableness of searches," but less is not to be expected when dealing with a Constitution, and, at any rate, "reasonableness is in the first instance for the [trial court] to determine."

It, therefore, plainly appears that the factual considerations supporting the failure of the Wolf Court to include the Weeks exclusionary rule when it recognized the enforceability of the right to privacy against the States in 1949, while not basically relevant to the constitutional consideration, could not, in any analysis, now be deemed controlling.

Some five years after Wolf, in answer to a plea made here Term after Term that we overturn its doctrine on applicability of the Weeks exclusionary rule, this Court indicated that such should not be done until the States had "adequate opportunity to adopt or reject the [Weeks] rule.". . . Today we once again examine Wolf's constitutional documentation of the right to privacy free from unreasonable state intrusion, and, after its dozen years on our books, are led by it to close the only courtroom door remaining open to evidence secured by official lawlessness in flagrant abuse of that basic right, reserved to all persons as a specific guarantee against that very same unlawful conduct. We hold that all evidence obtained by searches and seizures in violation of the Constitution is, by that same authority, inadmissible in a state court.

Since the Fourth Amendment's right of privacy has been declared enforceable against the States through the Due Process Clause of the Fourteenth, it is enforceable against them by the same sanction of exclusion as is used against the Federal Government. Were it otherwise, then just as without the Weeks rule the assurance against unreasonable federal searches and seizures would be "a form of words," valueless and undeserving of mention in a perpetual charter of inestimable human liberties, so too, without that rule the freedom from state invasions of privacy would be so ephemeral and so neatly severed from its conceptual nexus with the freedom from all brutish means of coercing evidence as not to merit this Court's high regard as a freedom "implicit in 'the concept of ordered liberty.'" At the time that the Court held in Wolf that the Amendment was applicable to the States through the Due Process Clause, the

cases of this Court, as we have seen, had steadfastly held that as to federal officers the Fourth Amendment included the exclusion of the evidence seized in violation of its provisions. Even Wolf "stoutly adhered" to that proposition. The right to privacy, when conceded operatively enforceable against the States, was not susceptible of destruction by avulsion of the sanction upon which its protection and enjoyment had always been deemed dependent. . . . Therefore, in extending the substantive protections of due process to all constitutionally unreasonable searches—state or federal—it was logically and constitutionally necessary that the exclusion doctrine—an essential part of the right to privacy—be also insisted upon as an essential ingredient of the right newly recognized by the Wolf case. In short, the admission of the new constitutional right by Wolf could not consistently tolerate denial of its most important constitutional privilege, namely, the exclusion of the evidence which an accused had been forced to give by reason of the unlawful seizure. To hold otherwise is to grant the right but in reality o withhold its privilege and enjoyment. Only last year the Court itself recognized that the purpose of the exclusionary rule "is to deter—to compel respect for the constitutional guaranty in the only effectively available way—by removing the incentive to disregard it."

Indeed, we are aware of no restraint, similar to that rejected today, conditioning the enforcement of any other basic constitutional right. The right to privacy, no less important than any other right carefully and particularly reserved to the people, would stand in marked contrast to all other rights declared as "basic to a free society." This Court has not hesitated to enforce as strictly against the States as it does against the Federal Government the rights of free speech and of a free press, the rights to notice and to a fair, public trial, including, as it does, the right not to be convicted by use of a coerced confession, however logically relevant it be, and without regard to its reliability. And nothing could be more certain than that when a coerced confession is involved, "the relevant rules of evidence" are overridden without regard to "the incidence of such conduct by the police," slight or frequent. Why should not the same rule apply to what is tantamount to coerced testimony by way of unconstitutional seizure of goods, papers, effects, documents, etc.? We find that, as to the Federal Government, the Fourth and Fifth Amendments and, as to the

States, the freedom from unconscionable invasions of privacy and the freedom from convictions based upon coerced confessions do enjoy an "intimate relation" in their perpetuation of "principles of humanity and civil liberty [secured] . . . only after years of struggle." The philosophy of each Amendment and of each freedom is complementary to, although not dependent upon, that of the other in its sphere of influence—the very least that together they assure in either sphere is that no man is to be convicted on unconstitutional evidence.

Moreover, our holding that the exclusionary rule is an essential part of both the Fourth and Fourteenth Amendments is not only the logical dictate of prior cases, but it also makes very good sense. There is no war between the Constitution and common sense. Presently, a federal prosecutor may make no use of evidence illegally seized, but a State's attorney across the street may, although he supposedly is operating under the enforceable prohibitions of the same Amendment. Thus the State, by admitting evidence unlawfully seized, serves to encourage disobedience to the Federal Constitution which it is bound to uphold. Moreover, "[t]he very essence of a healthy federalism depends upon the avoidance of needless conflict between state and federal courts." Such a conflict, hereafter needless, arose this very Term, in Wilson v. Schnettler, in which . . . we gave full recognition to our practice in this regard by refusing to restrain a federal officer from testifying in a state court as to evidence unconstitutionally seized by him in the performance of his duties. Yet the double standard recognized until today hardly put such a thesis into practice. In non-exclusionary States, federal officers, being human, were by it invited to and did, as our cases indicate, step across the street to the State's attorney with their unconstitutionally seized evidence. Prosecution on the basis of that evidence was then had in a state court in utter disregard of the enforceable Fourth Amendment. If the fruits of an unconstitutional search had been inadmissible in both state and federal courts, this inducement to evasion would have been sooner eliminated. There would be no need to reconcile such cases as . . . Schnettler, pointing up the hazardous uncertainties of our heretofore ambivalent approach. . . .

There are those who say, as did Justice (then Judge) Cardozo, that under our constitutional exclusionary doctrine "[t]he criminal is to go free because the constable has blundered." *People v. Defore.* In some cases this will undoubtedly be the result. But . . . "there is another consideration—the imperative of judicial integrity." The criminal goes free, if he must, but it is the law that sets him free. Nothing can destroy a government more quickly than its failure to observe its own laws, or worse, its disregard of the character of its own existence. Nor can it lightly be assumed that, as a practical matter, adoption of the exclusionary rule fetters law enforcement. Only last year this Court expressly considered that contention and found that "pragmatic evidence of a sort" to the contrary was not wanting. . . . Moreover, the experience of the states is impressive. . . . The movement towards the rule of exclusion has been halting but seemingly inexorable.

The ignoble shortcut to conviction left open to the State tends to destroy the entire system of constitutional restraints on which the liberties of the people rest. Having once recognized that the right to privacy embodied in the Fourth Amendment is enforceable against the States, and that the right to be secure against rude invasions of privacy by state officers is, therefore, constitutional in origin, we can no longer permit that right to remain an empty promise. Because it is enforceable in the same manner and to like effect as other basic rights secured by the Due Process Clause, we can no longer permit it to be revocable at the whim of any police officer who, in the name of law enforcement itself, chooses to suspend its enjoyment. Our decision, founded on reason and truth, gives to the individual no more than that which the Constitution guarantees him, to the police officer no less than that to which honest law enforcement is entitled, and, to the courts, that judicial integrity so necessary in the true administration of justice.

The judgment of the Supreme Court of Ohio is reversed and the cause remanded for further proceedings not inconsistent with this opinion.

Reversed and remanded.

MR. JUSTICE HARLAN, whom MR. JUSTICE FRANKFURTER and MR. JUSTICE WHITTAKER join, dissenting.

In overruling the Wolf case the Court, in my opinion, has forgotten the sense of judicial restraint which, with due regard for *stare decisis*, is one element that should enter into deciding whether a past decision of this Court should be overruled. Apart from that I also believe that the Wolf rule represents sounder Constitutional doctrine than the new rule which now replaces it.

From the Court's statement of the case one would gather that the central, if not controlling, issue on this appeal is whether illegally state-seized evidence is Constitutionally admissible in a state prosecution, an issue which would of course face us with the need for re-examining Wolf. However, such is not the situation. For, although that question was indeed raised here and below among appellant's subordinate points, the new and pivotal issue brought to the Court by this appeal is whether . . . [the Ohio law] making criminal the *mere* knowing possession or control of obscene material, and under which appellant has been convicted, is consistent with the rights of free thought and expression assured against state action by the Fourteenth Amendment. That was the principal issue which was decided by the Ohio Supreme Court, which was tendered by appellant's Jurisdictional Statement, and which was briefed* and argued in this Court.

In this posture of things, I think it fair to say that five members of this Court have simply "reached out" to overrule Wolf. With all respect for the views of the majority, and recognizing that *stare decisis* carries different weight in Constitutional adjudication than it does in nonconstitutional decision, I can perceive no justification for regarding this case as an appropriate occasion for re-examining Wolf. . . .

Since the demands of the case before us do not require us to reach the question of the validity of Wolf, I think this case furnishes a singularly inappropriate occasion for consideration of that decision, if reconsideration is indeed warranted. Even the most cursory examination will reveal that the doctrine of the Wolf case has been of continuing importance in the administration of state criminal law. Indeed,

certainly as regards its "nonexclusionary" aspect, Wolf did no more than articulate the then existing assumption among the States that the federal cases enforcing the exclusionary rule "do not bind [the States], for they construe provisions of the Federal Constitution, the Fourth and Fifth Amendments, not applicable to the States." People v. Defore. Though, of course, not reflecting the full measure of this continuing reliance, I find that during the last three Terms, for instance, the issue of the inadmissibility of illegally state-obtained evidence appears on an average of about fifteen times per Term just in the *in forma pauperis* cases summarily disposed of by us. This would indicate both that the issue which is now being decided may well have untoward practical ramifications respecting state cases long since disposed of in reliance on Wolf, and that were we determined to re-examine that doctrine we would not lack future opportunity. . . .

Thus, if the Court were bent on reconsidering Wolf, I think that there would soon have presented itself an appropriate opportunity in which we could have had the benefit of full briefing and argument. In any event, at the very least, the present case should have been set down for reargument, in view of the inadequate briefing and argument we have received on the Wolf point. To all intents and purposes the Court's present action amounts to a summary reversal of Wolf, without argument.

I am bound to say that what has been done is not likely to promote respect either for the Court's adjudicatory process or for the stability of its decisions. Having been unable, however, to persuade any of the majority to a different procedural course, I now turn to the merits of the present decision. . . .

I would not impose upon the States this federal exclusionary remedy. The reasons given by the majority for now suddenly turning its back on Wolf seem to me notably unconvincing.

First, it is said that "the factual grounds upon which Wolf was based" have since changed, in that more States now follow the Weeks exclusionary rule than was so at the time Wolf was decided. While that is true, a recent survey indicates that at present one-half of the States still adhere to the common-law non-exclusionary rule, and one, Maryland, retains the rule as to felonies. But in any case surely all

---

*The appellant's brief did not urge the overruling of Wolf. Indeed it did not even cite the case. The brief of the appellee merely relied on Wolf in support of the State's contention that appellant's conviction was not vitiated by the admission in evidence of the fruits of the alleged unlawful search and seizure by the police. The brief of the American and Ohio Civil Liberties Unions, as *amici*, did in one short concluding paragraph of its argument "request" the Court to re-examine and overrule Wolf, but without argumentation. . . .

this is beside the point, as the majority itself indeed seems to recognize. Our concern here, as it was in Wolf, is not with the desirability of that rule but only with the question whether the States are Constitutionally free to follow it or not as they may themselves determine, and the relevance of the disparity of views among the States on this point lies simply in the fact that the judgment involved is a debatable one. Moreover, the very fact on which the majority relies, instead of lending support to what is now being done, points away from the need of replacing voluntary state action with federal compulsion.

The preservation of a proper balance between state and federal responsibility in the administration of criminal justice demands patience on the part of those who might like to see things move faster among the States in this respect. Problems of criminal law enforcement vary widely from State to State. One State, in considering the totality of its legal picture, may conclude that the need for embracing the Weeks rule is pressing because other remedies are unavailable or inadequate to secure compliance with the substantive Constitutional principle involved. Another, though equally solicitous of Constitutional rights, may choose to pursue one purpose at a time, allowing all evidence relevant to guilt to be brought into a criminal trial, and dealing with Constitutional infractions by other means. Still another may consider the exclusionary rule too rough-and-ready a remedy, in that it reaches only unconstitutional intrusions which eventuate in criminal prosecution of the victims. Further, a State after experimenting with the Weeks rule for a time may, because of unsatisfactory experience with it, decide to revert to a non-exclusionary rule. And so on. From the standpoint of Constitutional permissibility in pointing a State in one direction or another, I do not see at all why "time has set its face against" the considerations which led Mr. Justice Cardozo, then chief judge of the New York Court of Appeals, to reject for New York in People v. Defore, the Weeks exclusionary rule. For us the question remains, as it has always been, one of state power, not one of passing judgment on the wisdom of one state course or another. In my view this Court should continue to forbear from fettering the States with an adamant rule which may embarrass them in coping with their own peculiar problems in criminal law enforcement.

Further, we are told that imposition of the Weeks rule on the States makes "very good sense," in that it will promote recognition by state and federal officials of their "mutual obligation to respect the same fundamental criteria" in their approach to law enforcement, and will avoid "'needless conflict between state and federal courts.'". . . .

An approach which regards the issue as one of achieving procedural symmetry or of serving administrative convenience surely disfigures the boundaries of this Court's functions in relation to the state and federal courts. Our role in promulgating the Weeks rule . . . was quite a different one than it is here. There, in implementing the Fourth Amendment, we occupied the position of a tribunal having the ultimate responsibility for developing the standards and procedures of judicial administration within the judicial system over which it presides. Here we review state procedures whose measure is to be taken not against the specific substantive commands of the Fourth Amendment but under the flexible contours of the Due Process Clause. I do not believe that the Fourteenth Amendment empowers this Court to mould state remedies effectuating the right to freedom from "arbitrary intrusion by the police" to suit its own notions of how things should be done. . . .

In conclusion, it should be noted that the majority opinion in this case is in fact an opinion only for the *judgment* overruling Wolf, and not for the basic rationale by which four members of the majority have reached that result. For my Brother BLACK is unwilling to subscribe to their view that the Weeks exclusionary rule derives from the Fourth Amendment itself. . . .

I regret that I find so unwise in principle and so inexpedient in policy a decision motivated by the high purpose of increasing respect for Constitutional rights. But in the last analysis I think this Court can increase respect for the Constitution only if it rigidly respects the limitations which the Constitution places upon it, and respects as well the principles inherent in its own processes. In the present case I think we exceed both, and that our voice becomes only a voice of power, not of reason.

The application of the exclusionary rule provides yet another example of the Warren Court's revolutionary treatment of the rights of the criminally accused. It also illustrates the highly politicized nature of criminal law. Since 1961, when the Court informed states that they must adopt it, the rule has been attacked and defended by scholars, lawyers, and judges. Opponents of the rule argue that letting a guilty person go free is too great a price for society to pay just because a police officer violated search and seizure guidelines. Supporters fear that if the exclusionary rule is eliminated, police will have no incentive to respect the law.

Disagreement over the exclusionary rule, expressed in academic circles and the public, also was evident among the justices. Six voted to overturn Mapp's conviction, but only five expressed full support for the exclusionary rule. Stewart, who voted with the majority, explicitly did so on other grounds. When Chief Justice Warren left the Court and was replaced by the law and order–minded Warren Burger in 1969, legal scholars predicted that the Court might well overrule *Mapp*. With each additional Court appointment by Richard Nixon and then later by Ronald Reagan, speculation on the end of the exclusionary rule increased.

At first, predictions of the reversal of *Mapp* were proven unfounded. Between 1969 and 1983 the justices made no significant move to alter the exclusionary rule. In case after case, however, they interpreted the rule very narrowly, and the Court refused to extend the rule to other stages of the criminal process (for example, to grand jury hearings).[12] In spite of these decisions, the exclusionary rule remained substantially intact.

By the mid-1980s, however, the situation had changed. The Court became dominated by more conservative justices appointed during the Nixon, Ford, and Reagan administrations. The national mood had turned quite conservative, and there was significant political pressure to alter liberal, Warren Court rulings. The time seemed ripe for change.

In 1984 the Court heard arguments supporting two

different exceptions to the exclusionary rule. The first argument was presented in the cases of *United States v. Leon* and *Massachusetts v. Sheppard.* Both cases involved similar controversies. In *Leon,* California police had received a tip from an informant of unproven reliability regarding certain drug transactions. Police followed up on this information, placed the suspects under observation, and received information from another informant. Based upon this investigation, officers obtained a warrant to search the automobiles and residences of the suspects. The search yielded a quantity of illegal drugs. At the trial defense attorneys argued that the evidence should be excluded because the initial information that had led to the issuing of the warrant was provided by a source of dubious credibility whose information was several months old. The trial court judge agreed and excluded the evidence gathered pursuant to the search warrant. In *Sheppard,* a man was accused of killing his former girlfriend, discarding her body in a vacant lot, and setting the corpse on fire. After obtaining considerable information pointing to his guilt, police obtained a warrant to search Sheppard's residence, a search which led to significant physical evidence further implicating Sheppard in the murder. The trial judge, however, declared the warrant technically invalid because of some inadvertent minor wording errors.

In both cases the Supreme Court rejected the position that the defendant's rights had been violated. Although the Court conceded that there might have been some technical defects in the issuance of the warrants, the justices also found that the police had done everything reasonable to comply with the law and respect the rights of suspects in question. They had relied on a warrant issued by a detached magistrate and had made a "good faith" effort to act within the dictates of the Constitution. According to Justice White's majority opinions in the two cases, the primary goal of the exclusionary rule is to impose a deterrent to police searches that abuse individual rights. Cases in which law enforcement officers act in good faith in-

---

12. See, for example, *United States v. Calandra* (1974).

volve no misbehavior by the police, and consequently the exclusionary rule should not be applied. Hence was born the "good faith exception" to the exclusionary rule. If police do everything reasonable to observe the Fourth Amendment rights of the suspect, then the exclusionary rule will not be applied if it later turns out that there was a defect, for example, in the form of the warrant.

The second argument was offered in *Nix v. Williams.* The case involved the abduction and murder of a ten-year-old girl whose body was discarded in an Iowa field. While a search party of some 200 volunteers searched the area for the body, Robert Anthony Williams, the prime suspect, turned himself in to police. During the process of transporting Williams to the Des Moines police station, officers conducted an illegal interrogation which led him to provide information concerning the location of the body. With that information, the girl's body was quickly found. Williams's attorneys argued that since the girl had been found as a result of an illegal interrogation, the exclusionary rule should apply and evidence from the body should not be admitted.

The Supreme Court rejected this argument and in doing so approved the "inevitable discovery exception" to the exclusionary rule. The justices reasoned that since the body was abandoned in an area directly in the search party's path, the volunteers inevitably would have found the body even if Williams had not provided information about its location. Under such conditions, the exclusionary rule should not be applied.

The good faith and inevitable discovery exceptions poked significant holes in the exclusionary rule. All three cases included a six-person majority consisting of four Nixon appointees (Blackmun, Burger, Powell, and Rehnquist), a Reagan appointee (O'Connor), and a Kennedy appointee (White). In two of the cases (*Sheppard* and *Williams*) this coalition was joined by Justice Stevens, a Ford appointee.

The Court's most liberal members, Justices Mar-shall and Brennan, dissented from all three decisions and were joined by Stevens in *Leon.* Brennan, the only remaining member of the *Mapp* majority, sharply criticized the creation of such exceptions. He attacked the majority for its "zealous efforts to emasculate the exclusionary rule," and its "determined strangulation of the rule."

Finally, given the appointments to the Court since *Leon,* would you predict any additional changes in the Court's interpretation of the exclusionary rule? On the one hand, Brennan's and Marshall's departures surely have weakened support for the exclusionary rule or, at least, for a broad application of it. On the other hand, it is possible that Justice Ginsburg, who replaced White, and Justice Breyer, who holds Blackmun's seat, will take a position similar to that advocated by Brennan and Marshall. If so, the status quo will prevail, for there does not seem to be strong support among the current justices for the elimination of the exclusionary rule. The Warren Court's decision in *Mapp* remains good law, but, according to Justice Brennan's dissent in *Leon,* in a much watered down form.

THE FIFTH AMENDMENT AND SELF-INCRIMINATION

As we have seen, the Fourth Amendment governs the procedures by which police obtain evidence—generally physical evidence. But evidence used to make an arrest is not always physical or material. Very often arrests, and ultimately convictions, hinge on verbal evidence—testimony, confessions, and the like—the gathering of which is governed by the Fifth Amendment's Self-Incrimination Clause: "No person . . . shall be compelled in any criminal case to be a witness against himself." Taken together, the Fourth (physical) and Fifth (verbal) Amendments dictate the procedures police use to gather most evidence against individuals.

The Self-Incrimination Clause is violated by the presence of two elements. First, there must be some form of testimonial evidence that incriminates the person who provides it, and, second, the testimonial evidence must somehow be compelled by the government.

The protection against self-incrimination most commonly applies in two situations. First, it means that no person may be forced to give testimony in any court case or other governmental hearing in which the truthful answering of questions will implicate the witness in a criminal act. For this reason a witness may decline to answer any questions that would lead to self-incriminating answers. Furthermore, a defendant in a criminal case is exempt from testifying at all, and no inferences of guilt may be made on the basis of a decision not to take the witness stand.

The second common situation for which the Fifth Amendment is relevant involves police interrogation of suspects prior to trial. Certainly, police must be able to ask questions during the investigation of crimes, but if their interrogation tactics involve compulsion constitutional questions arise. These issues have posed very difficult and controversial questions for the Court.

Even before the 1960s, the Supreme Court had established certain guidelines for police interrogations. For the most part, these guidelines dealt with the concept of coercion. Principles of self-incrimination and due process of law are violated, the Court held, when confessions are forced from a suspect by physical torture or psychological coercion.[13] These traditional guidelines curtailed the most blatant forms of police coercion, but they left considerable latitude for investigators to pry confessions out of poorly educated or naive suspects.

Several of the justices on the Warren Court felt that the balance was tipped decidedly in favor of the police. There were too many opportunities for police to obtain self-incriminating statements from unsuspect-

ing defendants. As a consequence, the justices handed down two particularly important decisions in the mid-1960s designed to provide additional protections to the criminally accused.

The first of the two was *Escobedo v. Illinois* (1964). The accused was Danny Escobedo, a twenty-two-year-old of Mexican extraction and limited formal education. The case began when Escobedo's brother-in-law was found fatally shot in a Chicago alley on January 19, 1960. The police quickly identified three potential suspects: Escobedo, his friend Benedict DiGerlando, and his sister. The crime was motivated, police believed, by the deceased's long history of physically abusing his wife.

In the ten days following the murder all three suspects at various times were taken into custody for questioning. Finally, on January 30, DiGerlando told police that Escobedo had fired the fatal shots. As a consequence, police arrested Escobedo, told him what DiGerlando had said, and began a lengthy interrogation. Escobedo, feeling overpowered by the situation, asked to have his attorney present. Police told Escobedo that his attorney did not want to see him, in spite of the fact that the lawyer had arrived at the police station and was requesting to see his client. The questioning lasted over fourteen hours, at the end of which Escobedo made statements that implicated himself in the crime. There was no overt physical or psychological coercion during this period. Against his attorney's objections, the incriminating statements, along with other evidence, were introduced at Escobedo's trial and he was convicted of murder.

On appeal, Escobedo argued that his rights had been violated. The atmosphere at the police station surrounding the interrogation had been overpowering. Without having his attorney present to provide advice, Escobedo broke down and made incriminating statements. Under such conditions, the incriminating statements could be considered the product of coercion in violation of the Fifth Amendment.

By a 5–4 vote the Warren Court ruled that Escobe-

---

13. See, for example, *Brown v. Mississippi* (1936); *Spano v. New York* (1959).

Danny Escobedo's 1960 arrest and conviction for the murder of his brother-in-law led to a Supreme Court decision that expanded constitutional protections for criminal defendants during police interrogations. This photograph of Escobedo was taken as he awaited processing on charges of burglarizing a hot dog stand not long after the Supreme Court issued its landmark ruling in *Escobedo v. Illinois* in 1964.

do's statements had been compelled. Coercion, the majority concluded, may take place even if overt physcial or psychological pressure is not present. When arrested and brought to the police station for questioning, a suspect does not stand on equal footing with the law enforcement authorities. There is a clear power imbalance in favor of the police. Poor and uneducated defendants are especially at a disadvantage. Under such circumstances, the suspect may break down and make incriminating statements.

The justices decided to remedy this situation by using the right to counsel as a method of protecting the defendant's Fifth Amendment rights. The Court held that suspects have the right to have an attorney present during any custodial interrogation. As stated in Justice Arthur Goldberg's opinion for the Court:

We hold, therefore, that where, as here, the investigation is no longer a general inquiry into an unsolved crime but has begun to focus on a particular suspect, the suspect has been taken into police custody, the police carry out a process of interrogations that lends itself to eliciting incriminating statements, the suspect has requested and been denied an opportunity to consult with his lawyer, and the police have not effectively warned him of his absolute constitutional right to remain silent, the accused has been denied "the Assistance of Counsel" in violation of the Sixth Amendment to the Constitution as "made obligatory upon the States by the Fourteenth Amendment," and that no statement elicited by the police during the interrogation may be used against him at a criminal trial. . . .

Danny Escobedo had been denied his right to counsel, and the majority found this right to be a primary defense against violations of the Self-Incrimination Clause. If an attorney is present, it is not likely that police will employ even subtle methods to coerce confessions from suspects. The *Escobedo* majority held that the right to counsel begins at the accusatory stage of the process, defined as the point at which the investigation ceases to be general and focuses on a specific individual. The right is in effect for every critical stage of the process, which includes all interrogations. But once the Court ruled this way, it was faced, in *Miranda v. Arizona*, with a more difficult and far-reaching question. How should this new right be enforced?

Miranda v. Arizona

384 U.S. 436 (1966)

Vote: 5 *(Black, Brennan, Douglas, Fortas, Warren)*
    4 *(Clark, Harlan, Stewart, White)*

Opinion of the Court: Warren
Opinion dissenting in part: Clark
Dissenting opinions: Harlan, White

Ernesto Miranda, a twenty-three-year-old indigent, nearly illiterate truck driver, allegedly kidnapped and raped a young woman outside of Phoenix, Arizona. Ten days after the incident, police arrested him, took him to the station, and interrogated him. Within two hours of questioning, Miranda confessed. There was no evidence of any police misbehavior during the interrogation, and at no point during questioning did Miranda request an attorney. Because of the decision in *Gideon v. Wainwright* (1963) *(see Chapter 17),* which mandated that all indigent criminal defendants receive a defense attorney at government expense, the trial judge appointed a lawyer to defend Miranda against the charges. Unfortunately, that attorney provided an inadequate defense—he hoped to prove Miranda insane or mentally defective—and Miranda received a twenty- to thirty-year sentence. The conviction was based not only on the confession but also on the basis of other evidence, including the victim's positive identification of Miranda as her assailant.

Miranda obtained new attorneys, who presented wholly different arguments to the Supreme Court, where Miranda's appeal was combined with three others presenting similar issues.[14] The attorneys claimed that because the entire interrogation process is so inherently coercive that any individual will eventually break down, the Court should affirmatively protect the right against self-incrimination by adding to those protections already extended in *Escobedo.*

MR. CHIEF JUSTICE WARREN delivered the opinion of the Court.

The cases before us raise questions which go to the roots of our concepts of American criminal jurisprudence: the restraints society must observe consistent with the Federal Constitution in prosecuting individuals for crime. More specifically, we deal with the admissibility of statements obtained from an individual who is subjected to custodial police interrogation and the necessity for procedures which

14. Along with *Miranda,* the Court decided *Vignera v. New York, Westover v. United States,* and *California v. Stewart.*

assure that the individual is accorded his privilege under the Fifth Amendment to the Constitution not to be compelled to incriminate himself.

We dealt with certain phases of this problem recently in *Escobedo v. State of Illinois* (1964). . . .

This case has been the subject of judicial interpretation and spirited legal debate since it was decided two years ago. Both state and federal courts, in assessing its implications, have arrived at varying conclusions. A wealth of scholarly material has been written tracing its ramifications and underpinnings. Police and prosecutor have speculated on its range and desirability. We granted certiorari in these cases in order further to explore some facets of the problems, thus exposed, of applying the privilege against self-incrimination to in-custody interrogation, and to give concrete constitutional guidelines for law enforcement agencies and courts to follow.

We start here, as we did in *Escobedo,* with the premise that our holding is not an innovation in our jurisprudence, but is an application of principles long recognized and applied in other settings. We have undertaken a thorough reexamination of the *Escobedo* decision and the principles it announced, and we reaffirm it. That case was but an explication of basic rights that are enshrined in our Constitution—that "No person . . . shall be compelled in any criminal case to be a witness against himself," and that "the accused shall . . . have the Assistance of Counsel"—rights which were put in jeopardy in that case through official overbearing. . . .

It was necessary in *Escobedo,* as here, to insure that what was proclaimed in the Constitution had not become but a "form of words" in the hands of government officials. And it is in this spirit, consistent with our role as judges, that we adhere to the principles of *Escobedo* today.

Our holding will be spelled out with some specificity in the pages which follow but briefly stated it is this: the prosecution may not use statements, whether exculpatory or inculpatory, stemming from custodial interrogation of the defendant unless it demonstrates the use of procedural safeguards effective to secure the privilege against self-incrimination. By custodial interrogation, we mean questioning initiated by law enforcement officers after a person has been taken into custody or otherwise deprived of his freedom of action in any significant way. As for the procedural

Ernesto Miranda, right, pictured with his defense attorney, John L. Flynn, was convicted of kidnapping and rape after he confessed to the crimes while in police custody. In a landmark ruling, *Miranda v. Arizona* (1966), the Supreme Court reversed the conviction because Miranda had not been told he had the right to remain silent and to have an attorney present during questioning.

safeguards to be employed, unless other fully effective means are devised to inform accused persons of their right of silence and to assure a continuous opportunity to exercise it, the following measures are required. Prior to any questioning, the person must be warned that he has a right to remain silent, that any statement he does make may be used as evidence against him, and that he has a right to the presence of an attorney, either retained or appointed. The defendant may waive effectuation of these rights, provided the waiver is made voluntarily, knowingly and intelligently. If, however, he indicates in any manner and at any stage of the process that he wishes to consult with an attorney before speaking there can be no questioning. Likewise, if the individual is alone and indicates in any manner that he does not wish to be interrogated, the police may not question him. The mere fact that he may have answered some questions or volunteered some statements on his own does not deprive him of the right to refrain from answering any further inquiries until he has consulted with an attorney and thereafter consents to be questioned.

The constitutional issue we decide in each of these cases is the admissibility of statements obtained from a defendant questioned while in custody or otherwise deprived of his freedom of action in any significant way . . . .

An understanding of the nature and setting of this in-custody interrogation is essential to our decisions today. The difficulty in depicting what transpires at such interrogations stems from the fact that in this country they have largely taken place incommunicado. From extensive factual studies undertaken in the early 1930's, including the famous Wickersham Report to Congress by a Presidential Commission, it is clear that police violence and the "third degree" flourished at that time. In a series of cases decided by this Court long after these studies, the police resorted to physical brutality—beatings, hanging, whipping—and to sustained and protracted questioning incommunicado in order to extort confessions. The Commission on Civil Rights in 1961 found much evidence to indicate that "some policemen still resort to physical force to obtain confessions. . . . " Only recently in Kings County, New York, the police brutally beat, kicked and placed lighted cigarette butts on the back of a potential witness under interrogation for the purpose of securing a statement incriminating a third party.

The examples given above are undoubtedly the exception now, but they are sufficiently widespread to be the object of concern. Unless a proper limitation upon custodial interrogation is achieved—such as these decisions will advance—there can be no assurance that practices of this nature will be eradicated in the foreseeable future. . . .

Again we stress that the modern practice of in-custody interrogation is psychologically rather than physically oriented. As we have stated before, "[T]his Court has recognized that coercion can be mental as well as physical, and that the blood of the accused is not the only hallmark of an unconstitutional inquisition." *Blackburn v. State of Alabama* (1960). Interrogation still takes place in privacy. Privacy results in secrecy and this in turn results in a gap in our knowledge as to what in fact goes on in the interrogation rooms. A valuable source of information about present police practices, however, may be found in various police manuals and texts which document procedures employed with success in the past, and which recommend various other effective tactics. These texts are used by law enforcement agencies themselves as guides. It should be noted that these texts professedly present the most enlightened and effective means presently used to obtain statements through custodial interrogation. By considering these texts and other data, it is possible to describe the procedures observed and noted around the country.

The officers are told by the manuals that the "principal psychological factor contributing to a successful interrogation is privacy—being alone with the person under interrogation."...

To highlight the isolation and unfamiliar surroundings, the manuals instruct the police to display an air of confidence in the suspect's guilt and from outward appearance to maintain only an interest in confirming certain details. The guilt of the subject is to be posited as a fact. The interrogator should direct his comments toward the reasons why the subject committed the act, rather than court failure by asking the subject whether he did it. Like other men, perhaps the subject has had a bad family life, had an unhappy childhood, had too much to drink, had an unrequited desire for women. The officers are instructed to minimize the moral seriousness of the offense, to cast blame on the victim or on society. These tactics are designed to put the subject in a psychological state where his story is but an elaboration of what the police purport to know already—that he is guilty. Explanations to the contrary are dismissed and discouraged.

The texts thus stress that the major qualities an interrogator should possess are patience and perseverance....

The manuals suggest that the suspect be offered legal excuses for his actions in order to obtain an initial admission of guilt....

When the techniques described above prove unavailing, the texts recommend they be alternated with a show of some hostility....

The interrogators sometimes are instructed to induce a confession out of trickery....

Even without employing brutality, the "third degree" or the specific stratagems described above, the very fact of custodial interrogation exacts a heavy toll on individual liberty and trades on the weakness of individuals....

In the cases before us today, given this background, we concern ourselves primarily with this interrogation atmosphere and the evils it can bring. In No. 759, Miranda v. Arizona, the police arrested the defendant and took him to a special interrogation room where they secured a confession....

In these cases, we might not find the defendants' statements to have been involuntary in traditional terms. Our concern for adequate safeguards to protect precious Fifth Amendment rights is, of course, not lessened in the slightest. In each of the cases, the defendant was thrust into an unfamiliar atmosphere and run through menacing police interrogation procedures. The potentiality for compulsion is forcefully apparent, for example, in *Miranda,* where the indigent Mexican defendant was a seriously disturbed individual with pronounced sexual fantasies.... To be sure, the records do not evince overt physical coercion or patent psychological ploys. The fact remains that in none of these cases did the officers undertake to afford appropriate safeguards at the outset of the interrogation to insure that the statements were truly the product of free choice.

It is obvious that such an interrogation environment is created for no purpose other than to subjugate the individual to the will of his examiner. This atmosphere carries its own badge of intimidation. To be sure, this is not physical intimidation, but it is equally destructive of human dignity. The current practice of incommunicado interrogation is at odds with one of our Nation's most cherished principles— that the individual may not be compelled to incriminate himself. Unless adequate protective devices are employed to dispel the compulsion inherent in custodial surroundings, no statement obtained from the defendant can truly be the product of his free choice.

From the foregoing, we can readily perceive an intimate connection between the privilege against self-incrimination and police custodial questioning. . . .

Today, then, there can be no doubt that the Fifth Amendment privilege is available outside of criminal court proceedings and serves to protect persons in all settings in which their freedom of action is curtailed in any significant way from being compelled to incriminate themselves. We have concluded that without proper safeguards the process of in-custody interrogation of persons suspected or accused of crime contains inherently compelling pressures which work to undermine the individual's will to resist and to compel him to speak where he would not otherwise do so freely. In order to combat these pressures and to permit a full opportunity to exercise the privilege against self-incrimination, the accused must be adequately and effectively apprised of his rights and the exercise of those rights must be fully honored. . . .

At the outset, if a person in custody is to be subjected to interrogation, he must first be informed in clear and unequivocal terms that he has the right to remain silent. For those unaware of the privilege, the warning is needed simply to make them aware of it—the threshold requirement for an intelligent decision as to its exercise. More important, such a warning is an absolute prerequisite in overcoming the inherent pressures of the interrogation atmosphere. . . . Further, the warning will show the individual that his interrogators are prepared to recognize his privilege should he choose to exercise it.

The Fifth Amendment privilege is so fundamental to our system of constitutional rule and the expedient of giving an adequate warning as to the availability of the privilege so simple, we will not pause to inquire in individual cases whether the defendant was aware of his rights without a warning being given. Assessments of the knowledge the defendant possessed, based on information as to his age, education, intelligence, or prior contact with authorities, can never be more than speculation; a warning is a clearcut fact. More important, whatever the background of the person interrogated, a warning at the time of the interrogation is indispensable to overcome its pressures and to insure that the individual knows he is free to exercise the privilege at that point in time.

The warning of the right to remain silent must be ac-

companied by the explanation that anything said can and will be used against the individual in court. This warning is needed in order to make him aware not only of the privilege, but also of the consequences of forgoing it. It is only through an awareness of these consequences that there can be any assurance of real understanding and intelligent exercise of the privilege. Moreover, this warning may serve to make the individual more acutely aware that he is faced with a phase of the adversary system—that he is not in the presence of persons acting solely in his interest.

The circumstances surrounding in-custody interrogation can operate very quickly to overbear the will of one merely made aware of his privilege by his interrogators. Therefore, the right to have counsel present at the interrogation is indispensable to the protection of the Fifth Amendment privilege under the system we delineate today. Our aim is to assure that the individual's right to choose between silence and speech remains unfettered throughout the interrogation process. A once-stated warning, delivered by those who will conduct the interrogation, cannot itself suffice to that end among those who most require knowledge of their rights. A mere warning given by the interrogators is not alone sufficient to accomplish that end. Prosecutors themselves claim that the admonishment of the right to remain silent without more "will benefit only the recidivist and the professional." Even preliminary advice given to the accused by his own attorney can be swiftly overcome by the secret interrogation process. Thus, the need for counsel to protect the Fifth Amendment privilege comprehends not merely a right to consult with counsel prior to questioning, but also to have counsel present during any questioning if the defendant so desires.

The presence of counsel at the interrogation may serve several significant subsidiary functions as well. If the accused decides to talk to his interrogators, the assistance of counsel can mitigate the dangers of untrustworthiness. With a lawyer present the likelihood that the police will practice coercion is reduced, and if coercion is nevertheless exercised the lawyer can testify to it in court. The presence of a lawyer can also help to guarantee that the accused gives a fully accurate statement to the police and that the statement is rightly reported by the prosecution at trial.

An individual need not make a pre-interrogation request for a lawyer. While such request affirmatively secures his right to have one, his failure to ask for a lawyer does not constitute a waiver. No effective waiver of the right to counsel during interrogation can be recognized unless specifically made after the warnings we here delineate have been given. The accused who does not know his rights and therefore does not make a request may be the person who most needs counsel. . . .

Accordingly we hold that an individual held for interrogation must be clearly informed that he has the right to consult with a lawyer and to have the lawyer with him during interrogation under the system for protecting the privilege we delineate today. As with the warnings of the right to remain silent and that anything stated can be used in evidence against him, this warning is an absolute prerequisite to interrogation. No amount of circumstantial evidence that the person may have been aware of this right will suffice to stand in its stead. Only through such a warning is there ascertainable assurance that the accused was aware of this right.

If an individual indicates that he wishes the assistance of counsel before any interrogation occurs, the authorities cannot rationally ignore or deny his request on the basis that the individual does not have or cannot afford a retained attorney. The financial ability of the individual has no relationship to the scope of the rights involved here. The privilege against self-incrimination secured by the Constitution applies to all individuals. The need for counsel in order to protect the privilege exists for the indigent as well as the affluent. In fact, were we to limit these constitutional rights to those who can retain an attorney, our decisions today would be of little significance. The cases before us as well as the vast majority of confession cases with which we have dealt in the past involve those unable to retain counsel. While authorities are not required to relieve the accused of his poverty, they have the obligation not to take advantage of indigence in the administration of justice. Denial of counsel to the indigent at the time of interrogation while allowing an attorney to those who can afford one would be no more supportable by reason or logic than the similar situation at trial and on appeal struck down in Gideon v. Wainwright (1963).

In order fully to apprise a person interrogated of the extent of his rights under this system then, it is necessary to warn him not only that he has the right to consult with an attorney, but also that if he is indigent a lawyer will be appointed to represent him. Without this additional warning, the admonition of the right to consult with counsel would often be understood as meaning only that he can consult with a lawyer if he has one or has the funds to obtain one. The warning of a right to counsel would be hollow if not couched in terms that would convey to the indigent—the person most often subjected to interrogation—the knowledge that he too has a right to have counsel present. As with the warnings of the right to remain silent and of the general right to counsel, only by effective and express explanation to the indigent of this right can there be assurance that he was truly in a position to exercise it.

Once warnings have been given, the subsequent procedure is clear. If the individual indicates in any manner, at any time prior to or during questioning, that he wishes to remain silent, the interrogation must cease. At this point he has shown that he intends to exercise his fifth Amendment privilege; any statement taken after the person invokes his privilege cannot be other than the product of compulsion, subtle or otherwise. Without the right to cut off questioning, the setting of in-custody interrogation operates on the individual to overcome free choice in producing a statement after the privilege has been once invoked. If the individual states that he wants an attorney, the interrogation must cease until an attorney is present. At that time, the individual must have an opportunity to confer with the attorney and to have him present during any subsequent questioning. If the individual cannot obtain an attorney and he indicates that he wants one before speaking to police, they must respect his decision to remain silent. . . .

If the interrogation continues without the presence of an attorney and a statement is taken, a heavy burden rests on the government to demonstrate that the defendant knowingly and intelligently waived his privilege against self-incrimination and his right to retained or appointed counsel. . . .

The warnings required and the waiver necessary in accordance with our opinion today are, in the absence of a fully effective equivalent, prerequisites to the admissibility of any statement made by a defendant. No distinction can be drawn between statements which are direct confessions and statements which amount to "admissions" of part or all of an offense. The privilege against self-incrimination protects the individual from being compelled to incriminate himself in any manner; it does not distinguish degrees of incrimination. . . .

To summarize, we hold that when an individual is taken into custody or otherwise deprived of his freedom by the authorities in any significant way and is subjected to questioning, the privilege against self-incrimination is jeopardized. Procedural safeguards must be employed to protect the privilege and unless other fully effective means are adopted to notify the person of his right of silence and to assure that the exercise of the right will be scrupulously honored, the following measures are required. He must be warned prior to any questioning that he has the right to remain silent, that anything he says can be used against him in a court of law, that he has the right to the presence of an attorney, and that if he cannot afford an attorney one will be appointed for him prior to any questioning if he so desires. Opportunity to exercise these rights must be afforded to him throughout the interrogation. After such warnings have been given, and such opportunity afforded him, the individual may knowingly and intelligently waive these rights and agree to answer questions or make a statement. But unless and until such warnings and waiver are demonstrated by the prosecution at trial, no evidence obtained as a result of interrogation can be used against him.

A recurrent argument made in these cases is that society's need for interrogation outweighs the privilege. This argument is not unfamiliar to this Court. The whole thrust of our foregoing discussion demonstrates that the Constitution has prescribed the rights of the individual when confronted with the power of government when it provided in the Fifth Amendment that an individual cannot be compelled to be a witness against himself. That right cannot be abridged. . . .

In announcing these principles, we are not unmindful of the burdens which law enforcement officials must bear, often under trying circumstances. We also fully recognize the obligation of all citizens to aid in enforcing the criminal laws. This Court, while protecting individual rights, has always given ample latitude to law enforcement agencies in the legitimate exercise of their duties. The limits we have placed on the interrogation process should not constitute an undue interference with a proper system of law enforcement. . . . [O]ur decision does not in any way preclude police from carrying out their traditional investigatory functions. Although confessions may play an important role in some convictions, the cases before us present graphic examples of the overstatement of the "need" for confessions. . . .

Over the years the Federal Bureau of Investigation has compiled an exemplary record of effective law enforcement while advising any suspect or arrested person, at the outset of an interview, that he is not required to make a statement, that any statement may be used against him in court, that the individual may obtain the services of an attorney of his own choice and, more recently, that he has a right to free counsel if he is unable to pay. . . .

The practice of the FBI can readily be emulated by state and local enforcement agencies. The argument that the FBI deals with different crimes than are dealt with by state authorities does not mitigate the significance of the FBI experience. . . .

Judicial solutions to problems of constitutional dimension have evolved decade by decade. As courts have been presented with the need to enforce constitutional rights, they have found means of doing so. That was our responsibility when *Escobedo* was before us and it is our responsibility today. Where rights secured by the Constitution are involved, there can be no rule making or legislation which would abrogate them.

Reversed.

MR. JUSTICE WHITE, with whom MR. JUSTICE HARLAN and MR. JUSTICE STEWART join, dissenting.

That the Court's holding today is neither compelled nor even strongly suggested by the language of the Fifth Amendment, is at odds with American and English legal history, and involves a departure from a long line of precedent does not prove either that the Court has exceeded its powers or that the Court is wrong or unwise in its present reinterpretation of the Fifth Amendment. It does, however, underscore the obvious—that the Court has not discovered or found the law in making today's decision, nor has it derived it from some irrefutable sources; what it has done is to make new law and new public policy in much the same way that it has in the course of interpreting other great clauses of the Constitution. This is what the Court historically has done. Indeed, it is what it must do and will continue to do until and unless there is some fundamental change in the constitutional distribution of governmental powers.

But if the Court is here and now to announce new and fundamental policy to govern certain aspects of our affairs, it is wholly legitimate to examine the mode of this or any other constitutional decision in this Court and to inquire into the advisability of its end product in terms of the long-range interest of the country. At the very least the Court's text and reasoning should withstand analysis and be a fair exposition of the constitutional provision which its opinion interprets. Decisions like these cannot rest alone on syllogism, metaphysics or some ill-defined notions of natural justice, although each will perhaps play its part. In proceeding to such constructions as it now announces, the Court should also duly consider all the factors and interests bearing upon the cases, at least insofar as the relevant materials are available; and if the necessary considerations are not treated in the record or obtainable from some other reliable source, the Court should not proceed to formulate fundamental policies based on speculation alone.

First, we may inquire what are the textual and factual bases of this new fundamental rule. To reach the result announced on the grounds it does, the Court must stay within the confines of the Fifth Amendment, which forbids self-incrimination only if *compelled.* Hence the core of the Court's opinion is that because of the "compulsion inherent in custodial surroundings, no statement obtained from [a] defendant [in custody] can truly be the product of his free choice," absent the use of adequate protective devices as described by the Court. However, the Court does not point to any sudden inrush of new knowledge requiring the rejection of 70 years' experience. Nor does it assert that its novel conclusion reflects a changing consensus among state courts, see Mapp v. Ohio, or that a succession of cases had steadily eroded the old rule and proved it unworkable. Rather than asserting new knowledge, the Court concedes that it cannot truly know what occurs during custodial questioning, because of the innate secrecy of such proceedings. It extrapolates a picture of what it conceives to be the norm from police investigatorial manuals, published in 1959 and 1962 or earlier, without any attempt to allow for adjustments in police practices that may have occurred in the wake of more recent decisions of state appellate tri-

bunals or this Court. But even if the relentless application of the described procedures could lead to involuntary confessions, it most assuredly does not follow that each and every case will disclose this kind of interrogation or this kind of consequence. Insofar as appears from the Court's opinion, it has not examined a single transcript of any police interrogation, let alone the interrogation that took place in any one of these cases which it decides today. Judged by any of the standards for empirical investigation utilized in the social sciences the factual basis for the Court's premise is patently inadequate.

Although in the Court's view in-custody interrogation is inherently coercive, the Court says that the spontaneous product of the coercion of arrest and detention is still to be deemed voluntary. An accused, arrested on probable cause, may blurt out a confession which will be admissible despite the fact that he is alone and in custody, without any showing that he had any notion of his right to remain silent or of the consequences of his admission. Yet, under the Court's rule, if the police ask him a single question such as "Do you have anything to say?" or "Did you kill your wife?" his response, if there is one, has somehow been compelled, even if the accused has been clearly warned of his right to remain silent. Common sense informs us to the contrary. While one may say that the response was "involuntary" in the sense the question provoked or was the occasion for the response and thus the defendant was induced to speak out when he might have remained silent if not arrested and not questioned, it is patently unsound to say the response is compelled. . . .

If the rule announced today were truly based on a conclusion that all confessions resulting from custodial interrogation are coerced, then it would simply have no rational foundation. . . . *A fortiori* that would be true of the extension of the rule to exculpatory statements, which the Court effects after a brief discussion of why, in the Court's view, they must be deemed incriminatory but without any discussion of why they must be deemed coerced. Even if one were to postulate that the Court's concern is not that all confessions induced by police interrogation are coerced but rather that some such confessions are coerced and present judicial procedures are believed to be inadequate to identify the confessions that are coerced and those that are not, it would still not be essential to impose the rule that the Court has now fashioned. Transcripts or observers could be required, specific time limits, tailored to fit the cause, could be imposed, or other devices could be utilized to reduce the chances that otherwise indiscernible coercion will produce an inadmissible confession.

On the other hand, even if one assumed that there was an adequate factual basis for the conclusion that all confessions obtained during in-custody interrogation are the product of compulsion, the rule propounded by the Court would still be irrational, for, apparently, it is only if the accused is also warned of his right to counsel and waives both that right and the right against self-incrimination that the inherent compulsiveness of interrogation disappears. But if the defendant may not answer without a warning a question such as "Where were you last night?" without having his answer be a compelled one, how can the Court ever accept his negative answer to the question of whether he wants to consult his retained counsel or counsel whom the court will appoint? And why if counsel is present and the accused nevertheless confesses, or counsel tells the accused to tell the truth, and that is what the accused does, is the situation any less coercive insofar as the accused is concerned? The Court apparently realizes its dilemma of foreclosing questioning without the necessary warnings but at the same time permitting the accused, sitting in the same chair in front of the same policemen, to waive his right to consult an attorney. It expects, however, that the accused will not often waive the right; and if it is claimed that he has, the State faces a severe, if not impossible burden of proof.

All of this makes very little sense in terms of the compulsion which the Fifth Amendment proscribes. That amendment deals with compelling the accused himself. It is his free will that is involved. Confessions and incriminating admissions, as such, are not forbidden evidence; only those which are compelled are banned. I doubt that the Court observes these distinctions today. By considering any answers to any interrogation to be compelled regardless of the content and course of examination and by escalating the requirements to prove waiver, the Court not only prevents the use of compelled confessions but for all practical purposes forbids interrogation except in the presence of counsel. That is, instead of confining itself to protection of the right against compelled self-incrimination the Court has created

a limited Fifth Amendment right to counsel—or, as the Court expresses it, a "need for counsel to protect the Fifth Amendment privilege. . . ." The focus then is not on the will of the accused but on the will of counsel and how much influence he can have on the accused. Obviously there is no warrant in the Fifth Amendment for thus installing counsel as the arbiter of the privilege.

In sum, for all the Court's expounding on the menacing atmosphere of police interrogation procedures, it has failed to supply any foundation for the conclusions it draws or the measures it adopts.

Criticism of the Court's opinion, however, cannot stop with a demonstration that the factual and textual bases for the rule it propounds are, at best, less than compelling. Equally relevant is an assessment of the rule's consequences measured against community values. The Court's duty to assess the consequences of its action is not satisfied by the utterance of the truth that a value of our system of criminal justice is "to respect the inviolability of the human personality" and to require government to produce the evidence against the accused by its own independent labors. More than the human dignity of the accused is involved; the human personality of others in the society must also be preserved. Thus the values reflected by the privilege are not the sole desideratum; society's interest in the general security is of equal weight.

The obvious underpinning of the Court's decision is a deep-seated distrust of all confessions. As the Court declares that the accused may not be interrogated without counsel present, absent a waiver of the right to counsel, and as the Court all but admonishes the lawyer to advise the accused to remain silent, the result adds up to a judicial judgment that evidence from the accused should not be used against him in any way, whether compelled or not. This is the not so subtle overtone of the opinion—that it is inherently wrong for the police to gather evidence from the accused himself. And this is precisely the nub of this dissent. I see nothing wrong or immoral, and certainly nothing unconstitutional, in the police's asking a suspect whom they have reasonable cause to arrest whether or not he killed his wife or in confronting him with the evidence on which the arrest was based, at least where he has been plainly advised that he may remain completely silent. Until today, "the admissions or confessions of the prisoner, when voluntarily and freely made, have always ranked high in the scale of incriminating evidence." Particularly when corroborated, as where the police have confirmed the accused's disclosure of the hiding place of implements or fruits of the crime, such confessions have the highest reliability and significantly contribute to the certitude with which we may believe the accused is guilty. Moreover, it is by no means certain that the process of confessing is injurious to the accused. To the contrary it may provide psychological relief and enhance the prospects for rehabilitation.

This is not to say that the value of respect for the inviolability of the accused's individual personality should be accorded no weight or that all confessions should be indiscriminately admitted. This Court has long read the Constitution to proscribe compelled confessions, a salutary rule from which there should be no retreat. But I see no sound basis, factual or otherwise, and the Court gives none, for concluding that the present rule against the receipt of coerced confessions is inadequate for the task of sorting out inadmissible evidence and must be replaced by the per se rule which is now imposed. Even if the new concept can be said to have advantages of some sort over the present law, they are far outweighed by its likely undesirable impact on other very relevant and important interests.

The most basic function of any government is to provide for the security of the individual and of his property. These ends of society are served by the criminal laws which for the most part are aimed at the prevention of crime. Without the reasonably effective performance of the task of preventing private violence and retaliation, it is idle to talk about human dignity and civilized values.

The modes by which the criminal laws serve the interest in general security are many. First the murderer who has taken the life of another is removed from the streets, deprived of his liberty and thereby prevented from repeating his offense. In view of the statistics on recidivism in this country and of the number of instances in which apprehension occurs only after repeated offenses, no one can sensibly claim that this aspect of the criminal law does not prevent crime or contribute significantly to the personal security of the ordinary citizen.

Secondly, the swift and sure apprehension of those who refuse to respect the personal security and dignity of their neighbor unquestionably has its impact on others who might be similarly tempted. That the criminal law is wholly or partly ineffective with a segment of the population or with many of those who have been apprehended and convicted is a very faulty basis for concluding that it is not effective with respect to the great bulk of our citizens or for thinking that without the criminal laws, or in the absence of their enforcement, there would be no increase in crime. Arguments of this nature are not borne out by any kind of reliable evidence that I have seen to this date.

Thirdly, the law concerns itself with those whom it has confined. The hope and aim of modern penology, fortunately, is as soon as possible to return the convict to society a better and more law-abiding man than when he left. Sometimes there is success, sometimes failure. But at least the effort is made, and it should be made to the very maximum extent of our present and future capabilities.

The rule announced today will measurably weaken the ability of the criminal law to perform these tasks. It is a deliberate calculus to prevent interrogations, to reduce the incidence of confessions and pleas of guilty and to increase the number of trials. Criminal trials, no matter how efficient the police are, are not sure bets for the prosecution, nor should they be if the evidence is not forthcoming. Under the present law, the prosecution fails to prove its case in about 30% of the criminal cases actually tried in the federal courts. But it is something else again to remove from the ordinary criminal case all those confessions which heretofore have been held to be free and voluntary acts of the accused and to thus establish a new constitutional barrier to the ascertainment of truth by the judicial process. There is, in my view, every reason to believe that a good many criminal defendants who otherwise would have been convicted on what this Court has previously thought to be the most satisfactory kind of evidence will now, under this new version of the Fifth Amendment, either not be tried at all or will be acquitted if the State's evidence, minus the confession, is put to the test of litigation.

I have no desire whatsoever to share the responsibility for any such impact on the present criminal process.

Chief Justice Warren's majority opinion in *Miranda* is a tour de force on self-incrimination, creating the so-called Miranda warnings that police must read to suspects before any custodial interrogation. The *Miranda* decision, in combination with subsequent rulings, means that whenever a criminal suspect is taken into custody for any crime the police are required to precede interrogations with the warnings.[15] By "custody" the Court means any situation in which the suspect is under police control and may not freely leave—no matter where this may occur. Custody, therefore, is not confined to formal interrogation rooms at the police station.[16] Similarly, the justices have given a relatively broad interpretation of what is meant by "interrogation." While most interrogations conform to the standard question–answer format, the justices have ruled that any police action designed to elicit statements from a suspect fall under the definition of interrogation and must be preceded by Miranda warnings.[17]

The Warren Court premised its decision in *Miranda* on the unavoidable inequities between the accused and police during custodial interrogations. In 1966 the justices thought the likelihood was too high to ignore that individuals would forgo their privilege against self-incrimination under intense and ultimately coercive police questioning. Arguably, the justices operated under the implicit assumption that incriminating statements made in the absence of *Miranda* warnings would automatically violate the Fifth Amendment and that judges and/or juries should exclude them from consideration.

Beginning in 1971 and continuing into the 1990s, however, the Burger Court and the Rehnquist Court began to create exceptions to this rule. In *Harris v. New York* (1971), for instance, the Court held that incriminating statements made in the absence of *Miranda* warnings could be used by prosecutors to impeach the testimony of witnesses or the accused. Chief Justice Burger noted in his first major post-*Miranda*

decision: "The shield of *Miranda* cannot be perverted into a license to use perjury by way of defense." Three years later the Court added another exception. In *Michigan v. Tucker* (1974) the majority buttressed police investigation efforts, holding that leads from statements made without the benefit of *Miranda* warnings could be used to assist officials in developing their cases.

After *Tucker* the Court waited a decade to carve out a new exception to the *Miranda* ruling. But when it did, in *New York v. Quarles* (1984) and *Oregon v. Elstad* (1985), it went well beyond the limits previously established. In the first case, the justices scrutinized the following facts. In 1980 a woman approached two Queens, New York, police officers and reported that she had been raped by a tall black man, who was armed. The officers drove to the site, where they spotted the alleged assailant, Benjamin Quarles, who had entered a grocery store. One officer pursued Quarles, ordered him to stop, and frisked him. Quarles was wearing an empty gun holster, so the officer asked him where his gun was. Quarles answered, "The gun is over there." He nodded toward empty cartons where he had thrown the weapon while temporarily out of the officer's view. At this point the officer placed Quarles under arrest and read him his *Miranda* warnings.

A trial judge excluded Quarles's statement concerning the gun on the grounds that he made it prior to hearing his rights. The Supreme Court reversed. Writing for the Court, Justice Rehnquist established a public safety exception to *Miranda*, holding that

the need for answers to questions in a situation posing a threat to public safety outweighs the need for the prophylactic rule protecting the Fifth Amendment privilege.... We decline to place officers ... in the untenable position of having to consider ... whether it best serves society for them to ask the necessary question without *Miranda* ... or for them to give the warnings in order to preserve the admissibility of evidence ... but possibly damage or destroy their ability to obtain that evidence and neutralize the volatile situation confronting them.

15. *Berkemer v. McCarty* (1984)
16. *Orozco v. Texas* (1969).
17. See *Brewer v. Williams* (1977); *Rhode Island v. Innis* (1980).

PD 47
Rev. 8/73

METROPOLITAN POLICE DEPARTMENT
WARNING AS TO YOUR RIGHTS

You are under arrest. Before we ask you any questions, you must understand what your rights are.

You have the right to remain silent. You are not required to say anything to us at any time or to answer any questions. Anything you say can be used against you in court.

You have the right to talk to a lawyer for advice before we question you and to have him with you during questioning.

If you cannot afford a lawyer and want one, a lawyer will be provided for you.

If you want to answer questions now without a lawyer present you will still have the right to stop answering at any time. You also have the right to stop answering at any time until you talk to a lawyer.

WAIVER

1. Have you read or had read to you the warning as to your rights? _____

2. Do you understand these rights? _____

3. Do you wish to answer any questions? _____

4. Are you willing to answer questions without having an attorney present? _____

5. Signature of defendant on line below.

_____

6. Time _____   Date _____

7. Signature of Officer _____

8. Signature of Witness _____

One year later the majority agreed that additional limits on *Miranda* were needed. The case was *Oregon v. Elstad,* which originated from a 1981 burglary investigation. Police were told that eighteen-year-old Michael Elstad was involved in the crime. Two police officers went to Elstad's house with a warrant for his arrest, and his mother let them in. One officer went into the kitchen with Elstad's mother, and the other sat down in the living room with the suspect. The officer told Elstad that he was investigating a burglary and that he felt Elstad was involved. Elstad said, "Yes, I was there." *Miranda* warnings had not been given at this time.

Elstad was arrested and, at the police station approximately one hour later, he was advised of his rights. He said he understood his rights, waived them, and signed a confession. He was convicted based in part on the confession. At no time during the investigation did police engage in any overt actions to coerce a confession.

On appeal, Elstad's attorneys argued that the confession should not have been admitted into evidence. They claimed that the first incriminating statements made at Elstad's house were obtained in violation of *Miranda.* Because he had "let the cat out of the bag" in this initial questioning, Elstad felt psychological pressure not to disclaim his incriminating statements. According to this argument, the *Miranda* warnings administered prior to the second round of questioning were insufficient to immunize Elstad against being compelled to give a formal confession. The damage had already been done.

The Supreme Court did not agree, finding that the formal confession was not tainted by the failure of police to advise Elstad of his rights during the first interview. According to Justice Sandra Day O'Connor's opinion for the Court, the initial violation of the *Miranda* warning procedure was largely technical. There was no evidence of coercion. Elstad's statement that he was a participant in the crime was voluntarily given. Nonetheless, because he had not been advised of his rights, that initial statement was constitutionally flawed and could not be admitted. However, the Court held that "a suspect who has once responded to unwarned yet uncoercive questioning is not thereby disabled from waiving his rights and confessing after he has been given the requisite *Miranda* warnings." The formal, signed confession, therefore, was admissible.

O'Connor's opinion in *Elstad* imposed a major limitation on the meaning of *Miranda*. Although her opinion did not overrule *Miranda* and, in fact, proclaimed its continuing viability, the Court had narrowed its applicability.[18]

As the Court entered the 1990s the justices gave additional indications that they might weaken *Miranda* even further. The warning came in *Arizona v. Fulminante* (1991). Oreste Fulminante was suspected of murdering his stepdaughter, who went missing while her mother was in the hospital. He left Arizona but was later arrested in New York on firearms violations and was incarcerated in a federal prison. Fulminante was subjected to rough treatment by his fellow inmates, who had heard rumors that he might be a child murderer. But then he was befriended by another inmate, Anthony Sarivola, who promised to protect him in return for the truth. Fulminante confessed to Sarivola in great detail. Unknown to Fulminante, Sarivola was a paid FBI informant. After his release, Fulminante also confessed to Sarivola's wife. Based on these confessions, Arizona indicted Fulminante for murder, and, over his attorney's objections, the trial court allowed both confessions to be introduced as evidence. He was convicted and sentenced to death, but the Arizona Supreme Court reversed the conviction, holding that the confession to Sarivola was coerced.

The Supreme Court affirmed the decision of the Arizona high court. The justices ruled that the prison confession was obtained only because the informant promised to protect Fulminante from physical violence. Naturally, no Miranda warnings had been given before the informant obtained the confession. The majority concluded that the coerced confession had been a significant factor in the prosecution's case and, therefore, the conviction could not stand. However, five justices, led by Chief Justice Rehnquist, held that if there had been sufficient evidence to convict Fulminante independent of the tainted confession, a reversal of the conviction would not have been necessary. Under such circumstances the unconstitutional confession would have been considered a "harmless error." *Fulminante* was the first time a majority had applied the harmless error principle in a coerced confession case.

Now that you have a good understanding of how the Fifth Amendment's Self-Incrimination Clause governs out-of-court "testimony," let's return to the question we posed earlier in this section: Why is *Miranda* so controversial? Some continue to argue that the decision binds the hands of police. Moreover, they point to cases like *Fulminante*, in which a confessed murderer and other criminals go free simply because their confessions were the product of coercion. That Fulminante's conviction was overturned, even though he confessed to a murder, is precisely what concerned Justice White and the others who dissented in *Miranda*. Yet supporters of *Miranda* make equally strong arguments. As Marvin Zalman and Larry Siegel point out, *Miranda* has not, in fact, made it more difficult for police to obtain incriminating statements. Empirical investigations of the effect of *Miranda* in cities—both large and small—indicate that "equivalent proportions of confessions were obtained in the post-*Miranda* period as before and that police effectiveness did not appear to suffer."[19] Why this is the case is a matter of speculation, but the answer, in part, lies with the pervasiveness of *Miranda* in our society, as anyone who watches police dramas on television can confirm. Police and suspects alike have come to view *Miranda* as part and parcel of the criminal justice system. In light of the cases you have read, which side do you take in the debate?

---

18. In *Moran v. Burbine* (1986) the Court further narrowed *Miranda*'s scope, ruling that a confession need not be suppressed even though police failed to inform a suspect of his attorney's attempts to reach him by telephone.

19. *Criminal Procedure*, 501. For a review of some of these studies, see Welsh S. White, "Defending *Miranda:* A Reply to Professor Caplan," *Vanderbilt Law Review* 39 (1986): 1–22.

READINGS

Baker, Liva. *Miranda: Crime, Law, and Politics.* New York: Atheneum, 1983.

Canon, Bradley. "Testing the Effectiveness of Civil Liberties Policies at the State and Federal Levels: The Case of the Exclusionary Rule." *American Politics Quarterly* 5 (1977): 57–82.

Casper, Jonathan D. *American Criminal Justice: The Defendant's Perspective.* Englewood Cliffs, N.J.: Prentice Hall, 1972.

Creamer, J. Shane. *The Law of Arrest, Search and Seizure.* New York: Holt, Rinehart and Winston, 1980.

Eisenstein, James, Roy B. Fleming, and Peter F. Nardulli. *The Contours of Justice: Communities and Their Courts.* Boston: Little, Brown, 1988.

Jacob, Herbert. *Law and Politics in the United States.* Boston: Little, Brown, 1988.

Kamisar, Yale. "The Warren Court (Was It Really So Defense-Minded?), the Burger Court (Was It Really So Prosecution-Oriented?) and Police Investigatory Procedures." In *The Burger Court,* ed. Vincent Blasi. New Haven: Yale University Press, 1983.

Landynski, Jacob W. *Search and Seizure and the Supreme Court.* Baltimore: Johns Hopkins University Press, 1966.

Levy, Leonard W. *Against the Law: The Nixon Court and Criminal Justice.* New York: Harper and Row, 1974.

Medalie, Richard J. *From Escobedo to Miranda.* Washington, D.C.: Lerner Law Books, 1966.

Neubauer, David W. *America's Courts and the Criminal Justice System.* 3d ed. Pacific Grove, Calif.: Brooks/Cole, 1988.

Scheingold, Stuart. *The Politics of Law and Order.* New York: Longman, 1984.

CHAPTER 17
ATTORNEYS, TRIALS, AND PUNISHMENTS

THE FRAMERS clearly recognized the importance of fairness in evidence gathering, but they also realized the need to protect the integrity of the entire criminal process. Consequently, the Bill of Rights included specific guarantees to protect prosecuted defendants from abuse by the government. These rights are among those Americans hold most dear, such as the right to be represented by counsel, to be tried by an impartial jury of peers, and to be protected against punishments that are cruel and unusual. Other guarantees, less well known but no less important, also enjoy constitutional status—such as the right to a speedy and public trial and to confront an accuser in open court. Taken as a whole, these rights were designed to help achieve a universally valued goal—fair criminal trials.

THE RIGHT TO COUNSEL

The Sixth Amendment guarantees that "In all criminal prosecutions, the accused shall enjoy the right . . . to have the Assistance of Counsel for his defence." At the time these words were written, the law was relatively uncomplicated, and lawyers in the new nation were scarce. Some individuals charged with crimes sought the advice of counsel, but most handled their own cases. Still, the Framers understood the importance of legal representation well enough to include the right to counsel in the Bill of Rights.

Today probably no other right guaranteed to the criminally accused is more important than the right to counsel. Until recently, a lawyer representing a criminal client could do the job by appearing at trial and dealing with well-established principles of evidence and procedure. That has changed, and appearing at the trial is now only a small part of what a criminal defense attorney must do. As the Supreme Court emphasized repeatedly in the Fifth Amendment cases we reviewed in Chapter 16, the role of the defense attorney begins when police first interrogate a suspect. From arrest through appeal, there are critical and complicated stages during which a defendant's rights might be violated. It is the responsibility of counsel to ensure that the interests of the defendant are not jeopardized. The presence of the defense attorney, therefore, is the primary guarantee that all of the other rights of the criminal due process will be observed.

The provisions of the Sixth Amendment are clear, and there has been little controversy over the right of an individual to have legal representation throughout the various stages of the criminal process. Historically, however, it was the responsibility of the accused person to secure a lawyer and to pay for the services. The most prolonged controversy over legal represen-

The plight of the nine "Scottsboro boys," arrested in rural Alabama in 1931 for raping two white females, spawned numerous legal actions including *Powell v. Alabama* (1932), which expanded the rights of indigents to legal representation. Samuel Leibowitz, a prominent attorney and later a judge, handled the defendants' cases after their original conviction. He is shown here conferring with his clients.

tation in criminal matters has centered on the rights of those who do not have the money to pay for legal assistance.

Indigents and the Right to Counsel: Foundations

As the U.S. system of justice became increasingly complex, more people retained lawyers to handle their cases. But as soon as this practice took hold, complaints of economic discrimination were heard. Civil libertarians and reformers throughout the country argued that only those who could afford it were guaranteed the right to counsel; indigent defendants were denied their constitutional guarantee. Reformers claimed that the only way to eliminate this injustice was a Supreme Court decision that would force governments to appoint free counsel for poor defendants.

In *Powell v. Alabama* (1932) the Supreme Court scrutinized this claim for the first time.[1] The case began when nine young black men were charged with raping two white women while riding a freight train through Alabama. The defendants had little chance of avoiding a conviction. They were uneducated, poor,

1. For more on this case, see Dan T. Carter, *Scottsboro: A Tragedy of the American South* (New York: Oxford University Press, 1969).

and far away from home with no friends or relatives to help them. Because of the nature of the charges, they faced a very hostile environment. Much was at stake. Rape in Alabama at that time was punishable by death.[2]

The young men did not have the funds to secure the services of an attorney, but under state law defendants in capital cases were entitled to a lawyer at government expense. Rather than appoint a specific attorney to prepare a defense, however, the trial court judge assigned all the lawyers in the town to represent the defendants. Not surprisingly, no one lawyer would accept the responsibility. When the trial was about to begin, the defendants were still without meaningful representation. An out-of-town lawyer who was present at the time finally agreed to serve as counsel. His first request was for additional time to prepare. The request was denied, and the trial began. It should come as no surprise that the young men were convicted and sentenced to death.

With the assistance of civil rights groups and political organizations, the defendants appealed to the Supreme Court. The Court reversed the conviction, holding that the young men did not receive effective counsel. For the first time the justices held that the Constitution requires meaningful legal representation for indigent defendants. But the Court's decision was quite limited. Justice Sutherland's opinion for the Court stressed that the right to government-provided attorneys was restricted to extreme situations. *Powell* certainly presented extreme circumstances: capital case, racially hostile environment, illiterate and indigent defendants with no family or friends in the area. It is easy to see why the Court concluded that under such conditions a fair trial was not possible if the defendants were not provided with a competent lawyer.

Just six years after *Powell*, the Court went one step

further. In *Johnson v. Zerbst* it ruled that indigent defendants involved in federal criminal prosecutions must be represented by counsel. Federal criminal prosecutions comprise a very small portion of all criminal cases. Therefore, although *Johnson* was a major decision, its impact did not reach most criminal defendants. Understandably, criminal defense attorneys wanted the Court to extend *Johnson* to state criminal courts where the vast majority of prosecutions take place. The Court's first opportunity to do so occurred in *Betts v. Brady* (1942).

Indicted for robbery in Maryland, Smith Betts—a poor, uneducated (but literate) white man—requested that an attorney be provided at government expense. Like many states, Maryland provided indigents with counsel only in rape and murder cases. Betts conducted his own defense and was convicted. On appeal he asked the Supreme Court to apply *Johnson* to the states. The Court refused, 6–3. Writing for the majority, Justice Roberts compared Betts's claim to that of the Powell defendants and found that it came up short. Betts was not helpless or illiterate, and he could not have received the death penalty for his offense.

Justice Black dissented. He wrote:

Denial to the poor of the request for counsel in proceedings based on charges of serious crime has been long regarded as shocking to the "universal sense of justice" throughout this country. . . . Most . . . states have shown their agreement [and] assure that no man shall be deprived of counsel merely because of his poverty. Any other practice seems to me to defeat the promise of our democratic society to provide equal justice under law.

More than twenty years later, a Court more sympathetic to the rights of the criminally accused reevaluated the wisdom of *Betts v. Brady*. As you read the landmark case of *Gideon v. Wainwright*, think about these questions: Why did the Court extend the right to government-provided attorneys to indigents accused of state crimes? Did something distinguish *Gideon* from *Betts*, or did other factors come into play?

---

2. Many states had laws mandating the appointment of counsel for capital crimes such as rape. We should note, however, that in *Coker v. Georgia* (1977) the Supreme Court outlawed the use of the death penalty in rape cases.

Gideon v. Wainwright

372 U.S. 355 (1963)

*Vote: 9 (Black, Brennan, Clark, Douglas, Goldberg, Harlan,
    Stewart, Warren, White)*

        0

Opinion of the Court: Black
Concurring opinions: Clark, Douglas, Harlan

Florida officials charged Clarence Earl Gideon with breaking and entering a poolroom.[3] The trial court refused to appoint counsel for him because Florida did not provide free lawyers to those charged with less than a capital offense. Gideon (like Betts, a poor, uneducated white man) tried to defend himself but failed. After studying the law in a prison library and attempting a number of lower court actions, Gideon filed a petition for a writ of certiorari with the U.S. Supreme Court. The petition was handwritten on prison notepaper, but the justices granted it a review.

Because Gideon was without counsel, the Court appointed Abe Fortas, a well-known attorney (and future Supreme Court justice) to represent him. Twenty-two states filed an amicus curiae brief, which was written by Walter Mondale (then the attorney general of Minnesota and later vice president of the United States), supporting Gideon's argument. Clarence Gideon went from being a poor convict facing a lonely court battle to a man represented by some of the country's finest legal minds.

MR. JUSTICE BLACK delivered the opinion of the Court.

Since 1942, when Betts v. Brady was decided by a divided Court, the problem of a defendant's federal constitutional right to counsel in a state court has been a continuing source of controversy and litigation in both state and federal courts. To give this problem another review here, we

3. For a full account of this case see Anthony Lewis, *Gideon's Trumpet* (New York: Vintage Books, 1964).

granted certiorari. Since Gideon was proceeding *in forma pauperis*, we appointed counsel to represent him and requested both sides to discuss in their briefs and oral arguments the following: "Should this Court's holding in Betts v. Brady be reconsidered?"

The facts upon which Betts claimed that he had been unconstitutionally denied the right to have counsel appointed to assist him are strikingly like the facts upon which Gideon here bases his federal constitutional claim.... Since the facts and circumstances of the two cases are so nearly indistinguishable, we think the Betts v. Brady holding if left standing would require us to reject Gideon's claim that the Constitution guarantees him the assistance of counsel. Upon full reconsideration we conclude that Betts v. Brady should be overruled.

The Sixth Amendment provides, "In all criminal prosecutions, the accused shall enjoy the right ... to have the Assistance of Counsel for his defence." We have construed this to mean that in federal courts counsel must be provided for defendants unable to employ counsel unless the right is competently and intelligently waived. Betts argued that this right is extended to indigent defendants in state courts by the Fourteenth Amendment. In response the Court stated that, while the Sixth Amendment laid down "no rule for the conduct of the states, the question recurs whether the constraint laid by the amendment upon the national courts expresses a rule so fundamental and essential to a fair trial, and so, to due process of law, that it is made obligatory upon the states by the Fourteenth Amendment." In order to decide whether the Sixth Amendment's guarantee of counsel is of this fundamental nature, the Court in Betts set out and considered "[r]elevant data on the subject ... afforded by constitutional and statutory provisions subsisting in the colonies and the states prior to the inclusion of the Bill of Rights in the national Constitution, and in the constitutional, legislative, and judicial history of the states to the present date." On the basis of this historical data the Court concluded that "appointment of counsel is not a fundamental right, essential to a fair trial.". . .

We accept Betts v. Brady's assumption, based as it was on our prior cases, that a provision of the Bill of Rights which is "fundamental and essential to a fair trial" is made obligatory upon the States by the Fourteenth Amendment. We think the Court in Betts was wrong, however, in

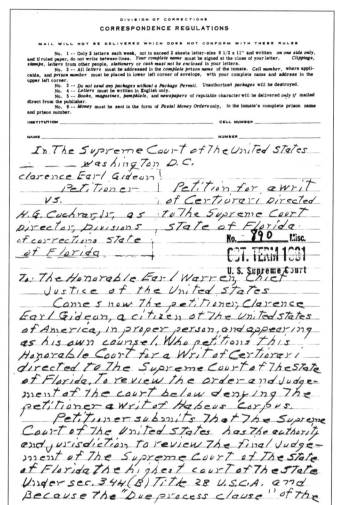

(left) Clarence Earl Gideon's handwritten petition to the Supreme Court. The Court ruled unanimously that indigent defendants must be provided counsel in state trials.

(above) Clarence Earl Gideon

concluding that the Sixth Amendment's guarantee of counsel is not one of these fundamental rights. Ten years before Betts v. Brady, this Court, after full consideration of all the historical data examined in Betts, had unequivocally declared that "the right to the aid of counsel is of this fundamental character." Powell v. Alabama (1932). While the Court at the close of its Powell opinion did by its language, as this Court frequently does, limit its holding to the particular facts and circumstances of that case, its conclusions about the fundamental nature of the right to counsel are unmistakable. Several years later, in 1936, the Court reemphasized what it had said about the fun-

damental nature of the right to counsel in this language:

"We concluded that certain fundamental rights, safeguarded by the first eight amendments against federal action, were also safeguarded against state action by the due process of law clause of the Fourteenth Amendment, and among them the fundamental right of the accused to the aid of counsel in a criminal prosecution." Grosjean v. American Press Co. (1936). . . .

In light of these and many other prior decisions of the Court, it is not surprising that the Betts Court, when faced with the contention that "one charged with crime, who is unable to obtain counsel, must be furnished counsel by the state," conceded that "[e]xpressions in the opinions of this court lend color to the argument. . . . " The fact is that in deciding as it did—that "appointment of counsel is not a fundamental right, essential to a fair trial"—the Court in Betts v. Brady made an abrupt break with its own well-considered precedents. In returning to these old precedents, sounder we believe than the new, we but restore constitutional principles established to achieve a fair system of justice. Not only these precedents but also reason and reflection require us to recognize that in our adversary system of criminal justice, any person haled into court, who is too poor to hire a lawyer, cannot be assured a fair trial unless counsel is provided for him. This seems to us to be an obvious truth. Governments, both state and federal, quite properly spend vast sums of money to establish machinery to try defendants accused of crime. Lawyers to prosecute are everywhere deemed essential to protect the public's interest in an orderly society. Similarly, there are few defendants charged with crime, few indeed, who fail to hire the best lawyers they can get to prepare and present their defenses. That government hires lawyers to prosecute and defendants who have the money hire lawyers to defend are the strongest indications of the widespread belief that lawyers in criminal courts are necessities, not luxuries. The right of one charged with crime to counsel may not be deemed fundamental and essential to fair trials in some countries, but it is in ours. From the very beginning, our state and national constitutions and laws have laid great emphasis on procedural and substantive safeguards designed to assure fair trials before impartial tribunals in which every defendant stands equal before the law. This noble ideal cannot be realized if the poor man charged with crime has to face his accusers without a lawyer to assist him. A defendant's need for a lawyer is nowhere better stated than in the moving words of Mr. Justice Sutherland in Powell v. Alabama:

"The right to be heard would be, in many cases, of little avail if it did not comprehend the right to be heard by counsel. Even the intelligent and educated layman has small and sometimes no skill in the science of law. If charged with crime, he is incapable, generally, of determining for himself whether the indictment is good or bad. He is unfamiliar with the rules of evidence. Left without the aid of counsel he may be put on trial without a proper charge, and convicted upon incompetent evidence, or evidence irrelevant to the issue or otherwise inadmissible. He lacks both the skill and knowledge adequately to prepare his defense, even though he have a perfect one. He requires the guiding hand of counsel at every step in the proceedings against him. Without it, though he be not guilty, he faces the danger of conviction because he does not know how to establish his innocence."

The Court in Betts v. Brady departed from the sound wisdom upon which the Court's holding in Powell v. Alabama rested. Florida, supported by two other States, has asked that Betts v. Brady be left intact. Twenty-two States, as friends of the Court, argue that Betts was "an anachronism when handed down" and that it should now be overruled. We agree. The judgment is reversed and the cause is remanded to the Supreme Court of Florida for further action not inconsistent with this opinion.

Reversed.

Beyond the legal significance of *Gideon*, the case is interesting for several reasons. First, *Gideon* provides another example of the Warren Court's revolution in criminal rights. The Court of 1963 took a carbon copy of *Betts* and came up with a radically different solution. *Gideon* completed a process of constitutional evolution in which the Court first applied a rule of law to the states and then reversed its position and brought the states under the rule's applicability.

Second, *Gideon* is a classic example of the importance of dissents. Justice Black's minority position in *Betts* was finally written into law when the Court reversed itself in *Gideon*. How fitting it was that Black was still on the Court twenty-one years later and was given the opportunity to write the majority opinion in *Gideon*.

Finally, *Gideon v. Wainwright* has had a tremendous impact on the U.S. criminal justice system, in which 75 percent of the criminally accused are indigent. To comply with the Court's ruling, states had to alter their public defender systems, creating mechanisms to provide lawyers for the accused.[4] Many localities have a public defender's office, which employs a staff of attorneys who are available to represent indigent defendants. Other areas use court-appointed attorney systems in which judges assign members of the legal community to represent the underprivileged.

For all its importance, however, *Gideon* left several questions unanswered. First, what crimes does the ruling cover? Does it cover just serious offenses, felonies, such as the one Gideon was accused of committing? Or does it apply to minor crimes as well? The Court answered this question in *Argersinger v. Hamlin* (1972), an appeal from a man sentenced to serve ninety days in jail for weapons violations. Writing for the majority, Justice Douglas developed a rule known as the loss of liberty rule: whoever is deprived of liberty even for one day is entitled to an attorney. By articulating such a standard, the Court rejected the argument of several states (including Florida once again) that only indigents facing jail sentences of more than six months are entitled to a lawyer at public expense.

Although *Argersinger* seemed to be the final statement on the question, the state of Illinois found a gap in this ruling. In *Scott v. Illinois* (1979) it argued that the loss of liberty standard should apply only when individuals receive a jail sentence, not when just the potential for imprisonment exists.[5]

The case arose when Illinois charged Aubrey Scott with theft, a crime carrying a maximum sentence of a $500 fine and/or one year in prison. Prior to trial the prosecutor announced that he had no intention of asking for a jail sentence if Scott was convicted. Without the assistance of counsel, Scott was tried, convicted, and fined $50. He appealed, claiming that he should have had a lawyer.

When the case reached the Supreme Court, the justices were presented with this question: Should the loss of liberty rule apply to those crimes for which the potential for imprisonment exists, but the accused does not receive a prison sentence? Writing for the Court, Justice Rehnquist read *Argersinger* to answer this question negatively. As he noted:

Although the intentions of the *Argersinger* Court are not unmistakably clear from its opinion, we conclude today that *Argersinger* did indeed delimit the constitutional right to appointed counsel in state criminal proceedings. Even were the matter *res nova* [a new issue], we believe that the central premise of *Argersinger*—that actual imprisonment is a penalty different in kind from fines or the mere threat of imprisonment—is eminently sound and warrants adoption of actual imprisonment as the line defining the constitutional right to appointment of counsel. *Argersinger* has proved reasonably workable, whereas any extension would create confusion and impose unpredictable, but necessarily substantial, costs on 50 quite diverse States. We therefore hold that the Sixth and Fourteenth Amendments to the United States Constitution require only that no indigent criminal defendant be sentenced to a term of imprisonment unless the State has afforded him the right to assistance of appointed counsel in his defense.

Justice Rehnquist draws a clear line for states to follow: they are constitutionally prohibited from imprisoning any indigent defendant who has not been represented by counsel.

A second unanswered question flowing from *Gideon* was to what stages of the process does the right to government-provided counsel apply? Justice Black's opinion in *Gideon* said that an indigent accused of a criminal offense must be represented by counsel at trial. What Black did not address was whether that right extended through the appellate process. And if so, did such a right apply only to obligatory appeals (usually the first appeal after a trial) or also to discretionary appeals (subsequent appeals

4. For more information on counsel for indigents, see David W. Neubauer, *America's Courts and the Criminal Justice System* (Monterey, Calif.: Brooks/Cole, 1984); Herbert Jacob, ed., *The Potential for Reform of Criminal Justice* (Beverly Hills, Calif.: Sage Publications, 1974); Lee Silverstein, *Defense of the Poor* (Chicago: American Bar Association, 1965). For an informative firsthand account of "what a criminal lawyer does and what it does to him," see Seymour Wishman, *Confessions of a Criminal Lawyer* (New York: Penguin Books, 1982).

5. The justices were aware that this argument would likely arise. In *Argersinger* Justice Lewis Powell's concurring opinion pressed the point that Douglas's "loss of liberty" analysis failed to consider the serious consequences resulting from some misdemeanor convictions even if a jail sentence is not imposed.

that the appellate court may or may not agree to hear)?

In *Douglas v. California* (1963) the Court answered part of this question, holding that the right indeed extended through the first obligatory appeal. Writing for the Court, Justice Douglas proclaimed:

[W]here the merits of *the one and only appeal* an indigent has as of right are decided without benefit of counsel, we think an unconstitutional line has been drawn between rich and poor. . . . There is lacking that equality demanded by the Fourteenth Amendment where the rich man, who appeals as of right, enjoys the benefit of the counsel's examination into the record, research of the law, and marshaling of arguments on his behalf, while the indigent . . . is forced to shift for himself.

Justice Douglas's opinion, however, left open the question of whether the Sixth Amendment right extends to the discretionary review stages, an issue the Burger Court took up in *Ross v. Moffitt* (1974). Here the Court ruled that the right to government appointed counsel is not constitutionally required at the discretionary appeals stages. In so holding, the justices of the Burger Court did not overrule revolutionary Warren Court decisions, but they shut the door on any further expansion of the right to counsel.

FAIR TRIALS

From a quantitative perspective, trials are insignificant; only about 5 percent of all criminal prosecutions go to trial. In the other 95 percent, the defendant pleads guilty, usually after arriving at a plea-bargaining agreement with the prosecutor. In such arrangements, the defendant waives the right to a jury trial and agrees to plead guilty in return for certain concessions made by the prosecutor. These concessions normally involve a reduction in the seriousness of the crimes charged, a reduction in the number of counts, or a recommendation for a lenient sentence. Although many citizens look at such arrangements unfavorably, the Supreme Court has sanctioned the practice, and it remains the most common way criminal prosecutions are settled.[6]

Qualitatively, however, trials are significant; the most serious crimes go to trial. In addition, trials serve a symbolic function and educate the public about crime and justice in the community. And they embody what Americans treasure so much—fundamental, objective, and open fairness.

The Framers of the Constitution clearly intended American trials to be the epitome of justice. They drafted the Sixth Amendment to correct the weaknesses they had observed in the English justice system, weaknesses that included closed proceedings, long delays, and few safeguards for defendants. Specifically, Sixth Amendment provisions governing trials state:

In all criminal prosecutions, the accused shall enjoy the right to a speedy and public trial, by an impartial jury of the State and district wherein the crime shall have been committed, which district shall have been previously ascertained by law, and to be informed of the nature and cause of the accusation; to be confronted with the witnesses against him; to have compulsory process for obtaining witnesses in his favor, and to have the Assistance of Counsel for his defence.

These fair trial provisions of the Sixth Amendment are supported by two important rights found in the Fifth: the right against self incrimination and the right to due process of law. The Constitution's fair trial guarantees provide strict guidelines for trial proceedings.

Speedy Trials

Individuals accused of crimes have the right to their day in court. But if justice is to be meaningful, trials must be scheduled in a timely fashion. The Framers considered it unfair for the government to levy criminal charges against suspects and then delay their trials for months, or even years. Consequently, the Sixth Amendment states that trials must be speedy.

6. See, for example, *North Carolina v. Alford* (1970).

But what constitutes "speedy"? The Court confronted this question in *Barker v. Wingo* (1972). In this case, two individuals, Willie Barker and Silas Manning, were charged with beating an elderly Kentucky couple to death with a tire iron. The prosecutor had a strong case against Manning, but not against Barker. To convict Barker, the prosecutor needed Manning to testify, but Manning refused on Fifth Amendment grounds. The prosecutor devised the following strategy: he would put Manning on trial first, and, after obtaining a conviction against Manning, he would try Barker and call Manning as a major witness. Manning would no longer be able to refuse to testify on Fifth Amendment grounds because, having already been convicted of murder, further incrimination would be impossible.

While this strategy was theoretically sound, it ran into difficulties. Getting Manning convicted took longer than the prosecutor had anticipated. In fact, because of hung juries, successful appeals, and subsequent retrials, it took several years. During this time, prosecutors had to ask the court to postpone Barker's trial sixteen times. Beginning with the twelfth continuance request, Barker's attorneys started asserting that the speedy trial provision of the Sixth Amendment was being violated. Finally, five years after he was indicted for murder, Barker went on trial. He was found guilty and sentenced to life in prison.

Barker's attorneys appealed the conviction on the grounds that the five-year delay was a violation of the Sixth Amendment. A unanimous Supreme Court, through an opinion by Justice Powell, refused to designate a specific length of time that would constitute unreasonable delay. Instead, the justices recognized that this period could vary from case to case. However, the Court established four criteria that should be considered in deciding questions of unreasonable delay:

–The length of the delay
–The reason for the delay

–The point at which the defendant begins asserting a Sixth Amendment violation
–Whether the delay prejudiced the defendant's case

As applied to Barker, the Court found no constitutional violation. While the five-year delay was admittedly long, the reason for the delay—the unavailability of an important witness—was sound. Furthermore, the defendant did not even register objections to the delay until well into the process. Finally, the Court was unable to see any prejudice suffered by the defendant due to the delay. Under Justice Powell's balancing test, defendants have a great deal to prove before the Court finds a violation of the speedy trial provision.[7]

Jury Trials

Like many other aspects of law and procedure, the Framers incorporated the British jury system into the U.S. Constitution. But what did the term *jury* mean to the Framers? We can speculate that they had in mind at least three aspects of the British system: that a jury be composed of the defendant's peers, that it consist of twelve persons, and that it reach unanimous verdicts. Today, none of these three guarantees is fully operative in criminal proceedings.

Jury Members. Presumably, in England being tried by a jury of one's peers meant that one would face members of one's social class. In other words, a commoner would be tried by a jury of commoners and a nobleman by a jury of noblemen. In the United States such class distinctions are not recognized; rather, a jury of one's peers means a jury that represents a cross-section of the community. To put together representative panels, most jurisdictions follow a procedure that works this way:

7. After *Barker*, as Neubauer notes, "There was considerable interest in putting some teeth into the guarantee of a speedy trial." In 1974 Congress passed the Speedy Trial Act, requiring indictment within thirty days of arrest, arraignment ten days after indictment, and trial sixty days after arraignment. Moreover, every state has enacted speedy trail laws of various sorts. See Neubauer, *America's Courts*, 394–395.

1. Individuals living within a specified geographical area are called for jury duty. Most localities select names from voter registration, property tax, or driver's license lists.

2. Those selected form the jury pool or venire, the group from which attorneys choose the actual jury.

3. The judge may conduct initial interviews excusing certain classes of people (felons, illiterates, the mentally ill) and certain occupational groups, as allowed under the laws of the particular jurisdiction.

4. The remaining individuals are available to be chosen to serve on a trial (petit) jury. In the final selection phase, the opposing attorneys interview the prospective jurors. This process is called *voir dire.* During voir dire attorneys can dismiss those individuals they believe would not vote in the best interests of their clients. The attorneys, therefore, select the jury.

During voir dire attorneys use two mechanisms or challenges to eliminate potential jurors. When a prospective juror appears to be unqualified to carry out the obligations of service, attorneys can *challenge for cause.* To do so they must explain to the judge their reason for eliminating that individual (for example, conflict of interest or expressions of extreme prejudice), and the judge must agree. Challenges for cause are unlimited. Attorneys also have a fixed number of *peremptory challenges,* which they may use to excuse jurors without stating a reason.

Traditionally, attorneys have been able to use their peremptory challenges in whatever way and for whatever reason they chose. While that general rule remains in effect, the Supreme Court has intervened to limit lawyers' discretion in two important ways.

First, in *Batson v. Kentucky* (1986) the Court ruled that prosecutors cannot use their peremptory challenges systematically to eliminate African Americans from the jury. The case involved James Batson, a black man charged with burglary. At his trial the prosecutor used his peremptory challenges to remove all four of the black people in the pool of potential jurors, result-

ing in an all-white jury. The prosecutor's behavior, the justices ruled, violated the Equal Protection Clause of the Fourteenth Amendment. Later, in *Powers v. Ohio* (1991), the Court extended the ruling to trials of white defendants, and in *Edmonson v. Leesville Concrete Co.* (1991) the Court extended it to civil cases. Finally in *Georgia v. McCollum* (1992), the Court prohibited defense attorneys from purposefully eliminating jurors on the basis of race. The end result of these decisions is to bar the use of peremptory challenges to exclude potential jurors on the basis of race.

Second, in *J. E. B. v. T. B.* (1994) the Court extended the ban against racial discrimination in jury selection to cover sex discrimination as well. The case grew from a paternity and child support complaint filed against James E. Bowman. The prosecution used nine of its ten peremptory challenges to remove men from the jury. As a consequence, Bowman was tried by an all-female jury. The jury ruled that he was the father of the child in question. The Supreme Court found the prosecutor's purposeful exclusion of men from the jury to offend the Constitution. For the majority Justice Blackmun concluded:

Today we reaffirm what, by now, should be axiomatic: Intentional discrimination on the basis of gender by state actors violates the [Equal Protection Clause], particularly where, as here, the discrimination serves to ratify and perpetuate invidious, archaic, and overbroad stereotypes about the relative abilities of men and women.

Jury Size. Another longstanding tradition Americans adopted from the British is jury size. Since the fourteenth century all English juries had twelve people. The origin of that number is disputed. Some suggest that it represents the twelve apostles; others claim it emanates from the twelve tribes of Israel. A point on which all agree is that the Framers accepted twelve as the proper number for a jury. Beginning in the mid-1960s, however, many states began to abandon this practice, substituting six-person juries in noncapital cases. These states reasoned that six-person juries would be more economical, faster, and more likely to reach a verdict. Was the use of less than twelve people consistent with the demands of the Sixth Amendment? The Court answered this question in *Williams v. Florida*, a 1970 appeal from a robbery conviction. For the Court, Justice White explained that the number twelve had no special constitutional significance. The traditional twelve-person jury was basically the result of historical accident. All the Constitution requires, according to the Court, is a jury sufficiently large to allow actual deliberation and to represent a cross-section of the community. The six-person jury used to convict Williams was sufficiently large to meet these standards.

White's reasoning has been closely scrutinized by legal scholars. In addition, numerous empirical investigations have tried to determine whether six-person juries reach conclusions that are significantly different from those of their twelve-person counterparts. Although the scholarly verdict is far from unanimous, many now agree that "research on the effects of panel size on jury performance indicates that the use of six-member juries does not result in significant differences in either trial outcome or deliberation quality."[8] A number of states have followed Florida's lead and now regularly use six-person juries, at least in some types of cases.

Jury Verdicts. Following the English tradition the Framers thought juries should reach unanimous verdicts or none at all. In the event that no verdict was reached, judges declared the jury hung, and the prosecutor could schedule a retrial or release the defendant. For the sake of efficient justice, some states altered the unanimity rule for twelve-person juries, requiring instead the agreement of nine or ten of the twelve.

Two cases, *Johnson v. Louisiana* and *Apodaca v. Oregon*, decided together in 1972, tested the constitution-ality of nonunanimous juries. The side in support of nonunanimity claimed that the alternative was excessive and obsolete in modern society, that because hung juries occurred regularly, the requirement of unanimity often led to miscarriages of justice. The other side pointed out that the very essence of jury decision making is that verdicts are based on doubt. If no reasonable doubt exists about a person's guilt, the jury is supposed to reach a guilty verdict; if doubt is present, the jury should come to the opposite conclusion. But if a jury is split 9–3 or 10–2, does that not indicate a reasonable doubt? According to Justice White, writing for the Court, less than unanimous verdicts do not violate the Sixth Amendment. A lack of unanimity is not the equivalent of doubt. He concluded:

[T]he fact of three dissenting votes to acquit raises no question of institutional substance about either the integrity or the accuracy of the majority vote of guilt.... [By obtaining] nine [votes] to convict, the State satisfied its burden of proving guilt beyond any reasonable doubt.

Although the Court's decisions on jury size prompted many states to use less than twelve person juries in some cases, the states have not embraced decision-making rules that allow a less than unanimous verdict. The overwhelming number of states have remained loyal to the unanimous verdict requirement.

Impartial Juries and the Press. As we have seen, Supreme Court decisions have led to jury practices that differ substantially from the vision of the Framers. But the controversies sparked by these pale in comparison with the furor over the notion of impartial juries.[9] Given the constitutional guarantees of a public trial and freedom of the press, how can judges see to it that defendants receive fair, impartial jury trials? This question has major constitutional importance because it forces courts to deal with conflicting rights. The Sixth Amendment requires judges to regulate trials, ensuring, among other things, that the

---

8. See, for example, Michael J. Saks, *Jury Verdicts* (Lexington, Mass.: Lexington Books, 1977); Reid Hastie et al., *Inside the Jury* (Cambridge, Mass.: Harvard University Press, 1983).

9. See *Patton v. Yount* (1984).

jury is impartial. In a highly publicized case, the judge's task can become arduous. The judge must deal with the media, who are exercising their constitutional guarantee of a free press. How can judges keep trials fair without interfering with the rights of the press and the public?

Before the mid-1960s no balance existed between freedom of the press and the right to an impartial jury—the former far outweighed the latter. In cases involving well-known individuals or otherwise of interest to the public, the press descended on courtrooms. Because there were no well-defined rules, reporters, accompanied by crews carrying bulky, noisy equipment, simply showed up and interviewed and photographed witnesses and other participants at will. These activities often disrupted trials and made objective, dispassionate analysis of evidence almost impossible for the jurors.

Not surprisingly, the Warren Court placed limitations on the media. In two important cases, *Estes v. Texas* (1965) and *Sheppard v. Maxwell* (1966), the Court reversed convictions on the basis of media misbehavior and chastised lower court judges for allowing the press to jeopardize the integrity of the trial. As a result, judges around the country policed their courtrooms much more vigilantly to ensure that the press did not compromise the right of the defendant to receive a fair trial.

Although judges have the obligation to impose limitations on the activities of the press in covering trials, they cannot go too far. The press is still protected by the First Amendment in gathering and reporting the news. The justices have supported free press rights as long as they are compatible with the right to a fair trial. For example, in *Richmond Newspapers v. Virginia* (1980), the Court held that a trial court judge could not close a trial in order to keep the press from observing it and reporting to the public. In controversial trials judges must often walk a very fine line, imposing some limitations on members of the press so that their activities do not deprive the defendant of a fair trial and yet preserving the right of the press to gather and report the news.

Confronting Witnesses

Among the Sixth Amendment protections is the right to confront witnesses. This provision includes a number of guarantees. First, it means that defendants have the right to be present during their trials. Unlike some countries, the United States does not permit trials in absentia.

Second, the Confrontation Clause requires that prosecution witnesses appear in open court in the presence of the defendant to give their testimony under oath. As a consequence, the prosecution cannot obtain a conviction based on anonymous testimony or upon information provided by witnesses who are unwilling to appear in court. Although this requirement appears to be both reasonable and necessary for most crimes, it has received considerable criticism for crimes such as rape and child abuse. Rape victims, for example, may refuse to report crimes, knowing that if they do so they will be required to give their testimony in open court. Similarly, many fear that children who have been abused will be traumatized by having to tell their stories in court with the person who abused them visibly present.

While the justices have generally adhered to the requirement that prosecution witnesses appear in court, they have been sympathetic to the situation facing children who may have been the victims of abuse. A good example is provided by *Maryland v. Craig* (1990). Sandra Ann Craig was charged by Maryland authorities with child abuse, sexual offenses, perverted sexual practice, assault, and battery. The alleged victim was a six-year-old girl who was enrolled for two years in a preschool that Craig owned and operated.

Maryland law allowed a special procedure to be invoked if the trial court judge determined that testifying in open court would cause a child serious emotional distress and reduce the child's ability to communicate. This procedure permitted the child to be questioned and cross-examined by the prosecutor and defense attorney in a room separate from the trial courtroom. Closed-circuit television transmitted the testimony to the courtroom, where the accused, the judge, and the jury would view it. This procedure was used at Craig's trial over her objections, and she was found guilty. She appealed, claiming that her Confrontation Clause rights had been violated.

The Court upheld the conviction. The majority's reasoning is well outlined by Justice O'Connor:

In sum, we conclude that where necessary to protect a child witness from trauma that would be caused by testifying in the physical presence of the defendant, at least where such trauma would impair the child's ability to communicate, the Confrontation Clause does not prohibit use of a procedure that, despite the absence of face-to-face confrontation, ensures the reliability of the evidence by subjecting it to rigorous adversarial testing and thereby preserves the essence of effective confrontation. Because there is no dispute that the child witnesses in this case testified under oath, were subject to full cross-examination, and were able to be observed by the judge, jury, and defendant as they testified, we conclude that, to the extent that a proper finding of necessity has been made, the admission of such testimony would be consonant with the Confrontation Clause. . . .

A third component of the right to confrontation is cross-examination. Not only does the prosecution have to produce witnesses who testify under oath in open court before the defendant, but those witnesses are subject to questioning by the defense. This requirement is based on the theory that a jury will best be able to discern the truth if testimony is tested by vigorous examination from the opposing side.

Self-Incrimination and Testimony

The defendant in a criminal case cannot be required to take the witness stand. This is because the Fifth Amendment's Self-Incrimination Clause prohibits the government from compelling a criminal defendant to give testimony. The Constitution, of course, does not preclude the defendant from giving

testimony; whether to take the witness stand is the defendant's choice.

If a witness refuses to answer questions on Fifth Amendment grounds, no inference of guilt may be made. Judges may not instruct jurors to consider a defendant's refusal to take the witness stand and deny guilt under oath; nor may prosecutors argue that a defendant's decision not to testify is evidence of wrongdoing. Such actions by judges or prosecutors would be clear violations of the Fifth Amendment. An individual's decision to invoke the Fifth Amendment privilege and not answer questions can be interpreted as nothing more than a decision to remain silent.

Furthermore, individuals must be free to exercise their Fifth Amendment rights. Governments may not coerce a person to testify. A prosecutor, for example, may not threaten a defendant that if he or she does not take the witness stand, the government will ask for a more severe sentence. Nor may the government use economic pressure to coerce an individual to waive the Fifth Amendment privilege. In *Garrity v. New Jersey* (1967) and *Gardner v. Broderick* (1968), for example, the Supreme Court ruled that public employees could not be threatened with the loss of their jobs if they did not testify in government investigations of corruption and wrongdoing. Citizens must be given the choice of exercising their rights against self-incrimination.

SENTENCING AND THE EIGHTH AMENDMENT

If a criminal defendant is convicted, the next stage of consequence is sentencing. While the Framers included many provisions in the Bill of Rights dealing with fair trials, there is only one section that focuses specifically on sentencing, the Eighth Amendment: "Excessive bail shall not be required, nor excessive fines imposed, nor cruel and unusual punishment inflicted."

The most significant section of this amendment is

its cruel and unusual punishment provision. Those who adopted the Bill of Rights clearly wanted to outlaw sentences that were not viewed as appropriate for a civilized society, those that were cruel and unusual. As a consequence, such punishments as crucifixion, the rack, drawing and quartering, tar and feathering, dismemberment, or the stocks are not practiced in the United States. By our standards of decency today, these would violate the prohibition against cruel and unusual punishments.

Defining Cruel and Unusual

The meaning of "cruel and unusual is open to interpretation. The Supreme Court turned its attention to this critical question in *Solem v. Helm* (1983), a case involving Jerry Helm, who over the years had been convicted of six nonviolent felonies in South Dakota. In 1979 he was charged with yet another offense—writing bad checks. Normally, that crime carries with it a maximum sentence of five years in prison and/or a $5,000 fine. But because of Helm's previous record, a South Dakota judge invoked a state recidivism law: if an individual is convicted of three felonies, the sentence can be that imposed for a Class 1 felony, which includes a life prison sentence (with no parole) and/or a $25,000 fine. Believing that Helm was beyond rehabilitation, the judge sentenced him to life imprisonment. After two years of trying to get the governor to commute his sentence, Helm turned to the courts, claiming that his punishment was cruel and unusual.

By a 5–4 vote, the justices found the life sentence violated the Cruel and Unusual Punishment Clause. Justice Powell's majority opinion held that the Eighth Amendment proscribes not only barbaric punishments but also sentences that are disproportionate to the crime committed. The justices held that this concept of proportionality could be traced back to the earliest development of English law. As applied in this case, life in prison was out of proportion to the bad check charges. With this case the Court provided a working definition of cruel and unusual. The justices seemed to abide by the old adage—let the punishment fit the crime.

The Death Penalty

The issue most frequently brought to the Court on Eighth Amendment grounds is the constitutionality of capital punishment. The death penalty cases have perplexed the Court for decades, presenting the justices with emotionally charged and legally complex questions.

The opinions in the death penalty cases tell us a great deal about what cruel and unusual punishment does and does not mean. Since 1947 the Court has held that the death penalty is inherently neither cruel nor unusual.[10] Never has a *majority* of the justices agreed that it is, but why not? The answer lies with the intent of the Framers (at the time of ratification, death penalties were in use) and with the Due Process Clauses of the Fifth and Fourteenth Amendments, which state that no person can be deprived of life without due process of law. Presumably, if due process is observed, life *can* be taken.

The majority of Americans also support use of the death penalty *(see Figure 17-1, page 634)*, but there are many interest groups working to eliminate it. These groups believe that the death penalty constitutes cruel and unusual punishment; but, recognizing the Court's unwillingness to agree, they have tried to convince the justices that the way the death penalty is applied violates due process norms.

One of the first attempts to implement a due process strategy was undertaken by the NAACP Legal Defense and Educational Fund (LDF) in *Furman v. Georgia* (1972). This case involved William Furman, a black man accused of murdering a white man, the father of five children. Under Georgia law, it was completely up to the jury to determine whether a convicted murderer should be put to death. This system, the LDF argued, led to unacceptable disparities in sen-

10. See *Louisiana ex rel. Frances v. Resweber* (1947).

tencing; specifically, blacks convicted of murdering whites were far more likely to receive the death penalty than whites convicted of the same crime.

A divided Supreme Court agreed with the LDF. In a short per curiam opinion, deciding *Furman* and two companion cases, the justices said, "The Court holds that the imposition and carrying out of the death penalty in these cases constitutes cruel and unusual punishment." Following this terse statement, however, were nine separate opinions (five in favor of the LDF's position and four against, running 243 pages—one of the longest in Court history).[11]

The views presented in the opinions of the five-member majority varied considerably—three justices (White, Stewart, and Douglas) thought capital punishment, as it was then imposed, violated the Constitution, and two (Brennan and Marshall) said it would be unconstitutional under all circumstances. Beyond these general groupings, the five justices agreed on only one major point of law: that the states that used capital punishment did so in an arbitrary manner, particularly with regard to race. However, they framed even this statement in divergent terms. Douglas said arbitrariness led to discriminatory sentencing. Brennan used arbitrariness as part of a four-part test designed to determine whether the death penalty was acceptable punishment. He found that it was (1) degrading, (2) arbitrary, (3) unacceptable to contemporary society, and (4) excessive. Marshall adopted a similar approach, but explained that arbitrariness was but one reason why capital punishment was cruel and unusual and "morally unacceptable." To Stewart, arbitrariness in sentencing meant that the death penalty was imposed in a "wanton" and "freak[ish] manner," akin to being struck by lightening. For White, arbitrariness led to the infrequency of imposition, which in turn made death a less than credible deterrent.

The dissenters, Blackmun, Burger, Rehnquist, and Powell (the four Nixon appointees), were more uniform in their critiques. To a lesser or greater extent, all expressed the view that the Court was encroaching on legislative turf and that Americans had not "repudiated" the death penalty. Justice Blackmun also lambasted the majority for expressing views wholly inconsistent with precedent. In particular, he noted that Stewart and White had previously found that it would be virtually impossible to create sentencing standards, but now they were striking laws in part because of the absence of such standards.

Chief Justice Burger's opinion raised a unique issue: he noted that the plurality (Douglas, Stewart, and White) had not ruled that capital punishment under all circumstances was unconstitutional and that it may be possible for states to rewrite their laws to meet their objections. As he asserted:

It is clear that if state legislatures and the Congress wish to maintain the availability of capital punishment, significant statutory changes will have to be made.... [L]egislative bodies may seek to bring their laws into compliance with the Court's ruling by providing standards for juries and judges to follow ... or by more narrowly defining crimes for which the penalty is imposed.

Privately, however, Burger thought his suggestion futile, lamenting later that "There will never be another execution in this country."[12]

This view was echoed in many quarters. A University of Washington law professor wrote, "My hunch is that *Furman* spells the complete end of capital punishment in this country."[13] LDF attorneys, predictably, were ecstatic. One called it "the biggest step forward criminal justice has taken in 1,000 years."[14]

As it turned out, the abolitionist celebration was a bit premature, for the Supreme Court was not fin-

11. We adopt this discussion from Lee Epstein and Joseph F. Kobylka, *The Supreme Court and Legal Change* (Chapel Hill: University of North Carolina Press, 1992), 78–80.

12. Bob Woodward and Scott Armstrong, *The Brethren* (New York: Simon and Schuster, 1979), 219.

13. John M. Junker, "The Death Penalty Cases: A Preliminary Comment," *Washington Law Review* 48 (1972): 109.

14. Quoted in Frederick Mann, "Anthony Amsterdam," *Juris Doctor* 3 (1973): 31–32.

ished with the death penalty. Just three years after *Furman*, the Court agreed to hear *Gregg v. Georgia* to consider the constitutionality of a new breed of death penalty laws written to overcome the defects of the old laws. Did these new laws reduce the chance for "wanton and freakish" punishment of the sort the Court found so distasteful in *Furman*? Consider this question as you read the facts and opinions in *Gregg v. Georgia*.

Gregg v. Georgia

428 U.S. 153 (1976)

Vote: 7 (Blackmun, Burger, Powell, Rehnquist, Stevens, Stewart, White)

2 (Brennan, Marshall)

Opinion announcing the judgment of the Court: Stewart

Concurring opinions: Blackmun, Burger and Rehnquist, White

Dissenting opinions: Brennan, Marshall

Taking cues from the justices' opinions in *Furman*, many states set out to revise their death penalty laws. Among the new plans was one proposed by Georgia (and other states). At the heart of this law was the "bifurcated trial," which consisted of two stages—the trial and the sentencing phase. The trial would proceed as usual, with a jury finding the defendant guilty or innocent. If the verdict was guilty, the prosecution could seek the death penalty at the sentencing stage, in which the defense attorney presents the mitigating facts and the prosecution presents the aggravating facts. Mitigating facts include the individual's age,[15] record, family responsibility, psychiatric reports, and chances for rehabilitation. Such data are not specified in law. The prosecution, on the other hand, has to

demonstrate that at least one codified aggravating factor exists.

The Georgia law specified ten aggravating factors, including: murders committed "while the offender was engaged in the commission of another capital offense," the murder of "a judicial officer ... or ... district attorney because of the exercise of his official duty," and murders that are "outrageously or wantonly vile, horrible, or inhumane." After hearing arguments in mitigation and aggravation, the jury determines whether the individual receives the death penalty. By spelling out the conditions that must be present before a death penalty can be imposed, the law sought to reduce the jury's discretion and eliminate the arbitrary application of the death penalty that the Court in *Furman* found unacceptable. As a further safeguard, the Georgia Supreme Court was to review all jury determinations of death. This new law was applied to Troy Gregg and was quickly challenged by abolitionist interests.

Gregg and a friend were hitchhiking north in Florida. Two men picked them up, and later the foursome was joined by another passenger who rode with them as far as Atlanta. The four then continued to a rest stop on the highway. The next day, the bodies of the two drivers were found in a nearby ditch. The individual let off in Atlanta identified Gregg and his friend as possible assailants. Gregg was tried under Georgia's new death penalty system. He was convicted of murder and sentenced to death, a penalty the state's highest court upheld.

Judgment of the Court, and opinions of
MR. JUSTICE STEWART, MR. JUSTICE POWELL, and
MR. JUSTICE STEVENS announced by
MR. JUSTICE STEWART.

The issue in this case is whether the imposition of the sentence of death for the crime of murder under the law of Georgia violates the Eighth and Fourteenth Amendments. ...

We address initially the basic contention that the pun-

---

15. In 1982 in *Eddings v. Oklahoma* the Court agreed that age constituted a mitigating factor, which does not mean that minors cannot receive the death penalty—just that juries and judges may consider age during the sentencing stage. In fact, the Court has held that those sixteen and older (at the time the crime was committed) can be executed; see *Thompson v. Oklahoma* (1988) and *Sanford v. Kentucky* (1989).

ishment of death for the crime of murder is, under all circumstances, "cruel and unusual" in violation of the Eighth and Fourteenth Amendments of the Constitution. . . . [W]e will consider the sentence of death imposed under the Georgia statutes at issue in this case.

The Court on a number of occasions has both assumed and asserted the constitutionality of capital punishment. In several cases that assumption provided a necessary foundation for the decision, as the Court was asked to decide whether a particular method of carrying out a capital sentence would be allowed to stand under the Eighth Amendment. But until *Furman v. Georgia* (1972), the Court never confronted squarely the fundamental claim that the punishment of death always, regardless of the enormity of the offense or the procedure followed in imposing the sentence, is cruel and unusual punishment in violation of the Constitution. Although this issue was presented and addressed in *Furman*, it was not resolved by the Court. Four Justices would have held that capital punishment is not unconstitutional *per se*; two Justices would have reached the opposite conclusion; and three Justices, while agreeing that the statutes then before the Court were invalid as applied, left open the question whether such punishment may ever be imposed. We now hold that the punishment of death does not invariably violate the Constitution.

The history of the prohibition of "cruel and unusual" punishment already has been reviewed at length. The phrase first appeared in the English Bill of Rights of 1689, which was drafted by Parliament at the accession of William and Mary. The English version appears to have been directed against punishments unauthorized by statute and beyond the jurisdiction of the sentencing court, as well as those disproportionate to the offense involved. The American draftsmen, who adopted the English phrasing in drafting the Eighth Amendment, were primarily concerned, however, with proscribing "tortures" and other "barbarous" methods of punishment.

In the earliest cases raising Eighth Amendment claims, the Court focused on particular methods of execution to determine whether they were too cruel to pass constitutional muster. The constitutionality of the sentence of death itself was not at issue, and the criterion used to evaluate the mode of execution was its similarity to "torture" and other "barbarous" methods.

But the Court has not confined the prohibition embodied in the Eighth Amendment to "barbarous" methods that were generally outlawed in the 18th century. Instead, the Amendment has been interpreted in a flexible and dynamic manner. The Court early recognized that "a principle to be vital, must be capable of wider application than the mischief which gave it birth." *Weems v. United States* (1910). Thus the Clause forbidding "cruel and unusual" punishments "is not fastened to the obsolete but may acquire meaning as public opinion becomes enlightened by a humane justice.". . .

It is clear from . . . these precedents that the Eighth Amendment has not been regarded as a static concept. As Mr. Chief Justice Warren said, in an oft-quoted phrase, "[t]he Amendment must draw its meaning from the evolving standards of decency that mark the progress of a maturing society." Thus, an assessment of contemporary values concerning the infliction of a challenged sanction is relevant to the application of the Eighth Amendment. As we develop below more fully, this assessment does not call for a subjective judgment. It requires, rather, that we look to objective indicia that reflect the public attitude toward a given sanction.

But our cases also make clear that public perceptions of standards of decency with respect to criminal sanctions are not conclusive. A penalty also must accord with "the dignity of man," which is the "basic concept underlying the Eighth Amendment." This means, at least, that the punishment not be "excessive." When a form of punishment in the abstract (in this case, whether capital punishment may ever be imposed as a sanction for murder) rather than in the particular (the propriety of death as a penalty to be applied to a specific defendant for a specific crime) is under consideration, the inquiry into "excessiveness" has two aspects. First, the punishment must not involve the unnecessary and wanton infliction of pain. Second, the punishment must not be grossly out of proportion to the severity of the crime.

Of course, the requirements of the Eighth Amendment must be applied with an awareness of the limited role to be played by the courts. This does not mean that judges have no role to play, for the Eighth Amendment is a restraint upon the exercise of legislative power . . . .

But, while we have an obligation to insure that constitutional bounds are not overreached, we may not act as judges as we might as legislators. . . .

Therefore, in assessing a punishment selected by a democratically elected legislature against the constitutional measure, we presume its validity. We may not require the legislature to select the least severe penalty possible so long as the penalty selected is not cruelly inhumane or disproportionate to the crime involved. And a heavy burden rests on those who would attack the judgment of the representatives of the people. . . .

In the discussion to this point we have sought to identify the principles and considerations that guide a court in addressing an Eighth Amendment claim. We now consider specifically whether the sentence of death for the crime of murder is a *per se* violation of the Eighth and Fourteenth Amendments to the Constitution. We note first that history and precedent strongly support a negative answer to this question.

The imposition of the death penalty for the crime of murder has a long history of acceptance both in the United States and in England. . . .

It is apparent from the text of the Constitution itself that the existence of capital punishment was accepted by the Framers. At the time the Eighth Amendment was ratified, capital punishment was a common sanction in every State. . . . The Fifth Amendment, adopted at the same time as the Eighth, contemplated the continued existence of the capital sanction by imposing certain limits on the prosecution of capital cases:

"No person shall be held to answer for a capital, or otherwise infamous crime, unless on a presentment or indictment of a Grand Jury . . . ; nor shall any person be subject for the same offense to be twice put in jeopardy of life or limb; . . . . nor be deprived of life, liberty, or property, without due process of law. . . . "

And the Fourteenth Amendment, adopted over three quarters of a century later, similarly contemplates the existence of the capital sanction in providing that no State shall deprive any person of "life, liberty, or property" without due process of law.

For nearly two centuries, this Court, repeatedly and often expressly, has recognized that capital punishment is not invalid *per se*. . . .

Four years ago, the petitioners in *Furman* and its companion cases predicated their argument primarily upon the asserted proposition that standards of decency had evolved to the point where capital punishment no longer could be tolerated. The petitioners in those cases said, in effect, that the evolutionary process had come to an end, and that standards of decency required that the Eighth Amendment be construed finally as prohibiting capital punishment for any crime regardless of its depravity and impact on society. This view was accepted by two Justices. Three other Justices were unwilling to go so far; focusing on the procedures by which convicted defendants were selected for the death penalty rather than on the actual punishment inflicted, they joined in the conclusion that the statutes before the Court were constitutionally invalid.

The petitioners in the capital cases before the Court today renew the "standards of decency" argument, but developments during the four years since *Furman* have undercut substantially the assumptions upon which their argument rested. Despite the continuing debate, dating back to the 19th century, over the morality and utility of capital punishment, it is now evident that a large proportion of American society continues to regard it as an appropriate and necessary criminal sanction.

The most marked indication of society's endorsement of the death penalty for murder is the legislative response to *Furman.* The legislatures of at least 35 States have enacted new statutes that provide for the death penalty for at least some crimes that result in the death of another person. And the Congress of the United States, in 1974, enacted a statute providing the death penalty for aircraft piracy that results in death. These recently adopted statutes have attempted to address the concerns expressed by the Court in *Furman* primarily (i) by specifying the factors to be weighed and the procedures to be followed in deciding when to impose a capital sentence, or (ii) by making the death penalty mandatory for specified crimes. But all of the post-*Furman* statutes make clear that capital punishment itself has not been rejected by the elected representatives of the people.

In the only statewide referendum occurring since *Furman* and brought to our attention, the people of California adopted a constitutional amendment that authorized capital punishment, in effect negating a prior ruling by the

Supreme Court of California that the death penalty violated the California Constitution.

The jury also is a significant and reliable objective index of contemporary values because it is so directly involved. . . . It may be true that evolving standards have influenced juries in recent decades to be more discriminating in imposing the sentence of death. But the relative infrequency of jury verdicts imposing the death sentence does not indicate rejection of capital punishment *per se.* Rather, the reluctance of juries in many cases to impose the sentence may well reflect the humane feeling that this most irrevocable of sanctions should be reserved for a small number of extreme cases. Indeed, the actions of juries in many States since *Furman* are fully compatible with the legislative judgments, reflected in the new statutes, as to the continued utility and necessity of capital punishment in appropriate cases. At the close of 1974 at least 254 persons had been sentenced to death since *Furman,* and by the end of March 1976, more than 460 persons were subject to death sentences.

As we have seen, however, the Eighth Amendment demands more than that a challenged punishment be acceptable to contemporary society. The Court also must ask whether it comports with the basic concept of human dignity at the core of the Amendment. Although we cannot "invalidate a category of penalties because we deem less severe penalties adequate to serve the ends of penology," the sanction imposed cannot be so totally without penological justification that it results in the gratuitous infliction of suffering.

The death penalty is said to serve two principal social purposes: retribution and deterrence of capital crimes by prospective offenders.

In part, capital punishment is an expression of society's moral outrage at particularly offensive conduct. This function may be unappealing to many, but it is essential in an ordered society that asks its citizens to rely on legal processes rather than self-help to vindicate their wrongs. . . . "Retribution is no longer the dominant objective of the criminal law," but neither is it a forbidden objective nor one inconsistent with our respect for the dignity of men. . . .

Statistical attempts to evaluate the worth of the death penalty as a deterrent to crimes by potential offenders have occasioned a great deal of debate. The results simply have been inconclusive. . . .

Although some of the studies suggest that the death penalty may not function as a significantly greater deterrent than lesser penalties, there is no convincing empirical evidence either supporting or refuting this view. We may nevertheless assume safely that there are murderers, such as those who act in passion, for whom the threat of death has little or no deterrent effect. But for many others, the death penalty undoubtedly is a significant deterrent. There are carefully contemplated murders, such as murder for hire, where the possible penalty of death may well enter into the cold calculus that precedes the decision to act. And there are some categories of murder, such as murder by a life prisoner, where other sanctions may not be adequate.

The value of capital punishment as a deterrent of crime is a complex factual issue the resolution of which properly rests with the legislatures, which can evaluate the results of statistical studies in terms of their own local conditions and with a flexibility of approach that is not available to the courts. Indeed, many of the post-*Furman* statutes reflect just such a responsible effort to define those crimes and those criminals for which capital punishment is most probably an effective deterrent.

In sum, we cannot say that the judgment of the Georgia Legislature that capital punishment may be necessary in some cases is clearly wrong. Considerations of federalism, as well as respect for the ability of a legislature to evaluate, in terms of its particular State, the moral consensus concerning the death penalty and its social utility as a sanction, require us to conclude, in the absence of more convincing evidence, that the infliction of death as a punishment for murder is not without justification and thus is not unconstitutionally severe.

Finally, we must consider whether the punishment of death is disproportionate in relation to the crime for which it is imposed. There is no question that death as a punishment is unique in its severity and irrevocability. When a defendant's life is at stake, the Court has been particularly sensitive to insure that every safeguard is observed. But we are concerned here only with the imposition of capital punishment for the crime of murder, and when a life has been taken deliberately by the offender, we cannot say that the punishment is invariably disproportionate to the crime. It is an extreme sanction, suitable to the most extreme of crimes.

We hold that the death penalty is not a form of punishment that may never be imposed, regardless of the circumstances of the offense, regardless of the character of the offender, and regardless of the procedure followed in reaching the decision to impose it.

We now consider whether Georgia may impose the death penalty on the petitioner in this case.

While *Furman* did not hold that the infliction of the death penalty *per se* violates the Constitution's ban on cruel and unusual punishments, it did recognize that the penalty of death is different in kind from any other punishment imposed under our system of criminal justice. Because of the uniqueness of the death penalty, *Furman* held that it could not be imposed under sentencing procedures that created a substantial risk that it would be inflicted in an arbitrary and capricious manner. . . .

Furman mandates that where discretion is afforded a sentencing body on a matter so grave as the determination of whether a human life should be taken or spared, that discretion must be suitably directed and limited so as to minimize the risk of wholly arbitrary and capricious action. . . .

Jury sentencing has been considered desirable in capital cases in order "to maintain a link between contemporary community values and the penal system—a link without which the determination of punishment could hardly reflect 'the evolving standards of decency that mark the progress of a maturing society.'" But it creates special problems. Much of the information that is relevant to the sentencing decision may have no relevance to the question of guilt, or may even be extremely prejudicial to a fair determination of that question. This problem, however, is scarcely insurmountable. Those who have studied the question suggest that a bifurcated procedure—one in which the question of sentence is not considered until the determination of guilt has been made—is the best answer. . . . When a human life is at stake and when the jury must have information prejudicial to the question of guilt but relevant to the question of penalty in order to impose a rational sentence, a bifurcated system is more likely to ensure elimination of the constitutional deficiencies identified in *Furman*.

But the provision of relevant information under fair procedural rules is not alone sufficient to guarantee that the information will be properly used in the imposition of punishment, especially if sentencing is performed by a jury.

Since the members of a jury will have had little, if any, previous experience in sentencing, they are unlikely to be skilled in dealing with the information they are given. To the extent that this problem is inherent in jury sentencing, it may not be totally correctible. It seems clear, however, that the problem will be alleviated if the jury is given guidance regarding the factors about the crime and the defendant that the State, representing organized society, deems particularly relevant to the sentencing decision.

The idea that a jury should be given guidance in its decisionmaking is also hardly a novel proposition. Juries are invariably given careful instructions on the law and how to apply it before they are authorized to decide the merits of a lawsuit. It would be virtually unthinkable to follow any other course in a legal system that has traditionally operated by following prior precedents and fixed rules of law. When erroneous instructions are given, retrial is often required. It is quite simply a hallmark of our legal system that juries be carefully and adequately guided in their deliberations.

While some have suggested that standards to guide a capital jury's sentencing deliberations are impossible to formulate, the fact is that such standards have been developed. . . . While such standards are by necessity somewhat general, they do provide guidance to the sentencing authority and thereby reduce the likelihood that it will impose a sentence that fairly can be called capricious or arbitrary. Where the sentencing authority is required to specify the factors it relied upon in reaching its decision, the further safeguard of meaningful appellate review is available to ensure that death sentences are not imposed capriciously or in a freakish manner.

In summary, the concerns expressed in *Furman* that the penalty of death not be imposed in an arbitrary or capricious manner can be met by a carefully drafted statute that ensures that the sentencing authority is given adequate information and guidance. As a general proposition these concerns are best met by a system that provides for a bifurcated proceeding at which the sentencing authority is apprised of the information relevant to the imposition of sentence and provided with standards to guide its use of the information.

We do not intend to suggest that only the above-described procedures would be permissible under *Furman* or that any sentencing system constructed along these general lines would inevitably satisfy the concerns of *Furman*, for each distinct system must be examined on an individual basis. Rather, we have embarked upon this general exposition to make clear that it is possible to construct capital-sentencing systems capable of meeting *Furman*'s constitutional concerns.

We now turn to consideration of the constitutionality of Georgia's capital-sentencing procedures. In the wake of *Furman*, Georgia amended its capital punishment statute, but chose not to narrow the scope of its murder provisions. Thus, now as before *Furman*, in Georgia "[a] person commits murder when he unlawfully and with malice aforethought, either express or implied, causes the death of another human being." All persons convicted of murder "shall be punished by death or by imprisonment for life."

Georgia did act, however, to narrow the class of murderers subject to capital punishment by specifying 10 statutory aggravating circumstances, one of which must be found by the jury to exist beyond a reasonable doubt before a death sentence can ever be imposed. In addition, the jury is authorized to consider any other appropriate aggravating or mitigating circumstances. The jury is not required to find any mitigating circumstance in order to make a recommendation of mercy that is binding on the trial court, but it must find a *statutory* aggravating circumstance before recommending a sentence of death.

These procedures require the jury to consider the circumstances of the crime and the criminal before it recommends sentence. No longer can a Georgia jury do as *Furman*'s jury did: reach a finding of the defendant's guilt and then, without guidance or direction, decide whether he should live or die. Instead, the jury's attention is directed to the specific circumstances of the crime. . . . In addition, the jury's attention is focused on the characteristics of the person who committed the crime. . . . As a result, while some jury discretion still exists, "the discretion to be exercised is controlled by clear and objective standards so as to produce nondiscriminatory application."

As an important additional safeguard against arbitrariness and caprice, the Georgia statutory scheme provides for automatic appeal of all death sentences to the State's Supreme Court. That court is required by statute to review each sentence of death and determine whether it was imposed under the influence of passion or prejudice, whether the evidence supports the jury's finding of a statutory aggravating circumstance, and whether the sentence is disproportionate compared to those sentences imposed in similar cases.

In short, Georgia's new sentencing procedures require as a prerequisite to the imposition of the death penalty, specific jury findings as to the circumstances of the crime or the character of the defendant. Moreover, to guard further against a situation comparable to that presented in *Furman*, the Supreme Court of Georgia compares each death sentence with the sentences imposed on similarly situated defendants to ensure that the sentence of death in a particular case is not disproportionate. On their face these procedures seem to satisfy the concerns of *Furman*. No longer should there be "no meaningful basis for distinguishing the few cases in which [the death penalty] is imposed from the many cases in which it is not.". . . .

The basic concern of *Furman* centered on those defendants who were being condemned to death capriciously and arbitrarily. Under the procedures before the Court in that case, sentencing authorities were not directed to give attention to the nature or circumstances of the crime committed or to the character or record of the defendant. Left unguided, juries imposed the death sentence in a way that could only be called freakish. The new Georgia sentencing procedures, by contrast, focus the jury's attention on the particularized nature of the crime and the particularized characteristics of the individual defendant. While the jury is permitted to consider any aggravating or mitigating circumstances, it must find and identify at least one statutory aggravating factor before it may impose a penalty of death. In this way the jury's discretion is channeled. No longer can a jury wantonly and freakishly impose the death sentence; it is always circumscribed by the legislative guidelines. In addition, the review function of the Supreme Court of Georgia affords additional assurance that the concerns that prompted our decision in *Furman* are not present to any significant degree in the Georgia procedure applied here.

For the reasons expressed in this opinion, we hold that the statutory system under which Gregg was sentenced to death does not violate the Constitution. Accordingly, the judgment of the Georgia Supreme Court is affirmed.

MR. JUSTICE WHITE, with whom THE CHIEF JUSTICE and MR. JUSTICE REHNQUIST join, concurring in the judgment.

In *Furman v. Georgia* (1972), this Court held the death penalty as then administered in Georgia to be unconstitutional. That same year the Georgia Legislature enacted a new statutory scheme under which the death penalty may be imposed for several offenses, including murder. The issue in this case is whether the death penalty imposed for murder on petitioner Gregg under the new Georgia statutory scheme may constitutionally be carried out. I agree that it may. . . .

The threshold question in this case is whether the death penalty may be carried out for murder under the Georgia legislative scheme consistent with the decision in *Furman v. Georgia.* In *Furman,* this Court held that as a result of giving the sentencer unguided discretion to impose or not to impose the death penalty for murder, the penalty was being imposed discriminatorily, wantonly and freakishly, and so infrequently that any given death sentence was cruel and unusual. Petitioner argues that, as in *Furman,* the jury is still the sentencer; that the statutory criteria to be considered by the jury on the issue of sentence under Georgia's new statutory scheme are vague and do not purport to be all-inclusive; and that, in any event, there are *no* circumstances under which the jury is required to impose the death penalty. Consequently, the petitioner argues that the death penalty will inexorably be imposed in as discriminatory, standardless, and rare a manner as it was imposed under the scheme declared invalid in *Furman.*

The argument is considerably overstated. . . . The Georgia Legislature has plainly made an effort to guide the jury in the exercise of its discretion, while at the same time permitting the jury to dispense mercy on the basis of factors too intangible to write into a statute, and I cannot accept the naked assertion that the effort is bound to fail. As the types of murders for which the death penalty may be imposed become more narrowly defined and are limited to those which are particularly serious or for which the death penalty is peculiarly appropriate as they are in Georgia by reason of the aggravating-circumstance requirement, it becomes reasonable to expect that juries—even given discretion *not* to impose the death penalty—will impose the death penalty in a substantial portion of the cases so

defined. If they do, it can no longer be said that the penalty is being imposed wantonly and freakishly or so infrequently that it loses its usefulness as a sentencing device. There is, therefore, reason to expect that Georgia's current system would escape the infirmities which invalidated its previous system under *Furman.* However, the Georgia Legislature was not satisfied with a system which might, but also might not, turn out in practice to result in death sentences being imposed with reasonable consistency for certain serious murders. Instead, it gave the Georgia Supreme Court the power and the obligation to perform precisely the task which three Justices of this Court, whose opinions were necessary to the result, performed in *Furman:* namely, the task of deciding whether in fact the death penalty was being administered for any given class of crime in a discriminatory, standardless, or rare fashion.

. . . Indeed, if the Georgia Supreme Court properly performs the task assigned to it under the Georgia statutes, death sentences imposed for discriminatory reasons or wantonly or freakishly for any given category of crime will be set aside. Petitioner has wholly failed to establish, and has not even attempted to establish, that the Georgia Supreme Court failed properly to perform its task in this case or that it is incapable of performing its task adequately in all cases; and this Court should not assume that it did not do so.

MR. JUSTICE BRENNAN, dissenting.

My opinion in *Furman v. Georgia* concluded that . . . the punishment of death, for whatever crime and under all circumstances, is "cruel and unusual" in violation of the Eighth and Fourteenth Amendments of the Constitution. I shall not again canvass the reasons that led to that conclusion. I emphasize only that foremost among the "moral concepts" recognized in our cases and inherent in the Clause is the primary moral principle that the State, even as it punishes, must treat its citizens in a manner consistent with their intrinsic worth as human beings—a punishment must not be so severe as to be degrading to human dignity. A judicial determination whether the punishment of death comports with human dignity is therefore not only permitted but compelled by the Clause.

I do not understand that the Court disagrees that "[i]n

comparison to all other punishments today . . . the deliberate extinguishment of human life by the State is uniquely degrading to human dignity." For three of my Brethren hold today that mandatory infliction of the death penalty constitutes the penalty cruel and unusual punishment. I perceive no principled basis for this limitation. Death for whatever crime and under all circumstances "is truly an awesome punishment. The calculated killing of a human being by the State involves, by its very nature, a denial of the executed person's humanity. . . . An executed person has indeed 'lost the right to have rights.'" Death is not only an unusually severe punishment, unusual in its pain, in its finality, and in its enormity, but it serves no penal purpose more effectively than a less severe punishment; therefore the principle inherent in the Clause that prohibits pointless infliction of excessive punishment when less severe punishment can adequately achieve the same purposes invalidates the punishment.

The fatal constitutional infirmity in the punishment of death is that it treats "members of the human race as nonhumans, as objects to be toyed with and discarded. [It is] thus inconsistent with the fundamental premise of the Clause that even the vilest criminal remains a human being possessed of common human dignity." As such it is a penalty that "subjects the individual to a fate forbidden by the principle of civilized treatment guaranteed by the [Clause]." I therefore would hold, on that ground alone, that death is today a cruel and unusual punishment prohibited by the Clause.

MR. JUSTICE MARSHALL, dissenting.

In *Furman v. Georgia* (1972) (concurring opinion), I set forth at some length my views on the basic issue presented to the Court in these cases. The death penalty, I concluded, is a cruel and unusual punishment prohibited by the Eighth and Fourteenth Amendments. That continues to be my view.

I have no intention of retracing the "long and tedious journey," that led to my conclusion in *Furman*. My sole purposes here are to consider the suggestion that my conclusion in *Furman* has been undercut by developments since then, and briefly to evaluate the basis for my Brethren's holding that the extinction of life is a permissible form of punishment under the Cruel and Unusual Punishments Clause.

In *Furman* I concluded that the death penalty is constitutionally invalid for two reasons. First, the death penalty is excessive. And second, the American people, fully informed as to the purposes of the death penalty and its liabilities, would in my view reject it as morally unacceptable.

Since the decision in *Furman*, the legislatures of 35 States have enacted new statutes authorizing the imposition of the death sentence for certain crimes, and Congress has enacted a law providing the death penalty for air piracy resulting in death. I would be less than candid if I did not acknowledge that these developments have a significant bearing on a realistic assessment of the moral acceptability of the death penalty to the American people. But if the constitutionality of the death penalty turns, as I have urged, on the opinion of an informed citizenry, then even the enactment of new death statutes cannot be viewed as conclusive. In *Furman*, I observed that the American people are largely unaware of the information critical to a judgment on the morality of the death penalty, and concluded that if they were better informed they would consider it shocking, unjust, and unacceptable. A recent study, conducted after the enactment of the post-*Furman* statutes, has confirmed that the American people know little about the death penalty, and that the opinions of an informed public would differ significantly from those of a public unaware of the consequences and effects of the death penalty.

Even assuming, however, that the post-*Furman* enactment of statutes authorizing the death penalty renders the prediction of the views of an informed citizenry an uncertain basis for a constitutional decision, the enactment of those statutes has no bearing whatsoever on the conclusion that the death penalty is unconstitutional because it is excessive. An excessive penalty is invalid under the Cruel and Unusual Punishments Clause "even though popular sentiment may favor." The inquiry here, then, is simply whether the death penalty is necessary to accomplish the legitimate legislative purposes in punishment, or whether a less severe penalty—life imprisonment—would do as well.

The two purposes that sustain the death penalty as nonexcessive in the Court's view are general deterrence and retribution. In *Furman*, I canvassed the relevant data on the deterrent effect of capital punishment. . . . The available evidence, I concluded in *Furman*, was convincing that "capital punishment is not necessary as a deterrent to crime in our society.". . .

The evidence I reviewed in *Furman* remains convincing, in my view, that "capital punishment is not necessary as a deterrent to crime in our society." The justification for the death penalty must be found elsewhere.

The other principal purpose said to be served by the death penalty is retribution. The notion that retribution can serve as a moral justification for the sanction of death finds credence in the opinion of my Brothers STEWART, POWELL, AND STEVENS, and that of my Brother WHITE. . . . See also *Furman v. Georgia* (BURGER, C.J., dissenting). It is this notion that I find to be the most disturbing aspect of today's unfortunate decisions.

The concept of retribution is a multifaceted one, and any discussion of its role in the criminal law must be undertaken with caution. On one level, it can be said that the notion of retribution or reprobation is the basis of our insistence that only those who have broken the law be punished, and in this sense the notion is quite obviously central to a just system of criminal sanctions. But our recognition that retribution plays a crucial role in determining who may be punished by no means requires approval of retribution as a general justification for punishment. It is the question whether retribution can provide a moral justification for punishment—in particular, capital punishment—that we must consider.

My Brothers STEWART, POWELL, AND STEVENS, offer the following explanation of the retributive justification for capital punishment:

"'The instinct for retribution is part of the nature of man, and channeling that instinct in the administration of criminal justice serves an important purpose in promoting the stability of a society governed by law. When people begin to believe that organized society is unwilling or unable to impose upon criminal offenders the punishment they "deserve," then there are sown the seeds of anarchy—of self-help, vigilante justice, and lynch law."

This statement is wholly inadequate to justify the death penalty. As my Brother BRENNAN stated in *Furman*,

"[t]here is no evidence whatever that utilization of imprisonment rather than death encourages private blood feuds and other disorders." It simply defies belief to suggest that the death penalty is necessary to prevent the American people from taking the law into their own hands. . . . The death penalty, unnecessary to promote the goal of deterrence or to further any legitimate notion of retribution, is an excessive penalty forbidden by the Eighth and Fourteenth Amendments. I respectfully dissent from the Court's judgment upholding the sentences of death imposed upon the petitioners in these cases.

Despite the many opinions in *Gregg*, the majority of justices agreed that the Georgia law was constitutional; indeed, some members of the Court referred to it as a model death penalty scheme. But what accounts for the abrupt change in the law between *Furman* and *Gregg*? Given that some scholars and even justices thought that *Furman* had brought an end to capital punishment, this about-face is all the more puzzling.[16] Analysts offer several explanations. Some point to the membership change on the Court that occurred between the two cases: William Douglas, who had voted with the five-person *Furman* majority, had been replaced by John Paul Stevens, who voted with the seven-person *Gregg* majority.

Other explanations focus on the shift in the political environment between 1972 and 1976. As Figure 17-1 shows, public opinion became more supportive of capital punishment. Around the time of the *Furman* decision, Americans were relatively divided on the issue. By November 1972, the number of respondents in favor of capital punishment had jumped by 7 percentage points; by 1974, roughly two-thirds of Americans supported legal executions. Given this trend in public opinion, state legislators could barely wait to reconvene after *Furman* and pass new laws designed to limit arbitrariness in sentencing. Indeed, almost every

16. We derive this discussion from Epstein and Kobylka, *The Supreme Court and Legal Change*, chap. 4.

FIGURE 17-1 Support for Capital Punishment, 1971–1991

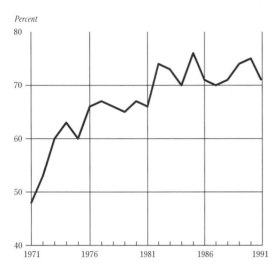

Percent

DATA SOURCES: Harold W. Stanley and Richard G. Niemi, *Vital Statistics on American Politics*, 4th ed. (Washington, D.C.: CQ Press, 1994), 33; Lee Epstein, Jeffrey A. Segal, Harold J. Spaeth, and Thomas G. Walker, *The Supreme Court Compendium: Data, Decisions, and Developments* (Washington, D.C.: Congressional Quarterly, 1994), Table 8-6.

state that had a death penalty prior to *Furman* had reinstated it prior to 1976. And the national government even got into the act. The day after *Furman* came down, President Nixon seized on Burger's dissent in noting that the Court had not completely ruled out capital punishment. He subsequently sent to Congress a bill calling for the death penalty in certain federal crimes.

It is not surprising that some scholars suggest that the Court merely succumbed to public pressure in this area: Americans wanted the death penalty and the justices caved in, or so the argument goes. Even Justice Marshall, in his *Gregg* dissent, acknowledged that post-*Furman* "developments have a significant bearing on a realistic assessment of the moral acceptability of the death penalty to the American people." (But recall that he also maintained that "the American people are largely unaware of the information critical to a

judgment on the morality of the death penalty, and . . . if they were better informed they would consider it shocking, unjust, and unacceptable.")

Yet another set of explanations centers on the new laws themselves and the way attorneys tried to challenge them. To put it simply, abolitionist lawyers may have overestimated the degree of their victory in *Furman*. In their arguments to the Court, they asserted that "death is different." But this view was held only by two justices in *Furman*—Brennan and Marshall. Remember that the others, especially White and Stewart, were more concerned with the arbitrariness of death penalty sentencing than with the constitutionality of the death penalty. In the end, as Justice White's concurrence in *Gregg* indicates, abolitionist attorneys were unable to convince the majority that the new laws—which explicitly sought to eliminate arbitrariness in sentencing by limiting jury discretion—were unconstitutional.

Whatever the explanation for the Court's change of heart, the results were clear. Many states adopted Georgia's death penalty law, and executions increased accordingly. During the 1970s, only three people were legally executed in the United States; between 1990 and 1994, that figure was 159.

In the Aftermath of Gregg

In some ways, *Gregg* settled the death penalty issue: the Court asserted that capital punishment did not violate the Constitution, a position to which it still adheres. But opponents of the death penalty have not given up. They have continued to bring lawsuits, many of which have been aimed at narrowing the application of capital punishment. In other words, this litigation has challenged procedural practices adopted by the states, not the constitutionality of the death penalty.

A good number of these procedural cases involved this question: What factors should sentencers consider in their deliberations? Occasionally, the Court has

Warren McCleskey based the appeal of his death sentence on a study showing that someone convicted for killing a white person was four times more likely to receive the death penalty than someone convicted for killing a black person. His appeal was rejected in *McCleskey v. Kemp* (1987), and he was executed in 1991.

ruled for defendants in these disputes; in *Eddings v. Oklahoma* (1982) it held that a trial court judge could not refuse to hear mitigating evidence pointing to the defendant's youth, troubled childhood, and history of mental problems. But the Court generally has taken a pro–death penalty posture in post-*Gregg* disputes.

A prime example is *McCleskey v. Kemp* (1987), which some observers consider the most significant capital punishment case since *Gregg*. The case began on May 13, 1978, when Warren McCleskey, a black man, and three accomplices attempted to rob a furniture store in Atlanta, Georgia. One of the employees hit a silent alarm button, which was answered by a white, thirty-one-year-old police officer. As the officer entered the store, he was shot and killed. Several

weeks later, when police arrested him on another charge, McCleskey confessed to the robbery. At his trial, McCleskey was identified by one of the accomplices as the individual who killed the officer. The prosecution also entered evidence indicating that McCleskey had bragged about the shooting.

Three months after the robbery, a jury of eleven whites and one black convicted McCleskey and sentenced him to death. At that point, the NAACP LDF took over his defense. The LDF based its appeal in the federal courts on a 1986 study showing that blacks convicted of murdering whites received death sentences at disproportionately high rates. The study centered on a statistical examination by several professors of the application of Georgia's death penalty.[17] Named after one of the researchers, David Baldus, the study was based on data consisting of 2,484 Georgia murder cases from 1973 to 1979, coded for some 230 variables. To analyze this mammoth amount of data, Baldus used a multivariate technique, which allows researchers to demonstrate the effects of possible explanatory variables (such as the race of the defendant or victim) on outcomes (such as the decision to sentence to death).[18]

Baldus's conclusions were dramatic. Among the most noteworthy were the following:

–The chances of receiving a death sentence were 4.3 times greater for defendants whose victims were white than for defendants whose victims were black.

–Of the 128 cases in which death was imposed, 87 percent (108) involved white victims.

–Prosecutors sought the death penalty in 70 percent of cases involving black defendants and white victims, but in only 32 percent in which both the defendant and the victim were white.

–Black defendants were 1.1 times more likely than other defendants to receive death sentences.

17. We adopt this discussion from ibid.. 123–125.

18. For more on this study, see David Baldus, George G. Woodworth, and Charles Pulaski, *Equal Justice and the Death Penalty* (Boston: Northeastern University Press, 1990).

Armed with this study, the LDF tried to convince the justices once and for all that the disparate application of death penalty laws led to unacceptable violations of the Equal Protection and Due Process Clauses.

The Supreme Court rejected the LDF's argument. McCleskey, the majority found, relied too heavily on the general statistics of the Baldus study and had failed to prove that there was purposeful discrimination in his case. Justice Powell wrote:

At most, the Baldus study indicates a discrepancy that appears to correlate with race. Apparent disparities in sentencing are an inevitable part of our criminal justice system.... Despite these imperfections, our consistent rule has been that constitutional guarantees are met when "the mode [for determining guilt or punishment] itself has been surrounded with safeguards to make it as fair as possible." Where the discretion that is fundamental to our criminal process is involved, we decline to assume that what is unexplained is invidious. In light of the safeguards designed to minimize racial bias in the process, the fundamental value of jury trial in our criminal justice system, and the benefits that discretion provides to criminal defendants, we hold that the Baldus study does not demonstrate a constitutionally significant risk of racial bias affecting the Georgia capital-sentencing process.

Before the Court handed down McCleskey, some observers speculated that if the justices had agreed with the LDF, they might have found that capital punishment was an inherently arbitrary form of punishment which could never be imposed fairly. Such a decision would have, in effect, resurrected Furman. But it was not to be. Although McCleskey divided the justices, the majority of the Court upheld the constitutionality of the death penalty. In short, the LDF's ace in the hole, the Baldus study, did not ensure victory.

Since the 1987 McCleskey decision the prospects for the abolition of the death penalty have grown dimmer. Justices Marshall and Brennan, the two most consistent opponents of the death penalty, left the Court. Justice Blackmun, who joined Brennan and Marshall in dissent in McCleskey, also stepped down.

Presidents Bush and Clinton, both supporters of the death penalty, certainly did not seek replacements who expressed firm opposition to capital punishment. Justice Steven Breyer, appointed by President Clinton in 1994, for example, expressed the view at his confirmation hearings that the death penalty was "settled law."

Breyer may well have been correct. Justices who hold that the death penalty is not unconstitutional are in the majority, and prospects for major changes in this area are negligible. This does not mean, however, that the members of the Court do not have fierce disagreements over the issue. Consider the material in Box 17-1. It presents a 1994 exchange between Justices Blackmun and Scalia over the death penalty. The debate between the two shows the intellectual and emotional fire that the death penalty sparks within the Court.

POST-TRIAL STAGES

Individuals convicted of crimes can appeal their convictions in the hope that appellate judges will find errors in the trial court's handling of the case. Under the American concept of due process, someone convicted of a criminal offense is entitled to at least one appeal. A new trial might be granted if new evidence is discovered that brings into serious question the guilt of the defendant, although such instances are rare.

An additional guarantee governing the post-trial stage is the Fifth Amendment's ban against double jeopardy: "nor shall any person be subject for the same offence to be twice put in jeopardy of life or limb." The clause reflected the Framers' belief that it is essentially unfair for any person to be tried twice for the same criminal charge. The government should have one attempt, and one attempt only, to convince a jury that the accused is guilty. A person who already has been acquitted of an offense by a court of law cannot be tried a second time for that same offense. Also,

BOX 17-1   JUSTICES BLACKMUN AND SCALIA ON THE
DEATH PENALTY

Below are excerpts from Justice Blackmun's dissent from the Court's denial of review in *Callins v. Collins* (1994) and Justice Scalia's response.

JUSTICE BLACKMUN

On February 23, 1994, at approximately 1:00 A.M., Bruce Edwin Callins will be executed by the State of Texas. Intravenous tubes attached to his arms will carry the instrument of death, a toxic fluid designed specifically for the purpose of killing human beings. The witnesses, standing a few feet away, will behold Callins, no longer a defendant, an appellant or a petitioner, but a man, strapped to a gurney, and seconds away from extinction.

Within days, or perhaps hours, the memory of Callins will begin to fade. The wheels of justice will churn again, and somewhere, another jury or another judge will have the unenviable task of determining whether some human being is to live or die. We hope, of course, that the defendant whose life is at risk will be represented by competent counsel— someone who is inspired by the awareness that a less-than-vigorous defense truly could have fatal consequences for the defendant. We hope that the attorney will investigate all aspects of the case, follow all evidentiary and procedural rules, and appear before a judge who is still committed to the protection of defendants' rights—even now, as the prospect of meaningful judicial oversight has diminished. In the same vein, we hope that the prosecution, in urging the penalty of death, will have exercised its discretion wisely, free from bias, prejudice, or political motive, and will be humbled, rather than emboldened, by the awesome authority conferred by the State.

But even if we can feel confident that these actors will fulfill their roles to the best of their human ability, our collective conscience will remain uneasy. Twenty years have passed since this Court declared that the death penalty must be imposed fairly, and with reasonable consistency, or not at all, see *Furman v. Georgia* (1972), and, despite the effort of the States and courts to devise legal formulas and procedural rules to meet this daunting challenge, the death penalty remains fraught with arbitrariness, discrimination, caprice, and mistake....

... Having virtually conceded that both fairness and rationality cannot be achieved in the administration of the death penalty, see *McCleskey v. Kemp* (1987), the Court has chosen to deregulate the entire enterprise, replacing, it would seem, substantive constitutional requirements with mere aesthetics, and abdicating its statutorily and constitutionally imposed duty to provide meaningful judicial oversight to the administration of death by the States.

From this day forward, I no longer shall tinker with the machinery of death. For more than 20 years I have endeavored—indeed, I have struggled—along with a majority of this Court, to develop procedural and substantive rules that would lend more than the mere appearance of fairness to the death penalty endeavor. Rather than continue to coddle the Court's delusion that the desired level of fairness has been achieved and the need for regulation eviscerated, I feel morally and intellectually obligated simply to concede that the death penalty experiment has failed. It is virtually self-evident to me now that no combination of procedural rules or substantive regulations ever can save the death penalty from its inherent constitutional deficiencies. The basic question—does the system accurately and consistently determine which defendants "deserve" to die?—cannot be answered in the affirmative.... The problem is that the inevitability of factual, legal, and moral error gives us a system that we know must wrongly kill some defendants, a system that fails to deliver the fair, consistent, and reliable sentences of death required by the Constitution....

There is little doubt now that *Furman's* essential holding was correct. Although most of the public seems to desire, and the Constitution appears to permit, the penalty of death, it surely is beyond dispute that if the death penalty cannot be administered consistently and rationally, it may not be administered at all....

Delivering on the *Furman* promise, however, has proved to be another matter. *Furman* aspired to eliminate the vestiges of racism and the effects of poverty in capital sentencing; it deplored the "wanton" and "random" infliction of death by a government with constitutionally limited power. *Furman* demanded that the sentencer's discretion be directed and limited by procedural rules and objective standards in order to minimize the risk of arbitrary and capricious sentences of death.

In the years following Furman, serious efforts were made to comply with its mandate. State legislatures and appellate courts struggled to provide judges and juries with sensible and objective guidelines for determining who should live and who should die....

Unfortunately, all this experimentation and ingenuity yielded little of what Furman demanded. It soon became apparent that discretion could not be eliminated from capital sentencing without threatening the fundamental fairness due a defendant when life is at stake....

Perhaps one day this Court will develop procedural rules or verbal formulas that actually will provide consistency, fairness, and reliability in a capital-sentencing scheme. I am not optimistic that such a day will come. I am more optimistic, though, that this Court eventually will conclude that the effort to eliminate arbitrariness while preserving fairness "in the infliction of (death) is so plainly doomed to failure that it and the death penalty must be abandoned altogether." I may not live to see that day, but I have faith that eventually it will arrive. The path the Court has chosen lessens us all. I dissent.

JUSTICE SCALIA

Convictions in opposition to the death penalty are often passionate and deeply held. That would be no excuse for reading them into a Constitution that does not contain them, even if they represented the convictions of a majority of Americans. Much less is there any excuse for using that course to thrust a minority's views upon the people. JUSTICE BLACKMUN begins his statement by describing with poignancy the death of a convicted murderer by lethal injection. He chooses, as the case in which to make that statement, one of the less brutal of the murders that regularly come before us—the murder of a man ripped by a bullet suddenly and unexpectedly, with no opportunity to prepare himself and his affairs, and left to bleed to death on the floor of a tavern. The death-by-injection which JUSTICE BLACKMUN describes looks pretty desirable next to that. It looks even better next to some of the other cases currently before us, which JUSTICE BLACKMUN did not select as the vehicle for his announcement that the death penalty is always unconstitutional—for example, the case of the 11-year-old girl raped by four men and then killed by stuffing her panties down her throat.... How enviable a quiet death by lethal injection compared with that! If the people conclude that such more brutal deaths may be deterred by capital punishment; indeed, if they merely conclude that justice requires such brutal deaths to be avenged by capital punishment; the creation of false, untextual and unhistorical contradictions within "the Court's Eighth Amendment jurisprudence" should not prevent them.

the government cannot prosecute a convicted person a second time in the hope of obtaining a more severe sentence. Once a trial on a given criminal charge is completed, the defendant is protected against any subsequent trial on that charge that might lead to more adverse consequences.

A great deal of the confusion surrounding the Double Jeopardy Clause stems from the words "same offence." If a man sets fire to an apartment building, killing five residents, has he committed one homicide or five? If a man spends an evening robbing a series of liquor stores, has he committed a single offense or several? What does the Double Jeopardy Clause mean when it prohibits trying a person more than once for the same offense? We find a partial answer in *Ashe v. Swenson* (1970). Here a group of individuals playing poker one night were robbed by three or four masked men. Several months later Bob Ashe was charged with the robbery. The prosecutor first placed him on trial for robbing one of the card players. The jury found him not guilty because of insufficient evidence. Then the prosecutor charged him with robbing a second poker player. Ashe objected, claiming the second trial would violate the Double Jeopardy Clause. On appeal the Supreme Court agreed. The robbing of the poker party was a single act, and once acquitted of robbing the first poker player, Ashe could not be tried for robbing another member of the group that same evening. In Justice Stewart's words, the Fifth Amendment "surely protects a man who has been acquitted from having to 'run the gauntlet' a second time."

READINGS

Baldus, David C., George G. Woodworth, and Charles A. Pulaski, Jr. *Equal Justice and the Death Penalty.* Boston: Northeastern University Press, 1990.

Eisenstein, James, and Herbert Jacob. *Felony Justice.* Boston: Little, Brown, 1977.

Epstein, Lee, and Joseph F. Kobylka. *The Supreme Court and Legal Change.* Chapel Hill: University of North Carolina Press, 1992.

Hastie, Reid, Steven D. Penrod, and Nancy Pennington. *Inside the Jury.* Cambridge: Harvard University Press, 1983.

Heumann, Milton. *Plea Bargaining.* Chicago: University of Chicago Press, 1978.

Kalven, Harry, Jr., and Hans Zeisel. *The American Jury.* Boston: Little, Brown, 1966.

Lewis, Anthony. *Gideon's Trumpet.* New York: Vintage Books, 1964.

Meltsner, Michael. *Cruel and Unusual: The Supreme Court and Capital Punishment.* New York: Random House, 1973.

Sigler, Jay A. *Double Jeopardy: The Development of Legal and Social Policy.* Ithaca, N.Y.: Cornell University Press, 1969.

Simon, Rita James. *The Jury: Its Role in American Society.* Lexington, Mass.: Lexington Books, 1980.

Way, Frank H. *Criminal Justice and the American Constitution.* North Scituate, Mass.: Duxbury Press, 1980.

Wishman, Seymour. *Confessions of a Criminal Lawyer.* New York: Penguin Books, 1982.

PART VII
CIVIL RIGHTS

CIVIL RIGHTS AND THE CONSTITUTION

18. DISCRIMINATION

19. VOTING AND REPRESENTATION

CIVIL RIGHTS AND THE CONSTITUTION

I N MARKED CONTRAST to the colonial period, in which most Americans had British roots, today the citizens of the United States have many different backgrounds. Immigration has diversified the population, and this trend is expected to continue. Americans are a people of wide-ranging religions, races, ethnic backgrounds, and levels of wealth. The slogan, "e pluribus unum" or "one from many," often appears to be more of a challenge than a statement of fact. In spite of the differences, however, the nation has pledged itself to fairness and equality. All Americans are to be free from unconstitutional discrimination, to have equal opportunity, and to participate fully in the political process.

Many times people feel they have been mistreated by government policies or by the actions of public officials, not because of what they have done but because of who they are. They claim that discrimination has occurred because of race, creed, national origin, sex, economic status, or some other characteristic that government should not use as a basis for policy. When disputes arise, the court system provides a venue for their resolution. In this part, we discuss the civil rights of Americans and how the Supreme Court has interpreted them. By civil rights we mean the legal provisions that emanate from the concept of equality. Unlike civil liberties issues, which focus on personal

freedoms protected by the Bill of Rights, civil rights issues involve the status of persons with shared characteristics who historically have been disadvantaged in some way. Civil rights laws attempt to guarantee full and equal citizenship for such persons and to protect them from arbitrary and capricious treatment. Chapter 18 examines discrimination, and Chapter 19 discusses the rights of political participation. Before we confront those subjects, however, a review of some basic concepts of history and law might be useful.

THE CONSTITUTION AND THE CONCEPT OF EQUALITY

Americans have become accustomed to hearing not only about charges of discrimination, but also about Supreme Court rulings on the proper meaning of the Constitution with regard to such issues. A general concern about such matters is comparatively recent. Although "equality" in the United States was relatively advanced from the beginning, colonial Americans discriminated in a number of ways that people today consider abhorrent. The most significant breach of fundamental equality was the institution of slavery. Notwithstanding the Declaration of Independence, which proclaimed all men to be created equal, the enslavement of Africans brought to North

America against their will was politically accepted, although not universally supported. The Constitution recognized this form of inequality, stipulating in Article I that a slave would be counted as three-fifths of a person for representation purposes; it also gave slavery a degree of protection by prohibiting any federal restrictions on the importation of slaves until 1808. Other forms of discrimination were also common. Voting qualifications, for example, were quite restrictive: only men could vote, and in some states only men who owned property.

Guarantees of equality did not officially become part of the Constitution until after the Civil War. When the Radical Republicans took control of the legislative branch, three constitutional amendments were proposed and ratified that would change dramatically the concept of civil rights in the United States. These amendments, the Thirteenth, Fourteenth, and Fifteenth, are generally referred to as the Civil War Amendments (*see Box VII-1*). They incorporated into the Constitution what had been won on the battlefield.

The Thirteenth Amendment was ratified in 1865. The language of the amendment unambiguously ended the institution of slavery. Although there have been some disputes over the prohibition of involuntary servitude (in relation, for example, to the military draft), the slavery issue, over which the nation had been divided since the Constitutional Convention, was finally put to rest.

The Fourteenth Amendment is unlike the other two because of its length and complexity. The first section is the most significant. In that passage, United States citizenship is accorded superior status to state citizenship, constitutionally reinforcing the Civil War outcome of national superiority over states' rights. This idea was a dramatic change from the pre–Civil War concept that national citizenship was dependent upon state citizenship. The first section also includes the Due Process and Privileges and Immunities Clauses we have discussed in earlier chapters, as well as the Equal Protection Clause, which forms the basis of constitutional protections against discrimination. The remaining sections of the Fourteenth Amendment require the former slaves to be fully counted for representational purposes, impose universal adult male suffrage, restrict the civil rights of certain participants in the rebellion, and guarantee the public debt resulting from the war. The amendment was ratified in 1868.

The Fifteenth Amendment removed race as a condition by which the right to vote could be denied. Unlike the Thirteenth Amendment, which was almost self-executing, the policy expressed so clearly in the Fifteenth Amendment in 1870 did not become a reality until almost a century later. Stubborn resistance by the southern states denied black citizens full participatory rights. It was not until the 1960s, when the nation renewed its commitment to civil rights, that equality in voting rights was substantially achieved.

Although the nation's leaders seemed unshakably committed to equality right after the Civil War, they soon turned their attention to other matters. Issues ranging from political corruption to the nation's industrialization moved to the top of the political agenda. At the same time, the white power structure of the prewar South began to reassert itself. Although forced to accept the Civil War Amendments as a condition of rejoining the union, the southern states survived Reconstruction and, once freed from the direct supervision of their victors, began to reinstitute discriminatory laws. Slavery was never again seriously considered, but, in its place, racial segregation became the official policy. For years the federal legislative and executive branches showed little interest in pursuing civil rights issues, and the Supreme Court dealt with such matters only on occasion. It was not until the civil rights movement gained momentum in the 1960s that the nation again turned its attention to freedom from discrimination and full participatory rights for all.

BOX VII-1   THE CIVIL WAR AMENDMENTS

AMENDMENT 13
(Ratified December 6, 1865)

SECTION 1. Neither slavery nor involuntary servitude, except as a punishment for crime whereof the party shall have been duly convicted, shall exist within the United States, or any place subject to their jurisdiction.

SECTION 2. Congress shall have power to enforce this article by appropriate legislation.

AMENDMENT 14
(Ratified July 9, 1868)

SECTION 1. All persons born or naturalized in the United States, and subject to the jurisdiction thereof, are citizens of the United States and of the State wherein they reside. No State shall make or enforce any law which shall abridge the privileges or immunities of citizens of the United States; nor shall any State deprive any person of life, liberty, or property, without due process of law; nor deny to any person within its jurisdiction the equal protection of the laws.

SECTION 2. Representatives shall be apportioned among the several States according to their respective numbers, counting the whole number of persons in each State, excluding Indians not taxed. But when the right to vote at any election for the choice of electors for President and Vice President of the United States, Representatives in Congress, the Executive and Judicial officers of a State, or the members of the Legislature thereof, is denied to any of the male inhabitants of such State, being twenty-one years of age, and citizens of the United States, or in any way abridged, except for participation in rebellion, or other crime, the basis of representation therein shall be reduced in the proportion which the number of such male citizens shall bear to the whole number of male citizens twenty-one years of age in such State.

SECTION 3. No person shall be a Senator or Representative in Congress, or elector of President or Vice President, or hold any office, civil or military, under the United States, or under any State, who, having previously taken an oath, as a member of Congress, or as an officer of the United States, or as a member of any State legislature, or as an executive or judicial officer to any State, to support the Constitution of the United States, shall have engaged in insurrection or rebellion against the same, or given aid or comfort to the enemies thereof. But Congress may by a vote of two-thirds of each House, remove such disability.

SECTION 4. The validity of the public debt of the United States, authorized by law, including debts incurred for payment of pensions and bounties for services in suppressing insurrection or rebellion, shall not be questioned. But neither the United States nor any State shall assume or pay any debt or obligation incurred in aid of insurrection or rebellion against the United States, or claim for the loss or emancipation of any slave; but all such debts, obligations and claims shall be held illegal and void.

SECTION 5. The Congress shall have power to enforce, by appropriate legislation, the provisions of this article.

AMENDMENT 15
(Ratified February 3, 1870)

SECTION 1. The rights of the citizens of the United States to vote shall not be denied or abridged by the United States or by any State on account of race, color, or previous condition of servitude.

SECTION 2. The Congress shall have power to enforce this article by appropriate legislation.

THE SUPREME COURT AND EQUAL PROTECTION OF THE LAWS

The Equal Protection Clause of the Fourteenth Amendment is the Constitution's most important passage with respect to issues of discrimination. An analysis of the wording of this brief provision will help us understand what it covers and what its limitations are. It says, "[N]or shall any State . . . deny to any person within its jurisdiction the equal protection of the laws."

The first significant element of the clause is the word *state*. The members of Congress who drafted the Fourteenth Amendment were concerned primarily that the states (especially those in the South) would impose discriminatory laws. Since the Radical Republicans, who were deeply committed to an abolition ideology, had complete control of Congress, the legislators were not afraid that the federal government would impose discriminatory policies. Consequently, the prohibitions of the clause apply only to the states and their political subdivisions, such as counties and cities.

Second, the amendment protects all persons within a state's jurisdiction. Although the authors of the amendment were primarily interested in the treatment of former slaves, the wording of the amendment is not restricted to them. Quite early in the history of disputes over the amendment, the Supreme Court acknowledged its broad applicability. In *Yick Wo v. Hopkins* (1886), a dispute over the enforcement of fire safety regulations in San Francisco, the Court held that the Equal Protection Clause applies to persons other than black Americans, including noncitizens who are the target of discrimination by the state.

Finally, the clause outlaws a denial of equal protection of the laws; in other words, it prohibits discrimination. Any person within a state's jurisdiction is constitutionally entitled to be treated equitably, to be free from arbitrary and unreasonable treatment at the hands of the state government.

The wording of the Equal Protection Clause means that before an individual can legitimately assert a claim that the clause has been violated, two important elements must be demonstrated. First, the aggrieved party must prove some form of unequal treatment or discrimination. Second, there must be state action; that is, the discrimination must have been initiated or supported by the state or its local governments. These two requirements have undergone substantial interpretation by the justices of the Supreme Court, and we need to understand what is included in each requirement.

Discrimination

Discrimination simply means distinguishing between people or things. It occurs in many forms, not all of which are prohibited by the Constitution. For example, in administering an admissions program, a state university must discriminate among its applicants. It admits some, rejects others. Decisions usually are based on an applicant's high school grades, standardized test scores, and letters of recommendation. The university admits those who, based on valid predictors of performance, have the best chance to succeed. Those who are rejected usually accept the decision because the university's admissions criteria appear reasonable. But the reaction would be quite different if an applicant received a letter that said, "In spite of your demonstrated potential for college studies, we cannot admit you because of our policy not to accept students of your ethnic background." In this case, the rejected applicant would rightly feel victimized by unreasonable discrimination.

What rule of law distinguishes acceptable discrimination from that which violates the Constitution? The Supreme Court answered this question by declaring that the Equal Protection Clause goes no further than prohibiting "invidious discrimination."[1] By invidious discrimination, the Court means discrimination that is arbitrary and capricious, unequal treatment that has no rational basis. Reasonable discrimination, on the other hand, is not unconstitutional. When the state treats two individuals differently, we need to ask upon what criteria the state is distinguishing them. What if you had consulted with two surgeons about an operation you might need and you liked both of them. Suddenly one is arrested and put in jail. At first you might be shocked and feel that the imprisoned person had not been treated fairly. But if you learned that this "surgeon" had never been to medical school, your opinion would change. Here the state would be "discriminating" on the basis of legiti-

---

1. See *Williamson v. Lee Optical* (1955).

mate, reasonable criteria. The Equal Protection Clause demands that similarly situated persons be treated equally. The two surgeons, because of their vastly different qualifications, are not similarly situated, and consequently the Constitution does not require that they be treated the same.

Almost every government action involves some form of discrimination. Most are perfectly legitimate, although perhaps not all those affected would agree. For example, when a state government passes an income tax law that imposes a higher rate on the wealthy than it does on the poor (that is, a "progressive" tax), the rich may feel they are the target of unconstitutional discrimination. When individuals believe they have been denied equal protection at the hands of the state, the courts must decide if the government's discrimination runs afoul of the Fourteenth Amendment. For taxes, the courts have ruled that progressive rate structures are not invidious but reasonable.

To assist the judiciary in deciding such disputes, the Supreme Court has developed three basic tests of the Equal Protection Clause. Which test is applied in any given case is determined by the alleged discrimination and the government interests at stake.

The traditional test used to decide discrimination cases is the "rational basis" test. Using this approach to the Constitution, the justices ask: Is the challenged discrimination rational? Or is it arbitrary and capricious? If a state passes a law that says a person must be at least eighteen years old to enter a legally binding contract, it is imposing age-based discrimination. Individuals under eighteen are not granted the right to consummate legal agreements; those over eighteen are. If a dispute over the validity of this law were brought to court, the judge would have to decide whether the state had acted reasonably to achieve a legitimate government objective.[2] Using the rational basis test, the Court generally defers to the state and pre-

sumes the validity of the government's action. The burden of proof rests with the party challenging the law to establish that the statute is irrational. Unless the Court has determined otherwise, discrimination claims proceed according to the rules of the rational basis test.

The second test is the "suspect class" or "strict scrutiny" test. This test is used when the state discriminates on the basis of a criterion that the Supreme Court has declared to be inherently suspect or when there is a claim that a fundamental right has been violated. A suspect classification is based on characteristics assumed to be irrational. The Supreme Court has ruled, for example, that race is a suspect class. Laws that discriminate on racial grounds are given strict scrutiny by the courts. The reason for moving racial discrimination from the rational basis test to the suspect class test is that the Supreme Court has concluded that racial criteria are inherently arbitrary, that compelling state interests are rarely (if ever) served by treating people differently according to race. For a law to be valid under strict scrutiny, it must be found to advance a compelling state interest by the least restrictive means available. When the suspect class test is used, the Court presumes that the state action is unconstitutional, and the burden of proof is on the government to demonstrate that the law is rational.

Given the rules associated with these two tests, it should be obvious that it is much easier to establish that a violation of the Constitution has occurred if the suspect class test is used. Therefore, many cases before the Supreme Court have been filed by attorneys representing groups seeking that classification. The Court has ruled that suspect class status should be accorded only to those groups that constitute discrete and insular minorities that have experienced a history of unequal treatment and a lack of political power.[3] Applying such criteria is difficult and has given rise to sharp divisions of opinion among the justices.

2. See *McGowan v. Maryland* (1961).

3. See *United States v. Carolene Products* (1938); *San Antonio Independent School District v. Rodriguez* (1973).

TABLE VII-1 Equal Protection Tests

Test	Examples of Applicability	Validity Standard
Rational basis test	General discrimination claims	The law must be a *reasonable* measure designed to achieve a *legitimate* government purpose.
Intermediate ("heightened") scrutiny test	Sex discrimination	The law must be *substantially related* to the achievement of an *important* objective.
Suspect class (strict scrutiny) test	Racial discrimination; cases involving fundamental rights (e.g., voting)	The law must be the *least restrictive* means available to achieve a *compelling* state interest.

Legal battles over what rules should apply to sex discrimination cases were particularly difficult for the Court to resolve.[4] A majority could not agree to elevate sex to suspect class status, but there was substantial opinion that the rational basis test was also inappropriate for dealing with sex discrimination. This conflict gave rise to a third test of the Equal Protection Clause, the "intermediate (or heightened) scrutiny" test. This test holds that to be valid the unequal treatment must serve important government objectives and must be substantially related to the achievement of those objectives.[5] As such, this test falls squarely between the rational basis test and the suspect class test *(see Table VII-1)*.

To be sure, this three-tiered approach can be confusing, and the Supreme Court has been neither clear nor consistent in applying the principles. Justice Marshall in *Dunn v. Blumstein* (1972) acknowledged that the tests do not have the "precision of mathematical formulas." Justice White hinted that in reality the Court may be using a spectrum of tests rather than three separate tests. Frustration over the status of the Equal Protection Clause tests prompted Justice Stevens to claim in his concurring opinion in *Cleburne v. Cleburne Living Center* (1985) that a continuum of standards was being used. Not persuaded of the wisdom of the Court's approach, Stevens has argued that

a single test should be adopted for all equal protection claims. In spite of these criticisms, the Court has stuck to the three-tiered approach, which reflects the belief that the more historically disadvantaged and politically powerless a class of people has been, the greater justification government must provide for any state action that discriminates against the members of that class.

State Action

As we have noted, the Equal Protection Clause specifically prohibits discrimination by any state. The Supreme Court has interpreted the concept of discrimination to include a wide array of state actions—statutes, the enforcement and administration of statutes, and the actions of state officials. For example, in *Yick Wo v. Hopkins* the Court struck down a fire safety regulation that was racially neutral as written but was enforced in a discriminatory manner against Chinese laundry operators. State action includes the policies of political subdivisions such as towns, cities, counties, and special purpose agencies. The states may not engage in invidious discrimination either directly or indirectly. A city, for example, may not run its municipal swimming pools in a racially segregated manner, nor may it donate the pools to a private organization that will restrict pool use to a particular racial group.

4. See, for example, *Frontiero v. Richardson* (1973).
5. *Craig v. Boren* (1976).

Some element of state action must be shown before a violation of the Equal Protection Clause occurs. This requirement means that discrimination by purely private individuals or organizations is not prohibited by the Equal Protection Clause. A white apartment house owner who refuses to rent to a black family is not in violation of the Constitution; neither is a restaurant manager who will not serve Hispanics, a private club that will not admit women, nor an employer who will not hire applicants over forty years of age. In each of these cases there is ample evidence of irrational discrimination, but no state action. The discrimination is conducted by private individuals or organizations. These forms of discrimination may well violate any number of state or federal statutes, but they do not offend the Equal Protection Clause of the Fourteenth Amendment.

Moreover, because it is restricted to the states, the Equal Protection Clause does not prohibit the federal government from engaging in discrimination. The Supreme Court, therefore, faced a difficult situation in 1954 in the school desegregation cases. The best-known case is *Brown v. Board of Education of Topeka, Kansas,* but *Brown* was only one of several cases involving the same basic issue. In *Bolling v. Sharpe* the Court faced the thorny issue of racial segregation in the Washington, D.C., public schools. The District of Columbia is not a state. In the 1950s, as now, Congress was the ultimate authority over Washington. The Equal Protection Clause was not applicable there. Given the political situation at the time, the Court had to find a way to declare *all* segregated schools unconstitutional.

The justices found a solution in the Due Process Clause of the Fifth Amendment, which states, "No person shall . . . be deprived of life, liberty, or property, without due process of law." This guarantee of essential fairness applies to the federal government and was used by the justices in *Bolling* as a bar to racial discrimination. Chief Justice Warren explained for a unanimous Court:

The Fifth Amendment, which is applicable in the District of Columbia, does not contain an equal protection clause as does the Fourteenth Amendment which applies only to the states. But the concepts of equal protection and due process, both stemming from our American ideal of fairness, are not mutually exclusive. The "equal protection of the laws" is a more explicit safeguard of prohibited unfairness than "due process of law," and, therefore, we do not imply that the two are always interchangeable phrases. But, as this Court has recognized, discrimination may be so unjustifiable as to be violative of due process.

While Warren cautioned that the Due Process Clause and the Equal Protection Clause could not be used interchangeably, the Court has consistently ruled that both provisions stand for the same general principles. In most areas of discrimination law (but not all), the justices have applied the same standards to both state and federal governments by using these two constitutional provisions. As a rule, any discriminatory action by a state found to be in violation of the Equal Protection Clause would also be a violation of the Fifth Amendment if engaged in by the federal government. However, we should understand which provision of the Constitution is offended when invidious discrimination is practiced by the different levels of government. If the U.S. National Park Service were to institute racially segregated campgrounds at Yellowstone, it would violate the Due Process Clause of the Fifth Amendment; if a state were to do the same at a state park, it would violate the Equal Protection Clause of the Fourteenth Amendment.

CONGRESSIONAL ENFORCEMENT OF CIVIL RIGHTS

The civil rights of Americans are defined and protected by more than the Constitution alone. Over the years Congress has passed laws designed to enforce and extend constitutional guarantees *(see Box VII-2).* These laws expand prohibitions against discriminatory behavior, give the federal executive branch authority to enforce civil rights protections, and enlarge the opportunities for aggrieved parties to seek redress in the courts. The rules of evidence and procedure in some of these laws make it easier for litigants to prevail by proving a violation of a civil rights statute rather than a constitutional violation.

The authority for Congress to pass such laws can be found in several constitutional provisions. The Civil War Amendments each contain a section granting Congress the power to enforce the amendment with appropriate legislation. Consequently, these amendments have had considerable impact not only because of their basic substantive content, but also because they give Congress new legislative power. Immediately following the Civil War, Congress used this authority to pass laws intended to give the new amendments teeth. For example, the Civil Rights Act of 1866, passed over the veto of President Andrew Johnson, guaranteed blacks the right to purchase, lease, and use real property. The Supreme Court upheld the law, ruling that the Thirteenth Amendment's enforcement section gave Congress the power not only to outlaw slavery but also to legislate against the "badges and incidents of slavery."[6] Much of the federal regulation on fair housing is based on this authority.

Congress learned by trial and error to ground legislation in the correct Civil War Amendment. In 1883 the Supreme Court handed down its decisions in the *Civil Rights Cases*, which involved challenges to the Civil Rights Act of 1875, a statute based on the Fourteenth Amendment that made discrimination in public accommodations unlawful. Because the law covered privately owned businesses, the owners of hotels, entertainment facilities, and transportation companies claimed that Congress had exceeded the authority granted to it by the amendment. The Court, with only one justice dissenting, struck down the statute, holding that any legislation based on the Fourteenth Amendment could regulate only discrimination promoted by state action. Discrimination by private individuals was not covered by the amendment and, therefore, Congress could not prohibit it through an enforcement statute.

Congress eventually was able to pierce the private discrimination veil by finding a different constitutional grant of power upon which to base the Civil Rights Act of 1964. The most comprehensive civil rights statute ever, the law regulated discrimination in employment, education, and public accommodations. It placed restrictions on federal appropriations and programs to ensure that nondiscrimination principles were followed in any activity supported by the U.S. government. The act outlawed discrimination based not only on race but on other factors as well, such as sex, national origin, and religion. Much of what was regulated by the statute was private behavior, including prohibitions of discrimination by restaurants, hotels, and other privately run public accommodations. Rather than the Fourteenth Amendment, Congress used the Commerce Clause of Article I as authorization to pass such legislation *(see Chapter 7)*. That clause gives the national legislature the power to regulate interstate commerce, and the provisions of the 1964 Civil Rights Act apply to all activities in interstate commerce. The Supreme Court upheld the constitutionality of the law and gave it increased effectiveness by broadly defining what is considered to be within interstate commerce.[7] The same commerce power has allowed Congress to pass additional statutes that extend civil rights protection beyond what was intended by the Civil War Amendments.

The Fifteenth Amendment, prohibiting states from denying the right to vote on the basis of race, also has extended significant powers to the federal government to preserve fairness and equality in the political process. So too have the Nineteenth, Twenty-fourth, and Twenty-sixth Amendments, which expanded the electorate by limiting state discrimination based on sex, the ability to pay a tax, and age. From

---

6. *Jones v. Alfred H. Mayer, Inc.* (1968).

7. See *Heart of Atlanta Motel v. United States* (1964); *Katzenbach v. Mc-Clung* (1964).

BOX VII-2   MAJOR CIVIL RIGHTS ACTS

CIVIL RIGHTS ACTS OF 1866, 1870, 1871, AND 1875.

Laws passed by Congress after the Civil War to guarantee the rights of blacks. The public accommodation provisions of the 1875 law were declared unconstitutional by the Supreme Court in the Civil Rights Cases (1883), as a federal invasion of private rights. Other provisions of these laws were struck down by the courts or repealed by Congress. Today, a few major provisions remain from the acts of 1866 and 1871. One makes it a federal crime for any person acting under the authority of a state law to deprive another of any rights protected by the Constitution or by laws of the United States. Another authorizes suits for civil damages against state or local officials by persons whose rights are abridged. Others permit actions against persons who conspire to deprive people of their rights.

CIVIL RIGHTS ACT OF 1957.

The first civil rights law passed by Congress since Reconstruction, designed to secure the right to vote for blacks. Its major feature empowers the Department of Justice to seek court injunctions against any deprivation of voting rights, and authorizes criminal prosecutions for violations of an injunction. In addition, the act established a Civil Rights Division, headed by an Assistant Attorney General in the Department of Justice, and created a bipartisan Civil Rights Commission to investigate civil rights violations and to recommend legislation.

CIVIL RIGHTS ACT OF 1960.

A law designed to further secure the right to vote for blacks and to meet the problems arising from racial upheavals in the South in the late 1950s. The major provision authorizes federal courts to appoint referees who will help blacks to register after a voter-denial conviction is obtained under the 1957 Civil Rights Act, and after a court finding of a "pattern or practice" of discrimination against qualified voters. Other provisions: (1) authorize punishment for persons who obstruct any federal court order, such as a school desegregation order, by threats or force; (2) authorize criminal penalties for transportation of explosives for the purpose of bombing a building; (3) require preservation of voting records for twenty-two months, and authorize the Attorney General to inspect the records; (4) provide for schooling of children of armed forces personnel in the event that a school closes because of an integration dispute.

CIVIL RIGHTS ACT OF 1964.

A major enactment designed to erase racial discrimination in most areas of American life. Major provisions of the act: (1) outlaw arbitrary discrimination in voter registration and expedite voting rights suits; (2) bar discrimination in public accommodations, such as hotels and restaurants, that have a substantial relation to interstate commerce; (3) authorize the national government to bring suits to desegregate public facilities and schools; (4) extend the life and expand the power of the Civil Rights Commission; (5) provide for the withholding of federal funds from programs administered in a discriminatory manner; (6) establish the right to equality in employment opportunities; and (7) establish a Community Relations Service to help resolve civil rights problems. The act forbids discrimination based on race, color, religion, national origin, and, in the case of employment, sex. Techniques for gaining voluntary compliance are stressed in the act, and the resolution of civil rights problems through state and local action is encouraged. Discrimination in housing is not covered by the law, but is prohibited by the Civil Rights Act of 1968.

Significance. The Civil Rights Act of 1964 is the most far-reaching civil rights legislation since Reconstruction. It was passed after the longest debate in Senate history (eighty-three days) and only after cloture was invoked for the first time to cut off a civil rights filibuster. Compliance with the act's controversial provisions on public accommodations and equal employment opportunities has been widespread. Title VI of the act, which authorizes the cutoff of federal funds to state and local programs practicing discrimination, proved to be the most effective provision of the act. For example, a dramatic jump in southern school integration took place when the national government threatened to withhold federal funds from schools failing to comply with desegregation orders. All agencies receiving federal funds are required to submit assurance of compliance with the 1964 act. Hundreds of grant-in-aid programs are involved, amounting to 20 percent of all state and local revenues.

CIVIL RIGHTS ACT OF 1968.

A law which prohibits discrimination on the advertising, financing, sale, or rental of housing, based on race, religion, or national origin and, as of 1974, sex, but provided limited and ineffective enforcement powers. A major amendment to the act in 1988 extended coverage to the handicapped and to families with children and added enforcement machinery through either administrative en-

BOX VII-2   MAJOR CIVIL RIGHTS ACTS *(continued)*

forcement by the Department of Housing and Urban Development (HUD) or by suits filed in federal court, with the choice of forums left to either party in the dispute. The law covers about 80 percent of all housing. Major exclusions are owner-occupied dwellings of four units or less and those selling without services of a broker.

VOTING RIGHTS ACT

A major law enacted by Congress in 1965 and renewed and expanded in 1970, 1975, and 1982 that has sought to eliminate restrictions on voting that have been used to discriminate against blacks and other minority groups. A major provision of the 1965 act suspended the use of literacy and other tests used to discriminate. The act also authorized registration by federal registrars in any state or county where such tests had been used and where less than 50 percent of eligible voters were registered. Seven southern states were mainly affected by these provisions. The act also authorized a legal test of poll taxes in state elections, and the Supreme Court in 1966 declared payment of poll taxes as a condition of voting to be unconstitutional. Major provisions of the 1965 act were upheld by the Court as a valid exercise of power under the Fifteenth Amendment. The Voting Rights Act of 1970: (1) extended the 1965 act for five years; (2) lowered the minimum age for all elections from twenty-one to eighteen; (3) prohibited the states from disqualifying voters in presidential elections because of their failure to meet state residence requirements beyond thirty days; and

(4) provided for uniform national rules for absentee registration and voting in presidential elections. In 1970 the Court upheld the eighteen-year-old vote for national elections but found its application to state and local elections unconstitutional. In 1975 the act was continued for seven years. Federal voting protection was extended to all parts of ten additional states, bilingual ballots were required, election law changes in states covered by the act were required to be approved by either a United States attorney or a federal court, and legal protection of voting rights was extended to Spanish-Americans, Alaskan natives, American Indians, and Asian-Americans. The 1982 act extends the law for twenty-five years, authorizes a "bailout" for covered states showing a clear record for ten years, and provides the intent to discriminate need not be proven if the results demonstrate otherwise.

CIVIL RIGHTS ACT OF 1991.

A reaffirmation and expansion of protection against discrimination in employment. The main purpose of the legislation was to overturn several 1989 Supreme Court decisions that made it harder for employees to challenge or prove discrimination, that narrowly interpreted the scope of civil rights laws, and that limited access to the courts.

SOURCE: Jack C. Plano and Milton Greenberg, *The American Political Dictionary* (Fort Worth, Texas: Harcourt Brace Jovanovich, 1993).

the enforcement provisions of these four voting rights amendments, Congress has passed a number of statutes ensuring the integrity of the election process. The most important of these is the Voting Rights Act of 1965, which has been strengthened by amendment over the years. This statute provided the machinery for federal enforcement and prosecution of voting rights violations. Its provisions have been the catalyst for significant growth in voter registration rates among segments of the population where political participation historically has been depressed.

Because this volume deals with constitutional law, our discussion of the various forms of discrimination focuses on the civil rights guarantees provided by the nation's fundamental law. Keep in mind, however, that in many areas Congress has passed statutes that extend those constitutional provisions to create various legal rights that go well beyond protections included in the Constitution itself.

CHAPTER 18
DISCRIMINATION

D ISCRIMINATION HAS BEEN a difficult and persistent problem for the United States from the start. Although the Founders were considered the vanguard of enlightened politics, differential treatment of individuals according to race, economic status, religious affiliation, and sex was the rule in the colonies. Since those early years of nationhood, issues of discrimination have been prominent on the country's political agenda. During the nation's first three-quarters of a century, slavery eroded national unity. Although the slavery issue was officially settled by the Civil War and the constitutional amendments that followed, racial inequity did not disappear. Many of today's social and political problems stem from racial discrimination.

The twentieth century also has seen the national spotlight turn to claims of unfair treatment by women, the poor, aliens, ethnic minorities, the handicapped, and other disadvantaged segments of society. Attempts to address these claims have given rise to arguments that a government that becomes overly sensitive to the needs of minorities will deprive the majority of their rights. With each new claim and counterclaim, the issues become more complex. This chapter explores how the justices of the Supreme Court have interpreted the Constitution in response to conflicting claims of discrimination. We first con-

centrate on three categories of discrimination, race, sex, and economics, and then discuss remedies used to eliminate discrimination and its effects.

RACIAL DISCRIMINATION

The institution of slavery is a blight on the record of a nation that otherwise has led the way in protecting individual rights. From 1619, when the first slaves were brought to Jamestown, to the ratification of the Civil War Amendments 250 years later, people of African ancestry were considered an inferior race; they could be bought, sold, and used as personal property. Although some states extended various civil and political rights to emancipated slaves and their descendants, the national Constitution did not recognize black Americans as full citizens. In *Scott v. Sandford* (1857), Chief Justice Taney, delivering the opinion of the Court, described the prevailing view of the black race at the time the Constitution was drafted and ratified:

They had for more than a century before been regarded as beings of an inferior order, and altogether unfit to associate with the white race, either in social or political relations; and so far inferior, that they had no rights which the white man was bound to respect; and that the negro might justly and lawfully be reduced to slavery for his benefit. He was bought and sold, and treated as an ordinary article of merchandise and traffic, whenever a profit could be made by it. This opinion was at that time fixed and universal in the civilized portion of the white race.

The Court's decision in *Scott* interpreted the Constitution consistent with this view and helped set the stage for the Civil War. The ruling, which held that a black slave could not become a full member of the political community and be entitled to all of the constitutional privileges of citizens, undermined the legitimacy of the Court and forever damaged Taney's reputation. Only because the Union army won on the battlefield was the Constitution later amended to end slavery and confer full national citizenship on black Americans.

Congress moved with dispatch to give force to the new amendments, but the Supreme Court was much slower. Although the justices supported the claims of newly emancipated black Americans in some cases, they did not construe the new amendments broadly, nor did they enthusiastically support new legislation designed to enforce them. In the *Slaughterhouse Cases* (1873) for example, the Court interpreted the Fourteenth Amendment's Privileges and Immunities Clause quite narrowly. In *United States v. Harris* (1883) and the *Civil Rights Cases* (1883), the justices nullified major provisions of the Ku Klux Klan Act of 1871 and the Civil Rights Act of 1875 for failure to confine statutory provisions to discriminatory actions by the state. It was clear that the battle for legal equality of the races was not over.

By the end of the nineteenth century, the Supreme Court still had not answered what was perhaps the most important question arising from the Fourteenth Amendment: What is equal protection? As the vitality of the Reconstruction Acts and federal efforts to enforce them gradually waned, the political forces of the old order began to reassert control in the South. From the 1880s to the 1950s, a period known as the Jim Crow era, the progress that had been made to achieve racial equality not only came to a halt but also began to run in reverse. The South, where 90 percent of the African American population lived, began to enact laws that reimposed an inferior legal status on blacks and commanded a strict separation of the races. Northern liberals were of little help. The battle against slavery having been won, they turned their attention to other issues. With more conservative political forces gaining power in Congress, it was left to the Court, still smarting from the *Scott* debacle, to give meaning to the constitutional guarantee of equal protection of the laws.

The most important case of this period was *Plessy v. Ferguson*, in which the justices were forced to confront directly the meaning of equality under the Constitution. At odds were the Equal Protection Clause of the Fourteenth Amendment and a host of segregation statutes by then in force in the southern and border states. While reading the *Plessy* decision, note that the Court uses the reasonableness standard (rational basis test) to interpret the Equal Protection Clause. Ironically, the majority opinion upholding the separation standards of the South was written by Justice Henry B. Brown, a Lincoln Republican, who had grown up in New England and supported the abolitionist movement. The lone dissent was registered by Justice John Marshall Harlan, an aristocratic Kentuckian whose family had owned slaves. Harlan's dissent is considered a classic and one of the most prophetic ever registered.

Plessy v. Ferguson

163 U.S. 537 (1896)
Vote: 7 (Brown, Field, Fuller, Gray, Peckham, Shiras, White)
        1 (Harlan)
Opinion of the Court: Brown
Dissenting opinion: Harlan
Not participating: Brewer

In 1890 Louisiana, following the lead of Florida, Mississippi, and Texas, passed a statute commanding the separation of the races on all railroads. The act was opposed by an organized group of New Orleans residents of black and mixed-race heritage, with the support of the railroads. Attempts to have the judiciary invalidate the statute were partially successful when the Louisiana Supreme Court struck down the law as applied to passengers crossing state lines for placing an unconstitutional burden on interstate commerce. This decision, however, left unanswered the question of segregated travel wholly within the state's borders.

On June 7, 1892, as part of the litigation strategy, Homer Adolph Plessy, who described himself as "of seven-eighths Caucasian and one-eighth African blood," bought a first-class rail ticket from New Orleans to Covington, Louisiana. He took a seat in a car reserved for white passengers. The conductor demanded that Plessy, under pain of ejection and imprisonment, move to a car for black passengers. Plessy refused. With the help of a police officer, Plessy was taken off the train and held in a New Orleans jail to await trial.

His lawyer moved to block the trial on the grounds that the segregation law was in violation of the U.S. Constitution. Judge John Ferguson denied the motion, and appeal was taken to the Louisiana Supreme Court. The state high court, under the leadership of Chief Justice Francis Tillou Nicholls, who as governor had signed the segregation statute into law, denied Plessy's petition, and the case moved to the U.S. Supreme Court.

MR. JUSTICE BROWN delivered the opinion of the Court.

This case turns upon the constitutionality of an act of the General Assembly of the State of Louisiana, passed in 1890, providing for separate railway carriages for the white and colored races. . . .

By the Fourteenth Amendment, all persons born or naturalized in the United States, and subject to the jurisdiction thereof, are made citizens of the United States and of the State wherein they reside; and the States are forbidden from making or enforcing any law which shall abridge the privileges or immunities of citizens of the United States, or shall deprive any person of life, liberty or property without due process of law, or deny to any person within their jurisdiction the equal protection of the laws. . . .

The object of the amendment was undoubtedly to enforce the absolute equality of the two races before the law, but in the nature of things it could not have been intended to abolish distinctions based upon color, or to enforce social, as distinguished from political equality, or a commingling of the two races upon terms unsatisfactory to either. Laws permitting, and even requiring, their separation in places where they are liable to be brought into contact do not necessarily imply the inferiority of either race to the other, and have been generally, if not universally, recognized as within the competency of the state legislatures in the exercise of their police power. The most common instance of this is connected with the establishment of separate schools for white and colored children, which has been held to be a valid exercise of the legislative power even by courts of States where the political rights of the colored race have been longest and most earnestly enforced.

One of the earliest of these cases is that of *Roberts v. City of Boston,* in which the Supreme Judicial Court of Massachusetts held that the general school committee of Boston had power to make provision for the instruction of colored children in separate schools established exclusively for them, and to prohibit their attendance upon the other schools. . . .

Laws forbidding the intermarriage of the two races may be said in a technical sense to interfere with the freedom of contract, and yet have been universally recognized as within the police power of the State.

The distinction between laws interfering with the political equality of the negro and those requiring the separation of the two races in schools, theatres and railway carriages has been frequently drawn by this court. Thus in *Strauder v. West Virginia* [1880] it was held that a law of West Virginia limiting to white male persons, 21 years of age and citizens of the State, the right to sit upon juries, was a discrimination which implied a legal inferiority in civil society, which lessened the security of the right of the colored race, and was a step toward reducing them to a condition of servility. Indeed, the right of a colored man that, in the selection of jurors to pass upon his life, liberty, and property, there shall be no exclusion of his race, and no discrimination against them because of color, has been asserted in a number of cases. . . .

So far, then, as a conflict with the Fourteenth Amendment is concerned, the case reduces itself to the question whether the statute of Louisiana is a reasonable regulation, and with respect to this there must necessarily be a large discretion on the part of the legislature. In determining the question of reasonableness it is at liberty to act with reference to the established usages, customs and traditions of the people, and with a view to the promotion of their comfort, and the preservation of the public peace and good order. Gauged by this standard, we cannot say that a law which authorizes or even requires the separation of the two races in public conveyances is unreasonable, or more obnoxious to the Fourteenth Amendment than the acts of Congress requiring separate schools for colored children in the District of Columbia, the constitutionality of which does not seem to have been questioned, or the corresponding acts of state legislatures.

We consider the underlying fallacy of the plaintiff's argument to consist in the assumption that the enforced separation of the two races stamps the colored race with a badge of inferiority. If this be so, it is not by reason of anything found in the act, but solely because the colored race chooses to put that construction upon it. The argument necessarily assumes that if, as has been more than once the case, and is not unlikely to be so again, the colored race should become the dominant power in the state legislature, and should enact a law in precisely similar terms, it would thereby relegate the white race to an inferior position. We imagine that the white race, at least, would not acquiesce in this assumption. The argument also assumes that social prejudices may be overcome by legislation, and that equal rights cannot be secured to the negro except by an enforced commingling of the two races. We cannot accept this proposition. If the two races are to meet upon terms of social equality, it must be the result of natural affinities, a mutual appreciation of each other's merits and a voluntary consent of individuals. . . . Legislation is powerless to eradicate racial instincts or to abolish distinctions based upon physical differences, and the attempt to do so can only result in accentuating the difficulties of the present situation.

If the civil and political rights of both races be equal one cannot be inferior to the other civilly or politically. If one race be inferior to the other socially, the Constitution of the United States cannot put them upon the same plane. . . .

The judgment of the court below is, therefore,

Affirmed.

MR. JUSTICE HARLAN dissenting.

In respect of civil rights, common to all citizens, the Constitution of the United States does not, I think, permit any public authority to know the race of those entitled to be protected in the enjoyment of such rights. Every true man has pride of race, and under appropriate circumstances when the rights of others, his equals before the law, are not to be affected, it is his privilege to express such pride and to take such action based upon it as to him seems proper. But I deny that any legislative body or judicial tribunal may have regard to the race of citizens when the civil rights of those citizens are involved. Indeed, such legislation, as that here in question, is inconsistent not only with that equality of rights which pertains to citizenship, National and State, but with the personal liberty enjoyed by every one within the United States.

The Thirteenth Amendment does not permit the withholding or the deprivation of any right necessarily inhering in freedom. It not only struck down the institution of slavery as previously existing in the United States, but it prevents the imposition of any burdens or disabilities that constitute badges of slavery or servitude. It decreed universal civil freedom in this country. This court has so adjudged. But that amendment having been found inadequate to the protection of the rights of those who had been in slavery, it was followed by the Fourteenth Amendment, which added greatly to the dignity and glory of American citizenship, and to the security of personal liberty. . . . These two amendments, if enforced according to their true intent and meaning, will protect all the civil rights that pertain to freedom and citizenship. Finally, and to the end that no citizen should be denied, on account of his race, the privilege of participating in the political control of his country, it was declared by the Fifteenth Amendment that "the right of citizens of the United States to vote shall not be denied or abridged by the United States or by any State on account of race, color or previous condition of servitude."

These notable additions to the fundamental law were welcomed by the friends of liberty throughout the world. They removed the race line from our governmental systems. They had, as this court has said, a common purpose, namely, to secure "to a race recently emancipated, a race that through many generations have been held in slavery, all the civil rights that the superior race enjoy.". . .

If a State can prescribe, as a rule of civil conduct, that whites and blacks shall not travel as passengers in the same railroad coach, why may it not so regulate the use of the streets of its cities and towns as to compel white citizens to keep on one side of a street and black citizens to keep on the other? Why may it not, upon like grounds, punish whites and blacks who ride together in street cars or in open vehicles on a public road or street? Why may it not require sheriffs to assign whites to one side of a court-room and blacks to the other? And why may it not also prohibit the commingling of the two races in the galleries of legislative halls or in public assemblages convened for the consideration of the political questions of the day? Further, if this statute of Louisiana is consistent with the personal liberty of citizens, why may not the State require the separation in railroad coaches of native and naturalized citizens of the United States, or of Protestants and Roman Catholics?. . .

The white race deems itself to be the dominant race in this country. And so it is, in prestige, in achievements, in education, in wealth and in power. So, I doubt not, it will continue to be for all time, if it remains true to its great heritage and holds fast to the principles of constitutional liberty. But in view of the Constitution, in the eye of the law, there is in this country no superior, dominant, ruling class of citizens. There is no caste here. Our Constitution is color-blind, and neither knows nor tolerates classes among citizens. In respect of civil rights, all citizens are equal before the law. The humblest is the peer of the most powerful. The law regards man as man, and takes no account of his surroundings or of his color when his civil rights as guaranteed by the supreme law of the land are involved. It is, therefore, to be regretted that this high tribunal, the final expositor of the fundamental law of the land, has reached the conclusion that it is competent for a State to regulate the enjoyment by citizens of their civil rights solely upon the basis of race.

In my opinion, the judgment this day rendered will, in time, prove to be quite as pernicious as the decision made by this tribunal in the *Dred Scott case*. . . .

I am of opinion that the statute of Louisiana is inconsistent with the personal liberty of citizens, white and black, in that State, and hostile to both the spirit and letter of the Constitution of the United States. If laws of like character should be enacted in the several States of the Union, the effect would be in the highest degree mischievous. Slavery, as an institution tolerated by law would, it is true, have disappeared from our country, but there would remain a power in the States, by sinister legislation, to interfere with the full enjoyment of the blessings of freedom; to regulate civil rights, common to all citizens, upon the basis of race; and to place in a condition of legal inferiority a large body of American citizens, now constituting a part of the political community called the People of the United States, for whom, and by whom through representatives, our government is administered. Such a system is inconsistent with the guarantee given by the Constitution to each State of a republican form of government, and may be stricken down by Congressional action, or by the courts in the discharge of their solemn duty to maintain the supreme law of the land, anything in the constitution or laws of any State to the contrary notwithstanding.

For the reasons stated, I am constrained to withhold my assent from the opinion and judgment of the majority.

The *Plessy* decision's separate but equal doctrine ushered in full-scale segregation in the southern and border states. According to the Court, separation did not constitute inequality under the Fourteenth Amendment; as long as facilities and opportunities were somewhat similar, the Equal Protection Clause permitted the separation of the races. Encouraged by the ruling, the legislatures of the South passed a wide variety of statutes to keep blacks segregated from the white population. The segregation laws affected transportation, schools, hospitals, parks, public rest rooms and water fountains, libraries, cemeteries, recreational facilities, hotels, restaurants, and almost every other public and commercial facility. These laws, coupled with segregated private lives, inevitably resulted in two separate societies.

During the first half of the twentieth century, the separate but equal doctrine dominated race relations law. The southern states continued to pass and enforce segregationist laws, largely insulated from legal attack. Over the years, however, it became clear that the "equality" part of the separate but equal doctrine was being ignored.

Segregated public facilities became increasingly unequal, and the blacks became more and more disadvantaged. Although this disparity extended to almost every area of life, education became the center of attention. Whites and blacks were given access to public schools, but the black schools, at all levels, received support and funding far inferior to that of white institutions.

These conditions spurred the growth of civil rights groups dedicated to eradicating segregation. None was more prominent than the National Association for the Advancement of Colored People (NAACP) and its affiliate, the Legal Defense and Educational Fund (LDF). Thurgood Marshall, who had been associated with the NAACP since he graduated first in his class at Howard University Law School, became the head of the Legal Defense Fund in 1940 and initiated a twenty-year campaign in the courts to win equal rights for black Americans. During those years, Marshall and his staff won substantial victories in the Supreme Court in housing, voting rights, public education, employment, and public accommodations. Marshall also served as a judge on the court of appeals and as U.S. solicitor general before being appointed in 1967 to the Supreme Court. He was the first African American to serve on the Court (see Box 18-1).

When Marshall took over leadership of the Legal Defense Fund, the rule set in *Plessy* was already on less than firm ground. In 1938 the Court had handed segregationist forces a significant defeat in *Missouri ex rel. Gaines v. Canada.* Lloyd Gaines, a Missouri resident who had graduated from the all-black Lincoln University, applied for admission to the University of Missouri's law school. He was denied admission because of his race. Although Missouri did not have a law school for its black citizens, the state offered to finance the education of qualified black students who would attend law school in a neighboring state that did not have segregationist policies. The Supreme Court, 7–2, concluded that the Missouri plan to provide opportunities out of state did not meet the obligations imposed by the Equal Protection Clause. The state then moved to establish a law school for blacks at Lincoln. Although this ruling imposed little substantive change, it served notice that segregation policies were about to undergo close evaluation.

The Supreme Court's message was reinforced in 1948 when in two cases, *Sipuel v. Board of Regents* and *Fisher v. Hurst,* the justices unanimously demanded that states provide equal facilities for blacks pursuing a legal education. Two years later the justices followed up with *Sweatt v. Painter,* in which the Court ruled that the Constitution had been violated by the University of Texas when its law school refused to admit a black applicant. The state had argued that its newly created law school for blacks met the separate but equal requirement and allowed the state to continue to run the University of Texas law school on a whites-only basis. The justices concluded, however, that quality differences between the two schools were such that the black law school did not provide an education equal to that of the white law school. The same day the Court decided *Sweatt,* it also issued a ruling in *McLaurin v. Oklahoma State Regents* (1950), which took another step toward racial equality in higher education.[1] Oklahoma, to comply with court orders, admitted some black students to graduate programs at the University of Oklahoma. However, the university kept the minority students segregated in special areas of the classrooms, libraries, and dining halls. The Supreme Court unanimously found this segregated system in violation of the Equal Protection Clause.

---

1. For a discussion of this issue, see Richard Kluger, *Simple Justice* (New York: Random House, 1976), especially chap. 12.

Under the rule of law established in *Plessy v. Ferguson* (1896), states could require racial separation if facilities for blacks and whites were of equal quality. In public education black schools were not always equal to those reserved for whites.

Pictured on the steps of the U.S. Supreme Court are the NAACP Legal Defense Fund lawyers who argued the school segregation cases that resulted in the May 17, 1954, *Brown v. Board of Education* precedent. Left to right: Howard Jenkins, James M. Nabrit, Jr., Spottswood W. Robinson III, Frank Reeves, Jack Greenberg, Special Counsel Thurgood Marshall, Louis Redding, U. Simpson Tate, and George E. C. Hayes. Missing from the photograph is Robert L. Carter, who argued the Topeka, Kansas, case.

BOX 18-1   THURGOOD MARSHALL
(1967–1991)

Thurgood Marshall was born July 2, 1908, in Baltimore, Maryland. He was the son of a primary teacher and a club steward. In 1926 he left Baltimore to attend the all-black Lincoln University in Chester, Pennsylvania, where he developed a reputation as an outstanding debater. After graduating cum laude in 1930, Marshall decided to study law and entered Howard University in Washington, D. C.

During his law school years, Marshall developed an interest in civil rights. After graduating first in his class in 1933, he began a long and historic involvement with the National Association for the Advancement of Colored People (NAACP). In 1940 he became the head of the newly formed NAACP Legal Defense and Educational Fund, a position he held for more than twenty years.

Over those two decades, Marshall coordinated the fund's attack on segregation in voting, housing, public accommodations, and education. The culmination of his career as a civil rights attorney came in 1954 as chief counsel in a series of cases grouped under the title *Brown v. Board of Education*. In that historic case, civil rights advocates convinced the Supreme Court to declare segregation in public schools unconstitutional.

Marshall married Vivian Burey, September 4, 1929. They had two sons. Vivian Marshall died in February 1955, and Marshall married Cecilia Suyat, December 17, 1955.

In 1961 Marshall was appointed by President John F. Kennedy to the Second Circuit Court of Appeals, but because of heated opposition from southern Democratic senators, he was not confirmed for a year.

Four years after he was named to the appeals court, Marshall was chosen by President Lyndon B. Johnson to be solicitor general. Marshall was the first black to serve in that capacity. During his years as the government's chief advocate before the Supreme Court, Marshall scored impressive victories in the areas of civil and constitutional rights. He won Supreme Court approval of the 1965 Voting Rights Act, voluntarily informed the Court that the government had used eavesdropping devices in two cases, and joined a suit that successfully overturned a California constitutional amendment that prohibited open housing legislation.

On June 13, 1967, President Johnson nominated Marshall to the seat vacated by Justice Tom C. Clark, who retired. Marshall was confirmed by the Senate, 69–11, August 30, 1967. Marshall, the first black justice of the Supreme Court, retired on October 1, 1991. He died January 24, 1993, at the age of 84.

SOURCE: Adapted from Elder Witt, *Guide to the U.S. Supreme Court*, 2d ed. (Washington, D.C.: Congressional Quarterly, 1990), 875.

As the nation entered the 1950s, the conditions were ripe for a final assault on the half-century-old separate but equal doctrine. Civil rights groups continued to marshal legal arguments and political support to eliminate segregation. Legal challenges to a wide array of discriminatory laws were filed through-out the country, and the Justice Department under President Truman supported these efforts. The Supreme Court, through its unanimous rulings in favor of racial equality in higher education, appeared on the verge of seriously considering an end to *Plessy*. In addition, there had been an important leadership

This photograph of Linda Brown, plaintiff in *Brown v. Board of Education*, was taken in 1952 when she was nine years old.

change on the Court. Chief Justice Vinson died September 8, 1953, and was replaced by Earl Warren, a former governor of California, who was much more comfortable with activist judicial policies than was his predecessor *(see Box 18-2)*.

All of these factors combined to produce *Brown v. Board of Education of Topeka* (1954), considered by many to be the Supreme Court's most significant decision of the twentieth century. Unlike earlier civil rights cases that involved relatively small professional and graduate education programs, the *Brown* case challenged official racial segregation in the nation's primary and secondary public schools. The decision affected thousands of school districts concentrated primarily in southern and border states. In addition,

it was apparent to all that the precedent to be set for public education would be extended to other areas as well.

As you read Warren's opinion for a unanimous Court, note how the concept of equality has changed. No longer does the Court examine only physical facilities and tangible items such as buildings, libraries, teacher qualifications, and funding levels; instead, it emphasizes the intangible negative impact of racial segregation on children. Warren's opinion includes a footnote listing social science references as authorities for his arguments. This opinion was criticized for citing sociological and psychological studies to support the Court's conclusions rather than confining the analysis to legal arguments. Are these criticisms valid? Should the Court take social science evidence into account in arriving at constitutional decisions? Consider how similar Warren's opinion is to Justice Harlan's lone dissent in the *Plessy* decision.

Brown v. Board of Education of Topeka

347 U.S. 483 (1954)
Vote: 9 (Black, Burton, Clark, Douglas, Frankfurter, Jackson,
Minton, Reed, Warren)
0
Opinion of the Court: Warren

Brown v. Board of Education was one of five cases involving similar issues consolidated by the Court for consideration at the same time. As part of the desegregation litigation strategy orchestrated by Thurgood Marshall and funded by the NAACP, these cases challenged the segregated public schools of Delaware, Virginia, South Carolina, and the District of Columbia, in addition to Topeka, Kansas. The most prominent lawyers in the civil rights movement, Spottswood Robinson III, Louis Redding, Jack Greenberg, Constance Baker Motley, Robert Carter, and James Nabrit,

BOX 18-2   EARL WARREN

(1953–1969)

Earl Warren, the son of Scandinavian immigrant parents, was born on March 19, 1891, in Los Angeles, California. Soon after his birth, the family moved to Bakersfield, where his father worked as a railroad car repairman.

Warren worked his way through college and law school at the University of California. After graduating in 1914, he worked in law offices in San Francisco and Oakland, the only time in his career that he engaged in private practice.

Warren married Nina P. Meyers, October 14, 1925. They had three daughters and three sons.

In 1938, after Warren had become active in politics, his father was bludgeoned to death in a crime that was never solved.

From 1919 until his resignation from the Supreme Court in 1969, Warren served without interruption in public office. His first post was deputy city attorney for Oakland. Then he was named a deputy district attorney for Alameda County, which embraces the cities of Oakland, Alameda, and Berkeley.

In 1925 Warren was appointed district attorney when the incumbent resigned. He won election to the post in his own right in 1926, 1930, and 1934. During his fourteen years as district attorney, Warren developed a reputation as a crime fighter, sending a city manager and several councilmen to jail on graft charges and smashing a crooked deal on garbage collection.

A Republican, Warren decided in 1938 to run for state attorney general. He cross-filed and won three primaries—his own party's as well as the Democratic and Progressive party contests.

In 1942 Warren ran for governor of California. Although he was an underdog, he wound up defeating incumbent Democratic governor Culbert Olson by a margin of 342,000, winning 57.1 percent of the total votes cast. He was twice reelected, winning the Democratic as well as the Republican nomination in 1946 and defeating Democrat James Roosevelt, son of President Franklin D. Roosevelt, by an almost two-to-one margin in 1950.

At first viewed as a conservative governor—he denounced "communist radicals" and supported the wartime federal order to move all persons of Japanese ancestry away from the West Coast—Warren developed a progressive image after the war. In 1945 he proposed a state program of prepaid medical insurance and later championed liberal pension and welfare benefits.

Warren made two bids for national political office. In 1948 he ran for Vice President on the Republican ticket with Gov. Thomas E. Dewey of New York. In 1952 he sought the Republican presidential nomination. But with little chance to win he threw his support at a crucial moment behind Gen. Dwight D. Eisenhower, helping him win the battle with Sen. Robert A. Taft of Ohio for the nomination.

That support resulted in Eisenhower's political indebtedness to Warren, which the president repaid in 1953 with a recess appointment to the Supreme Court. Warren replaced Chief Justice Fred M. Vinson, who had died. Warren was confirmed by the Senate March 1, 1954, by a voice vote. Eisenhower, reflecting on his choice years later in the light of the Warren Court's liberal record, called the appointment "the biggest damn-fool mistake I ever made."

In addition to his work on the Court, Warren headed the commission that investigated the assassination of President John F. Kennedy.

In 1968 Warren submitted his resignation, conditional on confirmation of a successor. But the Senate got bogged down in the fight to confirm President Lyndon B. Johnson's nomination of Justice Abe Fortas to succeed Warren, so Warren agreed to serve another year. In 1969, when Richard Nixon assumed office, he chose Warren E. Burger as the new chief justice, and Warren stepped down. He died July 9, 1974.

SOURCE: Adapted from Elder Witt, *Guide to the U.S. Supreme Court*, 2d ed. (Washington, D.C.: Congressional Quarterly, 1990), 869–870.

BOX 18-3

ONE CHILD'S SIMPLE JUSTICE

Linda Brown Buckner, now a Head Start teacher in Topeka, Kansas, was eight years old in 1951 when her father, Oliver, included her in a lawsuit to desegregate public schools that led to the Supreme Court's landmark *Brown v. Board of Education* decision in 1954.

"I was just starting school when the local NAACP was recruiting people to join its case. Topeka had eighteen elementary schools for whites and four for African Americans. The closest school to my family was four blocks away, the Sumner School. But I went to Monroe Elementary School, which was two and a half miles across town. Often, I came home crying because it was so cold waiting for the bus.

"My father hadn't been involved with the NAACP, but he was upset with the distance I had to go. One of his childhood friends was Charles Scott, one of the attorneys for the case, and Dad agreed to try to enroll me at the Sumner School. Dad's name wasn't first alphabetically, and my sister Cheryl always suspected there was sexism involved in his name coming first in the court records: among the twelve other plaintiffs, he was the only man.

"The day the decision was handed down, my mother was home and heard it on the radio. The news was shared with the family, and there was a rally that evening at the Monroe School. But I never did go to the Sumner School. That fall I went to the junior-high school, which had been integrated in Topeka since 1879."

SOURCE: Copyright *U.S. News and World Report*, October 25, 1993, 34.

---

dent Warren G. Harding. About this same time Davis had represented the steel mills in *Youngstown Sheet and Tube Co. v. Sawyer* (1952), the Korean War steel seizure case *(see his photo on page 178)*.

Linda Carol Brown was an eight-year-old black girl, whose father, Oliver, was an assistant pastor of a Topeka church. The Browns lived in a predominantly white neighborhood only a short distance from the local elementary school. Under state law, cities with populations over 15,000 were permitted to administer racially segregated schools. The Board of Education in Topeka required its elementary schools to be racially divided. The Browns did not want their daughter to be sent to the school reserved for black students. It was far from home, and they considered the trip dangerous. In addition, their neighborhood school was a good one, and the Browns wanted their daughter to be educated in integrated schools. They filed suit challenging the segregated school system as violating their daughter's rights under the Equal Protection Clause of the Fourteenth Amendment.

The *Brown* appeal was joined by those from the other four suits. The cases were originally argued in December 1952, but the following June the Court issued an order for the cases to be reargued in December 1953 with special emphasis to be placed on a series of questions dealing with the history and meaning of the Fourteenth Amendment. This delay also allowed the newly appointed Earl Warren to participate fully in the decision. Six months later, on May 17, 1954, the Court issued its ruling.

MR. CHIEF JUSTICE WARREN delivered the opinion of the Court.

In each of the cases, minors of the Negro race, through their legal representatives, seek the aid of the courts in obtaining admission to the public schools of their community on a nonsegregated basis. In each instance, they had been denied admission to schools attended by white children under laws requiring or permitting segregation according to race. This segregation was alleged to deprive the plaintiffs

---

Jr., prepared them. As Marshall had expected, the suits were unsuccessful at the trial level, where the lower courts relied on *Plessy* as precedent. The leading lawyer for the states was John W. Davis, a prominent constitutional lawyer who had been a Democratic candidate for president in 1924. Davis had reportedly once been offered a nomination to the Court by Presi-

of the equal protection of the laws under the Fourteenth Amendment. . . .

The plaintiffs contend that segregated public schools are not "equal" and cannot be made "equal," and that hence they are deprived of the equal protection of the laws. Because of the obvious importance of the question presented, the Court took jurisdiction. Argument was heard in the 1952 Term, and reargument was heard this Term on certain questions propounded by the Court.

Reargument was largely devoted to the circumstances surrounding the adoption of the Fourteenth Amendment in 1868. It covered exhaustively consideration of the Amendment in Congress, ratification by the states, then existing practices in racial segregation, and the views of proponents and opponents of the Amendment. This discussion and our own investigation convince us that, although these sources cast some light, it is not enough to resolve the problem with which we are faced. At best, they are inconclusive. . . .

An additional reason for the inconclusive nature of the Amendment's history, with respect to segregated schools, is the status of public education at that time. In the South, the movement toward free common schools, supported by general taxation, had not yet taken hold. Education of white children was largely in the hands of private groups. Education of Negroes was almost nonexistent, and practically all of the race were illiterate. In fact, any education of Negroes was forbidden by law in some states. Today, in contrast, many Negroes have achieved outstanding success in the arts and sciences as well as in the business and professional world. It is true that public school education at the time of the Amendment had advanced further in the North, but the effect of the Amendment on Northern States was generally ignored in the congressional debates. Even in the North, the conditions of public education did not approximate those existing today. The curriculum was usually rudimentary; ungraded schools were common in rural areas; the school term was but three months a year in many states; and compulsory school attendance was virtually unknown. As a consequence, it is not surprising that there should be so little in the history of the Fourteenth Amendment relating to its intended effect on public education.

In the first cases in this Court construing the Fourteenth Amendment, decided shortly after its adoption, the Court interpreted it as proscribing all state-imposed discriminations against the Negro race. The doctrine of "separate but equal" did not make its appearance in this Court until 1896 in the case of *Plessy v. Ferguson,* involving not education but transportation. American courts have since labored with the doctrine for over half a century. . . .

Here, unlike *Sweatt v. Painter,* there are findings below that the Negro and white schools involved have been equalized, or are being equalized, with respect to buildings, curricula, qualifications and salaries of teachers, and other "tangible" factors. Our decision, therefore, cannot turn on merely a comparison of these tangible factors in the Negro and white schools involved in each of the cases. We must look instead to the effect of segregation itself on public education.

In approaching this problem, we cannot turn the clock back to 1868 when the Amendment was adopted, or even to 1896 when *Plessy v. Ferguson* was written. We must consider public education in the light of its full development and its present place in American life throughout the Nation. Only in this way can it be determined if segregation in public schools deprives these plaintiffs of the equal protection of the laws.

Today, education is perhaps the most important function of state and local governments. Compulsory school attendance laws and the great expenditures for education both demonstrate our recognition of the importance of education to our democratic society. It is required in the performance of our most basic public responsibilities, even service in the armed forces. It is the very foundation of good citizenship. Today it is a principal instrument in awakening the child to cultural values, in preparing him for later professional training, and in helping him to adjust normally to his environment. In these days, it is doubtful that any child may reasonably be expected to succeed in life if he is denied the opportunity of an education. Such an opportunity, where the state has undertaken to provide it, is a right which must be made available to all on equal terms.

We come then to the question presented: Does segregation of children in public schools solely on the basis of race, even though the physical facilities and other "tangible" factors may be equal, deprive the children of the minority group of equal educational opportunities? We believe that it does.

In *Sweatt v. Painter*, in finding that a segregated law school of Negroes could not provide them equal educational opportunities, this Court relied in large part on "those qualities which are incapable of objective measurement but which make for greatness in a law school." In *McLaurin v. Oklahoma State Regents*, the Court, in requiring that a Negro admitted to a white graduate school be treated like all other students, again resorted to intangible considerations: ". . . his ability to study, to engage in discussions and exchange views with other students, and, in general, to learn his profession." Such considerations apply with added force to children in grade and high schools. To separate them from others of similar age and qualifications solely because of their race generates a feeling of inferiority as to their status in the community that may affect their hearts and minds in a way unlikely ever to be undone. The effect of this separation on their educational opportunities was well stated by a finding in the Kansas case by a court which nevertheless felt compelled to rule against the Negro plaintiffs:

"Segregation of white and colored children in public schools has a detrimental effect upon the colored children. The impact is greater when it has the sanction of the law; for the policy of separating the races is usually interpreted as denoting the inferiority of the negro group. A sense of inferiority affects the motivation of a child to learn. Segregation with the sanction of law, therefore, has a tendency to [retard] the educational and mental development of negro children and to deprive them of some of the benefits they would receive in a racial[ly] integrated school system."

Whatever may have been the extent of psychological knowledge at the time of *Plessy v. Ferguson*, this finding is amply supported by modern authority.* Any language in *Plessy v. Ferguson* contrary to this finding is rejected.

*K. B. Clark, Effect of Prejudice and Discrimination on Personality Development (Midcentury White House Conference on Children and Youth, 1950); Witmer and Kotinsky, Personality in the Making (1952), c. VI; Deutscher and Chein, The Psychological Effects of Enforced Segregation: A Survey of Social Science Opinion, 26 J. Psychol. 259 (1948); Chein, What Are the Psychological Effects of Segregation Under Conditions of Equal Facilities?, 3 Int. J. Opinion and Attitude Res. 229 (1949); Brameld, Educational Costs, in Discrimination and National Welfare (MacIver, ed., 1949), 44–48; Frazier, The Negro in the United States (1949), 674–681. And see generally Myrdal, An American Dilemma (1944).

We conclude that in the field of public education the doctrine of "separate but equal" has no place. Separate educational facilities are inherently unequal. Therefore, we hold that the plaintiffs and others similarly situated for whom the actions have been brought are, by reason of the segregation complained of, deprived of the equal protection of the laws guaranteed by the Fourteenth Amendment . . . .

It is so ordered.

Of obvious importance to the Court in *Brown* was public acceptance of the ruling. The Court has no formal enforcement powers, and the justices expected resistance, especially in the South. Chief Justice Warren went to great pains to obtain a unanimous vote and to unite the Court in a single opinion, written by him, demonstrating that the justices wanted to speak with all the authority they could muster in the hopes of encouraging voluntary compliance.

In the years following *Brown*, the Supreme Court regularly confronted questions of racial discrimination. The death of the separate but equal doctrine had widespread ramifications for American society because a number of states and local governments had laws that mandated segregated facilities. Other rules and restrictions, while not segregating the races, discriminated directly or indirectly against African Americans. Civil rights groups launched attacks on many of these discriminatory policies, as did the Justice Department, especially during the Kennedy and Johnson administrations.

As such challenges were brought before the Supreme Court, the justices faithfully applied the *Brown* precedent. If a case presented intentional discrimination by the government, the justices were not reluctant to declare that the Constitution had been violated. The Court presumed that racial classifications used to discriminate against black Americans violated the Equal Protection Clause of the Fourteenth Amendment (state government discrimination) or the Due

Process Clause of the Fifth (federal government discrimination). Attempts to justify such actions faced a heavy burden of proof. As members of a suspect class, black litigants enjoyed the advantages of the strict scrutiny test. These factors made it difficult for federal, state, and local governments to withstand the attacks made against discriminatory policies and practices. One by one the legal barriers between the races fell.

Since 1954 the Court has developed constitutional doctrine in many areas related to race. Some of these, such as the civil rights protesters' freedom of expression, we have already discussed; others, such as affirmative action and voting rights, will be covered in this chapter and the next. The justices have not always agreed, especially on how to eliminate the effects of past discrimination. But throughout the Court's post-*Brown* history, the justices have said consistently that the Constitution does not permit government classifications that penalize historically disadvantaged racial minorities or that impose distinctions that imply the racial inferiority of any group.

SEX DISCRIMINATION

The number of lawsuits based on claims of sex discrimination has increased dramatically since the 1970s. Before then such cases were rare, and those that reached the Supreme Court ended in decisions that reinforced traditional views of sex roles. In *Bradwell v. Illinois* (1873), for example, the Court heard a challenge to an action by the Illinois Supreme Court denying Myra Bradwell a license to practice law solely because of her sex. The Court, with only Chief Justice Salmon P. Chase dissenting, upheld the state action. Justice Joseph P. Bradley's concurring opinion, which Justices Noah H. Swayne and Stephen J. Field joined, illustrates the attitude of the legal community toward women. Bradley said that he gave his "heartiest concurrence" to contemporary society's "multiplication of avenues for women's advancement," but he added,

Myra Bradwell studied law with her husband, a judge, and edited and published the *Chicago Legal News*, the most important legal publication in the Midwest. Although she passed the bar exam, the Illinois Supreme Court refused to admit her to the state bar because of her sex. She appealed to the U.S. Supreme Court, but lost.

"The natural and proper timidity and delicacy which belongs to the female sex evidently unfits it for many of the occupations of civil life." This condition, according to Bradley, was the product of divine ordinance—that is, God's law.

Similar decisions followed. In 1875 the Court in *Minor v. Happersett* upheld Missouri's denial of voting rights to women, a precedent in effect until ratification of the Nineteenth Amendment in 1920. As late as 1948, the Court upheld the right of the state to ban women from certain occupations. In *Goesaert v. Cleary*, decided that year, the justices declared valid a Michigan law that barred women from becoming bartenders unless they belonged to the immediate family of the bar owner. In explaining the ruling, Justice Frankfurter wrote:

The fact that women may now have achieved the virtues that men have long claimed as their prerogatives and now indulge in vices that men have long practiced, does not preclude the States from drawing a sharp line between the sexes, certainly in such matters as the regulation of the liquor traffic.

In a comparatively modern case, *Hoyt v. Florida* (1961), the justices upheld a Florida law that automatically exempted women from jury duty unless they asked to serve.

During the first half of this century, the Court upheld a number of state laws enacted to protect women in the workplace. These laws dealt with matters such as hours, working conditions, physical demands, and compensation. At the time of their implementation these statutes were seen as a progressive response to the problems faced by the growing number of women employed outside the home. Today these protective laws are considered paternalistic, based as they are on the assumption that women are not the equals of men.

Social change in the 1950s and 1960s, and the growing strength of the women's movement, prompted major alterations in the law. Congress passed a number of federal statutes extending equal rights to women, among them the Equal Pay Act of 1963 and various amendments to the 1964 Civil Rights Act. Many states have passed similar laws to eliminate discriminatory conditions in the marketplace and in state legal codes.

In addition to these legislative actions, in 1972 Congress proposed an amendment to the Constitution. Known as the Equal Rights Amendment, it declared, "Equality of rights under the law shall not be denied or abridged by the United States or by any State on account of sex." The amendment failed to be approved by the required number of states, even though Congress extended the deadline for ratification.

In addition to working for changes in the Constitution and laws, women turned to the courts for redress of their grievances. Many in the women's movement believed that the Due Process and Equal Protection Clauses held the same potential for ensuring women's rights as they had for black Americans, and they began organizing to assert their claims in court.

The Supreme Court issued its first major sex discrimination decision of the contemporary period in 1971. In *Reed v. Reed* the justices considered the validity of an Idaho inheritance statute that used sex classifications. The statute was challenged on the grounds that it was in violation of the Equal Protection Clause of the Fourteenth Amendment. It was clear from the outset that the same requirements that had developed in race relations cases would apply here; that is, the statute's challenger would have to demonstrate both invidious discrimination and state action before a violation could be found.

What was not so clear was what standard of scrutiny the justices would use. In the racial discrimination cases, the Court had declared strict scrutiny the appropriate standard. Racial minorities were considered a suspect class, and, therefore, classifications based on race were presumed to be unconstitutional. The state had a heavy burden of proof if it wished to show that a law based on race was the least restrictive means to achieve a compelling state interest. Much of the success enjoyed by civil rights groups resulted from this favorable legal status. The advocates of equal rights for women, especially American Civil Liberties Union (ACLU) attorneys such as Ruth Bader Ginsburg *(see Box 18-4)*, hoped the Court would adopt the same standard for sex discrimination claims.

BOX 18-4 RUTH BADER GINSBURG

(1993–)

When President Bill Clinton nominated Ruth Bader Ginsburg in 1993 to fill the vacancy left by retiring justice Byron White, the president was enjoying the first such opportunity for a Democrat in more than a quarter century. Ginsburg became the second woman to sit on the Court and the first Jewish justice since the resignation of Abe Fortas in 1969. She brought to the Court a sterling record as a law professor, advocate, and federal judge. She earned a reputation as the "Thurgood Marshall of sex discrimination law" for her pioneering work in that field.

Ginsburg was born in Brooklyn, New York, in 1933 to Nathan and Celia Bader. In 1950 she began her undergraduate studies at Cornell University, where she met her future husband, Martin Ginsburg. After her graduation in 1954, the Ginsburgs lived briefly in Oklahoma where Martin was stationed in the army and Ruth worked for the Social Security Administration. In 1956 they moved to Cambridge, Massachusetts, to attend Harvard Law School. After graduation Martin accepted a job in New York City and Ruth transferred to Columbia Law School to finish her legal training. She graduated from Columbia in 1959, tied for first in her class and having the distinction of serving on the law review staffs at both Harvard and Columbia.

In spite of her academic credentials, Ginsburg's attempts to obtain employment in a major law firm were unsuccessful. She later explained these rejections by noting: "To be a woman, a Jew and a mother to boot, that combination was a bit much." She secured a clerkship with federal district judge Edmund Palmieri, where she worked from 1959 to 1961. She then joined a Columbia University research project on civil law procedures in other countries and became an expert on the Swedish legal system. Ginsburg joined the law faculty at Rutgers University where she worked up the ranks from assistant professor to full professor. In 1972 she returned to Columbia University as professor of law and became the first woman to be awarded tenure at that school.

While on the faculty at Columbia, Ginsburg served as general counsel for the American Civil Liberties Union, heading the Women's Rights Project. In that capacity she was in the vanguard of sex discrimination cases of the 1970s. Her legal arguments before the Supreme Court had a profound impact on the development of sex discrimination law. Of the six cases she argued before the justices, she was successful in five. She participated in *Reed v. Reed* (1971), *Frontiero v. Richardson* (1973), *Kahn v. Shevin* (1974), *Weinberger v. Wiesenfeld* (1975), and *Craig v. Boren* (1976).

In 1980 President Jimmy Carter nominated Ginsburg for the Court of Appeals for the District of Columbia. She was later joined on that court by Clarence Thomas and Antonin Scalia who would precede her to the Supreme Court. In thirteen years as a federal appellate judge, Ginsburg developed a reputation as an intelligent, highly competent jurist with a moderate political ideology.

Ginsburg's nomination to the Supreme Court met with broad, bipartisan approval. She received the highest rating of the American Bar Association. On August 3, 1993, by a vote of 96–3 the Senate confirmed Ruth Bader Ginsburg as the Supreme Court's 107th justice.

SOURCE: "Ruth Ginsburg: Carving a Career Path Through a Male-Dominated Legal World," *Congressional Quarterly Weekly Report*, July 17, 1993, 1876–1877.

Reed v. Reed

404 U.S. 71 (1971)

Vote: 7 (Blackmun, Brennan, Burger, Douglas, Marshall, Stewart, White)

o

Opinion of the Court: Burger

Richard Reed was the adopted child of Sally and Cecil Reed. He died March 29, 1967, in Ada County, Idaho, leaving no will. Richard's parents, who had separated before his death, became involved in a legal dispute over who should administer their son's estate. The estate was insignificant, consisting of a few personal items and a small savings account. The total value was less than $1,000. The probate court judge named Cecil Reed administrator of the estate, in accordance with Idaho law. Section 15-312 of the Idaho code stipulated that when a person died intestate (without a will) an administrator would be appointed according to a list of priority relationships. First priority went to a surviving spouse, second priority to children, third to parents, and so forth. Section 15-314 of the statute stated that in the case of competing petitions from otherwise qualified individuals of the same priority relationship, "males must be preferred to females."

Sally Reed challenged the law as a violation of the Equal Protection Clause of the Fourteenth Amendment. The state district court agreed with her argument, but the Idaho Supreme Court reversed. With assistance of Ginsburg and other ACLU attorneys, Sally Reed took her case to the U.S. Supreme Court.

MR. CHIEF JUSTICE BURGER delivered the opinion of the Court.

Having examined the record and considered the briefs and oral arguments of the parties, we have concluded that the arbitrary preference established in favor of males by § 15-314 of the Idaho Code cannot stand in the face of the Fourteenth Amendment's command that no State deny the equal protection of the laws to any person within its jurisdiction.

Idaho does not, of course, deny letters of administration to women altogether. Indeed, under §15-312, a woman whose spouse dies intestate has a preference over a son, father, brother, or any other male relative of the decedent. Moreover, we can judicially notice that in this country, presumably due to the greater longevity of women, a large proportion of estates, both intestate and under wills of decedents, are administered by surviving widows.

Section 15-314 is restricted in its operation to those situations where competing applications for letters of administration have been filed by both male and female members of the same entitlement class established by § 15-312. In such situations, § 15-314 provides that different treatment be accorded to the applicants on the basis of their sex; it thus establishes a classification subject to scrutiny under the Equal Protection Clause.

In applying that clause, this Court has consistently recognized that the Fourteenth Amendment does not deny to States the power to treat different classes of persons in different ways. The Equal Protection Clause of that amendment does, however, deny to States the power to legislate that different treatment be accorded to persons placed by a statute into different classes on the basis of criteria wholly unrelated to the objective of that statute. A classification "must be reasonable, not arbitrary, and must rest upon some ground of difference having a fair and substantial relation to the object of the legislation, so that all persons similarly circumstanced shall be treated alike." The question presented by this case, then, is whether a difference in the sex of competing applicants for letters of administration bears a rational relationship to a state objective that is sought to be advanced by the operation of §§ 15-312 and 15-314.

In upholding the latter section, the Idaho Supreme Court concluded that its objective was to eliminate one area of controversy when two or more persons, equally entitled under § 15-312, seek letters of administration and thereby present the probate court "with the issue of which one should be named." The court also concluded that where such persons are not of the same sex, the elimination of females from consideration "is neither an illogical nor arbitrary method devised by the legislature to resolve an issue that would otherwise require a hearing as to the relative merits . . . of the two or more petitioning relatives. . . . "

Clearly the objective of reducing the workload on probate courts by eliminating one class of contests is not without some legitimacy. The crucial question, however, is whether § 15-314 advances that objective in a manner consistent with the command of the Equal Protection Clause. We hold that it does not. To give a mandatory preference to members of either sex over members of the other, merely to accomplish the elimination of hearings on the merits, is to make the very kind of arbitrary legislative choice forbidden by the Equal Protection Clause of the Fourteenth Amendment; and whatever may be said as to the positive values of avoiding intrafamily controversy, the choice in this context may not lawfully be mandated solely on the basis of sex.

We note finally that if § 15-314 is viewed merely as a modifying appendage to § 15-312 and aimed at the same objective, its constitutionality is not thereby saved. The objective of § 15-312 clearly is to establish degrees of entitlement of various classes of persons in accordance with their varying degrees and kinds of relationship to the intestate. Regardless of their sex, persons within any one of the enumerated classes of that section are similarly situated with respect to that objective. By providing dissimilar treatment for men and women who are thus similarly situated, the challenged section violates the Equal Protection Clause. The judgment of the Idaho Supreme Court is reversed and the case remanded for further proceedings not inconsistent with this opinion.

Reversed and remanded.

The Court's unanimous decision in *Reed* applied two important principles to sex discrimination. First, the Court refused to accept Idaho's defense of its statute. The state had contended that it was inefficient to hold full court hearings on the relative merits of competing candidates to administer estates, especially small estates. Imposing arbitrary criteria saved court time and avoided intrafamily squabbles. The Supreme Court held that administrative convenience is no justification for violating the Constitution. Sec-

ond, defenders of the Idaho law argued that the arbitrary favoring of males over females made sense because, in most cases, the male will have had more education and experience in financial matters than the competing female. In rejecting this argument, the justices said that laws containing overbroad, sex-based assumptions violate the Equal Protection Clause.

The *Reed* case also signaled that the justices were receptive to sex discrimination claims and would not hesitate to strike down state laws that imposed arbitrary sex classifications. While *Reed* was certainly good news for women's rights advocates, the standard used in the case was not. Chief Justice Burger clearly articulated the rational basis test, holding that laws based on gender classifications must be reasonable and have a rational relationship to a state objective. The Idaho law was sufficiently arbitrary to fail the rational basis test, but other laws and policies might well survive it.

Predictably *Reed v. Reed* encouraged a great deal of sex discrimination litigation. Over the next several years a number of appeals reached the Supreme Court.[2] While these cases dealt with differing subject matter, the most important question explicitly or implicitly presented to the justices had to do with the proper standard of scrutiny to use in sex discrimination cases. Women's rights organizations were committed to persuading the Court to elevate sex discrimination to suspect class test status. The justices were closely divided on the issue, however, and until 1976 no change occurred. In that year the Court decided *Craig v. Boren*, which was to change sex discrimination law fundamentally.

In *Craig v. Boren* the justices adopt an entirely new standard of scrutiny for sex discrimination cases. This test, known as intermediate or heightened scrutiny, requires that laws that classify on the basis of sex be substantially related to an important government ob-

---

2. See, for example, *Frontiero v. Richardson* (1973); *Kahn v. Shevin* (1974); *Stanton v. Stanton* (1975).

jective. It was originally suggested as a compromise solution by attorneys for women's rights groups who feared that the Court majority would remain committed to rational basis. It appealed especially to justices in the center of the Court who were not happy with either the more conservative rational basis test or the liberal suspect class test. Observe how Brennan, writing for the Court, justifies the new test as being consistent with *Reed* and how he treats the use of social science evidence. Also, read carefully Rehnquist's dissenting opinion rejecting the new test, especially as beneficially applied to men.

Craig v. Boren

429 U.S. 190 (1976)
Vote: 7 (Blackmun, Brennan, Marshall, Powell, Stevens, Stewart, White)
2 (Burger, Rehnquist)
Opinion of the Court: Brennan
Concurring opinions: Powell, Stevens
Opinion concurring in judgment: Stewart
Opinion concurring in part: Blackmun
Dissenting opinions: Burger, Rehnquist

In 1972 Oklahoma passed a statute setting the age of legal majority for both males and females at eighteen. Before then, females reached legal age at eighteen and males at twenty-one. The equalization statute, however, contained one exception. Men could not purchase beer, even with the low 3.2 percent alcohol level, until they reached twenty-one; women could buy beer at eighteen. The state differentiated between the sexes in response to statistical evidence indicating a much greater tendency for men in the eighteen-to-twenty-one age bracket to be involved in alcohol-related traffic accidents, including fatalities. Curtis Craig, a man in the restricted age category, joined forces with a beer vendor to challenge the statute as a violation of the Equal Protection Clause. A three-judge district court found the statute valid under the rational basis test. With help from Ginsburg and the ACLU, Craig appealed.

MR. JUSTICE BRENNAN delivered the opinion of the Court.

Analysis may appropriately begin with the reminder that *Reed* emphasized that statutory classifications that distinguish between males and females are "subject to scrutiny under the Equal Protection Clause." To withstand constitutional challenge, previous cases establish that classifications by gender must serve important governmental objectives and must be substantially related to achievement of those objectives. Thus, in *Reed*, the objectives of "reducing the workload on probate courts" and "avoiding intrafamily controversy" were deemed of insufficient importance to sustain use of an overt gender criterion in the appointment of administrators of intestate decedents' estates. Decisions following *Reed* similarly have rejected administrative ease and convenience as sufficiently important objectives to justify gender-based classifications. . . .

Reed v. Reed has also provided the underpinning for decisions that have invalidated statutes employing gender as an inaccurate proxy for other, more germane bases of classification. Hence, "archaic and overbroad" generalizations could not justify use of a gender line in determining eligibility for certain governmental entitlements. Similarly, increasingly outdated misconceptions concerning the role of females in the home rather than in the "marketplace and world of ideas" were rejected as loose-fitting characterizations incapable of supporting state statutory schemes that were premised upon their accuracy. In light of the weak congruence between gender and the characteristic or trait that gender purported to represent, it was necessary that the legislatures choose either to realign their substantive laws in a gender-neutral fashion, or to adopt procedures for identifying those instances where the sex-centered generalization actually comported with fact.

In this case, too, "*Reed*, we feel, is controlling. . . . " We turn then to the question whether, under *Reed*, the difference between males and females with respect to the purchase of 3.2% beer warrants the differential in age drawn by the Oklahoma statute. We conclude that it does not.

The District Court recognized that *Reed v. Reed* was controlling. In applying the teachings of that case, the court found the requisite important governmental objective in the traffic-safety goal proffered by the Oklahoma Attorney General. It then concluded that the statistics introduced by the appellees established that the gender-based distinction was substantially related to achievement of that goal.

. . . Clearly, the protection of public health and safety represents an important function of state and local governments. However, appellees' statistics in our view cannot support the conclusion that the gender-based distinction closely serves to achieve that objective and therefore the distinction cannot under *Reed* withstand equal protection challenge.

The appellees introduced a variety of statistical surveys. First, an analysis of arrest statistics for 1973 demonstrated that 18-20-year-old male arrests for "driving under the influence" and "drunkenness" substantially exceeded female arrests for that same age period. Similarly, youths aged 17–21 were found to be overrepresented among those killed or injured in traffic accidents, with males again numerically exceeding females in this regard. Third, a random roadside survey in Oklahoma City revealed that young males were more inclined to drive and drink beer than were their female counterparts. Fourth, Federal Bureau of Investigation nationwide statistics exhibited a notable increase in arrests for "driving under the influence." Finally, statistical evidence gathered in other jurisdictions, particularly Minnesota and Michigan, was offered to corroborate Oklahoma's experience by indicating the pervasiveness of youthful participation in motor vehicle accidents following the imbibing of alcohol. . . .

Even were this statistical evidence accepted as accurate, it nevertheless offers only a weak answer to the equal protection question presented here. The most focused and relevant of the statistical surveys, arrests of 18-20-year-olds for alcohol-related driving offenses, exemplifies the ultimate unpersuasiveness of this evidentiary record. Viewed in terms of the correlation between sex and the actual activity that Oklahoma seeks to regulate—driving while under the influence of alcohol—the statistics broadly establish that .18% of females and 2% of males in that age group were arrested for that offense. While such a disparity is not trivial in a statistical sense, it hardly can form the basis for em-

ployment of a gender line as a classifying device. Certainly if maleness is to serve as a proxy for drinking and driving, a correlation of 2% must be considered an unduly tenuous "fit." Indeed, prior cases have consistently rejected the use of sex as a decisionmaking factor even though the statutes in question certainly rested on far more predictive empirical relationships than this.

Moreover, the statistics exhibit a variety of other shortcomings that seriously impugn their value to equal protection analysis. Setting aside the obvious methodological problems, the surveys do not adequately justify the salient features of Oklahoma's gender-based traffic-safety law. None purports to measure the use and dangerousness of 3.2% beer as opposed to alcohol generally, a detail that is of particular importance since, in light of its low alcohol level, Oklahoma apparently considers the 3.2% beverage to be "nonintoxicating." Moreover, many of the studies, while graphically documenting the unfortunate increase in driving while under the influence of alcohol, make no effort to relate their findings to age-sex differentials as involved here. Indeed, the only survey that explicitly centered its attention upon young drivers and their use of beer—albeit apparently not of the diluted 3.2% variety—reached results that hardly can be viewed as impressive in justifying either a gender or age classification.

There is no reason to belabor this line of analysis. It is unrealistic to expect either members of the judiciary or state officials to be well versed in the rigors of experimental or statistical technique. But this merely illustrates that proving broad sociological propositions by statistics is a dubious business, and one that inevitably is in tension with the normative philosophy that underlies the Equal Protection Clause. Suffice to say that the showing offered by the appellees does not satisfy us that sex represents a legitimate, accurate proxy for the regulation of drinking and driving. In fact, when it is further recognized that Oklahoma's statute prohibits only the selling of 3.2% beer to young males and not their drinking the beverage once acquired (even after purchase by their 18-20-year-old female companions), the relationship between gender and traffic safety becomes far too tenuous to satisfy *Reed*'s requirement that the gender-based difference be substantially related to achievement of the statutory objective.

We hold, therefore, that under *Reed*, Oklahoma's 3.2%

beer statute invidiously discriminates against males 18-20 years of age.

MR. JUSTICE REHNQUIST, dissenting.

The Court's disposition of this case is objectionable on two grounds. First is its conclusion that *men* challenging a gender-based statute which treats them less favorably than women may invoke a more stringent standard of judicial review than pertains to most other types of classifications. Second is the Court's enunciation of this standard, without citation to any source, as being that "classification by gender must serve *important* governmental objectives and must be *substantially* related to achievement of those objectives." (Emphasis added.) The only redeeming feature of the Court's opinion, to my mind, is that it apparently signals a retreat by those who joined the plurality opinion in *Frontiero v. Richardson* (1973) from their view that sex is a "suspect" classification for purposes of equal protection analysis. I think the Oklahoma statute challenged here need pass only the "rational basis" equal protection analysis expounded in cases such as *McGowan v. Maryland* (1961) and *Williamson v. Lee Optical Co.* (1955), and I believe that it is constitutional under that analysis.

In *Frontiero v. Richardson*, the opinion for the plurality sets forth the reasons of four Justices for concluding that sex should be regarded as a suspect classification for purposes of equal protection analysis. These reasons center on our Nation's "long and unfortunate history of sex discrimination," which has been reflected in a whole range of restrictions on the legal rights of women, not the least of which have concerned the ownership of property and participation in the electoral process. Noting that the pervasive and persistent nature of the discrimination experienced by women is in part the result of their ready identifiability, the plurality rested its invocation of strict scrutiny largely upon the fact that "statutory distinctions between the sexes often have the effect of invidiously relegating the entire class of females to inferior legal status without regard to the actual capabilities of its individual members."

Subsequent to *Frontiero*, the Court has declined to hold that sex is a suspect class, and no such holding is imported by the Court's resolution of this case. However, the Court's application here of an elevated or "intermediate" level scrutiny, like that invoked in cases dealing with discrimina-

tion against females, raises the question of why the statute here should be treated any differently from countless legislative classifications unrelated to sex which have been upheld under a minimum rationality standard.

Most obviously unavailable to support any kind of special scrutiny in this case, is a history or pattern of past discrimination, such as was relied on by the plurality in *Frontiero* to support its invocation of strict scrutiny. There is no suggestion in the Court's opinion that males in this age group are in any way peculiarly disadvantaged, subject to systematic discriminatory treatment, or otherwise in need of special solicitude from the courts.

The Court does not discuss the nature of the right involved, and there is no reason to believe that it sees the purchase of 3.2% beer as implicating any important interest, let alone one that is "fundamental" in the constitutional sense of invoking strict scrutiny. Indeed, the Court's accurate observation that the statute affects the selling but not the drinking of 3.2% beer further emphasizes the limited effect that it has on even those persons in the age group involved. There is, in sum, nothing about the statutory classification involved here to suggest that it affects an interest, or works against a group, which can claim under the Equal Protection Clause that it is entitled to special judicial protection.

It is true that a number of our opinions contain broadly phrased dicta implying that the same test should be applied to all classifications based on sex, whether affecting females or males. However, before today, no decision of this Court has applied an elevated level of scrutiny to invalidate a statutory discrimination harmful to males, except where the statute impaired an important personal interest protected by the Constitution. There being no such interest here, and there being no plausible argument that this is a discrimination against females, the Court's reliance on our previous sex-discrimination cases is ill-founded. It treats gender classification as a talisman which—without regard to the rights involved or the persons affected—calls into effect a heavier burden of judicial review.

The Court's conclusion that a law which treats males less favorably than females "must serve important governmental objectives and must be substantially related to achievement of those objectives" apparently comes out of thin air. The Equal Protection Clause contains no such language, and none of our previous cases adopt that standard.

I would think we have had enough difficulty with the two standards of review which our cases have recognized—the norm of "rational basis," and the "compelling state interest" required where a "suspect classification" is involved—so as to counsel weightily against the insertion of still another "standard" between those two. How is this Court to divine what objectives are important? How is it to determine whether a particular law is "substantially" related to the achievement of such objective, rather than related in some other way to its achievement? Both of the phrases used are so diaphanous and elastic as to invite subjective judicial preferences or prejudices relating to particular types of legislation, masquerading as judgments whether such legislation is directed at "important" objectives or, whether the relationship to those objectives is "substantial" enough.

I would have thought that if this Court were to leave anything to decision by the popularly elected branches of the Government, where no constitutional claim other than that of equal protection is invoked, it would be the decision as to what governmental objectives to be achieved by law are "important," and which are not. As for the second part of the Court's new test, the Judicial Branch is probably in no worse position than the Legislative or Executive Branches to determine if there is *any* rational relationship between a classification and the purpose which it might be thought to serve. But the introduction of the adverb "substantially" requires courts to make subjective judgments as to operational effects, for which neither their expertise nor their access to data fits them. And even if we manage to avoid both confusion and the mirroring of our own preferences in the development of this new doctrine, the thousands of judges in other courts who must interpret the Equal Protection Clause may not be so fortunate.

The heightened scrutiny test was adopted by a narrow margin. Although six justices joined the opinion, Powell's and Stevens's concurring views indicated that their agreement with Brennan's new standard was qualified. Nevertheless, the elevated level of scrutiny was established and since has been used in sex discrimination cases. The battle between strict scrutiny advocates and rational basis proponents thus ended with neither side able to claim victory. The strict scrutiny justices were forced to moderate their position just enough to capture sufficient votes to adopt an intermediate level test.

Heightened scrutiny was a compromise solution that did not fully please those who preferred strict scrutiny or those who favored the rational basis approach. Under such circumstances, the compromise may be temporary, lasting only as long as neither side has sufficient votes to adopt its preferences. In the sexual harassment case of *Harris v. Forklift Systems, Inc.* (1993) Justice Ginsburg signaled that the battle over appropriate standards for sex discrimination cases may be fought again. Consider the following statement contained in a footnote of Ginsburg's concurring opinion in that case: "Indeed, even under the Court's equal protection jurisprudence, which requires 'an exceedingly persuasive justification' for a gender-based classification, it remains an open question whether 'classifications based on gender are inherently suspect.'" Her assertion that gender classification standards remain an open question is a clear indication that at least for Ginsburg the issue is not yet settled. The fact that she included this statement in her first published opinion as a Supreme Court justice may well reflect the importance of this issue to her. Recall that Justice Ginsburg was a prominent sex discrimination litigator prior to her appointment as a federal judge, and she had been involved as an attorney in *Craig v. Boren.*

In the years following *Craig* the Court confronted many claims of unconstitutional discrimination on the basis of sex. In general, the Court continued to strike down laws and government actions that treated individuals differently on the basis of sex simply because it was administratively convenient to do so. The Court also has taken a dim view of laws that include overbroad sex-based assumptions, particularly if a presumption of female inferiority appears to be the basis for the statute. For example, in *Orr v. Orr* (1979) the justices struck down an Alabama law that permitted courts to impose alimony obligations on husbands but not on wives. The law, according to Justice Brennan speaking for the majority, contained an outdated stereotype that women are dependent upon men. Similarly, in *Mississippi University for Women v. Hogan* (1982) the Court struck down the all-female admissions standard used by a state university on the grounds that it was based on a presumption that female students were inferior and in order to succeed needed an academic environment without competition from males.

In other cases, however, the Court found some laws that discriminated between males and females to be valid because they recognized legitimate differences between the sexes. For example, in *Michael M. v. Superior Court of Sonoma County* (1981) the justices, by a 5–4 vote, upheld a statutory rape law that applied to males only. The fact that only females can become pregnant was a significant sex difference that the majority took into account. In *Rostker v. Goldberg* (1981) the Court upheld the federal draft law that required men, but not women to register for military service. Here the justices deferred to the judgment of the military and Congress that the nation required a system for quickly raising combat forces, for which men were better suited.

ECONOMIC DISCRIMINATION

As with matters of race and gender, society's views on economic status have changed. In the nation's early days, wealth was considered a reflection of individual worth. The poor were thought to be less deserving. The free enterprise philosophy that emphasized personal economic responsibility discouraged public policies designed to help the poor. The fact that people could be imprisoned for failure to pay debts (as opposed to today's more lenient treatment under the bankruptcy laws) reflects that period's hard-line approach to economic failure. Even a sitting Supreme Court justice, James Wilson, was imprisoned in 1796 because of a failure to satisfy his creditors. In *City of New York v. Miln* (1837) the Court supported the power of the state to take "precautionary measures against the moral pestilence of paupers."

As American society has evolved, the plight of the poor has become a major public policy concern. Although opinions differ widely on the proper role of government in poverty, housing, and health care, the U.S. political system has developed social programs that would have been inconceivable to leaders during the nation's formative years. Moreover, economic disadvantage is no longer seen as a justification for denying a person full political and social rights. The Supreme Court has ruled in a number of areas with respect to economic status. For example, we have discussed cases in which the Court extended certain rights, such as government-provided attorneys, to indigent criminal defendants. In the next chapter, we will examine the Court's response to states' limiting the right to vote on the basis of economic status. Here we deal with the Supreme Court's position on government policies that directly affect the poor. Among such cases none is more important than *San Antonio Independent School District v. Rodriguez* (1973).

The *Rogriguez* decision is significant for a number of reasons. First, the case involved the right of children to receive a public education, the surest way for the disadvantaged to improve their prospects for economic and social advancement. Second, the case attacked the constitutionality of the Texas method of funding public schools. Education is the most expensive of all state programs, and any change in the method of distributing school funds can have a tremendous impact. Third, the Texas system challenged here was similar to schemes used by most states in determining the allocation of education dollars. Whatever the Court decided, this case was going to be significant economically and socially.

At the heart of this case was the contention that the Texas system for funding schools discriminated against the poor. It was undeniable that children who lived in wealthy school districts had access to a higher quality education than children in poor districts. But does this difference violate the Constitution? In large measure, the answer to that question rests on which equal protection standard is used. Under strict scrutiny the Texas funding system almost certainly would fall. But before strict scrutiny can be applied, one of two requirements has to be met. Either the poor, like black Americans in the racial discrimination cases, would have to be declared a suspect class, or education would have to be declared a fundamental right. If the Court failed to support one of these positions, the rational basis test would control, and the state plan likely would stand. As you read Justice Powell's decision, think about his reasoning and conclusions on these two points.

San Antonio Independent School District v. Rodriguez

411 U.S. 1 (1973)

Vote: 5 (Blackmun, Burger, Powell, Rehnquist, Stewart)
    4 (Brennan, Douglas, Marshall, White)
Opinion of the Court: Powell
Concurring opinion: Stewart
Dissenting opinions: Brennan, Marshall, White

Demetrio Rodriguez and other Mexican-American parents whose children attended the public schools of the Edgewood Independent School District in San Antonio, Texas, were concerned about the quality of the local schools. The Edgewood district was about 90 percent Mexican-American and quite poor. Efforts to improve their children's schools were unsuccessful because the money was not available. Since the state formula for distributing education funds resulted in

Demetrio Rodriguez and other Mexican-American parents challenged the Texas public school financing system as discriminatory on the basis of economic status, but in 1973 the Supreme Court ruled against them.

low levels of financial support for economically depressed districts, the parents filed suit to declare the state funding system in violation of the Equal Protection Clause. The funding program guaranteed each child in the state a minimum basic education by appropriating funds to local school districts through a complex formula designed to take into account economic variations across school districts. Local districts levied property taxes to meet their assigned contributions to the state program but could use the property taxing power to obtain additional funds.

The Edgewood district had an assessed property value per pupil of $5,960, the lowest in the San Antonio area. The district taxed its residents at a rate of

$1.05 per $100 in assessed valuation, the area's highest rate. This local tax yielded $26 per pupil above the contributions that had to be made to the state for the 1967–1968 school year. Funds from the state added $222 per pupil, and federal programs contributed $108. These sources combined for a total of $356 per pupil for the year. In the nearby Alamo Heights district, property values amounted to $49,000 per pupil; property was taxed at a rate of $.85 per $100 of assessed valuation. These property taxes yielded $333 additional available revenues per pupil. Combined with $225 from state funds and $36 from federal sources, Alamo Heights enjoyed a total funding level of $594 per pupil.

The suit filed by Rodriguez and the other parents was based on these disparities. Although the residents of Edgewood taxed themselves at a much higher rate, the yield from local taxes in Alamo Heights was almost thirteen times greater. To achieve equal property tax dollars with Alamo Heights, Edgewood would have had to raise its tax rate to $13 per $100 in assessed valuation, but state law placed a $1.50 ceiling on such taxes. There was no way for the Edgewood parents to achieve funding equality.

A three-judge federal court agreed with the Rodriguez suit, finding that the Texas funding program invidiously discriminated against children on the basis of economic status. According to the federal court, the poor were a suspect class, and education was a fundamental right. The state appealed to the Supreme Court. Twenty-five states filed amicus curiae briefs supporting the Texas funding system. Groups such as the NAACP, the American Civil Liberties Union, and the American Education Association filed briefs backing Rodriguez.

MR. JUSTICE POWELL delivered the opinion of the Court.

Texas virtually concedes that its historically rooted dual system of financing education could not withstand the strict judicial scrutiny that this Court has found appropriate in reviewing legislative judgments that interfere with fundamental constitutional rights or that involve suspect classifications. If, as previous decisions have indicated, strict scrutiny means that the State's system is not entitled to the usual presumption of validity, that the State rather than the complainants must carry a "heavy burden of justification," that the State must demonstrate that its educational system has been structured with "precision," and is "tailored" narrowly to serve legitimate objectives and that it has selected the "less drastic means" for effectuating its objectives, the Texas financing system and its counterpart in virtually every other State will not pass muster. The State candidly admits that "[n]o one familiar with the Texas system would contend that it has yet achieved perfection." Apart from its concession that educational financing in Texas has "defects" and "imperfections," the State defends the system's rationality with vigor and disputes the District Court's finding that it lacks a "reasonable basis."

This, then, establishes the framework for our analysis. We must decide, first, whether the Texas system of financing public education operates to the disadvantage of some suspect class or impinges upon a fundamental right explicitly or implicitly protected by the Constitution, thereby requiring strict judicial scrutiny. If so, the judgment of the District Court should be affirmed. If not, the Texas scheme must still be examined to determine whether it rationally furthers some legitimate, articulated state purpose and therefore does not constitute an invidious discrimination in violation of the Equal Protection Clause of the Fourteenth Amendment.

The District Court's opinion does not reflect the novelty and complexity of the constitutional questions posed by appellees' challenge to Texas' system of school financing. In concluding that strict judicial scrutiny was required, that court relied on decisions dealing with the rights of indigents to equal treatment in the criminal trial and appellate processes, and on cases disapproving wealth restrictions on the right to vote. Those cases, the District Court concluded, established wealth as a suspect classification. Finding that the local property tax system discriminated on the basis of wealth, it regarded those precedents as controlling. It then reasoned, based on decisions of this Court affirming the undeniable importance of education, that there is a fundamental right to education and that, absent some compelling state justification, the Texas system could not stand.

We are unable to agree that this case, which in significant aspects is *sui generis,* may be so neatly fitted into the conventional mosaic of constitutional analysis under the Equal Protection Clause. Indeed, for the several reasons that follow, we find neither the suspect-classification nor the fundamental-interest analysis persuasive.

The wealth discrimination discovered by the District Court in this case, and by several other courts that have recently struck down school-financing laws in other States, is quite unlike any of the forms of wealth discrimination heretofore reviewed by this Court. Rather than focusing on the unique features of the alleged discrimination, the courts in these cases have virtually assumed their findings of a suspect classification through a simplistic process of analysis: since, under the traditional systems of financing public schools, some poorer people receive less expensive educations than other more affluent people, these systems discriminate on the basis of wealth. This approach largely ignores the hard threshold questions, including whether it makes a difference for purposes of consideration under the Constitution that the class of disadvantaged "poor" cannot be identified or defined in customary equal protection terms, and whether the relative—rather than absolute—nature of the asserted deprivation is of significant consequence. Before a State's laws and the justification for the classifications they create are subjected to strict judicial scrutiny, we think these threshold considerations must be analyzed more closely than they were in the court below. . . .

First, in support of their charge that the system discriminates against the "poor," appellees have made no effort to demonstrate that it operates to the peculiar disadvantage of any class fairly definable as indigent, or as composed of persons whose incomes are beneath any designated poverty level. Indeed, there is reason to believe that the poorest families are not necessarily clustered in the poorest property districts. A recent and exhaustive study of school districts in Connecticut concluded that . . . the poor were clustered around commercial and industrial areas—those same areas that provide the most attractive sources of property tax income for school districts. Whether a similar pattern would be discovered in Texas is not known, but

there is no basis on the record in this case for assuming that the poorest people—defined by reference to any level of absolute impecunity—are concentrated in the poorest districts.

Second, neither appellees nor the District Court addressed the fact that, unlike each of the foregoing cases, lack of personal resources has not occasioned an absolute deprivation of the desired benefit. The argument here is not that the children in districts having relatively low assessable property values are receiving no public education; rather, it is that they are receiving a poorer quality education than that available to children in districts having more assessable wealth. Apart from the unsettled and disputed question whether the quality of education may be determined by the amount of money expended for it, a sufficient answer to appellees' argument is that, at least where wealth is involved, the Equal Protection Clause does not require absolute equality or precisely equal advantages. . . .

However described, it is clear that appellees' suit asks this Court to extend its most exacting scrutiny to review a system that allegedly discriminates against a large, diverse, and amorphous class, unified only by the common factor of residence in districts that happen to have less taxable wealth than other districts. The system of alleged discrimination and the class it defines have none of the traditional indicia of suspectness: the class is not saddled with such disabilities, or subjected to such a history of purposeful unequal treatment, or relegated to such a position of political powerlessness as to command extraordinary protection from the majoritarian political process.

We thus conclude that the Texas system does not operate to the peculiar disadvantage of any suspect class. But in recognition of the fact that this Court has never heretofore held that wealth discrimination alone provides an adequate basis for invoking strict scrutiny, appellees have not relied solely on this contention. They also assert that the State's system impermissibly interferes with the exercise of a "fundamental" right and that accordingly the prior decisions of this Court require the application of the strict standard of judicial review. It is this question—whether education is a fundamental right, in the sense that it is among the rights and liberties protected by the Constitution—which has so consumed the attention of courts and commentators in recent years.

In Brown v. Board of Education (1954) a unanimous Court recognized that "education is perhaps the most important function of state and local governments.". . . This theme, expressing an abiding respect for the vital role of education in a free society, may be found in numerous opinions of Justices of this Court writing both before and after *Brown* was decided.

Nothing this Court holds today in any way detracts from our historic dedication to public education. We are in complete agreement with the conclusion of the three-judge panel below that "the grave significance of education both to the individual and to our society" cannot be doubted. But the importance of a service performed by the State does not determine whether it must be regarded as fundamental for purposes of examination under the Equal Protection Clause. . . .

Education, of course, is not among the rights afforded explicit protection under our Federal Constitution. Nor do we find any basis for saying it is implicitly so protected. As we have said, the undisputed importance of education will not alone cause this Court to depart from the usual standard for reviewing a State's social and economic legislation. It is appellees' contention, however, that education is distinguishable from other services and benefits provided by the State because it bears a peculiarly close relationship to other rights and liberties accorded protection under the Constitution. Specifically, they insist that education is itself a fundamental personal right because it is essential to the effective exercise of First Amendment freedoms and to intelligent utilization of the right to vote. In asserting a nexus between speech and education, appellees urge that the right to speak is meaningless unless the speaker is capable of articulating his thoughts intelligently and persuasively. The "marketplace of ideas" is an empty forum for those lacking basic communicative tools. Likewise, they argue that the corollary right to receive information becomes little more than a hollow privilege when the recipient has not been taught to read, assimilate, and utilize available knowledge. . . .

We need not dispute any of these propositions. The Court has long afforded zealous protection against unjustifiable governmental interference with the individual's rights to speak and to vote. Yet we have never presumed to possess either the ability or the authority to guarantee to the citizenry the most *effective* speech or the most *informed* electoral choice. That these may be desirable goals of a system of freedom of expression and of a representative form of government is not to be doubted. These are indeed goals to be pursued by a people whose thoughts and beliefs are freed from governmental interference. But they are not values to be implemented by judicial intrusion into otherwise legitimate state activities. . . .

It should be clear, for the reasons stated above and in accord with the prior decisions of this Court, that this is not a case in which the challenged state action must be subjected to the searching judicial scrutiny reserved for laws that create suspect classifications or impinge upon constitutionally protected rights.

We need not rest our decision, however, solely on the inappropriateness of the strict-scrutiny test. A century of Supreme Court adjudication under the Equal Protection Clause affirmatively supports the application of the traditional standard of review, which requires only that the State's system be shown to bear some rational relationship to legitimate state purposes. This case represents far more than a challenge to the manner in which Texas provides for the education of its children. We have here nothing less than a direct attack on the way in which Texas has chosen to raise and disburse state and local tax revenues. We are asked to condemn the State's judgment in conferring on political subdivisions the power to tax local property to supply revenues for local interests. In so doing, appellees would have the Court intrude in an area in which it has traditionally deferred to state legislatures. This Court has often admonished against such interferences with the State's fiscal policies under the Equal Protection Clause. . . .

Thus, we stand on familiar grounds when we continue to acknowledge that the Justices of this Court lack both the expertise and the familiarity with local problems so necessary to the making of wise decisions with respect to the raising and disposition of public revenues. Yet, we are urged to direct the States either to alter drastically the present system or to throw out the property tax altogether in favor of some other form of taxation. No scheme of taxation, whether the tax is imposed on property, income, or purchases of goods and services, has yet been devised which is free of all discriminatory impact. In such a complex arena in which no perfect alternatives exist, the Court does well not to impose too rigorous a standard of scrutiny lest all local fiscal schemes become subjects of criticism under the Equal Protection Clause.

In addition to matters of fiscal policy, this case also involves the most persistent and difficult questions of educational policy, another area in which this Court's lack of specialized knowledge and experience counsels against premature interference with the informed judgments made at the state and local levels. Education, perhaps even more than welfare assistance, presents a myriad of "intractable economic, social, and even philosophical problems." The very complexity of the problems of financing and managing a statewide public school system suggests that "there will be more than one constitutionally permissible method of solving them," and that, within the limits of rationality, "the legislature's efforts to tackle the problems" should be entitled to respect. . . .

It must be remembered, also, that every claim arising under the Equal Protection Clause has implications for the relationship between national and state power under our federal system. Questions of federalism are always inherent in the process of determining whether a State's laws are to be accorded the traditional presumption of constitutionality, or are to be subjected instead to rigorous judicial scrutiny. While "[t]he maintenance of the principles of federalism is a foremost consideration in interpreting any of the pertinent constitutional provisions under which this Court examines state action," it would be difficult to imagine a case having a greater potential impact on our federal system than the one now before us, in which we are urged to abrogate systems of financing public education presently in existence in virtually every State.

The foregoing considerations buttress our conclusion that Texas' system of public school finance is an inappropriate candidate for strict judicial scrutiny. These same considerations are relevant to the determination whether that system, with its conceded imperfections, nevertheless bears some rational relationship to a legitimate state purpose. . . .

In sum, to the extent that the Texas system of school financing results in unequal expenditures between children who happen to reside in different districts, we cannot say that such disparities are the product of a system that is so irrational as to be invidiously discriminatory. Texas has acknowledged its shortcomings and has persistently endeavored—not without some success—to ameliorate the differences in levels of expenditures without sacrificing the benefits of local participation. The Texas plan is not the result of hurried, ill-conceived legislation. It certainly is not the product of purposeful discrimination against any group or class. On the contrary, it is rooted in decades of experience in Texas and elsewhere, and in major part is the product of responsible studies by qualified people. . . .

These practical considerations, of course, play no role in the adjudication of the constitutional issues presented here. But they serve to highlight the wisdom of the traditional limitations on this Court's function. The consideration and initiation of fundamental reforms with respect to state taxation and education are matters reserved for the legislative processes of the various States, and we do no violence to the values of federalism and separation of powers by staying our hand. We hardly need add that this Court's action today is not to be viewed as placing its judicial imprimatur on the status quo. The need is apparent for reform in tax systems which may well have relied too long and too heavily on the local property tax. And certainly innovative thinking as to public education, its methods, and its funding is necessary to assure both a higher level of quality and greater uniformity of opportunity. These matters merit the continued attention of the scholars who already have contributed much by their challenges. But the ultimate solutions must come from the lawmakers and from the democratic pressures of those who elect them.

Reversed.

MR. JUSTICE MARSHALL . . . dissenting.

The Court today decides, in effect, that a State may constitutionally vary the quality of education which it offers its children in accordance with the amount of taxable wealth located in the school districts within which they reside. The majority's decision represents an abrupt departure from the mainstream of recent state and federal court decisions concerning the unconstitutionality of state educational financing schemes dependent upon taxable local wealth. More unfortunately, though, the majority's holding can only be seen as a retreat from our historic commitment to equality of educational opportunity and as unsupportable acquiescence in a system which deprives children in their earliest years of the chance to reach their full potential as citizens. The Court does this despite the absence of any substantial justification for a scheme which arbitrarily channels educational resources in accordance with the fortuity of the amount of taxable wealth within each district.

In my judgment, the right of every American to an equal start in life, so far as the provision of a state service as important as education is concerned, is far too vital to permit state discrimination on grounds as tenuous as those presented by this record. Nor can I accept the notion that it is sufficient to remit these appellees to the vagaries of the political process which, contrary to the majority's suggestion, has proved singularly unsuited to the task of providing a remedy for this discrimination. I, for one, am unsatisfied with the hope of an ultimate "political" solution sometime in the indefinite future while, in the meantime, countless children unjustifiably receive inferior educations that "may affect their hearts and minds in a way unlikely ever to be undone." I must therefore respectfully dissent.

The decision in *Rodriguez* was a blow to civil rights advocates. It had a substantial impact on education by validating financing systems that perpetuated inequity. Several states, however, reacted by adjusting their financing schemes to reduce funding disparities, and a few state supreme courts even found unequal funding systems to be in violation of state constitutional provisions.

In terms of constitutional development, the ruling introduced problems for future litigation. The Court expressly held that the poor were not a suspect class. Unlike other groups, such as black Americans and aliens, that were granted such status, the poor were neither an easily identified group nor politically powerless; as a group they did not have a history of overt discrimination. The decision not to elevate the poor to suspect class status meant that a rational basis test would be used in economic discrimination cases. As we know, this test provides the government with an advantage in demonstrating that challenged laws are valid. In the years that followed, the Court, increasing-

ly dominated by Reagan and Bush appointees, continued to refrain from expanding constitutional protections for the poor.

In addition, the Court in *Rodriguez* held that education was not a fundamental right under the Constitution. This holding also created potential problems for future cases. Civil rights advocates have concentrated their efforts on education because of its crucial role in human development. By not according it fundamental right status, the Court made litigation in the education field more difficult.

REMEDIES FOR DISCRIMINATION

Creating appropriate standards for interpreting the equal protection principles of the Constitution and determining when governments have engaged in impermissible discrimination are exceedingly difficult tasks. But even when they have been accomplished, the Court's business is not finished. In addition to condemning unconstitutional discrimination, the Court confronts the problem of remedies. To do so means considering acceptable ways to eliminate the discrimination, to implement nondiscriminatory policies, and to compensate the victims of discrimination.

For some discrimination issues remedial action is minimal: striking down a statute may be sufficient. For example, nullifying Idaho's discriminatory inheritance statute in *Reed v. Reed* required no remedial action. The state simply had to decide future estate administration issues without regard to sex.

For other discrimination issues, however, the enforcement of the Court's orders can be a lengthy, complex process. Timetables for change, compliance standards, and methods of implementation pose troublesome choices, and conditions are exacerbated when the affected population resists the change. Furthermore, the Supreme Court not only has created rules for implementing its own equal protection decisions, but also has heard cases challenging the antidiscrimination policies imposed by Congress and the state legislatures.

Issues of remedial action for discrimination are especially troublesome for the Court. The justices, like the nation generally, have been deeply divided over the appropriate actions to take. There is little agreement on what the Constitution requires and what it prohibits. In this final section of the chapter we deal with the two most significant controversies in creating remedies for unconstitutional discrimination: school desegregation and affirmative action.

School Desegregation

Brown v. Board of Education (1954) is a clear example of a judicial decision that required massive efforts for implementation. To agree that the separation of races in the public schools was unconstitutional was far easier than to decide how to end that practice and what would replace it. After all, areas that segregated the races did not enthusiastically embrace a change to fully integrated schools. When the justices issued their unanimous ruling, they instructed the attorneys in *Brown* and the accompanying cases to return the next year and argue the issue of remedies. The result, commonly referred to as *Brown II* (1955), set the stage for the public school desegregation battles that were to dominate the national agenda for the next quarter century and still linger in some districts.

The Court's ruling in *Brown II* focused on two basic questions. The first dealt with who was responsible for implementing desegregation; here the justices held that the primary duty for ending segregation rested with local school boards. These political bodies carried out the general administration of the schools, and they should be responsible for implementing desegregation. The Court, however, was aware that many school boards would resist the change. After all, in most states, board members were elected by the people, and desegregation was very unpopular with the electorate.

To ensure that the school boards acted properly, the Court gave oversight responsibilities to the federal district courts, the trial courts of general jurisdiction for the federal system. Because they are the federal courts closest to the people, their judges understand local conditions. In addition, district court judges enjoy life tenure; they are appointed, not elected. When school boards failed to live up to the expectation of *Brown I*, district judges were instructed to use their equity jurisdiction to fashion whatever remedies were necessary to achieve desegregation. This grant of authority allowed the judges to impose plans especially tailored to meet the specific conditions of the district's schools.

The second question was about the schedule for desegregation. Thurgood Marshall, the chief lawyer for those challenging the segregated schools, requested an immediate end to racial separation. Representatives of the federal government recommended a specific timetable for school boards to develop their desegregation plans. Attorneys for the southern states cited the substantial difficulties standing in the way of compliance and requested a gradual implementation. Chief Justice Warren, speaking for a unanimous Court, did not set a specific schedule, but instead ordered that desegregation take place "with all deliberate speed." This standard acknowledged that the situation in each district would determine how rapidly desegregation could progress. It was also a necessary compromise among the justices to achieve a unanimous ruling.

The combination of massive southern resistance, the vague with-all-deliberate-speed timetable, and the wide latitude granted to district judges in fashioning desegregation plans gave rise to many battles over implementing *Brown*. In each, the justices held steadfast in their desegregation goals. In 1958, for example, in *Cooper v. Aaron* the Court responded firmly to popular resistance in Arkansas by declaring that violence or threats of violence would not be allowed to slow the progress toward full desegregation. Some of the state legislatures and local governments were most creative in devising ways to evade integration. In *Griffin v. Prince Edward County School Board* (1964) the Court stopped a Virginia plan to close down public schools rather than integrate them. In *Green v. School Board of New Kent County* (1968) the justices struck down a "freedom of choice" plan as failing to bring about a nondiscriminatory school system. But by the mid-1960s the justices had begun to lose patience. Justice Black remarked in his opinion for the Court in *Griffin* that "there has been entirely too much deliberation and not enough speed" in enforcing *Brown's* desegregation mandate. The Court made it increasingly clear that dilatory tactics would not be tolerated.[3]

The freedom given to district judges to approve desegregation plans fostered a number of schemes, some of which were criticized by school officials for going too far, and some by civil rights advocates for not going far enough. The specific methods of integration commonly were attacked for exceeding the powers of the district courts. To clear up the confusion, in 1971 the Supreme Court accepted an appeal, which it saw as a vehicle for the declaration of authoritative rules to govern the desegregation process. The case, *Swann v. Charlotte-Mecklenburg County Board of Education*, involved challenges to a desegregation plan imposed by a district judge on North Carolina's largest city. In reading Chief Justice Burger's opinion for a unanimous Court, pay attention to the wide range of powers the Court approves for imposing remedies once a violation of the Constitution has been demonstrated.

---

3. See *Alexander v. Holmes County Board of Education* (1969).

Swann v. Charlotte-Mecklenburg County Board of Education

402 U.S. 1 (1971)

Vote: 9 (Black, Blackmun, Brennan, Burger, Douglas, Harlan, Marshall, Stewart, White)

0

Opinion of the Court: Burger

This case resulted from a longstanding legal dispute over the desegregation of schools in Charlotte, North Carolina. As part of the efforts to bring the district into compliance, the Charlotte schools were consolidated with the surrounding Mecklenburg County schools. The combined district covered 550 square miles, with 107 schools and an enrollment of 84,000 children. Seventy-one percent of the students were white and 29 percent black.

As a result of a plan imposed by the courts in 1965, desegregation began in earnest, but the results were not satisfactory. Of the 21,000 black students in the city of Charlotte, two-thirds attended schools that were at least 99 percent black. All parties agreed that the plan was not working, but there was considerable controversy over what to do. When the school board failed to submit a suitable plan, the district court appointed John Finger, an educational consultant, to devise one. The minority members of the school board and the U.S. Department of Health, Education and Welfare also offered plans. After considerable legal maneuvering, the district court imposed the Finger plan, part of which was later approved by the court of appeals. Both the plaintiffs and the school board appealed to the Supreme Court.

MR. CHIEF JUSTICE BURGER delivered the opinion of the Court.

Nearly 17 years ago this Court held, in explicit terms, that state-imposed segregation by race in public schools denies equal protection of the laws. At no time has the Court deviated in the slightest degree from that holding or its constitutional underpinnings. . . .

Over the 16 years since *Brown II,* many difficulties were encountered in implementation of the basic constitutional requirement that the State not discriminate between public school children on the basis of their race. Nothing in our national experience prior to 1955 prepared anyone for dealing with changes and adjustments of the magnitude and complexity encountered since then. Deliberate resistance of some to the Court's mandates has impeded the good-faith efforts of others to bring school systems into compliance. The detail and nature of these dilatory tactics have been noted frequently by this Court and other courts. . . .

The problems encountered by the district courts and courts of appeals make plain that we should now try to amplify guidelines, however incomplete and imperfect, for the assistance of school authorities and courts. The failure of local authorities to meet their constitutional obligations aggravated the massive problem of converting from the state-enforced discrimination of racially separate school systems. This process has been rendered more difficult by changes since 1954 in the structure and patterns of communities, the growth of student population, movement of families, and other changes, some of which had marked impact on school planning, sometimes neutralizing or negating remedial action before it was fully implemented. Rural areas accustomed for half a century to the consolidated school systems implemented by bus transportation could make adjustments more readily than metropolitan areas with dense and shifting population, numerous schools, congested and complex traffic patterns.

The objective today remains to eliminate from the public schools all vestiges of state-imposed segregation. Segregation was the evil struck down by *Brown I* as contrary to the equal protection guarantees of the Constitution. That was the violation sought to be corrected by the remedial measures of *Brown II.* That was the basis for the holding in *Green* that school authorities are "clearly charged with the affirmative duty to take whatever steps might be necessary to convert to a unitary system in which racial discrimination would be eliminated root and branch."

If school authorities fail in their affirmative obligations under these holdings, judicial authority may be invoked.

Once a right and a violation have been shown, the scope of a district court's equitable powers to remedy past wrongs is broad, for breadth and flexibility are inherent in equitable remedies. . . .

This allocation of responsibility once made, the Court attempted from time to time to provide some guidelines for the exercise of the district judge's discretion and for the reviewing function of the courts of appeals. However, a school desegregation case does not differ fundamentally from other cases involving the framing of equitable remedies to repair the denial of a constitutional right. The task is to correct, by a balancing of the individual and collective interests, the condition that offends the Constitution.

In seeking to define even in broad and general terms how far this remedial power extends it is important to remember that judicial powers may be exercised only on the basis of a constitutional violation. Remedial judicial authority does not put judges automatically in the shoes of school authorities whose powers are plenary. Judicial authority enters only when local authority defaults.

School authorities are traditionally charged with broad power to formulate and implement educational policy and might well conclude, for example, that in order to prepare students to live in a pluralistic society each school should have a prescribed ratio of Negro to white students reflecting the proportion for the district as a whole. To do this as an educational policy is within the broad discretionary powers of school authorities; absent a finding of a constitutional violation, however, that would not be within the authority of a federal court. As with any equity case, the nature of the violation determines the scope of the remedy. In default by the school authorities of their obligation to proffer acceptable remedies, a district court has broad power to fashion a remedy that will assure a unitary school system. . . .

We turn now to the problem of defining with more particularity the responsibilities of school authorities in desegregating a state-enforced dual school system in light of the Equal Protection Clause. Although the several related cases before us are primarily concerned with problems of student assignment, it may be helpful to begin with a brief discussion of other aspects of the process.

In *Green,* we pointed out that existing policy and practice with regard to faculty, staff, transportation, extracurricular activities, and facilities were among the most important indicia of a segregated system. Independent of student assignment, where it is possible to identify a "white school" or a "Negro school" simply by reference to the racial composition of teachers and staff, the quality of school buildings and equipment, or the organization of sports activities, a *prima facie* case of violation of substantive constitutional rights under the Equal Protection Clause is shown.

When a system has been dual in these respects, the first remedial responsibility of school authorities is to eliminate invidious racial distinctions. . . .

The construction of new schools and the closing of old ones are two of the most important functions of local school authorities and also two of the most complex. . . .

In ascertaining the existence of legally imposed school segregation, the existence of a pattern of school construction and abandonment is thus a factor of great weight. In devising remedies where legally imposed segregation has been established, it is the responsibility of local authorities and district courts to see to it that future school construction and abandonment are not used and do not serve to perpetuate or reestablish the dual system. When necessary, district courts should retain jurisdiction to assure that these responsibilities are carried out.

The central issue in this case is that of student assignment, and there are essentially four problem areas:

(1) to what extent racial balance or racial quotas may be used as an implement in a remedial order to correct a previously segregated system;

(2) whether every all-Negro and all-white school must be eliminated as an indispensable part of a remedial process of desegregation;

(3) what the limits are, if any, on the rearrangement of school districts and attendance zones, as a remedial measure; and

(4) what the limits are, if any, on the use of transportation facilities to correct state-enforced racial school segregation.

(1) Racial Balances or Racial Quotas.

The constant theme and thrust of every holding from *Brown I* to date is that state-enforced separation of races in public schools is discrimination that violates the Equal Protection Clause. The remedy commanded was to dismantle dual school systems. . . .

Our objective in dealing with the issues presented by these cases is to see that school authorities exclude no pupil of a racial minority from any school, directly or indirectly, on account of race; it does not and cannot embrace all the problems of racial prejudice, even when those problems contribute to disproportionate racial concentrations in some schools.

In this case it is urged that the District Court has imposed a racial balance requirement of 71%-29% on individual schools. . . .

As the voluminous record in this case shows, the predicate for the District Court's use of the 71%-29% ratio was twofold: first, its express finding, approved by the Court of Appeals and not challenged here, that a dual school system had been maintained by the school authorities at least until 1969; second, its finding, also approved by the Court of Appeals, that the school board had totally defaulted in its acknowledged duty to come forward with an acceptable plan of its own, notwithstanding the patient efforts of the District Judge who, on at least three occasions, urged the board to submit plans. As the statement of facts shows, these findings are abundantly supported by the record. . . .

We see therefore that the use made of mathematical ratios was no more than a starting point in the process of shaping a remedy, rather than an inflexible requirement. From that starting point the District Court proceeded to frame a decree that was within its discretionary powers, as an equitable remedy for the particular circumstances. As we said in *Green*, a school authority's remedial plan or a district court's remedial decree is to be judged by its effectiveness. Awareness of the racial composition of the whole school system is likely to be a useful starting point in shaping a remedy to correct past constitutional violations. In sum, the very limited use made of mathematical ratios was within the equitable remedial discretion of the District Court.

(2) One-race Schools.

The record in this case reveals the familiar phenomenon that in metropolitan areas minority groups are often found concentrated in one part of the city. In some circumstances certain schools may remain all or largely of one race until new schools can be provided or neighborhood patterns change. Schools all or predominantly of one race in a district of mixed population will require close scrutiny to determine that school assignments are not part of state-enforced segregation.

In light of the above, it should be clear that the existence of some small number of one-race, or virtually one-race, schools within a district is not in and of itself the mark of a system that still practices segregation by law. The district judge or school authorities should make every effort to achieve the greatest possible degree of actual desegregation and will thus necessarily be concerned with the elimination of one-race schools. No *per se* rule can adequately embrace all the difficulties of reconciling the competing interests involved, but in a system with a history of segregation the need for remedial criteria of sufficient specificity to assure a school authority's compliance with its constitutional duty warrants a presumption against schools that are substantially disproportionate in their racial composition. Where the school authority's proposed plan for conversion from a dual to a unitary system contemplates the continued existence of some schools that are all or predominately of one race, they have the burden of showing that such school assignments are genuinely nondiscriminatory. The court should scrutinize such schools, and the burden upon the school authorities will be to satisfy the court that their racial composition is not the result of present or past discriminatory action on their part. . . .

(3) Remedial Altering of Attendance Zones.

The maps submitted in these cases graphically demonstrate that one of the principal tools employed by school planners and by courts to break up the dual school system has been a frank—and sometimes drastic—gerrymandering of school districts and attendance zones. An additional step was pairing, "clustering," or "grouping" of schools with attendance assignments made deliberately to accomplish the transfer of Negro students out of formerly segregated Negro schools and transfer of white students to formerly all-Negro schools. More often than not, these zones are neither compact nor contiguous; indeed they may be on opposite ends of the city. As an interim corrective measure, this cannot be said to be beyond the broad remedial powers of a court.

Absent a constitutional violation there would be no basis for judicially ordering assignment of students on a racial basis. All things being equal, with no history of discrimination, it might well be desirable to assign pupils to schools nearest their homes. But all things are not equal in a system that has been deliberately constructed and maintained to enforce racial segregation. The remedy for such segregation may be administratively awkward, inconvenient, and even bizarre in some situations and may impose burdens on some; but all awkwardness and inconvenience cannot be avoided in the interim period when remedial adjustments are being made to eliminate the dual school systems. . . .

We hold that the pairing and grouping of noncontiguous school zones is a permissible tool and such action is to be considered in light of the objectives sought. . . . Conditions in different localities will vary so widely that no rigid rules can be laid down to govern all situations.

(4) Transportation of Students.

The scope of permissible transportation of students as an implement of a remedial decree has never been defined by this Court and by the very nature of the problem it cannot be defined with precision. No rigid guidelines as to student transportation can be given for application to the infinite variety of problems presented in thousands of situations. Bus transportation has been an integral part of the public education system for years, and was perhaps the single most important factor in the transition from the one-room schoolhouse to the consolidated school. Eighteen million of the Nation's public school children, approximately 39%, were transported to their schools by bus in 1969–1970 in all parts of the country. . . .

The importance of bus transportation as a normal and accepted tool of educational policy is readily discernible in this . . . case. . . . The Charlotte school authorities did not purport to assign students on the basis of geographically drawn attendance zones until 1965 and then they allowed almost unlimited transfer privileges. The District Court's conclusion that assignment of children to the school nearest their home serving their grade would not produce an effective dismantling of the dual system is supported by the record.

Thus the remedial techniques used in the District Court's order were within that court's power to provide equitable relief; implementation of the decree is well within the capacity of the school authority.

The decree provided that the buses used to implement the plan would operate on direct routes. Students would be picked up at schools near their homes and transported to the schools they were to attend. The trips for elementary school pupils average about seven miles and the District Court found that they would take "not over 35 minutes at the most." This system compares favorably with the transportation plan previously operated in Charlotte under which each day 23,600 students on all grade levels were transported an average of 15 miles one way for an average trip requiring over an hour. In these circumstances, we find no basis for holding that the local school authorities may not be required to employ bus transportation as one tool of school desegregation. Desegregation plans cannot be limited to the walk-in school.

An objection to transportation of students may have validity when the time or distance of travel is so great as to either risk the health of the children or significantly impinge on the educational process. District courts must weigh the soundness of any transportation plan in light of what is said in subdivisions (1), (2), and (3) above. It hardly needs stating that the limits on time of travel will vary with many factors, but probably with none more than the age of the students. The reconciliation of competing values in a desegregation case is, of course, a difficult task with many sensitive facets but fundamentally no more so than remedial measures courts of equity have traditionally employed.

The Court of Appeals, searching for a term to define the equitable remedial power of the district courts, used the term "reasonableness.". . . . On the facts of this case, we are unable to conclude that the order of the District Court is not reasonable, feasible and workable. However, in seeking to define the scope of remedial power or the limits on remedial power of courts in an area as sensitive as we deal with here, words are poor instruments to convey the sense of basic fairness inherent in equity. Substance, not semantics, must govern, and we have sought to suggest the nature of limitations without frustrating the appropriate scope of equity.

Order of District Court affirmed.

The Court's decision in *Swann* reaffirmed the broad powers of district courts in implementing desegregation. Plans imposed by the courts can affect the placement of teachers, the construction and maintenance of schools, the assignment of staff members, and the equalization of funding among schools within the district. Judges may use the overall racial composition of the district's students to set goals for racial balance in individual schools. Courts are empowered to use a wide arsenal of strategies to assign students to schools, including the rearrangement of attendance zones and the politically unpopular imposition of forced busing.

Although district judges were granted sweeping powers, a careful reading of Burger's opinion reveals certain limits. First, this judicial authority can be used only when the courts have determined that a particular district has violated the Constitution. These powers are remedial. Questions of school administration are to be left to local school officials unless unconstitutional discrimination has occurred and the districts have not made the necessary corrections. Second, the remedy imposed must be tailored to the violation. In Burger's terms, "The nature of the violation determines the scope of the remedy."

These limits have at times been obstacles to achieving effective integration, especially in large metropolitan areas in the North where many independent school districts may be in operation, and some may be composed of one race. True integration can take place only if multiple districts are brought into a single plan. But before a desegregation plan can be imposed on a district, unconstitutional discrimination must be found to have occurred within that particular district. Violations are difficult to prove in northern cities where segregation laws never were in effect and single race neighborhoods grew up without obvious government involvement.

That description fit Detroit, Michigan, in 1972. A district judge ordered a desegregation plan embracing

Detroit and fifty-three suburban school districts. To achieve the integration of the predominantly black central city schools with the largely white suburbs, the judge ordered massive busing. The plan required the purchase of almost 300 school buses and the appropriation of millions of dollars to fund the transportation system. On appeal, the Supreme Court ruled in *Millikin v. Bradley* (1974) by a vote of 5–4 that the district court had exceeded its authority by imposing a desegregation plan on school districts for which there had been no finding of constitutional violations.

The scope and limits of judicial authority to impose remedies for racial segregation remain open and controversial. The desegregation of contemporary metropolitan areas may require overwhelming dislocation and staggering sums of money. District judges often are forced to impose orders that jurisdictions can ill afford. When judges see such desegregation plans as the only way to comply with the Constitution, disputes are likely to follow.

A case in point is the 1989 decision in *Missouri v. Jenkins.* This suit arose out of attempts to attain satisfactory desegregation levels in the public schools of Kansas City, Missouri. The longstanding controversy focused on implementation of the district court's desegregation plan, at the heart of which was an expensive magnet school program. At various times the district judge had imposed spending orders to activate the plan, including $142.7 million for the magnet schools and $187.5 million for capital improvements. Because the state's law imposed certain property tax ceilings, the Kansas City school district could not raise its share of the money. The district judge, therefore, doubled the property tax rate. The state challenged his order, claiming that the district judge had abused his powers. The Supreme Court agreed that the district judge had exceeded his proper discretion, that he could not raise the taxes himself, but he could order city authorities to raise them.

Many school districts have been under court supervision since the early days of *Brown.* Judges still monitor all significant actions taken by these districts to ensure that desegregation efforts continue and that resegregation is not encouraged. How long should such judicial supervision continue, and what standards must school districts meet to be free of it?

The Supreme Court provided a partial answer to these questions in *Board of Education of Oklahoma City Public Schools v. Dowell* (1991). The Oklahoma City schools had been under various levels of judicial supervision since the 1970s. As the 1980s drew to a close, it looked as if the school district was becoming resegregated. The supervising district judge ruled that the court's desegregation decree should be dissolved because the district was in compliance; any resegregation could be traced to residential patterns, not intentional actions taken by school officials. The court of appeals reversed, and the controversy over the appropriate standard came to the Supreme Court. A five-justice majority held that judicial supervision would be ended when, after considering every facet of school operations, the court finds that the elements of state-sanctioned discrimination have been removed "as far as practicable." This standard was attacked by the dissenters (Marshall, Blackmun, and Stevens) as too lenient; they thought districts should remain under court control until all feasible means of removing racial concentrations have been exhausted.

To many observers the Oklahoma City case was an indication that the Rehnquist Court was gradually reducing—perhaps eliminating—close judicial supervision of the public schools on desegregation matters. This conclusion was reinforced one year later when the justices issued their ruling in *Freeman v. Pitts* (1992), a dispute concerning the extent to which the federal courts should maintain supervision over the public schools in DeKalb County, Georgia. The schools in this suburban Atlanta district had been under court supervision since 1969. In 1986 school officials petitioned the district court to release the school system from judicial supervision on the grounds that the county had made sufficient progress toward desegregation. The district court held that the county had achieved satisfactory desegregation in the areas of student assignments, transportation, physical facilities, and extracurricular activities.

The judge noted that the schools were becoming resegregated because of changing residential patterns, but found that such racial imbalances were the result of independent demographic changes unrelated to actions taken by the county. Based on these findings the judge declared that no additional remedial actions would be necessary in the areas where satisfactory progress had been made. However, the judge found inadequate progress in the areas of the assignment of faculty and the allocation of resources. Here, the district court refused to relinquish control and ordered additional remedial steps. The court of appeals reversed, holding that until full compliance was achieved the district court must continue supervision of the entire school system.

On appeal, the Supreme Court upheld the authority of the district court to reduce supervision over desegregation efforts on an incremental basis. It was within the trial court judge's discretion to reduce or eliminate judicial control over areas in which the district had attained compliance with the principles of *Brown,* and to retain control over those areas where compliance had not yet been achieved. The Court, therefore, rejected the more stringent enforcement called for by the appeals court. The vote in the case was unanimous, although in a strongly worded concurring opinion three justices, Blackmun, Stevens, and O'Connor, cautioned that the judiciary must not abdicate its responsibility to ensure that all state-sponsored racial segregation in the public schools be eliminated.

In 1995 the justices gave yet another signal that strict supervision of schools could be eased. The case, *Missouri v. Jenkins,* involved another examination of Kansas City's desegregation progress, which by that time had become the nation's most expensive desegregation effort. The Court held that desegregation plans ordered by federal courts can be ended even if minority students continue to underachieve as measured by standardized tests. The school district has the obligation only to make a good-faith effort at compliance with federal guidelines and to provide all students the same opportunities. In this case Chief Justice Rehnquist, for the majority, concluded that the district had already done more than was constitutionally required.

Although the Rehnquist Court seems eager to reduce the role of the federal courts in running public education systems, the justices remain willing to hand down tough desegregation rulings when necessary. A case in point is *United States v. Fordice* (1992), a challenge to the public universities in Mississippi. The lower federal courts supervising the system had concluded that the state had proceeded in good faith to dismantle the segregated system and that sufficient progress had been made. The Supreme Court, however, disagreed, finding that the system remained segregated in many ways and that additional affirmative efforts to achieve a fully integrated system were needed.

Segregated schools are not the only arena for battles over racial discrimination. Legal confrontations have occurred over housing,[4] employment,[5] admission policies in higher education,[6] and public accommodations.[7] In most of these areas federal civil rights statutes and the government's enforcement of them have played the dominant role. Historically, the Su-

---

4. See, for example, *Reitman v. Mulkey* (1967); *Village of Arlington Heights v. Metropolitan Housing Development Corporation* (1977); *Hills v. Gautreaux* (1976); *Spallone v. United States* (1990).

5. See, for example, *Sheet Metal Workers v. EEOC* (1986); *Wards Cove Packing Company v. Atonia* (1989); *Martin v. Wilks* (1989); *Patterson v. McLean Credit Union* (1989).

6. See, for example, *Regents of the University of California v. Bakke* (1978).

7. See, for example, *Heart of Atlanta Motel v. United States* (1964); *Katzenbach v. McClung* (1964).

preme Court has supported congressional legislation to extend fair treatment to racial minorities. The Burger and Rehnquist Courts, however, handed down some rulings that members of Congress saw as excessively limiting the opportunities of blacks and other disadvantaged groups to assert their statutory rights. In response, Congress has passed or amended laws to counteract the Court's decisions.

Affirmative Action

Few issues of constitutional law have sparked as much controversy as affirmative action. Based on the notion that the principles of the Equal Protection Clause cannot be supported by the simple termination of illegal discrimination, affirmative action programs direct government and private institutions to take positive measures to ensure that equality becomes a reality. This action is necessary, it is argued, because decades of race, sex, and ethnic discrimination have so held back certain segments of the population that special intervention is needed, at least temporarily, to level the playing field.

The affirmative action philosophy takes issue with Justice Harlan's assertion in his *Plessy v. Ferguson* dissent that the Constitution is "color blind," holding instead that characteristics associated with disadvantaged status must be considered and taken into account. Special programs and incentives for people from disadvantaged groups are warranted to eradicate and compensate for the effects of past discrimination. At its core, affirmative action is an attempt to help those who belong to groups that have suffered from longstanding, systematic bias.

Opponents of such special programs, however, see the situation very differently. Many valued goods and opportunities in society—jobs, promotions, contracts, and admission to education and training programs—are scarce. When factors such as race and sex are used (rather than merit alone) to determine who has access to these limited opportunities, the losers may themselves feel victimized and claim reverse dis-

crimination. The principles of equal protection, affirmative action opponents assert, should prohibit discrimination against whites and men just as they prohibit discrimination against blacks and women. Those who have been negatively affected by affirmative action view it as inconsistent with the nation's commitment to equal opportunity.

Affirmative action programs have their roots in presidential orders, issued as early as the 1940s, that expanded government employment opportunities for African Americans. These programs received their most significant boost, however, in 1965 when President Johnson issued Executive Order 11246 instructing the Labor Department to ensure that businesses that contracted with the federal government were nondiscriminatory. To meet the requirements, government contractors altered their employment policies and recruited minority workers. Over the years, these requirements were strengthened and expanded. Failure to comply with the government's principles of nondiscriminatory employment was grounds for stripping any business or institution of its federal contract or appropriated funds. State and local governments adopted similar programs, many aggressively establishing numerical standards for minority participation. Some private businesses voluntarily adopted programs to increase the numbers of women and minorities, especially in positions where their numbers historically had been low. In addition, courts began imposing affirmative action plans on public employers.

Legal obstacles to affirmative action programs arise from two sources. The first is the Constitution. The Equal Protection Clause of the Fourteenth Amendment and the Due Process Clause of the Fifth could be interpreted to prohibit the government from giving special consideration to individuals because of their race, sex, or national origin. The second is the Civil Rights Act of 1964 and related statutes. For example, Title VII specifies, with respect to private employment, that race, color, religion, sex, and national origin cannot be used to discriminate against any employee. It further holds:

It shall be an unlawful employment practice for an employer. . . . to limit, segregate, or classify his employees or applicants for employment in any way which would deprive or tend to deprive any individual of employment opportunities or otherwise adversely affect his status as an employee, because of such individual's race, color, religion, sex, or national origin.

Title VI of the same statute contained similar provisions for state and local government programs that received federal funding. These provisions were originally meant to prohibit discrimination against members of groups that historically have been the victims of prejudice. Whether giving preference to such individuals, at the possible expense of others, also violates these constitutional or statutory provisions remained for the Supreme Court to determine.

Undoubtedly, the most significant decision in establishing the law of affirmative action was *Regents of the University of California v. Bakke* (1978), an Equal Protection Clause challenge to a public university's policy to admit a specific number of minority applicants. The stakes were high. For civil rights groups, the case represented a threat to the best way yet devised to eliminate the effects of past discrimination and promote minority students into professional positions. For opponents of affirmative action, the case presented an opportunity to overturn the growing burden of paying for the sins of the past and return to a system based on merit. Fifty-seven friend of the court briefs were filed by various organizations and interested parties.

The Supreme Court was deeply divided over this case. Four justices gave strong support to affirmative action programs, four others had serious reservations about them, and Justice Powell found himself in the middle. Portions of his opinion announcing the judgment of the Court were supported by one set of four justices, and other parts were joined by an entirely different group of four. As the "swing" justice in this case,

Powell was effectively able to determine what the Constitution means with respect to affirmative action programs.

Regents of the University of California v. Bakke

438 U.S. 265 (1978)
Vote:5 (Burger, Powell, Rehnquist, Stevens, Stewart)
*   4 (Blackmun, Brennan, Marshall, White)*
Opinion announcing the judgment of the Court: Powell
Opinion concurring in part and dissenting in part: Blackmun, Brennan, Marshall and White
Separate opinion: White
Separate opinion: Marshall
Separate opinion: Blackmun
Opinion concurring in part and dissenting in part: Stevens

The medical school of the University of California at Davis began operations in 1968. In its first two years, it admitted only three minority students, all Asians. To improve minority participation, the school developed two admissions programs to fill the 100 seats in its entry class—a regular admissions program and a special admissions program. The regular admissions program worked in the customary way, in which applicants were evaluated on the basis of undergraduate grades, standardized test scores, letters of recommendation, extracurricular activities, and an interview. The special admissions program was for applicants who indicated that they were economically or educationally disadvantaged, or were black, Chicano, Asian, or Native American. Such applicants could choose to go through the regular admissions process or to be referred to a special admissions committee. Special admissions applicants were judged on the same characteristics as the regular applicants, but they competed only against each other. The school reserved sixteen seats to be filled from the special admissions pool. Many white applicants, claiming poverty, indicated a desire to be considered by the

Twice rejected for admission to the medical school of the University of California at Davis, Allan Bakke (center) filed suit challenging school policy that admitted minority students with grades and test scores lower than his. Bakke's suit led to the Supreme Court's first major statement on the constitutionality of affirmative action programs. Bakke was awarded his medical degree from the university in 1982.

special admissions committee, but none was admitted. All specially admitted students were members of the designated minority groups.

Allan Bakke was a white man of Scandinavian descent. He graduated with honors in engineering from the University of Minnesota and was a veteran of the Vietnam War. He worked for the National Aeronautics and Space Administration and received his master's degree in engineering from Stanford. When he developed an interest in pursuing a medical career, Bakke took extra science courses and did volunteer work in a local hospital. At age thirty-three, he applied for admission to the 1973 entry class of the medical school at Davis. He was rejected. He applied in 1974 and was again rejected. Because applicants admitted under the special admissions program were, at least statistically, less qualified than he *(see Table 18-1)*,

Bakke sued for admission, claiming that the university's dual admissions program violated the Equal Protection Clause of the Fourteenth Amendment.

The state trial court struck down the special program, declaring that race could not be constitutionally taken into account in deciding who would be admitted, but the court refused to order Bakke's admission. Both Bakke and the university appealed. The California Supreme Court found the special admissions program unconstitutional, holding that "no applicant may be rejected because of his race, in favor of another who is less qualified, as measured by standards applied without regard to race." The state supreme court's order to admit Bakke was stayed, pending the university's appeal to the U.S. Supreme Court.

TABLE 18-1 Admissions Data for the Entering Class of the Medical School of the University of California at Davis, 1973 and 1974

Class Entering in 1973

| | SGPA[a] | OGPA[b] | Verbal | MCAT (Percentiles) | | |
				Quantitative	Science	Gen. Infor.
Bakke	3.44	3.46	96	94	97	72
Average of regular admittees	3.51	3.49	81	76	83	69
Average of special admittees	2.62	2.88	46	24	35	33

Class Entering in 1974

| | SGPA[a] | OGPA[b] | Verbal | MCAT (Percentiles) | | |
				Quantitative	Science	Gen. Infor.
Bakke	3.44	3.46	96	94	97	72
Average of regular admittees	3.36	3.29	69	67	82	72
Average of special admittees	2.42	2.62	34	30	37	18

SOURCE: *Regents of the University of California v. Bakke* (1978).

NOTES: a. Science grade point average.

b. Overall grade point average.

MR. JUSTICE POWELL announced the judgment of the Court.

Petitioner does not deny that decisions based on race or ethnic origin by faculties and administrations of state universities are reviewable under the Fourteenth Amendment. For his part, respondent does not argue that all racial or ethnic classifications are *per se* invalid. The parties do disagree as to the level of judicial scrutiny to be applied to the special admissions program. Petitioner argues that the court below erred in applying strict scrutiny, as this inexact term has been applied in our cases. That level of review, petitioner asserts, should be reserved for classifications that disadvantage "discrete and insular minorities." Respondent, on the other hand, contends that the California court correctly rejected the notion that the degree of judicial scrutiny accorded a particular racial or ethnic classification hinges upon membership in a discrete and insular minority and duly recognized that the "rights established [by the Fourteenth Amendment] are personal rights."

En route to this crucial battle over the scope of judicial review, the parties fight a sharp preliminary action over the proper characterization of the special admissions program. Petitioner prefers to view it as establishing a "goal" of minority representation in the Medical School. Respondent, echoing the courts below, labels it a racial quota.

This semantic distinction is beside the point: The special admissions program is undeniably a classification based on race and ethnic background. To the extent that there existed a pool of at least minimally qualified minority applicants to fill the 16 special admissions seats, white applicants could compete only for 84 seats in the entering class, rather than the 100 open to minority applicants. Whether this limitation is described as a quota or a goal, it is a line drawn on the basis of race and ethnic status.

The guarantees of the Fourteenth Amendment extend to all persons. Its language is explicit: "No State shall . . . deny to any person within its jurisdiction the equal protection of the laws." It is settled beyond question that the "rights created by the first section of the Fourteenth Amendment are, by its terms, guaranteed to the individual. The rights established are personal rights." The guarantee of equal protection cannot mean one thing when applied to one individual and something else when applied to a person of another color. If both are not accorded the same protection, then it is not equal. . . .

Racial and ethnic distinctions of any sort are inherently suspect and thus call for the most exacting judicial examination. . . .

Although many of the Framers of the Fourteenth Amendment conceived of its primary function as bridging the vast distance between members of the Negro race and the white "majority," the Amendment itself was framed in universal terms, without reference to color, ethnic origin, or condition of prior servitude. . . .

Petitioner urges us to adopt for the first time a more restrictive view of the Equal Protection Clause and hold that discrimination against members of the white "majority" cannot be suspect if its purpose can be characterized as "benign." The clock of our liberties, however, cannot be turned back to 1868. It is far too late to argue that the guarantee of equal protection to *all* persons permits the recognition of special wards entitled to a degree of protection greater than that accorded others. "The Fourteenth Amendment is not directed solely against discrimination due to a 'two-class theory'—that is, based upon differences between 'white' and Negro." . . .

If it is the individual who is entitled to judicial protection against classifications based upon his racial or ethnic background because such distinctions impinge upon personal rights, rather than the individual only because of his membership in a particular group, then constitutional standards may be applied consistently. Political judgments regarding the necessity for the particular classification may be weighed in the constitutional balance, but the standard of justification will remain constant. This is as it should be, since those political judgments are the product of rough compromise struck by contending groups within the democratic process. When they touch upon an individual's race or ethnic background, he is entitled to a judicial determination that the burden he is asked to bear on that basis is precisely tailored to serve a compelling governmental interest. The Constitution guarantees that right to every person regardless of his background. . . .

We have held that in "order to justify the use of a suspect classification, a State must show that its purpose or interest is both constitutionally permissible and substantial, and that its use of the classification is 'necessary. . . . to the accomplishment' of its purpose or the safeguarding of its interest." The special admissions program purports to serve the purposes of: (i) "reducing the historic deficit of traditionally disfavored minorities in medical schools and in the medical profession"; (ii) countering the effects of societal discrimination; (iii) increasing the number of physicians who will practice in communities currently underserved; and (iv) obtaining the educational benefits that flow from an ethnically diverse student body. It is necessary to decide which, if any, of these purposes is substantial enough to support the use of a suspect classification.

If petitioner's purpose is to assure within its student body some specified percentage of a particular group merely because of its race or ethnic origin, such a preferential purpose must be rejected not as insubstantial but as facially invalid. Preferring members of any one group for no reason other than race or ethnic origin is discrimination for its own sake. This the Constitution forbids.

The State certainly has a legitimate and substantial interest in ameliorating, or eliminating where feasible, the disabling effects of identified discrimination. The line of school desegregation cases, commencing with *Brown*, attests to the importance of this state goal and the commitment of the judiciary to affirm all lawful means toward its attainment. In the school cases, the States were required by court order to redress the wrongs worked by specific instances of racial discrimination. That goal was far more focused than the remedying of the effects of "societal discrimination," an amorphous concept of inquiry that may be ageless in its reach into the past.

We have never approved a classification that aids persons perceived as members of relatively victimized groups at the expense of other innocent individuals in the absence of judicial, legislative, or administrative findings of constitutional or statutory violations. After such findings have been made, the governmental interest in preferring members of the injured groups at the expense of others is substantial, since the legal rights of the victims must be vindicated. In such a case, the extent of the injury and the consequent remedy will have been judicially, legislatively, or administratively defined. Also, the remedial action usually remains subject to continuing oversight to assure that it will work the least harm possible to other innocent persons competing for the benefit. Without such findings of constitutional or statutory violations, it cannot be said that the government has any greater interest in helping one individual than in refraining from harming another. Thus, the government has no compelling justification for inflicting such harm.

Petitioner does not purport to have made, and is in no position to make, such findings. Its broad mission is education, not the formulation of any legislative policy or the adjudication of particular claims of illegality. . . . Before relying upon these sorts of findings in establishing a racial classification, a governmental body must have the authority and capability to establish, in the record, that the classification is responsive to identified discrimination. Lacking this capability, petitioner has not carried its burden of justification on this issue.

Hence, the purpose of helping certain groups whom the faculty of the Davis Medical School perceived as victims of "societal discrimination" does not justify a classification that imposes disadvantages upon persons like respondent, who bear no responsibility for whatever harm the beneficiaries of the special admissions program are thought to have suffered. To hold otherwise would be to convert a remedy heretofore reserved for violations of legal rights into a privilege that all institutions throughout the Nation could grant at their pleasure to whatever groups are perceived as victims of societal discrimination. That is a step we have never approved.

Petitioner identifies, as another purpose of its program, improving the delivery of health-care services to communities currently underserved. It may be assumed that in some situations a State's interest in facilitating the health care of its citizens is sufficiently compelling to support the use of a suspect classification. But there is virtually no evidence in the record indicating that petitioner's special admissions program is either needed or geared to promote that goal. . . .

Petitioner simply has not carried its burden of demonstrating that it must prefer members of particular ethnic groups over all other individuals in order to promote better health-care delivery to deprived citizens. Indeed, petitioner has not shown that its preferential classification is likely to have any significant effect on the problem.

The fourth goal asserted by petitioner is the attainment of a diverse student body. This clearly is a constitutionally permissible goal for an institution of higher education. Academic freedom, though not a specifically enumerated constitutional right, long has been viewed as a special concern of the First Amendment. The freedom of a university to make its own judgments as to education includes the selection of its student body. . . .

The atmosphere of "speculation, experiment and creation"—so essential to the quality of higher education—is widely believed to be promoted by a diverse student body. As the Court noted in *Keyishian* [*v. Board of Regents of the University of the State of New York*, 1967] it is not too much to say that the "nation's future depends upon leaders trained through wide exposure" to the ideas and mores of students as diverse as this Nation of many peoples.

Thus, in arguing that its universities must be accorded the right to select those students who will contribute the most to the "robust exchange of ideas," petitioner invokes a countervailing constitutional interest, that of the First Amendment. In this light, petitioner must be viewed as seeking to achieve a goal that is of paramount importance in the fulfillment of its mission.

It may be argued that there is greater force to these views at the undergraduate level than in a medical school where the training is centered primarily on professional competency. But even at the graduate level, our tradition and experience lend support to the view that the contribution of diversity is substantial. . . . Physicians serve a heterogeneous population. An otherwise qualified medical student with a particular background—whether it be ethnic, geographic, culturally advantaged or disadvantaged— may bring to a professional school of medicine experiences, outlooks, and ideas that enrich the training of its student body and better equip its graduates to render with understanding their vital service to humanity.

Ethnic diversity, however, is only one element in a range of factors a university properly may consider in attaining the goal of a heterogeneous student body. Although a university must have wide discretion in making the sensitive judgments as to who should be admitted, constitutional limitations protecting individual rights may not be disregarded. Respondent urges—and the courts below have held—that petitioner's dual admissions program is a racial classification that impermissibly infringes his rights under the Fourteenth Amendment. As the interest of diversity is compelling in the context of a university's admissions program, the question remains whether the program's racial classification is necessary to promote this interest. . . .

It may be assumed that the reservation of a specified number of seats in each class for individuals from the preferred ethnic groups would contribute to the attainment of considerable ethnic diversity in the student body. But petitioner's argument that this is the only effective means of serving the interest of diversity is seriously flawed. In a most fundamental sense the argument misconceives the nature of the state interest that would justify consideration of race or ethnic background. It is not an interest in simple ethnic diversity, in which a specified percentage of the student body is in effect guaranteed to be members of selected ethnic groups, with the remaining percentage an undifferentiated aggregation of students. The diversity that furthers a compelling state interest encompasses a far broader array of qualifications and characteristics of which racial or ethnic origin is but a single though important element. Petitioner's special admissions program, focused *solely* on ethnic diversity, would hinder rather than further attainment of genuine diversity.

Nor would the state interest in genuine diversity be served by expanding petitioner's two-track system into a multitrack program with a prescribed number of seats set aside for each identifiable category of applicants. Indeed, it is conceivable that a university would thus pursue the logic of petitioner's two-track program to the illogical end of insulating each category of applicants with certain desired qualifications from competition with all other applicants. . . .

In such an admissions program, race or ethnic background may be deemed a "plus" in a particular applicant's file, yet it does not insulate the individual from comparison with all other candidates for the available seats. The file of a particular black applicant may be examined for his potential contribution to diversity without the factor of race being decisive when compared, for example, with that of an applicant identified as an Italian-American if the latter is thought to exhibit qualities more likely to promote beneficial educational pluralism. Such qualities could include exceptional personal talents, unique work or service experience, leadership potential, maturity, demonstrated com-

passion, a history of overcoming disadvantage, ability to communicate with the poor, or other qualifications deemed important. In short, an admissions program operated in this way is flexible enough to consider all pertinent elements of diversity in light of the particular qualifications of each applicant, and to place them on the same footing for consideration, although not necessarily according them the same weight. Indeed, the weight attributed to a particular quality may vary from year to year depending upon the "mix" both of the student body and the applicants for the incoming class.

This kind of program treats each applicant as an individual in the admissions process. The applicant who loses out on the last available seat to another candidate receiving a "plus" on the basis of ethnic background will not have been foreclosed from all consideration for that seat simply because he was not the right color or had the wrong surname. It would mean only that his combined qualifications, which may have included similar nonobjective factors, did not outweigh those of the other applicant. His qualifications would have been weighed fairly and competitively, and he would have no basis to complain of unequal treatment under the Fourteenth Amendment. . . .

In summary, it is evident that the Davis special admissions program involves the use of an explicit racial classification never before countenanced by this Court. It tells applicants who are not Negro, Asian, or Chicano that they are totally excluded from a specific percentage of the seats in an entering class. No matter how strong their qualifications, quantitative and extracurricular, including their own potential for contribution to educational diversity, they are never afforded the chance to compete with applicants from the preferred groups for the special admissions seats. At the same time, the preferred applicants have the opportunity to compete for every seat in the class.

The fatal flaw in petitioner's preferential program is its disregard of individual rights as guaranteed by the Fourteenth Amendment. Such rights are not absolute. But when a State's distribution of benefits or imposition of burdens hinges on ancestry or the color of a person's skin, that individual is entitled to a demonstration that the challenged classification is necessary to promote a substantial state interest. Petitioner has failed to carry this burden. For this reason, that portion of the California court's judgment holding petitioner's special admissions program invalid under the Fourteenth Amendment must be affirmed.

In enjoining petitioner from ever considering the race of any applicant, however, the courts below failed to recognize that the State has a substantial interest that legitimately may be served by a properly devised admissions program involving the competitive consideration of race and ethnic origin. For this reason, so much of the California court's judgment as enjoins petitioner from any consideration of the race of any applicant must be reversed.

With respect to respondent's entitlement to an injunction directing his admission to the Medical School, petitioner has conceded that it could not carry its burden of proving that, but for the existence of its unlawful special admissions program, respondent still would not have been admitted. Hence, respondent is entitled to the injunction, and that portion of the judgment must be affirmed.

The *Bakke* decision held that absent a history of racial discrimination demanding a strong remedy, affirmative action programs that set quotas for particular racial or ethnic groups violate the Equal Protection Clause. But minority status may play a role in the admissions process. Universities may seek to assemble a diverse student body by giving minority applicants special consideration. Race and ethnic background may permissibly be deemed a plus, but they cannot be the only factor determining admissions outcomes.

But what if a history of racial discrimination is present, or if certain racial, ethnic, or gender groups historically have been excluded from particular programs, occupations, and so forth? Does the Constitution or federal law prohibit the use of racial classifications as a means of correcting the situation? Under such circumstances the Court has generally permitted strong affirmative action program in both the public[8] and the private sector.[9] Occasionally, when

8. See, for example, *Johnson v. Transportation Agency of Santa Clara County, California* (1987).

9. *United Steelworkers of America v. Weber* (1979).

the situation has demanded it, the Court has even allowed the use of quotas that it condemned in *Bakke.*

United States v. Paradise (1987) provides a good example. This dispute centered on the hiring practices of the Alabama Department of Public Safety. In 1972 a district judge found the department in violation of the Equal Protection Clause: in the thirty-seven years since its inception, the department had not hired a single black state trooper. Blacks had been employed only as laborers. The district court imposed a strict 50 percent black hiring quota for all troopers and instructed the department to rid itself of all discriminatory practices, including those involving promotions. During the next twelve years, however, the department failed to achieve that goal. By 1984 only four blacks had been promoted to corporal, and none had been promoted to major, captain, lieutenant, or sergeant. In response to this lack of progress, the district court imposed a temporary 50 percent black quota for promotion to corporal and a similar, though conditioned, quota for promotions to the higher ranks.

The Reagan administration, which was opposed to the imposition of strict racial quotas, objected to the district court's order. Attempts to block the plan were unsuccessful at the court of appeals level, and the government asked the Supreme Court for review. In a 5–4 vote, the Court upheld the promotion quotas. The plurality opinion, issued by Justice Brennan, stressed the long history of discrimination by Alabama officials and the lack of progress made since the district court's first finding of constitutional violations. The remedy imposed here, according to the majority, was necessary given the extreme nature of the violations. The plan was temporary and flexible, and it did not overly burden innocent parties. Writing for the dissenters, Justice O'Connor said that less extreme plans might have been just as effective and should have been considered before the imposition of quotas.

A variation of the traditional affirmative action

programs is the minority set-aside. Minority set-asides attempt to enhance the prospects of disadvantaged groups by granting them special considerations in the awarding of government contracts and benefits. The justification for such programs is the long history of discrimination against minority-owned businesses in general commercial activity and in providing goods and services for the government. Set-asides are based on the principle that just eliminating discrimination in the letting of government contracts will not result in more business for minority-owned firms. Because of past discrimination, many minority businesses lack capital, management experience, and eligibility for bonding. They cannot compete successfully with more solid, better-financed white firms. Consequently, minority set-aside programs propose for a time to reserve a percentage of government business and contracts for minority-owned enterprises.

Set-aside programs received their first significant review by the Court in 1980 in *Fullilove v. Klutznick.* The Court's deliberations reveal that the justices were no more able to reach consensus here than they had on affirmative action issues. *Fullilove* concerned the Public Works Employment Act passed by Congress in 1977. A provision of that law directed that in federally financed state public works projects 10 percent of the goods and services had to be procured from minority-owned businesses. A minority-owned business was defined as a company at least 50 percent owned by citizens of the United States who were black, Spanish-speaking, Asian, Native American, Eskimo, or Aleut. The constitutionality of the statute was attacked by a group of contractors who claimed that enforcement of the statute had injured them economically.

The Supreme Court upheld the validity of the law as a remedial action to correct a history of discrimination in government contracting. Although the vote in the case was 6–3, the divisions among the justices were many and deep. Five different opinions were written, and no opinion garnered the support of more than three justices. Burger, Powell, and White held that the law was constitutional as a necessary means of advancing a compelling government interest. In their view, the law was a narrow and carefully tailored measure to eliminate a particular type of discrimination. Marshall, Brennan, and Blackmun also supported the law's validity. They adhered to the views they had expressed in *Bakke* giving strong support for the use of quotas as a means to alleviate discrimination. Stewart, Rehnquist, and Stevens dissented. Stewart wrote a strong opinion arguing that the Constitution should be hostile to all racial classifications.

Despite the divisions, six justices voted in *Fullilove* to uphold the federal set-aside program. This decision encouraged state and local governments that wanted to use the same kind of remedial approach. In *City of Richmond v. J. A. Croson Co.* (1989) the Court reviewed such a plan enacted by the city of Richmond, Virginia.

In 1983 the Richmond City Council, consisting of five black and four white members, adopted the Minority Utilization Plan, which required the city's prime contractors to award subcontracts of at least 30 percent of the dollar amount of the total contract to one or more minority business enterprises (MBEs). Minority contractors were defined as businesses at least 51 percent owned by persons who were black, Spanish-speaking, Asian, Native American, Eskimo, or Aleut. The minority business did not have to be located in Richmond.

The plan was developed to correct the effects of racial discrimination. Richmond's population was 50 percent black, but between 1978 and 1983 only .678 percent of the city's construction business had been awarded to minority contractors. There was no specific finding that the city had discriminated in awarding contracts to minority businesses; the problem stemmed largely from a lack of minority-owned contracting businesses in the Richmond area.

The Croson company was the only bidder on a project to install plumbing fixtures at the city jail, but the company had difficulty finding a minority subcontractor to supply the materials. Once Croson located a qualified company willing to participate, the projected price was too high. Croson requested a waiver from the set-aside requirements or permission to raise the cost of the project. The city refused and elected to re-bid the contract. Croson sued to have the set-aside program declared unconstitutional as a violation of the Equal Protection Clause of the Fourteenth Amendment.

The Supreme Court struck down the set-aside program. In a strongly worded opinion written by Justice O'Connor, the majority found numerous defects in the Richmond plan. First, there had been no finding based on evidence that the situation in the Richmond's construction industry was the result of any constitutional violation that required a remedial response. Second, the program included groups for which there was no evidence whatever of discrimination in Richmond (specifically, Hispanics, Asians, Native Americans, Eskimos, or Aleuts). Third, the program allowed contracting dollars to be given to out-of-state minority firms, hardly a strategy that was tailored to remedy discrimination against Richmond firms. Fourth, there was no evidence that the city of Richmond had considered race-neutral alternatives. Fifth, the 30 percent figure appeared to have been arbitrarily set. Sixth, the plan was not a temporary one to correct a specific constitutional violation. Along with these fatal defects, the Court ruled that such programs had to meet strict scrutiny standards of review.

The Court's strong condemnation of Richmond's minority set-aside program was a clear signal to other state and local governments that plans to increase business for minority-owned enterprises were going to be difficult to justify. The decision also gave encouragement to those majority-owned businesses that wanted to challenge such plans.

One year later, however, the Court heard another case involving the constitutionality of a plan to promote minority businesses, *Metro Broadcasting v. FCC* (1990). Attacked here was an affirmative action program created by the Federal Communications Commission to increase the number of minority-owned radio and television stations. Applications for broadcasting licenses submitted by minority-owned businesses were given special preferences, and in some cases minority firms were allowed to purchase a license at less than market value. In this case the justices seemingly pulled back from the attitudes expressed in *Croson* and upheld the plan. Furthermore, the justices held that the federal government's affirmative action and minority set aside program only had to meet the standards of intermediate scrutiny.

Needless to say, the result of these decisions was considerable confusion. Not only did the standard of scrutiny seem to vary from case to case, but the affirmative action and minority set aside cases were being decided consistently by 5–4 or 6–3 votes, which indicated that the state of the law was very unstable. Adding to the problem was personnel turnover on the Court. Between 1990 and 1994 Justices Brennan, Marshall, Blackmun, and White retired. These justices accounted for four of the five votes that made up the Metro Broadcasting majority. This left the affirmative action question in considerable doubt.

It was not until 1995 that the Court accepted its next major affirmative action/minority set-aside dispute. The case attracted a great deal of attention. As you read the Court's decision in *Adarand Constructors, Inc. v. Pena* (1995), pay close attention to the various positions expressed. Justice O'Connor's opinion for the majority returns the Court to the hard-line position she took in *Croson*, but the concurring opinions of Justices Scalia and Thomas take an even more negative approach to race-based remedial programs. The four dissenters, however, strongly defend federal minority set aside programs.

Adarand Constructors, Inc. v. Pena

___ U.S. ___ (1995)
Vote: 5 *(Kennedy, O'Connor, Rehnquist, Scalia, Thomas)*
     4 *(Breyer, Ginsburg, Souter, Stevens)*
Opinion of the Court: O'Connor
Concurring opinions: Scalia, Thomas
Dissenting opinions: Ginsburg, Souter, Stevens

This legal action challenges the validity of certain minority preferences in federal construction projects. At issue is a preference clause used in contracts issued by the Federal Highway Division under the Federal Construction Procurement Program and ultimately authorized by the Small Business Act (SBA) and the Surface Transportation and Uniform Relocation Assistance Act of 1987 (STURAA). The preference policy allows the prime contractor a monetary bonus if at least 10 percent of the overall contract amount is subcontracted to "disadvantaged business enterprises" (DBEs). All small businesses owned and operated by African Americans, Hispanics, Asians, Native Americans, as well as several other national origin groups are considered DBEs.

In 1989 the Federal Highway Division awarded a prime contract for highway work in Colorado to Mountain Gravel and Construction Company. Adarand Constructors, owned and operated by a white man, submitted the lowest subcontract bid to do guardrail work on the project. However, the guardrail contract was issued to Gonzales Construction, a minority-owned firm. Because Mountain Gravel awarded the subcontract to a DBE, it received a $10,000 bonus.

Adarand filed suit against Secretary of Transportation Federico Pena claiming that the preference policy violated the equal protection component of the Due Process Clause of the Fifth Amendment. The federal program was upheld at the trial level. The Tenth Circuit Court of Appeals affirmed, holding that Supreme

Randy Pech, owner of a guardrail installation company in Colorado Springs, challenged a federal minority set-aside program in *Adarand Constructors, Inc. v. Pena.*

Court precedent allowed more latitude to the federal government in implementing race-conscious programs (*Metro Broadcasting*) than was permitted the states (*Croson*). Adarand requested Supreme Court review.

JUSTICE O'CONNOR announced the judgment of the Court and delivered an opinion . . . which is for the Court except insofar as it might be inconsistent with the views expressed in JUSTICE SCALIA'S concurrence . . .

Adarand's claim arises under the Fifth Amendment to the Constitution, which provides that "No person shall . . . be deprived of life, liberty, or property, without due process of law." Although this Court has always understood that

Clause to provide some measure of protection against arbitrary treatment by the Federal Government, it is not as explicit a guarantee of equal treatment as the Fourteenth Amendment, which provides that "No State shall . . . deny to any person within its jurisdiction the equal protection of the laws." Our cases have accorded varying degrees of significance to the difference in the language of those two Clauses. We think it necessary to revisit the issue here. . . .

In *Bolling v. Sharpe* (1954), the Court for the first time explicitly questioned the existence of any difference between the obligations of the Federal Government and the States to avoid racial classifications. . . . *Bolling*'s facts concerned school desegregation, but its reasoning was not so limited. The Court's observations that "[d]istinctions between citizens solely because of their ancestry are by their very nature odious," *Hirabayashi [v. United States* (1943)], and that "all legal restrictions which curtail the civil rights of a single racial group are immediately suspect," *Korematsu [v. United States* (1944)], carry no less force in the context of federal action than in the context of action by the States—indeed, they first appeared in cases concerning action by the Federal Government. . . .

Later cases in contexts other than school desegregation did not distinguish between the duties of the States and the Federal Government to avoid racial classifications. Consider, for example, the following passage from *McLaughlin v. Florida*, a 1964 case that struck down a race-based state law:

"[W]e deal here with a classification based upon the race of the participants, which must be viewed in light of the historical fact that the central purpose of the Fourteenth Amendment was to eliminate racial discrimination emanating from official sources in the States. This strong policy renders racial classifications 'constitutionally suspect,' *Bolling v. Sharpe;* and subject to the 'most rigid scrutiny,' *Korematsu v. United States;* and 'in most circumstances irrelevant' to any constitutionally acceptable legislative purpose, *Hirabayashi v. United States."*

McLaughlin's reliance on cases involving federal action for the standards applicable to a case involving state legislation suggests that the Court understood the standards for federal and state racial classifications to be the same.

Cases decided after *McLaughlin* continued to treat the equal protection obligations imposed by the Fifth and the Fourteenth Amendments as indistinguishable. . . . *Loving v.*

Virginia [1967], which struck down a race-based state law, cited *Korematsu* for the proposition that "the Equal Protection Clause demands that racial classifications . . . be subjected to the 'most rigid scrutiny.'" The various opinions in *Frontiero v. Richardson* (1973), which concerned sex discrimination by the Federal Government, took their equal protection standard of review from *Reed v. Reed* (1971), a case that invalidated sex discrimination by a State, without mentioning any possibility of a difference between the standards applicable to state and federal action. Thus, in 1975, the Court stated explicitly that "[t]his Court's approach to fifth Amendment equal protection claims has always been precisely the same as to equal protection claims under the Fourteenth Amendment." *Weinberger v. Wiesenfeld;* see also *Buckley v. Valeo* (1976); *United States v. Paradise* (1987). . . .

Most of the cases discussed above involved classifications burdening groups that have suffered discrimination in our society. In 1978, the Court confronted the question whether race-based governmental action designed to benefit such groups should also be subject to "the most rigid scrutiny." *Regents of Univ. of California v. Bakke* involved an equal protection challenge to a state-run medical school's practice of reserving a number of spaces in its entering class for minority students. The petitioners argued that "strict scrutiny" should apply only to "classifications that disadvantage 'discrete and insular minorities.'" *Bakke* did not produce an opinion for the Court, but Justice Powell's opinion announcing the Court's judgment rejected the argument. . . .

Two years after *Bakke,* the Court faced another challenge to remedial race-based action, this time involving action undertaken by the Federal Government. In *Fullilove v. Klutznick* (1980), the Court upheld Congress' inclusion of a 10% set-aside for minority-owned businesses in the Public Works Employment Act of 1977. As in *Bakke,* there was no opinion for the Court. Chief Justice Burger, in an opinion joined by Justices White and Powell, observed that "[a]ny preference based on racial or ethnic criteria must necessarily receive a most searching examination to make sure that it does not conflict with constitutional guarantees.". . .

In *Wygant v. Jackson Board of Ed.* (1986), the Court considered a Fourteenth Amendment challenge to another form of remedial racial classification. The issue in *Wygant* was whether a school board could adopt race-based preferences in determining which teachers to lay off. Justice Powell's plurality opinion observed that "the level of scrutiny does not change merely because the challenged classification operates against a group that historically has not been subject to governmental discrimination." . . . In other words, "racial classifications of any sort must be subjected to 'strict scrutiny.'" (O'Connor, J., concurring in part and concurring in judgment). . . .

The Court's failure to produce a majority opinion in *Bakke, Fullilove,* and *Wygant* left unresolved the proper analysis for remedial race-based governmental action. . . .

The Court resolved the issue, at least in part, in 1989. *Richmond v. J. A. Croson Co.* concerned a city's determination that 30% of its contracting work should go to minority-owned businesses. A majority of the Court in *Croson* held that "the standard of review under the Equal Protection Clause is not dependent on the race of those burdened or benefited by a particular classification," and that the single standard of review for racial classifications should be "strict scrutiny." . . .

With *Croson,* the Court finally agreed that the Fourteenth Amendment requires strict scrutiny of all race-based action by state and local governments. But *Croson* of course had no occasion to declare what standard of review the Fifth Amendment requires for such action taken by the Federal Government. . . .

Despite lingering uncertainty in the details, however, the Court's cases through *Croson* had established three general propositions with respect to governmental racial classifications. First, skepticism: "'[a]ny preference based on racial or ethnic criteria must necessarily receive a most searching examination,'" *Wygant, Fullilove, McLaughlin, Hirabayashi.* . . . Second, consistency: "the standard of review under the Equal Protection Clause is not dependent on the race of those burdened or benefited by a particular classification," *Croson, Bakke.* . . . And third, congruence: "[e]qual protection analysis in the Fifth Amendment area is the same as that under the Fourteenth Amendment," *Buckley v. Valeo, Weinberger v. Wiesenfeld, Bolling v. Sharpe.* Taken together, these three propositions lead to the conclusion that any person, of whatever race, has the right to demand that any governmental actor subject to the Constitution justify any racial classification subjecting that per-

son to unequal treatment under the strictest judicial scrutiny. . . .

A year later, however, the Court took a surprising turn. *Metro Broadcasting, Inc. v. FCC* (1990) involved a Fifth Amendment challenge to two race-based policies of the Federal Communications Commission. In *Metro Broadcasting,* the Court repudiated the long-held notion that "it would be unthinkable that the same Constitution would impose a lesser duty on the Federal Government" than it does on a State to afford equal protection of the laws, *Bolling.* It did so by holding that "benign" federal racial classifications need only satisfy intermediate scrutiny, even though *Croson* had recently concluded that such classifications enacted by a State must satisfy strict scrutiny. . . .

By adopting intermediate scrutiny as the standard of review for congressionally mandated "benign" racial classifications, *Metro Broadcasting* departed from prior cases in two significant respects. First, it turned its back on *Croson*'s explanation of why strict scrutiny of all governmental racial classifications is essential. . . .

Second, *Metro Broadcasting* squarely rejected one of the three propositions established by the Court's earlier equal protection cases, namely, congruence between the standards applicable to federal and state racial classifications, and in so doing also undermined the other two—skepticism of all racial classifications, and consistency of treatment irrespective of the race of the burdened or benefited group. Under *Metro Broadcasting,* certain racial classifications ("benign" ones enacted by the Federal Government) should be treated less skeptically than others; and the race of the benefited group is critical to the determination of which standard of review to apply. *Metro Broadcasting* was thus a significant departure from much of what had come before it.

The three propositions undermined by *Metro Broadcasting* all derive from the basic principle that the Fifth and Fourteenth Amendments to the Constitution protect persons, not groups. It follows from that principle that all governmental action based on race—a group classification long recognized as "in most circumstances irrelevant and therefore prohibited," *Hirabayashi,*—should be subjected to detailed judicial inquiry to ensure that the personal right to equal protection of the laws has not been infringed.

These ideas have long been central to this Court's understanding of equal protection, and holding "benign" state and federal racial classifications to different standards does not square with them. "[A] free people whose institutions are founded upon the doctrine of equality," *ibid.*, should tolerate no retreat from the principle that government may treat people differently because of their race only for the most compelling reasons. Accordingly, we hold today that all racial classifications, imposed by whatever federal, state, or local governmental actor, must be analyzed by a reviewing court under strict scrutiny. In other words, such classifications are constitutional only if they are narrowly tailored measures that further compelling governmental interests. To the extent that *Metro Broadcasting* is inconsistent with that holding, it is overruled. . . .

Because our decision today alters the playing field in some important respects, we think it best to remand the case to the lower courts for further consideration in light of the principles we have announced. . . .

It is so ordered.

JUSTICE SCALIA, concurring in part and concurring in the judgment.

I join the opinion of the Court . . . except insofar as it may be inconsistent with the following: In my view, government can never have a "compelling interest" in discriminating on the basis of race in order to "make up" for past racial discrimination in the opposite direction. Individuals who have been wronged by unlawful racial discrimination should be made whole; but under our Constitution there can be no such thing as either a creditor or a debtor race. That concept is alien to the Constitution's focus upon the individual. . . . To pursue the concept of racial entitlement—even for the most admirable and benign of purposes—is to reinforce and preserve for future mischief the way of thinking that produced race slavery, race privilege and race hatred. In the eyes of government, we are just one race here. It is American.

It is unlikely, if not impossible, that the challenged program would survive under this understanding of strict scrutiny, but I am content to leave that to be decided on remand.

JUSTICE THOMAS, concurring in part and concurring in the judgment.

That these programs may have been motivated, in part, by good intentions cannot provide refuge from the principle that under our Constitution, the government may not make distinctions on the basis of race. As far as the Constitution is concerned, it is irrelevant whether a government's racial classifications are drawn by those who wish to oppress a race or by those who have a sincere desire to help those thought to be disadvantaged. There can be no doubt that the paternalism that appears to lie at the heart of this program is at war with the principle of inherent equality that underlies and infuses our Constitution.

These programs not only raise grave constitutional questions, they also undermine the moral basis of the equal protection principle. Purchased at the price of immeasurable human suffering, the equal protection principle reflects our Nation's understanding that such classifications ultimately have a destructive impact on the individual and our society. Unquestionably, "[i]nvidious [racial] discrimination is an engine of oppression." It is also true that "[r]emedial" racial preferences may reflect "a desire to foster equality in society." But there can be no doubt that racial paternalism and its unintended consequences can be as poisonous and pernicious as any other form of discrimination. So-called "benign" discrimination teaches many that because of chronic and apparently immutable handicaps, minorities cannot compete with them without their patronizing indulgence. Inevitably, such programs engender attitudes of superiority or, alternatively, provoke resentment among those who believe that they have been wronged by the government's use of race. These programs stamp minorities with a badge of inferiority and may cause them to develop dependencies or to adopt an attitude that they are "entitled" to preferences. . . .

In my mind, government-sponsored racial discrimination based on benign prejudice is just as noxious as discrimination inspired by malicious prejudice. In each instance, it is racial discrimination, plain and simple.

JUSTICE STEVENS, with whom JUSTICE GINSBURG joins, dissenting.

The Court's concept of "consistency" assumes that there is no significant difference between a decision by the majority to impose a special burden on the members of a minority race and a decision by the majority to provide a benefit to certain members of that minority notwithstanding its incidental burden on some members of the majority. In my opinion that assumption is untenable. There is no moral or constitutional equivalence between a policy that is designed to perpetuate a caste system and one that seeks to eradicate racial subordination. Invidious discrimination is an engine of oppression, subjugating a disfavored group to enhance or maintain the power of the majority. Remedial race-based preferences reflect the opposite impulse: a desire to foster equality in society. No sensible conception of the Government's constitutional obligation to "govern impartially," *Hampton v. Mow Sun Wong* (1976), should ignore this distinction. . . .

The Court's concept of "congruence" assumes that there is no significant difference between a decision by the Congress of the United States to adopt an affirmative-action program and such a decision by a State or a municipality. In my opinion that assumption is untenable. It ignores important practical and legal differences between federal and state or local decisionmakers. . . .

Ironically, after all of the time, effort, and paper this Court has expended in differentiating between federal and state affirmative action, the majority today virtually ignores the issue. It provides not a word of direct explanation for its sudden and enormous departure from the reasoning in past cases. Such silence, however, cannot erase the difference between Congress' institutional competence and constitutional authority to overcome historic racial subjugation and the States' lesser power to do so. . . .

In my judgment, the Court's novel doctrine of "congruence" is seriously misguided. Congressional deliberations about a matter as important as affirmative action should be accorded far greater deference than those of a State or municipality.

The Court's concept of stare decisis treats some of the language we have used in explaining our decisions as though it were more important than our actual holdings. In my opinion that treatment is incorrect.

This is the third time in the Court's entire history that it has considered the constitutionality of a federal affirmative-action program. On each of the two prior occasions,

the first in 1980, *Fullilove v. Klutznick,* and the second in 1990, *Metro Broadcasting, Inc. v. FCC,* the Court upheld the program. Today the Court explicitly overrules *Metro Broadcasting* (at least in part), and undermines *Fullilove* by recasting the standard on which it rested and by calling even its holding into question. . . .

The Court's holding in *Fullilove* surely governs the result in this case. . . . In no meaningful respect is the current scheme more objectionable than the 1977 Act. Thus, if the 1977 Act was constitutional, then so must be the SBA and STURAA. Indeed, even if my dissenting views in *Fullilove* had prevailed, this program would be valid. . . .

My skeptical scrutiny of the Court's opinion leaves me in dissent. The majority's concept of "consistency" ignores a difference, fundamental to the idea of equal protection, between oppression and assistance. The majority's concept of "congruence" ignores a difference, fundamental to our constitutional system, between the Federal Government and the States. And the majority's concept of stare decisis ignores the force of binding precedent. I would affirm the judgment of the Court of Appeals.

JUSTICE SOUTER, with whom JUSTICE GINSBURG and JUSTICE BREYER join, dissenting.

. . . I agree with Justice Stevens's conclusion that stare decisis compels the application of *Fullilove.* Although *Fullilove* did not reflect doctrinal consistency, its several opinions produced a result on shared grounds that petitioner does not attack: that discrimination in the construction industry had been subject to government acquiescence, with effects that remain and that may be addressed by some preferential treatment falling within the congressional power under section 5 of the Fourteenth Amendment. Once *Fullilove* is applied, as Justice Stevens points out, it follows that the statutes in question here (which are substantially better tailored to the harm being remedied than the statute endorsed in *Fullilove*) pass muster under Fifth Amendment due process and Fourteenth Amendment equal protection. . . .

. . . The Court has long accepted the view that constitutional authority to remedy past discrimination is not limited to the power to forbid its continuation, but extends to eliminating those effects that would otherwise persist and skew the operation of public systems even in the absence of current intent to practice any discrimination. This is so whether the remedial authority is exercised by a court, the Congress, or some other legislature. Indeed, a majority of the Court today reiterates that there are circumstances in which Government may, consistently with the Constitution, adopt programs aimed at remedying the effects of past invidious discrimination.

When the extirpation of lingering discriminatory effects is thought to require a catch-up mechanism, like the racially preferential inducement under the statutes considered here, the result may be that some members of the historically favored race are hurt by that remedial mechanism, however innocent they may be of any personal responsibility for any discriminatory conduct. When this price is considered reasonable, it is in part because it is a price to be paid only temporarily; if the justification for the preference is eliminating the effects of a past practice, the assumption is that the effects will themselves recede into the past, becoming attenuated and finally disappearing. Thus, Justice Powell wrote in his concurring opinion in *Fullilove* that the "temporary nature of this remedy ensures that a race-conscious program will not last longer than the discriminatory effects it is designed to eliminate."

JUSTICE GINSBURG, with whom JUSTICE BREYER joins, dissenting.

The divisions in this difficult case should not obscure the Court's recognition of the persistence of racial inequality and a majority's acknowledgement of Congress' authority to act affirmatively, not only to end discrimination, but also to counteract discrimination's lingering effects. Those effects, reflective of a system of racial caste only recently ended, are evident in our workplaces, markets, and neighborhoods. . . . Bias both conscious and unconscious, reflecting traditional and unexamined habits of thought, keeps up barriers that must come down if equal opportunity and nondiscrimination are ever genuinely to become this country's law and practice.

Given this history and its practical consequences, Congress surely can conclude that a carefully designed affirmative action program may help to realize, finally, the "equal protection of the laws" the Fourteenth Amendment has promised since 1868.

BOX 18-5

AFFIRMATIVE ACTION/MINORITY
SET-ASIDE PRINCIPLES

The Supreme Court's affirmative action and minority set-aside decisions have been criticized for failing to develop a consistent and coherent set of legal principles. The unstable majorities that have controlled these cases surely have contributed to this result. The justices have not provided a rule of law in one clear test that would allow a reasonably accurate indicator of what is constitutionally defective. While there are no absolutes, there are certain characteristics that clearly make minority enhancement plans more acceptable.

An affirmative action or minority set-aside program is more likely to be found constitutional if it:

1. is enacted as a response to clear and demonstrable acts of unconstitutional or illegal discrimination;

2. is narrowly tailored to respond to acts of illegal discrimination or to the continuing effects of that illegal discrimination;

3. is designed to assist only those groups who have been the victim of illegal discrimination;

4. is not based on racial, ethnic, or gender stereotypes, or presumes the inferiority of such groups;

5. avoids the use of quotas and does not absolutely bar any group from competing or participating;

6. is temporary, with clear indicators of plan termination when certain thresholds are met;

7. seeks to eliminate racial imbalance, not maintain racial balance;

8. is based on data from relevant labor pools or other appropriate statistical comparisons;

9. does not trammel the rights of the majority;

10. seeks to achieve balance by providing new benefits to minorities rather than taking already earned benefits away from the majority;

11. is imposed by a federal court as a remedy for demonstrated constitutional violations.

The Court's decision to apply the same strict standards to the federal government as to state and local governments is an important one. While the ruling in *Adarand* certainly does not strike down all affirmative action programs, it does hold them to very exacting standards. The decision also demonstrates that the more conservative members of the Court continue to have a controlling influence over affirmative action policy. The 5–4 vote in this case is significant, however. It means that the Court's doctrine on affirmative action issues is not indelibly written, but may fluctuate with a single vote. A single new justice could radically change the Court's position.

READINGS

Baer, Judith. *Equality Under the Constitution*. Ithaca, N.Y.: Cornell University Press, 1983.

Glazer, Nathan. *Affirmative Discrimination*. New York: Basic Books, 1975.

Goldstein, Leslie Friedman. *The Constitutional Rights of Women*. 2d ed. Madison: University of Wisconsin Press, 1988.

Graglia, Lino A. *Disaster by Decree: The Supreme Court's Decisions on Race and the Schools*. Ithaca, N.Y.: Cornell University Press, 1976.

Kluger, Richard. *Simple Justice*. New York: Knopf, 1976.

Mezey, Susan Gluck. *In Pursuit of Equality*. New York: St. Martin's Press, 1992.

Rhode, Deborah L. *Justice and Gender*. Cambridge: Harvard University Press, 1989.

Ross, Susan Deller, and Ann Barcher. *The Rights of Women*. New York: Bantam Books, 1984.

Schwartz, Bernard. *Swann's Way: The School Busing Case and the Supreme Court*. New York: Oxford University Press, 1986.

Sindler, Allan P. *Bakke, DeFunis, and Minority Admissions*. New York: Longman, 1978.

Smith, Christopher E. *The Courts and the Poor*. Chicago: Nelson Hall, 1991.

Vose, Clement E. *Caucasians Only: The Supreme Court, the NAACP, and the Restrictive Covenant Cases*. Berkeley: University of California Press, 1959.

Wilkinson, J. Harvie. *From Brown to Bakke: The Supreme Court and School Integration 1954–1978*. New York: Oxford University Press, 1979.

CHAPTER 19
VOTING AND REPRESENTATION

F OR ANY GOVERNMENT built on a foundation of popular sovereignty, voting and representation are of critical importance. Through these mechanisms the people express their political will and ultimately control the institutions of government. Representative democracy can function properly only when the citizenry has full rights to regular and meaningful elections and when the system is structured so that public officials act on behalf of their constituents. If any segment of society is denied the right to vote or is denied legitimate representation, the ideals of a republican form of government are not completely realized. Because elections and representation are the primary links between the people and their government, it is not surprising that the history of American constitutional law is replete with disputes over rights of political participation.

VOTING RIGHTS

When the Framers met at the Philadelphia Convention of 1787, the states already had election systems, with their own requirements for qualifying voters and procedures for selecting state and local officials. By European standards, the states were quite liberal in extending the right to vote.[1] But suffrage was

not universal. Ballot access generally was granted only to free adult men, and in several states only to men who owned sufficient property. Women, slaves, Indians, minors, and the poor could not vote. Some states prohibited Jews and Catholics from voting.

With state systems in place, the Framers saw no reason to create a separate set of qualifications for participating in federal elections. Because there was little uniformity from state to state and qualifications often changed, the addition of a new body of federal voting requirements could cause conflict. In addition, under the constitution drafted at Philadelphia, only one agency of the new national government, the House of Representatives, was to be elected directly by the people, further reason why the federal government need not develop its own voter rolls. In Article I, Section 2, the Constitution says with respect to House elections that "the Electors in each State shall have the Qualifications requisite for Electors of the most numerous Branch of the State Legislature." If citizens were qualified to cast ballots in their state's legislative elections, they were also qualified to vote in congressional elections.

Only one constitutional provision gave the federal government any regulatory authority over elections. Section 4 of Article I stipulates, "The Times, Places and Manner of holding Elections for Senators and

---

1. Melvin I. Urofsky, *A March of Liberty* (New York: Knopf, 1988), 294.

Representatives, shall be prescribed in each State by the Legislature thereof; but the Congress may at any time by Law make or alter such Regulations, except as to the Places of chusing Senators." Congress took only modest advantage of this authority. In 1842 it passed a law requiring that representatives be elected from specific constituencies, rather than from the state at large; and in 1866 it clarified the procedures to be used in the selection of senators by the state legislatures. These statutes dealt essentially with procedural matters; they did not speak to the question of voter qualifications. During the first half of the nation's history, this authority remained in the hands of the states, where the electorate was expanding and barriers to suffrage gradually were being reformed. Following the Civil War, however, power over voting rights began steadily shifting toward the federal government.

Ratification of four constitutional amendments substantially limited the states' authority to restrict the right to vote. The first of these was the Fifteenth Amendment in 1870. Part of the Reconstruction package initiated by the Radical Republicans after the Civil War, the Fifteenth Amendment removed from the states the power to deny voting rights on the basis of race, color, or previous condition of servitude. It prohibits such discrimination by either the federal government or the states, but the obvious target was the South. Most members of the reconstructionist Congress reasoned that unless some action was taken to protect the political rights of the newly freed slaves, the white majority would reinstitute measures to deny black citizens full participation.

Fifty years later the Constitution was again amended to expand the electorate. The Nineteenth Amendment, ratified in 1920, stipulated that the right to vote could not be denied on account of sex. This amendment was the culmination of decades of effort by supporters of women's suffrage. Although a number of states had already modified their laws to allow women to vote, a change in the Constitution was necessary to extend that right uniformly across the nation. This amendment nullified the Supreme Court's unanimous 1875 decision in *Minor v. Happersett* in which the justices rejected Virginia Minor's contention that the Missouri constitution's granting of voting rights only to men violated the Privileges and Immunities Clause of the Fourteenth Amendment.

The third voter qualification amendment went into effect in 1964. The Twenty-fourth Amendment denied the federal government and the states the power to impose a poll tax as a voter qualification for federal elections. The levying of a tax on the right to vote was a common practice in the South and was identified by Congress as one of many tactics used to keep blacks from voting, and thereby circumventing the clear intent of the Fifteenth Amendment.

In 1971 the last of the voting rights amendments, the Twenty-sixth, was ratified. It set eighteen years as the minimum voting age for all state and federal elections. Before 1971 individual states determined the minimum voting age, which ranged from eighteen to twenty-one. Earlier, Congress had attempted to impose the eighteen-year minimum through legislation. The constitutionality of that act was challenged in *Oregon v. Mitchell* (1970). In a 5–4 vote, the justices held that Congress had the power under Article I to set a minimum age for voting in federal elections but was without the constitutional authority to impose an age standard on state and local elections. Rather than face the possible confusion of conflicting sets of qualifications, Congress abrogated the *Mitchell* ruling by proposing the Twenty-sixth Amendment.

Each of these four constitutional changes altered the balance of authority over the establishment of voter qualifications. The states retained the basic right to set such qualifications, but with restrictions. States may no longer abridge voting rights by denying access to the ballot on the basis of race, sex, age, or ability to pay a tax; any actions by the states affecting voting rights are also constrained by the Fourteenth Amendment's guarantee of equal protection of the laws.[2] In addition to limiting state power, the voting rights amendments increased congressional authority. The Fourteenth, Fifteenth, Nineteenth, Twenty-fourth, and Twenty-sixth Amendments declare: "The Congress shall have the power to enforce this article by appropriate legislation." These enforcement clauses grant Congress authority over an area that had been left entirely to the states.

Congress has not been reluctant to use its enforcement authority. Shortly after ratification of the Fourteenth and Fifteenth Amendments, it demonstrated the federal government's interest in extending the franchise to African Americans by passing the Enforcement Act of 1870. This statute made it unlawful for state election officials to discriminate against black citizens in the application of state voting regulations. It also made acts of electoral corruption, including bribery, violence, and intimidation, federal crimes. The following year Congress passed the Enforcement Act of 1871, which allowed for federal supervision of congressional elections. The federal government also intervened to stem the growing incidence of private intimidation of black voters with the Ku Klux Klan Act of 1871, which gave the president broad powers to combat conspiracies against voting rights.

The Supreme Court's response to these post–Civil War enforcement statutes was mixed. In some of its decisions the justices questioned the breadth of the congressional actions that regulated state elections beyond the specific racial purposes of the Fifteenth Amendment. For example, in *United States v. Reese* (1876) the justices declined to uphold the indictment of a Kentucky election official who refused to register a qualified black voter for a state election. The Court justified its conclusion on the ground that the Enforcement Act of 1870 was too broadly drawn. On the same day as *Reese,* and for the same reason, the Court in *United States v. Cruikshank* dismissed the federal indictments of ninety-six Louisiana whites who were charged with intimidating potential black voters by shooting them.

The Court also was reluctant to approve sanctions under the Ku Klux Klan Act when the prosecution centered on purely private behavior (*United States v. Harris,* 1883). However, in *Ex parte Yarbrough* (1884) the justices gave strong support to federal enforcement actions against even private behavior when the right to vote in national elections was abridged. Similarly, in *Ex parte Clark* (1880), *Ex parte Siebold* (1880), and *United States v. Gale* (1883) the Court approved criminal charges against state officials who compromised the integrity of federal elections.

Although these enforcement measures had an impact on the South, their influence was short-lived. By the time the nation entered the 1890s, the zeal behind the Reconstruction efforts had waned. White southerners had regained control of their home states and began passing measures to restrict black participation in state and federal elections. The Jim Crow era had begun. The Civil War amendments officially had reduced the power of the states to discriminate and had given regulatory authority to the federal government, but full voting rights were not a reality until after the struggles of the civil rights movement of the mid-twentieth century.

State Racial Restrictions on Voting

In 1869, during the congressional debate over the Fifteenth Amendment, Sen. Waitman T. Willey, a Republican from West Virginia, proclaimed from the Senate floor:

This amendment, when adopted, will settle the question for all time of negro suffrage in the insurgent States, where it

---

2. The Fourteenth Amendment also contained a provision that stipulated that any state denying voting rights to any male citizens over the age of twenty-one could have its representation in the U.S. House reduced. This provision, however, has never had a practical impact and has been largely superseded by the ratification of the other voting rights amendments.

has lately been extended under the pressure of congressional legislation, and will preclude the possibility of any future denial of this privilege by any change in the constitutions of those States.

In retrospect, it would be hard to imagine a more overly optimistic prediction of the impact of the Fifteenth Amendment. While ratification meant that the states were constitutionally prohibited from engaging in racial discrimination in extending the right to vote, the southern states, once out from under the policies of Reconstruction, acted to keep blacks out of the voting booth.

Actions by the Southern states to limit black participation in voting took many forms. They included such tactics as "white only" voting in Democratic Party primary elections, poll taxes, difficult registration requirements, literacy and understanding tests, and outright intimidation. These strategies were very effective. Black participation at the ballot box in the South was negligible well into the middle of the twentieth century.

Beginning in the 1960s the federal government undertook to reduce racial discrimination in voting. All three branches were involved: Congress passed legislation to enforce voting rights and remove legal barriers to the ballot box; the executive branch brought suits against state governments and election officials who deprived blacks of their rights; and the judiciary heard legal disputes over claims of voting discrimination.

As you read Justice Black's opinion for the Court in *Louisiana v. United States* (1965), a dispute over the use of "understanding tests," pay close attention to his account of the many obstacles the state placed in the way of suffrage and how effective they were.

Louisiana v. United States

380 U.S. 145 (1965)

Vote: 9 (Black, Brennan, Clark, Douglas, Goldberg, Harlan, Stewart, Warren, White)

0

Opinion of the Court: Black
Concurring opinion: Harlan

The U.S. government brought suit in the federal District Court for the Eastern District of Louisiana against the state of Louisiana and members of the state Board of Registration. The government charged the defendants with enforcing state laws denying black citizens the right to vote in violation of the Fourteenth and Fifteenth Amendments. The suit centered on the use of "interpretation" or "understanding" tests. These devices, commonly used throughout the South, required any citizens applying for voter registration to pass a test demonstrating a proper understanding of any section of the Louisiana or U.S. Constitution. The test had no objective standards: the local voting registrar selected the passage to be interpreted by the potential voter and determined whether sufficient understanding had been demonstrated. The state justified this requirement as a means of ensuring a well-informed, qualified electorate. The fact that the Board of Registration developed the interpretation test in cooperation with the state Segregation Committee indicated that other goals were intended as well. The test was quite effective in denying blacks, even those with graduate and professional degrees, the right to vote. The district court ruled in favor of the federal government, and the state appealed.

MR. JUSTICE BLACK delivered the opinion of the Court.

The complaint alleged, and the District Court found, that beginning with the adoption of the Louisiana Constitution of 1898, when approximately 44% of all the registered voters in the State were Negroes, the State had put into effect a successful policy of denying Negro citizens the right to vote because of their race. The 1898 constitution adopted what was known as a "grandfather clause," which imposed burdensome requirements for registration thereafter but exempted from these future requirements any person who had been entitled to vote before January 1, 1867, or who was the son or grandson of such a person. Such a transparent expedient for disfranchising Negroes, whose ancestors had been slaves until 1863 and not entitled to vote in Louisiana before 1867, was held unconstitutional in 1915 as a violation of the Fifteenth Amendment, in a case involving a similar Oklahoma constitutional provision. Guinn v. United States. Soon after that decision Louisiana, in 1921, adopted a new constitution replacing the repudiated "grandfather clause" with what the complaint calls an "interpretation test," which required that an applicant for registration be able to "give a reasonable interpretation" of any clause in the Louisiana Constitution or the Constitution of the United States. From the adoption of the 1921 interpretation test until 1944, the District Court's opinion stated, the percentage of registered voters in Louisiana who were Negroes never exceeded one percent. Prior to 1944 Negro interest in voting in Louisiana had been slight, largely because the State's white primary law kept Negroes from voting in the Democratic Party primary election, the only election that mattered in the political climate of that State. In 1944, however, this Court invalidated the substantially identical white primary law of Texas, and with the explicit statutory bar to their voting in the primary removed and because of a generally heightened political interest, Negroes in increasing numbers began to register in Louisiana. The white primary system had been so effective in barring Negroes from voting that the "interpretation test" as a disfranchising devise had been ignored over the years. Many registrars continued to ignore it after 1944, and in the next dozen years the proportion of registered voters who were Negroes rose from two-tenths of one percent to approximately 15% by March 1956. This fact, coupled with this Court's 1954 invalidation of laws requiring school segregation, prompted the State to try new devices to keep the white citizens in control. The Louisiana Legislature created a committee which became known as the "Segregation Committee" to seek means of accomplishing this goal. The chairman of this committee also helped to organize a semiprivate group called the Association of Citizens Councils, which thereafter acted in close cooperation with the legislative committee to preserve white supremacy. The legislative committee and the Citizens Councils set up programs, which parish voting registrars were required to attend, to instruct the registrars on how to promote white political control. The committee and the Citizens Councils also began a wholesale challenging of Negro names already on the voting rolls, with the result that thousands of Negroes, but virtually no whites, were purged from the rolls of voters. Beginning in the middle 1950's registrars of at least 21 parishes began to apply the interpretation test. In 1960 the State Constitution was amended to require every applicant thereafter to "be able to understand" as well as "give a reasonable interpretation" of any section of the State or Federal Constitution "when read to him by the registrar." The State Board of Registration in cooperation with the Segregation Committee issued orders that all parish registrars must strictly comply with the new provisions.

The interpretation test, the court found, vested in the voting registrars a virtually uncontrolled discretion as to who should vote and who should not. Under the State's statutes and constitutional provisions the registrars, without any objective standard to guide them, determine the manner in which the interpretation test is to be given, whether it is to be oral or written, the length and complexity of the sections of the State or Federal Constitution to be understood and interpreted, and what interpretation is to be considered correct. There was ample evidence to support the District Court's finding that registrars in the 21 parishes where the test was found to have been used had exercised their broad powers to deprive otherwise qualified Negro citizens of their right to vote; and that the existence of the test as a hurdle to voter qualification has in itself deterred and will continue to deter Negroes from attempting to register in Louisiana.

Because of the virtually unlimited discretion vested by the Louisiana laws in the registrars of voters, and because in the 21 parishes where the interpretation test was applied that discretion had been exercised to keep Negroes from voting because of their race, the District Court held the interpretation test invalid on its face and as applied, as a violation of the Fourteenth and Fifteenth Amendments to the United States Constitution and of 42 U.S.C. § 1971(a). The District Court enjoined future use of the test in the State, and with respect to the 21 parishes where the invalid interpretation test was found to have been applied, the District Court also enjoined use of a newly enacted "citizenship" test, which did not repeal the interpretation test and the validity of which was not challenged in this suit, unless a reregistration of all voters in those parishes is ordered, so that there would be no voters in those parishes who had not passed the same test.

We have held this day in United States v. Mississippi that the Attorney General has power to bring suit against a State and its officials to protect the voting rights of Negroes guaranteed by 42 U.S.C. § 1971(a) and the Fourteenth and Fifteenth Amendments. There can be no doubt from the evidence in this case that the District Court was amply justified in finding that Louisiana's interpretation test, as written and as applied, was part of a successful plan to deprive Louisiana Negroes of their right to vote. This device for accomplishing unconstitutional discrimination has been little if any less successful than was the "grandfather clause" invalidated by this Court's decision in Guinn v. United States 50 years ago, which when that clause was adopted in 1898 had seemed to the leaders of Louisiana a much preferable way of assuring white political supremacy. The Governor of Louisiana stated in 1898 that he believed that the "grandfather clause" solved the problem of keeping Negroes from voting "in a much more upright and manly fashion" than the method adopted previously by the States of Mississippi and South Carolina, which left the qualification of applicants to vote "largely to the arbitrary discretion of the officers administering the law." A delegate to the 1898 Louisiana Constitutional Convention also criticized an interpretation test because the "arbitrary power, lodged with the registration officer, practically places his decision beyond the pale of judicial review; and he can enfranchise or disfranchise voters at his own sweet will and pleasure without let or hindrance."

But Louisianans of a later generation did place just such arbitrary power in the hands of election officers who have used it with phenomenal success to keep Negroes from voting in the State. The State admits that the statutes and provisions of the state constitution establishing the interpretation test "vest discretion in the registrars of voters to determine the qualifications of applicants for registration" while imposing "no definite and objective standards upon

registrars of voters for the administration of the interpretation test." And the District Court found that "Louisiana . . . provides no effective method whereby arbitrary and capricious action by registrars of voters may be prevented or redressed." The applicant facing a registrar in Louisiana thus has been compelled to leave his voting fate to that official's uncontrolled power to determine whether the applicant's understanding of the Federal or State Constitution is satisfactory. As the evidence showed, colored people, even some with the most advanced education and scholarship, were declared by voting registrars with less education to have an unsatisfactory understanding of the Constitution of Louisiana or of the United States. This is not a test but a trap, sufficient to stop even the most brilliant man on his way to the voting booth. The cherished right of people in a country like ours to vote cannot be obliterated by the use of laws like this, which leave the voting fate of a citizen to the passing whim or impulse of an individual registrar. Many of our cases have pointed out the invalidity of laws so completely devoid of standards and restraints. Squarely in point is Schnell v. Davis, in which we affirmed a district court judgment striking down as a violation of the Fourteenth and Fifteenth Amendments an Alabama constitutional provision restricting the right to vote in that State to persons who could "understand and explain any article of the Constitution of the United States" to the satisfaction of voting registrars. We likewise affirm here the District Court's holding that the provisions of the Louisiana Constitution and statutes which require voters to satisfy registrars of their ability to "understand and give a reasonable interpretation of any section" of the Federal or Louisiana Constitution violate the Constitution. And we agree with the District Court that it specifically conflicts with the prohibitions against discrimination in voting because of race found both in the Fifteenth Amendment and 42 U.S.C. § 1971(a) to subject citizens to such an arbitrary power as Louisiana has given its registrars under these laws.

Affirmed.

The Voting Rights Act of 1965

Although decisions such as *Louisiana v. United States* defined the constitutional rights of minority voters and condemned efforts by the states to depress black voting participation, court rulings alone were insufficient to prompt major changes. Too many alternative measures, many of them informal, were available to block or delay the effective exercise of the right to vote. Registration numbers in the southern states highlight the fact that court victories did not necessarily translate into social change. According to Justice Department statistics, between 1958 and 1964 black voter registration in Alabama rose to 19.4 percent from 14.2 percent. From 1956 to 1965 Louisiana black registration increased only to 31.8 percent from 31.7 percent. And in Mississippi the ten years from 1954 to 1964 saw black registration rates rise to only 6.4 percent from 4.4 percent. In each of these states the registration rates for whites was 50 percentage points or more ahead of black rates. Figures such as these convinced Congress that its strategy of passing legislation to expand opportunities for taking civil rights claims to court had been ineffective and that a more aggressive policy was required. President Lyndon Johnson is reported to have instructed Attorney General Nicholas Katzenbach to "write the goddamnedest, toughest voting rights act that you can devise."[3] The result was the Voting Rights Act of 1965, the most comprehensive statute ever enacted by Congress to enforce the guarantees of the Fifteenth Amendment.

The provisions of the Voting Rights Act did not apply equally to all sections of the country. Instead, the act targeted certain areas. The coverage formula stipulated that the most stringent provisions of the statute would govern all states or counties that met the following criteria: (1) that a discriminatory test or device was in operation in November 1964; and (2) that less than 40 percent of the voting age population was registered to vote or voted in the 1964 presidential general election.

3. Howard Ball, "The Voting Rights Act of 1965," in *The Oxford Companion to the Supreme Court of the United States*, ed. Kermit L. Hall, James W. Ely, Jr., Joel B. Grossman, and William M. Wiecek (New York: Oxford University Press, 1992), 903.

In 1965 the states covered were Alabama, Alaska, Georgia, Louisiana, Mississippi, South Carolina, and Virginia, as well as portions of North Carolina, Arizona, Hawaii, and Idaho. A state could be removed from the list by convincing the District Court for the District of Columbia that no discrimination had been practiced for five years. The act's most significant provision authorized the U.S. attorney general to appoint federal examiners to supervise registration and voting procedures when the Justice Department determined that low black participation rates were a probable result of racial discrimination. The law prohibited literacy tests and stipulated that any changes in state election laws had to be approved by the attorney general before they could take effect. The 1965 Voting Rights Act was Congress's most comprehensive intervention into the state's traditional powers over voter qualifications, and it was not surprising that it was almost immediately challenged as exceeding constitutional limits on federal power.

South Carolina v. Katzenbach

383 U.S. 301 (1966)

Vote: 8 (Brennan, Clark, Douglas, Fortas, Harlan, Stewart, Warren, White)

   1 (Black)

Opinion of the Court: Warren

Opinion concurring in part and dissenting in part: Black

To gain a review of the Voting Rights Act, South Carolina instituted legal action against Attorney General Nicholas Katzenbach, asking that he be enjoined from enforcing the act's provisions. Because in the dispute a state was suing a citizen of another state and because of the importance of the issues involved, the Supreme Court accepted the case under its original jurisdiction. The hearing before the Supreme Court involved not only South Carolina and the federal government but also other states invited by the Court to participate. Five states (all southern) appeared in support of South Carolina, and twenty-one states submitted legal arguments urging the Court to approve the act.

MR. CHIEF JUSTICE WARREN delivered the opinion of the Court.

The Voting Rights Act was designed by Congress to banish the blight of racial discrimination in voting, which has infected the electoral process in parts of our country for nearly a century. The Act creates stringent new remedies for voting discrimination where it persists on a pervasive scale, and in addition the statute strengthens existing remedies for pockets of voting discrimination elsewhere in the country. Congress assumed the power to prescribe these remedies from § 2 of the Fifteenth Amendment, which authorizes the National Legislature to effectuate by "appropriate" measures the constitutional prohibition against racial discrimination in voting. We hold that the sections of the Act which are properly before us are an appropriate means for carrying out Congress' constitutional responsibilities and are consonant with all other provisions of the Constitution. We therefore deny South Carolina's request that enforcement of these sections of the Act be enjoined.

The constitutional propriety of the Voting Rights Act of 1965 must be judged with reference to the historical experience which it reflects. Before enacting the measure, Congress explored with great care the problem of racial discrimination in voting. The House and Senate Committees on the Judiciary each held hearings for nine days and received testimony from a total of 67 witnesses. More than three full days were consumed discussing the bill on the floor of the House, while the debate in the Senate covered 26 days in all. At the close of these deliberations, the verdict of both chambers was overwhelming. The House approved the bill by a vote of 328–74, and the measure passed the Senate by a margin of 79–18.

Two points emerge vividly from the voluminous legislative history of the Act contained in the committee hearings and floor debates. First: Congress felt itself confronted by an insidious and pervasive evil which had been perpetuated in certain parts of our country through unremitting and ingenious defiance of the Constitution. Second: Congress

concluded that the unsuccessful remedies which it had prescribed in the past would have to be replaced by sterner and more elaborate measures in order to satisfy the clear commands of the Fifteenth Amendment. . . .

The Voting Rights Act of 1965 reflects Congress' firm intention to rid the country of racial discrimination in voting. The heart of the Act is a complex scheme of stringent remedies aimed at areas where voting discrimination has been most flagrant. Section 4(a)–(d) lays down a formula defining the States and political subdivisions to which these new remedies apply. The first of the remedies, contained in § 4(a), is the suspension of literacy tests and similar voting qualifications for a period of five years from the last occurrence of substantial voting discrimination. Section 5 prescribes a second remedy, the suspension of all new voting regulations pending review by federal authorities to determine whether their use would perpetuate voting discrimination. The third remedy, covered in §§ 6(b), 7, 9, and 13(a), is the assignment of federal examiners on certification by the Attorney General to list qualified applicants who are thereafter entitled to vote in all elections.

Other provisions of the Act prescribe subsidiary cures for persistent voting discrimination. Section 8 authorizes the appointment of federal poll-watchers in places to which federal examiners have already been assigned. Section 10(d) excuses those made eligible to vote in sections of the country covered by § 4(b) of the Act from paying accumulated past poll taxes for state and local elections. Section 12(e) provides for balloting by persons denied access to the polls in areas where federal examiners have been appointed.

The remaining remedial portions of the Act are aimed at voting discrimination in any area of the country where it may occur. Section 2 broadly prohibits the use of voting rules to abridge exercise of the franchise on racial grounds. Sections 3, 6(a), and 13(b) strengthen existing procedures for attacking voting discrimination by means of litigation. Section 4(e) excuses citizens educated in American schools conducted in a foreign language from passing English-language literacy tests. Section 10(a)–(c) facilitates constitutional litigation challenging the imposition of all poll taxes for state and local elections. Sections 11 and 12(a)–(d) authorize civil and criminal sanctions against interference with the exercise of rights guaranteed by the Act. . . .

These provisions of the Voting Rights Act of 1965 are

challenged on the fundamental ground that they exceed the powers of Congress and encroach on an area reserved to the States by the Constitution. . . .

The ground rules for resolving this question are clear. The language and purpose of the Fifteenth Amendment, the prior decisions construing its several provisions, and the general doctrines of constitutional interpretation, all point to one fundamental principle. As against the reserved powers of the States, Congress may use any rational means to effectuate the constitutional prohibition of racial discrimination in voting. . . .

Section 1 of the Fifteenth Amendment declares that "[t]he right of citizens of the United States to vote shall not be denied or abridged by the United States or by any State on account of race, color, or previous condition of servitude." This declaration has always been treated as self-executing and has repeatedly been construed, without further legislative specification, to invalidate state voting qualifications or procedures which are discriminatory on their face or in practice. . . . [T]he Fifteenth Amendment expressly declares that "Congress shall have power to enforce this article by appropriate legislation.". . . Accordingly, in addition to the courts, Congress has full remedial powers to effectuate the constitutional prohibition against racial discrimination in voting.

Congress has repeatedly exercised these powers in the past, and its enactments have repeatedly been upheld. . . . On the rare occasions when the Court has found an unconstitutional exercise of these powers, in its opinion Congress had attacked evils not comprehended by the Fifteenth Amendment.

The basic test to be applied in a case involving § 2 of the Fifteenth Amendment is the same as in all cases concerning the express powers of Congress with relation to the reserved powers of the States. Chief Justice Marshall laid down the classic formulation, 50 years before the Fifteenth Amendment was ratified:

"Let the end be legitimate, let it be within the scope of the constitution, and all means which are appropriate, which are plainly adapted to that end, which are not prohibited, but consist with the letter and spirit of the constitution, are constitutional." McCulloch v. Maryland.

The Court has subsequently echoed his language in describing each of the Civil War Amendments:

"Whatever legislation is appropriate, that is, adapted to carry out the objects the amendments have in view, whatever tends to enforce submission to the prohibitions they contain, and to secure to all persons the enjoyment of perfect equality of civil rights and the equal protection of the laws against State denial or invasion, if not prohibited, is brought within the domain of congressional power." Ex parte Virginia.

. . . We therefore reject South Carolina's argument that Congress may appropriately do no more than to forbid violations of the Fifteenth Amendment in general terms—that the task of fashioning specific remedies or of applying them to particular localities must necessarily be left entirely to the courts. Congress is not circumscribed by any such artificial rules under § 2 of the Fifteenth Amendment. . . .

Congress exercised its authority under the Fifteenth Amendment in an inventive manner when it enacted the Voting Rights Act of 1965. First: The measure prescribes remedies for voting discrimination which go into effect without any need for prior adjudication. This was clearly a legitimate response to the problem, for which there is ample precedent under other constitutional provisions. . . . Second: The Act intentionally confines these remedies to a small number of States and political subdivisions which in most instances were familiar to Congress by name. This, too, was a permissible method of dealing with the problem. Congress had learned that substantial voting discrimination presently occurs in certain sections of the country, and it knew no way of accurately forecasting whether the evil might spread elsewhere in the future. In acceptable legislative fashion, Congress chose to limit its attention to the geographic areas where immediate action seemed necessary. . . .

After enduring nearly a century of widespread resistance to the Fifteenth Amendment, Congress has marshalled an array of potent weapons against the evil, with authority in the Attorney General to employ them effectively. Many of the areas directly affected by this development have indicated their willingness to abide by any restraints legitimately imposed upon them. We here hold that the portions of the Voting Rights Act properly before us are a valid means for carrying out the commands of the Fifteenth Amendment. Hopefully, millions of nonwhite Americans will now be able to participate for the first time on an equal basis in the government under which they live. We may finally look forward to the day when truly "[t]he right of citizens of the United States to vote shall not be denied or abridged by the United States or by any State on account of race, color, or previous condition of servitude."

The bill of complaint is dismissed.

TABLE 19-1 Percentage of Eligible Blacks Registered to Vote, 1940–1984

Year	South	Peripheral South	Deep South
1940	3%	5%	1%
1947	12	17	8
1956	25	29	21
1964	43	52	30
1966	52	58	46
1968	62	67	57
1976	63	62	64
1984	59	58	59

SOURCE: Earl Black and Merle Black, *Politics and Society in the South* (Cambridge, Mass.: Harvard University Press, 1987), 137. Reprinted by permission.

NOTE: South: the eleven Peripheral and Deep South States. Peripheral South: Arkansas, Florida, North Carolina, Tennessee, Texas, Virginia. Deep South: Alabama, Georgia, Louisiana, Mississippi, South Carolina.

With the Court's approval of the Voting Rights Act, the federal government was free to launch a vigorous campaign to make the goals of the Fifteenth Amendment a reality. The executive branch actively enforced the law, and Congress periodically strengthened and extended its provisions. These efforts, coupled with large-scale voter registration drives conducted by civil rights organizations, have resulted in southern blacks being registered to vote at rates only slightly below those of whites. Consider Table 19-1, which shows black registration rates two decades before and after passage of the 1965 Voting Rights Act. Clearly the legislation was a significant factor in expanding voting participation by minority citizens in the South— more than a full century after the ratification of the Fifteenth Amendment constitutionally declared voting equality.

Property, Taxation, and Residency

Aside from race, states have imposed several other limitations on voting participation. Inevitably such restrictions have been challenged, usually as violations of the Equal Protection Clause. As a rule the Supreme Court has been very skeptical of any limitation placed on voting rights.

Property ownership as a voting requirement is one such restriction that the justices have confronted. In the early part of U.S. history it was common for suffrage to be tied to property ownership, but in the 1960s property qualifications again became an issue. With the postwar baby boom in full force and a growing need to improve education and other social programs, governments greatly expanded public services and raised taxes to pay for them. At the local level, the primary means of raising revenue was the property tax. Issuing various kinds of revenue bonds and increasing the property tax rate were the usual methods of raising revenue. Many states required that such increases be approved by the voters. Citizens opposed to tax increases were dismayed that individuals who would not have to pay the increased property taxes were allowed to vote in such elections. Obviously, those who did not own property would tend to favor the projected improvement in facilities and services because the cost would be borne by others. Property owners considered this situation unfair, and some states laws were passed restricting the right to vote in property tax and related elections to those who owned or rented real property. In *Kramer v. Union Free School District* (1969), however, the Supreme Court struck down such laws, finding that property ownership as a voting requirement violated the Equal Protection Clause of the Fourteenth Amendment.

Another form of the voting/economics relationship was the state-imposed tax on the privilege of casting a ballot. Where levied, the poll tax was nominal. States nonetheless claimed that the tax improved the quality of the electorate by weeding out those who did not sufficiently appreciate the right to vote and who probably would not be well informed on the issues and the candidates. In 1937, in *Breedlove v. Suttles,* the Supreme Court heard a challenge to the constitutionality of the poll tax. At that time, the justices rejected the idea that the Georgia poll tax violated the Equal Protection Clause of the Fourteenth Amendment.

With the rise of the civil rights movement two decades later, the poll tax began to attract increasing criticism. The poll-tax states were in the South, and many saw the tax as just another way of depressing black voting participation. Although large numbers of whites also forfeited the right to vote by failure to pay the poll tax, proportionately the requirement hit blacks harder, and civil rights and other interest groups targeted the poll tax for elimination. In response, Congress proposed the Twenty-fourth Amendment outlawing the poll tax as a requirement for voting in any federal election. The amendment did not cover state elections because opposition by southerners in Congress and by a number of states was judged sufficient to jeopardize its passage. Those who proposed the elimination of the tax were confident that if the requirement were removed as a condition for voting in federal elections, state elections would likely follow. It would be too costly and cumbersome, they reasoned, for the states to maintain two separate voting rolls. The amendment was ratified in 1964.

Shortly thereafter, all but four states rescinded the poll tax on state elections. Alabama, Texas, and Virginia retained their poll taxes of $1.50, and Mississippi continued its $2 tax. Having failed to obtain a constitutional amendment that completely rid the nation of these taxes, opponents sought relief in the courts. In *Harper v. Virginia State Board of Elections* (1966) the Supreme Court invalidated state taxes on the privilege to vote in state and local elections. As Justice Douglas summarized, "We conclude that a State violates the Fourteenth Amendment whenever it makes the affluence of the voter or payment of any fee an electoral standard."

Traditionally, the states have had the authority to restrict voting to individuals who were truly citizens and residents of the community, and state legislatures usually require individuals to be residents for a certain period of time before they can vote. States also normally require potential voters to register prior to election day. These restrictions have been based on the principle that only bona fide residents should have a voice in making political decisions for the community. They also help prevent fraud: candidates cannot recruit large numbers of nonresident supporters to present themselves on election day and demand the right to vote. Although these limitations do not have the same connotations as restricting access to the ballot box on the basis of race or economic status, the Supreme Court has taken steps to ensure that states do not unreasonably deny the right to vote.

The Court, for example, has ruled that individuals moving into a community must have a reasonable opportunity to obtain resident status. *Carrington v. Rash* (1965) provides a good illustration. The Court struck down a Texas regulation that imposed too great a burden on military personnel. Texas, home to numerous military bases, feared that the large numbers of armed services personnel transferred into the state for relatively short assignments would have a disproportionate impact on local elections. The state argued that it was very difficult to determine whether these individuals were bona fide residents. Texas therefore imposed a blanket exclusion on service personnel, stipulating that members of the armed forces who moved into Texas could not vote there while they remained in the military. The Court refused to accept the placement of such a burden on an entire class of individuals, holding that the Equal Protection Clause demands a more precise test to determine whose residence in the state is bona fide.

But the Court has never seriously questioned the authority of the state to limit voting to bona fide residents, and, in fact, many states require that individuals live in the state and the local community for a minimum period of time before they are eligible to vote. In 1970 Congress amended the Voting Rights Act to outlaw residency requirements longer than thirty days for voting in presidential elections. This change was based on the rationale that the length of time one lived in a particular state or locality had no reasonable connection to being qualified to vote for the federal executive. However, many states retained their time requirements for state and local elections. In 1972, the Supreme Court's decision in *Dunn v. Blumstein* sharply curtailed the ability of the state to impose lengthy residency requirements. Here the justices struck down Tennessee's requirement that an individual live in the state for at least one year and in the county for a minimum of thirty days before being eligible to vote. The Court ruled that these minimums were entirely too long and suggested that the state could accomplish its goals by reducing the residency requirement to no longer than thirty days.

The combined effects of constitutional amendments, federal enforcement legislation, and judicial decisions have taken away most of the states' discretion to determine qualifications for voting. The states retain responsibility for administering the voting process, but contemporary political and legal notions of universal suffrage have left them little else. The state may still deny individuals the right to vote if for legitimate considerations (for example, mental illness) they are demonstrably unqualified. The Court also has ruled that states may strip convicted felons of the right to vote. In some states, such bans last only until the convicted criminals complete all aspects of their sentences. In *Richardson v. Ramirez* (1974), however, the justices upheld a California law that forever disenfranchised individuals found guilty of felonies.

POLITICAL REPRESENTATION

Having the right to vote does not guarantee that people share equally in political influence. The United States is not a direct democracy; consequently, few

In 1812 Elkanah Tinsdale lampooned the political maneuverings of Gov. Elbridge Gerry of Massachusetts, who deftly engineered the construction of constituency boundaries to aid in the election of a member of his own party. Because the district resembled a mythological salamander in the cartoonist's illustration, the term *gerrymander* has come to mean the drawing of political district lines for partisan advantage.

public policy decisions are made in the voting booth. In a republican form of government, most political decisions are made by officials who are elected by the people from defined geographical districts. The duty of these officials is to represent the interests of their constituencies in the policy-making process.

How well and how equitably this representational process works depend in part on how the boundary lines of political units are drawn. These issues are not easy to resolve, as history shows. Much of the debate at the Constitutional Convention centered on representation. The smaller states wanted representation in Congress based on statehood, with each of the thirteen states having equal voting powers. The larger states argued for legislative representation based on size of population. The convention compromised by accepting both ideas in a bicameral Congress.

Because district lines determine political representation, the authority to draw those boundaries carries with it a great deal of political power. Skillful construction of political subdivisions can be used to great advantage, and politicians have never been reluctant to use this power to advance their own interests. Since 1812 the art of structuring legislative districts to ensure political success has been known as gerrymandering. The term refers to the political maneuverings of Gov. Elbridge Gerry of Massachusetts, who convinced the state legislature to draw district lines so that his partisan supporters would have a high probability of reelection. Gerrymandered districts frequently are characterized by the rather strange geographical configurations necessary to achieve the desired political ends.

Establishing or modifying the district lines historically has been a political matter. Battles over drawing the boundaries of political subdivisions usually are fought within the halls of the state legislatures. However, serious legal or even constitutional questions may arise when officials use inappropriate criteria for drawing boundaries, or when the process results in the discriminatory treatment of certain groups of voters. In such cases the courts may be called upon to intervene in what is otherwise a legislative duty.

The Reapportionment Controversy

In drafting Article I of the Constitution, the Framers clearly intended that representation in the lower house of Congress would be based upon population. Each state was allotted at least one representative, with additional seats based upon the number of persons residing within its boundaries.[4]

The Constitutional Convention wisely anticipated that the nation would undergo considerable growth and population shifts and consequently determined that the number of congressional seats allocated to each state would be reformulated every ten years following completion of the national census. States that grew in population would gain increased congressional representation, and those that lost population would lose representation. This process remains relatively unchanged today. The number of seats in the House of Representatives is fixed by federal law, currently at 435. Every ten years, when the Census Bureau completes its work, the allocation of those 435 seats among the states must be recalculated to reflect changes since the previous population count.

Following the census, each state is told the number of representatives it will have for the next decade. The state legislature then geographically divides the state into separate congressional districts, each of which elects a member of Congress. This scheme is known as the single-member constituency system of representation.[5] Political representation is equitable only if the state legislature constructs its congressional districts so that each contains approximately the same number of residents.

The process of devising the legislative districts is called apportionment. When the legislature creates equally populated districts, the system is properly apportioned. But when the districts are not in proper balance, when some districts are substantially larger than others, they are said to be malapportioned. A state can be malapportioned if the legislature does not draw the district lines properly or fails to adjust boundaries to keep pace with population shifts.

Representational districts are used not only for congressional seats but also for other government units. The state legislatures, for example, generally are based on a single-member constituency system, as are many county commissions and city councils. Even special purpose commissions, such as boards of education and public utility districts, often follow the

---

4. Originally, population was determined by the number of free persons, including indentured servants, but excluding Indians not taxed, plus three-fifths of the slaves. This formula was changed with ratification of the Fourteenth Amendment in 1868 to define population as the whole number of persons, excluding Indians not taxed.

5. During the first half century of the nation's history it was common for the states to select their delegates to the House of Representatives on an at-large basis rather than using the single-member constituency plan.

same scheme. In each case, a legislative body must create districts from which representatives will be selected. The same apportionment concepts apply to these bodies as apply to Congress.

The constitutional issues regarding apportionment rose to the surface after World War II. Spurred by industrialization, two major wars, and an economic depression, major population shifts had occurred during the first half of the twentieth century. Large numbers of people moved from rural areas and small towns into larger urban centers. Cities grew rapidly and agricultural areas declined, but state legislatures failed to respond adequately to these migration patterns by reapportioning their congressional and state legislative districts. The more state legislatures came to be dominated by rural interests, the less incumbent legislators wished to consider redistricting. To apportion the districts properly would mean fewer legislative seats for the rural areas, and that meant abolishing some seats held by incumbents. At the midpoint of the century, many states had not reapportioned since the 1900 census.

The first major apportionment case to come before the Supreme Court was *Colegrove v. Green* (1946), a challenge to the congressional districts in Illinois, where the largest district had almost nine times as many residents as the smallest. This imbalance was challenged on the grounds that it resulted in a system that violated the Constitution's guarantee of a republican form of government. The Supreme Court, however, refused to rule on the case, holding that reapportionment was a political issue that should be resolved at the ballot box and not in court.

The Court's admonishment presented an insurmountable problem for urban residents living in disproportionately large districts. Many states were so badly malapportioned and the dominant rural interests so opposed to change that electing enough state legislators sympathetic to reapportionment was almost impossible. But the Court maintained its position that reapportionment questions were outside the purview of judicial scrutiny. Meanwhile, the census figures for 1950 and 1960 indicated that the malapportionment problem was growing.

As the nation entered the 1960s, the Supreme Court's position began to soften. This change was prompted by a greater awareness of the problems associated with malapportionment and by significant changes in the makeup of the Court. Of the four votes comprising the majority in *Colegrove*, only Justice Frankfurter remained on the bench. The justices, now under the leadership of Earl Warren, expressed a much greater willingness to address claims of violated rights.

In 1962 the Court radically changed its position. In *Baker v. Carr,* a challenge to the badly malapportioned Tennessee state legislature, the justices ruled that apportionment issues raise serious Equal Protection questions that are justiciable *(see Chapter 3)*. In effect, the Court announced that it would welcome reapportionment challenges.

The first reapportionment dispute heard by the Supreme Court following *Baker* was *Wesberry v. Sanders* (1964), which involved a challenge to the way Georgia apportioned its congressional districts. Although this case involved only Georgia, the malapportionment there was typical of that found in most states following the 1960 census and the 1962 congressional elections.

This suit was filed by James P. Wesberry and other qualified voters of Georgia's Fifth Congressional District against Gov. Carl Sanders and other state officials. The plaintiffs claimed that the state's congressional districting system violated the federal Constitution. The Fifth (metropolitan Atlanta) was the largest of Georgia's ten congressional districts, with a population of 823,680. By comparison the Ninth District had only 272,154 residents, and the population of the average district was 394,312. This inequality meant that the Fifth District's legislator represented two to three times as many people as the other members of Congress from Georgia. The districting scheme had been enacted by the state legislature in 1931, and no effort to bring the districts into balance had occurred since then.

The justices held that this condition of significant malapportionment violated Article I, Section 2, of the Constitution, which says, "The House of Representatives shall be composed of Members chosen every second Year by the People of the several States." To satisfy that constitutional provision, the Court ruled, the congressional districts within a state must be as equal in population as possible. The decision required the state legislature to redraw its congressional districts to meet this standard.

Wesberry, however, did not resolve the reapportionment controversy. A more difficult and politically charged issue centered on malapportionment within the state legislatures. It was one thing to command the state legislators to alter the boundaries of congressional districts, but another to require them to reapportion their own legislative districts. Many states would regard such an action as an infringement of their sovereignty. In addition, the wholesale alteration of state legislative districts would mean that many state representatives would lose their districts or become politically vulnerable, and legislative power would shift from rural to urban interests. That the state legislatures were less than enthusiastic about such prospects is hardly surprising.

It did not take the Supreme Court long to address the dilemma of the state legislatures. Only four months after the *Wesberry* ruling, the Court announced its decision in *Reynolds v. Sims.* While *Reynolds* shares with *Wesberry* questions of representational equality, the legal basis for the two cases is very different. Article I, Section 2, of the Constitution, upon which the *Wesberry* outcome rested, deals only with the U.S. House of Representatives. Consequently, a challenge to state representational schemes had to be based on other grounds. In addition, all state legislatures except Nebraska's are bicameral, leaving open for dispute whether both houses of the state assembly must be based on population. Notice in Chief Justice Warren's majority opinion in *Reynolds* how the Court reaches a conclusion consistent with *Wesberry* while using entirely different constitutional grounds. Also, consider the Court's holding on the issue of bicameralism. Is this ruling reasonable? Or should the states be allowed to base representation in one house of the legislature on interests other than population alone? How compelling is Justice Harlan's dissent?

Reynolds v. Sims

377 U.S. 533 (1964)
Vote: 8 (Black, Brennan, Clark, Douglas, Goldberg, Stewart,
   Warren, White)
   1 (Harlan)
Opinion of the Court: Warren
Concurring opinions: Clark, Stewart
Dissenting opinion: Harlan

Alabama's 1901 constitution authorized a state legislature of 106 House members and 35 senators. These legislators were to represent districts created generally on the basis of population. Although obliged to reapportion following each national census, the legislature had never altered the districts that were originally drawn following the 1900 census. Because of population shifts and a state constitutional requirement that each county, regardless of size, have at least one representative, Alabama had become severely malapportioned. For the state House of Representatives, the most populous legislative district had sixteen times as many people as the least populous. Conditions in the state Senate were even more inequitable. The largest senatorial district had a population forty-one times the population of the smallest. As was the case in other states, rural areas enjoyed representation levels far in excess of what their populations warranted. For example, urban Jefferson County's single senator represented more than 600,000 residents, while rural

Lowndes County had one senator for its 15,417 citizens.

Voters in urban counties filed suit to have the Alabama system declared unconstitutional as a violation of the Equal Protection Clause of the Fourteenth Amendment. Pressured by the threat of legal action in light of the Supreme Court's decision in *Baker v. Carr*, the state legislature offered two reapportionment plans to improve the situation. A three-judge district court declared the existing system unconstitutional and the proposed reforms inadequate. A temporary reapportionment plan was imposed by the trial court judges, and the state appealed to the Supreme Court. The *Reynolds* case was one of six state legislative reapportionment disputes the Supreme Court heard at the same time. The others came from Maryland, Delaware, Virginia, New York, and Colorado. The justices used the opinion in *Reynolds* as the primary vehicle for articulating the Court's position on the state redistricting issue.

MR. CHIEF JUSTICE WARREN delivered the opinion of the Court.

Legislators represent people, not trees or acres. Legislators are elected by voters, not farms or cities or economic interests. As long as ours is a representative form of government, and our legislatures are those instruments of government elected directly by and directly representative of the people, the right to elect legislators in a free and unimpaired fashion is a bedrock of our political system. It could hardly be gainsaid that a constitutional claim had been asserted by an allegation that certain otherwise qualified voters had been entirely prohibited from voting for members of their state legislature. And, if a State should provide that the votes of citizens in one part of the State should be given two times, or five times, or 10 times the weight of votes of citizens in another part of the State, it could hardly be contended that the right to vote of those residing in the disfavored areas had not been effectively diluted. It would appear extraordinary to suggest that a State could be constitutionally permitted to enact a law providing that

certain of the State's voters could vote two, five, or 10 times for their legislative representatives, while voters living elsewhere could vote only once. And it is inconceivable that a state law to the effect that, in counting votes for legislators, the votes of citizens in one part of the State would be multiplied by two, five, or 10 while the votes of persons in another area would be counted only at face value, could be constitutionally sustainable. Of course, the effect of state legislative districting schemes which give the same number of representatives to unequal numbers of constituents is identical. Overweighting and overvaluation of the votes of those living here has the certain effect of dilution and undervaluation of the votes of those living there. The resulting discrimination against those individual voters living in disfavored areas is easily demonstrable mathematically. Their right to vote is simply not the same right to vote as that of those living in a favored part of the State. Two, five, or 10 of them must vote before the effect of their voting is equivalent to that of their favored neighbor. Weighting the votes of citizens differently, by any method or means, merely because of where they happen to reside, hardly seems justifiable. One must be ever aware that the Constitution forbids "sophisticated as well as simple-minded modes of discrimination." . . .

Logically, in a society ostensibly grounded on representative government, it would seem reasonable that a majority of the people of a State could elect a majority of that State's legislators. To conclude differently, and to sanction minority control of state legislative bodies, would appear to deny majority rights in a way that far surpasses any possible denial of minority rights that might otherwise be thought to result. Since legislatures are responsible for enacting laws by which all citizens are to be governed, they should be bodies which are collectively responsive to the popular will. And the concept of equal protection has been traditionally viewed as requiring the uniform treatment of persons standing in the same relation to the governmental action questioned or challenged. With respect to the allocation of legislative representation, all voters, as citizens of a State, stand in the same relation regardless of where they live. Any suggested criteria for the differentiation of citizens are insufficient to justify any discrimination, as to the weight of their votes, unless relevant to the permissible purposes of legislative apportionment. Since the achieving of fair and effective representation for all citizens is concededly the basic aim of legislative apportionment, we conclude that the Equal Protection Clause guarantees the opportunity for equal participation by all voters in the election of state legislators. Diluting the weight of votes because of place of residence impairs basic constitutional rights under the Fourteenth Amendment just as much as invidious discriminations based upon factors such as race or economic status. . . .

We are told that the matter of apportioning representation in a state legislature is a complex and many-faceted one. We are advised that States can rationally consider factors other than population in apportioning legislative representation. We are admonished not to restrict the power of the States to impose differing views as to political philosophy on their citizens. We are cautioned about the dangers of entering into political thickets and mathematical quagmires. Our answer is this: a denial of constitutionally protected rights demands judicial protection; our oath and our office require no less of us. . . . To the extent that a citizen's right to vote is debased, he is that much less a citizen. The fact that an individual lives here or there is not a legitimate reason for overweighting or diluting the efficacy of his vote. The complexions of societies and civilizations change, often with amazing rapidity. A nation once primarily rural in character becomes predominantly urban. Representation schemes once fair and equitable become archaic and outdated. But the basic principle of representative government remains, and must remain, unchanged—the weight of a citizen's vote cannot be made to depend on where he lives. Population is, of necessity, the starting point for consideration and the controlling criterion for judgment in legislative apportionment controversies. A citizen, a qualified voter, is no more nor no less so because he lives in the city or on the farm. This is the clear and strong command of our Constitution's Equal Protection Clause. This is an essential part of the concept of a government of laws and not men. This is at the heart of Lincoln's vision of "government of the people, by the people, [and] for the people." The Equal Protection Clause demands no less than substantially equal state legislative representation for all citizens, of all places as well as of all races.

We hold that, as a basic constitutional standard, the Equal Protection Clause requires that the seats in both houses of a bicameral state legislature must be apportioned on a population basis. Simply stated, an individual's right to vote for state legislators is unconstitutionally impaired when its weight is in a substantial fashion diluted when compared with votes of citizens living in other parts of the State. . . .

Legislative apportionment in Alabama is signally illustrative and symptomatic of the seriousness of this problem in a number of the States. At the time this litigation was commenced, there had been no reapportionment of seats in the Alabama Legislature for over 60 years. Legislative inaction, coupled with the unavailability of any political or judicial remedy, had resulted, with the passage of years, in the perpetuated scheme becoming little more than an irrational anachronism. Consistent failure by the Alabama Legislature to comply with state constitutional requirements as to the frequency of reapportionment and the bases of legislative representation resulted in a minority stranglehold on the State Legislature. Inequality of representation in one house added to the inequality in the other. . . . Since neither of the houses of the Alabama Legislature, under any of the three plans considered by the District Court, was apportioned on a population basis, we would be justified in proceeding no further. However, one of the proposed plans, that contained in the so-called 67-Senator Amendment, at least superficially resembles the scheme of legislative representation followed in the Federal Congress. Under this plan, each of Alabama's 67 counties is allotted one senator, and no counties are given more than one Senate seat. Arguably, this is analogous to the allocation of two Senate seats, in the Federal Congress, to each of the 50 States, regardless of population. Seats in the Alabama House, under the proposed constitutional amendment, are distributed by giving each of the 67 counties at least one, with the remaining 39 seats being allotted among the more populous counties on a population basis. This scheme, at least at first glance, appears to resemble that prescribed for the Federal House of Representatives, where the 435 seats are distributed among the States on a population basis, although each State, regardless of its population, is given at least one Congressman. Thus, although there are substantial differences in underlying rationale and results, the 67-Senator Amendment, as proposed by the Alabama Legislature, at least arguably presents for consideration a scheme analogous to that used for apportioning seats in Congress. . . .

We agree with the District Court, and find the federal analogy inapposite and irrelevant to state legislative districting schemes. Attempted reliance on the federal analogy appears often to be little more than an after-the-fact rationalization offered in defense of maladjusted state apportionment arrangements. The original constitutions of 36 of our States provided that representation in both houses of the state legislatures would be based completely, or predominantly, on population. And the Founding Fathers clearly had no intention of establishing a pattern or model for the apportionment of seats in state legislatures when the system of representation in the Federal Congress was adopted. . . .

The system of representation in the two Houses of the Federal Congress is one ingrained in our Constitution, as part of the law of the land. It is one conceived out of compromise and concession indispensable to the establishment of our federal republic. Arising from unique historical circumstances, it is based on the consideration that in establishing our type of federalism a group of formerly independent States bound themselves together under one national government. . . .

Political subdivisions of States—counties, cities, or whatever—never were and never have been considered as sovereign entities. Rather, they have been traditionally regarded as subordinate governmental instrumentalities created by the State to assist in the carrying out of state governmental functions. . . . The relationship of the States to the Federal Government could hardly be less analogous.

Thus, we conclude that the plan contained in the 67-Senator Amendment for apportioning seats in the Alabama Legislature cannot be sustained by recourse to the so-called federal analogy. Nor can any other inequitable state legislative apportionment scheme be justified. . . .

By holding that as a federal constitutional requisite both houses of a state legislature must be apportioned on a population basis, we mean that the Equal Protection Clause requires that a State make an honest and good faith effort to construct districts, in both houses of its legislature, as nearly of equal population as is practicable. We realize that it is a practical impossibility to arrange legislative districts so that each one has an identical number of residents, or citizens, or voters. Mathematical exactness or precision is hardly a workable constitutional requirement. . . .

A State may legitimately desire to maintain the integrity of various political subdivisions, insofar as possible, and provide for compact districts of contiguous territory in designing a legislative apportionment scheme. Valid considerations may underlie such aims. Indiscriminate districting, without any regard for political subdivision or natural or historical boundary lines, may be little more than an open invitation to partisan gerrymandering. Single-member districts may be the rule in one State, while another State might desire to achieve some flexibility by creating multimember or floterial districts. Whatever the means of accomplishment, the overriding objective must be substantial equality of population among the various districts, so that the vote of any citizen is approximately equal in weight to that of any other citizen in the State.

History indicates, however, that many States have deviated, to a greater or lesser degree, from the equal-population principle in the apportionment of seats in at least one house of their legislatures. So long as the divergences from a strict population standard are based on legitimate considerations incident to the effectuation of a rational state policy, some deviations from the equal-population principle are constitutionally permissible with respect to the apportionment of seats in either or both of the two houses of a bicameral state legislature. But neither history alone, nor economic or other sorts of group interests, are permissible factors in attempting to justify disparities from population-based representation. Citizens, not history or economic interests, cast votes. Considerations of area alone provide an insufficient justification for deviations from the equal population principle. . . .

We find, therefore, that the action taken by the District Court in this case, in ordering into effect a reapportionment of both houses of the Alabama Legislature for purposes of the 1962 primary and general elections, by using the best parts of the two proposed plans which it had found, as a whole, to be invalid, was an appropriate and well-considered exercise of judicial power. Admittedly, the lower court's ordered plan was intended only as a temporary and provisional measure and the District Court correctly indicated that the plan was invalid as a permanent apportionment. In retaining jurisdiction while deferring a hearing on the issuance of a final injunction in order to give the provisionally reapportioned legislature an opportunity to act effectively, the court below proceeded in a proper fashion. . . .

Affirmed and remanded.

MR. JUSTICE HARLAN, dissenting.

In these cases the Court holds that seats in the legislatures of six States are apportioned in ways that violate the Federal Constitution. Under the Court's ruling it is bound to follow that the legislature in all but a few of the other 44 States will meet the same fate. These decisions, with Wesberry v. Sanders, involving congressional districting by the States, and Gray v. Sanders, relating to elections for statewide office, have the effect of placing basic aspects of state political systems under the pervasive overlordship of the federal judiciary. Once again, I must register my protest.

Today's holding is that the Equal Protection Clause of the Fourteenth Amendment requires every State to structure its legislature so that all the members of each house represent substantially the same number of people; other factors may be given play only to the extent that they do not significantly encroach on this basic "population" principle. Whatever may be thought of this holding as a piece of political ideology—and even on that score the political history and practices of this country from its earliest beginnings leave wide room for debate . . . I think it demonstrable that the Fourteenth Amendment does not impose this political tenet on the States or authorize this Court to do so.

The Court's constitutional discussion, found in its opinion in the Alabama cases, is remarkable . . . for its failure to address itself at all to the Fourteenth Amendment as a whole or to the legislative history of the Amendment pertinent to the matter at hand. Stripped of aphorisms, the Court's argument boils down to the assertion that appellees' right to vote has been invidiously "debased" or "diluted" by systems of apportionment which entitle them to vote for fewer legislators than other voters, an assertion which is tied to the Equal Protection Clause only by the constitutionally frail tautology that "equal" means "equal."

Had the Court paused to probe more deeply into the matter, it would have found that the Equal Protection Clause was never intended to inhibit the States in choosing any democratic method they pleased for the apportionment of their legislatures. This is shown by the language of the Fourteenth Amendment taken as a whole, by the understanding of those who proposed and ratified it, and by the political practices of the States at the time the Amendment was adopted. It is confirmed by numerous state and congressional actions since the adoption of the Fourteenth Amendment, and by the common understanding of the Amendment as evidenced by subsequent constitutional amendments and decisions of this Court before Baker v. Carr made an abrupt break with the past in 1962.

The failure of the Court to consider any of these matters cannot be excused or explained by any concept of "developing" constitutionalism. It is meaningless to speak of constitutional "development" when both the language and history of the controlling provisions of the Constitution are wholly ignored. Since it can, I think, be shown beyond doubt that state legislative apportionments, as such, are wholly free of constitutional limitations, save such as may be imposed by the Republican Form of Government Clause (Const., Art. IV, § 4), the Court's action now bringing them within the purview of the Fourteenth Amendment amounts to nothing less than an exercise of the amending power by this Court.

So far as the Federal Constitution is concerned, the complaints in these cases should all have been dismissed below for failure to state a cause of action because what has been alleged or proved shows no violation of any constitutional right.

Harlan's dissent in *Reynolds* predicting that the legislatures of all the states would be affected by the Court's one person, one vote principle proved to be accurate. At first, there was some disagreement with the Court's ruling. State advocates began a movement to amend the Constitution to provide states the authority to have at least one house of their legislatures based on factors other than population, but the proposal failed to garner sufficient support. As the states began the Court-imposed reapportionment process, opposition started to wane. Today, reapportionment of congressional and state legislative districts occurs each decade following the national census. In addition, the reapportionment rulings have been extended to representation systems used at the local level, expanding the influence of decisions such as *Wesberry* and *Reynolds*. The first effect of the reapportionment rulings was to shift a significant amount of political power from the rural areas to the cities. In more recent years, consistent with demographic changes, the suburban areas have been the beneficiaries of the Court's redistricting policies. In the near future, increased representation for minority citizens, especially for the rapidly growing Hispanic population, undoubtedly will occur.

Upon his retirement, Chief Justice Warren said that, in his opinion, the reapportionment decisions were the most significant rulings rendered during his sixteen-year tenure. That statement was remarkable, considering that under his leadership the Court handed down landmark decisions on race relations, criminal justice, obscenity, libel, and school prayer.

Political Representation and Minority Rights

So long as the one person, one vote principle is observed, the Supreme Court generally has allowed the states freedom in constructing representational districts. That latitude, however, is not without limit. The Court always has been aware that representational schemes that satisfy standards of numerical equality may still offend basic constitutional principles. Plans that discriminate on the basis of race or ethnicity have been of particular concern. The justices have served notice that boundary lines cannot be drawn in a way that dilutes the political power of minorities.

An early example of how lines can be drawn to change the influence of minorities is *Gomillion v. Lightfoot* (1960). Prior to 1957 the city limits of Tuskegee, Alabama, were in the shape of a square that covered the entire urban area. With the growing civil rights activism of the time and the increasing tendency of black citizens to vote, the white establishment in Tuskegee feared a loss of political control. Conse-

quently, members of the Alabama legislature sympathetic to the city's white leaders successfully sponsored a bill that changed the boundary lines. No longer a square, the altered city limits formed, in Justice Felix Frankfurter's words, "an uncouth twenty-eight-sided figure."

The effect of the redistricting was phenomenal. The law removed from the city all but 4 or 5 of its 400 black voters, but no white voters. The black plaintiffs, now former residents of Tuskegee, claimed that their removal from the city denied them the right to vote on the basis of race and, therefore, violated their Fifteenth Amendment rights. The city did not deny that race was at issue, but claimed that the state of Alabama had an unrestricted right to draw city boundaries as it saw fit and that the courts could not intervene to limit that authority. A unanimous Supreme Court ruled to the contrary, holding that when an otherwise lawful exercise of state power is used to circumvent a federally protected right, the courts may indeed intervene. A legislative act that removes citizens from the municipal voting rolls in a racially discriminatory fashion violates the Fifteenth Amendment.

Beginning in the 1970s the issue of race and representation took on a new twist when legislatures started to enact districting plans designed to ensure the election of minority officials. This was done through the creation of "majority-minority" districts, representational units in which a majority of the residents were members of a particular minority group. These districts virtually insured the election of minority officeholders. In *United Jewish Organizations of Williamsburgh v. Carey* (1977), the Supreme Court upheld such legislative actions. For the Court Justice White declared:

[T]he Constitution does not prevent a State subject to the Voting Rights Act from deliberately creating or preserving black majorities in particular districts ... [N]either the Fourteenth nor the Fifteenth Amendment mandates any per se rule against using racial factors in districting and apportionment.... The permissible use of racial criteria is not confined to eliminating the effects of past discriminatory districting or apportionment.

United Jewish Organizations and subsequent decisions encouraged state legislatures to engage in such racially aware districting practices. Civil rights groups and other liberal organizations had been advocating this practice as the only meaningful way to guarantee African Americans, Hispanics, and other minorities a fair share of legislative seats.

In promoting this cause, advocates of increasing the political power of minorities received significant support from the Justice Department under Presidents Reagan and Bush. Why would a Republican administration back efforts to increase the number of black representatives, especially since these legislators probably would be Democrats? The answer is simple. When lines are drawn to create districts with high concentrations of black voters, the other districts become more white and more Republican. In other words, by creating a few districts that are dominated by minorities, the state legislatures also fashion districts that are more likely to elect Republicans.

In many states the reapportionment battles that followed the 1990 census were not over one person, one vote issues; rather, they focused on drawing district boundary lines in a manner that would increase the number of minority officeholders. The successful creation of districts with heavy concentrations of racial and ethnic minorities had its intended effect. In the 1992 congressional elections, sixteen new black representatives were elected, bringing the total membership of the Black Caucus to forty. Eight newly elected Hispanic representatives also took their seats after the 1992 elections.

To draw these new majority-minority districts, state legislatures often had to engage in very creative districting methods. Critics contended that legislators went too far, frequently establishing district boundaries that were highly irregular in shape and sprawled across large areas. It was one thing, they argued, to

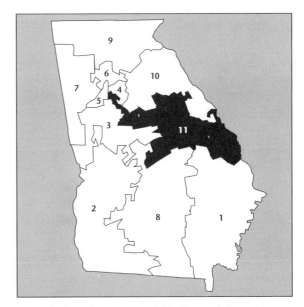

Georgia's Eleventh Congressional District was challenged in *Miller v. Johnson* (1995). Although the district is not generally irregular in shape, note the thin fingerlike extensions in the northwestern, northeastern, and western sections of the district. These were designed to incorporate high concentrations of black voters in Savannah, Augusta, and Atlanta.

SOURCE: *Congressional Quarterly Weekly Report*, July 1, 1995, 1945

create districts that did not purposefully dilute minority voting strength, but a much different thing to base representational boundaries exclusively on race. As a consequence, lawsuits filed in Florida, Georgia, Louisiana, North Carolina, and Texas challenged the constitutionality of many new districts.

The first appeal to reach the Supreme Court was *Shaw v. Reno* (1993), a challenge to two majority-minority congressional districts in North Carolina. The decision in that case shocked the civil rights community when the Court ruled that congressional districts created to maximize minority representation under some circumstances may be unconstitutional. At constitutional risk were district lines that created bizarrely shaped configurations explainable in racial terms only. After establishing this new standard, the justices sent the case back down to the lower courts for additional proceedings.

It was only a matter of time before the Court would receive an appeal requiring it to apply the *Shaw* principles. How much latitude would the Court give state legislatures in fashioning districts designed to enhance minority voting strength? To what extent would the *Shaw* standard allow race to be taken into account? The Court was not clear in *Shaw*, and its 5–4 vote left the districting waters muddy. It did not take long, however, for the Court to respond. The first appeal to reach the justices was a 1995 case challenging a majority-minority district in Georgia. As you read *Miller v. Johnson*, pay close attention to the different views expressed.

Miller v. Johnson

___ U.S. ___ (1995)

Vote: 5 (Kennedy, O'Connor, Rehnquist, Scalia, Thomas)
*   4 (Breyer, Ginsburg, Souter, Stevens)*
Opinion of the Court: Kennedy
Concurring opinion: O'Connor
Dissenting opinions: Ginsburg, Stevens

Following the 1990 census it was necessary for the state of Georgia to redraw the lines of its eleven congressional districts. The first plan, passed by the state legislature in 1991, included two districts that had a majority of black voters. Because Georgia is subject to the provisions of the 1965 Voting Rights Act, the plan was submitted to the Justice Department for approval ("preclearance"). The Justice Department rejected the plan, holding that it did not give sufficient attention to black voting strength. The state revised its apportionment plan, but the new version also included only two majority black districts. This plan also failed to receive Justice Department approval. Finally, in 1992 the state passed and the Justice Department approved

a new districting plan. This legislation created three majority black districts: the Second (southwest Georgia), the Fifth (Atlanta), and the district challenged in this case, the Eleventh.

The Eleventh District ran diagonally across the state from the edge of Atlanta to the Atlantic ocean. It included portions of urban Atlanta, Savannah, and Augusta, as well as sparsely populated, but overwhelmingly black, rural areas in the central part of the district. The Eleventh covered 6,784 square miles, splitting eight counties and five cities along the way. There were numerous narrow land bridges used to incorporate areas with significant black populations into the district. The district was 60 percent black. In the 1992 and 1994 congressional elections district voters sent Cynthia McKinney, a black Democrat, to the House of Representatives.

In 1994 five white voters from the Eleventh District, including Davida Johnson, filed suit claiming that the legislature violated the Equal Protection Clause of the Fourteenth Amendment by adopting a redistricting plan driven primarily by considerations of race. A three judge federal court, applying principles articulated in *Shaw v. Reno*, struck down the district. The Constitution was violated, the judges ruled, because race was the overriding, predominant factor employed to determine the lines of the district. Governor Zell Miller, on behalf of the state, appealed to the Supreme Court.

JUSTICE KENNEDY delivered the opinion of the Court.

The Equal Protection Clause of the Fourteenth Amendment provides that no State shall "deny to any person within its jurisdiction the equal protection of the laws." Its central mandate is racial neutrality in governmental decisionmaking. See, e.g., *Loving v. Virginia* (1967); *McLaughlin v. Florida* (1964); see also *Brown v. Board of Education* (1954). Though application of this imperative raises difficult questions, the basic principle is straightforward: "Racial and ethnic distinctions of any sort are inherently suspect and thus call for the most exacting judicial examination. . . . This perception of racial and ethnic distinctions is rooted in our Nation's constitutional and demographic history." *Regents of Univ. of California v. Bakke* (1978) (opinion of Powell, J.). This rule obtains with equal force regardless of "the race of those burdened or benefited by a particular classification." *Richmond v. J. A. Croson Co.* (1989) (plurality opinion). Laws classifying citizens on the basis of race cannot be upheld unless they are narrowly tailored to achieving a compelling state interest.

In *Shaw v. Reno* [1993] we recognized that these equal protection principles govern a State's drawing of congressional districts, though, as our cautious approach there discloses, application of these principles to electoral districting is a most delicate task. Our analysis began from the premise that "[l]aws that explicitly distinguish between individuals on racial grounds fall within the core of [the Equal Protection Clause's] prohibition." This prohibition extends not just to explicit racial classifications, but also to laws neutral on their face but "'unexplainable on grounds other than race.'" Applying this basic Equal Protection analysis in the voting rights context, we held that "redistricting legislation that is so bizarre on its face that it is 'unexplainable on grounds other than race,'... demands the same close scrutiny that we give other state laws that classify citizens by race."

This case requires us to apply the principles articulated in *Shaw* to the most recent congressional redistricting plan enacted by the State of Georgia. . . .

. . . Just as the State may not, absent extraordinary justification, segregate citizens on the basis of race in its public parks, buses, golf courses, beaches, and schools, so did we recognize in *Shaw* that it may not separate its citizens into different voting districts on the basis of race. The idea is a simple one: "At the heart of the Constitution's guarantee of equal protection lies the simple command that the Government must treat citizens 'as individuals, not as simply components of a racial, religious, sexual or national class.'" *Metro Broadcasting, Inc. v. FCC* (1990) (O'Connor, J., dissenting). When the State assigns voters on the basis of race, it engages in the offensive and demeaning assumption that voters of a particular race, because of their race, "think alike, share the same political interests, and will prefer the same candidates at the polls." *Shaw;* see *Metro Broadcasting* (Kennedy, J., dissenting). Race-based assignments "embody stereotypes that treat individuals as the product of their race, evaluating their thoughts and efforts—their very worth as citizens—according to a criterion barred to the Government by history and the Constitution." *Metro Broadcasting* (O'Connor, J., dissenting). They also cause society serious harm. As we concluded in *Shaw:*

"Racial classifications with respect to voting carry particular dangers. Racial gerrymandering, even for remedial purposes, may balkanize us into competing racial factions; it threatens to carry us further from the goal of a political system in which race no longer matters—a goal that the Fourteenth and Fifteenth Amendments embody, and to which the Nation continues to aspire. It is for these reasons that race-based districting by our state legislatures demands close judicial scrutiny."

Our observation in *Shaw* of the consequences of racial stereotyping was not meant to suggest that a district must be bizarre on its face before there is a constitutional violation. Nor was our conclusion in *Shaw* that in certain instances a district's appearance (or, to be more precise, its appearance in combination with certain demographic evidence) can give rise to an equal protection claim, a holding that bizarreness was a threshold showing, as appellants believe it to be. Our circumspect approach and narrow holding in *Shaw* did not erect an artificial rule barring accepted equal protection analysis in other redistricting cases. Shape is relevant not because bizarreness is a necessary element of the constitutional wrong or a threshold requirement of proof, but because it may be persuasive circumstantial evidence that race for its own sake, and not other districting principles, was the legislature's dominant and controlling rationale in drawing its district lines. The logical implication, as courts applying *Shaw* have recognized, is that parties may rely on evidence other than bizarreness to establish race-based districting.

Our reasoning in *Shaw* compels this conclusion. We recognized in *Shaw* that, outside the districting context, statutes are subject to strict scrutiny under the Equal Protection Clause not just when they contain express racial classifications, but also when, though race neutral on their face, they are motivated by a racial purpose or object. . . .

Shaw applied these same principles to redistricting. "In some exceptional cases, a reapportionment plan may be so highly irregular that, on its face, it rationally cannot be understood as anything other than an effort to 'segregat[e] . . . voters' on the basis of race." In other cases, where the district is not so bizarre on its face that it discloses a racial design, the proof will be more "difficul[t]." Although it was not necessary in *Shaw* to consider further the proof required in these more difficult cases, the logical import of our reasoning is that evidence other than a district's bizarre shape can be used to support the claim. . . .

In sum, we make clear that parties alleging that a State has assigned voters on the basis of race are neither confined in their proof to evidence regarding the district's geometry and makeup nor required to make a threshold showing of bizarreness. Today's case requires us further to consider the requirements of the proof necessary to sustain this equal protection challenge.

. . . Electoral districting is a most difficult subject for legislatures, and so the States must have discretion to exercise the political judgment necessary to balance competing interests. Although race-based decisionmaking is inherently suspect, until a claimant makes a showing sufficient to support that allegation the good faith of a state legislature must be presumed. The courts, in assessing the sufficiency of a challenge to a districting plan, must be sensitive to the complex interplay of forces that enter a legislature's redistricting calculus. Redistricting legislatures will, for example, almost always be aware of racial demographics; but it does not follow that race predominates in the redistricting process. The distinction between being aware of racial considerations and being motivated by them may be difficult to make. This evidentiary difficulty, together with the sensitive nature of redistricting and the presumption of good faith that must be accorded legislative enactments, requires courts to exercise extraordinary caution in adjudicating claims that a state has drawn district lines on the basis of race. The plaintiff's burden is to show, either through circumstantial evidence of a district's shape and demographics or more direct evidence going to legislative purpose, that race was the predominant factor motivating the legislature's decision to place a significant number of voters within or without a particular district. To make this showing, a plaintiff must prove that the legislature subordinated traditional race-neutral districting principles, including but not limited to compactness, contiguity, respect for po-

litical subdivisions or communities defined by actual shared interests, to racial considerations. Where these or other race-neutral considerations are the basis for redistricting legislation, and are not subordinated to race, a state can "defeat a claim that a district has been gerrymandered on racial lines." *Shaw.* These principles inform the plaintiff's burden of proof at trial. . . .

In our view, the District Court applied the correct analysis, and its finding that race was the predominant factor motivating the drawing of the Eleventh District was not clearly erroneous. The court found it was "exceedingly obvious" from the shape of the Eleventh District, together with the relevant racial demographics, that the drawing of narrow land bridges to incorporate within the District outlying appendages containing nearly 80% of the district's total black population was a deliberate attempt to bring black populations into the district. Although by comparison with other districts the geometric shape of the Eleventh District may not seem bizarre on its face, when its shape is considered in conjunction with its racial and population densities, the story of racial gerrymandering seen by the District Court becomes much clearer. Although this evidence is quite compelling, we need not determine whether it was, standing alone, sufficient to establish a *Shaw* claim that the Eleventh District is unexplainable other than by race. The District Court had before it considerable additional evidence showing that the General Assembly was motivated by a predominant, overriding desire to assign black populations to the Eleventh District and thereby permit the creation of a third majority-black district. . . .

The court found that "it became obvious," both from the Justice Department's objection letters and the three preclearance rounds in general, "that [the Justice Department] would accept nothing less than abject surrender to its maximization agenda." It further found that the General Assembly acquiesced and as a consequence was driven by its overriding desire to comply with the Department's maximization demands.

In light of its well-supported finding, the District Court was justified in rejecting the various alternative explanations offered for the District. Although a legislature's compliance with "traditional districting principles such as compactness, contiguity, and respect for political subdivisions" may well suffice to refute a claim of racial gerrymandering,

Shaw, appellants cannot make such a refutation where, as here, those factors were subordinated to racial objectives. Georgia's Attorney General objected to the Justice Department's demand for three majority-black districts on the ground that to do so the State would have to "violate all reasonable standards of compactness and contiguity." This statement from a state official is powerful evidence that the legislature subordinated traditional districting principles to race when it ultimately enacted a plan creating three majority-black districts, and justified the District Court's finding that "every [objective districting] factor that could realistically be subordinated to racial tinkering in fact suffered that fate."

Nor can the State's districting legislation be rescued by mere recitation of purported communities of interest. The evidence was compelling "that there are no tangible 'communities of interest' spanning the hundreds of miles of the Eleventh District." A comprehensive report demonstrated the fractured political, social, and economic interests within the Eleventh District's black population. It is apparent that it was not alleged shared interests but rather the object of maximizing the District's black population and obtaining Justice Department approval that in fact explained the General Assembly's actions. A State is free to recognize communities that have a particular racial makeup, provided its action is directed toward some common thread of relevant interests.... But where the State assumes from a group of voters' race that they "think alike, share the same political interests, and will prefer the same candidates at the polls," it engages in racial stereotyping at odds with equal protection mandates.

Race was, as the District Court found, the predominant, overriding factor explaining the General Assembly's decision to attach to the Eleventh District various appendages containing dense majority-black populations. As a result, Georgia's congressional redistricting plan cannot be upheld unless it satisfies strict scrutiny, our most rigorous and exacting standard of constitutional review.

To satisfy strict scrutiny, the State must demonstrate that its districting legislation is narrowly tailored to achieve a compelling interest. *Shaw*. There is a "significant state interest in eradicating the effects of past racial discrimination." *Shaw*. The State does not argue, however, that it created the Eleventh District to remedy past discrimination, and with good reason: there is little doubt that the State's true interest in designing the Eleventh District was creating a third majority-black district to satisfy the Justice Department's preclearance demands.... Whether or not in some cases compliance with the Voting Rights Act, standing alone, can provide a compelling interest independent of any interest in remedying past discrimination, it cannot do so here. As we suggested in *Shaw*, compliance with federal antidiscrimination laws cannot justify race-based districting where the challenged district was not reasonably necessary under a constitutional reading and application of those laws. The congressional plan challenged here was not required by the Voting Rights Act under a correct reading of the statute....

We do not accept the contention that the State has a compelling interest in complying with whatever preclearance mandates the Justice Department issues. When a state governmental entity seeks to justify race-based remedies to cure the effects of past discrimination, we do not accept the government's mere assertion that the remedial action is required. Rather, we insist on a strong basis in evidence of the harm being remedied. "The history of racial classifications in this country suggests that blind judicial deference to legislative or executive pronouncements of necessity has no place in equal protection analysis." *Croson*. Our presumptive skepticism of all racial classifications, prohibits us as well from accepting on its face the Justice Department's conclusion that racial districting is necessary under the Voting Rights Act. Where a State relies on the Department's determination that race-based districting is necessary to comply with the Voting Rights Act, the judiciary retains an independent obligation in adjudicating consequent equal protection challenges to ensure that the State's actions are narrowly tailored to achieve a compelling interest. See *Shaw*. Were we to accept the Justice Department's objection itself as a compelling interest adequate to insulate racial districting from constitutional review, we would be surrendering to the Executive Branch our role in enforcing the constitutional limits on race-based official action. We may not do so....

The Voting Rights Act, and its grant of authority to the federal courts to uncover official efforts to abridge minorities' right to vote, has been of vital importance in eradicating invidious discrimination from the electoral process and enhancing the legitimacy of our political institutions. Only if our political system and our society cleanse themselves of that discrimination will all members of the polity share an equal opportunity to gain public office regardless of race. As a Nation we share both the obligation and the aspiration of working toward this end. The end is neither assured nor well served, however, by carving electorates into racial blocs. "If our society is to continue to progress as a multiracial democracy, it must recognize that the automatic invocation of race stereotypes retards that progress and causes continued hurt and injury." *Edmondson v. Leesville Concrete Co.* (1991). It takes a shortsighted and unauthorized view of the Voting Rights Act to invoke that statute, which has played a decisive role in redressing some of our worst forms of discrimination, to demand the very racial stereotyping the Fourteenth Amendment forbids.

The judgment of the District Court is affirmed, and the case is remanded for further proceedings consistent with this decision.

It is so ordered.

JUSTICE GINSBURG, with whom JUSTICES STEVENS, BREYER ... and ... SOUTER join, dissenting.

Legislative districting is highly political business. This Court has generally respected the competence of state legislatures to attend to the task. When race is the issue, however, we have recognized the need for judicial intervention to prevent dilution of minority voting strength. Generations of rank discrimination against African-Americans, as citizens and voters, account for that surveillance.

Two Terms ago, in *Shaw v. Reno* (1993), this Court took up a claim "analytically distinct" from a vote dilution claim. *Shaw* authorized judicial intervention in "extremely irregular" apportionments in which the legislature cast aside traditional districting practices to consider race alone—in the *Shaw* case, to create a district in North Carolina in which African-Americans would compose a majority of the voters.

Today the Court expands the judicial role, announcing that federal courts are to undertake searching review of any district with contours "predominantly motivated" by race: "strict scrutiny" will be triggered not only when traditional districting practices are abandoned, but also when those practices are "subordinated to"—given less weight than—race. Applying this new "race-as-predominant-factor" standard, the Court invalidates Georgia's districting plan even though Georgia's Eleventh District, the focus of today's dispute, bears the imprint of familiar districting practices. Because I do not endorse the Court's new standard and would not upset Georgia's plan, I dissent. . . .

Before *Shaw v. Reno* this Court invoked the Equal Protection Clause to justify intervention in the quintessentially political task of legislative districting in two circumstances: to enforce the one-person-one-vote requirement, see *Reynolds v. Sims* (1964); and to prevent dilution of a minority group's voting strength.

In *Shaw*, the Court recognized a third basis for an equal protection challenge to a State's apportionment plan. The Court wrote cautiously, emphasizing that judicial intervention is exceptional: "[S]trict [judicial] scrutiny" is in order, the Court declared, if a district is "so extremely irregular on its face that it rationally can be viewed only as an effort to segregate the races for purposes of voting."

"[E]xtrem[e] irregular[ity]" was evident in *Shaw*, the Court explained. . . .

. . . The problem in *Shaw* was not the plan architects' consideration of race as relevant in redistricting. Rather, in the Court's estimation, it was the virtual exclusion of other factors from the calculus. Traditional districting practices were cast aside, the Court concluded, with race alone steering placement of district lines.

The record before us does not show that race similarly overwhelmed traditional districting practices in Georgia. Although the Georgia General Assembly prominently considered race in shaping the Eleventh District, race did not crowd out all other factors, as the Court found it did in North Carolina's delineation of the *Shaw* district.

In contrast to the snake-like North Carolina district inspected in *Shaw*, Georgia's Eleventh District is hardly "bizarre," "extremely irregular," or "irrational on its face." Instead, the Eleventh District's design reflects significant consideration of "traditional districting factors (such as keeping political subdivisions intact) and the usual political process of compromise and trades for a variety of nonracial reasons.". . .

Nor does the Eleventh District disrespect the boundaries of political subdivisions. Of the 22 counties in the District, 14 are intact and 8 are divided. That puts the Eleventh District at about the state average in divided counties. . . .

Evidence at trial similarly shows that considerations other than race went into determining the Eleventh District's boundaries. For a "political reason"—to accommodate the request of an incumbent State Senator regarding the placement of the precinct in which his son lived—the DeKalb County portion of the Eleventh District was drawn to include a particular (largely white) precinct. The corridor through Effingham County was substantially narrowed at the request of a (white) State Representative. In Chatham County, the District was trimmed to exclude a heavily black community in Garden City because a State Representative wanted to keep the city intact inside the neighboring First District. The Savannah extension was configured by "the narrowest means possible" to avoid splitting the city of Port Wentworth.

Georgia's Eleventh District, in sum, is not an outlier district shaped without reference to familiar districting techniques. . . .

The Court suggests that it was not Georgia's legislature, but the U. S. Department of Justice, that effectively drew the lines, and that Department officers did so with nothing but race in mind. . . .

And although the Attorney General refused preclearance to the first two plans approved by Georgia's legislature, the State was not thereby disarmed; Georgia could have demanded relief from the Department's objections by instituting a civil action in the United States District Court for the District of Columbia, with ultimate review in this Court. Instead of pursuing that avenue, the State chose to adopt the plan here in controversy—a plan the State forcefully defends before us. We should respect Georgia's choice by taking its position on brief as genuine.

Along with attention to size, shape, and political subdivisions, the Court recognizes as an appropriate districting principle, "respect for . . . communities defined by actual shared interests." The Court finds no community here, however, because a report in the record showed "fractured political, social, and economic interests within the Eleventh District's black population."

But ethnicity itself can tie people together, as volumes of social science literature have documented—even people with divergent economic interests. For this reason, ethnicity is a significant force in political life. . . .

To accommodate the reality of ethnic bonds, legislatures have long drawn voting districts along ethnic lines. Our Nation's cities are full of districts identified by their ethnic character—Chinese, Irish, Italian, Jewish, Polish, Russian, for example. . . .

To separate permissible and impermissible use of race in legislative apportionment, the Court orders strict scrutiny for districting plans "predominantly motivated" by race. No longer can a State avoid judicial oversight by giving—as in this case—genuine and measurable consideration to traditional districting practices. Instead, a federal case can be mounted whenever plaintiffs plausibly allege that other factors carried less weight than race. This invitation to litigate against the State seems to me neither necessary nor proper.

The Court derives its test from diverse opinions on the relevance of race in contexts distinctly unlike apportionment. The controlling idea, the Court says, is "'the simple command [at the heart of the Constitution's guarantee of equal protection] that the Government must treat citizens as individuals, not as simply components of a racial, religious, sexual or national class.'" . . .

In adopting districting plans, however, States do not treat people as individuals. Apportionment schemes, by their very nature, assemble people in groups. States do not assign voters to districts based on merit or achievement, standards States might use in hiring employees or engaging contractors. Rather, legislators classify voters in groups—by economic, geographical, political, or social characteristics—and then "reconcile the competing claims of [these] groups." *Davis v. Bandemer* (1986) (O'Connor, J., concurring in judgment).

That ethnicity defines some of these groups is a political reality. Until now, no constitutional infirmity has been seen in districting Irish or Italian voters together, for example, so long as the delineation does not abandon familiar apportionment practices. If Chinese-Americans and Russian-Americans may seek and secure group recognition in the delineation of voting districts, then African-Americans should not be dissimilarly treated. Otherwise, in the name of equal protection, we would shut out "the very minority group whose history in the United States gave birth to the Equal Protection Clause." See *Shaw* (Stevens, J., dissenting). . . .

Democratic representatives protesting the Court's decision in *Miller v. Johnson*. From left to right, Charles B. Rangel of New York; Cynthia A. McKinney, whose Georgia district was invalidated by the decision; and Bobby L. Rush and Luis V. Gutierrez of Illinois.

SOURCE: *Congressional Quarterly Weekly Report*, July 1, 1995, 1947.

Only after litigation—under either the Voting Rights Act, the Court's new *Miller* standard, or both—will States now be assured that plans conscious of race are safe. Federal judges in large numbers may be drawn into the fray. This enlargement of the judicial role is unwarranted. The reapportionment plan that resulted from Georgia's political process merited this Court's approbation, not its condemnation. Accordingly, I dissent.

Not only does *Miller v. Johnson* call into question the validity of many of the majority-minority congressional districts created over the last decade, but its rationale can also be applied to numerous districts at the state and local levels. Furthermore, the opinion of the Court is highly critical of efforts by the Justice Department to encourage states to maximize black representation, and it implies that the Voting Rights Act has been misinterpreted by the federal government. The political fallout, particularly in the South and Southwest, is likely to be substantial. Americans can expect to witness an avalanche of redistricting litigation in the coming years.

READINGS

Alfange, Dean, Jr. "Gerrymandering and the Constitution: Into the Thorns of the Thicket at Last." *Supreme Court Review* (1986): 175–257.

Bullock, Charles S., and Charles M. Lamb. *Implementation of Civil Rights Policy*. Monterey, Calif.: Brooks/Cole, 1984.

Cortner, Richard C. *The Apportionment Cases*. Knoxville: University of Tennessee Press, 1970.

Dixon, Robert G. *Democratic Representation: Reapportionment in Law and Politics*. New York: Oxford University Press, 1968.

Grofman, Bernard. *Political Gerrymandering and the Courts*. New York: Agathon Press, 1990.

Hamilton, Charles V. *The Bench and Ballot: Southern Federal Judges and Black Voters*. New York: Oxford University Press, 1973.

Lewinson, Paul. *Race, Class and Party: A History of Negro Suffrage and White Politics in the South*. New York: Grosset and Dunlap, 1959.

Maveety, Nancy. *Representation Rights and the Burger Court Years*. Ann Arbor: University of Michigan Press, 1991.

Montague, Bill. "The Voting Rights Act Today." *ABA Journal* 74 (August 1988): 52–58.

Thernston, Abigail. *Whose Votes Count?* Cambridge, Mass.: Harvard University Press, 1987.

REFERENCE MATERIAL

APPENDICES

1. CONSTITUTION OF THE UNITED STATES
2. FEDERALIST, NO. 78
3. U.S. PRESIDENTS
4. THUMBNAIL SKETCH OF THE SUPREME COURT'S HISTORY
5. THE JUSTICES
6. NATURAL COURTS
7. THE AMERICAN LEGAL SYSTEM
8. THE PROCESSING OF CASES
9. SUPREME COURT CALENDAR
10. BRIEFING SUPREME COURT CASES
11. GLOSSARY

CONSTITUTION OF THE UNITED STATES

We the People of the United States, in Order to form a more perfect Union, establish Justice, insure domestic Tranquility, provide for the common defence, promote the general Welfare, and secure the Blessings of Liberty to ourselves and our Posterity, do ordain and establish this Constitution for the United States of America.

ARTICLE I

Section 1. All legislative Powers herein granted shall be vested in a Congress of the United States, which shall consist of a Senate and House of Representatives.

Section 2. The House of Representatives shall be composed of Members chosen every second Year by the People of the several States, and the Electors in each State shall have the Qualifications requisite for Electors of the most numerous Branch of the State Legislature.

No Person shall be a Representative who shall not have attained to the age of twenty five Years, and been seven Years a Citizen of the United States, and who shall not, when elected, be an Inhabitant of that State in which he shall be chosen.

[Representatives and direct Taxes shall be apportioned among the several States which may be included within this Union, according to their respective Numbers, which shall be determined by adding to the whole Number of free Persons, including those bound to Service for a Term of Years, and excluding Indians not taxed, three fifths of all other Persons.][1] The actual Enumeration shall be made within three Years after the first Meeting of the Congress of the United States, and within every subsequent Term of ten Years, in such Manner as they shall by Law direct. The Number of Representatives shall not exceed one for every thirty Thousand, but each State shall have at Least one

Representative; and until such enumeration shall be made, the State of New Hampshire shall be entitled to chuse three, Massachusetts eight, Rhode-Island and Providence Plantations one, Connecticut five, New-York six, New Jersey four, Pennsylvania eight, Delaware one, Maryland six, Virginia ten, North Carolina five, South Carolina five, and Georgia three.

When vacancies happen in the Representation from any State, the Executive Authority thereof shall issue Writs of Election to fill such Vacancies.

The House of Representatives shall chuse their Speaker and other Officers; and shall have the sole Power of Impeachment.

Section 3. The Senate of the United States shall be composed of two Senators from each State, [chosen by the Legislature thereof,][2] for six Years; and each Senator shall have one Vote.

Immediately after they shall be assembled in Consequence of the first Election, they shall be divided as equally as may be into three Classes. The Seats of the Senators of the first Class shall be vacated at the Expiration of the second Year, of the second Class at the Expiration of the fourth Year, and of the third Class at the Expiration of the sixth Year, so that one third may be chosen every second Year; [and if Vacancies happen by Resignation, or otherwise, during the Recess of the Legislature of any State, the Executive thereof may make temporary Appointments until the next Meeting of the Legislature, which shall then fill such Vacancies.][3]

No Person shall be a Senator who shall not have attained to the Age of thirty Years, and been nine Years a Citizen of the

---

1. The part in brackets was changed by section 2 of the Fourteenth Amendment.

2. The part in brackets was changed by the first paragraph of the Seventeenth Amendment.

3. The part in brackets was changed by the second paragraph of the Seventeenth Amendment.

United States, and who shall not, when elected, be an Inhabitant of that State for which he shall be chosen.

The Vice President of the United States shall be President of the Senate, but shall have no Vote, unless they be equally divided.

The Senate shall chuse their other Officers, and also a President pro tempore, in the Absence of the Vice President, or when he shall exercise the Office of President of the United States.

The Senate shall have the sole Power to try all Impeachments. When sitting for that Purpose, they shall be on Oath or Affirmation. When the President of the United States is tried, the Chief Justice shall preside: And no Person shall be convicted without the Concurrence of two thirds of the Members present.

Judgment in Cases of Impeachment shall not extend further than to removal from Office, and disqualification to hold and enjoy any Office of honor, Trust or Profit under the United States: but the Party convicted shall nevertheless be liable and subject to Indictment, Trial, Judgment and Punishment, according to Law.

Section 4. The Times, Places and Manner of holding Elections for Senators and Representatives, shall be prescribed in each State by the Legislature thereof; but the Congress may at any time by Law make or alter such Regulations, except as to the Places of chusing Senators.

The Congress shall assemble at least once in every Year, and such Meeting shall [be on the first Monday in December],[4] unless they shall by Law appoint a different Day.

Section 5. Each House shall be the Judge of the Elections, Returns and Qualifications of its own Members, and a Majority of each shall constitute a Quorum to do Business; but a smaller Number may adjourn from day to day, and may be authorized to compel the Attendance of absent Members, in such Manner, and under such Penalties as each House may provide.

Each House may determine the Rules of its Proceedings, punish its Members for disorderly Behaviour, and, with the Concurrence of two thirds, expel a Member.

Each House shall keep a Journal of its Proceedings, and from time to time publish the same, excepting such Parts as may in their Judgment require Secrecy; and the Yeas and Nays of the Members of either House on any question shall, at the Desire of one fifth of those Present, be entered on the Journal.

Neither House, during the Session of Congress, shall, without the Consent of the other, adjourn for more than three days, nor to any other Place than that in which the two Houses shall be sitting.

Section 6. The Senators and Representatives shall receive a Compensation for their Services, to be ascertained by Law, and paid out of the Treasury of the United States. They shall in all

4. The part in brackets was changed by section 2 of the Twentieth Amendment.

Cases, except Treason, Felony and Breach of the Peace, be privileged from Arrest during their Attendance at the Session of their respective Houses, and in going to and returning from the same; and for any Speech or Debate in either House, they shall not be questioned in any other Place.

No Senator or Representative shall, during the Time for which he was elected, be appointed to any civil Office under the Authority of the United States, which shall have been created, or the Emoluments whereof shall have been encreased during such time; and no Person holding any Office under the United States, shall be a Member of either House during his Continuance in Office.

Section 7. All Bills for raising Revenue shall originate in the House of Representatives; but the Senate may propose or concur with Amendments as on other Bills.

Every Bill which shall have passed the House of Representatives and the Senate, shall, before it become a Law, be presented to the President of the United States; If he approve he shall sign it, but if not he shall return it, with his Objections to that House in which it shall have originated, who shall enter the Objections at large on their Journal, and proceed to reconsider it. If after such Reconsideration two thirds of that House shall agree to pass the Bill, it shall be sent, together with the Objections, to the other House, by which it shall likewise be reconsidered, and if approved by two thirds of that House, it shall become a Law. But in all such Cases the Votes of both Houses shall be determined by yeas and Nays, and the Names of the Persons voting for and against the Bill shall be entered on the Journal of each House respectively. If any Bill shall not be returned by the President within ten Days (Sundays excepted) after it shall have been presented to him, the Same shall be a Law, in like Manner as if he had signed it, unless the Congress by their Adjournment prevent its Return, in which Case it shall not be a Law.

Every Order, Resolution, or Vote to which the Concurrence of the Senate and House of Representatives may be necessary (except on a question of Adjournment) shall be presented to the President of the United States; and before the Same shall take Effect, shall be approved by him, or being disapproved by him, shall be repassed by two thirds of the Senate and House of Representatives, according to the Rules and Limitations prescribed in the Case of a Bill.

Section 8. The Congress shall have Power To lay and collect Taxes, Duties, Imposts and Excises, to pay the Debts and provide for the common Defence and general Welfare of the United States; but all Duties, Imposts and Excises shall be uniform throughout the United States;

To borrow Money on the credit of the United States;

To regulate Commerce with foreign Nations, and among the several States, and with the Indian Tribes;

To establish an uniform Rule of Naturalization, and uniform

Laws on the subject of Bankruptcies throughout the United States;

To coin Money, regulate the Value thereof, and of foreign Coin, and fix the Standard of Weights and Measures;

To provide for the Punishment of counterfeiting the Securities and current Coin of the United States;

To establish Post Offices and post Roads;

To promote the Progress of Science and useful Arts, by securing for limited Times to Authors and Inventors the exclusive Right to their respective Writings and Discoveries;

To constitute Tribunals inferior to the supreme Court;

To define and punish Piracies and Felonies committed on the high Seas, and Offences against the Law of Nations;

To declare War, grant Letters of Marque and Reprisal, and make Rules concerning Captures on Land and Water;

To raise and support Armies, but no Appropriation of Money to that Use shall be for a longer Term than two Years;

To provide and maintain a Navy;

To make Rules for the Government and Regulation of the land and naval Forces;

To provide for calling forth the Militia to execute the Laws of the Union, suppress Insurrections and repel Invasions;

To provide for organizing, arming, and disciplining, the Militia, and for governing such Part of them as may be employed in the Service of the United States, reserving to the States respectively, the Appointment of the Officers, and the Authority of training the Militia according to the discipline prescribed by Congress;

To exercise exclusive Legislation in all Cases whatsoever, over such District (not exceeding ten Miles square) as may, by Cession of particular States, and the Acceptance of Congress, become the Seat of the Government of the United States, and to exercise like Authority over all Places purchased by the Consent of the Legislature of the State in which the Same shall be, for the Erection of Forts, Magazines, Arsenals, dock-Yards, and other needful Buildings;—And

To make all Laws which shall be necessary and proper for carrying into Execution the foregoing Powers, and all other Powers vested by this Constitution in the Government of the United States, or in any Department or Officer thereof.

Section 9. The Migration or Importation of such Persons as any of the States now existing shall think proper to admit, shall not be prohibited by the Congress prior to the Year one thousand eight hundred and eight, but a Tax or duty may be imposed on such Importation, not exceeding ten dollars for each Person.

The Privilege of the Writ of Habeas Corpus shall not be suspended, unless when in Cases of Rebellion or Invasion the public Safety may require it.

No Bill of Attainder or ex post facto Law shall be passed.

No Capitation, or other direct, Tax shall be laid, unless in Proportion to the Census or Enumeration herein before directed to be taken.[5]

No Tax or Duty shall be laid on Articles exported from any State.

No Preference shall be given by any Regulation of Commerce or Revenue to the Ports of one State over those of another; nor shall Vessels bound to, or from, one State, be obliged to enter, clear, or pay Duties in another.

No Money shall be drawn from the Treasury, but in Consequence of Appropriations made by Law; and a regular Statement and Account of the Receipts and Expenditures of all public Money shall be published from time to time.

No Title of Nobility shall be granted by the United States: And no Person holding any Office of Profit or Trust under them, shall, without the Consent of the Congress, accept of any present, Emolument, Office, or Title, of any kind whatever, from any King, Prince, or foreign State.

Section 10. No State shall enter into any Treaty, Alliance, or Confederation; grant Letters of Marque and Reprisal; coin Money; emit Bills of Credit; make any Thing but gold and silver Coin a Tender in Payment of Debts; pass any Bill of Attainder, ex post facto Law, or Law impairing the Obligation of Contracts, or grant any Title of Nobility.

No State shall, without the Consent of the Congress, lay any Imposts or Duties on Imports or Exports, except what may be absolutely necessary for executing it's inspection Laws: and the net Produce of all Duties and Imposts, laid by any State on Imports or Exports, shall be for the Use of the Treasury of the United States; and all such Laws shall be subject to the Revision and Controul of the Congress.

No State shall, without the Consent of Congress, lay any Duty of Tonnage, keep Troops, or Ships of War in time of Peace, enter into any Agreement or Compact with another State, or with a foreign Power, or engage in War, unless actually invaded, or in such imminent Danger as will not admit of delay.

ARTICLE II

Section 1. The executive Power shall be vested in a President of the United States of America. He shall hold his Office during the Term of four Years, and, together with the Vice President, chosen for the same Term, be elected, as follows

Each State shall appoint, in such Manner as the Legislature thereof may direct, a Number of Electors, equal to the whole Number of Senators and Representatives to which the State may be entitled in the Congress: but no Senator or Representative, or Person holding an Office of Trust or Profit under the United States, shall be appointed an Elector.

---

5. The Sixteenth Amendment gave Congress the power to tax incomes.

[The Electors shall meet in their respective States, and vote by Ballot for two Persons, of whom one at least shall not be an Inhabitant of the same State with themselves. And they shall make a List of all the Persons voted for, and of the Number of Votes for each; which List they shall sign and certify, and transmit sealed to the Seat of the Government of the United States, directed to the President of the Senate. The President of the Senate shall, in the Presence of the Senate and House of Representatives, open all the Certificates, and the Votes shall then be counted. The Person having the greatest Number of Votes shall be the President, if such Number be a Majority of the whole Number of Electors appointed; and if there be more than one who have such Majority, and have an equal Number of Votes, then the House of Representatives shall immediately chuse by Ballot one of them for President; and if no Person have a Majority, then from the five highest on the list the said House shall in like Manner chuse the President. But in chusing the President, the Votes shall be taken by States, the Representation from each State having one Vote; A quorum for this Purpose shall consist of a Member or Members from two thirds of the States, and a Majority of all the States shall be necessary to a Choice. In every Case, after the Choice of the President, the Person having the greatest Number of Votes of the Electors shall be the Vice President. But if there should remain two or more who have equal Votes, the Senate shall chuse from them by Ballot the Vice President.] [6]

The Congress may determine the Time of chusing the Electors, and the Day on which they shall give their Votes; which Day shall be the same throughout the United States.

No Person except a natural born Citizen, or a Citizen of the United States, at the time of the Adoption of this Constitution, shall be eligible to the Office of President; neither shall any Person be eligible to that Office who shall not have attained to the Age of thirty five Years, and been fourteen Years a Resident within the United States.

In Case of the Removal of the President from Office, or of his Death, Resignation, or Inability to discharge the Powers and Duties of the said Office,[7] the Same shall devolve on the Vice President, and the Congress may by Law provide for the Case of Removal, Death, Resignation or Inability, both of the President and Vice President, declaring what Officer shall then act as President, and such Officer shall act accordingly, until the Disability be removed, or a President shall be elected.

The President shall, at stated Times, receive for his Services, a Compensation, which shall neither be encreased nor diminished during the Period for which he shall have been elected, and he shall not receive within that Period any other Emolument from the United States, or any of them.

Before he enter on the Execution of his Office, he shall take the following Oath or Affirmation:—"I do solemnly swear (or affirm) that I will faithfully execute the Office of President of the United States, and will to the best of my Ability, preserve, protect and defend the Constitution of the United States."

Section 2. The President shall be Commander in Chief of the Army and Navy of the United States, and of the Militia of the several States, when called into the actual Service of the United States; he may require the Opinion, in writing, of the principal Officer in each of the executive Departments, upon any Subject relating to the Duties of their respective Offices, and he shall have Power to grant Reprieves and Pardons for Offences against the United States, except in Cases of Impeachment.

He shall have Power, by and with the Advice and Consent of the Senate, to make Treaties, provided two thirds of the Senators present concur; and he shall nominate, and by and with the Advice and Consent of the Senate, shall appoint Ambassadors, other public Ministers and Consuls, Judges of the supreme Court, and all other Officers of the United States, whose Appointments are not herein otherwise provided for, and which shall be established by Law: but the Congress may by Law vest the Appointment of such inferior Officers, as they think proper, in the President alone, in the Courts of Law, or in the Heads of Departments.

The President shall have Power to fill up all Vacancies that may happen during the Recess of the Senate, by granting Commissions which shall expire at the End of their next Session.

Section 3. He shall from time to time give to the Congress Information of the State of the Union, and recommend to their Consideration such Measures as he shall judge necessary and expedient; he may, on extraordinary Occasions, convene both Houses, or either of them, and in Case of Disagreement between them, with Respect to the Time of Adjournment, he may adjourn them to such Time as he shall think proper; he shall receive Ambassadors and other public Ministers; he shall take Care that the Laws be faithfully executed, and shall Commission all the Officers of the United States.

Section 4. The President, Vice President and all civil Officers of the United States, shall be removed from Office on Impeachment for, and Conviction of, Treason, Bribery, or other high Crimes and Misdemeanors.

ARTICLE III

Section 1. The judicial Power of the United States, shall be vested in one supreme Court, and in such inferior Courts as the Congress may from time to time ordain and establish. The Judges, both of the supreme and inferior Courts, shall hold their Offices during good Behaviour, and shall, at stated Times, re-

6. The material in brackets has been superseded by the Twelfth Amendment.

7. This provision has been affected by the Twenty-fifth Amendment.

ceive for their Services, a Compensation, which shall not be diminished during their Continuance in Office.

Section 2. The judicial Power shall extend to all Cases, in Law and Equity, arising under this Constitution, the Laws of the United States, and Treaties made, or which shall be made, under their Authority;—to all Cases affecting Ambassadors, other public Ministers and Consuls;—to all Cases of admiralty and maritime Jurisdiction;—to Controversies to which the United States shall be a Party;—to Controversies between two or more States;—between a State and Citizens of another State;[8]—between Citizens of different States;—between Citizens of the same State claiming Lands under Grants of different States, and between a State, or the Citizens thereof, and foreign States, Citizens or Subjects.[8]

In all Cases affecting Ambassadors, other public Ministers and Consuls, and those in which a State shall be Party, the supreme Court shall have original Jurisdiction. In all the other Cases before mentioned, the supreme Court shall have appellate Jurisdiction, both as to Law and Fact, with such Exceptions, and under such Regulations as the Congress shall make.

The Trial of all Crimes, except in Cases of Impeachment, shall be by Jury; and such Trial shall be held in the State where the said Crimes shall have been committed; but when not committed within any State, the Trial shall be at such Place or Places as the Congress may by Law have directed.

Section 3. Treason against the United States, shall consist only in levying War against them, or in adhering to their Enemies, giving them Aid and Comfort. No Person shall be convicted of Treason unless on the Testimony of two Witnesses to the same overt Act, or on Confession in open Court.

The Congress shall have Power to declare the Punishment of Treason, but no Attainder of Treason shall work Corruption of Blood, or Forfeiture except during the Life of the Person attainted.

ARTICLE IV

Section 1. Full Faith and Credit shall be given in each State to the public Acts, Records, and judicial Proceedings of every other State. And the Congress may by general Laws prescribe the Manner in which such Acts, Records and Proceedings shall be proved, and the Effect thereof.

Section 2. The Citizens of each State shall be entitled to all Privileges and Immunities of Citizens in the several States.

A Person charged in any State with Treason, Felony, or other Crime, who shall flee from Justice, and be found in another State, shall on Demand of the executive Authority of the State from which he fled, be delivered up, to be removed to the State having Jurisdiction of the Crime.

[No Person held to Service or Labour in one State, under the Laws thereof, escaping into another, shall, in Consequence of any Law or Regulation therein, be discharged from such Service or Labour, but shall be delivered up on Claim of the Party to whom such Service or Labour may be due.][9]

Section 3. New States may be admitted by the Congress into this Union; but no new State shall be formed or erected within the Jurisdiction of any other State; nor any State be formed by the Junction of two or more States, or Parts of States, without the Consent of the Legislatures of the States concerned as well as of the Congress.

The Congress shall have Power to dispose of and make all needful Rules and Regulations respecting the Territory or other Property belonging to the United States; and nothing in this Constitution shall be so construed as to Prejudice any Claims of the United States, or of any particular State.

Section 4. The United States shall guarantee to every State in this Union a Republican Form of Government, and shall protect each of them against Invasion; and on Application of the Legislature, or of the Executive (when the Legislature cannot be convened) against domestic Violence.

ARTICLE V

The Congress, whenever two thirds of both Houses shall deem it necessary, shall propose Amendments to this Constitution, or, on the Application of the Legislatures of two thirds of the several States, shall call a Convention for proposing Amendments, which, in either Case, shall be valid to all Intents and Purposes, as Part of this Constitution, when ratified by the Legislatures of three fourths of the several States, or by Conventions in three fourths thereof, as the one or the other Mode of Ratification may be proposed by the Congress; Provided [that no Amendment which may be made prior to the Year One thousand eight hundred and eight shall in any Manner affect the first and fourth Clauses in the Ninth Section of the first Article; and][10] that no State, without its Consent, shall be deprived of its equal Suffrage in the Senate.

ARTICLE VI

All Debts contracted and Engagements entered into, before the Adoption of this Constitution, shall be as valid against the United States under this Constitution, as under the Confederation.

This Constitution, and the Laws of the United States which shall be made in Pursuance thereof; and all Treaties made, or which shall be made, under the Authority of the United States, shall be the supreme Law of the Land; and the Judges in every State shall be bound thereby, any Thing in the Constitution or Laws of any State to the Contrary notwithstanding.

---

8. These clauses were affected by the Eleventh Amendment.

9. This paragraph has been superseded by the Thirteenth Amendment.
10. Obsolete.
11. The part in brackets has been superseded by section 3 of the Twentieth

The Senators and Representatives before mentioned, and the Members of the several State Legislatures, and all executive and judicial Officers, both of the United States and of the several States, shall be bound by Oath or Affirmation, to support this Constitution; but no religious Test shall ever be required as a Qualification to any Office or public Trust under the United States.

ARTICLE VII

The Ratification of the Conventions of nine States, shall be sufficient for the Establishment of this Constitution between the States so ratifying the Same. Done in Convention by the Unanimous Consent of the States present the Seventeenth Day of September in the Year of our Lord one thousand seven hundred and Eighty seven and of the Independence of the United States of America the Twelfth. IN WITNESS whereof We have hereunto subscribed our Names,

George Washington,
President and deputy from Virginia.

New Hampshire:	John Langdon,
	Nicholas Gilman.
Massachusetts:	Nathaniel Gorham,
	Rufus King.
Connecticut:	William Samuel Johnson,
	Roger Sherman.
New York:	Alexander Hamilton.
New Jersey:	William Livingston,
	David Brearley,
	William Paterson,
	Jonathan Dayton.
Pennsylvania:	Benjamin Franklin,
	Thomas Mifflin,
	Robert Morris,
	George Clymer,
	Thomas FitzSimons,
	Jared Ingersoll,
	James Wilson,
	Gouverneur Morris.
Delaware:	George Read,
	Gunning Bedford Jr.,
	John Dickinson,
	Richard Bassett,
	Jacob Broom.
Maryland:	James McHenry,
	Daniel of St. Thomas Jenifer,
	Daniel Carroll.
Virginia:	John Blair,
	James Madison Jr.
North Carolina:	William Blount,
	Richard Dobbs Spaight,
	Hugh Williamson.
South Carolina:	John Rutledge,
	Charles Cotesworth Pinckney,
	Charles Pinckney,
	Pierce Butler.
Georgia:	William Few,
	Abraham Baldwin.

[The language of the original Constitution, not including the Amendments, was adopted by a convention of the states on September 17, 1787, and was subsequently ratified by the states on the following dates: Delaware, December 7, 1787; Pennsylvania, December 12, 1787; New Jersey, December 18, 1787; Georgia, January 2, 1788; Connecticut, January 9, 1788; Massachusetts, February 6, 1788; Maryland, April 28, 1788; South Carolina, May 23, 1788; New Hampshire, June 21, 1788.

Ratification was completed on June 21, 1788.

The Constitution subsequently was ratified by Virginia, June 25, 1788; New York, July 26, 1788; North Carolina, November 21, 1789; Rhode Island, May 29, 1790; and Vermont, January 10, 1791.]

AMENDMENTS

Amendment I
(First ten amendments ratified December 15, 1791.)

Congress shall make no law respecting an establishment of religion, or prohibiting the free exercise thereof; or abridging the freedom of speech, or of the press; or the right of the people peaceably to assemble, and to petition the Government for a redress of grievances.

Amendment II

A well regulated Militia, being necessary to the security of a free State, the right of the people to keep and bear Arms, shall not be infringed.

Amendment III

No Soldier shall, in time of peace be quartered in any house, without the consent of the Owner, nor in time of war, but in a manner to be prescribed by law.

Amendment IV

The right of the people to be secure in their persons, houses, papers, and effects, against unreasonable searches and seizures, shall not be violated, and no Warrants shall issue, but upon probable cause, supported by Oath or affirmation, and particularly describing the place to be searched, and the persons or things to be seized.

Amendment V

No person shall be held to answer for a capital, or otherwise infamous crime, unless on a presentment or indictment of a Grand Jury, except in cases arising in the land or naval forces, or in the Militia, when in actual service in time of War or public danger; nor shall any person be subject for the same offence to be twice put in jeopardy of life or limb; nor shall be compelled in any criminal case to be a witness against himself, nor be deprived of life, liberty, or property, without due process of law; nor shall private property be taken for public use, without just compensation.

Amendment VI

In all criminal prosecutions, the accused shall enjoy the right to a speedy and public trial, by an impartial jury of the State and district wherein the crime shall have been committed, which district shall have been previously ascertained by law, and to be informed of the nature and cause of the accusation; to be confronted with the witnesses against him; to have compulsory process for obtaining witnesses in his favor, and to have the Assistance of Counsel for his defence.

Amendment VII

In Suits at common law, where the value in controversy shall exceed twenty dollars, the right of trial by jury shall be preserved, and no fact tried by a jury, shall be otherwise re-examined in any Court of the United States, than according to the rules of the common law.

Amendment VIII

Excessive bail shall not be required, nor excessive fines imposed, nor cruel and unusual punishments inflicted.

Amendment IX

The enumeration in the Constitution, of certain rights, shall not be construed to deny or disparage others retained by the people.

Amendment X

The powers not delegated to the United States by the Constitution, nor prohibited by it to the States, are reserved to the States respectively, or to the people.

Amendment XI

(Ratified February 7, 1795)

The Judicial power of the United States shall not be construed to extend to any suit in law or equity, commenced or prosecuted against one of the United States by Citizens of another State, or by Citizens or Subjects of any Foreign State.

Amendment XII

(Ratified June 15, 1804)

The Electors shall meet in their respective states and vote by ballot for President and Vice-President, one of whom, at least, shall not be an inhabitant of the same state with themselves; they shall name in their ballots the person voted for as President, and in distinct ballots the person voted for as Vice-President, and they shall make distinct lists of all persons voted for as

President, and of all persons voted for as Vice-President, and of the number of votes for each, which lists they shall sign and certify, and transmit sealed to the seat of the government of the United States, directed to the President of the Senate;—The President of the Senate shall, in the presence of the Senate and House of Representatives, open all the certificates and the votes shall then be counted;—The person having the greatest number of votes for President, shall be the President, if such number be a majority of the whole number of Electors appointed; and if no person have such majority, then from the persons having the highest numbers not exceeding three on the list of those voted for as President, the House of Representatives shall choose immediately, by ballot, the President. But in choosing the President, the votes shall be taken by states, the representation from each state having one vote; a quorum for this purpose shall consist of a member or members from two-thirds of the states, and a majority of all the states shall be necessary to a choice. [And if the House of Representatives shall not choose a President whenever the right of choice shall devolve upon them, before the fourth day of March next following, then the Vice-President shall act as President, as in the case of the death or other constitutional disability of the President.][11] The person having the greatest number of votes as Vice-President, shall be the Vice-President, if such number be a majority of the whole number of Electors appointed, and if no person have a majority, then from the two highest numbers on the list, the Senate shall choose the Vice-President; a quorum for the purpose shall consist of two-thirds of the whole number of Senators, and a majority of the whole number shall be necessary to a choice. But no person constitutionally ineligible to the office of President shall be eligible to that of Vice-President of the United States.

Amendment XIII

(Ratified December 6, 1865)

Section 1. Neither slavery nor involuntary servitude, except as a punishment for crime whereof the party shall have been duly convicted, shall exist within the United States, or any place subject to their jurisdiction.

Section 2. Congress shall have power to enforce this article by appropriate legislation.

Amendment XIV

(Ratified July 9, 1868)

Section 1. All persons born or naturalized in the United States, and subject to the jurisdiction thereof, are citizens of the United States and of the State wherein they reside. No State shall make or enforce any law which shall abridge the privileges or immunities of citizens of the United States; nor shall any State de-

---

11. The part in brackets has been superseded by section 3 of the Twentieth Amendment.

prive any person of life, liberty, or property, without due process of law; nor deny to any person within its jurisdiction the equal protection of the laws.

Section 2. Representatives shall be apportioned among the several States according to their respective numbers, counting the whole number of persons in each State, excluding Indians not taxed. But when the right to vote at any election for the choice of electors for President and Vice President of the United States, Representatives in Congress, the Executive and Judicial officers of a State, or the members of the Legislature thereof, is denied to any of the male inhabitants of such State, being twenty-one years of age,[12] and citizens of the United States, or in any way abridged, except for participation in rebellion, or other crime, the basis of representation therein shall be reduced in the proportion which the number of such male citizens shall bear to the whole number of male citizens twenty-one years of age in such State.

Section 3. No person shall be a Senator or Representative in Congress, or elector of President and Vice President, or hold any office, civil or military, under the United States, or under any State, who, having previously taken an oath, as a member of Congress, or as an officer of the United States, or as a member of any State legislature, or as an executive or judicial officer of any State, to support the Constitution of the United States, shall have engaged in insurrection or rebellion against the same, or given aid or comfort to the enemies thereof. But Congress may by a vote of two-thirds of each House, remove such disability.

Section 4. The validity of the public debt of the United States, authorized by law, including debts incurred for payment of pensions and bounties for services in suppressing insurrection or rebellion, shall not be questioned. But neither the United States nor any State shall assume or pay any debt or obligation incurred in aid of insurrection or rebellion against the United States, or any claim for the loss or emancipation of any slave; but all such debts, obligations and claims shall be held illegal and void.

Section 5. The Congress shall have power to enforce, by appropriate legislation, the provisions of this article.

Amendment XV

(Ratified February 3, 1870)

Section 1. The right of citizens of the United States to vote shall not be denied or abridged by the United States or by any State on account of race, color, or previous condition of servitude.

Section 2. The Congress shall have power to enforce this article by appropriate legislation.

Amendment XVI

(Ratified February 3, 1913)

The Congress shall have power to lay and collect taxes on incomes, from whatever source derived, without apportionment among the several States, and without regard to any census or enumeration.

Amendment XVII

(Ratified April 8, 1913)

The Senate of the United States shall be composed of two Senators from each State, elected by the people thereof, for six years; and each Senator shall have one vote. The electors in each State shall have the qualifications requisite for electors of the most numerous branch of the State legislatures.

When vacancies happen in the representation of any State in the Senate, the executive authority of such State shall issue writs of election to fill such vacancies: *Provided,* That the legislature of any State may empower the executive thereof to make temporary appointments until the people fill the vacancies by election as the legislature may direct.

This amendment shall not be so construed as to affect the election or term of any Senator chosen before it becomes valid as part of the Constitution.

[Amendment XVIII

(Ratified January 16, 1919)

Section 1. After one year from the ratification of this article the manufacture, sale, or transportation of intoxicating liquors within, the importation thereof into, or the exportation thereof from the United States and all territory subject to the jurisdiction thereof for beverage purposes is hereby prohibited.

Section 2. The Congress and the several States shall have concurrent power to enforce this article by appropriate legislation.

Section 3. This article shall be inoperative unless it shall have been ratified as an amendment to the Constitution by the legislatures of the several States, as provided in the Constitution, within seven years from the date of the submission hereof to the States by the Congress.][13]

Amendment XIX

(Ratified August 18, 1920)

The right of citizens of the United States to vote shall not be denied or abridged by the United States or by any State on account of sex.

Congress shall have power to enforce this article by appropriate legislation.

---

12. See the Nineteenth and Twenty-sixth Amendments.

13. This Amendment was repealed by section 1 of the Twenty-first Amendment.

Amendment XX

(Ratified January 23, 1933)

Section 1. The terms of the President and Vice President shall end at noon on the 20th day of January, and the terms of Senators and Representatives at noon on the 3d day of January, of the years in which such terms would have ended if this article had not been ratified; and the terms of their successors shall then begin.

Section 2. The Congress shall assemble at least once in every year, and such meeting shall begin at noon on the 3d day of January, unless they shall by law appoint a different day.

Section 3.[14] If, at the time fixed for the beginning of the term of the President, the President elect shall have died, the Vice President elect shall become President. If a President shall not have been chosen before the time fixed for the beginning of his term, or if the President elect shall have failed to qualify, then the Vice President elect shall act as President until a President shall have qualified; and the Congress may by law provide for the case wherein neither a President elect nor a Vice President elect shall have qualified, declaring who shall then act as President, or the manner in which one who is to act shall be selected, and such person shall act accordingly until a President or Vice President shall have qualified.

Section 4. The Congress may by law provide for the case of the death of any of the persons from whom the House of Representatives may choose a President whenever the right of choice shall have devolved upon them, and for the case of the death of any of the persons from whom the Senate may choose a Vice President whenever the right of choice shall have devolved upon them.

Section 5. Sections 1 and 2 shall take effect on the 15th day of October following the ratification of this article.

Section 6. This article shall be inoperative unless it shall have been ratified as an amendment to the Constitution by the legislatures of three-fourths of the several States within seven years from the date of its submission.

Amendment XXI

(Ratified December 5, 1933)

Section 1. The eighteenth article of amendment to the Constitution of the United States is hereby repealed.

Section 2. The transportation or importation into any State, Territory, or possession of the United States for delivery or use therein of intoxicating liquors, in violation of the laws thereof, is hereby prohibited.

Section 3. This article shall be inoperative unless it shall have been ratified as an amendment to the Constitution by conventions in the several States, as provided in the Constitution, within seven years from the date of the submission hereof to the States by the Congress.

Amendment XXII

(Ratified February 27, 1951)

Section 1. No person shall be elected to the office of the President more than twice, and no person who has held the office of President, or acted as President, for more than two years of a term to which some other person was elected President shall be elected to the office of the President more than once. But this Article shall not apply to any person holding the office of President when this Article was proposed by the Congress, and shall not prevent any person who may be holding the office of President, or acting as President, during the term within which this Article become operative from holding the office of President or acting as President during the remainder of such term.

Section 2. This article shall be inoperative unless it shall have been ratified as an amendment to the Constitution by the legislatures of three-fourths of the several States within seven years from the date of its submission to the States by the Congress.

Amendment XXIII

(Ratified March 29, 1961)

Section 1. The District constituting the seat of Government of the United States shall appoint in such manner as the Congress may direct:

A number of electors of President and Vice President equal to the whole number of Senators and Representatives in Congress to which the District would be entitled if it were a State, but in no event more than the least populous State; they shall be in addition to those appointed by the States, but they shall be considered, for the purposes of the election of President and Vice President, to be electors appointed by a State; and they shall meet in the District and perform such duties as provided by the twelfth article of amendment.

Section 2. The Congress shall have power to enforce this article by appropriate legislation.

Amendment XXIV

(Ratified January 23, 1964)

Section 1. The right of citizens of the United States to vote in any primary or other election for President or Vice President, for electors for President or Vice President, or for Senator or Representative in Congress, shall not be denied or abridged by the United States or any State by reason of failure to pay any poll tax or other tax.

Section 2. The Congress shall have power to enforce this article by appropriate legislation.

---

14. See the Twenty-fifth Amendment.

Amendment XXV

(Ratified February 10, 1967)

Section 1. In case of the removal of the President from office or of his death or resignation, the Vice President shall become President.

Section 2. Whenever there is a vacancy in the office of the Vice President, the President shall nominate a Vice President who shall take office upon confirmation by a majority vote of both Houses of Congress.

Section 3. Whenever the President transmits to the President pro tempore of the Senate and the Speaker of the House of Representatives his written declaration that he is unable to discharge the powers and duties of his office, and until he transmits to them a written declaration to the contrary, such powers and duties shall be discharged by the Vice President as Acting President.

Section 4. Whenever the Vice President and a majority of either the principal officers of the executive departments or of such other body as Congress may by law provide, transmit to the President pro tempore of the Senate and the Speaker of the House of Representatives their written declaration that the President is unable to discharge the powers and duties of his office, the Vice President shall immediately assume the powers and duties of the office as Acting President.

Thereafter, when the President transmits to the President pro tempore of the Senate and the Speaker of the House of Representatives his written declaration that no inability exists, he shall resume the powers and duties of his office unless the Vice President and a majority of either the principal officers of the executive department or of such other body as Congress may by law provide, transmit within four days to the President pro tempore of the Senate and the Speaker of the House of Representatives their written declaration that the President is unable to discharge the powers and duties of his office. Thereupon Congress shall decide the issue, assembling within forty-eight hours for that purpose if not in session. If the Congress, within twenty-one days after receipt of the latter written declaration, or, if Congress is not in session, within twenty-one days after Congress is required to assemble, determines by two-thirds vote of both Houses that the President is unable to discharge the powers and duties of his office, the Vice President shall continue to discharge the same as Acting President; otherwise, the President shall resume the powers and duties of his office.

Amendment XXVI

(Ratified July 1, 1971)

Section 1. The right of citizens of the United States, who are eighteen years of age or older, to vote shall not be denied or abridged by the United States or by any State on account of age.

Section 2. The Congress shall have power to enforce this article by appropriate legislation.

Amendment XXVII

(Ratified May 7, 1992)

No law varying the compensation for the services of the Senators and Representatives shall take effect, until an election of Representatives shall have intervened.

SOURCE: *United States Government Manual, 1993–94* (Washington, D.C.: Government Printing Office, 1993), 5–20.

FEDERALIST, NO. 78

A VIEW OF THE CONSTITUTION OF THE JUDICIAL DEPARTMENT IN RELATION TO THE TENURE OF GOOD BEHAVIOUR

We proceed now to an examination of the judiciary department of the proposed government.

In unfolding the defects of the existing Confederation, the utility and necessity of a federal judicature have been clearly pointed out. It is the less necessary to recapitulate the considerations there urged as the propriety of the institution in the abstract is not disputed; the only questions which have been raised being relative to the manner of constituting it, and to its extent. To these points, therefore, our observations shall be confined.

The manner of constituting it seems to embrace these several objects: 1st. The mode of appointing the judges. 2nd. The tenure by which they are to hold their places. 3rd. The partition of the judiciary authority between different courts and their relations to each other.

First. As to the mode of appointing the judges: this is the same with that of appointing the officers of the Union in general and has been so fully discussed in the two last numbers that nothing can be said here which would not be useless repetition.

Second. As to the tenure by which the judges are to hold their places: this chiefly concerns their duration in office, the provisions for their support, the precautions for their responsibility.

According to the plan of the convention, all judges who may be appointed by the United States are to hold their offices *during good behavior;* which is conformable to the most approved of the State constitutions, and among the rest, to that of the State. Its propriety having been drawn into question by the adversaries of that plan is no light symptom of the rage for objection which disorders their imaginations and judgments. The standard of good behavior for the continuance in office of the judicial magistracy is certainly one of the most valuable of the modern improvements in the practice of government. In a monarchy it is an excellent barrier to the despotism of the prince; in a republic it is a no less excellent barrier to the encroachments and oppressions of the representative body. And it is the best expedient which can be devised in any government to secure a steady, upright, and impartial administration of the laws.

Whoever attentively considers the different departments of power must perceive that, in a government in which they are separated from each other, the judiciary, from the nature of its functions, will always be the least dangerous to the political rights of the Constitution; because it will be least in a capacity to annoy or injure them. The executive not only dispenses the honors but holds the sword of the community. The legislature not only commands the purse but prescribes the rules by which the duties and rights of every citizen are to be regulated. The judiciary, on the contrary, has no influence over either the sword or the purse; no direction either of the strength or of the wealth of the society, and can take no active resolution whatever. It may truly be said to have neither FORCE nor WILL but merely judgment; and must ultimately depend upon the aid of the executive arm even for the efficacy of its judgments.

This simple view of the matter suggests several important consequences. It proves incontestably that the judiciary is beyond comparison the weakest of the three departments of power; that it can never attack with success either of the other two; and that all possible care is requisite to enable it to defend itself against their attacks. It equally proves that though individual oppression may now and then proceed from the courts of justice, the general liberty of the people can never be endangered from that quarter; I mean so long as the judiciary remains truly distinct from both the legislature and the executive. For I agree that "there is no liberty if the power of judging be not separated from the legislative and executive powers." And it proves, in the last place, that as liberty can have nothing to fear from the judiciary alone, but would have everything to fear from its union with either of the other departments; that as all the effects of such a union must ensue from a dependence of the former on the latter, notwithstanding a nominal and apparent separation; that as, from the natural feebleness of the judiciary, it is in continual jeopardy of being overpowered, awed, or influenced by its co-ordinate branches; and that as nothing can contribute so much to its firmness and independence as permanency in office, this quality may therefore be justly regarded as an indispensable ingredient in its constitution, and, in a great measure, as the citadel of the public justice and the public security.

The complete independence of the courts of justice is peculiarly essential in a limited Constitution. By a limited Constitution, I understand one which contains certain specified exceptions to the legislative authority; such, for instance, as that it shall pass no bills of attainder, no *ex post facto* laws, and the like. Limitations of this kind can be preserved in practice no other way than through the medium of courts of justice, whose duty it must be to declare all acts contrary to the manifest tenor of the Constitution void. Without this, all the reservations of particular rights or privileges would amount to nothing.

Some perplexity respecting the rights of the courts to pronounce legislative acts void, because contrary to the Constitution, has arisen from an imagination that the doctrine would imply a superiority of the judiciary to the legislative power. It is urged that the authority which can declare the acts of another void must necessarily be superior to the one whose acts may be declared void. As this doctrine is of great importance in all the American constitutions, a brief discussion of the grounds on which it rests cannot be unacceptable.

There is no position which depends on clearer principles than that every act of a delegated authority, contrary to the tenor of the commission under which it is exercised, is void. No legislative act, therefore, contrary to the Constitution, can be valid. To deny this would be to affirm that the deputy is greater than his principal; that the servant is above his master; that the representatives of the people are superior to the people themselves; that men acting by virtue of powers may do not only what their powers do not authorize, but what they forbid.

If it be said that the legislative body are themselves the constitutional judges of their own powers and that the construction they put upon them is conclusive upon the other departments it may be answered that this cannot be the natural presumption where it is not to be collected from any particular provisions in the Constitution. It is not otherwise to be supposed that the Constitution could intend to enable the representatives of the people to substitute their *will* to that of their constituents. It is far more rational to suppose that the courts were designed to be an intermediate body between the people and the legislature in order, among other things, to keep the latter within the limits assigned to their authority. The interpretation of the laws is the proper and peculiar province of the courts. A constitution is, in

fact, and must be regarded by the judges as, a fundamental law. It therefore belongs to them to ascertain its meaning as well as the meaning of any particular act proceeding from the legislative body. If there should happen to be an irreconcilable variance between the two, that which has the superior obligation and validity ought, of course, to be preferred: or, in other words, the Constitution ought to be preferred to the statute, the intention of the people to the intention of their agents.

Nor does this conclusion by any means suppose a superiority of the judicial to the legislative power. It only supposes that the power of the people is superior to both, and that where the will of the legislature, declared in its statutes, stands in opposition to that of the people, declared in the Constitution, the judges ought to be governed by the latter rather than the former. They ought to regulate their decisions by the fundamental laws rather than by those which are not fundamental.

This exercise of judicial discretion in determining between two contradictory laws is exemplified in a familiar instance. It not uncommonly happens that there are two statutes existing at one time, clashing in whole or in part with each other and neither of them containing any repealing clause or expression. In such a case, it is the province of the courts to liquidate and fix their meaning and operation. So far as they can, by fair construction, be reconciled to each other, reason and law conspire to dictate that this should be done; where this is impracticable, it becomes a matter of necessity to give effect to one in exclusion of the other. The rule which has obtained in the courts for determining their relative validity is that the last in order of time shall be preferred to the first. But this is a mere rule of construction, not derived from any positive law but from the nature and reason of the thing. It is a rule not enjoined upon the courts by legislative provision but adopted by themselves, as consonant to truth and propriety, for the direction of their conduct as interpreters of the law. They thought it reasonable that between the interfering acts of an *equal* authority that which was the last indication of its will should have the preference.

But in regard to the interfering acts of a superior and subordinate authority of an original and derivative power, the nature and reason of the thing indicate the converse of that rule as proper to be followed. They teach us that the prior act of a superior ought to be preferred to the subsequent act of an inferior and subordinate authority; and that accordingly, whenever a particular statute contravenes the Constitution, it will be the duty of the judicial tribunals to adhere to the latter and disregard the former.

It can be of no weight to say that the courts, on the pretense of a repugnancy, may substitute their own pleasure to the constitutional intentions of the legislature. This might as well happen in the case of two contradictory statutes; or it might as well happen in every adjudication upon any single statute. The courts must declare the sense of the law; and if they should be disposed to exercise WILL instead of JUDGMENT, the consequence would equally be the substitution of their pleasure for that of the legislative body. The observation, if it proved anything, would prove that there ought to be no judges distinct from that body.

If, then, the courts of justice are to be considered as the bulwarks of a limited Constitution against legislative encroachments, this consideration will afford a strong argument for the permanent tenure of judicial offices, since nothing will contribute so much as this to that independent spirit in the judges which must be essential to the faithful performance of so arduous a duty.

This independence of the judges is equally requisite to guard the Constitution and the rights of individuals from the effects of those ill humors which the arts of designing men, or the influence of particular conjunctures, sometimes disseminate among the people themselves, and which, though they speedily give place to better information, and more deliberate reflection, have a tendency, in the meantime, to occasion dangerous innovations in the government, and serious oppressions of the minor party in the community. Though I trust the friends of the proposed Constitution will never concur with its enemies in questioning that fundamental principle of republican government which admits the right of the people to alter or abolish the established Constitution whenever they find it inconsistent with their happiness; yet it is not to be inferred from this principle that the representatives of the people, whenever a momentary inclination happens to lay hold of a majority of their constituents incompatible with the provisions in the existing Constitution, would, on that account, be justifiable in a violation of those provisions; or that the courts would be under a greater obligation to connive at infractions in this shape than when they had proceeded wholly from the cabals of the representative body. Until the people have, by some solemn and authoritative act, annulled or changed the established form, it is binding upon themselves collectively, as well as individually; and no presumption, or even knowledge, of their sentiment can warrant their representatives in a departure from it prior to such an act. But it is easy to see that it would require an uncommon portion of fortitude in the judges to do their duty as faithful guardians of the Constitution, where legislative invasions of it had been instigated by the major voice of the community.

But it is not with a view to infractions of the Constitution only that the independence of the judges may be an essential safeguard against the effects of occasional ill humors in the society. These sometimes extend no farther than to the injury of the private rights of particular classes of citizens, by unjust and partial laws. Here also the firmness of the judicial magistracy is of vast importance in mitigating the severity and confining the operation of such laws. It not only serves to moderate the immedi-

ate mischiefs of those which may have been passed but it operates as a check upon the legislative body in passing them; who, perceiving that obstacles to the success of an iniquitous intention are to be expected from the scruples of the courts, are in a manner compelled, by the very motives of the injustice they meditate, to qualify their attempts. This is a circumstance calculated to have more influence upon the character of our governments than but few may be aware of. The benefits of the integrity and moderation of the judiciary have already been felt in more States than one; and though they may have displeased those whose sinister expectations they may have disappointed, they must have commanded the esteem and applause of all the virtuous and disinterested. Considerate men of every description ought to prize whatever will tend to beget or fortify that temper in the courts; as no man can be sure that he may not be tomorrow the victim of a spirit of injustice, by which he may be a gainer today. And every man must now feel that the inevitable tendency of such a spirit is to sap the foundations of public and private confidence and to introduce in its stead universal distrust and distress.

That inflexible and uniform adherence to the rights of the Constitution, and of individuals, which we perceive to be indispensable in the courts of justice, can certainly not be expected from judges who hold their offices by a temporary commission. Periodical appointments, however regulated, or by whomsoever made, would, in some way or other, be fatal to their necessary independence. If the power of making them was committed either to the executive or legislature there would be danger of an improper complaisance to the branch which possessed it; if to both, there would be an unwillingness to hazard the displeasure of either; if to the people, or to persons chosen by them for the special purpose, there would be too great a disposition to consult popularity to justify a reliance that nothing would be consulted but the Constitution and the laws.

There is yet a further and weighty reason for the permanency of the judicial offices which is deducible from the nature of the qualifications they require. It has been frequently remarked with great propriety that a voluminous code of laws is one of the inconveniences necessarily connected with the advantages of a free government. To avoid an arbitrary discretion in the courts, it is indispensable that they should be bound down by strict rules and precedents which serve to define and point out their duty in every particular case that comes before them; and it will readily be conceived from the variety of controversies which grow out of the folly and wickedness of mankind that the records of those precedents must unavoidably swell to a very considerable bulk and must demand long and laborious study to acquire a competent knowledge of them. Hence it is that there can be but few men in the society who will have sufficient skill in the laws to qualify them for the stations of judges. And making the proper deductions for the ordinary depravity of human nature, the number must be still smaller of those who unite the requisite integrity with the requisite knowledge. These considerations apprise us that the government can have no great option between fit characters; and that a temporary duration in office which would naturally discourage such characters from quitting a lucrative line of practice to accept a seat on the bench would have a tendency to throw the administration of justice into hands less able and less well qualified to conduct it with utility and dignity. In the present circumstances of this country and in those in which it is likely to be for a long time to come, the disadvantages on this score would be greater than they may at first sight appear; but it must be confessed that they are far inferior to those which present themselves under the other aspects of the subject.

Upon the whole, there can be no room to doubt that the convention acted wisely in copying from the models of those constitutions which have established *good behavior* as the tenure of their judicial offices, in the point of duration; and that so far from being blamable on this account, their plan would have been inexcusably defective if it had wanted this important feature of good government. The experience of Great Britain affords an illustrious comment on the excellence of the institution.

PUBLIUS [Hamilton]

U.S. PRESIDENTS

PRESIDENT	POLITICAL PARTY	TERM OF SERVICE
George Washington	Federalist	April 30, 1789–March 4, 1793
George Washington	Federalist	March 4, 1793–March 4, 1797
John Adams	Federalist	March 4, 1797–March 4, 1801
Thomas Jefferson	Democratic Republican	March 4, 1801–March 4, 1805
Thomas Jefferson	Democratic Republican	March 4, 1805–March 4, 1809
James Madison	Democratic Republican	March 4, 1809–March 4, 1813
James Madison	Democratic Republican	March 4, 1813–March 4, 1817
James Monroe	Democratic Republican	March 4, 1817–March 4, 1821
James Monroe	Democratic Republican	March 4, 1821–March 4, 1825
John Q. Adams	Democratic Republican	March 4, 1825–March 4, 1829
Andrew Jackson	Democrat	March 4, 1829–March 4, 1833
Andrew Jackson	Democrat	March 4, 1833–March 4, 1837
Martin Van Buren	Democrat	March 4, 1837–March 4, 1841
W. H. Harrison	Whig	March 4, 1841–April 4, 1841
John Tyler	Whig	April 6, 1841–March 4, 1845
James K. Polk	Democrat	March 4, 1845–March 4, 1849
Zachary Taylor	Whig	March 4, 1849–July 9, 1850
Millard Fillmore	Whig	July 10, 1850–March 4, 1853
Franklin Pierce	Democrat	March 4, 1853–March 4, 1857
James Buchanan	Democrat	March 4, 1857–March 4, 1861
Abraham Lincoln	Republican	March 4, 1861–March 4, 1865
Abraham Lincoln	Republican	March 4, 1865–April 15, 1865
Andrew Johnson	Republican	April 15, 1865–March 4, 1869
Ulysses S. Grant	Republican	March 4, 1869–March 4, 1873
Ulysses S. Grant	Republican	March 4, 1873–March 4, 1877
Rutherford B. Hayes	Republican	March 4, 1877–March 4, 1881
James A. Garfield	Republican	March 4, 1881–Sept. 19, 1881
Chester A. Arthur	Republican	Sept. 20, 1881–March 4, 1885

PRESIDENT	POLITICAL PARTY	TERM OF SERVICE
Grover Cleveland	Democrat	March 4, 1885–March 4, 1889
Benjamin Harrison	Republican	March 4, 1889–March 4, 1893
Grover Cleveland	Democrat	March 4, 1893–March 4, 1897
William McKinley	Republican	March 4, 1897–March 4, 1901
William McKinley	Republican	March 4, 1901–Sept. 14, 1901
Theodore Roosevelt	Republican	Sept. 14, 1901–March 4, 1905
Theodore Roosevelt	Republican	March 4, 1905–March 4, 1909
William H. Taft	Republican	March 4, 1909–March 4, 1913
Woodrow Wilson	Democrat	March 4, 1913–March 4, 1917
Woodrow Wilson	Democrat	March 4, 1917–March 4, 1921
Warren G. Harding	Republican	March 4, 1921–Aug. 2, 1923
Calvin Coolidge	Republican	Aug. 3, 1923–March 4, 1925
Calvin Coolidge	Republican	March 4, 1925–March 4, 1929
Herbert Hoover	Republican	March 4, 1929–March 4, 1933
Franklin D. Roosevelt	Democrat	March 4, 1933–Jan. 20, 1937
Franklin D. Roosevelt	Democrat	Jan. 20, 1937–Jan. 20, 1941
Franklin D. Roosevelt	Democrat	Jan. 20, 1941–Jan. 20, 1945
Franklin D. Roosevelt	Democrat	Jan. 20, 1945–April 12, 1945
Harry S. Truman	Democrat	April 12, 1945–Jan. 20, 1949
Harry S. Truman	Democrat	Jan. 20, 1949–Jan. 20, 1953
Dwight D. Eisenhower	Republican	Jan. 20, 1953–Jan. 20, 1957
Dwight D. Eisenhower	Republican	Jan. 20, 1957–Jan. 20, 1961
John F. Kennedy	Democrat	Jan. 20, 1961–Nov. 22, 1963
Lyndon B. Johnson	Democrat	Nov. 22, 1963–Jan. 20, 1965
Lyndon B. Johnson	Democrat	Jan. 20, 1965–Jan. 20, 1969
Richard Nixon	Republican	Jan. 20, 1969–Jan. 20, 1973
Richard Nixon	Republican	Jan. 20, 1973–Aug. 9, 1974
Gerald R. Ford	Republican	Aug. 9, 1974–Jan. 20, 1977
Jimmy Carter	Democrat	Jan. 20, 1977–Jan. 20, 1981
Ronald Reagan	Republican	Jan. 20, 1981–Jan. 20, 1985
Ronald Reagan	Republican	Jan. 20, 1985–Jan. 20, 1989
George Bush	Republican	Jan. 20, 1989–Jan. 20, 1993
William J. Clinton	Democrat	Jan. 20, 1993–

THUMBNAIL SKETCH OF THE SUPREME COURT'S HISTORY

THE JUSTICES

COURT ERA	CHIEF JUSTICES	DEFINING CHARACTERISTICS	MAJOR COURT CASES
Developmental Period (1789–1800)	John Jay (1789–1795) John Rutledge (1795) Oliver Ellsworth (1796–1800)	Low prestige: spotty attendance by justices, resignations for more "prestigious positions," hears about fifty cases Business of the Court: largely admiralty and maritime disputes Use of seriatim opinion practice	*Chisholm v. Georgia* (1793) *Ware v. Hylton* (1796) *Hylton v. United States* (1796)
The Marshall Court (1801–1835)	John Marshall (1801–1835)	Establishment of Court's role in governmental process Strong Court support for national powers (especially commerce) over states' rights Use of "Opinions of the Court," rather than seriatim practice Beginning of systematic reporting of Court opinions Despite the importance of its opinions interpreting the Constitution, the business of the Court continues to involve private law issues (maritime, property, contracts)	*Marbury v. Madison* (1803) *Fletcher v. Peck* (1810) *Dartmouth College v. Woodward* (1819) *McCulloch v. Maryland* (1819) *Cohens v. Virginia* (1821) *Gibbons v. Ogden* (1824)
Taney and Civil War Courts (1836–1888)	Roger Taney (1836–1864) Salmon Chase (1864–1873) Morrison Waite (1874–1888)	Continued assertion of federal power over states (with some accommodation for state police powers) Growing North–South splits on the Court Court showdowns with Congress at the onset and conclusion of the Civil War Growth of Court's caseload, with the majority of post–Civil War cases involving private law issues and war litigation Congress fixes Court size at nine	*Charles River Bridge v. Warren Bridge* (1837) *New York v. Miln* (1837) *Luther v. Borden* (1849) *Scott v. Sandford* (1857) *Ex parte Milligan* (1866) *Ex parte McCardle* (1869) *Civil Rights Cases* (1883)
Conservative Court Eras (1889–1937)	Melville Fuller (1888–1910) Edward White (1910–1921) William Howard Taft (1921–1930) Charles Evans Hughes (1930–1937)	But for a brief period reflecting progressivism, the Courts of this era tended to protect business interests over governmental police powers Court sets "civil rights" policy of "separate but equal" Congress relieves justices of circuit-riding duty	*United States v. E. C. Knight* (1895) *Pollock v. Farmers' Loan* (1895) *Plessy v. Ferguson* (1896) *Allgeyer v. Louisiana* (1897) *Lochner v. New York* (1905) *Hammer v. Dagenhart* (1918) *Schenck v. United States* (1919)

COURT ERA	CHIEF JUSTICES	DEFINING CHARACTERISTICS	MAJOR COURT CASES
		Congress, in 1925 Judiciary Act, gives Court greater discretion over its docket Despite Judiciary Act, Court's docket continues to grow, with many cases reflecting economic issues (e.g., congressional power under the Commerce Clause) Some important construction of Bill of Rights guarantees (protection of rights increases after WW I) Showdown with FDR over New Deal legislation: Court continues to strike down New Deal leading the president to propose a Court-packing plan	*Adkins v. Children's Hospital* (1923) *Near v. Minnesota* (1931) *Powell v. Alabama* (1932) *Schechter Poultry v. United States* (1935)
The Roosevelt and World War II Court Eras (1937–1953)	Charles Evans Hughes (1937–1941) Harlan Fiske Stone (1941–1946) Fred Vinson (1946–1953)	With the "switch in time that saved nine" the Court begins to uphold federal regulations under the Commerce Clause, as well as state use of police powers Expansion of rights and liberties, until WW II and ensuing cold war Increases in nonconsensual behavior (dissents and concurrences) among the justices	*NLRB v. Jones & Laughlin Steel* (1937) *United States v. Carolene Products* (1938) *Korematsu v. United States* (1944) *Dennis v. United States* (1951) *Youngstown Sheet & Tube v. Sawyer* (1952)
The Warren Court Era (1953–1969)	Earl Warren (1953–1969)	Expansion of rights, liberties, and criminal justice Establishment of the right to privacy Emergence of Court as national policy maker Continued increase in Court's docket, with steady growth in the number of *in forma pauperis* petitions Growth in the percentage of constitutional cases on Court's plenary docket First black (Marshall) appointed to the Court	*Brown v. Board of Education* (1954) *Roth v. United States* (1957) *Mapp v. Ohio* (1961) *Baker v. Carr* (1962) *Abington School District v. Schempp* (1963) *Gideon v. Wainwright* (1963) *Heart of Atlanta Motel v. United States* (1964) *New York Times v. Sullivan* (1964) *Griswold v. Connecticut* (1965) *Miranda v. Arizona* (1966)
Republican Court Eras (1969–)	Warren Burger (1969–1986) William Rehnquist (1986–)	Attempts in some areas (e.g., criminal law) to limit or rescind Warren Court rulings Expansion of women's rights, including right to abortion Some attempt to increase state power Legitimation of limited affirmative action policies Court increasingly called on to resolve intergovernmental disputes, involving separation of powers or the authority of one branch of government over another Appointment of first woman (O'Connor) to the Court Rejected state-imposed term limits for members of Congress. Tightened standards for the creation of legislative districts designed to enhance minority representation	*Reed v. Reed* (1971) *New York Times v. United States* (1971) *Roe v. Wade* (1973) *Miller v. California* (1973) *United States v. Nixon* (1974) *Buckley v. Valeo* (1976) *Gregg v. Georgia* (1976) *Regents of the University of California v. Bakke* (1978) *United States v. Leon* (1984) *Garcia v. SAMTA* (1985) *Planned Parenthood of Southeastern Pennsylvania v. Casey* (1992) *R.A.V. v. City of St. Paul* (1992) *U.S. Term Limits v. Thornton* (1995) *Adarand Constructors v. Pena* (1995)

The justices of the Supreme Court are listed below in alphabetical order, with their birth and death years, state from which they were appointed, political party affiliation at time of appointment, educational institutions attended, appointing president, confirmation date and vote, date of service termination, and significant preappointment offices and activities.

Baldwin, Henry (1780–1844). Pennsylvania. Democrat. Yale. Nominated associate justice by Andrew Jackson; confirmed 1830 by 41–2 vote; died in office 1844. U.S. representative.

Barbour, Philip Pendleton (1783–1841). Virginia. Democrat. College of William and Mary. Nominated associate justice by Andrew Jackson; confirmed 1836 by 30–11 vote; died in office 1841. Virginia state legislator, U.S. representative, U.S. Speaker of the House, state court judge, federal district court judge.

Black, Hugo Lafayette (1886–1971). Alabama. Democrat. Birmingham Medical College, University of Alabama. Nominated associate justice by Franklin Roosevelt; confirmed 1937 by 63–16 vote; retired 1971. Alabama police court judge, county solicitor, U.S. senator.

Blackmun, Harry Andrew (1908–). Minnesota. Republican. Harvard. Nominated associate justice by Richard Nixon; confirmed 1970 by 94–0 vote; retired 1994. Federal appeals court judge.

Blair, John, Jr. (1732–1800). Virginia. Federalist. College of William and Mary; Middle Temple (England). Nominated associate justice by George Washington; confirmed 1789 by voice vote; resigned 1796. Virginia legislator, state court judge, delegate to Constitutional Convention.

Blatchford, Samuel (1820–1893). New York. Republican. Columbia. Nominated associate justice by Chester A. Arthur; confirmed 1882 by voice vote; died in office 1893. Federal district court judge, federal circuit court judge.

Bradley, Joseph P. (1813–1892). New Jersey. Republican. Rutgers. Nominated associate justice by Ulysses S. Grant; confirmed 1870 by 46–9 vote; died in office 1892. Private practice.

Brandeis, Louis Dembitz (1856–1941). Massachusetts. Republican. Harvard. Nominated associate justice by Woodrow Wilson; confirmed 1916 by 47–22 vote; retired 1939. Private practice.

Brennan, William Joseph, Jr. (1906–). New Jersey. Democrat. University of Pennsylvania, Harvard. Received recess appointment from Dwight Eisenhower to be associate justice 1956; confirmed 1957 by voice vote; retired 1990. New Jersey Supreme Court.

Brewer, David Josiah (1837–1910). Kansas. Republican. Wesleyan, Yale, Albany Law School. Nominated associate justice by Benjamin Harrison; confirmed 1889 by 53–11 vote; died in office 1910. Kansas state court judge, federal circuit court judge.

Breyer, Stephen G. (1938–). Massachusetts. Democrat. Stanford, Oxford, Harvard. Nominated associate justice by William Clinton; confirmed 1994 by 87–9 vote. Law professor; chief counsel, Senate Judiciary Committee; federal appeals court judge.

Brown, Henry B. (1836–1913). Michigan. Republican. Yale, Harvard. Nominated associate justice by Benjamin Harrison; confirmed 1890 by voice vote; retired 1906. Michigan state court judge, federal district court judge.

Burger, Warren Earl (1907–1995). Minnesota. Republican. University of Minnesota, St. Paul College of Law. Nominated chief justice by Richard Nixon; confirmed 1969 by 74–3 vote; retired 1986.   Assistant U.S. attorney general, federal appeals court judge.

Burton, Harold Hitz (1888–1964).   Ohio.   Republican. Bowdoin College, Harvard.   Nominated associate justice by Harry Truman; confirmed 1945 by voice vote; retired 1958. Ohio state legislator, mayor of Cleveland, U.S. senator.

Butler, Pierce (1866–1939).   Minnesota.   Republican. Carleton College.   Nominated associate justice by Warren G. Harding; confirmed 1922 by 61–8 vote; died in office 1939. Minnesota county attorney, private practice.

Byrnes, James Francis (1879–1972).   South Carolina. Democrat.   Privately educated.   Nominated associate justice by Franklin Roosevelt; confirmed 1941 by voice vote; resigned 1942.   South Carolina local solicitor, U.S. representative, U.S. senator.

Campbell, John Archibald (1811–1889).   Alabama. Democrat.   Franklin College (University of Georgia), U.S. Military Academy.   Nominated associate justice by Franklin Pierce; confirmed 1853 by voice vote; resigned 1861.   Alabama state legislator.

Cardozo, Benjamin Nathan (1870–1938).   New York. Democrat.   Columbia.   Nominated associate justice by Herbert Hoover; confirmed 1932 by voice vote; died in office 1938. State court judge.

Catron, John (1786–1865).   Tennessee.   Democrat.   Self-educated.   Nominated associate justice by Andrew Jackson; confirmed 1837 by 28–15 vote; died in office 1865.   Tennessee state court judge, state chief justice.

Chase, Salmon Portland (1808–1873).   Ohio.   Republican.   Dartmouth.   Nominated chief justice by Abraham Lincoln; confirmed 1864 by voice vote; died in office 1873.   U.S. senator, Ohio governor, U.S. secretary of the Treasury.

Chase, Samuel (1741–1811).   Maryland.   Federalist.   Privately educated.   Nominated associate justice by George Washington; confirmed 1796 by voice vote; died in office 1811. Maryland state legislator, delegate to Continental Congress, state court judge.

Clark, Tom Campbell (1899–1977).   Texas.   Democrat. University of Texas.   Nominated associate justice by Harry Truman; confirmed 1949 by 73–8 vote; retired 1967.   Texas local district attorney, U.S. attorney general.

Clarke, John Hessin (1857–1945).   Ohio.   Democrat. Western Reserve University.   Nominated associate justice by Woodrow Wilson; confirmed 1916 by voice vote; resigned 1922. Federal district judge.

Clifford, Nathan (1803–1881).   Maine.   Democrat.   Privately educated.   Nominated associate justice by James Buchanan; confirmed 1858 by 26–23 vote; died in office 1881. Maine state legislator, state attorney general, U.S. representative, U.S. attorney general, minister to Mexico.

Curtis, Benjamin Robbins (1809–1874).   Massachusetts.

Whig.   Harvard.   Nominated associate justice by Millard Fillmore; confirmed 1851 by voice vote; resigned 1857.   Massachusetts state legislator.

Cushing, William (1732–1810).   Massachusetts.   Federalist.   Harvard.   Nominated associate justice by George Washington; confirmed 1789 by voice vote; died in office 1810. Massachusetts state court judge, electoral college delegate.

Daniel, Peter Vivian (1784–1860).   Virginia.   Democrat. Princeton.   Nominated associate justice by Martin Van Buren; confirmed 1841 by 22–5 vote; died in office 1860.   Virginia state legislator, state Privy Council, federal district court judge.

Davis, David (1815–1886).   Illinois.   Republican. Kenyon College, Yale.   Nominated associate justice by Abraham Lincoln; confirmed 1862 by voice vote; resigned 1877.   Illinois state legislator, state court judge.

Day, William Rufus (1849–1923).   Ohio.   Republican. University of Michigan.   Nominated associate justice by Theodore Roosevelt; confirmed 1903 by voice vote; resigned 1922.   Ohio state court judge, U.S. secretary of state, federal court of appeals judge.

Douglas, William Orville (1898–1980).   Connecticut. Democrat.   Whitman College, Columbia.   Nominated associate justice by Franklin Roosevelt; confirmed 1939 by 62–4 vote; retired 1975.   Law professor, Securities and Exchange Commission.

Duvall, Gabriel (1752–1844).   Maryland. Democratic/Republican.   Privately educated.   Nominated associate justice by James Madison; confirmed 1811 by voice vote; resigned 1835.   Maryland state legislator, U.S. representative, state court judge, presidential elector, comptroller of the U.S. Treasury.

Ellsworth, Oliver (1745–1807).   Connecticut.   Federalist. Princeton.   Nominated chief justice by George Washington; confirmed 1796 by 21–1 vote; resigned 1800.   Connecticut state legislator, delegate to Continental Congress and Constitutional Convention, state court judge, U.S. senator.

Field, Stephen J. (1816–1899).   California.   Democrat. Williams College.   Nominated associate justice by Abraham Lincoln; confirmed 1863 by voice vote; retired 1897.   California state legislator, California Supreme Court.

Fortas, Abe (1910–1982).   Tennessee.   Democrat. Southwestern College, Yale.   Nominated associate justice by Lyndon Johnson; confirmed 1965 by voice vote; resigned 1969. Counsel for numerous federal agencies, private practice.

Frankfurter, Felix (1882–1965).   Massachusetts.   Independent.   College of the City of New York, Harvard.   Nominated associate justice by Franklin Roosevelt; confirmed 1939 by voice vote; retired 1962.   Law professor, War Department law officer, assistant to secretary of war, assistant to secretary of labor, War Labor Policies Board chairman.

Fuller, Melville Weston (1833–1910).   Illinois.   Democrat.   Bowdoin College, Harvard.   Nominated chief justice by Grover Cleveland; confirmed 1888 by 41–20 vote; died in office 1910.   Illinois state legislator.

Ginsburg, Ruth Bader (1933–   ).   New York.   Democrat.   Columbia.   Nominated associate justice by William Clinton; confirmed 1993 by 96–3 vote.   Professor, federal court of appeals judge.

Goldberg, Arthur J. (1908–1990).   Illinois.   Democrat.   Northwestern.   Nominated associate justice by John Kennedy; confirmed 1962 by voice vote; resigned 1965.   Secretary of labor.

Gray, Horace (1828–1902).   Massachusetts.   Republican.   Harvard.   Nominated associate justice by Chester A. Arthur; confirmed 1881 by 51–5 vote; died in office 1902.   Massachusetts Supreme Court.

Grier, Robert Cooper (1794–1870).   Pennsylvania.   Democrat.   Dickinson College.   Nominated associate justice by James Polk; confirmed 1846 by voice vote; retired 1870.   Pennsylvania state court judge.

Harlan, John Marshall (1833–1911).   Kentucky.   Republican.   Centre College, Transylvania University.   Nominated associate justice by Rutherford B. Hayes; confirmed 1877 by voice vote; died in office 1911.   Kentucky attorney general.

Harlan, John Marshall (1899–1971).   New York.   Republican.   Princeton, Oxford, New York Law School.   Nominated associate justice by Dwight Eisenhower; confirmed 1955 by 71–11 vote; retired 1971.   Chief counsel for New York State Crime Commission, federal court of appeals.

Holmes, Oliver Wendell, Jr. (1841–1935).   Massachusetts.   Republican.   Harvard.   Nominated associate justice by Theodore Roosevelt; confirmed 1902 by voice vote; retired 1932. Law professor, justice, Supreme Judicial Court of Massachusetts.

Hughes, Charles Evans (1862–1948).   New York.   Republican.   Colgate, Brown, Columbia.   Nominated associate justice by William Howard Taft; confirmed 1910 by voice vote; resigned 1916; nominated chief justice by Herbert Hoover; confirmed 1930 by 52–26 vote; retired 1941.   New York governor, U.S. secretary of state, Court of International Justice judge.

Hunt, Ward (1810–1886).   New York.   Republican.   Union College.   Nominated associate justice by Ulysses S. Grant; confirmed 1872 by voice vote; retired 1882.   New York state legislator, mayor of Utica, state court judge.

Iredell, James (1751–1799).   North Carolina.   Federalist.   English schools.   Nominated associate justice by George Washington; confirmed 1790 by voice vote; died in office 1799.   Customs official, state court judge, state attorney general.

Jackson, Howell Edmunds (1832–1895).   Tennessee.   Democrat.   West Tennessee College, University of Virginia, Cumberland University.   Nominated associate justice by Benjamin Harrison; confirmed 1893 by voice vote; died in office 1895.   Tennessee state legislator, U.S. senator, federal circuit court judge, federal court of appeals judge.

Jackson, Robert Houghwout (1892–1954).   New York.   Democrat.   Albany Law School.   Nominated associate justice by Franklin Roosevelt; confirmed 1941 by voice vote; died in office 1954.   Counsel for Internal Revenue Bureau and Securities and Exchange Commission, U.S. solicitor general, U.S. attorney general.

Jay, John (1745–1829).   New York.   Federalist.   King's College (Columbia University).   Nominated chief justice by George Washington; confirmed 1789 by voice vote; resigned 1795.   Delegate to Continental Congress, chief justice of New York, minister to Spain and Great Britain, secretary of foreign affairs.

Johnson, Thomas (1732–1819).   Maryland.   Federalist.   Privately educated.   Nominated associate justice by George Washington; confirmed 1791 by voice vote; resigned 1793.   Delegate to Annapolis Convention and Continental Congress, governor, state legislator, state court judge.

Johnson, William (1771–1834).   South Carolina.   Democratic/Republican.   Princeton.   Nominated associate justice by Thomas Jefferson; confirmed 1804 by voice vote; died in office 1834.   South Carolina state legislator, state court judge.

Kennedy, Anthony McLeod (1936–   ).   California.   Republican.   Stanford, London School of Economics, Harvard.   Nominated associate justice by Ronald Reagan; confirmed 1988 by 97–0 vote.   Federal appeals court judge.

Lamar, Joseph Rucker (1857–1916).   Georgia.   Democrat.   University of Georgia, Bethany College, Washington and Lee.   Nominated associate justice by William Howard Taft; confirmed 1910 by voice vote; died in office 1916.   Georgia state legislator, Georgia Supreme Court.

Lamar, Lucius Quintus Cincinnatus (1825–1893).   Mississippi.   Democrat.   Emory College.   Nominated associate justice by Grover Cleveland; confirmed 1888 by 32–28 vote; died in office 1893.   Georgia state legislator, U.S. representative, U.S. senator, U.S. secretary of the interior.

Livingston, Henry Brockholst (1757–1823).   New York.   Democratic/Republican.   Princeton.   Nominated associate justice by Thomas Jefferson; confirmed 1806 by voice vote; died in office 1823.   New York state legislator, state court judge.

Lurton, Horace Harmon (1844–1914).   Tennessee.   Democrat.   University of Chicago, Cumberland.   Nominated associate justice by William Howard Taft; confirmed 1909 by voice vote; died in office 1914.   Tennessee Supreme Court, federal court of appeals judge.

McKenna, Joseph (1843–1926).   California.   Republican.   Benicia Collegiate Institute.   Nominated associate justice by William McKinley; confirmed 1898 by voice vote; retired 1925.   California state legislator, U.S. representative, federal court of appeals judge, U.S. attorney general.

McKinley, John (1780–1852).   Alabama.   Democrat.

Self educated.   Nominated associate justice by Martin Van Buren; confirmed 1837 by voice vote; died in office 1852.   Alabama state legislator, U.S. senator, U.S. representative.

McLean, John (1785–1861).   Ohio.   Democrat.   Privately educated.   Nominated associate justice by Andrew Jackson; confirmed 1829 by voice vote; died in office 1861.   U.S. representative, Ohio Supreme Court, commissioner of U.S. General Land Office, U.S. postmaster general.

McReynolds, James Clark (1862–1946).   Tennessee.   Democrat.   Vanderbilt, University of Virginia.   Nominated associate justice by Woodrow Wilson; confirmed 1914 by 44–6 vote; retired 1941.   U.S. attorney general.

Marshall, John (1755–1835).   Virginia.   Federalist.   Privately educated, College of William and Mary.   Nominated chief justice by John Adams; confirmed 1801 by voice vote; died in office 1835.   Virginia state legislator, minister to France, U.S. representative, U.S. secretary of state.

Marshall, Thurgood (1908–1993).   New York.   Democrat.   Lincoln University, Howard University.   Nominated associate justice by Lyndon Johnson; confirmed 1967 by 69–11 vote; retired 1991.   NAACP Legal Defense Fund, federal court of appeals judge, U.S. solicitor general.

Matthews, Stanley (1824–1889).   Ohio.   Republican.   Kenyon College.   Nominated associate justice by Rutherford B. Hayes; no Senate action on nomination; renominated associate justice by James A. Garfield; confirmed 1881 by 24–23 vote; died in office 1889.   Ohio state legislator, state court judge, U.S. attorney for southern Ohio, U.S. senator.

Miller, Samuel Freeman (1816–1890).   Iowa.   Republican.   Transylvania University.   Nominated associate justice by Abraham Lincoln; confirmed 1862 by voice vote; died in office 1890.   Medical doctor, private law practice, justice of the peace.

Minton, Sherman (1890–1965).   Indiana.   Democrat.   Indiana University, Yale.   Nominated associate justice by Harry Truman; confirmed 1949 by 48–16 vote; retired 1956.   U.S. senator, federal court of appeals judge.

Moody, William Henry (1853–1917).   Massachusetts.   Republican.   Harvard.   Nominated associate justice by Theodore Roosevelt; confirmed 1906 by voice vote; retired 1910.   Massachusetts local district attorney, U.S. representative, secretary of the navy, U.S. attorney general.

Moore, Alfred (1755–1810).   North Carolina.   Federalist.   Privately educated.   Nominated associate justice by John Adams; confirmed 1799 by voice vote; resigned 1804.   North Carolina legislator, state attorney general, state court judge.

Murphy, Francis William (1880–1949).   Michigan.   Democrat.   University of Michigan, London's Inn (England), Trinity College (Ireland).   Nominated associate justice by Franklin Roosevelt; confirmed 1940 by voice vote; died in office

1949.   Michigan state court judge, mayor of Detroit, governor of the Philippines, governor of Michigan, U.S. attorney general.

Nelson, Samuel (1792–1873).   New York.   Democrat.   Middlebury College.   Nominated associate justice by John Tyler; confirmed 1845 by voice vote; retired 1872.   Presidential elector, state court judge, New York Supreme Court chief justice.

O'Connor, Sandra Day (1930–   ).   Arizona.   Republican.   Stanford.   Nominated associate justice by Ronald Reagan; confirmed 1981 by 99–0 vote.   Arizona state legislator, state court judge.

Paterson, William (1745–1806).   New Jersey.   Federalist.   Princeton.   Nominated associate justice by George Washington; confirmed 1793 by voice vote; died in office 1806.   New Jersey attorney general, delegate to Constitutional Convention, U.S. senator, governor.

Peckham, Rufus Wheeler (1838–1909).   New York.   Democrat.   Albany Boys' Academy.   Nominated associate justice by Grover Cleveland; confirmed 1895 by voice vote; died in office 1909.   New York local district attorney, city attorney, state court judge.

Pitney, Mahlon (1858–1924).   New Jersey.   Republican.   Princeton.   Nominated associate justice by William Howard Taft; confirmed 1912 by 50–26 vote; retired 1922.   U.S. representative, New Jersey state legislator, New Jersey Supreme Court, Chancellor of New Jersey.

Powell, Lewis Franklin, Jr. (1907–   ).   Virginia.   Democrat.   Washington and Lee, Harvard.   Nominated associate justice by Richard Nixon; confirmed 1971 by 89–1 vote; retired 1987.   Private practice, Virginia State Board of Education, American Bar Association president, American College of Trial Lawyers president.

Reed, Stanley Forman (1884–1980).   Kentucky.   Democrat.   Kentucky Wesleyan, Yale, Virginia, Columbia, University of Paris.   Nominated associate justice by Franklin Roosevelt; confirmed 1938 by voice vote; retired 1957.   Federal Farm Board general counsel, Reconstruction Finance Corporation general counsel, U.S. solicitor general.

Rehnquist, William Hubbs (1924–   ).   Arizona.   Republican.   Stanford, Harvard.   Nominated associate justice by Richard Nixon; confirmed 1971 by 68–26 vote; nominated chief justice by Ronald Reagan; confirmed 1986 by 65–33 vote.   Private practice, assistant U.S. attorney general.

Roberts, Owen Josephus (1875–1955).   Pennsylvania.   Republican.   University of Pennsylvania.   Nominated associate justice by Herbert Hoover; confirmed 1930 by voice vote; resigned 1945.   Private practice, Pennsylvania local prosecutor, special U.S. attorney.

Rutledge, John (1739–1800).   South Carolina.   Federalist.   Middle Temple (England).   Nominated associate justice by

George Washington; confirmed 1789 by voice vote; resigned 1791.   Nominated chief justice by George Washington August 1795 and served as recess appointment; confirmation denied and service terminated December 1795.   South Carolina legislator, state attorney general, governor, chief justice of South Carolina, delegate to Continental Congress and Constitutional Convention.

Rutledge, Wiley Blount (1894–1949).   Iowa.   Democrat. Maryville College, University of Wisconsin, University of Colorado.   Nominated associate justice by Franklin Roosevelt; confirmed 1943 by voice vote; died in office 1949.   Law professor, federal court of appeals judge.

Sanford, Edward Terry (1865–1930).   Tennessee.   Republican.   University of Tennessee, Harvard.   Nominated associate justice by Warren G. Harding; confirmed 1923 by voice vote; died in office 1930.   Assistant U.S. attorney general, federal district court judge.

Scalia, Antonin (1936–   ).   District of Columbia.   Republican.   Georgetown, Harvard.   Nominated associate justice by Ronald Reagan; confirmed 1986 by 98–0 vote.   Assistant U.S. attorney general, federal court of appeals judge.

Shiras, George, Jr. (1832–1924).   Pennsylvania.   Republican.   Ohio University, Yale.   Nominated associate justice by Benjamin Harrison; confirmed 1892 by voice vote; retired 1903. Private practice.

Souter, David Hackett (1939–   ).   New Hampshire.   Republican.   Harvard, Oxford.   Nominated associate justice by George Bush; confirmed 1990 by 90–9 vote.   New Hampshire attorney general, state court judge, federal appeals court judge.

Stevens, John Paul (1920–   ).   Illinois.   Republican. Chicago, Northwestern.   Nominated associate justice by Gerald Ford; confirmed 1975 by 98–0 vote.   Federal court of appeals judge.

Stewart, Potter (1915–1985).   Ohio.   Republican.   Yale, Cambridge.   Received recess appointment from Dwight Eisenhower to be associate justice in 1958; confirmed 1959 by 70–17 vote; retired 1981.   Cincinnati city council, federal court of appeals judge.

Stone, Harlan Fiske (1872–1946).   New York.   Republican.   Amherst College, Columbia.   Nominated associate justice by Calvin Coolidge; confirmed 1925 by 71–6 vote; nominated chief justice by Franklin Roosevelt; confirmed 1941 by voice vote; died in office 1946.   Law professor, U.S. attorney general.

Story, Joseph (1779–1845).   Massachusetts.   Democratic/Republican.   Harvard.   Nominated associate justice by James Madison; confirmed 1811 by voice vote; died in office 1845.   Massachusetts state legislator, U.S. representative.

Strong, William (1808–1895).   Pennsylvania.   Republican.   Yale.   Nominated associate justice by Ulysses S. Grant;

confirmed 1870 by voice vote; retired 1880.   U.S. representative, Pennsylvania Supreme Court.

Sutherland, George (1862–1942).   Utah.   Republican. Brigham Young, University of Michigan.   Nominated associate justice by Warren G. Harding; confirmed 1922 by voice vote; retired 1938.   Utah state legislator, U.S. representative, U.S. senator.

Swayne, Noah Haynes (1804–1884).   Ohio.   Republican. Privately educated.   Nominated associate justice by Abraham Lincoln; confirmed 1862 by 38–1 vote; retired 1881.   Ohio state legislator, local prosecutor, U.S. attorney for Ohio, Columbus city council.

Taft, William Howard (1857–1930).   Ohio.   Republican. Yale, Cincinnati.   Nominated chief justice by Warren G. Harding; confirmed 1921 by voice vote; retired 1930.   Ohio local prosecutor, state court judge, U.S. solicitor general, federal court of appeals judge, governor of the Philippines, secretary of war, U.S. president.

Taney, Roger Brooke (1777–1864).   Maryland.   Democrat.   Dickinson College.   Nominated associate justice by Andrew Jackson; nomination not confirmed 1835; nominated chief justice by Andrew Jackson; confirmed 1836 by 29–15 vote; died in office 1864.   Maryland state legislator, state attorney general, acting secretary of war, secretary of the Treasury (nomination later rejected by Senate).

Thomas, Clarence (1948–   ).   Georgia.   Republican. Holy Cross, Yale.   Nominated associate justice by George Bush; confirmed 1991 by 52–48 vote.   Department of Education, Equal Employment Opportunity Commission, federal appeals court judge.

Thompson, Smith (1768–1843).   New York.   Democratic/Republican.   Princeton.   Nominated associate justice by James Monroe; confirmed 1823 by voice vote; died in office 1843.   New York state legislator, state court judge, secretary of the navy.

Todd, Thomas (1765–1826).   Kentucky.   Democratic/Republican.   Liberty Hall (Washington and Lee).   Nominated associate justice by Thomas Jefferson; confirmed 1807 by voice vote; died in office 1826.   Kentucky state court judge, state chief justice.

Trimble, Robert (1776–1828).   Kentucky.   Democratic/Republican.   Kentucky Academy.   Nominated associate justice by John Quincy Adams; confirmed 1826 by 27–5 vote; died in office 1828.   Kentucky state legislator, state court judge, U.S. attorney, federal district court judge.

Van Devanter, Willis (1859–1941).   Wyoming.   Republican.   Indiana Asbury University, University of Cincinnati. Nominated associate justice by William Howard Taft; confirmed 1910 by voice vote; retired 1937.   Cheyenne city attorney, Wyoming territorial legislature, Wyoming Supreme Court, assistant U.S. attorney general, federal court of appeals judge.

Vinson, Frederick Moore (1890–1953). Kentucky. Democrat. Centre College. Nominated chief justice by Harry Truman; confirmed 1946 by voice vote; died in office 1953. U.S. representative, federal appeals court judge, director of Office of Economic Stabilization, secretary of the Treasury.

Waite, Morrison Remick (1816–1888). Ohio. Republican. Yale. Nominated chief justice by Ulysses S. Grant; confirmed 1874 by 63–0 vote; died in office 1888. Private practice, Ohio state legislator.

Warren, Earl (1891–1974). California. Republican. University of California. Recess appointment as chief justice by Dwight Eisenhower 1953; confirmed 1954 by voice vote; retired 1969. California local district attorney, state attorney general, governor.

Washington, Bushrod (1762–1829). Virginia. Federalist. College of William and Mary. Nominated associate justice by John Adams; confirmed 1798 by voice vote; died in office 1829. Virginia state legislator.

Wayne, James Moore (1790–1867). Georgia. Democrat. Princeton. Nominated associate justice by Andrew Jackson; confirmed 1835 by voice vote; died in office 1867. Georgia state legislator, mayor of Savannah, state court judge, U.S. representative.

White, Byron Raymond (1917–   ). Colorado. Democrat. University of Colorado, Oxford, Yale. Nominated associate justice by John Kennedy; confirmed 1962 by voice vote; retired 1993. Deputy U.S. attorney general.

White, Edward Douglass (1845–1921). Louisiana. Democrat. Mount St. Mary's College, Georgetown. Nominated associate justice by Grover Cleveland; confirmed 1894 by voice vote; nominated chief justice by William Howard Taft; confirmed 1910 by voice vote; died in office 1921. Louisiana state legislator, Louisiana Supreme Court, U.S. senator.

Whittaker, Charles Evans (1901–1973). Missouri. Republican. University of Kansas City. Nominated associate justice by Dwight Eisenhower; confirmed 1957 by voice vote; retired 1962. Federal district court judge, federal appeals court judge.

Wilson, James (1742–1798). Pennsylvania. Federalist. University of St. Andrews (Scotland). Nominated associate justice by George Washington; confirmed 1789 by voice vote; died in office 1798. Delegate to Continental Congress and Constitutional Convention.

Woodbury, Levi (1789–1851). New Hampshire. Democrat. Dartmouth, Tapping Reeve Law School. Nominated associate justice by James Polk; confirmed 1846 by voice vote; died in office 1851. New Hampshire state legislator, state court judge, governor, U.S. senator, secretary of the navy, secretary of the Treasury.

Woods, William B. (1824–1887). Georgia. Republican. Western Reserve College, Yale. Nominated associate justice by Rutherford B. Hayes; confirmed 1880 by 39–8 vote; died in office 1887. Ohio state legislator, Alabama chancellor, federal circuit court judge.

NATURAL COURTS

Natural court[a]	Justices[b]	Dates	U.S. Reports[c]
Jay 1	Jay (*o* October 19, 1789), J. Rutledge (*o* February 15, 1790), Cushing (*o* February 2, 1790), Wilson (*o* October 5, 1789), Blair (*o* February 2, 1790)	October 5, 1789–May 12, 1790	2
Jay 2	Jay, Rutledge (*r* March 5, 1791), Cushing, Wilson, Blair, Iredell (*o* May 12, 1790)	May 12, 1790–August 6, 1792	2
Jay 3	Jay, Cushing, Wilson, Blair, Iredell, T. Johnson (*o* August 6, 1792; *r* January 16, 1793)	August 6, 1792–March 11, 1793	2
Jay 4	Jay (*r* June 29, 1795), Cushing, Wilson, Blair, Iredell, Paterson (*o* March 11, 1793)	March 11, 1793–August 12, 1795	2–3
Rutledge 1	J. Rutledge (*o* August 12, 1795; *rj* December 15, 1795), Cushing, Wilson, Blair (*r* January 27, 1796), Iredell, Paterson	August 12, 1795–February 4, 1796	3
No chief justice	Cushing, Wilson, Iredell, Paterson, S. Chase (*o* February 4, 1796)	February 4, 1796–March 8, 1796	3
Ellsworth 1	Ellsworth (*o* March 8, 1796), Cushing, Wilson (*d* August 21, 1798), Iredell, Paterson, S. Chase	March 8, 1796–February 4, 1799	3
Ellsworth 2	Ellsworth, Cushing, Iredell (*d* October 20, 1799), Paterson, S. Chase, Washington (*o* February 4, 1799)	February 4, 1799–April 21, 1800	3–4
Ellsworth 3	Ellsworth (*r* December 15, 1800), Cushing, Paterson, S. Chase, Washington, Moore (*o* April 21, 1800)	April 21, 1800–February 4, 1801	4
Marshall 1	Marshall (*o* February 4, 1801), Cushing, Paterson, S. Chase, Washington, Moore (*r* January 26, 1804)	February 4, 1801–May 7, 1804	5–6
Marshall 2	Marshall, Cushing, Paterson (*d* September 9, 1806), S. Chase, Washington, W. Johnson (*o* May 7, 1804)	May 7, 1804–January 20, 1807	6–7
Marshall 3	Marshall, Cushing, S. Chase, Washington, W. Johnson, Livingston (*o* January 20, 1807)	January 20, 1807–May 4, 1807	8
Marshall 4	Marshall, Cushing (*d* September 13, 1810), S. Chase (*d* June 19, 1811), Washington, W. Johnson, Livingston, Todd (*o* May 4, 1807)	May 4, 1807–November 23, 1811	8–10

Natural court [a]	Justices [b]	Dates	U.S. Reports [c]
Marshall 5	Marshall, Washington, W. Johnson, Livingston, Todd, Duvall (*o* November 23, 1811)	November 23, 1811–February 3, 1812	11
Marshall 6	Marshall, Washington, W. Johnson, Livingston (*d* March 18, 1823), Todd, Duvall, Story (*o* February 3, 1812)	February 3, 1812–February 10, 1824	11–21
Marshall 7	Marshall, Washington, W. Johnson, Todd (*d* February 7, 1826), Duvall, Story, Thompson (*o* February 10, 1824)	February 10, 1824–June 16, 1826	22–24
Marshall 8	Marshall, Washington (*d* November 26, 1829), W. Johnson, Duvall, Story, Thompson, Trimble (*o* June 16, 1826; *d* August 25, 1828)	June 16, 1826–January 11, 1830	25–27
Marshall 9	Marshall, W. Johnson (*d* August 4, 1834), Duvall (*r* January 14, 1835), Story, Thompson, McLean (*o* January 11, 1830), Baldwin (*o* January 18, 1830)	January 11, 1830–January 14, 1835	28–33
Marshall 10	Marshall (*d* July 6, 1835), Story, Thompson, McLean, Baldwin, Wayne (*o* January 14, 1835)	January 14, 1835–March 28, 1836	34–35
Taney 1	Taney (*o* March 28, 1836), Story, Thompson, McLean, Baldwin, Wayne	March 28, 1836–May 12, 1836	35
Taney 2	Taney, Story, Thompson, McLean, Baldwin, Wayne, Barbour (*o* May 12, 1836)	May 12, 1836–May 1, 1837	35–36
Taney 3	Taney, Story, Thompson, McLean, Baldwin, Wayne, Barbour, Catron (*o* May 1, 1837)	May 1, 1837–January 9, 1838	36
Taney 4	Taney, Story, Thompson, McLean, Baldwin, Wayne, Barbour (*d* February 25, 1841), Catron, McKinley (*o* January 9, 1838)	January 9, 1838–January 10, 1842	37–40
Taney 5	Taney, Story, Thompson (*d* December 18, 1843), McLean, Baldwin (*d* April 21, 1844), Wayne, Catron, McKinley, Daniel (*o* January 10, 1842)	January 10, 1842–February 27, 1845	40–44
Taney 6	Taney, Story (*d* September 10, 1845), McLean, Wayne, Catron, McKinley, Daniel, Nelson (*o* February 27, 1845)	February 27, 1845–September 23, 1845	44
Taney 7	Taney, McLean, Wayne, Catron, McKinley, Daniel, Nelson, Woodbury (*o* September 23, 1845)	September 23, 1845–August 10, 1846	44–45
Taney 8	Taney, McLean, Wayne, Catron, McKinley, Daniel, Nelson, Woodbury (*d* September 4, 1851), Grier (*o* August 10, 1846)	August 10, 1846–October 10, 1851	46–52
Taney 9	Taney, McLean, Wayne, Catron, McKinley (*d* July 19, 1852), Daniel, Nelson, Grier, Curtis (*o* October 10, 1851)	October 10, 1851–April 11, 1853	53–55
Taney 10	Taney, McLean, Wayne, Catron, Daniel, Nelson, Grier, Curtis (*r* September 30, 1857), Campbell (*o* April 11, 1853)	April 11, 1853–January 21, 1858	56–61
Taney 11	Taney, McLean (*d* April 4, 1861), Wayne, Catron, Daniel (*d* May 31, 1860), Nelson, Grier, Campbell (*r* April 30, 1861), Clifford (*o* January 21, 1858)	January 21, 1858–January 27, 1862	61–66
Taney 12	Taney, Wayne, Catron, Nelson, Grier, Clifford, Swayne (*o* January 27, 1862)	January 27, 1862–July 21, 1862	66
Taney 13	Taney, Wayne, Catron, Nelson, Grier, Clifford, Swayne, Miller (*o* July 21, 1862)	July 21, 1862–December 10, 1862	67

Natural court [a]	Justices [b]	Dates	U.S. Reports [c]
Taney 14	Taney, Wayne, Catron, Nelson, Grier, Clifford, Swayne, Miller, Davis (o December 10, 1862)	December 10, 1862–May 20, 1863	67
Taney 15	Taney (d October 12, 1864), Wayne, Catron, Nelson, Grier, Clifford, Swayne, Miller, Davis, Field (o May 20, 1863)	May 20, 1863–December 15, 1864	67–68
Chase 1	S. P. Chase (o December 15, 1864), Wayne (d July 5, 1867), Catron (d May 30, 1865), Nelson, Grier (r January 31, 1870), Clifford, Swayne, Miller, Davis, Field	December 15, 1864–March 14, 1870	69–76
Chase 2	S. P. Chase, Nelson (r November 28, 1872), Clifford, Swayne, Miller, Davis, Field, Strong (o March 14, 1870), Bradley (o March 23, 1870)	March 14, 1870–January 9, 1873	76–82
Chase 3	S. P. Chase (d May 7, 1873), Clifford, Swayne, Miller, Davis, Field, Strong, Bradley, Hunt (o January 9, 1873)	January 9, 1873–March 4, 1874	82–86
Waite 1	Waite (o March 4, 1874), Clifford, Swayne, Miller, Davis (r March 4, 1877), Field, Strong, Bradley, Hunt	March 4, 1874–December 10, 1877	86–95
Waite 2	Waite, Clifford, Swayne, Miller, Field, Strong (r December 14, 1880), Bradley, Hunt, Harlan I (o December 10, 1877)	December 10, 1877–January 5, 1881	95–103
Waite 3	Waite, Clifford, Swayne (r January 24, 1881), Miller, Field, Bradley, Hunt, Harlan I, Woods (o January 5, 1881)	January 5, 1881–May 17, 1881	103
Waite 4	Waite, Clifford (d July 25, 1881), Miller, Field, Bradley, Hunt, Harlan I, Woods, Matthews (o May 17, 1881)	May 17, 1881–January 9, 1882	103–104
Waite 5	Waite, Miller, Field, Bradley, Hunt (r January 27, 1882), Harlan I, Woods, Matthews, Gray (o January 9, 1882)	January 9, 1882–April 3, 1882	104–105
Waite 6	Waite, Miller, Field, Bradley, Harlan I, Woods (d May 14, 1887), Matthews, Gray, Blatchford (o April 3, 1882)	April 3, 1882–January 18, 1888	105–124
Waite 7	Waite (d March 23, 1888), Miller, Field, Bradley, Harlan I, Matthews, Gray, Blatchford, L. Lamar (o January 18, 1888)	January 18, 1888–October 8, 1888	124–127
Fuller 1	Fuller (o October 8, 1888), Miller, Field, Bradley, Harlan I, Matthews (d March 22, 1889), Gray, Blatchford, L. Lamar	October 8, 1888–January 6, 1890	128–132
Fuller 2	Fuller, Miller (d October 13, 1890), Field, Bradley, Harlan I, Gray, Blatchford, L. Lamar, Brewer (o January 6, 1890)	January 6, 1890–January 5, 1891	132–137
Fuller 3	Fuller, Field, Bradley (d January 22, 1892), Harlan I, Gray, Blatchford, L. Lamar, Brewer, Brown (o January 5, 1891)	January 5, 1891–October 10, 1892	137–145
Fuller 4	Fuller, Field, Harlan I, Gray, Blatchford, L. Lamar (d January 23, 1893), Brewer, Brown, Shiras (o October 10, 1892)	October 10, 1892–March 4, 1893	146–148
Fuller 5	Fuller, Field, Harlan I, Gray, Blatchford (d July 7, 1893), Brewer, Brown, Shiras, H. Jackson (o March 4, 1893)	March 4, 1893–March 12, 1894	148–151
Fuller 6	Fuller, Field, Harlan I, Gray, Brewer, Brown, Shiras, H. Jackson (d August 8, 1895), E. White (o March 12, 1894)	March 12, 1894–January 6, 1896	152–160

Natural court[a]	Justices[b]	Dates	U.S. Reports[c]
Fuller 7	Fuller, Field (r December 1, 1897), Harlan I, Gray, Brewer, Brown, Shiras, E. White, Peckham (o January 6, 1896)	January 6, 1896–January 26, 1898	160–169
Fuller 8	Fuller, Harlan I, Gray (d September 15, 1902), Brewer, Brown, Shiras, E. White, Peckham, McKenna (o January 26, 1898)	January 26, 1898–December 8, 1902	169–187
Fuller 9	Fuller, Harlan I, Brewer, Brown, Shiras (r February 23, 1903), E. White, Peckham, McKenna, Holmes (o December 8, 1902)	December 8, 1902–March 2, 1903	187–188
Fuller 10	Fuller, Harlan I, Brewer, Brown (r May 28, 1906), E. White, Peckham, McKenna, Holmes, Day (o March 2, 1903)	March 2, 1903–December 17, 1906	188–203
Fuller 11	Fuller, Harlan I, Brewer, E. White, Peckham (d October 24, 1909), McKenna, Holmes, Day, Moody (o December 17, 1906)	December 17, 1906–January 3, 1910	203–215
Fuller 12	Fuller (d July 4, 1910), Harlan I, Brewer (d March 28, 1910), E. White, McKenna, Holmes, Day, Moody, Lurton (o January 3, 1910)	January 3, 1910–October 10, 1910	215–217
No chief justice	Harlan I, E. White (p December 18, 1910), McKenna, Holmes, Day, Moody (r November 20, 1910), Lurton, Hughes (o October 10, 1910)	October 10, 1910–December 19, 1910	218
White 1	E. White (o December 19, 1910), Harlan I (d October 14, 1911), McKenna, Holmes, Day, Lurton, Hughes, Van Devanter (o January 3, 1911), J. Lamar (o January 3, 1911)	December 19, 1910–March 18, 1912	218–223
White 2	E. White, McKenna, Holmes, Day, Lurton (d July 12, 1914), Hughes, Van Devanter, J. Lamar, Pitney (o March 18, 1912)	March 18, 1912–October 12, 1914	223–234
White 3	E. White, McKenna, Holmes, Day, Hughes, Van Devanter, J. Lamar (d January 2, 1916), Pitney, McReynolds (o October 12, 1914)	October 12, 1914–June 5, 1916	235–241
White 4	E. White, McKenna, Holmes, Day, Hughes (r June 10, 1916), Van Devanter, Pitney, McReynolds, Brandeis (o June 5, 1916)	June 5, 1916–October 9, 1916	241
White 5	E. White (d May 19, 1921), McKenna, Holmes, Day, Van Devanter, Pitney, McReynolds, Brandeis, Clarke (o October 9, 1916)	October 9, 1916–July 11, 1921	242–256
Taft 1	Taft (o July 11, 1921), McKenna, Holmes, Day, Van Devanter, Pitney, McReynolds, Brandeis, Clarke (r September 18, 1922)	July 11, 1921–October 2, 1922	257–259
Taft 2	Taft, McKenna, Holmes, Day (r November 13, 1922), Van Devanter, Pitney (r December 31, 1922), McReynolds, Brandeis, Sutherland (o October 2, 1922)	October 2, 1922–January 2, 1923	260
Taft 3	Taft, McKenna, Holmes, Van Devanter, McReynolds, Brandeis, Sutherland, Butler (o January 2, 1923)	January 2, 1923–February 19, 1923	260
Taft 4	Taft, McKenna (r January 5, 1925), Holmes, Van Devanter, McReynolds, Brandeis, Sutherland, Butler, Sanford (o February 19, 1923)	February 19, 1923–March 2, 1925	260–267
Taft 5	Taft (r February 3, 1930), Holmes, Van Devanter, McReynolds, Brandeis, Sutherland, Butler, Sanford, Stone (o March 2, 1925)	March 2, 1925–February 24, 1930	267–280
Hughes 1	Hughes (o February 24, 1930), Holmes, Van Devanter, McReynolds, Brandeis, Sutherland, Butler, Sanford (d March 8, 1930), Stone	February 24, 1930–June 2, 1930	280–281
Hughes 2	Hughes, Holmes (r January 12, 1932), Van Devanter, McReynolds, Brandeis, Sutherland, Butler, Stone, Roberts (o June 2, 1930)	June 2, 1930–March 14, 1932	281–285

Natural court[a]	Justices[b]	Dates	U.S. Reports[c]
Hughes 3	Hughes, Van Devanter (r June 2, 1937), McReynolds, Brandeis, Sutherland, Butler, Stone, Roberts, Cardozo (o March 14, 1932)	March 14, 1932–August 19, 1937	285–301
Hughes 4	Hughes, McReynolds, Brandeis, Sutherland (r January 17, 1938), Butler, Stone, Roberts, Cardozo, Black (o August 19, 1937)	August 19, 1937 January 31, 1938	302–303
Hughes 5	Hughes, McReynolds, Brandeis, Butler, Stone, Roberts, Cardozo (d July 9, 1938), Black, Reed (o January 31, 1938)	January 31, 1938–January 30, 1939	303–305
Hughes 6	Hughes, McReynolds, Brandeis (r February 13, 1939), Butler, Stone, Roberts, Black, Reed, Frankfurter (o January 30, 1939)	January 30, 1939–April 17, 1939	306
Hughes 7	Hughes, McReynolds, Butler (d November 16, 1939), Stone, Roberts, Black, Reed, Frankfurter, Douglas (o April 17, 1939)	April 17, 1939–February 5, 1940	306–308
Hughes 8	Hughes (r July 1, 1941), McReynolds (r January 31, 1941), Stone (p July 2, 1941), Roberts, Black, Reed, Frankfurter, Douglas, Murphy (o February 5, 1940)	February 5, 1940–July 3, 1941	308–313
Stone 1	Stone (o July 3, 1941), Roberts, Black, Reed, Frankfurter, Douglas, Murphy, Byrnes (o July 8, 1941; r October 3, 1942), R. Jackson (o July 11, 1941)	July 3, 1941–February 15, 1943	314–318
Stone 2	Stone, Roberts (r July 31, 1945), Black, Reed, Frankfurter, Douglas, Murphy, R. Jackson, W. Rutledge (o February 15, 1943)	February 15, 1943–October 1, 1945	318–326
Stone 3	Stone (d April 22, 1946), Black, Reed, Frankfurter, Douglas, Murphy, R. Jackson, W. Rutledge, Burton (o October 1, 1945)	October 1, 1945–June 24, 1946	326–328
Vinson 1	Vinson (o June 24, 1946), Black, Reed, Frankfurter, Douglas, Murphy (d July 19, 1949), R. Jackson, W. Rutledge, Burton	June 24, 1946–August 24, 1949	329–338
Vinson 2	Vinson, Black, Reed, Frankfurter, Douglas, R. Jackson, W. Rutledge (d September 10, 1949), Burton, Clark (o August 24, 1949)	August 24, 1949–October 12, 1949	338
Vinson 3	Vinson (d September 8, 1953), Black, Reed, Frankfurter, Douglas, R. Jackson, Burton, Clark, Minton (o October 12, 1949)	October 12, 1949–October 5, 1953	338–346
Warren 1	Warren (o October 5, 1953), Black, Reed, Frankfurter, Douglas, R. Jackson (d October 9, 1954), Burton, Clark, Minton	October 5, 1953–March 28, 1955	346–348
Warren 2	Warren, Black, Reed, Frankfurter, Douglas, Burton, Clark, Minton (r October 15, 1956), Harlan II (o March 28, 1955)	March 28, 1955–October 16, 1956	348–352
Warren 3	Warren, Black, Reed (r February 25, 1957), Frankfurter, Douglas, Burton, Clark, Harlan II, Brennan (o October 16, 1956)	October 16, 1956–March 25, 1957	352
Warren 4	Warren, Black, Frankfurter, Douglas, Burton (r October 13, 1958), Clark, Harlan II, Brennan, Whittaker (o March 25, 1957)	March 25, 1957–October 14, 1958	352–358
Warren 5	Warren, Black, Frankfurter, Douglas, Clark, Harlan II, Brennan, Whittaker (r March 31, 1962), Stewart (o October 14, 1958)	October 14, 1958–April 16, 1962	358–369
Warren 6	Warren, Black, Frankfurter (r August 28, 1962), Douglas, Clark, Harlan II, Brennan, Stewart, B. White (o April 16, 1962)	April 16, 1962–October 1, 1962	369–370
Warren 7	Warren, Black, Douglas, Clark, Harlan II, Brennan, Stewart, B. White, Goldberg (o October 1, 1962; r July 25, 1965)	October 1, 1962–October 4, 1965	371–381

Natural court [a]	Justices [b]	Dates	U.S. Reports [c]
Warren 8	Warren, Black, Douglas, Clark (*r* June 12, 1967), Harlan II, Brennan, Stewart, B. White, Fortas (*o* October 4, 1965)	October 4, 1965–October 2, 1967	382–388
Warren 9	Warren (*r* June 23, 1969), Black, Douglas, Harlan II, Brennan, Stewart, B. White, Fortas (*r* May 14, 1969), T. Marshall (*o* October 2, 1967)	October 2, 1967–June 23, 1969	389–395
Burger 1	Burger (*o* June 23, 1969), Black, Douglas, Harlan II, Brennan, Stewart, B. White, T. Marshall	June 23, 1969–June 9, 1970	395–397
Burger 2	Burger, Black (*r* September 17, 1971), Douglas, Harlan II (*r* September 23, 1971), Brennan, Stewart, B. White, T. Marshall, Blackmun (*o* June 9, 1970)	June 9, 1970–January 7, 1972	397–404
Burger 3	Burger, Douglas (*r* November 12, 1975), Brennan, Stewart, B. White, T. Marshall, Blackmun, Powell (*o* January 7, 1972), Rehnquist (*o* January 7, 1972)	January 7, 1972–December 19, 1975	404–423
Burger 4	Burger, Brennan, Stewart (*r* July 3, 1981), B. White, T. Marshall, Blackmun, Powell, Rehnquist, Stevens (*o* December 19, 1975)	December 19, 1975–September 25, 1981	423–453
Burger 5	Burger (*r* September 26, 1986), Brennan, B. White, T. Marshall, Blackmun, Powell, Rehnquist (*p* September 26, 1986), Stevens, O'Connor (*o* September 25, 1981)	September 25, 1981–September 26, 1986	453–478
Rehnquist 1	Rehnquist (*o* September 26, 1986), Brennan, B. White, T. Marshall, Blackmun, Powell (*r* June 26, 1987), Stevens, O'Connor, Scalia (*o* September 26, 1986)	September 26, 1986–February 18, 1988	478–484
Rehnquist 2	Rehnquist, Brennan (*r* July 20, 1990), B. White, T. Marshall, Blackmun, Stevens, O'Connor, Scalia, Kennedy (*o* February 18, 1988)	February 18, 1988–October 9, 1990	484–498
Rehnquist 3	Rehnquist, B. White, T. Marshall (*r* October 1, 1991), Blackmun, Stevens, O'Connor, Scalia, Kennedy, Souter (*o* October 9, 1990)	October 9, 1990–October 23, 1991	498–501
Rehnquist 4	Rehnquist, B. White (*r* July 1, 1993), Blackmun, Stevens, O'Connor, Scalia, Kennedy, Souter, Thomas (*o* October 23, 1991)	October 23, 1991–August 10, 1993	502–
Rehnquist 5	Rehnquist, Blackmun (*r* August 3, 1994), Stevens, O'Connor, Scalia, Kennedy, Souter, Thomas, Ginsburg (*o* August 10, 1993)	August 10, 1993–August 3, 1994	
Rehnquist 6	Rehnquist, Stevens, O'Connor, Scalia, Kennedy, Souter, Thomas, Ginsburg, Breyer (*o* August 3, 1994)	August 3, 1994	

SOURCE: Lee Epstein, Jeffrey A. Segal, Harold J. Spaeth, Thomas G. Walker, *The Supreme Court Compendium: Data, Decisions, and Developments* (Washington, D.C.: Congressional Quarterly, 1994), Table 5-2.

NOTES: The term *natural court* refers to a period of time during which the membership of the Court remains stable. There are a number of ways to determine the beginning and end of a natural court. Here a natural court begins when a new justice takes the oath of office and continues until the next new justice takes the oath. When two or more justices join the Court within a period of fifteen or fewer days, we treat it as the beginning of a single natural court (for example, Marshall 9, Chase 2, White 1, and Stone 1).

a. Numbered sequentially within the tenure of each chief justice.

b. The name of the chief justice appears first, with associate justices fol-

lowing in order of descending seniority. In addition, the date a justice left the Court, creating a vacancy for the next justice to be appointed, is given, as well as the date the new justice took the oath of office. *o*=oath of office taken, *d*=died, *r*=resigned or retired, *rj*=recess appointment rejected by Senate, *p*=promoted from associate justice to chief justice.

c. Volumes of *United States Reports* in which the actions of each natural court generally may be found. Because of the way decisions were published prior to the twentieth century, these volume numbers may not contain all of the decisions of a given natural court. They do, however, provide a general guide to the location of each natural court's published decisions. Natural courts of short duration may have little business published in the reports.

THE AMERICAN LEGAL SYSTEM

FEDERAL COURTS	STATE COURTS
HIGHEST APPELLATE COURT	
U.S. Supreme Court	State Supreme Court[1]
INTERMEDIATE APPELLATE COURTS	
U.S. Court of Appeals	Courts of Appeals[2]
Court of Appeals for the Federal Circuit	
TRIAL COURTS OF GENERAL JURISDICTION	
U.S. District Courts	District Courts[3]
TRIAL COURTS OF LIMITED JURISDICTION	
Examples include:	*Examples include:*
Rail Reorganization Court	Juvenile Court
Court of Federal Claims	Family Court
Court of International Trade	Traffic Court
Tax Court	Small Claims Court
	Justice of the Peace
	Magistrate Court

1. Sometimes called Supreme Judicial Court or Court of Appeals.
2. These courts exist in about two-thirds of all states. They are sometimes called Superior or District Courts.
3. Sometimes called circuit courts, superior courts, or supreme courts.

THE PROCESSING OF CASES

OCCURS THROUGHOUT TERM

Court Receives Requests for Review (4,000-6,000)
- appeals (e.g., suits under the Civil Rights and Voting Rights Acts)
- certification (requests by lower courts for answers to legal questions)
- petitions for writ of certiorari (most common request for review)
- requests for original review

OCCURS THROUGHOUT TERM

Cases Are Docketed
- original docket (cases coming under its original jurisdiction)
- appellate docket (all other cases)

OCCURS THROUGHOUT TERM

Justices Review Docketed Cases
- Chief justice, in consultation with the associate justices and their staffs, prepares discuss lists (approximately one quarter of docketed cases)
- Chief justice circulates discuss lists prior to conferences

FRIDAYS

Conferences
- selection of cases for review, for denial of review
- Rule of Four: Four or more justices must agree to review most cases

BEGINS MONDAYS AFTER CONFERENCE

Announcement of Action on Cases

Clerk Sets Date for Oral Argument
- usually not less than three months after the Court has granted review

Attorneys File Briefs
- appellant must file within forty-five days from when Court granted review
- appellee must file within thirty days of receipt of appellant's brief

SEVEN TWO-WEEK SESSIONS, FROM OCTOBER THROUGH APRIL ON MONDAYS, TUESDAYS, WEDNESDAYS

Oral Arguments
- Court typically hears four cases per day, with each case receiving one hour of Court's time

WEDNESDAY AFTERNOONS, FRIDAYS

Conferences
- discussion of cases
- tentative votes

Assignment of Majority Opinion

Drafting and Circulation of Opinions

Issuing and Announcing of Opinions

Reporting of Opinions
- U.S. Reports (U.S.) (official reporter system)
- Lawyers' Edition (L.Ed.)
- Supreme Court Reporter (S.Ct.)
- U.S. Law Week (U.S.L.W.)
- electronic reporter systems (WESTLAW, LEXIS)
- Project Hermes (accessed though bitnet, internet, or National Public Telecomputing Network)

SOURCE: Lee Epstein, Jeffrey A. Segal, Harold J. Spaeth, Thomas G. Walker, *The Supreme Court Compendium: Data, Decisions, and Developments* (Washington, D.C.: Congressional Quarterly, 1994), Figure 1-1.

SUPREME COURT CALENDAR

Activity	Time
Start of term	First Monday in October
Oral argument cycle	October–April: Mondays, Tuesdays, Wednesdays in seven two-week sessions
Recess cycle	October–April: two or more consecutive weeks after two weeks of oral argument; Christmas, Easter holidays
Conferences	Wednesday afternoon following Monday oral arguments (discussion of four Monday cases)
	Friday following Tuesday, Wednesday oral arguments (discussion of eight Tuesday–Wednesday cases; certiorari petitions)
	Friday before two-week oral argument period
Majority opinion assignment	Following oral arguments/conferences
Opinion announcement	Throughout term with bulk coming in spring/summer
Summer recess	Late June/early July until first Monday in October
Initial conference	Late September (resolve old business, consider certiorari petitions from the summer)

BRIEFING SUPREME COURT CASES

1. **What is the name of the case?**
   The name is important because it *generally* reveals which party is asking the Court to review the case. The name appearing first is usually (but not always) the appellant/petitioner, the party that lost in the court below.

2. **In what year did the Supreme Court decide the case?**
   The year is important because it will help to put the case into a legal and historical context. See Appendix 4 for more detail.

3. **What circumstances triggered the dispute?**

4. **What statute or action triggered the dispute?**

5. **What provision of the Constitution is at issue?**

6. **What is the basic legal question(s) the Court is being asked to address?**

7. **What was the outcome of the dispute?**

8. **How did the majority reach its decision? What was its legal reasoning?**

9. **What legal doctrine, standards, or policy did the majority announce?**

10. **What other views (dissents, concurrences) were expressed?**

AN EXAMPLE: *National League of Cities v. Usery* (1976)

1. Case Name. *National League of Cities v. Usery*
2. Year Case Decided by Supreme Court. *1976*
3. Facts that Triggered the Dispute. *In 1974 Congress required the states and their subdivisions to abide by established minimum wage and maximum hour work requirements. The National League of Cities, along with another organization and various cities and states, brought this action against Secretary of Labor W. J. Usery to challenge the constitutionality of the congressional enactment.*
4. Statute. *National League of Cities et al. launched this suit to challenge 1974 amendments to the Fair Labor Standards Act of 1938 (FLSA). This amendment expanded the scope of the FLSA's minimum wage and maximum hour provisions so that virtually all state public employees, who were excluded in the original legislation, were brought under its reach.*
5. Provision of the Constitution. *National League of Cities et al. alleged that the 1974 amendments, enacted by Congress under its power to regulate commerce, infringed on states' rights under the Tenth Amendment.*
6. Legal Question. *Do the 1974 amendments to the Fair Labor Standards Act constitute an infringement on states' rights?*
7. Outcome. *In a 5–4 ruling, the Court held for National League of Cities et al.*
8. Legal Reasoning of the Majority. *In delivering the opinion of the Court, Justice William H. Rehnquist held that:*
   a. there are "attributes of sovereignty attaching to every state government which may not be impaired by Congress, not because Congress may lack an affirmative grant of legislative authority to reach the matter, but because the Constitution prohibis it from exercising the authority in that manner."
   b. in this instance, the amendments fall within the reach of the commerce clause. But they infringe, to an impermissible degree, on State sovereignty. That is, they impair the State's "ability to function

State sovereignty. That is, they impair the State's "ability to function effectively in a federal system."

9. Legal Doctrine. The majority:

a. *established a legal standard that prohibited the exercise of congressional power "so as to force directly upon the States its choices as to how essential decisions regarding the conduct of integral governmental function are to be made."*

b. *did not specify precisely the meaning of the term "integral governmental functions," but wrote that Congress could not displace functions that are "essential to [the] separate and independent existence of the states." It also provided some examples of activities outside of congressional authority: fire prevention, sanitation, public health, and parks and recreation.*

c. *overruled a previous decision* (Maryland v. Wirtz, *1968) in which the Court ruled that Congress could prescribe regulations for employees, regardless of whether their employer is a state.*

10. Other Points of View.

a. Justice Blackmun concurred: *the Court is adopting a "balancing approach" to federal-state relations.*

b. Justice Brennan (joined by White and Marshall) dissented: *the majority repudiates well-settled principles of constitutional interpretation.*

1. *"Nothing in the Tenth Amendment constitutes a limitation on congressional exercise powers delegated by the Constitution to Congress," including the authority to regulate commerce.*

2. *The majority opinion is a "usurpation of the role reserved for the political process by their purported discovery in the Constitution of a restraint derived" from state sovereignty on congressional power under the commerce clause. It "can only be regarded as a transparent cover for invalidating a congressional judgment with which they disagree."*

c. Justice Stevens dissented: *the majority's opinion means that Congress "may not interfere with a sovereign State's inherent right to pay a substandard wage to the janitor at the state capitol. The principle on which the holding rests is difficult to perceive."*

A fortiori With greater force or reason.

Abstention A doctrine or policy of the federal courts to refrain from deciding a case so that the issues involved may first be definitively resolved by state courts.

Acquittal A decision by a court that a person charged with a crime is not guilty.

Advisory opinion An opinion issued by a court indicating how it would rule on a question of law should such a question come before it in an actual case. Federal courts do not hand down advisory opinions, but some state courts do.

Affidavit A written statement of facts voluntarily made under oath or affirmation.

Affirm To uphold a decision of a lower court.

Aggravating circumstances Conditions that increase the seriousness of a crime but are not a part of its legal definition.

Amicus curiae "Friend of the court." A person (or group), not a party to a case, who submits views (usually in the form of written briefs) on how the case should be decided.

Ante Prior to.

Appeal The procedure by which a case is taken to a superior court for a review of the lower court's decision.

Appellant The party dissatisfied with a lower court ruling who appeals the case to a superior court for review.

Appellate jurisdiction The legal authority of a superior court to review and render judgment on a decision by a lower court.

Appellee The party usually satisfied with a lower court ruling against whom an appeal is taken.

Arguendo In the course of argument.

Arraignment A formal stage of the criminal process in which the defendants are brought before a judge, are confronted with the charges against them, and enter a plea to those charges.

Arrest Physically taking into custody or otherwise depriving freedom of a person suspected of violating the law.

Attainder, Bill of A legislative act declaring a person or easily identified group of people guilty of a crime and imposing punishments without the benefit of a trial. Such legislative acts are prohibited by the United States Constitution.

Bail A security deposit, usually in the form of cash or bond, which allows those accused of crimes to be released from jail and guarantees their appearance at trial.

Balancing test A process of judicial decision making in which the court weighs the relative merits of the rights of the individual against the interests of the government.

Bench trial A trial, without a jury, conducted before a judge.

Bicameral A legislature, such as the U.S. Congress, with two houses.

Bona fide Good faith.

Brandeis brief A legal argument that stresses economic and sociological evidence along with traditional legal authorities. Named after Louis Brandeis, who pioneered its use.

Brief A written argument of law and fact submitted to the court by an attorney representing a party having an interest in a lawsuit.

Case law Law that has evolved from past court decisions, as opposed to law created by legislative acts.

Case or controversy rule The constitutional requirement that courts may only hear real disputes brought by adverse parties.

Case A legal dispute or controversy brought to a court for resolution.

Certification A procedure whereby a lower court requests that a superior court rule on specified legal questions so that the lower court may correctly apply the law.

Certiorari, Writ of An order of an appellate court to an inferior court to send up the records of a case that the appellate court has elected to review. The primary method by which the U.S. Supreme Court exercises its discretionary jurisdiction to accept appeals for a full hearing.

Circuit courts of appeal The intermediate level appellate courts in the federal system having jurisdiction over a particular region.

Civil law Law that deals with the private rights of individuals (e.g., property, contracts, negligence), as contrasted with criminal law.

Class action A lawsuit brought by one or more persons who represent themselves and all others similarly situated.

Collateral estoppel A rule of law that prohibits an already settled issue from being relitigated in another form.

Comity The principle by which the courts of one jurisdiction give respect and deference to the laws and legal decisions of another jurisdiction.

Common law Law that has evolved from usage and custom as reflected in the decisions of courts.

Concurrent powers Authority that may be exercised by both the state and federal governments.

Concurring opinion An opinion that agrees with the result reached by the majority, but disagrees as to the appropriate rationale for reaching that result.

Consent decree A court-ratified agreement voluntarily reached by parties to settle a lawsuit.

Constitutional court A court created under authority of Article III of the Constitution. Judges serve for terms of good behavior and are protected against having their salaries reduced by the legislature.

Contempt A purposeful failure to carry out an order of a court (civil contempt) or a willful display of disrespect for the court (criminal contempt).

Contraband Articles that are illegal to possess.

Criminal law Law governing the relationship between individuals and society. Deals with the enforcement of laws and the punishment of those who, by breaking laws, commit crimes.

Curtilage The land and outbuildings immediately adjacent to a home and regularly used by its occupants.

De facto In fact, actual.

De jure As a result of law or official government action.

De minimis Small or unimportant. A de minimis issue is considered one too trivial for a court to consider.

De novo New, from the beginning.

Declaratory judgment A court ruling determining a legal right or interpretation of the law, but not imposing any relief or remedy.

Defendant A party at the trial level being sued in a civil case or charged with a crime in a criminal case.

Demurrer A motion to dismiss a lawsuit in which the defendant admits to the facts alleged by the plaintiff but contends that those facts are insufficient to justify a legal cause of action.

Deposition Sworn testimony taken out of court.

Dicta; Obiter dicta Those portions of a judge's opinion that are not essential to deciding the case.

Directed verdict An action by a judge ordering a jury to return a specified verdict.

Discovery A pretrial procedure whereby one party to a lawsuit gains access to information or evidence held by the opposing party.

Dissenting opinion A formal written expression by a judge who disagrees with the result reached by the majority.

Distinguish A court's explanation of why a particular precedent is inapplicable to the case under consideration.

District courts The trial courts of general jurisdiction in the federal system.

Diversity jurisdiction The authority of federal courts to hear cases in which a party from one state is suing a party from another state.

Docket The schedule of cases to be heard by a court.

Double jeopardy The trying of a defendant a second time for the same offense. Prohibited by the Fifth Amendment to the Constitution.

Due process Government procedures that follow principles of essential fairness.

En banc An appellate court hearing with all the judges of the court participating.

Enjoin An order from a court requiring a party to do or refrain from doing certain acts.

Equity Law based on principles of fairness rather than strictly applied statutes.

Error, Writ of An order issued by an appeals court commanding a lower court to send up the full record of a case for review.

Ex parte A hearing in which only one party to a dispute is present.

Ex post facto law A criminal law passed by the legislature and made applicable to acts committed prior to passage of the law. Prohibited by the U.S. Constitution.

Ex rel Upon information from. Used to designate a court case instituted by the government but instigated by a private party.

Ex vi termini From the force or very meaning of the term or expression.

Exclusionary rule A principle of law that illegally gathered evidence may not be admitted in court.

Exclusive powers Powers reserved for either the federal government or the state governments, but not exercised by both.

Federal question A legal issue based on the U.S. Constitution, laws, or treaties.

Felony A serious criminal offense, usually punishable by incarceration of one year or more.

Grand jury A panel of twelve to twenty-three citizens who review prosecutorial evidence to determine if there are sufficient grounds to issue an indictment binding an individual over for trial on criminal charges.

Guilty A determination that a person accused of a criminal offense is legally responsible as charged.

Habeas corpus "You have the body." A writ issued to determine if a person held in custody is being unlawfully detained or imprisoned.

Harmless error An error occurring in a court proceeding that is insufficient in magnitude to justify the overturning of the court's final determination.

In camera A legal hearing held in the judge's chambers or otherwise in private.

Indictment A document issued by a grand jury officially charging an individual with criminal violations and binding the accused over for trial.

Information A document, serving the same purpose as an indictment, but issued directly by the prosecutor.

In forma pauperis "In the form of a pauper." A special status granted to indigents that allows them to proceed without payment of court fees and to be exempt from certain procedural requirements.

Injunction A writ prohibiting the person to whom it is directed from committing certain specified acts.

In re "In the matter of." The designation used in a judicial proceeding in which there are no formal adversaries.

In rem An act directed against a thing and not against a person.

Immunity An exemption from prosecution granted in exchange for testimony.

Incorporation The process whereby provisions of the Bill of Rights are declared to be included in the due process guarantee of the Fourteenth Amendment and made applicable to state and local governments.

Infra Below.

Interlocutory decree A provisional action that temporarily settles a legal question pending the final determination of a dispute.

Inter alia Among other things.

Judgment of the court The final ruling of a court, independent of the legal reasoning supporting it.

Judicial activism A philosophy that courts should not be reluctant to review and if necessary strike down legislative and executive actions.

Judicial restraint A philosophy that courts should defer to the legislative and executive branches whenever possible.

Judicial review The authority of a court to determine the constitutionality of acts committed by the legislative and executive branches and to strike down acts judged to be in violation of the Constitution.

Jurisdiction The authority of a court to hear and decide legal disputes and to enforce its rulings.

Justiciable Capable of being heard and decided by a court.

Legislative court A court created by Congress under authority of Article I of the Constitution to assist in carrying out the powers of the legislature.

Litigant A party to a lawsuit.

Magistrate A low level judge with limited authority.

Mandamus "We command." A writ issued by a court commanding a public official to carry out a particular act or duty.

Mandatory jurisdiction A case that a court is required to hear.

Marque and reprisal An order from the government of one country requesting and legitimizing the seizure of persons and property of another country. Prohibited by the Constitution.

Merits The central issues of a case.

Misdemeanor A less serious criminal act, usually punishable by less than one year of incarceration.

Mistrial A trial that is prematurely ended by a judge because of procedural irregularities.

Mitigating circumstances Conditions that lower the moral blame of a criminal act, but do not justify or excuse it.

Moot Unsettled or undecided. A question presented in a lawsuit that cannot be answered by a court either because the issue has resolved itself or conditions have so changed that the court is unable to grant the requested relief.

Motion A request made to a court for a certain ruling or action.

Natural law Laws considered applicable to all persons in all nations because they are thought to be basic to human nature.

Nolle prosequi The decision of a prosecutor to drop criminal charges against an accused.

Nolo contendere No contest. A plea entered by a criminal defendant in which the accused does not admit guilt but submits to sentencing and punishment as if guilty.

Opinion of the court An opinion announcing the judgment and reasoning of a court endorsed by a majority of the judges participating.

Order A written command issued by a judge.

Original jurisdiction The authority of a court to try a case and to decide it, as opposed to appellate jurisdiction.

Per curiam An unsigned or collectively written opinion issued by a court.

Per se In and of itself.

Petitioner A party seeking relief in court.

Petit jury A trial court jury to decide criminal or civil cases.

Plaintiff The party who brings a legal action to court for resolution or remedy.

Plea bargain An arrangement in a criminal case in which the defendant agrees to plead guilty in return for the prosecutor reducing the criminal charges or recommending a lenient sentence.

Plurality opinion An opinion announcing the judgment of a court with supporting reasoning that is not endorsed by a majority of the justices participating.

Police powers The power of the state to regulate for the health, safety, morals, and general welfare of its citizens.

Political question An issue more appropriate for determination by the legislative or executive branch than the judiciary.

Precedent A previously decided case that serves as a guide for deciding a current case.

Preemption A doctrine under which an area of authority previously left to the states is, by act of Congress, brought into the exclusive jurisdiction of the federal government.

Prima facie "At first sight." A case that is sufficient to prevail unless effectively countered by the opposing side.

Pro bono publico "For the public good." Usually refers to legal representation done without fee for some charitable or public purpose.

Pro se A person who appears in court without an attorney.

Quash To annul, vacate, or totally do away with.

Ratio decidendi A court's primary reasoning for deciding a case the way it did.

Recuse The action of a judge not to participate in a case because of conflict of interest or other disqualifying condition.

Remand To send a case back to an inferior court for additional action.

Res judicata A legal issue that has been finally settled by a court judgment.

Respondent The party against whom a legal action is filed.

Reverse An action by an appellate court setting aside or changing a decision of a lower court.

Ripeness A condition in which a legal dispute has evolved to the point where the issues it presents can be effectively resolved by a court.

Selective incorporation The policy of the Supreme Court to decide incorporation issues on a case-by-case, right-by-right basis.

Solicitor general Justice Department official whose office represents the federal government in all litigation before the U.S. Supreme Court.

Standing; standing to sue The right of parties to bring legal actions because they are directly affected by the legal issues raised.

Stare decisis "Let the decision stand." The doctrine that once a legal issue has been settled it should be followed as precedent in future cases presenting the same question.

State action An action taken by an agency or official of a state or local government.

Stay To stop or suspend.

Strict construction Narrow interpretation of the provisions of laws.

Subpoena ad testificandum An order compelling a person to testify before a court, legislative hearing, or grand jury.

Subpoena duces tecum An order compelling a person to produce a document or other piece of physical evidence that is relevant to issues pending before a court, legislative hearing, or grand jury.

Sub silentio "Under silence." A court action taken without explicit notice or indication.

Summary judgment A decision by a court made without a full hearing or without receiving briefs or oral arguments.

Supra Above.

Temporary restraining order A judicial order prohibiting certain challenged actions from being taken prior to a full hearing on the question.

Test A criterion or set of criteria used by courts to determine if certain legal thresholds have been met or constitutional provisions violated.

Three-judge court A special federal court made up of appellate and trial court judges created to expedite the processing of certain issues made eligible for such priority treatment by congressional statute.

Ultra vires Actions taken that exceed the legal authority of the person or agency performing them.

Usus loquendi The common usage of ordinary language.

Vacate To void or rescind.

Vel non "Or not."

Venireman A juror.

Venue The geographical jurisdiction in which a case is heard.

Voir dirè "To speak the truth." The stage of a trial in which potential jurors are questioned to determine their competence to sit in judgment of a case.

Warrant A judicial order authorizing an arrest or search and seizure.

Writ A written order of a court commanding the recipient to perform or not to perform certain specified acts.

SUBJECT INDEX

Abernathy, M. Glenn, 365n7, 526n2
Abortion, 547–570
  amicus curiae briefs, 566
  consent requirements, 559 (table), 560, 568, 569
  constitutional amendment proposals, 19, 558
  exclusionary rule case, 586
  funding restrictions, 560–561
  jurisdiction change proposal, 82 (table)
  justices' approaches, 361, 569 (table)
  justices' diminishing support (table), 566
  mandatory wait period, 568 (box), 569
  mootness concept, 85
  privacy right, 525, 526, 547–558
  protest demonstrations, 474, 475
  public opinion, 78, 558 (chart)
  regulation by pregnancy stage (table), 556
  restrictive approaches (box), 564
  state legislative action (chart), 548
  substantive due process, 338
Abraham, Henry J., 46n62, 366n13, 368n19, 369n21
Absolutist standard (speech rights), 457 (table)
ACLU See American Civil Liberties Union
"Actual malice" standard, 522–523
Ad Hoc Balancing standard (speech rights),
    448–449, 457 (table)
Adamany, David, 75–78
Adams, John, 56, 66–67, 97, 150–151, 172
Adams, Samuel, 13, 580
Adarand Constructors, Inc., 700
Admiralty issues, 64
Advisory opinions, 83–84
Affirmative action, 690–706
  government contractors, 690, 698–705
  higher education, 691–697
  judicial principles (box), 705
  opposition, 690–691
  police promotions, 697
African Americans See Racial discrimination; Slav-
    ery
Age Discrimination Act, 211 (table)
Agenda allocations
  civil liberties focus, 446
  solicitor general's role, 46
  substantive rights cases (graph), 361
Agnew, Spiro, 154
Agricultural Adjustment Act of 1933, 232, 275–277
Agricultural Adjustment Act of 1938, 246, 247 (table)
Agricultural policies

  commerce regulation, 246, 247 (table), 256
  tax and spend power, 275–277
Aguillar, Don, 409
Air Force Dress Code, 375–377
Airport solicitation, 475
Akron Center for Reproductive Health, 563
Alabama Department of Public Safety, 697
Alcoholic beverage regulation
  commerce regulation, 227
  Prohibition repeal amendment, 17
  sex discrimination, 671
  substantive due process, 314, 317–318
  tax and spend power, 271, 277–280
Aliens, 85
Alimony, 675
Allgeyer Co., 320
Allied Structural Steel Co., 308–309
Ambassadors, 168, 171
American Association of University Women, 550
American Bar Association, 368, 369n20
American Civil Liberties Union (ACLU)
  abortion cases, 547, 550, 562, 563
  congressional investigations, 130
  criminal rights, 578, 587n11
  economic discrimination, 677
  history, 436, 444, 476
  press freedoms, 491, 506
  privacy cases, 537
  religious establishment issues, 409, 419
  sex discrimination cases, 667, 668, 669, 671
  speech rights cases, 443, 445, 462–463, 476, 478
  Women's Rights Project, 50
American College of Obstetricians and Gynecolo-
    gists, 550, 565
American Education Association, 677
American Federation of Labor-Congress of Industri-
    al Organizations (AFL-CIO), 368n19
American Jewish Congress, 478
American Sugar Refining Co., 227
American Union Against Militarism, 436, 444
Amicus curiae, 46–51, 566, 587n11
  brief citation by justice (table), 51
  opinions containing briefs (graph), 48
  solicitor general's success rate (table), 47
  summary (box), 49
Amish people, 374, 375
Amnesty, 81–82
Anarchy laws, 442, 445, 454

Anderson, C. Ian, 327n13, 327n15
Animal sacrifice, 386–387
Anti-Defamation League of B'nai B'rith, 478
Anti-evolutionary laws, 406–408
Anti-Federalists, 13, 65–66, 261
Anti-Semitism, 470–471, 490
Antitrust legislation, 225, 226–228
Appeals
  right of, 576, 636
  right to counsel, 616–617
Appeals courts
  criminal rights, 576
  en banc hearings, 375n23
  establishment, 64, 65, 66
Appellate jurisdiction
  authority, 63 (box), 65
  constraints, 79–82
  elimination proposals (table), 82
Appointment power, 63, 163–165
Appointments Clause, 164, 165
Apportionment of legislatures, 86–88, 719–725
Apportionment of taxes, 261–263
Armbands, 462
Armstrong, Scott, 624n12
Arms manufacturing, 374–375
Arms sales, 133, 169–170
Arraignment, 575
Arrest, searches incident to, 581, 585
Articles of Confederation
  accomplishments, 4–5
  amendment process, 17
  commerce regulation, 4, 218–219
  congressional powers, 4, 8, 97–99
  economic liberty, 288, 292
  executive powers, 149
  federal-state relations, 4, 10
  structure, powers of government, 4, 5 (chart), 55
  tax and spend power, 4, 99, 259–260
Ashe, Bob, 638
Asian American Legal Defense and Education Fund,
    478
Asian Law Caucus, 478
Asian Pacific American Legal Center, 478
Assembly right, 22, 445
Assistance, writs of, 580
Assisted suicide, 540, 547
Association of American Publishers, 478
Association rights, 33, 34, 43

abortion, 548
  privacy right, 525
At-large constituencies, 708, 719n5
Attorneys *See* Counsel, right to
Attorneys, U.S., 575
Automobiles
  license plate slogans, 487–488
  search and seizure protections, 584
Aviation
  foreign arms sales, 133

Bad Tendency test (speech restrictions), 442, 443,
    447–448, 449, 453, 457 (table)
Bail, 22n, 575
Bailey, J.W., 274
Bailey, John, 102 (table)
Baker, John S., 365n10
Bakery workers, 321–322, 527
Bakke, Allan, 692
Balanced budget amendment, 17, 21
Balanced Budget and Emergency Deficit Control Act
    of 1985, 146 (box), 155–156
Balancing of interests, 34–35
  religious exercise, 373
  speedy trial, 618
  substantive due process, 318, 320
Baldus, David, 635
Baldus study, 635–636
Baldwin, Henry, 100 (table)
Baldwin, Roger, 444
Ball, Howard, 713n3
Bank of the United States, 118–121, 193–196, 197
Bankruptcy laws, 292, 294–295
Banning, Lance, 4
Barber, Sotirios, 137
Barbour, Phillip P., 100 (table)
Bardes, Barbara A., 5n
Barenblatt, Lloyd, 130–131
Barker, Lucius J., 506n9
Barker, Twiley W. Jr., 506n9
Barker, Willie, 618
Barnette family, 368–369, 483–487
Barnum, David G., 420n48, 421n49
Barron, Clarence W., 329 (box)
Barron, John, 340
Batson, James, 619
Baum, Lawrence, 33n34, 45n61, 47nn65–66, 78–79
Baxter, Maurice G., 298n
Beacon Press, 114–116
Beard, Charles A., 7, 285
Becker, Frank, 420
Belz, Herman, 98, 330n17
Berger, Victor L., 102 (table)
Beth, Loren, 265
Betts, Smith, 612
Bible-reading in schools, 394 (table), 419 (table), 420
Bicameral legislatures, 97–98, 718, 721
Bifurcated trials, 625
Bill of Rights *See also* specific amendments
  applied to states, 21–23, 25, 340–341
  Constitution ratification debates, 11, 14–17, 364
  criminal rights, 573, 579
  Preferred Freedoms philosophy, 35, 446
Bill of Rights Committee (ABA), 369n20
Bills of attainder, 15
Birkby, Robert, 420
Birth control
  information dissemination, 43, 337–338, 506
  privacy right, 525, 526, 528, 529–539
Biskupic, Joan, 171n4
Bituminous Coal Conservation Act of 1935, 232, 237
Black Americans *See* Racial discrimination; Slavery

Black Caucus, 727
Black, Earl, 716n
Black, Galen, 379
Black, Hugo, 3
  amicus curiae brief citations, 51 (table)
  career, 3, 28, 230
  on congressional powers, 131 (box)
  on criminal rights, 613–615, 616
  ideology, 36 (table)
  legislation overturn votes, 40 (table)
  legislative experience, 100 (table)
  on press freedoms, 496
  on privacy right, 531–534, 535, 555
  on religious establishment, 392–393, 394, 395, 419,
    421
  on religious exercise, 369
  on school desegregation, 683
  on speech rights, 27–29, 451–452, 453, 457 (table),
    462
  on *stare decisis*, 33–34
  on voting rights, 710–712
  on war powers, 176–179
Black, Merle, 716n
Black Monday, 231
Blackmun, Harry A., 161 (illus.)
  on abortion, 550–569
  affirmative action, 698
  amicus curiae brief citations, 51 (table)
  career, 456, 557, 699
  on criminal rights, 594, 619
  on death penalty, 624, 636, 637–638
  on federal-state relations, 210, 212–214, 215–216
  legislation overturn votes, 40 (table)
  on press freedoms, 496–497
  on privacy right, 538–540, 544–547
  on property takings, 351, 354–355
  on religious establishment, 402 (table), 416–418,
    422, 428–429, 432
  on religious exercise, 373–374, 377, 385–388
  school desegregation, 688, 689
  on substantive due process, 338
Blacks *See* Racial discrimination; Slavery
Blair, John Jr., 100 (table)
Blaisdell, John and Rosella, 303–304
Blatchford, Samuel
  on substantive due process, 318
Blue laws, 370–373
Bork, Robert
  Court nomination, 565
  Cox dismissal, 159
  on federal-state relations, 209
  on original intent, 25, 26
Bowman, James E., 619
Bowsher, Charles A., 155
Bradley, Joseph P.
  on sex discrimination, 666
  on substantive due process, 312, 315–316, 317
Bradwell, Myra, 666
Brandeis Brief, 329
Brandeis, Louis D., 441
  career, 246, 328–329
  on federal-state relations, 185
  on judicial power constraints, 93–94
  New Deal decisions, 230, 232, 240
  on privacy right, 526, 528–529, 536, 540
  on speech rights, 440, 443, 457 (table)
  on substantive due process, 312, 329–330, 331
    (table)
Brandenburg, Clarence, 456
Branzburg, Paul M., 498
Braunfeld, Abraham, 370
Brennan, William J. Jr., 161 (illus.)

abortion cases, 563, 566 (table), 567
affirmative action programs, 697, 698
amicus curiae brief citations, 51 (table)
on balancing, minority interests, 35
career, 454, 505, 567, 699
on criminal rights, 584, 594
on death penalty, 624, 631–632, 634, 636
on federal-state relations, 210, 216
legislation overturn votes, 40 (table)
original intent doctrine, 26
on political questions, 88–90
on press freedoms, 496, 504, 506–507, 512–513,
    516–522
on privacy right, 43, 530–531, 534, 535 (table),
    538–540, 544–547
on property takings, 344–346, 351
on religious establishment, 409–412, 416, 422
on religious exercise, 371, 372–373, 377, 378,
    382–385, 388 (table)
on sex discrimination, 671–673, 675
on speech rights, 464–467
on tax and spend power, 272
Brenner, Saul, 42n51
Brewer, David J.
  on substantive due process, 319
Breyer, Stephen
  abortion cases, 569
  affirmative action programs, 704–705
  career, 578, 594
  on death penalty, 636
  on federal-state relations, 216 (table)
  on minority legislative districts, 732–734
  religious establishment, 414, 418
  religious exercise, 388 (table)
Bribery
  speech or debate cases, 115 (table)
  Teapot Dome scandal, 127
  Yazoo land fraud, 293–294
Brigham, John, 365
Brown, Henry B.
  on racial discrimination, 654, 655–656
Brown, John Y., 102 (table)
Brown, Linda Carol, 661 (photo), 663
Brown, Oliver, 663
Brown, Robert E., 7n20
Brownell, Herbert, 577
Bryan, William Jennings, 407
Bryant, Paul, 522–523
Buckner, Linda Brown, 663 (box)
Budget process, 155–156
Building permits, 355
Burger Court
  amicus curiae citations, 50
  criminal rights cases, 576 (graph), 606, 617
  economic, civil liberties decisions, 38 (graph)
  federal-state relations, 192 (table)
  First Amendment claims, 360 (graph)
  legislation overturns, 40
  obscenity standards (table), 512
  precedents overruled, 33 (table)
  privacy right cases, 540
  religious establishment cases, 389, 395–403,
    420–424
  religious exercise cases, 373–377
  speech rights cases, 463
  standing to sue, 93
Burger, Warren, 161 (illus.)
  on abortion, 556, 563, 565, 566 (table), 569
  affirmative action programs, 698
  amicus curiae brief citations, 51 (table)
  Blackmun career, 557
  career, 307, 456, 508, 577, 578, 662

on criminal rights, 593, 594, 606
on death penalty, 624, 631
on executive privilege, 158, 160–163
on federal-state relations, 216 (table)
ideology, 37
judicial role, 39
legislation overturn votes, 40 (table)
on legislative vetoes, 144–145
on press freedoms, 496, 508–512
on property takings, 346
on religious establishment, 396–397, 398–401, 402
    (table), 403, 415, 422, 423–424
on religious exercise, 373–374
on school desegregation, 683–687
on sex discrimination, 669–670
on speech rights, 488
Burr, Aaron, 151, 158
Burton, Harold H.
    amicus curiae brief citations, 51 (table)
    legislation overturn votes, 40 (table)
    legislative experience, 100 (table)
Bush administration
    abortion cases, 566
    military base closings, 146 (box)
    minority legislative districts, 727
    religious establishment issues, 424, 425
    solicitor general's briefs, 47
Bush, George
    death penalty, 636
    flag desecration, 19, 468
    presidential succession, 153 (box)
    special prosecutors, 165
    Supreme Court appointments, 567
    war powers, 172
"Business affected with a public interest" doctrine,
    317, 332
Butchers' Benevolent Assn., 315
Butler, Pierce
    career, 246
    New Deal decisions, 230, 231, 232, 237–240, 245
    on substantive due process, 331 (table), 333
Butler, William M., 275–276
Butterfield, Alexander, 159
Butts, Wally, 522–523
Buxton, C. Lee, 529
Byrnes, James F., 100 (table)

Caldeira, Gregory A., 48n69, 23, 239n8
Calhoun, John C., 196
California Coastal Commission, 351
Campbell, John A.
    legislative experience, 100 (table)
    on substantive due process, 315
Capital gains taxes, 347–348
Capital punishment See Death penalty
Capitation taxes, 260, 263
Caplan, Lincoln, 563n25
Cardozo, Benjamin
    career, 230, 246
    on criminal rights, 586
    on delegated powers, 139, 140
    New Deal decisions, 230, 231, 240
Carriage taxes, 66, 261–263
Carswell, G. Harrold, 556
Carter administration
    legislative veto, 142–143
    solicitor general as amicus curiae, 47 (table)
Carter, Dan T., 611n1
Carter, James W., 237
Carter, Jimmy
    judicial appointments, 668
    on legislative veto, 142

treaty power, 89
Carter, Robert L., 659 (photo), 661
"Case and controversy" doctrine, 83
Casper, Jonathan, 45
Catholic church
    aid to hospitals, 389, 392
    holiday displays, 416
Catholic schools
    aid, religious establishment issues, 392, 395,
        397–401
    compulsory school attendance, 365–366
Catron, John, 296
Censorship
    justified imposition, 495
    Nazi Skokie march, 476–477
    prior restraint, 490–497
Census, 86, 719
Center for Constitutional Rights, 562
Center for Individual Rights, 478
Central Intelligence Agency, 92
Certiorari, writ of, 613
Chadha, Jagdish Rai, 142–143
Chafee, Zechariah Jr., 436n, 514n13
Chaplains
    military dress code, 375–377
    prayer in legislatures, 421–422
Chaplinsky, Walter, 469
Charities
    property tax exemption, 396
Charles River Bridge, 297–298
Chase, Harold, 20n23, 140n57, 210n16, 319n12,
    332n21
Chase, Salmon P.
    on jurisdiction, 79–82
    legislative experience, 100 (table)
    sex discrimination case, 666
Chase, Samuel, 210n10
    legislative experience, 100 (table)
    tax and spend power, 263
    on war powers, 175
Checks and balances
    constitutional principles, 8–10, 56, 57
    foreign policy powers, 170–171
    habeas corpus right, 174
    judicial constraints, 77–78
Chicago, Milwaukee, and St. Paul Railway, 318
Chicago Seven, 497
Chicago Tribune, 491
Child abuse
    victim testimony, 621
Child Labor Amendment, 18 (box), 19–20
Child labor regulation
    commerce regulation, 19n22, 201–206
    constitutional amendment proposal, 18 (box),
        19–20
    minimum wage, 330
    street sales, 369–370
    tax and spend power, 274
Child Labor Tax Act of 1919, 274
Children
    death penalty, 625n15
    obscenity standard, 506, 507
    parental notice, consent to abortion, 559, 560,
        562, 568 (box), 569
Children's Hospital of the District of Columbia, 330
Chilling effect
    press freedoms, 498, 504, 514
    speech rights, 438, 459–460
Chinese laundries, 648
Christmas displays, 415–418
Church-state separation See Religious establishment
Circuit Court Act of 1801, 66

Circuit courts See Appeals courts
Citizenship
    blacks, 199–201, 653–654
    national-state relationship, 644
Civil cases
    jury trial, 22n
    peremptory juror challenges, 619
Civil liberties See also specific rights and freedoms
    balancing in judicial decisions, 34–35
    constitutional principles, 10–11
    contrasted to civil rights, 643
    Supreme Court trends, 37 (table), 38 (graph), 132,
        360–361, 446
    war powers disputes, 173–177, 436
Civil Liberties Bureau, 444
Civil Rights Act of 1866, 650, 651
Civil Rights Act of 1870, 651
Civil Rights Act of 1871, 475, 651
Civil Rights Act of 1875, 650, 651, 654
Civil Rights Act of 1957, 651
Civil Rights Act of 1960, 651
Civil Rights Act of 1964
    affirmative action, 690–691
    commerce regulation, 250–252, 650
    sex discrimination, 667
    text, 651
Civil Rights Act of 1991, 47, 652
Civil rights movement See also School desegregation
    demonstrations, 456, 461, 471–474
    flag desecration, 462
    libel cases, 514–522, 523
    Marshall career, 660
    NAACP campaigns, 49–50, 658
    public accommodations integration, 249–252, 650
    Supreme Court support, 644, 660, 665–666
    voting rights, 713, 716, 717, 726
Civil Rights of Institutionalized Persons, 142 (box)
Civil War
    civil liberties, 436
    events leading to (table), 197
    federal debt, 263, 644
    federal-state relations, 187, 201
    war powers disputes, 172–175
Civil War Amendments, 644–645, 650
Clarendon Foundation, 478
Clark, David, 202–203
Clark, Tom C.
    amicus curiae brief citations, 51 (table)
    career, 448, 660 (box)
    on commerce regulation, 250–252
    on congressional investigations, 131 (box)
    on criminal rights, 587–590
    legislation overturn votes, 40 (table)
    privacy right, 535 (table)
    on religious establishment, 394–395, 419–420
    speech rights, 472
Clarke, John H.
    speech rights, 439–440, 442, 457 (table)
    substantive due process, 331 (table)
Clay, Henry, 3
Clear and Present Danger test (speech rights)
    439–440, 442–443, 445–447, 449, 457 (table)
Clear and Probable Danger standard (speech
    rights), 448, 449–453, 457 (table)
Cleland, John, 507
Clifford, Nathan
    legislative experience, 100 (table)
    on war powers, 175
Clinton administration
    abortion issues, 569
    separation of powers cases, 146 (box)
    solicitor general's briefs, 47

Clinton, Bill
  death penalty, 636
  executive immunity, 157–158
  special prosecutors, 165
  Supreme Court appointments, 578, 668
Clymer, Adam, 386n29
Coal industry regulation, 237, 309, 350
Coastal Licensing Act of 1793, 221
Coercion
  consent searches, 582
  religious establishment, 402 (table), 418, 432
  right not to speak, 482–488
  self-incrimination, 82 (table), 595–608, 622
Coffee, Linda, 549–550
Coke, Edward, 75
Cold war era, 448–449
Colleges and universities
  affirmative action, 691–697
  desegregation, 658, 689
  hate speech, 477
  religious establishment issues, 404, 406, 414
  sex discrimination, 675
Collins, Bruce Edward, 637–638
Collusive suits, 84–85
Commander in chief
  constitutional authority, 171
  executive powers, 168
  line of authority, 153 (box)
Commerce regulation, 218–258
  child labor, 19n22, 202
  congressional powers, 117, 138–140, 141 (table),
    218–225
  evolution of doctrine, 225–228, 248 (table)
  expansion of powers, 1937–1941 (table), 247
  federal police powers, 249–252
  federal-state relations, 201–207
  Marshall definition, 30–31, 219–225
  minority set-asides, 698–706
  New Deal developments, 229–249
  original intent, 218–219, 249–252, 256
  racial discrimination, 650, 655
  state powers, 252–257, 280, 283
  state restrictions struck (table), 257
  state taxes, 281–282
Communications regulation, 141 (table), 699
Communists
  congressional investigations, 128–132
  jurisdiction change proposals, 82 (table)
  labor union regulation, 448, 455
  speech rights, 436–437, 442–443
Community Education Program, 405
Compelling state interest
  abortion, 548, 550, 555, 563–564
  equal protection tests, 647
  privacy right, 528, 534
  religious exercise restrictions, 373–374, 377–378,
    386
  speech restrictions, 459
Complete Auto Transit, 282
Comptroller general, 155–156
Compulsory process, 22, 574 (table), 482
Comstock Act, 506
"Concurrent majority" doctrine, 196, 199
Confederate sympathizers, 173–175
Confederation government See Articles of Confederation
Confessions See Self-incrimination protection
Confrontation Clause, 22, 574 (table), 621–622
Congress See also House of Representatives; Senate
  appointment power, 164–165
  composition, structure, 97–98
  Confederation powers, 5 (chart)

constitutional authority, 7 (chart), 8–10, 57–58
  enumerated, implied powers, 117–126
  foreign policy powers, 170–171
  inherent powers, 132–136
  internal affairs, 101–116
  investigations, 32, 33, 34, 126–132
  powers summarized, 98–99, 116–117
  removal power, 166
  war powers, 171–172
Congress, members of See also Legislative representation
  compensation, 17
  elections, 707–708, 709
  excluded members (table), 102
  military commissions, 92
  qualifications for office, 101
  seating and discipline, 101–113
  speech and debate, 114–116
Congress of Industrial Organizations (CIO), 447
Congress of Racial Equality, 473–474
Congressional Budget Office, 155
Congressional districts
  apportionment issues, 719, 720–721, 725
  minority districts, 728–734
Congressional-executive relations
  checks and balances, 9 (chart)
  delegated powers, 137–140
  law enforcement, 155
  legislative veto, 140–147
  separation of powers cases (box), 146
Congressional-judicial relations
  checks and balances, 9 (chart), 47, 77
  delegated powers, 138
  jurisdiction change, 47, 80
Conscientious Objectors, Bureau of (ACLU), 444
Consent searches, 582
Constitution, U.S. See also specific amendments
  Art. I, 8, 30, 57, 86, 96–99, 644
  Art. I, Sec. 2, 101, 260, 707, 721
  Art. I, Sec. 3, 101
  Art. I, Sec. 4, 106, 707–708
  Art. I, Sec. 5, 101, 103
  Art. I, Sec. 6, 92, 101, 114
  Art. I, Sec. 8, 8, 91, 96, 99, 116–117, 171, 219, 260,
    295
  Art. I, Sec. 9, 15, 92, 174, 260
  Art. I, Sec. 10, 261, 280, 288, 292
  Art. II, 8, 57, 149, 150, 152
  Art. II, Sec. 2, 164, 168, 171
  Art. II, Sec. 3, 154, 168
  Art. III, 8, 57, 62–64, 79, 83, 90
  Art. III, Sec. 2, 63, 64, 79–80
  Art. IV, 86–87
  Art. V, 17, 19–20
  Art. VI, 99, 364
  Art. VII, 187
  principles, 8–11
  ratification, 13–17
Constitutional amendments See also specific amendments
  amendment process, 17–19
  Constitution flexibility, 7
  Court instigation, 19
  Court interpretation, 19–21
  methods (table), 18
  overturned Court decisions (box), 20
  proposed by Congress, rejected by states (box), 18
Constitutional Convention, 5–6, 13. See also Original intent
  delegate characteristics, 6–7, 62, 288
  delegates on Supreme Court, 263
  prayer session, 364, 422

Contempt citations
  congressional investigation power, 127–128, 129,
    130, 131
Content discrimination (speech restrictions), 460,
  475, 482
Continental Congress, 3–4
Contraceptives See Birth control
Contract obligations, 291–310
  corporate charters, 295–296
  definition, 292
  liberty of contract, 314–315, 320–336, 527
  Marshall interpretation, 293–295
  mortgage relief, 303–307
  original intent, 288, 291–293
  regulation for public good, 296–303, 307–310
Contract with America, 106
Cooley, Aaron, 253
Cooley, Thomas M., 316, 318–319
Cooperative federalism, 191–196, 206–216
Copperheads, 173–174
Copyrights, 271
Corporate charters, 120n20, 295–296
Corporate income taxes
  revenue impact of 16th Amendment, 269 (table)
Corsi, Jerome R., 468n25
Cortner, Richard C., 88n48, 366n14, 549n18
Corwin, Edward S., 76
Council of Revision, 63–64, 76
Counsel, right to
  appeals, 616–617
  applied to states by 14th Amendment, 22
  arraignment, 575
  criminal justice system summaries, 574 (table), 610
  indigent defendants, 597, 611–616
  jury selection, 619
  Miranda warnings, 607
  original intent, 610
  self-incrimination protection, 595–606
Court-appointed attorneys, 616
Courts See Judiciary
Cover, Albert D., 38n46
Covey, Frank Jr., 49n1
Cox, Archibald, 159
Cox, B. Elton, 473
Craig, Barbara Hinkson, 570n30
Craig, Curtis, 671
Craig, John, 340
Craig, Sandra Ann, 621–622
Creationism, 394, 406–414
Crescent City Live Stock Landing and Slaughter
  House Co., 315
Criminal rights See also Counsel, right to; Jury trial;
    Search and seizure protections; Self-incrimination protection
  constitutional basis (tables), 22, 574
  criminal justice system summary, 574–576
  Miranda warnings, 605–606, 607
  original intent, 573, 579–580, 610, 617, 618, 620,
    623, 636
  sentences, 622–638
  Supreme Court trends, 576–578
  voting, 718
Criminal speech, 458
Criminal syndicalism laws, 442, 443, 445, 456
Cross burnings, 361, 456, 477–482
Cross-examination of witnesses, 22, 622
Crosskey, W.W., 29–30
Crowninshield, Richard, 294–295
Cruel and unusual punishment, 22, 574 (table),
  622–623. See also Death penalty
Cruzan, Lester and Joyce, 542–547
Cruzan, Nancy Beth, 542–547

Curfews, 176–177
Currency motto, 415, 419
Curtis, Benjamin R.
  on commerce regulation, 253–255
  legislative experience, 100 (table)
Curtiss-Wright Export Corp., 132–133, 169
Cushing, William, 263n2
Cushman, Robert F., 262n1
Customs duties
  regulatory power, 273
  revenue impact of 16th Amendment, 269 (table)

Dagenhart, John, 202–203
Dagenhart, Reuben, 202–203
Dagenhart, Roland, 202–203
Dahl, Robert, 78
Dairy See Milk and dairy industry regulation
Danbury Baptist Association, 365, 388
Danelski, David J., 41, 42n51
Daniel, Peter, 100 (table)
Darby, Fred W., 206
Darrow, Clarence, 407, 408
Dartmouth College, 295
Darwinism
  Scopes trial, 407
  Social Darwinism, 316
Daugherty, Harry M., 127
Daugherty, Mally S., 127–128
Davis, David
  legislative experience, 100 (table)
  on war powers, 173, 175
Davis, John W. Jr., 178 (photo), 203, 663
Day, William R.
  on child labor regulation, 203–205
  on collusive suits, 84
  on criminal rights, 585
  substantive due process, 331 (table)
Days, Drew S. III, 47
Dean, John III, 159
Death penalty
  aggravating, mitigating facts, 625, 634
  constitutionality, 623–634
  precedents importance, 32–33
  public support, 77, 623, 633–634
  racial discrimination, 623–624, 635–636
  rape, 612n2
  right to counsel, 612, 613
Debs, Eugene V., 439, 468
Debtor-creditor relations, 292, 294–295, 301, 675
Declaration of Independence
  adoption, 3
  derivation of powers, 16
  equality concept, 643
Defense Department
  presidential succession, 153 (box)
  whistleblower case, 157
Democratic-Republicans (Jeffersonians), 118, 121,
    151, 295
DeFunis, Marco Jr., 85
DeJonge, Dirk, 445
Delau, Carl, 586–587
Desegregation See School desegregation
Devins, Neal, 527nn3–4, 569n29
Dies Committee, 129
DiGerlando, Benedict, 595
Direct taxes
  constitutional basis, 260
  definition, 261–263
  judicial review, 66
Dirksen, Everett, 17n20
Disabled persons
  aid to religious schools, 405

Discretionary appeals, 616–617
Discrimination See also Racial discrimination; Sex
    discrimination
  constitutional prohibition, 645–649
  equality approach to abortion, 569
  hate crimes, 39, 361, 474–482
  remedies, 681–706
Discrimination in education
  affirmative action, 691–697
  desegregation, 649, 658–665, 682–689
  school funding, 675–681
  sex discrimination, 675
Discrimination in employment
  affirmative action, 690–691, 697
  racial discrimination, 689
  sex discrimination, 39, 327–330, 332–333, 666–667
Discrimination in housing, 49–50, 650, 660 (box), 689
Discrimination in public accommodations,
    249–252, 650, 655, 689
Discrimination in taxation, 261, 272, 281–284, 647
District attorneys, 575
District courts
  establishment, 64, 65, 66
  school desegragation, 82 (table), 682–689
District of Columbia
  congressional representation, 18 (box)
  judicial appointments, 67
  school desegregation, 649
  school system investigation, 115 (table)
Dolan, Florence, 355
Dole, Elizabeth, 277
Domestic Tranquility Clause, 469
Dorrites, 86
Double jeopardy protection, 22, 574 (table), 576,
    636, 638
Douglas, William O.
  abortion cases, 562, 566 (table)
  amicus curiae brief citations, 51 (table)
  on appellate jurisdiction, 82
  on criminal rights, 616, 617
  on death penalty, 624, 633
  ideology, 36 (table)
  legislation overturn votes, 40 (table)
  on press freedoms, 496
  on privacy right, 43, 528n9, 529, 530, 534–535
  on religious establishment, 395, 396, 402 (table),
    415, 419, 421–422
  on religious exercise, 369
  on speech rights, 453–453, 457 (table), 471, 472
  on stare decisis, 32n31, 33
  on substantive due process, 337
  on voting rights, 717
Draft See Military draft
Drug control
  exclusionary rule, 593
  peyote in religious exercise, 378–386
  press reporters' privilege, 498
  regulatory taxes, 275
Dual federalism, 191, 192, 196–206, 314, 331–332
Ducat, Craig, 20n23, 140n57, 210n12, 319n12, 332n21
Due notice of criminal charges, 22, 574 (table)
Due Process Clause (5th Amendment)
  affirmative action, 690, 700
  commerce regulation, 231, 249
  death penalty, 623
  discrimination prohibition, 649, 665–666
  privacy right, 526–527
  substantive due process, 313, 314, 330
Due Process Clause (14th Amendment)
  abortion, 555, 558
  Bill of Rights applied to states, 22, 23, 442, 586
  death penalty, 623, 636

economic liberties, 288–289
  privacy right, 525–535, 540, 547
  property takings, 340–341
  sex discrimination, 667
  substantive due process, 312–338
  unincorporated rights, 22n, 575
Duval, Gabriel, 100 (table)

Eastland, Terry, 105 cap.
Economic discrimination
  right to counsel, 611–617
  school funding, 675–681
Economic liberties See also Contract obligations;
    Property rights; Substantive due process
  agenda allocations, 289 (graph), 290, 293
  congressional powers, 99
  summary, 287–290
  Supreme Court trends, 37 (table), 38 (graph)
Economic Stabilization Act of 1970, 209 (box)
Education See Colleges and universities; Private
    schools; Public schools
Eighth Amendment
  criminal rights, 573, 574 (table)
  provisions incorporated by 14th Amendment, 22
  punishment standards, 45, 622–623
  unincorporated provisions, 22n
Eisenhower administration
  solicitor general as amicus curiae, 47 (table)
Eisenhower, Dwight D., 455
  judicial appointments, 132, 454, 505 (box), 662
  on legislative veto, 142
  removal power, 168
Elastic Clause See Necessary and Proper Clause
Elections
  of executive, 150–151
  of representatives, 707–708, 709
  Electoral college, 58, 150–151
Elementary and Secondary Education Act of 1965, 91
Eleventh Amendment, 20 (box), 63n
Elliot, Martha J.H., 122n28, 125n31, 529n30, 587n10
Ellsworth, Oliver, 263n2
  legislative experience, 100 (table)
  resignation, 67
Elstad, Michael, 607
Elving, Ronald D., 172n5
Ely, John Hart, 29n11, 338, 558
Emergency Banking Act of 1933, 230
Emerson, John, 199
Emerson, Thomas I., 442n7, 529
Eminent domain power, 339, 340, 341
  state exercise, 340, 347
Employment See also Child labor regulation; Dis-
    crimination in employment; Labor relations reg-
    ulation; Wage and hour regulation
  religious conflicts, 371–373, 374–386
En banc hearings, 375n23
Encroachment principle (speech restrictions), 459
Endangered Species Act of 1973, 92
Endo, Mitsuye, 177
Energy policies, 307–308
Enforcement Acts of 1870, 1871, 709
Enforcement of judicial decisions
  Brown implementation, 665, 682–683
  executive powers, 157
  political influences, 44–45, 46
Environmental policies
  amicus curiae briefs, 48–49, 50
  property takings, 342, 351–355
  standing to sue, 92, 93
Environmental Protection Agency, 155
Epperson, Susan, 408
Epstein, Lee, 33n32, 37n, 38n, 40n, 44n56, 45n63,

47nn, 48nn, 50n72, 51n, 59n1, 80n31, 90n50, 174n7, 202n11, 360n, 421n, 444n, 541n, 549n18, 558n, 560n22, 561n24, 624n11, 633n16, 634n, 645n17
Equal Pay Act of 1963, 667
Equal Protection Clause (14th Amendment)
  abortion, 548, 569
  affirmative action, 690–697, 699
  commerce regulation, 249
  death penalty, 636
  discriminatory school funding, 676–681
  jury selection, 619
  legislative apportionment, 720, 722
  minority legislative districts, 728
  racial discrimination, 92, 644, 645–649, 650, 654–666
  reapportionment, 87–88
  sex discrimination, 667–674
  voting rights, 708–709, 716, 717
Equal Rights Amendment, 18 (box), 19, 20–21, 667
Erlich, Walter, 200n7
Escobedo, Danny, 595–596
Eskridge, William N., 47nn65, 67, 59, 77n21, 147n65
Espionage Act of 1917, 436, 437, 439
Establishment Clause See Religious establishment
Estate administration law, 669–670, 681
Ethics in Government Act of 1978, 146 (box), 164–165
Everson, Arch, 392
Evidence
  exclusionary rule, 585–594
  search and seizure, 580–594
  self-incrimination protections, 594–608, 622
  witnesses, 621–622
Evidence-loss searches, 581–582
Evolutionary theory, 394 (table), 406–414
  Scopes trial, 407
Ex post facto laws, 15
Exceptions Clause (Article III), 80–82
Excise taxes
  agricultural products, 275–276
  constitutional basis, 260
  direct tax definition, 261–263
  regulatory power, 273–275
  revenue impact of 16th Amendment, 269 (table)
Exclusion from Congress (table), 102
Exclusionary rule, 22, 585–594
Executive
  constitutional authority, 7 (chart), 8–10, 57, 58
  eligibility, 150
  immunity, 156–158
  selection, 150–151
  succession, 152–154
  tenure, 151–152
  voting qualifications, 718
Executive Committee of Southern Cotton Manufac-
    turers, 202, 205
Executive-judicial relations
  checks and balances, 9 (chart)
  habeas corpus constraint, 174
  politics in judicial decision making, 45–47
Executive powers
  appointment, removal, 163–168
  constitutional authority, 154
  foreign policy, 168–171, 496–497
  law enforcement, 154–156
  pardons, 81–82
  war powers, 171–182
Executive privilege, 158–163
Expression See Speech and expression rights

Fair housing, 650, 660 (box)
Fair Labor Standards Act of 1938, 18 (box), 28, 205, 208–216

Fair trial See Jury trial
Fairman, Charles, 80n33
Fanny Hill, 507
Farber, Daniel A., 4n10, 6, 13n2, 14nn, 15n9, 16nn, 62n2, 63nn5–6, 64, 83n40, 97n3, 99nn7,10, 122n30, 205n13, 364nn4–5
Farmers' Loan and Trust Co., 264
Faux, Marion, 549n18
Federal Bureau of Investigation, 535–536
Federal Child Labor Act, 202
Federal Communications Commission, 141 (table), 699
Federal Construction Procurement Program, 700
Federal contractors
  affirmative action, 690
  minority set-asides, 698, 699–705
  taxes, 271
Federal courts See Judiciary
Federal Election Campaign Act Amendments of 1974, 146 (box), 164
Federal Election Commission, 146 (box), 164
Federal employees and officials
  affirmative action, 690
  appointment, 163–165
  religious tests, 364
  removal, 165–168
  separation of powers, 146 (box), 155, 164
Federal Highway Administration, 700
Federal judges
  appointment, 63
  impeachment, 30
  salaries, 64
  special prosecutors, 164–165
Federal lands
  income taxes, 271
Federal Railway Act, 211 (table)
Federal-state relations
  amicus curiae briefs, 51
  cases between National League and Garcia (table), 211
  commerce regulation, 252–257
  constitutional powers allocation (table), 188
  constitutional principles, 10, 98
  doctrinal cycles (table), 192
  dual/cooperative federalism compared (table), 192
  inherent powers, 135–136
  judicial power constraints, 86
  legal standards, 191–216
  liberal voting by chief justices, 37 (table)
  original intent, 186–187
  subversive activity control, 454
  summary, 185–189, 191–192
  Supreme Court personnel changes (table), 216
  tax and spend power, 277–280
  tax immunity, 270–272
  Tenth Amendment, 187–189
  voting rights, 707–709, 713, 716–718
Federal Trade Commission, 141 (table), 167, 231
Federal Water Pollution Control Act Amendments of 1972, 154–155
Federalism See Federal-state relations
Federalist Papers, 13
  on commerce regulation, 219
  on contract obligations, 293
  on federal-state relations, 187–188
  inherent powers, 136
  on judiciary, 48, 62, 75–76
  removal power, 166
  on tax and spend power, 261
Federalists, 13–14, 63–67, 118, 121, 261, 295, 435–436
Feeley, Malcolm M., 288n3, 337n27, 442n6, 447n15
Feinberg Act (New York), 453n18

Feiner, Irving, 471
Ferejohn, John A., 59n1, 147n65
Ferguson, John, 655
Fidelity Manufacturing Co., 202
Field, Stephen J., 442
  legislative experience, 100 (table)
  on sex discrimination, 666
  on substantive due process, 312, 315, 316, 317
  tax and spend power, 265
  on war powers, 175
Fifteenth Amendment
  discrimination prohibition, 650–652
  enforcement, 709, 713–716
  legislative representation, 726
  ratification, 644, 709–710
  text, 645
  voting rights, 708
Fifth Amendment
  affirmative action, 690, 700
  commerce regulation, 231, 232, 249
  criminal rights, 573, 574 (table), 575, 576
  death penalty, 623
  double jeopardy, 636, 638
  economic liberties, 289
  fair trial, 617, 622
  privacy right, 525, 526, 528n9
  property takings, 79, 339–355
  provisions incorporated by 14th Amendment, 22
  racial discrimination, 649, 665–666
  self-incrimination protections, 594–608
  substantive due process, 312, 314, 330
  unincorporated provisions, 22n
"Fighting words" doctrine, 470–471, 472, 474, 476, 477–482
Filburn, Roscoe, 246
Finger, John, 683
Firearms
  regulation, 247, 275
  safety searches, 582–583
  unincorporated rights, 22n
First Amendment See also Press freedom; Religious establishment; Religious exercise; Speech and ex-pression rights
  association rights, 33, 34, 43
  judicial interpretations, 359–361
  privacy right, 525, 529, 534, 536, 540
  provisions incorporated by 14th Amendment, 22, 442
  Supreme Court support (graph), 360
First Bank of the United States, 118–121
First Congress
  Bill of Rights ratification, 16, 17
  executive departments, 166
  judiciary establishment, 63
  legislative chaplains, 422
Fiscal powers See Tax and spend power
Fish Committee, 129
Fish, Hamilton Jr., 129
Fisher, Louis, 32n25, 61n1, 114n16, 141n58, 147nn63, 65–66, 332n22, 377n25, 527nn3–4, 569n29
Fitzgerald, A. Ernest, 157
Fitzsimmons, Morris, 99
Flag desecration, 19, 29, 368, 462–468
Flag Protection Act of 1989, 468
Flag salute, 367–369, 483–487
Flammang, Janet A., 9n
Fleming, James E., 31n20, 288nn4–5, 316nn5–6
Fletcher, Robert, 294
Ford administration
  solicitor general as amicus curiae, 47 (table)
Ford, Gerald R.
  presidential succession, 154

Fordney-McComber Act, 138
Foreign embassies, 475
Foreign language instruction, 527
Foreign policy
  executive powers, 168–171
  inherent powers, 133
  press restraints, 496–497
Foreign trade
  Civil War blockade, 173
  delegated powers, 138
  state taxes, 280–281
  taxes, 260–261
Fortas, Abe
  amicus curiae brief citations, 51 (table)
  career, 557, 578, 662, 668
  legislation overturn votes, 40 (table)
  on religious establishment, 395, 408, 414–415
  right to counsel, 613
Foster, William Z., 449n16
Four Horsemen of the Apocalypse, 230, 237–240,
  245, 331
Fourteenth Amendment *See also* Due Process
  Clause; Equal Protection Clause
  commerce regulation, 249
  discrimination prohibition, 644, 645–649, 650,
    654, 665
  economic liberties, 288–289
  enforcement clause, 709
  legislative representation formula, 719n4
  property takings, 341
  qualifications for Congress, 101
  ratification, 644
  reapportionment, 87–88
  Supreme Court decision overturns, 19, 20 (box)
  text, 645
  women's voting rights, 708
Fourth Amendment
  criminal rights, 573, 574 (table), 581–594
  press privilege, 502–503
  privacy right, 525, 526, 529, 534, 535–536, 540
  provisions incorporated by 14th Amendment, 22,
    586
Framers' intent *See* Original intent
Franchise *See* Voting rights
Frankfurter, Felix
  amicus curiae brief citations, 51 (table)
  on appellate jurisdiction, 82
  balancing of interests, 34
  on criminal rights, 586, 590–592
  ideology, 36 (table)
  judicial role, 39–40, 41, 76
  legislation overturn votes, 40 (table)
  on legislative apportionment, 87, 88, 720
  on religious exercise, 368, 369
  on removal power, 168
  on ripeness concept, 85
  on sex discrimination, 667
  on speech rights, 448, 457 (table), 487
Franklin, Benjamin, 364, 422
Franklin, Charles H., 78, 558
Fraud, 293–294
Frazier-Lemke Act of 1934, 231, 232
Free Exercise Clause *See* Religious exercise
Freedom of expression *See* Speech and expression
  rights
Freedom of religion *See* Religious establishment; Re-
  ligious exercise
Freedom of speech *See* Speech and expression rights
Freedom of the press *See* Press freedom
Freedom to Read Foundation, 478
Freivogel, William H., 47n64
Frenzel, Bill, 105n

Fried, Charles, 565
Friendly, Fred W., 122n28, 125n31, 490nn1–2, 490n3,
  529n10, 587n10
Frothingham, Harriet, 90–91
Full Employment and Balanced Growth Act of 1978,
  142 (box)
Fuller, Melville W.
  on commerce regulation, 227, 248
  legislative experience, 100 (table)
  on tax and spend power, 265–267
Fulminante, Oreste, 608
Fulton, Robert, 220–221
Furman, William, 623

Gag orders, 491
Gaines, Lloyd, 658
Gallatin, Albert, 102 (table)
Gambling regulation, 275, 302
  privacy cases, 535–536
Garcia, Joe G., 211
Gedicks, Frederick Mark, 386n28
Gender issues *See* Sex discrimination
General Accounting Office, 155
General Motors, 282
General welfare
  contract obligation limits, 296–310
  tax and spend power, 275–280
George, Tracey E., 33n32
Gerry, Elbridge, 718 cap., 719
Gerrymandering, 89, 718 (illus.), 719
Gibbons, Henry J., 437–438
Gibbons, Thomas, 221, 222
Gibson, James L., 39n47
Gibson, John, 76
Gideon, Clarence Earl, 613–615
Gift tax, 269 (table)
Gillman, Howard, 327n14
Gilman, Benjamin, 377
Ginsburg, Ruth Bader
  on abortion, 361, 569
  affirmative action programs, 703–705
  career, 578, 594, 668
  federal-state relations, 216 (table)
  on minority legislative districts, 732–734
  religious establishment, 414, 418, 432
  on religious exercise, 376, 387–388
  on sex discrimination, 667, 669, 671, 674
Gitlow, Benjamin, 442
Gladstone, William, 3
Glasser, Ira, 580n3
Glenn, John, 377
Glick, Henry R., 541n16
Gobitas, Lillian, 367–368
Gobitas, Walter, 367–368
Gobitas, William, 367–368
Goldberg, Arthur
  amicus curiae brief citations, 51 (table)
  on criminal rights, 596
  legislation overturn votes, 40 (table)
  on privacy right, 530–531, 534–535
  speech rights, 473–474
Goldman, S. Simcha, 375–377
Goldman, Sheldon, 32, 42n51, 290n7, 311n1, 317n8,
  443
Gonzales Construction, 700
"Good faith" exception (exclusionary rule), 593–594
Grain storage regulation, 316–317
Gramm-Rudman-Hollings Act *See* Balanced Budget
  and Emergency Deficit Control Act
Grand Central Terminal, New York, 343–346
Grand juries, 22n, 574 (table), 575, 593
Grant, Ulysses S., 166

Gravel, Mike, 114–116
Gray, Horace, 441
Great Depression, 229, 275, 303, 332
Greenberg, Jack, 659 (photo), 661
Greenberg, Milton, 652n
Greenhouse, Linda, 105n
Gregg, Troy, 625
Grier, Robert
  on war powers, 173, 175
Griswold, Erwin, 462
Griswold, Estelle, 529
Guarantee Clause (Article IV), 86–88
Guilty pleas, 574, 575, 617
Gun-Free School Zones Act, 247, 249
Gunn, James, 294
Guns *See* Firearms
Gunther, Gerald, 15n11, 82nn, 83, 121n21,
  122nn25,27, 196n2, 314n3
Gutierrez, Luis V., 734 (photo)
Gutterman, Leslie, 424–425

Habeas Corpus Act of 1867, 80
Habeas corpus rights
  Civil War disputes, 174–175
  writs, 15, 80
Haig, Alexander M. Jr., 153 (box)
Hall, Kermit L., 62nn3–4, 63n6, 314, 318n9
Hamilton, Alexander, 5, 13
  on Bill of Rights, 11, 15
  on commerce regulation, 219
  on contract obligations, 293
  on House qualifications, 103
  on inherent powers, 136
  on judicial review, 75–76
  on judiciary, 62
  on national bank, 118–120, 122, 125
  on removal power, 166
  on Supreme Court, 48
  on tax and spend power, 261, 262–263, 275, 276
Hammer, William C., 203
Hancock, John, 14
Hand, Augustus, 506
Hand, Learned, 453n17
Handicapped *See* Disabled persons
Hanukkah displays, 416–418
Harbison, Winfred A., 98, 330n17
Harding, Warren G.
  Supreme Court appointments, 331, 663
Hardwick, Michael, 536–540
Harlan, John Marshall (1877–1911)
  on commerce regulation, 227–228
  on racial discrimination, 654, 656–657, 690
  on tax and spend power, 265, 267
Harlan, John Marshall (1955–1971)
  amicus curiae brief citations, 51 (table)
  balancing of interests, 34, 35
  career, 454
  on congressional investigation power, 131
  on criminal rights, 590–592, 602–605
  legislation overturn votes, 40 (table)
  on legislative apportionment, 725
  on press freedoms, 496–497, 504, 523
  on privacy right, 528–529, 531, 535, 536, 555
  on religious exercise, 373, 378
  on speech rights, 454
  on substantive due process, 337–338
Harrington, James, 56
Harris, William F. II, 31n21, 288nn4–5, 316nn5–6
Harrison, Cynthia, 64nn8–9, 65n, 66nn10–11
Hastie, Reid, 620n8
Hatch, Orrin, 386
Hate speech, 361, 474–482

Hawaii Housing Authority, 348
Hayden, Carl, 152 (photo), 153
Hayes, George E.C., 659 (photo)
Haynesworth, Clement F., 557
Head tax, 260, 263
Health and safety regulation
    abortion, 555, 556 (table), 565
    contract obligations, 301–302
    property takings, 342
    substantive due process, 320–330, 337
Healy, Jonathan, 284
Heart of Atlanta Motel, 250
"Heightened scrutiny" test
    minority set-asides, 699
    sex discrimination, 648, 670–674
Heller, Joseph, 233 (photo)
Helm, Jerry, 623
Henken, Louis, 136
Henry Street Group, 444
Hentoff, Nat, 504n8
Herblock, 238 (ill.)
Hershey, Marjorie Randon, 105n
Hicklin test, 505–506
Hill, Arthur, 329 (box)
Hinckley, John, 153 (box)
Hirabayashi, Gordon, 176
Hispanic Americans, 727
Hiss, Alger, 139
Historic preservation, 342–346
Holding, 33
Holiday displays, 414–418
Holmes, Oliver Wendell Jr.
    career, 441
    on child labor regulation, 205
    on commerce regulation, 228, 248
    on logical reasoning, 32
    on property takings, 342
    on speech rights, 438–442, 443, 445, 447, 453, 457
        (table), 472, 504
    on substantive due process, 312, 326–327, 331
Holy Names Society (Pittsburgh), 416
Home Building and Loan Assn., 303–304
Home mortgages, 303–307
Home Owners Loan Act of 1933, 232
Homosexual relations, 536–540
Hook, Janet, 105n
Hoosac Mills Corp., 276
Hoover, Herbert, 229, 332
    legislative veto, 141
    Supreme Court appointments, 230
Hospital aid, 389, 392
Hot pursuit searches, 583–584
Hours of work *See* Wage and hour regulation
House of Representatives
    appointment power, 164
    apportionment, 86–88, 719–721
    impeachment power, 152
    legislative veto suit, 143–144
    presidential selection, 150, 151
    qualifications for office, 89, 101, 102–105
Housing discrimination, 49–50, 650, 660 (box), 689
Hovey, Alvin, 174, 175
Howard, J. Woodford, 41, 42n51
Hudson and Manhattan Railroad, 307
Hughes, Charles Evans
    on commerce regulation, 226, 234–236, 241–243,
        248
    on constitutional amendment process, 19–20
    on contract obligations, 304–306
    Holmes retirement, 441
    ideology, 36 (table)
    New Deal decisions, 230, 232, 240

on press freedoms, 490, 491–495, 497
    on Roosevelt Court plan, 239
    speech rights, 445
    on substantive due process, 334–336
    on tax and spend power, 276
Humphrey, William E., 167
Hung juries, 620
Hunt, Ward, 100 (table)
Hutchinson, Ronald R., 116
Hyde Amendment, 560–562
Hylton, Daniel, 261–262

Idelson, Holly, 146n
Ideology in judicial decisions, 36–39, 44–45
Immigration and Nationality Act, 143
Immigration and Naturalization Service, 142–143
Immigration policy, 85
Immunity
    of executive, 156–158
    press reporters' privilege, 498–502
Impartial juries, 620–621
Impeachment
    of judges, 30
    of president, 152, 160, 163, 166–167
    Senate powers, 30, 89, 90
Import taxes
    constitutional basis, 260, 261
    regulatory power, 273
    state power restrictions, 280–281
Impounded appropriations, 155
Incest
    abortion law, 547, 561n23
"Incident to arrest" searches, 581, 585
Income tax
    constitutionality, 84, 263–269, 647
    intergovernmental immunity, 271
    judges' exemption, 441
    revenue impact, 269 (table)
    16th Amendment, 20 (box)
Independent counsel *See* Special prosecutors
Indians
    land law, 84
    peyote in religious use, 378–386, 387
Indictments, 575
Individual rights
    balancing of interests, 34–35
    Constitution principles, 10–11
Industrial Workers of the World, 444
"Inevitable discovery" exception (exclusionary rule),
    594
Informations, 575
Inheritance law, 669–670, 681
Inheritance tax, 269 (table)
Insurance company regulation, 319–320
Interest groups
    effects on Supreme Court, 48–53
    religious exercise, 386
    standing to sue, 90–93
"Intermediate scrutiny" test
    minority set-asides, 699
    sex discrimination, 648, 670–674
Internal Security Subcommittee, Senate, 129
International Development and Food Assistance Act
    of 1975, 142 (box)
"Interpretation tests" for voter registration, 710–712
Interstate commerce *See* Commerce regulation
Interstate Commerce Act of 1887, 219, 225–226
Interstate Commerce Commission, 141 (table), 226
Investigations Subcommittee, Senate Permanent,
    129
Iran-Contra affair, 165
Iraq, 172, 497

Iredell, James
    on tax and spend power, 263
Irons, Peter H., 140n56, 176nn8–9, 233n7, 333,
    367n15, 368n17, 537n13
Isle of Palms, 351, 352

Jackson, Andrew
    federal-state relations, 196, 197, 199
    Supreme Court appointments, 296
Jackson, Howell E.
    income tax case 264–265
    legislative experience, 100 (table)
Jackson, Robert H.
    amicus curiae brief citations, 51 (table)
    career, 454
    on First Amendment rights, 35
    legislation overturn votes, 40 (table)
    on original intent, 26–27
    on religious establishment, 393
    on religious exercise, 368–369
    on speech rights, 483, 484–487
    on war powers, 177, 179–181
Jacob, Herbert, 616n4
Jacobellis, Nico, 507
Jahnige, Thomas P., 42n51
James, Leonard F., 203n
Japanese-American relocation, 29, 43–44, 175–177,
    662
Jaworski, Leon, 160
Jay, John, 13, 67
Jay Treaty, 158
Jefferson, Thomas
    advisory opinions, 83
    on amending conventions, 21
    on Constitution ratification, 14–15
    executive privilege, 157
    judicial review, 66–68, 73–75
    on national bank, 118–120, 122
    presidential elections, 151
    on religious establishment, 388–395, 402, 423
    on religious exercise, 365
    Sedition Act pardons, 514
    on speech rights, 435–436
    Yazoo land fraud, 294
Jeffersonians *See* Democratic-Republicans
Jehovah's Witnesses, 366–370, 374–375, 446–447,
    469, 483–488
Jenkins, Howard, 659 (photo)
Jews
    Nazi Skokie march, 476
    religious exercise, 370–371, 375–377
Jim Crow laws *See* Segregation
Johnson (Lyndon) administration
    racial discrimination, 665
    solicitor general as amicus curiae, 47 (table)
Johnson, Andrew, 80
    civil rights statutes, 650
    executive immunity, 156
    impeachment, 152, 166–167
    removal power, 166
    war powers, 174–175
Johnson, Davida, 728
Johnson, Gregory Lee, 464, 474
Johnson, Lyndon B.
    affirmative action, 690
    presidential succession, 152 (photo), 153
    Supreme Court appointments, 578, 660, 662
    Vietnam War, 456
    on voting rights, 713
    war powers, 172
Johnson, Paul E., 6n18, 7n, 185n3, 186n4, 188n
Johnson, William, 100 (table)

Jones & Laughlin Steel Corp., 240
Jones, Paula, 157–158
Judicial activism, 39–41, 76
    abortion, 556
    substantive due process, 312, 313, 319, 527
Judicial branch See Judiciary
Judicial decision making, 24–52
    attitudes, 36–39
    balancing of interests, 34–35
    extralegal approaches, 35–52
    interest group effects, 48–51
    legal approaches, 24–35
    literalism, 27–31
    logical reasoning, 31–32
    original intent doctrine, 25–27
    partisan politics effects, 45–47
    policy based approaches, 36–41
    political factors, 43–52
    public opinion effects, 43–45
    roles, 39–41
    stare decisis, 32–34
    strategic approaches, 41–43
Judicial power constraints, 79–94
    enforcement, 157
    jurisdiction, 79–82
    justiciability, 83–90
    standing to sue, 90–94
Judicial restraint, 34, 39–41, 76–77
Judicial review, 61–62, 66–79
    enforcement of decisions, 46
    number of provisions struck, 41 (graph)
    original intent, 75–76
Judiciary, 61–95. See also Supreme Court
    checks and balances, 9 (chart)
    constitutional authority, 7 (chart), 8–10, 57, 58
    federal courts established, 63–65
    jurisdiction, 63 (box)
    original intent, 63–64
Judiciary Act of 1789, 62, 63, 64–66, 68, 73–75, 80, 138
Judiciary Committee, House, 160
Junker, John M., 624n13
Jurisdiction
    authority, 63 (box), 64–66
    changes, 47
    elimination proposals, 82 (table), 131–132
    as judicial power constraint, 79–82
Jury service
    challenges, 619
    sex discrimination, 47 667
Jury trial
    civil cases, 22n
    constitutional basis, 22, 574 (table), 576
    exclusionary rule, 585–594
    impartiality, 620–621
    jury selection, 618–619
    jury size, 619–620
    press access, 503–504, 621
    testimony, 621–622
    unanimous verdicts, 620
"Just compensation," 22, 341
Justice Department, U.S.
    abortion restrictions, 565
    child labor regulation, 203
    legislative veto, 142–143
    minority legislative districts, 727, 728–734
    Pentagon Papers, 114
    racial discrimination, 660, 665
    special prosecutors, 164–165
    sugar industry regulation, 227
    voting rights enforcement, 713
    Watergate scandal, 159
Justiciability, 83–90

Kammen, Michael, 3n1, 21n26
Katz, Charles, 535–536
Katzenbach, Nicholas, 713
Keating-Owen Act of 1916, 274
Keenan, J.T., 5n14, 14n5, 17n19, 18n, 20n
Kelly, Alfred H., 98, 330n17
Kennedy administration
    racial discrimination, 665
    solicitor general as amicus curiae, 47 (table)
Kennedy, Anthony
    on abortion, 566–569
    amicus curiae brief citations, 51 (table)
    federal-state relations, 216 (table)
    legislation overturn votes, 40 (table)
    on minority legislative districts, 728–732
    property takings, 351
    on religious establishment, 402 (table), 414, 418,
        425–428, 432
    religious exercise, 388 (table)
    speech rights, 468
Kennedy, Edward M., 386
Kennedy, John F., 662
    judicial appointments, 660
    presidential succession, 153
Kevorkian, Jack, 547
Kilbourn, Hallett, 127
King, Don, 587
Kluger, Richard, 658n1
Knox, Bishop, 432
Kobylka, Joseph F., 44n56, 206n15, 210n17, 211n,
    396n36, 423, 549n18, 560n22, 561n24, 624n11,
    633n16, 635n17
Korean War, 172
    steel mill seizure, 177–182
Korematsu, Fred, 176
Kosaki, Liane, 78, 558
Krislov, Samuel, 49n2, 288n3, 337n27, 442n6,
    447n15
Ku Klux Klan, 28, 366, 418, 455–456
Ku Klux Klan Act of 1871, 654, 709
Kurtzman, David, 397
Kutler, Stanley J., 446n13, 453n19, 456n26

Labor Department, U.S., 211, 690
Labor-Management Relations Act of 1947, 448
Labor relations regulation See also Child labor regu-
    lation; Wage and hour regulation
    collective bargaining rights, 240–245
    delegated powers, 141 (table)
    steel mill seizure, 177–178
Labor unions
    communist affiliation, 448, 455
    picketing restrictions, 460–461
    speech rights, 447
Lacayo, Richard, 21n17
Laissez-faire economic philosophy
    federal-state relations, 201–206
    legal tools (table), 313
    substantive due process, 312, 316, 319, 327, 332, 527
Lamar, Joseph R., 100 (table), 328
Lamar, L.C.Q., 100 (table)
Land reform, 347–350
Landon, Alf, 238
La Noue, George, 395
Law enforcement power, 154–156
    habeas corpus constraint, 174
Lawrence, Susan E., 50n70
Lawyers See Counsel, right to
Laycock, Douglas, 378n26, 386n27
League for Infants, Fetuses, and the Elderly, 550
League of Women Voters, 105
"Least restrictive means" test

discrimination prohibition, 647
privacy right, 528
religious exercise restrictions, 373, 377
speech restrictions, 459
Lee, Rex E., 563
Lee, Robert E., 424–425
Legal Defense and Educational Fund (NAACP),
    49–50, 658, 659 (photo), 660 (box), 623–624,
    635–636
Legislation overturn decisions
    justices' votes, 40 (table),
    number of provisions, 41 (graph)
Legislative branch See Congress
Legislative chaplains, 421–422
Legislative representation See also Congress, mem-
    bers of
    apportionment issues, 86–88, 719–726
    District of Columbia, 18 (box)
    historical background, 97
    minority districts, 726–734
    original intent, 7 (chart), 98, 718, 719
    proportion to population, 17, 18 (box)
    reduction option, 709n2
Legislative veto, 61, 76, 140–147
    examples, 142 (box)
"Legitimate purpose" standard (speech restrictions),
    459
Leibowitz, Samuel, 611 (photo)
Lemon, Alton, 397
Lerner, Max, 32n24
Les Amants, 507
Leuchtenburg, William E., 240n10, 333n26
Levy, Leonard W., 365n10, 423n51, 514n13
Libel, 513–524
    "actual malice" standard, 522–523
    privacy right, 526
    speech or debate case, 115 (table), 116
    unprotected expression, 458, 459, 513
Liberty interest
    abortion, 567–568
    privacy right, 526–529
    right to die, 540, 547
Liberty of contract, 314–315, 320–336, 527
Libya, 172
Lieberman, Jethro, 118n18, 120n20, 121n22, 122n29
Lincoln, Abraham, 18 (box), 80, 201
    speech rights, 436
    war powers, 173–175
Lincoln University, 658
Lippman, Matthew Ross, 468n25
Lipscomb, Andrew A., 74n14
Literacy tests for voter registration, 713
Literalism, 27–31
Living wills, 547
Livingston, Henry B., 100 (table)
Livingston, Robert R., 220–221
Lobbying, 48
Lochner, Joseph, 321–322, 527
Lopez, Alfonzo Jr., 247
Lord's Prayer, 394 (table)
"Loss of evidence" searches, 581–582
"Loss of liberty" rule, 616
Lotteries, 302
Louisville Courier Journal, 498
Loyalty issues
    Burger career, 577
    Civil War era, 101–102, 173–175
    Japanese-American relocation, 175–177
    speech rights, 453
    "un-Americanism" investigations, 128–129
Lucas, David, 48–49, 351–355
Luther, Martin (Dorrite), 86

McCardle, William, 80
McCarthy, Joseph, 128, 129, 448, 455
McCleskey, Warren, 635–636
McConnell, Michael W., 365n8
McCord, James Jr., 159
McCormack, John, 103, 129, 152 (photo), 153
McCorvey, Norma, 85, 549
McCulloch, James, 122, 193
McDowell, John, 128 (photo)
McGlen, Nancy, 20n24
McHenry, James, 99
McKay, Robert B., 35n41
McKenna, Joseph
   legislative experience, 100 (table)
   on substantive due process, 330
McKinley, John, 100 (table)
McKinney, Cynthia A., 728, 734 (photo)
McLarin, Kimberly J., 418n43
McLean, John, 100 (table)
McReynolds, James Clark
   career, 246
   on commerce regulation, 243–245
   ideology, 36 (table)
   New Deal decisions, 230, 231, 232, 237–240, 245
   substantive due process, 331 (table)
Madison, James, 5, 13
   on advisory opinions, 83
   Bill of Rights, 14, 16, 21, 23, 364
   on commerce regulation, 219
   on contract obligations, 293
   on economic liberties, 287
   executive departments, 166
   on federal-state relations, 186–188, 205
   on House qualifications, 103
   judicial review 63–64, 67
   on power concentration, 57
   on property takings, 340
   on religious establishment, 389, 390–393, 402, 423
   on state law vetoes, 99
   on tax and spend power, 260, 275
Magnet schools, 688
Majority-minority legislative districts, 726–734
Malbin, Michael, 97n4, 389
Management and Budget, Office of, 155
Mandamus writs, 65, 67–68
Mann, Frederick, 624n14
Mann, Thomas E., 105n
Manning, Silas, 618
Manufacturing
   commerce regulation, 226–228, 248
   excise taxes, 260
   maximum hours of work, 330
Manwaring, David, 368n18, 484n27
Mapp, Dollree, 586–587
Marbury, William, 67–68
Margarine, 273–274
Marital relations
   privacy right, 528–529
   spousal consent to abortion, 559, 560, 568
Marshall Court
   composition, 199 (table)
   on contract obligations, 288, 296
   federal-state relations, 192 (table), 198
   judicial review, 46
Marshall, John
   career, 67, 72–73
   on commerce power, 30–31, 117, 219–225, 248, 249, 252
   on congressional powers, 122–126, 138
   Constitution interpretation approach, 30, 31, 296
   on contract obligations, 293–296, 298
   on federal-state relations, 192–196, 197

   on judicial review, 64, 68–73, 74–75
   legislative experience, 100 (table)
   on opinion writing, 263n3
   original jurisdiction, 80
   on political questions, 86
   on property takings, 340
   on state power constraints, 25
   on tax and spend power, 270, 272, 280
Marshall, Thomas, 44, 77
Marshall, Thurgood
   abortion cases, 563, 566 (table), 567
   affirmative action programs, 698
   amicus curiae brief citations, 51 (table)
   career, 351, 567, 658, 660 (box), 699
   on criminal rights, 594
   on death penalty, 624, 632–633, 634, 636
   economic discrimination, 680–681
   on equal protection, 648
   on federal-state relations, 211 (table), 216
   on Framers, 6–7
   judicial vote shifting, 42
   legislation overturn votes, 40 (table)
   press freedoms, 496, 513
   on privacy right, 536, 538–540, 544–547
   on racial discrimination, 658–663
   religious establishment, 402 (table), 416, 422
   on religious exercise, 377, 382–385, 388 (table)
   school desegregation, 682, 688
   speech rights, 461–462
Martial law, 174
Martin, Luther, 122
Mason, Alpheus T., 14n6, 15n8, 446
Mason, George, 15
Mass transit systems, 307–308
Matthews, Stanley J., 100 (table), 319
Maynard, George and Maxine, 487–488
Meat and poultry industry regulation, 228, 233–237
Medicaid funding for abortion, 561
Medical care
   right to die, 540–547
Meese, Edwin III, 25n2, 26, 565
Memoirs of a Woman of Pleasure, 507
Mencken, H.L., 407
Menorah displays, 416–418
Meredith, James, 462–463, 523
Michelin Tire Corp., 281
Midkiff, Frank, 348
Military base closings, 146 (box)
Military draft
   draft-card burning, 461–462
   resistance, 437, 444
   sex discrimination, 675
   speech rights, 436, 439
Military forces
   congressional commissions, 92
   constitutional authority, 89, 168, 170, 171–172
   dress codes, 375–377
   quartering, 22n
   voting rights, 717
Military tribunals, 174–175
Milk and dairy industry regulation, 273–274, 283–284, 332, 445
Miller, Marvin, 508
Miller, Samuel
   war powers, 173, 175
   on substantive due process, 315–316, 317, 319, 336, 338
Miller, Zell, 728
Milligan, Lambdin, 174
Minimum drinking age, 277
Minimum voting age, 20 (box), 708
Minimum wage, 206, 330–336

Mining industry regulation, 320–321
Ministerial actions, 157
Minnesota Civil Liberties Union, 478
Minnesota Mortgage Moratorium Act, 303
Minnesota Private Pension Benefits Act, 308
"Minnesota Twins," 557
Minor, Virginia, 708
Minority interests
   and balancing approach, 35
   equal protection tests, 647, 666
   hate speech, 477
   legislative representation, 726–734
   Preferred Freedoms doctrine, 446
   separation of powers, 56
   Supreme Court role, 78
Minority set-aside programs, 698–706
   judicial principles (box), 705
Minors *See* Children
Minton, Sherman
   amicus curiae brief citations, 51 (table)
   career, 448, 454, 505
   legislation overturn votes, 40 (table)
   legislative experience, 100 (table)
Miranda, Ernesto, 597–605
Miranda warnings, 605–606, 607, 608
Mishler, William, 44nn55
Mississippi Agricultural, Educational, and Manufacturing Aid Society, 302
Missouri Compromise, 79, 199, 200–201
Missouri Staats Zeitung, 439
Mitchell, William D., 141
Mondale, Walter, 613
"Monkey trial," 407, 408
Monopoly regulation, 225, 226–228, 315
Montesquieu, Charles de, 56
Moody, William, 100 (table)
Moore, Alfred, 100 (table)
Mootness, 85
Morgan, Richard E., 366n13
Mormons, 365, 374
Mortgage relief, 301, 303–307
Motley, Constance Baker, 661
Mountain Gravel and Construction Co., 700
Movie industry
   obscenity issues, 507, 512–513
Muller, Curt, 327
Municipal Bankruptcy Act, 232
Murphy, Francis W.
   career, 448
   ideology, 36 (table)
   Japanese-American relocation, 177
   on religious exercise, 369
   speech rights, 460–461, 469–470
Murphy, Walter F., 31n20, 41, 42n51, 142, 288nn4–5, 316nn5–6
Muskrat, David, 84
Myers, Frank, 167

NAACP *See* National Association for the Advancement of Colored People
Nabrit, James M. Jr., 659 (photo), 661
Narcotics taxes, 275
Narrow construction standard (speech restrictions), 459
National Academy of Sciences, 409
National Asian Pacific American Bar Association, 478
National Association for the Advancement of Colored People (NAACP), 368n19
   death penalty, 623–624, 635–636
   discriminatory school funding, 677
   hate speech, 478

racial discrimination opposition, 49–50, 658–661, 663 (box)
National Association for the Repeal of Abortion Laws, 547–548
National banks, 118–121, 193–196, 197, 273
National Bituminous Coal Conservation Act of 1935, 232, 237
National Black Women's Health Project, 478
National Civil Liberties Bureau, 444
National Command Authority, 153 (box)
National Conference of Christians and Jews, 424
National Consumers' League, 329–330, 333, 334
National Federation for Constitutional Liberties, 447
National Governors' Conference, 209
National Guard, 89
National Industrial Recovery Act, 138, 140, 206, 230–233
National Labor Relations (Wagner) Act of 1935, 240, 247 (table)
National Labor Relations Board, 141 (table), 240, 448
National League of Cities, 209–210
National Organization for Women, 20
National Prison Project (ACLU), 444
National Right to Life Committee, 550
National security
  press restraints, 495, 495
  speech rights, 435, 449, 456–457, 458
  unprotected expression, 504
National Security Act of 1947, 153 (box)
National Socialist party, 476
National Women's party, 333
Native American church, 378–386, 387
Native Americans See Indians
Native Hawaiians, 347–350
Nativity scenes, 415–417
Navigation, as commerce, 30–31, 221–225, 253–256
Nazi march in Skokie, 476–477
Near, Jay, 490–497
Nebbia, Leo, 332
Necessary and Proper Clause (Article I)
  federal-state relations, 187, 191, 192 (table), 195–196
  national bank, 119–120, 122–126
  original intent, 99, 117–119
Neier, Aryeh, 476n26
Nelson, Samuel
  war powers, 175
Nelson, Steve, 454
Neubauer, David W., 616n4, 618n7
Neubauer, Mark, 497n5
Nevins, Allan, 172n7
New Deal
  commerce regulation, 227–246
  contract obligations, 303–307
  delegation of powers, 135, 138–140, 206
  economic legislation (box), 229
  legislation upheld, 47, 140
  opponents views, 319
  substantive due process, 332–336, 527
  tax and spend power, 275–277
  unconstitutional legislation, 43, 58, 84, 232
"New federalism," 208
New Jersey Plan, 6, 7, 149
New York Civil Liberties Union, 419
New York Milk Control Board, 332
New York Times, 495–497, 514–522
Newmyer, R. Kent, 197
Nicholls, Francis Tillow, 655
Niemi, Richard G., 41n, 208n, 421n, 578n1, 634n
Nineteenth Amendment, 650, 708, 709
Ninth Amendment

abortion, 549
  privacy right, 22n, 525, 529, 534–535, 555
  provisions incorporated by 14th Amendment, 22
Nixon administration
  legislative veto, 142
  papers, tapes, 146 (box)
  press freedoms, 497
  solicitor general as amicus curiae, 47 (table)
  Watergate scandal, 158–160
Nixon, Richard M.
  ACLU history, 444
  clean water projects funding, 155
  on criminal rights, 578
  on death penalty, 633–634
  executive immunity, 157
  executive privilege, 158–163
  federal-state relations, 208
  impeachment threat, 152, 160, 163
  minimum voting age, 20 (box)
  presidential succession, 154
  Supreme Court appointments, 45, 307, 396, 456, 508, 557, 577, 578, 594, 624, 662
  un-American activities investigations, 128 (photo), 129
  war powers, 172
  Watergate crisis, 58, 158–160, 163
Nixon, Walter L. Jr., 30
Nollan, James and Marilyn, 350–351
Nolo contendere pleas, 575
Norpoth, Helmut, 45
Northern Securities Co., 441
Northwest Fertilizing Co., 301
Notification Clause (6th Amendment), 22, 574 (table)
Nuclear Non-Proliferation Act of 1978, 142 (box)
Nugent, John, 497
Nullification crisis, 196–197

Oaths of witnesses, 621–622
Obligatory appeals, 616
O'Brien, David, 461–462, 468, 476
O'Brien, David M., 570n30
Obscenity, 504–513
  community standards test, 507
  judicial standards, 505–508, 512 (table)
  prior restraint, 495
  privacy right, 536
  search and seizure case, 587
  social value test, 507
  unprotected expression, 29, 458, 459
Occupational health and safety
  bakery workers' hours, 322–327
  manufacturing, 330
  miners' liberty of contract, 320–321
  sex discrimination, 327–330, 667
O'Connor, Karen, 20n24, 444n
O'Connor, Sandra Day
  on abortion, 562–569
  affirmative action programs, 697, 699, 700–703
  amicus curiae brief citations, 51 (table)
  on criminal rights, 594, 607–608, 622
  on federal-state relations, 214–215, 216
  judicial vote shifting, 42
  legislation overturn votes, 40 (table)
  legislative experience, 100 (table)
  on privacy right, 547
  on property takings, 348–350
  on religious establishment, 402 (table), 416, 418, 422, 423–424, 428–430, 432
  on religious exercise, 377, 382–384, 386, 387, 388 (table)
  school desegregation, 689

on speech rights, 467–468
  on tax and spend power, 272, 279, 280
Ogden, Aaron, 220, 221
Ohio Butterine Co., 273
Oil industry regulation, 138–140, 230–231, 271
Oleomargarine Act of 1886, 273
Olson, Theodore B., 165
"One person, one vote" principle, 87 (box), 725, 726
Opinion writing
  Marshall practice, 263n3
  vote shifting, 42–43
Oregon Waste Systems, 283
Organic Act, 67
Original intent
  commerce regulation, 219
  contract obligations, 291–293
  criminal rights, 573, 579–580, 610, 617, 618, 620, 623, 636
  doctrine, 25–27, 118–120
  economic liberties, 287–288, 289
  executive, 149, 150
  federal-state relations, 186–187
  House qualifications, 103
  individual rights, 15
  judicial review, 75–76, 79, 80
  press freedoms, 489, 503, 504
  religious establishment, 388–391, 393, 422, 423–424
  religious exercise, 365
  separation of powers, 57–58
  speech rights, 435–436
  tax and spend power, 259–261, 263
  voting rights, 707–708
  war powers, 171
"Original package" doctrine, 280
Orthodox Jews, 370–371, 375–377
Otis, James, 75, 580
Overbroad legislation
  sex discrimination, 670, 674–675
  speech restrictions, 459

Pacelle, Richard L. Jr., 289n, 290n8, 361n, 446n14
Pacificism, 436
Packers and Stockyard Act of 1921, 228
Pardons, 81–82
Parental consent to abortion, 559, 560, 562, 568 (box), 569
Paris Adult Theatre, 512–513
Parker, John J., 368, 483
Parrish, Elsie, 333–334
Patents
  income taxes, 271
Paterson, William
  legislative experience, 100 (table)
  on tax and spend power, 263
Paul, Arnold M., 319n10
Pech, Randy, 700 (photo)
Peck, John, 294
Peckham, Rufus W.
  on substantive due process, 320, 322–326
Peltason, J.W., 3n5, 4nn8,13, 8n21, 96n1, 117n, 185n1, 188n, 215–216
Pena, Federico, 700
Penn Central Transportation Co., 343–346
Pension benefits
  contract obligations, 308
  retirement income taxation, 272
Pentagon Papers, 114–116, 495–497
Peremptory juror challenges, 619
Perlman, Philip B., 178
Persian Gulf War, 172, 497
Peters, John F., 577

Petition right, 22
Peyote, 378–386, 387
Pfeffer, Leo, 395n35, 398n38, 409n41, 421n49
Physical evidence, 580–594
Picketing, 460–461, 475
Pinckney, Charles, 15
Pinkney, William, 122
Pitney, Mahlon
  legislative experience, 100 (table)
  substantive due process, 331 (table)
Pitt, William, 580
"Plain view" doctrine, 583
Planned Parenthood groups, 529, 550, 562
Plano, Jack C., 652n
Plea bargaining, 574, 617
Pledge of Allegiance, 367–368, 483
Plessy, Homer Adolph, 655
Police and law enforcement agencies
  affirmative action, 697
  criminal justice system summary, 574–575
  evidence search and seizure, 581–585
  interrogation guidelines, 595–608
Police powers
  federal powers, 249–252
  property takings, 342, 352
  rational basis test, 527–528
  religious exercise, 370, 379
  speech restriction, 469–470
  state regulation for public good, 301–310
  substantive due process as limit, 317, 321–330
  taxation as regulation, 272–275
Political issues
  influences on Supreme Court, 43–53
  judicial power constraints, 86–90
Poll taxes, 708, 716–717
Pollock, Charles, 264
Polygamy, 102 (table), 365
Populist party, 263–264, 319
Pornography, 506–513
Port Authority of New York, 307–308
Postal service
  obscenity issues, 506
Postmasters, 167
Poverty
  affirmative action, 691–692
  discriminatory school funding, 675–681
  right to counsel, 597, 611–617
Powell, Adam Clayton Jr., 89, 102–105
Powell, Lewis Franklin Jr.
  on abortion, 561, 563, 564, 566 (table)
  affirmative action programs, 691, 693–697, 698
  amicus curiae brief citations, 51 (table)
  career, 456, 565, 566
  on criminal rights, 594, 616n5, 618, 623
  on death penalty, 624, 625–630, 636
  on discriminatory school funding, 677–680
  on executive immunity, 157
  on federal-state relations, 214–215, 216 (table)
  judicial role, 39
  legislation overturn votes, 40 (table)
  on political questions, 89
  on privacy right, 540
  religious establishment, 402 (table), 403, 422, 423
Precedent See Stare decisis
Preferred Freedoms standard, 34–35, 445–446,
  447–449, 457 (table), 463
Pregnancy See Abortion
Preliminary hearings, 575
President See Executive
Presidential Recordings and Materials Preservation
  Act of 1974, 146 (box)
Press freedom, 489–524. See also Libel; Obscenity

access, 503–504
applied to states by 14th Amendment, 22
jury impartiality, 620–621
original intent, 489, 503, 504
prior restraint, 489, 490–497
reporters' privilege, 497–502
Prince, Sarah, 369
Prior restraint
  hate speech, 477
  justifications, 497
  press freedoms, 489, 490–497
  speech restrictions, 460
Prisons
  press access, 503
  right to counsel, 616
  search and seizure protections, 584
Pritchett, C. Herman, 3, 4n9, 16n15, 19n21, 30,
  35n40, 36–37, 80n32, 84, 90n49, 99nn8–9, 114,
  118n19, 126n34, 127n38, 131n42, 132n43, 132n45,
  186n5, 188n, 205, 210n18, 317n7, 497, 502,
  514nn11,13
Privacy rights, 525–569
  abortion, 547–558
  birth control, 43, 529–535
  constitutional basis, 22, 27, 359, 525–529, 535
  homosexual relations, 536–540
  obscenity possession, 536
  right to die, 540–547
  search and seizure protections, 584–585
  substantive due process, 314, 337–338, 526–529
  wiretaps, 535–536
Private schools
  compulsory school attendance, 365–366, 374
  religious establishment issues, 394 (table),
    397–401, 403–406
  textbook loans, 393, 394 (table), 395, 404, 405, 406
  transportation aid, 392, 394 (table), 404, 405
Privilege
  executive privilege, 158–163
  press reporters, 497–502
Privileges and Immunities Clause (14th Amendment)
  racial discrimination, 654
  substantive due process, 315
  women's voting rights, 708
Procedural due process, 311, 312
Pro-choice See Abortion
Progressive movement, 368n19
  compulsory school attendance, 365–366
  social welfare legislation, 319, 321
  speech rights cases, 436, 444
Prohibition repeal amendment, 17
Pro-life See Abortion
Property ownership
  Indian distributions, 84
  Native Hawaiians, 347
  voting rights, 716
Property rights See also Contract obligations; Property takings; Substantive due process
  freed slaves, 650
  original intent, 288
  speech right limits, 458
  steel mill seizure, 177–182
Property takings, 339–355
  definition, 341–346
  public use requirement, 347–350
  Rehnquist Court decisions, 350–355
  state restrictions, 22
Property taxes
  direct tax definition, 260, 263, 264–269
  discriminatory school funding, 676–677
  imported articles, 281

increase approval, 716
religious exemptions, 396–397
school desegregation, 688
Proportionality of sentences, 622
Prosecutors, 575, 619
  special prosecutors, 146 (box), 164–165
Prosser, William I., 526n1
Protected speech See Speech and expression rights
Protest demonstrations, 459, 461, 471–474, 475
Proxmire, William, 116
Public accommodations
  discrimination ban, 249–252, 650, 655, 689
Public defenders, 615–616
Public officials See also Federal employees and
  officials; State employees and officials
  libel, 521
  self-incrimination protection, 622
Public opinion
  abortion, 556–558, 570
  death penalty, 623, 633–634
  effect on Supreme Court decision making, 43–45,
    77–78, 436, 443, 508
  right to die, 541
  Roosevelt Court plan (chart), 239
Public order and safety
  Miranda exception, 605
  speech restrictions, 468–474, 475
Public schools See also School desegregation; School
  prayer
  Bible readings, 419, 420
  compulsory attendance, 365–366, 374
  discriminatory funding, 675–681
  education as fundamental right, 675–676, 677, 681
  flag salute, 367–368
  holiday displays, 418
  religious establishment cases, 394 (table)
  religious teaching, 406–414
Public trial, 22, 620–621
Public use requirement, 347–350
Public Utility Regulatory Policies Act, 211 (table)
Public Works Employment Act of 1977, 698
Pulaski, Charles, 635n18
Pusey, Merlo J., 245n13, 246n14

Qualifications Clause (Article I), 101–105
Qualifications for office
  members of Congress, 101
  president, 150
  religious tests, 364
Quarles, Benjamin, 606
Quinlan, Karen, 541

Racial discrimination, 653–666. See also Civil rights
  movement; School desegregation
  affirmative action, 690–706
  black citizenship, 199–201, 653–654
  commerce regulation, 249–252, 655
  constitutional protections, 644, 645–649
  death penalty, 611–612, 623–624, 635–636
  hate speech, 361, 476, 477–482
  Japanese-American relocation, 175–177
  juror challenges, 619
  legislative representation, 726–734
  "separate but equal" doctrine, 654–660
  statutory bans, 649–652
  "suspect class" test, 647, 666
  tax-exempt status, 92
  voting rights, 7, 707–716, 717
  zoning, 93
Racial quotas, 691–697
Racketeer Influenced and Corrupt Organizations
  Act, 475

Radical Republicans, 47, 80, 156, 166, 174–175, 644, 645–646, 708
Railroad regulation, 225–226, 227, 256, 318, 655
Railroad Retirement Act of 1934, 231, 232
Randolph, Edmund, 15, 118
Rangel, Charles B., 734 (photo)
Rankin, John, 128 (photo)
Rape
    abortion law, 549, 553n19, 561n23
    death penalty, 612n2
    right to counsel, 612
    sex discrimination, 675
    victim testimony, 621
Ratio decidendi, 33
"Rational basis" tests
    abortion, 555–556, 564 (box), 569 (table)
    discriminatory school funding, 676, 681
    economic regulation, 336–337, 527–528
    racial discrimination, 647, 654
    sex discrimination, 670–674
    substantive due process, 318, 320–327, 329
Reagan administration
    abortion cases, 563–565
    affirmative action programs, 697
    minority legislative districts, 727
    original intent doctrine, 26
    religious establishment, 422
    solicitor general as amicus curiae, 47 (table)
    special prosecutors, 165
Reagan, Ronald, 464
    abortion issue, 562
    budget deficit control, 155
    federal-state relations, 215
    judicial restraint, 76
    legislative veto, 143
    presidential succession, 153 (box)
    on school prayer, 420–421
    subminimum wage, 18 (box)
    Supreme Court appointments, 565, 566, 578
    war powers, 172
Reapportionment, 86–88, 719–725
Reasonableness standards *See* "Rational basis" tests
Recidivism laws, 623
Reconstruction
    appellate jurisdiction, 80
    civil rights amendments, 644–646, 650
    congressional-judicial relations, 47
    executive immunity, 156–157
    removal power, 166
    voting rights, 708–709
    war powers disputes, 174–175
Reconstruction Acts, 156–157
Redding, Louis, 659 (photo), 661
Reed, Cecil, 669
Reed, Richard, 669
Reed, Sally, 669
Reed, Stanley F.
    amicus curiae brief citations, 51 (table)
    ideology, 36 (table)
    legislation overturn votes, 40 (table)
    on speech rights, 448
Reeves, Frank, 659 (photo)
Regulatory agencies
    delegated powers (table), 141
    removal power, 167–168
Rehnquist Court
    abortion cases, 565–570
    amicus curiae citations, 50
    criminal rights cases, 576, 578, 606
    economics, civil liberties decisions, 38 (graph), 289–290
    First Amendment claims, 360 (graph)

on judicial impeachments, 30
legislation overturns, 40
minority interest protection, 78
precedents overruled, 33 (table)
privacy right, 540
on property takings, 49, 350–355
religious establishment, 389, 414, 424–433
religious exercise cases, 377–388
school desegregation, 688–689
speech rights cases, 474, 475 (table)
substantive due process, 337
Rehnquist, William H.
    on abortion, 553–569
    affirmative action programs, 698
    amicus curiae brief citations, 51 (table)
    career, 456
    on commerce regulation, 247
    on criminal rights, 578, 594, 606, 608, 616
    on death penalty, 624, 631
    on federal-state relations, 209–210, 214–216
    hate crimes sentencing, 482
    ideological attitudes, 37
    on judicial impeachments, 30
    judicial vote shifting, 42
    legislation overturn votes, 40 (table)
    political questions, 89
    on privacy right, 542–544
    on property takings, 346, 350, 355
    on protected expression, 25
    on religious establishment, 402 (table), 403, 412–414, 418, 422, 423–424, 430–432
    on religious exercise, 376–377, 378, 388 (table)
    school desegregation, 689
    on sex discrimination, 671, 673–674
    on special prosecutors, 165
    on speech rights, 467–468
    on substantive due process, 337
    on tax and spend power, 277–279
Religious apparel, 375–377
Religious establishment, 388–433. *See also* School prayer
    accomodationist-separationist positions compared, 389, 390–391, 393, 394 (table)
    applied to states by 14th Amendment, 22
    aid to religious schools, 91, 92, 403–406
    coercion standard, 402 (table), 418, 432
    colonial practices, 363–364
    endorsement standard, 402 (table), 416–418, 423, 432
    excessive entanglement test, 396–397, 401 (table), 402 (table), 423
    holiday displays, 414–418
    Lemon test roots (table), 401
    major cases *Everson* thru Warren Court (table), 394
    neutral effect test, 394–395, 396, 401 (table), 402 (table), 405, 408, 414–415, 423
    nonpreferentialism standard, 389, 390–391, 402 (table), 423, 432
    original intent, 388–391, 393, 422, 423–424
    property transfer, 92
    religious teaching in public schools, 406–414
    secular purpose test, 393, 394–395, 401 (table), 402 (table), 414, 415–416, 423
    standards advocated, 402 (table)
    wall of separation, 365n10, 388, 392–395, 423
Religious exercise, 364–388
    applied to states by 14th Amendment, 22
    belief-action dichotomy, 365, 366, 370, 372–373
    compelling state interest standard, 373, 374, 377, 378, 379, 386, 387
    least restrictive means approach, 371, 373, 377, 379, 386

original intent, 365
    and speech rights, 368–369, 386, 446–447, 483–487
    valid secular policy test, 366–373
Religious Freedom Restoration Act of 1993, 386, 388
Religious instruction
    time-release programs, 394 (table)
Religious mottoes, 415, 419
Religious organizations
    tax exemption, 396–397
Religious schools
    federal aid, 403–406
    major cases, 1947–94 (table), 404–405
Religious tests, 364
Removal power, 165–168
Rent control, 337
Reporters' privilege, 497–502
Reproductive Freedom Project (ACLU), 444
Reproductive rights *See* Abortion
Residency requirements for voting, 717–718
Retirement *See* Pension benefits
Reverse discrimination, 85, 690
Reynolds, George, 365
Rhode Island Civil Liberties Union, 415
Rice, Robert, 38n44
Richmond Inquirer, 196
Right to die, 540–547
Right to life *See* Abortion
Ripeness concept, 85
Roane, Spence, 196
Roberts, Brigham H., 102
Roberts, Owen Josephus
    career, 230
    ideology, 36 (table)
    Japanese-American relocation, 177
    New Deal decisions, 230, 232, 238, 240, 245–246
    on religious exercise, 366–367
    on right to counsel, 612
    on speech rights, 447
    on substantive due process, 332, 333
    tax and spend power, 276
Robinson, Spottswood W. III, 659 (photo), 661
Rockefeller, Nelson, 154
Rodberg, Leonard, 114–116
Rodriguez, Demetrio, 676–677
Rogge, O. John, 471
Rohde, David W., 30n15, 31nn, 32n23, 33nn35–36, 37n43
Roman Catholics *See* Catholic church
Roosevelt, Franklin D. *See also* New Deal
    advisory opinions, 83
    on Constitution, 3
    Court-packing plan, 28, 47, 237–240, 333
    elections, 43, 229, 332
    foreign arms sales, 133, 169
    Japanese-American relocation, 29, 175
    presidential tenure, 151–152
    removal power, 167–168
    separation of powers, 58
    Supreme Court appointments, 28, 230, 246
Roosevelt, Theodore, 441
Rosen, Lawrence, 433
Rossiter, Clinton, 13n4, 171n3
Rossum, Ralph A., 32, 131n41, 287nn1–2, 337n28, 443n8
Roth, Samuel, 506
Rowland, C.K., 50n72
Rubin, Eva, 549n18
Rush, Bobby L., 734 (photo)
Rutherford, Joseph, 367
Rutledge, John
    legislative experience, 100 (table)
Rutledge, Wiley B.

career, 448
on religious establishment, 364, 393
on religious exercise, 364, 369, 370
on speech rights, 447, 457 (table)

Sabbath observance, 370–373
Safety searches, 582–583
Saks, Michael J., 620n8
San Antonio Metropolitan Transit Authority,
    210–216
Sanford, Edward T.
    career, 230
    speech rights, 457 (table)
    substantive due process, 331 (table)
Sanford, John, 199–200
Santeria religion, 386–387
Sarivola, Anthony, 608
Saturday Evening Post, 522–523
"Saturday Night Massacre," 159–160
Saturday Press, 490
Sawyer, Charles, 177
Scalia, Antonin
    on abortion, 566–567, 569
    affirmative action programs, 699, 703
    amicus curiae brief citations, 51 (table)
    career, 668
    on death penalty, 636, 638
    federal-state relations, 216
    ideological attitudes, 38
    legislation overturn votes, 40 (table)
    judicial vote shifting, 42
    on property takings, 289, 350, 351, 352–354
    on religious establishment, 402 (table), 412–414,
        418, 430–432
    on religious exercise, 376, 379–382, 385–386, 387,
        388 (table)
    on speech rights, 468, 479–481
Schechter Poultry Corp., 233–237
Schenck, Charles, 437
Schlesinger, Arthur M. Jr., 26, 455n20, 456n22
Schmidhauser, John, 436, 439
Schmidt, Steffen W., 5n
School attendance, 365–366, 373–374
School busing, 82 (table), 687, 688
School desegregation
    court implementation, 82 (table), 682–689
    District of Columbia, 649
    elementary and secondary schools, 660–665
    interest groups, 49–50
    law, graduate schools, 658
    university affirmative action, 85, 691–697
    Walker libel case, 523
School prayer, 418–433
    graduation ceremonies, 424–432
    jurisdiction change proposal, 82 (table)
    major religious establishment cases, 394 (table)
    proposed amendment, 19, 420, 421
    public opinion, 77, 419, 420 (graph)
    silent meditation, voluntary prayer, 422
    state-written prayers, 419–420
Schools *See also* Private schools; Public schools
    foreign language instruction, 527
Schubert, Glendon, 37n43
Schwartz, Bernard, 43n53, 201n9, 312n, 407n,
    420n45, 528n8, 534n11
Scopes trial, 407, 408
Scott, Aubrey, 616
Scott, Charles, 663 (box)
Scott, Dred, 199–201
"Scottsboro boys," 611–612
Search and seizure protections
    applied to states by 14th Amendment, 22

colonial practices, 580
    criminal rights summary, 574 (table)
    exclusionary rule, 585–594
    levels of protection, 584
    precedents importance, 33
    press privilege, 510–503
    privacy right, 525, 526, 535–536
    reasonable searches, 581–585
Second Amendment, 22n
Second Bank of the United States, 120–121, 193, 197
Secrecy
    executive privilege, 158
Secular humanism, 409
Sedition Act of 1798, 435–436, 514, 521
Sedition Act of 1918, 436
Seditious libel, 514, 521
Segal, Jeffrey A., 26, 29, 32, 33nn, 37nn, 38nn, 40,
    46n63, 47n, 51n, 75n15, 76n20, 360n, 420n47,
    421n, 541n, 558n, 634n
Segregation *See also* School desegregation
    post-Reconstruction South, 644, 654
    "separate but equal" doctrine, 654–660
Seizure *See* Property takings; Search and seizure pro-
    tections
Selected exclusiveness doctrine, 255
Selective incorporation doctrine, 23
Selective Service Act, 439, 461–462
Self-incrimination protection, 594–608
    applied to states by 14th Amendment, 22
    constitutional basis, 594–595
    criminal justice system summary, 574 (table)
    Miranda warnings, 82 (table), 605–606, 607
    police interrogation, 595–608
    privacy right, 525, 526
    trial testimony, 622
Senate, U.S.
    appointment, removal power, 164, 166–167
    foreign policy powers, 171
    impeachment power, 30, 89, 152
    legislative veto suit, 143–144
    qualifications for office, 101
    vice presidential selection, 150
Sentences *See also* Death penalty
    bifurcated trials, 625
    criminal rights summary, 575–576
    federal guidelines, 77
    hate crime enhancements, 39, 482
    punishment standards, 45, 622–623
"Separate but equal" doctrine, 657–659, 665
Separation of church and state *See* Religious estab-
    lishment
Separation of powers, 55–60
    appointment power, 164
    budget deficit control, 155–156
    checks and balances (chart), 9
    commerce regulation, 233–237
    Constitution principles, 8–10
    delegated powers, 137–140, 141
    judicial activism/restraint, 39
    legislative veto, 140–147
    recent cases (box), 146
Seventeenth Amendment, 58, 98
Seventh Amendment, 22n
Seventh-Day Adventists, 371, 377–378
Sex discrimination, 666–675
    employment, 666–667
    equal protection tests, 648, 667–674
    Equal Rights Amendment, 18 (box)
    hours of work, 39, 327–330, 332–333
    interest group effects, 50
    jury selection, 47, 619
    minimum wage, 333

speech or debate case, 115 (table)
    voting rights, 644, 666, 708
Sexual harassment, 674
    executive immunity, 157–158
Sexual relations
    obscenity issues, 507–513
    privacy right, 529, 536–540
Shared Time Program, 405
Shays, Daniel, 5, 219
Shays's Rebellion, 5
Sheehan, Reginald S., 44nn, 50–51
Shelley, Mack. C. II, 5n
Sheppard-Towner Maternity Act, 90–91
Sherbert, Adell, 371–372
Sherman Anti-Trust Act of 1890, 225–228
Sherry, Suzanna, 4n10, 6, 13n2, 14nn, 15n9, 16nn,
    62n2, 63nn5–6, 64, 83n40, 97n3, 99nn7,10,
    122n30, 205n13, 364nn4–5, 418n44
Shiras, George
    on tax and spend power, 265
Shreveport Doctrine, 225–226, 248
Sick Chicken Case, 233–237
Siegel, Larry, 580n2, 583n5, 608
Silverstein, Lee, 616n4
Simmons, Betty, 369
Simon, Dennis, 142
Simpson, W.D., 102 (table)
Single-member constituencies, 708, 719
Six-person juries, 619–620
Sixteenth Amendment
    passage, 20 (box), 269–270
    revenue impact (table), 269
Sixth Amendment
    criminal rights, 573, 574 (table), 576
    fair trial, 617–621
    provisions incorporated by 14th Amendment, 22
    right to counsel, 610, 617
Skokie march, 476–477
Slavery
    abolition by 13th Amendment, 644, 645, 650
    characteristics, 643–644, 653
    Constitution changes, 7, 644
    Dred Scott decision, 20 (box), 26, 79, 199–201, 314,
        653–654
    proposed proslavery amendment, 18 (box)
    three-fifths formula, 199, 644
Small Business Act, 700
Smith, Alfred, 379
Smith Act of 1940, 449–453, 454, 455
Snake-handling, 365n17
Social Darwinism, 316, 327
Social science evidence, 329, 661, 671
Social Security
    compulsory participation, 375
    tax and spend power, 276–277
Social Security Act, 247 (table)
Socialists, 436–438, 439, 442
Society of Sisters, 366
Sodomy, 536–540
Solicitation regulation, 369–370, 446–447, 475
Solicitor general, U.S., 46–47, 51
Songer, Donald, 50–51
Sorauf, Frank, 393, 396n37, 419n
Souter, David
    on abortion, 567–568, 569 (table)
    affirmative action programs, 704–705
    amicus curiae brief citations, 51 (table)
    federal-state relations, 216 (table)
    legislation overturn votes, 40 (table)
    on minority legislative districts, 732–734
    on religious establishment, 402 (table), 414, 418,
        424, 429–430, 432

religious exercise, 388 (table)
South Carolina Coastal Commission, 351–355
Southern Pacific Co., 256
Southern University, 473
Spaeth, Harold J., 26, 29, 30n15, 31, 32, 33nn, 37n,
    37n43, 38nn, 40, 43n63, 47n, 51n, 75n15, 76n20,
    36on, 420n47, 421n, 541n, 558n, 634n
Spannaus, Warren, 308
Specter, Arlen, 146 (box)
Speech and expression rights, 434–488. See also Li-
    bel; Press freedoms
  abortion, 548
  applied to states by 14th Amendment, 22, 442
  coerced expression, 482–488
  heirarchy of protection, 458
  legal standards summary (table), 457
  limiting principles, 458–460
  original intent, 25, 27–29, 435–436
  Preferred Freedoms doctrine, 34–35, 446
  public forums, 468–474, 475
  and religious freedom, 368–369, 386, 414, 418,
    483–487
  "time, place, and manner" doctrine, 459, 474
  unprotected expression, 504
Speech or Debate Clause, 114–116
Speedy Trial Act, 618n7
Speedy Trial Clause, 22, 574 (table), 617–618
Special interests See Interest groups
Special prosecutors, 146 (box), 164–165
Spence, Harold, 463
Spencer, Herbert, 316, 319, 327
Springer, William M., 263
St. Clair, James, 161 (illus.)
St. Paul Bias-Motivated Crime Ordinance, 477–482
Standing to sue, 90–94
Stanford Daily, 502–503
Stanley, Harold W., 41n, 208n, 421n, 578n1, 634n
Stanley, Robert, 536
Stanton, Edwin M., 166
Stare decisis, 32–34
  precedents overruled (table), 33
Starr, Kenneth, 376
State and local government
  bonds, 264, 272
  contract obligations, 293–294
  minority set-asides, 698–699
State constitutions
  Dorrite dispute, 86
  judicial review, 75
  rights enumerations, 15
State courts
  advisory opinions, 84n45
  federal judicial review, 65–66, 73–74, 76
State Department, U.S., 166
State employees and officials
  affirmative action, 697
  income taxes, 271
  labor standards, 191, 208–216
  standing to sue, 92
State laws
  congressional veto, 99
  discrimination ban, 645–649
  federal judicial review, 78–79, 294
  interstate commerce restrictions struck (table), 257
State legislatures
  apportionment, 87–88, 719–725
  chaplains' prayer, 421–422
  congressional elections, 98, 707–708
  presidential selection, 150
State mottoes, 487–488
State powers
  Articles of Confederation, 5 (chart)

Bill of Rights constraints, 21–23, 25
  commerce regulation, 252–257
  Constitution principles, 10
  constitutional amendment process, 17–19
  contract obligation limits for public good, 296–310
  eminent domain, property takings, 340, 342, 347,
    352
  federal relations, 185–189, 191–216
  obscenity definition, 512, 513
  substantive due process limits, 317, 321–330
  taxation, 260–261, 280–284
  voting rights, 707–709, 716–718
State taxes
  foreign commerce, 280–281
  interstate commerce, 281–282
Statutory rape, 675
Steel industry
  labor relations, 240–245
  seizure suit, 27, 29, 177–182
Stephenson, D. Grier Jr., 15n8, 446
Stevens, John Paul
  on abortion, 562, 563, 566 (table), 567, 569
  affirmative action programs, 698, 703–704
  amicus curiae brief citations, 51 (table)
  on criminal rights, 594
  on death penalty, 625–630, 633
  on equal protection, 648
  federal-state relations, 216 (table)
  judicial vote shifting, 42
  legislation overturn votes, 40 (table)
  on minority legislative districts, 732–734
  on privacy right, 538–540
  on property takings, 346, 350
  on religious establishment, 402 (table), 414, 416,
    418, 422, 428–430, 432
  religious exercise, 388 (table)
  school desegregation, 688, 689
  on speech rights, 468
  on term limits, 106–112
Stewart, Potter
  abortion issues, 556, 562, 566 (table)
  affirmative action programs, 698
  amicus curiae brief citations, 51 (table)
  on contract obligations, 309
  on criminal rights, 593, 602–605, 638
  on death penalty, 624, 625–630, 634
  federal-state relations, 216 (table)
  ideology, 132
  legislation overturn votes, 40 (table)
  on press freedoms, 496, 502, 513
  on privacy right, 531–534, 535, 536
  religious establishment, 402 (table), 419
  on religious exercise, 371, 373
  on speech rights, 472
Stites, Francis N., 67n12
Stone, Harlan Fiske
  career, 448
  on federal-state relations, 207
  ideology, 36 (table)
  New Deal decisions, 230, 232, 240
  on speech rights, 445–446, 457 (table)
  on stare decisis, 32
  on war powers, 176
Stone, John B., 302
Stoner, Joey, 582
Story, Joseph, 122
  career, 197
  on contract obligations, 294, 296, 300–301
  on federal-state relations, 186
  on inherent powers, 132
  on judicial review, 74
  legislative experience, 100 (table)

Strategic approaches of justices, 41–43
"Stream of commerce" doctrine, 228, 237, 248
"Strict scrutiny" test
  abortion, 564 (box), 568–569
  discriminatory school funding, 676
  minority set-asides, 699
  privacy right, 528, 534
  racial discrimination, 647, 666, 667
  sex discrimination, 670–674
Stromberg, Yetta, 445, 468
Strong, William, 100 (table)
Sturges, Josiah, 294
Subpoenas See also Compulsory process
  press privilege, 497–498
Substantive due process, 311–338, 526–528
  definition, 311, 312
  economic liberties summary, 288–289
  initial decisions, 314–316
  noneconomic applications, 314, 337–338, 527, 534,
    555–556
  "reasonableness" of statutes, 312, 318, 320,
    321–327, 329
  regulatory legislation struck, 318–320, 321–327,
    330–333
  regulatory legislation upheld, 316–318, 320–321,
    327–330, 332, 333–336
Subversive activities
  Civil War disputes, 173
  Japanese-American relocation, 175–177
  seditious libel, 514, 521
  speech rights cases, 435, 442, 445, 448–455
  un-Americanism investigations, 129–132
Subversive Activities Control Act of 1950, 455
Succession of executive, 152–154
Succession Act of 1947, 153 (box)
Suffrage See Voting rights
Sugar industry regulation, 227–228
Suicide, 540, 547
Sullivan, L.B., 514–516, 522 (photo)
Sumner, Charles, 201
Sunday closing laws, 370–373
"Superlegislature," Court as, 312, 315, 317
Supremacy Clause (Article VI), 99
  federal-state relations, 187, 189, 191, 192 (table), 196
Supreme Court See also Judicial decision making; Ju-
  dicial review; specific Courts by name of chief
  justice
  civil liberties agenda, 361 (graph), 445–446
  Constitution flexibility, 7–8, 9–10
  constitutional amendment process, 19–23
  decisions overturned by Congress, 377, 387
  decisions overturned by constitutional amend-
    ment (box), 20
  First Amendment claims, 360 (graph)
  jurisdiction, 63 (box), 65
Supreme Court justices
  blocked nominations, 368n19, 557, 565, 578, 662
  ideology, 1939–41 (graph), 36
  legislative experience (table), 100
  number, 64
  Roosevelt Court-packing plan, 28, 47, 237–240, 333
Surface Mining and Reclamation Act of 1977, 211
  (table)
Surface Transportation and Uniform Relocation Assistance Act of 1987, 700
"Suspect class" test
  discriminatory school funding, 676, 677, 681
  racial discrimination, 647, 666, 667
  sex discrimination, 648, 670
Sutherland, George
  career, 246
  on commerce regulation, 248

on contract obligations, 303, 306–307
on foreign policy powers, 168, 169–170
on inherent powers, 134–135
legislative experience, 100 (table)
New Deal decisions, 230, 231, 232, 237–240, 245
on right to counsel, 612
on standing to sue, 90–91
on substantive due process, 331
Swayne, Noah H.
   on contract obligations, 302
   legislative experience, 100 (table)
   on sex discrimination, 666
   on substantive due process, 315
   war powers, 173, 175
Sweeping Clause *See* Necessary and Proper Clause
Symbolic speech, 460–468
Synar, Mike, 155
Syndicalism laws, 442, 443, 445, 456

Taft-Hartley Act of 1946, 178
Taft, William Howard, 230
   on Brandeis, 328–329
   commerce regulation evolution, 248
   on delegated powers, 138
   on removal power, 167
   substantive due process, 331 (table)
   on tax and spend power, 274
Take Care Clause, 154
Takings Clause (5th Amendment)
   economic liberties summary, 289–290
   property takings, 339–355
Taney Court
   composition, 199 (table)
   on contract obligations, 288, 296–301
   federal-state relations, 192 (table), 197–201
Taney, Roger B.
   appointment, 197, 296
   career profile, 198
   on contract obligations, 296–300
   legislative experience, 100 (table)
   on political questions, 86
   on slavery, 20 (box), 26, 79, 200, 314, 653–654
Tariffs, 138, 196
Tarr, G. Alan, 32, 131n41, 287nn1–2, 337n28, 442n7
Tate, C. Neal, 45n60
Tate, U. Simpson, 659 (photo)
Tax and spend power
   constitutional basis, 99, 119, 259–261
   direct and income taxes, 261–270
   federal-state relations, 270–272, 280–284
   regulatory aspects, 272–275
   revenue impact of 16th Amendment, 269 (table)
   welfare purposes, 275–280
Taxpayer suits, 90–92
Teachers
   salaries, 404, 405
   subversive activities, 453n18
Teapot Dome scandal, 127–128
Telephone privacy, 526, 535–536
Televised testimony, 621–622
Tennessee Valley Authority, 230
Tenth Amendment
   federal-state relations, 187–189, 191–216, 314
   inherent powers, 136
   New Deal legislation, 232
   term limits issue, 106
Tenure
   constitutional authority, 57–58
   of executive branch officials, 165–168
   of justices, 43
   of president, 151–152

Tenure of Office Act of 1867, 166–167
Term limits
   arguments pro/con (box), 104–105
   of Congress, 104–113
   of president, 58
   proposed amendment, 19, 21, 106, 113
Terminiello, Arthur, 470–471
Terry stops, 582–583
Test Oath Law of 1862, 101–102
Testimonial evidence, 594–608
Textbooks
   religious establishment issues, 393, 394 (table),
      395, 404, 405, 406
Thanksgiving holiday, 415
Third Amendment
   privacy right, 525, 529, 534
   unincorporated provisions, 22n
Thirteenth Amendment
   property rights guarantees, 650
   ratification, 644
   text, 645
Thomas, Clarence
   abortion cases, 569 (table)
   affirmative action programs, 699, 703
   amicus curiae brief citations, 51 (table)
   career, 567, 668
   federal-state relations, 216
   legislation overturn votes, 40 (table)
   original intent doctrine, 26
   on property takings, 351
   religious establishment, 402 (table), 418, 430–432
   religious exercise, 388 (table)
   on tax and spend power, 283
   on term limits, 112–113
Thomas, Phillip F., 102
Thomas, R.J., 447
Thompson, Smith, 100 (table)
Thornhill, Byron, 460
Thornton, Ray, 105
Three-fifths formula, 199, 644
Tinker, John and Mary, 462
Tinsdale, Elkanah, 718 (illus.)
Tipaldo, Joseph, 332–333
Tires, 281
Titles of nobility, 18 (box)
Tocqueville, Alexis de, 363
Toll bridges, 297
Tonkin Gulf Resolution of 1964, 172
Towell, Pat, 146n
Train, Russell, 155
Transportation regulation, 141 (table), 210–212,
   219–225, 282
Treaty power
   congressional powers, 171
   executive powers, 168
   political questions, 89
Trespass, 459
Trial by jury *See* Jury trail
Tribe, Laurence, 406n40, 541nn15,17
Trimble, Robert, 100 (table)
Truman administration
   racial discrimination, 660
Truman, Harry S.
   on congressional investigation power, 126
   steel mill seizure, 27, 29, 177–178
Twelfth Amendment, 150, 151
Twenty-fifth Amendment, 152–154
Twenty-first Amendment, 17, 277
Twenty-fourth Amendment, 650, 708, 709, 717
Twenty-second Amendment, 152
Twenty-seventh Amendment, 17

Twenty-sixth Amendment, 20 (box), 650, 708, 709
Twenty-third Amendment, 18 (box)

UGP Properties, 343
Ulysses case, 506
Un-American Activities, House Committee on,
   128–132
Unanimity rule (jury trial), 620
"Understanding tests" for voter registration, 710–712
"Undue burden" standard (abortion restrictions),
   563–564, 567–569
Unemployment compensation, 371–373, 374–375,
   378–386
United States Trust Co., 307–308
United Steelworkers Union, 177
University of Alabama, 522–523
University of California at Davis, 691–693
University of Georgia, 522–523
University of Mississippi, 523
University of Missouri, 658
University of Oklahoma, 658
University of Texas, 658
Urban renewal projects, 347
Urofsky, Melvin I., 6, 8, 9n23, 13n3, 16nn14,16,
   76n19, 120n, 121, 122n25, 141n59, 142n61, 143n62,
   147n64, 200nn6–7, 262n1, 421n50, 580n1, 707n1
U.S. Term Limits, 105–113

Vagueness standard (speech restrictions), 459
"Valid arrest" searches, 581
"Valid secular policy" test, 366–373
Van Buren, Martin, 296n4
Van Devanter, Willis
   career, 28, 245
   on congressional investigation power, 127
   legislative experience, 100 (table)
   New Deal decisions, 230, 231, 232, 237–240, 245
   substantive due process, 331 (table)
Vanderbilt, Arthur T., 505 (box)
Vanderbilt, Cornelius, 221, 222
Veazie Bank, 273
Verdicts, 620
Vice president
   eligibility, selection, 150
   succession, 152–154
Vietnam War, 172, 456
Vietnam War protest movement, 456, 471
   ACLU history, 444
   armbands, 462
   draft resistance, 461–462
   flag desecration, 463
   Pentagon Papers case, 114–116, 495–497
   standing to sue, 92
Vinson, Fred M.
   career, 448, 454
   legislative experience, 100 (table)
   on speech rights, 448–449, 450–451, 457 (table),
      471
   on war powers, 177, 181–182
Violence
   advocacy, 442, 444, 445, 449, 456, 458
   black voter intimidation, 709
   press freedoms, 495
   speech restrictions, 462, 463, 469–470, 472–473
Virginia Plan, 6, 7 (chart), 62, 63, 97–99
Virtual representation, 97
Voir dire, 619
Vose, Clement E., 19n22, 329n16, 330n18, 331,
   332n23, 333n24, 366n12
Vote changes of justices, 42
Voting rights

apportionment issues, 87, 719–726
  constitutional basis, 644, 650–652, 707–708
  military personnel, 717
  minimum age, 20 (box), 708
  minority representation, 726–734
  poll taxes, 708, 716–717
  property ownership, 716
  racial discrimination, 708, 709–716
  residency requirements, 717–718
  "understanding tests," 710–712
  women, 666, 708
Voting Rights Act of 1965, 652, 660 (box), 712–716,
  718, 728, 734

Wage and hour regulation, 39
  child labor, 201–205
  New Deal legislation, 233, 240
  state employees, 191, 208–216
  substantive due process, 320–336, 527
Wages, W.L., 281
Wagner Act *See* National Labor Relations Act of
  1935
Waite, Morrison R.
  legislative experience, 100 (table)
  on religious exercise, 365, 374
  on substantive due process, 317, 319, 332, 336–337
Wald, Kenneth D., 363n3
Walker, Edwin, 523
Walker, Thomas G., 4nn6,11, 6n15, 37n, 38n, 40n,
  43n63, 47nn, 51n, 59n1, 80n31, 102n14, 174n7,
  360n, 421n, 541n, 558n, 634n
"Wall of separation," 365n10, 388, 392–395, 423
Wallace, George, 208
Walsh, Lawrence E., 165
Walsh, Thomas J., 329 (box)
Walz, Frederick, 396–397
War Claims Commission, 168
War declaration, 170, 171–172, 173
War powers
  Civil War disputes, 172–175
  constitutional authority, 171–172
  Korean War, 177–182
  World War II, 175–177
War Powers Act of 1973, 142 (box), 172
Warehouse taxes, 280–281
Warren Bridge Co., 297–298
Warren, Charles, 67n13, 201nn8,10
Warren Court
  amicus curiae citations, 50
  criminal rights cases, 396, 576 (graph), 578,
    592–593, 595–596, 606, 615, 617, 621
  economic, civil liberties decisions, 58, 38 (graph)
  First Amendment claims, 360 (graph)
  legislative apportionment, 720
  obscenity standards, 512 (table)
  precedents overruled, 33 (table)
  privacy right, 540
  religious establishment cases, 394–395, 419–420
  speech rights cases, 453–456, 462–463
  standing to sue, 93
Warren, Earl
  amicus curiae brief citations, 51 (table)
  career, 87 (box), 454, 456, 661, 662
  on congressional investigation power, 131 (box)
  on criminal rights, 597–602, 605

  on equal protection, 649
  on First Amendment rights, 32
  on House qualifications, 103, 105
  ideological attitudes, 37
  justiciability, 83
  legislation overturn votes, 40 (table)
  on legislative apportionment, 720, 721–725, 726
  privacy right, 530–531, 534, 535 (table)
  on racial discrimination, 661, 663–665, 682
  on religious establishment, 396, 419
  on religious exercise, 370–371
  on speech rights, 454, 462
  on taxpayer suits, 91
  on voting rights, 714–716
Warren, Samuel D. Jr., 328, 526n1
Wasby, Stephen L., 32nn29,31, 79n29, 215
Washington, Bushrod, 100 (table)
Washington, George
  advisory opinions, 83
  Bill of Rights, 16–17, 19
  executive privilege, 158
  national bank issue, 118, 120
  presidential elections, 150–151
  presidential tenure, 151
Washington Post, 495–497
Waste management, 283, 301–302
Watergate scandal, 58, 158–163, 497
Watkins, John T., 32, 33, 130–131
Wayne, James M.
  Dred Scott case, 200
  legislative experience, 100 (table)
  war powers, 173, 175
Webber, Howard, 114–115
Webster, Daniel
  career, 122, 298 (box)
  commerce regulation, 221, 222, 225
  contract obligations, 295–296, 297–298
Weddington, Sarah, 549–550
Weeks, Freemont, 585
Weisman, Daniel, 425
Weisman, Deborah, 425
Wesberry, James P., 720
West Lynn Creamery, 283–284
Wheeler, Burton, 239
Wheeler, Russell R., 64nn8–9, 65n, 66nn10–11
Wheelock, John, 295
White, Byron R., 161 (ill.)
  on abortion, 554, 556, 563, 565–567
  affirmative action programs, 698
  amicus curiae brief citations, 51 (table)
  career, 668, 699
  on criminal rights, 593–594, 602–605, 608, 620
  on death penalty, 624, 631, 634
  on equal protection, 648
  federal-state relations, 216
  legislation overturn votes, 40 (table)
  on legislative veto, 61, 145–147
  on minority legislative districts, 726–727
  on press freedoms, 496, 498–502, 503
  on privacy right, 535, 537–538, 540
  on religious establishment, 395, 402 (table), 403,
    418, 422, 423, 430–432
  on religious exercise, 387–388
  on speech or debate clause, 116
  on speech rights, 467–468

White, Edward D.
  legislative experience, 100 (table)
  on speech rights, 436
  substantive due process, 331 (table)
White, Welsh S., 608n19
Whitney, Charlotte, 442–443
Whittaker, Charles
  amicus curiae brief citations, 51 (table)
  on criminal rights, 590–592
  ideology, 132
  legislation overturn votes, 40 (table)
  on tax and spend power, 267–269, 274
Whittemore, Benjamin F., 102 (table)
Wickard, Claude R., 246
Wiener, Myron, 168
Willey, Waitman T., 709–710
Williams, Robert Anthony, 594
Wills, Garry, 363
Wilson-Gorman Tariff Act of 1894, 264
Wilson, James, 15–16, 263n2, 263n4, 675
Wilson, John A., 102 (table)
Wilson, Woodrow
  on congressional investigation power, 126
  removal power, 167
  Supreme Court appointments, 328–329
Wiretaps, 526, 535–536
Wirt, William, 221
Wishman, Seymour, 616n4
Witnesses
  congressional investigations, 32, 33, 34, 126–128,
    482
  criminal trials, 22, 482, 621–622
Witt, Elder, 28n, 73n, 84–85, 100n, 146n, 198n,
    239n9, 288n6, 290n9, 329n, 441n, 443n11, 505n,
    557n, 577n, 660n, 662n
Witte, John F., 263n5
Woll, Peter, 126n33, 319, 435n1
Women *See* Sex discrimination
Women's Rights Project (ACLU), 50, 444, 668
Wood, Frederick, 233 (photo)
Wood, Stephen B., 202n11
Woodbury, Levi, 100 (table)
Woods, William B., 100 (table)
Woodward, Bob, 624n12
Woodward, William, 295
Woodworth, George C., 635n18
World War I
  speech rights cases, 436–443
World War II
  Japanese-American relocation, 175–177
Wright, Benjamin F., 293n2
Wright, John R., 48n69
Writs *See* specific type of writ

Yarbrough, Tinsley E., 27n9
Yarmulkes, 375–377
Yates, Oleta O'Connor, 454
Yazoo land fraud, 293–294
Young Communist League, 445
Young, John D., 102 (table)
Young Progressives, 471

Zalman, Marvin, 580n2, 583n5, 608
Zamora, Rigoberto, 387 (photo)
Zoning regulations, 92, 93, 342

CASE INDEX

Boldface indicates excerpted case.

Abington Township, School District of v. Schempp, 374 U.S. 203 (1963), 19, 82 (table), 394–395, 396–397, 401 (table), 404, 420, 422, 432

Abrams v. United States, 250 U.S. 616 (1919), 439–440, 442, 457 (table)

Adarand Constructors v. Pena, —U.S.— (1995) 78, **699–705**

Addystone Pipe and Steel Co. v. United States, 175 U.S. 211 (1899), 227n4

Adkins v. Children's Hospital, 261 U.S. 525 (1923), 330–331, 333, 336

Adler v. Board of Education, City of New York, 342 U.S. 485 (1952), 453n18

Aguilar v. Felton, 473 U.S. 402 (1985), 405

Akron v. Akron Center for Reproductive Health, 462 U.S. 416 (1983), 559, 562–569

Alabama v. King and Boozer, 314 U.S. 1 (1941), 271n12

Albertson v. Subversive Activities Control Board, 382 U.S. 70 (1965), 455

Alexander v. Holmes County Board of Education, 396 U.S. 19 (1969), 683n3

Allen v. Wright, 468 U.S. 737 (1984), 92

Allgeyer v. Louisiana, 165 U.S. 578 (1897), 313 (table), 319, 320

Allied Structural Steel Co. v. Spannaus, 438 U.S. 234 (1978), 307, 308–309

American Communication Association v. Douds, 339 U.S. 382 (1950), 448–449

Anderson v. Dunn, 6 Wheat. 204 (1821), 126n36

Apodaca v. Oregon, 406 U.S. 404 (1972), 620

Aptheker v. Secretary of State, 378 U.S. 500 (1964), 455

Argersinger v. Hamlin, 407 U.S. 25 (1972), 22, 616

Arizona v. Fulminante, 499 U.S. 279 (1991), 608

Arlington Heights v. Metropolitan Housing Corporation, 429 U.S. 252 (1977), 93

Ashe v. Swenson, 397 U.S. 436 (1970), 638

Ashton v. Cameron County District Court, 298 U.S. 513 (1936), 232

Ashwander v. Tennessee Valley Authority, 297 U.S. 288 (1936), 93, 94

Associated Press v. Walker, 388 U.S. 130 (1967), 522, 523

Bailey v. Drexel Furniture Co., 259 U.S. 20 (1922), 274, 313 (table)

Baker v. Carr, 369 U.S. 186 (1962), 87–90, 720, 722

Barenblatt v. United States, 360 U.S. 109 (1959), 33, 34, 35, 130–132

Barker v. Wingo, 407 U.S. 514 (1972), 618

Barron v. Baltimore, 7 Pet. 243 (1833), 25, 340

Batson v. Kentucky, 476 U.S. 79 (1986), 619

Beal v. Doe, 432 U.S. 438 (1977), 561

Belchertown v. Saikewicz, 370 N.E. 2d 417 (1977), 541n17

Bellotti v. Baird, 443 U.S. 622 (1979), 559

Benton v. Maryland, 395 U.S. 784 (1969), 22

Berkemer v. McCarty, 468 U.S. 420 (1984), 606n15

Bethel School District No. 403 v. Fraser, 478 U.S. 675 (1986), 330

Betts v. Brady, 316 U.S. 455 (1942), 612, 615

Bibb v. Navajo Freight Lines, 386 U.S. 976 (1959), 257

Board of Airport Commissioners of Los Angeles v. Jews for Jesus, Inc., 482 U.S. 569 (1987), 475

Board of Education v. Allen, 392 U.S. 236 (1968), 393, 394 (table), 395, 402, 403, 404

Board of Education of Kiryas Joel Village School District v. Grumet, 512 U.S. — (1994), 405

Board of Education of Oklahoma City Public Schools v. Dowell, 498 U.S. 237 (1991), 688

Bolling v. Sharpe, 347 U.S. 497 (1954), 649

Boos v. Barry, 485 U.S. 312 (1988), 475

Bowers v. Hardwick, 478 U.S. 186 (1986), **536–540**

Bowsher v. Synar, 478 U.S. 714 (1986), 146 (box), 155

Bradfield v. Roberts, 175 U.S. 291 (1899), 389, 392

Bradwell v. Illinois, 16 Wall. 130 (1873), 666

Brandenburg v. Ohio, 395 U.S. 444 (1969), 455–456, 477

Branzburg v. Hayes, 408 U.S. 665 (1972), **498–502,** 503

Braunfeld v. Brown, 366 U.S. 599 (1961), 370–373

Bray v. Alexandria Women's Health Clinic, 506 U.S. 263 (1993), 475

Breedlove v. Suttles, 302 U.S. 277 (1937), 717

Brewer v. Williams, 430 U.S. 387 (1977), 606n17

Brewster; United States v., 408 U.S. 501 (1972), 115 (table)

Bronson v. Kinzie, 1 How. 311 (1843), 301

Brown v. Board of Education of Topeka, 347 U.S. 483 (1954), 131, 249, 649, 659 (photo), 660 (box), **661–666,** 682

Brown v. Board of Education of Topeka, 349 U.S. 294 (1955), 682–683

Brown v. Mississippi, 297 U.S. 278 (1936), 595n13

Brown v. Maryland, 12 Wheat. 419 (1827), 280

Brown; United States v., 381 U.S. 437 (1965), 455

Brushaber v. Union Pacific Raliroad, 240 U.S. 1 (1916), 270

Buckley v. Valeo, 424 U.S. 1 (1976), 146 (box), 164

Bumper v. North Carolina, 391 U.S. 543 (1968), 582

Bunting v. Oregon, 243 U.S. 426 (1917), 330, 331

Butler v. Michigan, 372 U.S. 380 (1957), 506

Butler; United States v., 297 U.S. 1 (1936), 232, 276, 277, 280, 313 (table)

C & A Carbone, Inc. v. Town of Clarkstown, New York, — U.S. — (1994), 257

Calandra; United States v., 414 U.S. 338 (1974), 593n12

California v. Stewart, 384 U.S. 436 (1966), 597n14

Cantwell v. Connecticut, 310 U.S. 296 (1940), 22, 366–367, 371, 386

Capitol Square Review Board v. Pinette, — U.S. — (1995), 418

Carolene Products Co.; United States v., 304 U.S. 144 (1938), 445–446, 457 (table), 647n3

Carrington v. Rash, 380 U.S. 89 (1965), 717

Carroll v. United States, 267 U.S. 132 (1925), 584

Carter v. Carter Coal Co., 298 U.S. 238 (1936), 84, 232, 237, 246, 248, 313 (table)

Causby; United States v., 328 U.S. 256 (1946), 341–342

Chambers v. Maroney, 399 U.S.42 (1970), 584n8

Chaplinsky v. New Hampshire, 315 U.S. 568 (1942), **469–470,** 474, 514n12

Charles River Bridge v. Warren Bridge, 11 Pet. 420 (1837), **296–301**

Chicago Board of Trade v. Olsen, 262 U.S. 543 (1923), 228

Chicago, Burlington & Quincy Railroad v. Chicago, 166 U.S. 226 (1897), 22, 341

Chicago, Milwaukee & St. Paul Railway v. Minnesota, 134 U.S. 418 (1890), 318–319, 320

Church of the Lukumi Babalu Aye Inc. v. City of Hialeah, 508 U.S. — (1993), 386–388

City of New York v. Miln, 11 Pet. 102 (1837), 675

City of Richmond v. J. A. Croson Co., 488 U.S. 469 (1989), 78, 698–699, 700

Civil Rights Cases, 100 U.S. 3 (1883), 650, 654

Clark, Ex parte, 100 U.S. 399 (1880), 709

Cleburne v. Cleburne Living Center, 473 U.S. 432 (1985), 648

Cohens v. Virginia, 6 Wheat. 264 (1821), 74, 75, 298 (box)

Coker v. Georgia, 433 U.S. 583 (1977), 612n2

Cole v. Arkansas, 333 U.S. 196 (1948), 22

Colegrove v. Green, 328 U.S. 459 (1946), 87, 88, 720

Coleman v. Miller, 307 U.S. 433 (1939), 19–20

Collector v. Day, 11 Wall. 113 (1871), 271

Collins v. Collins, — U.S. — (1994), **637–638**

Committee for Public Education and Religious Liberty v. Nyquist, 413 U.S. 756 (1973), 403, 404

Committee for Public Education and Religious Liberty v. Regan, 444 U.S.646 (1980), 405

Communist Party of the United States, United States v., 377 U.S. 968 (1964), 455

Complete Auto Transit v. Brady, 430 U.S. 274 (1977), 281–282

Consolidated Edison Co. v. NLRB, 305 U.S. 197 (1938), 247 (table)

Cooley v. Board of Wardens, 12 How. 229 (1852), **253–255**

Cooper v. Aaron, 358 U.S. 1 (1958), 682–683

County of Allegheny v. ACLU, 492 U.S. 573 (1989), 416–418, 422, 432

Cox v. Louisiana, 379 U.S. 559 (1965), 473–474

Craig v. Boren, 429 U.S. 190 (1976), 648n5, 668, 670, **671–674**

Crist v. Bretz, 437 U.S. 28 (1978), 22

Cruikshank; United States v., 92 U.S. 542 (1876), 709

Cruzan v. Director, Missouri Department of Health, 497 U.S. 261 (1990), 540, **541–547**

Curtis Publishing Co. v. Butts, 388 U.S. 139 (1967), 522–523

Curtiss-Wright Export Corp.; United States v., 299 U.S. 304 (1936), **132–136,** 137–138, **168–170**

Dalton v. Specter, — U.S. — (1994), 146 (box)

Darby Lumber; United States v., 312 U.S. 100 (1941), **206–207,** 209 (box), 246, 247 (table)

Dartmouth College, Trustees of v. Woodward, 4 Wheat. 518 (1819), 295–296, 298 (box)

Davidson v. New Orleans, 96 U.S. 97 (1878), 316n4

Davis v. Bandemer, 478 U.S. 109 (1986), 89

Davis v. Michigan Department of Treasury, 489 U.S. 803 (1989), 272

Davis v. Passman, 442 U.S. 228 (1979), 115 (table)

Dean Milk Co. v. Madison, 346 U.S. 343 (1951), 257

Debs v. United States, 249 U.S. 211 (1919), 439, 442

DeFunis v. Odegaard, 416 U.S. 312 (1974), 85

DeJonge v. Oregon, 229 U.S. 353 (1937), 22, 445

Dennis v. United States, 341 U.S. 494 (1951), **449–453,** 455 (table), 457 (table)

Dobbins v. Commissioners of Erie County, 16 Pet. 435 (1842), 271

Doe v. Bolton, 410 U.S. 179 (1973), 549, 553n19, 555, 558

Doe v. McMillan, 412 U.S. 306 (1973), 115 (table)

Dolan v. City of Tigard, — U.S. — (1994), 355

Doremus; United States v., 249 U.S. 86 (1919), 275

Douglas v. California, 372 U.S. 353 (1963), 617

Duncan v. Louisiana, 391 U.S. 145 (1968), 22

Dunn v. Blumstein, 405 U.S. 330 (1972), 648, 718

E. C. Knight Co.; United States v., 156 U.S. 1 (1895), 227–228, 237, 246, 248

Eakin v. Raub, 12 Sergeant and Rowle 330 Pa. (1825), 76

Earley v. DiCenso, 403 U.S. 602 (1971), **397–401,** 404

Eastland v. U.S. Servicemens' Fund, 421 U.S. 491 (1975), 115 (table)

Eddings v. Oklahoma, 455 U.S. 104 (1982), 625n15, 635–645

Edmonson v. Leesville Concrete Co., 500 U.S. 614 (1991), 619

Edwards v. Aguillard, 482 U.S. 578 (1987), **408–414**

Edwards v. California, 314 U.S. 160 (1941), 257

Edwards v. South Carolina, 372 U.S. 229 (1963), 472, 473–474

Eichman; United States v., 496 U.S. 310 (1990), 468

Elfbrandt v. Russell, 384 U.S. 11 (1966), 455

Employment Division, Department of Human Resources of Oregon v. Smith, 494 U.S. 872 (1990), **378–386,** 387–388

Endo, Ex parte, 323 U.S. 283 (1944), 177

Energy Reserves Group, Inc. v. Kansas Power and Light Co., 459 U.S. 400 (1983), 309

Engel v. Vitale, 370 U.S. 421 (1962), 19, 82 (table), 394 (table), 419–420, 421, 422, 432

Epperson v. Arkansas, 393 U.S. 97 (1968), 394 (table), 408, 414

Equal Employment Opportunity Commission v. Wyoming, 460 U.S. 226 (1983), 211 (table)

Escobedo v. Illinois, 378 U.S. 478 (1964), 595–596

Estes v. Texas, 381 U.S. 532 (1965), 621

Everson v. Board of Education, 330 U.S. 1 (1947), 22, 364, 392–393, 394 (table), 395, 396, 401 (table), 402, 403, 404, 406, 408, 423

Ex parte *See* specific name of party

Exxon Corp. v. Eagerton, 462 U.S. 176 (1983), 309n5

FEC v. National Rifle Ass'n Political Victory Fund, — U.S. — (1994), 146 (box)

Federal Energy Regulatory Commission v. Mississippi, 456 U.S. 742 (1982), 211 (table)

Feiner v. New York, 340 U.S. 315 (1951), 470, 471, 472–473

Ferguson v. Skrupa, 372 U.S. 726 (1963), 408n, 528n7

First English Evangelical Lutheran Church of Glendale v. County of Los Angeles, 482 U.S. 304 (1987), 350

Fisher v. Hurst, 333 U.S. 147 (1948), 658

Fiske v. Kansas, 274 U.S. 380 (1927), 443n9

Flast v. Cohen, 392 U.S. 83 (1968), 83n39, 91–93

Fletcher v. Peck, 6 Cr. 87 (1810), 293–294

Fordice; United States v., 505 U.S. 717 (1992), 689

Forsyth County, Georgia v. Nationalist Movement, 505 U.S. 123 (1992), 475

Freeman v. Pitts, 503 U.S. 467 (1992), 688–689

Frisby v. Schultz, 487 U.S. 474 (1988), 475

Frohwerk v. United States, 249 U.S. 204 (1919), 439, 442

Frontiero v. Richardson, 411 U.S. 677 (1973), 648n4, 668, 670n2

Frothingham v. Mellon, 262 U.S. 447 (1923), 90–93

Fry v. United States, 421 U.S. 542 (1975), 209 (box)

Fullilove v. Klutznick, 448 U.S. 448 (1980), 698

Furman v. Georgia, 408 U.S. 238 (1972), 623–625, 633–634, 636

Gale; United States v., 109 U.S. 65 (1883), 709

Garcia v. San Antonio Metropolitan Transit Authority, 469 U.S. 578 (1985), 191, **210–216**

Gardner v. Broderick, 392 U.S. 273 (1968), 622

Garrity v. New Jersey, 385 U.S. 493 (1967), 622

Georgia v. McCollum, 505 U.S. 42 (1992), 619

Gertz v. Welch, 418 U.S. 323 (1974), 523

Gibbons v. Ogden, 9 Wheat. 1 (1824), 30, 117, **220–225,** 248, 249, 252, 298 (box)

Gideon v. Wainwright, 372 U.S. 335 (1963), 22, 597, **613–615,** 616

Gillespie v. Oklahoma, 257 U.S. 501 (1922), 271n9

Gilligan v. Morgan, 413 U.S. 1 (1973), 89

Gitlow v. New York, 268 U.S. 652 (1925), 22, 442, 443

Glidden Co. v. Zdanok, 370 U.S. 530 (1962), 82n37

Goesaert v. Cleary, 335 U.S. 465 (1948), 666–667

Goldman v. Secretary of Defense, 739 F. 2d 657 (1984), 376n24

Goldman v. Weinberger, 475 U.S. 503 (1986), 375–377, 378, 385, 387–388

Goldwater v. Carter, 444 U.S. 996 (1979), 89

Gomillion v. Lightfoot, 364 U.S. 339 (1960), 726

Grand Rapids School District v. Ball, 473 U.S. 373 (1985), 405, 406n39

Gravel v. United States, 408 U.S. 606 (1972), 114–116

Graves v. New York ex rel. O'Keefe, 306 U.S. 466 (1939), 271

Great Atlantic and Pacific Tea Co. v. Cottrell, 424 U.S. 366 (1976), 257

Green v. School Board of New Kent County, 391 U.S. 430 (1968), 683

Green v. United States, 356 U.S. 165 (1958), 33–34

Gregg v. Georgia, 428 U.S. 153 (1976), **625–633,** 634–635

Griffin v. Prince Edward County School Board, 377 U.S. 218 (1964), 683

Griswold v. Connecticut, 381 U.S. 479 (1965), 22, 43, 337–338, 526, **529–535,** 536, 547, 548, 550, 555, 556, 558

H. L. v. Matheson, 451 U.S. 398 (1981), 559

Hague v. C.I.O., 307 U.S. 496 (1939), 22

Hammer v. Dagenhart, 247 U.S. 251 (1918), 19n22, **201–206,** 228, 274, 313 (table)

Hampton & Co. v. United States, 276 U.S. 394 (1928), 138, 140

Harden v. Tennessee, 216 S.W. 2d 708 (1949), 365n7

Harper v. Virginia State Board of Elections, 383 U.S. 663 (1966), 717

Harris v. Forklift Systems, Inc., 510 U.S. — (1993), 674

Harris v. McRae, 448 U.S. 297 (1980), 561 (table), 562

Harris v. New York, 401 U.S. 222 (1971), 606

Harris; United States v., 106 U.S. 629 (1883), 654, 709

Hawaii Housing Authority v. Midkiff, 467 U.S. 229 (1989), **347–350**

Healy v. Beer Institute, 491 U.S. 324 (1989), 257

Heart of Atlanta Motel v. United States, 379 U.S. 241 (1964), **250–252,** 650n7, 689n7

Helstoski; United States v., 442 U.S. 264 (1979), 115 (table), 116

Helvering v. Davis, 301 U.S. 609 (1937), 247 (table), 276

Helvering v. Gerhardt, 304 U.S. 405 (1938), 271

Hills v. Gautreaux, 425 U.S. 284 (1976), 689n4

Hirabayashi v. United States, 320 U.S. 81 (1943), 176

Hobbie v. Unemployment Appeals Commission of Florida, 480 U.S. 136 (1987), 377, 379

Hodel v. Virginia Surface Mining & Reclamation Ass'n, 452 U.S. 264 (1981), 216n22

Hodgson v. Minnesota, 497 U.S. 417 (1990), 559

Holden v. Hardy, 169 U.S. 366 (1898), 320–321, 327

Home Building and Loan Ass'n v. Blaisdell, 290 U.S. 398 (1934), **303–307**

Hopkins Savings Ass'n v. Cleary, 296 U.S. 315 (1935), 232

Houchins v. KQED, Inc., 438 U.S. 1 (1978), 503

Houston, E. & W. Texas Railway Co. v. United States, 234 U.S. 342 (1914), 226, 248

Hoyt v. Florida, 368 U.S. 57 (1961), 667

Hudson v. Palmer, 468 U.S. 517 (1984), 584n7

Hughes v. Oklahoma, 441 U.S. 322 (1979), 257

Humphrey's Executor v. United States, 295 U.S. 602 (1935), 167–168, 231

Hunt v. McNair, 413 U.S. 734 (1973), 404

Hunt v. Washington State Apple Advertising Comm'n, 432 U.S. 333 (1977), 256

Hutchinson v. Proxmire, 443 U.S. 111 (1979), 115 (table), 116

Hylton v. United States, 3 Dall. 171 (1796), 66, 261

Illinois Central Railroad Co. v. ICC, 206 U.S. 41 (1907), 226n3

Illinois ex rel. McCollum v. Board of Education, 333 U.S. 293 (1948), 394 (table), 419

Immigration and Naturalization Service v. Chadha, 462 U.S. 919 (1983), 61, **142–147**

Indian Motorcycle Co. v. United States, 238 U.S. 501 (1931), 271n10

International Longshoreman's Union v. Boyd, 347 U.S. 222 (1954), 85

International Society for Krishna Consciousness v. Lee, 505 U.S. 672 (1992), 475

Interstate Circuit v. Dallas, 390 U.S. 676 (1968), 504n7

Interstate Commerce Comm'n v. Alabama-Midland Railway Co., 168 U.S. 144 (1897), 226n2

Interstate Commerce Comm'n v. Brimson, 154 U.S. 447 (1894), 226n2

Interstate Commerce Comm'n v. Cincinnati, New Orleans & Texas Pacific Railway Co., 167 U.S. 479 (1897), 226n2

J. E. B. v. T. B., — U.S. — (1994), 619

Jackson, Ex parte, 96 U.S. 727 (1878), 506

Jacobellis v. Ohio, 378 U.S. 184 (1964), 507, 508 (box)

Johnson v. Louisiana, 406 U.S. 356 (1972), 620

Johnson v. Transportation Agency of Santa Clara County, California 480 U.S. 646 (1987), 697n8

Johnson v. Zerbst, 304 U.S. 458 (1938), 612

Jones v. Alfred H. Mayer, Inc. (1968), 650n6

Jones v. Opelika, 316 U.S. 584 (1942), 369n21

Kahn v. Shevin, 416 U.S. 351 (1974), 668, 670n2

Kahriger; United States v., 345 U.S. 22 (1953), 275

Karcher v. May, 484 U.S. 72 (1987), 92

Kassell v. Consolidated Freightways, 450 U.S. 662 (1981), 257

Katz v. United States, 389 U.S. 347 (1967), 535–536, 585n9

Katzenbach v. McClung, 379 U.S. 294 (1964), 650n7, 689n7

Keystone Bituminous Coal Ass'n v. DeBenedictis, 480 U.S. 470 (1987), 309n6, 350

Kidd v. Pearson, 128 U.S. 1 (1888), 227

Kilbourn v. Thompson, 103 U.S. 168 (1881), 114, 126–127, 128

Klein; United States v., 80 U.S. 128 (1872), 81, 82

Klopfer v. North Carolina, 386 U.S. 213 (1967), 22

Kokinda; United States v., 497 U.S. 720 (1990), 475

Koremato v. United States, 323 U.S. 214 (1944), 29n12, 43–44, 176–177

Kovacs v. Cooper, 336 U.S. 77 (1949), 448, 457 (table)

Kramer v. Union Free School District, 395 U.S. 621 (1969), 716

Lee v. Weisman, 505 U.S. 577 (1992), **424–432,** 433

Lee; United States v., 435 U.S. 252 (1982), 375, 386

Lemon v. Kurtzman, 403 U.S. 602 (1971), **397–401,** 402–403, 404–405, 406, 414, 415–416, 418, 421–425, 432–433

Leon; United States v., 468 U.S. 897 (1984), 593, 594

Levitt v. CPEARL, 413 U.S. 472 (1973), 404

License Cases, 5 How. 504 (1847), 199

Lochner v. New York, 198 U.S. 45 (1905), 312, 313 (table), **321–330,** 527, 534, 535, 555

Long v. Rockwood, 277 U.S. 142 (1928), 271n9

Lopez; United States v., — U.S. — (1995), 216 cap., 247–248

Louisiana ex rel. Francis v. Resweber, 329 U.S. 459 (1947), 22, 623n10

Louisiana v. United States, 380 U.S. 145 (1965), **710–712**

Louisville Bank v. Radford, 295 U.S. 555 (1935), 231n6, 232

Lucas v. South Carolina Coastal Council, 505 U.S. 1003 (1992), 48–49, 50, **351–355**

Lujan v. Defenders of Wildlife, — U.S. — (1992), 92

Luther v. Borden, 7 How. 1 (1849), 86–88, 298 (box)

Lynch v. Donnelly, 465 U.S. 668 (1984), 402 (table), 415, 417, 418

McCardle, Ex parte, 7 Wall. 506 (1896), 79n30, **80–81,** 82

McCleskey v. Kemp, 481 U.S. 279 (1987), 635–636

McCray v. United States, 195 U.S. 27 (1904), 273, 274

McCullagh; United States v., 221 Fed. 288 (1915), 318

McCulloch v. Maryland, 4 Wheat. 316 (1819), 31, **118–126, 193–196,** 197, 270, 298 (box)

McGowan v. Maryland, 366 U.S. 420 (1961), 647n2

McGrain v. Daugherty, 273 U.S. 135 (1927), 127–128

McLaurin v. Oklahoma State Regents for Higher Education, 339 U.S. 637 (1950), 658

Madsen v. Women's Health Center, Inc., 512 U.S. — (1994), 474, 475

Maher v. Roe, 432 U.S. 464 (1977), 561

Malloy v. Hogan, 378 U.S. 1 (1964), 22

Mapp v. Ohio, 367 U.S. 643 (1961), 22, **586–592,** 593

Marbury v. Madison, 1 Cr. 137 (1803), 31, 46, 64, 65, **66–75,** 76, 80, 86

Marsh v. Chambers, 463 U.S. 783 (1983), 421–422

Martin v. Hunter's Lessee, 1 Wheat. 304 (1816), 74, 80, 186n6

Martin v. Wilks, 490 U.S. 755 (1989), 689n5

Maryland v. Craig, 497 U.S. 836 (1990), 621–622

Maryland v. Wirtz, 392 U.S. 183 (1968), 209–210

Massachusetts v. Sheppard, 468 U.S. 981 (1984), 593, 594

Meek v. Pittenger, 421 U.S. 349 (1975), 404, 406

Memoirs v. Massachusetts, 383 U.S. 413 (1966), 507, 508 (box)

Metro Broadcasting, Inc. v. FCC, 497 U.S. 547 (1990), 699, 700

Meyer v. Nebraska, 262 U.S. 390 (1923), 527, 528n9

Michael M. v. Superior Court of Sonoma County, 450 U.S. 464 (1981), 675

Michelin Tire Corp. v. Wages, 423 U.S. 276 (1976), 281

Michigan v. Tucker, 417 U.S. 433 (1974), 606

Miller v. California, 413 U.S. 15 (1973), **508–512,** 513

Miller v. Johnson, — U.S. — (1995), 727 (map), **728–734**

Milligan, Ex parte, 4 Wall. 2 (1866), 80n34, 174–175

Millikin v. Bradley, 418 U.S. 717 (1974), 688

Minersville School District v. Gobitis, 310 U.S. 586 (1940), 367–368, 369, 388, 483

Minor v. Happersett, 21 Wall. 162 (1875), 666, 708

Miranda v. Arizona, 384 U.S. 436 (1966), 82 (table), **596–605,** 606–608

Mississippi v. Johnson, 4 Wall. 475 (1867), 156–157, 163

Mississippi University for Women v. Hogan, 458 U.S. 718 (1982), 675

Missouri ex rel. Gaines v. Canada, 305 U.S. 237 (1938), 658

Missouri v. Jenkins, 491 U.S. 274 (1989), 688, 689

Mistretta v. United States, 488 U.S. 361 (1989), 77

Monongahela Navigation Co. v. United States, 148 U.S. 132 (1893), 79

Moran v. Burbine, 475 U.S. 412 (1986), 608n18

Morehead v. New York ex rel. Tipaldo, 298 U.S. 587 (1936), 240n11, 313 (table), 332–333, 334

Morrison v. Olson, 487 U.S. 654 (1988), 146 (box), 164–165

Mueller v. Allen, 463 U.S. 388 (1983), 405

Mugler v. Kansas, 123 U.S. 623 (1887), 317–318, 319

Mulford v. Smith, 307 U.S. 38 (1939), 247 (table), 276n13

Muller v. Oregon, 208 U.S. 412 (1908), 39, 327, 329–330, 331

Munn v. Illinois, 94 U.S. 113 (1877), 316–317, 320, 336–337

Muskrat v. United States, 219 U.S. 346 (1911), 84

Myers v. United States, 272 U.S. 52 (1926), 167–168

NAACP v. Button, 371 U.S. 415 (1963), 35

National Labor Relations Board v. Fainblatt, 306 U.S. 601 (1939), 247 (table)

National Labor Relations Board v. Friedman-Harry Marks Clothing Co., 301 U.S. 58 (1937), 247 (table)

National Labor Relations Board v. Fruehauf Trailer Co., 301 U.S. 49 (1937), 247 (table)

National Labor Relations Board v. Jones & Laughlin Steel Corp., 301 U.S. 1 (1937), **240–245,** 248, 249

National League of Cities v. Usery, 426 U.S. 833 (1976), 191, 208–210, 211, 215–216

National Mutual Insurance Co. v. Tidewater Transfer Co., 337 U.S. 582 (1949), 82n36

National Organization for Women v. Scheidler, 510 U.S. — (1994), 475

National Socialist Party v. Skokie, 432 U.S. 43 (1977), 476–477

Near v. Minnesota, 283 U.S. 697 (1931), **490–495**

Nebbia v. New York, 291 U.S. 502 (1934), 245n12, 332, 333, 527n5

New England Power Co. v. New Hampshire, 455 U.S. 331 (1982), 257

New State Ice Co. v. Liebmann, 285 U.S. 262 (1932), 185n2

New York v. Cathedral Academy, 434 U.S. 125 (1977), 405

New York v. Quarles, 467 U.S. 649 (1984), 606

New York Times Co. v. Sullivan, 376 U.S. 254 (1964), **514–522,** 523–524

New York Times Co. v. United States, 403 U.S. 713 (1971), 495–497

Nigro v. United States, 276 U.S. 332 (1928), 275

Nix v. Williams, 467 U.S. 431 (1984), 594

Nixon v. Fitzgerald, 457 U.S. 731 (1982), 157

Nixon v. General Services Administration, 433 U.S. 425 (1977), 146 (box)

Nixon v. Herndon, 273 U.S. 536 (1927), 778
Nixon v. United States, 506 U.S. 224 (1993), 30, 89, 90
Nixon; United States v., 418 U.S. 683 (1974), **158–163**
Nollan v. California Coastal Comm'n, 483 U.S. 825 (1987), 350–351
North Carolina v. Alford, 400 U.S. 25 (1970), 617
Northern Pipeline Construction Co. v. Marathon Pipe Line Co., 458 U.S. 50 (1982)
Northern Securities Co. v. United States, 193 U.S. 197 (1904), 227
Northwest Fertilizing Co. v. Hyde Park, 97 U.S. 256 (1878), 301–302
NOW v. Idaho, 459 U.S. 809 (1982), 20–21

O'Brien; United States v., 391 U.S. 367 (1968), 461–462
Ogden v. Saunders, 12 Wheat. 213 (1827), 295n3, 298 (box)
Ohio v. Akron Center for Reproductive Health, 497 U.S. 502 (1990), 559
Oliver, In re, 333 U.S. 257 (1948), 22
Oliver v. United States, 466 U.S. 170 (1984), 584n6
Olmstead v. United States, 277 U.S. 438 (1928), 526, 536, 540
One Book Called "Ulysses"; United States v., 72 F.2d 705 (1934), 506
O'Neill v. Synar, 478 U.S. 714 (1986), 146 (box)
Oregon v. Elstad, 470 U.S. 298 (1985), 606, 607–608
Oregon v. Mitchell, 400 U.S. 112 (1970), 708
Oregon Waste Systems v. Department of Environmental Quality of the State of Oregon, — U.S. — (1994), 283
Orozco v. Texas, 394 U.S. 324 (1969), 606n16
Orr v. Orr, 440 U.S. 268 (1979), 674–675
Osborn v. Bank of the United States, 9 Wheat. 783 (1824), 298 (box)
Owen v. Owen, 500 U.S. 305 (1991), 42

Panama Refining Co. v. Ryan, 293 U.S. 388 (1935), 133, 138–140, 230–231, 232, 246, 313 (table)
Panhandle Oil Co. v. Mississippi, 277 U.S. 218 (1928), 271n9
Paradise; United States v., 480 U.S. 149 (1987), 697
Paris Adult Theatre I v. Slaton, 413 U.S. 49 (1973), 512–513
Patterson v. McLean Credit Union, 491 U.S. 164 (1989), 689n5
Patton v. Yount, 467 U.S. 1025, (1984), 620
Penn Central Transportation Co. v. City of New York, 438 U.S. 104 (1978), **342–346,** 350
Pennell v. City of San Jose, 485 U.S. 1 (1988), 337
Pennsylvania v. Nelson, 350 U.S. 497 (1956), 453–454, 455
Pennsylvania Coal Co. v. Mahon, 260 U.S. 393 (1922), 342
People v. Defore, 242 U.S. 13 (1926), 586
Philadelphia v. New Jersey, 437 U.S. 617 (1978), 257
Pierce v. Society of Sisters, 268 U.S. 510 (1925), 365–366
Pike v. Bruce Church, 397 U.S. 137 (1970), 257
Piqua Branch of the State Bank of Ohio v. Knoop, 16 How. 369 (1854), 301
Pittsburgh Press Co. v. Pittsburgh Commission of Human Relations, 413 U.S. 376 (1973), 296
Planned Parenthood Association of Kansas City v. Ashcroft, 462 U.S. 476 (1983), 559
Planned Parenthood of Central Missouri v. Danforth, 428 U.S. 52 (1976), 559, 560, 562

Planned Parenthood of Southeastern Pennsylvania v. Casey, 559, 567–570
Plessy v. Ferguson, 163 U.S. 537 (1896), **654–657,** 658–661, 690
Poe v. Ullman, 367 U.S. 497 (1961), 528, 529, 535
Poelker v. Doe, 432 U.S. 519 (1977), 561
Pointer v. Texas, 380 U.S. 400 (1965), 22
Pollock v. Farmers' Loan & Trust Co., 158 U.S. 601 (1895), 84, **264–269,** 271, 272
Powell v. Alabama, 287 U.S. 45 (1932), 611–612
Powell v. McCormack, 395 U.S. 486 (1969), 89, 102–105, 106, 113
Powers v. Ohio, 499 U.S. 400 (1991), 619
Prince v. Massachusetts, 321 U.S. 296 (1940), 369–370, 374, 376
Prize Cases, 2 Black 635 (1863), 173

Quinlan, In re, 355 A.2d 647 (1976), 541

R.A.V. v. City of St. Paul, Minnesota, 505 U.S 377 (1992), **477–482**
Railroad Retirement Board v. Alton Railroad Co., 295 U.S. 230 (1935), 231n5, 232
Raymond Motor Transportation v. Rice, 434 U.S. 429 (1978), 257
Reed v. Reed, 404 U.S. 71 (1971), 667, 668, **669–670**
Reese; United States v., 92 U.S. 214 (1876), 709
Regents of the University of California v. Bakke, 438 U.S. 265 (1978), 689n6, **691–697,** 698
Regina v. Hicklin, L.R. 3 Q.B. 360 (1868), 505–506
Reitman v. Mulkey, 387 U.S. 369 (1967), 689n4
Reynolds v. Sims, 377 U.S. 533 (1964), 17n20, 87 (box), 393n32, **721–725,** 726
Reynolds v. United States, 98 U.S. 145 (1879), 365, 374, 376, 385–386
Rhode Island v. Innis, 446 U.S. 291 (1980), 606n17
Richardson v. Ramirez, 418 U.S. 24 (1974), 718
Richardson; United States v., 418 U.S. 166 (1974), 92
Richmond Newspapers v. Virginia, 448 U.S. 555 (1980), 503–504, 621
Robel; United States v., 389 U.S. 258 (1967), 455
Rock Royal Cooperative; United States v., 307 U.S. 533 (1939), 247 (table)
Roe v. Wade, 410 U.S. 113 (1973), 19, 41, 78, 82 (table), 85, 338, 526, 547, **549–555,** 556–570
Roemer v. Maryland Public Works Board, 426 U.S. 736 (1976), 404
Rosenberger v. University of Virginia, — U.S. — (1995), 414
Ross v. Moffitt, 417 U.S. 600 (1974), 617
Ross; United States v., 456 U.S. 798 (1982), 584n8
Rostker v. Goldberg, 453 U.S. 57 (1981), 675
Roth v. United States, 354 U.S. 476 (1957), 457 (table), 506–507, 508 (box), 512, 513
Rumely; United States v., 345 U.S 41 (1953), 32

San Antonio Independent School District v. Rodriguez, 411 U.S. 1 (1973), 647n3, **675–681**
Sanchez; United States v., 340 U.S. 42 (1950), 275
Sanford v. Kentucky, 492 U.S. 361 (1989), 625n15
Santa Cruz Fruit Packing v. NLRB, 303 U.S. 453 (1938), 247 (table)
Scales v. United States, 367 U.S. 203 (1961), 455
Schechter Poultry Corp. v. United States, 295 U.S. 495 (1935), 138–140, 206, 231, 232, **233–237,** 313 (table)
Schenck v. United States, 249 U.S. 47 (1919), **437–438,** 439, 442, 445, 453, 457 (table), 472, 504
Schlesinger v. Reservists Committee to Stop the War, 418 U.S. 208 (1974), 92

Schneider v. Irvington, 308 U.S. 147 (1939), 446–447
Schware v. Board of Bar Examiners, 353 U.S. 232 (1957), 82 (table)
Scott v. Illinois, 440 U.S. 367 (1979), 616
Scott v. Sandford, 19 How. 393 (1857), 20 (box), 79, 175, 199–201, 314, 653–654
SCRAP; United States v., 412 U.S. 669 (1973), 93
Shaw v. Reno, 509 U.S. — (1993), 727–728
Sheet Metal Workers v. EEOC, 478 U.S. 501 (1986), 689n5
Sheppard v. Maxwell, 384 U.S. 333 (1966), 621
Sherbert v. Verner, 374 U.S. 398 (1963), 371–373, 374–375, 377–378, 379, 385–386, 388 (table)
Shreveport Rate Case, 234 U.S. 342 (1914), 226, 248
Siebold, Ex parte, 100 U.S. 371 (1880), 709
Sierra Club v. Morton, 405 U.S. 727 (1972), 93
Sipuel v. Board of Regents of the University of Oklahoma, 332 U.S. 631 (1948), 658
Slaughterhouse Cases, 16 Wall. 36 (1873), 315–320, 336, 338, 654
Smith v. California, 361 U.S. 147 (1959), 29
Solem v. Helm, 463 U.S. 277 (1983), 623
Sonzinsky v. United States, 300 U.S. 506 (1937), 275
South Carolina v. Baker, 485 U.S. 505 (1988), 272
South Carolina v. Katzenbach, 383 U.S. 301 (1966), **713–716**
South Carolina v. United States, 199 U.S. 437 (1905), 271n11
South Dakota v. Dole, 483 U.S. 203 (1987), **277–280**
Southern Pacific Co. v. Arizona, 325 U.S. 761 (1945), 256
Spallone v. United States, 493 U.S. 265 (1990), 689n4
Spano v. New York, 360 U.S. 315 (1959), 595n13
Spence v. Washington, 418 U.S. 405 (1974), 463
Springer v. United States, 102 U.S. 586 (1881), 263
Stafford v. Wallace, 258 U.S. 495 (1922), 228, 248
Stanley v. Georgia, 394 U.S. 557 (1969), 536, 540
Stanton v. Stanton, 421 U.S. 7 (1975), 670n2
State of Wyoming v. State of Oklahoma, 502 U.S. 437 (1992), 257
Steward Machine Co. v. Davis, 301 U.S. 548 (1937), 247 (table), 276, 277
Stone v. Mississippi, 101 U.S. 814 (1880), 302
Stoner v. California, 376 U.S. 483 (1964), 582
Street v. New York, 394 U.S. 576 (1969), 462–463
Stromberg v. California, 283 U.S. 359 (1931), 445, 460, 462
Sturges v. Crowninshield, 4 Wheat. 122 (1819), 294–295
Swann v. Charlotte-Mecklenburg County Board of Education, 402 U.S. 1 (1971), 82 (table), **683–687**
Sweatt v. Painter, 339 U.S. 629 (1950), 658
Swift v. Tyson, 16 Pet. 1 (1842), 298 (box)
Swift & Co. v. United States, 196 U.S. 375 (1905), 228, 248

T. W. In re, 551 So. 2d (1989), 569
Terminiello v. Chicago, 337 U.S. 1 (1949), 470–471, 472, 473
Terry v. Ohio, 392 U.S. 1 (1968), 582–583
Texas v. Johnson, 491 U.S. 397 (1989), 19, **463–468**
Thomas v. Collins, 323 U.S. 516 (1945), 447, 448, 457 (table)
Thomas v. Review Board of Indiana Employment Security Division, 450 U.S. 707 (1981), 374–375, 377–378, 379
Thompson v. Oklahoma, 487 U.S. 815 (1988), 625n15

Thornburgh v. American College of Obstetricians and Gynecologists, 476 U.S. 747 (1986), 564–565, 566 (table), 568

Thornhill v. Alabama, 310 U.S. 88 (1940), 460–461

Tilton v. Richardson, 403 U.S. 672 (1971), 404

Time, Inc. v. Firestone, 424 U.S. 448 (1976), 523–524

Tinker v. Des Moines, 393 U.S. 503 (1969), 462

Train v. City of New York, 420 U.S. 35 (1975), 155

Trop v. Dulles, 356 U.S. 349 (1958), 45n57

Trustees of Dartmouth College v. Woodward, 4 Wheat. 518 (1819), 295–296, 298 (box)

U.S. Term Limits v. Thornton, — U.S. — (1995), **105–113**

Underwriters Ass'n; United States v., 322 U.S. 533 (1944), 32n27

United Jewish Organizations of Williamsburgh v. Carey, 430 U.S. 144 (1977), 726–727

United States v. Brewster, 408 U.S. 501 (1972), 114n16, 115 (table)

United States v. Brown, 381 U.S. 437 (1965), 455

United States v. Butler, 297 U.S. 1 (1936), 232, 276, 277, 280, 313 (table)

United States v. Calandra, 414 U.S. 338 (1974), 593n12

United States v. Carolene Products Co., 304 U,S. 144 (1938), 445–446, 457 (table), 647n3

United States v. Causby, 328 U.S. 256 (1946), 341–342

United States v. Communist Party of the United States, 377 U.S. 968 (1964), 455

United States v. Cruikshank, 92 U.S. 542 (1876), 709

United States v. Curtiss-Wright Export Corp., 299 U.S. 304 (1936), **132–136,** 137–138, **168–170**

United States v. Darby Lumber, 312 U.S. 100 (1941), **206–207,** 209 (box), 246, 247 (table)

United States v. Doremus, 249 U.S. 86 (1919), 275

United States v. E. C. Knight Co., 156 U.S. 1 (1895), 227–228, 237, 246, 248

United States v. Eichman, 496 U.S. 310 (1990), 468

United States v. Fordice, 505 U.S. — (1992), 689

United States v. Gale, 109 U.S. 65 (1883), 709

United States v. Harris, 106 U.S. 629 (1883), 654, 709

United States v. Helstoski, 442 U.S. 264 (1979), 115 (table), 116

United States v. Kahriger, 345 U.S. 22 (1953), 275

United States v. Klein, 80 U.S. 128 (1872), 81, 82

United States v. Kokinda, 497 U.S. 720 (1990), 475

United States v. Lee, 435 U.S. 252 (1982), 375, 386

United States v. Lefkowitz, 285 U.S. 452 (1932),

United Slates v. Leon, 468 U.S. 897 (1984), 593

United States v. Lopez, — U.S. — (1995), 216 cap., 247–248

United States v. Nixon, 418 U.S. 683 (1974), **158–163**

United Slates v. O'Brien, 391 U.S. 367 (1968), 461–462

United States v. One Book Called "Ulysses," 72 E2d 705 (1934), 506

United States v. Paradise, 480 U.S. 149 (1987), 697

United States v. Reese, 92 U.S. 214 (1876), 709

United States v. Richardson, 418 U.S. 166 (1974), 92

United States v. Robel, 389 U.S. 258 (1967), 455

United States v. Rock Royal Cooperative, 307 U.S. 533 (1939), 247 (table)

United States v. Ross, 456 U.S. 798 (1982), 584n8

United States v. Sanchez, 340 U.S. 42 (1950), 275

United States v. SCRAP, 412 U.S. 669 (1973), 93

United States v. Underwriters Ass'n, 322 U.S. 533 (1944), 32n27

United States Senate v. Synar, 478 U.S. 714 (1986), 146 (box)

United States Trust Co. v. New Jersey, 431 U.S. 1 (1977), 307

United Steelworkers of America v. Weber, 444 U.S. 193 (1979), 697n9

United Transportation Union v. Long Island Rail Road, 455 U.S. 678 (1982), 210, 211 (table)

Valley Forge Christian College v. Americans United for Separation of Church and State, 454 U.S. 464 (1982), 92

Veazie v. Moor, 14 How. 568 (1853), 226–227

Veazie Bank v. Fenno, 8 Wall. 533 (1869), 273

Vignera v. New York, 384 U.S. 436 (1966), 597n14

Village of Arlington Heights v. Metropolitan Housing Development Corp., 429 U.S. 252 (1977), 689n4

Wabash, St. Louis & Pacific Railway Co. v. Illinois, 118 U.S. 557 (1886), 226n1

Wallace v. Jaffree, 472 U.S. 38 (1985), 402 (table), 422–423

Walz v. Tax Commission of the City of New York, 397 U.S. 664 (1970), 396–397, 401 (table), 402

Ward v. Rock Against Racism, 491 U.S. 781 (1989), 475

Warden v. Hayden, 387 U.S. 294 (1967), 583–584

Wards Cove Packing Co. v. Atonio, 490 U.S. 642 (1989), 689n5

Warth v. Seldin, 422 U.S. 490 (1975), 92

Washington v. Texas, 388 U.S. 14 (1967), 22

Watkins v. United States, 354 U.S. 178 (1957), 32, 33, 130–131

Wayman v. Southard, 10 Wheat. 1 (1825), 138, 140

Webster v. Reproductive Health Services, 492 U.S. 490 (1989), 565–567, 569

Weeks v. United States, 232 U.S. 383 (1914), 585

Weinberger v. Wiesenfeld, 420 U.S. 636 (1975), 668

Wesberry v. Sanders, 376 U.S. 1 (1964), 720–721, 726

West Coast Hotel v. Parrish, 300 U.S. 379 (1937), 240, 245, **333–336**

West Lynn Creamery v. Healy, — U.S. — (1994), 283

West River Bridge Co. v. Dix, 6 How. 530 (1848), 298 (box)

West Virginia Board of Education v. Barnette, 319 U.S. 624 (1943), 34, 35, 368–369, 386, **483–487**

Westover v. United States, 384 U.S. 436 (1966), 597n14

Wheaton v. Peters, 8 Pet. 491 (1834), 298 (box)

Whitehill v. Elkins, 389 U.S. 54 (1967), 455

Whitney v. California, 274 U.S. 357 (1927), 442–443, 456

Wickard v. Filburn, 317 U.S. 111 (1942), 246, 252, 276n13

Wiener v. United States, 357 U.S. 349 (1958), 168

Williams v. Florida, 399 U.S. 78 (1970), 620

Williamson v. Lee Optical Co., 348 U.S. 483 (1955), 337, 528n6, 646n1

Wisconsin v. Mitchell, 508 U.S. 476 (1993), 39, 482

Wisconsin v. Yoder, 406 U.S. 205 (1972), 373–374, 375, 385, 388 (table)

Witters v. Washington Department for Services for the Blind, 474 U.S. 481 (1986), 405

Wolf v. Colorado, 338 U.S. 25 (1949), 22, 586, 587n11

Wolman v. Walter, 433 U.S. 229 (1977), 404, 406

Wooley v. Maynard, 430 U.S. 705 (1977), 487–488

Wynehamer v. People of New York, 13 N.Y. 378 (1856), 314

Yarborough, Ex parte, 110 U.S. 651 (1884), 709

Yates v. United States, 354 U.S. 298 (1957), 454, 455 (table)

Yerger, Ex parte, 8 Wall. 85 (1869), 82n38

Yick Wo v. Hopkins, 118 U.S. 356 (1886), 646, 648

Youngstown Sheet and Tube Co. v. Sawyer, 343 U.S. 579 (1952), 26–27, **177–182**

Zobrest v. Catalina Foothills School, 509 U.S. 1 (1993), 405

Zorach v. Clauson, 343 U.S. 306 (1952), 394 (table)

Zurcher v. Stanford Daily, 436 U.S. 547 (1978), 502–503

ILLUSTRATION CREDITS

28	Supreme Court of the United States
67	Lisa Biganzoli, National Geographic Staff
68	Maryland Historical Society
72	Library of Congress
128	Library of Congress
152	LBJ Library
159	National Archives
161	UPI/Bettmann
163	Bettmann
176	AP/Wide World
178	Bettmann
198	Supreme Court of the United States
202	Library of Congress
220	Courtesy of the New York Historical Society
221	Georgia Historical Society
222	Drew University Library Archives
231	(all) Library of Congress
233	Bettmann
238	(left) Washington Post; (right) Franklin Delano Roosevelt Library
245	Supreme Court of the United States
268	Library of Congress
276	UPI/Bettmann
297	Goodspeed's Bookshop/ Supreme Court Historical Society
298	Library of Congress
312	Library of Congress
321	(both) From the collection of Joseph Lochner, Jr., by Dante Tranquille
328	Library of Congress
343	Bettmann
351	M.L. Miller-SIPA
387	Tom Salyer
409	AP/Wide World
417	(left) Thomas Ordney; (right) Andy Starnes
425	Providence Journal Bulletin Photo
437	Bettmann
441	Library of Congress
461	Bettmann
464	Bill Pierce
472	Associated Press/ Washingtoniana Division, D.C. Public Library
491	Minnesota Historical Society
505	National Geographic Society
515	New York Times
522	Bettmann
529	Ted Eastwood
537	AP/Wide World Photos
548	Bettmann
556	Supreme Court Historical Society
587	The Plain Dealer, Cleveland Ohio
596	Bettmann
598	Bettmann
611	The Brown Brothers
614	(left) Supreme Court Historical Society; (right) Flip Schulke, Life Magazine
635	Marlene Karas, The Atlanta Constitution
659	(top) Library of Congress; (bottom) NAACP
660	Supreme Court of the United States
661	AP/Wide World Photos
666	Library of Congress
668	R. Michael Jenkins, Congressional Quarterly
676	Institute of Texan Cultures
692	AP/Wide World Photos
700	AP
718	Library of Congress
727	Congressional Quarterly
734	Scott J. Ferrell, Congressional Quarterly